GLAMORGAN COUNTY HISTORY

Henry Herbert, second earl of Pembroke (*c.* 1534–1601)

(Artist unknown)

GLAMORGAN COUNTY HISTORY

General Editor: GLANMOR WILLIAMS
General Editor's Assistant: M. FAY WILLIAMS, M.A.

VOLUME IV
EARLY MODERN GLAMORGAN

from the Act of Union to the Industrial Revolution

Edited by GLANMOR WILLIAMS, M.A., D.Litt.,
Professor of History, University College of Swansea

CARDIFF
Published by the Glamorgan County History Trust Limited
and distributed by the University of Wales Press
1974

PRINTED BY QUALITEX PRINTING LIMITED, CARDIFF

FOREWORD

BY

SIR CENNYDD TRAHERNE, K.G.

Her Majesty's Lord-Lieutenant for the Counties of Glamorgan
Chairman of the Glamorgan County History Trust Limited

THREE YEARS ago I had the pleasure of welcoming the publication of Volume III of the Glamorgan County History and the reprint of Volume I. The reception given to Volume I and Volume III by reviewers and general readers has been very encouraging, and I hope that Volume IV will be just as warmly received. I should like to express my profound and sincere thanks to the editor of this volume and all his contributors for the sterling work they have undertaken over a long period of years to bring their studies to fruition.

In the meantime, since Volume III was published, changes have been made in the organisation of the Glamorgan County History. Early in 1974, a new non-profit-making Trust, the Glamorgan County History Trust Limited, was established in order to facilitate the task of publishing Volume IV and succeeding volumes of the County History. To all those who were involved in the protracted and sometimes complicated procedures necessary to set up the Trust, and expecially to Mr. T. V. Walters, Mr. D. B. Starke, Dr. R. A. Griffiths and Mr. J. H. Vanstone, I offer our best thanks.

Until 31st March 1974, the Glamorgan County History continued to be as indebted as ever to the Glamorgan County Council for its splendid moral and financial support. On behalf of the Trust I should like to record our deepest sense of gratitude for all the sustained help we received from the County Council from 1956 onwards. Since the reorganisation of Local Government, the three successor authorities of Mid, South and West Glamorgan have given great encouragement and pleasure to us by indicating their willingness to assume responsibility for supporting the County History Trust. We should like to thank them in the warmest terms for doing so. We have every expectation that representatives of the new County Councils will soon become members of the Trust. We look forward to working as closely and fruitfully with them and their authorities as we did with their predecessors in an effort to produce a History worthy of the people of the Counties of Glamorgan.

EDITOR'S PREFACE

THE two-and-a-half centuries lying between the Act of Union and the Industrial Revolution covered a crucial and formative period in the history of Glamorgan. An era of stability and well-being for the most part, it saw a considerable growth in population, the evolution of prosperous agriculture and thriving trade, and the creation of the bases of modern industry. Landed estates were extended and consolidated; many new houses were built and old ones remodelled; the modern patterns of farm and field took shape; ports and market towns revived and expanded; and mineral and metallurgical resources were exploited on a significant scale. For the gentry it was a golden age, when some of the county's most famous families — Herberts, Stradlings, Mansels, Lewises, Mathews, Aubreys, Bassetts, Carnes, and others—left their mark writ large on Glamorgan life. But it was also a period from which enough evidence has survived to enable us, for the first time, to write in some depth and detail of the everyday condition of other ranks in society: of yeoman and parson, merchant and husbandman, industrialist and shopkeeper, vagabond and pauper. In a way never possible for earlier centuries we can begin to discern what life was like for the peasant farmer, the rural craftsman, the industrial worker, and the hired labourer.

Politically and administratively, Glamorgan was absorbed along with the rest of Wales into the orbit of the English state. The county became the basic unit of politics, justice, and administration; and the new machinery created by the Tudor monarchy for parliamentary representation, county government, and local lawcourts in Wales was gradually put into tolerably effective working order by the families of county gentry, into whose hands power was largely entrusted. Nor were the religious changes introduced by the Tudors any less significant. The institutions of the medieval Church were in large measure swept away or reconstructed, and the new Church 'by law established' introduced a Protestant liturgy and a vernacular prayer book, though not without meeting stubborn resistance from Roman Catholic recusants and demands for more radical reform from Puritan critics.

The greater degree of internal peace, order, and prosperity slowly achieved in the century before 1642 was rudely shattered by the alarms and excursions of the Civil Wars, which bore hardly on staunchly-royalist Glamorgan as on many another county. They were followed by the confused and rapid changes of the Interregnum, in the course of which a series of experiments in politics, government, religion, and education were embarked upon, though most of these proved to be abortive and short-lived.

After the restoration of the monarchy, life in the county showed remarkable resilience. Mixed farming in the Vale and livestock husbandry in the Uplands continued to flourish; and Glamorgan's trade across the Bristol Channel and farther afield recovered its buoyancy. Rural industries like weaving, stocking-knitting, and tanning remained active and widespread, but it was the development of the heavy industries of coal, iron, and copper which was soon to show the remarkable acceleration that put Glamorgan industrialists among the pacemakers of the early phases of the Industrial Revolution.

Political and administrative authority came back into the hands of the traditional families, though some men who 'had done well out of the war' survived with their gains intact. The gap between the major families and those of the minor gentry and yeomen now grew markedly wider, and changes in the balance of political and social forces made eighteenth-century Glamorgan an arena of lively political rivalries and manoeuvres. The Anglican Church, though restored with the monarchy and strongly buttressed by its close alliance with the landowners, never again enjoyed its position of complete dominance despite all its commendable efforts with the charity and circulating schools. Dissent, firmly rooted during the Interregnum, throve in spite of persecution between 1660 and 1688 and became the faith of a significant minority; while in the eighteenth century the swift success of the Methodist Revival brought an exciting new dimension to the county's religious experience.

It was crisis and jeopardy, however, that during these centuries overtook the Welsh literary tradition which had been so healthy and virile in the fifteenth century. The cult of gentryhood and Renaissance ideals of culture and education found eager acolytes in Glamorgan, but increasingly at the expense of the patronage of Welsh literature. English education and English books were gaining ground among the upper class and, as they did so, the traditional Welsh strict-metre poetry, and the bardic order which had been its guardian, withered to the point of extinction. Nor was there sufficient compensatory vitality infused into Welsh free-metre verse or Welsh prose to make good the loss. Yet the hold of the native language and custom on the mass of the population was never broken; and in the eighteenth century a revival of interest germinated in Welsh poetry. A handful of enthusiasts—'grammarians', lexicographers, antiquarians, and poets—gave the old indigenous literary culture a new lease of life and energy.

Not the least striking feature of these centuries is the emergence from Glamorgan of a galaxy of interesting and gifted individuals who made a notable contribution to the life of England and Wales. The statesmen, Sir Robert Mansel and Sir Leoline Jenkins, and that towering intellectual, Richard Price, played their part on the stage of British, even European, politics, as did the diplomats Sir Edward Carne and Sir John Herbert. Fighting-men like Sir Rice Mansel, Sir Thomas Button, Colonel

Philip Jones, and Admiral Thomas Matthews, were widely known outside Glamorgan, as were the lawyers, David Jenkins of Hensol and Evan Seys of Boverton, or the businessmen, Sir Humphrey Mackworth and Sir Humphrey Edwin, or the Puritans William Erbery and Samuel Jones of Brynllywarch. Sir Edward and Sir John Stradling were considerable figures in the world of letters and scholarship, Rice Merrick and Thomas Wilkins accomplished antiquarians, and Thomas Richards and John Walters major contributors to Welsh-language studies. Perhaps the most talented of them all, as he was certainly the most wayward, was that enigmatic genius, Iolo Morganwg, so appropriately dubbed by the late Professor Griffith John Williams as 'the Walter Scott of Glamorgan'. Who but Iolo could ever have so comprehensively refashioned the old pastoral Glamorgan in his own image, or transmitted with such unblushing conviction to the rhapsodic and unsuspecting patriots of the industrial Glamorgan of Victoria's reign his blissful Arcadia of an immemorial and rose-tinted past?

In the process of compiling this volume I have incurred many debts which I should like gratefully to acknowledge here. First of all my warmest thanks must go to all the contributors to this volume for their devoted efforts over many years. In the nature of the case some chapters were completed much sooner than others, and I am particularly grateful to those contributors who have waited with exemplary patience to see their work published. I should also like to thank Mrs. Glenys Bridges, of the Department of Geography, University College of Swansea, who drew all the maps except one and was a model of speed and efficiency. Mr. Roger Davies of the University College of Swansea, Dr. G. O. Jones, Director of the National Museum of Wales, Mr. David Jenkins, Librarian of the National Library of Wales, Mrs. Patricia Moore of the Glamorgan Record Office, Sir Hugo Boothby, Mr. Christopher Methuen-Campbell, Miss Joanna Methuen-Campbell, and Sir Cennydd Traherne, all gave me a great deal of help with the illustrations. So, too, did Mr. Stewart Williams, who also allowed me to borrow a number of blocks in his possession. Mr. Peter Smith, Secretary of the Royal Commission on Ancient Monuments for Wales, was so exceptionally kind in choosing, supplying, and annotating the illustrations for Glamorgan houses that he deserves a special word of gratitude. I have received a great deal of kindness and co-operation at the hands of the Librarians and Staffs of the National Library of Wales, the Cardiff Central Library, the University College of Swansea, and the Archivists and Staff of the Glamorgan County Record Office. I am deeply indebted to a number of my former research pupils for discussing their work with me and allowing me to make extensive use of their theses: Dr. F. G. Cowley, Ph.D., and Mr. Gareth E. Jones, M.A., M.Ed., of the University College of Swansea, Mr. C. Mervyn Thomas, M.A., of Cardiff, Dr. W. S. K. Thomas, Ph.D., of Brecon, and Canon T. J. Prichard, M.A., of Neath. Four other authors of unpublished postgraduate theses from whose work I derived a great deal of benefit were Miss Megan Thomas, M.A., of the University College of Wales, Aberystwyth, Mrs. Margaret O'Keeffe, M.A., of the University College of Galway, Mr. David Cole, M.A., of the University of Birmingham, and the late Ieuan Jeffreys-Jones, M.A., Warden of Coleg Harlech. I owe a great deal also to the knowledge and advice of my old friend, Mr. I. J. Hopkins of the Cardiff Central Library.

Once again I have owed much to the support and collaboration of the members of the former Glamorgan County History Executive Committee, now the Glamorgan County History Trust Limited. It is difficult for me to speak too highly of the consistent friendship and encouragement of the Chairman, Sir Cennydd Traherne, K.G., the former Treasurer, Mr. T. V. Walters, the present Treasurer, Mr. D. B. Starke, or the Secretary, Dr. R. A. Griffiths, who has not only removed many administrative burdens from my shoulders but has also given me the benefit of his extensive historical scholarship. Nor could an editor have wished for more careful, attentive, or constructive printers; it has been a delight and edification for me to work with Mr. Robert Sansom of Qualitex Printing Limited. My friend, Dr. R. Brinley Jones, Director of the University of Wales Press, has been characteristically generous, co-operative, and prudent in his advice on publishing problems. My wife has helped immeasurably at every stage of the work; her contribution is beyond praise and my debt to her beyond redemption.

GLANMOR WILLIAMS

CONTENTS

LIST OF DIAGRAMS, MAPS and PLATES

DIAGRAMS

MAPS

PLATES

LIST OF ABBREVIATIONS

AAFCT.	*Anglesey Antiquarian and Field Club Transactions.*
Agric. HR.	*The Agricultural History Review.*
APC.	*The Acts of the Privy Council.*
Arch. Camb.	*Archaeologia Cambrensis.*
Badm. MSS.	Badminton (Beaufort) Manuscripts, National Library of Wales.
BBCS.	*The Bulletin of the Board of Celtic Studies.*
BGA.	Rice Merrick, *A Booke of Glamorganshires Antiquities* (ed. J. A. Corbett, London, 1887).
BIHR.	*The Bulletin of the Institute of Historical Research.*
BM.	The British Museum.
Bowen, *Statutes*	*The Statutes of Wales* (ed. Ivor Bowen, London, 1908).
CAgH., IV	*The Agrarian History of England and Wales: Volume IV*, 1500–1640 (ed. Joan Thirsk, Cambridge, 1967).
Cambrian Register	*The Cambrian Register* (3 vols., London, 1796–1818).
Cardiff Records	*Records of the County Borough of Cardiff* (ed. J. H. Matthews, 6 vols., Cardiff, 1898–1911).
CCC.	*Calendar of the Proceedings of the Committee for Compounding, etc.*, 1643–1660 (ed. M. A. Everett Green, 1 vol. in 5, London, 1889–92).
CCL.	Cardiff Central Library.
CCSP.	*Calendar of the Clarendon State Papers* (4 vols., London, 1872).
CHST.	*Caernarvonshire Historical Society Transactions.*
CJ.	*The Journals of the House of Commons.*
Clarendon, *History*	Edward Hyde, earl of Clarendon, *The History of the Rebellion and Civil Wars in England* (ed. W. D. Macray, 6 vols., Oxford, 1888).
Clark, *Cartae*	G. T. Clark, *Cartae et Alia Munimenta quae ad Dominium de Glamorgancia Pertinent* (2nd. ed., 6 vols., Cardiff, 1910).
CPR.	*Calendar of the Patent Rolls.*
CSPD.	*Calendar of State Papers, Domestic Series.*
CSP. Rome	*Calendar of State Papers . . . preserved principally at Rome.*
CSP. Span.	*Calendar of . . . State Papers . . . relating to the Negotiations between England and Spain.*
CSP. Ven.	*Calendar of State Papers . . . existing in the Archives and Collections of Venice.*
Dillwyn, *Contributions*	Lewis W. Dillwyn, *Contributions towards a History of Swansea* (Swansea, 1840).
DNB.	*The Dictionary of National Biography.*
DWB.	*The Dictionary of Welsh Biography down to* 1940 (London, 1959).
Econ. HR.	*The Economic History Review.*
EHR.	*The English Historical Review.*
F. and R.	C. H. Firth and R. S. Rait, *Acts and Ordinances of the Interregnum*, 1642–60 (3 vols. London , 1911).
Glam. Hist.	*The Glamorgan Historian* (ed. Stewart Williams, Barry, 1963 ff.).
GRO.	The Glamorgan County Record Office, Cardiff.
Harl. MSS.	Harleian Manuscripts.
Hen Gwndidau	*Hen Gwndidau, Carolau a Chywyddau* (ed. L. J. Hopkin-James and T. C. Evans, Bangor, 1910).
HMC.	The Historical Manuscripts Commission.
Hopkiniaid Morganwg	*Hopkiniaid Morganwg* (ed. Lemuel James, Bangor, 1909).
IAW.	Iolo Aneurin Williams Manuscripts, National Library of Wales.
JCMHS.	*The Journal of the Calvinistic Methodist Historical Society.*

[xvii]

JHSCW.	. . .	*The Journal of the Historical Society of the Church in Wales.*
JWBS.	. . .	*The Journal of the Welsh Bibliographical Society.*
L. and P.	. . .	*Letters and Papers, Foreign and Domestic, of the Reign of Henry VIII* (23 vols., London, 1862–1929).
LCR.	. . . .	*The Report of the Royal Commission on Land in Wales and Monmouthshire* (London, 1896).
Leland, *Itin. Wales*	.	*The Itinerary in Wales of John Leland in or about the Years* 1536–1539 (ed. L. Toulmin Smith, London, 1906).
Limbus	. .	G. T. Clark, *Limbus Patrum Morganiae et Glamorganiae* (London, 1886).
Llandaff Records	.	*Llandaff Records* (ed. J. A. Bradney and R. Rickards, 5 vols., Cardiff and London, 1905–14).
Merrick's Glam. Antiqs.	.	Rice Merrick, *Morganiae Archaiographia; A Booke of Glamorganshires Antiquities* (ed. J. A. Corbett, London, 1887).
ML.	. . .	*The Letters of Lewis, Richard, William, and John Morris of Anglesey* (ed. J. H. Davies, 2 vols., Aberystwyth, 1907–09).
Myv. Arch.[1]	. .	*The Myvyrian Archaiology of Wales* (ed. Owen Jones, Edward Williams, and William Owen [-Pughe], 2nd edition, Denbigh, 1870).
NLW.	. . .	The National Library of Wales.
NLWJ.	. .	*The National Library of Wales Journal.*
P. and M. Orig. Corr.	.	Penrice and Margam Original Correspondence, National Library of Wales.
PCC.	. . .	The Prerogative Court of Canterbury (records now deposited at the Public Record Office).
Penrice and Margam MSS.		W. de Gray Birch, *A Descriptive Catalogue of the Penrice and Margam Manuscripts, Series I–IV* (London, 1893–1905).
P.R. (Ll.)	. .	Probate records of the diocese of Llandaff, National Library of Wales.
P.R. (S.D.)	. .	Probate records of the diocese of St. David's, National Library of Wales.
PRO.	. . .	The Public Record Office.
RCAM., Wales	.	The Royal Commission on Ancient Monuments for Wales.
Rees, *Cardiff*	.	William Rees, *Cardiff: a History of the City* (Cardiff, 1962).
RWM.	. .	*Report on Manuscripts in the Welsh Language* (ed. J. Gwenogvryn Evans, 2 vols. in 7 parts, Historical Manuscripts Commission, 1898–1910).
Sociol. Rev.	. .	*The Sociological Review.*
Stradling Correspondence		*The Stradling Correspondence: a Series of Letters written in the Reign of Queen Elizabeth* (ed. J. M. Traherne, London, 1840).
S. Wales and Mon. R.S.	.	*The South Wales and Monmouthshire Record Society Publications.*
TDHS.	. .	*The Transactions of the Denbighshire Historical Society.*
TLlM.	. .	G. J. Williams, *Traddodiad Llenyddol Morgannwg* (Caerdydd, 1948).
Trans. Cymm.	.	*The Transactions of the Honourable Society of Cymmrodorion.*
TRHS.	. .	*The Transactions of the Royal Historical Society.*
UCS.	. . .	The University College of Swansea.
Val. Eccl.	. .	*Valor Ecclesiasticus temp. Henrici VIII Auctoritate Regia Institutus* (ed. J. Caley and J. Hunter, 6 vols., London, 1810–34).
VCH.	. . .	*The Victoria County History.*
Warburton, *Memoirs*	.	Eliot Warburton, *Memoirs of Prince Rupert and the Cavaliers* (3 vols., London, 1849).
WHR.	. .	*The Welsh History Review.*

CHAPTER I

The Economic Life of Glamorgan, 1536-1642

By GLANMOR WILLIAMS

i.

LIFE ON THE LAND

IN all parts of Tudor and Stuart Glamorgan—upland *Blaenau* no less than low-lying *Bro*, peninsular Gower like hilly Llangyfelach Hundred —most of the inhabitants had one basic interest in common: they looked to the land for a living. Even the one in twelve or so who lived in the little towns were, as we shall see (below, pp. 42–6), directly or indirectly dependent on the fortunes of farming. Such a community had an all-pervading interest, often a literally life-and-death concern, in those matters that have preoccupied farmers from time immemorial: the fertility of the soil, the state of the weather, the quality of the harvest, the well-being of livestock, and the prices that crops, animals, land, and labour could command. Theirs was an economy in which people pressed hard on resources that never enjoyed great reserves. Only a minority of gentlemen and substantial farmers and town-dwellers could feel reasonably sure that they were unlikely ever to be pinched by want and hunger. In a society composed mostly of small subsistence farmers and wage-earners, perhaps as many as one-third of the population lived just above the poverty-line and another third on or below it. For paupers who depended on charity, labourers who had to spend 80 or 90 per cent of their income on food and drink, and peasants whose holdings were barely large enough to support themselves and their families, the state of the harvest, and the resultant prices reached by corn and other food-stuffs, were the fundamental facts of economic life. In the worst years most of them would probably go hungry; some of them might not even survive.[1]

Nearly all of them were engaged in farming, but the way they farmed depended on where they lived and the vagaries of climate and terrain. Hence the emphasis which contemporary observers placed on the geographical characteristics and the farming potential of Glamorgan. The first of these commentators was one of the most interesting of Tudor travellers, 'the King's antiquary', John Leland. This pioneer topographer, some time during the years from 1536 to 1539, undertook those journeys through Wales of which he left so lively a record. He was well aware of the difference between north and south Glamorgan, between *Blaenau* and *Bro*. In the north he found 'many hills . . . and woods good plenty' but 'few villages or corn except in a few small valleys', though in the mountains were 'some red deer, kids plenty, oxen and sheep'. Down in the south, however, was 'meetly good corn ground . . . and very good fruit for orchards' in Llandaff commote, while in the Ely valley the soil was 'very good for corn and grass and meetly woody . . . a flat soil without any high hills'; and he was equally complimentary about a number of places in the Vale.[2]

Some forty years later than Leland one of Glamorgan's own sons, Rice Merrick or Rhys Amheurug, the antiquary of Cottrell, drew an even more explicit contrast between Vale and Upland in his *Booke of Glamorganshires Antiquities* (1578). The *Bro*, 'the low country' or 'the Country in the Vale', 'always renowned . . . for the fertility of the soil and the abundance of all things serving to the necessity or pleasure of man, as also for the temperature and wholesomeness of the air', was 'for the most part . . . a plain, even soil, saving low swelling hills . . . and near towards the plains, pleasant meadows and . . . pastures, the plains fruitful and apt for tillage, bearing abundance of all kinds of grain'. The desirability of the Vale, so Merrick claimed, had attracted the Norman Fitzhamon there centuries before and had made men the more willing to serve him, 'for that the fame and praise of Glamorgan, although it was fertile, exceeded the goodness thereof'. In the north, divided from the lowlands by 'almost a continual direct ridge, or hill, in length from the East toward the West', lay the *Blaenau*, 'being three times double as much and more in quantity as the low country', but with soil much more barren among its 'many great hills and high mountains', though apt enough for 'great breeding of cattle, horses and sheep' and in 'nourishing and bringing up tall, mighty and active men'.[3]

The distinction drawn by Merrick was echoed by the prince of all Elizabethan antiquaries, William Camden, who, following Merrick, seemed partially to anticipate the modern geographers' concept of the transitional zone of the Border Vale lying between the Uplands and the Vale proper (see Map II). 'On the north', wrote Camden, 'it is very rugged with mountains, which inclining towards the South become by degrees more tillable; at the roots whereof we have a spacious Vale or plain open to the South-Sun . . . For this part of the County is exceeding pleasant, both in regard to the fertility of the soil and the number of towns and villages.' This same kind of geographical distinction can be applied in the western lordship of Gower, added to the old lordship of Glamorgan to form the new county in 1536. There, too, exists a lowland coastal plateau in the peninsula of Gower, a transitional border area across the neck of the peninsula, and the hill and moorland country to the north-east, forming the upland hundred of Llangyfelach[4] (see Map II).

THE PASTORAL FARMING OF THE UPLANDS

The upland districts of the *Blaenau* and Llangyfelach Hundred, with their wetter, cooler climate, steep hills and narrow valleys, and more barren and marshy soil, were a region where the emphasis could not but lie on the rearing of flocks and herds. Here there was an abundance of pasture and rough grazing, where there was 'always great breeding of cattle, horses and sheep' (Merrick), so characteristic of much of Wales. The essentially pastoral character of hill-country farming finds confirmation at the very outset of our period in the *Valor Ecclesiasticus*, the survey of church possessions and income compiled in 1535 for Henry VIII (below, pp. 206-7). Extracting the information it gives for three representative parishes in the uplands, Merthyr Tydfil, Gelli-gaer, and Llantrisant, we find that the tithes paid on livestock and their products form distinctly the highest proportion of the incumbent's income. At Merthyr the tithe on lambs and wool (£3 13s. 4d.) and on calves and cheese (£6 15s. 0d.) came to rather more than half the total of £20 11s. 8d. At Gelli-gaer the tithe on lambs and wool (£7 13s. 4d.), on cheese and calves (£6 3s. 4d.), and on pigs, geese and goats (5s.) amounted to an even higher proportion of £14 1s. 8d. out of a total of £20 17s. 0d. Figures for Llantrisant are incomplete, but the tithes on lambs and wool (£10 13s. 4d.) and on pigs and geese (1s. 8d.) come to £10 15s. 0d. out of £14 5s. 0d. A comparable emphasis on pastoralism in the hill country is described by Merrick, Camden, and John Speed, and it is further borne out by the inventories of early-seventeenth-century farmers living in the *Blaenau* and the hill country of west Glamorgan.[5]

First in order of importance in this pastoral economy was the breeding of cattle. Upland Glamorgan, said John Speed, was 'replenished with cattle, which is the best means unto wealth that this shire doth afford; upon whose hills you may behold whole herds of them feeding'. The persistent cause for concern which cattle-stealing in some of the upland hundreds of Glamorgan caused the Council in the Marches and the Court of Great Sessions is testimony to the value of cattle in their economy as well as to the continuation of old nefarious habits. Inventories of livestock in the early-seventeenth-century wills show that store cattle raised for beef normally made up about one-third of a farmer's livestock in the *Blaenau*. But the large tithes paid on cheese in hill parishes suggest that milk production from dairy cattle must have been of primary importance early in the sixteenth century, and this is attested by the seventeenth-century inventories which show that dairy cattle formed about a quarter (28 per cent) of the hill farmer's livestock. Late in our period, one very big Merthyr Tydfil stockbreeder, Lewis William Lewis (d. 1603), had 65 dairy cattle and only 41 stores. He also carried 360 sheep. This last figure, together with the substantial amounts paid in tithe on lambs and wool, underlines the importance of sheep-rearing in the hills. In the earlier part of the sixteenth century sheep may well have closely rivalled cattle in value, though by the seventeenth century they seem to have formed only 28.4 per cent of the hill-farmer's stock, perhaps because wool prices had not risen as much as other prices in the sixteenth century (below, p. 19). Sheep, valued not only for their wool but also as a source of meat, tallow, skins, and milk for cheese, were hardy and adaptable, and they had the additional advantage of low labour costs. They were the 'most profitable cattle that a man can have', in the opinion of that expert on Tudor husbandry, Fitzherbert. Horses were of lesser importance, though Leland singled out Hirwaun and Aberdare for having 'a great race and breadth of horses'. They may have been coming into use as draught animals in place of oxen by the end of the century, and there was a growing demand for them as pack animals arising out of the growth of coal mining and other industrial activities within the county, so it is not surprising to find them accounting for 8.5 per cent of hill farmers' livestock in the early-seventeenth century. Pigs, geese, and goats were occasionally thought to be of sufficient value to be mentioned in the *Valor Ecclesiasticus*, where they are ordinarily lumped together and the tithe on them valued at a few shillings. The inventories accord them an even more marginal place and value. Leland made specific mention of 'kids plenty' in the *Blaenau*, and William Harrison referred with some enthusiasm to the goats of the 'rocky hills of Wales', 'by whom the owners do reap no small advantage', but in the inventories they amount to no more than 0.1 per cent of the livestock.[6]

The prevailing pastoralism of upland Wales was not without its critics. Leland spoke sternly of its farmers 'studying more to pasturage than tillage, as favourers of their consuete idleness'; the Elizabethan poet, Thomas Churchyard, chided them more gently for neglecting the plough because 'most of Wales likes better ease and rest'; and an Italian observer declared that they attended to agriculture 'only so far as it is necessary for their subsistence'. These critics hardly took sufficient account of the handicaps of climate and soil under which hill farmers laboured, nor did they pay as much attention as they might to the grain crops that were grown in the hill districts. In the parish of Merthyr Tydfil the tithe of corn was worth £4 6s. 8d. out of a total of £20 11s. 8d., and in Gelli-gaer £5 out of £20 17s. 0d. Leland did, in fact, describe the Upper Taff valley as a 'good valley for corn and grass' and the southernmost parts of Glynrhondda as 'meetly good for barley and oats but little wheat'. Hardy oats were, doubtless, the main crop grown in the hills, having a particular value as a source of winter fodder for the animals, as well as for the making of that oatmeal bread eaten by 'almost all the inhabitants of Wales' and praised for its excellent qualities by John Major in 1521. Small quantities of wheat and barley may also have been grown by bigger farmers, the wheat for bread corn, and the barley for malt. As the sixteenth century went on, however, there were some signs that increasing attention was paid to corngrowing in the uplands. Merrick tells us that whereas in 'the elder time' they grew 'but small stores of corn', 'the mountains in my remembrance be far bettered by good husbandry, toil and travail taken both in liming the ground and enclosing it', so that 'now of late years' 'there groweth more plenty of grain'. As a result, 'the people live more delicately', 'they feed upon bread made of wheat, and drink ale and beer, leaving off the . . . using of oaten bread and small drink'. Not that Merrick altogether approved of the consequences: whereas the mountains had at one time bred 'the tallest and valianter men', he now found 'the people do degenerate from their ancestors both in tallness of person and activity and lustiness'. Neither Merrick nor other contemporaries give us much clue as to the nature of the fields in which corn was grown, but in all probability the normal highland pattern of infield-outfield production prevailed: that is, the corn was grown mainly in small infields, lying near the homestead or hamlet, sometimes cultivated for the individual, sometimes in common for the whole of the tiny township. The ground chosen for cultivation was enclosed and the animals folded on it during the months from mid-March to November, when the land would be ploughed in preparation for sowing the oats in the following March. This process went on annually until the soil was exhausted. Another method of preparing the soil for an arable crop was 'beating and burning' turf prior to the sowing of the corn.[7]

In much of the northern Border Vale and in the *Blaenau* proper at this time we have to envisage a landscape in which trees were much thicker on the ground than people. Leland described the north-western corners of the county as having 'woods good plenty', the upper reaches of the Taff and Cynon as 'very woody', and in the northern half of Miskin commote 'all this way is hills and woods'. The forest of Coedffranc extended from the Vale of Neath to the river Cynon with only an occasional break. A survey of Tir Iarll taken in 1588 abounds with forest names, and the inhabitants there clearly lived in scattered clearings that had been laboriously won from densely-wooded country. Even today, in what used to be Coety Wallia, as in other parts of northern Glamorgan, the country is redolent of former woodland names: *Allt*-y-rhiw, *Coed*-y-mwstwr, Pen*coed*, and Cefn Hir*goed*; while in the former lordship of Talyfan not only have forest names survived from the thirteenth century but a large part of the area is now managed by the Forestry Commission; a remarkable example of the continuity of geographical control. Although Rice Merrick was much concerned about the 'many forests and woods' in the neighbourhood of ironworks that were 'spoiled and consumed' and his son-in-law, Miles Button, deplored 'several woods and forests . . . of late years brought to destruction', much of northern Glamorgan remained a handsomely-timbered region until the coming of eighteenth-century industry. As late as 1833 the Rhondda valleys were still luxuriously wooded, and tradition had it that a squirrel might make his way from the top of the valley to the sea without ever once needing to descend to the ground.[8]

Given the pastoral and wooded nature of the upland zone, its settlement pattern, as was to be expected, was that of dispersed and thinly-spread tiny hamlets and individual, often isolated, homesteads. The parishes were vast and sprawling (*ante*, III, 117–8, Map 4), bounded by major rivers and having within them no nucleated villages. This would be as true of parishes within the Border Vale, like St. Bride's Minor or Pendoylan, as of the *Blaenau* proper. Far more of the tenants in the uplands were freeholders than was usual in the lowlands, where customary tenure was much more prevalent. In this matter of tenure, history had reinforced geography, when the Norman conquerors of Glamorgan drew a distinction between the upland Welshries and the lowland Englishries (*ante*, III, 11–27); but the real difference was an economic not a racial or administrative one: it was the contrast between the pastoralists of the uplands and the mixed farmers of the lowlands. Even so, we must not suppose that no connexions existed between the two. Enterprising and sharp-eyed individuals had, long before the end of the Middle Ages, appreciated how the woodland and pasture resources of the Welshry complemented those of the Englishry (*ante*, III, 309–11). In the disturbed conditions of the fourteenth and fifteenth centuries many of the Welsh from the north of the county moved into the fertile south to penetrate into the Vale of Glamorgan and the Gower peninsula. These processes of mutual interpenetration and exchange between lowland and upland would continue and expand during our period.

The Mixed Farming of the Lowlands

The essential contrast between the pastoral farming of the uplands and the mixed farming of the lowlands is strikingly brought out in the parish-by-parish surveys of the *Valor Ecclesiasticus*. Whereas in the parishes of the *Blaenau* the tithe on corn was worth only about a quarter of the incumbent's income, in the lowland parishes it was nearly always worth about half; sometimes more, even in parishes within the Border Vale like Llansannor (£5 6s. 8d. out of £8) or Llanharry (£3 3s. 0d. out of £5 7s. 4d.). Down in the southernmost and most favoured parishes of the Vale it might amount to two-thirds, as at Gilestone (£4 out of £5 18s. 0d.), or even three-quarters at Newton Nottage (£12 13s. 4d. out of £17 6s. 4d.). The Vale was traditionally the classical corn-growing country of the manorial open fields, 'champion and open country, without great store of enclosures'. Some of these open fields still survived although, as will be seen (below, pp. 26–8), enclosures were increasing apace during the sixteenth and seventeenth centuries.

Of the suitability of the Vale for corn, contemporaries had no doubt. 'A very principal good corn ground', Leland thought it; 'the plains fruitful and apt for tillage, bearing abundance of all kinds of grain', was Merrick's verdict; but the much-quoted description of the Vale as the corn-growing 'Garden of Wales', though true, comes not from the pen of sixteenth-century Sir Edward Mansel but from eighteenth-century Iolo Morganwg's. What kinds of corn were grown in the Vale, and in what proportions, it is more difficult to tell. The *Valor Ecclesiasticus* is chary of details in this respect, but it does record that in St. Fagan's parish wheat, oats, and barley were grown, on which tithes of £3 10s. 0d., £3 6s. 4d., and 15s., respectively, were paid, while in more northerly Pentyrch wheat brought in a tithe of 8s., rye 1s. 8d., barley 10s. 8d., and oats £2 18s. 4d. How typical these were of the rest of lowland Glamorgan at this time it is impossible to say; but in early-Stuart Gower, oats were the crop most extensively grown, with wheat next in terms of acreage, and barley close behind. The only other crop cultivated in virtually every parish was hay, though in the parish returns of the *Valor*, the tithe on it amounts only to a fraction of that on corn in value. It has been suggested that hay crops may have been slight because cattle were rarely stall-fed in winter and remained on the commons or on 'fogged' pastures near the farm buildings, where straw, crushed furze, or reed could be fed to them. Flax and hemp were included in the *Valor* returns for a number of parishes, producing trifling sums of a shilling or two in tithes, and they may have been cultivated in other parishes as well, though they went unrecorded because the sums involved were so small. Peas and beans are recorded in the inventories of a number of seventeenth-century farmers.[9]

Yet this was a region of mixed farming, and Glamorgan's plains were as famous for their excellent livestock as for their grain. Indeed, without the regular supply of humus from the animals' dung, the intensive production of corn would not have been possible. Fifteenth-century Glamorgan had rung with the praises of Welsh poets for the strength, size, weight, and healthy appearance of its cattle. As early as this, apparently, attention was being given to selective breeding, for the poet Deio ab Ieuan Ddu, extolling the virtues of a specially-chosen bull and heifer, looked forward to the day when these and their offspring would produce prodigious quantities of calves and milk. This poetic tradition persisted into the sixteenth century. Moreover, Glamorgan men were proverbial for the care they lavished on their beasts, and many of their customary practices for the welfare of their animals did not become extinct until the nineteenth century. The larger Tudor landowners, taking advantage of the abundant common pasture of the many Glamorgan downs as well as of their own meadows, possessed numerous flocks and herds, as their wills often reveal. Sir Thomas Stradling (d. 1573) could afford to leave 17 milch kine for 17 poor married couples with none of their own, another 17 for fatherless maidens, yet another 17 for fatherless boys, and 3 for 'fatherless innocents'. Jenkin Carne of Sully (d. 1561), not by any means one of the largest gentry, could bequeath 3 bulls, 32 milch kine, 22 cattle, 6 oxen, 140 sheep, and 30 ewes with lambs, for the upkeep of his wife and two daughters. David Evans of the Gnoll, Neath (will dated 1567), who left his eldest daughter 30 kine, 18 oxen, and 500 sheep, and a further 40 kine and 200 sheep apiece to two other daughters, on top of handsome provision for his widow and eldest son, reminds us how the families of the Vale of Neath, of Aberpergwm and Ynysarwed, Ynys-y-gerwn and the Gnoll, almost rivalled those of the Vale of Glamorgan. Those shrewd landlords, the Mansels of Margam, with an ever-open eye for a good profit, always reckoned to make more from livestock than they did from crops. In 1572 they made £229 15s. 10d. from livestock, while their crops brought them £145 5s. 0d.; by 1638–9, their profits from livestock were £622 2s. 6d., as compared with £354 5s. 0d. from crops.[10]

A splendidly-detailed analysis of the livestock reared in early-seventeenth-century Gower has been provided by Mr. F. V. Emery on the basis of the numerous wills and inventories surviving from all classes of society there. Most valuable were the dairy cattle kept by all but the smallest farmers. The annual profit from 40 of them was reckoned to be worth £24 6s. 8d. more than that from 400 sheep; but to achieve such results called for careful breeding and well-controlled grazing. Dairy cattle were not only indispensable for breeding young cattle but their milk also produced a handsome profit in cheese and butter. Store cattle of up to three years old, too, were much prized, being driven overland or shipped to the West Country for sale. In addition, most farmers kept their patient oxen as draught animals or for the plough, where yoked in teams of four, six, or eight, they performed their essential task to the songs of the *geilwad*, some of which survived into the nineteenth century and have been preserved for us. Glamorgan had its own breeds of cattle, the reds and the blacks; but a good deal of cross-breeding had taken place. Next to cattle in importance came sheep. 'Three-quarters of all farmers, from the peasant living close to the margins of subsistence to the rising free-holder with a hand in the corn and cattle markets, had their flocks', ranging from an average 20–30 among the smallest peasants to over 200 among the biggest farmers. The native breed of Glamorgan Down sheep enjoyed a high reputation for their mutton and their wool. Horses were by this time much more common in Gower, with an average of from three to seven on even the smallest farms. Pigs, oddly enough, were found mostly on farms in the middling range, despite the tradition of the poor man having a pig or two in his sty; and poultry, too, were generally found on these farms. Many a farm kept its beehives, for honey was invaluable for sweetening; and in the *Valor* a number of parishes thought it worth including an item of a shilling or two for a tithe on wax and honey. Rabbits were bred by some landowners who had their own coney warrens, not just for the table but also for their handsome and valuable furs.[11]

Lowland settlement patterns reflected the region's age-old concentration on corn-growing. Here was a land of small, compact parishes and nucleated villages, geared to the effective production of grain. Each parish usually had one main cluster of dwellings grouped around church, manor house, parsonage, and inn, the whole lying somewhere near the centre of the great open fields, meadows, and waste, on which the life of the whole community depended and to which all its members must have reasonably easy access. Some of the larger parishes might have outlying hamlets, as for example Llancadle, Moulton, Liege Castle, and Pennon, all within Llancarfan parish; and there might be individual farmsteads, whose holdings had been arduously hacked out of woodland or waste. Lowland villages, too, might exhibit minor differences of emphasis. Some straggled untidily in linear or ribbon development, like Coychurch, Laleston, or Marcross; or even climbed a steep hill like Llanbleddian or Newcastle (Bridgend). Others were more compactly grouped around a village green, like St. Bride's Major or Reynoldston, or clustered round a castle like St. Fagan's, Coety, or Dinas Powys. Some might be down in a dingle like Llancarfan, others might be up on the ridge like Penmark. The advantages of life in such nucleated villages were warmly advocated by Iolo Morganwg, who knew the old villages of Glamorgan as few others have ever done. Farmers in such villages, he declared, were 'much more affable and sociable, much less sullen and arrogant, and more intelligent than those who live more solitary lives in the middle of their farms'.[12]

One of the most remarkable traits of settlement boundaries near the southern coast of Glamorgan was the way in which a calculated effort appeared to have been made to ensure that some part, however small, of as many parishes as possible had access to the sea-coast. The most plausible reason suggested for this was the value set upon the brown sea-weeds of the sea-coast as manure, and, after burning, as kelp. Yet, along many stretches of the Glamorgan coast, proximity to the shifting sands had led to a serious problem long before the end of the Middle Ages. Leland found Newton Nottage, Kenfig, and the land between the rivers Neath and Afan seriously encroached upon, and in Gower, at Pennard on the south coast and Llanmadog on the north, sand was a severe hazard. An Act of Parliament touching the Sea Sands in Glamorgan, of 1553, designed to tackle the problem by the appointment of six commissioners, seems to have left no trace of having served its purpose. More to the point were the attempts made by local inhabitants to plant sedges and maintain sea-walls, though even these were far from being either consistent or successful.[13]

LORDSHIPS AND MANORS

Though the manor had long since broken down as an economic unit (*ante*, III, 308-11), it continued to retain its force as a legal and tenurial institution, on which much of the life of the countryside still centred. Landowners continued to be the possessors of this or that manor or lordship, and tenants held their lands of them by a variety of tenures to be discussed below. Every tenant owed suit of court at the three-weekly court baron, presided over by the steward and having cognisance of all matters relating to the custom of the manor and copyhold lands, and again at the six-monthly court leet, in which the lord or his steward was judge in all personal actions under £2. Non-attendance at these courts could lead to fines upon the offender. 'Thus the manor, with its various courts, its registration of conveyances, its promulgation and enforcement of by-laws, and its administration of customary law, was an essential institution in the life of most of the countryside'. One contemporary asked if every manor were not a 'little commonwealth, whereof the tenants are not the members, the land the body and the lord the head'?[14]

The boundaries of the manor and the parish so often coincided in the Vale and south Gower as to be the more usual state of affairs. But it did not always work that way; Newton Nottage parish was divided into three manors, so too were Llantwit Major and St. Athan, while Llancarfan had no fewer than five: Walterston, Wrinston, Llancadle, Moulton, and Pennon. Ordinarily a manor might expect to have a single lord; but the manor of St. Nicholas had three—the earl of Pembroke, the Buttons of Dyffryn, and the Merricks of Cottrell—and that of Pen-llin had four, not to mention its two parish churches and three courts baron. Within the manors the pattern of tenancies might vary widely. For our knowledge of them we are chiefly indebted to the assiduity of Rice Lewis, who compiled his invaluable 'Breviat of Glamorgan' between 1596 and 1600. In it he surveyed some 140 Glamorgan manors and detailed the nature of the tenancies found within them. Much the commonest pattern was that found in 42 manors, situated mostly in the Vale of Glamorgan and south Gower, in which there were demesnes (not necessarily held in hand by the lord), free tenancies, and copyholds. There were 22 others, many of them in Gower, which had leaseholders, free tenants, and copyholders; and 17 more with only freeholders and copyholders. Customary tenures survived on only 9 manors, while many of the old northern lordships and Welshries had only leaseholders and free tenants, and two—Llandyfodwg and Llangeinor—had free tenants only. A detailed record of the manors' boundaries, customs, tenancies, resources, rights, and privileges was regularly and minutely kept in the surveys, many of which are still extant and a priceless source of information for the local historian. The survey was a court of inquiry taken by the lord or his steward through commissioners appointed by him, assisted by a sworn jury of knowledgeable tenants. In answer to an extensive set of interrogatories they compiled a mass of information concerning the manor: boundaries; suit of court; demesnes, parks, and woods; the names, tenures, ranks and services of tenants; common rights and encroachments on commons and wastes; forfeitures; miscellaneous rights and royalties—waifs, strays, felons' goods, wrecks, and the like; advowsons; mills; fisheries; markets and fairs; mines and quarries; military responsibilities and beacons; all these and other miscellaneous oddments came within the purview of the survey.[15]

Of Glamorgan's manorial lords the most powerful were absentees of distinguished rank who lived outside the county. The most illustrious landowner, though not the most extensive, was the sovereign, by virtue of his possession of the duchy of Lancaster manors within the county. Overshadowing all others in the number and value of the manors held by them ever since Edward VI's reign were the earls of Pembroke. William Herbert (d. 1570), the first earl, had begun to accumulate lands and offices in Glamorgan in the last years of Henry VIII's reign, but it was the grants made to him in 1550 for his part in putting down 'that rebellion raised by desperate men in Devon' (1549) and his creation as earl of Pembroke and Lord Herbert of Cardiff in 1551 that set the seal on his ascendancy. They made him lord of the six boroughs of Cardiff, Kenfig, Llantrisant, Cowbridge, Aberafan, and Neath, and of 36 manors, many of them 'in the best part in that country, and all as finable as any other and so every man knoweth'. Other absentee magnates were the earls of Worcester, lords of Gower and Swansea, and possessors of a number of manors—mostly in the west of the county, Lord St. John, lord of Fonmon castle and a compact group of productive manors in the vicinity, and the Herberts of Montgomery, whose interests lay in Gower. The marriage of Robert Sidney, later Viscount Lisle and earl of Leicester, to Barbara Gamage, heiress of the Gamages of Coety, added another absentee magnate to the list in 1584.[16]

However, all but nine of the 42 manorial lords listed by Rice Lewis were resident in the county. They came from a diversity of backgrounds. Some were from well-established *Advenae* families of Norman or English immigrants (below, pp. 79–80), like the Stradlings of St. Donat's, the Turbervilles of Pen-llin, the Bassetts of Beaupré, or the Mansels of Margam and Oxwich. Others, among them the Lewises of Y Fan, the Mathews of Llandaff and Radyr, and the Thomases of Brocastle, were of old Welsh *uchelwyr* stock within the county, who had moved into the more fertile south (*ante*, III, 306–11, 328–31). A few were newcomers attracted into the county by sixteenth-century opportunities, like the Herberts of Swansea, the Vaughans of Dunraven, and the Aubreys of Llantriddyd, all of whom made successful marriages with Glamorgan heiresses. The manors they possessed varied from one another considerably in size, resources, and wealth; but, quite apart from that, possession of manors in itself was not a sure index of the wealth and status of a family. The Lewises of Y Fan, for instance, were credited only with the manor of Roath Keynsham, which gives no inkling of the wide range of their interests in the east and north-east of the county that led to their being accounted the wealthiest of all the resident gentry of

Glamorgan by 1645 (below, p. 82). Possession of manors, nevertheless, was in general synonymous with wealth and power. The Stradlings and the Mansels were, by any standards, among the two or three most influential families in Glamorgan; they were also the largest owners of manors among the resident gentry. Sir Edward Stradling (d. 1609), in addition to his extensive properties on the English side of the Bristol Channel, was the lord, in whole or in part, of eleven manors in Glamorgan. His ancestral home at St. Donat's had been in his family's hands since the end of the thirteenth century, though some of the intervening generations of Stradlings had lived in England; a marriage to the heiress of the Berkerolles in the mid-fourteenth century added a number of valuable manors to the family's holding; but Nash and Llantwit had been bought only after the dissolution of the monasteries, Sully in 1558, and part of Pen-llin in 1573 (below, pp. 31–2). The Mansels had been in Gower since the early-fourteenth century; prudent marriages gained them a number of small Gower manors before the end of the Middle Ages; but it was the brilliant Sir Rice Mansel (d. 1559) who turned them into squires of the front rank when he bought the lion's share of Margam abbey's estates in the 1540s and 1550s (below, p. 32). Others owed an equal debt to the glittering opportunities of the sixteenth century. The Carnes of Ewenni came of old and gentle stock, but they acquired most of their manors as the result of the success of Sir Edward Carne (d. 1561) as a diplomat and his well-judged investments in monastic lands (below, pp. 209–10). Sir Richard Herbert's advancement came from his marriage to the heiress of Sir Mathew Cradock of Swansea; and her fine inheritance of manors in the west, middle, and east of the county was the means of founding a line of Herberts at Neath and Cogan Pill as well as at Swansea.[17]

Tenures

Ever since the medieval manor had broken down in the fourteenth and fifteenth centuries (*ante*, III, 308–11) under the pressures of economic depression, pestilence, and rebellion, a variety of tenures, indeed a bewildering confusion of them, had come into existence. Lords' demesnes, no longer directly farmed in most cases, had been rented out in a variety of ways. Some might be let *en bloc* to a single farmer or a group of substantial farmers. Or they might be divided up into smaller parcels of varying sizes and rented out by lease, copyhold, yearly letting, or tenancy-at-will. It was possible for a tenant to hold two or three parcels of demesne under different tenures. In the resultant confusion, demesnes tended to become drastically reduced in size, or even to disappear altogether by being merged with freehold, copyhold, or leasehold lands. In a majority of manors demesnes were still retained in name. They were, potentially, much more valuable resources in the sixteenth century as the result of the growing demand for land. The way in which they were exploited would depend on the absence or presence of the lord. If he were an absentee he would normally farm out the demesne. To do this as profitably as possible, attempts were increasingly made to consolidate demesne holdings so as to be able to charge an economic rent. The rentals of the earl of Pembroke for the splendid demesnes of Boverton provide a good example of this. These excellent lands, which are often said, on the basis of a somewhat ambiguous statement of Rice Lewis, to have been held in hand, were actually leased to a number of substantial tenants. In 1570 they included Sir Edward Stradling, Anthony Mansel, and John Turberville; by 1614 Edward Van alone farmed 400 acres of these demesnes and John Turberville 142 acres. Where the lord of the manor was resident, however, and demesnes could be profitably worked under his own direction, it might pay him to keep as much as possible in his own hands. Commenting on the practice of direct farming by the gentry, William Harrison observed that 'so far from suffering their farmers to have any gains at all . . . they themselves became graziers, butchers, tanners, sheepmasters, woodmen, and *denique quid non*, merely to enrich themselves'. The best-documented instance of more intensive demesne farming comes from the Mansel estates. This family abandoned the direct exploitation of their Gower estates when they left Oxwich for Margam; but at Margam they reversed the monastic policy of leasing out demesnes and took back several tenant holdings into their own hands. And no wonder! In 1537 the demesne was valued at no more than £13 4s. 8d.; by 1572 it was worth £445 in a year; and by 1638 livestock alone were bringing in £622 and crops a further £354. Even allowing for the inflation of these years, the Mansels had made a spectacular success of their demesne farming. Nor is there any reason to suppose they were alone in doing so, even though details are not available for other estates.[18]

The main categories of tenure within the manors were freehold, customary, and leasehold. Freehold tenancy allowed a tenant to hold his lands in socage tenure in perpetuity, for which he rendered suit of court, homage, fealty, and a small fixed rent, usually in money but occasionally in kind. Freehold tenants were most numerous in the former Welsh lordships of the north of the county, where servile or customary tenants had been unknown. In the lordship of Glynrhondda as late as 1661 the fixed rents of the 129 freeholders came to a total of only £5 11s. 0½d., as compared with the £3 5s. 10d. paid by the free tenants of 1596 and the £3 5s. 4d. paid by those of 1570. Freeholders in these areas were also liable to the payment of a heriot of the best beast at death. Freeholders were still commonly found at the beginning of the seventeenth century in a Border Vale parish like Pendoylan, where it was not until the eighteenth and nineteenth centuries that they became swallowed up in the estates of the Aubreys of Llantriddyd and the Jenkinses of Hensol. Welsh freehold tenure had also penetrated into, or perhaps survived in, some lowland manors like Newcastle and Newton Nottage, where about half the land was held in freehold tenures in the seventeenth century. In most of the manors of the Vale, however, free tenants numbered only a fraction of the population and accounted for an even smaller proportion of the manorial rents. On Leckwith manor in 1570 they paid 11s. 8d. rent out of a total of £26 9s. 11½d., at Llanbleddian £2 0s. 3d. out of £65 13s. 11½d., and at Boverton and Llantwit £9 4s. 5½d. out of £85 7s. 1½d. On the Margam manors of the Mansels in 1633 there were only three free tenants out of 385.[19]

Freehold tenants being everywhere a minority, except in the north, the majority of manorial tenants, especially in the corn-growing areas, held their lands by customary tenures. These were lands that had previously been occupied by the servile population of the medieval manor in return for labour services and renders in kind. Such services and renders had long since been commuted into money rents, though vestiges of them might still survive. The tenants of Coed-y-mwster in 1611 had to find 34 capons, four hens, and 18 days' labour service in addition to their rents totalling £55 7s. 8d., and in Gower many tenants had to render quantities of coal and/or lime on top of the rent and the usual pair of capons or geese. All customary tenants were liable to suit of court and to grind their corn at the manorial mill, and were often obliged to give their labour to 'fetch home to the lord's mill the mill-stones, and also all such timber as shall be needful towards the repairing of the floodgates and the wheels, and also ought to cleanse the millpond'. There were many different kinds of customary tenure; everything depended on 'the custom of the manor'. There were customary tenants like those of the manor of Caergurwen who were 'customary holders and do hold their lands by the virge or rod to them and their heirs for ever, and . . . they are neither freeholders nor copyholders otherwise than aforesaid'. At a number of other places in Glamorgan there were similar customary holders by inheritance, enjoying considerable protection from the custom of the manor, such as fixed rents per acre—3d. at Newton Nottage, 6d. at Newcastle, and 6½d. at Llanbleddian.[20]

The more usual customary tenure, nevertheless, was that of copyhold, i.e. land held by a copy of the manorial court roll with conveyance by surrender and admission in the lord's court. Though copyhold for a term of years was not unknown, copyhold for three lives was the commonest practice, with inheritance normally passing to the eldest son, or to daughters for want of male heirs, though there are examples of inheritance by the youngest son, as at Ogmore. But at least one Glamorgan landlord, Mathew Price of Cwrt-y-carnau, thought it worth his while fighting a lawsuit not to have to recognize the claim of his tenants to copyholds for three lives and sought to establish his right to dispose of them as he saw fit at the death of every tenant. In addition to copyholds there were tenancies-at-will or yearly tenancies of customary land. Though these were becoming far less common than they had been in the days of the land-glut of the medieval period, they numbered no less than one-third of the tenancies on a group of Mansel manors in 1633.[21]

All customary holdings were normally liable to the payment of a heriot at death and a fine at entry, a fine which was rarely fixed in amount and was usually arbitrable between lord and tenant. No stigma attached to customary land, and ever since the fifteenth century enterprising men, from the gentry and yeomen as well as from lower social groups, had been seizing the opportunity of acquiring customary land and, where possible, consolidating their holdings. Nor were customary tenants as defenceless or as vulnerable to pressure as used to be thought. 'Copyholders stand upon a sure ground', wrote Edward Coke, 'now they weigh not their lords' displeasure, they shake not at every sudden blast of wind.' Had they not enjoyed considerable security it is unlikely that men from the higher social reaches would have been so willing to take on customary holdings. A good deal of pressure was exerted on copyholders to convert their tenures into leasehold; but many of Glamorgan's customary tenures proved to be surprisingly resistant and survived all vicissitudes to flourish as late as the nineteenth century, and even the twentieth, in places as different from one another as Wick, Llanharry, or Pentyrch.[22]

The tenure becoming increasingly common and important on sixteenth-century manors was leasehold. Whereas in an earlier age it was demesne land which was chiefly let out by indenture, during our period leasehold was being increasingly substituted for copyhold, tenancy-at-will, and other forms of customary tenure. Leases in Tudor Glamorgan, like those of the western parts of the kingdom generally, were for three lives, which was usually thought of as the equivalent of the twenty-one-year lease regarded as normal elsewhere. This was a term deemed long enough to encourage improvement by the tenants and to justify a higher rent or entry fine on the part of the landlord. In a county where so many copyholds were for three lives anyway, an indenture for a similar term would be almost indistinguishable. Still, such a changeover had its advantages, especially for those who were tenants-at-will; it represented enfranchisement and it stipulated more precisely the obligations of a lord to a tenant. It was not unknown for the tenant to take the initiative in the changeover, 'for good consideration given to the lord'. But it also carried the risk of a considerably-raised rent and/or a stiff entry fine. The horrific picture given by George Owen of such a situation in not-so-distant Pembrokeshire recalls how 'the poor tenant . . . is taught to sing unto his lord a new song . . . and now the world is so altered with the poor tenant . . . that two or three years ere his lease end he must bow to his lord for a new lease and must pinch it out many years before to keep money together'.[23]

Nothing like a full account of the degree of letting that went on emerges from manorial rentals and surveys. They record only the transactions between the lord of the manor and those tenants who held directly of him; they shed no light on the incalculable number of transactions concluded between the tenants and the undertenants to whom they in turn sublet. Many manorial freeholds were held by well-to-do landowners who had no intention of working the land themselves and whose only concern was for the rent they could raise from subtenants. The process had begun in the fifteenth century and was well advanced by the early Tudor period. An unusually apt illustration of this is afforded by the holdings of Edward Lewis Y Fan within the lordships and manors of the earl of Pembroke (*ante*, III, 328–31). By 1570 he dominated the lordships of Senghennydd Supra and Subtus. In the former he held 32 tenements for which he paid the annual rent and *cymmortha* of £9 18s. 5½d., and in the latter 52 tenements (some of them jointly with his kinsman Edward ap Richard) for which he paid £5 11s. 1d. In addition he had got hold of 12 tenements in Whitchurch and 13 in Rudry. They varied in value from cottages worth a few pence to the old family home of the Lewises at Tir y Cwrt in Merthyr Tydfil, which was rented at 27s. 10d. There can be no doubt that they were all let to undertenants, whose names are recorded in the rental; but what we do not know are the conditions on which they were let. By 1625 Edward Lewis's grandson, another Edward, is estimated to have held two-fifths of the tenements in Senghennydd Supra and nearly half in Senghennydd Subtus, and he died leaving in all 300 miscellaneous holdings.[24]

Nor was it only freeholds that could be let in this way; subletting by leaseholders to undertenants presented no difficulties either. The undertenancy was usually held on the same sort of conditions as those operating for the tenancy itself: regular payment of rent, keeping the buildings in good repair, and not entering into any bargains without the lessor's consent. The subletting of customary land varied from manor to manor. In some manors there was almost complete freedom; in others the lord's licence was needed in varying circumstances; but in all it seemed possible to sublet without undue difficulty. Customary tenants who sublet might be allowed to remain outside the manor, provided they were bound by an obligation to make all their houses tenantable and to keep them so during their lifetime. In all cases of subletting we are probably safe in assuming that the lessors arrived at a contract which ensured them as large a profit as they could negotiate. If a lease granted by Richard Seys to an undertenant, one of the few to survive, be any guide, some bargains must have been distinctly remunerative. Seys demanded of his subtenant a cash rent, capons, and day's work, and in addition insisted that he discharge all chief rents and other obligations falling on Seys in respect of the property.[25]

The artificially neat division of tenures into the categories given above should not be allowed to conceal the confusion and overlapping that often existed in practice. Acquisition, encroachment, exchange, consolidation, and enclosure were known among all ranks of the population except the very lowest, but they were obviously commonest among the most powerful. A member of the gentry might be simultaneously a manorial lord, freeholder, leaseholder, and customary tenant, with his interests scattered over half-a-dozen parishes—no fewer than 30 if he were a Stradling—while he would have, in perhaps as many parishes, a small army of undertenants holding of him by an equal variety of tenures. Farming on a vastly smaller scale, a peasant farmer might nevertheless have his holdings scattered in a number of separate parcels within the same parish or one or two neighbouring ones, without necessarily holding them all on the same conditions of tenure. Out of 82 tenants at Newton Nottage in the seventeenth century, nearly half held their land in three or more separate quillets, and at Llancadle in 1622 there was one tenant who held some 40 acres in 21 scattered parcels. But changes had long been in the offing, and for the most part they worked in the interests of the bigger and wealthier men.[26]

ii.

CHANGES OF THE CENTURY FROM 1536 TO 1642

CLIMATE, HARVESTS, AND PRICES

Hitherto, much of our discussion has necessarily given the impression of a static and unchanging society. Of course, there was much that could not change; in neither this nor any other century could the basic facts of climate, contour, and soil, which set such close limits to the economic possibilities of pre-industrial society, be fundamentally altered. Some marginal change in climate there does, however, appear to have been. Climatic conditions seem to have deteriorated all over western Europe during the latter half of the sixteenth century and became perceptibly cooler and wetter. This must have contributed to the worsening of harvests, which fluctuated a good deal over the period. About one really bad harvest in six could be expected on an average; but, because of the meagre crop yields of about 1 : 3 or 4, much of what should have been kept as seed corn had to be eaten in a year of poor harvest, leaving less to plant and thus creating a tendency for bad harvests to run in series. Just such a succession of bad harvests came in the early 1550s and led to the famine of 1556; there was another bad run in the 1590s, culminating in a great European famine; but probably the worst years of all were those between 1620 and 1623 and practically the whole decade of the 1630s, which may well have been among the worst eras of dearth in the whole history of England and Wales. The chief cause of bad harvests—excessive rain—tended to add to the hardships by bringing heavy mortality among livestock, thus pushing up still further the price of all foodstuffs. So, for example, the price levels of consumables are estimated to have risen from 193 in 1548 to 409 in 1557, from 396 in 1590 to 685 in 1597, and from 510 in 1629 to 707 in 1638. The effects upon a society in which so many of its members lived near or below the poverty line could be disastrous. In these black years many went close to the edge of starvation; a few may have gone over it. Many more died of disease brought on by malnutrition, as they did in the appalling influenza epidemic of 1556–8, which may well have begun in Wales, or in the decimating outbreak of plague which came hard on the heels of the shortages of 1620–3.[27]

Just how all this affected Glamorgan is difficult to tell. If parish registers had survived in larger numbers our task might have been a great deal easier. However, only the merest handful of Glamorgan registers survive from the sixteenth century. In those which have come down to us there are long gaps, with the records for many years missing, and even for those years which were covered we have no means of knowing how conscientious the clergy were in including all the entries which ought to have been there. The evidence of these registers cannot, therefore, be taken as conclusive. For what it is worth, however, it reveals no disastrous increase in mortality between about 1570 and 1640. During the difficult years from 1590 to 1596 there was a significant but not catastrophic increase in the number of burials recorded for the two parishes of Wenvoe and Pendoylan; in the former, burials rose from an average of 6.9 a year to 13.3, and in the latter from 7.2 to 12.4. Yet in the small parishes of St. Donat's and Llandough-juxta-Cowbridge the average number of burials only was recorded. Conversely, during another lean period from 1623 to 1627, the burials at St. Donat's rose from an average of 2.2 a year to 4.5, but at Wenvoe and Pendoylan for the same period they remained at almost exactly the normal yearly average. The cold statistics taken from parish registers do not tell the whole story, however. In many of the popular religious verses of Glamorgan, the *cwndidau*, the fear of hunger, disease, and death recurs with sombre insistence. Though the verse in these poems is not to be compared with Shakespeare's celebrated description of a bad harvest—generally thought to refer to the harvest crises of the 1590s—in *A Midsummer Night's Dream*, Act II, Sc. i, ll. 93–108, 111–14, in its own less accomplished but nevertheless moving way it communicates much of the sense of vulnerability which the people felt in the face of bad harvests and of the suffering they brought in their wake. 1535 was a particularly bad year and is thought to have been the subject of a poem which describes how nine months of unbroken rain alternated with nine months of parching heat. As a result, the price of bread and cheese, the common man's staple food, soared in *Bro* and *Blaenau*, with the rich hogging what food there was, and the poor having to subsist on the leavings. One of the years of Mary's reign—1557 possibly—was even grimmer; the worst year of famine anyone could remember, according to the poet. Many were desperate for sustenance, and the privations of the

Welsh were so acute as to revive in their minds rancorous animus against the English as ancient usurpers of Welsh lands.[27A]

Food shortages and high prices were not solely, or even chiefly, the results of bad harvests. Quite independently of the acute short-term crises provoked by crop failures and animal mortality there appears to have been a general long-term rise in prices throughout England and Wales from about the second decade of the sixteenth century to the eve of the Civil Wars. The statistics compiled by economic historians for sixteenth-century price levels must be used with due caution, as they themselves are the first to warn us; but on present evidence it seems likely that, following a long period of stable prices during the fifteenth century, inflation began c. 1510, when the level of prices is put at 103. Already by 1540 the price-index had gone up to 158, and over the next century it had quadrupled, reaching 607 by 1639. It had not risen in a smooth, steady movement. There had been two periods of particularly convulsive upward leaps; the one during the 1540s and '50s and the other during the 1590s, when in each case the combination of heavy government expenditure on wars and the pressure of bad harvests had pushed prices up drastically. Even when the short-term crisis had subsided and prices had fallen again, they remained at a higher level than they had reached before the crisis, and in general continued their upward movement. By the 1630s, in a decade of unusually heavy pressure, the price-index had climbed to unprecedentedly high levels, reaching 707 in 1638.[28]

The rise in levels as between one commodity and another was uneven. Grain prices rose from an index of 154 in 1540 to 569 in 1639, while that of wool only doubled from 190 (in 1540) to 371 (1639); cattle prices quadrupled from 152 (1540) to 622 (1639), but sheep prices trebled from 190 (1540) to 577 (1639); timber prices rose from 105 (1540) to 510 (1639), but the industrial index moved only from 110 (1530-9) to 281 (1630-9). Differences in the levels and movements of prices between one region and another must also have been considerable; but, unfortunately, as far as Glamorgan is concerned insufficient data are available to enable us to measure their importance. However, when we recall how much more closely Glamorgan was responding to wider market conditions, or the general character of economic development in the county during the period, it is difficult to suppose that conditions there differed very widely from the five-to-six-fold increase in prices observed in parts of England between the accession of Henry VIII and the Civil Wars. Nor is it likely that the relative levels of wage-rates and purchasing power were far out of line. Between the decade 1510-19 and that of 1630-39 the index level of an agricultural labourer's wages had nearly trebled, moving from 101 to 287; but during the same interval the 'cost-of-living index' had jumped from 114 to 609, so that the labourer's purchasing power had fallen from 89 to 47. In short, his 'real' wages had been cut by a half, and so had those of a building craftsman, for whose wages similar data are available.[29]

The severity of inflation was unmistakable; it was unquestionably the most rapid and painful rise in prices experienced in this country before the twentieth century, and it was all the more grievously felt because it followed a long period of stable prices. A completely satisfying explanation of the causes for it is not available, and perhaps never will be, because all the data needed for the purpose simply do not survive. But in the light of the evidence at present available to scholars it is suggested that the most important cause of inflation was the rise in population and the consequent growth of demand. Other contributory factors were the inflationary effects of the debasement of the coinage in the 1540s, heavy government expenditure on war in the 1540s and 1590s, the influx of Spanish silver from the New World, the expansion of credit facilities, and Reformation changes which led to the melting of much silver plate and the end of investment in non-productive activities like church-building, chantries, or post-funerary masses. Whatever the exact causes of the price-rise may have been, its effects were all too plain and readily recognizable to contemporaries and constituted for them perhaps the most inescapable fact of economic life.[30]

Inflation turned a painful screw on all men and, whatever their social degree, there were none who were oblivious of its squeeze. Some felt it more sorely than others, nonetheless. The paupers, urban labourers, and agrarian labourers who grew little or none of their own food experienced it most sharply of all. Small farmers and cottage-labourers, who could not produce enough for all their needs and were in danger of losing their pitiful holdings, were not much better off. The most substantial husbandmen and yeomen had to pit all their wits against rising prices; and not even the gentry could be indifferent, especially in an age which acquainted them with a greatly enlarged range of new luxuries that quickly became regarded as necessities. But inflation brought new opportunities as well as hardship in its train. The stimulus of growing demand, soaring prices, and mounting land values raised a tempting prospect of attractive profits and advancement for those who had the energy and initiative to seize them. Enterprise and hard work were not confined to one social degree, nor were ill-luck, sloth and mismanagement; and men of all ranks moved downward to poverty as well as upward to affluence. All the same, the dice were much more heavily loaded in favour of some than of others. Gentlemen who had the power to change tenants' tenures and raise their rents and fines, to exploit the resources of demesne and estate to the full, and to capitalize on influence and office; freeholders, yeomen, and the bigger tenant farmers, who could keep their overheads down and gear production to the needs of the most profitable markets; and all those who had the skill and the capital to invest in more land and better techniques; to these was given a flying start in the race against prices. They reacted to inflation in a variety of ways: individuals became harder and more grasping under economic pressures, or so contemporaries alleged; more land was brought under effective use; crops, livestock, and other agricultural products were more intensively produced by specialization and improved methods; holdings were enlarged and enclosed, mainly at the expense of the poorer peasants; among all classes there was an almost inappeasable land-hunger; old estates were enlarged and new ones rose and flourished; all the resources of the land, including non-agrarian ones, were fostered. Each of these characteristic reactions will be examined in more detail in what follows.

Of the spirit of the age as it affected the majority we can know little. The nearest we come to gaining some insight into it is in the popular religious poems, the *cwndidau* (*ante*, III, 526–33). The authors of these poems had no love for most of what they saw in their own society. Over and over again they depict a harsh, greedy, acquisitive world in which men were insatiable and unrestrained in their cupidity for wealth, land, possessions, luxuries, imposing houses, and fine clothing—'these are our gods', complained Hopcyn Twm Phylip, 'and what poor ones they are!' Greed for gain had become the mainspring of human life, according to Ieuan ap Rhys, and just as Judas had sold Christ for lucre, so now all men with authority—bishops, sheriffs, bailiffs, lawyers—were prepared to serve any man's turn for money; even the common people 'took pains to labour with the bad against the good for some trifling amount of gain'. True charity was gone from the world, sighed Thomas Llywelyn, and in its place pride, avarice, hypocrisy, and self-seeking were enthroned. Some of the poets were not surprised that there should so often be bad harvests, hard times, high prices, and food shortages: these 'are portents for us that our sins are grievous; famine has come into the world and the grain crop fails; it is our sins which are the cause', warned Harri Brydydd Bach. When these hardships befell a community it was the poor who suffered most, said the poets. To the plight of the pauper, men were blind, and to his pleas unheeding, 'conscience went to the hedge; a penniless, needy and starving pauper got no welcome but was sent away bare-backed'. A similar lack of pity to the beggar Lazarus and the dire fate that it brought to Dives were held up by the poets as an awful warning to the hard-faced men of their own age. In their own simpler and more unsophisticated way the *cwndidwyr* of Glamorgan were echoing the criticisms and concern of the pamphlets and sermons of the Commonwealth men in England. However, we have to be on our guard against accepting too uncritically their portrait of a society unrelievedly grasping and devoid of compassion. Behind the sixteenth-century *cwndid* lay a long medieval moralistic tradition of fiercely denouncing, in bardically rhetorical vein, corrupt officials and sinful obsession with the pleasures and profits of earthly existence (*ante*, III, 154–5, 512–15). This could be merged with a bardic motif of a very different kind, that of attacking the greed of a low-bred 'miser' unwilling to give as freely as any gentleman worthy of the name should. Moreover, these popular poems survive in bulk for the first time only from the sixteenth century and may give a distorted picture of that age as compared with an earlier one. Even so, the way these notes were persistently sounded and the frequency with which they were reiterated suggest that they voiced an underlying reality which cannot be ignored.[31]

Intensified and Commercialized Farming

It is not only poetic evidence which points to an intensified and more energetic search for new economic opportunities. An unmistakable symptom was the bringing into use of additional land. Much land had been abandoned in the later Middle Ages as a result of economic decline, falling population, and rebellion; and signs of this earlier decay were still visible to Leland's discerning eye in 1536–9, especially in the market towns (*ante*, III, 350–60). When demand revived again in the sixteenth century there was no shortage of possibilities for taking up old land and new. In most parts of the county, lowland as well as upland, there was a reserve of neglected land, waste, heath, and woodland that could be brought into more productive use. The lordship of Ogmore affords an unusually well-documented illustration of the way in which an area hard hit by the disasters of the later Middle Ages, where cultivation was at a low ebb in the first half of the fifteenth century (*ante*, III, 302–4), experienced a marked revival. Surveys of the group of six manors of Pittcoed, Southerndown, Sutton, St. Bride's, Wick and Broughton, and Northdown, taken in 1429, 1502, 1615, and 1637 tell an interesting story. In 1429 there were only 420 acres of customary land rented to 30 tenants; by 1502 there had already been a remarkable recovery to 697 acres and 42 tenants; comparable figures for 1615 were 848 acres and 73 tenants; and in 1637 they were up to 862 and 78 respectively. Other surveys, especially of upland lordships like Senghennydd and Miskin, show marked encroachments on wastes and commons. In the 10 years before 1623, 260 acres had been encroached on and enclosed from the wastes and demesnes of Miskin alone. Very often they were undertaken surreptitiously without the lord's permission. The rights of both lords and tenants might suffer as a consequence of these illicit encroachments, and it might be in the best interests of both to ensure that they were recorded in the surveys.[32]

But manorial surveys could be far from telling the whole truth about old and new land brought under occupation by tenants, who sometimes had the strongest reasons for not wanting the real state of affairs brought to light. In Gower the earls of Worcester became convinced that they had suffered serious losses at the hands of their tenants. A survey of the whole lordship was taken in 1583 by a powerful commission set up by William, third earl of Worcester, and headed by Edward, Lord Herbert. It failed to bring all the facts to light, as surveys frequently did, for the very good reason that members of the jury of presentment used for the survey were themselves parties to the abuses. In 1590, accordingly, the fourth earl, Edward, instituted an immensely long and complex Chancery suit against his tenants, in the course of which he complained he had lost no less than 3,000 acres by tenants' encroachments. This was, without doubt, an exaggeration; but equally there is no doubt that he had been deprived of large acreages, and he gives a plausible explanation of the ways in which this could have been brought about. Much of the waste within his lordship was known by general place-names covering large areas in which some of his tenants held small tenements. When they intended to encroach upon some of the earl's wastes 'they would dig furze and turf beforehand from the place which they intended to enclose, saying that it was appurtenant to their tenements. After some time, with the collusion of negligent officers who were themselves tenants and parties to these practices, the tenants encroached the lands concerned.' Those accused of being involved in these encroachments were said by the earl to be 1,000 in number and to have ranged from small tenants to one of the most powerful men in the county, Sir William Herbert of Swansea, against whom the earl cherished a particular animus even though he was the grandson of Sir George Herbert, a former steward of the lordship. The earl of Worcester was not the only absentee landlord who believed himself to be defrauded in this way. The earl of Pembroke suffered losses, and so did Lord St. John, who declared himself the victim of 'concealments and encroachments' connived at by corrupt officers (below, pp. 33–4). The lengthy and complex litigation over the burrows of Merthyr Mawr between Sir Edward Stradling and his adversaries illustrates to what lengths of ingenuity and unscrupulousness men might go to acquire economic advantage for themselves when, as in this case, the rightful owners had been somewhat lax in maintaining their rights over waste and common. Extra land might also be brought into use for farming for the first time as the result of extensive timber-felling for industrial fuel. The forest of Talyfan had become 'a fair and large sheep leaze' by 1596, after much of the timber had been felled for iron-working.[33]

Taking in new or formerly neglected land was important, but using land more intensively and effectively was even more significant. As population increased, if the growing needs of townsfolk were to be met and the extra mouths in every country parish were to be fed, then the soil had to be more fruitfully cultivated and more livestock raised. To this end there was plenty of helpful literature available for those who could buy and read books. Master Fitzherbert's *Book of Husbandry*, Thomas Tusser's *Five Hundred Points of Good Husbandry*, and Barnaby Googe's *Four Books of Husbandry*, were only the most popular of many handbooks on improved agricultural methods. In Welsh there were translations of

Walter of Henley's popular medieval treatise and Sir John Price's useful hints in *Yn y Llyfr Hwn* (1547). We cannot tell how many Glamorgan readers there were for such works, nor do we know whether or not there were Glamorgan gentlemen who made such rigorous observations of agricultural practice and such meticulous assessments of the profits of husbandry as George Owen of Pembrokeshire, though the Mansels certainly kept careful accounts which have survived. But among a gentry so intellectually alert, alive, and practical in other respects (below, pp. 113–21), it would be astonishing if there were none who kept themselves informed of the best contemporary agricultural practice and theory. In any case, whether or not they kept abreast of theory, the accumulated wisdom of many generations had given them a working knowledge of what was best for their lands. What mattered most was the will, capital, and incentive to step up yields.[34]

No one doubted that to bear better crops land had to be kept in good heart with plenty of humus and improved, when necessary, with the use of lime, marl, and other fertilizers. Lime was already well-known and easily obtainable in Glamorgan. Some manorial tenants had long enjoyed the same rights as those of Oxwich, Nicholaston, or Penrice 'to dig limestones . . . and to burn lime for their own use as often as they had occasion'. Furthermore, a more efficient fuel for burning the lime in the kilns was at hand as larger supplies of coal were mined in the county. Lime was being used in greater quantities even in the *Blaenau* where, 'since the knowledge or use of liming, there groweth more plenty of grain'. From well-endowed Gower, lime was shipped by lighters to the less fortunate places along the shores of Glamorgan and Carmarthenshire and even to the West Country. From Oystermouth quarries it was sent across Swansea Bay to Neath and the opposite shore, ultimately destined for the 'small, sloping fields, damp, shaded, and often acid-soiled' in the foothills of the *Blaenau*. Gower farmers mixed lime with earth to form what they called marl; otherwise there seems no evidence of the widely-recommended marl, though it is unlikely that Glamorgan farmers were ignorant of its valuable properties. Near the sea-coast seaweed was highly prized and widely used as a fertilizer. Intensified crop production had to be matched by rearing a greater number of livestock. When it came to raising more and better animals Glamorgan men had long known the value of selective breeding. Testimony to the high reputation of their milch-kine is that in 1578 Sir John Perrott, one of the biggest land-owners in south Pembrokeshire, perhaps the most progressive farming region in Wales, should solicit Sir Edward Stradling's help in buying dairy stock in Glamorgan.[35]

To obtain the maximum profits in return for their efforts producers had to become increasingly commercial in their outlook and to specialize in those commodities they were best-fitted to produce, in order to meet the demands of the wider market as well as local needs. Down to the

1620s, at least, there was a lively and expanding market at home in the county and further afield in Bristol and the West of England, France, and Ireland, to all of which Glamorgan had convenient access by sea, indispensable when land transport was so primitive. Corn, dairy produce, meat, hides, and wool were obviously the products in which the county was well qualified to specialize. Corn supplies were customarily more than adequate for its own needs, though there might always be the bad year like 1585, when there were complaints about the excessive number of Glamorgan corn-dealers going into Somerset and endangering supplies and prices there—every region was always acutely sensitive to any threat to its corn supplies. A very good market for Glamorgan corn was Bristol, and Tewkesbury and Gloucester were also willing to buy it. Some small quantities went to France, and during the wars in Ireland at the end of Elizabeth's reign the county was called upon to supply the troops there with corn and butter. Butter and cheese were a particularly important specialism. Along with Suffolk and the Whitby-Stockton area, Glamorgan was one of the three biggest butter-and-cheese producing regions in the kingdom, having a large and flourishing export trade. With meat, too, in brisk demand in Bristol and the West of England, Glamorgan cattle and sheep were quickly and easily shipped in large numbers to West Country fairs and markets. The other typical by-products of mixed and pastoral farming—hides and wool—found valuable outlets within local leather and woollen industries as well as among buyers outside. Sheep may well have become less valuable than cattle because wool prices, especially for some of the rather coarser Welsh wools, failed to rise as high over the century as those of other agricultural products (for a more detailed treatment of trade and exports, below, pp. 58–68).[36]

ENGROSSMENT AND ENCLOSURE

Commercial and specialized farming put a premium on large holdings. In the absence of a striking break-through in farming techniques the easiest way to get bigger surpluses was by taking in more land. The Mansels farmed 473 acres of arable, 142 acres of meadow, 190 acres of pasture, and 160 acres of sheep-walks in their profitable venture at Margam and Hafod-y-porth. At Y Fan, when Thomas Lewis died in 1595, he left 200 acres of arable, 80 acres of meadow, 60 acres of pasture, and 40 acres of woodland. On the demesnes of Boverton Edward Van farmed 400 acres. In the upland lordships of Glamorgan there was an unmistakable movement towards engrossing. At Ynysafan in Afan Wallia, though the number of freehold tenements remained unchanged at 41 between 1601 and 1631, the number of freeholders dropped from 18 to 9. Similarly at Neath Citra, whereas in 1611 there were 39 freeholders in possession of 60 tenements, by 1628 their number had fallen to 21, and by 1654 to 16; and parallel circumstances existed in other lordships. A handful of powerful freeholders, or even a single one, were usually responsible for the engrossing. At Ynysafan the man concerned was Lewis Thomas, who was also extremely active in the same fashion in Glynrhondda; and at Neath Citra it was Bussy Mansel, who held 28½ freehold tenements himself by 1654, in addition to 8 copyholds and 4 tenancies-at-will. Such purchasers tried to acquire adjacent tenements wherever possible in order to consolidate their holdings. In the lowland manors similar processes were taking place, not only by purchase or exchange of freehold lands but also by reorganizing demesnes and, to a lesser extent, customary lands for the benefit of the bigger leaseholders. In Pentyrch the Mathews of Castell-y-mynach had been only one family of freeholders among a number of others for most of the sixteenth century; but between the years 1595 and 1608 the aggressive acquisitions of Thomas Mathew ('Mathew Tew') gave them complete supremacy. He whittled down the number of other freeholders by half, got hold of much of the copyhold land, and rented all the demesne, much of which was subsequently converted into the family's freehold possession. The same sort of story is told by the Boverton rental of 1614. It reveals that while there were 87 freeholds within the manor the bulk of the land was held by fewer than 10 tenants, all of whom belonged to the local families of gentry, leaving over four-fifths of the tenantry in possession only of cottages and a few acres of freehold. At the same time, five out of 95 customary tenants held 28.5 per cent of the manor's customary land. This customary land had distinct advantages attaching to it; the rent per acre was fixed, so were the fines, and lands could be sublet without licence for up to 99 years. In Gower many smaller men had benefited by engrossing demesne or customary land to build up their holdings to a level of from 15–25 acres.[37]

Engrossment and consolidation became most effective if accompanied by enclosure, by means of hedging or ditching. All the contemporary authors on agriculture were agreed that enclosures improved the value of land and increased the chances of its being better managed. Only after enclosing could a farmer be sure of being able fully to control his resources in his own interest and manage crops and livestock free from hindrance by lazier or less efficient neighbours. Within his enclosed lands the cultivator could decide what crops they were best fitted for, could plough more easily and fertilize less wastefully. The livestock farmer could separate the vigorous from the weakly animals and breed selectively with greater hopes of success. Enclosures were changing the face of lowland Glamorgan in Tudor times, as Rice Merrick noted in a well-known passage. Whereas it had been 'champion and open country, without great store of enclosures', old men said that their forefathers told them that great part of th'enclosures was made in their days'. Merrick's depiction of the rapid spread of enclosures in the sixteenth century has been splendidly illustrated in detail by the researches of the late Ieuan Jeffreys-Jones. He has shown that enclosures began on the manorial demesnes, some of which Professor William Rees traced as having been laid down to pasture in the mid-fourteenth century. The movement towards enclosure of demesnes was encouraged still further by the tendency to farm them out in large blocks, though less markedly in Glamorgan than in Monmouthshire.[38]

Freehold land, like demesnes, was susceptible to enclosure because of the absence of any restrictions on methods of cultivating it and because of greater security of tenure, though enclosure of freeholds in the uplands may have been retarded by the Welsh practice of *cyfran*, or partible inheritance. Customary land on the open fields of the manor was, by its very nature, more resistant to enclosure. Vestiges of the open fields, with their unenclosed landsets or strips, survived well into the seventeenth century and beyond. Even in the former open fields, however, enclosures had made remarkable progress, as Merrick's comments indicate. Manorial plans of the manors of Llancadle, Fonmon, and Barry survive from the year 1622 and, on the basis of their evidence, Ieuan Jeffreys-Jones was able to show how far the process of enclosure had proceeded. Although open fields survived in all three they had been modified almost out of existence by the consolidation of strips which had gone on apace and had been followed by the splitting up of the open field into enclosed holdings or closes. At Llancadle 85.5 per cent of the cultivated land of the manor was enclosed into 162 closes extending over 486 acres and held by 22 tenants; but the valuable meadows were still held in common. At Fonmon the meadow was completely enclosed, along with 92.5 per cent of the arable land, while at Barry enclosure was virtually complete, with 90 closes covering an area of 368 acres. At Penmark, in the same group of manors, no map is known to have survived, but something like 90–95 per cent of the land was enclosed. At Coety Anglia in 1631 the process was far less advanced. Only 289 acres of arable land out of 1,207 acres of freehold land, together with 289 acres of arable and 60 acres of meadow out of the 600 acres of customary land, had been enclosed. Even here, the difference may be more apparent than real, because the acreage of freehold land was very imprecisely defined.[39]

Even the commons had been enclosed in some of the manors of the Vale, including Llancadle, Fonmon, Barry, Sully, and Dinas Powys. Enclosure of the commons, which created such a furore in parts of Tudor England, evoked little protest in Wales. Not because pasture was of less consequence in Wales; there, as in England, a great many holdings would have been too small to have been viable if there had been no rights of common pasture attaching to them. Added to which, the more intensively arable was cultivated, the more humus it needed to maintain its fertility, and that meant more livestock. If a holding was at an unhandy distance from common pasture, as was John Grove's in Paviland, the tenant had to reduce the area cropped by him, even though, like John Grove, he might be the biggest copyholder in the area. On the occasions when common rights were seriously threatened in Glamorgan the predictable riots and protests were forthcoming. In a dispute between the tenants of Talyfan and their lord, Anthony Mansel, they went to the Court of Requests and claimed that they were no longer able to maintain themselves as the result of Mansel's enclosure of 120 acres at Tir Porthmon. At Milwood near Swansea in 1571, at Llandeilo Tal-y-bont in 1578 and 1584, and at Cadoxton-juxta-Neath in 1583, protests went beyond words, and hedges were thrown down. At Llandeilo Tal-y-bont amid 'great rejoicing and triumphing' a substantial band of yeomen declared with 'great and loud voices' that they would not desist as long as 'one hedge or mound were there standing, growing or being'. Between 1575 and 1579 there was serious friction between the tenants of Wick and those of Southerndown and St. Bride's over common rights in the duchy of Lancaster manors, and more discord in the same manors in the 1590s, when this time it was the tenants of St. Bride's and Southerndown who strongly resented the attempts at enclosures there. These troubles in Glamorgan were small beer compared with those in the neighbouring counties of Monmouthshire and Carmarthenshire. Such enclosures as there were may have caused less upheaval because of the relative abundance of common pasture in the county—there were still 107,200 acres of unenclosed commons as late as 1795—and because enclosures had taken place by mutual consent and agreement. Steps had to be taken, however, to avert a different kind of threat to the commons by overstocking them with strangers' cattle. It became customary in a number of manors to introduce 'stinting', i.e. to control the number of beasts being pastured on the commons. This was achieved at some places by restricting rights of grazing to tenants and residents only. At Llanharry they restricted the number of cattle each tenant was allowed in proportion to the value of his holding, and at Hafod-y-porth and Pyle tenants were made to pay for common rights of grazing.[40]

All the developments so far discussed point to the existence of a deep and compulsive craving for land and incessant competition for it, in all parts of Glamorgan. Land-hunger was a universal characteristic of the age in the whole of England and Wales. 'Do not all strive to enjoy the land?', asked Gerrard Winstanley, 'The gentry strive for land, the clergy strive for land, the common people strive for land; and buying and selling is an art whereby people endeavour to cheat one another of the land.' Among even the humblest tenants there might be keen rivalry for agricultural holdings. From nearby Pembrokeshire, a county similar to Glamorgan in many ways, George Owen commented that 'the world is so altered with the poor tenant that he standeth so in bodily fear of his greedy neighbour, that two or three years ere his lease end he must bow to his lord for a new lease and must pinch it out many years before to heap money together'. Fines and rents were going up steeply, not only because of inflation or because landlords were anxious to force them up, but also because tenants, in the scramble for holdings, were offering sums higher than they could readily afford. How much alternative had they in a peasant society where agricultural and industrial labourers were already over-plentiful? They clung tenaciously on, yet many of them were doomed to lose the struggle. Apart from all the vicissitudes of personal deficiencies or domestic misfortune, of sickness or premature death, to which the poor were always most prone in an age of widespread disease and low life-expectation, it was they who suffered most from the rise of prices and were least able to take advantage of it. They had least to offer for stepped-up rents and increased fines, were nearest the margin of financial indebtedness and insolvency which all the minor courts so frequently record, and were most at the mercy of pressures from economic forces and powerful neighbours. How many of them were able to retain their holdings or to cling on as subtenants of bigger men who acquired them, it is impossible to say, but one suspects that a number must have fallen into the ranks of the labourers and paupers. Higher up the scale, among freeholders and less impoverished husbandmen, the search for extra land was no less keen and has left its traces in the hundreds of deeds which have come down from this age to record innumerable small transactions for the purchase, lease, mortgage, and exchange of land. One particularly interesting indicator is the increasing care with which the terms of marriage settlements entered into by all classes of society were recorded.[41]

THE GROWTH OF ESTATES

In the free-for-all in land it was the gentry and yeomen who participated from positions of strength. They were the ones with the secure economic base, the knowledge, influence, and money; and it was they who made the most striking gains. Land was for them not only a valuable material investment but also a source of social power and prestige. No one who has any acquaintance with the records or the material remains of this age can fail to recognize as one of its salient characteristics the rise of gentry estates, great and small. The process of accumulation had begun for many families in the fifteenth century and was well under way when the first Tudor sat on the throne. The sixteenth century and the early Stuart era were the most creative phase, nevertheless; this was when incentives were at their most impelling and opportunities most numerous.

The old and well-tried expedients for accumulating land were still much in evidence: purchase, lease, exchange, and marriage. When it came to making purchases in a land market that had become more fluid and expensive, it was men with the longest purses who could snap up the best opportunities. They, too, could most confidently enter the keener and more prevalent competition to bargain for the growing number of leases available from landlords letting lands in larger units and at higher rates. Marriage to an heiress was one of the oldest and most successful methods of acquiring an estate and founding a family. But a suitor who came empty-handed had little to hope for; only those who brought wealth, rank, or influence, better still all three, could hope to acquire heiresses in marriage. It was an art at which the Herberts were unusually adept; the cadet members of that thrustful and prolific clan showed what G. T. Clark called 'a more than Austrian success in wedding heiresses and establishing themselves in the seats of the older gentry'. The most famous heiress in Tudor Glamorgan was Barbara, heiress to the Gamages of Coety, through whom Robert Sidney gained a valuable stake in the county (below, pp. 183–6). Other gentry families founded largely on the success of a good marriage were the Loughors of Tythegston, the Vaughans of Dunraven, the Morgans of Ruperra, and the Mansels of Briton Ferry.[42]

Tudor policies were newer factors assisting the process of estate-building. The Act of Union got rid of *cyfran* and so made it easier to acquire land formerly held under Welsh tenure and to bequeath it undivided. Not that *cyfran* had ever been much of a hindrance to ambitious families even before Union, though its survival among some smaller freeholders despite the Act could have served to make their tenements more unviable and vulnerable to the pressure of powerful engrossers. Union also entrusted offices of local justice and administration to the native gentry and put them in a situation of influence and advantage over lesser men. Reformation changes released an immense amount of former ecclesiastical possessions onto the market for lease and for sale; but it was only the most successful of the gentry who had the cash, credit, or connexions to be able to afford to invest in this property (below, pp. 209–10). The same was true of other crown lands. Those vast estates in Glamorgan once in Jasper Tudor's hands were very largely acquired by William, first earl of Pembroke, for his services to the crown. Royal favour was almost indispensable in the building of the biggest estates. Nearly every one of the leading Glamorgan families had at least one of their number who had served the state with distinction—a Thomas Stradling, Rice Mansel, Edward Carne, John Herbert, or David Jenkins. On a smaller scale, service to a leading aristocratic family with big interests in the county might be potentially a very valuable asset. Installed in such offices, men were in a key position to acquire leases or other advantages in their own interest, sometimes to the detriment of their aristocratic patrons. One would like to know how much the Lewises of Y Fan owed to their loyal attachment to the Herbert interest throughout Elizabeth's reign. Another ladder to fortune might be remarkable success in a profession, nearly always the law in Glamorgan, followed by investment of the profits in land. Judge David Jenkins of Hensol came from old Welsh gentle stock but it was his own highly successful career as lawyer and judge that put him among the wealthiest of Glamorgan gentry in the 1640s. It was also Dr. William Aubrey's flourishing law practice that no doubt had much to do with the marriage of his second son, Thomas, to the heiress of Llantriddyd, while John Thomas Bassett of Bonvilston, from whose fortune the Llantriddyd estate largely derived, was very much a self-made lawyer. Though many of the Glamorgan gentry were interested in trade and industry their income from these sources was not the decisive factor in creating their estates, although Evan 'yr halen' (Evan 'the salt'), father of David Evans of the Great House, Neath, made a good deal of money out of the salt trade, which contributed not a little to his family's subsequent rise.[43]

To trace, even in outline, the rise of more than a handful of the most prominent families would be impracticable, so a series of rapid impressions must here suffice. The biggest estates in Glamorgan were those of the earls of Worcester and Pembroke. The ascendancy of the earls of Worcester in Glamorgan under the early Tudors had been unrivalled, and details of their rapid rise by successful marriage, relationship to the Tudors, and royal favour have already been given in an earlier volume (ante, III, 558-60). By mid-century, however, the Worcesters' position was overshadowed by that of the earl of Pembroke. His unparalleled success is the most telling demonstration of how, as a result of exceptional favour for extraordinary service, a vast estate could be created at a stroke. The grants given to the earl in 1550-1 made him 'the greatest lord that ever owned lands in Glamorgan either before or after Iestyn ap Gwrgan's time'. Reckoned by the crown to be worth £371 10s. 4d. when granted, in return for an annual payment of £100, they were worth well over £1,000 to him and his descendants in Queen Elizabeth's reign. The Herberts had been given more than half the area of the county, and no other acquisition on that scale was, or could be, made again. It was rare for any family to make its fortunes in one generation, except by a fortunate marriage or a rapid rise in a profession. The process usually extended over a number of generations, with one or two crucial turning-points.[44]

The Stradlings had been at St. Donat's since the end of the thirteenth century. In the fifteenth century a prudent marriage with the heiress of the Berkerolles family had brought the manors of St. Athan, Merthyr Mawr, and Lampha. In the sixteenth century Sir Thomas Stradling (d. 1573), capitalized on the more fluid and favourable circumstances of the middle decades of the century to advance the family's fortunes. He was active in the service of the crown and in public life, which no doubt helped him in his successful pursuit of Nash manor and other lands formerly belonging to Neath abbey in St. Bride's, Wick, and Marcross (1542) and the former Tewkesbury manor of Llantwit (1543). In 1558, by Queen Mary's favour, he acquired the reversion of the manor of Sully and, in 1573, at the very end of his life, bought part of the manor of Pen-llin. His son, Sir Edward (d. 1609), though he

[31]

D

appears to have added nothing very much to the estate, had a well-deserved reputation as a vigilant, enterprising, and prudent landlord and estate-manager.[45]

The rise of the Mansels is not dissimilar in pattern to that of the Stradlings. The first of them can be traced in Gower as early as 1310. A careful eye for the matrimonial main chance had won them a whole clutch of neighbouring manors, Scurlage, Oxwich, Penrice, Port Eynon, and Nicholaston; but they remained a relatively obscure west Gower brood. Again, it was the emergence of an able and energetic representative, taking advantage of the exceptional opportunities of those disturbed decades of the 1540s and 1550s which proved to be decisive. It was the career of the crown's loyal soldier-servant, Sir Rice Mansel (d. 1559), which gave his family their real rise to fortune. Over a period of seventeen years he bought the pick of Margam abbey's rich endowment of granges and manors (below, pp. 209–10). They put him in the front rank of the county gentry and kept his descendants there. His less gifted son, Edward (d. 1595), far from being able to extend the estate, was hard put to fend off a long and determined challenge to his undivided possession of it from relatives by one of his father's three marriages. The immensely tortuous Chancery case, arising out of a marriage settlement made by Sir Rice in 1517, was fought out in the 1570s and became a legal *cause célèbre*. Fortunately for his posterity Edward Mansel emerged successful. The next heir, Sir Thomas (d. 1631), was in a much stronger position than his father. He acquired an enormous number of small plots of land most of which he left to his grandson, Bussy, heir to his second son, Arthur. He had a penchant for investing heavily in tithe income, which formed the most significant of his additions to the main family estate, and he made a mint of money out of mortgages.[46]

Of all the leading families of Glamorgan the Lewises of Y Fan yield to none in having the most consistently successful record in acquiring land, for which they had a marvellous propensity in generation after generation. The early coups of Edward Lewis in getting hold of property in Senghennydd lordship have already been noted. It was he, too, who bought the monastic lands of Roath Keynsham and Moor Grange, moved the family home to Y Fan, and enclosed the park there. When his son, Thomas, died in 1593 he left, in addition to his capital messuage at Y Fan, his manors of Roath and Moor, valuable interests at Cefn-tre-paen in Miskin manor, and no fewer than 300 messuages, cottages and tenements in a dozen Glamorgan parishes, not to mention very large estates in Monmouthshire. He was followed by his son, Sir Edward, an indefatigable litigant and a major purchaser of land. He bought from William Herbert the manor of St. Fagan's, to which he moved the family's headquarters. His other purchases included Penmark Place and Splott from William Bawdrip, the manors and lands of the Wildgoose family in Llancarfan, Bonvilston, Wenvoe, and Sydmerstone, and Sir

George Mathew's former possessions at Corntown near Ewenni and the house and park of Radyr. The catalogue of his lands and possessions in his Inquisition Post Mortem is strikingly longer than the impressive list in his father's some thirty years previously. The Lewises had become the ranking Glamorgan family in terms of wealth, and Sir Edward was able to make the most handsome provision for all his sons [47] (below, p. 94).

To build up an estate needed good fortune as well as determination and enterprise. A failure of heirs, or a long minority, or a rapid succession of heirs at a crucial time might make all the difference to a family's success. The Mathew family of Castell-y-mynach, seemingly well-placed early in the sixteenth century, was held back until nearly the end of the century when it came into its own again with the gains of Mathew Tew (above, p. 26). Even Rice Mansel's fine estates might have been halved had his son by Anne Bridges, Philip, or the latter's son, Rice, survived to inherit the Gower estates of the family as the old knight had originally intended.[48]

THE MANAGEMENT OF ESTATES

Just as vital for successful land tenure as the acquisition of new estates was the effective management of what had already been won. Acquisition and management were inextricably linked, insofar as successful management laid the ground for fresh acquisition, and the latter was barren without the former. A large part of the recipe for efficient management lay in residence by the landowner himself and his ability to apply himself with acumen and diligence to the task of overseeing, either in person or through his agents, all activities on his own and his tenants' lands. Even temporary absence from his estates could be highly damaging, as Lady Mansel plaintively reminded Thomas Cromwell when her husband was on service in Ireland in 1535: 'as things are not done to his profit he sustains many losses', and she mournfully prophesied that unless he were allowed to return home she and her 'poor children' would be 'utterly undone'. A century later, another Lady Mansel, Jane of Briton Ferry, urged her son, Bussy, that 'you will be resolved to come and live in the country and not go abroad to consume and waste your estate and discomfort your poor friends and tenants'. To be more or less permanently absent from their Glamorgan estates, as a number of the greatest landowners were, created serious difficulties for them. 'Myself being so far off', lamented Oliver Lord St. John to Sir Edward Stradling in 1576, 'as that for want of good oversight I do sustain many damages.' The best safeguard against such losses was to be able to appoint a powerful and dependable member of the neighbouring gentry to act as steward, as St. John did with Sir Edward Stradling in 1576. Hardly less indispensable was a sound choice of the understeward on whom the burden of day-to-day responsibility must fall. He must be a man 'wise, learned and stout . . . to govern such a great number of rude and froward people

[33]

as appeareth before him at every court and leet', or else the landowner might be 'diversely abused', as St. John believed he had been 'through certain concealments and encroachments made upon my lands, as also through other disorders which have been winked at and not redressed'. It was, indeed, a question of *Quis custodiat ipsos custodes* from whose misfeasance lords and tenants alike might suffer. No Glamorgan landowners were worse done by at the hands of unjust stewards than the earls of Worcester, whose negligent and corrupt officers did permanent damage to their Gower estates. The Worcesters' kinsman, Sir George Herbert, steward from 1526 to 1560, was a tyrannical individual whose hand fell harsh and heavy on tenants (*ante*, III, 278–81); but he seems to have avoided financial arrears until the last two years of his tenure. It was his successor, Sir Edward Mansel, who proved to be the great disaster. Although he was appointed as a favour to help him out of personal adversities, he incurred arrears between the years 1562 and 1567 to the tune of £1,570 1s. 8½d., none of which was subsequently repaid. Only protracted and expensive litigation by the earl between 1590 and 1596 could partially make good the neglect of decades. Yet too much sympathy should not be expended on the earl, who was aware of Mansel's deficiencies but was unwilling to take the necessary steps to end them. Nor should we suppose that there were never any pressures on tenants from stewards and understewards. A few snatches of evidence surviving from the administration of the Sidney estates in Glamorgan by local agents suggest that they were well versed in the techniques of not-so-gentle persuasion and bargaining with tenants.[49]

To the alert and business-like estate manager a number of sources of income lay open, but they all needed careful nursing and regular attention. Among the possibilities were: direct farming; rents and fines; tithe income; mills, timber, and fisheries; industrial and mineral resources; curial income and other manorial prerogatives; tolls, markets, and fairs; and the proceeds and perquisites of office.

Direct farming was indispensable to every landowner. It provided his household with basic foodstuffs, supplemented and diversified as they were by fruit from his orchards, vegetables and herbs from his garden, venison from his deer park if he had one, conies from his warren, fish from his pond or estuary fisheries, and wildfowl and other game from the teeming woods and marshes. But his demesne, if large enough and properly managed, also enabled him to produce profitably for the market. In 1572 the Mansels were getting an income of £375 from their demesnes, and by 1638–9 an income of £976. Unfortunately, we have no comparable figures for other estates, but there is no reason to suppose that the Mansels were exceptional in anything other than the survival of their accounts.[50]

Rents and fines were usually the major source of revenue. The general tendency everywhere was for landlords to push up rents wherever they could as a hedge against inflation. This was not always easy, since the rents of freeholders and customary tenants by inheritance were protected. So landlords were obliged to recoup on such rents as they could, and to bring pressure to bear on tenants to change the nature of their tenures. Allegations of excesses on the part of landlords do exist in some court proceedings, though examples of lawsuits of this kind are not very numerous. Tenants at Boverton complained in Star Chamber in Henry VIII's reign that Rice Mansel and John Mathew were raising rents and fines 'at such exceeding prices' that the tenants were not 'able to pay the same but of necessity to leave'. Tenants of Talyfan brought Rice Mansel's son, Anthony, to the Court of Requests for having levied excessive fines, hoping thereby to make them 'weary of the occupation' of their tenancies. There are other similar examples but not many. Landlords were doubtless helped by the ardent competition for holdings and the reluctance of tenants to go to court except when *in extremis*, but the absence of litigation also suggests that most rents were being raised by processes within the law.[51]

Documenting the nature and extent of the movement in rent is not easy in relation to the estates of the Herberts and the Mansels; for the others it is virtually impossible. The following table on page 36 gives some indication of the movement of rents on the Herbert estates.[52]

The figures yield a fairly clear overall picture of the upward movement of rent, with the rental of 1570 recording a total of £449 19s. 3¾d. for these manors and lordships and that of 1631 £1,169 9s. 9d. The rate of increase as between individual units was very uneven, as can readily be seen, ranging from a 5 per cent increase for Whitchurch between 1570 and 1631 and one of 461 per cent for Neath Ultra. In Glynrhondda there was a fairly steady increase over the period of nearly a century, and this was true of a few other manors between 1570 and 1631. In Miskin and Miskin Forest, on the other hand, there was a very big jump in the level of rents between 1595-96 and 1631. The same holds good for Neath Ultra, Neath Citra, Ruthin, Llantrisant Borough, Senghennydd Supra, and Pentyrch and Clun; all of them, it may be noted, were in upland country or areas bordering upon it, and were situated in some of those hundreds of the county where population seems to have shown the fastest rate of growth during the period (below, pp. 75-6). However, some lowland manors—Cosmeston, Michaelston, and Llantwit Raleigh—also showed a sharp increase between 1595-6 and 1631. It was leasehold rents which were chiefly responsible for the rise. No significant increase could be made in freehold rents or in the rents of customary lands by inheritance; but there were some startling increases in leasehold revenue in both hill and lowland estates. In Miskin it jumped from £18 19s. 10d. in 1570 to £114 7s. 0d. in 1631, and from £41 14s. 10d. to £156 17s. 2d. at Boverton and Llantwit in the same period, thus more than keeping pace with inflation. These same years witnessed persistent pressure on copyholders, tenants-at-will, and

GLAMORGAN

THE EARL OF PEMBROKE'S RENTS IN SOME
GLAMORGAN LORDSHIPS AND MANORS, 1540–1631

Manor/Lordship	1540			1570			1588–9			1595–6			1631			Percentage increase between 1570 & 1631
	£	s.	d.	£	s.	d.	£	s.	d.	£	s.	d.	£	s.	d.	
Senghennydd Supra				39	14	10	35	18	3½	38	3	0	80	5	9½	102
Senghennydd Subtus				26	19	4	29	9	6	29	11	9	32	18	4	23
Senghennydd Forest				2	3	4	2	0	0	4	0	0	7	4	0	235
Caerphilly Burgus	81	4	9½	1	7	0	3	8	7	3	19	7	3	19	7	192
Whitchurch				12	6	5¼	12	14	8¼	12	17	3	12	18	8¼	5
Rudry				5	1	7½	4	11	7½	4	17	4½	12	11	3½	148
Miskin	32	10	1	37	1	2½	54	13	7	44	2	5	158	18	4	328
Miskin Forest	3	8	0	9	0	0	10	16	0	18	16	8	38	17	8	332
Glynrhondda	10	11	3	29	2	7½	38	1	9	45	13	8½	57	5	2	97
Cosmeston				11	14	0	18	19	11	19	19	11	55	10	11	375
Walterston				13	5	10	12	18	2	13	5	10	19	1	10	43
Leckwith				26	9	11½	27	3	6	30	0	0	39	15	3	50
Michaelston				8	19	9	8	7	7	8	0	2½	24	6	5	170
St. George's				42	13	8	54	18	5	50	5	6	60	6	7	41
St. Nicholas				16	12	11½	18	1	3½	21	13	1½	29	0	2½	75
Boverton & Llantwit				86	0	7½	149	11	3¾	149	11	3¾	211	3	1¼	145
Spittle				7	2	4	8	10	4	9	4	4	15	9	4	117
Newton Nottage				5	9	6	5	19	11¾	7	11	5½	9	13	1	77
Llantrisant Burgus				2	11	6	3	2	1	3	12	6	12	5	5	380
Caerau				4	1	8½	4	0	0½	4	1	8½	7	2	11	75
Llantwit Raleigh				8	10	9½	9	14	7½	12	5	3½	21	1	5	148
Kenfig				8	18	5½	8	12	3¾	9	6	9¾	15	1	4¾	70
Neath Ultra				19	13	7½	22	7	5½	41	18	2	110	7	8½	461
Neath Citra				5	7	1½	5	5	7½	6	13	11½	27	1	1	406
Ruthin				11	2	6½	13	6	8½	14	5	2½	34	9	5½	210
Pentyrch				4	3	11½	10	7	7½	10	9	3	72	14	10	156
Clun				24	4	7	30	13	11	31	19	5				
TOTAL				449	19	3¾	591	14	11	646	5	7	1169	9	9	160

annual tenants to change to leasehold tenure, and at Senghennydd, Miskin and Whitchurch, these older categories of tenant had disappeared altogether by 1631. The process may not have been due entirely to landlord pressure. Tenants could hope to gain from the greater certainty and legal security which leasehold tenure conferred. Landlords, however, stood to benefit even more, for at each new letting the rent could be fixed in accordance with the progress of inflation, the state of the market, and the keenness of competition. The measure of increment that a landlord could derive can be gauged from the fact that in Senghennydd in 1631 some 350 freehold tenements produced between them an annual revenue of no more than £53 16s. 10½d., while 56 leasehold tenements yielded £82, or half as much again. Pushing up copyhold rents, too, was a major factor in augmenting revenue on other Herbert manors. At Walterston, for instance, they rose from £6 15s. 0d. in 1570 to £17 11s. 10d. by 1631, at St. Nicholas from £10 7s. 0d. to £18 2s. 11d., and at St. George's from £18 18s. 11d. to £37 2s. 11d.

The Mansels' records shed further light on rents. On their Gower lands in the first half of the sixteenth century there was a slow but steady increase in rents down to 1559, the total income increasing from £87 11s. 9d. in 1510 to £105 16s. 9d. in 1534-9, and £106 1s. 4d. in 1559, though as this last figure is taken from an Inquisition Post Mortem it may well be an underestimate. Between 1559 and 1632 there was a drastic upward leap, outpacing inflation, from £106 to £400. Rises on individual manors diverged widely, ranging from a 50 per cent increase at Penrice through 150 per cent at Port Eynon and 400 per cent at Oxwich to no less than 1,100 per cent at Scurlage. As the figure for Scurlage was made up entirely of demesne rents it suggests that it was this kind of rent that had contributed most to the general increase. It seems very likely that the main increases in Gower, as in other parts of Glamorgan, did not come until the end of the sixteenth century or the early part of the seventeenth century. Figures for the Mansels' Margam estates are more scanty, but they show an even bigger overall increase from £109 2s. 7d. in mid-century to £1,098 9s. 8½d. in 1632, though here, too, the increases are extraordinarily unevenly divided as between individual manors. Here, also, the main increase may well not have come until late in the sixteenth century or early in the seventeenth, though the scantiness of the sources makes it impossible to be certain. The pushing up of rents was accompanied by a strong drive towards extending leasehold tenure, especially of the sort that was known as *per notam* tenancy. Another particularly interesting feature of Margam policy on tenures was the unmistakable tendency to reimpose labour services and renders in kind on a limited scale. Farming as large a demesne as they did, the Mansels may well have found this a valuable device for keeping down labour and maintenance costs in an effort to make the estate more profitable.[53]

[37]

Increasing entry fines was an important adjunct of raising rents. There were limits to the powers of the lords in this respect, however. In the upland regions it was the practice not to demand fines, and in some of the lowland manors fines were fixed at so much per acre, e.g. 1*d.* an acre at Llanbleddian, or double the annual rent at Colwinston. Freeholders and customary tenants by inheritance enjoyed a large measure of protection from common law or the custom of the manor against arbitrary or unreasonable fines; but leaseholders, copyholders by lives, or tenants-at-will were much more vulnerable. It was tempting for landowners to go for money in hand in the shape of a large fine, and men of substance were at an advantage as would-be tenants in being more likely to be able to offer a relatively large sum as a fine with no significant increase in the rent. Glamorgan evidence is decidedly thin, but examination of the Mansels' estate practice between 1600 and 1632 shows that fines were certainly levied on their Gower estates during those years and produced a handsome return. A reliable estimate gives the annual rental as yielding £360 10*s.* 4*d.* and fines £1,672 3*s.* 4*d.* A similar estimate for their Margam estates in 1633 gives £801 2*s.* 5½*d.* for rents and £2,270 13*s.* 0*d.* for fines. Although the evidence for the years before 1600 is scanty, what there is suggests that the annual rental was normally supplemented by the periodic collection of entry fines. Fragments of information from elsewhere help to attest this. In the manor of Llystalybont the annual rent totalled £35 2*s.* 0*d.* as compared with £253 income from fines. Even in the upland areas entry fines were not unknown by the beginning of the seventeenth century, though in Miskin in 1630 they amounted to only £50 16*s.* 8*d.* as compared with rent of £144 2*s.* 4*d.* Many of the fines levied at the higher levels must have been too large to have been paid in a single instalment and must have been spread over a period of years, for all practical purposes not unlike an additional rent.[54]

MISCELLANEOUS SOURCES OF INCOME

In an age of rising prices for agrarian products, control of tithe could be nearly as profitable as demesne farming, especially in parishes that were conveniently close to the gentry's houses for tithe collection to be relatively easy and inexpensive. Many of the Glamorgan land-owners became lay impropriators of tithe on a big scale after the dissolution of the monasteries, and some of the most favoured and productive parishes came into their hands (below, pp. 227–8). Other tithes were leased by them for long terms at favourable rents. The potentially huge increment deriving from such tithes is illustrated by the struggle between the chapter of Llandaff and tithe lessees to be discussed later (below, pp. 243–5). Some inkling of the value of tithes as an investment may also be gleaned from the eagerness of that shrewd man of business and mortgagor, Sir Thomas Mansel, to put his money into them. In 1613 he acquired additional interests in the tithes of Laleston, Newcastle, and Tythegston; in 1623 the tithes which Robert, earl of Leicester, had at Pen-y-fai, Cwrt Colman, Cefn Cribwr, Horgrove and Treannell came Sir Thomas's way, as well as interests in the vicarages of Llangynwyd, Llangyfelach, Newcastle and Glyncorrwg, and the chapels of Laleston, Tythegston and Betws.[55]

On a number of estates there were non-agrarian sources of income. Mills could often be profitably rented, like the two corn-mills, the Castle Mills, which stood under a single roof on the castle moat near the West Gate at Cardiff, and were rented for £15 a year. The earl of Pembroke's fisheries in the 'rivers of Rhymney, Taff, Ely ,"Ki", Ogmore, Afan, and Neath', were 'very profitable by the year, for the fishing only of Taff hath been set out for some years past at £24 per annum', according to Rice Lewis. Many parts of Glamorgan were thickly-wooded, and timber was a valuable commodity much in demand for domestic fuel, building, ship-building, industry, and a range of other uses. It was becoming scarcer, and as early as the 1530s Leland had occasion to comment on the scarcity of wood in a number of parts of the county. Much of the timber found within Glamorgan was of too poor a quality and too far from centres of population to be of any commercial value except as a source of fuel for the iron industry which, consuming the timber from an acre of woodland for every three tons of iron smelted, had an almost unassuageable appetite for fuel. The woods of Dinas Powys had been disposed of to an iron merchant of Bristol, and those of Ogmore were, by 1596, 'reserved to the ironworks'. The earl of Pembroke's woods in Talyfan and Ruthin were 'sold to the ironworks', and other timber fellings on his estates in Glamorgan and Monmouthshire usually brought him anything from £50 to £100 a year. Robert Sidney also entered into agreements with ironmasters to lease out rights of working iron and felling timber on his estates at Coety. Some landowners were themselves heavily committed to industrial enterprises. Sir Henry Sidney and Edmund Mathew had a major interest in ironworking, and the earl of Pembroke was a leading shareholder in the Mines Royal. In the west of the county, where the mining and exporting of coal were becoming intensively developed, families like the Mansels, the Evanses of the Gnoll, the Prices of Briton Ferry, and Thomases of Dan-y-graig and others had a big stake in the industry's fortunes (see below, pp. 49-50).[56]

Manorial lords enjoyed a number of miscellaneous minor sources of revenue. There were the proceeds of courts leet and baron, heriots, mises, avowry fees, and survivals of medieval dues and payments like 'chence' and *cymorth*; but none of these amounted to any very substantial sum and they remained almost static throughout the period. Quay dues payable at some of the little ports like the Stradlings' harbours at Aberthaw and Ogmore, the St. John creek at Barry, or the Mansels' preserves at

Oxwich and Port Eynon, were of growing value in view of the flourishing state of trade at the ports. At the Gower creeks 2*d.* was levied on every horse, 1*d.* on cattle, ½*d.* on swine, and ¼*d.* on sheep, with a keelage on every outgoing vessel that had a cockboat, and a bushel of salt or grain being demanded from every such cargo entering harbour. Wrecks, and goods cast up along the shore, could be valuable for the manorial lord. Sir Edward Stradling used a main yard cast up at Merthyr Mawr to 'make the rails of many ceilings' and to beautify the wainscot of his dining room at St. Donat's. But a lord had got to make sure that these windfalls were not 'sinisterly . . . embezzled and conveyed away by his own tenants', as happened to Lord St. John in 1579. Wrecks might, indeed, be a source of revenue, but they could be an even greater source of conflict and expense. Contention and violence between Mansels and Herberts first broke out over their respective rights to a French ship wrecked at Oxwich in 1557, and another sharp quarrel occurred between them in 1584 over a ship wrecked near the mouth of the river Afan. Both episodes led to Star Chamber suits (below, pp. 176–7, 183). The smouldering bitterness between the two families over maritime rights burst into flames yet again in 1630–1 over a ship at Swansea.[57]

Most of the gentry of any consequence sought to hold office, paid or unpaid, under the Crown (for detailed treatment, below, chapter III). Ordinarily, the aspirants for patronage far exceeded the number of jobs available; a well-informed guess estimates that among the aristocracy the ratio was 2:1, among the leading county families 5:1, and among the parish gentry it was as high as 30:1. Only a minority could, therefore, expect to add to their income from the proceeds of office, and it was unknown for any but the greatest figures, secure at Court and well friended by the Crown, to make vast sums out of office. In south-east Wales the earls of Worcester and Pembroke alone came into this category. Office seems to have been more important to them as a source of income and influence during the first half of our period than the second. Henry, second earl of Worcester, at the time of his death in 1549 held royal and other offices worth £450 a year, many of which were farmed out to deputies in return for large capital sums, with singularly detrimental consequences for the efficiency and honesty of administration and justice. The first earl of Pembroke was another to whom office was lavishly granted in Edward VI's reign, and his son did nearly as well under Elizabeth. Both held, at various times, the most important and prestigious office in Wales, that of President of the Council in the Marches. Not very much lower down the scale came Sir Rice Mansel, who acquired a number of important posts, including that of Chamberlain and Chancellor of South Wales, which were worth in all £154 a year to him, an amount not far short of the £215 which his Inquisition Post Mortem showed him as deriving from his Margam and Oxwich estates in 1559. Yet it may be doubted whether the actual income which men like Mansel or Edward Carne or Thomas Stradling derived from the public service was as important in the long run as the opportunities which office gave them for acquiring crown lands by lease or purchase. Not that occupying even the highest office in itself necessarily made the holder outstandingly powerful as a landowner. Sir John Herbert, the Glamorgan gentleman to rise highest in the service of the crown in early Stuart times (below, pp. 117–8), did not, in consequence, become the possessor of a particularly large or wealthy estate. Nor, on a much lower level, did the corrupt customs officers of Glamorgan (below, pp. 60–2), make any appreciable mark in contemporary society. Conversely, the wealthiest family in early Stuart Glamorgan, the Lewises Y Fan, had never been particularly significant office-holders under the crown, while the Mansels, when at their wealthiest under Sir Thomas Mansel, owed very little to the proceeds of office. Prestigious office could, indeed, be a source of debilitating expense, and it is significant that it was Robert Sidney, earl of Leicester and holder of some very elevated positions, who was in serious financial embarrassment over the marriage-settlement between his daughter and the son of Sir Thomas Mansel, and not the squire of Margam (below, p. 109; cf. also the experience of William Carne of Nash, below, pp. 165–6).[58]

Most gentry families could, at best, hope for nothing more than relatively minor offices under the crown which could never have been more than a trifling source of income. Some public offices, such as that of sheriff or justice of the peace, carried no remuneration and were valued chiefly for the status and authority they conferred. There were, in addition, many minor offices in the service of the great landowners, particularly that of the earl of Pembroke. They ranged in value from the £20 per annum paid to the steward to sums of a few shillings paid to bailiffs and other underlings. Contemporary rentals and accounts show that some of the county gentry as well as a large number of the minor gentry did not consider it beneath their dignity to be thus employed. Some of the more important among them, like Thomas Lewis Y Fan, steward for a time to the earl of Pembroke, or Edward Mansel, steward to the earl of Worcester (p. 34), could make sizeable sums out of the office, especially when, like Mansel, they were more concerned to use their position to meet their own financial exigencies than those of their employer. Another who seems to have become a man of affluence early in the seventeenth century was Sir Thomas Morgan of Ruperra, (pp. 124, 129). Himself the seventh son of a not-very-wealthy Monmouthshire family, Sir Thomas founded his prosperity on the combination of a marriage to a rich heiress, his position as steward of the Pembroke estates, and as Surveyor of the Woods to James I. However, most of these officials, great and small, though no doubt appreciative enough of the fees and perquisites accruing from their offices, may have valued them less as a source of income than as a fount of influence over other tenants and a means of gaining advantages in leases and tenancies for themselves, their kinsmen and allies.[58A]

iii.

THE TOWNS

The towns of Glamorgan had always been small and none of them wealthy. During the fourteenth and fifteenth centuries they had been subjected to many adversities from which some of them had never really recovered (*ante*, III, 348ff.). Caerphilly, Llantrisant, and Loughor, whose economic viability must always have been extremely precarious, had shrunk to the condition of insignificant country villages. Kenfig, choked with encroaching sand, and Aberafan, threatened by sand, sea, and river flooding, were ghosts of their former selves and survived as boroughs in hardly more than name. Neath and Cowbridge, though hard pressed in the fifteenth century, had managed to survive rather better, the former by reason of its shipping and the latter as a market centre for the fertile Vale of Glamorgan. Even the two largest and most flourishing towns, Cardiff and Swansea, the *capita* until 1536 of the lordships of Glamorgan and Gower respectively, had not escaped unscathed. They had been included along with Cowbridge in an Act of Parliament of 1544 which referred to a number of towns of south Wales as being decayed and in need of rehabilitation. It may be symptomatic of the still greater decline of all other Glamorgan towns that they were not deemed worthy of inclusion in the Act at all.[59]

Despite this Act of 1544, insofar as there could be said to be any concentrations of wealth in the Glamorgan of that era, it was in the towns that they were to be found. In the first major Tudor tax assessment available for the county, the Lay Subsidy of 1543–4, the 174 taxpayers of the town of Cardiff were liable for the sum of £42 3s. 8d., as compared with the £18 4s. 10d. for the rest of the whole hundred of Cardiff, or even the £63 8s. 1d. raised in the whole of the relatively rich and densely-populated hundred of Dinas Powys, made up of two dozen fertile parishes. Or again, in the opposite end of the county, the 111 taxpayers of Swansea contributed about one-third (£23 16s. 2d.) of the total taxation (£70 3s. 2d.) of the 20 parishes of the hundred of Swansea, while the average tax burden of each taxpayer in Swansea was three times as heavy as that of the average rural taxpayer. Comparable figures for the smaller towns show less affluence in them. Cowbridge could muster 67 taxpayers contributing £9 10s. 0d. between them, and Neath 73 assessed at £6 1s. 0d. Aberafan had only 30, who were liable for no more than £1 9s. 4d., and Loughor was down to as few as 15 paying 5s. 8d. No comparison between these conditions prevailing at the outset of our period with those obtaining at the end of it can be made, because no sources comparable in quality and detail to the subsidy assessment of

1543-4 exist. Nevertheless, there is every reason to believe that the larger towns were on the threshold of a century of growth in the 1540s. They served one or both of two main economic functions: as centres of markets, fairs, and services for their rural hinterland, and as the main ports for the region. Both functions were to grow in importance during the century following the Act of Union. The swelling demand for agricultural produce and for the products of crafts and industries associated with agriculture stimulated activities at markets and fairs. Furthermore, if the larger output of Glamorgan agriculture and industry was successfully to be channelled to meet the enhanced demand for it within the Bristol Channel area and further afield, it had to be sent by sea from the ports, since land transport would never have served to meet the need (below, pp. 59ff). Cardiff, as the county town, fulfilled yet another function as the administrative and judicial centre of the county, where Great Sessions, Quarter Sessions, parliamentary elections, and other comparable public activities were held. Contemporary observers waxed eloquent in their praises of the town. It was 'very well compacted, beautified with many fair houses and large streets', testified Rice Merrick in 1578; and a generation later George Owen and John Speed declared it to be 'the fairest town of all south Wales'. Nor need we wonder that Cardiff should deem it only compatible with its status and dignity to seek from the crown the renewal of its charter, in 1600 and 1608.[60]

All the towns were inextricably associated with the agrarian life of their rural hinterland. Many townsmen were themselves engaged in farming pursuits for their own and their families' subsistence. In an age of rising prices they were only too glad to meet as much of their food needs as possible from their own resources. The ordinances of Cowbridge regarded it as normal practice that cattle kept in the town should be driven daily to and from their pastures—but they must not be milked in the town's streets! Cardiff's townsmen cultivated small patches of corn and harvested hay on Portman's Moor, later known as East Moor, and grazed their animals on the common pastures of the Great and Little Heath. A number of Swansea's early-seventeenth-century inhabitants, drawn from a variety of occupations, left in their wills and inventories a record of their possessions in corn, livestock, and farming implements. In 1603 and 1617 the town's records refer with some anxiety to complaints that the common pastures at Cefn Coed and Townhill were becoming overstocked because of the growing number of beasts being kept by the townsfolk.[61]

More essential to the rural economy than the direct participation in agriculture of towndwellers was the function of the towns as venues of markets and fairs. Glamorgan was unusually well supplied with markets, for a Welsh county, and few farmers in the Vale lived more than five miles away from one. Markets were held twice weekly at Cardiff (Wednesday and Saturday) and Cowbridge (Tuesday and Saturday), and once weekly at Bridgend (Saturday), Llantrisant (Friday), Neath (Wednesday), and Swansea (Saturday), while at Merthyr Tydfil (Monday) and Caerphilly (Thursday) there were markets only between May and Christmas. At these markets corn, meat, general provisions, and cloth were the commodities chiefly offered for sale. At Cardiff the meat market was held in the space under the Gild or Booth Hall in the High Street, and the corn and cloth market near the town cross at the south end of the town hall. 'The market for more general produce was held on Wednesday and Saturdays in the High Street to the north of the hall, the stalls lining the streets as far as the castle.' The high markets for sale of stock were held from March to October on the second Wednesday of the month. At the market the bailiff was required to proclaim at the market cross what goods were for sale and what prices had been fixed for them.[62]

Fairs were another main feature of a town's commercial life. The grant of market rights ordinarily carried with it the privilege of holding fairs, and all the principal market towns held two or three fairs a year. The fairs usually fell during the summer and autumn, and were chiefly designed to facilitate private sales of livestock, which were conducted on a much bigger scale in the fairs than in the open markets. If the financial accounts surviving from some Swansea fairs of the early-seventeenth century are any guide, there were only a few standings at the fairs, mostly taken by hatters, glovers, and pedlars, and set up in the churchyard, where they brought in a few shillings to be recorded in the churchwardens' account. Many fairs were conducted outside the towns, at places like Ewenni, St. Mary Hill, St. Nicholas, or Waun Hill near Merthyr Tydfil. These fairs, the haunts of many doubtful characters, were associated in the public mind with disorder and unruly conduct. It may be of some significance that of the 'seven dangerous places' in Glamorgan listed by Rice Merrick—Llandaff, Llantrisant, Llantwit, Bridgend, Caerphilly, Neath and St. Mary Hill—all but two, Caerphilly and Llantwit, were entitled to hold fairs. It is certainly true that Ewenni fair was the scene of serious violence in 1574 and 1597 and that Ffair y Waun, near Merthyr, had an unsavoury reputation as a haunt of cattle thieves.[63]

The Tudor town offered a wide variety of trades, wares, and services provided by its merchants, shopkeepers, and craftsmen. The most comprehensive sketch of the characteristic occupations of a Glamorgan town comes from Swansea, where the municipal records and the wills and inventories of its citizens have been better preserved than those of any other town. The various trades represented there should not be too finely differentiated from one another because of the possibility of overlapping between them, but there are some broad categories which emerge. The food and drink trades were well represented, by millers, bakers, vintners, brewers, victuallers, innkeepers, butchers, fishmongers, cutlers, and pewterers. Nearly as important were the many crafts of the clothing trades: shoemakers, cobblers, lastmakers, tailors, buttonmakers, seamstresses, hatters, and cappers. Closely linked to them were the powerful and well-organized leather trades of tanners and saddlers, curriers and glovers, and the textile trades of weavers, dyers, tuckers, and feltmakers. A variety of crafts were associated with the building trades: carpenters, joiners, masons, plumbers, tilers, paviers, and glaziers. Merchants, mercers, and pedlars were involved in the distributive trades, and mariners, shipbuilders, and fishermen in the seafaring trades. Professional men included clergymen, lawyers, and doctors. Other miscellaneous occupations were those of yeomen, husbandmen, tinkers, barbers, colliers, ironworkers, and a large number of general labourers and paupers, together with a sprinkling of gentry. The town was also regularly visited by itinerant dealers and pedlars, like that Evan ap David, chapman of Caerleon, who died in 1616, and had debts owing to him, mostly for tobacco, linen, and cloth, from merchants in Swansea, Neath, Cowbridge, Lampeter, Llandovery, Devon, and Somerset, as well as the towns of his native Monmouthshire. All the facilities provided by traders, shopkeepers, craftsmen and others at Swansea were at least paralleled and, probably, exceeded in the wealthier county town of Cardiff, where a number of the county gentry kept town houses and where the needs for hospitality and accommodation were considerably greater. Other smaller towns may be supposed to have offered a broadly similar but more restricted range of services.[64]

Some of the crafts mentioned above had long been organized in guilds which regulated their activities and protected their interests. Leatherworkers appear to have been particularly prominent in Glamorgan (below, pp. 47–8). Cardiff's medieval guild of cordwainers had its chapel of St. Piran in St. Mary's church, and the town's glovers had their chapel at St. John's church. The glovers of Swansea had their chapel at St. Mary's church within the town. Cardiff's cordwainers were faced with a crisis in 1550, when their chapel of St. Piran was threatened with confiscation as part of the campaign against chantries. Six irate members of the guild of cordwainers tried forcibly to retain possession of the chapel, only to be haled before the courts for their temerity. Their protest was not without its effect, however, for although the religious aspect of the guild's activities was suppressed, it succeeded in retaining its chapel as a secular hall, in which the cordwainers were now joined by the glovers. As late as 1589 the particular rights and privileges of the Cardiff cordwainers and glovers to exclusive pursuit of their craft within the borough, originally granted in 1323–4, were solemnly reaffirmed by Queen Elizabeth. The leatherworkers of Cardiff and Swansea continued to number in their midst some of the wealthiest and most prosperous of the citizens of both towns, as is amply attested by some of their surviving wills and inventories (below, p. 129).[65]

[45]

All the economic activities conducted within a Tudor borough were, in theory, strictly controlled by a body of by-laws, ordinances or regulations laid down by its corporation. These codes had originated in the Middle Ages and were often reaffirmed in the sixteenth and seventeenth centuries. They have come down to us, in whole or in part, from Cowbridge, Kenfig, Neath, and Swansea. Broadly speaking, all were aimed at securing much the same sort of ends: ensuring the quality of commodities offered for sale; checking the accuracy of weights and measures used; regulating the hours and conditions of trading; achieving some rudimentary measure of public health and cleanliness; prohibiting buying and selling outside the market; maintaining peace and good order; and safeguarding the economic privileges of the burgesses (who formed only a small minority of the whole population of the town) of freedom from tolls, exclusive trading, and rights of pre-emption. Two or three short quotations may convey something of the flavour of these regulations. Cowbridge required every baker to 'bake good and sufficient bread' and brewers to 'brew good and wholesome ale, third drink, and small drink'. It insisted that 'no butcher shall cast no heads, feet, nor other garbage in the high street' and 'no taverner keep no open taverns in the annoyance of his neighbour after 10 of the clock at night'; and it ordered that 'no stranger shall buy any corn in the market until the time that the bailiffs, aldermen, and burgesses be served'. All Tudor legislators were notoriously better able to lay down regulations than to implement them, and no doubt many municipal ordinances were more honoured in the breach than the observance. On the other hand, the Swansea records provide many instances of burgesses being disfranchised for offences against the town's orders and by-laws. Similarly, a number of the inhabitants of Cardiff were proceeded against in the Court of Great Sessions for committing the same kind of offences, mostly relating to the unlawful sale of drink and the use of fraudulent weights and measures. This would seem to suggest that the paternalistic controls cherished by the Tudor state were exercised *in parvo* within the municipalities.[66]

iv.

INDUSTRY IN GLAMORGAN

The Wool and Leather Industries

In the century between Union and Civil War the pulse of industrial activity in Glamorgan, as in many other parts of England and Wales, beat perceptibly quicker and more robustly. Industries like the wool and leather trades, having already been firmly established in the Middle Ages, grew out of the rural economy of the county. They probably continued to employ more people and to contribute more to the wealth of the county than any other industry. Nevertheless, new developments in 'heavy' industry, especially the growth of the coal and iron industries, themselves existing in embryo in the Middle Ages, prepared the way in this century for the immense industrial expansion later to be associated with the Industrial Revolution.

Sheep farming had long provided ample raw materials for by-employment in the form of woollen cloth weaving. In the fifteenth century cloth had been woven in both town and country but had been processed in the towns. Swansea then boasted four or five mills for fulling cloth. The continued existence there in the sixteenth century of a large number of dyers, tuckers, and felt-makers, and the prominence of hatters and cappers at its fairs, together with a similar prevalence in seventeenth-century Cardiff of men engaged in the same callings, suggest that both towns were important centres of the wool trade. An Exchequer suit brought in 1600-1 shows that woollen cloth was made and sold in the towns of Cardiff, Swansea, and Bridgend, but not always with a proper respect for the multifarious statutory regulations intended to control its manufacture. Hugh George, farmer of the office of Alnager (i.e. officer for the inspection of woollen cloth) complained that defendants from these towns illegally placed an official seal on cloth made contrary to statute and prevented him and his deputies from carrying out their official duties. Although raw wool was being exported from Glamorgan in growing quantities to supply the clothiers of the west of England, a good deal was still being worked within the county. The Mansels, for instance, sold most of their wool to two Swansea hatters, John Harris and Harry John. Generally, enough wool was being kept and spun within Glamorgan to provide valuable by-employment for farmers and their wives. Weaving and stocking-knitting, so well illustrated by the large number of seventeenth- and eighteenth-century inventories (below, pp. 338-43), continued to be an important, possibly indispensable, source of income to the farming community. However, suggestions that cloth-making ought to be extended to the *Blaenau*, among other mountainous parts of south Wales, do not seem to have met with much response until later in the seventeenth century.[67]

The leather industry is far less well-known in British history than the woollen industry, yet it was second only to cloth-making during this period. It flourished particularly in those pastoral regions where calf-skins and sheepskins were in ample supply and farmers much in need of supplementary sources of income. Leather products were indispensable for the farmer, providing him and his family with boots and shoes, gloves, and other items of clothing, and with saddles, cart saddles, horse collars, and other essential equipment. Leather was becoming additionally popular for use in the more luxurious furnishings of the Tudor period. The tanning and fashioning of leather had already been widely established within medieval Glamorgan, but especially in the towns of Cardiff and Swansea, where leatherworkers constituted a powerful vested interest.

E

Safeguards for the leather interest were built into Swansea's indenture of 1532 agreed with Henry, earl of Worcester, whereby the portreeve was to appoint two burgesses to examine all leather brought into the town or tanned there, with provision for the forfeiture of any faulty leather and a stiff fine of 6s. 8d. for any defective hide. The Swansea Common Hall Book, 1549–1665, regularly notes the appointment every year of an officer appointed for the 'searching, sealing, and registering of tanned leather', and the same source shows that boys apprenticed by the town to shoemakers and glovers far outnumbered those placed in any other trade. Glamorgan towns enjoyed many advantages for the making of leather goods. All the raw materials needed for tanning leather were readily available: hides and skins from the flourishing live-stock farming; plentiful supplies of oak-bark from the county's forests, especially where they were being stripped for ironworking; lime burned from the local limestone with the use of increasingly abundant locally-mined coal; and salt brought from Rochelle as a return cargo for the coal exported from Glamorgan. When necessary, local leather supplies could be supplemented by superior leather from Bristol. The tanners' wills and those of other leatherworkers leave us in no doubt about their ample wealth and high economic standing.[68]

THE COAL INDUSTRY[69]

The coal deposits of Glamorgan were known and worked as early as Roman times, judging by small quantities of unburnt coal found at the Roman sites of Gelli-gaer, Ely, and Llantwit Major. Nor were the men of the Middle Ages unfamiliar with the working of coal seams. The sharp-eyed Cistercians of Margam and Neath were alive to the value of coal; it was mined by laymen on a big scale at Llansamlet, where there was a flourishing enterprise from the fourteenth century onwards; and there were workings at Cefn Carn and Rudry in the east of the county. On some manors, freeholders and tenants succeeded in retaining their rights to dig for coal on the manorial commons and wastes in face of a persistent tendency to restrict mining rights in the interests of the manorial lord.

An organized coal industry, producing on a relatively large scale for home and export markets, came into being only from the second half of the sixteenth century onwards. This resulted from the operation of many forces which combined to create a vastly-increased demand for coal. It arose partly from a pressing shortage of timber, caused to some extent by extensive clearance of woodland to make way for farming and still more by the voracious appetite for fuel of metal smelting. With wood in such short supply, more coal had to be used for heating homes, many of which were now being built with adequate fireplaces and stone chimneys; and even if Sir Henry Sidney voiced the widespread prejudice of contemporaries against that 'noxious mineral, pit-coal',

George Owen could urge its merits as 'very good and sweet to roast and boil meat' and not requiring 'a man's labour to cleave wood and feed the fire continually'. Quite independently of the consequences of a timber shortage there was an expanding range of uses for coal in relation to agriculture and industry. On the land, before lime could be used as a fertilizer it had to be burnt in kilns, which were being increasingly fired by coal and culm. Many industries were making greater use of coal, among them malting, salt-refining, soap-making, brick and tile manufacture, glass-making, dyeing, and the preparation of saltpetre, copperas, and alum. Nearly the whole of this kind of demand for coal came from outside the county. Nor was it confined to England and Wales; a flourishing export market, further encouraged by mercantilist notions of the need for a favourable balance of trade, grew up in France, the Channel Islands, and Ireland.[70]

Glamorgan was in a position to respond readily to the demand. Its coal deposits were rich and extensive, and some of them outcropped near the sea. The latter advantage was crucial, because mining techniques were too primitive to work deep seams, and inland transport was so poor that the exploitation of coal at any distance away from the sea or a navigable river would be fruitless. Some of the coal-working remained on a small scale. Individual farmers like William ap William of Llanrhidian, who died in 1609, leaving £5 worth of 'coals above the ground already wrought' and 'one vein of coals whereupon is two pits open', might mine coal on their own land. Similarly, many of the burgesses of the borough of Neath early in the seventeenth century exercised their individual right to mine coal within the borough, with the result that they impeded one another's works, causing great difficulties and many lawsuits. However, if coal was to be mined on a commercial scale, men with deeper pockets had to take the industry in hand. Coalmining could necessitate heavy outlay on trial borings, sinking pits, digging water courses, erecting colliery buildings, and organizing transport. Furthermore, in the Swansea district many of the mines were described as being situate in 'clay and slimy ground', which required much expenditure on timber supports. These needs for greater capital resources and bigger-scale operation brought major changes to the industry. Ambitious entrepreneurs drawn from the ranks of the gentry and other wealthy men were attracted to coalmining enterprises; the rights of manorial lords were more strictly enforced as against those of the tenants; coal-bearing lands formerly belonging to the abbeys of Neath and Margam and the Order of St. John passed into the hands of more enterprising lessees for long terms; and the typical sixteenth-century leases, which tended to limit the size and output of pits, gave way to those of the seventeenth century, which allowed unrestricted production on condition of the payment of royalties. The kind of family which came to dominate the scene was one like the Evanses of the Gnoll, who had taken over the working of coal from the burgesses of Neath in 1620 on condition of providing them with coal at favourable rates; an arrangement which led to a big expansion of coal production within the borough, but only at the price of securing the lion's share of the profits for David Evans and of placing the administration of the borough of Neath almost completely under the control of Evans and his nominees. Allies and kinsmen of the Evanses were the Prices of Briton Ferry, who had extensive coal interests in Briton Ferry, Neath, and Kilvey. These passed to a younger branch of the Mansels when Sir Anthony Mansel married Jane, the heiress of the Prices, early in the seventeenth century. The senior Mansel line were themselves interested in coal mines near their main residence at Margam which came down to them from the monks, and also in Gower. Swansea families with a stake in coal included the Herberts of Swansea and Neath abbey, and the Seys and Thomas families. In the east of the county the Mathews of Castell-y-mynach worked coal at Hirwaun Wrgan in the 1630s.[71]

The main centres of coal-mining were found on the south-western fringes of the coalfield in the vicinity of Neath and Swansea, where experience of mining coal was most extensive and conditions for winning and exporting it most propitious. It was worked at a number of points within and around the borough of Neath, on the former Neath abbey lands at Cadoxton, in the lordship of Neath Ultra near Onllwyn, within the parish of Llantwit-juxta-Neath, in the lordship of Neath Citra, and again at a number of points in the neighbournood of Briton Ferry and Baglan. The lordships of Gower and Kilvey also had a number of mines within their boundaries. In east Gower there were the long-established pits at Kilvey and Llansamlet. There were others in Sketty and the parish of St. John on the Milwood manors previously owned by the Order of St. John, at Clyne Forest near Swansea, and on the former Neath abbey lands at Grange in the parish of Oystermouth. Other mines lay along the north Gower coast at Llanrhidian, Landimore, and Weobley, some of them on lands once belonging to Neath abbey and others on lands always in secular possession. Near Loughor and Llandeilo Tal-y-bont there were coal workings on the old Neath grange at Cwrt-y-carnau. Coal was also dug at Gwaun-cae-gurwen, where tenants stubbornly maintained their right to it in a survey of 1610. All other coalmining regions in Glamorgan were at this time less important than those in the west. In the middle of the county, on the former Margam abbey lands, coal continued to be worked under the aegis of the Mansels at Penhydd, Ffrwdwyllt, Hafod-y-porth, and Cefn Cribwr. Elsewhere in Glamorgan, although coal was mined at some favourable sites along the south and south-eastern edges of the coalfield at Cefn Carn and Rudry, Llanharry and Llanharan, and at a few scattered points along the northern rim, at places like Hirwaun, Glyn Cynon, the outskirts of Aberdare, and the Waun near Dowlais, the smallness of local demand

and the difficulties of getting coal away any distance from these areas precluded any major expansion.[72]

We have no contemporary description of the working methods and conditions in the Glamorgan mines of this age, but it is likely that George Owen's celebrated description of the Pembrokeshire coalpits of the late-sixteenth century is equally applicable to those of Glamorgan. Whereas the shallower workings of an earlier age were approached by means of a slope or drift, by Owen's day a shaft, some six or seven feet square and lined with timber, was being sunk to a depth of anything from 12 to 20 fathoms (70 to 120 feet) to reach the coal. The coal seam was usually no more than five or six feet wide, of which one foot was left undug at the bottom to provide a foundation. The roof was timbered and was also supported by pillars of unworked coal. Each hewer of coal worked in his own 'stall' and was attended by one or more bearers, boys who carried the coal in baskets in relays to the shaft. There it was riddled to separate the small coal and culm from the larger lumps, then hauled to the surface. In an average pit, Owen tells us, there would have been a labour force of three hewers, seven bearers, one filler, four winders, and two riddlers; a team capable of producing about 80 to 100 barrels of coal a day. Their work was exhausting and dangerous. Because of the narrowness of the seams the hewers had to cut coal from a sitting position, and the bearers were obliged to stoop when carrying it on their backs. They worked from 6.0 a.m. to 6 p.m. with an hour off at noon to eat their meal, consisting of a 'half-pennyworth of bread to every man and 4d. of drink among a dozen men . . . on the charge of the pit'. Danger was never far away, and colliers worked in the knowledge that death or crippling injury from water, gas, roof-falls, and accidents on ladders or from rope-breaks in the shaft might easily befall them. Small wonder that they were superstitious and backward-looking in George Owen's eyes: 'the workmen observe all abolished holy days and cannot be weaned from that folly'. No doubt they were glad to get as many days' respite from their back-breaking toil as they could and had no wish to take any chance of offending supernatural powers that might protect them in their hazardous occupation. Despite the perils of the miners' calling, the industry seemed to be able to recruit them without difficulty, judging by the fact that in west Glamorgan coal-mining became a full-time occupation, and not a by-employment, and also by the noticeable increase in the population of the mining districts of the neighbourhood of Neath, Swansea, and north Gower. Additionally, the sharp rise in the export of coal (below, pp. 65–7) gives no indication of the expansion of the industry being held back by labour shortages.[73]

THE IRON INDUSTRY

Iron, like coal, had been known in Glamorgan since Roman times, evidence of iron-working having been found in the Roman villa at

[51]

Ely and the Mwyndy mine, Llantrisant. In the thirteenth century the alert monks of Margam had spotted the possibilities of iron-working at Cornelly, and there had been other tiny medieval enterprises at Pen-y-fai, Llantrisant, and near Neath. Their output had been too small even to meet the modest needs of the smiths working in the county. In the Tudor age iron-working assumed a new importance with the advent of cannon for use on land and at sea, when it became the basis of the contemporary armaments industry. As early as 1521 Henry VIII took the first tentative steps along the road to national self-sufficiency by setting up a commission under a German expert, Peter son of Almain, to search for possible sources of iron, lead, and copper within the kingdom. It was probably as a follow-up to this report that work was begun on the mining and smelting of lead and iron at Llantrisant in 1531.[74]

Not until Elizabeth's reign did the major developments in iron-working come. They were brought about by the acute shortage of timber already referred to and the legislation (i Eliz., c.15) designed to prevent any further deforestation. Scarcity of fuel led a number of Sussex ironmasters, the foremost iron producers in the country, to turn their eyes to Glamorgan and Monmouthshire. Here they found three compelling attractions: luxuriant woodlands to provide charcoal; iron-stones in the coal measures which were workable by 'patching' or 'scouring', and convenient limestone; and numerous streams to provide water-power for the wheels which operated the bellows that 'blew' the blast into the furnaces and for working the tilt hammers which fashioned the refined iron in the forges. Among the more notable Sussex ironmasters who established enterprises in Glamorgan were Sir Henry Sidney of Robertsbridge and his partners, William Relfe, Anthony and William Morley, James Robson, Robert Martin, and Thomas Mynyffee. A few local men were attracted by the possibilities of the industry; foremost among them the formidable Edmund Mathew of Radyr, Lewis Price, who borrowed from Bristol merchants to set up in business, and Anthony Mansel. The Sussex ironmasters were largely dependent for technical expertise on Germans, some of whom were sent to south Wales, like John Bowde and three other Germans sent by Sir Henry Sidney to his works near Cardiff in 1565. Some English craftsmen also migrated to Glamorgan, one of whom, at least, died of fever or exhaustion after four years of exile.[75]

The ironmasters established their works in three main areas: the lower Taff valley, the upper Taff and Cynon valleys, and mid-Glamorgan. Somewhere in the lower Taff valley, on a site near Cardiff so far unidentified but possibly in the neighbourhood of Radyr-Pentyrch, Sir Henry Sidney established a forge and furnace in 1564. By a piece of good fortune the accounts for these works for the years 1564–8 still survive in the De L'Isle and Dudley manuscripts to tell us much about the labour force, the wages paid, and working methods. The enterprise employed miners, fillers, founders, and charcoal burners; a skilled man like the master founder being paid the high wage of 9s. 6d. a week and the filler 6s. for a smelting, which normally took six days. Each smelting produced about 8 tons of cast iron at £2 7s. od. a ton, for which 10 tons of ore, 1 *load* of limestone, 4 *loads* of marl, and 32-35 *loads* of charcoal were needed. Every 3 tons of cast iron produced 2 tons of wrought iron at the forge, at a cost of £8 3s. 8d. a ton. Large quantities of plate iron were transported to Cardiff, at 3s. 4d. a ton, and conveyed from there by sea to Rye, to be made into steel at Robertsbridge. With the decline of activity at Robertsbridge in the 1570s this Glamorgan works lost much of its importance, though it found an alternative outlet in Ireland for a time.[76]

There had already been iron-working at Radyr-Pentyrch in the Middle Ages, and it was in this area that one of Henry Sidney's partners at Robertsbridge, Edmund Roberts, was operating in the 1560s. But the man principally associated with the works in this locality was Edmund Mathew, son of Sir George Mathew of Radyr and eventual heir to his estate in 1600. Mathew appears to have been an aggressive individual with few scruples, who was accused in 1574 of the illegal export of ordnance. In 1602 he was again accused of having illicitly sent abroad 150 tons of ordnance between the years 1582 and 1600, having taken advantage of the officers of the port of Cardiff who were too poor to dare displease him, so the Privy Council was informed. Partly because he had been detected in his illegalities, partly because he was in debt to the tune of £16,000, he had leased his interest in the works to Peter Semayne, a Cardiff merchant possibly of Dutch origin, but he seems to have kept a finger in the pie himself. Semayne and Mathew were birds of a feather, and they may well have been jointly responsible for breaches of the law, when the former was accused in 1609, 1614 and 1616 of the illegal export of ordnance. Semayne, who also had a shady record as an illegal importer of wine, was described by Sir John Throckmorton in 1614 as 'a pestilent fellow in these and suchlike businesses' [illegal export of ordnance] 'making an infinite gain thereof besides the arming of all the world with our artillery against us'.[77]

In much the same part of the Taff valley, but on the east bank of the river at Tongwynlais, ironworks may have been established as early as 1560 by one Hugh Lambert of Tonbridge. But the first positive reference to their existence is one of 1625 to a furnace in the possession of Thomas Hackett, who had already established himself at Machen.[78]

In the upper reaches of the Taff and its tributary, the Cynon, the Sussex ironmaster, William Relfe, settled in the parish of Llanwynno in Elizabeth's reign and established works at Pontygwaith and Dyffryn (modern Mountain Ash). It was the depredations of these works which doubtless led a contemporary Welsh poet to deplore in tones of sad indignation the sacrilege of 'cutting the woods of Glyn Cynon' ('torri coed Glyn Cynon' (cf. below, pp. 565–6). After Relfe's death he was followed by Anthony Morley, whose business was so bedevilled by debt and litigation that his interest was sold to yet another Sussex master, Thomas Mynyffee, in 1586. Mynyffee himself died in 1589 leaving a widow heavily encumbered with debts and with legal claims against her of Talmudic complexity. Further north in the locality Anthony Morley is known to have had a forge, possibly at Pontyryn (Abercannaid), where the remains of an early furnace can still be seen. It has even been claimed on the strength of an early iron fireback bearing the date 1555 found in the district that iron-working had begun there as early as that. However, the earliest ironmasters certainly known to have had interests in the area were Anthony Morley in the 1580s and Bartholomew Maskell in 1593. By 1625 Thomas Erbury had a furnace and forge at Pontyryn.[79]

In mid-Glamorgan, iron-working near Angelton in the lordship of Coety Anglia owed its existence to the initiative and encouragement of Robert Sidney, son of Sir Henry. In 1589 he encouraged two ironmasters named John Cross and John Thornton to migrate from Cleobury Mortimer to Glamorgan. They ran into difficulties and by 1600 had been succeeded by two Sussex ironmasters, Willard and Bullen.[80]

Traces of two or three of the furnaces used by the pioneer ironmasters can still be detected in Glamorgan. The most celebrated of them are those at Blaencannaid near Merthyr Tydfil and Cwm Aman near Aberdare to which William Llewellin drew attention over 100 years ago, though it ought to be added that there can be no complete certainty that either of these sites goes back to the period 1558–1625. A third site, thought to be associated with Robert Sidney's ventures, exists at Angelton. What remains of these furnaces suggests that they were built into sloping ground in order that they might be more easily filled from above with raw materials, with sometimes a stone platform built at this level to make the operation still more convenient. At ground level, in the front wall of the furnace, was an opening which was stopped up during the smelting process but through which the molten metal was subsequently allowed to flow. At Cwm Aman, where the sandstone furnace was about 24 feet square and the outer walls 16 feet high, there were still, in the 1860s, traces of the watercourse that once conveyed water from the local stream to the water-wheel. These and similar furnaces were part of a technical progression which transformed the industry as it passed from the stage of pygmy bloomeries blown by small leather hand bellows to that of big furnaces in which blast was produced by a large bellows driven by water-power. The former type could be easily constructed almost anywhere, whereas the latter needed careful location near streams and on a slope; it also called for sounder construction, a larger labour force, and a much bigger capital investment. In the process the industry became more commercialized, no longer simply producing for paltry local requirements but with an eye on a more extensive market within England

and Wales and abroad—if necessary at the risk of breaking the law. Of the success which was achieved, the trade statistics of the port books give at least a partial indication.[81]

Yet grave difficulties remained to be overcome. The multiplicity and acrimony of the lawsuits spawned by the industry point to some of the failures of the entrepreneurs. They still had much to learn about methods of successful production, in particular the techniques of realistic costing and financing. A number of them overreached their resources in their initial outlay, and others failed to fulfil their contracts on time. The costly litigation in which they became involved only compounded their difficulties. The extravagant felling of woodlands, though it solved an immediate fuel problem, made timber a fast-wasting asset. Transport of the bulky finished product to the coast was still cumbersome and expensive; and sea voyages could be hazardous and lead to delay, as William Mathew and Thomas Mynyffee discovered, when a gale in the Bristol Channel prevented them from shipping a consignment of iron from Cardiff on time to a Bristol merchant, who promptly sued them. The first steps might have been taken towards the major iron industry of the future, but progress was still slow and faltering.[82]

COPPER SMELTING

During the Elizabethan age the crown firmly insisted upon its exclusive rights to 'mines royal', i.e. the ores of those metals needed for coinage: gold, silver, quicksilver, copper, and tin. Royal policy towards them was to encourage their discovery and exploitation in the wider interests of national wealth, employment, and economic self-sufficiency. To achieve these ends, German experts were encouraged to settle in the country, their technical operations to be financed by native capital. The situation was formalized in 1568 by the creation of two joint-stock chartered companies, that of the Mines Royal and of the Mineral and Battery Works, which, between them, were given monopoly rights to discover and work 'mines royal' throughout England and Wales. The Mines Royal company, enjoying a monopoly in the whole of Wales, except Monmouthshire, in 1580 leased its mining rights in the north of England, Wales, Devon, and Cornwall to Thomas Smythe and his partners. In 1584 one of Smythe's associates, probably Thomas Weston, who had spent some time engaged on Smythe's interests in Wales, or William Carnsew, a Cornish squire who had married one of the Stradlings, mooted the idea of building a smelting house near Neath to smelt Cornish copper. The choice of site had much to recommend it. Copper smelting demanded large quantities of coal and timber for charcoal as fuel, neither of which were readily available in Cornwall but existed in abundance round Neath. In addition, the site chosen at Aberdulais was secluded—if secrecy of operation were needed, it had easy access to the sea along the river, and it had a strong fall of water in the Dulais cascade to provide water-power. As an added bonus the chief landlord in the area was the earl of Pembroke, himself associated with the Mines Royal.[83]

Two furnaces were raised at Aberdulais, capable of dealing with 560 tons of ore in 40 weeks. They had a possible daily output of 24 cwt.—the product of seven hours' smelting and the consumption of 89 sacks of charcoal and three horse-loads of coal. To supervise the operations a German expert, who had previously worked in the copper mines at Keswick and Cornwall, Ulrich Frosse, supported by a master copper-maker, a qualified under-smelter, and a German carpenter, was brought to Neath. Frosse, though a somewhat melancholic, thin-skinned man and a born worrier, was a capable and conscientious technician. It has been claimed for him that he achieved a 'marked advance towards the creation of the reverberatory furnace' for smelting and that he should be assigned a 'conspicuous place in the development of copper smelting processes'. However, the concern at Neath was confronted with formidable problems which proved too much for it. Deliveries of ore supplies from Cornwall were uncertain and uneven, and their sulphide composition made them particularly difficult and expensive to analyse and smelt. Nor was the supplementary source of supply, the copper and lead mines at Cwmsymlog, Cardiganshire, adequate to make good the deficiencies in the 1590s. There were serious drawbacks over timber supplies from Coed Iarll, which led to legal actions. Finance was a particularly worrying source of weakness, especially after the illness of Thomas Smythe in 1591. There was a shortage of ready cash at the works and a suggestion was made that the high wages paid to Frosse should be reduced. By the time Smythe's lease ran out in 1598 he was not sorry to relinquish his interest to the celebrated London-Welsh merchant, Thomas Myddelton. The latter, however, was faced with demands for added rent and an entry fine by the local landlord, Thomas ap Hopkins. Following an appeal by Myddelton to the Privy Council, a commission of Glamorgan gentry was set up to ensure that he was given a lease on reasonable terms, but the outcome is not known. What does seem certain is that very little smelting was afterwards undertaken at Neath, though there is a record of copper being exported from there as late as 1605. The significance of the venture lay in what it portended not what it achieved. The laying of solid foundations for the future greatness of Neath and Swansea as the centres of copper smelting had to await the coming of Sir Humphrey Mackworth at the end of the seventeenth century (below, pp. 364–6). Even so, Frosse's smelting-house is a highly interesting episode exemplifying three distinctive characteristics of Elizabethan industrial venture: the exploitation of new or neglected resources; the employment of alien technical expertise; and the creation of inter-regional economic dependence.[84]

MISCELLANEOUS INDUSTRIES

Some lesser known minor industries had survived from the Middle Ages to flourish in the sixteenth century and beyond. One of the more important of them was ship-building, of which Swansea seems to have been the most active centre within the county. The town's medieval charters had contained provisions granting the citizens the right to cut down timber to build 'four great ships . . . at the same time', and 'as many small vessels as they will, able to carry 20 hogsheads of wine or less'. An added fillip to ship-building was given by the rapid rise of a coal export trade in the sixteenth century. Of at least 37 local ships known to have plied in and out of Swansea and Mumbles between 1558 and 1640 many, if not all, must have been locally built. The Swansea Common Attorneys' accounts of the early-seventeenth century show a busy scene on the Strand at Swansea, with many barques and pinnaces being built there. So brisk had the 'building of barques and boats at the New Quay and several places on the Strand' become by 1652 that it caused 'great annoyance and several inconveniences' to shipping using the port, with the result that the town authorities felt it necessary to prohibit boat-building on the corporation quay. Other pointers to the flourishing state of the ship-building industry in Swansea are the large amounts of canvas, tar, pitch, and oakum imported into the town. Neath, like Swansea a busy coal port and sited in a well-timbered locality, also appears to have had its ship-builders. In a letter to Sir Edward Stradling of 1582 William Carnsew referred to a Cornish merchant, Richard Vivian, having been 'about the parts of Neath in Wales, and there making his ship anew, which he accounted to do with less charges than here in our county Cornwall, by reason of the good store of timber, which is not so plentiful [here]'. A small but busy port like Aberthaw had a number of ships built in the seventeenth century at the Booth and Marsh House. 'The business was mainly in the hands of local merchants, namely the Hollands, the Cottons, the Powels, the Walters of west Aberthaw, and the Batsleys, as well as the Spencers. These merchants employed local carpenters and shipwrights.' Doubtless there was similar activity in Cardiff and the other ports.[85]

Fishing, both on the river estuaries and at sea, was another medieval occupation which retained its importance. The letting of sites for 'henges' (stationary nets) along the banks of the Taff and the Rhymney provided a useful supplementary source of income for the lord of Glamorgan. As late as the eighteenth century the Taff was a river in which 'prodigious quantities' of salmon were taken. Fishermen are frequently referred to in the Cardiff and Swansea records, and Glamorgan inventories sometimes note shares held in small boats and tackle. Along the shores, also, seaweeds had long been burnt so that their ashes might be used either to nourish the soil or in the making of soft soap and for other cleaning purposes, and in 1517 a customs duty of 1½*d*. a ton had been levied on ashes in Swansea. The practice undoubtedly continued during our period, but it is more clearly illustrated for the later seventeenth century (below, pp. 346–8). Another minor industry which may have been a valuable by-employment for shore-dwellers was the gathering of marram grass to make rush mats. It was claimed that on the lower burrows of Merthyr Mawr some 'ten thousand yards of fine mat yearly after 40*s*. the thousand' were made.[86]

Among other industries which may have gained ground during this period were brewing, salt-refining, lime-burning, potteries, and glass-making. All had one thing in common: each was making greater use of coal, a commodity becoming increasingly plentiful in Glamorgan. Tantalizing glimpses of them are all we derive from the contemporary records, which suggests that they can hardly have been operating on a very big scale. Cardiff brewers, like Anne Andrews and William Nailer, were certainly importing sizeable consignments of barley-malt in the Elizabethan era. Large quantities of salt, too, were being brought into Cardiff and Swansea, and the existence of smaller cargoes of salt among the exports from Cardiff may possibly point to the refining locally of the salt, while an Exchequer suit of 1615 refers to a 'salt works' at Barry which had supplied salt to Gloucester. Lime-burners figure frequently in the parochial records of Cardiff, and may be assumed to have supplied the needs of prosperous farmers in the vicinity. For the manufacture of pottery the only uncertain clue we have is a reference by the eighteenth-century antiquary, Iolo Morganwg, who tells us that suitable brick clay for pottery was found within Glamorgan only at the Great Heath near Cardiff, Pencoed, and especially Ewenni, where he describes the manufacture of brown pottery as having, 'from time immemorial been carried on on a pretty large scale, supplying half south Wales nearly with this useful article'. The evidence for glass-making is much more tenuous, consisting as it does of a tradition that Sir Robert Mansel, after failing in a glass-making venture at Milford Haven in 1615, was similarly unsuccessful at Swansea. There was, undoubtedly, a flourishing glass industry in Swansea later in the century (below, pp. 346–7).[87]

v.

TRADE PATTERNS

It is a commonplace of British economic history that successive Tudor régimes were much preoccupied with the need to foster trade. Wales, brought more closely by the Tudors within the orbit of their realm, gained from the effects of the Navigation Acts, the Act of Union, the appointment of vice-admirals along the coast, and other measures designed to encourage commerce. Such royal solicitude would have availed little had there not been new energies independently coursing through the economic life of the country. In Glamorgan both agriculture and industry were responding in lively fashion to the attractions of the wider market as well as local demand. The resultant increases in production were mirrored in the trade patterns of the county. The commodities sent out were the fruits of its mixed and pastoral farming: corn, livestock, dairy produce, hides, and wool; but a mounting volume of its industrial production—coal especially; iron, copper, and lead to a lesser extent—was also being exported. Though most of the county's output was directed to destinations within England and Wales, a significant proportion of its industrial goods went to foreign markets. The return traffic made good some of the deficiencies of Glamorgan's own agricultural production by imports such as malt and fruit from the West Country and the Severn basin, and it also brought in necessities like salt or luxuries like wine from European countries, either directly or by re-exports from English ports.

Little of the county's thriving trade was carried on overland. From the north of Glamorgan some livestock may have been driven along familiar drovers' routes into the Midlands, and some of the coal and iron was brought by pack-horse to be used locally or on its short haul to the ports. In general, however, the state of the roads and tracks was too bad to allow much land transport. Even within the county town and its immediate environs local inhabitants were frequently summoned to answer to the Court of Great Sessions for the insufficiency of highways and bridges. It was on river and sea communications that Glamorgan had perforce to depend for conducting the great bulk of its commerce. The county prospered, like Pembrokeshire, the other main entrepôt of south Wales trade, because it was blessed with easy outlets to the sea through the many harbours and creeks, great and small, along its coastline. These pulsating arteries of water-borne trade were what made Glamorgan a flourishing member of the busy commercial zone of the Bristol Channel and Severn basin.[88]

Glamorgan's natural havens at the mouth of almost every river and stream had been used since prehistoric times. During the Middle Ages the score of multifarious creeks and harbours* were the scene of busy activity, since water carriage was much the most convenient form of transport. From these ports and creeks a vigorous coast-wise and foreign trade grew up under the aegis of the Marcher lords. Though the harbours

---

*The names of the ports and creeks listed by Dr. Thomas Phaer in 1552-3 are Cardiff, Penarth, Sully, Barry, Aberthaw, Newton, Neath, Swansea, Mumbles, Oxwich, Port Eynon, and Worm's Head. Others noted in Elizabethan documents are Ogmore, Baglan, Briton Ferry, Llangennydd, Loughor, and three obscure 'pills' (streams)—'Mondies', 'Trascons', and 'Hookes'. Kenfig was at this time almost completely choked with sand, and Colhugh was in decay.

were not excluded from statutes enforcing the payment of customs duties
to the crown, the various expedients devised from time to time for the
collection of these duties proved unavailing. Following the union of
England and Wales changes were gradually introduced in an effort to
control the trade of these ports. A prime object in the uniting of Wales
to England was the enhancement of royal revenues, and it can hardly
be a coincidence that in 1545 Henry VIII appointed John Cole as
searcher at the port of Cardiff and other ports in Glamorgan, though
his tenure of office proved to be short and unproductive. There followed
in 1552–3 a report prepared for the crown by Dr. Thomas Phaer,
which revealed that the whole coast of Glamorgan and Monmouthshire
was controlled by the earls of Pembroke and Worcester. Such tolls as
were collected went to the earls, but a large quantity of butter and
hides was exported without paying any toll. Not until early in Elizabeth's
reign was a serious effort made to rationalize the customs organization
of Welsh ports, when all the harbours of Wales were grouped under the
three head ports of Chester, Milford, and Cardiff, which was to be the
head port for all the ports and creeks from Chepstow to Worm's Head,
with customs houses at Cardiff and Swansea. The intention was unmistakably to place in the appropriate ports the main customs officers:
the controller, customer, searcher, and surveyor.[89]

The actual appointment of such officers in Glamorgan was a tardy
process. In June 1559 Henry Morgan was appointed searcher at Cardiff
but no other officer was installed there. Morgan found himself faced
with stiff opposition and, during 1560–1, he reported to the Exchequer
a number of cases of customs evasion, none of which appears to have
been brought to trial. In 1563 the much more forceful John Leek was
appointed customer at Cardiff. He soon found himself coming up against
the well-entrenched vested interests of the earls of Pembroke and Worcester
and their representatives. At Swansea the earl of Worcester's agent,
Leyshon Price, J.P., of Briton Ferry, instructed the town's officers to
ignore Leek and to continue to load and discharge ships without royal
warrant, payment of customs, or search. When Leek tried to enforce
his authority Price had him arrested. This led to a meeting between
Lord Treasurer Winchester and the earl of Worcester, at which the
latter conceded the right of the crown to levy tonnage and poundage
at the ports under his control. There was similar contention over the
earl of Pembroke's ports of Cardiff, Sully, and Neath. In 1566 the
earl's claim to tonnage and poundage was rejected by the Barons of
the Exchequer, as was his son's in 1572. Effectively, the crown's right
to levy customs in the Glamorgan ports was 'established and in some
measure enforced from 1565 onwards'. Other obstacles still remained.
Some Bristol merchants were evading the payment of customs at home
by unloading in south Wales ports and trans-shipping to Bristol, and
others were engaged in the illegal export of goods from south Wales.

To eliminate such practices the ports of Glamorgan and Monmouthshire were put under the control of the port of Bristol in 1567, an expedient that was short-lived and unsuccessful. The customer at Cardiff, John Leek, was himself not above reproach. In 1571 he was dismissed from office and, shortly afterwards, proceedings were taken against him for compounding with persons exporting or importing goods without paying customs duties, releasing goods or vessels seized for offences after compounding with their owners, failing to prosecute for offences, and blackmailing non-offenders into compounding with him.[90]

Only from about 1573 onwards do tonnage and poundage appear to have been levied with some regularity at Cardiff and its member ports. Tonnage represented a payment of 3s. per tun on all wines imported. Poundage consisted of an *ad valorem* subsidy duty of 12d. in the £ payable on all merchandise exported and imported, along with an additional *ad valorem* custom of 3d. in the £ payable by all alien merchants. But for a long time after 1573 the situation was far from satisfactory from the Crown's point of view. There were frequent complaints of opposition to the payment of customs, of illegality, evasion and corruption on the part of merchants and customs officers, and of violence offered to customs officials. In 1585 the inhabitants of south Wales fiercely objected to the new impost on wine because 'the traffic of strangers' was now sorely decayed to 'their great impoverishment'; yet, conversely, as late as 1619 Bristol merchants were no less insistent that their profitable Gascon wine trade was being ruined 'for that out of ports in Wales impost free most of their customers for wines were being served at a lower rate than could be by Bristol merchants afforded'. Some evasion of customs may have been taking place at smaller ports still under the control of their manorial lords, such as Aberthaw, of which Sir Edward Stradling claimed that he and his ancestors had been the 'only lords and possessioners since the Norman Conquest', or Ogmore, where they had taken 'duties without contradiction or interruption of boats arriving in the river Ogmore'. In an undated letter to Sir Edward, Nathaniel Morgan, a customs officer, informed him—not without deferential circumspection —that he had been obliged to take action at Aberthaw against a boat from Port Eynon landing salt there without inspection or payment of custom. But evidence exists, too, of the illegal departure of leather and butter on a considerable scale from the two biggest ports, Cardiff and Swansea.[91]

The gravest allegations, unparalleled elsewhere in Wales, were made against those very port officials whose function it should have been to detect and prevent illegal trade and the evasion of customs duties. In 1598 a controller of Cardiff, John Millom, alleged to be unable to read or write, was found guilty of 'sundry foul and notorious misdemeanours and offences' by the Court of Star Chamber, fined £200, and put in the pillory. A few years later, in 1609, Peter Semayne, whose clandestine export of ordnance along with Edmund Mathew has already been referred to, was accused, together with a number of other Cardiff men, of unlawfully importing wine, and, a short time later, in 1617, of bribing Matthew Price, the customer of Cardiff, though it is fair to add that the Attorney General did not believe he had sufficient evidence to proceed very far with this accusation. A year or two previously, however, in November 1615 he had brought very serious charges against Matthew Price, Edward Jordan, the controller at Cardiff, and Hopkin Davy, deputy controller at Swansea. All three were accused, as John Leek had been in 1571, of accepting bribes, rewards, and favours, of concealing forfeitures, of allowing the export of cloth, wool, lead, tallow, butter, cheese, hemp, and flax without payment of custom, and the import of Gascon wine without payment of duty. They were also charged with having issued, in return for bribes, blank warrants allowing the transport overseas of prohibited goods. Their answers to these charges were not very convincing. Even less convincing were the replies of Thomas Williams, former searcher at the port of Cardiff, and his brother, Philip, who succeeded him, to accusations brought against them by the Attorney General in 1618. Thomas Williams was charged with having conspired with Bristol merchants during the years from 1614 to 1616 to export illegally 10,000 kilderkins (a kilderkin was a cask holding 16 to 18 gallons or the equivalent in butter) to France, Portugal, and other countries, on which Williams got 1s. per kilderkin for himself. Later, his brother, Philip, ' "noseled" and bred up' by Thomas, had accepted bribes from merchants in Bristol, London, Cardiff, and Newport, for the illegal export of a further 10,000 kilderkins. Thomas Williams's only reply to these charges was a plea that he had the king's pardon for all offences committed by him before November 1617, and Philip replied that he was already facing charges in the Court of Exchequer. In 1622, Edmund Morgan, then customer of Cardiff, brought an action in the Exchequer against Morgan Harry, deputy collector at Swansea, in which he accused him of preventing the customer from having proper access to the custom house at Swansea, of making illegal compositions and issuing illegal documents to merchants in 'alehouses and other private and obscure places', and of conniving at and even encouraging the illicit export of a 'great quantity of leather and other prohibited goods'. Unfortunately, no answer by Morgan Harry to this bill of complaint has survived. Yet a customs official's life could also be a hazardous one; a lesson fatally learned by Matthew Giles, customer at Aberthaw, when he was murdered by some French seamen there in 1618.[91A]

In view of what has already been written about the shortcomings in the customs administration and its officials it is hardly to be wondered at that the records kept by them, the port books, are an imprecise instrument for measuring the nature and volume of Glamorgan trade. Quite apart from the misdeeds of the officers themselves, there are other difficulties connected with the use of port books for studying contemporary trade. The purpose of the books was to keep a financial not a trading record; they take no account of widely-prevalent smuggling, evasion of duties, or the malpractice of officials; they give us little or no information about the smaller havens or creeks; they do not record the movement of livestock; and there are long periods for which no port books have survived. Nonetheless, whatever their imperfections, when supplemented by other sources they succeed in giving us almost for the first time an invaluable broad picture of Glamorgan trade and some of the ships and merchants that participated in it. Overall, they give an impression of buoyant and expanding trade.[92]

The testimony of the port books is reinforced by the evident care with which municipalities and individuals tried to maintain and improve the facilities available for shipping at quays and havens. The Swansea records give us a unique account of the corporation's unremitting concern for the proper upkeep of harbour resources and their extension whenever appropriate. Regularly each year the town appointed a 'layer-keeper' to supervise the 'layer', or mud-bank, in the river Tawe, where vessels could lie high and dry without fear of damage when the tide ran out. Regulations designed to prevent the indiscriminate discharge of ballast on the 'layer' were stringently enforced and stiff fines imposed on those who infringed them. New quays were built in 1585 and 1597, and another in 1616 by an alert and energetic portreeve, Walter Thomas, who himself had a big stake in the coal trade of the area. Expenditure on the regular maintenance of the quays is frequently noted in the town records. Private initiative was responsible for the docks built in Swansea by Edmund Rich and Sir Thomas Mansel in the 1620s. Though infinitely less is known about the town quay at Cardiff there is no reason to believe that the citizens were less solicitous for its welfare than those of Swansea were for theirs. In 1552 Cardiff people declared that 'a great part of the common wealth of the town and country resteth only in the maintenance' of the quay, to which they had often been obliged to divert income from one of the town's chantries. A quite small and insignificant haven like Port Eynon had its new quay 'lately builded' by Sir Edward Mansel, with the 'aid of the country of Gower', according to Rice Merrick in 1578; and among the claims to fame of Sir Edward Stradling were his efforts to strengthen the sea-wall in his harbour of Aberthaw and to construct a tiny harbour at Ogmore.[93]

GLAMORGAN'S EXPORTS

The outward trade of Glamorgan consisted to a large extent of the products and by-products of her farming. For the most part these goods formed the county's coastwise traffic, though there are instances of cargoes of cloth, butter, barley, and rye going from Cardiff to Rochelle

F

and Brittany, and of cloth and barley going from Swansea to France. Corn supplies in the county were often more than adequate for local consumption and could be used to supply others' needs. A particularly valuable market was Bristol, a regional capital of major status, easily the largest city in the West of England, and one whose population had doubled from 6,000 in 1546 to 12,000 in 1600. To supply its needs Bristol depended heavily on Glamorgan among other counties, and it exercised a pull on the county's farming resources similar to that exerted on many English counties by London, though on a smaller scale. In 1630 the mayor and aldermen of Bristol explained to the Privy Council that their city 'containing 18 parishes and being very populous hath heretofore had provision of all sorts of corn and grain brought into it in small barques and vessels . . . from the counties of Devon, Cornwall, Pembroke, and Glamorgan, for the necessary provision and relief of the inhabitants'. Nor was it only Bristol that took Glamorgan corn; Tewkesbury and Gloucester were also willing to buy it, and small amounts went to France. During the wars in Ireland at the end of Elizabeth's reign heavy demands were made on Glamorgan to supply the troops there with corn and butter, notwithstanding the risks that these goods might be illegally shipped out of the country on the pretext of being exported to Ireland. Out of 70 cargoes shipped from Cardiff in 1600, no fewer than 25 were destined for Ireland, as compared with 21 for Bristol.[94]

A big market for meat also existed in Bristol and the West of England. Large numbers of Glamorgan cattle and sheep were shipped across the Bristol Channel from Sully to Uphill, Aberthaw and Newton to Minehead and Watchet, and Oxwich and Port Eynon to Combe. From the ports they were driven overland by their drovers to the fairs of Somerset, Devon, and Bristol. On the short crossing between Aberthaw and Minehead there was an almost daily traffic when tides and weather were favourable, with passengers and livestock being brought over. As many as 240 sheep might be transported in a boat of 20 tons; and it was claimed that one south Wales cattle-dealer made 20 journeys from Wales to Somerset between June 1622 and May 1623, bringing at least 20 beasts on each trip. An act of 1555 required cattle-drovers to be licensed, and some of the earliest surviving licences date from this period. The drovers' trade was evidently a flourishing one, for by 1637–40 the Mansels of Margam who had, in 1572, been heavily committed to dairy produce, seem to have been dealing almost exclusively in cattle for the graziers.[95]

But if the Mansels had given up dairy produce, it remained a prime source of income for many other Glamorgan producers. In 1552–3 Thomas Phaer reported on the 'great lading of butter and cheese along the Glamorgan coast', and Defoe's statement that southern Glamorgan supplied Bristol with butter 'just as Suffolk does the city of London' could well have been just as true a century and a half before he made it.

Undoubtedly, great quantities of butter and cheese are shown by the port books to have been exported to Bristol and other western ports. It was valuable enough a trade for members of the Bristol Society of Merchant Venturers to obtain, in 1619, a share in the patent allowing the export of a certain amount of butter overseas to Spain, Portugal, and France. It was in Glamorgan and Monmouthshire that most of the butter was bought for this purpose. In 1639 there was a record of local buyers being appointed in Cardiff and Swansea, assisted by Bristol coopers to 'visit, search and allow of the goodness of the said butter and the sufficiency of cooping and trimming the cask'. Serious breaches of the patent were alleged by the Merchant Venturers in 1620. This was hardly surprising, since illegal export of butter and corn had been common in Glamorgan 40 or 50 years earlier, some of it going un-punished, and some of the men responsible being detected in their offences and punished for them by Special Commission of the Exchequer and in the Court of Great Sessions. Obviously the trade in butter was of the utmost value to Glamorgan farmers. When shipping carrying Glamorgan butter to France and Ireland was preyed on by Barbary pirates in 1625-6, the deputy-lieutenants of the county maintained to the king's government that the farmers could not pay their rent and the whole county was impoverished.[96]

Wool, hides, leather, and tallow left the Glamorgan ports in smaller quantities than butter and cheese. Even so, Dr. Moelwyn Williams has cogently argued that Bristol merchants believed it to be worth their while establishing the same sort of monopoly over Glamorgan wool as they enjoyed over its butter. Dr. Thomas Phaer, in his report of 1552-3, commented that along the Glamorgan coast went 'away much leather and tallow to the ships of Bristol and so forth over seas without search or any controlment'. An Exchequer suit of 1594 reveals how merchants from the Channel Islands, alleging that they were loading 200 dickers of tanned leather at Swansea for Plymouth, in fact intended it to be taken illegally to Spain. The elusive glimpses of more lawful and normal trade that we get from the port books in the years 1599-1600 and 1601-2, two years which, for once in a way, are fairly fully-documented, indicate that most of the wool was exported from Aberthaw and Newton to Minehead and from Cardiff to Bristol. Most of the skins, hides, and tallow then recorded went from Cardiff to Bristol.[97]

When it came to industrial exports, coal was unquestionably king. The basis was provided for a lucrative coal export trade two centuries before the coming of the Industrial Revolution. It was largely con-centrated in the western ports of the county. True, there were some exports from Cardiff to Rochelle and an occasional cargo from Barry and Aberthaw, but the great bulk of the coal went from Swansea, with Neath as an important secondary outlet. The absence of port books for such long stretches makes it impossible to give precise statistics, but the following table of estimates compiled by Professor J. U. Nef gives an approximation of the growth of the trade:

Estimated annual coal shipments, 1550–1640

Port	1551–60	1591–1600	1631–40
Swansea	1,800 tons	3,000 tons	} 12,000 tons
Neath	600 tons	1,000 tons	

Another way of illustrating the same development is to give available figures for the number of cargoes leaving these ports:

Year	Swansea	Neath
1580	21	8
1588	42	—
1600	47	46
1607	76	15

A large proportion of the outgoing cargoes went in foreign trade, especially to France, where coal had now almost completely superseded Glamorgan's medieval trade in woollen cloths. Most of the coal destined for France went to the Breton ports, with smaller amounts going to Normandy. Jersey and Guernsey were also substantial customers. It was a trade profitable to exporters and importers. Despite the rise in prices from 3s. to 6s. a chaldron in Elizabethan Wales, foreign buyers were charged double these amounts; but even then they made a fat profit, selling the coal in France for as much as £2 a chaldron (c. 2 tons) and even £4 in 1630. Most of the foreign cargoes were carried in vessels from France or the Channel Islands, many of which arrived in ballast. There were, however, some vessels from Swansea and Neath engaged in carrying coal to Rochelle and bringing salt and wine in return. Voyages direct to the Channel Islands might take up to six or seven days and those to France a few days longer; so shipping usually avoided making the voyages during the winter months of November, December, and January, with their short days and adverse weather. The coal trade was handicapped to some extent by the imposition of additional taxes. In 1599 an additional tax of 5s. per chaldron of coal was imposed on foreign exports; but some uncertainty exists about how far the trade was affected by this imposition. Quite apart from any unauthorized evasion of duty which may have occurred, there is no evidence in the Swansea port book of 1606–7 that the tax was being imposed on coal leaving the port, and in 1608 the Isle of Man, Jersey and Guernsey were declared exempt from it. On the other hand, the deputy controller of the port of Swansea, in an Exchequer suit of 1615, testified that the farmer of the imposition on coal had a resident deputy at Swansea 'who diligently looketh to all duties' due upon it. An additional tax raised on coal in 1620 and another in 1634, together with the levies raised to meet the cost of protecting coal exports during the French war of 1628, undoubtedly had an adverse effect on the foreign trade. It has been estimated that by 1640, out of 12,000 tons of coal being exported from Swansea and Neath, only about 2,000 tons were intended for foreign ports. This fall in foreign traffic may have stimulated the coast-wise trade, which had been of growing value since Elizabethan times. It had been directed to a multiplicity of West Country ports: Barnstaple, Bideford, Ilfracombe, Clovelly, Lynmouth, and Minehead in north Devon and Somerset; Fowey, Falmouth, and Looe in Cornwall; Plymouth, Dartmouth, and Salcombe in south Devon; and occasional cargoes had gone to Southampton, London, Dover, Yarmouth, and Ireland.[98]

Iron came a poor second to coal among industrial exports. It was dispatched by sea from Cardiff to Rye in the 1560s at Sir Henry Sidney's instance, as has been seen. Other small cargoes, mainly from Cardiff to Bridgwater, are recorded in the Elizabethan port books. Most interesting is the occasional note of exports of ordnance from Cardiff, among which those of Edmund Mathew stand out. In May 1600 he despatched to London 48 pieces of iron ordnance called 'sakers and mynions'.* Swansea does not appear to have shared in this iron trade in the sixteenth century, but in the seventeenth century it began to export iron to Bristol and other ports in the West and South of England, and by 1629–30 was shipping the relatively large amount of 107 tons to Bristol and 12 tons to Barnstaple. No record exists in the Elizabethan port books of the export of any copper from Glamorgan, but there are one or two references to small cargoes of lead from Cardiff and Swansea.[99]

GLAMORGAN'S IMPORTS

Our sources show a miscellany of imports arriving at Glamorgan ports, both from foreign countries and coastwise from Bristol and other West Country ports. Of the foreign countries concerned France was easily the largest supplier and provided the two most significant imports, salt and wine. Salt, essential for the preserving of meat, butter, and fish, and for tanning leather, came in large amounts and frequent crossings from Rochelle to Cardiff, Neath, and Swansea. Other commodities brought from France included paper, canvas, treger cloth and other cloths, pitch, tar, oakum, rosin, starch, fish, honey, sugar, vinegar, prunes, raisins, currants, and figs, and re-exports of Spanish iron. Spain sent raisins, oranges, lemons, and a little salt, and Portugal cane sugar, calico, and some salt. Holland was a source of hops, pulse, grain, pitch, cable ropes, and yarn, Ireland of yarn, linen, dye, fish, skins, and hides, and Newfoundland of a little train oil and fish. From Bristol and the West of England came quantities of high-quality leather, barley, wheat,

---

* A 'saker' was a form of small cannon much employed in sieges and on ships. A 'minion' was a small cannon of about 3-inch calibre.

and rye to make good any local shortfall, malt for brewing, apples, pears, peas and beans, and re-exports of cloth, pitch, tar, rice, salt, and wine. An interesting new item among the seventeenth-century imports was tobacco. In March 1603 the first recorded cargo of 1,000 lb. was unloaded at Swansea from the 400-ton *Samson* of Rotterdam. In the next few decades the little port of Aberthaw became well-known for its imports of tobacco direct from St. Kitt's in the West Indies, and in 1638 a local vessel of 200 tons, *Long Thomas*, arrived there 'with about eight score thousand weight of tobacco'.[100]

SHIPS AND MERCHANTS

One of the features of the trade of the period was how small and numerous were the ships engaged in it. Vessels plying coast-wise were usually between 15 and 20 tons, but some as small as 5 or 6 tons are known to have participated. They tended to get bigger in the seventeenth century, but the coasters that left Swansea between Christmas 1629 and Christmas 1630 had an average burden of only 29 tons and those from Neath 27 tons. The size of these vessels was largely determined by the attitude of the customs officials, who sternly discouraged the building of larger coasting ships in case they should be illegally used for foreign trade. In 1636 the Swansea customers brought an action against Bridgwater shipowners on the grounds that they had illegally adapted coasters for sailing to foreign parts in the hope of evading duties payable. Even so, when considering vessels of 30 tons it is worth reminding ourselves that each of them could carry as much as 100 horses. Larger vessels were used for the foreign trade. In the seventeenth century ships like *Long Thomas* (200 tons) and *Great Thomas* (100 tons) plied from Aberthaw to Ireland, France, Spain and even across the Atlantic to the West Indies. Yet many of the Glamorgan vessels engaged on the run to and from France were no bigger than the 40–50 ton *William* or *Moses* of Cardiff, or the 40-ton *Jonas* of Swansea, which made at least half-a-dozen round trips between Swansea and Rochelle in 1587–8. Because the ships were small the trade of even a little port was shared by many of them. At Neath, in the year ending Michaelmas 1600 there were 46 outward shipments made by 32 boats, of which 23 made one voyage each, 6 made 2, 2 made 3, and 1 made 5. Similarly, in the year ending Michaelmas 1602, Cardiff's 28 outward shipments were shared among 15 boats and its 17 inward shipments by 10. Some 23 local vessels have been traced to Swansea during the last decades of the sixteenth century, and 10 to Cardiff. Provisioning, supplying, repairing, and loading and unloading foreign and local vessels must have been a useful source of income and employment for local merchants, shopkeepers, shipwrights, and labourers. Unfortunately, we get no more than the rarest glimpse of this aspect of the logistics of sea-borne trade. But we do know that when *Long Thomas*, a very large vessel, was unloaded at Aberthaw in 1637, 32 men and women were employed for over nine days at 6*d.* a day for the men and 4*d.* a day for the women in unloading her.[101]

The trade carried to and from the Glamorgan ports was directed and organized in a variety of ways, though the inadequacies of the port books, in respect both of continuity and of the details they record, make it difficult to generalize with much confidence. The voyages of nearly all the foreign and English ships calling at Glamorgan destinations were, of course, organized by foreign or English masters or merchants. Many of the county's own ships were commanded by masters who were themselves merchants. From Christmas 1629 to Christmas 1630 the 7 shipments of coal from Neath and all but 15 out of 57 shipments from Swansea were carried by masters acting on their own account. Such men might carry for themselves on one trip and for a merchant on another. In January 1587 the *Mary David* of Swansea, master John Rogers, carried a cargo of coal on Rogers's account; the next time we hear of her, Rogers was bringing in salt from Rochelle for Richard Clement, merchant; and when she appears again, captained this time by John Clement, she was once more carrying salt for Richard Clement. Another Swansea vessel of the same period, the *Jonas*, appears to have been on a regular run from Swansea to Rochelle and back, with John Jenkins as her master acting on behalf of Richard Sadler, merchant, almost without exception.[102]

Merchants themselves were drawn from a mixture of backgrounds and had widely differing degrees of commitment to maritime trade. Not a few of them shipped only a single cargo in a year, e.g. at Cardiff in 1602, 14 merchants are recorded as having supplied only one outward cargo apiece. Some might be farmers interested in small individual cargoes. Craftsmen or traders, like cordwainers, might be responsible for cargoes of leather, as were the Froudes of Cardiff. The brewers of Cardiff, in 1602, commissioned a number of inward cargoes of malt, among them the 6 out of 17 inward cargoes in the name of Anne Andrews, a considerable property-owner as her will reveals, who shipped 106 weys of barley malt from Gloucester to Cardiff, employing three different ships for the purpose. Industrialists like Edmund Mathew or Sir Henry Sidney might have a hand in the trade. Some of the biggest figures were merchants pure and simple—if such adjectives can ever be applied to the merchants of this period! Some, like Richard Sadler of Swansea, specialized in key commodities like coal and salt. But his contemporary, John Tanner of Cardiff, had a finger in a multiplicity of pies. Dealing with only the biggest ships, the *William* (40 tons) and *Moses* (50 tons) of Cardiff, and the *Margaret* (40 tons) of Rochelle, he imported salt, pitch, tar, wine, rosin, figs, and prunes at various times, and exported coal, lead, cloth, and butter. Close connexions existed between merchants on both sides of the Bristol Channel. Cardiff men entered into partnerships with men on the English side of the Channel, and a number of

Glamorgan merchants and apprentices settled in Bristol, while Bristol merchants were very active in Glamorgan. The commercial relationships of the Bristol Channel knew no national boundaries between England and Wales.[103]

PIRACY

Commerce had grown and blossomed in face of many adversities. To the discouragements of tolls and dues and the normal seafarers' hazards of storm and shipwreck were added the depredations of pirates. As trade multiplied in value, so did the swarm of predators who lurked around the western coasts to batten on shipping. They had existed throughout the sixteenth century but were at their most active in the 1570s. Prime targets of their assaults were French and Spanish ships which carried fish, grain, iron, and especially salt and wine, though more exotic cargoes were not unknown. The pirates, having overcome what little resistance there was, brought the captured ships, crews, and cargoes to ports where the complicity and connivance of local officials ensured them of a sympathetic reception and trouble-free disposal of their loot at prices well below what such goods would ordinarily command. Among the ports most favoured by them was Cardiff, described by a Pembrokeshire justice of the peace as 'the general resort of pirates and there they are sheltered and protected'. Cardiff's own citizens were forced to admit that their town had so bad a reputation for associating with pirates that its merchants, when travelling elsewhere, dared not 'avow the place of their dwelling at Cardiff'.[104]

Cardiff's notoriety as a pirates' haunt came about for two reasons: first because of the partiality shown for the town by the foremost pirate, John Callice, 'a notorious malefactor [who] hath committed sundry great piracies', and secondly because of the collusion between him and the leading men of the town and neighbourhood, above all those of the unchallengeable Herbert clan, with whom Callice himself appears to have had some kinship. Ordinary inhabitants of Cardiff found themselves in an unhappy and ambivalent state; they disliked the arrogant ways of the pirates and the notoriety they brought on the town, but at the same time they liked buying stolen goods cheap and they had a 'great fear of some of note' who were hand in glove with the freebooters. Between 1574 and 1576 Callice and his cronies sold in Cardiff and elsewhere the cargoes of at least three ships they had seized, and did so with such brazenness that one whole meeting of the Privy Council was taken up with a discussion of their misdeeds. From the end of 1576 Cardiff was placed under close surveillance, and no fewer than four lots of enquirers into piracy were set to work there by the Privy Council in 1576–7. First came John Croft, next Judge David Lewis, then the two-man team of Fabian Phillips and Thomas Lewis Y Fan, and finally the three-man commission of Sir Edward Stradling, Sir Edward Mansel, and William Mathew. A number of prisoners, mostly small fry, were taken and confessions extracted. In the course of the investigations there was unfolded a bizarre story of the relationships between pirates and local gentry, of mutual visits to homes on land and pirates' ships offshore, and of gay old times in 'taverns and tippling houses in Penarth and Cardiff'. Even Thomas Lewis Y Fan, one of the inquisitors, turned out to be deeply implicated with a number of pirates.[105]

Gradually, some improvement was effected. Early in 1578 the sheriff of Glamorgan, Nicholas Herbert, and other ringleaders involved with pirates were heavily fined and bound over not to repeat their offences. Later in the same year another notorious pirate, Tom Clarke, ventured into Penarth Roads and still managed to find allies among the Herberts and their friends; but on this occasion the pirates were not as warmly welcomed as they had been and had to exercise some compulsion to re-victual their ships. In 1581 a Special Commission of the Court of Great Sessions tried six men in Cardiff for piracy and hanged one. Three years later 11 strangers were put on trial, and these may be the same men as were involved in the piracy of a Barnstaple ship, seized near Lands End and brought to the mouth of the river Ely, about which Sir Edward Stradling was written to for his help. However, an episode of 1586-87 shows how easy it still was for a pirate to evade capture. A pirate called Beere put into Penarth with a valuable Scottish prize. Stradling and his fellow-commissioners were soon on Beere's track, but with the connivance of Cardiff bailiffs, he got away. Irritated by his escape and perhaps suspecting some of the Herberts as well as the bailiffs of complicity, the Privy Council put pressure on the second earl of Pembroke, Lord President of the Council in the Marches as well as lord of Cardiff, to act firmly. It was typical of the sense of personal honour and family loyalty of the age that the earl's reaction should be to write a testy letter to Stradling, Mansel, and Mathew about their dealings with Beere, reproaching them for having proceeded rather 'from malice to me, or contempt of me, than from an upright meaning to redress offences or punish offenders'. He got back rather better than he had given, in a courteous but firm letter from Stradling and Mathew, in the course of which they damningly indicted the Cardiff bailiffs for their partiality to pirates: 'we never learned of any pirate arrived in this road wherein they have not showed their inclination'. After this episode the records are silent about any piracy in Cardiff.[106]

In none of the other Glamorgan ports was piracy as prevalent as at Cardiff and Penarth. Swansea was the one that might have been expected to be as attractive to pirates, and some faint suggestions of piratical activity there do emerge from two letters in Sir Edward Stradling's correspondence. The first, written to him in 1575 by Sir Richard Grenville, briefly mentions the capture of a pirate at Mumbles, and the other, from Sir John Arundel in 1581, seeks to explain that

Arundel's ship, recently berthed at Swansea, had been confiscated from a previous owner for piracy and subsequently entrusted to Arundel. A better-documented visit to Swansea by a pirate ship is that of the *Primrose*, captained by Philip Smith, which sailed into Swansea in 1581 with a cargo of tropical luxuries—brazil wood, cotton, pepper, monkeys, and parrots. These, according to Smith, had been bought from a well-known pirate, Stephen Haynes, whom he had by chance encountered in Torbay. His improbable story was accepted by the piracy commissioners, rendered less critical, perhaps, by the gift of a monkey apiece to Sir Edward Stradling and William Herbert and two parrots to Henry Watkins, customer of Swansea. Cleared at Swansea, the *Primrose* sailed to Neath, where some of her cargo was traded for a lading of coal. This was not the end of her story. The goods she had brought into Swansea had, in reality, been pirated from a French merchant, Adrian le Seigneur of Rouen, whose long and tenacious memory enabled him eventually to bring a suit at the Court of Admiralty against his despoilers. No subsequent record of piracy at Swansea is known to exist for nearly half a century until, in 1629, a pirate vessel was driven ashore at Oystermouth; but the question of piracy was soon overshadowed by the furious and dangerous quarrel over the custody of the ship which broke out between William Herbert of Swansea and Thomas Mansel.[107]

By the early Stuart era it was the Barbary pirates, using subsidiary bases in Ireland, who were terrifying the inhabitants of western Britain with their devastating raids on shipping, carried out in long, light, formidably-armed ships, all too perfectly designed to give chase. Their raids on Glamorgan ships carrying butter have already been noted (above, p. 65) and in 1626 the justices of the peace for the county further lamented that 'within the space of little more than one year now last past, five several good barques within the port of Cardiff and the creeks thereof in this county have been taken by the Turkish pirates of "Sallie" to the utter undoing of many poor merchants here and discouragement of all others'. Let us hope it was of some comfort to Glamorgan men to know that one of the county's sons, Sir Thomas Button, was praised by Bristol merchants as being pre-eminent in trying to suppress 'those common enemies of humane society, the Turkish pirates', and this although his ship, *Phoenix*, had 'incurred imminent danger . . . for want of men, the coast of Ireland and Channel of Severn being very dangerous in winter time'.[108]

CHAPTER II

Glamorgan Society, 1536-1642

By GLANMOR WILLIAMS

i.

POPULATION

THE size of the population of England and Wales, and the nature and rate of any change in it, are notoriously difficult to estimate at any time before the last century, when regular censuses were first taken. Any discussion of population problems for an earlier period must be a hazardous operation which can, at best, provide no more than rough estimates open to a wide degree of error. However, on the basis of such sources as are available to them, historians are generally agreed that the population of England increased substantially during the sixteenth and early-seventeenth centuries. It is difficult to determine just when this rise in population began because of the great uncertainty which still exists concerning population changes during the fifteenth century. However, it seems likely that after the catastrophic drop in population during the fourteenth century and the early part of the fifteenth there was some measure of recovery after about 1450. But the really significant upward trend began in the second or third decade of the sixteenth century. For about a century afterwards population continued to increase, though its growth may have been checked from time to time, especially by the outbreak of a very serious influenza epidemic in the 1550s. The increase may have continued until the 1630s, when there was a marked slowing down, which appears to have been succeeded by stagnation or even a slight decline in population from the 1640s to about 1690. Estimates for the population of Wales during the period tend to show that it followed a similar pattern to that of England, as may be seen from the following figures:

Estimates of the Population of Wales, 1536–1670[1]

1536: 278,000	1630: 405,000
1570: 325,000	1670: 408,000
1600: 379,000	

Turning from these more general estimates to those compiled for the county of Glamorgan, we find that all the sources available for such an exercise are, to a greater or lesser degree, unsatisfactory. Four main sources exist for the purpose: the subsidy rolls of 1543–5; the chantry certificates of 1545; the bishops' returns of 1563; and the bishops' certificates of 1603. To these may also be added a dim additional light cast by a few parish registers.

Of these sources the subsidy rolls are the fullest and most detailed, listing as they do the names of all those who paid the first subsidy levied in Wales. Undoubtedly, they provide the names of the great majority of householders in Glamorgan; but what we do not know is what categories of the population were too poor to be liable for the payment of tax, though it would probably be reasonable to assume that the only people who fell outside its scope were the poorest labourers and domestic servants, and the paupers of course. We do not know, either, what proportion of the total population the non-taxpayers constituted. There is good reason for believing that in Glamorgan, where most of the landholdings were small and worked largely by family labour, farm-labourers did not form as large a proportion of the population as they did in many parts of England. It seems equally probable that within Glamorgan itself labourers formed a smaller fraction of the community in the pastoral uplands than they did in the mixed-farming lowlands. However, even if we knew for certain what percentage of non-taxpayers had to be added to those who paid, we should still be left with only the number of households in the county and not the total population. In order to calculate the latter from the former, a multiplier of five is usually employed, on the assumption that an average household consisted of five persons; a reasonable estimate, but one which can, at best, provide only an approximation.[2]

All the other sources are ecclesiastical returns of one kind or another, and they are less detailed and more unsatisfactory than the subsidy rolls. Chantry certificates of 1545 give estimates of the number of 'houseling people', i.e. communicants, but do so for only a very few parishes. Here again we are faced with the difficulty of deciding what multiplier to use in order to assess the total population from the number of communicants. The one most usually employed has been 1.5, but it has recently been suggested that a multiplier of $\frac{10}{6}$ or $\frac{100}{56}$ might be more accurate. The bishops' returns of 1563 purported to give the number of households in every parish, but we may reasonably doubt whether the figures given are anything more than rough estimates, hastily compiled. In any case, as far as Glamorgan is concerned, they exist only for the deanery of Gower, which lay within the diocese of St. David's. Figures for the diocese of Llandaff, if they were ever compiled, have not survived. In a letter to the Privy Council on the subject, Bishop Kitchen of Llandaff explained that it 'was so great a matter, and of such difficulty, and the time so short that I nor my officers are able to certify your honours without conference had with parsons, vicars, curates, and some honest men of every parish and hamlet'. Conceivably, such a 'conference' never took place and no return was ever made. A return for 1603 does, however, exist, when Bishop Godwin returned the number of communicants and recusants within his diocese. The number of communicants then recorded for Glamorgan was 20,453, plus 45 recusants and 137 'non-communicants'. The total of 20,635 multiplied by $\frac{100}{56}$ would give an estimated population of nearly 37,000—a figure reasonably in line with what might be expected in the light of estimates for 1545-63 and 1670 (below, p. 76). The evidence of the parish registers, though scrappy and limited to a few parishes, confirms that of other sources in suggesting a steady rise in the population over the period. The birth-rate seems to have been distinctly higher than the death rate in most of those parishes where enough evidence exists to measure the difference. In St. Donat's parish over a period from 1571 to 1637 the average annual number of baptisms, at 3.7, was considerably higher then the average number of burials at 2.2. In Pendoylan the comparable figures over a period from 1569 to 1611 were 11.3 baptisms to 7.9 burials, and at Wenvoe from 1589 to 1631 the figures were 9.7 and 6.9 respectively. By contrast, the little parish of Llandough-juxta-Cowbridge had rather more burials in an average year (2.7) than baptisms (2.2), but its register between 1583 and 1640 has a great many gaps.[3]

The most detailed estimates for the population of individual hundreds within the county were those made by the late Leonard Owen, and they are reproduced in the following table:

POPULATION OF GLAMORGAN[4]

| Hundreds and towns | 1545/63 | | 1670 | | % change |
	House-holds	Popu-lation	House-holds	Popu-lation	
Cardiff	253	1,349	467	2,491	86
Caerphilly	452	2,411	848	4,523	88
Meisgyn	421	2,245	791	4,219	88
Dinas Powys	786	4,192	935	4,987	19
Cowbridge	556	2,965	969	5,168	75
Ogmore	424	2,261	657	3,504	55
Llangyfelach	437	2,331	607	3,237	40
Newcastle	546	2,912	1,057	5,637	91
Neath	550	2,933	975	5,200	77
Swansea	736	3,925	1,211	6,458	68
Cardiff town	189	1,008	332	1,771	75
Swansea town	180	960	325	1,733	80
TOTALS	5,530	29,493	9,174	48,928	66

The figures given above were based mainly on the first subsidy returns for the county and on the hearth-tax returns of 1670 (below, pp. 311–12). In order to take account of those too poor to pay tax, ten per cent was added to the number of taxpayers and the whole was multiplied by $5\frac{1}{3}$. The number of households supplied by the bishop of St. David's in 1563 were also taken into account for the hundreds of Swansea and Llangyfelach. On the basis of Leonard Owen's calculations Glamorgan, with an estimated population of 29,493, would have been one of the most densely-populated counties of Wales, second only in aggregate to Carmarthenshire (34,374), a county considerably larger in area than Glamorgan. As compared with the estimates of population based on the chantry certificates or bishops' returns, the figures derived from the subsidy rolls appear to be rather low. Cardiff and Swansea, for instance, on the basis of the subsidy rolls would have had a population of 1,008 and 650 respectively; but the chantry certificates' estimates of the number of communicants multiplied by $\dfrac{100}{56}$ would give totals of 1,340 and 1,070 respectively; and on the basis of the bishop's return of 1563 Swansea would have a population of c. 900–960. By 1670, estimates based on the hearth-tax returns suggest that the population of the county may have risen by 66 per cent to as high a total as 48,928, which made it the most populous Welsh county at that date. A more cautious estimate, based on the same returns but using a multiplier of 4.5 to 5 per household, would give a population of between 40 and 45,000 (below, pp. 311–12). While there would appear to be no reason to doubt that the population of Glamorgan, like that of England and Wales generally, had increased substantially during our period, we have to beware of placing too firm a reliance on estimates which may conceal a wide margin of error.[5]

Our sources may be used with more confidence to illustrate the distribution of population within the county than to compute its total population. They show, as might be expected, a marked difference in density between the population of the mixed-farming lowlands and that of the pastoral uplands. The hundred of Dinas Powys, with an estimated population of 4,192 or 65 persons per square mile, was one of the most thickly-populated hundreds in Wales, whereas in the northern hundreds of the county population ranged between 15 and 29 persons per square mile. Similarly in the two westernmost hundreds of Swansea and Llangyfelach, there was a dramatic difference between the one taxpayer to every 59.2 acres in the former and the one taxpayer to 155.2 in the latter; and the differences between individual parishes were ranged in even wider extremes, from the one taxpayer to 23.2 acres in Nicholaston parish to the one taxpayer to 216.4 acres in hilly Llan-giwg. We can also glean some impression of the relative proportion of town to country dwellers in Glamorgan at this time. Only four centres of population were really big enough to qualify as towns: Cardiff, Swansea, Neath, and Cowbridge. Others, like Aberafan or Llantrisant, were so decayed that they cannot properly be regarded as towns. Cardiff and Swansea, as we have seen, had populations of 1,008 and 650, or 1,340 and 1,070, depending on whether we use the subsidy rolls or the chantry certificates for computation. Neath and Cowbridge were much smaller. The use of subsidy rolls as a basis gives them an estimated population of 425 and 380; using the chantry certificates we get an estimate of 715 and 470. However, since we do not have chantry certificates for all the Glamorgan parishes we are obliged to use the estimates derived from the subsidy rolls as our basis for comparison with the rural areas. On this showing, the four towns had a population of about 2,463 out of a total of 29,493, or a ratio of about 1:12. Although there may have been some movement into the towns during the period up to 1670, their population does not seem to have increased significantly faster than that of the surrounding countryside. By 1670 the estimated population of Cardiff and Swansea had risen to 1,770 and 1,733 respectively, an increase of 75 and 80 per cent; but this, although slightly greater than the overall increase of 66 per cent for the county, fell below the increase of 91 per cent and 88 per cent for the fastest-growing hundreds of Newcastle, Meisgyn, and Caerphilly. However, if we take Swansea's population on the basis of the subsidy return of 1545 as 650, then by 1670 it had grown by 166 per cent, which may more truly reflect the relatively rapid growth of the coal industry around the town and of coal exports from the port. Once again, however, what becomes plainly apparent is that our figures are not sufficiently well founded to place too much reliance upon them.[6]

ii.

THE SOCIAL DEGREES

THE GENTRY

The one basic social distinction which overrode all others was that which existed between those who were of gentle status and those who were not. To define what constituted a gentleman is not easy. Perhaps the most accurate, as well as the simplest, way of doing so is to say that a gentleman was a man who considered himself to be one and was accepted as such by the community around him. On the face of it, the distinction should have been straightforward enough: a gentleman ought to have been someone who could trace back his descent from gentle stock for many generations. This, however, could be something of an embarrassment in Wales, where there were a relatively large number of the population who could claim descent from families of Welsh *uchelwyr*. The passionate interest of the Welsh in genealogy, their intense pride in their pedigree, and their acute sensitivity on the subject, were all a source of amusement to their English contemporaries. Many of the Welsh gentry were notoriously poor in everything except their family pride. To console themselves for what might be their humble status they fell back on their gentle, even princely, lineage. When the antiquary, John Leland, came to Neath, he encountered 'one Leyshon, a gentleman of ancient stock, but now of mean lands about £40 by the year'. In terms of income this man cut a poor figure, but that did not prevent him from airing to Leland his family's proud boast that they had been 'there in fame before the conquest of the Normans'; a claim that obviously left a deep impression on the antiquary. The family in question, the Leyshons of Baglan, claimed descent from Iestyn ap Gwrgant (*ante*, III, chap. i), an eleventh-century ruler of Glamorgan. There were many others in the county even poorer than the Leyshons, who were just as proudly conscious of their descent from Iestyn, or Gwaethfoed, or Einion ap Collwyn, or one of the other ancient progenitors of the county's gentle stocks.[7]

Two kinds of gentle descent were honoured in Glamorgan, broadly speaking. The one derived from native Welsh families, the other from immigrant Norman or English stocks, the *Advenae*. The Welsh families traced their lineage back to one of four or five main progenitors. Some of the oldest and most reliable Welsh pedigrees were those deriving from Gwaethfoed who, though not readily identifiable, must have been a considerable figure in early Gwent and Morgannwg. From him some of the foremost families of Tudor and Stuart Glamorgan claimed descent, including the Mathews of Llandaff and Radyr and their numerous cadets, the Thomases of Llanbradach, the Lewises of Y Fan and their offshoots, and the Prichards of Llancaeach. Two others claimed as major founders of many Glamorgan lines were Iestyn ap Gwrgant and Einion ap Collwyn, both of whom were reputed to have played so conspicuous a role in Glamorgan history at the time of the first Norman invasions. Iestyn's progeny included a prominent group of families in the west of the county, among them the Leyshons of Baglan, the Evanses of the Gnoll, the Prices of Briton Ferry and Cwrt-y-carnau, the Williamses of Blaen Baglan and Aberpergwm (who also cherished Iestyn's famous motto 'A ddioddefws a orfu' ('He who suffered conquered') as their own), the Thomases of Betws and Llanfihangel, the Thomases of Brigan, and the Loughors of Tythegston. To the more shadowy, possibly mythical, Einion ap Collwyn, the families of Gibbon of Trecastle, Prichard of Collenna, Price of Glyn Neath and its multifarious junior branches, Powel of Llwydarth and Llandow, and others, traced their origins. Maenarch, from whom other Glamorgan families were sprung, was lord of Brycheiniog, and his most influential descendants were settled in Breconshire; but among the most prominent Glamorgan families who looked to him as their ancestor were Jenkins of Hensol, Jones of Fonmon, Seys of Boverton, and Vaughan of Dunraven. Similarly,

Bleddri ap Cadifor was best-known as the founder of the prolific Morgan clans of Gwent, some of whom, like the Morgans of Ruperra and Rhiwbina, settled in Glamorgan. Remembering the deep dynastic attachment of these families and the power of oral tradition and the influence of the bardic order in their midst, the late Professor Griffith John Williams argued strongly that we have good grounds for thinking that these Welsh pedigrees may be reasonably accurate.[8]

Of the families of *Advenae* who had been associated with FitzHamon or his immediate successors in the conquest of Glamorgan, none had any surviving representatives left in Glamorgan. Knightly families like the de Londres, de Cardiffs, Le Sores, or Umfravilles, so conspicuous in the early medieval period, were now all extinct. With the exception of the Turbervilles—and even they had not survived in direct line—none of the prominent *Advenae* families of the sixteenth century can be traced in the county much before the beginning of the fourteenth century. That did not deter many of them from seeking to establish an earlier and more illustrious connection. Sir Edward Stradling's first ancestor to have any connection with the county came there in the thirteenth century; but in his manuscript history of the winning of Glamorgan by the Norman FitzHamon, the squire of St. Donat's linked himself and his forbears with Sir William le Esterling, one of the legendary twelve knights alleged to have been companions-in-arms of FitzHamon. The Buttons of Worlton, who probably established themselves there late in the fourteenth century or early in the fifteenth, claimed as their ancestor a duke of Seville who was said to have married a daughter of Richard de Clare, earl of Gloucester. The Mansels of Oxwich and Margam, wrapped in obscurity before the early fourteenth century, tried to give themselves a longer and more glorious line of descent by associating themselves with a variety of families of name similar to their own and having a more legitimate claim to ancient lineage. The Kemeys of Cefnmabli, despite the obvious Welshness of such names as Iorwerth or Meurig in the earliest stages of their pedigree, claimed for themselves a Norman origin. Nevertheless, the *Advenae*, though relatively recently arrived in the county, numbered among them some of the most vigorous and successful of Glamorgan families, including among them the Aubreys, Bassetts, Carnes, Flemings, Gamages, and Vans, as well as those named already.[9]

Pride in lineage had long been fostered in Glamorgan by the medieval poets, who had traced and eulogized the descent not only of families sprung from native Welsh stock but also of the Cymricized families of the *Advenae*, many of whom, as the result of intermarriages, had as much Welsh as alien blood in their veins (*ante*, III, chap. x). This practice continued into Tudor times, when interest in genealogy had become a positive craze. Long-established families wanted to reassure themselves of their superiority over upstarts; the more newly-arrived

G

were anxious to acquire for themselves family trees as lengthy and distinguished as those claimed by older stocks. Gentlemen with anti-quarian tastes, no less than bards and heralds, were enthralled by genea-logical studies. Their most notable representatives in Glamorgan were Sir Edward Mansel, Rice Merrick, Anthony Powel of Llwydarth, and Sir Edward Stradling of St. Donat's. The last-named was frequently consulted on matters genealogical by other gentlemen with tastes similar to his own, like Henry Vernon who, asking for Stradling's advice, took the opportunity of paying himself and his correspondent a delicate compliment, 'that you yourself being of great antiquity and worship have a mind to maintain and prefer such personages as are like unto yourself'. Stradling's most distinguished correspondent on these matters was the great William Cecil himself, who shared his contemporaries' passion for genealogy. He was desperately anxious to find for himself an ancestor who had been a companion to Robert FitzHamon and, judging by notes in his own hand surviving in the Hatfield archives and purporting to show Cecil descent from one Robert de Sitsilt, who was with FitzHamon at the conquest of Glamorgan, we may conclude that with Stradling's help Burghley convinced himself that he had succeeded in his quest. Stradling and Sir Edward Mansel were also thought to have been mainly responsible for helping the herald Lewis Dwn to obtain the patent granted to him on February 3, 1585 to conduct his visitations in Wales. When Dwn and Twm Siôn Cati (Thomas Jones of Fountain Gate), another of the leading Welsh genealogists of the day, came to Glamorgan on their visits, both Stradling and Mansel were particularly helpful to them (below, pp. 590, 595).[10]

Descent alone, however, unfortified by economic sufficiency, can hardly have been enough to have supported gentle status for long at any time. Certainly, by the sixteenth century, the test was becoming increasingly an economic one; perhaps the very zeal with which men busied themselves with genealogy was itself partly designed to cloak this disagreeable fact. Not that everyone was afraid to face this unpleasant reality. In a classic definition of a gentleman given by Sir Thomas Smith in 1582 he made no bones about what constituted a gentleman:

> In these days he is a gentleman who is commonly taken and reputed. And whosoever studieth in the universities, who professeth the liberal sciences, and to be short, who can live idly and without manual labour and will bear the port, charge, and countenance of a gentleman shall be called master.

However addicted the Welsh might be to genealogy, the concept under-lying Sir Thomas Smith's definition that a gentleman was someone who did not have to work with his own hands was becoming increasingly prevalent in Wales, especially as union with England and closer contact with that country made the greater Welsh gentry better acquainted with the life-style of their English counterparts. As for pedigrees, no man of wealth need worry about them. Compliant heralds were only too willing to oblige with ready-made ones, as Sir Thomas Smith pointed out:

> And if need be, a King of Heralds shall give him for money arms newly-made and invented with crest and all: the title whereof shall pretend to have been found by the said herald in perusing and viewing old registers.

It was just as well for no less a family than the Herberts that heralds were so obligingly inventive. The Herberts had risen very swiftly in the fifteenth and sixteenth centuries, but their descent was decidedly obscure. This was readily remedied by providing them with an elaborate but bogus family tree which ostensibly traced them back to Herbert the chamberlain of Henry I. Any deficiencies in pedigree could much more easily be made good than any shortfall in income.[11]

Looking back on the rise of the gentry traced in an earlier chapter (pp. 29–33), we can quickly observe that the crucial factor in accounting for their success was not their lineage but the degree of skill with which they were able to seize the economic opportunities of the period and avoid its pitfalls. It was not their claim to descent from Gwaethfoed, which they shared with many others, that brought the Lewises Y Fan or the Mathews of Llandaff to the forefront, but their energy and acumen in pressing their interests in the disturbed but fluid conditions of the fifteenth century. Again, Thomas ap William of Betws held himself to be descended from the lords of Afan and Iestyn ap Gwrgant, but he himself was looked down upon as a cooper. The success of his two sons owed little to their gentle blood: the elder, Lewis, was a prodigiously wealthy sheep-farmer, careful to the point of miserliness; and the younger, William, was a successful barrister and husband of Ann, daughter and heiress of the Thomases of Llanfihangel, whose son, Edward Thomas, of Betws and Llanfihangel, was one of the only four Glamorgan baronets before the Civil Wars. Those who might have been expected to be most sensitive to, and alarmed by, the tendency for money to become more esteemed than lineage were the poets; and, indeed, warning notes against what they saw as the supplanting of the generous patrician by the low-bred money-grabber are common in their verse. One of the poems on this theme with the sharpest edge is that by Tomos Brwynllys (c. 1580–90) to the 'Miser and the Usurer', and at one point he sums up his own fears and those of many of his fellows thus:

> Llawn travael yw r dyn haelwych
> Ar okrwr ydiw r gwr gwych;
> Gwaed isel a godysent
> A sy yn pryny pob rent.

> ('The fine and generous man is sorely troubled, and the usurer is become the great man; low blood has been exalted and is buying up every rent.')

Moreover, it was very noticeable that almost all the really successful gentry, whatever their genealogical or geographical background, sooner or later established themselves in or near the Vale of Glamorgan, where economic opportunities were at their most promising. Those who remained in the uplands, no matter how distinguished or ancient their ancestry, never rose above the status of minor gentry. Undoubtedly the only men who could expect to play a leading role in the political and administrative life of the county were the most wealthy landowners, (below, pp. 161–75). The economic circumstances of most of the Glamorgan gentry families were, admittedly, distinctly modest as compared with those of the gentry in many English counties. Even so, when Symonds gave his list of the county gentry in 1645 he was able to name 35 heads of families whom he considered to be worth £300 a year or more and to refer to upwards of 100 unnamed families with an income of £40–200 a year. It may be worth noting that Symonds seems to have been interested only in the income of these families not their lineage. Yet, descent continued to count for a good deal. There were many men whose possessions were smaller than those of yeomen or farmers but who would nevertheless be accounted as 'gentlemen' (below, pp. 86–7).[12]

Within the ranks of the upper class itself there were differences of degree. At the top of the social order came the peerage. In Glamorgan at this time there were no resident peers, though at rare intervals the earls of Pembroke and Worcester paid fleeting visits to the county. Just below the peers came the baronets, first created by James I in 1611. This inflation of honours by the king gave rise to a fierce scramble in many counties for the prestige of becoming the first families within the county to attain the honour. Two Glamorgan notabilities, Sir John Stradling and Sir Thomas Mansel, on whose tomb the distinction was carefully recorded, were made baronets by James I in the first creation on May 22, 1611. Two more were created by Charles I in 1642: Sir Nicholas Kemeys of Cefnmabli and Sir Edward Thomas of Betws and Llanfihangel. Knighthoods were an older dignity but had not been very common in Glamorgan in the sixteenth century. The only two families the head of which was regularly knighted in each generation from the reign of Henry VIII onwards were the Stradlings and the Mansels, which had doubtless constituted very strong grounds for making them baronets in 1611. Sir George Herbert of Swansea and two of his grandsons, William and John, were knighted. The Aubreys of Llantriddyd, who did not enter the county until Elizabeth's reign, were regularly knighted in each generation, and Sir John Aubrey became a baronet in 1660. Not until 1603 was one of the Lewises of Y Fan knighted, but then James I made up for lost time by knighting Edward Lewis senior and his son, another Edward. Two younger sons of Edward Lewis senior, Sir William of Cilfach-Bargoed and Sir Thomas of Penmark Place, were also knighted later. The Mathew family of Llandaff, many of whose members were knighted in the fifteenth century, seemed to pass into eclipse in the sixteenth century. So, too, did the Radyr branch of the Mathews after the death of Sir George Mathew in 1557. The only other families to enter the magic circle of knights were the Carnes, two of whom, Sir Edward and his grandson John, were knighted, and the Morgans of Ruperra. Two distinguished individuals who were knighted for their services on sea were Sir Robert Mansel and Sir Thomas Button. The heads of a number of other families were dignified with the title of esquire, which was customarily bestowed upon the younger sons of peers and on deputy-lieutenants, sheriffs, and justices of the peace. Thirty-three of them were included for Glamorgan in an official list of Charles I's reign. All these families who could boast the rank of esquire or better could be said to constitute the county gentry, in whose hands the local government and justice of the shire very largely rested (for detailed analysis, below, pp. 161–75).[13]

Below the county gentry came a large number of lesser families of gentry, the minor or parish gentry. Because they appear far less frequently in the records than do the county gentry we know a good deal less about them. Glimpses that we do get of some of them, however, suggest that they were often attractive and influential figures in their own locality. They could in most cases boast of a pedigree at least as long and honourable as that of the county gentry and they were usually intensely proud of their family origins. The famous family of Glyn Nedd which later adopted the surname of Price are a particularly attractive example of a family that must count under our classification as lesser gentry; yet they had been, and remained, one of the best-known families in the west of the county. Descendants of the lords of Glyn Nedd and claiming to spring from Richard ab Einion ap Collwyn, lord of Meisgyn, they were surrounded by numerous offshoots from their line. They had, for centuries, maintained a life-style appropriate to their dignity and honour. Renowned for their princely hospitality and patronage of poetry, they had welcomed to their hearth not only the leading Glamorgan bards but also famous poets from other parts of Wales. Here were no bucolic backwoods squirelings but men of taste and discernment with a deep attachment to the native culture. In Elizabethan Glamorgan there were literally dozens of families who kept up a traditional pattern of living, entertained liberally, patronized the bards in the free and fixed metres, and delighted in hearing their pedigrees elaborated and their patrician virtues praised. Some were themselves poets, like Hopcyn Twm Phylip or Thomas Llywelyn; and others, like Llywelyn Siôn, were manuscript-copiers and collectors.[14]

An outstanding example of a gifted and widely-cultivated man, of minor gentry origins, was Rice Merrick or Rhys Amheurug of Cottrell. Through his father he claimed descent from a 'royal' ancestor, Caradog Freichfras, thought to have lived in what is now northern Radnorshire, but whose descendants had settled in the medieval lordship of Meisgyn, where eight generations of them before Rice Merrick had lived on their freeholds. His own father, Meurug ap Hywel ap Phylip, had managed to acquire the manor of Trehill in 1546. In 1554 it passed to his son, Rice, who added to it by purchasing the adjoining manor of Bonvilston, so that by his death in 1587 he possessed the nucleus of an attractive estate, mainly in the parishes of St. Nicholas and Bonvilston. He probably practised as an attorney and was made clerk of the peace in Glamorgan by two successive *custodes rotulorum*, the first and second earls of Pembroke. He was a generous friend and patron of the poets, but he is best known as one of the most learned, accomplished, and intelligent antiquaries, topographers, and genealogists of his age (below, pp. 597–603). A man of considerable practical as well as intellectual gifts he was obviously sufficiently successful to hoist himself into the ranks of the county gentry in the course of his lifetime (below, p. 175). Undoubtedly there existed among many of the lesser gentry a reservoir of latent energy and ambition which enabled some of them, given the opportunity, to achieve great things—a David Jenkins, John Gibbon, or Leoline Jenkins to become famous lawyers; a Philip Jones or a Rowland Dawkins to become eminent parliamentary commanders.[15]

In addition to the members of the landed families, major and minor, others who might come within the scope of the contemporary definition of gentry were those who belonged to the learned professions of the law, the Church, and medicine. There was a large number of Glamorgan lawyers who made a success of their careers (above, pp. 30–1 and below, pp. 97–8); but almost without exception they were drawn from gentry families. Their success in their profession did not make gentlemen of them; it enhanced their social status only insofar as it gave them a more substantial income and broader acres. Broadly speaking, the same was true of the clergy. Many of the parish clergy, though perhaps treated with the respect due to their sacred calling, were too poor to rank as gentlemen. Those in their midst who were accorded that status seem to have been drawn from the younger sons of existing gentry families, whose clerical income together with any patrimony they enjoyed enabled them to maintain their position as gentlemen (below, pp. 227, 246). Physicians were very much less numerous at this time than lawyers or parsons, and almost nothing is known about them in Glamorgan. However, the Nichol family of Llantwit Major numbered at least three generations of surgeons in its midst in the sixteenth and early-seventeenth centuries and seems to have been recognized as a family of minor gentry.[16]

The Non-Gentle Orders

At the head of those who fell below the ranks of the gentlemen came the yeomen, the only men among the non-gentle orders who were dignified with the status name of 'yeoman' as opposed to a merely occupational one like 'husbandman' or 'carpenter' or 'labourer'. The yeomen are a difficult group to pin down. They were usually identified with those freeholders who were not substantial enough to be regarded as gentlemen, and Rice Merrick in his detailed survey of some of the parishes of east Glamorgan ranked nearly all the freeholders within them who were not gentlemen as yeomen. Yet it was possible for men of yeoman status not to own any freehold land at all but to be large-scale leasehold tenants or copyholders. For instance, Richard Love of Penmark, who died in June 1639, was a copyholder who farmed 120 acres in all, and he left behind him in his fine eight-roomed house, with its separate milkhouse and bakehouse, household stuff worth £38 10s., including a quantity of pewter and silver spoons. His economic prosperity and his standard of living put him clearly as being of yeoman status. Though Love would have had no pretensions to gentle birth, many of the yeomen of the county did, especially in those parts of the county where Welsh tenures prevailed and where there was a large proportion of freeholders. Wherever they existed, they constituted a kind of *élite* among the farming population. Conscious of their descent from old *uchelwyr* stock and their free status, proud of having maintained their virtual independence from Norman rule and alien custom, and glorying in their own particular *mores* of 'moes a defod', as Rice Merrick described them, they enjoyed a status which set them apart from the small farmers or husbandmen. In some such cases it might be virtually impossible to separate them from minor gentry. In the parish of Pendoylan, a stronghold of freeholders, the two leading families were Gibbon of Brynhelygen and Llywelyn of Caerewigau, whose solid Tudor house still stands with some of its original features intact. These two families could be regarded as either minor gentry or substantial yeomen. Both claimed ancient descent, the former from Einion ap Collwyn and the latter from Iestyn; both were big freeholders, open-handed in their hospitality and much loved by the bards. Identification in such cases is not helped by the way in which the same man may be variously described as 'gentleman', 'yeoman', and 'freeholder'. In the last resort it probably came down to what status a family considered it enjoyed and whether or not its own assessment was accepted by its neighbours. However, there is reason to believe that the freeholder-yeoman group may have constituted a very considerable proportion of the population of the county. In a contested election of coroners of 1570, in which only freeholders were allowed to participate, it was estimated that there were about 1,000 of them present. This estimate, it is true, was made by a party that had a strong interest in placing the figure as high as possible; and, of course, many freeholders were ranked as gentry. On the other hand many yeomen were not freeholders; so, on balance, it may not be unreasonable to conclude that there were several hundred yeomen families in Glamorgan. Further attestation for this suggestion comes from the large number of solidly-built houses still surviving in the county, which must have been put up by small gentry and yeomen (below, pp. 126-9).[17]

Below the yeomen came the 'husbandmen', the bulk of the tenant farmers. In terms of social classification they would also have included the more prosperous rural craftsmen, many of whom would have a smallholding as well. It was this group which contained the largest single section of the community. This becomes readily apparent from the analyses which have been made of the first subsidy returns for Glamorgan. Most of those paying tax fell into two categories: those who paid tax on goods valued at £1–5, and those who paid on goods worth £5–10. The first category may have included a minority of self-employed craftsmen and small shopkeepers, and a small number of labourers and domestic servants; but most of those included in the two categories must have been tenant farmers. In the poor upland hundred of Llangyfelach 81 per cent of the taxpayers paid on goods worth from £1–5 and a further 12 per cent on goods worth £5–10; in Swansea Hundred the figures were 68 per cent and 19 per cent respectively; and in a sample of eighteen parishes in east Glamorgan they were 63 per cent and 21–3 per cent. While we cannot be sure what proportion of the population was not paying tax at all, or what proportion of those who did pay were small farmers, we should probably be justified in concluding that husbandmen made up the large majority of the taxpayers and that they and their families constituted a clear majority of the population as a whole. Unfortunately we have no sources of a kind that would enable a direct comparison to be made between conditions revealed by the tax returns with those which prevailed a hundred years later in the early Stuart period. However, an analysis of inventories surviving from the decade from 1630 to 1640 —and it was only the more well-to-do husbandmen who tended to leave them—shows that 76 per cent of them recorded possessions worth less than £50, which must classify those who left them as medium to small farmers. Within the ranks of these husbandmen, however, there might be wide variations in the acreage of holdings, size of income, and standard of living. Acreages might vary from 5 to 50 or 60, with an average of about 20–30 acres, though mere size was in itself far less important than the quality and situation of the land held. Possessions, too, as valued in the numerous inventories for west Glamorgan, ranged from £10 to £89, in which amounts allotted to household goods varied from £2 8s. 4d. to £11 3s. 4d. Just as it would be difficult to tell a yeoman from a member of the minor gentry, so it might be equally difficult to tell a yeoman or even a minor gentleman from a prosperous and rising tenant simply in terms of the possessions which each enjoyed. The average value of possessions left by yeomen in west Glamorgan was £71 13s. 1d.; that of husbandmen's possessions was only a little way behind at £70 4s. 6d.; but it has to be remembered that most yeomen would leave an inventory, whereas a great many of the smaller husbandmen would not. Nevertheless, when John Beynon, husbandman of Llanddewi in Gower, died in 1576 he left behind him possessions worth £76, which put him well above a yeoman of Llangyfelach, Richard Lloyd, who died leaving possessions worth £10 6s. 6d. and even men like Morgan Bennett of Loughor (£18 1s. 8d.) or Thomas Rees of Llandeilo Tal-y-bont (£57 7s. 8d.), both of whom were accounted to be gentlemen.[18]

Beneath the husbandmen came the labouring population. Here again there was no sharp dividing-line between the two groups, and the one merged gradually into the other. Towards the lower end of the husbandmen's scale were men whose holdings were so small, and many craftsmen whose earnings were so meagre, that they might be obliged to seek occasional employment as labourers. These were not easily distinguishable from cottagers who had a tiny holding of perhaps two to four acres, enjoyed common rights, and kept a few livestock, but were mainly dependent on employment as labourers. Labourers of this kind and their wives, together with the smallest farmers and their wives, were also the mainstays of the cottage industries already noted. However, many—perhaps the majority—of the labourers had no land or stock to speak of, and had no hedge against inflation or adversity other than what they could precariously earn in by-employment. More secure and better-off were the servants kept in the large gentry households. Surer of regular employment and meals, they were also usually remembered in their masters' wills. Sir Rice Mansel left all his servants a year's wages and a coat apiece, and Thomas Carne of Ewenni provided that his old and infirm servant, Thomas Chambers, should keep his chamber where he lay for the term of his natural life, together with 'such yearly wage and allowance as he now hath'. Just what proportion of the whole population was made up of labourers and servants it seems impossible to tell. In England they constituted about one-quarter to one-third of the population; but proportions varied widely from region to region according to the nature of the farming practised, and in upland areas they were usually far fewer than in corn-growing lowlands. In Glamorgan the need for labour must have been much greater in the Vale, especially in the intensively-cultivated demesne-farming, than in the Uplands. Operations in arable farming, particularly at harvest time, called for a large labour-force, e.g. in Pembrokeshire George Owen mustered 240 people to get his harvest in; a fact which underlines the seasonal nature of much agricultural employment and the consequent high incidence of under-employment among agricultural labourers.[19]

On the basis of the information available to us for Glamorgan, it does not appear possible to make a reliable estimate of the size of the labouring population within the county. In some areas it must have been large. At Boverton and Llantwit in 1614, for example, cottage holdings of four acres and less accounted for 43 per cent of all tenant holdings. Many of their occupants must have depended heavily on labourers' earnings to make ends meet; and in addition to these cottagers there may well have been a good many more landless labourers. On the other hand, in Hafod-y-porth and Margam in 1633, cottage holdings made up only 18.3 per cent of the total, and on the St. John estates about the same time only 16 per cent. That the number of labourers in the county increased, both absolutely and relatively, as the result of economic changes discussed in an earlier chapter, seems very probable. Yet we should not exaggerate the extent of this trend, since it is quite evident that even in the eighteenth century many of Glamorgan's farmers were still small men employing mainly family labour (below, pp. 320–1).[20]

The lot of the poorer and landless labourers was a hard one in an era of inflation, when the level of wages was lagging behind that of prices. Their working conditions were also arduous. They were required by the Statute of Artificers of 1563, which presumably only gave statutory form to the kind of conditions which already existed in practice, to work from 5.0 a.m. to 7.0 or 8.0 p.m., from March to September, and from dawn to dusk during the rest of the year, with breaks for meals and rest, which must not exceed two and a half hours. Women and children were obliged to join in whatever work was open to them in order to make up the family's skimpy pittance. The Pembrokeshire squire, George Owen, was struck by the weatherbeaten appearance of labourers and the adverse effect on their physique of the 'continual labour in tilling the land, burning of lime, digging of coals, and other slaveries and extreme toils', though it must be doubted whether the smaller farmers and their families were any less toilworn than the labourers and theirs. The grinding pressures exerted on the poorer classes are further revealed, indirectly, by the extremely high incidence of theft revealed by the records of the Great Sessions. Hardly a session went by without a number of petty thieves being tried and convicted; and in years of dearth and depression, like 1586–87 or the years from 1592–1598, cases of theft showed a steep increase in number. The social class or background of many of those indicted is not given, but a very high proportion of those involved are specifically identified as labourers from Glamorgan, and a number of others appear to be wandering outcasts from elsewhere in Wales and the West of England. A surprisingly large body of women as well as men were accused of theft—usually of small sums of money or minor items of finery, clothing or food. In view of the savage penalties inflicted on culprits of either sex who were convicted of theft (below, pp. 105–6), it seems difficult to resist the conclusion that many of them were driven to crime by desperation. Not that this elicited much sympathy for them from judges, as two Cardiff labourers discovered in 1596 when they were hanged for stealing ten loaves of bread. We must, however, be careful not to overstress the consequences of poverty, drudgery, and degradation on the old pre-industrial labouring population of Glamorgan, or their inability to rise above their daunting circumstances. Iolo Morganwg, who knew and loved them so well, gives an attractive picture of them:

The cottagers are most of them of gentle and tractable dispositions, addicted to no great nor many vices, yet not very ceremonious in their manners, though not harsh, and so much cleanliness can hardly be found among the lower classes in any other part of the kingdom. Rural mechanics or artists in general good; masons, carpenters, thatchers surpassingly so; smiths tolerably good in general, weavers good &c. Labourers in agriculture do their work well, and even neatly. Ploughing, mowing, reaping, fencing, stacking generally well done &c.; women very neat in general.

Iolo was, admittedly, the staunchest of local patriots, impenitently wedded to applauding the virtues of his native county and its sons and daughters; but he was also a man of strong democratic sympathies, not lacking in concern for the poor or unwilling to denounce injustice or malpractice where he saw them.[21]

Lowest of all came the poor, among whom contemporaries recognized three main categories. The first of these, the 'poor by impotency', included the aged, widowed, orphaned, and those permanently sick, infirm or disabled. Then there were the 'poor by casualty', made up of the 'wounded soldier, the decayed householder, and the sick persons visited with grievous and painful diseases'. These two categories were thought to cover the 'deserving poor'. The third category consisted of the able-bodied poor, usually branded by the ruling classes as the 'thriftless poor' and treated as though they comprised only wastrels, vagabonds, rogues, and strumpets. Yet they numbered in their midst many un-fortunates who were involuntarily reduced to poverty because they could find no employment at all or too little to prevent them from having to beg their bread. The plight of this sort found little sympathy or understanding among the authorities, who were prone to dismiss them all as nothing better than 'sturdy rogues and vagabonds'. The swelling ranks of paupers and vagrants became a major social problem in Tudor England and Wales, to cope with which a series of statutes was devised, culminating in the great Poor Law Acts of 1598 and 1601. Broadly speaking, this legislation tried to distinguish between the deserving poor, for whom a system of charitable relief was gradually evolved, and the 'sturdy beggars', for whom a savage regimen of punishment and deterrence was prescribed.

Glamorgan was not unfamiliar with the problem of pauperdom, as is plain from some of the popular poetry of the period (above, pp. 21–2). The authors of these *cwndidau* were sharp in their condemnation of harsher attitudes prevailing towards the poor. Siôn Hywel Siôn, in particular, denounced the inhumanity of the penalties laid down under statute—a reference, very probably, to the working of the very severe poor law of the first year of Edward VI's reign—whereby even a man in his late sixties might be branded on hand or ear and half-naked beggars be whipped, then clapped into the stocks. In the country parishes, paupers depended for relief more on the charity dispensed by their well-disposed neighbours than on the working of the poor law. Glamorgan bards laid particular emphasis on the gentlemanly virtue of giving generously to the poor. When, for instance, one of his patrons, Thomas ap William Siancyn, died the poet Thomas ab Ieuan ap Rhys singled out for praise above all else his unsurpassed generosity to the poor, to whom he had dispensed food and drink in their need, gifts when they married, and shrouds and decent burial when they died. Similarly, in an anonymous biography of Sir Lewis Mansel his secular qualities were described as 'but the glimmering of the moon' if compared with the sun of his 'silent liberality towards the poor'. Many of the contemporary wills included customary bequests to the needy, though in 1634 Sir John Stradling voiced misgivings in his will about the effect of some of these bequests and expressly desired to be buried without 'funeral pomp and common dole, which in these days is found to be a maintenance of wandering beggars'. Nevertheless, true to the exceptionally generous tradition of the Stradlings, he left money for the poor in all those parishes where he held lands. Stray references afford momentary glimpses of the kind of unfortunate wretches who might be drifting around the rural parishes—out-of-work labourers, poor women and their children deserted by husbands and fathers, runaway scallawags of various kinds, and other social flotsam, many of them from the West of England as well as south Wales. But most of the paupers filtered into the towns, where they were less conspicuous among many others of their kind. There, they created an intractable problem for the municipal authorities (below, pp. 91–2).[22]

THE URBAN SOCIAL ORDER

The structure of society in the towns was, *mutatis mutandis*, not very different from that which existed in the countryside. A small group of resident gentry dominated the society and government of each town (see below, pp. 157–61). In Cardiff the Herberts and their allies were masters of the town, though other prominent families, including the Stradlings, Mansels, Lewises, and Morgans of Ruperra, maintained town houses there as well. In Swansea, Sir George Herbert and his descendants were the leading figures, and in Neath the Evanses of the Gnoll. Around these dominant figures were grouped a handful of lesser gentry and leading merchants who controlled municipal institutions. Although these townsmen were acutely conscious of the power of the earls of Pembroke and Worcester, the non-resident lords of the towns, they were not always prepared to submit tamely to them, and there is evidence of incipient friction between the lords and their representatives on the one hand and some of the leading townsmen on the other (below, pp. 99–100). Beneath the ruling group of gentry and merchants came a middle group consisting of the tradesmen, shopkeepers, and craftsmen, and also the yeomen and husbandmen who lived in the town but farmed in the adjacent countryside. Then came the manual workers: mariners, general labourers, colliers, and the like. Finally, there was the growing body of paupers and vagrants.[23]

Towns were unhealthy, and their population, decimated by periodic attacks of plague and other sicknesses, could not usually be maintained by natural increase. They had always depended on a considerable influx of population from the countryside, and in the sixteenth century this was more pronounced than ever. Some Glamorgan people were moving out of the county altogether into a big city like Bristol. In the ten years from 1532 to 1542 as many as 32 boys from a diversity of social backgrounds went from Glamorgan to Bristol to be apprenticed to a variety of trades. Many people, however, were moving into the Glamorgan towns themselves. Among them was a decidedly larger number of Welsh-speaking people than had been usual in the Middle Ages. Place-names and personal names in both Cardiff and Swansea indicate this, and the demand for more religious services in Welsh at Swansea (below, pp. 252-3) is another symptom of the same trend.[24]

However, the influx into their midst that worried the townsmen was that of vagrants and paupers. Harsh measures to deter these unwanted immigrants were taken in Cardiff on a number of occasions between 1545 and 1584, and they included the branding and flogging which had so stirred the indignation of the poet Siôn Hywel Siôn. The year 1576, following shortly after a statute of 1572 which laid down savage punishments, was one in which the justices of the Great Sessions came down extremely severely on a large number of vagrants from different parts of Glamorgan, like the hapless Joan Powell of Cardiff, described as having 'not any lands, neither exerciseth any lawful merchandise, craft, or industry, whereby she may gain her livelihood, nor can give a reason or account in what manner she useth to gain her livelihood'. In Swansea the town records reveal a good deal of anxiety about the problem of poverty. Following an Act of Parliament of 1563, a 'benevolence for the poor' was regularly collected at St. Mary's church. It usually amounted to about 3s. 6d. to 4s. a week and was disbursed to much the same group of about sixteen paupers every week. People who did not contribute regularly and promptly to the poor rate were ordered to have their goods distrained in 1595. Following an Act of Parliament of 1576 for the building within every county of a house of correction where the poor could be put to work, the corporation made an annual contribution of 4s. 10d. towards its upkeep. By 1603, however, it expressed its profound concern at the 'great toleration and sufferance of strangers' who, on account of their 'evil lives, debt, picking, and cozening', had drifted into Swansea. As a result, there had ensued not only 'ungodly living, and unlawful keeping of disordered alehouses, playing, and other disorders but also great loss unto the burgesses'. To try to check the influx of too many paupers, 'fearing that by poverty or sickness they may become chargeable unto the town, as many hath

[91]

become before', 'by reason of so many poor decayed people which doth resort hither to inhabit', the corporation tried to insist that such new-comers should either depart, even if they were cripples or pregnant women, or else find sureties to guarantee that they would not become a burden on the town. Other measures taken to help the poor were to try to keep the price of corn down in time of shortage, to distribute food and clothing as poor relief, and to administer the many bequests left by townsmen to relieve the poor or to place boys in apprenticeships. Following the royal command of 1631 that rogues and vagabonds must be severely punished, poor people set to work, and poor children placed as apprentices, brisk efforts were made in Swansea to carry out these injunctions, especially those for apprentices. Many benefactors, during their lifetime and/or in their wills, made contributions for the relief of the poor, but no other in Glamorgan is known to have achieved quite so remarkable a public tribute for his philanthropy as Hopkin David of Swansea (d. 1626), whose epitaph, long since vanished, read in characteristically flowery rhyme:

> Marvail not, Reader, though thou doest see
> This shrine so much frequented be.
> The reliques of a Saint here lie
> Who spent his days in Piety;
> The Poor here come and raise their cry,
> To feel their alms deeds with him die.[25]

iii.

SOCIAL MOBILITY

In an overwhelmingly rural and largely static society the dead weight of custom was brought heavily to bear on the acceptance of the existing social order and the maintenance of its differences of degree. Custom was formidably reinforced by religious teaching; in collect, catechism, and homily, men were regularly and solemnly adjured to respect estab-lished authority and to accept that station in life into which it had pleased God to call them. Yet, whatever might be the nature of social theory and religious sanction, in practice there were many factors at work in the sixteenth century tending to make economic conditions more volatile and thereby to destabilize society. In these more fluid conditions it was possible for families and individuals to move up and down the social scale, though success usually left a more obvious and indelible mark on the records and is far easier to spot than failure.

As we have seen it was the gentry who were best able to take advantage of the opportunities to move upwards. Indeed, there appears to be no single instance of a leading family dropping out of sight except through failure of male heirs. Though it is impossible to estimate precisely the increase in the number of relatively wealthy gentry families during the period there is no doubt that it was considerable. It can be seen unmistakably in the establishment of gentry at a number of points where they had never hitherto been: the Herberts at Neath abbey, Cogan Pill, and the Friars, Cardiff; the Lewises at Y Fan; the Mansels at Margam; the Turbervilles at Sker; the Carnes at Ewenni; the Meyricks at Cottrell; and the Prices at Cwrt-y-carnau, to name but a few. Just as striking was the extraordinary success achieved by many families in founding new collateral and cadet branches. This branching-out of existing families is, indeed, much more in evidence than the emergence of completely new ones. The Herberts showed a talent for proliferation amounting almost to genius, though most of their offshoots are not found in Glamorgan. In the list compiled by Symonds in 1645 of 35 leading gentry, no fewer than six belonged to the Lewis family; four of them were brothers, the sons of Sir Edward Lewis, and two others were closely related. The Mathews of Llandaff established successful offshoots at Radyr and Castell-y-mynach; and scions of Castell-y-mynach were in turn set up at Maes-mawr and Saint-y-nyll, which in due course gave rise to the Mathews of Roos and Aberaman, not to mention other lesser ramifications of the family. There were Mansels at Briton Ferry, Llantriddyd, Llanddewi in Gower, and Muddlescombe, Carmarthenshire, as well as the main family at Margam. Nor was it only the biggest families that succeeded in multiplying themselves in this way. Smaller houses might be equally adept at the process—the lords of Glyn Nedd, who were surrounded by a galaxy of satellite lines, or the Powels of Llwydarth, themselves a junior branch of the Glyn Nedd house, who managed to establish their descendants at Maesteg, Pen-y-fai, Llanharan, Llyswyrnwy, Ton-du, and elsewhere. Even sons born outside wedlock, of whom there were not a few, might on occasion be suitably set up as heads of new lines. The immediate ancestor of as highflying and powerful a stock as the Herberts of Glamorgan and Wilton—Sir Richard Herbert of Ewias, father of Sir George Herbert of Swansea and his younger brother, the earl of Pembroke—was himself a bastard. The Stradling family too, in Henry VIII's reign had in its midst a number of illegitimate sons, whom the countess of Worcester denounced as having no living 'but by extortion and pilling of the king's subjects'. Nevertheless, two of these were married to heiresses: Edward to the daughter of Robert Raglan, thus becoming the founder of the Stradlings of Roath, and Robert, who founded the Stradlings of Llantwit Major. Further evidence of the increase in the number of families eager to assert their status as gentry is provided by the remarkable extension in the range and number of poetic patrons in the second half of the sixteenth century. Families which had never previously been known to welcome poets were now only too ready to acquire a bardic certificate of gentility in the eyes of the community. Among the many new sponsors of the poets traced by

Professor Griffith John Williams were the Meyricks of Cottrell, the Prichards of Llancaeach, the Bawdrips of Splott, the Powels of Llandow, the Llywelyns of Caerewigau, the Gibbons of Brynhelygen, the Thomases of Llanfihangel, the Llywelyns of Rhydlafar, and many others. Equally impressive testimony to the rise of gentry families is the progressive growth in the number of the justices of the peace from an average of about fifteen in 1570 to 33 in 1642 and the inclusion by that date of a representative from a number of families who never reached the commission of the peace in earlier days (below, pp. 169–75).[26]

Ordinarily, the main family estates passed to the eldest son; a practice that drew an acid complaint from a contemporary, Sir Thomas Wilson, that fathers had 'such fond desire' to leave 'a great show of the stock of their house' that the eldest brother 'must have all, and all the rest that which the cat left on the malt heap'. Many of the Glamorgan gentry, however, like those of other counties remote from London, were anxious to do a great deal better for their younger sons than Wilson's disparaging remarks about fathers would have suggested. In the course of their lifetime many were active in seeking to acquire additional interests which could be passed on to their younger sons. The massive acquisitions made by Sir Thomas Mansel and Sir Edward Lewis have already been remarked upon (above, pp. 32–3). When the latter made his will in January 1624 he provided handsomely for each of his four younger sons. The second son, Sir William, who had married Anne, heiress of Edmund Williams of Gelli-gaer, was left lands bought by his father in the parishes of Llanwynno and Aberdare. To the third son, Nicholas, went the manors of Moulton, Leach Castle, and Llancarfan, the capital messuage of Carnllwyd and the mill of Llancarfan, purchased by his father from Sir John Wildgoose. The manor of Odyn's Fee, in the parish of Penmark, bought from William Bawdrip, and the Whittons in Llancarfan, acquired from Morgan Meyrick, were to go to the fourth son, Thomas the elder, though possession of the Whittons was switched to Nicholas in a later codicil. Even the fifth son, Thomas the younger, was given lands bought in the parish of Eglwysilan and Caerphilly. Sir John Stradling (d. 1637) explained in his will that he had bought the manor of Lampha in the parishes of St. Bride's and Ewenni, together with 100 acres of land at Pitcot, for the benefit of his second son, Thomas, and had already made over the deeds to his son but wished to confirm the transaction in his will. Where a smaller squire had a number of younger sons of whom to take account, he might have to exercise considerable ingenuity. James Thomas of Llanfihangel in his will of 1565 left the bulk of his estates to his eldest son, John; Robert was given a lease of lands at Cowbridge, James an interest in Burry Hill, Francis and Richard were to divide the farm of Brocastle between them, and the youngest, Edmund, was to get £40 and was to be kept at school by his mother until he was twenty-one. Provisions of this kind are normal in most of the surviving gentry wills. Men of humbler status were even more concerned as a rule to deal equitably with all their children. Wills of well-to-do freeholders, yeomen, and husbandmen, though usually singling out the eldest son for the most favoured treatment and leaving him the family homestead and a larger share of the father's possessions, normally make provision in land, livestock, and household possessions for younger sons.[27]

Daughters as well as sons had to be provided for. They could not marry without a dowry, as the careful marriage settlements of the age make abundantly clear. Surviving wills, too, contain bequests to daughters in cash, livestock, and possessions, designed to enable them to marry as well as they could, or at least to have a modest competence. Typical legacies of an average farmer were those of Howell ap Richard of Coychurch (d. 1597), who left his eldest daughter eight kine, one bull, a yearling and a calf (worth £11 18s. 4d.), his second daughter six kine and a calf (worth £8 10s. 0d.), the third a cow (worth £1 6s. 8d.) and £6 13s. 4d., and the youngest £3 6s. 8d. In addition, each daughter was left two blankets, a coverlet and a bolster. Gentry legacies might range from those included in the will of John Giles of Llancarfan (d. 1564), who bequeathed his two daughters 19 kine and a bull, all the corn and oats growing on parts of his estates, as much ground and grass as would keep the cattle for a year, a featherbed and six silver spoons each, to the £3,000 left by a county magnate like Sir Lewis Mansel (1638) to one of his daughters, along with £2,500 left to each of two others, and £100 to a married daughter who had already had her portion. In his will dated 1621 William Thomas of Llanfihangel apologized to his daughters, Mary and Agnes, for not being able to leave them more than £600 and £400 respectively, and requested his brother, Lewis, to increase their capital as best he might during their minority.[28]

Nevertheless, however far-seeing, prudent or affectionate a father might be, there were inevitably many younger children who could not be provided for in such a way as to preserve their gentry status. Gentlemen's families tended to be large, and possibly were increasing in size (below, p. 113). The more sons and daughters who survived into adult life the greater was the likelihood that some of them might have to find a niche in society lower than that into which they had been born. Where there was not enough left of the father's estate to enable a son to live like a gentleman, he had the choice of entering trade or one of the professions, or of becoming a working farmer. In the process of thus being thrown in at the deep end like so many kittens they did not all sink. To quote Thomas Wilson once more, 'this doth us good some ways, for it makes us industrious to apply ourselves to letters or to arms, whereby many times we become my master elder brothers' masters'. Some younger sons of Glamorgan families did, indeed, achieve great things; notably the great admiral, Sir Robert Mansel, the dashing explorer, Sir Thomas Button, and Sir John Herbert, secretary of state (below, pp. 117-8).

H

Many of them, however, simply drifted into the service of great aristocratic families or the households of leading county gentry, or hung around at home, often frustrated and resentful. Glamorgan found itself with too many of these would-be gentlemen who attached themselves as retainers and hangers-on. Judge David Lewis delivered himself of some harsh strictures upon them when writing to Sir Francis Walsingham in 1576. Blaming the excessive number of retainers for much of the turbulence of the county, he drew Walsingham's attention to the fact that too many of the gentry had about them foster-brothers, idle kinsmen, and other hangers-on who did nothing but 'play at cards and pick and steal and kill or hunt any man when they will have them, and yet themselves will wash their hands thereof when the ill fact is done'. George Owen also commented on the 'great troops of retainers that follow every gentleman'. The general tenor of the Penrice and Margam correspondence, which is itself almost wholly taken up with the contemporary quarrels, suggests that the gentry were themselves not unaware of the dangers caused by the touchiness and rashness of many of their entourage (below, pp. 106–8). It may well be that not the least reason for the thin-skinned sensitivity of some of these retainers was their anxiety to preserve the status and honour of a gentleman in a world in which it was increasingly difficult for them as younger sons to maintain their rank, and even more so for their sons in turn. Younger branches of a family tried to give their sons a good education or an apprenticeship in trade but were not able to maintain it beyond the second generation, if indeed they kept it up that far. Moreover, by the seventeenth century, opportunities for younger sons in trade, the Church, the law, or in soldiering, were decidedly less plentiful than they had been.[29]

The other group apart from the gentry that was most successful in climbing the social ladder was that of yeoman-freeholders. Economic conditions were favourable to men of this kind, many of whom aspired to take full advantage of their opportunities. It was commonly reputed that they 'are able and daily do buy the lands of unthrifty gentlemen, and setting their sons to school at the universities, to the law of the realm or otherwise leaving them sufficient lands whereon they may live without labour, do make their said sons by those means gentlemen'. They were heavily involved in the numerous land transactions of the period and were among the most eager purchasers, lessees, and exchangers of land. The most enterprising among them had pretensions to buying manors, just as Thomas ap Llywelyn, yeoman, bought the manor of Llanharan in 1550, or William ap John, yeoman, joined with David ap Ievan Seys, ancestor of the Seys family but at this time described as a burgess of Cowbridge, to buy half the manor of Eglwys Brewys in 1522. Occasionally it is possible to trace the status of a yeoman family rising with its economic fortunes. Before Rice Merrick's father bought the manor of Trehill he was referred to merely as freeholder (*frankelanus*), but after the purchase he appears as *generosus* (gentleman). It was the yeoman, William ap John, who bought an interest in Eglwys Brewys, but when his son, Edward William, came to sell it to the Seys family he was described as a gentleman. The Bennetts of Penrice in Gower rose from an even humbler base, and their elevation is unusually well documented. In 1546 William Bennett was no more than a 'husbandman'; but by 1587 his son, John, was a 'yeoman'; and in 1638, the grandson, another William, had attained the dignity of 'gentleman'. Not far away from the Bennetts lived the Lucas family of Stouthall, who have been described as an 'ideal example of the rising yeoman'; 'wealthy farmers in Elizabethan times, they became squires in the following century, and a family of considerable standing among the Georgian gentry'. This success of the Bennetts or the Lucases should not, however, be allowed to conceal the fact that there were many yeomen who were neither particularly successful nor wealthy. As we have already seen the overall average value of the possessions of west Glamorgan yeomen as reflected in their inventories was only fractionally higher than that for husbandmen. The failure of yeomen and their decline into the ranks of husbandmen or labourers leave virtually no trace in the records; but in an age when the old Welsh practice of equal partition of the inheritance, which had contributed powerfully to the maintenance of a large class of freeholders, had been much weakened by provisions of the Act of Union, the younger sons of many members of that social group must have found it increasingly difficult, if not impossible, to maintain their fathers' status.[30]

Families founded on wealth derived from the proceeds of trade or industry, which were common enough in parts of the kingdom, were not apparent in Glamorgan. Although men from the county migrated to great trading centres like London or Bristol, they seemed to have lacked either the capital or the inclination to buy estates in their native county. Glamorgan's own towns were too small to produce merchants with profits large enough to invest heavily in land, though a Cardiff cordwainer, one Richard Careles, in his will dated 1604, was able to bequeath his reputed daughter the manor of Hyde, alias 'Glassenburye', which he had bought from William and Anne Gascoigne of Cardiff. Other families, it is true, had a big stake in industry (above, pp. 48–58), but this was not the main source of their income nor had they risen to the rank of gentry on the basis of it. Of the professions, only the law contributed significantly to the creation of landed families. The complaint widely heard of lawyers was that 'by the ruin of their neighbours' contentions [they] are grown so rich and so proud that no other sort dare meddle with them . . . the numbers of the lawyers are so great they undo the country people and buy up all the lands that are to be sold'. These allegations of the wealth, covetousness, sharp practice, and ambition of lawyers found an echo in Glamorgan in Sir John Stradling's contention that he saw lawyers 'loth to be troubled with anything except taking money, wherein they have a great facility . . . they be not so scrupulous as other people in receiving money, so it be gold'; and he described them preying on a young man as 'the eagles do on a carrion'. Whether or not their methods were as dubious as those just described, we cannot say, but some Glamorgan legal luminaries did very well. The rise of the Bassetts and Aubreys of Llan-triddyd and the Jenkinses of Hensol has already been described (above, pp. 30–1). David Evans, of the Great House, Neath, second member of parliament for the Glamorgan boroughs and attorney-general for Wales, was another who owed much to his success as a lawyer, as did Roger Seys of Boverton, Elizabeth's attorney-general for Wales. Two other successful lawyers who became members of parliament for the Glamorgan boroughs were Leyshon Price, of Ynys-y-maerdy, Briton Ferry, and his son, William. John Gibbon, LL.D., whose father had been apprenticed to a skinner in Bristol, made enough out of the law to purchase the manor of St. Fagan's and to build the many-gabled manor-house there which is now the National Folk Museum of Wales.[31]

But if there was a fair amount of social mobility in the upper reaches of society, what of the great majority of the people, that 80 per cent or more of the population that was made up of husbandmen, craftsmen, labourers, and paupers? The sad truth is that they were so large, amorphous, and unrecorded a mass that it becomes unsafe to make too many generalizations about them. Much as we should like to be able to trace in some detail the fortunes of this majority, the materials that would enable us to do so simply do not exist. Yet we are surely justified in concluding that for most of them there could be little or no prospect of moving up in the world. Only a fortunate minority of the bigger husbandmen, capable of hard work and shrewd judgement, and blessed with good luck in health and harvest, could hope to add sufficiently to their capital and their holdings for them or their descendants to rise to the status of yeomen, or even, in a few exceptionally favoured instances, to become minor gentlemen. For every upthrusting Bennett or Lucas family there were almost certainly twenty others or more who counted themselves lucky if they could hold their own and remain in that station of life in which it had pleased God to place them. At the lower end of this scale there must have been many who lay under the ever-present threat of drifting downwards. The contemporary portents already outlined reveal the pressures exerted upon the poorer classes: the growth of population, inflation of prices and rents, engrossing and consolidation of holdings, erosion of common rights, and the existence of many holdings already so small that further subdivisions made them economically unviable. The combined operation of these conditions can hardly have failed to augment the numbers of landless labourers and paupers. Add to this that their lives were short, their health precarious, their labour backbreaking, their wages insufficient, their housing insanitary, and their diet inadequate, and it becomes difficult not to believe that such social mobility as existed among them was more likely to have been in a downwards than an upwards direction. We need not wonder that municipal authorities became greatly agitated about the poor, or that poets were moved to eloquent protests at the callous and unchristian indignity with which these unfortunates were often treated.

iv.

SOCIAL RELATIONSHIPS

Tudor and Stuart society was strongly hierarchical. It was universally believed and preached that the powers that be were ordained of God, that men of every social degree had their appointed place in the divinely-arranged scheme of things, and that all must accept, as a religious duty as well as a social obligation, the responsibilities no less than the privileges of that station of life into which they had been born. Authority ramified downwards from the king through the aristocracy and the gentry; it was their responsibility to rule and the duty of their inferiors to obey. Of the situation of the mass of the populace, including small farmers, shop-keepers, craftsmen, and labourers, Sir Thomas Smith wrote in his *Commonwealth of England*: 'These have no voice nor authority in our Commonwealth and no account is made of them, but only to be ruled and not to rule other'. The same hierarchical concept of authority ran through all social institutions: it gave the king the right to rule his subjects, the gentry their tenants, masters their servants, husbands their wives, and fathers their families. Unless the proper respect and obedience due to rank and authority were observed, then the whole fabric of ordered society would be in danger of decay and destruction, or in the sonorous periods of the Book of Homilies: 'where there is no right order, there reigneth all abuse, carnal liberty, enormity, sin, and babylonical confusion . . . and there must needs follow all mischief and utter destruction, both of souls, bodies, goods and commonwealths'.[32]

Given this view of social relationships it was inevitable that the men with the most far-reaching influence over Glamorgan society were its two greatest aristocratic landowners, the earls of Pembroke and Worcester. In addition to their exalted rank and their huge landed possessions they enjoyed towering prestige from their prominent position at Court. Their power fell most directly on the towns, where their stewards, drawn from their own or allied families, very largely ruled the roost in their interest. Ordinarily, townsmen could be expected to defer to the wishes of their overlords without demur. But Tudor burgesses were not spineless creatures; there were times when they were prepared to bare their teeth at their masters. The earl of Worcester complained of the Swansea Corporation in a letter of 1566, written to his steward, Edward Mansel, in a state of high dudgeon: 'for they that will bear their money against me in any suit, I think they might as well come to cut my throat, as they

[99]

were ready to bear their money against me. Therefore I am loth to deal with them in any kind of way, for I take them to be careless but only to serve their own turn.' The opposition encountered at Cardiff by the Herbert family in the course of the rumbustious turmoils there during 1596, some of the most notorious examples of overbearing behaviour encountered anywhere in Tudor Wales, are fully discussed in a later chapter (below, pp. 188–91). The bad feelings then aroused obviously rankled for some years, for there exists an indignant protest of 1602 on the part of the dowager countess of Pembroke, who held the lordship of Glamorgan as part of her jointure, against what she alleged to be the high-handed insolence, violence, and sharp practice of the bailiffs and recorder at Cardiff. A year or two later she launched a Star Chamber suit against the bailiffs and a number of the burgesses of the town, and against Edmund Mathew, whom she believed to be their ally and backer. Her main cause of complaint was that the borough court, hitherto held in the earl of Pembroke's name, was now being held in the king's name, an encroachment which the burgesses admitted, though they claimed that they had changed their practice only after taking counsel's opinion.[33]

Unlike the townsmen, the gentry were not directly under the rule of the earls; but they were predictably anxious to keep on good terms with these influential aristocrats and to have them as their patrons. Sir Edward Mansel, writing of the earl of Pembroke in 1581, at a time when he and the earl were on very bad terms with one another, nevertheless averred that Pembroke had in Glamorgan 'more servants (as I believe) than in any other county, more loving kinsmen than servants, more tenants than of both: and, I assure myself, he had double the number of all the rest in well-wishers.' But clientage was a two-way process, and the earls on their side were no less aware of the value to themselves of maintaining a strong gentry following in the county. The second earl of Pembroke deemed it prudent as well as hospitable, when the Queen came to visit his house in 1572, to invite Sir Edward Stradling—and, no doubt, other Glamorgan notabilities as well—to 'come and be merry there'. Later, when the earl and his countess visited Wales they were 'honourably received' by 'the most part of the gentlemen of Glamorgan and Monmouthshires, and with like entertainment brought to the castle of Cardiff, where, keeping a very honourable and sumptuous house to all comers, they continued for the space of . . . days, riding abroad, and visiting their friends, and viewing the country'. Similarly, in 1596, the earl of Pembroke as president of the Council in the Marches, kept 'a grand Christmas in the castle of Ludlow', 'among such honourable and gentlemanly company', that a young gentleman of Glamorgan was expected to have learned 'as much good behaviour and manners as should have stuck by him ever after whilst he lived'. Sir Edward Stradling's unique correspondence reveals that a leading county gentleman of his status did not confine his friendship to those peers like Pembroke or

Worcester or St. John who were connected with his county. He might have a wide range of patrons and friends at Court and in the country. Stradling was on terms of easy friendship with such eminent figures at Court as Lords Burghley, Buckhurst, and Mountjoy, Sir Francis Walsingham, Sir Henry Sidney, Sir Francis Drake, Sir James Croft, and Sir Humphrey Gilbert, as well as with many of the gentry of south Wales and the west of England. The Mansel correspondence is not dissimilar in character, though it is less comprehensive in the range of topics and correspondents embraced by it. Nevertheless, if more correspondence like that of Sir Edward Stradling had survived, he would probably not have been found to be alone in the breadth and distinction of his circle of friends and contacts.[34]

Men as spirited and self-confident as the Glamorgan gentry were not prepared to buy the friendship of aristocrats at any price. The turbulent local politics of the county and the endemic feuds between some of the gentry and the earl of Pembroke, discussed in the next chapter, leave us in no doubt about their willingness to stand their ground defiantly against him if they believed their honour or their interest, or both, demanded it of them. The temerity of one of their number, Sir Edward Mansel, called down upon him a pompous rebuke from no less Olympian a figure than Robert Dudley, earl of Leicester. Writing to Mansel in 1581 he criticised the tone of Mansel's letter to him, which he thought savoured of 'faction' (Leicester's own family and career should have made him a good judge of that!) and emanated from 'such a mind as will take upon it to control the High Court of Parliament' (possibly such presumption had not been entirely absent from Leicester's thinking at times!). He loftily reminded Mansel of the gulf which existed between a belted earl and a mere knight: as long as Pembroke continued in his customary duty and allegiance to the Queen 'there will be made a difference between his Lordship and Sir Edward Mansel'; and Leicester ended his letter by washing his hands of Mansel and leaving him to his own devices. Obviously it took more than Leicester's strictures *de haut en bas* to deflate Mansel. In a letter to Sir William Herbert, undated but almost certainly written after Leicester's to him, he wrote that he had no wish to offend the earl of Pembroke, 'yet I confess if my dear father had then been living and party against my country [i.e. Glamorgan in the context of this letter], though he had been of estate as high as the prince of "Praga" I would and ought to have opposed myself against him'.[35]

Within their own localities the major gentry exercised an almost unquestioned dominance. Fortified by wealth, influence, and public office, they took their supremacy as their birthright, were intensely aware of it, and spared no effort to manifest, underline, and uphold it among those around them. Their lineage, real and fictitious, was inscribed in book and manuscript, and extolled by bard and herald. Their family arms and motto were emblazoned in hall and church, on fireplace and

window, ceiling and panel, hatchment and tomb, in portrait and effigy,
wood and stone, glass and paint. Sir Edward Stradling even left a silver
ring 'with my whole arms and crest' as a family heirloom. Only the lone
voice of Henry Vaughan, the Silurist, comes down to us reproaching the
gentry for their inordinate pride:

> O why so vainly do some boast
> Their birth and blood, and a great host
> Of ancestors, whose coats and creasts
> Are some ravenous birds or beasts?

Yet by our own age no more than a few material fragments of this once
omnipresent expression of family pride remain to revive for us some faint
flavour of the departed greatness of the Tudor and Stuart squires. On the
unique and graceful italianate porch of Beaupré built in 1600 by Richard
Bassett, the Bassetts, whose proud motto was 'gwell angau na chywilydd'
('better death than shame'), have left their arms of the chevron between
bugle-horns, and on the crumbling gatehouse at Oxwich Castle is a panel
bearing the Mansels' chevron between three maunches (ladies' sleeves)
and the great Sir Rice's initials (Pl. XXI). In Llanmihangel Place the
fine oak-panelled hall has a mantelpiece on which several coats of arms
can still be seen, but a few miles away at Llantriddyd, those 'magnificent
staircases, embossed and panelled ceilings, carved chimney pieces and
armorial embellishments of the most splendid' which, a century ago,
were 'fast sinking into ruin', have now quite disappeared (Pl. XVII).
However, within the church adjoining is the ornate and impressive, but
over-large, tomb of John Bassett and his wife, raised by their son-in-
law, Anthony Mansel, in gratitude, perhaps, for having married their
wealthy heiress, Elizabeth (Pl. VI). St. John's church, Cardiff, houses a
particularly fine and characteristic Jacobean tomb of two of the Herberts,
William (d. 1609) and John (d. 1617), whose effigies lie side by side
in an unusual all-male pair (Pl. VI). In Margam abbey's south aisle
stands the most beautiful and striking group of all Glamorgan tombs,
the splendid monuments of four generations of Mansels: Sir Rice, Sir
Edward, Sir Thomas, and finally Sir Lewis (Pl. VII). All were made
to the same general pattern, with their elegantly-carved effigies and little
troupes of supporting 'weepers', all were worked in the same white
marble, now weathered to a darker cream, and all must presumably have
been erected at the same time as a pious tribute to her husband's family
by the sorrowing wife of Sir Lewis Mansel, the second baronet (d. 1638).[36]

Of the many portraits that were probably painted at this time
scarcely more than half-a-dozen have survived. From the walls of the
tiny Stradling chapel in St. Donat's church the portraits of three Stradling
knights have looked down on the congregation since they were placed
there in 1590 by Sir Edward Stradling (d. 1609). Only the portrait of
the donor himself, clad in dark Elizabethan costume, with a scroll above
his head bearing the legend 'Vertues hole praise consisteth in doing' has

any pretensions to being a portrait from life. The best pictorial record of a family has been left by the Mansels, some of whose portraits still hang on the walls of Penrice Towers, the home of their descendants. The first baronet, Sir Thomas, survives in two portraits, the one on his own and the other of him and his wife and daughter in characteristic Jacobean costume (Pl. IV). They are not great works of art, and they have justly been stigmatized as stiff, formal, and aloof. Yet as social documents they are revealing; they were 'made for limited and clearly envisaged purposes of domestic assertion and dynastic prestige'. Though we learn little of Sir Thomas as an individual personality from his portrait, he obviously wanted himself depicted as strong, dignified, and confident; the posture of a man who has no doubt of his own place in society or his fitness to occupy and enjoy it. How sad it is that more of these material remains of the past, which can often reveal so much more at a glance than pages of words, have not survived.[37]

Around each squire was a household of kinsmen, retainers and servants, as large as he believed his social status warranted and his purse could be made to stretch to. On his manors and estates were a body of freeholders, burgesses, and tenants, ranging perhaps from a few dozen to several hundred. Over all of them he exercised the authority of lord and master, and from all of them he expected obedience and support. Even as late as 1647, after all the upheaval, dislocation and defeat of the Civil War, the ordinary people of Wales publicly and stubbornly insisted that they 'would not offend their landlords come what may'. The ways in which squires treated their dependants varied widely, and were conditioned, as all human relationships always are, by differences of personality and temperament. Instances are not lacking of men who were brutal and arrogant, and who rode roughshod over tenantry, for whose rights they had neither regard nor compunction. Sir George Herbert had no scruple about indulging in blackmail and even judicial murder in relation to one of his tenants (*ante*, III, 280). Others were accused of being grasping to the point of tyranny: Anthony Mansel was alleged by his tenants in a suit they brought against him in the Court of Requests to be 'a man in those parts of great kindred, power and authority [who] doth by all ways and means devise . . . to make his tenants weary of the occupation' of their holdings. Yet it is unlikely that such high-handed and inequitable treatment was the norm, if only because the more substantial freeholders and tenants, pushed too far, were themselves willing to offer resistance by force or litigation (above, pp. 27–8). A very different picture of the relationship between lord and men emerges from other sources. Although it presents the same impression of the landowner's unquestioned sense of his divine right to supremacy, it also conveys a parallel awareness on his part that authority over tenants and dependants carried with it the obligation of justice and protection and must be exercised in a patriarchal sense of responsibility. The earl of Worcester, in 1570, adjured his steward, Edward Mansel, to be 'careful how the inhabitants within these towns of mine which are franchised with liberties may peaceably enjoy their common quiet, as also by government be reformed, if among them happen any occasion of disorder'. Or there is the dying Jane Mansel's charge to her son Bussy: 'be ruled by your [step] father . . . for he never injured any tenant or neighbour since he came among them . . . Consider that your poor servants and friends will be utterly undone if they be bereaved of your [step] father to protect them from the injuries and oppression of others . . . I charge you, as you shall answer before God, to use [your poor friends and tenants] well and conscionably, and not to wrong or oppress them in any way.' Lest it be thought that these were simply the pious aspirations of a religious woman on her deathbed, there can be compared with them an extract from a letter written under no such pressure by Lord St. John to Edward Stradling in 1585: 'it hath been informed me that since your coming out of the country, great oppression and bad dealing hath been used against some of my tenants by means of your want to assist and speak for them; which hard course being like to continue towards them, it standeth upon me to provide for redress thereof . . . [I] would be loth to have the place of my high steward unfurnished to the hurt of my tenants and prejudice of myself'. Or there was a similar request from Sir Thomas Mansel to Stradling that, during Mansel's absence from home, he would take upon him 'the protection of [Mansel's] poor neighbours and friends in preventing that the rich shall not oppress the poor, and that the poor injure not the wealthy', and assuring him that Mansel would perform a similar favour for him in time of need. Other letters in the same correspondence breathe much the same spirit of solicitude and concern, as well as self-interest, in relation to the treatment of tenants. Sir Edward Stradling's own will revealed a particularly scrupulous and honourable attitude towards tenants, laying down that any agreements arrived at between him and them, even if only by word of mouth, must be honoured and tenants allowed 'peaceably to occupy and enjoy the same'.[38]

It was inevitable in this highly competitive world and acquisitive society with its numerous gentle families, proud and acutely sensitive on points of honour, tenacious of their economic interests and social position, and appalled by the prospect of any loss of face in the eyes of either their peers or underlings, that there should be constant jostling for position and advantage, in the course of which quarrels were bound to break out from time to time between individuals and factions. Old habits of violence, prevalent in late-medieval Glamorgan (*ante*, III, ch. xi), died hard, and survived long after the Acts of Henry VIII's reign which were hopefully intended to bring about a more law-abiding state of society. The gentry and many of their followers, fiery, mettlesome, quick to take offence and slow to relinquish a grudge, impatient of any slight, real or imagined, and accustomed to carrying weapons—swords, daggers, bills, bows and arrows, cudgels, and pikestaves for the most part, though by the seventeenth century firearms were not unknown—were still prone to move very quickly from words to blows. The womenfolk could be as determined as the men in these quarrels. When a serjeant-at-arms came to execute a commission at Edmund Mathew's house at Llandaff in 1611, having demanded that the inmates should come forth and deliver possession of it, he was answered by a 'gentlewoman at a window, being one of Edmund Mathew's daughters, that they had received commandment from their father and mother not to deliver it, neither would they, but would rather die together'. Concluding that the house was not to be won 'without ordnance to batter it, and shedding of much blood', the serjeant withdrew in dismay.[39]

Neither was violence the prerogative of one social class; it was common among all ranks of society. The surviving court books of manor and lordship, whether it be of the upland country of Senghennydd or lowlying Ewenni, show that rarely did a session pass without at least one instance of affray or assault among the tenants. Great Sessions records also reveal the existence of an enormous amount of violent crime. Homicides were distressingly common; hardly a session went by without one, and in March 1617 there were no fewer than five for the single county of Glamorgan. There were, in addition, very many cases of stealing cattle, sheep, horses, and other livestock, and frequent instances of highway robbery, burglary, and housebreaking. Punishments for these offences were intended to be ferociously deterrent and were themselves primitive and violent. Even trivial thefts, by culprits of either sex, were punishable by flogging and pillorying, while offences more serious than these carried the death penalty. It is true that many more people than might have been expected were sufficiently literate to escape execution for a first conviction by successfully pleading benefit of clergy and were branded with an 'ff' on the left hand. No woman was hanged, either, until it had been ascertained that she was not pregnant. But even so, not a year went by without a number of hangings being publicly carried out in the county. For a particularly odious offence, that of poisoning a husband, two women were burnt in Cowbridge in 1562; and for killing his wife by suffocation in 1573 David ap Hopkin of Llandeilo Tal-y-bont was executed by having his body loaded with as much stone and iron as it would carry and being fed with bread and water of the worst kind on alternate days until he died. Amid men and women so conditioned and inured to violence, with such a low emotional flashpoint, there was always a serious risk that bad feelings might explode into open violence whenever men congregated together and rival groups or hostile individuals were likely to meet—in markets, fairs, taverns, elections, sessions, county court, and even in church. An expressive letter from James Turberville conveys something of the readiness with which inflamed emotion could be translated into physical assault. In the heat of a quarrel between Sir Edward Mansel and Turberville's father-in-law, Turberville had felt that 'if the matter took not such effect as it ought, I would not be the last should draw my sword against you [Mansel], which thing nature and duty bound me thereunto'. One observer had believed that Turberville was so infuriated that he had intended to kill Mansel, but Turberville himself repudiated this as being the report of a 'dissembling sycophant'.[40]

From a number of sources—contemporary comment, letters, and especially court proceedings—we derive a distinct impression that the gentry's followers, in their zeal to uphold their masters' honour and their own prestige, were often more to blame for instigating and exacerbating disputes than anyone else (above, pp. 95–6). 'This I know', wrote Sir Edward Mansel to Sir William Herbert, 'that our men's pride will not be bridled till either our dispositions to quietness, or our smarts for their lewdness, press us severely to chastise our followers when they attempt the breach of amity between gentlemen.' But once the retainers had become involved, whatever the rights and wrongs of the issue, their lords usually felt obliged to uphold them. As the domineering Sir George Herbert, in the course of his quarrel with the Mansels in 1557, insisted to the would-be peacemaker, Anne Mansel, it was not the fate of the wrecked French cargo which had incensed him. 'Tush, tush, it is not for that!' he protested, 'But I will not suffer my officers, which are as good gentlemen as your nephew [Edward Mansel], to be louted and misused at his hand. I will make him know the worst servant of my house that I send to do my commandment.' Or again, after the violent Cardiff riots of 1596 Sir William Herbert openly said 'at the bench in great choler and heat in upholding and countenancing his said servants that the bailiffs of Cardiff before that time were not wont nor durst imprison his men but leave the same to him, and that if the earl of Pembroke did not stick close unto them he would make there should be but few bailiffs in Cardiff thereafter'. The highly-coloured and unashamedly partisan language of the court proceedings which often followed these quarrels conveys a lurid picture of unbridled physical force that must not be taken too literally; but as the next chapter will show there is no doubt that factiousness, degenerating into violence, was rife among the Glamorgan gentry and their entourages in Tudor times.[41]

Many of the quarrels, of course, were not fought by force of arms but by litigation. One of the features of a society which is moving from a violent phase in its history to a more law-abiding one tends to be excessive litigiousness; feuds which were previously settled by physical encounter became transferred to the lawcourt. It was a golden age for lawyers when men went to law so often and for so long. Some of their suits, like the tremendous tug-of-war over the Mansel inheritance, were matters of life and death and justified the energy and fees spent on them. There were others where the effort involved hardly seemed worth while, except that it became a point of honour not to be worsted by an adversary because, in a litigious age, it was presumably a matter of great importance for any man of property not to acquire a reputation of being a 'soft option' for any of the sharp-eyed, malicious suitors in which the age abounded. Oliver Lord St. John found his suit over the parsonage of Penmark 'long delayed' and 'tedious' but still expressed his determination never to leave it 'till I have brought the same to some perfection'. Many other suits have been 'wholly obliterated and buried in oblivion', or at least neglected in the dusty records of the lawcourts, as Sir John Stradling feared the long legal battle over the lower burrows of Merthyr Mawr would have been, had he not recorded that now-famous encounter in writing. The sand-blown lands in dispute were not of particularly great value, but the case dragged on for many years. Its particular interest for us is that Sir John's animated and colourful prose presents us with so lively a cameo of the methods and attitudes of the Elizabethans in their legal proceedings. Both parties to the dispute were tenacious, ingenious, and unscrupulous. Sir John's dyed-in-the-wool partisan's account, of course, indicts only his opponents with being prepared to use violence, chicanery, corruption, pickpocketing, abuse of office, and any and every other device that came to hand. But his modern editor has justly observed, 'the ethics of litigation were not then what they have become since modern reforms', and 'neither side can claim any great merit on the grounds of scrupulousness'. The truth was that for the men of that age all was fair in love and lawsuits; there was no equivalent of the Queensberry rules in the vendettas of the gentry and their followers. They were partisan and they made no bones about it. If they were in office and could empanel a partial jury, or intimidate under-sheriffs or witnesses, or in some other way influence the course of justice, they did so without any qualms; though few of them would have gone to such extremes as that most notorious of Elizabethan sheriffs, Edward Kemeys, of whom it has been said that he 'abused every function which it was left to him as sheriff to commit' and had to be 'removed out of the commission of the peace until the right honourable the Lord Keeper should be better satisfied of his behaviour'. Not that the gentry were unduly oppressed by any sense of apprehension about remonstrances from above. Thomas Lewis Y Fan, in deep disgrace with the Council in the Marches for having gerrymandered the choice of Glamorgan coroners in 1570, dismissed the consequences, even 'if the worse happen', as 'but a money matter and the paying of a fine to which it is also affirmed a number have promised to contribute with him whatsoever the penalty be'.[42]

Yet it is fair to say that by the beginning of the seventeenth century there was a greater chance than ever before of well-born offenders being brought before the courts to answer for their misdemeanours and to be punished for them. We know of many of the most dangerous and riotous conflicts between them because the participants were subsequently brought to answer for them in the Court of the Star Chamber and even the Privy Council (below, pp. 175–91). The risk of appearing before such august tribunals did not, however, in itself deter the gentry from squaring up to their enemies and standing by their friends, nor prevent their dependants from lining up behind them. In their quarrels, whether political or economic or personal, the reputation of a gentleman was reckoned not only by his own strength and courage in maintaining his honour but also by the number and combativeness of his followers and his allies. It was a kind of social bond and cohesion which was to be elevated from the level of county squabbles to the dignity of the highest loyalty to king and church in the tumultuous years between 1642 and 1645.

Almost all of the clashes within society of which we have any knowledge were vertical not horizontal in character. They were conflicts between town and country, between yeoman and yeoman, and, most frequently of all, between individual gentlemen or factions of gentlemen. They were not a war between rich and poor. Yet we know that for a century before 1642 the propertied classes in England and Wales had been apprehensive about the perennial possibility of a violent upheaval from below, and the successive poor law statutes were designed to contain if not remove the danger. Glamorgan men were, perhaps, haunted by the same dread, but if they were, it has left little or no trace of itself in the records. Insofar as the poets who protested so articulately against the treatment of the poor were concerned, it was retribution in the life hereafter not in the present that they seemed to predict; men who were rich and callous on earth would be punished in the eternal world like the rich man, Dives, in the parable. The periodically harsh clamp-down on vagrants and paupers gave some hints of an anxiety to ensure the severity of fierce deterrent measures. But the overtly-expressed concern about the possibility of a head-on clash between rich and poor expressed by the earl of Worcester to Sir Edward Mansel in 1570 seems unique. In his letter the earl referred to tensions which had arisen in Swansea 'partly through the wilful disobedience of the meaner sort towards their superiors, and partly also by the wealthier sort meaning to suppress their inferiors by ravine'. Perhaps the risks of violent uprisings by the paupers and the propertyless were not really as great as they sometimes appeared in the fevered and frightened imaginations of some of the upper classes. In a county like Glamorgan the poor and downtrodden, conditioned to accept the superiority of the upper classes, dependent on charity, ill-fed and ill-armed, poor in health and in spirit, lacked the will, numbers, organization, or force to put themselves in armed opposition to their rulers. Only in the biggest cities did the able-bodied beggars exist in large bands which might possibly burst out in dangerous concerted action. Even there, the appalling mortality among the poorest caused by the periodic visitations of plague acted as 'a veritable shears of Fate, which cut off the fringe of poverty as it grew from time to time', and prevented their numbers from getting wholly out of hand.[43]

v.

MARRIAGE AND THE FAMILY

During the period under discussion 'marriage was not a personal union for the satisfaction of psychological and physical needs; it was an institutional device to ensure the perpetuation of the family and its property' (Lawrence Stone). Among the propertied classes in society, therefore, marriages were usually carefully arranged by parents and were the subject of meticulously detailed legal settlements, normally in the form of a contract between the fathers of the bride and groom, and the settlement of lands by the father of the groom—or the groom himself if the father were dead—to trustees for uses. A number of such settlements have survived in the voluminous Margam archives, some relating to various members of the Mansel family itself, others to members of other gentry families, and a number drawn up by yeomen families. An excellent example of a major marriage settlement is that so carefully drawn up between Sir Thomas Mansel and Henry, earl of Manchester, whereby the former's son and heir, Lewis, was to marry the latter's daughter, Elizabeth. Sir Thomas agreed to settle a number of manors and lands in Mid Glamorgan and Gower on trustees along with £300 yearly, and also agreed to a jointure of £400 during the widowhood of the Lady Elizabeth if this should come about. Wives were expected to bring to their husbands dowries appropriate to their station. The Lewis Mansel already mentioned had married as his first wife, Katherine, daughter of Robert and Barbara Sidney, and the illustrious father-in-law got into difficulties over the payment of his daughter's dowry. 'I am at my wits' ends what to do', he wrote to his wife in 1607, 'I am not able to give Sir Thomas Mansel any satisfaction and that, I fear, will be a reason to make him use my poor daughter the worse.' Nearly two years later his steward in Glamorgan was urging him to pay the debt by six-monthly instalments of £200: 'this I take it will content him [Mansel] and less than this your honour cannot tender'.[44]

At the opposite end of the social scale we find a poor tenant from Tir Iarll having his case taken up by the earl of Pembroke. The tenant, described by the earl as an 'old poor man', had a daughter who had been got with child; nevertheless, if the seducer would agree to marry the girl her old father would struggle to give them 'four kine and forty sheep in marriage, being more than he was well worth'. The large body of documents in the Cardiff Central Library's series of Glamorgan deeds show the great care that was taken in drawing up marriage settlements, with each stage in the process carefully recorded in a deed. Almost invariably, one part of the property was reserved to the use of the parents as long as they lived, with remainder to the newly-married couple and their heirs, whilst the rest of the property was conveyed directly to the use of the newly-married couple for their lives, with remainder to their heirs.[44A]

Many of the wills of the period include bequests in cash and kind to unmarried girls to provide them with dowries. But Sir Edward Stradling specified that the £100 he left to each of the six unmarried daughters of Lambrook Stradling should only be paid if they married in accordance with their parents' wishes. Occasionally, if an agreement had already been arrived at in principle, the will stipulated the name of the individual that the daughter or son was to marry. John Thomas Bassett of Llantriddyd bequeathed two parts of the manor and the great mill at Bonvilston to his daughter, Elizabeth, on condition she married Thomas Bassett, one of the sons of William Bassett of Beaupré; and John Fleming required his son, Christopher, to fulfil the covenants agreed between Fleming senior and William Bassett for Christopher's marriage to Anne Bassett. After the parents' death, if the children were young enough to be in wardship, it was one of the prerogatives of their guardians to arrange prospective marriages for them. Lewis Thomas of Betws, who had three heiresses, his nieces, as his wards, became so angry when the eldest of them married a young man not of his choosing as soon as she was old enough to do so that he took the matter to the Star Chamber. In other cases it seems to have fallen to the lot of the eldest brother to see his sisters married. Sir Edward Stradling's aunt, Margaret Howard, wrote to him conveying her pleasure that his somewhat wayward sister, Gwenllian, was now willing to be married according to his wishes: 'she yields herself thus much unto you in all things, and in all to be governed by you'. Where no brother existed to take the responsibility, a senior male kinsman might take it upon himself to arrange an orphan daughter's marriage, as Sir Edward Stradling did with Barbara Gamage (below, pp. 183–4).[45]

The successful conclusion of a marriage settlement depended on what each party had to offer in the way of property and/or status. A very rich heiress like Barbara Gamage could become the subject of fierce competition between rival suitors, who would appear to have had more influence than wealth to offer her (below, pp. 183–6). Sir Edward Stradling's difficult sister had a suitor, Robert Giles, whose friends testified to his moral worth but whose possessions fell short, and the knight of St. Donat's was eloquently urged to open his 'purse awide to the present augmentation' of his sister's fortune. We cannot tell whether it was because Sir Edward loosened his purse-strings or not, but his sister became Mistress Giles and was left a legacy in his will. There was always a risk that to help one party's matrimonial prospects there might be overoptimistic assessments or even conscious deceit. William Thomas

of Eglwysilan felt so strongly that he had been grossly cheated by
Charles Kemeys, a younger son of Cefnmabli, that he took him to the
Court of Exchequer where he accused him of having defaulted on
his marriage settlement with Thomas's daughter, Anne, of having
received from Thomas over £300 in 'money and money worth', and
of having lived at Thomas's expense and in his household for three and
a half years until Anne's death; accusations largely denied by Kemeys
who, in turn, accused Thomas of not having fulfilled his promises concerning Anne's marriage portion. There was the further risk of the
abduction and forced marriage of adolescent heiresses, and this despite
the existence of legislation prohibiting the taking-away of heiresses
under the age of sixteen. Five Star Chamber suits relating to Glamorgan
tell of episodes where this was alleged to have happened. The conflicting
nature of the surviving testimony makes it very difficult to know exactly
what took place, but in only one of these suits does it seem likely that
there was a genuinely violent abduction. That was when John David
Griffith, tailor of Llangynwyd—the complainant in the suit, ironically
enough!—would appear to have forcibly carried off the fifteen-year-old
Gwenllian, daughter and heiress of Thomas Griffith of Betws, in February
1594 and compelled her to marry him.[46]

Because of the nature of the property interests involved, it was
usual for marriages to take place between men and women of the same
social status. Contemporaries were extremely sensitive of the need to
avoid a *mésalliance* that would lead to one of the partners being 'in any
sort impeached or disparaged in reputation', as one Glamorgan lawsuit
expressed it. Most of the gentry's children were married to sons and
daughters of comparable families. Such alliances were usually contracted
within the same county, which was the normal unit of upper-class society,
though it might often be that marriages were arranged with families in
neighbouring counties like Monmouthshire, especially with the prolific
Herbert and Morgan clans of that county, in Breconshire and Carmarthenshire to a lesser extent, and, not uncommonly, in Somerset conveniently
near across the Channel. It was rare, but by no means unknown, for one
of the gentry to venture further afield for a partner, as when Jane Stradling
married a Gruffydd of the Penrhyn in Caernarvonshire, a union that
created immense pleasure and interest among the bards, or when Sir
John Carne of Ewenni married the daughter of Sir Walter Hungerford
of Farley. The rapid rise of some of the most eminent county families
by the beginning of the seventeenth century awoke in them aspirations
to link themselves in marriage with members of the peerage. The second
Sir Edward Lewis married the widow of Lord Beauchamp and daughter
to Robert Sackville, earl of Dorset. Three successive generations of the
Mansels married into the peerage: Sir Edward Mansel married Jane,
daughter of the second earl of Worcester, Sir Thomas married the daughter
of Lord Mordaunt, and Sir Lewis married as his first wife the daughter

of the earl of Leicester, and as his second, the daughter of the earl of Manchester.[47]

The precariousness of life and health in the sixteenth and seventeenth centuries, and especially the dangers to women of a succession of child-births, gave rise to many short-lived unions; and second and third marriages were not uncommon. It was rare for any man or woman of property to remain widowed for long. A man with a household of any size dependent on him could not easily do without a wife to look after his children, oversee the household servants, and supervise the domestic chores in an establishment expected to be largely self-sufficient. A woman left widowed with a family of young children found it virtually impossible to manage property and tenants in that disturbed age without the support and protection of a man, though provision made for wives in a number of wills is dependent on their remaining unmarried. The contemporary records hardly ever afford us any intimate glimpses of the nature of the relationship between husband and wife. Yet the fact that the marriage was essentially a business contract, with the parties to it being chosen for one another by parents or relatives without any consideration of later conceptions of romantic love, did not necessarily mean that the partnerships were devoid of a deep and genuine affection. The happy survival of letters which passed between Barbara Gamage and her husband after their marriage reveals a rare and delicate attachment between them despite the indecent scramble for her hand that had preceded their union. A very different picture of acute married discord is presented by the suit which Anne Lloyd brought against her husband, the squire of Llandeilo Tal-y-bont, in which she successfully claimed separation from him on grounds of extreme cruelty; though her husband, it is fair to add, complained that she had refused to prepare his meals, had recklessly spent money on his step-children, and had called him abusive names. A more light-hearted vignette of matrimonial tensions comes in Thomas ab Ieuan ap Rhys's poem 'Cân Cymhortha'. His was the age-old situation of an old husband being henpecked by a young wife, and Thomas described with self-mocking satire, tinctured by just the right touch of pathos, how his young termagant's rasping tongue hectored him into going to look for corn in the Vale. In many of the contemporary wills a kinder note is struck when many husbands refer to their 'beloved' or 'well-beloved' wives. This may have been no more than an amiable convention, but when John Carne of Ewenni in 1617 not only referred to his loving wife 'whom I have always found kind and faithful and obedient to me' but also added voluntarily to her jointure, or when Sir Edward Lewis of Y Fan (1628) mentioned 'my well-beloved wife with whom I have lived in the blessed state of matrimony for about nine and thirty years' and bequeathed to her, as a mark of gratitude, his coach, four coach horses and 'all the furniture thereto belonging', this clearly seemed to show an affection for the wives going beyond mere testamentary clichés. References by wives to husbands are much rarer because of the fewness of wills made by women. Nevertheless, Lady Jane Mansel of Margam could write of her 'dear and loving husband' and Lady Agnes Stradling expressed her wish to be buried with her 'late dear husband'. No doubt, there were then, as now, marital relationships which ranged over the whole spectrum of human emotions from fervent detestation through stolid unconcern to profound devotion. Where relations between husband and wife were unsatisfactory the man, at least, often found consolation with another partner, judging by the large number of illegitimate children included among gentry pedigrees and referred to in records relating to paupers and vagrants.[48]

The size and structure of families at this time are largely a closed book. The pedigrees of the gentry can, however, provide us with a rough index of the average number of children born to them. Taking a representative sample of 20 such Glamorgan families, whose pedigrees appear to be fully recorded for at least four generations during our period, we find a total of 82 generations yielding between them 574 children, of whom at least 34 were illegitimate. Absolute accuracy cannot be claimed for these figures. Quite apart from any inaccuracy in the pedigrees themselves, we have no means of knowing how many children who died in infancy went unrecorded, nor can we be sure how many of those recorded grew up into adults. However, the resultant average of just over seven children per gentry family would not seem to be far out of line with what little is known of family sizes. How this figure compared with that for the average family of poorer households it is at present impossible to tell in the absence of parish registers for most of the Glamorgan parishes. Almost certainly, the average for the gentry would have been markedly higher than that for people of lower social rank. The gentry usually married earlier and lived longer, were better fed and housed, and lost fewer children in infancy than the mass of the population; but just how great the difference between family sizes was, must as yet remain a matter of conjecture.[49]

vi.

EDUCATION AND CULTURE

The most epoch-making cultural change of the sixteenth century was the acceptance by the laity of the need for academic training. In earlier centuries education had been, in the main, the prerogative of youths destined for the clergy, from whose midst came the great majority of those who entered grammar school and university. Though it had not been unknown for a layman to proceed to the university or the inns of court in preparation for a career as a lawyer or merely as an introduction to the social graces, this had been a relatively rare phenomenon. What transformed the situation in the sixteenth century was the diminished emphasis on the previously dominant need for military expertise in the service of the state or overlord and the increased demand for men appropriately trained in legal and administrative skills. As the Tudor state expanded the scope of its activities, both at the centre and in the counties, so it needed more men who had at least enough education effectively to shoulder the responsibility of public office and local administration and justice. As members of parliament, deputy-lieutenants, sheriffs, justices of the peace, and in other capacities (below, ch. iii), they were being given a constantly extended range of function and influence, for which, however, their educational attainments must be adequate. Moreover, if they were younger sons of gentry, or sprung from yeoman stock, and cherished ambitions to make their fortune by entering either the public service or the professions, they had no hope of doing so without first climbing the rungs of the educational ladder. Undoubtedly it was these practical considerations of education as the avenue to office, influence, and affluence that were uppermost in determining men to seek it.

There was another impetus of a more distinctively cultural kind that was given by the metamorphosis of the concept of a gentleman. Borne from Italy on the wings of admiration and emulation came the ideal of the Renaissance man; the all-rounder depicted in books like Castiglione's *Il Cortegiano*: the courtier, man of affairs, and soldier; scholar, man of letters, and connoisseur; as virtuous as he was brave; as supple, strong and disciplined in mind as in body; as sensitive to the delights of the intellect as he was accomplished in public affairs; a just magistrate and a generous patron. Only a handful may have sensed its appeal in full, and even fewer came anywhere to achieving it in practice. Yet it percolated to Glamorgan and was not without its influence in moulding the cultural and educational ethos of the county. Out of such needs and aspirations, practical and theoretical, sprang the dramatic increase in the numbers of laymen proceeding to grammar schools, universities and inns of court from about the middle of the sixteenth century onwards. Nearly all the aspirants for the benefits of education were recruited from among the sons of either the gentry or the more ambitious burgesses and yeomen, who alone could afford to do without the labour or the earning capacity of their children for long years of full-time education, or subsequently to help provide them with opportunities to make full use of their education after it had been completed.[50]

Many youngsters received their first education from a tutor or schoolmaster hired by their parents for the purpose. Sir Rice Mansel made provision in his will for the maintenance for the space of twenty years out of the revenues of Laleston manor of 'one honest and learned man' to educate his grandchildren, great-nephews and 'three or four of the aptest children' of his tenants, provided their parents went responsible for their food and clothing, at some covenient place in Margam. In the 1630s the widow of Sir Edward Lewis of Y Fan was maintaining three tutors for her son, to teach him Latin, French, and Welsh respectively. A girl, no less than a boy, in a well-to-do household would be given some instruction, being carefully brought 'up at her book, needle and other things fitting for her calling and degree', as a contemporary lawsuit put it. Though no endowed grammar schools, so numerously established in the sixteenth century, were found in Tudor Glamorgan, one of Rice Merrick's observations informs us that there were schools of one sort or another in existence in Elizabethan times at Cardiff, Llandaff, St. Nicholas, Cowbridge (*not* as yet Cowbridge Grammar School), Neath, Swansea, and Llantwit (Major). A school of this kind is known to have been kept by Gervase Babington, himself an accomplished scholar and at one time chaplain to Mary Sidney, countess of Pembroke, before he became bishop of Llandaff, so these institutions in the hands of men like him may have imparted education of a high standard. It was, perhaps, schools of this sort that testators had in mind when they made provision for their sons, especially younger ones, to be 'kept at school', though when James Thomas of Llanfihangel required his wife to keep their fourth son, Edmund, 'at school' until he was twenty-one he must surely have been thinking of something more ambitious for him, including a career at university or inns of court.[51]

Not until the reign of James I was Glamorgan's first, and for a long time only, permanently endowed grammar school founded at Cowbridge. It was originally envisaged by that ornament of the county's cultural life, Sir Edward Stradling; but when the old knight died in 1609 work on his proposed foundation was still 'inchoate and unfinished'. It must have been completed shortly afterwards by his heir, Sir John Stradling, himself a productive, if not inspired, poet and prose-author (below, pp. 120-1). He had acquired a house in Cowbridge from a mercer called Griffith, and he established as the first schoolmaster there one of his own kinsmen, a cleric and capable Latinist called Walter Stradling. The latter was paid a salary of £20 per annum to instruct in classical grammar such sons of the local gentry and yeomen who were placed in his care and also, very probably, sons of the poorer burgesses of the town of Cowbridge. Of its earliest pupils there are two of whom we can be sure. The one was Evan Seys of Boverton, scion of a family that had already made something of a name for itself in legal circles by the career of Evan's grandfather, Roger, Queen Elizabeth's attorney-general for Wales. Evan Seys himself proceeded to Christ Church, and graduated M.A., Ll.D., became a bencher of Lincoln's Inn, recorder of Gloucester, and member of parliament for Glamorgan in 1659 and Gloucester, 1661-81. The other Cowbridge *alumnus*, Leoline Jenkins (1625-85), was the son of a Glamorgan yeoman and a pupil at Cowbridge in the 1630s. He was later to be principal of Jesus College, Oxford, a distinguished judge, diplomat, secretary of state, and the re-founder of his old school.[52]

Having been grounded in classical grammar at home, at school in Glamorgan, or in a grammar school outside the county, many young men proceeded to the university, usually at the age of about sixteen or seventeen. In their choice of university Glamorgan men showed the same overwhelming preference for Oxford as most of their fellow-Welshmen. Even during the most flourishing decades for university education between 1600 and 1642, only two Glamorgan names have been traced at Cambridge, while at Oxford during the same period there were at least 114 Glamorgan men, an average of nearly three new entrants a year. The colleges to which they were chiefly attracted were Jesus College and Brasenose particularly, and Christ Church and New College to a lesser extent. Among the students at Oxford were members of a number of leading Glamorgan gentry families. A notable example was set for them by the two great aristocratic houses associated with the county; the second earl of Pembroke was an *alumnus* of Oxford and Cambridge, and his sons, William and Philip, were both sent to New College; and both the fourth and fifth earls of Worcester went to Oxford, together with the fifth earl's two brothers. Some of the gentry families of the county were better represented at the university than others. Among the Aubreys, Stradlings, and Carnes of Ewenni there was a strong tradition that the heir should proceed to the university; a practice far from common, as can be seen from the fact that out of Symonds's list of 35 heads of families in 1645, only seven were university-educated. Other families with numerous graduates in their midst, especially among younger sons, were the Bassetts, Gamages, Lewises, and Mansels.

A number of students were also attracted to the 'third university', the inns of court. Many went there after graduating, but others proceeded directly to the inns. Between 1600 and 1642 55 Glamorgan names were entered upon their admission registers: 7 of them at the Middle Temple, 20 at Lincoln's Inn, and 28 at Gray's Inn. Lincoln's Inn had been the most favoured institution down to 1625, but it became decidedly less popular thereafter because it was reputed to be a nursery of Puritanism. A spell at an inn of court had much to recommend it. Obviously those who were bent on practising law as a career went there for the most advanced professional training. Many others who had no intention of becoming lawyers by profession went there to be initiated into the mysteries of the law and lawcourts, a highly desirable acquisition in so litigious an age, and to avail themselves of the general education in public affairs, conduct of business, and polite behaviour, which the inns of court were reputed to provide.

When all this formal and informal instruction at university or inn of court was concluded, a fortunate and favoured few rounded off their education with a spell of foreign travel. Sir Edward Stradling, as a young man of nineteen or twenty, travelled in Germany and France, and in 1548–9 was in Italy as the companion of Sir Thomas Hoby, who was later to become famous for his translation of *Il Cortegiano* into English. In 1578, the young Thomas Mansel, son and heir of Sir Edward, was at Pisa, where he picked up news of Sir Thomas Stukeley's dealings with the pope and the king of Portugal which he sent home to his father, who in turn forwarded it to Burghley. When Henry Somerset, fifth earl of Worcester (*c.* 1577–1646), made the grand tour, he set out a Protestant and returned a Catholic. Fears of such subversive conversions as the result of travel in Catholic countries persisted for a long time, and they explain the wording of a pass for John Mathew of Llandaff and John Prichard of Llancaeach, which still survives among the State Papers for 1635. It allowed them 'to travel into foreign parts' for three years and allowed them to take with them 'a servant, their trunks of apparel and other necessities', but only on condition 'they repair not to the city of Rome'.[53]

The value of the new kind of academic training as a preparation for service to the state was exemplified in the careers of some of the most gifted sons of Tudor and Stuart Glamorgan. An early representative of the new kind of highly-educated layman, eager to play his part in affairs of state and equipped to do so, was Sir Edward Carne (*c.* 1500–1561). Characteristically, he was a younger son, the second son of Hywel Carne of Nash, who aimed at making his own way in the world by means of the legal profession. Educated at Oxford, he became principal of Greek Hall and graduated D.C.L. in 1524. He was later employed by Henry VIII in proceedings designed to annul the king's marriage, he took part in the dissolution of the monasteries, was the first sheriff of Glamorgan after the Act of Union, and sat in the Parliament of 1554 as member for the county. Together with Lord Montague and the bishop of Ely he was nominated by Queen Mary to make the submission of England to the pope, and he ended his career in the highly responsible position of ambassador to Rome (below, p. 232). Another second son, and also trained as a lawyer, Sir John Herbert (1550–1617), son of Mathew Herbert of Swansea, rose even higher in the royal service. Educated at Oxford, he later became a well-known judge in the Courts of Admiralty and Requests. A brilliant linguist, he was actively engaged on behalf of the Queen's government in a number of trade and diplomatic missions to Denmark, Poland, Brandenburg, the Low Countries, and France. He sat in parliament on a number of occasions from 1586 to 1611, including once (1601) as member for Glamorgan. In 1600 he became the first man to hold the office of second secretary of state and was created a privy councillor; but he did not enjoy much of the confidence or favour of James I, and he was bitterly disappointed not to succeed his master and patron, Robert Cecil, earl of Salisbury, as secretary of state when the latter died in 1610. His fine tomb at Cardiff shows him in effigy, fittingly wearing his lawyer's gown. The most brilliant Glamorgan man of them all was Sir Robert Mansel (1573–1656), fourth son of Sir Edward

Mansel of Margam. Having entered Brasenose College in 1587, at the tender age of fourteen, he subsequently became one of the most eminent naval commanders of his generation. He is first known to have participated in a naval action during the expedition of 1596 to Cadiz. From then onwards, down to about 1612–13, he had an active and distinguished naval career. From 1604 to 1618 he was treasurer of the navy, and in 1620–1 commanded a large-scale expedition against the pirates of Algiers. However, the intense dislike which he and the royal favourite, Buckingham, cherished for one another prevented his being employed in naval commands at a time when his powers might have been expected to have been at their peak. In addition to his naval career, Sir Robert was active in politics, sitting in nearly all the parliaments between 1601 and 1628, including two spells (1623 and 1625, and 1627–8) as a member for Glamorgan. He was also deeply interested in the manufacture of glass, for which he held monopoly rights.[54]

The seminal influences of the better education being received by laymen were also apparent among the gentlemen resident in the county. The new-style Renaissance education, far from killing off traditional Welsh cultural modes, seemed to give them new impetus—in the short run at least. The customary 24 feats expected of men of birth and breeding in medieval Wales were not at all incompatible with the newer notions. They emphasized physical strength and dexterity, accomplished handling of weapons, and skill in the arts of the chase, but they also required a man to show an appreciative knowledge of poetry, harping, genealogy, and heraldry (below, p. 137). Here was a sturdy and honourable enough stock into which to graft the more sophisticated and ambitious Renaissance ideal; and at its best it was to bear choice and abundant fruit. Though the formal training the gentry received in grammar schools, university, and inns of court was conducted in English or Latin, they seemed to have no difficulty in preserving their knowledge of Welsh. Indeed, the indications are that if they married English wives, the latter were obliged to make some effort to learn Welsh in order to be able to cope effectively with their servants and their households. These Welsh-speaking gentlemen, great and small, continued to be the patrons of Welsh poets, in the fixed and free metres, and some of them were themselves poets and copyists, as well as collectors of books and manuscripts. If the quality of Welsh poetry composed within the county showed a marked decline at this time, this was not, in the first instance, because the gentry had become anglicized and no longer extended their patronage. Even a poet like Dafydd Benwyn (*flor. c.* 1550–1600), whose work was distinctly second-rate as compared with that of earlier poets, actually had a wider range and greater number of patrons in all parts of Glamorgan and Monmouthshire than his more accomplished predecessors had had, with some 60 to 70 of them in Glamorgan alone. Some of these patrons were discriminating judges of poetry, as Sir John

Stradling's well-known story of the encounter between the poet Meurug Dafydd and old William Bassett, squire of Beaupré, reminds us (below, pp. 539–40). One group of gentlemen, including Sir Edward Stradling Sir Edward Mansel, Anthony Powel, and Rice Merrick, were deeply immersed in the study of antiquities, history, genealogy, and heraldry (for fuller details on all these themes, see below, pp. 592–608).[55]

It is also symptomatic of the times that Sir Edward Stradling's correspondence should be liberally sprinkled with Latin quotations and classical references, or that William Mathew, writing to Sir Edward Mansel in 1575, could casually introduce into his letter allusions to classical and scriptural history: 'The troublesome state of our country (i.e. Glamorgan) hath ministered matter sufficient to write not letters only but volumes of infamy . . . Cicero by his wisdom and industry was able to repress the rebellion of Catilinus, but when the time was accomplished that the empire should prevail, what eloquence in Cicero or wisdom in Cato was able to prevail?' He urged that the Glamorgan gentry must not despair, however; like the citizens of Nineveh they must repent in response to godly preaching, and Edward Mansel was adjured to put his 'helping hand to repair the broken walls of Jerusalem'. Other patrons kept up an interest in music. The Stradling correspondence gives us a quick snapshot of Thomas Richards, the family harpist at St. Donat's, who was skilled enough a performer on an instrument 'stringed with wires' as well as the harp, to be warmly recommended to so illustrious a patron as Sir Philip Sidney, by whom he was summoned to Salisbury to play in the presence of an 'honourable assembly' and 'receipt of many gentlemen of good calling'. In west Glamorgan there was a master of several instruments, including harp, viol, organ and virginals, in the person of Thomas ap William ap Hywel of Cilffriw, near Neath, so Watcyn ap Hywel's poetic elegy to him tells us.[55A]

The completest embodiment of the Renaissance ideal of the gentleman in Glamorgan and one of the most notable examples of the type anywhere in Wales was Sir Edward Stradling (1529–1609). The enlightened, capable, and fair-minded owner of one of the largest estates in Glamorgan, he entertained his extensive circle of friends and acquaintances with a proverbial lavishness, gratitude for which reverberates through his correspondence. Inevitably, he was one of the foremost figures in local justice and administration; sheriff three times, justice of the peace, and deputy-lieutenant. A man of uncommon probity and good sense, he was extensively employed by the Crown on special commissions, and he frequently tried to use his good offices to mediate in the numerous quarrels among the local gentry, though he was never shy of standing up to the earl of Pembroke when he thought right and honour demanded it of him. His help was constantly being solicited by a wide range of correspondents in an extraordinary *mélange* of requests concerning matters public and private, important and trivial. What marks

[119]

him off from most of his fellows, however, was the range and seriousness of his intellectual interests. Not for nothing had he been educated at Oxford and then travelled widely on the Continent, especially in Italy. He returned imbued with Renaissance ideals but contrived to marry them happily with the native culture of Glamorgan and Wales. This 'Maecenas', as Dr. Siôn Dafydd Rhys dubbed him, was not only a generous patron of Welsh poets and harpists but also arranged for the publication in 1592, at his own expense, of 1,250 copies of a new Welsh grammar by Siôn Dafydd Rhys, *Cambrobrytannicae Linguae Institutiones*, for which, the grateful author declared, Stradling had been praised in 'more worshipful speeches . . . than about any one thing that ever you did in all your life'. It led another accomplished Elizabethan scholar, Thomas Wiliems, to describe Stradling as the 'chief guardian of our Welsh language in south Wales'. Reputedly the master of seven languages, Stradling assiduously collected books and manuscripts, including such lost treasures as the Register of Neath Abbey, for his library at St. Donat's, which was easily the finest in Glamorgan and possibly the best in Wales. The whole splendid collection, later to be much admired by Archbishop Usher in 1645, Stradling bequeathed to his heir, together with what appear to have been large and, probably, choice collections of armour, weapons, firearms, and 'Roman and ancient coins'. In his attitude towards his collections there was nothing self-centred about Sir Edward. Himself an enthusiastic scholar, he readily responded to a similar passion in others and was generous in sharing his books and manuscripts with them. His own celebrated account of the 'winning of Glamorgan', compiled some time between 1561 and 1566 at Burghley's instigation, went the rounds of other scholars and was extensively used by Sir Edward Mansel and Rice Merrick in their writings. There was in Stradling a largeness of mind and spirit recognized both by humble suitors for patronage like William Fleming, who spoke of Stradling's courtesy 'which carefully respecteth the causes of poor scholars and university men' and by someone more nearly his equal like Rice Merrick, who paid him this remarkable tribute: 'you refuse things which others most fervently crave and desire, viz. gains and profit . . . in respect of the zeal ye bear to the public commodity of your country before your own private wealth'. The maxim Sir Edward had incorporated in his portrait in St. Donat's church, 'Virtue's whole praise consisteth in doing', was for him no empty platitude.[56]

Sir Edward's heir, the first baronet, Sir John Stradling (1563-1629), was another interesting figure in the Glamorgan cultural scene. He was not Sir Edward's son, but was the grandson of Henry Stradling, second son of Sir Thomas Stradling (d. 1480), who had found a good match for himself in Jane Jubb, daughter and heiress of a successful Bristol attorney. John Stradling was, by instinct, training and accomplishment, a man after Sir Edward's own heart. As an undergraduate at Brasenose

College and Magdalen Hall he was 'accounted a miracle for his forwardness in learning and pregnancy of parts'. He later became a fellow of All Souls College and subsequently travelled widely on the Continent. Having entered the inns of court he was closely associated with such leading intellectuals as William Camden, John Harrington, and Thomas Leyshon. The first books he published were translations from the Latin works of the neo-Stoicist philosopher, Justus Lipsius, *A Direction for Travellers* (1592) and *Two Books of Constancy* (1594). In 1597 he published a Latin prose work, *De Vita et Morte Contemnenda Libri Duo*, and in 1607 a volume of Latin epigrams, many of which were addressed to his kinsmen, friends, and neighbours in south Wales, as well as to a large number of prominent individuals, including Elizabeth I, James I, leading politicians, commanders, intellectuals, and poets. In 1623 Stradling published his *Beati Pacifici*, a 'divine poem' addressed to James I, applauding the king's exertions as a peace-maker. His last and most ambitious published work, *Divine poems in Seven Several Classes, written to his most Excellent Majesty Charles I*, appeared in 1625. It is a volume of some 290 pages, divided into seven parts, each containing 200 six-lined stanzas. The two books are of some interest as an index to Stradling's political attitudes and values as a warm supporter of the Stuarts and especially of James's peace policies, but the quality of the verse is pedestrian and uninspired. Much more lively and readable are two prose works which Stradling left in manuscript form. The one, 'The Story of the Lower Burrows', was published in this century by Professor William Rees and the late Dr. H. J. Randall, and it is easily accessible in print. The other, 'A politic discourse or dialogue between a Knight of the Commons-house of Parliament and a Gent. his friend, being a moderate Roman Catholic', now preserved in the National Library of Wales as Manuscript 5666, is based on the author's experiences as a member in the parliaments of 1623–4, 1625, and 1625–6, in the last-named of which he sat as the member for Glamorgan. No claims can be made for Stradling as a poet or prose-author of the first rank; but he has a secure place in the cultural history of the county as an outstandingly intelligent, learned, and cultivated member of its new intelligentsia, and as the founder of Cowbridge Grammar School.[57]

vii.

THE MATERIAL STANDARD OF LIVING

The increase in production, trade and wealth during this century was accompanied by a steep and unmistakable rise in the living standards of many individuals and social groups. The fortunate ones who prospered attained superior levels of creature comfort in the shape of better houses, more luxurious furnishings and household goods, finer and more sumptuous clothing, and a richer and more varied diet. There was nothing new in lavish expenditure on housing, household, entertainment, and personal finery, of course. Such spending had long been a central characteristic of the image of the medieval magnate; but it was increased and diversified in the sixteenth century, not merely as a result of higher incomes but also of the diffusion of new and more expensive concepts, derived from Renaissance Europe, of the *mise-en-scène* and life-style appropriate to an aristocrat. Along with the ideas came a tide of luxury imports. The resultant craze for splendour and ostentation in accommodation, hospitality, food and drink, costume, adornment, display, and recreation was at its most feverish among the great luminaries of the Court, the peerage, and London; and over-indulgence in its vanities brought some illustrious figures in their midst to disaster. Its modes and manners, in reduced and more modest guise, spread to the provinces where they found willing exponents among those who could afford in some measure to indulge in these novelties. In the main it was the gentry who followed these fashions, but even among soberer and more cautious merchants and yeomen the ways of their social superiors to some extent rubbed off. Evidence of the actual impact of these changes on Glamorgan families and individuals is not easy to come by. Certainly there is no clear sign that any leading county family became so obsessed with conspicuous consumption as to slide over the brink into financial ruin or, as far as can be judged, to come anywhere near doing so. On the other hand, those poets who were critical of contemporary society, much as they adored open-handed benefactors and despised close-fisted 'usurers', did regularly condemn the incessant pursuit of worldly comfort and magnificence by their contemporaries and their boundless cupidity for fine houses, possessions, food and clothing. There seems little doubt, as we shall see, that where there was a rise in the incomes of Glamorgan families it was in general matched, as one would expect, by greater expenditure on improved material well-being. As the disparity between the incomes of the prosperous and the poor grew wider, so too did the chasm which existed between their standards of living.

HOUSING

In no sphere can the improvement in standards be seen more clearly than in that of housing. When the Act of Union was passed, all the housing in Glamorgan was medieval in character. A hundred years later, at the outbreak of the Civil War, most of the dwellings occupied by the well-to-do had undergone a revolution; they were either completely new or had been drastically modified. Glamorgan, too, had had its share of the 'great rebuilding' that had characterized many parts of England and Wales between 1550 and 1640. The new or reconstructed buildings then put up had been designed to secure more privacy, convenience, comfort, warmth, and light. To achieve these ends, new houses with two or more storeys were built to provide more private rooms, bedrooms and storage-space; and the halls of older medieval houses, hitherto open to the roof, had ceilings inserted, upper floors created, and stairways installed. Windows were enlarged, mullioned, and glazed; and stone fireplaces and chimneys installed. This spate of new and remodelled houses flowed from a society which was becoming more populous, prosperous and secure; and the better housing conditions which resulted may, in themselves, have contributed significantly to a healthier and larger population. Such building was expensive, as Sir John Stradling had cause to observe in his caustic comment on Nicholas Williams's 'very sumptuous new house' at Llantwit, 'more than three quarters finished at the lawyer's cost, whereas the one quarter thereof had been sufficient to dispend their whole living in, and more too'. The costs of such ventures could be borne only by those who had benefited most from the economic progress of the age: the gentry, yeomen, merchants, and the more thriving husbandmen and shopkeepers. One thing all these successful men, great and small, tended to have in common was that as soon as they could afford to build a new house or transform an old one they did so.[58]

The largest medieval houses with which Glamorgan was familiar were its numerous castles and its less frequent tower-houses like Candleston castle (*ante*, III, ch. ix). In the more ordered and secure days of the sixteenth century their military function was redundant; and as early as Leland's time, 1536-9, many of them were already written off as ruins. Only a handful of them were still inhabited by wealthy and powerful families, who transformed them into mansions, where the accent was less on strength than ease, and more on luxury than security. Cardiff castle, of which Rice Merrick gives an excellent contemporary description, was taken in hand by Henry, second earl of Pembroke, who 'repaired and translated the form of all the rooms within the castle' in the 1570s, and fragmentary accounts exist for further work undertaken there again in 1590, though the earl can only very rarely have been in residence within its walls. However, at St. Donat's castle, which continued to be the Stradlings' main residence, three generations of the family—Sir Thomas, Sir Edward and Sir John—exerted themselves to turn the castle into a country house of fitting dignity and comfort for one of the county's premier families. Fonmon castle, on the other hand, was not improved until Col. Philip Jones acquired it. In an early-seventeenth-century survey the manor house there was described as being 'of the old fabric' of the castle but no better than a good farmhouse in condition. Even though the castles were no longer needed as military bastions, the prestige of castellation outlived its usefulness and some of the more important new houses were built in quasi-castellated style. At Oxwich the Mansels raised a large and impressively-crenellated building called Oxwich Castle; but the large, spacious, mullioned windows of the tall four-storeyed ruin reveal that it was a new-style palatial country mansion, not a baronial stronghold, that was being built (Pl. XV). The largest and architecturally the most attractively-designed house erected in Glamorgan between the Act of Union and the Civil War, Ruperra Castle, built early in the seventeenth century by Sir Thomas Morgan from plans provided for him by John Thorpe, was itself another castellated building (Pl. XIX).[59]

A medieval abbey provided the nucleus for some of the houses. Sir Edward Carne adapted the conventual buildings of Ewenni priory into a commodious country house for himself and his descendants, which was not rebuilt until the beginning of the last century. An inventory of 1650 shows the house as having a hall, dining-room, a new, old, and little parlour, study, gallery, 16 bedrooms, a cockloft, two kitchens, pantry, larder, buttery, wine-cellars, wash-house, brew-house, two dairies, and a 'bunting house'. At Neath, Abbot Thomas Leyshon's fine house, greatly enlarged and extended, made excellent accommodation for a gentleman, and it passed in turn from Sir John Herbert to his daughter's husband, Sir William Dodington, and finally to the Hoby family. The two friaries at Cardiff provided stone for the earl of Pembroke's repairs at Cardiff castle and for the elegant town house built by his kinsman, Sir William Herbert, and called the Friary. The Mansels created one of the county's finest seats from the former Cistercian abbey at Margam. The earliest description of it, unfortunately, does not come before 1684, by which time the house may well have been the scene of post-Restoration improvements. However, at that date, Dinely spared no praise for this 'very noble seat', with its 'summer banqueting house, built after the Italian, whose regular symmetry, excellent sculpture, delicate graving, and an infinity of good Dutch and other paintings make a lustre not to be imagined'. Former monastic granges provided the site and, possibly, the materials for new houses. At Sker, formerly a possession of Neath abbey, the Turbervilles built their large house, lonely and gaunt in outline but compellingly attractive too, near the bleak and sandy wastes of Kenfig Burrows, where it still stands, part of it inhabited by a farmer and his family, but most of it a desolate ruin, its state-rooms with their once richly-moulded plaster ceilings the haunt and nesting-place of owls (Pl. XVIII).[60]

By 1640, in all parts of the county but especially in the thriving lowlands, hundreds of new or remodelled houses, their owners' pride and joy, were in existence. Some were the 'great houses' of Glamorgan, of which a number survive. Cefnmabli is now a hospital, but some of its oak-panelling and massive roof timbers remain in place. The National Folk Museum is housed in the handsome Tudor manor house built by Dr. John Gibbon to take the place of the ruinous medieval castle, some of whose earlier fortifications are built into its exterior walls. Llansannor manor house, a private residence still, stands in dignified seclusion, with its little church nestling beside it, though internally the house no longer preserves much of its original character (Pl. XX). But Llan-mihangel Place, built in the first Elizabeth's time by James Thomas, who needed a big house to accommodate his sixteen children, has its fine oak-panelled dining-room and its Tudor fireplace all the while (Pl. XVI). Flemingston Court, now a farmhouse, can boast a noble Jacobean hall and a splendid fireplace (Pl. XXVI). Another farmhouse, Castell-y-mynach, was originally a stone hall-house, probably built in the fifteenth century by Robert Mathew, the coroner. Later, this structure was enlarged and modernized by the addition of two storeys, of which only one now remains, and the construction of a great new chimney. Early in the seventeenth century, in the Mathew family's most flourishing phase, Thomas Mathew added a fine new wing to the house in contemporary seventeenth-century style. Other houses have had a more unhappy fate and have disappeared or been reduced to ruins. One of the saddest is the old house at Y Fan, where Edward Lewis (*temp*. Henry VIII) enclosed a park and probably built the oldest part of the manor-house, to which his son, Thomas (*temp*. Elizabeth) added the great gallery and porch. So successful were the Lewises, however, that Sir Edward Lewis (d. 1630) turned his eyes to Wiltshire, where he rented the manor and priory of Edlington, 'to the neglect of Y Fan'.[61]

Around a number of the greater houses were deer parks, in which the owners and their friends could indulge in the delights of the chase, which gave them so much pleasure. These parks could mean a serious loss to agriculture, not merely in terms of the destruction caused to crops but also by the withdrawal of much land from farming. In some parts of the country they were gradually being extinguished in the sixteenth century in favour of more productive uses; and in Glamorgan a number had been disparked, including two at Clun, which had had to give way to ironmaking, so Leland noted. Most of the major landowners insisted on having a deer park, however, and some, like the one at Y Fan, were brought into existence for the first time in the sixteenth century. Some houses, including Ewenni and St. Donat's, had two parks, one for red and the other for fallow deer. The St. Donat's herds were held in particularly high esteem; the second earl of Pembroke craved the gift of deer from there to stock his own new park in 1578, and Sir Edward Stradling's correspondence is peppered with solicitations for gifts of his excellent venison and with the thanks of grateful recipients. When Thomas Dinely visited Margam in 1684 he described the deer there as being of 'extraordinary weight and fatness'. Other adjuncts of these bigger houses might also be coney-warrens, dovecotes, and fishponds, though only Margam appears to have been able to boast all three. Flower and herb gardens, too, and even a vineyard, might be a further source of pleasure and refreshment. In an ecstatic moment Thomas Leyshon, in one of his Latin poems, vowed that the roses at St. Donat's were so delightful that they would have drawn Neptune and Thetis from their deep salt-water haunts to savour their perfume.[62]

Numerously interspersed among these larger gentry houses were smaller but craftsman-built stone houses, the homes of minor gentry, yeomen, and successful husbandmen, a large number of which still survive, though often drastically modified, into our own day. Among these houses Mr. Peter Smith has identified two main versions of a regional type that was very common in Glamorgan and the rest of south-east Wales. The first was planned so that the entrance was behind the main hall fireplace. This seems to have been the more common type and is frequently encountered in Monmouthshire, Breconshire and Carmarthenshire as well as Glamorgan. Plans of some examples of this kind of house, prepared by Mr. Smith, are given on the following page.

The second version, perhaps derived from the first, had the entrance opposite the main fireplace, so that there was a small lobby giving onto the 'hall' on the one side and a secondary room on the other. This second type seems to be common only in Glamorgan, as far as south Wales goes. Its plan is, however, generally similar to that found among the wooden houses of Montgomeryshire, except that whereas in Montgomeryshire any second fireplace is usually built backing onto the first, so that there is only one stack, in Glamorgan any second fireplace is usually built onto a gable wall forming a second stack. There are in addition a small number of houses which have the main fireplace on the side wall. Such lateral chimney houses (of which Flemingston in the parish of that name is a classical example) generally have fairly marked upper-class associations. Examples of this kind of house are also given on page 128.

Both kinds of house might vary a good deal in the size and scope of their lay-out. Some were single-unit dwellings with hall only; others were of a two-unit plan, with hall and parlour (i.e. bed-chamber on the ground floor); and others might be more ambitious again, having a three-unit plan, with the hall placed between an inner and outer room. In all, more than 1,000 of these sixteenth- and seventeenth-century houses, new and reconstructed, have been traced in Glamorgan by the staff of the Royal Commission on Ancient Monuments for Wales, in whose forthcoming Inventories we may expect to see the subject exhaustively described and discussed. The existence of such large numbers of houses of this sort in the Glamorgan countryside is, in itself, a most important piece of ocular evidence for social conditions; it points unmistakably to what Mr. Smith has described as a 'comparatively large class of small independent proprietors living in conditions of peace and prosperity'.[63]

Nor was it only in the countryside that such rebuilding was going on; the towns must have presented an almost equally busy scene of building craftsmen at work. Though virtually all their handiwork has disappeared from our modern townscapes, enough evidence survives

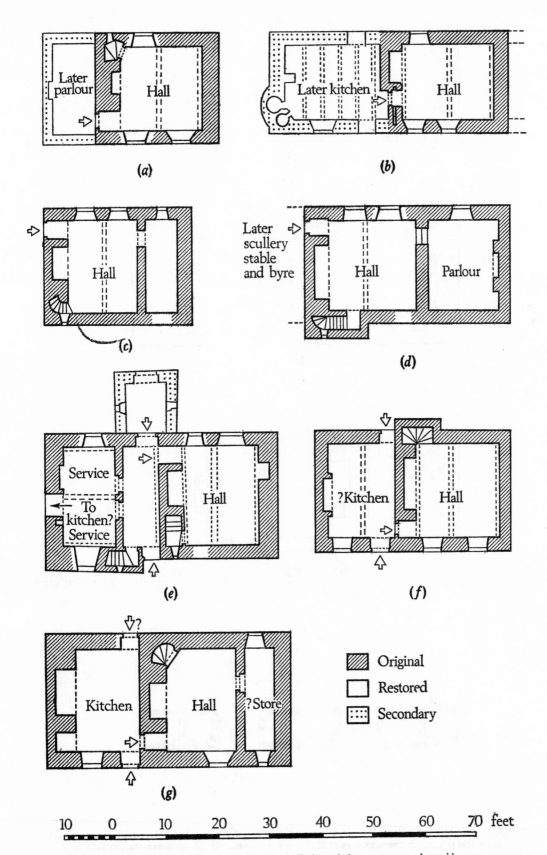

Fig. 1. Regional houses type B, with end entry to the hall through lower room, and outside cross-passage. *a* and *b* originally single-unit (hall only); *c* and *d* two-unit, hall with inner room; *e* and *f* two-unit, hall with outer room; *g* three-unit, hall between inner and outer room. (*a*) House on Cowbridge Road, Llantwit Major, Glam. (*b*) Cottage, Lampha, Ewenny, Glam. (*c*) Pentre-hwnt, Lampha, Ewenny, Glam. (*d*) Clements Farm, Tythegston, Glam. (*e*) Church House, Newcastle Hill, Bridgend, Glam. (*f*) The Bush Inn, St. Hilary, Glam. (*g*) Gadlys, Llanmaes, Glam. (*e* after C. N. Johns).

[127]

J

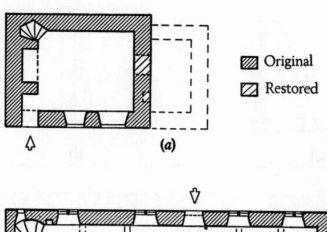

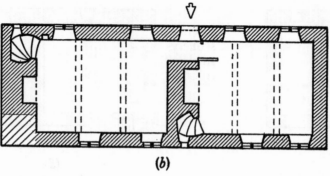

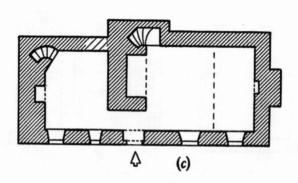

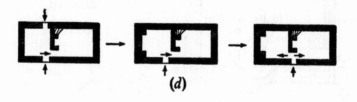

10   0   10   20   30   40   50   60   70 feet

Fig. 2. Central-chimney houses type D, with main chimney opposite entry but secondary chimney on end wall. (a) Duffryn-maelog Llysworney, Glam. (b) Walterston-fawr, Walterston, Glam. (c) Limpert, Gileston, Glam. (d) Possible origin of central-chimney house type D from type B.

Figs. 1 and 2 were originally published in *CAgH.*, IV, 795, 801. They are reproduced here by kind permisson of Mr. Peter Smith, Dr. Joan Thirsk, and the Cambridge University Press.

among the records to give us important clues to the kind of activity prevailing in the towns between 1540 and 1640. Cardiff's 'many fair houses and large streets' owed much to the dwellings built within its walls by leading families of gentry. In addition to the Herberts' work there, Thomas Lewis Y Fan in Elizabeth's time built 'a large square house, with a central court, and a garden extending to the Taff', which stood in the town until the middle of the last century. Another well-known Cardiff house was the Red House (the 'Cardiff Arms' still commemorated in the name of the famous football ground), which was put up by Sir Thomas Morgan, the builder of Ruperra Castle; and though the sum of £19,999 19s. 9d. which both residences are said to have cost him may be too neatly rounded to be true, it nevertheless gives some indication, however imprecise, of the kind of money the wealthier classes were reputed to be willing to spend to satisfy their craze for building. Neither were the traders to be left out of the picture. A rare surviving inventory of a Cardiff cordwainer, that of Edward Collins (d. 1637), shows him as having occupied a well-furnished house with several rooms, including a shop, parlour, four chambers (i.e. upstairs bedrooms), two other rooms, and a cockloft. For Swansea we have rather more information. Its biggest and finest house was Sir George Herbert's splendid mansion in the middle of the town, 'New Place', which lasted until Victorian times when it was pulled down to make way for the well-known Swansea store of Ben Evans. The will and inventory of a lesser gentleman, John Moris (d. 1608), listed his spacious house as having, along with a quantity of luxurious furnishings, a hall, parlour, seven chambers, shop, buttery, kitchen, and cellar. Merchants within the town may have been more circumscribed in their ambitions. The wealthiest of their number traced by Dr. W. S. K. Thomas in early-Stuart Swansea was Thomas Hopkin, a tanner, who left possessions worth £753 6s. 0d., or nearly two-and-a-half times as much as John Moris (£322); but he lived in a house described as having only one very large store-room and one other room. Not all his fellows were as modest—or as miserly—in their tastes as Hopkin. John Symonds (d. 1605), a shoemaker, lived in a house with hall, chamber, loft, and shop; while Francis After (d. 1646) died leaving a house with hall, little hall, five chambers, kitchen, shop, and cellar. However, out of 55 wills and inventories surviving from the Swansea of this period no fewer than 44 list no rooms at all, which suggests that many of those dwellings they record had only a hall, which may perhaps have had a lightweight partition to form a parlour for sleeping, with an open loft above the parlour to provide sleeping accommodation for the children and servants, if there were any.[64]

This brings us to re-emphasize the point that the bigger and better housing was available only to the more prosperous in town and country alike. The majority of the population continued to live as they always had done, in miserable one-roomed hovels, with earthen floors and open hearths, built by their own efforts. It is doubtful whether they had advanced much, if at all, beyond the 'small huts made of boughs of trees twisted together, constructed with little labour and expense, and sufficient to endure throughout the year', described in the twelfth century by Gerald of Wales. Even as late as the middle of the last century some Glamorgan rural cottages were stigmatized as 'deplorable . . . old thatched buildings, very low, with one living-room, a portion of which is generally partitioned off for a pantry, and a general garret or sleeping-room for the whole of the family'. Squalid as these were, it has to be remembered that they must have been of markedly better standard than most of the hovels of the sixteenth century to have been inhabited at all in Victorian times.[65]

The interiors of the bigger households were richly embellished. The more important rooms—hall, dining-room, gallery, and best chamber —were often panelled and wainscotted, their ceilings might be plaster-moulded, and their windows brightened with coats of arms in coloured glass. Some walls might be enlivened with frescoes like the exuberant and colourful scenes of legendary classical themes, wonderfully preserved and still alive with warmth and vitality, on the walls at Castell-y-mynach. Others might be hung with tapestries, the 'arrases' often singled out for mention in the wills of the more important landowners; but only bare hints of their crumbled glories survive in those intriguing titles of the twelve 'pieces of verdure of broad leaves with my lord's arms', or the nine-piece story of Bacchus, and the three pieces of 'poetical fantasies' which, along with a number of others, were placed in Cardiff castle in 1581. Pictures graced the walls, too; not merely family portraits, but a 'Christ in Resurrection', possibly by a Flemish painter, which aroused suspicions concerning Sir Thomas Stradling's religious loyalties, or Sir George Herbert's portrait of Lucrece, or the wide range of paintings at Margam abbey already referred to. Furniture and furnishings were becoming richer and more abundant. Two lengthy inventories, accessible in print, will give an interested reader minute details of the contents of a gentleman's household in country and town. That of Edward Carne of Ewenni (1650) included a vast quantity of miscellaneous household furniture, furnishings, cloths, linens, utensils, tools, and implements typical of a county gentleman's household. They were worth in all £245 3s. 4d., £150 worth of which was accounted for by the contents of the gallery with its silk carpets, many and luxurious cushions, brass andirons, seven pieces of Arras, and fifteen pictures (was it the last-named, one wonders, which made the contents of the gallery so valuable?). John Moris of Swansea (d. 1608) was a gentleman of considerably less consequence than Edward Carne, but he lived as well as Carne and in greater style and affluence than any other Glamorgan townsman of this period of whom we have details. He left behind him a large list of luxurious furniture and furnishings, including a Spanish bed, Turkish carpet, rugs, carved and embroidered chairs, cushions of gilted leather, taffeta curtaining, and a mass of clothing. He also possessed much silver plate and a number of silver spoons, a status symbol of some consequence as well as a valuable investment, to which nearly all the gentry aspired and which is carefully detailed in many of their surviving wills. Sir Thomas Stradling, predictably, left an inordinately long list of silver plate, including a silver basin parcel gilt of 42 ounces and another of 26 ounces; but even a minor figure like William Carne of Sully, who died as early as 1555, could leave his daughter, Bess, silver worth 100 marks in the days before the inflation of the age had proceeded very far. Some of the most affluent townsmen also boasted an impressive stock of silver. Morgan Williams, alderman and merchant of Cardiff (1621) bequeathed to his wife and each of his three daughters a substantial quantity of silver, and still left a large unlisted residue to his son, while Hopkin David Edwards of Swansea (1626), as well as providing amply for his two daughters, singled out for his grandson a number of particularly valuable items—a basin and ewer of silver, his 'biggest silver pot', 'fairest silver salt cellar', and 'bowl of silver', two silver wine bowls and six silver spoons.[66]

In these matters of furnishing, as of housing, there is a clear line of distinction to be drawn between the rich and the rest. Even the yeomen and the merchants spent far less on furnishing their houses than did the gentry, and usually left a far smaller proportion of their possessions in household goods than in livestock or the tools of their trade. These groups could, nevertheless, follow from afar the lead of the gentry in their search for greater comfort and ampler possessions. Though the inventories of their household goods and furnishings are usually disappointingly vague, lumping all the furniture and utensils under a single heading of household stuff, we do get plenty of indications of the widening range of their possessions. Feather beds, once a great luxury, were becoming widespread in the sixteenth century, and with them came coverlets, flannel blankets, and sheets—fine and coarse. Tables, cupboards, benches, forms, chairs, stools, chests, and coffers, made by joiners and carpenters, were increasingly common among them, too; and they could usually rise to table-cloths, napkins, curtains, and rugs. Platters and mugs were frequently made of pewter, and rooms were additionally brightened by brass or pewter candlesticks. Their kitchenware often boasted brass or copper pans, and iron cauldrons, pots, skillets, gridirons, spits, dripping-pans, bakestones, and other utensils, as well as earthenware crockery and dishes. Even quite small farmers might leave more than just the barest necessities. Moses David of Nash in 1627 left livestock and other goods which were worth only the modest sum of £17 6s. 2d. in all, but he had a feather bed, bolster, and sheets, two other bedsteads, a chest, a table, small table, cupboard, and coffer, as well as his household utensils. For the poorest smallholders, the lowlier craftsmen, and labourers, however, these things were too much to hope for. They ate and drank from wooden vessels and platters, lay on straw, and had only the barest minimum of belongings. Because they almost never left wills and inventories, we get scarcely any inkling of the number and nature of their possessions. One such rare insight comes from the inventory of Owen Griffith, a mason of Pentyrch, who died in 1632, leaving one of the most meagre of all Glamorgan inventories. His livestock and goods were worth only £3 8s. od. in all, of which his household stuff was priced at 10s. Apart from two kine, a calf, three sheep, and 6s. od. worth of corn, the only things he appears to have had worth leaving were an iron crock, a coffer and a rake for his son, and a coffer, skillet, bakestone, pail, and standard (a large candlestick) for his daughter. Yet there must have been in Glamorgan a great many men as poor as, or poorer than, Owen Griffith, pathetically scanty though his worldly goods were.[67]

Costume and Jewellery

Much is known and has been written about clothing, especially the costume of the *bon ton*, during this period. It was an age when new fashions, inspired by the leading European arbiters of style and taste in Italy, France, and Spain, were introduced into England and widely copied; and a wide spectrum of sumptuous and colourful clothing materials—high-quality fur, velvet, camlet, sarcanet, silk, satin, taffeta, cloth of gold and of silver, and fine lace and linen—became available at luxury prices. Sumptuary laws passed by Elizabeth's parliaments, and designed to restrict the wearing of the most luxurious clothing to the very rich only, went largely unheeded. For the impact of all this on Glamorgan, however, the evidence is very tenuous. The Glamorgan *cwndidwr* Siôn Hywel Siôn, commenting acidly in broad terms on rich men's love of fine clothing, had this to say:

> ny chaiff goludog vyth, tra vytho chwyth na dannedd,
> hanner digon or byd pring, nes mynd i gyving ddaerfedd;
> er kael dillad gwychion glan, ag aur ag sidan wisgedd,
> ar y byd ny thyrr e chwant, be gaffei gant o ynysedd.

('The rich man will never have, as long as he has breath or teeth, half enough of what is scarce in the world before he goes to his narrow grave; although he has fine and beautiful clothes, and garments of gold and satin, his worldly greed will never be sated, though he were to get a hundred islands.')

And another poet, Thomas Siencyn ab Ieuan, drew a pointed contrast between the 'poor flannel' in which the infant Christ was wrapped and the 'dainty holland, lawn and cambric' he would have found in a rich man's home.[68]

The handful of surviving portraits and effigies on tombs seem to indicate that members of the wealthier families—when sporting their finery, at least—were richly and fashionably dressed (Pls. IV–V). Sir Thomas Button is resplendent in yellow embroidered doublet and green breeches, with a dashing white sash knotted on his shoulder. Sir Thomas Mansel appears in handsome white doublet, with his wife in a black and white gown, and both they and their little daughter, charmingly dressed in pink, are wearing the most delicate lace collars and cuffs. Wills give us a few further glimpses of the kind of clothing worn. Many of the testators were proud enough of their clothing to leave it as bequests; but it is very rare to find them giving such precise details of the individual items as those given by Sir Rice Mansel. To his son Edward's wife, Jane, he left an 'upper habiliment of goldsmith's work and a gown of purple cloth of silver, a gown of green velvet, and a gown of black velvet'. His daughters, Catherine and Elizabeth, and his niece, Elizabeth, got a gown of damask apiece, and his niece, Mary, a taffeta gown. But the choicest items, perhaps, were reserved for his daughter, Mary,—'a crimson velvet gown, the second black velvet gown, and a satin gown' that had belonged to his wife. The crimson gown was, almost certainly, the one his wife had worn at Queen Mary's coronation, where she was given a place of honour and made an impressive figure in the coronation procession, 'dressed in crimson velvet, in a chariot and horses trapped with the same'. Dame Joan Babington, widow of Gervase Babington, former bishop of Llandaff, was one of the few who gave some details of the wardrobe she was leaving behind her. She passed on to her daughter, Margaret, wife of Sir Rowland Morgan, 'one black velvet gown and his mantle . . . one black satin gown and his mantle . . . one taffeta gown and his mantle . . . and one satin petticoat and one damask cloak'.[69]

It seems highly likely that Welsh people beneath the rank of gentry were now better and more amply dressed than they had been in an earlier age. An English poet of the fourteenth century had been astonished, not to say appalled, at the scantiness of Welshmen's attire:

> They be clothed wonder well
> In a shirt and mantell,
> A crisp breech well fain,
> Both in wind and rain.

In this attenuated garb they worked, played, fought and slept.

> Without surcoat, gown, coat, and kirtle, . . .
> Without lace and chaplet in their laps,
> Without hood, hat, or caps
> And alway with bare legs.

By Tudor times, however, those days were long since past. We have a record of rich Welsh yeomen aping their betters in their fine shirts edged with gold, handsome doublets lined with orange sarcanet, purple Venetian hose, and white woollen stockings. Wives of the same class were no less well or colourfully turned out with frieze gown, red petticoat and blue mantle. Farmers wore 'solid leather shoes, knitted woollen stockings, and a doublet or jerkin of fustian, canvas or frieze, the whole attire being set off by a felt hat or cap'. Even a humble Glamorgan carpenter, Rinald Thomas of Llystalybont, near Llandaff, could bequeath to his brother, Thomas, his 'best hose and doublet', to another brother, Morgan, the 'waistcoat and hose that is next to the best . . . together with my best shoes and stockings', and to a third brother, Howell, his 'grey jerkin'.[70]

It was not only costume but precious metals and jewellery which could also lend adornment and magnificence, as well as being one of the safer and more favoured forms of investment. Along with that crimson gown he bequeathed his daughter, Sir Rice Mansel also passed on to her 'a diamond pointed, which the Queen Mary gave to my wife, a ring with a cross of turquoises, a tablet laid with stones, a pair of beads of gold, . . . and my wife's wedding ring'. When Mansel's grandson's wife, Lady Jane Mansel, had her portrait painted about 1614 she was wearing a splendid string of pearls. Her son, Lewis, was in 1635 to buy from Sir Edward Stradling for £400 'one chain of pearls containing nine links and having on every link the number of 400 pearls or there-abouts and one great or m(aste)r pearl besides'. An earlier Stradling, Sir Thomas, had had as one of his most treasured possessions, which he left to his younger son, David, 'a great chain of gold containing 400 links and weighing about three score and six ounces'. Such chains were a status symbol of more than ordinary value and dignity, and it must have gone hard with Thomas Carne of Ewenni to have to part with his 'chain of gold with a button' to Dame Elizabeth Dennys in 1563, not to mention the 'jewel with an unicorn's horn and three diamonds' that went with it. A number of Glamorgan testators refer to plate, jewels, and rings, but without specifying in detail the nature of these heirlooms.[71]

That very large sums were spent on clothing and adornment, especially by the upper classes, is quite certain. The expenditure involved evoked censure from a number of contemporary observers, one critic going so far as to claim that excessive outgoings of this kind were deterring many gentlemen from properly maintaining their traditional hospitality to their equals and to the poor:

> I hold this excessive costly apparel a great cause why gentlemen cannot maintain their wonted and accustomed bounty and liberality in housing and housekeeping—for, whenas the mercer's book shall come *item* for so many yards of cloth of gold, of silver, velvet, satin, taffeta, or suchlike ware; the goldsmith's *debet* for chains, rings, jewels, pearls, and precious stones; the tailor's bill, so much for such a suit of laced satin and suchlike superflous charges, amounting in one year to more than the revenues of his lands.

Many of the gentlemen of Glamorgan, it can hardly be doubted, were familiar with the situation of being dunned for such high-priced items; but in the seemingly complete absence of household and personal accounts we have no means of knowing certainly whether or not they overtaxed their resources by incurring such expenses. Whatever they may have spent in this manner, however, there is good reason to believe that it did not prevent most of them from continuing to keep up their customary good cheer and warm welcome at hearth and home, as we shall see in the next section.[72]

FOOD AND DRINK

In the Middle Ages the Welsh had always set very great store on the virtue of *perchentyaeth*—the practice of hospitality, of keeping an open house with an abundance of food and drink and of extending an unstinted welcome to guests and a ready bounty to the poor. In the sixteenth century the practice appears to have remained a *sine qua non* for any gentleman worthy of the name, amid the Welsh families and the *Advenae*. Many of Sir Edward Stradling's letters resound with thanks of grateful guests for his princely entertainment at St. Donat's. Typical of their general tone were those of Sir Humphrey Gilbert, who offered Sir Edward and Lady Stradling 'a million of commendations' for their kindness, or Edward Halfacre, who wrote of 'the great courtesy and kindness I received from you, myself being a stranger and in no way deserving that favour which I found'. The poets, too, waxed eloquent about the profusion, diversity, and quality of the fare offered them by their patrons. Thomas ab Ieuan ap Rhys, mourning the loss of one of the Leyshons, Thomas ap William Siancyn, claimed that he had kept as well-laden a board as any in Wales, with the most delicate viands, the finest white bread, red and white wine, beer, ale and metheglin (a spiced form of mead peculiar to Wales). In another poem to Sir Walter Herbert the same poet vowed that even the king's kitchen did not provide more roasts at greater cost than Sir Walter's. Bards were, of course, notoriously committed to overstatement and embellishment when lauding their benefactors' *perchentyaeth*, and their rhetorical flights have to be to some extent deflated. Even so, their testimony, taken together with that of the Stradling letters, gives confirmation that the Glamorgan gentry, as we might have supposed from contemporary accounts of upper-class life in general, enjoyed a wide variety of meat, venison, poultry, fish, game and other delicacies, many of which came from their own estates (p. 34). The imports of exotic fruits and foreign wines that came into Glamorgan ports may also be presumed to have found their way mainly to the gentry's tables.[73]

Merchants, yeomen, and better-off farmers were also reported by general observers like William Harrison to eat heartily and well, and what we have already seen of the improving living standards of such groups in Glamorgan suggests that they were unlikely to have fared significantly worse than their fellows in England. Even the smallest farmers in the neighbouring county of Pembrokeshire enjoyed a surprisingly good diet, according to George Owen: 'the poorest husbandman liveth upon his own travail, having corn, butter, cheese, beef, mutton, poultry, and the like of his own sufficient to maintain his house . . . Their diet is as the English people use, as the common food is; beef, mutton, pig, goose, lamb, veal, and kid, which usually the poorest husbandman doth daily feed on'. George Owen here gives us a rather more favourable picture of the life of the poorer farmers than is usual, and we ought perhaps not to overlook the fact that he was a staunch local patriot where his own county was concerned. What he says of Pembrokeshire may have been true of Glamorgan, especially of the Vale. We have no direct evidence of this; but it may be recalled that Rice Merrick commented on the greatly improved standards of eating and drinking among the inhabitants of even the poorer areas of the *Blaenau* (above, pp. 4–5), who were by his day eating white bread and drinking ale and beer. All classes ate two meals a day: the gentry at eleven o'clock and between five o'clock and six; the merchants at noon and six o'clock; and the farmers at noon and between seven and eight o'clock. It was also generally accepted that on special occasions like Christmas or the *gwylmabsant* (feast of the patronal saint of the parish) or other major feasts, and at family celebrations such as weddings and christenings, there would be a great deal of additional eating and drinking—not infrequently to excess, which may be the source of the criticisms by bardic moralists of the widespread insobriety and gluttony among their fellows.[74]

Yet it is by no means certain that the poorest classes of crofters, labourers, and paupers ever partook of much, if any, of this good living even in normal times, and certainly not in times of dearth. They ate little or no roast meat, and depended largely on such white meats, i.e. butter, cheese, and milk, as they could get. Bread was their staple food; not made of white flour, of course, but of oatmeal or rye, or substitutes made from peas, beans, and even, in really hard times, acorns. Where they were fortunate enough to have a strip of ground in which to grow vegetables, they relied heavily on cabbages, parsnips, carrots, onions, and other vegetables from which, together with any occasional scraps of meat they might get hold of, they made *cawl* and broth. They also depended a good deal on whatever left-overs and charity they could beg from their wealthier neighbours. However, as with so many aspects of the life of the poor, their diet remains largely shrouded in obscurity.[75]

viii.

PASTIMES, RECREATIONS, AND FOLK-CUSTOMS

Most of what we know about this subject has to be derived from accounts which were compiled by eighteenth- and nineteenth-century observers. At the time when they wrote, Glamorgan seems to have had a richer corpus of folk tradition than almost any part of Wales, with an astonishingly variegated and exuberant mass of popular games, practices, entertainment, lore, and culture still surviving abundantly. As the county was then accounted to be one of those most tenacious of the past—'the most old-fashioned county in Wales', was how Iolo Morganwg described it—there seems to be a sound basis for supposing that many of these folk activities stretched back to Tudor and even medieval times. Unfortunately, evidence concerning them during the earlier periods is regrettably tenuous. Of one thing, however, we can be sure: that those 24 feats which in the Middle Ages had been regarded as the hall-mark of a man of good breeding were still known and admired in the sixteenth century. The poet, Thomas ab Ieuan Madog, hailed one of his patrons as a 'foremost exponent of the 24 feats and the lamp of the multitude', and there are other similar references. These accomplishments are interesting enough to be listed in detail: 1. strength, 2. running, 3. leaping, 4. swimming, 5. wrestling, 6. horsemanship, 7. archery, 8. fencing with sword and buckler, 9. fencing with two-handed sword, 10. using the quarter staff, 11. hunting with greyhounds, 12. fishing, 13. hawking, 14. poetry, 15. harping, 16. reading Welsh, 17. singing *cywydd* with harp, 18. *penillion* singing, 19. drawing coats of arms, 20. heraldry, 21. chess, 22. backgammon, 23. dice, and 24. harp notation.[76]

Of these exercises, hawking and hunting were a passion with the upper class, many of whom, like Sir Edward Stradling, kept their own deer parks and eyries. In the poem mentioned above Thomas ab Ieuan Madog recalled how his dead patron had been, throughout his life, an inveterate hunter of the hart over the wooded slopes with his crossbow. Many of the other feats of physical strength and dexterity were widely esteemed among other classes; and contests of running, leaping, wrestling, and throwing quoits, heavy stones and iron bars, were often held on Sundays and other holidays in summer. Prowess in archery, too, had long been established as one of the outstanding accomplishments of the men of south-east Wales, and, despite the advent of fire-arms, Tudor governments made every effort to keep up the practice of it. Other manly sports of the age, played with immense vigour and not a little violence, were football and *bando* or *bandy*, a kind of primitive hurling, both of which might often be played as contests between rival parishes. Some very ancient games, like 'broch yng nghôd' ('badger in the bag') and 'cnau i'm llaw' ('nuts in my hand'—a kind of guessing game of 'he loves me, he loves me not'), were also played and were to survive into the last century. Tennis and bowls were newer games; they are known to have been played but seem to have been confined largely to gentlemen and yeomen. Some of the 'spectator sports' of the age were the brutal but very popular cockfighting and, in the towns, bull-baiting.[77]

The indoor games of chess and backgammon were being increasingly overshadowed by the popularity of cards and dice. The last-named were obnoxious in the eyes of the government of the time because of the growing craze for gambling associated with them. Attempts to make all games of chance illegal met with little success, and the bardic critics of contemporary society were more than usually stern in their condemnation of the vices associated with gambling. Thomas Siencyn ab Ieuan adjured his hearers to remember:

Gwsnaethy r klaivon ywr siars, nid chwarau kars twylledig;
kladdy r mairw trwy air e, nid tawly dise n ffrolig

('We are charged with ministering to the sick not playing with deceitful cards, and with burying the dead according to his word and not frivolously throwing dice.')

In the eyes of the devoted Catholic poet and copyist, Llywelyn Siôn, many of the worst evils of the day sprang from playing cards and dice:

Mi wela r byd, gwedy symyd
o waith chwarau, kards a disau.
Maen hwyn magy, llid a thyngy,
llesgedd a lladd, a gwyr ymladd,
trachwant meddwi, glwth diogi,
kynfigen kas, okr diras,
nodi r karde, kogo r dise,
a thawly n llonn, ddisau ffailston,
chwaigain mewn llid, ar un ergid,
a llawer dyn, mewn tost newyn.

('I see the world changed as the result of playing cards and dice. They breed anger and cursing, debility and killing, and fights among men, the craving of drunkenness, the gluttony of sloth, hateful envy, graceless money-grabbing, marking the cards, cheating with dice; and they will gaily throw false dice, betting ten shillings a throw in anger, while many a man is in sore need.')

It is interesting to note that a man like Llywelyn Siôn, whose religious sympathies were wholly Catholic, could be as 'puritanical' in his criticism in this respect as convinced Protestants.[78]

Poetry and singing, accompanied by *crwth* (fiddle) and harp, were universally enjoyed; and the itinerant bards, fiddlers, and minstrels were everywhere welcomed. In addition to the poetry of the fixed metres and the *cwndidau*, Glamorgan was famous for its unique folk-verses, the *tribannau*. Composed for every kind of occasion and vicissitude in the life of men, sad and gay, serious and trivial, they have as one of their most endearing characteristics a heartfelt love of the charms of Glamorgan. They persisted up to the twentieth century and they constitute, in the words of Professor Griffith John Williams, one of the 'chief glories of the popular literature of the Welsh nation'. Many of the folk-songs, especially those of the plough-boys at their work, were unusually attractive and did not become extinct until the last century. The harpists and fiddlers who accompanied the verse and song were also welcomed for the part they played in the dancing which was a feature of every public jollification. The companies of Morris dancers, so popular and vigorous in the eighteenth and nineteenth centuries, very probably went back to a much earlier age. They survived the Reformation and the disapproval of Puritans and Methodists. How far the performance of late-medieval religious and morality plays, once very common in Glamorgan, also survived the Reformation it is impossible to say; but the municipal accounts show that Swansea, at least, was visited by wandering companies of secular players. They, or their audiences perhaps, were more boisterous in their behaviour than the town authorities might have wished, since on more than one occasion they were required to pay for windows in the town hall broken in the course of their visits. No doubt the fairs, too, attracted wandering shows and performers, though we cannot now discover any material about them specifically relating to Glamorgan.[79]

Much of the popular recreation of the age was centred on the tavern. By the eighteenth century tavern-keepers had a well-known propensity for organizing many of the games, revels, and festivities for their own profit even more than for the delectation of their customers. Their precursors of the sixteenth and seventeenth centuries may have done the same. The moralists of the age were certainly gravely perturbed about the insidious seductions of the tavern and the inability of men of all ranks to withstand them. The Tavern, in Thomas Llywelyn's famous dialogue between the Church and the Tavern, taunted the Church thus:

> Ynof j i bydd meibion
> goreugwyr cyfoethogion;
> Ynof j y bydd crefftwyr
> yr awr eu bônt yn segur;
> a chwareuŵyr a gwilliaid . . .
> nid oes ynod ddim dynion,
> ond yr hên bobloedd feirwon.

('To me come sons of the best and wealthy, craftsmen as soon as they are at leisure, and players and robbers . . . no one comes to you but old dead people.')

The Church found it impossible to deny the infinitely greater popularity of the Tavern; all it could do was to deplore that fact that the fuller a tavern was, the greater was its capacity for doing social and moral damage:

> Y prŷd ei bŷch di lawnaf,
> dyna'r prŷd ei byddy gwaethaf . . .
> yn wir ni fedrwn enwi
> hanner yr holl ddrygioni
> a sy'n y bŷd estyddieu
> gan amled yw'r tafarneu.

('The time when you are fullest is the time that you are at your worst . . . indeed I could not name half of all the wickedness that has been in the world for a long time because taverns are so numerous.')

Then followed, later in the poem, a familiar catalogue of the moral and physical ills which taverns were said to encourage: drunkenness, dissolution, waste, ill-health, anger, and neglect of religious and domestic obligations; and along with this came a rather horrifying account of the adulterated ingredients which tavern-keepers were alleged to brew in their drink in an unholy concoction 'like the cauldron of the old witch, Ceridwen'. Less apprehensive about such immoral or foolish conduct than about the dangers of violence or poverty arising from the existence of an excessive number of taverns or alehouses, many of them unlicensed, the Council in the Marches made efforts to reduce their number (below p. 155). The local courts also regularly record penalties inflicted on those who kept unlicensed alehouses. Yet we need hardly wonder at the popularity of taverns then and since. The poetic critics themselves, for all their strictures, could not help revealing how attractive taverns were to a hard-working populace with simple needs and uncomplicated tastes. In the absence of other social amenities, the taverns set out to provide warmth, comfort, light, food and drink, dice and cards, gay music from the fiddle and harp, and, as one of the poets said, 'all other needs' so that 'everyone could stay in them day and night' ('a phob cyfraid yn barod' 'fal y gallo pawb aros ynof i ddydd a nos'). There, the inhabitants of thinly-populated and badly-housed rural communities could, for a short while, escape from the toil, hardship and dreariness of much of their daily round into the cheerful company of their fellows or the oblivion of alcoholic stupor. At this distance of time we cannot know in detail what their tavern-going habits were; but many of them cannot have gone particularly frequently or over-indulged too regularly, since it seems improbable they would have had the money to do so.[80]

Many of the most treasured folk customs were linked with the great events of the church calendar and the seasons of the year. The rejoicings and festivities of Christmas and the New Year came at the slackest times of the farmer's year, and the weeks between Christmas and Candlemas (February 2) were the 'loitering time', when poets went on the rounds to declaim their verses and receive their rewards. Twelfth Night (January 6), which fell near the middle of this period, was associated with such well-loved pastimes as the visits of the wassailers and the *Mari Lwyd* mummers, with their gaily-bedecked horse's head; groups who were familiar figures in many parts of Glamorgan up to the present century. In spring and early summer came the exhilaration and high spirits of *Calan Mai* (Mayday), the *taplas haf* ('summer revel') and *y fedwen haf* ('summer birch'), bright with ribbons and garlands, and set up in most Glamorgan parishes on the eve of St. John, Midsummer Day (June 24), to the accompaniment of music, dancing and all kinds of merry-making. Still later in the year came all the practices associated with the harvest season, when there were harvest feasts and celebrations; and a few weeks later All Hallows Eve (October 31) and *Calan Gaeaf* (November 1) came round, accompanied by many games and customs, some of them involving divination of future sweethearts and other kinds of fortune telling. A wealth of lore and activities also surrounded the great milestones of human existence—birth, courtship and marriage, and death. Many of them were very ancient in origin, and not a few were intimately associated with medieval Catholic practice which had nevertheless triumphantly survived the Reformation. To recount all aspects of this folk lore and custom in detail would require a volume in itself, though little of its contents could be drawn from sixteenth- and seventeenth-century sources and would have to be constructed from later materials. Judging by the unmistakably archaic nature of these survivals, however, and knowing the conservativism and tenacity of a peasant population, we may reasonably conclude that behind the vitality and resilience of the lore and custom which lent so much gaiety, warmth, colour, and sense of community to the rural population of the eighteenth century lay a continuity that was centuries-old. This same kind of folk-culture must surely have given just as much meaning, variety, delight, and integration to the life of the parishes of Tudor and Stuart Glamorgan.[81]

CHAPTER III

The Political and Administrative History of Glamorgan, 1536-1642

By PENRY WILLIAMS

i.

THE POLICY OF UNION

IN the generation before the Acts of Union the social and political affairs of Glamorgan were dominated by the earls of Worcester.[1] Charles Somerset, the first earl, had acquired the lordships of Gower and Kilvey by marriage to Elizabeth Herbert and had received several crown offices by favour of Henry VII and Henry VIII: in particular he had been granted the sheriffwick of Glamorgan in 1509. This office, together with the lordships, he passed on to his son Henry in 1526. Unlike his father, Henry Somerset was not attracted to the court and therefore had both the incentive and opportunity to devote closer attention to Welsh affairs. Yet his rule in Glamorgan was at once lax and oppressive. The coroner and other royal officials were alleged to have defrauded the crown of fines and forfeitures. The earl's steward, George Herbert, hanged a sixteen-year-old boy whose father had dared to complain about Herbert to the Council in the Marches. The lordship of Magor, where the earl acted as steward for the King, became a haven for murderers and thieves under the corrupt aegis of Walter Herbert, Worcester's deputy.[2] The sessions in eyre were said to be more like instruments of lordly exaction than of justice: rather than suffer the demands of the lord's judges, the inhabitants preferred to 'redeem', or buy off, the sessions; and thus the principal law-courts of the region seldom so much as attempted to administer the law.[3]

Any prospect that the Council in the Marches might purge this administration of its abuses was dimmed by the age and indolence of its president, Bishop Vesey. Appointed to lead the Council in 1525, Vesey allowed theft and disorder to spread over much of his jurisdiction. Complaints came to the crown from most parts of Wales and the Marches, and Henry VIII attributed the lawlessness to 'the remiss and slack looking-upon' by Vesey and his colleagues. Such a situation would by itself have made reform imperative, in Glamorgan as in the rest of Wales.

[143]

In the 1530s it was made more urgent by the risks inherent in the breach with Rome and more likely by the presence of Thomas Cromwell, an imaginative and determined administrator, at the side of the King.[4]

In 1534 one of Cromwell's political friends, Bishop Rowland Lee, replaced Vesey as President of the Council in the Marches. A tough, vigorous and worldly cleric, fearing no-one but Cromwell, Lee travelled up and down the border country, searching out criminals, hanging thieves and bringing home to everyone his determination that the law be enforced. To help him in controlling and tightening the existing system of government various statutes were enacted: jurors giving a false verdict were to be punished; the passages over the Severn were to be carefully watched for thieves; the justices of assize in the English shires were empowered to try various offences committed within Marcher lordships; and criminals who fled from one lordship to another were to be handed back on command of the Council in the Marches.[5]

Such measures attempted no more than an improvement of the existing system. But in the winter of 1535–6 the crown decided on a radical policy that would bring the government of Wales and its Marches much more nearly into line with the English system. Bishop Lee was thoroughly opposed to such a change: the Welsh, he said, were unfit to be justices of the peace, 'for there be very few Welshmen in Wales above Brecknock that may dispend ten pound land, and, to say truth, their discretion less than their lands'.[6] His indignant opposition was, however, ignored and his master, Thomas Cromwell, evidently preferred to listen to other advisers, whose identity we cannot certainly know: John ap Rhys, Sir Richard Herbert of Montgomery, and Thomas Holt are among the possible candidates. Cromwell's reasons can only be guessed in the broadest of terms. He was certainly anxious to bring under direct royal government all those parts of the realm which had hitherto escaped such control: the bishopric of Durham and the county palatine of Chester also felt the impact of his determination that 'one order of ministering of his [the King's] laws should be had observed and used in the same as in other places of this realm of England is had and used'. Perhaps those words are the best indication of Cromwell's motives: desire for an efficient and therefore a uniform administrative machine at a time when both the problems and expectations of government were being magnified by the break with Rome.[7]

The critical changes were contained in four acts of parliament, three carried in 1536 and the fourth in 1543. Of the three earlier statutes, one established justices of the peace in the counties of the Principality and in Pembroke and Glamorgan, the second transferred to the crown the judicial authority of the Marcher lands, while the third laid down the general lines of the union between the Principality, the Marches and England.[8] Between 1536 and 1543 the crown's policy was marked by hesitancy and alteration; but finally, in 1543, the second Act of

Union filled in the details and completed the process. This is not the place to discuss the changes of policy during those years, and we shall only attempt here an analysis of the general effect of those acts.[9] Geographically, the principal achievement was the addition of seven new shires—Monmouth,[10] Brecknock, Radnor, Montgomery, Denbigh, Pembroke, and Glamorgan—to the existing Welsh counties of Anglesey, Caernarvon, Merioneth, Flint, Cardigan, and Carmarthen.[11] The nucleus of the new county of Glamorgan was formed, naturally enough, by the medieval lordship of that name, to which were added, rather less naturally, the lordships of Gower and Kilvey. One might have expected the crown to join these lordships to Carmarthenshire rather than to Glamorgan, for they had always had stronger links with the west than with the east. Probably the crown's decision arose from a wish to keep intact—at least for the time being—the sphere of influence of Henry, second earl of Worcester, who held the lordships of Gower and Kilvey and administered the lordship of Glamorgan on behalf of the crown.[12]

Into the newly-formed shires was imported the whole apparatus of English county government. The separate act of 1536 had already authorised justices of the peace for much of Wales although none was named until later: that of 1543 created the rest. Sheriffs and their bailiffs, escheators, coroners, clerks of the peace, high constables, petty constables now appeared. Each shire in Wales was given the right to send a knight to parliament; and, except in Merioneth, 'every borough being a shire town' was to send a burgess. The old Marcher lordships were not, however, abolished: instead they were absorbed into the new shires, with their independence much reduced. The powers of their lords, while greatly diminished, were still valuable. True, they could no longer try pleas of the crown; but they continued to hold courts-leet and courts-baron, to receive their ancient rents and to claim the rights of treasure-trove and wreck. By the act of 1536 they were allowed half the forfeited goods of all convicted felons, and although this concession was abolished in 1543 it was restored by Queen Mary in 'an act to confirm the liberties of the Lords Marcher in Wales'.[13] That the rights remaining to the lords were real enough is fully confirmed by the later history of tension and conflict.

Thus the lordships of Gower, Kilvey, and Glamorgan remained in existence. As we have seen, the first two of these were, at the time of the Union, in the hands of the earl of Worcester, who was also sheriff of Glamorgan. Worcester's office of sheriff was preserved by the first Act of Union but abolished in 1540 by a statute annulling all existing appointments to sheriffdoms in Wales: the protection extended over his interests in 1536 was thus short-lived.[14] Under Edward VI most of the smaller lordships which had in the past gone to make up the lordship of Glamorgan were granted to Worcester's cousin, William Herbert, created earl of Pembroke in 1551. Although the house of Worcester continued to hold the lordships of Gower and Kilvey, its authority in the county of Glamorgan began from this time to pass to the house of Pembroke.[15]

Although the various statutes which formed the Union tended to bring the administration of Wales into line with that of England, they did not go all the way. In two respects Wales and the Marches remained separate from the rest of Henry's realm. The Council in the Marches of Wales, founded under Edward IV, strengthened by Rowland Lee and Cromwell, was now given statutory power to 'hear and determine, by their wisdoms and discretions, such causes and matters as be or hereafter shall be assigned to them by the King's Majesty, as heretofore hath been accustomed and used'.[16] The common law jurisdiction over the Welsh shires was entrusted, not to the law courts at Westminster, but to newly created courts of Great Sessions. Wales was divided into four circuits—Glamorgan being joined with Brecknock and Radnor—over which the judges toured twice a year. Thus, between the central government in London and the local agencies of the shire there was interposed a regional administration.[17]

Two other provisions of the Union must be mentioned. First, the act of 1543 laid down that the inheritance of all lands in Wales was to be by the English system of primogeniture, not by the Welsh custom of *cyfran* or partible inheritance; and second, it stipulated that the English language be used in all legal proceedings and that no-one could hold office unless he could speak English.[18] These two clauses have sometimes been seen as a radical break with native tradition, an attempt to destroy Welsh institutions and culture. The truth is probably less dramatic. For some generations past English principles of land tenure had been gaining ground throughout Wales and a class of landed gentry had long been visible.[19] The Act of Union neither initiated a new departure, nor completed the process of development, since traces of the older system remained for many years to come. The language clauses cannot be seen as a serious attempt to destroy the Welsh tongue, for they were not very rigorously enforced. But just as the provisions for land tenure helped on their way existing tendencies, so the language clauses hindered Welsh at a time when social and economic pressures were against it.[20]

For two hundred years the gentry of Wales had looked to the English crown for advancement and had become more and more closely involved with English society and administration.[21] The crown itself, since the struggles of York and Lancaster, had been bringing the Marcher lordships directly under its own control: Brecknock, the last great lordship in the possession of a subject, had fallen into royal hands at the execution of the duke of Buckingham, fifteen years before the first Act of Union. Thus in a sense the general direction of Welsh history had been set well before the 1530s. Nevertheless, the union had real significance for the administrative machinery, although its effects varied from one part of Wales to another. In Caernarvonshire and the rest of the old Principality a shire system had long existed and the break with the past was gentle. By contrast the area to become Monmouthshire had, before 1536, no unity at all, being a complex mass of small lordships. Glamorgan stood somewhat between these two extremes: it had not been a county in the English sense, even though described as one by the act; but the lordship had for long formed a powerful block with a developing administration of its own.

ii.

THE MACHINERY OF LOCAL GOVERNMENT

The remainder of this chapter falls into three parts. The first describes the machinery of local government; the second reviews the major families of the county and holders of the principal offices; and the third analyses the political conflicts of the century between Union and Civil War. The treatment of these parts is determined largely by the chance survival or destruction of records. The quarter sessions records for Glamorgan, the essential source for describing the machinery of county government, have perished, and our account of this part of the subject has consequently to be based upon what we know of other shires whose records have survived.[22] What is said here on the matter can present little that is new and is therefore designed only as a necessary background to the second and third parts. Here we are much more fortunate. Two sets of letters, the correspondence of the Mansel and Stradling families,[23] tell us a good deal about the landed gentlemen of the time; and their many bitter conflicts are set out in the records of the court of Star Chamber. Untrustworthy as these court proceedings are, they form an invaluable source for county history, since even in the most conflicting stories of a dispute, given by the two sides in the action, one can usually find some common denominator of truth.

THE ORGANS OF CENTRAL GOVERNMENT

An analysis of county administration must start with the institutions of central and regional government. At the peak of the hierarchy stood the Privy Council.[24] So many and varied were its functions that one cannot easily summarise them—and in trying to do so one might easily give too cut-and-dried an impression of a complicated and varied business. What one can say is that the Privy Council operated, when it wished, in every field of governmental concern, from the most general to the most particular. If it was not technically a court of law, it often looked very much like one, calling miscreants or litigants before it and trying to settle the business.[25] More often the Privy Council, rather than settle the matter itself, would make sure that justice was done by the proper agencies. For instance, in 1591, it was told, 'by the better sort of her majesty's justices of the peace within the said county' of Glamorgan, that the sheriff was showing partiality in the handling of a case. The Council wrote to the justices of assize telling them to ensure that an impartial jury be empanelled 'such as would not for need or favour charge their consciences'.[26] The Council also, of course, dealt with administrative as well as judicial business—though it would not have recognised the distinction. At the most general level it was concerned with the execution of 'policy'—to use an anachronistic word—sending down its orders to the county, often through the Council in the Marches of Wales, less often directly. Justices of the peace were to see to 'the serving of the markets with corn', to prevent the export of butter and other foodstuffs, to enforce the laws 'for the true and sufficient tanning of leather' and to put down piracy off the Welsh coast—to give only a few illustrations.[27] Sometimes the Privy Council would descend from the level of general instruction to the smallest details of administration. In 1596 it sent special orders to Sir Thomas Mansel and John Gwynne, telling them to search the house of a suspected recusant, and wrote them a letter of thanks when they had finished their task.[28] In 1592 it ordered the sheriff of Glamorgan to allow Hugh Williams and Gabriel Lewis to enjoy the exercise of bailiwicks granted them by letters patent.[29]

Glamorgan was exempt from the jurisdiction of the two principal common law courts at Westminster, common pleas and king's bench, since their functions were performed in Wales by the courts of Great Sessions. But several London courts did exercise a jurisdiction over Glamorgan. The courts of first fruits and of augmentations while they existed, the court of wards, the court of admiralty and the court of requests all heard Glamorgan cases. More important than these were exchequer, chancery and Star Chamber. The jurisdiction of the court of exchequer covered suits involving crown lands, debts, revenues and officers: in practice its authority was rather wider than this suggests, since plaintiffs who wished for tactical reasons to use the court often sought ways of bringing their private disputes to its notice.[30] The court of chancery exercised a jurisdiction in equity over civil cases. Its strength lay in the relative simplicity of its procedure, which, at least in its early days, freed its decisions from the technicalities of the common law courts. Parallel to chancery on the criminal side was the court of Star Chamber. Its jurisdiction was principally over such misdemeanours as perjury, riot, forcible entry, and unlawful assembly. But cognizance of these offences allowed it to develop a much wider jurisdiction, since litigants often included charges of riot in their accusation in order to get the Star Chamber to hear what were basically civil disputes. The great advantages of Star Chamber were its independence from a jury that might be bribed or bullied, the use of interrogation to bring material evidence to light, a procedure that was relatively quick and relatively free from technicalities, and its power to get its decisions enforced. Not surprisingly it was in great demand: in the reigns of Elizabeth I and James I about 240 Glamorgan cases were taken to Star Chamber. Probably only a fraction of that number would actually have been heard by Star Chamber, the rest being delegated to commissioners or to other courts; and consequently its impact on county government may have been less than its massive records might suggest. But whatever its impact on the shire its impact on historical writing has been great, since its archives, recording the complaints, assertions and counter-assertions of contemporaries, are excellent witnesses for the local contests and quarrels of the time.[31]

REGIONAL GOVERNMENT

Between the central and the local authorities were interposed two organs of regional government. The higher of these was the Council in the Marches of Wales, which probably acquired its shape and definition at about the time of the Act of Union. Primarily it was a law-court, wielding a civil jurisdiction roughly equivalent to that of chancery, a jurisdiction over misdemeanours roughly equivalent to that of Star Chamber, and by virtue of its commission of *oyer et terminer* a criminal jurisdiction over felony, murder and treason. Its task was to fill the gaps in the common law system and to provide an authority of enforcement stronger than the justices of the peace or the judges of assize. Initially it was intended for the 'preservation of the common tranquillity and public peace', but gradually its civil jurisdiction—for 'mitigating . . . of all extremities and rigorousness of the common law'[32]—came to encroach upon its time until, by the early-seventeenth century, it was hearing twice as many civil actions as criminal. The Council's secondary function was administration. At the humblest level it acted as an entrepôt for orders from the Privy Council to the local justices of the peace, receiving the orders, copying them seventeen times, and then dispatching them to the *custos rotulorum* in each shire. Rather more significant than this were the Council's police duties: not only did it sit in judgment as a law-court, it also investigated crimes, arrested criminals and tried to prevent disorders; and it acted, too, as the general supervisor of local officials, seeing that justices of the peace were effectively organized and drawing their attention to particular abuses. Perhaps most important of all was the Council's say in the choice of sheriffs, deputy-lieutenants and justices of the peace. Efficient local government rested, obviously enough, upon intelligent selection of these officers and the Council was in a key position for advising the crown about suitable candidates.[33]

The other regional institutions were the courts of Great Sessions. In each of the four circuits into which Wales was divided the justices of Great Sessions went on assizes twice a year, holding their courts in the county towns for six days at a time. Throughout this period none of the justices on the Brecknock circuit, in which Glamorgan was included, came from the county: they thus supplied an element of outside supervision. The jurisdiction of the Great Sessions was very wide, since they combined in themselves the civil and criminal jurisdictions of king's bench and common pleas, together with a power 'to relieve in cases of equity'. In the counties within their circuit the Great Sessions judges had, like the assize judges in England, a good deal of supervisory power. They could summon cases from the Quarter Sessions to their own courts, prevent the Quarter Sessions from proceeding with a case or order them to take action. Not surprisingly the courts became extremely busy and a second justice had to be added to each circuit in 1576. In practice, however, although the number of cases was large, their range was small. On the civil side most were for debt, while on the criminal side the Great Sessions seem to have dealt with few cases of real importance. Since the Great Sessions were poorly equipped to counter local influence and corruption, most cases of difficulty were probably sent to the Council in the Marches or to London.[34]

Defence and Military Arrangements

One of the most important parts of county government concerned the raising of troops to keep order, to defend the country if it were invaded, and to form an army overseas. By various medieval statutes all able-bodied men between the ages of sixteen and sixty were compelled to bear arms, and this militia provided a pool from which armies could be formed for foreign service. However, this system was ineffective in providing a trained body of soldiers, and later medieval kings all had to resort to the system known, rather inappropriately, as 'bastard feudalism': prominent noblemen and gentlemen were asked by the King to supply soldiers from among their tenants, retainers, and followers. Such a system had the obvious disadvantage of allowing the great men of the country to build up private armies with which they could threaten the peace of the countryside, and even, in the fifteenth century, the throne itself. Therefore part of the Tudor problem was to establish an effective fighting force without having to rely too heavily upon these private bands. The obvious expedient, a permanent standing army, was out of the question for a monarchy so poor as England's, and the Tudors turned in the end to the militia.

In the first half of the sixteenth century the crown still raised troops either by issuing *ad hoc* commissions of array to the sheriff and other local gentlemen for the levy of men from the militia, or by ordering landowners to assemble their tenants and retainers. One can see both systems operating in early-Tudor Glamorgan. In 1544 the government prepared a large muster-book, showing which nobles and gentlemen could supply soldiers for the royal service. Nine Glamorgan landowners were named: Sir Thomas Gamage, William Herbert, Sir George Herbert, Thomas Stradling, John Bassett, Edward Lewis, George Mathew, Miles Mathew, and Sir Rice Mansel.[35] Again, in 1557, William Herbert of Cogan Pill was despatched to Glamorgan with orders to raise 500 men from among the tenants and friends of the earl of Pembroke, lately appointed commander of the expedition to France.[36] By contrast, in 1545 five muster commissioners were ordered to assemble the men of the shire, ready to attend the lord privy seal.[37] The disadvantages of the crown's dependence on retainers were obvious to all; but as yet the militia was unable to take their place. For the system of *ad hoc* muster commissioners failed to provide a permanent military organisation in the counties or to fix responsibility firmly on a single man.

However, in the course of the century, two steps were taken to improve the militia. Under Edward VI there appeared a new official, the lord lieutenant, created to muster the levies, to keep order, and to raise men for royal service. His first appearance was in 1549, a critical year of riot and rebellion, when the office was developed by the duke of Northumberland in order to strengthen his own political control.[38] But the system did not at once develop into a permanent institution: under Mary and in the early years of Elizabeth commissions of lieutenancy were only issued in years of emergency. In Wales it made little practical difference whether a commission of lieutenancy was in force or not. If it were, then it was held, from 1558–1601, by the lord president of the Council in the Marches; if it were not, then the president, aided by his council, performed the supervisory duties of a lord lieutenant. After 1585 the lieutenancies became permanent and were exercised for the twelve Welsh shires by the earl of Pembroke, lord president until his death in 1601. There was then a break with tradition, as far as Glamorgan and Monmouth were concerned, when the earl of Worcester became lord-lieutenant until the earl of Bridgwater won the post back for the presidency.

Nominally, the lords president were responsible for supervising the musters, encouraging archery and horse-breeding, maintaining the county armouries, and levying men for foreign service. In practice the control that one man, even supported by a council, could exercise over twelve counties was remote and therefore local machinery was needed in each shire.[39] To begin with, the crown and the Council in the Marches continued to operate the old system of temporary *ad hoc* commissioners: in 1569 William Herbert, Edward Mansel and the sheriff were ordered to take charge of the county armoury; and in 1570, following the discovery during the northern rebellion that men were not keeping their required numbers of horses and equipment, the Privy Council appointed commissioners to review all the troops in their counties.[40] Sir Henry Sidney took the view that this did not produce the control that he wished and in 1572 he complained to the Privy Council that the situation was then much worse than it had been in 1561–62 when he had used his own officials to train the soldiers.[41] However, his protest had no immediate effect and the use of *ad hoc* commissioners continued for some years. But eventually a more permanent form came with the creation of deputy-lieutenants. These had been appointed in some shires and for short periods from early in Elizabeth's reign; but it was probably not until 1585, or thereabouts, that they became permanent officials. The first deputy-lieutenants in Glamorgan may have been appointed as early as 1579, but we cannot be sure of the date; by 1590 the deputy-lieutenancy was firmly established.[42] Beneath it there gradually grew up a more sophisticated machinery, at whose centre was the muster-master, a professional soldier who was supposed to provide the expertise lacking in the amateur gentry. The muster-master was to be a 'practick soldier and expert in the wars abroad'; and his job was to see that fit men were chosen for trained bands, to inspect their arms and to supervise training.[43]

The other important innovation was the trained band. Two enactments of Mary's reign did something to bring the Statute of Winchester up to date by assigning more modern arms to the different classes of able-bodied men.[44] The Elizabethan muster-commissioners were, however, still faced with the large mass of armed but untrained militia; and to train them all would have been a hard, perhaps an impossible, task. The dangers of relying for home security and defence upon a force of this kind were brought home to the crown by the rising of the northern earls in 1569 and by the crisis in Anglo-Spanish relations between 1568 and 1572. In the early 1570s the government began the practice of choosing from the whole mass of the militia a small fraction for selective training; the rest then served as a pool from which levies could be drawn for foreign campaigns. In Glamorgan this system was in operation by 1573 when the muster-commissioners reported that there were 600 able-bodied men in the county, of whom 100 were trained and 100 chosen for foreign service. From that date on, the distinction seems to have been clearly established.[45]

LOCAL OFFICIALS:

The Sheriff

Of the many officials concerned with civil government, the most ancient was the sheriff.[46] Originally the most powerful county agent of the crown, he had come during the later middle ages to have his authority severely shorn, so that by the time of the Union he was far weaker than he once had been. But certain duties and some powers remained. In the early days after 1536 he was associated with the muster-commissioners in raising the county levies, but as the lieutenancy developed this role disappeared. Throughout the period he collected the ancient revenues of the crown—rents from royal estates, profits of justice and casual windfalls; and although these duties were largely formal for much of the century following the Union, they came in the 1630s to have a disquieting significance when the sheriff was called upon to levy ship-money.[47]

The sheriff still held county and hundred courts. The first of these, which sat monthly, was authorised to hear a wide range of civil disputes —such as debt, trespass, detaining of chattels—provided that the value of the goods concerned was below forty shillings. But although the county court had some prestige, for the sheriff presided and the coroners were normally in attendance, it usually had little to do. George Owen of Henllys said that it 'is so decayed that you shall scarce have a dozen persons at a county court'. Only when parliamentary elections occurred did it regain any of its old signficance: for the knights of the shire were chosen in the county court and the sheriff's role as returning officer gave him the opportunity to influence the voters' choice. Owen attributed the decline of county courts largely to the increasing use of the fortnightly hundred courts, held nominally by the sheriff, but in practice by his deputy. According to Owen, although the hundred courts had no valid legal authority, they drew 'a multitude of suits and suitors, twenty times more than in the county'. Their proceedings were, in his opinion, disorderly, partial, and corrupt. Unfortunately, there is no record of the proceedings of these courts in Glamorgan; and it may be that in some hundreds they were abolished during Elizabeth's reign. But where they survived they may well have been familiar and important institutions for the great bulk of the shire's inhabitants.[48]

The principal part of the sheriff's duties lay in his relations with other law-courts, central and local. It was his task to execute writs, processes and orders issued by the Westminster courts, the Council in the Marches, the Great Sessions, and the Quarter Sessions, to act as the executive officer of Quarter Sessions and Great Sessions, gaoling prisoners, levying fines, sending priests to London, and so on. While much of this work was obviously mechanical, the machinery itself was complex enough to require from the sheriff and his officers a detailed knowledge of the law.[49] Nor was it all a matter of routine, for the sheriff would often be asked to help or hinder litigants by his handling of the writs. For instance, Edmund Walter, judge of Great Sessions, requested the sheriff, Sir Edward Stradling, as a personal favour to postpone until the next assizes the execution of an order from the Council in the Marches; and Judge Bromley called upon Stradling to execute a process for 'a friend of mine', Mrs. Blount.[50] The sheriff's influence could be brought to bear still more effectively in his choice of jurymen. Oliver St. John once asked Stradling to help him in 'the procuring of an indifferent and wise jury' and later showed his belief in the sheriff's influence by demanding that Stradling advise him whom he should 'make suit for to be preferred into the office of high sheriff within the county of Glamorgan, that I might make account of to be an indifferent friend, not being of my kin'. For, St. John explained, if the sheriff were a kinsman he would not be allowed to empanel the jury: an 'indifferent friend' would suit his book perfectly. It is a revealing phrase.[51]

To help him in his duties the sheriff had a small staff. His principal assistant was the under-sheriff, responsible for collecting money and other routine duties.[52] Below him were placed the county gaoler, the sheriff's bailiff—a kind of messenger—and the hundred bailiff. The bailiwick of a hundred was apparently regarded as a useful perquisite. According to George Owen, these bailiffs were a rapacious and extortionate lot 'who with all greediness by colour of these courts (the hundred courts) pill and poll the poor people'. Part of their oppression sprang, in his opinion, from the yearly rotation of the office. Forced to pay £10 or £20 for the post, a bailiff must be vigorous and unscrupulous if he were to make a profit within twelve months. There is not much evidence about their activities in Glamorgan. But one piece of evidence suggests that the office was prized: when Sir Edward Stradling became sheriff in 1582 he was solicited by both Sir James Croft and the earl of Pembroke to give the bailiwick of Llantrisant to one of their servants.[53]

The Justices of the Peace

The main part of the civil government of the shire was carried on by the authority of various commissions issued from the crown. Of these much the most important was the commission of the peace. Unhappily, since the county's quarter sessions records for the period have disappeared, there is very little evidence for the working of this commission in Glamorgan and we can give only a generalized account, based on archives of other counties, in the hope and belief that this applies also to Glamorgan.[54] The core of the work done by the justices of the peace lay, of course, in the court of Quarter Sessions. Although the sessions had extremely wide powers, which authorized them to try almost all felonies, in practice as the sixteenth century went on the more important and difficult cases, in particular those carrying the death penalty, tended to be transferred to the assizes, leaving to Quarter Sessions only petty larcenies and misdemeanours. This may well have been the result of deliberate crown policy, for the local magistrates, lacking the prestige of the assize judges, were probably less successful in persuading juries to convict.[55]

Be that as it may, the reduction in the number of felonies heard by justices of the peace was more than balanced by increasing administrative duties. Of these the most important was the execution of the various poor laws. These laws, as they ultimately crystallized in the statutes of 1598, imposed on the justices the task of dealing with four classes of poor.[56] Pauper children were if possible to be maintained up to the age of twelve by their fathers, and much of the justices' time was taken up in hearing bastardy cases and attributing paternity; after the age of twelve the children were to be apprenticed. Vagrants were either to be returned to their place of settlement or to be punished and found employment in a house of correction: it was the task of the justices to find the money for such houses. Those unemployed through no fault of their own were to be provided with materials on which they could work. The aged, infirm and maimed were to be supported in almshouses or provided with pensions. All these projects had to be financed either out of private charity or out of the county rate.[57]

Apart from supervising the relief of the poor, justices of the peace were generally responsible for law-enforcement and for social and economic regulation. When the Council in the Marches heard that people in Wales were 'terrified to travel on or about their necessary affairs and business for fear of being robbed', it ordered the justices throughout the region to report to it within twenty days of the event of any robbery committed by three men or more.[58] Justices of the peace were also to reduce the number of alehouses, where 'thieves, murderers and women of light conversation are harboured, rogues and vagabonds maintained, whoredom, filthy and detestable life much frequented, unlawful games such as tables, dice, cards, bowls, kayles, quoits and such like commonly exercised'. They were to restrain persons who, 'without any charitable respect to the sustentation of their poor neighbours, exported grain and thus raised prices'.[59] They were to take bonds from the owners of tanneries for keeping the regulations of the industry, and from soap-makers for preventing the manufacture of 'speckled soap', said to be 'both more wasteful and more unwholesome for man's body, only profitable to the manufacturer'. They were to enforce the laws against eating of meat during Lent and to appoint persons to inspect butchers' shops: 'persons notoriously sick or otherwise weak of stomach' were, however, allowed to have meat dressed in their own houses.[60]

The effect of this growing burden of administration, drastically increased during the 1630s, was to emphasize the work of the justices acting 'out of sessions'.[61] Quarter Sessions remained, of course, the central co-ordinating agency, the core of county government, but more and more of the actual work was done by justices of the peace acting alone or in pairs; and slowly an organization developed to meet this new role. In Glamorgan the justices were first allocated to divisions in 1573, some of these divisions being single hundreds, others groups of hundreds; and from this system of grouping there developed in time the petty sessions.[62] To help them in their work the justices had a small central permanent staff, headed by the clerk of the peace, who drafted and preserved the records of Quarter Sessions. Locally, there was a chief constable in every hundred and a petty constable in every parish. These men and their duties remain obscure. In general they were responsible for police and administrative work, levying certain taxes, calling out the musters, arresting criminals; very occasionally when something went wrong, one of them emerged from the dim background, as when Philip Ingram had to arrest Thomas Williams, keep him in custody and convey him to London, all at his own expense, which he pointed out was too heavy for him to bear.[63]

Special Commissions

Although the commission of the peace was certainly the most powerful, it was by no means the only commission issued for the government of the shire. For a great deal of the business of Tudor administration was done through commissions issued for special purposes. For instance, subsidy commissioners had to be appointed for raising the principal direct tax of the time, and special commissioners were appointed to enquire into the illegal export of grain and butter.[64] Perhaps the most interesting of all these special commissions were those for the suppression of piracy, which may serve to illustrate the piecemeal nature of Tudor government. In 1565 the Privy Council became worried at the activities of pirates along the English and Welsh coast. Commissioners were appointed for almost every coastal shire—William Herbert of Swansea, Edward Mansel, William Bassett and Thomas Lewis being chosen for Glamorgan; they were ordered to appoint deputies in every port or creek and to inspect those deputies monthly. The commissioners and their deputies were to make a census of all landing-places and ships, to prevent any ship from going to sea without a licence, to prohibit certain goods from being shipped on board, to control the sale of all goods and, in short, to supervise the affairs of every port so closely that nothing could be done without their knowledge.[65] About ten years later piracy again became an urgent problem when the well-known pirate Callice was operating off British shores. The Privy Council began by issuing a commission to Sir John Perrott, Fabian Phillips and Thomas Lewis, of whom only Lewis came from Glamorgan, and another to John Croft, specifically for the arrest of Callice. Early in 1577 a third commission was given to Sir William Herbert, Thomas Lewis and William Mathew for restoring to a merchant goods that had been seized by some pirates. By this time the connivance of Cardiff burgesses with the pirates had become so notorious that merchants from the town doing business overseas 'dare not well be known or to avow the place of their dwelling at Cardiff'. In November 1577 more general commissions were issued for every coastal shire, Sir Edward Mansel, Sir Edward Stradling and William Mathew being named for Glamorgan. This commission remained in operation for at least ten years.[66]

Besides these commissions for dealing with general tasks, many others were issued from the exchequer or the Council in the Marches for particular purposes; and any prominent gentleman might expect to receive a large number of these. For instance, in 1580, the president of the Council in the Marches ordered Sir Edward Stradling and Sir William Herbert to examine the causes of 'some brawls and contentions betwixt the surnamed Thomases and Johnes'. Because of their family alliances, he said, 'there is very likely to fall out partaking, and more harm grow than were to be wished'; and therefore the commissioners were to 'deal so by your wisdoms and discretions as the matter may take some good end'.[67] A little later in the same year Henry Townshend, second justice of Chester, wrote to Stradling telling him that in a suit about the theft of a cow the defendant had objected to the commission issued. A new one was then sent to Stradling with the injunction that his proceedings be 'such as no party shall have just cause to be grieved therewith'. 'For that I hear the matter is borne by gent' of good account', wrote Townshend, 'I heartily pray you to have special care to foresee that revenge of privy malice be not sought to prejudice the poor man'.[68] All this for one cow!

These commissions were official orders from recognized institutions. But a great deal of administration was carried on by means of informal requests and personal favours; and the operation of this network can be understood from three examples. In 1582 the earl of Pembroke, who had then no 'official' standing in the shire except as a Marcher lord and a county magnate, wrote to Sir Edward Stradling of some 'enorme' dealing by members of the Bassett family. He asked Stradling and William Bassett, cousin to the offenders, to try out the truth and 'administer such indifferent justice as I may be served harmless'.[69] The very next day Pembroke wrote again to Stradling asking for his help in a quite different kind of case. Jevan Llewellyn was said to have got pregnant the daughter of one of Pembroke's tenants. The girl's father wanted Llewellyn to marry the girl—'for satisfying his duty towards the world and God'—and was prepared to endow them with forty sheep and four kine. 'If by your means', said Pembroke, 'the party may be brought to marry her, or otherwise to sustain punishment, and to keep the child, with some recompense to her father according to the laws of the realm, if you find him faulty, the old man will reckon himself bound to pray for you and be ready to do any service that he can'.[70] Pembroke had no authority to issue official commissions for examining cases, but he had at least great standing in the shire. The other two examples concern requests from outside Glamorgan. In 1585 a certain J. Stowell of Cotheleston asked Stradling to arrest a servant of his 'one Ellis Bagge, a young man without a beard, his left leg maimed', who had left his service contrary to law and gone into Wales.[71] He promised to do any service for Stradling in return. Finally, in 1576, Sir Arthur Champernoun of Dartington, Devonshire, asked Stradling to redress the robbery of £80 13s. 0d. from his household chaplain the year before. The chaplain was able to tell Stradling the names of the thieves and the money was apparently returned.[72]

BOROUGH GOVERNMENT

Borough government may best be described by taking first the specific example of Swansea, which has more records for this period than any other Glamorgan town. At the summit of Swansea's administration was the lord of Gower, who was throughout this period the earl of Worcester. To act as his agent in the town the lord appointed a steward, usually one of the local gentry, whose most important duty was to preside with the portreeve over the two courts-leet held in Swansea each year, when borough officers were elected and burgesses admitted.[73] While lord and steward exercised a supervision from without, the most important internal officer was the portreeve, the town's chief executive, corresponding to the mayors and bailiffs of other boroughs. He was chosen annually by the steward from two aldermen elected by the burgesses.[74] Next in stature to the portreeve was the council of twelve aldermen, which acted as an executive committee. The aldermen were elected for life by the whole body of burgesses, but could be removed from the bench if they were absent from the town for a year and a day.[75] This council was responsible for running most of the town's affairs; in particular they were empowered to make bye-laws and ordinances. However, they were by no means as powerful or as exclusive a body as the aldermen of some other towns, since the burgesses as a whole had a considerable say in what was to be done. The burgesses had a voice in the election of the portreeve; they had complete control, at least in theory, over the election of aldermen; and they often took part in the voting of bye-laws and ordinances.[76]

This did not mean that the constitution of the town was, by modern standards, democratic, since the burgesses represented only a small proportion of the town's inhabitants, perhaps eight per cent of the total population. To become a burgess a man had to be married; he had also either to be the son of a burgess or to have served an apprenticeship in the town, or, if a newcomer to the town, he had to live there for at least a year before he could qualify.[77] Even these rules did not satisfy the exclusive instincts of the town's élite. Sometimes specific conditions were laid down: for instance, in 1583, two Irishmen were admitted as burgesses only if they promised not to go about the countryside with 'wallets and fardels', peddling goods; and they were warned that 'if they shall become outrageous and rave, brawl, and fight with any body out of course', without provocation, they would be expelled. Some years later, in 1613, the men of power and influence became alarmed at the number of burgesses too poor to hold office, 'by reason of admitting of all sorts of people to be burgesses, as well strangers as inhabitants, some for little and some for nothing at all'; and it was therefore decreed that in future burgesses should be admitted only with the consent of the portreeve, aldermen and common attorneys, and that aspirants who were not burgesses' sons or ex-apprentices should pay 20s. to the town's coffers.[78]

Portreeve, aldermen and burgesses formed the main sources of power. Beneath them were ranged a host of minor officers, some appointed for life, some for a year. Most responsible of these were the common attorneys, who administered the town's finances. Then there were the serjeant-at-mace, who arrested miscreants, the constables, whose main task seems to have been the collection of *ad hoc* taxes, and such lesser men as the ale-tasters, waiters of the market, haywards, 'layer-keepers', 'cardiners' of the market, and hewers of the mountain and the burrows.[79]

What did the town government do? One must bear in mind that its resources were very limited. Its principal revenue, paid to the common attorneys from rents and from sale of merchandise, averaged only about £23 *per annum* in the 1630s; and the expenditure on this account was smaller still.[80] Even though this revenue excludes the regular levies for the poor, which provided on average another £9 or £10 *p.a.*,[81] the total sum was small.

The records of the aldermen in council and the Common Hall are principally concerned with two spheres of action: the regulation of trade and the treatment of the poor. Burgesses alone could trade within the borough; they were also exempt from the various tolls on merchandise brought into the town; any goods brought by ship must be taken first to the town-hall, where they would be offered for sale to the burgesses alone; and 'foreign' merchants could not sell to non-burgesses for fifteen days after their arrival in the port.[82] The enforcing of burgess-privilege and the elaboration of detailed regulations on the subject take up a good deal of space in the Council records. Even more space was taken up with the problem of the poor. The Poor Law Act of 1563 enjoined on every parish the collection of a benevolence for the poor, and from then on collections were made every Sunday. An average of 3s. 8d. was collected each week and distributed to an average of sixteen people.[83] This was not the only source of relief, for various benefactors had left money to the town: some of these bequests were lent without interest to deserving craftsmen and tradesmen, others were lent at interest, the income being devoted to the poor. But the direct relief of the poor was not the only concern of borough government. One of the duties most strictly enjoined upon it by the Privy Council was the placing of children as apprentices; another was the control of corn prices.[84] Yet another was the purchase by the portreeve and the common attorneys of up to one-third of all goods brought to the town hall and its subsequent re-sale, presumably at fair prices, to the poor.[85] But the borough authorities were not concerned only with helping the poor within the town; they were most anxious to keep them outside it if possible. In 1603 the aldermen reported that the town had been much pestered with immoral persons; they regretted that strumpets who bore children within the walls could not be expelled; and they ordered that no strangers could be allowed to inhabit the town unless the portreeve was informed of their presence and security given by townsmen that the strangers would not become a burden on the town's poor-rate.[86]

Beyond the protection of their trade and the regulation of the poor the town government did not show itself very active. It tried to keep

L

the streets clean; it made some regulations about the use of commons; and it provided some public entertainment in the form of bull-baiting and travelling players.[87]

Life in the borough of Swansea was often violent and disorderly: for instance, in 1581, William Thomas, a saddler, was threatened by some armed men who reviled him and his wife, beat his mare and eventually beat his wife—all, according to Thomas, out of 'some mortal malice'.[88] Sometimes the town fell out with the earl of Worcester, its lord, who complained that the answer of the burgesses to one of his demands was slight and undeserving of any favour. Once, at least, there is a sign of some dissension among the burgesses themselves, 'partly through the wilful disobedience of the meaner sort towards their superiors, and partly also by the wealthier sort meaning to suppress their inferiors by ravine', to use the words of the earl of Worcester. But by and large there seem to have been few serious tensions and conflicts of interest within the town, nothing at any rate to match the competition for power within some English boroughs at this time.[89]

There is much less information about the government of Cardiff, although it came eventually to be a more powerful and a more independent borough than Swansea. In the earlier part of this period the town must have been governed under much the same system as in the later middle ages: two portreeves, later known as bailiffs, acted as the executive officers, assisted by a body of twelve aldermen who sat for life and were perpetuated by co-optation.[90] Although the Acts of Union would seem at first to have much reduced the power of the lord of Cardiff and his deputy, the constable of the castle, the wide authority granted by Edward VI to William Herbert, earl of Pembroke, made him a dominating influence in the borough, for he had the final choice of bailiffs, confirmed the election of aldermen and received the town rents.[91] But it is only with the charter of 1608 that the system of government in Cardiff becomes really clear. Executive power was then confirmed in two bailiffs, the new version of the medieval reeves: the whole body of burgesses elected four men from whom the lord or the constable chose two as bailiffs. A new body of twelve capital burgesses was created to reinforce the aldermen; and together with the bailiffs these two groups formed the common council, empowered to make decrees and ordinances for the town. Cardiff was also authorized to appoint a lawyer to the new office of steward, who acted with the constable, the bailiffs and a senior alderman as justices of the peace for the borough. For Cardiff now became almost independent of the shire commission of the peace and special Quarter Sessions were held for the town. Only in the offences of murder, treason and felony did the shire justices of the peace have any authority, and it is likely that in practice they left such matters to the Great Sessions. There were also of course certain minor officers. Financial affairs were conducted as in Swansea by the common attorneys; two serjeants-at-the-mace served writs, summoned juries and so on; a constable was assigned to each of the two wards; and there were various officials attached to the markets.[92]

MANORIAL COURTS

At the bottom of the structure of shire government—below Great Sessions, Quarter Sessions, county courts, hundred courts and borough councils—were the courts-baron and courts-leet of the lordships and manors. In the words of George Owen, the courts-baron dealt with 'small debts and wrongs which are under 40s.', the courts-leet with such minor misdemeanours as 'affrays, assaults, rescues, bloodsheddings, pound breaches, stopping highways, false weights and measures, and divers other annoyances in the commonwealth'. According to Owen the leets, not being concerned with disputes between parties, worked well enough; but the courts-baron were ruled by 'ignorant judges' and greatly injured the poorer people. In the present state of the evidence this assertion is not easily tested, but we should remember that the judgements in courts-baron were given by the suitors to the court, not by the lord's steward, who merely presided. Some measure of self-government probably persisted in what Sir Edward Coke called 'little commonwealths'. In a period when the poor bought most of their necessities on credit, especially during the winter months, suits for petty debt were a major feature of life; and we have to remember that however trivial such cases may seem today, for the humbler inhabitants of Glamorgan these courts were probably far more important than the more prestigious organs of government.[93]

iii.

THE RULING FAMILIES (Map IV)

Which were the leading families of Glamorgan? How were the principal offices of the shire distributed? What was the general structure of power and influence? In answering these questions we shall try to describe the political anatomy of the county.[94]

THE HERBERTS

One great clan, the Herberts, had spread over the whole shire and must be given precedence in this survey.[95] They had a common ancestor in Sir William ap Thomas of Raglan, whose elder son William Herbert received the earldom of Pembroke in 1468 in return for his services to the Yorkists. On his death in 1469 he was succeeded by his son, another William, who died in 1491 leaving only a daughter, Elizabeth. She married Sir Charles Somerset, illegitimate son of the third duke of Somerset and servant to Henry VII, and thus the senior branch of the clan were Somersets by name, though Herberts in descent. Sir Charles himself was granted several important offices in south Wales, most notably the sheriffwick of Glamorgan in 1509, was created earl of Worcester in 1513 or 1514, and acquired through his wife Elizabeth most of the Herbert lands, including the lordships of Gower and Kilvey. Thus, although the principal seat of the family was throughout this period at Raglan castle, Monmouthshire, they held substantial interests in Glamorgan. From Charles Somerset the earldom descended in the direct male line for generations, but few of its members were as effective or as influential as the founder. Henry, the second earl, who succeeded his father in 1526, allowed much of the family influence to decay; and the sheriffwick of Glamorgan and Morgannwg lapsed in 1540. On the second earl's death in 1549 most of his offices were granted to William Herbert, later earl of Pembroke, and the process of decline continued under the third earl, who died in 1589. It was left to the fourth earl, Edward, and his son, Henry, to restore some of the family's influence in Wales: this was in part achieved in 1602 when the fourth earl took over the lieutenancy of Glamorgan and Monmouth from the lord president of the Marches. But in spite of this resurgence the Somerset family was always more important in Monmouth than in Glamorgan.[96]

The other branch of the Herberts to be important in Glamorgan affairs descended from the first earl of Pembroke's bastard son, Richard Herbert of Ewyas in Herefordshire. Illegitimacy was no bar to the advancement of an able man and Richard succeeded in marrying the daughter of the influential Sir Mathew Cradock of Swansea. Although both Richard's sons founded important families, it turned out that the descendants of the younger were the more famous. The elder son was George Herbert of Swansea, who probably inherited many of his Cradock grandfather's lands and certainly succeeded that grandfather in 1526 as steward to the lordships of Gower and Kilvey. From the Union until his death in 1570 he was an important Glamorgan dignitary: a member of the first commission of the peace for the shire, knight of the shire in 1542, sheriff in 1540 and 1552. His son, Mathew, was a rather shadowy figure: he managed to attain the commission of the peace only for a very brief period, but fathered five sons, of whom three were influential in Glamorgan. The eldest of these, Sir William, although distinguished from the multitude of other William Herberts by the epithet 'of Swansea', seems rather confusingly to have lived for most of his life in Cardiff, where he built a 'sumptuous house' on the site of the Grey Friars' buildings. For most of the reign of Elizabeth he was one of the dominant figures in the county: justice of the peace from 1554 until his death in 1609; deputy-lieutenant from about 1579; five times sheriff; and knight of the shire in 1559. He was vigorously supported in Glamorgan politics by his brother, Nicholas, who lived at Cogan Pill, near Cardiff, was intermittently on the commission of the peace from 1573 until the end of the century, was twice sheriff and was member of parliament for Cardiff in 1584. Support came also from the third brother, Sir John Herbert of Neath, who had a distinguished career at court and ended as second secretary of state to Elizabeth and to James I. On the death of Sir William Herbert without heirs in 1609 the family's influence seems to have been much reduced, the property passing to the descendants of his brother, Nicholas. William Herbert, grandson of Nicholas, however achieved some fame as a royalist M.P., killed at Edgehill.[97]

One more descendant of Sir George Herbert has to be mentioned, albeit briefly. This is his son, William, younger brother to Mathew, uncle to Sir William of Swansea. This William lived at Cogan Pill, which passed on the death of his son, George, to his nephew Nicholas. He was on the commission of the peace from 1561 until 1569, was sheriff in 1551 and 1566 and was knight of the shire in 1558 and 1572.[98]

We can now return to the second son of Richard Herbert of Ewyas. This was yet another William Herbert, who left south Wales early in his life and joined the service of Sir Charles Somerset, earl of Worcester. Very quickly he was making a career for himself at court. Under Henry VIII he received grants of lordships in Monmouthshire; and in 1547 he became a privy councillor and obtained two lordships in Glamorgan. His critical year came in 1549 when he helped to put down the rebels in Devon and Cornwall, and then joined Warwick in the overthrow of Protector Somerset. This brought him a grant of the remaining lordships of Glamorgan, the Wiltshire estates of the Protector, most of the offices held in Wales by the second earl of Worcester, and the title of earl of Pembroke. Having first given support to Northumberland's plan for putting Lady Jane Grey on the throne, Pembroke was quick to see which way things were going and led the cheering after Queen Mary was proclaimed in London on July 19, 1553. Like most of Mary's other lay councillors he survived without difficulty the accession of Elizabeth, although he was under some suspicion of conspiracy shortly before his death in March, 1570. Thus the younger son of a bastard rose to be one of the most powerful magnates in the kingdom. In Glamorgan his influence was enormous since he was lord of almost the entire county, excluding only the Worcester lordships of Gower and Kilvey and the Gamage lordship of Coety.[99]

His successors came to exercise this influence less and less directly, since the family seat was at Wilton in Wiltshire. The first earl had been more at home in Welsh than in English;[100] his son Henry, the second earl, was certainly more an Englishman than a Welshman. Nevertheless, he intervened constantly in Glamorgan affairs and from 1586 until he died in 1601 wielded the major power in Wales by virtue of his office of lord president of the Council in the Marches. The third earl, William, was best known for his patronage of Shakespeare and his opposition to the duke of Buckingham: his principal concern in Glamorgan was the exercise of parliamentary patronage in order to develop his faction in the House of Commons.[101] He was succeeded by his brother, Philip, first earl of Montgomery and fourth earl of Pembroke, who allowed the links with Glamorgan to get slacker still, although he maintained the electoral influence.

To conclude a complicated survey: the descendants of William Herbert, first earl of Pembroke of the first creation, formed three branches of relevance to Glamorgan—though many other branches were significant elsewhere. The senior line was that of the Somersets, earls of Worcester, heirs to most of the original Herbert lands in south Wales, potentially powerful through their lordships of Gower and Kilvey, but declining in authority from the time of the Acts of Union. Much more powerful were the earls of Pembroke of the second creation, whose influence over Glamorgan was formed in the reign of Edward VI. Although their power was mainly exercised from outside the shire, it was all the greater for their influence at court. Within the county there were the descendants of Sir George Herbert, headed by his grandson, William, who had great strength in the county until his death in 1609.

The Resident Gentry

We shall discuss the other families of Glamorgan by taking a geographical sweep from the western part of the county through the Vale to the east. The most westerly family were the Mansels of Oxwich and Margam. They had long been settled in the Gower at Penrice castle and during the fifteenth century had been working their way up as landowners and local politicians. Although they were deprived of their lands by the Yorkists, their estates were restored by Henry Tudor. At the time of the Union the head of the family was Sir Rice Mansel, who had served at sea with Sir Mathew Cradock, his uncle, and in Ireland with Sir William Skeffington. He made three marriages, of which two were important for his career: the first of them, with Eleanor, daughter of James Bassett of Beaupré, near Cowbridge, brought him a link with another influential Glamorgan family; the third, with Cecily Daubridge-court, made him the husband of one of the gentlewomen of Princess Mary. Irish service and court influence put Sir Rice in a position to lease and then to buy the large estates of Margam abbey, thus making himself one of the richest landowners in south Wales. When Princess Mary came to the throne his influence increased still further with the grant of the offices of chamberlain and chancellor of south Wales, Cardiganshire and Carmarthenshire. He was on the commission of the peace for Glamorgan in 1543 and remained on it until his death in 1559.[102]

Sir Rice's son, Edward, was a much less interesting and capable man, but his possessions and status automatically qualified him for a leading position in the shire, a position which was confirmed by his marriage to Jane, daughter of the second earl of Worcester. He was a justice of the peace from 1555 until his death, knight of the shire in 1554, sheriff in 1575. Of his children one was outstanding: Sir Robert Mansel, vice-admiral of England and parliamentary opponent of the duke of Buckingham. But the heir was Thomas Mansel, who followed his father's example in occupying most of the important local offices: justice of the peace from 1585 until his death in 1631, deputy-lieutenant from 1590, knight of the shire in 1597, 1605, 1614, and three times sheriff. Sir Thomas was succeeded by his eldest son, Lewis, justice of the peace from 1607, deputy-lieutenant from 1631, and Lewis by his son, Henry.[103]

The only other family of much significance in the western part of the county were the Prices of Briton Ferry. The founder of their short-lived fortunes seems to have been Leyshon Price, a barrister, who was on the commission of the peace from 1561 until his death in about 1586. His son William, justice of the peace from 1601 to 1625, was linked to the Herbert interest and managed some of the Pembroke estates in the shire. Having sat for the earl's pocket borough of Old Sarum he became knight of the shire for Glamorgan in 1621 and member for Cardiff in 1624, 1625 and 1626. After his death in the early years of Charles I's reign the property passed to a branch of the Mansels, through the marriage of his daughter, Jane, to Arthur Mansel, who was the father of Bussy Mansel, the parliamentary commander.[104]

In the central part of the vale of Glamorgan lived the largest concentration of gentry families. Of these the most westerly were the Carnes of Ewenni, the junior, but more important, of the two branches of the Carne family. Its founder was Sir Edward Carne, who had graduated from Oxford with a D.C.L., entered the royal service under Henry VIII and been entrusted with several important diplomatic missions. On its dissolution he bought Ewenni priory near Bridgend, where he built what Rhys Lewis described a little later as 'a goodly house' with two deer parks. Under Mary he was sent first on an embassy to the emperor and then to Rome as permanent ambassador to the Pope: he was still en poste in Rome when Elizabeth succeeded and was detained there until his death in 1561. Since he was a professed Catholic, this absence abroad at an awkward moment may well have helped the family to weather the change in religion. In spite of his state service Sir Edward played some part in county affairs: he was a justice of the peace from 1542 until his death, knight of the shire in 1554, and twice sheriff. His son, Thomas, continued the tradition of Catholic sympathy and service to the shire: he was intermittently on the commission of peace from 1573 until 1605, knight of the shire in 1586 and 1588, and once sheriff. In 1590 he was considered for the post of deputy-lieutenant but rejected as unsuitable, possibly on account of his earlier religious dis-affection.[105] His son and grandson, both named John, followed much the same pattern: they were on the commission for long stretches, were both twice sheriff, but never reached parliament or the rank of deputy-lieutenant. The senior branch of this family, the Carnes of Nash, were a good deal less influential. They appear intermittently as justices of the peace and sheriffs, but only one of them, Sir Edward, teller of the exchequer and receiver-general in south Wales, was on the commission for any length of time. Sir Edward's son, William, continued in the post of teller of the exchequer, which he sold to his younger brother, when he himself bought for £6,000 a 'six clerkship' in chancery. But this incursion into national administration did the Carnes of Nash no good, and William eventually retreated from it in debt.[106]

A mile or so north-east of Bridgend lived the Gamages, established at Coety castle since the fourteenth century. At the time of the Union the head of the family was Sir Thomas, whose status can be judged from his own and his children's marriages. He himself married first into the St. John family and then into the Crofts of Croft castle; his elder son, Robert, married Joan Champernowne, sister-in-law of Sir Walter Raleigh; one daughter married Sir Thomas Stradling and the other William, Lord Howard of Effingham. But with the death of Sir Thomas, the Gamages seem to have lost influence. Robert Gamage was on the commission of peace from 1549 to 1564 but his son John did not reach it until just before his death in 1584. That brought the main line of the family to an end, for John left only a daughter, Barbara, whose marriage was to cause one of the most interesting disputes of the period. With Barbara's marriage to Sir Robert Sidney the Gamage properties passed to that family until the eighteenth century.[107]

South-east of Bridgend, near Llantwit Major, lived the Stradlings of St. Donat's, next to the Herberts, and along with the Mansels, the most influential family in the county. They had first come to England from the continent in the reign of Edward I and were by the fifteenth century firmly established among the landowners of Glamorgan. In the 1530s the family was headed by Sir Edward Stradling, who seems to have had little ability or desire to control his many and disreputable sons: 'there are', said the countess of Worcester, 'twelve brothers, most of them bastards, and they have no living but by extortion and pilling of the King's subjects'.[108] But on Sir Edward's death the property came to a much more solid citizen, his eldest son Thomas, married to Catherine Gamage. Under Edward VI Sir Thomas allied with the more 'conservative' wing at court under the earl of Arundel and fell with his patron in 1551, when several of his local offices went to William Herbert, first earl of Pembroke, who had joined the victorious faction of Northumberland. With the accession of Mary, Stradling recovered his authority in the county. From 1542 until 1558/59 he was usually on the commission of the peace, but from 1559 until his death in 1571 he was excluded, presumably on account of his Catholic sympathies. Although the recusant tradition was maintained by his younger son, David, and by a daughter who entered a convent in Bruges, the main branch of the family, under Thomas's son, Sir Edward, conformed to the Anglican settlement. Sir Edward was a leader of Glamorgan society: continuously a justice from 1569 until his death in 1609; twice or three times sheriff; and deputy-lieutenant from 1590. But he was more than this, for he collected a fine library of books and manuscripts at St. Donat's and was described by one of his contemporaries as 'chief guardian of our Welsh language in south Wales'. He died childless and left his estates to an adopted cousin, Sir John Stradling, who continued the tradition of local service and literary interest. Sir John's son Edward, who succeeded to the property in 1637, had been a justice of the peace since 1621 and a deputy-lieutenant since 1631. He represented the shire in the short parliament of 1640, fought for the king in the civil war and died as a prisoner at Oxford.[109]

The Bassetts of Beaupré (or St. Hilary), also near Cowbridge, were closely linked with the Mansels. Elinor, daughter of James Bassett, was married to Sir Rice Mansel, while James's nephew, William, who inherited the property, married Sir Rice's daughter, Catherine. For most of the period a Bassett was on the commission of the peace, though there were occasions after the death of the head of the house when his son had to wait some years before being appointed. William Bassett was knight of the shire in 1563 and 1571, and his son, Richard, was appointed deputy-lieutenant in 1590.[110]

The Aubreys of Llantriddyd, two miles east of Beaupré, were newcomers to the county at the end of the sixteenth century. William Aubrey of Abercynrig, Brecon, had a distinguished career as a civil lawyer under Elizabeth, having been helped at the start by the first earl of Pembroke. He was himself on the Glamorgan commission of the peace from 1578 to 1594 and had friendly contacts with Sir Edward Stradling. His second son, Thomas, founded the Glamorgan branch of the family by marrying the daughter and co-heiress of Antony Mansel, brother of Sir Edward Mansel, and thus acquiring the Llantriddyd property on his father-in-law's death. He seems to have been settled in the county before then, since he was appointed to the commission of the peace in 1595. By the reign of Charles I his influence had risen to such a height that he could be made deputy-lieutenant. His son, John, who succeeded him on the bench and in the deputy-ship, fought for Charles I and gained a baronetcy at the Restoration.[111]

The Buttons of Dyffryn House, St. Nicholas, a few miles west of Cardiff, are best known for the career of Admiral Sir Thomas Button, the explorer of Hudson's Bay in the reign of James I. The family seems to have originated in Wiltshire and to have leased their principal seat from the bishop of Llandaff. The admiral's grandfather, James Button, was made justice of the peace in 1555 and sheriff the following year; he seems not to have returned to the bench. James's son, Miles, had a longer career on the bench, from 1561 until 1594, and was three times sheriff. There was then a gap of ten years until Miles's son Edward was put on the commission in 1604. After he disappeared from the commission in 1624 the Buttons had no further representative there before 1642, when Robert was placed. The Buttons were perhaps typical of the gentry family whose head was usually, but by no means always, on the commission of the peace, but which could not aspire to represent the shire in Parliament or to hold the post of deputy-lieutenant.[112]

The Mathew family of Llandaff and Radyr owed its descent and prominence to Sir David Mathew (*fl.* 1428–84), a follower of the Nevilles, and to the patronage after 1485 of Sir Rhys ap Thomas. In the first half of the sixteenth century both branches of the family were influential and prestigious. But the Llandaff line seems to have been unimportant after the Union, although most of the eldest sons reached the commission of the peace for a part at least of their lives. The Radyr branch was certainly powerful in the lifetime of Sir George Mathew, who was on the commission from 1542 until his death in 1557 and was probably the knight of the shire in 1553. His eldest son, William, was also of some consequence and was helped by his marriage to Margaret, daughter of Sir George Herbert. He was on the commission of the peace from 1569 until 1585 and was elected knight of the shire in 1577. But William quarrelled with the earl of Pembroke and died in disfavour in 1587. Thereafter the family power was not what it had been: his brothers, Henry and Edmund, who succeeded him, both became justices of the peace but do not seem otherwise to have been of much account, and Edmund's son, George, sold Radyr and went to Ireland.[113]

The Lewises of Y Fan first became significant with Edward Lewis, who built what Leland called 'a fair place called Vann' half a mile from Caerphilly and married the daughter of Sir William Morgan of Pencoed, Monmouthshire. Edward was three times sheriff and was justice of the peace from 1542 until 1575. His son, Thomas, made two useful marriages —one to the daughter of Sir Robert Gamage, the other to the daughter of Sir George Mathew of Radyr—built the family house in Cardiff, sat on the commission of the peace from 1564 until his death in 1594 and acted, with Sir William Herbert of Swansea, as one of the first two deputy-lieutenants for the county. His son Edward, knighted in 1603, continued the tradition of strong local power: he added to the property by buying St. Fagan's castle, sat on the commission from about 1590 and acted as deputy-lieutenant from about 1595. His successor, another Edward, survived his father for only two years, dying in 1630. But the next heir, William, who had been on the bench since 1613, stepped into the deputyship in 1631. Their record puts the Lewises clearly into the county élite: the head of the family was on the commission of the peace with an unbroken run from 1542 and three of them held the much more distinguished post of deputy-lieutenant.[114]

Most easterly of all the important Glamorgan families were the Kemeyses of Cefnmabli, near the Monmouthshire border. They were an old family, with lands and some influence in both Glamorgan and Monmouthshire, but they rose to real significance only at the end of the period. Edward Kemeys was intermittently on the commission of the peace from 1573 to 1608 and was four times sheriff. He was succeeded by his nephew David who sat on the commission for only about a year and was once sheriff. Much more powerful was David's brother, Nicholas Kemeys of Llanvair castle, who ultimately inherited the Cefnmabli estate from his nephew Edward. Nicholas was on the commission of the peace from 1636, acted as sheriff in 1638, became deputy-lieutenant in 1640 and fought vigorously for the king during the civil war.[115]

These were not of course the only families whose members sat on the bench or held the office of sheriff; and several others ran them close in importance. One might mention here the Evanses of Gnoll House, near Neath; the Gwyns of Llansannor and the Thomases of Llanfihangel, both near Cowbridge; the Seys's of Boverton, near Llantwit Major; the Mathews of Castell-y-mynach near Llantrisant; the Morgans of Ruperra, east of Caerphilly; and the Prichards of Llancaeach, near Treharris. The heads of all these families were men of some consequence. There were also families from outside the county who played a part in its affairs, in particular the Morgans of Machen in Monmouthshire; Sir Robert Sidney of Penshurst, who had acquired Coety through his wife; the Lords St. John of Bletsoe who held lands at Fonmon; besides, of course, the earls of Worcester and of Pembroke, who have already been discussed. One point is worth making before we leave this account of the families. The influential men of the county almost all lived in the swathe of lowland territory which runs from the Gower peninsula through the Vale of Glamorgan to Cardiff and on to the lower course of the Rhymney. Only four important houses lay in the more mountainous part of the shire: the Lewises of Y Fan and of Ruperra, the Morgans of Ruperra, the Prichards of Llancaeach; and of these only the last-named lived in the innermost reaches of Glamorgan. Within the lowland region the greatest concentration of powerful families was to be found between Bridgend on the west and Cardiff on the east.

OFFICES OF LOCAL GOVERNMENT

From the major families we can turn to the offices that they held: the deputy-lieutenancy, the sheriffwick, the commission of the peace and membership of Parliament. The office of deputy-lieutenant carried most prestige, but since few records of appointment have survived it is impossible to give a complete list of its holders. The first two deputies to be named were Sir William Herbert of Swansea and Thomas Lewis of Y Fan in 1579. When the war against Spain demanded greater military effort three more were added in 1590: Sir Edward Stradling, Sir Thomas

Mansel and Richard Bassett. On Thomas Lewis's death in 1594 he was replaced by his son, Edward. By 1600 Bassett seems to have dropped out, but Herbert, Stradling, Mansel, and Edward Lewis were still acting. There is then a large gap in our knowledge until 1626 when we find Sir Thomas Mansel, Sir John Stradling, Sir Edward Lewis, and Sir Thomas Aubrey acting as deputies. In the course of the next five years Mansel and Stradling were each replaced by their sons, Lewis by his grandson, William; and early in the 1630s Sir Thomas Lewis of Penmark Place, fourth son of Sir Edward, was added to the office. In 1640, or thereabouts, the crown, faced with major military commitments against the Scots, increased the number of deputies to eight: to the five men in office in 1637 were added Nicholas Kemeys, Sir Thomas Mathew, and Antony Mansel, with Sir John Aubrey replacing his father. Thus up to 1640, when the post became rather less exclusive, it was virtually the preserve of the Lewis, Herbert, Stradling, Mansel, and Aubrey families.[116]

Welsh sheriffs were pricked annually by the sovereign from a list of three names submitted by the lord president and the Council in the Marches. The post clearly carried enough power to arouse some competition, as we have already seen,[117] but it may have been the kind of office that one liked to see one's friends in rather than to occupy oneself. At any rate there were signs in the 1630s of some reluctance to hold it: James Turberville, for instance, petitioned the lord keeper in 1636 that his name be left off the roll.[118] The men chosen as sheriffs were drawn from the major gentry families of the county, but from a much wider group than were the deputy-lieutenants. We have the details of ninety-six appointments between 1540 and 1641. These were held by sixty-two men in all, some important landowners like Sir William Herbert of Swansea being pricked three, four or even five times. Members of the Herbert family were pricked eleven times, the Mansels and the Carnes of Ewenni nine times each, the Lewises eight times, the Stradlings and the Kemeys's six times each, and the Bassetts, Buttons and Mathews of Radyr five times each. Almost all the Herbert sheriffs were pricked before 1603, the Kemeys sheriffs all after 1558.[119]

Those figures add a few rather crude strokes to our profile of the county establishment: the image becomes clearer when we look at the office of justice of the peace. It is not easy, indeed it is impossible, to make a complete and accurate roll of all those men who were appointed to the commission in this period. There are lists only for some of the years and many of the lists extant are probably defective. Even so, our sources do provide material for some firm conclusions: they may not enable us to say positively whether such and such a man was or was not a justice at a particular time; they do tell us the size of the bench and which families were most usually to be found upon it.[120] The commission for each of the Welsh counties usually included a number of purely formal appointments, such as the members of the Council in the Marches, the lord keeper of the great seal, and various other officers of the central government: these 'honorary' justices have been excluded, as far as is possible, from the analysis that follows. The Act of Union laid down that eight justices should be appointed for each shire, but this figure was soon exceeded. The list of 1542 contained eleven names; in the 1570s the average was about fifteen; in the late 1590s it was about twenty; in 1625 there were twenty-five justices; and in 1642 there were thirty-three. By the end of the period there were, therefore, families appearing on the commission who had never reached it in the earlier days. In all 128 justices are named on the surviving lists, excluding the 'honorary' appointments. Of these men about ten cannot be identified and seven were normally resident outside the shire. About 110 came from established Glamorgan families. Of the justices identified, four are known to have been clerics, seven professional lawyers, two office-holders in the central government. The remainder, a far higher proportion than was usual in English counties, belonged to the landed gentry.[121]

Members of the Herbert family of Swansea sat on the commission without interruption from 1542 until 1607 and then again from 1610 until 1642. The Lewises of Y Fan were there continuously, except for a brief interval between 1548 and 1554. With a few very short breaks, which may in fact be errors in the records, Mansels were justices from 1542 until 1642. There were some years between 1542 and 1569 when neither Sir Thomas Stradling nor his son, Edward, were on the commission; from 1569 onwards the Stradlings were always there. Those four families held perhaps the most remarkable records. The Carnes of Ewenni, however, were not far off, though there were four periods of a few years each when they were not justices. The Aubreys of Llantriddyd entered Glamorgan society late; but once there they were soon important, for one of the family was on the commission without a break from 1595 to the end.

The heads of several other families could expect to be appointed to the bench at some point in their lives, but could not achieve the almost unbroken succession from father to son of the Herberts, Stradlings, Mansels, and Lewises. The Evans family of Gnoll House, Neath, provides an example: David Evans was a justice from the middle of Mary's reign until 1564; there was no member of the family on the commission from then until 1590, when his son Leyshon was appointed; Leyshon was a justice until 1597 and was then reappointed from 1602 until 1610. There was another break before his son, David, appeared on the lists in 1608. The Bassetts of Beaupré, the Buttons of St. Nicholas, the Carnes of Nash, the Kemeys's of Cefnmabli, the Mathews of Llandaff, the Prices of Briton Ferry, and the Thomases of Llanfihangel all produce a similar pattern of appointment throughout the century from 1542 to 1642. The Gamages of Coety were on the commission at intervals from 1542 until 1584 when the male line ended, and the Mathews of Radyr from 1542 until 1605/6, after which the property was sold. By the late-sixteenth century other families which had not earlier laid claim to a place on the commission now began to appear on it, in particular the Gwyns of Llansannor, the Prichards of Llancaeach, the Seys's of Boverton, and the Thomases of Betws.

There were thus about six families who would have a member on the bench at almost any time—though this was not true of the Aubreys before 1595. By the reign of James I the heads of a further twelve families could expect to become justices at some point in their lives; and this had earlier been true of the Gamages of Coety and the Mathews of Radyr. The remaining justices came from about fifteen families which supplied a very occasional member: such families were more often to be found on the bench under the early Stuarts than under the Tudors.

Appointment to the commission of the peace was not for life. When pricked as a sheriff a man had to leave the bench, but he was usually reinstated the following year. Occasionally there were less formal and longer interruptions. Sir Thomas Stradling was left off for the last twelve years of his life. Members of other families had occasional breaks in service. But except in Stradling's case there is little sign that the commission was manipulated for political or religious ends. Even in the rapidly altering circumstances of the mid-sixteenth century the justices almost always survived a change of régime.[122]

PARLIAMENTARY REPRESENTATION

From 1536 Glamorgan sent two members to Parliament, one for the shire and the other for the combined boroughs of Cardiff, Llantrisant, Kenfig, Aberavan, Neath, Swansea, and Loughor. Over the whole period, 1536–1640, twenty-seven election results are recorded for the shire, in which eight families were successful: Mansels eight times; Herberts seven times; Carnes three times; Mathews, Sidneys, Stradlings, and Bassetts twice; Prices once.[123] Up to 1601 the Herbert interest dominated the shire: Sir George Herbert was returned in 1541/42, his second son, William of Cogan, in 1558 and 1572, his eldest grandson, Sir William of Swansea, in 1559, his younger grandson, Sir John of Neath, the secretary of state, in 1601. But this was not all. William Mathew, knight of the shire from 1577 to 1581, had married Sir George Herbert's daughter; and Sir Robert Sidney, M.P. in 1584 and 1593, was the brother-in-law of Henry Herbert, earl of Pembroke. Mathew's alliance with the Herbert clan is conjectural; but Sidney's is amply demonstrated, for Pembroke wrote in his support in 1584, and Sidney himself asked Pembroke's agent to canvass on his behalf in 1592/93.[124] Out of eighteen known returns between 1536 and 1601 eight may therefore be credited to the Herberts, and ultimately perhaps to the influence of the earls of Pembroke. In this period the Mansels were returned three times, their allies the Bassetts of Beaupré twice, the Carnes three times.

After 1601 the descendants of Sir George Herbert disappeared from the returns, but the Pembroke interest remained strong. Sir Philip Herbert, younger brother of the third earl, later to be first earl of Montgomery and then fourth earl of Pembroke, was returned in 1604, while his son, another Philip, was member for the shire in the Long Parliament. The member in 1621, William Price of Briton Ferry, also belonged to the Pembroke entourage, for he was manager of some of the earl's estates and had sat in the past for the pocket borough of Old Sarum. Sir John Stradling, member in 1626, had also been returned for Old Sarum in 1625. However, the Mansel interest came in the early-Stuart period almost to match the Herbert, largely because Sir Robert Mansel, the vice-admiral, was returned three times. It is worth noting that of the ten returns made for the shire between 1604 and 1640 five were for men who lived outside Glamorgan.[125]

In the borough constituency Herbert influence was again strong. Nicholas Herbert, M.P. in 1584, was a grandson of Sir George; Mathew Davies, M.P. in 1604 and 1614, sat in the Pembroke interest and was given a Wiltshire seat in 1624;[126] William Herbert of Cardiff, M.P. in 1621, was certainly returned with Pembroke help, since he wrote that the countess had recommended him to the bailiffs and burgesses, and that they were ready to elect him;[127] William Price, M.P. in 1624, 1625, 1626, has already been noted as a Pembroke supporter; and finally Nicholas Herbert's grandson, William, sat for the boroughs in both the Short and Long Parliaments.[128] The only other important family to have a footing in the borough elections was Lewis of Y Fan, some of whose lesser members sat in 1586, 1589 and 1601. In the Tudor period most of the borough members were obscure men whose affiliations are hard to trace; but from 1604 the borough seat was sought by better-known men with clear affiliations to the leading family of the shire. Herbert influence, visible but not striking before 1604, became almost monopolistic under the early Stuarts, when the magnates of England laid the foundations of their electoral domains.

What did Glamorgan M.P.s do when they got to Westminster? For the first fifty years almost the only members for either shire or borough to sit on a parliamentary committee were Sir Edward Carne of Ewenni in 1554 and Sir Thomas Mansel in 1597.[129] Sir John Herbert, knight of the shire in 1601, was an active parliamentarian but owed his status in the Commons to his position as second secretary of state rather than to his standing in the county. Under the early Stuarts Glamorgan men became a good deal more prominent. With Pembroke's backing and protection Mathew Davies and William Price both spoke often, and Price in particular was critical of the administration. More important than either of these was Sir Robert Mansel. The mismanagement of naval affairs by Buckingham set him strongly against the favourite and he became one of the Commons' most informed critics of the government's handling of the war. Eventually, when Mansel's criticism looked like getting him into trouble, he came under the protection of Buckingham's enemy, Pembroke—a powerful linking of two Glamorgan interests. The only other Glamorgan M.P. to make a mark was Sir John Stradling, who seems to have maintained a moderate support for the king.[130]

The main features of Glamorgan's political anatomy are now revealed. The posts of deputy-lieutenant, justice of the peace and sheriff were held by the members of from thirty-five to forty families—the number depending on whether or not one counts cadet branches separately from the main family. These families make up the élite of the country's gentry; but it is an élite that can itself be divided into three strata. In the top level were six families whose heads were almost always on the bench and might hope to become deputy-lieutenants or knights of the shire. Up to 1609 this small group was led by the Herberts of Swansea, strongly represented in parliament, on the commission of the peace, in the sheriffwick and in the lieutenancy, supported in the county and at court by their kinsmen, the earls of Pembroke. After 1609 the descendants of Sir George Herbert were less important in the county and Pembroke influence was largely directed towards parliamentary elections. Next to the Herberts, Mansels and Stradlings played the largest part, with an influence that lasted throughout the century. The Lewises of Y Fan were not far behind, powerful as justices, sheriffs, and deputy-lieutenants, but having to be content with the borough seat in parliament. The Carnes of Ewenni deserve a place in this top group, although their recusancy kept them out of the lieutenancy and thus reduced their influence. Finally the Aubreys of Llantriddyd, latecomers to the shire, established their importance by sitting continually on the bench and by holding a deputy-lieutenancy throughout the reign of Charles I.

In the middle stratum we find those fifteen families whose heads could fairly expect to reach the commission of the peace at some point in their lives. At the top of this group the Mathews of Radyr, in the early part of the period, the Bassetts of Beaupré, the Kemeys's of Cefnmabli, the Buttons of St. Nicholas, the Prices of Briton Ferry are outstanding. The families of Carne of Nash, Evans of Gnoll, Gamage of Coety, Gwyn of Llansannor, Mathew of Llandaff, Mathew of Castell-y-mynach, Prichard of Llancaeach, Seys of Boverton, Thomas of Llanfihangel and of Betws make up the rest.

The third stratum contains about seventeen families which occasionally had members on the bench or in the sheriffwick but could by no means count on this. The Turbervilles of Pen-llin belong here, although one might have expected to find them in the middle stratum: Christopher Turberville was twice sheriff and justice only in 1543 and 1564; his descendant was sheriff in 1615 but never on the bench. Probably their recusancy prevented them from achieving the standing to which their lands and birth might have entitled them. More typical perhaps were the Meyricks of Cottrell. Rice Meyrick, a distinguished antiquarian, was clerk of the peace in Glamorgan under Elizabeth until he died in 1587, but never reached the bench; his son Morgan, however, was a justice of the peace from 1601 to 1623. Thereafter the family seems to have died out.[131] For the rest we find here Bassett of Llantriddyd and of Broviskin, Bawdripp of Splott, Franklin of Gower, Gibbon of St. Fagan's, Jones of Frampton, Lewis of Llanishen and Ruperra, Leyshon of Baglan, Loughor of Tythegston, Mathew of Aberamman, Thomas of Swansea and of Wenvoe, Vann of Marcross, and Williams of Blaen Baglan.[132]

iv.

CONFLICTS AND RIVALRIES

From anatomy we can move to pathology; to a description of the conflicts and rivalries which divided the county between the Union and the Civil War. Inevitably this description will be episodic. There is no single theme that can give unity to this story and the search for one would only distort. But certain general lines of dispute emerge and the episodes in the chronicle enable us to sense the prevailing climate of local politics, to glimpse the reasons why men quarrelled and the ways in which they fought.

FROM THE UNION TO THE ACCESSION OF ELIZABETH

The evidence about Glamorgan politics between the Union and the accession of Elizabeth is unhappily sparse. In the years immediately following the Union the principal rivalry seems to have been between the earl of Worcester and his allies on one side, and the Carne family on the other. Possibly the earl and his friends resented the favour shown by Lord Chancellor Audley to his protégé, Roger Carne of Sully. At any rate, open conflict broke out in February 1537, when, according to Roger Carne, some servants of Sir Rice Mansel set upon William Carne and then took refuge in Llandaff cathedral. A few months later Roger Carne himself was involved in an affray at Cowbridge with the servants of George Herbert of Swansea, Worcester's steward. From the jumble of conflicting testimony two points stand out: first, that Herbert was in some way allied with Mansel; second, that there was sword-fighting between the two groups, who then shot arrows at one another, though not to any great effect.[133]

Three years later another member of the Carne family was involved in dispute with the Herberts. John Carne of Sully, Roger's cousin, was watching his man ploughing, when there appeared some servants of Walter Herbert, son of Sir George Herbert of St. Julian's and first cousin to George Herbert of Swansea. One of them, William David, said to the ploughman, 'Thou thief, what doest here in my master's close ground',

[175]

M

and then struck at him. Carne went to his servant's rescue and was in turn hit on his head by John Thomas William. The miscreants fled to Cardiff castle and Carne died. His widow accused Walter Herbert of protecting the killers, for he was then deputy-keeper of Cardiff castle under the earl of Worcester. Herbert, while admitting that the murderer had been a servant of his, denied all complicity and said of Carne that he 'loved him right well'. Herbert's testimony is very far from forthcoming, but, while the evidence about the murder itself is clear enough, there is no direct testimony to prove the accusations against him. All one can say for certain is that the incident shows some resentment against the Herberts, and may perhaps have been connected with the gradual displacement from power of the earl of Worcester.[134]

By the end of Mary's reign this displacement was more or less complete and the earl of Pembroke had come to play the central role in Glamorgan politics. The first clash in which Pembroke was involved followed his appointment to the command of an expeditionary force to France in 1557. In June of that year his nephew, William Herbert of Cogan Pill, brought down to Glamorgan a commission authorising him to raise on Pembroke's behalf a contingent of five hundred men fully equipped for war. He was joined in this commission by his father, Sir George Herbert of Swansea, and by Edward Lewis and James Button. After the commission had finished its work Sir Thomas Stradling of St. Donat's, already resentful about Pembroke's usurpation of some offices, brought a Star Chamber action against William Herbert for exceeding his authority, which only extended to the tenants and friends of Pembroke, for taking money for armour, for receiving bribes, and for distraining goods—all for 'his own private lucre and gain'. The evidence reveals that large sums of money were certainly raised, that William Herbert took bribes ranging from 10s. to 30s. for letting enrolled men stay at home, and that the levy was thoroughly unpopular—the tax was paid only with 'murmur and grudge'. But it is not possible to be certain that William Herbert was guilty of exceeding his commission, as Stradling alleged.[135]

By this time relations between the Herberts and the Mansels were becoming strained, perhaps because Sir Rice had been granted the office of Chamberlain of South Wales in 1553.[136] Bad feeling turned into open violence in December 1557, when a French ship was wrecked on the shore of Oxwich Bay in Gower. The local villagers, led by Sir Rice Mansel's steward, collected the cargo, sharing some of it among themselves and giving the rest to Mansel. On the following day Sir George Herbert, steward to the earl of Worcester, lord of Gower, got news of the wreck and sent two men to claim it on behalf of his master. Naturally the villagers insisted on keeping their loot and Herbert had to take firmer steps. He began to search houses in the parish and to seize forcibly what he could find. When that had been done his search party went to Oxwich Castle, which was occupied by Edward Mansel, Rice's son, and by Lady Anne Mansel, Edward's aunt, Sir Rice himself being away. Herbert obviously wanted to show young Mansel his place, said that 'he was but a boy that would never be a man' and boasted that he would send him to his father trussed like a cock. Edward as obviously wanted to show his own mettle in his father's absence and stood at the castle gates when Herbert approached. There is some conflict of evidence on what happened next, but in the fighting that broke out Anne Mansel was hit on the head by a stone, from which she died on New Year's Day. Herbert and his men were summoned before the Privy Council, which eventually fined them and ordered the restoration of the goods to Mansel. Watkin John ap Watkin, whose stone-throwing killed Lady Anne, was later pardoned.[137]

Towards the end of Mary's reign animosity began to grow against the head of the Herbert clan, the earl of Pembroke himself. Following his grant of Cardiff castle and the twelve member-lordships of Glamorgan in 1551, Pembroke claimed the rights of a Marcher lord, including the right to demand a 'mise' from the inhabitants. The nature of a 'mise' was at this time obscure and ambiguous. Originally it had been a contribution exacted by a Marcher lord on first succeeding to his lordship; and in Glamorgan and Morgannwg it amounted to 1,000 marks.[138] But by the reign of Mary it was confused with the fine paid by the inhabitants for redeeming the sessions in eyre, a levy which had been abolished by the Act of 1543. Pembroke seems to have been claiming no more than the 1,000 marks due to him in 1551 on change of lord. While his opponents did not deny that such a levy was due, they asserted that it belonged to the monarch, not to the earl. On Elizabeth's accession they were able to argue that Pembroke's claim was an attempt to defraud the Queen, and they thus presented the curious spectacle of subjects loudly clamouring to be allowed to pay the Queen a tax.

Why were they so anxious to be mulcted by the monarch rather than the earl? The dispute over mises evidently reflected deeper fears among the Glamorgan gentry. If Pembroke were able to establish his claim as lord of Glamorgan, he might wield still wider powers, in particular the right to demand a fine for the redemption of the sessions in eyre, which, they said were 'only a comfort and maintenance of wicked and evil-disposed persons'.[139] Pembroke's opponents used two principal arguments against him. First they asserted, on legal and historical grounds, that the lordships granted him in 1551 had always been members of the principal lordships of Glamorgan and Morgannwg, which had been retained in the hands of the crown. Second, they contended that grave practical consequences would follow if Pembroke's claim were allowed. The Queen would lose substantial revenues from mises, fines, escheats, rents and wardships. Justice would be perverted by the appointment of bailiffs of liberties in place of sheriffs, for such bailiffs would empanel corrupt jurors, postpone the execution of writs and allow criminals to escape.[140]

THE 1560s AND 1570s

The fight against the Pembroke interest was begun towards the end of Mary's reign by Morgan Mathew and the men of Glynrhondda and Miskin.[141] A few years after Elizabeth's accession a much stronger, county-wide opposition was formed under the leadership of the Mansels and the Stradlings, who posed as the protectors of the monarch's rights.[142] The legal battle was fought out locally and at Westminster. Pembroke was lucky to have the case heard in the mid-1560s when two of his kinsmen were sheriff: William Herbert of Cogan Pill in 1566/67 and William Mathew, who had married his niece, in 1567/68. This case seems never to have been settled in the first earl's lifetime. But there are signs that it was going against him: Edward Mansel wrote to Sir Thomas Stradling that the earl had been told by Sir Walter Mildmay that he could not gain his ends by *quo warranto* since the claim would be contrary to statute. He might, however, pretend to surrender the case, allow his opponents' attorneys to go home and then persuade the Queen to give him a fresh grant.[143] There is no sign that this happened and in any event the case soon moved on to a fresh stage with the death of the first earl in 1570. Two servants of Edward Mansel and Edward Stradling alleged that Henry, the second earl, had usurped the Queen's rights. Nine years later, in 1580, the case had still not been settled; and there is some evidence that the second earl continued to exact regalian rights until his death in 1601.[144] The dispute was always in the background of the politics of Elizabeth's reign, and seems to have dragged on, in some form or other, until the nineteenth century.[145] Pembroke's general influence was a constant source of attraction and alarm: in most issues of Glamorgan politics under Elizabeth his power was visible in the background, while occasionally specific issues were raised about his Marcher rights.

In 1570, just after the death of the first earl, there began a dispute which had, at the start, nothing to do with Pembroke but came in the end, like so many other conflicts, to involve him. In June of that year William Gerard, justice of Great Sessions for the Glamorgan circuit, acting on the advice of the local justices of the peace, reported to the Lord Keeper that the two coroners, John Llewellyn and Rees Jones, were unfit for office: they were 'serving men convicted before the Council in the Marches of divers affrays'; they were on such bad terms that one of them had lately almost killed the other; and they had made no presentment of murdered persons to Gerard that year.[146] The Lord Keeper accordingly issued writs for the election of two new officers and on October 2, 1570 the freeholders of the county assembled at Llandaff. Although there was wide agreement on the choice of Thomas Turberville and John ap Harry to fill the posts, the sheriff, Thomas Lewis of Y Fan, refused to accept the decision and ordered a fresh election at Llandaff in a month's time. This produced a strong protest from most of the county's leading gentry, who asserted that Lewis wanted both coroners to come from his own part of the shire, the eastern end, and was deliberately putting the western part to inconvenience by calling the meeting once again at Llandaff.

Lewis was then ordered by the Council in the Marches either to admit the newly elected coroners to office or to appear before it. He was soon reported to be refusing to comply with this order, saying that it would merely involve the payment of a fine. At the next county day his ally, William Herbert of High Street, Cardiff, 'as captain of all the inhabitants in or about the same town', paraded the able-bodied men of the town, 'armed in warlike manner', and tried to secure the election of the sheriff's two brothers-in-law.[147] This was refused by the freeholders, who failed, nevertheless, to get their own candidates sworn in. Lewis's next move was to pretend sickness in order to avoid appearing before the Council in the Marches. When the Council sent its own messenger to him he 'at once feigned himself sick in bed', although he had only the day before been 'continually riding about and in perfect health'. Surprisingly enough this delaying tactic seems to have gained Lewis his point. For one of the old coroners, Rees Jones, managed to persuade members of the Privy Council to write to Ludlow on his behalf, urging that he should not be displaced until he had had a chance to answer the charges against him. The Council in the Marches therefore reversed its previous stand and ordered the Glamorgan justices of the peace to send in writing the precise faults committed by the old coroners, who were meanwhile to continue in office.

In the event John Llewellyn remained as coroner until his death and Rees Jones was still in office in 1574. For neither of them were these final years of office very peaceful. Llewellyn was murdered in September 1573 and Jones hurried back from Shrewsbury, where he was attending the Council in the Marches, to hold a view of the body. On Jones's story, which is unsupported by other evidence, he was about to swear in a jury for the inquest, when Rees Gwyn, son of Richard Gwyn, the sheriff, and servant of Sir Edward Mansel, sent him 'letters of defiance and challenge unto the field'. Although Rees Gwyn was imprisoned by the justices of the peace for this conduct, he was soon at large again, thanks to the influence of Mansel and his father, and was able to ambush Jones, who was severely wounded and only escaped with the help of some servants of Sir Edward Stradling.[148] That, at least, is Jones's story.

The death of John Llewellyn gave the earl of Pembroke an opportunity to assert his influence over the choice of a successor. Pembroke's servant, Robert Grove, wrote to Sir Edward Stradling and Sir Edward Mansel asking them not to allow the election of a new coroner

[179]

until the earl was able to consider a candidate who might be both suitable and 'resident in that part of the shire, as is most necessary in that respect'. It looks as if the earl was proposing to support the claims of the eastern parts of the county. Grove pointed out that the earl was a freeholder, a justice of the peace, and *custos rotulorum* in the county, and moreover that he intended to live in Glamorgan: 'therefore there is some cause that his consent and mind should be received in that behalf'.[149] The reply given by Stradling and Mansel showed their alarm at this interference from the Marcher lord. They began by a rather unconvincing piece of evasion, saying that they had only two votes in the election, 'being sure there will be two or three thousand at the least, of whom every one hath as free voice in the choice as each of us'. That done they sharpened their tone, reminded Grove that there had been discussions over such a matter between their fathers and the first earl, and stated openly that they would not grant his request because they did not want the lawful liberties of their county abridged. One concession, they said, might lead to others; and they ended, with some tactical conciliation, by saying that they would not nominate anyone of whom Pembroke disapproved.[150] This, unfortunately, is as far as our evidence takes the story of the coroners, a story which reflects none too well upon the state of local administration.

About a year later the alliance between Stradling and Mansel had been destroyed in the course of various brawls between their kinsmen and followers. Bitter quarrels had broken out between the Stradlings, Turbervilles, Bawdripps and Mathews on one side, with the Mansels, Carnes and Bassetts on the other.[151] In part the trouble seems to have begun with Sir Edward Stradling's resentment that Antony Mansel should have taken one Jenkin Stradling into his service: this was apparently regarded as an insult to the Stradling family honour. Jenkin Stradling himself did not much help matters by 'shouldering' one of Sir Edward's men in the streets of Cowbridge and by saying that 'he would meet with more of the fellows of L. Turbill (Turberville)'. Indeed servants seem to have been responsible for much of the trouble: Antony Mansel's and Edward Stradling's men are described as frowning at one another during the assizes. Once a servant had got himself into a dispute the master felt bound to give support; and Antony Mansel said of Jenkin Stradling that 'while he serveth him (he intends) to defend him from wrong for his cause'.[152]

Details of the brawls are obscure and the different incidents seem to run one into another. The most fitting comment upon them was made by the Council in the Marches, which wrote that 'the chief parties' to the riots were the most to blame since they were men 'of such countenance as ought rather to be conservators of the peace than otherwise'.[153] Relations between Sir Edward Stradling and Thomas Carne became so embittered that the earl of Pembroke intervened in order to prevent what he called 'this boiling hatred'. On coming to Cardiff to pacify the county Pembroke told Stradling to attend with a small company only, 'and those of the most conformablest minds to quietness', leaving behind the men hurt in earlier frays, who might be expected to take revenge.[154]

By the end of 1575 Pembroke had apparently calmed the dispute between Edward Stradling and the Carnes. But other tensions were unresolved. On February 11, 1576 there was a riot at Cowbridge, with the followers of William Herbert and John Thomas on one side, and those of William Bassett and William Carne on the other. Several men, including a petty constable, were hurt, and the Council in the Marches complained that the affray was 'a great disquiet to the whole country and (as it is thought) likely by parts taking to work division in the country to renew their wonted malice and outrages'.[155] Rumblings of these disputes could still be heard in the following summer when one of the Bassetts threatened to stir up again all the controversies settled by the earl of Pembroke. Apparently Bassett had brought various legal actions against Stradling and his friends. This led Pembroke to promise his help to Stradling. He told Bassett that he heard 'ye go about to unrip all the controversies and variances agreed by me' and that he would stand in his way if Bassett went on with his law-suits.[156]

THE CARDIFF BRIDGE DISPUTE

The brawls of the gentry were, however, soon stilled by a major issue which affected their purses.[157] This was the prolonged controversy over payment for rebuilding the bridge which carried the road from Cardiff to Cowbridge over the river Taff. After its collapse in 1575, the Cardiff authorities insisted that they were not liable for the repair, since the bridge lay outside the town's boundaries, while the shire insisted that the bridge lay within those limits. The shire offered, however, to make a large *ex gratia* contribution of £500 without admitting any responsibility, and the town accepted this offer. All therefore seemed settled when, to the surprise of the leading gentlemen of Glamorgan, news came that the knight of the shire, William Mathew, was promoting a parliamentary bill to fix responsibility for payment upon the whole county. This was resisted by the shire, not so much to save the immediate cost of the present operation—for they were prepared to pay heavily towards it—as to prevent every other borough in Glamorgan from handing over responsibility. Cardiff Bridge thus became a test case.

The gentlemen of the shire mostly dropped their quarrels to fight this threat, and the lead was taken jointly by Sir Edward Mansel, Thomas Carne, and Sir Edward Stradling, while support was given by most of the other leading families of Glamorgan—Lewises, Bassetts, Buttons, Prices, and so on.[158] Only two heads of families stood out from this united front: William Mathew of Radyr and Sir William Herbert of Swansea. One can merely guess at their motives. Both of them were related to the earl of Pembroke, Herbert through his father and Mathew through his wife; and Pembroke as lord of Cardiff was disposed to protect the town. Thus the Herbert interest apparently stood with Cardiff against the rest of the shire.

The gentlemen of the county realized that the influence of the earl was likely to be decisive and they accordingly petitioned him to use his good offices with the borough, assuring him rather obsequiously that their original offer had been made, 'your lordship may assure yourself, in respect of you'.[159] To this Pembroke returned a very sharp answer, reprimanding Mansel for hindering the repairs. According to Mansel this reply only made the gentlemen of the shire more angry and a new meeting, called at Cowbridge in April 1579, refused at first to make even the *ex gratia* payment of £500. Mansel depicted himself as the mediating force in all this and asserted that by his efforts the meeting was persuaded to agree to £500 being raised while the judges were being consulted.

Pembroke and Sir Henry Sidney, lord president of the Council in the Marches, having consulted the judges, who pronounced in favour of the town, then proposed a compromise by which Cardiff should pay £30 for every £100 raised by the shire. To this the county rather grudgingly agreed on condition that no Act of Parliament should be promoted. However, an agreement in principle was one thing, actual collection of the money quite another, and in October 1580, ten months after this agreement, Sir Edward Stradling was complaining that the greater part of the levy was still uncollected. Probably as a result of this delay, the town of Cardiff, still without its bridge, reverted to the earlier plan of a private Act of Parliament. In February 1581, William Mathew and David Roberts, M.P. for the borough, brought in a bill to apportion the cost of repairs between county and town in the ratio of five to one, a proportion rather less favourable to the county than that agreed earlier. But the actual proportion was less important to the shire than the general principle that they would henceforth be under an obligation to contribute. The leading gentry urgently petitioned Sir Henry Sidney, the earl of Pembroke, the earl of Leicester and the Privy Council itself to prevent the bill going through. But their efforts failed and the bill became law at the end of the session.

Pembroke certainly resented the opposition of the shire and most of his anger fell upon Sir Edward Mansel, whose chief offence had been publicly to reveal the earl's promise that he would guarantee the shire against an Act of Parliament. Such a revelation was taken by Pembroke and his friends as a deliberate slight upon his honour. However strongly Mansel might argue that he had done nothing but remind the earl of his promise and that the real cause of all the trouble was the malice of William Mathew, the Herberts continued to accuse him of impugning Pembroke's credit and, equally serious, of urging 'this matter to a popular faction'.[160] The earl of Leicester, asked by Mansel to mediate for him, brushed aside the request with the curt dismissal that 'I cannot but marvel that a man of your experience would take such a course as you have done'.[161]

Several important elements are revealed within this conflict. The struggle between borough and county was a common one at that time, especially when the share of financial responsibility was in question. Superimposed upon it was the pattern of rivalry among the Glamorgan gentry: the Mathew-Herbert alliance was a significant element in the town's victory and Sir Edward Mansel certainly felt that William Mathew's personal malice had embroiled him with the earl of Pembroke. Above all the incident emphasises the weight of Pembroke's influence. Throughout the struggle his voice seems to have been decisive. When the leaders of the shire first offered an *ex gratia* payment they claimed that it was done out of respect to the earl; when Cardiff refused to compromise, the gentry petitioned Pembroke; and when Pembroke himself turned against them the gentry, by appealing to Sidney and Leicester for mediation, tried to win him back rather than oppose him. Only at the end, when the fight seemed desperate and Mansel's prestige as a county leader was at stake, did the gentry risk direct opposition to the earl.

QUARRELS OF THE 1580s

The principal episodes of the next decade all demonstrate the influence of Pembroke and the difficulty of opposing his will. The first of them again involved Sir Edward Mansel as the earl's principal antagonist; and curiously enough its occasion was another ship-wreck.[162] On December 28, 1583 a ship owned by the merchant Francis Shaxton was wrecked about two miles from Mansel's house at Margam. Mansel claimed that the site of the wreck lay within his manor of Hafod-y-porth and on December 29 his brother Antony went down to take possession of the goods. He soon met competition in the person of Pembroke's servant, George Williams, who swore that the wreck lay within his master's manor of Avan. Next day Sir Edward visited the ship with four servants, in order to keep Williams off. Each side later accused the other of using force, but in the welter of conflicting testimony one can say only that although there was probably some violence, the action was a good deal more restrained than the earlier affray at Oxwich Castle. The interests of the unfortunate Shaxton were for some time forgotten, until he appealed for help to the Privy Council. Letters were then sent to both Mansel and Pembroke ordering them to save as many of the goods as possible. Pembroke responded reasonably to this and appears to have given Shaxton back his goods; but Mansel refused to surrender anything until his dispute with the earl was ended. On the whole Pembroke comes better out of the limited evidence than his rival.

In the second episode of the 1580s, the struggle for the hand of Barbara Gamage, Pembroke's role lay in the background of the action, but may well have been decisive for the outcome.[163] As the sole heiress of John Gamage, lord of Coety, Barbara was thought an excellent match by several important families in south Wales and the Marches. She was courted by Thomas, heir to Sir Henry Jones of Abermarlais, Carmarthenshire, by Sir James Whitney, of Whitney, Herefordshire, and most significantly of all by Herbert Croft, grandson of Sir James Croft of Croft castle, Herefordshire. The Croft interest had several advantages over its rivals, for Sir James was not only the great-uncle of John Gamage and a man of influence in the Marches, but had a voice at court as privy councillor, comptroller of the royal household and political ally of Lord Burghley. It is thus not surprising to find that by the late summer of 1584 the Crofts were confident of success.

At this point—on September 8, 1584—Barbara's father died and the girl herself was taken into the custody of her cousin, Sir Edward Stradling, who had already promised his support to the Crofts. Herbert Croft then received a thoroughly disagreeable shock when he went down to visit his intended bride and was denied any sight of her by Lady Stradling. His grandfather's riposte was instantly to drum up support at court, and Stradling was bombarded with conflicting orders and advice. The Privy Council ordered him to hand Barbara over to George Herbert, the sheriff, who was thought to be favourable to the Crofts; Lord Burghley, acting as Master of the Court of Wards, commanded him to surrender her to Sir John Carne; and Barbara's two influential uncles, Sir Walter Raleigh and Lord Howard of Effingham, told Stradling to do nothing without their consent.

Faced with this barrage of admonition, Stradling might have been expected to walk cautiously and slowly. Instead, he allowed Barbara to be courted by an altogether new suitor, Robert Sidney, younger brother of the more famous Philip and son to Sir Henry Sidney, lord president of the Council in the Marches. Powerful as was Croft's backing in Wales and at court, the Sidney faction showed itself even stronger. Sir Henry himself had married Mary Dudley, sister to Robert, earl of Leicester, the principal favourite of the Queen, and his elder son, Philip, had married Frances, daughter to Sir Francis Walsingham, secretary of state. This allied him firmly with the Leicester faction at court, which had long been rivals to Lord Burghley and Sir James Croft. The clash over the hand of Barbara Gamage was thus in part a struggle between court factions; but it also involved more local rivalries, for Sir James Croft was one of Sidney's principal opponents in his government of the Marches.

The brief and bitter struggle ended with the marriage of Robert Sidney to Barbara Gamage on September 23. Why did Stradling ignore the commands of so many powerful courtiers, indeed of the Privy Council itself? The answer is clearly to be found in a letter to Stradling from Sir Francis Walsingham, who had previously ordered the instant dispatch

THE GAMAGES AND THEIR RELATIONS

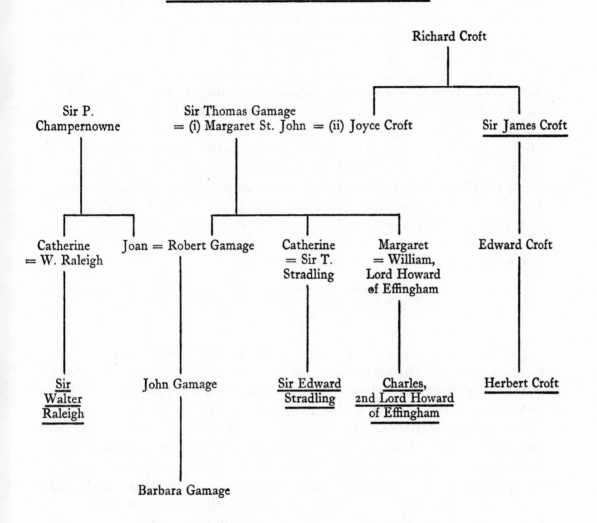

Those underlined took part in the marriage contest.

of the girl to court. Now Walsingham wrote to cancel this command: 'being now secretly given to understand that for the good will you bear unto the Earl of Pembroke, you mean to further what you may young Mr. Robert Sidney, I cannot but encourage you to proceed therein'.[164] His words give the key to Stradling's action, which apparently proceeded from 'the good will you bear unto the Earl of Pembroke'. For Pembroke had married Mary, the sister of Philip and Robert Sidney, and naturally gave his support to their cause. The speed and confidence with which Stradling acted, in defiance of all the orders from Court, are striking tribute to Pembroke's influence in Glamorgan.

The match ensured a useful niche in Glamorgan society for the Sidney family and was quickly followed by the election of Robert as knight of the shire for Glamorgan at the surprisingly youthful age of twenty-one. More important, it was the start of a long and happy married life for bride and bridegroom. Married within fifteen days of her father's death, as the result of political pressure, to a man that she had probably never seen before, Barbara Gamage made an excellent wife and mother. Robert Sidney's letters to her display an affection rare in husbands of that day; the beautiful family group at Penshurst shows her in the midst of her charming family; and Ben Jonson epitomised her virtue in his poem on the Sidney home at Penshurst:

> These, Penshurst, are thy praise and yet not all,
> Thy lady's noble, fruitful, chaste, withall.
> His children thy great lord may call his owne,
> A fortune, in this age, but rarely known.

Their respective parts in the Cardiff Bridge controversy and the Gamage match might have made William Mathew and Edward Stradling confident of Pembroke's lasting favour. But it was not to be. Pembroke's jealous concern about his rights in the shire and his protection of the privileges of Cardiff brought down his anger upon them both. In the summer of 1586 Stradling and Mathew, who held a joint commission to investigate pirates, ordered the bailiffs of Cardiff to send some suspects for questioning and appointed some townsmen to perform watch and ward. The bailiffs refused the first order and forbade the appointed men to watch. This recalcitrance, together with some earlier evidence, led Stradling and Mathew to conclude that the officers of Cardiff were in league with the pirates, and they reported in that sense to the Privy Council.[165]

Pembroke countered with a tirade. He was pleased, he said with ponderous irony, to hear of justices doing their duty, but he could only suppose that this particular report sprang from malice. Did Stradling and Mathew believe themselves to be the only conscientious officers? 'Are you alone carefully minded to respect the good of your country, or alone authorised to chasten such faults, or continually accustomed to use such integrity in your offices that neither you may be thought for favour to wink at, or for malice to pry into, offences?' On the contrary, it was known that 'some riots, unlawful assemblies, many frays and bloodsheds, yea peradventure bloody actions, have not been not only unpunished, but bolstered by you'—Pembroke's anger was such that he overloaded his sentence with negatives! He insisted that they should have first reported the matter to him, instead of implying to the Privy Council that he was incompetent. Moreover, he claimed that they were quite mistaken in supposing that Cardiff's resistance to their commands was a sign of guilt, and pronounced that the bailiffs were rightly jealous of the town's liberties and properly unwilling to 'allow of them for fit watchmen in the night, of whose unruly bloody behaviours they had of late certain experience in the day'.[166]

In reply Stradling and Mathew began with an appeal to the highest authority of all. At the Day of Judgment, they asserted, God would witness that they had meant no malice. Until then they could only point, as men unjustly accused, to the commission that they had held so long. As for the bailiffs of Cardiff, they were seeking to erect as a right what had previously been allowed as a convenience, when earlier commissioners, having no house in the area, had examined townsmen within the walls, a practice that imposed no obligation on their successors.[167]

Here the matter seems to have ended, for we hear no more of the dispute beyond the advice of Secretary Walsingham ten months later that Stradling should reconcile himself to the earl. As far as Sir Edward was concerned no great damage seems to have been done; but William Mathew was in harder case. A year before the piracy episode his followers had been involved in a brawl with the servants of Thomas Lewis of Y Fan, in which one of Lewis's men, Roger Phillip, had been killed. The queen's attorney at the Council in the Marches alleged that although indictments were made out against the murderers William Mathew had 'conferrated' with his followers 'to hide, conceal and cloak' the murder; and an action was accordingly brought against Mathew at Ludlow.[168] Mathew's defence was typical of his time. He began by refusing to attend the Council in the Marches, on the ground that he was too ill to travel so far. When even his own counsel refused to swear to the truth of this, he went up to London and asked help of the Privy Council. He told Lord Burghley that Pembroke was an unsuitable choice as President of the Council in the Marches in view of his interests in south Wales. The country, he said, did not need a 'great and mighty lord to terrify, but a temperate, prudent and a learned judge to govern us'.[169] In particular Mathew pointed out that the case in question had already been settled by Sir Henry Sidney, the previous Lord President. As a result of this protest the Privy Council ordered a stay of action by the Council in the Marches. But this was the limit of Mathew's success, for in May 1587 the Privy Council found him unable to prove any of his allegations and had him imprisoned. They also, at the request of the Lord President, transferred

[187]

the case from the Council in the Marches to the justices of assize. Mathew's next step was to demand a delay on the ground that the sheriff, Thomas Lewis of Y Fan, could not be trusted to empanel an impartial jury. This request was granted by the Privy Council, who thus aroused Pembroke's anger. This delay, he said, was prejudicial to justice and to the credit of the queen's officers. In his view the fact that the sheriff had been the master of the murdered man was less important than the face that might be lost if Mathew got his way. The Privy Council then decided to have the case heard by a Herefordshire jury, which would be more likely to be impartial.

Shortly after, William Mathew died and his heirs showed no objection to the trial of the case in Glamorgan. The Privy Council therefore switched it back again to that county. But now, according to Thomas Atkins, queen's attorney at the Council in the Marches, another change took place and Pembroke himself began to grow lukewarm in the prosecution. Atkins complained that 'my silence is now herein imposed, the expectation of the country for justice is deceived, my poor credit . . . is to be impaired'.[170] All this because, in his opinion, Pembroke had been bought off with the sum of £500 and the concession by the Mathew family of Pembroke's claim to the wardship of William Mathew of Llandaff. It is impossible to discover how much, if any, truth lay behind this charge.

THE CARDIFF RIOTS, 1593–98

The Mathew case saw Pembroke's last major appearance in Glamorgan politics: the principal episode of the 1590s, the Cardiff riots, concerned his cousin, Sir William Herbert of Swansea, rather than himself. These Cardiff riots form a series of affrays and disputes between 1593 and 1598. There is a great deal of evidence about them, but most of the testimony is unreliable and conflicting. We can be certain that violence was used, but we cannot always say who was to blame.

The first, rather isolated, incident was an affray in October 1593, arising presumably from the long-standing Lewis-Mathew feud, between the servants of Edmund Mathew and those of Thomas Lewis of Cardiff, ending in the death of one of the Lewis party, Thomas Comyn.[171] The offenders were first indicted in Herefordshire, but this case was moved to Glamorgan in order to give that unruly county a taste of justice. The grand jury found a true bill, but when the case came for trial the petty jury found the principal accused guilty only of manslaughter, so that he could and did plead benefit of clergy.

The second set of incidents came in February 1595 and had no apparent connection with the first.[172] Three servants of Sir William Herbert—John Miller, controller of the port of Cardiff, Phillip Jones, and Richard Thomas—were imprisoned by Nicholas Hawkins, one of the Cardiff bailiffs, for assault and contempt. When Sir William's brother,

Nicholas, heard of this he tried to persuade the bailiffs to allow bail and on their refusal sent about eighteen armed men to achieve his purpose. These men occupied the town hall and shouted to the bailiffs: 'you were offered bail for the said prisoners, but it would not be accepted, and therefore now we will bail them ourselves'.[173] Charles Froude, Hawkins's colleague, rang the town bell to summon his fellow burgesses to give help and a general mêlée followed, in which the prisoners were freed, a Herbert follower, Llewellyn David, 'did with his sword very cruelly cut and slit the nose of . . . (a) woman in such sort as the same did hang down over her lips',[174] and the same Llewellyn David was given a wound from which he later died. Sir William Herbert then persuaded his relative, Edward Kemeys the sheriff, to empanel a packed coroner's jury which falsely indicted Nicholas Hawkins of Llewellyn David's murder, while Herbert himself saw that the townsmen's accusation of riot was thrown out at a petty sessions, over which he himself presided.[175]

Behind these apparently purposeless brawls lay sharp hostility between the townspeople and the local gentry. One of the burgesses, Roger Spencer, was accused of saying 'that if the townsmen of Cardiff held together they were able to beat all the gentlemen in the shire'.[176] While he denied having said this he admitted to remarking that if the townsmen stuck together they would beat 'all the serving men in the town' into their masters' houses. Sir William Herbert, for his part, seems to have resented the town's independence from his control: he was reported to have said of the bailiffs that 'if the earl of Pembroke did not stick close unto them, he would make there should be but few bailiffs in Cardiff thereafter'.[177] There is no sign here of any friendship between the two branches of the Herbert clan: perhaps Pembroke's ill-health throughout the 1590s allowed the local gentry to interfere without inhibition in the affairs of Cardiff.

In the following September a third dispute broke out within the town, this time over the election of bailiffs. Hawkins and Froude, acting on the advice of Thomas Bawdripp, an ally of the Mathew family, managed to have Nicholas Herbert and two of his followers disfranchised. When Herbert forced his way into the town hall, where the election was being held, he was pushed out by the townsmen, who proceeded to elect Froude as bailiff for a further year.[178] Here is clear indication of the town's resentment at the influence of local gentry.

The fourth and most violent phase of the story came during the first five months of 1596, with a running fight between the Mathews on one side, and the Herberts and Lewises on the other. Charge and counter-charge were presented to the courts and without a judgment in Star Chamber one cannot for certain know the truth. But often one can find some common ground. Generally both sides agree about the place, date and fact of a riot; they differ on the question of blame and the numbers involved.

The first brawl came on Saturday January 31, 1596, when three Lewis servants, William Lambert, Watkin Mathew and Howell Evans, clashed with Lewis ap Evan Higgins, Walter Cook and Thomas ap John, followers of the Mathews. According to the Lewis version of the incident, Lambert was lured away by Higgins to Castle Green in Cardiff, set upon and left for dead, while Watkin Mathew, who tried to keep the peace, was assaulted and his 'very shin bone was beaten and broken into shivers'. In the Mathew story, Higgins was enticed away and assaulted, after which the rioters attacked Thomas ap John and smashed the house of Edmund Mathew.[179]

Various small affrays followed in February and March, but each of them is known only in the unsupported evidence of one side or the other. The next major riot, about which both factions have something to say, occurred on March 26. In the Mathew version, Edmund Mathew was returning to Cardiff from London when the Lewis faction, joined now by Sir William and Nicholas Herbert, tried to ambush him. When the ambush failed, Mathew escaped into his house, where he was besieged. The Lewis story is quite different. Edmund Mathew was marching towards Cardiff with a hundred armed men and on reaching Michaelston tried to lure out some of Lewis's men by playing a noisy game of football. When this failed he and his men marched on until they met a band of soldiers on their way to Ireland, having been pressed for service by Sir William Herbert and Edward Lewis. Mathew turned the soldiers about, entered Cardiff and assaulted some of Lewis's servants in Shoemaker Street.[180]

Throughout April the followers of the main protagonists assaulted, fought and ambushed one another, until the next major clash at Cowbridge Quarter Sessions on April 28. Unfortunately we have only the Mathew story of this episode. According to this version, all the justices of the peace left the Quarter Sessions, except Sir William Herbert, Nicholas Herbert and Edward Lewis, who struck out most of the names empanelled for the grand jury and put in men of their own, who found a true bill against one of the Mathew faction, John Thomas. At about the same time a muster was held, at which only the men needed for service abroad should have been paraded. In spite of this order Edward Lewis marched six or seven hundred men from Llandaff to St. Lythan's Down, 'observing all the way a very warlike form of marching', and brought them back into Llandaff, when Edmund Mathew and his friends shut themselves into the castle.[181]

The final incidents arose two years later out of the Star Chamber suit between the Herberts and the bailiffs of Cardiff. Two members of the Herbert faction, Edward Howell and William Jones, were said to have assaulted two of their accusers. The charge is unsupported and the story is of a familiar type.[182]

One feature of all these incidents is the constant resort by most of the contenders to the law-courts. Between 1594 and 1599 ten suits arising out of these quarrels were brought to Star Chamber alone. Unfortunately we know the results of only two of these actions, Hawkins and Froude *versus* Herbert, and Hawkins *versus* Kemeys. Sir William and his friends were all found guilty of their misdemeanours. He himself was fined 1,000 marks; Nicholas Herbert and Edward Kemeys were each fined £500 and removed from the commission of the peace; seven defendants were fined £200 each and ordered to stand in the pillory; and fifteen defendants were fined 100 marks each. In addition Sir William and Nicholas Herbert had between them to pay £200 damages to the bailiffs, while Kemeys had to pay 100 marks damages to Hawkins. Thus did the 'great blazing star commonly seen at high noon within the meridian of Middlesex' deal with the offenders.[183]

THE EARLY-SEVENTEENTH CENTURY

The period from about 1600 until the outbreak of the Civil War seems to have been much quieter than the reign of Elizabeth. Violent assaults were still, naturally enough, being made; but most of them were committed by lesser gentry and yeomen. For instance, in 1608 Thomas Williams, a yeoman of Wenvoe, complained that he had been assaulted near Cardiff Bridge by Thomas Philip, also a yeoman, Walter Cook, prominent as one of Edmund Mathew's followers in the Cardiff riots a few years before, and various others. The defendants admitted the fighting but alleged that it had been begun by Williams.[184] The early-Stuart period yields few examples of major feuds between the leading gentry.[185] A Chancery suit brought by Sir H. Billingsley against one of the Mathew family reached a climax in 1611 when Billingsley was given a warrant to enter the disputed house and lands. On the arrival of the serjeant-at-arms one of Edmund Mathew's daughters resisted the execution of the writ by throwing stones at the sheriff's men.[186] Later in James's reign Henry Dodington esquire, of Bristol, charged Sir Thomas Mansel with various offences, of which he was acquitted of all but one: the court found that 'he had for three years space set his coach in an out aisle of a large church where lime and rubbish was used to be laid', and fined him £100 for this.[187] But neither of these cases suggests a major feud.

The only significant feud was the prolonged quarrel between the Prichards of Gelli-gaer, near Merthyr Tydfil, and the followers of Lewis of Y Fan. The origin of this dispute seems to lie in the killing of one Lewis William in 1601. Edward William Lewis, kinsman to the dead man, succeeded in getting Thomas ap Evan Rees hanged for the offence and thus brought down on himself the anger of Rees's master, Edward Prichard, J.P. Edward William Lewis however found himself a strong protector by marrying his daughter to the second son of Sir Edward Lewis of Y Fan. There followed the usual sequence of charge and counter-charge, in which riots, assaults and ambushes were copiously alleged.[188]

[191]

N

Probably the quarrel between Edward Prichard's son, David, and William Bawdripp of Splott was connected with this dispute. In the course of it Bawdripp, according to Prichard, called him 'a scurvy, saucy fellow' and challenged him to a duel.[189]

The only other quarrel in this period worth mentioning was the charge brought by John Stradling of St. Donat's against the Bassett family. He alleged that while acting as sheriff he had tried to secure the arrest of William Bassett's servant, Rice Williams, and that Bassett had hindered his bailiffs.[190]

Compared with the frequent and bitter feuds of the Elizabethan period these bickerings are trivial; and the main dispute, between Lewises and Prichards, centred on the more mountainous and inaccessible part of the county. It is interesting to recall the comment made in 1609 by Lord Eure, President of the Council in the Marches, after he had toured Glamorgan and Monmouth, 'The gentlemen whereof (Glamorganshire especially)', he said, 'are well educated, of great livelihood, and very potent in the places where they inhabit'. 'I understood also', he went on, 'that the County of Monmouth was wholly divided almost into factions . . .'.[191] We can believe Eure when he says that the Glamorgan gentry were very powerful in their own localities; and we can believe also his implication that by the reign of James I they were less faction-ridden than their Monmouthshire neighbours.

THE STUART MONARCHY AND THE SHIRE

With the calming of the major feuds between the gentry, interest shifts to the impact of the central government upon the shire. At two points within the century 1536–1642 the crown made heavy demands upon the resources of Glamorgan. The first of these was the period of war between 1585 and 1604, when levies from the shire were required in large numbers to fill the English armies abroad.[192] As far as one can calculate 385 men were levied from Glamorgan for foreign service between 1593 and 1599. Then, from 1604 until 1624, there was a lull: few troops were needed and the government's interest in the militia amounted largely to the reiteration of pious hopes.[193]

With the government's commitment to war in 1624 and the succession of a more vigorous king in the following year a sharper and more urgent tone conveyed the Privy Council's orders to the shires. In October 1626 commissions were issued throughout the realm for loans to be raised for the crown from all men able to pay: those refusing to lend would be reported to the Privy Council. Over much of England there was sharp opposition: in Gloucestershire, for instance, the Lord President of the Council in the Marches found 'many that did refuse', some of whom 'refuse to subscribe, lend or to be bound to appear before Council to answer their contempts'.[194] But in Glamorgan by contrast Lord Herbert, son to the earl of Worcester, the lord-lieutenant of the shire, found the business going on cheerfully and successfully, with complaint directed, not against the King, but against the members of parliament who had 'failed in their promises and deceived His Majesty's expectation in not giving the supply necessary to a business of so high consequence'. Such acquiescence was to be typical of the Glamorgan gentry.[195]

The forced loan was only a prelude to the tougher measures of the 1630s. The aftermath of war, the disruption of trade and the poor harvests of 1629 and 1630 focused the government's attention upon the problems of poverty, famine and disorder; and in January 1631 the Privy Council issued its Book of Orders to the magistracy of every shire in the kingdom. Here was an unprecedented attempt to enforce upon the local governors a comprehensive policy for the effective operation of the poor laws, the punishment of offenders against penal statutes and the dispatch of regular progress reports to the Privy Council.[196] Only one such report has survived from Glamorgan and that one is made to the justices of assize. It reveals that the justices of the peace of the county met on March 24, 1631 and divided themselves into groups for monthly meetings. At the first of such meetings the justices of the peace for three of the eastern hundreds—Kibbor, Caerphilly and Llantrisant—called before them all chief constables, petty constables and overseers of the poor in the area, and ordered them to make reports on the execution of their office. The first results of such reports were then sent up: in Kibbor, to take one instance, sixty persons were apprehended as vagrants and returned to the place of their birth or their last abode; seven alehouses were suppressed; and forty-six persons were bound apprentice.[197] The signs are that the government's orders were being obeyed and that the justices of the peace were co-operating with good grace. Unfortunately there are no more signs thereafter. Whether this indicates that the Glamorgan gentry were slack in execution of their duty or whether the reports have been lost one cannot be sure; but the second seems more likely, since reports were made to justices of Great Sessions rather than to Privy Council and may thus more easily have disappeared.

Pressure on the militia was heavy from 1624. The first need was to provide levies for foreign service.[198] To this the deputy-lieutenants responded cheerfully, reporting that the hundred footmen levied for Buckingham's disastrous expedition of 1627 had been clothed in coats of good broad cloth lined with baize. They regretted only that they had been unable to include in the group any archers, as ordered, owing to the long neglect of that weapon; but they announced their joy that long-bows 'begin again to come into esteem'.[199] With the coming of peace attention turned from foreign levies to building up that 'perfect militia' of which the King and his privy councillors dreamed. On April 30, 1629 the council ordered a general review of the trained bands, with particular efforts to modernise equipment and to improve the standards of the cavalry; and in subsequent years these instructions were repeated.[200]

The Glamorgan deputy-lieutenants showed no resentment at these commands. They wrote on October 30, 1631 that they were carrying out the Council's order that weapons be 'according to the modern fashion', and in the following year they were able to report the task completed. They also said that men liable to serve in the bands were being compelled to parade in person, or in the person of sons and nephews, 'and not with servants'.[201] Year by year they announced that all was well, both with the trained bands and with the untrained men from whom levies for foreign service could be drawn. Such brief and complacent reports only arouse suspicion. The task of creating an effective militia in years of peace was exceptionally tough, bristling with obstacles and pitfalls. It is hardly credible that all these should have been so easily avoided.[202]

Since the Privy Council seems to have accepted without question these optimistic accounts, the training of the militia may well have been little burden on the local governors and the inhabitants of Glamorgan. Such was not the case with Ship Money. The first writ, issued in 1634, caused no stir. The second, of 1635, demanded more money and made clear to all that they were faced with an annual tax. The task of collection, thrown upon the sheriff, became a heavy load. In many counties of England opposition sprang up quickly: first, in the form of protest at the distribution of the tax between different areas; then in the refusal of individuals to pay; and finally in the reluctance of the sheriff and his officers to collect.[203] Glamorgan however, and indeed most of Wales, seemed remarkably acquiescent. In 1635 the sheriff, Watkin Loughor, reported on November 26 that he had collected the whole of the county's assessment of £1,389, demanded on August 12, though the £60 levied in Cardiff seems not to have been in his hands until a little later. He was soon commended by the Privy Council for his diligence—not surprisingly, since Glamorgan was among the earliest counties in the kingdom to have paid in full.[204] Next year, 1636, the same sum, £1,449, was levied on both shire and borough, and once more was paid in full within a few months; and in 1638/39 Glamorgan had paid its contribution before any other county in the kingdom.[205] John Carne, sheriff in 1639-40, was the first to voice a protest—but of the mildest possible kind. He said that he had been asked at first to pay the sum involved by April 1, 1640, and that then, on January 12, had come a letter demanding the full sum by 20 February. This had proved impossible; but, even so, all except the Cardiff contribution was in by March 22. Such compliance was perhaps typical of Wales, where Anglesey, Monmouth and Radnorshire showed themselves as punctilious as Glamorgan in the levy, and where only Pembrokeshire and Carmarthenshire showed any recalcitrance. It contrasts sharply with many English counties, where buck-passing and outright refusal dogged the efforts of the unlucky sheriffs.[206]

Even Glamorgan's anxiety to please was diminished by the next crisis. In February 1639 the King announced to his subjects that the rebellious posture of his Scottish subjects compelled him to raise an army in defence. Glamorgan was to levy 100 men, fifty fewer than the normal complement demanded from the shire in past years for Irish service; but in April Glamorgan's quota was raised to its more normal 150.[207] There is no sign of opposition to this demand and indeed the quality of the south Wales levies earned favourable comment. The military requirements of the Second Bishops' War in 1640 were to prove more testing. Wales was to supply 2,000 men—by contrast with the 600 finally asked in the previous year; and Glamorgan's share was raised to 200.[208] By May 20 the Glamorgan levies were assembled at Cardiff, ready to march north. Unfortunately the Privy Council had, too late, decided to put off the date of the northwards march, and the men were consequently kept inactive at the rendezvous. The deputy-lieutenants were now in a quandary, since their warrants only authorised them to levy coat-and-conduct money up to May 20. However they paid the soldiers out of their own pockets until further authority came to enable them to raise more money from the shire, 'notwithstanding the heavy groans of the complaining inhabitants'.[209] For a month the soldiers were allowed to disperse, with strict orders to assemble again on July 1. This they did; but the deputy-lieutenants were still left with the problem of coat-and-conduct money. It had been raised by the county in the first instance, on the optimistic understanding that it would be repaid by the crown. Sadly the deputies asked for the help of the Lord President at Ludlow, the earl of Bridgwater, 'tendering our humble suit in the behalf of a poor country complaining by reason of the heavy charges there already borne'.[210] It was the nearest that the local governors of the shire came to open protest during these years.

TOWARDS CIVIL WAR

In this summer of 1640 there occurred one other incident which may have been significant for Glamorgan history. On July 17 the King wrote to the earl of Bridgwater telling him to order his deputy-lieutenants in Herefordshire and south Wales to give all possible aid to the earl of Worcester, 'who has been entrusted with some secret service'.[211] When Bridgwater had taken office at Ludlow, some nine years before, the earl of Worcester had been deprived of his lieutenancy in Glamorgan and Monmouth, presumably on account of his recusancy. Worcester's son had then protested to the King against his father's indignity, stressing the affront put upon him by being termed a 'jack out of office', urging the value of the earl's past services and present loyalty, and pointing out the waste of the twelve 'great horses' which he kept in his stable. To this plea Charles had responded, in 1636, by ordering Bridgwater to treat Worcester with respect and to consult him on all appointments to deputy-lieutenant. Now, in 1640, he at last gave recognition to Worcester's loyalty and stature. We do not know what this 'secret service' involved; but there are grounds for thinking that its consequences were unfortunate for Charles, arousing as it did a general fear of a Catholic force under the earls of Strafford and Worcester.[212]

By September 1640 Charles was desperate enough to summon all the trained bands to the north; and Bridgwater was responding with gloomy comments on the state of Wales. Although his deputies assured him of their diligence, he thought that ill spirits had walked in his lieutenancy during the past year. Many feared that when the trained men left the country, 'mischief' might happen.[213]

There is nothing to connect Glamorgan in particular with this alarm. But an episode of the following year shows how low the authority of government had sunk, even in so loyal a county. Two special bailiffs were sent by the Council in the Marches into Glamorgan to arrest one Robert Russe of Llandeilo Tal-y-bont. Russe assembled round him about forty persons, who 'most of them being weaponed with staves, reaping hooks and other weapons, did not only then and there in forcible manner take away and rescue the said defendant (Russe) from the said special bailiffs, and thereby escaped, but did assault the said special bailiffs with their said weapons then and there, and gave them several blows upon their bodies . . .'.[214]

Even so, when war broke out Glamorgan was predominantly loyal to the King. True, the knight of the shire in the Long Parliament, Philip Herbert, son of the earl of Pembroke and Montgomery, fought for Parliament. But he hardly seems to have represented the shire in any real sense, for the Pembroke influence had been on the wane in Glamorgan since the succession in 1630 of the fourth earl, who evinced little interest in Welsh affairs. Thus deprived of any influential leadership on the spot, the Parliamentary cause was ineffective.[215] The shire's representative in the Short Parliament, Sir Edward Stradling, fought for the King; and William Herbert of Cogan Pill, M.P. for Cardiff in the Short and the Long Parliaments, was one of the hard royalist core which supported Strafford in 1640–41.[216] Sir Edward was captured at Edgehill and William Herbert died there. They were both typical of their county, for Bassetts, Aubreys, Carnes, Kemeys, and Mansels all followed the royal cause.

This survey of Glamorgan history in the years leading to the Civil War raises some interesting problems. We are used to envisaging the the great bulk of the political nation as standing opposed to the King's policy in 1640 and as dividing only when the parliamentary leaders pushed their demands to unacceptable lengths in the latter half of 1641; and in some regions such was undoubtedly the situation.[217] But Glamorgan was a county apparently little stirred to anger or even to reluctance by the demands of 'personal rule'. Of course, the evidence is incomplete: deprived of any corpus of political correspondence for this shire the historian has to rely for information upon state papers. But even when allowance has been made for this, the willing acquiescence of Glamorgan's local rulers in the burdens laid upon them stands in striking contrast to the foot-dragging, the grumbling and the downright opposition of many English shires.[218]

Why were the Glamorgan gentry so acquiescent? Perhaps this county, lying relatively far from the seat of government, was less heavily burdened and overseen than English shires of the midlands and the south, and certainly it escaped entirely one of the most distasteful grievances of the southern English counties—billeting. Perhaps, too, accident deprived it of any powerful leader, for Pembroke and his son were uninterested in Welsh affairs, while no one else combined the necessary standing at court with a sense of grievance: Glamorgan had no counterpart to Somerset's Sir Robert Phelips. Above all, it was relatively free from the two most powerful forces on the Parliamentary side—the influence of London and the ideology of Puritanism.[219]

v.

SUMMING UP: THE CENTURY IN PERSPECTIVE

It is time now to attempt some synthesis of this long and complicated survey of Glamorgan's history in the years between the Act of Union and the Great Rebellion. When this period opened the dominant power in the area still belonged to the earl of Worcester, by virtue partly of his possession of Gower and Kilvey, partly of his sheriffwick of Glamorgan. Even in the bishop's lordship of Llandaff it was reported in 1539 that 'all the gentlemen is retained to the earl of Worcester'.[220] Between 1540 and 1551 this power was sharply diminished; in part it was replaced by the machinery of English shire government, in part by the earl of Pembroke, who during the minority of Edward VI secured some of the influence wielded by the house of Worcester. The second half of the sixteenth century saw a transitional phase between the rule of the Marcher lords and the government of justices of the peace. Gradually the Pembroke influence weakened as the second earl grew ill and his successors lost interest in the affairs of the county. At the same time the system of shire government, in Wales as in England, grew more complex. A military machine of lord-lieutenant, deputy-lieutenants, captains and muster-masters replaced the *ad hoc* muster commissioners of the mid-sixteenth century. The work of the gentry élite increased in scope and in weight, while commissions multiplied; and as the work of the justices of the peace became more intricate they developed an organisation of their own.

What was the quality of the political life within this system? Despite the reduction of the Marcher lord's power, the influence of the earls of Pembroke remained impressive. Most of the major feuds of Elizabeth's reign touched the earl or his kinsmen at some point, and the gentry sought his support and patronage while opposing the extension of his power. The behaviour of William Mathew of Radyr illustrates the point. So anxious was he to please the earl in the Cardiff Bridge affair that he betrayed the county gentry whom he represented. Yet a few years later he was bitterly complaining of the earl's appointment as lord president of the Council in the Marches: 'I never heard it thought agreeable', he wrote, 'with the law of this, or of any country whatsoever . . . that such a one should hear . . . our capital causes of whom (in a manner) all our lands, especially within Monmouth and Glamorgan shires, are holden, and unto whom the escheat of all that ever we have, both lands and goods, do fall and belong'.[221]

The concern of the earls with Glamorgan explains, at least in part, the remarkable involvement of the court in the county's affairs. The earl of Leicester and the whole Privy Council were drawn into the business of Cardiff Bridge, while an even more remarkable galaxy of courtiers intervened in the Gamage marriage contest. Apparently minor details of local concern could often in the sixteenth century preoccupy the highest persons in the land: an individual or a town wanting support for a cause would almost automatically search through the channels of patronage for court backing.[222] So it was with Cardiff, where some of the tension between town and country may stem from the borough's knowledge that it could generally count upon the earl's help. But a protector could also be an encumbrance, as Cardiff found: sometimes the town appealed to the earl for support, sometimes it denied his claim to authority.[223]

By the beginning of the seventeenth century the influence of the earls upon Glamorgan affairs was on the wane. This seems to have been less the result of government policy than of their own personalities and preoccupations. The second earl was an ill man for most of the 1590s, disinclined to spend much time at Ludlow, intervening little in Glamorgan.[224] Although, after his death in 1601, the dowager countess strongly contested her rights in Cardiff, the family played little part in the government of the shire under the early Stuarts. They did, however, use their influence, more effectively even than in the sixteenth century, to procure seats in Parliament for their protégés. This shift of concern from the feuds of the county to electoral politics sets up a remarkable contrast between the two centuries.

When they were not opposing Pembroke's claim to regalian rights, the Glamorgan gentry occupied much of their energies, in the sixteenth century, by feuding among themselves. The rivalries of Mansel and Herbert, Stradling and Carne, Mathew and Lewis were violent and prolonged; and it is not surprising that Glamorgan had a bad reputation. Dr. David Lewis, judge in the Admiralty court, wrote to Walsingham in 1576: 'one thing more is to be remembered, and that is the late inordinate and unlawful assembly in Glamorganshire, and the excessive number of retainers there'.[225] George Owen of Henllys was also conscious of the problem. He commented on the people of Glamorgan that they were 'very tall and populous, impatient of injuries, and therefore often quarrels with great outrages; thefts in some parts too common; great troops of retainers follow every gentleman'.[226] Often violence seems to have been sparked off, not from any rational motive and not by the leading gentlemen themselves, but by their touchy and quarrelsome followers. It is easy to understand why the townsmen of Cardiff felt resentment against 'serving-men'.

The feuds of the gentry certainly had a corrupting effect upon local administration. Oliver St. John once remarked to Edward Stradling that 'I have seen the disposition of your country before this hath been much led by affection rather than equity of law'; and on another case he reported that 'the judges in all their experiments (experience?) and as far as they have read, never heard the like matter for the hindrance of justice'.[227] One of the weakest points in the machinery of local government was the sheriff. Time and again Glamorgan sheriffs were suspected or proved to be corrupt. Antony Mansel, sheriff in 1590–91, was twice reported to the Privy Council for partiality. When Sir William Herbert was sheriff in the following year some men indicted for murder were reported to be ready to stand trial, 'presuming to be acquitted by the countenance and favour of the High Sheriff, being servants to his brother-in-law'. Edmund Mathew, sheriff in 1592–93, was prosecuted in Star Chamber by the attorney-general for taking bribes, embezzling money and levying illegal fines 'in most cruel, tyrannous and unlawful manner'.[228] Above all, Edward Kemeys, four times sheriff, was accused in Star Chamber in 1585 of releasing a prisoner in return for a bribe, selling offices and wrongfully imprisoning the county gaoler, while in 1599 he was fined £500 in the same court and removed from the commission of the peace for his part in the Cardiff riots.[229]

Obstruction of the law and complicity with criminals are well illustrated in Cardiff's relations with pirates. Fabian Phillips and Thomas Lewis reported to the Privy Council in 1577 that their investigation of piracy was hindered by the townsmen who 'have taken a general rule that they will neither accuse one another' nor answer on oath to any questions that involved themselves. Part of their reluctance sprang from their own purchase of pirated goods, part from fear of the big men and officials who were friendly with the pirates. Nicholas Herbert, the sheriff, William Herbert of Cardiff High Street, David Roberts, the controller of the port, and Edward Kemeys yet again were all heavily involved.[230]

Yet violent, partial and obstructive as the officers of justice too often were, some improvement was apparent. When, before 1536, the Marcher lords had ruled in theory through sessions in eyre, and when in practice those sessions were more often redeemed than held, there simply was no adequate machinery of justice. The men of Hay put the point in 1518 when they protested that the custom of redeeming the sessions 'would cause great boldness to be in misruled people, which would regard no thing what they do, for that no justice should be ministered unto them'.[231] The men of Glamorgan reaffirmed this view later during their struggle against the earl of Pembroke: the appointment of itinerant justices before the union, they said, while 'seeming to have the face of an earnest administration of justice, was in effect to none other purpose but ungodly to exact great sums of money on the said inhabitants'.[232] Rice Merrick may well have had in mind the ambitions of Pembroke when he wrote of the government of Wales before the Union:[233]

> . . . how unorderly they were then governed—life and death,
> lands and goods, subject to the pleasure of peculiar lords:
> and how uncertain laws, customs, and usages . . . were ministered,
> a great number that live at this day can well remember and
> testify.

The structure of Council in the Marches, Great Sessions, Quarter Sessions and so on did at least provide law-courts that operated and in which impartial justice was occasionally possible. Even if lawlessness and violence were not at once eliminated, Tudor rule brought real benefits. Rice Merrick himself was in no doubt about its effects: ' . . . for now life and death, lands and goods, resteth in this monarchy, and not in the pleasure of a subject'.[234] His judgment of the Union was supported by George Owen of Henllys:[235]

> . . . then we the poor Welshmen that were cruelly oppressed
> by our governors . . . who had power to judge as pleased them
> and not to justify as we deserved, were very glad of these
> new laws, and embraced the same with joyful hearts . . .

From about 1600 the influence of the earls of Pembroke was restricted to electoral matters and the Glamorgan gentry were largely in control of their affairs, subject to the word of the central government. More important, violence among the leading gentry and their followers was certainly decreasing: Glamorgan was converted from an unruly county under Elizabeth to a relatively quiet one under the early Stuarts. How much difference this made to the ordinary man, to the merchant, shop-keeper, yeoman or husbandman it is difficult to tell. The nature of the evidence has necessarily focused our attention upon the upper stratum of county society. For the mass of the peasantry government and administration meant the sessions of hundredal and manorial courts, whose quality is not easily assessed. Probably the lives of husbandmen, artisans and labourers continued to be as violent as before; and the substitution of gentry rule for the authority of Marcher lords may not have seemed too great a change. But, while the gentry were often ready to use their power for their own ends, they could be and were checked. The Star Chamber sentence upon the Herberts in 1598 was a turning-point:

thereafter the gentry were not only more pacific, they seem also to have become less partial, corrupt and obstructive.

It is worth asking, in conclusion, how far Glamorgan was representative of the whole region. No county can be said to have had a typical pattern of politics; and the only feature common to all the Welsh and Marcher shires was that, except during the brief career of the earl of Essex, politics remained very much a county rather than a national or a regional affair. In some counties, like Monmouth, the struggle between Anglican and Catholic dominated the feuds of the gentry; in others, like Denbigh, the principal dispute was between east and west. In Herefordshire two great families, the Crofts and the Coningsbys, fought for precedence with little interference from outside the county; in north Wales the external influence, first of the earl of Leicester and then of the earl of Essex, did much to shape the structure of events. Glamorgan combined some, but not all, of these features. Religious strife played hardly any part in its politics, and the east-west struggle only a little. Rivalry between town and country was certainly important in Glamorgan, as it was also for instance in Brecknock. The feuds between the leading families were, of course, a common feature, but in Glamorgan about six families were in the forefront of the struggle, by contrast with the two great protagonists of Herefordshire. The role of the second earl of Pembroke was unique to Glamorgan. Unlike Essex and Leicester he was not an outsider, but he was not exactly an insider either. His position never produced a clear-cut struggle, since the Glamorgan gentry, however anxious they might be to oppose his pretensions, wanted also to exploit his favour and patronage.

Finally, improvements in law and order were not apparent only in Glamorgan. The increase of litigation at the Council in the Marches and at Star Chamber shows a general readiness to turn from violence to legal methods, a readiness upon which contemporaries commented; and Professor Stone has demonstrated that the titled peerage in England as a whole was becoming more peaceful in its attitudes.[236] Yet the transition may perhaps have been more remarkable in Glamorgan than elsewhere. To judge from the remarks of David Lewis and George Owen,[237] that county was unusually given to feuds and violence under Elizabeth. By the 1630s it seems to have been as peaceful as any other shire in Wales and the Marches.

CHAPTER IV

The Ecclesiastical History of Glamorgan, 1527-1642[1]

By GLANMOR WILLIAMS

i.

THE ROYAL SUPREMACY

FROM about 1527 to 1533 the kingdom of England was plunged into one of the profoundest crises in its history as a result of the king's determination to have his first marriage annulled so as to enable him to marry Anne Boleyn. King Henry VIII's 'great matter' led to a series of statutes passed between 1532 and 1534 which decisively and, as it ultimately turned out, permanently shattered papal authority over the Church in England and replaced it by a royal supremacy based on parliamentary statute. These same statutes had also begun the process of turning England and Wales into a Protestant country.

Of the reactions of people in Glamorgan to these epoch-making events we have surprisingly little evidence. To many of the king's ordinary subjects within the county the whole crisis may well have seemed remote and unreal; the affair of a powerful, god-like sovereign which impinged but little on their obscure existence. Insofar as they had any thoughts on the matter, these may have been accurately reported by Eustace Chapuys, ambassador to the Emperor Charles V, nephew to Queen Catherine and vitally interested in the proceedings against her. Chapuys informed his imperial master on a number of occasions between 1531 and 1534 of the sympathy of the Welsh for Queen Catherine and her daughter, their hatred of Anne Boleyn, and the possibility that they might make common cause with the Scots and Irish in a rebellion against the king. However, the ambassador was probably too prone to exaggerate the extent and intensity of such reactions in his anxiety to report all portents favourable to Queen Catherine and her cause.[2]

In Glamorgan itself there is very little sign of popular opposition to the king's proceedings during these years. When in June 1534 two Observant friars, men belonging to a religious order more stubborn than almost any other in its antagonism to Henry's measures, crossed from the West Country to Cardiff, they found neither security nor sympathy, being promptly arrested by the bailiffs and packed off to Westminster

[203]

as prisoners. Other Observant friars who found their way into the town were imprisoned at the order of the king. It is true that in January 1536 the bishop of Llandaff, George de Athequa, was reprimanded by the king for not having stopped the mouths of seditious preachers within his diocese, but this may have been no more than a stick with which to beat the unfortunate bishop.[3] There is more evidence of popular dislike of Anne Boleyn. It finds expression in a poem by Glamorgan's leading poet, Lewis Morgannwg. He attacked Anne Boleyn as the reincarnation of Rhonwen and Alice, who had for centuries been the classical symbols in Welsh verse of English treachery. He denounced her as a woman of low birth, unworthy of the king's trust, who had ended up by betraying him. Lewis may have been expressing a sentiment widely shared in Glamorgan, but he hardly dared to give tongue to it until after Anne's downfall. Any earlier resentment against her that there may have been appears to have left no trace in the records.[4]

However imperceptive or inarticulate many ordinary people may have been concerning these great affairs, there were a number of highly placed personages associated with Glamorgan who were well enough aware of the significance of what was going on. Foremost among them was George de Athequa, a Spanish friar who had been bishop of Llandaff since 1517. Confessor to Catherine of Aragon and her agent in confidential diplomatic missions, he had remained unshakably loyal to the queen and was still allowed to remain in residence with her. He resisted all attempts to make him connive at the annulment of the king's marriage and refused to take the oath under the Act of Supremacy. On January 7, 1536 he was at Catherine's deathbed and later officiated at her funeral. Immediately she was dead, he found the screws being turned on him. Henry VIII charged him with not silencing preachers in his diocese who criticized royal policy, and Cromwell reminded him of his duty to ensure the elimination of 'such abuses as by the corrupt and unsavoury teaching of the bishop of Rome and his disciples' had crept into the people's hearts. Athequa, defenceless and terrified, 'finding he could not live as a Catholic or preserve his soul in safety', made plans to escape to his native land. As he was on the point of boarding a Flemish vessel he was arrested, and was confined to the Tower until being released through the good offices of the ambassador, Chapuys, and allowed to return to Spain.[5]

The bishop's stand against the royal supremacy was a personal one which had a negligible effect on the remainder of the clergy within Glamorgan. There was one priest in Gower who had spoken hostile words against the king in 1536, but before he could be brought before the Council of the Marches to answer for it, he died. There is no evidence that any of the Glamorgan clergy refused to take the oath under the Act of Supremacy when it had been proffered to them in 1534. Inmates of the monasteries like the rest of the clergy were obliged to take an oath of their acceptance of the new régime, though only for the monks of Ewenni is there a surviving record of these proceedings. The Latin declaration made by Prior Thomas Bysley and two monks of Ewenni survives in full, and appears to have been a more comprehensive affirmation than that required of the parish clergy. It contains not only an oath of loyalty to the king, his queen, and their offspring, and acceptance of Henry as the head of the Church in England (*ecclesia Anglicana*), but also categorical rejection of any acknowledgement of papal authority. Such a declaration, or something very similar, was required of all those in monastic orders. Though no record survives from other Glamorgan monasteries there is every reason to suppose that their monks subscribed to it without demur.[6]

If Athequa's refusal to take the oath inspired no similar recalcitrance among his clergy, his own attitude, together with his absence from the diocese, may have led to lukewarmness in publicizing the royal supremacy. When Thomas Cromwell's visitors, Adam Becansaw and John Vaughan, arrived at Llandaff in November 1535 to visit the cathedral, they reported that because the bishop had been negligent they had assigned preachers for the task of expounding the royal supremacy. Early in January 1536 the king and Cromwell, as already described, urged upon Athequa the need to prevent disaffection and to establish the royal supremacy. The bishop, of course, had no intention of going to his diocese or of complying with instructions so repugnant to him. Meantime, in Llandaff itself, John Vaughan was trying to carry out Cromwell's injunctions; but on March 16, 1536 wrote despondently that the 'people were never so far out of frame concerning the spiritual jurisdiction by reason of naughty bishops and worse officers'. A short time later Bishop Hugh Latimer referred to Cromwell's attention an anonymous informant, 'an honest poor gentleman' who had travelled much in the diocese of Llandaff and was anxious to disclose what he believed to be in urgent need of reformation there; but no further details of the informant or his information are available.[7]

While the supremacy was thus being accepted and published by the clergy, however slowly and belatedly, the laity for their part had shown no serious disposition to reject it. Some leading figures among them must have been well-informed about the course of events. Dr. Edward Carne, after a distinguished university career, was in 1531 being employed as the king's *excusator* when Henry's suit for the annulment of his marriage had been revoked to Rome to the papal curia. He contrived to carry out this thankless commission without alienating his royal master and yet remaining on friendly terms with the pope. Carne was later to be a devoted son of the Roman church, but at this point he seems fully to have accepted the royal supremacy. The earl of Worcester was another whose family at a later stage was to have its full share of Roman Catholic loyalty; but he showed complete devotion to the king, taking part in Anne Boleyn's coronation and the christening of her baby daughter, the future Queen Elizabeth. By contrast, another leading Glamorgan gentleman, Sir Rice Mansel, married as his third wife, Cecily Daubridgecourt, who was one of the Princess Mary's ladies and confidantes. Mansel and his wife stood by the young princess in her years of shame and humiliation with commendable loyalty; but this did not prevent him from serving with distinction in the royal forces on land and sea, nor deter him from benefiting from the dissolution of the monasteries. Whatever reservations or misgivings the Glamorgan gentry may have had about the king's policies, none of them appears to have followed the example of Rhys ap Gruffydd, the young heir to the great Carmarthenshire house of Dynevor. He had been unwise enough among other things to criticize the king's relationship with Anne Boleyn, and for his mistakes he paid with his head in 1531. His fate may perhaps have served as a dire warning to the gentry of Glamorgan not to take the risk of opposing the king's will. In the absence of any opposition from them or the clergy, the rest of the Glamorgan populace were unlikely to give much trouble. So the first stage of the Reformation in England and Wales—the assertion and enforcement of the royal supremacy—had been successfully and smoothly accomplished in Glamorgan, as in most parts of Henry's Welsh domain. Exploitation of its financial possibilities could now be followed up.[8]

ii.

THE DISSOLUTION OF THE MONASTERIES

Some of Thomas Cromwell's memoranda compiled as early as 1534 suggest that he was turning over in his mind ambitious schemes for making his royal master one of the richest rulers of Christendom by means of expropriating ecclesiastical property. Whatever measures he might ultimately adopt, he would need at the outset as comprehensive and accurate a report on the property of the Church as he could get. At the beginning of 1535, therefore, he set in train all over England and Wales the commissions of inquiry that were to produce that extraordinary Domesday Book of the Church, the *Valor Ecclesiasticus*.[9]

On January 30, 1535 the Commissioners for the diocese of Llandaff were appointed. Headed by Bishop Athequa and Sir William Morgan, and drawn from among the leading gentry of the diocese, they numbered nineteen in all. Their task was to list all dignities, prebends, benefices, monasteries, and other ecclesiastical institutions, and to provide a full and accurate account of their possessions and revenues. The work was actually completed in four months from June to October 1535 by one man, Sir William Morgan, with some assistance from Master Quarr, the archdeacon of Llandaff. Unfortunately, the returns for Glamorgan are much slighter and less informative than those for Monmouthshire which are probably the best in Wales and justify Morgan's comment to Cromwell in October 1535, 'I have sent you a book of the Valor to the best of my abilities. It will rise above any previous estimation as Master Quarr, archdeacon of Llandaff, can inform you.'[10]

Cromwell now put another set of commissioners at work to visit the cathedrals and monasteries and report on the state of morals and discipline within them. His two visitors for Wales, Adam Becansaw and John Vaughan, arrived at Llandaff cathedral on November 11, 1535 and found plenty to criticize: 'the bishop and his archdeacon guilty not only of great ruin and decay of their mansions but of other great faults'. They took measures to remedy these defects and, also, 'in the negligence of the bishop to declare to the people the Word of God', to depute preachers for the work. Although they were in south Wales until as late as May 1536 and almost certainly visited Glamorgan monasteries, no record of their findings survives.[11]

Before these visitors had wound up their duties, the decision to suppress monasteries worth less than £200 a year had already been embodied in a bill brought before the Commons in March 1536. All the Glamorgan monasteries listed in the *Valor* were worth less than £200— Margam (£181), Neath (£120), and Ewenni (£59)—and were included in an official list of houses falling within the scope of the Act. The first Glamorgan monastery to go was Margam. It was dissolved on August 23-4, 1536 when Sir Rice Mansel took possession of it on the king's behalf. Abbot Lewis Thomas was given a pension, his monks were given the *peculia* or allowance due to them, the abbey servants were paid off, and a careful note was made of assets and debts.[12] At Ewenni an unusual arrangement was entered upon in February 1537, whereby Sir Edward Carne leased the priory and its possessions for a term of 99 years at a favourable rent, and in return agreed to maintain Prior Edmund Wotton and two monks. This arrangement lasted until the surrender of Ewenni's mother house, St. Peter's, Gloucester, in 1539.[13]

The remaining Glamorgan house, Neath, though worth less than £200 and poorer than Margam, in January 1537 was exempted from suppression on payment of a fine of £150, a large sum but one which was about normal in the circumstances. Houses like Neath were spared in order to accommodate some of the monks from other dissolved houses, but why Neath should thus have been singled out is not known, unless it was because its head, Leyshon Thomas, was the most estimable Cistercian abbot in Wales. Neath's reprieve did not last long. Its abbot found it hard to raise £150 despite issuing a number of leases of abbey lands on which he raised large entry fines. Finally, in February 1539, when the house was on the point of being surrendered, John Price wrote to Cromwell that the abbot had 'of late endangered himself and his friends very far with the redemption of his house. This should be considered in the moderation of his bill'. Abbot Thomas did, in fact, come off far better

[207]

o

than most Welsh abbots, being given a pension of £40 a year and the rectory of Cadoxton. Five of his monks got pensions of £4 apiece, and two more got £3 6s. 8d. each.[14]

The two Glamorgan friaries were extinguished in 1538 by Richard Ingworth, himself a former friar, the royal agent appointed to accept the surrender of the friaries.[15] By the time the visitor reached them on September 6, 1538 both Cardiff houses were in parlous condition, like most other friaries. The friars' houses were neglected, many of their goods were in pledge, and they themselves deep in debt. Cardiff Dominican friars owed a local victualler, Thomas Robert, £1 for provisions and their servant 7s. 6d. in wages. Vestments worth £7 were missing, and the visitors reported, 'there is gone many things of which we can have no knowledge, for the prior . . . be dead'. The visitor made an inventory of the articles still left and delivered it and the friary to the town bailiffs to keep on the king's behalf. The Cardiff Franciscans were treated in the same way. They were also in debt, and had been forced to raise money by pawning two of their chalices. Here, again, a careful record was kept of what little there was that might be turned to the king's profit: alabaster, vestments, plate, candlesticks, organs, and bells in the church; and cooking utensils, plates, tables, and the like in the kitchen, hall, and chamber. All told, it provided a poor enough haul for the visitor and the king. At the Dominican friary, where death had just carried off the prior, sub-prior, and a friar, there were seven friars left to sign the deed of surrender, as compared with nine Franciscans. All were now free to leave and make the best they could of it in the world outside, without the benefit of any pension such as some of the monks were allowed.[16]

The number of monks and friars within the county cannot have totalled more than about 35 to 40; and making provision for them did not represent a very serious problem. The three abbots were awarded pensions, and so were a number of monks. Others who got no pensions were able to acquire benefices or serve as stipendiary priests, but we have no means of tracing them with any certainty in Glamorgan. Nor can we tell whether or not any of them reverted to the secular life. It may be that some of the monks who had no strong vocation welcomed the opportunity of turning their backs on the cloisters. What we cannot measure, or even discover, is the possible mental and emotional distress caused to men who had taken a vow to live all their lives according to the rule of religion, by turning them out into a very different, if not more unsympathetic, world.[17]

The moveable or saleable contents of a dissolved monastery were quickly disposed of. Jewels, plate, cash, and valuable manuscripts were sent to the royal treasury. Other assets like glass, vestments, missals, candlesticks, organs, timber, and other furnishings were auctioned on the spot. Lead, bells, and any other removable metal were melted down into pigs. Buildings were rendered uninhabitable by removing roofs and stairs, and further demolition was often assisted by the eager, pillaging hands of local inhabitants. Depredations of this sort at both the Cardiff friaries led to suits at the Court of Augmentations, where there were complaints of the illicit removal of stone, timber, and windows.[18] Little was subsequently left of these two friaries: only the foundations of the Dominican friary can now be seen, while the remains of the Franciscan friary finally disappeared in the 1960s to make way for an office block. The three abbeys fared a good deal better. Ewenni church still survives for parish worship, and so does the nave of Margam. Margam's superb chapter house, a building of marvellous elegance and delicacy, also survives, though it was unfortunately allowed to fall into ruin in the eighteenth century. The church at Neath quickly became a gaunt and roofless ruin, but more of the abbey's conventual buildings, especially its fine abbot's house, have survived than those of any other Glamorgan abbey.[19]

More important than the fate of the buildings was the disposal of the estates and spiritual endowments of the monasteries. At first it seems to have been intended that they should all remain in the royal possession and would only be leased for a term of years. On February 29, 1537 the site and demesne of Margam was leased for 21 years to Sir Rice Mansel, and Ewenni was leased to Sir Edward Carne in the same month. But heavy government expenditure upon warfare in the 1540s led the crown to sell monastic lands outright. The first such sale in Glamorgan occurred when Sir Rice Mansel was allowed to buy some of Margam's possessions at 20 years' purchase in October 1540.[20]

None of this land in Glamorgan was given away to its new owners or sold at cheap rates. The only concession made was to remit £100 out of a total purchase price of £731 11s. 8d. paid by Rice Mansel for some Margam estates in 1543. Otherwise, all the rest was paid for at the normal market rate of 20 years' purchase, and sometimes more, as when Sir Edward Carne bought lands at Colwinston for 23 years' purchase, or when Sir Thomas Stradling bought the manor of Llantwit at 25 years' purchase. On the other hand, spiritual income, i.e. tithes, glebe, and the like could usually be bought at the rate of 10 years' purchase.[21]

Very little of the former monastic possessions came back to the Church. The newly-created chapter at Gloucester benefited to some extent when it was endowed with tithes at Tregough, Pennon, and Llancarfan, formerly belonging to St. Peter's, Gloucester, and with the rectories of Llantwit, Llanbleddian, Llantrisant, Penmark, and Cardiff, which Tewkesbury had for centuries possessed. By contrast, Tewkesbury's much more valuable manors at Llandough and Llantwit were sold in 1543 to Sir George Herbert (via Lord Clinton) and Thomas Stradling.[22]

Some of the land went to purchasers whose chief interests lay outside the county. Merchant interest was negligible, and no new Glamorgan landed family was founded on the basis of investment of merchant wealth in monastic estates. In almost every instance it was existing landed families who acquired new estates. Some, like Sir John St. John, had their main estates in other counties but had important interests in Glamorgan. St. John was an early purchaser of former Margam possessions when he bought the manor and rectory of Bonvilston and Greendown grange in February 1541. Sir Richard Cromwell, alias Williams, whose family had originally come from Glamorgan, now had his seat in Huntingdonshire. He acquired the bulk of the Neath estates in March 1542 but by October 1542 he had arranged to sell the grange at Nash and other estates to Thomas Stradling, and he sold the Sker grange to Christopher Turberville in March 1543. Sometimes, Glamorgan lands were bought by big-scale speculators who disposed of them quickly to local gentry. Sir Thomas Heneage bought Margam lands at Cibwr, Cardiff, Resolven, and Cwrt Colman on August 17, 1548, only to dispose of them a week later to two Monmouthshire brothers, James and William Gunter, who were acting as agents for Sir George Herbert of Swansea.[23]

The main beneficiaries from the dissolution, unquestionably, were a small group of leading local families: Mansels, Carnes, Stradlings, Lewises, and Herberts. The most strikingly successful was Sir Rice Mansel, who contrived to get hold of the bulk of the estates of Margam, Glamorgan's wealthiest abbey. The actual purchase was spread over seventeen years from 1540 to 1557, was carried out in four instalments, and cost in all £2,482 13s. 1d.[24] Sir Edward Carne was nearly as successful. His main acquisition was Ewenni priory, which he bought for £727 6s. 4d. in 1546, but he also bought lesser estates at Colwinston, Cardiff, and Llanfeithyn.[25] None of the other purchases compares with those of Mansel and Carne. The Stradlings got lands in Nash, St. Bride's, Wick, Marcross, and St. Donat's formerly belonging to Neath, and Tewkesbury's manor of Llantwit. Lewis Y Fan bought Keynsham's former manor at Roath and Moor grange near Cardiff. Sir George Herbert of Swansea came into possession of Tewkesbury's manor of Llandough, and its manors of Cardiff and Roath, and also acquired the two former friaries at Cardiff. Yet remembering how powerful the Herbert family was in south Wales at this time, it seems a little surprising that their acquisitions of monastic land were not substantially larger.[26]

No new families were created by the sales of monastic land in Glamorgan. The effect of the purchases was rather to increase the gap between the new owners and the rest of the gentry. It was made the more pronounced by the lease or purchase of other crown lands and by the gains to be made from serving the crown and holding office. It can hardly be coincidence that the two men who benefited most from the dissolution, Rice Mansel and Edward Carne, were distinguished royal servants, the former in war and the latter in diplomacy. Among the Glamorgan gentry an upper stratum of some half-a-dozen families was clearly emerging. The most important among them had all benefited from the erstwhile monastic lands to a greater or lesser extent.[27]

The overall loss or gain to Glamorgan life as a result of the disappearance of the monasteries is not easily assessed. The loss to art and architecture is undeniable. The monastic churches were the largest and, architecturally, the finest in the county; but only Ewenni survives largely intact to prove the point, though even the truncated nave of Margam is still deeply impressive. The monasteries must also have housed some of the best examples of medieval sculpture, woodwork, glass, plate, and vestments, all of which have gone. Of their books and manuscripts only a few straggling survivors remain: a Neath manuscript of the *Digestum Novum* at Hereford, Margam's *Annales* at Cambridge, other Margam manuscripts at the British Museum, and possibly another at Bruges.[28]

Economically and socially, the monasteries no longer had much to commend them. They were not, and for two centuries had not been, the pioneers of estate management, stockbreeding, wool production, mining, and metallurgy, that once they had been. They had long since ceased directly to exploit their lands, mills, and mineral resources; they were content to lease them out to laymen and live on the rents. Nor is there any evidence that as landlords they differed significantly in their methods or attitudes from surrounding laymen. Conversely there is little to suggest that the new proprietors who succeeded them were unduly harsh or oppressive in their treatment of tenants. The records of the great law courts reveal little trace of such behaviour, nor do the voluminous archives of the Margam collections. It looks as if many of the new owners, though not without an eye to business, were more concerned with the prestige than the profits accruing from their new estates. In addition to which, the crown had leaned over backwards when appropriating monastic land to confirm the validity of tenants' contracts entered into with their former landlords. Neither could the monks have been said to be conscientious rectors of those parishes whose tithes they largely pocketed. They treated their appropriated churches primarily as a source of profit and had a poor reputation for fulfilling such obligations as maintaining chancels in good repair and paying adequate stipends to vicars or chaplains. The laymen into whose hands the churches passed were admittedly no better. The most valid criticism to be applied here is of the state for failing to ensure that the appropriated tithe was returned to the parishes, from which it had originally come, to be devoted to worthwhile religious and educational ends.

The monks cannot be said to have fulfilled their social functions with much insight or vigour. It is true that they were still maintaining one or two corrodians (i.e., people given board and lodging in return for gifts to the monastery); and they were still dispensing alms, though Margam gave no more than £2 a year and maintained six almsmen, while Neath gave £3 and 'Our Lady's loaf of half a bushel of wheat weekly'. They probably maintained some hospitality, though we know little about it. Neath also had a reputation for learning; but Iolo Morganwg's fables about the existence of a 'university' there have to be dismissed out of hand. Both Neath and Margam were generous patrons of Welsh literature. Yet in all these respects much of the momentum had gone out of monastic life. Such charity as was dispensed was perfunctory, haphazard, and unrelated to need; and much of the hospitality had about it a secularized flavour quite out of keeping with the Rule of St. Benedict. Their patronage of literature had a laicized and not altogether admirable quality about it, and their contribution to education and learning was now negligible.[29]

In the last resort, however, it is as centres of religious and spiritual life that the monasteries must be judged. As such they had long since ceased to exercise a positive influence as a creative minority within the Church. Reduced in numbers, zeal, and morale, they were but a shadow of their former selves, incapable of giving a lead or inspiring devotion. They were not even strong enough in numbers to maintain a full round of their central task of worship and prayer. Those who sympathize with the monastic ideal may, nevertheless, argue that the life of the community was the poorer when this source of vicarious acts of worship and prayer, however diminished, was removed from its midst for ever. That may be so; but it is noteworthy that contemporary laymen who were to prove themselves to be some of the most devoted sons of the Roman Church in Glamorgan did not appear to think that their devotion ought to embrace the preservation of the monasteries. Sir Edward Carne was one of Glamorgan's most distinguished Roman Catholics; Sir Thomas Stradling went to the Tower for his papalist sympathies in Elizabeth's reign; and the Turbervilles were the most stubborn recusant family in the county; yet none of them hesitated about buying monastic land. In truth it would have been hard for them to have conceived a profound respect for the late-medieval monasteries as they ticked over lazily and unperturbedly. The monks were not, for the most part, degenerate or immoral, but they were certainly lax, luke-warm, and indolent; beset with a secularism that had long devitalized their proper function and dimmed their true vision.

iii.

THE PROGRESS OF THE REFORMATION,
1536–1547

During the later years of his reign Henry VIII's overriding objective was to maintain the unity of his realm, if necessary at the price of burning those heretics who denied transubstantiation while at the same time executing any traitors who still acknowledged the authority of Rome. Any changes he allowed must not be disruptive in their effect, nor be pushed to the point of endangering political cohesion. Some willingness to countenance cautious encouragement of change was occasionally shown in the choice of bishops. Cromwell and Cranmer were able to secure the elevation to the bench of a handful of men of known reforming sympathies. A mild and cautious man of this kind, Robert Holgate, was advanced to be bishop of Llandaff in March 1537. A Yorkshireman and a Cambridge graduate, formerly master of the English order of Gilbertines, Holgate was a man of thoughtful and scholarly bent, with a long and thorough university training. His later career proved him to be an administrator of more than ordinary competence, and, despite his lack of local connexions, he might have made a good bishop of Llandaff had he not been whipped away in 1538 to serve on the Council of the North. Thereafter Llandaff saw nothing of him.[30] Nor was the diocese any more fortunate in its suffragan, John Bird, who was sent on an embassy to Germany in 1539 and on his return made bishop of Bangor. No other suffragan was appointed in succession to him, so the diocese was obliged to make do without a resident bishop until the election of Anthony Kitchen in succession to Holgate in 1545.[31]

Kitchen was a complex individual who has fared badly at the hands of historians of Llandaff, ancient and modern. In 1603 Bishop Godwin stigmatized Kitchen as *fundi nostri calamitas* ('the calamity of our estate') and more recently Archdeacon Lawrence Thomas has described him as a 'student, a recluse, a child of the cloister. The rough and strenuous changes reduced him to a lethargic state of spiritless acquiesence.' Yet when Kitchen was first appointed bishop he came into the category of men of reformist sympathies who might be expected to be conscientious resident pastors of their sees. Kitchen, like Holgate, had a long and thorough training in theology at the university before becoming a monk. In 1528 he had been implicated in the clandestine traffic in Protestant books, but when caught he had characteristically retracted. He later became abbot of Eynsham and was active in the Convocation of Canterbury between 1529 and 1536. Like many monks who became bishops he showed a pronounced distaste for traditional ways and a marked sympathy for reforming doctrines. It is less than fair to suggest that men like Kitchen surrendered their abbeys solely from cynicism or spinelessness; an element of genuine conviction entered into it as well.[32]

Another step in the direction of reform, or at least away from long-cherished observances, was the campaign launched in 1538 against some of the more notable images which attracted a concourse of pilgrims, and particularly those associated with monasteries or cathedrals. Officially, the campaign was one directed against idolatry, but another compelling motive was the confiscation for the king's use of the rich treasures of the shrines. Easily the most celebrated shrine in Glamorgan was that of Pen-rhys, erected on a grange belonging to the former abbey of Llantarnam. It was widely known outside Wales, and Latimer, writing to Cromwell in June 1538, referred to the shrine of the Blessed Virgin at Pen-rhys as one of a number, including those at Worcester, Walsingham,

Ipswich, and Doncaster, that would make 'a jolly muster at Smithfield; they would not be all day in burning'. Cromwell took the hint. In August 1538 he wrote to William Herbert and the chancellor of Llandaff to take down the image. Fearing that public opinion, apparently unmoved by the dissolution of the monasteries, might react much more sharply in this instance, he gave instructions that the image should be taken down 'as secretly as it might be'. On September 26 the royal will was proclaimed at Pen-rhys and 'idolatry' denounced. The image was removed to London, burnt with a number of others, and the event celebrated in a ballad by William Gray, one of Cromwell's servants. Meantime, back in Glamorgan, the once-prosperous tavern at Pen-rhys fell into decay when pilgrims no longer thronged there.[33]

Another shrine now broken up was that of St. Teilo in the Lady Chapel at Llandaff cathedral. It was an elaborate and valuable piece of work, containing the images of Ss. Teilo, Dyfrig, and Euddogwy, made mostly of silver gilt, and surrounded by a mass of gold and silver treasures of many kinds. The canons tried to forestall royal expropriation by breaking up the shrine and dividing it among themselves. This is usually said to have happened in 1541–2, but the real date must certainly be earlier than June 1540, when Thomas Cromwell, who was prominently involved in the affair, fell from power. The most likely dates for the event are either late 1538 or early 1539, about the time of, or soon after, the break-up of the shrine of St. Thomas at Canterbury and St. David at St. David's. The canons did not escape with their pillage. Bishop Holgate got to hear of it and informed Cromwell. Holgate ordered the chancellor to recover the missing parts, and the latter succeeded in gathering up 4,000 or 5,000 ounces of plate. He told Holgate, however, that a 'great part of the said shrine was conveyed away'. He was right. The ringleader of the canons, Henry Morgan, fearing Cromwell more than Holgate, delivered a large part of the spoils directly to the former. He also gave Cromwell to understand that Holgate had unlawfully pocketed some of the plate himself. Cromwell was unimpressed by these complaints, but Holgate felt impelled to present the cathedral with 'a pair of organs and divers suits of vestments' by way of compensation.[34]

A more constructive change in the direction of reform was the encouragement given to the use of the vernacular in worship and devotion, especially to the circulation of English versions of the Bible and English primers. There is no way of telling how widely they circulated in Glamorgan, nor how parishioners received the English litany printed in May 1544 and thereafter used in all the churches by royal command. To a great many Welsh-speaking people in Glamorgan, English was unlikely to have been much more intelligible than Latin. Yet there were many in the towns, the Vale, and south Gower for whom the English Bible and litany may have had an immediate and lively appeal. For instance the opening paragraph of the will of Sir Thomas Gamage of Coety castle, drawn up in June 1543 is unmistakably Protestant in tone: 'I recommend my soul to Almighty Jesu, my maker and redeemer, to whose blessed passion is all my trust of clear remission and forgiveness of sins'; and significantly it makes no provision for any prayers or masses to be said after death. Similarly, the Marian martyr, Rawlins White, gave the impression that he and his family and friends had been eagerly reading the vernacular Bible for some years, possibly since Henry VIII's reign. Others in the county who had read Tyndale's English Bible had made use of it in preparing a Welsh translation of a number of chapters of the New Testament for those who did not understand English (*ante*, III, 551). These Welsh speakers may also have benefited from reading the first Welsh book ever to be printed, Sir John Price's *Yny lhyvyr hwn* of 1546–7, which was, in effect, a Welsh primer. How many Glamorgan men and women availed themselves of this book or the English primers we cannot tell, but if a deep interest in providing Welsh religious literature be any guide, then no part of Wales was readier than Glamorgan to welcome and make use of such a publication.[35]

The prevailing atmosphere of these years was not innovation, however, but cautious conservatism. Open heresy met with condign punishment. In Cardiff at least one unfortunate religious rebel, Thomas Capper, was burned at the stake, presumably for denying transubstantiation. His fate is known only because of the chance survival of the bailiffs' account for 1542–3 recording a payment of 4s. 4d. being 'costs and expenses sustained in burning Thomas Capper, who was attainted of heresy at Cardiff . . . being in prison there by the space of 130 days'. He may have been an isolated individual; but it is possible that the decision to proceed to extremes with Capper was intended to terrify into orthodoxy a number of others who were disaffected by making a frightful example of one from their midst.[36]

iv.

THE EDWARDIAN REFORMATION, 1547–1553

During the six years of Edward VI's reign, under the direction first, of the duke of Somerset from 1547 to 1549, and later, of the still more radical and ruthless duke of Northumberland, the whole realm underwent a religious revolution, the repercussions of which radiated to the remotest corners of the kingdom. Its impact may be conveniently considered under two broad heads: first, the elimination of practices and beliefs associated with the Roman Church and the implanting of reformed doctrine and worship by means of the English Book of Common Prayer; and second, further expropriation of ecclesiastical property, for which the changes in doctrine were offered as a justification, though more truly they were little better than an excuse.

[215]

Almost immediately after seizing power Somerset repealed the conservative Six Articles Act, the measures against heresy, and restrictions on reading and circulating the English Bible. Early in 1548 traditional Catholic ceremonies were abrogated and the abolition of all images in churches decreed. In the same year an English *Order of Communion* was published. In 1549 came the first English Book of Common Prayer, the use of which was enforced from Whit Sunday (June 9) onwards by an Act of Uniformity. To many in Glamorgan the new order, though a startling novelty, was intelligible; to some it may have been warmly welcome. To most of the Welsh-speaking inhabitants it must have been largely alien, for no provision was at this time made for a Welsh version of the Prayer Book. We do not know how they, or a number of their priests, made shift with the English book. Possibly some of the priests resorted to subterfuges common enough elsewhere of mumbling the words indistinctly, so that no one knew quite what was being said, and of continuing to intone and chant in the old way. Not until 1551, with the publication of William Salesbury's translation of the Epistles and the Gospels, *Kynniver Llith a Ban*, was any part of the Prayer Book available in Welsh. Meantime, other major changes were going forward. In 1549 priests were allowed to marry. In 1550 it was ordered that altars should be replaced by tables, an outward reflection of a profound theological shift away from the concept of the mass as a sacrifice in the direction of a commemorative communion of believers. Finally, in 1552 came the Second Book of Common Prayer, a much more outspokenly and uncompromisingly Protestant document than the First.[37]

Changes in doctrine were accompanied by further raids on church property. Occasioned partly by changing spiritual values, they were even more obviously the product of thinly-veiled material incentives. Even before the end of Henry VIII's reign an Act had been passed in 1545 to dissolve all chantries, hospitals, and free chapels in order to finance the king's wars. No general dissolution was effected at this time, however, and a fresh Act was passed in 1547. A small commission of lay experts, appointed in February 1548, drew up a report in time for the Act to come into operation by Easter (April 1) 1548. The report not only gave valuable information about the larger chantries at Swansea, Cardiff, Llandaff, Cowbridge, and Llantwit Major, but also included a number of more modest endowments, sufficient only to maintain a light before an altar or an image, or to add a small contribution to a priest's income or towards the repair of the church. It also gave useful estimates of the number of communicants in some parishes and information about plate, vestments, and other possessions belonging to the chantries.[38]

All were now dissolved and were treated much as the monasteries had been. Most of the dispossessed priests were given pensions of £4–5; though, because of churchwardens' neglect, at least one Glamorgan priest, John Pylle, had to petition the Court of Augmentations for his. Readily realizable assets like plate, vestments, or jewels, were either sold locally or sent to London. Some chantries were richly furnished: St. John's, Cardiff, had valuables worth £7 2s. 0d. Houses or lands were leased or sold, with no shortage of buyers for compact blocks of property. Sir William Herbert was not slow to acquire former chantry land at Cowbridge and Llantwit, and his kinsman, George Herbert, did equally well out of the former Hospital of St. David at Swansea. Miles Mathew took possession of land belonging to Llandaff's former David Mathew chantry as his 'hereditary right'. Urban properties were not much sought after, and were leased only with difficulty because of their frequently ruinous and decayed condition. Not a little of this kind of property got 'lost' in the general confusion, as commissions of concealment, appointed well into the seventeenth century, reveal.[39]

Pious hopes expressed in the preamble to the Chantries Act that the proceeds of the dissolution would be used to found schools or be devoted to charity went unrealized. At least one school in Glamorgan was lost by the dissolution, because the priest of the former Mathew chantry had been obliged to teach twenty children as part of his duties. Nor did any secular institution take over care of the four aged poor maintained by the Hospital at Swansea. The townsmen of Cardiff, too, felt the loss of the chantry income which they had from time to time diverted to meet the heavy cost of repairing the town quay and the stone bridge over the River Taff. Chantries had impinged more directly than monasteries upon the religious and social life of ordinary people, especially in the towns, and their destruction and disappearance cannot but have been unpopular.[40]

If attacks on chantries were unpopular, the confiscation of the treasures of the parishes must have been even more detested. First mooted as early as 1551, the scheme was not implemented until April 1553, and was still incomplete when Edward VI died on July 6, 1553. Glamorgan was divided into four groups of hundreds: Swansea, Llangyfelach, and Neath; Newcastle and Ogmore; Cowbridge; Caerphilly, Llantrisant, Dinas Powys, and Cardiff. Eight lay commissioners, drawn from leading families of Glamorgan gentry, worked from Swansea, Newcastle (Bridgend), Cowbridge, and Cardiff. They summoned before them representatives from each parish to present an inventory of parish plate, ornaments, vestments, and any other valuables. Nearly all of these had now been rendered superfluous by the liturgical changes of the Second Prayer Book and were confiscated in the king's name. Ironically enough, the work was going on for some weeks after Edward had died—Llandaff's cathedral treasures, including the Book of Llandaff, were not removed until July 17, 1553—and was undertaken in the name of Queen Mary, to whom it was thoroughly abhorrent, and who was later to order a commission of inquiry into the whole sorry business. As late as 1558 it was revealed that John Smith, the archdeacon of Llandaff, had, in Edward VI's reign, sold 292 ounces of the cathedral's silver plate for £73, half its real value.[41]

Another grievous loss suffered by the diocese was that of the rich manor of Llandaff, which, in pre-Reformation times, had been worth £50 a year and had accounted for nearly one-third of the bishop's income. It was now leased in perpetuity at an accustomed rent, i.e. it was virtually granted away to Sir George Mathew by Bishop Kitchen, very late in the reign of Edward VI, on May 10, 1553. Such a transaction drastically impoverished the see for the future, and Kitchen has been understandably castigated for it. Before condemning him too harshly we should remember the background of other similar transactions in Edward VI's reign. Almost invariably they came about as the result of unscrupulous pressure on bishops by noblemen in favour with Northumberland. The man responsible in Llandaff was William Herbert, earl of Pembroke, into whose family George Mathew had married. There is no reason to suppose that Kitchen would willingly have parted with so valuable an asset as the manor of Llandaff; there are good grounds for thinking that George Mathew's powerful patrons gave the bishop no choice in the matter. The consequences for his diocese were very detrimental; well might Bishop Babington (1591–5) aver with rueful humour that he was bishop of Aff, for all the land had gone.[42]

Of the reactions of some Glamorgan people to this spate of change we have graphic evidence. Most of it comes from the *cwndidau* and shows them to be hotly opposed to the innovations. The severest critic was Thomas ab Ieuan ap Rhys, the most important *cwndidwr* of the first generation (below pp. 562–71). A scion of the most eminent bardic family in Glamorgan, he was thoroughly imbued with the vigorous ascetic tradition of medieval religious verse in the county. His response to the Edwardian Reformation was that of an unrelenting opponent; staunchly conservative, but not obscurantist nor unconcerned about the religious and moral health of the community around him. His hostility to the new order was so fierce and undisguised that it could hardly have been safe for him to make public such sentiments until after the Catholic Mary had come to the throne, even if the poems had been composed earlier.

He rejected with contumely the whole Protestant teaching as an alien English faith ('ffydd Sayson') imposed on the Welsh. Its effects on churches had been calamitous: God's temples had passed into laymen's hands and had become deserted, with their great altars cast down and replaced by tables like widows' boards. The country had become a Sodom and Gomorrha, having no prayer or fasting, no penance or assoiling, no confession or absolution, no Catholic baptism or burial, no incense or holy oil, no pax, nor rood, nor holy water. Above all he missed the mass: 'for after despoiling God and His house they caused His servants to hide His body and summoned the people to receive mere breadcrumbs'. 'Wales, bereft of the body of Christ, was sad indeed without it.' The new-style married clergy he regarded as pusillanimous, 'conceited goats', for whom he had nothing but contempt. All this depravity was associated in his mind with men's insensate craving after wealth and possessions, which had already brought down on their heads famine, high prices, bad weather, crop failures, dearth of game and livestock, and might bring direr punishments yet.[43]

Thomas ab Ieuan ap Rhys's testimony was clear and convincing. That he spoke for many of his fellow-Welshmen, we scarcely need doubt, for the Reformation presented in a strange tongue can have won few hearts among them. Others more familiar with English may not have been so tardy to accept new doctrines; the Marian martyr, Rawlins White, shared his Protestant convictions with a group of others in Cardiff. Not all the Welsh-speakers may have gone unconverted, either. A celebrated *cwndidwr* of the early Elizabethan period, Thomas Llywelyn, had learnt his poetic craft, but not his religious convictions, from Thomas ab Ieuan ap Rhys, for Thomas Llywelyn was as fervent in the reformed faith as his master had been in the opposite camp.

During Edward's reign there may have been a real danger of rebellion in Wales, and concern was expressed about the possibility of serious trouble, in 1549, 1550, and 1551. That it never came in Glamorgan cannot be due to any lack of dislike for the new régime. It may be attributed in large measure to the earl of Pembroke's growing hold over the county by virtue both of his enormous personal stake in Glamorgan and his office as president of the Council in the Marches. There was no one powerful or disaffected enough in south-east Wales to try conclusions with him; and as yet he was prepared to derive as much profit and influence as he could from the Protestant interest as represented by the duke of Northumberland.[44]

v.

THE MARIAN REACTION, 1553–1558

In the closing months of Edward VI's life the earl of Pembroke had been drawn into Northumberland's conspiracies for diverting the succession from Princess Mary to Lady Jane Grey. Pembroke's task was to have been to hold Wales securely in the Northumberland interest against any possible tumult when Mary was excluded from the throne. However, he seems never to have been more than a luke-warm participant in these schemes, and he quickly deserted Northumberland in favour of Mary. Thereafter a loyal supporter of the Queen, he had by his prompt defection made it certain that Glamorgan and the rest of south-east Wales would come into line behind Mary. Even without Herbert's change of front, it would probably have been found difficult to get Glamorgan men to side against her. The heads of at least three leading families in the county —Carne, Mansel, and Stradling—were strongly in sympathy with her, and were soon to be shown her favour. Moreover, *cwndidau* suggest that she was as genuinely popular in Glamorgan as she was elsewhere in Wales. As the heiress of the Tudors she was hailed with delight by Thomas ab Ieuan ap Rhys as 'bearing the crown of our island', 'justly derived from her father and mother'. This, he maintained, was achieved 'against the will of the English' ('o anfodd Sayson'), an oblique reference to Northumberland's conspiracies, presumably. Another *cwndid* similarly stressed the Welsh welcome for Mary and the earl of Pembroke's role in 'silencing the Saxons'.[45]

In Glamorgan it seems that the chief ingredient in Mary's successful appeal for popular support in 1553 was her claim to be the rightful Tudor heir. Another element in the loyal response accorded to her was religious sympathy. This was a less universal and more divisive sentiment, and perhaps consisted less of a positive attachment to Catholic doctrine, still less a loyalty to papal jurisdiction, than of revulsion against the over-hasty changes of the Edwardian régime. Innovation had been too hectic in pace, too incomprehensible in presentation, and too closely associated with bare-faced despoliation to command much respect or devotion. The indignant and hostile backlash was well summed up in the *cwndidau*. Nor was it a coincidence that Thomas ab Ieuan ap Rhys should link with his welcome to Queen Mary a lively expectation that she had been placed on the throne by the Blessed Virgin to take vengeance on the 'false heads' who 'had treated the son of God as badly as His enemies had done, by stripping him and leaving him naked'.[46]

Loyal as Mary was to her faith, she at first moved circumspectly in restoring it. Nevertheless, her actions, and especially her intention to marry Philip of Spain, provoked the highly dangerous Wyatt rebellion of 1554. In Glamorgan the earl of Pembroke and Sir Rice Mansel were not only able to prevent any uprising, but were also able to raise a large contingent of Welsh troops which Pembroke used to defeat the rebels decisively.[47] Following the suppression of Wyatt's rebellion, the marriage with Philip, and the return of Cardinal Pole, Mary embarked upon a more stringent religious policy. Between the spring of 1554 and that of 1555 active steps were taken against the married clergy, all anti-papal legislation passed since 1529 was repealed, the schism with Rome was ended, heresy laws were revived, and the burning of notorious heretics was begun. In some parts of the realm bitter resentment and opposition were aroused. The hard core of resistance was found among the Protestant bishops and higher clergy, and among middle-class laymen and artisans who had embraced reforming doctrines. These groups had few representatives in Glamorgan. Bishop Kitchen, whatever his earlier sympathies, was a timid, humane, and moderate man, increasingly mistrustful of extremes of any complexion. Unembarrassed by marriage or over-ardent espousal of Protestant doctrine, he did not seem to find any difficulty in conforming to the queen's demands. On the contrary, in March 1554, he was one of six bishops appointed to each of two commissions to inquire into the shortcomings of his episcopal brethren; the one to look into the case of married bishops and the other to examine those who were heretics.[48]

Kitchen's clergy may well have followed their bishop's example of acquiescence. There is no evidence of any resistance among his cathedral clergy, as there was in neighbouring St. David's diocese. Nor was there likely to have been much opposition among the parish clergy who, in most dioceses, were far less moved by issues of doctrine and conscience than their more exalted brethren. The rank-and-file clergy were chiefly affected by the reinstatement of clerical celibacy and the insistence that married priests must give up their wives or their benefices. In St. David's and Bangor dioceses, bishops' registers show that a large number of the clergy were married, but most of them gave up their wives, did penance, and were transferred to other parishes. Having no contemporary registers for Llandaff, we cannot tell if the same thing happened there. Only two Glamorgan priests deprived for marriage have been traced: John Lipyngton, rector of Bishopston in Gower, and Henry Morgan of Newton Nottage. There may have been a number of others deprived at this time, for we know from the *cwndidau* that a number of clergy had taken wives and thereby occasioned great scandal among the conservatively-minded. The fact that a cleric had got married did not, of course, necessarily mean that he was a heretic.[49]

Only one overt heretic is in fact recorded in Glamorgan during Mary's reign. He was Rawlins White, the Cardiff fisherman who held half a burgage on the site of present-day Westgate Street, and five 'henges' on the Taff and the sea-shore in 1542-3. We depend for almost all our knowledge of him on John Foxe's account in his *Book of Martyrs*. There he is portrayed as 'a good man . . . altogether unlearned and withal very simple', 'a great searcher-out of truth' when 'God of his mercy had raised up the light of his gospel through the blessed government of Edward VI'. Particularly affecting touches are those which depict this honest, simple fisherman sending his little boy to school so that he might be able to read the gospel to his father. The portrait is an unusually appealing one, which we are reluctant to reject or qualify. Yet on Foxe's own showing there must have been something considerably more to Rawlins White than an unsophisticated artisan-convert. According to Foxe, White had been in prison for a little over a year before his execution in March 1555. For him to have been imprisoned that early in Mary's reign, when only very notorious offenders were seized upon, suggests that he was a more extreme and dangerous heretic than Foxe would have us believe. The clue to his imprisonment may lie in his activities as a 'notable and open professor of the truth'. He sounds very like the leader of a group of believers which continued to meet after Mary had come to the throne. Foxe is careful not to attribute to him views any more advanced than a denial of transubstantiation and an avowal of the authority of the scriptures. Yet it has been pointed out that the loosening of traditional restraints during Edward VI's reign had given rise to many beliefs more radical than those warranted by the Book of Common Prayer. In view of the slenderness of the evidence in White's case this point should not be pressed, for it is perfectly possible that he got into trouble at Cardiff only because of the fewness of even moderate reformers in the diocese of Llandaff.[50]

Whatever the exact nature of White's beliefs, Bishop Kitchen was evidently very reluctant to make an example of him. Kitchen is easily dismissed as a turncoat and trimmer; but in his dealings with White he showed a degree of humanity and compassion all too rare in that age of fierce persecution. White was not easy to handle; he could be as opinionated and unamenable to persuasion as only a self-educated fanatic can be. When Kitchen, after vainly trying to reason with him, insisted upon praying for him before condemning him, White was plainly moved by this unusually charitable act, but could not desist from adding, 'Do you pray to your God, and I will pray to my God. I know that my God will hear my prayer and perform my desire'. Kitchen was slow to anger. He had White brought to his palace at Mathern and again tried to reason with him. Even when this failed and White was once more imprisoned at Cardiff, it seems to have been no very rigorous confinement, because his friends were allowed to visit him freely and derive consolation and exhortation from him. In the spring of 1555 when the net of persecution began to be pulled much tighter, Kitchen made last desperate efforts to save him, but all in vain. As White's end approached, his stubborn courage did not desert him. Although he confessed to the human weakness of 'a great fighting between the flesh and the spirit, and the flesh would fain have his swing', he died the horrible death at the stake with great courage and without recanting a word of his opinions. Tradition gives two possible sites as the place of his burning—one in High Street, near the opening of Church Street, the other in St. John's Square, just north of St. John's church.[51]

The fact that only one man was burned is not in itself conclusive proof of the absence of heretics. The intensity of persecution varied widely and depended not only on the number of heretics but also on the persecuting zeal of the bishop, and Kitchen was one of the least blood-thirsty of the prelates. Clearly there was no great problem of heresy in Glamorgan, but the account of White's martyrdom shows that there were others in and around Cardiff who shared his beliefs without being persecuted for them. Again, the rapid growth of Protestant *cwndidau* in Elizabeth's reign could hardly have taken place without having had some roots in an earlier period.

Mary's reign was not solely a time of reaction and persecution; it was also characterized by a programme of Catholic reform carried out by Pole and some of his bishops. They concentrated their efforts upon improving the quality of the clergy and curbing the rapacity of the laity. Not much could be expected of Kitchen on either count, and little was, indeed, achieved. There is no indication of his having held reforming synods or tightening discipline, and non-residence appears to have become worse. Some attempt was made, however, to repair the devastating loss of church goods. In 1555, following a petition to the Lord Chancellor, a commission of six local gentlemen was set up to make inquiries and report. Their findings recounted lamentable episodes of wholesale spoliation and embezzlement. Llandaff cathedral had been reduced to a deplorable state: services were irregular and drastically reduced in number; service-books were missing 'so that God cannot there be served for lack of books'; the canons had been negligent and unscrupulous in farming out chapter lands, with the result that vicars choral and curates could not be maintained; and the furnishings of the cathedral were bare and broken. The parish churches were in a hardly less desolate condition; 'sacked of goods, plate, and ornaments, they must have resembled empty barns'. Yet all the pillaging had hardly benefited the state at all; most of the proceeds had lined the pockets of George and William Herbert and Rice Mansel, and could not now be recovered.[52]

A more hopeful aspect of the Catholic reform movement was the production in Welsh of works of Catholic piety. Glamorgan was the most vigorous province in Wales in producing religious prose texts in Welsh. Unfortunately, no means exists of dating precisely when they were undertaken, still less of linking them positively with the Catholic reform movement of the Marian period. Yet it is difficult to avoid the conclusion that this Marian Catholic resurgence gave added impetus to a literary tradition which was a good deal older than the 1550s but would stretch far forward into the Elizabethan era, when adherents of the Roman faith would seek to circulate clandestinely both printed books and hand-copied manuscripts to serve their purposes.[53]

vi.

THE ELIZABETHAN CHURCH

In the spring of 1559 the Elizabethan Book of Common Prayer was published and enforced by the now familiar device of an Act of Uniformity. Since this book, with a few significant modifications, was the Second Edwardian Book, stiff opposition was offered to it by the bishops and many of the higher clergy. Among them, at first, was Bishop Kitchen, who voted against the restoration of royal supremacy and the Act of Uniformity, and initially refused the oath required of the bishops. But he was either too timorous or too weary to persist. On July 18, 1559

[223]

P

he agreed to take the oath, the only bishop to do so, much to the disgust of the Spanish ambassador, who dismissed him as a 'greedy old man with but little learning'.[54]

To administer the oath to the clergy under the Act of Supremacy, enforce the use of the prayer book and promulgate royal injunctions, a royal visitation was planned in the summer of 1559. For the purpose of the visitation the diocese of Llandaff was grouped with the other Welsh dioceses and those of Hereford and Worcester. The visitation articles for Llandaff survive, but they conform to the general run of such documents without showing any interesting individual characteristics. Llandaff gave the visitors less trouble than any other diocese. It is the only one in which not a single cleric appears to have been deprived for refusing to take the oath, though two Glamorgan priests, William Dawkins of Llansannor and Thomas Williams of Llanharry, may have been removed for recusancy within a year or two. Nor were the laity any less pliable than the clergy. Only two of the leading figures among them, Sir Edward Carne and Sir Thomas Stradling, of whom more later, gave serious grounds for concern. The parish churches, too, must soon have resumed a Protestant guise, if we may judge by Swansea's experience. Early in the new reign the churchwardens' accounts of St. Mary's church recorded the taking down of two stone altars and their replacement by a wooden communion table, for making which 14*d*. was paid to one John Thomas. At the same time 4*d*. was paid for the removal of the great rood from its loft, though the loft itself was retained as a singing gallery.[55]

The new religious settlement had been imposed with surprisingly little hindrance or opposition; but if its acceptance was to be anything more than outward compliance much would depend on the vigour and effectiveness with which its doctrines were propagated in the diocese. This in turn would be determined to a large extent by the quality of the episcopate. Llandaff was, by and large, fortunate in its Elizabethan bishops. Admittedly, Kitchen gave the new régime an uninspiring start, and when he died in 1563 there followed a dismal three-year vacancy, brought about perhaps by the queen's familiar tactic of keeping a diocese vacant as long as possible in order to augment the royal income. In the course of this vacancy Archbishop Parker received solicitous advice from the best of the Welsh bishops, Richard Davies of St. David's. Davies urged the choice of a bishop who might, 'by preaching the Word of God and living according to the same', 'set forth the glory of God and show light in these places of extreme darkness' which had, of all dioceses, 'most lacked good doctrine and true knowledge of God and where in matters of religion no reformation or redress had been since the time of the queen's majesty'.[56]

Kitchen, happily, was followed by a succession of better bishops. The first, Hugh Jones (1566–74) was an Oxford graduate, and a resident preacher and canon in the diocese before his election. He was the first

Welshman to become bishop of Llandaff for three centuries. He was followed by another Welshman, a native of the diocese, an Oxford man, and a resident parish priest and canon, the active and vigorous reformer, William Bleddyn (1575-90). Bleddyn's successor, Gervase Babington (1591-5), a very learned Cambridge graduate, was an excellent bishop. Though not a native of the diocese or of Wales, he had kept a school in the diocese of Llandaff and had been its treasurer before becoming bishop. He was succeeded by the most distinguished of all Welsh Elizabethan bishops, William Morgan (1595-1601), the translator of the Bible into Welsh. Morgan was not, as it happened, the first choice for Llandaff in 1595. The man originally intended as bishop was Richard Vaughan, who went instead to Bangor, and was later translated to Chester and London. Archbishop Whitgift warmly commended Morgan as a 'man of integrity, gravity, and great learning', and Gabriel Goodman, dean of Westminster, described him as 'the most sufficient man' in Wales, 'for his learning, government, and honesty of life' and especially for his translation of the Bible into Welsh.[57] All of these bishops were men of piety, integrity, and good intention; all were men of learning and two were distinguished scholars; all had previous experience of the condition and needs of the diocese; and all were resident and committed pastors of their flock. This could not have been said of any comparable group of Llandaff bishops for centuries. If there were shortcomings in the Elizabethan Church, this was not for want of an appropriate choice of bishops.

One of the most serious handicaps from which the Elizabethan Church suffered in Llandaff and elsewhere in Wales was its crippling poverty. In part this was the inescapable consequence of a relatively poor economy and was a legacy of medieval times. It had been made worse by the distressing effects of lay rapacity and clerical weakness or connivance, to which the Reformation changes had given rise. The memory of successful plunder of ecclesiastical wealth in Henrician and Edwardian times, and the prospect of further spoils to come, continued to whet the acquisitive instincts of laymen in the Elizabethan age. For instance, some time during the twenty-fourth year of the Queen's reign, (November 1581 to November 1582) Bishop Bleddyn, under pressure from Elizabeth, leased to her the manor and rectory of Bassaleg, and other churches for a term of no less than 100 years; and she in turn promptly leased them to Sir William Herbert for 60 years.[58]

The consequences were plain to see in the shrunken income of the bishops. Never lavish, it had now become quite insufficient to maintain a bishop on even the reduced scale to which Elizabethan prelates had to become accustomed. Bishop Babington complained with wry jocularity that he was only the bishop of Aff because all the land had gone. Bishop Morgan begged that the restitution of temporalities might date from the translation of his predecessor, 'for the revenue is very small and the charge is very great'. Bishop Godwin contended that his was by far the poorest bishopric in the land, and that a number of benefices in the diocese brought their incumbents more income than the see did to him. All the Elizabethan bishops of Llandaff had to be given other livings to hold *in commendam*, thus setting an unfortunate example of pluralism and non-residence which others were not slow to follow. Even the good Bishop Babington was obliged humbly to beg Sir Edward Stradling that he would confer the parsonage of St. Athan upon him to hold *in commendam* because 'my living is small and my charge great'. Bishops were also tempted to indulge in nepotism. Bishop Bleddyn made his sons, Morgan and Philemon, prebendaries of Llandaff, while Philemon was also vicar of Caerwent and rector of Shirenewton. Bishop Godwin was accused of selling the chancellorship and of disposing of whatever fell into his gift in favour of a son or daughter. Browne Willis commented with some asperity that notwithstanding the freedom Godwin took with other bishops' reputations, he was certainly 'a very great "symoniack"' who 'omitted no opportunity in disposing of his preferments'.[59]

The malign results of impoverishment, greed, and neglect were to be seen on the cathedral and its chapter. In 1576 Bishop Bleddyn, bent on thorough-going reform, condemned the cathedral as 'derelict and destitute of pastoral care', 'untidy, full of dirt, and almost beyond repair', a horrifying picture which is in large measure confirmed by Rice Merrick, who described the canons as non-resident 'and their houses almost in utter decay'. Bishop Bleddyn made strenuous efforts to improve the state of the cathedral and close, tighten up discipline, and insist upon more residence and preaching. He sharply censured the canons for their prodigal leases: 'To whom have you not granted large manors, many lordships and farms?' he asked. 'You have wasted everything; sweet-toned bells, books, precious vestments, golden vessels, unknown treasures. They are all reduced to nothing.' Laying down stricter conditions, he insisted that capitular lands could be leased only with the consent of the bishop and six canons, and that agreements must be signed only in the chapter-house and sealed with the chapter seal. Excellent provisions all of them; but Bleddyn himself can hardly have contributed much to their implementation when he leased Bassaleg, admittedly under pressure, for a term of 100 years, or the manor of Undy to his three sons for a term of lives.[60]

Later bishops were also much preoccupied with the state of the cathedral. In 1592 Babington and the chapter entered into an agreement with Bristol craftsmen to make the cathedral 'proof against all leaks, wet, or rain'. In 1594 he installed pews at his own expense for those inhabitants 'as by him were thought meet to kneel and sit in them'. At the same time he and his canons, deeply distressed by the cathedral's 'ruinous and decayed state', 'more like a desolate and profane place than like a house of prayer', gratefully accepted William Mathew's offer to have the north side paved and the window repaired. No more than ten years later, however, Bishop Godwin's injunctions of 1603 spoke of the cathedral as 'fallen into such decay as 500 marks will not repair the same, so that it must needs in short time fall to the ground without some extraordinary relief'. The state of the cathedral and its chapter's finances continued to be a source of anxiety for some generations to come.[61]

Poverty was also widespread among the parish clergy and serious in its effects. The general level of parochial income before the Reformation had been low. Reformation changes had completely extinguished some earlier sources of clerical income, like pilgrims' offerings, the sale of candles, or masses for the dead. In addition, the clergy having been given the right to marry now had to maintain a wife and family, though it should not be overlooked that many of them had been unofficially 'married' in the Middle Ages. Moreover, the century from 1540 to 1640 was one of rapid and painful inflation, when prices are estimated to have increased five fold. This pressure may not have borne too hardly on those parsons who farmed their own glebe and collected all the tithe due to them. Their income ought to have been elastic enough to keep pace with the rise in prices, though they had always to contend with the stubborn reluctance of the laity to pay tithe and their constant attempts to encroach upon glebe land, as a result of which, Bishop Godwin contended, 'much land is daily embezzled from the Church'. Some of the incumbents of the better rectories in Glamorgan were undoubtedly comfortably placed in their material circumstances. Morgan Nicholas, who ended his days as archdeacon of Llandaff, when he died in 1598 was able to leave his wife, sons, and other relatives, valuable landed interests and livestock, goods, and chattels worth £143, including household goods worth £35 and books and apparel valued at £5. Thomas Herbert, vicar of Llantrisant for much of Elizabeth's reign, and later chancellor of Llandaff, was a nephew of the first earl of Pembroke by an illegitimate line. Before his death, he sold most of his estate to the second earl, but was nevertheless able to leave a considerable fortune in his will. Thomas Evans, vicar of Coychurch, was another who contrived to bequeath his relatives a wide range of possessions in land, stock, goods, and money when he died. As far as is known, Lewis Philip, parson of Michaelston-super-Ely (d. 1611) never became a member of the cathedral clergy, but he must have lived and farmed on the scale of a wealthy yeoman if not a member of the minor gentry, with his 16 kine, 34 head of cattle, 59 sheep, 5 horses and mares, household goods worth £10, and total possessions of the order of £100 (see also, below, pp. 245–6).[62]

Not all clerics were as fortunate, however. Those who felt the pinch of poverty most keenly were the incumbents of impropriated livings which, for all practical purposes, had passed into the hands of the local gentry, either by purchase, or by lease, from the crown or the cathedral chapter. As a rule, only a relatively small proportion of the tithes of such a living came to the incumbent, or, what was worse, a fixed stipend, while the greater part of the profits passed to the lay impropriator. The diocese of Llandaff had an unduly large proportion of such livings by Welsh standards; and a return of 1603 gives us a graphic glimpse of conditions prevailing in them. There were 34 impropriations listed for Glamorgan, 24 of them endowed vicarages and ten of them stipendiary vicarages, making up in all about a third of the livings of the diocese. Their total value to impropriators (£1,185 10s. 0d.) was worth two-and-a-half times the share received by the incumbents (£455 16s. 0d.). The list of impropriators reads like a roll-call of leading gentry families: Herberts, Mansels, Carnes, Stradlings, Lewises, Mathews, and the rest. Heading the list was Anthony Mansel, impropriator of St. John's and St. Mary's, Cardiff, Llantrisant, Llanbleddian, Cowbridge, Penmark, and St. Mary Hill, worth in all £269 a year. Close on his heels came Sir William Herbert, with Cadoxton-juxta-Neath, Eglwysilan, Penarth, Lavernock, and Llanedern, worth £258 a year. Half of the vicars had incomes worth one-third or more of the value of the living. In many others the disparity between the impropriator's share and the incumbent's was very wide. The Cardiff livings were worth £100 to Anthony Mansel but the vicar got £20; Eglwysilan brought William Herbert £120, and left its parish priest £15; and Henry Dodington received £100 from Margam and paid the curate £10. In one instance, at Uchelolau (Highlight), Christopher St. John would not pay a curate at all, 'so the parish hath been without service these 30 years and more, and the church almost fallen down'. What made the situation all the more serious was that the impropriated livings were among the best in the county, in market-towns and centres of population like Cardiff, Cowbridge, Llantwit, Neath, Aberafan, and Swansea, and ought to have been supporting an able and well-educated clergy.[63]

The bishops' opportunities of presenting suitable men to these livings where the rights of advowson rested in lay hands were much curtailed. The less scrupulous among patrons and clergy were not above entering into doubtful bargains with one another, in which the one demanded and the other agreed to inducements that were not in the best interests of the Church. When Andrew Vayn, a cleric in the diocese, was a suitor to Sir Edward Stradling for the living of Sully in his gift, he referred to 'divers simonaical offers' made to Stradling, but hastened to add that both he and Bishop Bleddyn were convinced that Sir Edward preferred his 'credit before any worldly commodity, and the peace of a religious conscience before the perverse pelf of this transitory world'. This may have been true of Sir Edward, but the last-named was himself assured by another aspiring Glamorgan cleric, William Fleming, seeking his help on another occasion, that the 'door which leads men to any preferment be it never so mean can not be opened without the silver or golden key' and the key into the chaplaincy that he hoped for 'must be so ponderous that, if it weigh not ten pounds in silver, I shall have no entrance'.[63A]

All the bishops of Llandaff complained about impropriations, which made the poverty of the livings within the diocese even more pronounced. This added still further to the already formidable task of recruiting an adequately-trained clergy. To propagate reformed doctrine a constant supply of capable preachers was urgently needed; but the only men who could be licensed by the bishops for the responsible function of preaching were university graduates, preferably with a theological training. Men of this sort were nowhere plentiful, and it would be doubly difficult to attract them to poverty-stricken benefices in Llandaff where, in most instances, they would have to cope with the additional responsibility of preaching in Welsh. Bishops seem to have gone to some pains to try to secure the appointment of preachers. When Sir Edward Stradling's parsonage of Sully, which was able 'to maintain a preacher', went void, Bishop William Bleddyn, 'according to his duty, lest an unfit man for the room should attempt to obtain it', solicited Stradling's favour for Andrew Vayn, 'being a public preacher lawfully authorized'. But such bishops' reports as are available for Llandaff show how painfully few preachers there were in the diocese, especially during the earlier years of Elizabeth's reign. Bishop Kitchen's report of 1561 listed only five for the whole bishopric. In 1570 Bishop Hugh Jones bemoaned that only two livings in Glamorgan and two in Monmouthshire could sustain preachers; for the rest he had to procure preachers from other dioceses from time to time at his own expense.[64]

Poverty gave rise to other shortcomings. There was a good deal of pluralism among the higher clergy, though this was a practice of long standing. William Evans, treasurer of the cathedral in 1561, was also rector of St. Fagan's and vicar of Llangatwg-feibion-Afel in Monmouthshire; and John Smith, archdeacon of Llandaff, was not only rector of Merthyr Tydfil but was also chancellor of Exeter and had other livings in that diocese, where he normally resided. As for the unbeneficed clergy, unless they were markedly different from their fellows elsewhere in Wales, many of them had to hold a number of ill-paid curacies simultaneously in order to keep alive. Pluralism in turn led to non-residence and a failure to maintain hospitality in a way expected of the clergy. However, there appears to have been an improvement in this respect over the years. In Kitchen's first report of 1561, 23 incumbents were noted as non-resident, but in 1563 the number had dropped as low as five. In Hugh Jones's report of 1570, eight of the cathedral canons were reported as resident and four as non-resident, whereas in 1561 only the treasurer had been returned as resident.[65]

There are some signs of a slow improvement, too, in the quality of the clergy, though many of the shortcomings already referred to persisted well into the seventeenth century and beyond. The greater availability of grammar school education and university training led to an increase in the number of graduates being ordained within the diocese. This was reflected in a marked increase in the number of preachers by the end of Elizabeth's reign. By 1603, although Bishop Godwin was still gravely perturbed that not enough sermons were being preached in his diocese, he nevertheless was able to number 50 preachers among his clergy, which was just ten times as many as Llandaff could muster at the beginning of Elizabeth's reign. Furthermore, Glamorgan produced in greater numbers than any other county those 'sermons in song', the Welsh-language *cwndidau* (discussed below, pp. 566–76). They proved to be a singularly effective way of instructing the uneducated and illiterate in their moral and religious duties through the medium of their own language and they must have owed much to clerical patronage and encouragement.[66]

Insufficient means of instructing the Welsh in the vernacular had been one of the crippling limitations of the Elizabethan Church when it was first introduced into Wales. There were no Welsh versions of Bible or Prayer Book, which made the shortage of adequate preachers even more acute. When the Welsh New Testament and Prayer Book first arrived in 1567 they were marred by the strange views of their translator, William Salesbury, concerning language and orthography. Not until the publication of William Morgan's Bible of 1588 was the task satisfactorily accomplished. This, the supreme achievement of the Elizabethan Church in Wales, was greeted with rapture in *cwndid* and other verse within the diocese of Llandaff. It provoked a long and ecstatic poem by a Monmouthshire cleric, Thomas Jones, whose unbounded delight at the 'pure bread of life given by God to Welshmen' can probably be taken as typical of the reaction of many of his fellow-Welshmen in Glamorgan. But although there had been early translations in Glamorgan of parts of the New Testament, no significant contribution to the task of translating the Bible into Welsh was made within the county during Elizabeth's reign. Persistent stories that Thomas Llywelyn of Rhigos translated the whole Bible into Welsh before Bishop Morgan did so, originated with Iolo Morganwg and have no basis in fact.[67]

The output of religious verse in the form of *cwndidau*, however, was prolific. Some of them were written by clerics and many more were very likely commissioned by them; yet, as far as can be judged, the prime initiative came from laymen. Most of the content of these verses was non-controversial and consisted of stern moralizing and trenchant social criticism in a vein long made familiar by medieval religious poetry. It denounced with intense, puritanical fervour the unbridled sensual passion, rapacity, and oppression of men; the way they fell a ready prey to the three arch-enemies—the world, the flesh and the devil; the prevalence of the seven deadly sins in their midst; their frenetic pursuit of ephemeral worldly wealth, pleasure, and satisfaction; and their heedless trampling underfoot of the weak and the poor. Such themes were common ground to all the *cwndidwyr*. Some among them, however, continued to be conservative in their religious sympathies, their most notable representative being Llywelyn Siôn, the outstanding scribe and copyist of his age as well as a prominent poet. In a characteristic poem he denounced the Devil, mankind's betrayer since the Garden of Eden, for having deceived the men of his own generation into betraying the four evangelists and following the four false prophets, Luther, Zwingli, Calvin, and Beza. Llywelyn Siôn is less typical, however, than such leading figures as Thomas Llywelyn, Dafydd Benwyn, and Hopcyn Twm Philip, all of whom voiced their sympathy with the new doctrine, in keeping with the majority of their fellow-*cwndidwyr*. In their poems they placed a marked emphasis on the authority of the scriptures and showed a commendably wide and detailed knowledge of the Bible. More than one stressed the significance of faith in the believer, but almost without exception this was accompanied by a parallel emphasis on the absolute need for faith to bear fruit in good works. Thomas Llywelyn recalled with evident approval the insistence of St. James's epistle that faith without works is barren. Such emphasis was in keeping with the generally stern and austere tone of Llywelyn's writing, a flavour which may have accounted for Iolo Morganwg's legends about Thomas Llywelyn's alleged rôle as a pioneer of puritanism in Elizabethan Glamorgan (below, pp. 253–4). In Llywelyn's most celebrated poem, 'The Tavern and the Church', the evils of drink and its accompanying vices of sloth and loose-living came under heavy fire. Particularly interesting was the connexion which he sought to establish between the tavern and medieval religion. He put into the tavern's mouth sneers at the bareness of the churches 'now like a barn', bereft of the colour and adornment of earlier times, only to reply with crushing severity that the deceitful money-spinning practices associated with the mass and the images had been rightly replaced by the purer ideals of reformed religion.[68]

Protestant interpretations of history, as well as Protestant doctrine, had won currency among *cwndidwyr*. In Bishop Richard Davies's Address to the Welsh Nation, with which he prefaced the New Testament of 1567, he had adumbrated the notion that the church of the ancient Britons in their golden age, based on the authority of the scriptures, had been corrupted by Roman superstition, introduced at the point of the sword by the instigation of Augustine of Canterbury. Davies's main themes were followed faithfully and paraphrased by Thomas Jones in his poem welcoming the Welsh Bible of 1588 and by Dafydd Benwyn in his poems. Slowly, Protestant doctrines and ideas were gaining ground among the people of Glamorgan.[69]

The *cwndidau* and other evidence may provide signs of gradual permeation of new doctrines in Glamorgan; but the operative word is 'gradual'. There survived, and would continue to survive long after the sixteenth century, a mass of earlier practices and beliefs, and a still greater mass of poverty, ignorance, and apathy. A traveller through Wales in 1578 deplored the 'ignorance of God's word, petty thefts, idleness, and extreme poverty' which prevailed so widely. He went on to comment more particularly upon upland Glamorgan where, in common with other regions of the same kind, he found deep darkness, 'with neither college nor free school, neither any bishop or prelate which with his authority or fatherly love offereth one prebend to a foundation'.[70]

vii.

RECUSANCY IN ELIZABETHAN GLAMORGAN

A minority in Glamorgan pressed their sympathy with the old ways in religion to the point of open opposition to the new. Although no record has been found of overt conscientious opposition by the Elizabethan clergy to the Elizabethan settlement in 1559, a handful of Marian priests continued secretly to minister the sacraments according to the Roman rites; they must either have refused to conform in 1559 or made an outward show of obedience only. In 1577–8 when Bishop Bleddyn made his return of Catholic recusants within his diocese he included the names of five Catholic priests among them. The most amazing instance of such a priest continuing to minister in the diocese for more than a generation, is provided by the career of Walter Powell, sometimes dubbed the 'bishop of Llandaff'. It was reported of him as late as 1604 that he was 'a priest ordered in Queen Mary's days, and being some time beneficed in the diocese of Llandaff gave over his living some thirty years since, continuing all this space a recusant. And for many years . . . hath been accounted a common mass-monger'.[71]

Two prominent laymen also had scruples which would not allow them to accept the Elizabethan settlement. Sir Edward Carne of Ewenni, Queen Mary's ambassador at Rome, was reluctant—possibly even afraid—to return to Elizabeth's England, in view of his adherence to the Roman faith and his failure to secure recognition by the pope of the queen's title to the throne. Yet he feared that to obey the pope's command to remain at Rome and take charge of the English hospital there would so irritate the queen that she would deprive him and his wife and children of their revenues. A state paper presented to the pope urged him to allow Carne to 'go whither he please, provided he do not return to England, in which case the queen will readily allow him to retain his revenue, so long as he lives elsewhere than at Rome'. Death soon intervened to relieve Carne and the pope of their dilemma, and Sir Edward lies buried in a church at Rome, though his will was successfully proved in England. Another staunch Glamorgan papist was Sir Thomas Stradling of St. Donat's. Back in 1551 he had been imprisoned in the Tower by the Privy Council, possibly for religious reasons. Much in favour during

Mary's reign, he had been placed on a commission to inquire into heresy. The same steadfastness in his faith during Elizabeth's reign got him into trouble. In March 1559 when a great oak tree on his estate at St. Donat's was blown down it left an impression of a crucifix, thought by Catholic sympathizers to be miraculous. Sir Thomas fostered the belief by having four pictures made of the impression. News of the 'miracle of St. Donat's' spread far outside Glamorgan, disseminated principally by Stradling's exiled kinsfolk on the Continent, particularly by one of his daughters who was a nun. Elizabeth's ministers, understandably suspicious of Catholic propaganda, especially when it had links into Europe and was suspected of being part of a wider Catholic plot in England, indicted Stradling at Essex Assizes on June 3, 1561. He was clapped into the Tower from where he petitioned the queen in chastened tones, explaining that everything he had done was unmotivated by 'any seditious purpose or ill intent, but only of ignorance', and beseeching her, of her 'accustomed clemency, to bear with his ignorance'. Notwithstanding his pleas, he remained in prison until October 15, 1563, when he was released on a bond of 1,000 marks. He had not, as we shall see, abandoned his religious loyalties.[72]

The loyalty of other members of the gentry was distinctly suspect. In a report of 1564 on the religious soundness of the county's justices of the peace Archbishop Parker would commit himself no further than to say of the eleven justices listed by him: 'I know them not, and some times informers serve their own turn and gratify their friends'. Parker's caution was justified. Among the eleven justices were Thomas Lewis Y Fan, who was afterwards known to employ a recusant priest as school-master to his children, and Christopher Turberville, who belonged to what was to prove to be the most devotedly recusant family in Glamorgan.[73]

Yet overall in Glamorgan, as in most parts of the realm, the queen succeeded in achieving an almost universal and untroubled conformity to her settlement during the first decade or so of her reign. This engendered a deepening anxiety among dedicated Catholics, in whose eyes the need to reverse the drift away from Rome was becoming desperate. In response to these fears Cardinal Allen's seminary for training priests to reconvert England and Wales was founded at Douai in 1568. In 1569 the dangerous Catholic rising of the northern earls, followed early in 1570 by the papal bull excommunicating the queen, created a major crisis for the government. Measures to detect possible sources of dis-affection were hastily devised, and every bishop was required to report on any persons in his diocese who refused to join in common prayer and receive the sacrament. There were none such in Glamorgan according to Bishop Jones's return of January 28, 1570. A few months earlier, however, in November 1569 when all justices of the peace had been required to give a public declaration of loyalty to the Established Church

Sir Thomas Stradling was the only one in Wales who had refused. But he was now an old and ailing man of 71, and he had, oddly enough, been willing to attend his parish church to receive communion according to the Anglican rite, and even the preamble to his will, drafted in 1566, had the fervent phraseology more reminiscent of a Protestant than a Catholic testator. On the advice of his fellow-justices, the Privy Council left him unmolested as long as he observed his bond of 1563.[74]

The growth of recusancy during the 1570s continued to occasion grave concern. Catholicism, hitherto kept alive by ageing Marian priests, was now being given a fresh and potent injection by the activities of a small but growing number of young seminarists, thirteen of whom were to be recruited from the diocese of Llandaff during Elizabeth's reign. An alarming indictment of the dangers existing in Wales and the Marches came in 1577 from John Whitgift, then bishop of Worcester and vice-president of the Council in the Marches. The Privy Council was sufficiently impressed by this and other similar reports to call for an inquiry by each of the bishops into the state of his diocese. Bledddyn of Llandaff, in a return dated October 25, 1577, gave the names of 13 recusants, only two of whom came from Glamorgan, but hinted that if he had not been hindered by the laity from obtaining more reliable information the list might have run to 200 names. The chief Glamorgan recusant in 1577 was Thomas Carne, eldest son of Sir Edward Carne, who had not attended his parish church throughout Elizabeth's reign, though this did not prevent him from being a justice of the peace, from acting as sheriff of the county in 1562, 1572, and 1581, or from becoming knight of the shire in 1586 and 1588. The other recusant was William Winslade of St. Bride's Major, a refugee from Devon, where his father had been executed in 1549 for his part in the western rebellion. Other justices of the peace were suspected by Bleddyn of harbouring Catholic priests, of whom five were certainly known to be active in the diocese. Bleddyn, a man of Whitgift's own stern disciplinarian temperament, was quick to follow up the campaign against these priests. Early in 1579 he was given a commission to seize them, but he found to his frustration and anger that Catholic sympathies among his fellow-commissioners had led to the priests' being warned in advance. His persistence, however, appears to have made his diocese too hot to hold at least one of the recusant priests, George Morris, who withdrew to Rheims in 1581. Other leading families suspected by Bleddyn of recusant sympathies were the Lewises of Y Fan and the Kemeyses of Cefnmabli. Both these families were believed to have harboured priests and recusants. When Rowland Morgan, a Jesuit, came to Wales in 1584 he brought with him five sealed letters, one of which was addressed to Thomas Lewis. Moreover, Rowland's brother, Thomas Morgan, one of the most dangerous Catholic exiles on the Continent, advised him that a potentially good recruiting-ground for the 'toward youths' so urgently needed for the seminaries was the Fan estates.[75]

Pressure on the recusants was sharply stepped up in the 1580s and 1590s, with severe penal legislation being enacted against them in 1581, 1585, 1587, and 1593. The records of the Court of Great Sessions in Glamorgan from 1584 onwards, and the Recusant Rolls after 1591, testify to the tightening of the net around offenders. The numbers presented at Great Sessions rose from 4 in 1584 to 77 in 1587, a year when the nerves of all the queen's subjects were put most sharply on edge by the preparations for the Armada. Nor did the defeat of the great invasion force readily allay all fears. 1590 was another year when 72 were indicted, to be quickly followed by another 46 in 1591. Thereafter the numbers brought before the court tended to dwindle steadily, except for 1596, a year of great military activity, when there were 49 presented. By the year 1602 only 19 appeared.[76]

Yet during these years the authorities did not appear reassured or willing to relax their pressure. In 1592 the Privy Council warned the Council in the Marches that English recusants were fleeing into Wales and exhorted it to help in detecting them. In 1593 the Council in the Marches was ordered to prevent the Welsh from worshipping at the sites of former shrines. Three years later, the Privy Council required Sir Thomas Mansel of Margam to go to the home of the Turberville family at Pen-llin near Cowbridge secretly to search for two priests, Morgan Clynnog and Fisher, and also to confiscate 'seditious books' lately brought there 'in some quantity'. As a result, Jenkin Turberville and, possibly, his son, Lewis, spent some time in the Tower. As late as 1601 the Council in the Marches was still deeply disturbed by the 'great backsliding in religion in these parts'. When, in 1603, a comprehensive survey was made of all recusants in Wales, Llandaff diocese emerged with easily the highest number of recusants, and a still higher proportion of them in relation to total population, than any other diocese in Wales. There were 381 recusants in Llandaff out of 37,100 communicants, as compared with 250:53,188 in St. Asaph, 145:83,322 in St. David's, and 32:38,840 in Bangor. Within Llandaff diocese, however, it was the recusants of Monmouthshire, numbering 336 out of 381, and not those of Glamorgan, who were chiefly responsible for the very large total.[77]

The geographical distribution of Elizabethan recusants within the county reveals some interesting features. They were all confined to lowland Glamorgan; not one was at this period presented in the *Blaeneudir*. Within lowland Glamorgan itself they were concentrated in a relatively small number of parishes—Colwinston, Pen-llin, Llancarfan, Pyle and Kenfig, and Newcastle, most notably. Some of these parishes had had close contacts with former monasteries, but this mattered less than that within each of them were one or more families of gentry who gave their kinsmen, dependants, and tenants a lead and offered them protection. The most ardent and ubiquitous of these families were the Turbervilles.

Their main centres of strength were at Pen-llin and Colwinston; but offshoots of the family figure in every one of the strong recusant parishes. The Turbervilles were the only consistently recusant family who belonged to that class of gentry who could aspire to the office of the justice of the peace or sheriff, but though they held the shrievalty in 1569 they seem to have been excluded from all other office. Whether this was a consequence of the recusancy, or their recusancy a consequence of their exclusion, it seems impossible to tell. Certainly in the complex and sometimes riotous politics of Elizabethan Glamorgan they were as turbulent a family as any and were usually to be found ranged against the successful and conformist families of the 'establishment'. Yet at least one member of the Turbervilles, Richard Turberville, was among a number of hitherto hardened recusants who conformed in 1592, and by 1615 Christopher Turberville was pricked as sheriff[78].

A particularly interesting recusant personality was William Griffith, gentleman, of the parish of Llancarfan, who visited the Continent several times and was in touch with Campion and Parsons. His was a family destined to play a key rôle in the history of seventeenth-century recusancy, but in Herefordshire, not Glamorgan. More typical of the lesser, parish gentry was David ab Ieuan of Margam, who had a house near an old chapel of Margam, at which mass was celebrated in 1591 in the presence of 160 people, three-quarters of whom were women; an interesting episode which brought David himself and a number of others before the justices at the Carmarthenshire assizes. Around the recusant gentry of the kind described, there crystallized the support of lesser men in an allegiance that was frequently as much personal as religious. Most of these supporters were described as yeomen, though there was also a sprinkling of craftsmen and labourers. As striking a characteristic of recusant loyalty as any is the stubborn fidelity of many women. Jane, wife of William Thomas of Colwinston, was presented for recusancy no fewer than thirteen times, and the widow, Dionysia Lewis, of Newcastle parish, ten times.[79]

One of the most important reasons for the existence of a significant recusant minority in Glamorgan was the county's geographical position. It lay open to the movement of recusants and priests from England, from across the water in the West Country, and from major Catholic strongholds in border counties like Herefordshire. Most important of all, Glamorgan lay adjacent to Monmouthshire, relatively the strongest recusant county in the whole of England and Wales. Indeed, recusancy in Glamorgan was largely an overspill from Monmouthshire. It was in the latter county that there existed the big and influential recusant households, that of the Morgans at Llantarnam and, later, of the earls of Worcester at Raglan, described by a contemporary as 'able to command most in Monmouthshire'.[80] It was they who were primarily responsible for harbouring, organizing, and stiffening recusancy in south-east Wales.

Yet it is clear by the end of Elizabeth's reign that if recusancy had not completely failed in Glamorgan it enjoyed so limited a success as to render it impotent. The Glamorgan recusant with the best information and greatest initiative, William Griffith, seemed tacitly to have recognized this by withdrawing, accompanied by most of his family, early in the seventeenth century, to Herefordshire, where his home at The Cwm, Llanrothal, became a major centre of Catholic influence in Stuart times. This move, possibly part of a wide-scale plan for the strategic concentration of Catholic strength, certainly deprived Glamorgan of effective leadership as markedly as it enriched Herefordshire. The Griffith family were leaving behind them only a small contingent of recusants in Glamorgan. The proportion of recusants to communicants in the whole diocese of Llandaff in 1603 was only fractionally more than one per cent; in Glamorgan it was more like 0.15 per cent. There may have been, admittedly, many more secret sympathizers, 'church papists' too timid to come out into the open, like the father of David Augustine Baker of Abergavenny, who was reconciled to the faith on his death-bed by the seminary priest, Morgan Clynnog. But their numbers are not easy to estimate and their timorousness made them allies of doubtful value. The truth was that, by 1603, recusancy in Glamorgan, though it would survive for generations, had been successfully contained in small encapsulated cells of no great consequence. Only the accession of a Catholic successor to Elizabeth might have given them any real hope of dramatically expanding their numbers.[81]

The reasons for the lean fortunes of recusancy are not far to seek. On the one side were all the conditions favouring the Established Church: a monopoly of the means of public worship, instruction, and education; its association with legality, order, and patriotism; and the reward it could offer, in return for outward conformity, of security and prospects for advancement. To be set against this were all the disabilities under which recusancy laboured: it could be propagated only in secret and outside the law; it was smeared with suggestions of disloyalty, subversion, and conspiracy; and it debarred men from positions of power and brought them in danger of heavy fines and long imprisonment, even if the inadequacies of the fining system and the evasions of recusants managed to alleviate much of the full rigour of penal statutes. For recusancy to thrive in these circumstances it needed the protection of families of the first rank, and in Glamorgan it found none. There had been at one time a number of influential families which had seemed likely to act as patrons of recusants: the Stradlings of St. Donat's, the Lewises of Y Fan, the Kemeyses of Cefnmabli, the Carnes of Ewenni, and the Turbervilles. Apart from the Turbervilles, none were proof against the blandishments of the established régime. After the death of Sir Thomas Stradling, the squires of St. Donat's conformed, although Sir Edward's brother, David, was a Catholic exile in the 1570s and a pensioner of Philip II. Both

Thomas Lewis and Rice Kemeys dutifully signed the Bond of Association of 1584, and Lewis was in the 1590s thought sufficiently reliable to be recommended for membership of the Council in the Marches. Thomas Carne was presented for recusancy in 1577 but never afterwards; in 1586 and 1588 he was a member of parliament, which suggests that he, too, had conformed; and the preamble to his will (1602) was even more Protestant than that of Sir Thomas Stradling. The Turbervilles were loyal enough to the faith; but they held no office after 1569, and their influence was obviously too restricted to protect them or their friends against persecution and imprisonment. Jenkin Turberville was rigorously examined in prison in London, and this may have hastened his death. He had a brother, Richard, a prisoner in the Clink; and two other Turbervilles, James and Lewis, died of gaol fever at Cardiff in 1598. Many other Glamorgan recusants were, like the Turbervilles, confined to prison at a time when a gaol sentence was not far removed from a death penalty, so pestilential and overcrowded was Cardiff gaol in the 1590s.[82]

In these circumstances effectively maintaining the Roman faith became a task of heroic proportions. Of course, there survived among the people at large a mass of somewhat unthinking vestiges of medieval practices; but this did little to commend itself to ardent Catholics. What was essential for the spiritual health and nourishment of the faithful was the regular ministration of the sacraments by properly-ordained priests. But very few of them were available; it was extremely difficult for them to enter the country undetected; and, having got in, even more difficult for them to work in the utmost secrecy. Occasionally we get glimpses of them ministering in a household like that of the Turbervilles at Pen-llin, or making use of deserted monastic chapels like that formerly belonging to Margam at Hafod-y-porth, where a congregation of 160 gathered in 1591, among them an infant carried by its nurse on a two-day journey from Llandeilo Fawr to be christened. A few priests apostatized, others were quickly captured. A handful only of them managed to remain active over a long period. The most celebrated of these was Morgan Clynnog, nephew of the more famous Morys Clynnog. A native of Caernarvonshire, he was educated at the English College at Rome, and returned to Wales in 1582. Thereafter he continued active, mainly in Glamorgan and Carmarthenshire, until at least as late as 1619. During all that time we get nothing more than the briefest and most occasional glimpse of what must have been a long and intensely active career of ministering to the faithful, encouraging young men to proceed to the Continental seminaries, and working in harmony with Jesuits and other priests. Morgan Clynnog was the exception; no other seminary priest is known to have had anything like so active and successful a ministry in Glamorgan.[83]

The labours of these priests were seconded by campaigns for the dissemination of Catholic literature. Jenkin Turberville, it may be recalled, kept a quantity of 'seditious books' in his home in 1596; and as late as 1625 it was some such collection that converted John Woodhouse, who read them 'in the parish of Aberdare'. Some of this literature was doubtless the work of English Catholic apologists; other publications were almost certainly those Welsh books published by exiles on the Continent like Morys Clynnog or Gruffydd Robert. But some of this literature was undoubtedly produced and copied in Glamorgan. The central figure in this activity was Llywelyn Siôn (1540–1615), the greatest Welsh professional copyist of his age. His assiduity not only preserved a great body of the Catholic verse and prose of the medieval period but also made available crucially important contemporary Catholic writings like the *Drych Cristnogawl* ('Christian Mirror'), of which Llywelyn Siôn's copy is the only one that preserves all three parts of the work in its entirety. He was, in addition, himself a poet who made no pretence of concealing his religious sympathies. However, under the close and oppressive surveillance of the authorities—Llywelyn Siôn was brought before the Great Sessions more than once—and amid a population apathetic and largely illiterate the work of publishing and distributing Romanist books and manuscripts must always have been formidable, and, at times, heartbreaking.[84] All these difficulties considered, the wonder was not that at the end of Elizabeth's reign there should have been only a small number of Glamorgan recusants but that there should have been any at all.

viii.

THE CHURCH IN EARLY-STUART TIMES

One of the most marked contrasts between Llandaff diocese in the Elizabethan age and in early-Stuart times was that during the former most of the bishops appointed were Welsh and often had an earlier connexion with the diocese, whereas of the four bishops appointed to the see between 1601 and 1640 three were Englishmen and one was a Scot, and none appears to have had any previous connexion with the diocese. The Stuart bishops owed their position to the favour of the crown or of a great courtier and, apart from Morgan Owen (1640–45), do not appear to have had any special suitability for the diocese of Llandaff but were rewarded with a diocese that happened to be vacant. One of them, George Carleton (1617–19), was not unaware of his own lack of appropriate qualifications for the diocese to which he had been called. Writing to Sir David Carleton in November 1617 he explained that he had been appointed to the diocese by the king and the prince. He confessed his misgivings that he could do little good there from ignorance of the language and on account of the opposition of some 'great ones who hate the truth' (a reference, perhaps, to the earl of Worcester?). He was honest enough to add that he had accepted the diocese only because the favours of princes were not to be rejected.[85]

Q

The first of the Stuart bishops was Francis Godwin (1562–1633), who was bishop of Llandaff from 1601 to 1617. This distinguished student of church history was a friend of Camden, whom he had accompanied in 1590 on a tour of Wales in search of antiquities. In 1601 he published his *De Praesulibus Angliae Commentarius*, a history of the episcopal succession in the English Church which is his chief claim to distinction, though he himself wryly confessed that his 'delight in the study of history and antiquities' had been 'somewhat greater than was needful for a man that dedicated himself and his labours unto the service of God's church in the ministry'. As a reward, he was made bishop of Llandaff in succession to Bishop William Morgan, despite the urgent plea of Griffith Lewis, dean of Gloucester, and a native of the diocese of St. Asaph, that he be placed in that 'poor and small seat of Llandaff that now in mine old age I may do good in that my native country'. Little is known of Bishop Godwin's tenure of the see except that he was confronted with serious problems of recusancy and a shortage of ministers so acute that Lord Eure, president of the Council in the Marches, in 1609 reported that the bishop was obliged to allow laymen to officiate. Lord Eure went on to urge a project for six ministers to be paid from recusants' fines. Godwin, described by Anthony à Wood as a good preacher and 'a strict liver', seems to have spent most of his time at Llandaff engaged upon the revision of his famous book, a second edition of which appeared in 1615 and gained him translation to Hereford.[86]

Godwin's successor was George Carleton (1559–1628), bishop of Llandaff from 1617 to 1619. Born in Northumberland, Carleton was a pupil of the famous Puritan divine, Bernard Gilpin, 'Apostle of the North', and enjoyed a reputation at Oxford as a poet and orator as well as a theologian. In 1615 he entered the service of the Prince of Wales and, taken aback by the sycophancy of some clerics and resolving that he 'begged best who made his service speak for him', he allowed the see of Carlisle to pass to another candidate. In 1617, however, he overcame his scruples and accepted the diocese of Llandaff in spite of his own misgivings. At the Synod of Dort in 1618 he won golden opinions for his spirited defence of the bishops and the apostolic succession; his speeches being described as 'learned, devout, and the style masculous'. His reward for such an achievement was to be translated to Chichester in 1619.[87]

Theophilus Field (1574–1636), bishop of the diocese from 1619 to 1627, had a Puritan background like Carleton. He was the son of the very famous and active London Puritan leader of Elizabeth's reign, John Field. He proved, however, to be an unscrupulous individual, 'took no very exalted view of his profession, nor ever troubled himself much about its duties', and turned out to be the worst of the early-Stuart bishops of Llandaff. He first came to prominence as the chaplain and client of Sir Francis Bacon, and had acted as a kind of broker to the latter in his peculations. As the duke of Buckingham's star rose, Field transferred his allegiance to the royal favourite. In the words of a contemporary, Field 'hung about the court with shameless avidity watching for preferment' and, thanks to Buckingham's patronage, he was made bishop of Llandaff in 1619. In 1621 his malpractices in Bacon's service caught up with him when the Lord Keeper fell, and he was accused of bribery and jobbery in Parliament (below, p. 243). Fortunately for Field, Buckingham did not withdraw his favour and even defended him in Parliament. Field wrote to thank Buckingham effusively for his protection and to sue for the vacant diocese of London or Hereford, 'the next to mine, whither my predecessors have oft been moved', as a salve for his wounded reputation. Field got no reward for his pains on this occasion and was obliged to remain, disgruntled and nursing his grievances, in Llandaff for some years. In that space he achieved the unenviable distinction of losing from his diocese its most famous manuscript, the *Liber Landavensis*, in which Field was the last bishop of Llandaff to write his name. He lent the manuscript to the great antiquary, John Selden, from whom it passed to John Vaughan of Trawsgoed, Cardiganshire, and from the Vaughans it came to the house of Llannerch and Gwysaney. Field importuned Buckingham for translation with renewed urgency in 1626. Likening himself to 'old household-stuff, apt to be broke upon often removing', he asked for one final move to a worthwhile see, like Ely or Bath and Wells, and promised, 'I will spend the remainder of my days in writing an history of your good deeds to me and others'. Ely or Bath and Wells were prizes too big for Field to hope for, and he had to be content with Buckingham's consolation prize to him—another, and not-much-richer, Welsh diocese, that of St. David's, where he succeeded Bishop Laud.[88]

Field was succeeded by William Murray, B.D., a Scot, who was bishop from 1627 to 1639. Murray had previously been provost of Eton and bishop of Kilfenora in Ireland. But little is known of him or his episcopate at Llandaff. Generally considered to be a friend and protégé of Laud, he probably owed his translation to Llandaff to Laud's influence. It may well be significant of his devotion to Laudian ideals that his tenure of the see is characterized by attempts to improve the fabric of the cathedral and the order of worship there. How far his High Church tendencies may have contributed to the rise of Puritanism within his diocese it is impossible to tell, but it may be more than a coincidence that Murray was the first bishop to be confronted by overt and articulate Puritans like Wroth, Cradock, and Erbury (below, pp. 253-5). He died in March 1639 and was buried at Mathern.[88A]

The last of the bishops of Llandaff before the Civil Wars, Morgan Owen (*c.* 1585-1645), was even more closely associated with Laud than Murray had been. He was the son of a clergyman, Owen Rees, a native of Myddfai in Carmarthenshire and reputedly related to a famous family of physicians in that parish. He entered Jesus College, Oxford, in 1608, graduated B.A. in 1613 when chaplain of New College, proceeded M.A. in 1616 as a member of Hart Hall, and D.D. in 1636. A wealthy man and a close friend and admirer of Laud, Owen set up the porch of St. Mary's Oxford, with the image of the Blessed Virgin Mary and child upon it. Laud was thought to have inspired this action, and at his trial it was to form the basis of serious charges brought against him. Made bishop of Llandaff in March 1640 at Laud's instigation, Owen was to have only a short and unhappy tenure there. In 1641 he was imprisoned in the Tower for promulgating the canons enacted by Convocation in the early summer of 1640. Released after a time, he was once more imprisoned there for having signed the protest drawn up by twelve bishops in December 1641 that because they could only attend the House in danger of their lives, Parliament was unfree and all its proceedings illegal. After remaining in prison for about four months, Owen 'retired to his own country, whither his sufferings likewise followed him, as well for the sake of his patron, as of his order and loyalty'. He found his palace at Mathern seized by a citizen of Cardiff called Green, together with all the revenues deriving from his see. He withdrew in despair to his native Carmarthenshire, where he enjoyed Vicar Prichard's friendship. His death there in 1645 was said to have been hastened by the news of the execution of Archbishop Laud.[89]

The main problems confronting all these bishops continued to be the same as those which had beset their Elizabethan predecessors: the poverty of the diocese; the need for preaching and instruction, especially in Welsh; and the persistence of recusancy and Catholic sympathies. By the 1630s, however, there had emerged a new and vigorous form of Puritan nonconformity which was to challenge the Anglican Church in the future much more dangerously than recusancy had ever done.

THE POVERTY OF THE DIOCESE

Each of the Stuart bishops of Landaff was made pressingly aware of the meagreness of his income; how, indeed, could they fail to be in an age of continuing inflation? Bishop Godwin, in 1607, urged that he be given the archdeaconry of Gloucester because his see was so poor. Carleton hinted that the diocese was so unremunerative that the only reason for accepting it was that princes' favours must not lightly be declined. Field managed to combine a compliment to the king with a sly dig at the 'exility' of his preferment. In the preface to a tract published by him in 1624, *The Earth's Encrease, or a Communion Cup: presented to the King's Most Excellent Majesty for a New Year's Gift*, he wrote: 'Silver and gold have I none, such as I have I give or rather render', the gift being the treatise. This, he hoped, would be sufficiently acceptable to James I that 'by the next New Year's tide' he might be able to present the king with a 'cup indeed, reall and massie'.[90] Each of the bishops had to be allowed to retain other livings *in commendam*. Bishop Godwin retained the subdeanery of Exeter and his rectory of Kingston Seymour when he became bishop in 1601; two years later he added the rectory of Shirenewton in Monmouthshire; and in 1607 he begged to be allowed the archdeaconry of Gloucester. Even Morgan Owen, a conscientious Laudian and himself reputedly a wealthy man, nevertheless held the livings of Bedwas and Rudry *in commendam*, and he also became rector of Newton. Nor did some of the bishops escape criticism for their avarice and self-seeking. Of Francis Godwin the antiquary, Browne Willis, commented acidly that he 'omitted no opportunity in disposing of his preferments in order to provide for his children'. Three of Godwin's sons, Thomas, chancellor of Hereford, Morgan, archdeacon of Shropshire, and Charles, a Monmouthshire parson, as well as his son-in-law, Richard Bassett, chancellor of Llandaff and prebendary of Hereford, were left well enough provided for when the bishop died. Bishop Theophilus Field was the target of sharper censure than Godwin. He was reputed to have pestered the duke of Buckingham relentlessly with letters 'urging his poverty' and the needs of his large family. In 1621, two years after his election as bishop of Llandaff, he was impeached by the House of Commons for bribery and 'brocage' (i.e., the corrupt jobbing of offices) before his promotion. Cleared on the charge of bribery, he was severely admonished for his 'brocage' by the archbishop of Canterbury in a meeting of Convocation.[91]

The pressure of inadequate incomes weighed on the cathedral chapter as well as the bishops. Many of the canons continued to succumb to the temptation, so fiercely denounced by Bishop Bleddyn in 1576, of trying to lease their lands for long terms in return for large entry fines. Their management of their own finances was often improvident and negligent, seemingly designed to meet present need without much concern for future solvency. At one stage early in the seventeenth century their debts to their own archdeacon, arising out of the accounts for 1600, 1607, and 1608, amounted to £138 12s. 7d., a large sum in relation to the smallness of their income. Belated attempts at reform, periodically made by them, were not wholly successful. In 1598 they decreed that leases should no longer run for more than 21 years, following an example set them by Bishop Babington, who had leased the manors of Bishton, Dewstow, and Llanddewi to Thomas Lewis Y Fan for 21 years only in 1593, and in return for an entry fine of £100. For some years afterwards the chapter records seem to show that this policy was moderately successful, though there were leases for three lives by Bishop Godwin in January 1603 and January 1610, and by the chapter on a number of occasions after 1616.[92]

Some of the difficulties which the archdeacon and chapter encountered in their relations with the laity over the leasing of their possessions are pointed up in documents concerning disputes over the rectory of Eglwysilan in 1611. At this time the chapter claimed that the fruits of this rectory were worth £200 a year, though the rent for it provided in a lease concluded as far back as the 35th year of Henry VIII's reign was no more than £22. Not surprisingly, the chapter now wanted to let the rectory 'at the best and highest rate' without fine. However, Sir William Herbert of St. Julian's claimed to have an interest in the lease and offered the chapter a substantial entry fine if it would enter into a new agreement with him. It would not be easy to refuse him when, as the chapter itself admitted, he was a 'gentleman of great wealth, power and countenance', of whom 'many of the said chapter [were] dependants'. He was also, as it happened, a man deeply interested in divinity who had published an *Exposition of the Revelations*, though he hardly seems to have allowed himself to be guided by his New Testament studies in dealing with the chapter. For all Herbert's influence and authority, however, the chapter had the temerity to maintain that it had no record of his lease 'in any register book' and was prepared to contest its validity in a court of law. Before the issue between the two parties could be resolved Herbert had died and his claims were taken over by his nephew, William Herbert of Crindau. For all its brave talk, the chapter was no match for the power of a Herbert in the end. It was to the younger William Herbert that the rectory was re-leased in June 1612 upon surrender of the old lease. This time it was for a term of 21 years only, but the rent remained at £22. Perhaps the lease was agreed to only upon condition of a large entry fine, but if there was such a payment it went unrecorded in the chapter records.[93]

A further move to control leases was taken in 1619. The chapter laid down that no grant was to be made unless a majority of its members were present, and no proxies were to be allowed. In 1626 Bishop Field and eleven others signed in the chapter act book 'a most serious and solemn protestation to the glory of God and credit of the place and good' of their successors. Moved to this by consideration of the 'great decay' of Llandaff cathedral and the 'small means' of its prebends, they 'steadfastly resolved' not to renew the lease of Eglwysilan rectory but to 'convert the entire profits and annual rent (being not diminished by taking any fine) to the best use and most valuable advantage' of their church. Unfortunately, as an historian of the diocese commented, 'the resolution was not long observed notwithstanding the use of their ancient form, "Qui custodit custodiat, qui violat anathema sit" '. In 1629 yet more attempts were made by Bishop Murray and the chapter to secure a firmer grip on the resources of the see. In response to a petition directed by him to the king Bishop Murray seems to have managed to reserve control of the manor and rectory of Bassaleg which, thanks to the good offices of Queen Elizabeth, had been secured by Sir William Herbert, from whom it had passed to one Benjamin Valentine, who paid no rent. In 1629, also, the chapter decided to scrutinize more closely the rents and leases of no less a figure than the earl of Worcester, but what the outcome was is not clear. The insufficiency of all these attempts at reform becomes evident when as late as 1634 it was found necessary to send royal letters to the bishop and chapter urging stricter control over the practice of converting leases of chapter lands from a term of 21 years into one of three lives in order to make quick profits on the basis of larger entry fines. The letters were accompanied by a firm reminder that particular attention should be paid that no bishop, dean, or canon should agree to such a transaction after he knew that he himself was to be translated to other preferment. Not that it was at all easy to maintain discipline over members of the chapter. In 1619 in the course of Bishop Field's visitation, the archdeacon of Llandaff, Robert Robotham, claimed that he had the archbishop of Canterbury's authority for refusing to yield up documents and keys at the bishop's request. When angrily ordered by the bishop, 'Do all civilly and in good manners, else I will teach you manners', Robotham replied with equal heat, 'You cannot teach me manners', and stalked out.[94]

Some of the reforms and improvements embarked upon by the bishops and chapter after 1627 appear to be part of a drive by the Laudian bishop, William Murray, to improve the quality of the services and to raise the level of dignity and good order in worship and the appearance of the cathedral. In 1628 it was agreed by the chapter that on the first Sunday in every month one of the prebendaries, or a qualified deputy, should preach in the cathedral. Any one of them who failed to perform this duty was to be subject to a fine of 10s., of which 6s. 8d. was to go as a fee to a preacher and 3s. 4d. to the poor of Llandaff. In 1629 an organist was appointed. In 1630 efforts were made to ensure that when members of the chapter were meeting together they should come into the chapter-house 'wearing their gowns, hoods, and surplices', and money was set aside for the payment of 'six singing men' and 'four boys as choristers'. In the following year provision was made for the repair and upkeep of the bells, for the conduct of burials, and for announcements of the times when prebendaries would be preaching. In 1638 arrangements were made for the glazing of windows in the chancel, choir, chapels, chapter-house, library, schoolhouse, and consistory at the cathedral. But before any further progress could be achieved in beautifying the fabric and worship the Civil Wars had supervened.[95]

THE QUALITY OF THE CLERGY AND RELIGIOUS INSTRUCTION

The quality of the educational attainments of the clergy in England and Wales appears to have improved appreciably by the end of the sixteenth century and the beginning of the seventeenth. Their social status had risen, and more men of good family and university education were finding their way into the ranks of the priesthood. Jenkin Price, vicar of Baglan, 1587-1605, and parson of Briton Ferry, was a younger brother of Leyshon Price, lord of Briton Ferry. Richard Bassett, M.A., Ll.B. (d. 1644), a younger son of the squire of Beaupré, married the daughter of Bishop Godwin, and became vicar of Llantrisant, rector of Llandow, chancellor of Llandaff and prebendary of Hereford. His kinsman, Thomas Bassett (d. 1666), M.A., one of the Bonvilston Bassetts and the son of a cleric, another vicar of Llantrisant, was also rector of Leckwith, Llandough and Cogan, and prebendary of Llandaff. The Wilkins family of Llanquian provided a line of squire-parsons, three of whom were rectors of St. Mary Church in three successive generations spanning the whole of the seventeenth century. No fewer than seven members of various cadet lines of the Gamage family held preferment in early-Stuart Glamorgan. Four of them certainly owed their benefices to their connexion with their illustrious relative by marriage, the earl of Leicester, and the other three may also have been indebted to the same source. The existence of men of this kind among the clergy reminds us that the economic prospects for all seventeenth-century clergymen cannot have been utterly uninviting or they would never have attracted so many men of gentry stock. Many of them were nepotists, it is true, and not a few were pluralists, but at least it can be said in their favour that all of those mentioned above were graduates, like a large proportion of their fellow-clergy.[96]

However, some strange cases brought before the Court of High Commission in 1639 show how much the calibre of a clergyman appointed to a living, and his suitability, or otherwise, for serving the cure depended on lay patrons, whose choice could be distinctly unpredictable. In this episode of 1639 it was the Glamorgan living of Merthyr Dyfan which was the bone of contention. Almost certainly a mainly Welsh-speaking parish at this time, it had been held for 17 years by an Englishman, Laomedon Fowler, who had held it in plurality with the living of Cadoxton near Barry since 1626, though he possessed no dispensation for doing so. The irregularity was brought to light by one Thomas Maddocks, who laid information before the Lord Keeper and induced the latter to institute him to Merthyr Dyfan. However, the Lord Keeper had no authority to have done so, and while Llandaff was *sede vacante* in 1639 the patron of the living of Merthyr Dyfan, Sir Francis Popham, took advantage of the situation to present his own candidate, Oliver Chivers. It was a strange choice for him to have made. Chivers was not only an Englishman who knew no Welsh but he was also something of an anti-Puritan, whereas Popham was himself a man of marked Puritan sympathies. By the time Maddocks had taken the issue to the Court of High Commission for decision that body was on its last legs, and Chivers managed to retain Merthyr Dyfan. In the meantime Laomedon Fowler had been presented to Llantriddyd by Sir Thomas Aubrey.[97]

Unfortunately the absence of episcopal registers for this period, combined with the sparsity and bareness of entries for the diocese in the

Institution Books of the Court of Tenths and First Fruits, makes it impossible to generalize with much confidence about the nature and quality of most of the Llandaff clergy of this period. Where there were conscientious clergymen with a will to instruct their parishioners, they were finding better means at hand to enable them to do so. In addition to the vast output of English religious and devotional books for those who understood the language, there was also a modest trickle of books in Welsh. Already a Welsh Prayer Book and New Testament and Psalter had existed in each parish since 1567, and the whole Bible since 1588. In 1620 had come the excellent Authorised Version of the Welsh Bible and in 1621 the fourth re-issue of the Prayer Book. Even more significant in some ways was the publication in 1630 of the first Welsh Bible intended to reach men's homes, the octavo Bible, known affectionately as *Y Beibl Bach* ('The Little Bible'). Along with the Bible and the Prayer Book came a number of other works in Welsh designed to deepen and illumine popular devotion, ranging from Maurice Kyffin's translation of Bishop Jewel's *Apologia* to a slim volume designed for children bearing the title *Car-wr y Cymry*. Just how familiar Glamorgan priests and parishioners were with these publications we have almost no means of telling, though the fortunate survival of the Swansea churchwardens' accounts shows that in this urban parish reasonable care and diligence was shown in buying and repairing Bibles and service-books in Welsh and English.[98]

The only specific Glamorgan contribution to the preparation of Welsh religious literature was a major one: the translation of the Book of Homilies by Edward James (?1569–?1610), a Glamorgan man and chancellor of the diocese of Llandaff. An Oxford graduate, James held a number of livings in Monmouthshire before being made vicar of Cadoxton-juxta-Neath in 1603 and chancellor of Llandaff in 1606. His translation of the Homilies, published in 1606, has justly won high praise as a model of pure and dignified Welsh prose. It was deeply influenced by the standard set in the Bible of 1588 by Bishop William Morgan, who may well have encouraged James to undertake the work when he was bishop of Llandaff. James's grave and sonorous prose, intended to be read in Welsh churches, week in and week out, must have exercised down the generations an influence on the Welsh language second only to that of the Bible and Prayer Book. Surprisingly enough, James's translation of the Homilies owes little or nothing to the influence and inspiration of the native Glamorgan school of prose authors so active in the Middle Ages and the sixteenth century (*Ante*, III, ch. x). Almost the only point of contact between James and the earlier writers is that he, like the translator of 'Darn o'r Ffestial', a Welsh translation of some of John Mirk's sermons, was drawn to translate homilies into Welsh. Two reasons may account for this lack of continuity. There is, on the one hand, the powerful influence of the new kind of Welsh scholarly humanism exercised through the medium of university graduates and biblical translators like

William Salesbury, Richard Davies, and, above all, William Morgan, to which Edward James was particularly susceptible. On the other hand—and this in itself may be a consequence of the rise of the new-style humanism—the native Glamorgan prose tradition itself appears to have withered to the point of extinction, and no new additions were made to it in the seventeenth century.[99]

The other distinctive Glamorgan contribution to Welsh religious literature, the *cwndidau*, also became distinctly enfeebled in the seventeenth century, though without disappearing entirely. After the rich harvest of the Tudor Age, Professor Griffith John Williams drew attention to only two *cwndidwyr* during the early Stuart period, each of them no more than a minor figure. Both were laymen, and both came from the western side of the county. The one was William Price of Ynys-y-maerdy in Briton Ferry, member of parliament for Glamorgan in 1621–2 and for Glamorgan boroughs in 1624–6, and the other was Edward Dafydd of Margam, the last of the old-style poets of Glamorgan (below, pp. 554–8). Neither of them was a distinguished poet and they added little of note to the existing stock of religious verse. It does seem, however, as if free verse continued to maintain some hold over popular imagination and loyalty and did not become extinct until the eighteenth century. The impact of the local *cwndidau* may have been reinforced at this time by that of the highly popular religious and didactic verses of Vicar Prichard of Llandovery, composed in easily-intelligible, colloquial style and sung to popular tunes. Though the vicar's verses were best known and most influential in the neighbourhood of his home in Carmarthenshire they could easily have spread south-east into Glamorgan. Additional links between the vicar and Glamorgan may have been forged by Sir Thomas Mansel of Margam and Bishop Owen of Llandaff, both of whom are known to have been his close friends and admirers, and there may have been others in Glamorgan who were impressed by his homespun poetic aids to Christian belief and morality.[100]

Just why the springs of Christian literature which had flowed so copiously in the sixteenth century should have run dry in the next is not easily explained. Probably the most important reason is the ending of the medieval era in the life and organization of the professional bards and littérateurs, which had undoubtedly reached the end of its tether by the beginning of the seventeenth century; for although many gentlemen and clerics had been involved in the composition of literature in addition to bards and men-of-letters by calling, it was these professionals, nevertheless, who had been the heart and soul of literary tradition and continuity. Furthermore, the appointment of a succession of non-Welsh bishops and the existence among the higher clergy of a number of Englishmen could significantly have reduced the degree of patronage and encouragement previously enjoyed by Welsh writers; certainly, there was no one among the early Stuart chapter who would readily compare with William Evans, the Elizabethan treasurer of Llandaff, as a patron of literature. Finally, the gradual anglicization of the squires and the gentry may have contributed to the decline, though we ought not to overstress this point, for as late as the 1630s we know that the heir of a family as important as that of Lewis Y Fan had a schoolmaster to teach him Welsh, as well as two other tutors to instruct him in French and Latin.[101] Nor should we, either, make too gloomy an assessment of the effect of these literary changes on the quality and nature of religious instruction. When all was said and done, if the Welsh Bible, Prayer Book, and Homilies were being regularly read in the churches, they provided for Welsh people in their own tongue a much wider, more substantial, and more varied intellectual and religious diet, and one more systematically and universally purveyed, than ever the earlier *cwndidau* and prose translations could have done. Even so, it cannot but be a matter of regret that Glamorgan appeared to have lost the urge and creativity to make those original contributions to religious literature which once had characterized it.

RECUSANCY IN THE EARLY-SEVENTEENTH CENTURY

Whatever degree of success the parish clergy of Glamorgan may have achieved in grounding their parishioners in the essentials of the doctrine of the church 'by law established' there still remained a handful of men and women obdurate to all attempts by persuasion or persecution to wean them away from their loyalty to the Roman faith. The penalties and discomforts attaching to such an allegiance were no less in the seventeenth century than they had been in the previous one. At an earlier point in this chapter it was suggested that the only hope for a happier lot for recusants and for a substantial increase in their numbers was that a Roman Catholic ruler might come to occupy the throne. James I himself was not such a ruler, but the reputation that he enjoyed at his accession for being tolerant in religion raised keen expectations among his recusant subjects. Their hopes were still-born; and as early as 1604 the Elizabethan penal laws against them were re-enacted. Still more severe legislation followed in the wake of the alarm aroused by the Gunpowder Plot when, in 1606, two new statutes were passed; the one imposing stiffer fines on recusants, and the other requiring officers of local government to be stricter in compiling their lists of offenders. A few years later, in 1610, came the Oaths Act directed particularly against women devotees who had often formed the hard core of recusant resistance. The net effect of this more stringent code was to make the watch kept on recusants by the local authorities appreciably harsher and more sharp-eyed. More thorough-going vigilance is reflected in the gaol files of the Great Sessions and the Recusant Rolls which, between them, give us a fairly comprehensive list of Glamorgan recusants, especially during James I's reign, as may be seen from the following table:[102]

Year	Number of recusants	Year	Number of recusants
Sept. 1603	15	July 1611	33
Sept. 1604	8	1617	23
Feb. 1605	47	1622	27
April 1605	16	1629	48
Sept. 1609	24	1636	46

As may be seen from the table the overall number of Catholic recusants did not increase markedly during James I's reign. Even before the outbreak of the panic awakened by the Gunpowder Plot, 63 recusants were presented in the space of two months in the spring of 1605. On the whole, however, the number of recusants remains remarkably constant in Glamorgan down to the end of James I's reign, suggesting that the recusants could do no more than hold their own. Was it perhaps disgust at James's failure to relieve the lot of Catholics as well as at his moral delinquencies which provoked the exasperated and seditious outburst by Thomas William, a yeoman from that most persistently recusant of Glamorgan parishes, Colwinston? He was presented by a Cardiff grand jury in 1625 for having said, 'Mae dy frenin yn drewi ger bron Duw yn ei bechod fel ddoet ti, William Howell' ('Thy king stinks before God in his sin, as didst thou, William Howell').[103]

There seems to have been a mild upsurge in recusant numbers during Charles I's reign. The second Stuart ruler had a wife and a number of influential courtiers who were Roman Catholics. During his eleven years of personal rule, when he was freed from having to placate a puritanly-minded lower house of Parliament, something of the vigour may have gone out of the persecution of recusants. Encouraged by the milder atmosphere, recusants increased in number. In 1629 there were 48 recusants noted in Glamorgan and 46 in 1636. This represented a perceptible but undramatic increase over the numbers in James I's reign.

Throughout the early-Stuart period the pattern of recusancy continued to be broadly similar to what it had been in Elizabethan times; the stubborn and unyielding struggle of a tiny handful to maintain their beliefs in the face of repression by a hostile régime. Survival of the faith continued to depend on the courage and steadfastness of its devotees, sustained by the patronage of one or two landowning families and the zeal of a handful of dedicated priests. The most gifted Glamorgan recusant, William Griffith, was now living and working at the Cwm in Herefordshire but his native county may indirectly have benefited from his co-operation with Father Robert Jones when, between them, they virtually reorganized the Catholic missionary effort in Wales and the Marches. Deeply worried by the activities of this group of Catholics in south-east Wales and along the English border, and the comfort and succour they derived from Jesuits and priests, the puritanical Sir James Perrott urged upon Salisbury in March 1612 the desirability of sending into their midst some 'trusty professed Romanist', who might 'discover and reveal much of their haunts and practices'. Within Glamorgan itself, the geographical distribution of recusants showed the same concentration of resistance in or near the parishes of the Vale, notably in Colwinston, Margam, Pyle and Kenfig, Newcastle, and Newton Nottage. In other parishes where recusants had previously been found, like Llancarfan, Llyswyrnwy, Laleston, St. Bride's Major, Coety, and Aberafan, they seem to have disappeared by the seventeenth century. But in the western end of the county there were growing signs of resistance in the parishes of Cadoxton-juxta-Neath and Llantwit-juxta-Neath, which had been 'infected' from the 1590s onwards. Equally interesting was the appearance for the first time of recusancy in some of the upland parishes, Eglwysilan, Llanfabon, and Gelli-gaer. Whether this was the fruit of intensive missionary activity by the priests in these localities, or the result of closer scrutiny of the beliefs and practices of parishioners there by the officers of local administration, it does not seem possible to tell. It may well have been the latter, however, because the first indication of recusants in these parishes comes in the course of the concerted drive to uncover religious disaffection in the years 1604-5.[104]

Most of the recusants were drawn from the same kind of social background as in Elizabethan times. Pre-eminent among them still were the prolific and determined Turbervilles, one of whose representatives at least was found in each of the parishes with the longest and most unremitting history of recusancy. Two of the family, and possibly more, became Catholic priests. One of them, Humphrey Turberville, was at Valladolid in 1602 and later entered the Benedictine order, of which he remained an important member until his death in Glamorgan in 1645.[105] The other, Henry Turberville, matriculated at Douai in 1635. Around the Turbervilles were grouped a number of yeomen, farmers and labourers. But though the numbers showed a modest increase in Charles I's reign there was no likelihood of this being maintained. Only a complete change in the king's religious allegiance or of policy in favour of the Catholics could have transformed their prospects; but, High Churchman though Charles was, there was no chance of his going over to Rome. In the meantime there was one alarming sympton of decline from within the Catholic ranks. Unsparing though men like Father Robert Jones and other Catholic priests were in their efforts to minister to the faithful, this could not conceal the fact that there was a sharp decrease in the number of young men coming forward to offer themselves for the priesthood. During Elizabeth's reign 16 young men had gone from Llandaff to become priests; between 1603 and 1642 only four did so.[106] Figures for other Welsh dioceses are comparable. Yet without the commitment of the priests, recusancy must necessarily wither. Its decay from within was further being hastened from without by the rise of a new and more aggressive form of Protestantism in the shape of Puritan nonconformity.

The Emergence of Puritan Nonconformity

The terms 'Puritan' and 'Puritanism' are sometimes used in such a way as to denote only those who broke away from, or were driven out of, the Church of England to establish separate or 'gathered' congregations. This should not lead us to overlook the influence of those who would never seriously have thought of leaving the Established Church during the age of Elizabeth and the first two Stuart kings but who would, nevertheless, have wished to see it 'purified' of what they called 'the dregs of popery'. They wanted a simplified order of service nearer to that of Calvinist reformed churches in other countries, a stricter observance of Sundays, less emphasis on vestments and ritual, much greater attention to preaching, and a more scrupulous concern for personal sanctity of life. Though Wales as a whole was notoriously slow to respond to such promptings there were some minimal indications of their existence in Glamorgan during this period. They occur, predictably, in the more anglicized towns and parishes. In Cardiff there had already been some inklings of these tendencies in the persons of the martyrs, Thomas Capper and Rawlins White. Later, the records of the Great Sessions reveal that there were some people in Cardiff whose insistence upon carrying out burial services punctiliously according to Protestant rites gave offence to others more backward looking and was a common source of affrays in churchyards. Stricter observance of Sundays in the town led to the prosecution of Thomas Jenkin for being a 'vagrant and common player in the time of divine service' in 1584, of Rees Jones and others of Gelli-gaer 'for playing at tennis in the time of divine service' also in 1584 and of one Morgan, a labourer of Cardiff, 'for that he works upon the Lord's Day' in 1590.[107]

A favourite means of propagating moderate—and sometimes not-so-moderate—Puritanism was the appointment of 'lecturers', usually zealous young graduates who preached at parish churches at times other than those of the normal services, frequently on Sunday afternoons. In the Neath area, as early as 1580, David Hopkins of Neath House left money in his will for the preaching of sermons 'in our mother tongue' at Llangyfelach, Neath, Cadoxton, and Swansea. Later, Neath and its environs were to be deeply influenced by the Puritan preaching of Robert Powell, vicar of Cadoxton-juxta-Neath from 1620 to c. 1640. This 'very able preacher' was a 'great light in the country', of whom Vicar Prichard of Llandovery gave it as his opinion that he knew 'no church minister who had such care and regard to the interest of Christ'. Nor ought we to overlook the unmistakably Puritan flavour of the letter written by the dying Lady Jane Mansel in 1638 to her son, Bussy, later to be one of the foremost parliamentary commanders in Glamorgan during the Commonwealth. In it she adjured him 'first, and above all things to be diligent and careful in the service of my great God'. In the town of Swansea, too, some Puritan tendencies have been discerned. In 1593 the vicar of the town, John After, was presented in the consistory court at Carmarthen for failing to conduct services in Welsh, and he was required by the court to do so every third Sunday. In 1604 the churchwardens of Swansea made two contributions to the relief of the city of Geneva. Sermons were very much to the taste of the Swansea burgesses, whose accounts between 1613 and 1635 record payments made to a number of visiting preachers for their discourses. Two, at least, of these preachers, Evan Williams and Lewis Thomas, were men of pronounced Puritan sympathies. Furthermore, the first extant parish register of Swansea shows that in the 1630s, and possibly earlier, Swansea parents had developed a marked taste for giving their children biblical names, like Ruth or Rebecca, Moses or Isaac, not previously encountered among the names of townspeople.[108]

Not until the reign of Charles I, however, do we find radical Puritan opposition to the Established Church being taken to the point of open separation. A conspicuous feature of this break was that it was in those parts of Wales like the north-eastern border around Wrexham and in Flintshire, or even more particularly in Monmouthshire, where recusancy was strongest, best-organized, and most articulate, that an equally positive and eloquent expression of hard-core Puritanism manifested itself. One of the counties in which such Puritanism gained ground was Glamorgan. Before proceeding to trace its emergence, however, it is necessary to refer briefly to some hoary myths concerning the alleged origins of Glamorgan Puritanism. They originate, it need hardly be said, in some of Iolo Morganwg's ingenious inventions. Long discredited, they seem to persist in popular imagination with a tenacity not easily defeated. The origin of the legend lies in a letter in one of Iolo's manuscripts purporting to give an account of congregations of advanced Puritan believers founded in the recesses of Blaenau Morgannwg under the influence of that Thomas Llywelyn apocryphally claimed by Iolo to have translated the Bible into Welsh before Bishop William Morgan. These secret conventicles were even said to have enjoyed the inspiration and advice of John Penry, though that famous Welsh Puritan is not thought by historians to have made any real impact on his native land in his own lifetime or for centuries afterwards. The story adumbrated by Iolo was conveyed by him to Benjamin Malkin, author of a celebrated and widely-read account of a tour through Wales, from whom it found its way into the writings of a number of subsequent authors. Their often romantic and highly-coloured accounts of ardent believers dauntlessly holding secret meetings in lonely glens and remote farmhouses have no basis in any reliable historical record.[109]

We are on sure ground only when we come to the exertions of the undoubted pioneers of Puritan separatism in south Wales. The apostle of all the early Welsh Puritan churches was William Wroth (1576–1641), a man of Monmouthshire stock and an Oxford graduate, who was made rector of Llanfaches, a small Monmouthshire parish between Newport and Chepstow on July 17, 1617 at King James's presentation. For some twenty years before he came under censure from his bishop in the 1630s Wroth had, by means of his powerful preaching and personal sanctity, converted many from what a Puritan record calls 'their sinful courses in the world'. The same record informs us that he afterwards gathered his converts 'into the gospel order of church government'. Among the 'multitudes' who 'came with delight' to Llanfaches were believers not only from Monmouthshire but also from English border counties and from Welsh counties, among them Glamorgan. One of the Glamorgan men most deeply influenced by Wroth was William Erbery (1604–54). Son of a Roath merchant, graduate of both Oxford and Cambridge, Erbery was ordained a deacon in 1626 and was for some years a curate at Newport. Having become vicar of St. Mary's, Cardiff, in August 1633, Erbery began to preach Puritanism to his congregation with all the fervour of his excitable and unstable mind. Among his converts at Cardiff was the fifteen-year-old Christopher Love (1618–51), later to be a well-known Puritan, whose career at Oxford was financed by his mother and Erbery because Love's father was hostile to his son's Puritan convictions. Love himself was not very complimentary to his birthplace, which he referred to on the scaffold as an 'obscure country in Wales'. Erbery had as his curate at Cardiff one of the most talented of all early Welsh Puritans, Walter Cradock (?1610–1659), also a Monmouthshire man, an Oxford graduate, and a preacher of exceptional gifts.[110]

Although Erbery, Cradock, and Wroth especially, had been evangelizing for some years previously it was not until Archbishop Laud's drive against the Puritans that their activities began to emerge more clearly into the light of historical records. In 1634, under Laud's inspiration, Charles I issued instructions requiring each bishop to present an annual report to his metropolitan 'so that we may see how the whole church is governed and our commands obeyed'. Bishop Murray of Llandaff had been able to certify in his reply for the year 1633 that he had 'not one refractory, nonconformist, or schismatical minister' and only 'two lecturers, and they are both licensed preachers'. Murray's return for 1634, however, described both Erbery and Cradock as having 'preached very schismatically and dangerously to the people'. This had brought Erbery a stern warning from Murray; while Cradock, described by his bishop as 'a bold, ignorant fellow', had had his licence to preach taken away. The 'base and unchristian' passage in Cradock's sermon which seems to have given particular offence to the bishop and to the king himself when he heard of it was Cradock's declaration 'that God so loved the world that for it He sent His son to live like a slave and die like a beast'. Yet their censure of Cradock's preaching would seem to have been harsh in view of the exceptional reputation he enjoyed among Puritans for his 'wonderful faculty of coming down and bringing with him the things of God to the meanest of his auditors'.[111]

Murray's report for 1635 condemned the 'two noted schismatics, Wroth and Erbery, that led away many simple people after them'. Both were now proceeded against in the Court of High Commission, but the outbreak of sickness caused a long delay, and it was not until 1638 that Erbery, who would 'neither submit nor satisfy his parishioners, to whom he hath given public offence', was forced to resign his living. He did not leave Cardiff, however, but continued to preach there to those who sympathized with his views. Wroth was reported to Murray as having submitted. It has been suggested that in fact he resigned his living, but the Institution Books of Llandaff livings reveal no trace of this. In November of the following year, 1639, Wroth founded at Llanfaches the first Independent church in Wales, to which Cradock returned as Wroth's assistant after a temporary exile in north Wales and the Marches. This church at Llanfaches appeared in Puritan eyes to be 'like Antioch', 'the mother church in that Gentile country' of south Wales. Before the outbreak of the Civil War in 1642 another Independent church had been founded at Cardiff with William Erbery as its minister.[112]

A late but well-informed source on the development of Puritanism in Wales—the account written by the great Welsh Puritan leader, Henry Maurice, in 1675—assigns priority among the Puritan churches in Glamorgan to 'those of Merthyr, which is part now of Llanigon church. And also the church that meets at Swansea, gathered at first by Mr. Ambrose Mostyn'. Local tradition in Merthyr Tydfil maintained stoutly that the first gathering of Dissenters used to meet at the lonely farmstead at Blaencannaid from 1620 onwards and was constituted as a church about 1642. Historians of Merthyr and district have accepted the validity of the tradition, though their claims to reliability are weakened by their fondness for Iolo Morganwg's unfounded claims for Thomas Llywelyn as a Puritan pioneer and by their suggestion that the congregation worshipping there consisted of men of different religious standpoints, including Baptists, Independents, Presbyterians, and even Quakers—apparently before the Civil Wars! By the 1650s Merthyr was certainly a strong centre of Puritan and Quaker beliefs, and it is not out of the question that the nucleus of a Puritan church existed there before 1642; but in the absence of more and firmer evidence it would be unwise to express too dogmatic an opinion either way on the subject.[113]

Puritan stirrings in the western end of the county around Swansea are better documented. The report of Bishop Field of St. David's for

1636 drew attention to Marmaduke Matthews (1606–1683), vicar of Penmaen, a native of Llangyfelach and an Oxford graduate, who was said to have preached against the 'keeping of all holy days with divers other, as fond, of profane opinions'. He, too, was threatened with proceedings in the Court of High Commission, but he migrated in 1638 to New England, where he became a Puritan pastor. His departure was not the end of Puritanism in those parts, for in April 1642 Ambrose Mostyn (1610–63), a scion of the well-known Mostyn family of Flintshire and an Oxford graduate, was appointed lecturer in the parish of Pennard. It was an interesting appointment, the only one made in Wales by a committee set up by the Long Parliament to improve the state of religion. Mostyn was later to have a distinguished career in the Swansea area, which he turned into a stronghold of Puritan convictions. But before he could achieve anything worthwhile in 1642, the Civil War between King and Parliament had broken out. Royalist Glamorgan was no place for ardent Puritans, whose leaders now fled into exile to more congenial havens in England.[114]

CHAPTER V

The Civil Wars in Glamorgan

By C. MERVYN THOMAS[*]

THE history of the Civil War in Glamorgan, as elsewhere, is essentially a history of families. It is the history of that small, closely-knit group of people, the gentry, who in Tudor and Stuart times had risen to a dominant position at the county level where the work of local government was concerned. It is the account of their reaction to the problems that confronted them as King and Parliament contended for the supreme power in the land and plunged the country into civil war. It is the account of their response to the call to arms and, for those who remained faithful to their sovereign, of trial and tribulation after the defeat of the Royalist cause. The mass of the population, bound by patent ties of tenure and not so obvious but equally binding ties of servile association and loyalty, rarely acted in an independent manner but were generally content to follow, where compelled, the lead of the gentry, their betters and their masters.

SUPPORT FOR THE CROWN

The gentry of Glamorgan, for a variety of reasons, supported the King when the call to arms came. National pride and patriotism had bound them with strong ties of loyalty to the Tudor dynasty—a legacy which the Stuarts inherited. Then there were the more material gains derived from the Reformation and the Act of Union. The Reformation in Glamorgan, as elsewhere, had helped to advance the fortunes of the gentry who shared in the spoils that came their way consequent upon the dissolution of their county's monastic houses and the disposal of other ecclesiastical possessions. As for the Act of Union, its influence was to be experienced in both the economic and political fields. In the economic field it regularized the substitution of primogeniture for gavelkind which helped to promote the growth and consolidation of large landed estates in Glamorgan with, of course, the consequent economic aggrandisement of the gentry. In the political field the power of the gentry was further enhanced by parliamentary representation and the entrusting of local government and justice into their hands.

In religious matters neither Catholicism nor Puritanism commanded support among the ruling class of gentry. Almost imperceptibly they had drifted away from the old religion and slowly anchored themselves to the Anglican Church. The Turberville family was the last in Glamorgan

[257]

to cling to Catholicism and there is no evidence for believing that the gentry had espoused Puritan ideas, with the exception of the Price family of Gellihir and a probable member of the Carne family.[1] Indeed, it would seem that the Arminian trend under Laud coincided with the rather conservative attitude of the majority of the Welsh gentry and their tenants towards religion, thus strengthening Royalist sympathy.

For these and other reasons, then, the Glamorgan gentry were to follow the King when the call to arms came. In Glamorgan there is ample evidence to be found supporting A. H. Dodd's rebuttal of the old charge that the Welsh gentry rallied to the King out of 'blind, unreasoning loyalty'.[2] The Glamorgan gentry, keen, shrewd, and often unscrupulous, many of them educated at Oxford or one of the Inns of Court, had no great reason to be dissatisfied with the old order in Church and State. Their incomes were largely derived from agriculture and not from trade, and the continued levying of tonnage and poundage without consent of Parliament together with the increases in customs duties, which so embittered the merchant communities in England against the personal rule of the King, had no such repercussions in Glamorgan. Furthermore ship money, the most notorious and worst hated of Charles's exactions, was not as unpopular in Glamorgan as elsewhere, since the emergence of a strong navy could be expected to afford protection to the inhabitants of south Wales against the depredations of the Barbary pirates.[3]

The Royalist inclinations of the Glamorgan gentry would again have been strengthened by the influence of two powerful landowners within the county though they resided outside it, the marquis of Worcester and the earl of Pembroke. But while the marquis of Worcester was to champion the King's cause to the bitter end, the earl of Pembroke was to annoy the King over his attitude to the Strafford issue and this led to his being deprived of the office of Lord Chamberlain and joining the Parliamentarian camp. However, Pembroke's exalted position, wealth and the favour of the Crown which he had enjoyed hitherto, with Charles frequently visiting him at his Wilton seat, could not have failed to foster the loyalty which the people of Glamorgan, where some of his most extensive estates lay, by and large felt for the King. But when personal pique, commercial interests and contacts drew Pembroke over to champion the militant opposition, his predominance in Glamorgan political affairs disappeared.[4]

Neither did the earl of Pembroke's son and heir exert any influence over affairs in Glamorgan during those last months of peace. Philip, Lord Herbert, who had sat for Wiltshire in the Short Parliament, now filled the Glamorgan seat which had been held by Sir Edward Stradling of St. Donat's but who was abroad at election time. However, although Lord Herbert had been concerned with righting the wrongs done to Puritans by the Court of Star Chamber and with supporting measures for stripping the bishops of their political power,[5] he did not continue to render support to the Parliamentary side in the summer of 1642. Not only was he recovering from an illness but also his views seem to have undergone a change. So the fact that the greatest landowner in Glamorgan had entered the Parliamentary camp was to have little or no effect on the county, for he was an absentee, and his eldest son, the Glamorgan M.P. and Lord Lieutenant, did not share his father's views, which he confessed to 'haue an ill influence vpon ye whole famely . . .', and he himself was in any case indisposed during those critical months.[6] Indeed, on July 29, 1642 the earl of Pembroke replaced his son as Lord Lieutenant of Glamorgan and the project of sending the earl down to Glamorgan was actually considered by the House of Commons, but for some reason the idea was dropped.[7]

That the Glamorgan gentry, however, were stoutly loyal to the King was already apparent. The Stradling family had already rendered signal service to the King. Henry Stradling, brother of Sir Edward, held a command at sea and had had a hand in smuggling the Queen to the Continent to pawn the crown jewels. Incidentally he was one of only two captains that Parliament failed to win over.[8] Sir John Pennington had actually advised Charles to appoint Sir Robert Mansel of Margam, who had devoted his lifetime to the Navy, commanded its respect, and could be relied on to support the King, as Admiral of the 1642 fleet. But while Charles dithered on account of Mansel's age the fleet went over to Parliament.[9]

Events now moved rapidly towards civil war. The earl of Pembroke had been ordered by Parliament to grant forth his deputations for Glamorgan on July 29, 1642; but there was no organization on behalf of Parliament in Glamorgan, for the leading men were all opposed to it, and the Militia Ordinance was never put into operation in the county. The King, in turn, declaring Parliament's orders illegal, issued his own Commissions of Array under the Great Seal, and there is evidence that at one time or another most of the gentry served as Commissioners of Array.[10] Of these, one of the leading Royalists was Sir Edward Stradling of St. Donat's, who set about raising a regiment of foot, a thousand strong, to serve the King. He was a brother of Henry, the sea captain, and Thomas, who fought as a lieutenant-colonel under his elder brother at Edgehill. Two of Sir Edward's sons, Edward and John, the major-general, also actively supported the Royalist cause which was to bring greater tragedy to this family than to any in Glamorgan. Then again Sir George Vaughan, who had just sold Dunraven to Humphrey Windham, hastened to join the forces of Sir John Glemham then being raised for the King. Later on, in command of the Fourth Regiment of Foot, he was to distinguish himself at the Battle of Lansdowne in July 1643 but was severely wounded in the head by a pike thrust. Another gesture of loyalty was the presentation on August 1, 1642 of a Petition of the

Gentry, Ministers, Freeholders and other inhabitants of Glamorgan and all Wales to the King at York, a document which shows clearly that, while they welcomed the early reforms and changes brought about by the Long Parliament, they were now opposed to any further changes and not only desired to trust the King but were prepared to defend him with force if necessary.[11]

THE OUTBREAK OF WAR

With civil war now inevitable, on orders from the King, Cardiff castle and all other possessions of the earl of Pembroke in Glamorgan were seized and his rent collected by William Herbert of the Friars, a Commissioner of Array. Another Commissioner of Array, Sir Anthony Mansel of Margam or, more strictly, of Briton Ferry, the step-father of Bussy Mansel, became the first governor of Cardiff for the King. Various references testify to his strenuous adherence to the Royalist cause, and, with Sir Edward Stradling, to whom he was connected by marriage, he earned the reputation of being one of the first to join the King. At the same time Walter Thomas of Dan-y-graig was made Commissioner of Array and governor of the other garrison town in Glamorgan, Swansea, where he armed and arrayed the inhabitants and was no doubt responsible for the construction of a new magazine in the lower town hall.[12]

In the meantime Charles had raised his standard at Nottingham on August 22, 1642. From there, on September 13, he began his march westwards in search of reinforcements, and a week later he entered Shrewsbury, whence he dispatched his agents into Wales and neighbouring areas 'to quicken the levies of men which were making there'.[13] As Charles did not leave Shrewsbury until October 12 it was there, no doubt, that Sir Edward Stradling joined the Royalist forces, because he referred to the billeting of 500 soldiers of his regiment in Monmouthshire in a letter dated September 17 to Sir William Morgan of Tredegar. Sir Nicholas Kemeys of Cefnmabli is also supposed to have raised a regiment of horse at his own expense. That Sir Nicholas was active for the King's cause in Glamorgan and Monmouthshire is evident from an order issued by the Commons in September that he be sent for as a delinquent for executing the Commission of Array, but with little hope of getting the order carried out. And as a recognition of his services the King conferred a baronetcy on Sir Nicholas in the following November.[14]

In the meantime William Seymour, marquis of Hertford, to whom the King had given supreme command in the west, including the counties of south Wales, had been sorely pressed by the Parliamentary forces in Dorset and had surrendered Sherborne castle, whence he retreated with a small force of 400 men and 45 of his best horses to Minehead. There, at midnight on Friday September 23, he commandeered a number of Welsh coal boats in which he transported his men to Cardiff. Making Cardiff castle his headquarters, he joined with the Commissioners of Array in levying and equipping an army reputed to have been 7,000 strong. In this task he was also assisted by the marquis of Worcester and his son, Lord Herbert, who subsequently claimed that his father and he had expended £10,000 on this army. And as for equipping the levies, one source of arms, ordnance, and ammunition was the Parliamentary city of Bristol. This state of affairs resulted in action being taken by the House of Commons on October 8.[15]

However, if it was the intention of Hertford to join with the King's forces immediately, he was unable to put his plan into operation because Charles, intending to launch a direct attack on London, left Shrewsbury on October 12. But between Kineton and Edgcott he was intercepted by the earl of Essex, and the first important battle of the Civil War was fought at Edgehill on October 23. The army fielded by the King included the Glamorgan recruits under the command of Sir Edward Stradling as colonel, with his brother, Thomas, as lieutenant-colonel, and William Herbert of Cogan Pill, M.P. for Cardiff, also with a commission as lieutenant-colonel. The Glamorgan men, together with the other Welsh recruits, seem to have been inadequately equipped and to have lacked training and discipline, with the result that their conduct came in for censure and they themselves suffered heavy casualties. Indeed, the unenviable reputation won at Edgehill stuck to the Welsh soldier to the end of the war. That the Glamorgan regiment suffered severely is evident, for Sir Edward Stradling was taken prisoner and William Herbert of Cogan Pill killed on the field of battle. According to Carte one of the Button family fell there too. The regiment gave a better account of itself, however, at Brentford on November 12 as the King resumed his march on London, and it recovered its honour by assaulting the works and forcing the barricades. But on the next day the King's forces found their way effectively barred at Turnham Green by the London trained bands, and Charles had to fall back on Oxford, which now became his headquarters, and consider a new plan of campaign.[16]

MIXED FORTUNES, 1642-3

In the meantime the marquis of Hertford had continued to operate from Cardiff and in one probing sally he penetrated as far as Hereford with a force 2,000 strong, but was repulsed by the earl of Stamford.[17] Hereford had fallen into the hands of the Parliamentary army when Essex had sent a force from Worcester to occupy it at the end of September, and the earl of Stamford had been made governor. Subsequently, on or about November 4, the marquis of Hertford joined forces with Lord Herbert and set out to link up with the King at Oxford. But after being ferried across the Severn on November 15 and making for Tewkesbury, the force was intercepted on the following day by the earl of Stamford's army. Of the subsequent encounter we have only a rather flamboyant account written by a Parliamentary reporter. According to him, Hertford's hard core of Cavaliers who had made the escape from Minehead put up a strong resistance; but the ragged and inexperienced Welsh sought refuge in flight.[18] The shattered Royalists fell back again on Monmouthshire and in mid-November we have the first intimation that all was not well between Hertford and Herbert. Differences there were, and no doubt the Tewkesbury defeat had frayed nerves considerably. Lord Herbert desired to hold the command in south Wales which the King with-held from him because his Catholic beliefs would lay Charles open to the charge of popery. However, the differences did not immediately prevent Hertford and Herbert from working together and on November 27 another skirmish occurred between their forces and those of Stamford This also ended in a withdrawal.[19]

But some success Hertford did obtain. Early in the second week of December he had dispatched two letters to some Royalist sympathizers in Bristol, promising the city 'extraordinary kind usage' if it would admit his forces. Forestalled there by Essex's troops, however, he had to be content with occupying Worcester, which had been left by Essex.[20] This isolated Stamford and made his position at Hereford untenable, so that on December 14 he quit the city for Gloucester. Herefordshire then fell into Royalist hands, and late in December Hertford at last managed to reach Oxford. Hertford's absence from south Wales now enabled the King to soothe the feelings of Lord Herbert and in some way repay the debt he owed to the house of Worcester. Throwing discretion to the winds and laying himself wide open to the charge of popery, Charles appointed Lord Herbert as commander-in-chief in the absence of the marquis of Hertford. This appointment, a temporary one announced on January 5, 1643, was made permanent on April 6. Although Edward Hyde was strongly opposed to the appointment, the immediate prospects must have seemed attractive to the King since Herbert promised to raise a force at his own expense to reduce Gloucester.[21]

This was done in March; but the expedition suffered severely at the hands of Sir William Waller's forces outside the city. For this ignominious defeat of what he called 'that mushrump-army' Edward Hyde, possibly with a measure of personal animus, castigated the Lord Herbert, who was at Oxford at the time and not with his army; and Hyde concluded that if the money spent on this army had been used to better purpose the war might have been ended the next summer.[22] Early in April Waller marched for Wales in pursuit of Lord Herbert's forces, occupying Newnham and Ross and pressing on to Monmouth and Chepstow. With such a critical situation developing, Lord Herbert and his father, the marquis of Worcester, left a garrison to defend Raglan and set up their headquarters first at Cardiff, into which refugees with their 'estates portable' were streaming to seek protection, and then at Swansea. But the attack feared in Glamorgan never materialized. Waller, lacking sufficient troops to garrison the towns he had occupied and apprehensive of the possibility of tougher resistance ahead as the Welsh would be called upon to protect their own homesteads, was not unaware of the precariousness of his position. When news reached him that Prince Maurice had been sent from Oxford to fall on his rear, he withdrew to reach Gloucester safely on April 11. Thus disappeared the immediate threat to Glamorgan, and it was the Royalists and not the Parliamentarians who were now to do the attacking.[23]

THE SIEGE OF GLOUCESTER 1643

The King at this point planned a threefold attack upon London and in the summer opened his offensive to reduce the city. Within a short time and with the victories of Adwalton Moor and Roundway Down to the credit of the Royalist forces under the command of Newcastle and Hopton respectively, the threat to London became acute. It was in July, when the Parliamentary forces were reeling back before the onslaught, that Prince Rupert laid siege to the city of Bristol and after a sharp assault on July 26 it surrendered. Before advancing on London with his own forces the King now decided, after great deliberation, to reduce Gloucester. Gloucester, Plymouth, and Hull, added to what S. R. Gardiner has described as 'the fatal . . . predominance of local over national patriotism', were to spell disaster to the Royalist cause.[24] Yet the threat that such a powerful fortress as Gloucester could pose in the King's rear, if left untaken, cannot be minimized; and the Welsh forces, whilst they were ready and eager to attack Gloucester, refused to advance beyond the Severn with that city uncaptured. The decision to attack Gloucester was welcomed by them, and Lord Herbert stated that within fourteen days of receiving notice of the intended attack, he had raised 4,000 foot and 800 horse and conducted them to the siege, where they were concentrated under the command of Sir William Vavasour, who had recently been appointed governor of Hereford by the King.[25]

After having converged on Gloucester towards the end of the first week in August, the forces of the King, Rupert and Sir William Vavasour began the siege in earnest on August 10. On the following day the Welsh forces under Sir William Vavasour advanced and occupied the Vineyard, an ancient palace of the bishops of Gloucester some half a mile from the city, after it had been evacuated and fired by the garrison. The Glamorgan troops under Sir William's command were led by the high sheriff of the county, Richard Bassett, who had been directed by the King to raise forces for the assault on Gloucester and who had accompanied them in person.[26] Subsequently, more demands were made by the King on the manpower of the county but these were to meet opposition, especially from its western parts. It was Bussy Mansel, Walter Thomas, and William Thomas who apparently experienced most difficulty in raising more troops in the hundreds of Llangyfelach, Swansea, and Neath. But William Thomas's plea that the commissioners should spare his own 'remote' hundred of Llangyfelach elicited a sharp reprimand from Sir Anthony Mansel, the governor of Cardiff, who was to take the reinforcements to Gloucester. Demands for money, directed through Judge David Jenkins, were also apparently unsuccessful and were remitted by the King, who realized that he had pressed his supporters too far.[27]

On Tuesday, August 15, the commissioners at Cardiff received an undated letter from the sheriff, Richard Bassett, at the Vineyard giving details of the tasks performed by the Welsh before Gloucester. They had prevented any sallies from the west gate of the city and had been visited by the King, who 'did reioyce much at the Welshmen for they Did throwe their Capps and hallow with much Joye'. Bassett himself was presented to Charles who bestowed a kinghthood upon him. The letter also upbraided the commissioners for being 'soe slacke in advancinge' with the reinforcements and exhorted them to greater efforts; but it ended on an optimistic note, expecting the city to fall within three days (Pl. X). Another letter from Sir Richard Bassett, dated August 15, expected Gloucester to fall soon; but in the meantime, in London, Parliament had given top priority to the relief of the besieged city.[28] On Thursday, September 5, Essex and his relief force appeared and, to avoid being attacked in the rear, Charles raised the siege and withdrew. Three barrels of gunpowder alone remained in the city after the twenty-five-day siege. The King had come within an ace of success; but his failure at Gloucester was to cost him the war. It neutralized the success at Bristol, and the wealthiest and most populous part of Wales, instead of forming an integral part of the Royalist sphere of influence, was to remain isolated. The King had now lost the initiative and was driven to take what defensive measures he could, but not before he tried to cut Essex off from London. The move failed at the first Battle of Newbury on September 20, an action in which the Glamorgan troops who had fought at Gloucester were involved. This is established in the Results and Orders of the Glamorgan Commissioners of Array dealing with the maimed and wounded from the battle. The same source also established conclusively that Sir Anthony Mansel was killed in the same battle and not in the second one at Newbury. To Edward Hyde, subsequently earl of Clarendon and the great Royalist historian of the Civil War, there seemed to be something contrary to the order of nature in the achievements of the Parliamentarians at Newbury for, while they only lost some few obscure adherents, on the King's side unequal fate cut down men of honour.[29]

ROYALIST SETBACKS, 1643–1644

After Newbury there is evidence that some of the Welsh troops that proceeded under Sir William Vavasour to Hereford were recalcitrant and defected. Glamorgan men were amongst these, and the defection lends credence to the Parliamentary allegation that the Welsh were now beginning to realize that they were fighting for popery.[30] During the closing months of the year 1643 further demands were to be made on Glamorgan and, significantly, there are recurring references to separatists and delinquents. In the meantime Parliament succeeded in making an alliance with the Presbyterian majority in Scotland and, from the moment the Scots army began to cross the Tweed on January 19, 1644, the King's position deteriorated. Furthermore, the regiments brought over from Ireland by the Royalists were dispersed at Nantwich on January 25. To cope with the critical situation that was now developing a proposal to grant emergency powers to Prince Rupert was considered; but the suggestion to bestow upon him the title of President of Wales, thus presumably concentrating in his person the powers of the lord-lieutenancies of Wales, may never have been translated into actual fact because of the hostility of Lord Herbert of Raglan. Lord Herbert, quick to take offence, was an eminent example on the King's side of a commander who had to be tolerated for his wealth and influence, however limited his ability. However, emergency powers Rupert certainly did exercise at this critical juncture.[31]

In March Rupert left Shrewsbury for Newark. The task of marshalling Welsh resources he entrusted to certain officers, one of whom was Sir Thomas Dabridgecourt. The latter's letter of March 11, 1644 to Rupert from St. Pierre, near Chepstow, contains indications that Welsh loyalty was badly shaken. He apologizes for being unable to carry out Rupert's orders thus, 'if your Highness shall be pleased to command me to the Turk, or Jew, or Gentile, I will go on my bare feet to serve you, but from the Welch, good Lord, deliver me: and I shall beseech you to send me no more into this country, if you intend I shall do you any service, without a strong party to compel them, not to entreat them'.[32] That this refusal to collaborate on the part of the Welsh could in part have been due to high-handed action by Dabridgecourt himself is likely. Even so it could not be the whole explanation, and there is plenty of evidence that in Glamorgan the people, while still nominally remaining loyal to the King, were not prepared to make the increasing sacrifices which the Royalist cause was now demanding of them. Finally, there was the threat to Glamorgan from Pembrokeshire, where in mid-February the Parliamentarians, under Rowland Laugharne, went over from the defensive to the offensive.[33]

In April came the resignation of the earl of Carbery, the Royalist commander in west Wales, revealing the true extent to which the Royalist cause had crumbled. Immediate action was needed if complete disaster was to be avoided, and from Oxford on May 1 Rupert wrote to the Glamorgan commissioners that he was sending to their aid Colonel Charles Gerard, 'a person of such eminent Couradage and approved Conduct in Martiall affaires'.[34] Gerard now crossed into Glamorgan from Monmouthshire and united in his person the vacant commands formerly held by the earl of Carbery in the south-west and Lord Herbert in the south-east. His appearance was soon to prove effective, though his stay was to be but short-lived. On July 2 the King's defeat at Marston Moor was to make the Royalist situation desperate, with the north of England now virtually lost. The impact of this defeat must have been severe in Glamorgan as elsewhere; and money contributions from the county were not now readily forthcoming, nor were the recruits. The more serious the situation then, the less likely was the King to receive any aid from counties such as Glamorgan where the instinct of self-preservation was strong.[35]

The defeat at Marston Moor also led to the recall of Gerard and his forces from Wales. This was effected by August 22, but Gerard's work remained incomplete, with Pembroke and Tenby still in Parliamentary hands and the Royalists deprived of the crucial control of Milford Haven—a setback for Lord Herbert, who had been granted a secret commission by the King to secure support from the Irish Catholic Confederation and whose plans at this time were to land two Irish armies of 10,000 men each, one in north Wales and one in south Wales.[36] Also important was the resentment caused in Glamorgan and elsewhere by the attitude and conduct of Gerard and his men, which lost for the Royalist cause the sympathy of hitherto loyal adherents of the King. Under Gerard, with his continental military experience, south Wales had suffered the savagery and inhumanity of total war which often repelled friend and foe alike.[37] Gerard's actions indeed suggest that he had little faith in the ability of the local gentry to conduct the war. It seems almost certain from a statement of the Glamorgan Commissioners of Array that Gerard forced the resignation of Sir Nicholas Kemeys of Cefnmabli as governor of Cardiff and replaced him with one of his own nominees, an Englishman and a Gentleman of the Privy Chamber, Sir Timothy Tyrrell of Oakley, Buckinghamshire. At Swansea it seems likely that Walter Thomas, the governor of that town, was also removed by Gerard in favour of Colonel Richard Donnel.[38] But it is reputed that at least one supporter was found in Glamorgan for Gerard's activities, and that was none other than David Jenkins of Hensol, the Welsh judge, who rode with Gerard's men 'w[i]th his long rapier drawne, holding it on-end'.[39]

September 1644 saw a renewed threat to Glamorgan, this time from a Parliamentary force penetrating from south-west England under Colonel Edward Massey who, through the treachery of Lieutenant-colonel Kyrle, had captured Monmouth. There followed sharp skirmishes in Glamorgan's neighbouring county as Gerard's forces, which included Welsh levies from Glamorgan, struggled to regain possession of the town.[40] This was achieved in November and the pressure from the east was removed. It was no more than a temporary respite, for in the same month Laugharne, now reinforced by men and ammunition landed at

Milford Haven, began to take the offensive again. Of far greater consequence, however, were the defeat of Essex at Lostwithiel and Manchester's half-hearted encounter with the King at Newbury. These were to produce important changes in the Parliamentary leadership and, once Cromwell was in control, the days of the Royalists were numbered.

THE DEFEAT OF THE ROYALISTS

The continued advance of Laugharne out of Pembrokeshire led the King to order back to that area Sir Charles Gerard, who had, on March 17, 1645, helped to retake Beeston castle in Cheshire. Far from instilling confidence in the Glamorgan Commissioners of Array, news of Gerard's impending return caused misgivings and consternation amongst them. Their reaction was to insist that they should be consulted and should be allowed freedom of action to implement instructions from the King, that they should be allowed to debate freely all matters requisite to the King's service and the safety of the county, that payment to the garrisons at Cardiff and Swansea should be made out of the county contributions, and that no arms or troops should be commanded out of the county without their consent.[41] Gerard soon restored the situation, putting Laugharne's forces into full retreat towards Tenby and Pembroke, but indications that his temper was becoming rather frayed towards the Glamorgan commissioners are to be found in a letter he addressed to them repeating complaints about desertion by Glamorgan men.[42] However, Gerard was again recalled and marched towards Hereford to link up with the King, but by the time he had come out of Wales the decisive battle of the Civil War had been fought at Naseby on June 14, 1645. The defeated Royalist army then fell back on Hereford to link up with Gerard's forces, about 2,000 strong.

In this hour of crisis the King saw south Wales as his only hope of fielding a new force quickly and on July 1 he left Hereford for Monmouthshire, a move severely criticized by Edward Hyde: 'And nothing can be more wondered at, than that the King should amuse himself about forming a new army in counties which had been vexed and worn out with the oppressions of his own troops and the licence of those governors whom he had put over them, and not have immediately repaired into the west where he had an army already formed, and a people generally well devoted to his service, and whither General Gerard, and all his broken troops, might have transported themselves before Fayrefax could have given them any interruption.'[43] At Abergavenny Charles broke his journey to meet the Commissioners of Array for the south Wales counties who, according to report, promised him 'mountains'.[44] The King then retired to Raglan and spent the first fortnight of July as the guest of the marquis of Worcester, apparently confidently awaiting the fulfilment of the commissioners' promises. Finally, on Wednesday July 16 he set out for Cardiff where he supped with the governor, Sir Timothy Tyrrell.

The purpose of the visit, according to Symonds, was to meet the commissioners 'to rayse men, and settle the towne'. This statement about settling the town can be taken as further corroboration of the discontent and apathy spreading in Glamorgan, especially as Symonds mentions that Parliamentary ships had taken 'many of Swansey boates and some from Cardiffe' at this time.[45] It can be assumed, therefore, that the activities of the Parliamentary fleet under Captain Batten were having serious repercussions on morale in Glamorgan generally and in Cardiff in particular. In addition, the eventual defection of the south Wales counties was also hastened by the capture of the King's baggage at Naseby, which had revealed to the world the earl of Glamorgan's negotiations on Charles's behalf for the landing in Wales of Catholic forces from Ireland and the Continent.[46]

On July 17 the King reached an agreement with the Glamorgan Commissioners of Array concerning arrears of payment, future contributions, the provision of a thousand men by July 24 for a new undertaking and £800 to equip them, together with other details concerning corn supplies, the fortification of the garrison towns of Cardiff and Swansea, and finally the sending of commissioners to Hereford concerning an association and a new army against the Scots.[47] But on the same day news came that Montrose had beaten the Scots near Edinburgh, and Charles immediately left Cardiff for Raglan. To deal with the Scots' threat to Hereford, which still existed, the King called for a rendezvous of all Glamorgan men able to bear arms near that city on July 28, affirming that he would be there in person.[48] However, at this critical juncture Charles vacillated. Decisions were made, only to be set aside again. No sooner had the above communication been sent than Charles began to entertain thoughts of joining Prince Rupert at Bristol. This plan was discussed at a conference on July 22 which Rupert attended at Crick, near Chepstow. Two days later the King was at Blackrock ready to cross the Severn, only to receive intelligence that Bridgwater had fallen to Fairfax and that the Scots were advancing on Hereford.[49] The Welsh gentry pressed him to remain in south Wales; but it was the military setbacks that changed the King's mind for him, and he now wrote to Rupert that he planned to join Montrose in Scotland. Rupert's reaction was to write to the duke of Richmond that the King had now 'no way left to preserve his posterity, kingdom, and nobility, but by a treaty'.[50]

WAR-WEARINESS IN GLAMORGAN

Charles was not of like mind, and decided on another journey to Cardiff on July 29 after the Glamorgan gentry had failed to get their men to a rendezvous at Newport on the previous day. According to an eyewitness, a man named Smith had made a speech against Sir Timothy Tyrrell and consequently all the men had refused to stir. The King met the Glamorgan forces at St. Fagan's, the gentlemen on horseback and the levies drawn up in battle array. When Charles questioned their conduct he was answered that it was dictated by the need to preserve their country. It was then that the articles were handed to him demanding first, that papists be removed out of the county; second, that the English garrison be removed out of Cardiff and replaced by a governor and garrison of their own choice; and finally that the £7,000 arrears demanded by Gerard be remitted. To these demands Charles made a favourable reply, promising 'all reasonable contentment'. The assembled crowd refused to be satisfied, whereupon Charles desired to have a discussion with the gentry. The gentry, however, were solemnly warned by the rank and file 'not any way to ingage them without their consent'.[51]

After the King had returned to Cardiff the Glamorgan men continued at rendezvous at Cefn Onn, the high ridge between the rivers Taff and Rhymney, some four miles north of the town, on Wednesday and Thursday, July 30 and 31, and at Llantrisant on the Friday when they first called themselves the 'Peaceable Army'. In the meantime Charles demanded security to come and treat with them or that men should be sent to him with powers to treat. As a result, ten gentlemen and ten countrymen (an indication of radical tendencies) were sent to treat with the King, and the outcome was that the county agreed to furnish him with 1,000 men and £800 in money to arm them. At the demand of the countrymen Gerard was relieved of his command in Wales and replaced by Sir Jacob Astley. In addition, Sir Timothy Tyrrell was replaced as governor of Cardiff by one of the Glamorgan gentry, Sir Richard Bassett. When he left, Sir Timothy had to take with him his English garrison.[52]

This taking advantage of the King's dire straits in order to impose conditions before rallying to his cause was symptomatic of the strong underlying current of disaffection that was now prevalent in Glamorgan, and of this Charles could not but have been well aware. To be thus treated in the hour of his greatest need; to find that his own nephew, Prince Rupert, was now advocating peace; and to have news of fresh disasters brought to him—Pontefract castle, Scarborough, and Bath falling at the end of July, together with the routing of the Royalist forces under Stradling and Egerton on Colby Moor on August 1 by Laugharne: this was the ordeal that Charles had to undergo during his short stay at Cardiff. Yet in this period of trial and tribulation King Charles assumed for the first time those heroic qualities which for some people turned his subsequent execution into a martyrdom. Coming to recognize the inevitability of defeat and all that it would entail for himself, he wrote to Rupert from Cardiff as follows, 'God will not suffer rebels to prosper, or this cause to be overthrown; and whatsoever personal punishment He shall please to inflict upon me, must not make me repine, much less give over this quarrel'.[53] Only in the light of such convictions can Charles's subsequent career be understood.

[269]

The unhappy predicament in which Charles now found himself is described in the memoirs of Edmund Ludlow. According to him 'the generality of the country, that during his successes had subjected themselves even slavishly to his instruments, now fearing he might draw the army of the Parliament after him, and make their country the seat of war, began to murmur against him, and drew together a numerous body in the nature of a club-army, whispering amongst themselves as if they intended to seize his person, and deliver him to the Parliament to make their peace. Which being reported to the King, he thought fit to retire from thence with his forces . . . '. Since it was purposeless to delay any longer in Cardiff —even dangerous according to Ludlow—Charles left Cardiff on Tuesday, August 5, with the intention of linking up with Montrose's forces.[54]

To the veteran Sir Jacob Astley was left the thankless task of re-presenting the King in what was now fast becoming hostile territory. And the latest news—Colby Moor following upon Naseby—had crushed what fighting spirit the Glamorgan men had left after Gerard's period in power. Rumour and counter-rumour were rife and turbulence pre-vailed, and it is to Astley that we now turn for a first-hand account of the situation in Glamorgan as it appeared to the Royalist commander on the spot. On the King's departure, Astley had ordered the inhabitants of south Wales and Monmouthshire to meet him at Abergavenny on August 8, when the strategical necessity of preserving Hereford from the besieging Scots was outlined to them, but without any response. From Cardiff on August 11 he wrote to Prince Rupert that 'the county of Glamorgan so unquiet, as there is no good to be expected; shall strive as far as he can to put things in order, which he despairs of, because it must be power to rule these people, and not entreaties with cap in hand to such as deserve the halter'.[55] In further letters written from Newport and Abergavenny, Astley reported that the state of affairs in south Wales was rapidly deteriorating into open disaffection. He wrote of having had the 'infinitest trouble' with the Commissioners of Array, the majority of whom he believed to be false and secretly treating with Parliamentary ships, seven of which were lying between Swansea and Blackrock, and that in a few days the earl of Pembroke was expected to come amongst them. Such was the situation at the end of August; and Astley's exasper-ation can be further explained when it is observed that arrangements had been made for a meeting of Glamorgan, Brecon and Monmouthshire forces on August 29 for the relief of Hereford but that none had come from Glamorgan, though he had sent three several posts to them. On August 30 Astley wrote that he could see these people all inclining to fall off from their obedience, and as a postscript he added wryly that since he had come amongst them he had never received a penny of their money for any entertainment.[56]

In the meantime the King, whose journey northwards to link up with Montrose had come to nothing, returned to Hereford on September 4, the siege of which had been raised by the Scots two days previously. On September 7, he retired to Raglan where he was joined by Astley. The King now sent Astley's forces, together with those of Sir Marmaduke Langdale, against the Glamorgan Peace Army. Both armies met eight miles outside Cardiff and Astley's resolution to fight brought the Peace Army to heel for the time being.[57] Bussy Mansel of Margam, who with others had been in command of the Peace Army, was relieved of his commission but he tried to excuse his conduct and that of Colonel Humphrey Mathew of Castell-y-mynach by pleading that 'the madness of the multitude' prevented them from doing their duties. He was confident that the Peace Army would have disbanded but for the plundering of the soldiers marching out of the county and declared that he was going to Cornwall to clear up all doubts of his 'encouraging the people this way they are now upon'.[58] Mansel's pleas, however, could hardly have impressed Astley, who had stated categorically at Abergavenny that the common people were being led by the gentry.

Indeed, a day or two after Astley's intervention in Glamorgan, the Peace Army was supplied by sea with arms and ammunition from Pembrokeshire, and by this time also there is abundant proof that some of the Glamorgan gentry were now in direct contact with the Parliamentarians.[59] The capitulation of Bristol to the Parliamentary forces on August 11 led to further disaffection in Glamorgan which culminated on September 17 in Sir Richard Bassett's being forced to deliver up the town and castle of Cardiff to the Peace Army. With 200 men he marched thence, leaving in the castle 16 pieces of ordnance, between 300 and 400 arms, 10 barrels of powder, and other ammunition and provisions. And amongst the leaders of the Peace Army are now found the names of many prominent Glamorgan gentry, Commissioners of Array and others, including Edward Carne, Sir John Aubrey, Humphrey Mathew, and Bussy Mansel.[60] Disaffection had now spread everywhere in the county, and the appearance of Bussy Mansel's name belies his statement that he was about to go to Cornwall to prove his loyalty to the Crown. As for Swansea, it is not known exactly when it capitulated. It had not yielded at the same time as Cardiff, and the opposition there was stiffened by the presence of Sir John Winter and Judge David Jenkins.[61] Laugharne was at Carmarthen on October 12 and must have advanced on Swansea, but whether it had capitulated before his arrival is not known. However, the first entry in the Swansea Corporation records after Michaelmas 1645 (unfortunately undated) notes the provision of wine and beer to entertain General Laugharne.[62]

THE END OF THE FIRST CIVIL WAR

After the capture of Cardiff Lieutenant-colonel Thomas Carne, who had estates in Glamorgan but had fought against his kinsmen and fellow countrymen in the Civil War, together with Michael Oldsworth, M.P.

for Salisbury, acted as Parliamentary Commissioners in Glamorgan.[63] However, as the situation there became more favourable to Parliament, local people, who doubtless had been forward in encouraging the defection from the King, were promoted to share in the work of administration. On November 17 the Commons nominated and approved none other than Bussy Mansel, with his protestations of loyalty to the King now conveniently forgotten, to be commander-in-chief of the Glamorgan forces subordinate to Sir Thomas Fairfax. The Puritan Edward Prichard of Llancaeach was to be the new governor of Cardiff, and Philip Jones, an energetic young man who had espoused the Parliamentary cause, was appointed governor of Swansea. This was followed on December 3 by the Commons nominating and approving Colonel Edward Carne of Ewenni to be high sheriff of Glamorgan.[64]

If, however, Parliament believed that the Royalist cause in south Wales had now been completely crushed, it was in for a rude awakening. Captain Robert Moulton, who was watching developments from the fleet in the Channel, sounded a warning note about the condition of Glamorgan in a letter to the Commons on December 12.[65] From neighbouring Monmouthshire came further disquieting reports about the condition of that county. Indeed, by the beginning of January 1646 the Royalist forces operating from Raglan had taken the offensive against the Parliamentary forces in the county. This Royalist revival quickly assumed dangerous proportions and the first intimation of the serious repercussions it might have on Glamorgan came in a letter from Bussy Mansel and Edward Carne to Major-general Rowland Laugharne on January 26 seeking speedy assistance. Laugharne, who was besieging Aberystwyth castle, refused to give priority to their pleas and on Friday February 6, the storm broke.[66]

The troops under the command of Edward Carne began to quarrel and declared for the King, as did Carne himself. Some of the gentry of the Vale objected strongly to the religious policy pursued by the victorious party. They alleged that there had been a general agreement in the previous year to keep all parties out of Glamorgan but that this had been broken. At that time the purpose had been to remove 'insupportable grievances' caused by the conduct of Sir Charles Gerard and his soldiers. This had been achieved. But the movement, they alleged, had since been directed to other ends by the action of a few. Men of no social standing had been given authority while baronets, knights, and other gentlemen had been passed over. The county's monthly contribution had been raised from £67 to £162. These points might not arouse general indignation; but a wider issue was raised in a manifesto which the clergy in each parish were asked to read to their people and, where necessary, to explain in Welsh. It included two passages of special significance. It was asserted that 'the Common Prayer Book hath been commonly traduced, and several Sundays omitted in Cardiff, which we apprehend as a forerunner of its final rejection, had some their desires . . . '. This was amplified by the statement that 'schismatics of several kinds are of greatest trust with some in chiefest place of government in this county . . . '. Rather late in the day the painful truth had been forced on some of the Glamorgan men, led by Carne, that the civil war had shaken the very foundations of pre-war society and that the overthrow of the King could not be separated from social, economic, and religious repercussions little to their liking.[67]

Edward Carne's action created a critical position in Glamorgan and Edward Prichard, the governor of Cardiff, immediately wrote to Laugharne for assistance, stressing the danger that the Monmouthshire Royalists might join Carne's men who were now already besieging the town. Speedy assistance, however, came from another quarter. Vice-admiral Crowther landed provisions and a body of seamen to stiffen Prichard's opposition, and it was only on February 13 that the Parliamentarians were finally compelled to withdraw into the castle itself. Crowther then encouraged them to hold out by himself 'daily approaching as near as possible with six barks and boats, and firing upon the town with large ordnance',—an evident admission that there was now no contact between him and the garrison.[68]

The siege was not to continue for long, however. On Monday, February 16, Crowther, having received notification that relief was on the way, approached near enough to convey the good news to the besieged, which was done by hanging their colours within sight of the castle and shooting off six pieces of ordnance.[69] Then, on February 18, when Laugharne's own forces had approached within a mile of Cardiff, Carne drew his men off from the siege and marshalled them on the heath north of the town, together with the Monmouthshire forces under Sir Charles Kemeys, ready to give battle to the Parliamentary forces. There followed a sharp and violent encounter which ended in absolute victory for Laugharne. Before nightfall Carne and his shattered forces found themselves surrounded in the town of Cardiff with Parliamentarians not only around them but also occupying the castle itself.[70] On the next day, February 19, negotiations were opened between the Royalists and Edward Prichard in the castle. The terms were generous. The countrymen who had joined the rising were to return to their homes. Gentlemen and officers were to march away with their horses and their equipment to any Royalist garrison within fifty miles. More significant was the clause that no one was to be disturbed in the use of the Common Prayer Book and the general assurance that the clergy would be secure and encouraged, provided that they intermeddled 'only with the business of their vocations'. The negotiators clearly realized that the religious issue had played an important part in the rising.[71] Unfortunately this was not the end of the affair. On February 20, as Carne's men were withdrawing from Cardiff, some altercation arose and shots were exchanged. It developed into a general fight in which Laugharne was again victorious. In both actions, according to Laugharne, 250 of the enemy were killed and 800 were taken prisoner. Edward Carne himself was among the prisoners and was sent to Bristol and subsequently to London: a fine of £856 was levied on his estate.[72]

One report indicates that Swansea also had fallen into the possession of the Royalists at the same time as Cardiff. That this was true is highly likely, for the Compounding Papers reveal that William Thomas of Swansea and Sir Edward Thomas of Llanfihangel and Betws at this time laid siege to Briton Ferry House, the home of Bussy Mansel. The rebels were, however, defeated by the garrison and, if Swansea had defected, the defeat of Carne's men at Cardiff must soon have led to the position there being restored as well.[73] On August 19 Raglan castle fell and resistance in south Wales was over. The few remaining Royalist garrisons elsewhere, recognizing the futility of further resistance, also capitulated. To all intents and purposes the war was at an end.

THE AFTERMATH OF WAR

With the cessation of hostilities came the day of reckoning. In Glamorgan, however, those members of the gentry who had led the revolt against the King in 1645 were to escape punishment unless they had subsequently returned to their former allegiance. Those punished, about a dozen in all, naturally tried to minimize the part they had played. Some said that they had been nominated as Commissioners of Array without being asked; which was probably true. The question was whether they had acted in that capacity.

Sir Richard Bassett stated that the King appointed him a Commissioner of Array for Glamorgan when there was a regiment of 1,200 raised in the county. Subsequently, when he was made governor of Cardiff, he dared not refuse as the King was then in the town with a considerable force. But six weeks later, when summoned by some of the gentry and freeholders, he had yielded it up without any resistance on condition that he should go where he pleased.[74] It is understandable, of course, that here no mention is to be found of the knighthood conferred upon him by Charles at the siege of Gloucester.

Edward Carne's defence of his conduct over the February revolt was that he had been pressed into it by the multitude, which resented the pressures of the garrison at Cardiff. It is interesting to note, however, that Carne denied that he ever was sheriff of Glamorgan for Parliament or ever acted in that capacity, and an examination of the messenger who brought down the commission under the great seal from Parliament revealed that Carne never received it. This evidence resulted in the fine being reduced from a moiety to a sixth.[75]

William Thomas of Dan-y-graig represented himself as the victim of circumstances; he was made sheriff when Gerard was in power. After his attempt to summon Briton Ferry House in the 1646 revolt he had come in voluntarily to surrender to Laugharne.[76] Though there is no evidence that Walter Thomas, also of Swansea and father of the above-mentioned William, participated in the 1646 rising, his estate was nevertheless sequestered. He claimed that he was old and confined to his bed and had submitted before December 1, 1645.[77] On the strength of the evidence it is difficult to see why Walter Thomas's estate should have been sequestered at all unless he suffered for the sins of his son. Sir Edward Thomas of Llanfihangel and Betws also stood charged with summoning Briton Ferry House. He claimed that this was his only delinquency and pleaded that he was old, lame, and unable to travel.[78]

Whatever their pleas in extenuation, the above were fined a sum based on the estimated value of their estates. But Sir John Aubrey, although he had been involved in the 1646 rising, managed to evade sequestration for a time. How active he had been is not clear. He claimed that he had only done what others had done and could not help being made Commissioner of Array. In his defence was quoted his reputation for moderation and his having presented a petition to the King in the summer of 1645 and thus 'deserved the favor to be looked vpon as a p[er]son more tendring his Countryes safty than countenancing its disturbance'. But there were obviously some people not convinced of his innocence, for his estate was subsequently 'discovered' and sequestered in 1648.[79] Judge David Jenkins of Hensol alone remained defiant to the bitter end. Taken prisoner with Sir Richard Bassett at Hereford and committed to the Tower on a charge of high treason, Jenkins denied that his adherence to the King was treason, arguing that since the King was the fountain of justice, without his authority Parliament had no jurisdiction. Though moved from prison to prison he continued to deny Parliament's right to try him and he does not appear to have been released until the Restoration. His estate was sequestered and a part, if not all of it, was sold in 1652.[80]

As for the Kemeys family, Sir Charles had also been involved in the Carne rebellion and he petitioned to compound before December 1, 1647, when he also asked to be admitted to make composition for his father, Sir Nicholas Kemeys, who was sickly. But before they were to compound, Sir Charles and his father were to be involved in the Second Civil War in which Sir Nicholas was killed at Chepstow castle and Sir Charles was eventually taken prisoner at Pembroke castle.[81] Then there were two members of another staunch Glamorgan Royalist family taken prisoner at Oxford, true to their sovereign to the last. They were Sir Henry Stradling and Colonel John Stradling, but what fine, if any, they had to pay, is not known.[82] Neither is it known what fine, if any, was imposed on Edward Lewis of Y Fan whose name also appears in the Calendar of the Committee for Compounding.[83]

Laugharne had also had further trouble with the gentlemen of the Vale in June, 1647, after the Army took the bold step of seizing the King's person. When news of this coup reached Glamorgan, it seemed to some of the Royalist gentry of the Vale an opportune moment to stage a demonstration against the County Committee. They met at Cowbridge on June 13 and issued warrants to the high constables of the hundred of Miskin to summon all able-bodied men to assemble there with their arms. This they claimed they did in the names of the King and Sir Thomas Fairfax, the commander of the Army. They wrote to assure Laugharne, who was at Carmarthen, that their action was not intended to be any disrespect to him. Information had reached them that the County Committee intended to seize some of them and they had to act for their own security. Laugharne described the leaders as 'ancient malignants of a deep stain' who had no grievances. The County Committee, he declared, had justly administered the Ordinances of Parliament. But that was the rub. The leaders, with such countrymen as joined them, marched towards Cardiff and, at Llandaff, sent a challenge to Edward Prichard, who naturally demanded their authority for assembling the inhabitants in a martial way. The demands in their letter had been that they should enjoy their liberties and estates as fully as they had before the setting up of the Committee and that taxation should be suspended until the outcome of the present discussions between King, Parliament, and Army was ascertained. Laugharne acted promptly and was able to report from Cardiff on June 21 that the chief movers in the business, to the number of fifty, all well mounted, had fled the county at his approach. The ringleaders in this affair were Sir Henry Stradling and his brother, John Stradling of St. Donat's, Sir Edward Thomas of Llanfihangel and Betws, Sir Richard Bassett of Beaupré and Sir Thomas Not.[84]

THE SECOND CIVIL WAR

There is definite evidence that in January 1647, before the above outbreak, an attempt had been made to tamper with Laugharne's loyalty. He was invited to betray his trust by the King's secret agents; but he exhibited his good faith by sending the letters to the House of Commons and he subsequently dealt with the Vale rising. But a year later there were persistent rumours that Laugharne was involved in Royalist plots. He was summoned to London to answer these allegations and there he remained on parole from January to May 1648.[85] In the meantime Parliament had issued an order for the disbanding of supernumeraries, a heading under which Laugharne's troops came. John Poyer, Laugharne's brother-in-law and governor of Pembroke castle, refused to disband his men and precipitated a new struggle in the spring of 1648. His defiance was supported by part of the forces of Colonel Rice Powell, who had been Laugharne's right-hand man throughout the war. The old Parliamentarians in revolt then marched into Glamorgan to link up with the diehard Royalist elements there. Once again there was a threat to Cardiff. News of it reached Colonel Horton, the officer sent by Fairfax to deal with the trouble in Pembroke, when he was in Brecon. Alarmed by the danger to Cardiff, Horton left Brecon, and by forced marches he got to Llandaff, crossed the Taff, and threw himself between Powell's forces and Cardiff. The Welsh had already reached St. Nicholas after seizing Swansea and Neath, and were attempting to persuade Edward Prichard at Cardiff to throw in his lot with them.[86]

Laugharne had meanwhile escaped from London and had joined Powell on Thursday, May 4. The very location of Powell's forces at St. Nicholas is interesting. The entire area south-west of St. Fagan's containing Cottrell, St. Nicholas, and Dyffryn belonged to the Button family. And both Laugharne and Poyer were married to Miles Button's sisters, whilst Miles Button himself was married to a daughter of Sir Nicholas Kemeys. The Button family, no doubt, was the source through which Laugharne's loyalty had been tampered with, for it was to their territory that he now hurried.[87] He at once wrote to Horton to ask by what authority he had entered the district which Parliament had entrusted to himself. He complained that his troops had been attacked and that the disbandment had not been carried out in accordance with the instructions of Parliament. He called on Horton to withdraw his forces from the county. Horton naturally replied that he had entered Wales under orders from Fairfax, who was in command of all Parliamentary forces, and that Poyer's resistance to the ordinance for disbanding had made such intervention necessary. In conclusion Horton expressed his surprise that Laugharne should have taken the side of those who had so manifestly violated the authority of Parliament rather than offer his help.

Unfortunately our knowledge of what happened from Friday to Monday, May 5-8, comes from the Parliamentary side only. Horton stated that the Welsh withdrew from St. Nicholas to Llancarfan, Penmark, and Fonmon on Friday. No doubt they held a council of war and the fact that Cromwell was hastening to Wales and was expected to reach Gloucester by the week-end was, as Horton suggested, a decisive factor in favour of an immediate engagement. They advanced again to St. Nicholas on Sunday evening and on Monday morning the Welsh forces were actually drawn up near Cottrell, Miles Button's house on the hill and not far from the village of St. Fagan's. Horton had been on his guard that night, and early on Monday morning his scouts came in touch with the Welsh about a mile and a half from his quarters. So he drew up his forces in the best position he could select. Major Bethel was given command of the horse on the Parliamentary right, and Major Barton on the left; Colonel Okey's dragoons were divided between the two wings. Since the topographical indications are slight, it is hard to reconstruct the course of the action. Suffice it here to say that the ground was fiercely contested for a couple of hours, and that by ten o'clock, or soon after, Laugharne's forces were broken and the Parliamentarians were pressing in hot pursuit.

The battle of St. Fagan's was the most considerable engagement that took place in Wales during the Civil Wars. Horton estimated that Laugharne's forces numbered 8,000, horse and foot. Nearly half of them, however, consisted of clubmen armed with pikes and bills, and naturally these suffered heavy casualties in the retreat. The Parliamentary army was much smaller, probably under 3,000. But they were seasoned troops; in fact it was the one battle in Wales in which elements from the New Model Army played a part. The issue was at first by no means certain. Horton confessed that he felt himself in straits, outnumbered and without advantage of the ground. But the steadiness of trained men assisted by the superiority in cavalry eventually told in his favour. As a result of the battle, Laugharne could not again meet his adversaries in the field.[88] The Second Civil War was soon at an end and the Royalists of the Vale had to accept the policies of the Puritan party.

CHAPTER VI

Politics and Religion in Glamorgan during the Interregnum, 1649-1660

By ANTHONY M. JOHNSON

i

THE COMMONWEALTH ESTABLISHED

THE establishment of the Commonwealth in January 1649 had very little direct effect on the personnel of Glamorgan politics. Part of the reason was that unreliable men had been removed from positions of authority for their involvement in the abortive risings of 1648, but also, the government had good reason to be suspicious of the affiliations of the county during the past few years and continued to rely upon the support of a small group of about fifteen loyal county committeemen who had emerged during the First Civil War, led by Philip Jones, Rowland Dawkins, Bussy Mansel, and John Price. J.P.s were appointed almost exclusively from their ranks and thus, in their dual capacities as county committeemen and J.P.s, they kept Glamorgan politics and the new and traditional forms of county government firmly under their control.[1] There was, in fact, a marked degree of continuity in the membership of the governing group in Glamorgan throughout the Interregnum.

By the beginning of the Commonwealth the traditional pattern of county government was fully revived and co-existed alongside that which had evolved during the civil wars. The Great Sessions met regularly and without interruption, the only difference being that during the Commonwealth the Sessions were held in the name of the Keeper of the Liberties of England, and during the Protectorate, in the name of the Protector. The Glamorgan Quarter Sessions continued to perform their traditional functions. The old royal revenues, now diverted to the use of the state, were collected in time-honoured ways under the new régimes.[2]

Because of the difficulties of sequestration of delinquents before 1649 one of the first measures of the Rump Parliament was to pass on February 23, 1649 an Act for the Sequestration of South Wales and Monmouthshire, followed by a similar one for the northern counties in August. A fine totalling £20,500 was laid upon the south Wales counties, of which Glamorgan's contribution was set at £3,500. About one-quarter of the thirty-nine commissioners authorised to collect the fines were Glamorgan men, including the county's four most prominent committeemen. Of those exempted from the provisions of the Act eleven were former royalists or recent delinquents from Glamorgan, including the recusant Sir Charles Kemeys, Sir John Aubrey, Sir Richard Bassett, Sir Henry Stradling, and Sir Edward Thomas. These people were to submit to the central committee in accordance with former ordinances for sequestration. All other delinquents were to be discharged from all former obligations.[3]

Little is known about the actual collection of the fine, but it was probably set as a general assessment on land values in the south Wales counties. Half of the total sum was to be paid within ten weeks of the passing of the Act and the second moiety within the ten weeks following; all of which was probably achieved. The first £10,000 was sent to Bristol on the direction of the Council of State for the use of the Navy and arrived there before April 26, 1649. The second half of the sum was not due until July, but because there was an urgent need for the money the Council of State proposed that money should be raised on credit of that sum and used for the service of Ireland, to which end the south Wales commissioners were urged to get in the money as soon as possible.[4] Philip Jones was one of the commissioners against whom allegations were made of unfairness in collecting the fines, though in general the Act was well received in south Wales. On June 20, 1650 a petition was presented to the House of Commons said to have been signed by 19,000 persons giving thanks for the remission of their delinquency.[5]

Both the Commonwealth and Protectorate were minority régimes which were obliged to rely on men who, for the most part, were outsiders in county societies throughout England and Wales. To try to ensure the loyalty of the localities, some of whose support was doubtful, the Rump introduced on January 2, 1650 an Oath of Engagement to the Commonwealth to be taken by all males over the age of sixteen, though it met with a varied response throughout the country. Because of the precarious nature of the Commonwealth the localities had to be more closely controlled, and increased centralization by the government became an important feature of the Commonwealth period and continued to be so under the Cromwellian Protectorate. The tendency towards greater centralization was manifest from early in the life of the Commonwealth in the shape of two major developments which served to emasculate the power of the former county committees.

Firstly, the county committees, which hitherto had controlled all financial and military affairs, were replaced by assessment and militia commissioners. The government relied mainly on the assessment commissioners, though during the Interregnum power tended to move towards the militia commissioners. In practice, however, the effect of this division of function was often mitigated, because the leading personnel in the counties acted in a dual capacity. The Glamorgan militia commissioners were drawn from the well-established governing group, the most active being John Jones, Rowland Dawkins, Bussy Mansel, and John Price.[6]

Secondly, local committees were deprived of the power to sequester delinquents' estates. The general pattern adopted was that in the place of county sequestration committees the Rump named three persons in each county to sequester estates on behalf of the central government and made them directly answerable to it. The new sequestration commissioners were appointed by the central committee for compounding for the whole of the country in February 1650, and efforts were made to appoint, where possible, persons who had not previously sat on their local committees. In Wales, however, separate commissioners were not named for each county. Two bodies of sequestrators were appointed with responsibility for the north and south regions of the Principality respectively, though a separate group of commissioners was appointed for Monmouthshire. Six sequestration commissioners were named for south Wales, of whom two each were from Glamorgan and Carmarthenshire, while Brecon and Monmouthshire supplied the other two, even though Monmouthshire had its own sequestrators. The two Glamorgan sequestrators were Captain Thomas Evans of Eglwysilan, a Baptist, and William Morgan of Neath.[7]

The sequestrators took charge of the county or group of counties nearest their places of residence, so that Jenkin Francklin and John Hughes assumed responsibility for the counties of Carmarthenshire, Pembrokeshire, and Radnorshire. The commissioners, or some of them, met together every Thursday in Cardiff to co-ordinate their work, though they experienced considerable difficulties in discharging their tasks. They inherited a legacy of mismanagement from the previous committees and were particularly hampered by the paucity of accurate records; even the threat of a £20 fine upon all former sequestrators failing to produce a satisfactory statement of accounts.[7]

In addition, there was a good deal of uncertainty as to the extent of the authority of the sequestration commissioners, for by the Act for the Propagation of the Gospel in Wales of February 1650, the propagators were granted power to sequester clergy and manage their revenues, which led to confusion between the sequestrators and propagators. The Act for the General Fine on South Wales also raised the problem of which set of officials was responsible for sequestration, especially as many claimed they were exempt from sequestration as a result of the General Fine. The Committee for Compounding was itself uncertain at first as to how to direct the south Wales sequestrators, though eventually there evolved the principle that the benefits of the General Fine were confined to persons who were actually domiciled in Wales. The General Fine, however, made an appreciable difference to the potential revenue from sequestration in south Wales.[9]

The sequestration commissioners complained of the lack of an agent to help them in their work, and by the beginning of 1651 some of the commissioners asked to be relieved of their onerous duties. One modest concession was accorded the commissioners, however, when at their request William Lewis of Llanigon, Brecon, was officially appointed as agent by the central committee in London, though the commissioners for the counties of west Wales were apparently employing their own agent, William Rutland, at the time.[10]

From the very beginning the activities of the south Wales sequestration commissioners were subjected to criticisms led, and probably inspired by, Colonel Edward Freeman, attorney-general for south Wales. He accused the sequestrators of undervaluing estates and other disreputable practices. Freeman's allegations probably contained a measure of truth, for the central committee for compounding in London accepted on November 25, 1651 a list of new commissioners drawn up by Freeman which adopted the principle—as in England—of appointing three commissioners for each county. For Glamorgan, William Seys of Llanrhidian, Edward Bowen of Swansea, and Matthew Hopkins of Neath were originally on the list submitted by Freeman, though Bowen, who was 'taken prisoner by the French', and Hopkins, who was unable to take up the appointment, were replaced by Hugh Jones of Walterstone and Evan Prichard of Collenna, and the committee for compounding appointed Freeman himself to serve as a commissioner in the south Wales counties.[11]

Freeman's efforts achieved only temporary success, for when Major-General Harrison and Colonel Philip Jones were released from more pressing duties, they, together with Henry Herbert, nominated other sequestrators to whom Freeman took exception. Some, he claimed, were related to the old commissioners, while others were under age, debtors to the state and even non-resident.[12] Harrison's influence was too strong to be challenged, and several of Freeman's nominees were rejected, including his two for Glamorgan, who were replaced by Robert Thomas and Jenkin Williams. They, too, complained that their predecessors were behindhand with their accounts and would not supply sufficient relevant information, whereupon the committee for compounding ordered that a £20 fine should be imposed on each of the defaulters.[13]

There was no respite from regular taxation during the Commonwealth. The system of appointing commissioners to supervise the collection of assessments throughout the country established in 1647 remained in force and continued with little variation until the Restoration. The burden of assessments increased appreciably during the Commonwealth but was reduced during the Protectorate. The assessment for Glamorgan rose from £131 15s. 10d. in June 1647 to £197 13s. 9d. a month from March to June 1649. From the latter date to March 1650 the assessment was raised substantially to £590 a month. It fell to £393 6s. 8d. a month from December 1650 to April 1651, after which it doubled to £786 13s. 4d. a month and remained at that rate for the rest of the Commonwealth period. Early in the Protectorate the monthly assessment was reduced to the early Commonwealth figure of £590 per month and was reduced further in February 1655 to £393 6s. 8d. It continued at that rate for over two years until it was reduced again in June 1657 to £229 8s. 10d. for the next three years up to the Restoration.[14]

Though there is no evidence of the procedure of apportionment and collection of the monthly assessments in this period, it is not unreasonable to suppose that the commissioners continued levying the assessments according to the long-established procedure of the poundage rate upon the inhabitants of the ten hundreds of the county, whereby the most prosperous area, Dinas Powys hundred, contributed just over one-eighth of the tax, while the poorest hundred, Llangyfelach, contributed less than one-sixteenth of the assessment.[15] If the county followed the pattern of the rest of Wales the Glamorgan commissioners probably experienced difficulties in securing the required sums during the Commonwealth and found the task rather easier during the Protectorate, when the assessments were lower and economic conditions were generally improved. In a speech to Parliament in June 1657 Colonel Philip Jones stated that some counties in Wales paid 'one half, the least a fourth or fifth of the revenue yearly'.[16]

ii

THE PROPAGATION ERA

The Rump Parliament and the Commonwealth rested on extremely shaky foundations. The ardent Commonwealthsmen and radical M.P.s were in a minority and commanded very little support in the country at large. Parliament was in reality a collection of fluid groups of M.P.s who agreed on some issues and disagreed on others, which seriously inhibited the cherished hopes of the radicals for initiating a wide range of reforming legislation. The Rump's failure to introduce a comprehensive religious settlement was essentially the result of its own internal divisions, and it was only in Wales and the northern counties of England that significant progress was made in religious innovation in the cause of the godly reformation.[17]

Puritanism had made little headway in 'the dark corners of the land', especially in Wales, in spite of a great deal of Puritan missionary work since the sixteenth century. Even the efforts of dedicated men like Vavasor Powell and Walter Cradock in recent years failed to move the government to action.[18] No official attack on the problem was made until after the purge of Parliament by Colonel Pride in December 1648 had removed from the Commons most of the Welsh Presbyterian M.P.s who were unlikely to support demands for radical religious innovation.

[283]

Eventually, following pressure from Major-General Harrison, who had been appointed to the south Wales command in July 1649, two petitions, one from north Wales and one from the southern counties, the Propagation proposals came before the House in January 1650. By this time, Wales's few representatives in the Rump were mainly aristocrats like Algernon Sidney, Republican M.P. for Cardiff, whose interests lay outside Wales, or by radical M.P.s like Philip Jones, who entered Parliament as a new member early in February in time to help the Bill through the House.

The Act for the Propagation of the Gospel in Wales, drafted 'according to the plan laid down by Hugh Peter', was passed on February 22, 1650.[19] The Act, which was to be in force initially for three years until March 25, 1653, had two principal objectives: to puritanize Wales, and to establish schools in which children could be educated in a puritan atmosphere from an early age. Seventy-one commissioners were appointed with Harrison at their head. Of these, twenty-eight were put in charge of the north Wales counties, and forty-three of the southern counties.[20] They were a diverse body of men. A number were not Welsh and eleven came from the English border counties. The Commission also numbered a few who had been royalists and Anglicans before 1646. The majority of the commissioners came from outside the leading county families and were invariably trusted county committeemen. There was no attempt at equitable distribution of commissioners throughout the thirteen counties of Wales. Five of the most distinctively Welsh counties supplied only two members between them, while Glamorgan supplied about one-third of the commissioners for the six south Wales counties and Monmouthshire.[21] The commissioners were given power to examine and eject the incumbents of livings within the Principality for delinquency, malignancy, and non-residence, while those convicted of pluralism had to choose one living.

To fill the vacancies of the ejected ministers twenty-five approvers or triers were appointed to approve ministers, who were to receive a salary not exceeding £100, which was to derive from sequestered church and crown livings and sequestered estates of royalists.[22] The approvers were led and inspired by the zeal of Walter Cradock and Vavasor Powell. As in the case of the commissioners, many of the approvers were not Welsh in origin. At least six of them came from outside Wales and had no connexion with the Principality before the Propagation Act. Again, there was no attempt at equitable distribution of the approvers among the counties. Four approvers worked in Glamorgan: David Walter and Morris Bidwell, William Seaborn and one Miles, of whom the latter two came from the English border counties.[23]

The commissioners divided their activities between north and south Wales and acted quite separately. They began their work very soon after the passing of the Act and, as early as June 1650, Bulstrode Whitelocke relates, many malignant and scandalous ministers had been ejected in north Wales.[24] It can be assumed that the same was true in the southern counties. In three years there were ejected two hundred and seventy-eight persons, eighty-two from north Wales, one hundred and fifty-one from south Wales, of whom twenty were ejected in Glamorgan, and forty-five from Monmouthshire. One hundred and twenty-seven ministers were left in their places.[25] There is only one record of the commissioners following the suggestion under the Act to the effect that parishes might unite for purposes of public worship; this was done at Roath, Cardiff, the day after the Act had technically expired.[26]

Although forty-three commissioners were nominated for south Wales the work of propagation was effectively carried out by a much smaller group of about fifteen persons under the leadership of the four Glamorgan men who were in the ascendant in south Wales during the Interregnum: Colonel Philip Jones, Rowland Dawkins, Bussy Mansel, and John Price. Price acted as treasurer and John Creed, not named in the Act, served as registrar.[27] The south Wales commissioners held meetings in various parts of the region, including Neath and Cowbridge, though the most usual rendezvous was Swansea. Within a short time because of the growth of business especially in Monmouthshire, Pembrokeshire, and Glamorgan, the bulk of propagation work was carried out by residents in these counties. After about a year Glamorgan itself was divided into two districts, the east and west of the county, with officials of the western part exercising their authority in the eastern part of Carmarthenshire also.[28]

Each county in Wales had its own sequestrator or agent appointed at a salary of £40 per annum and a collector to gather in rents and profits. Each county kept separate accounts, though the accounts of the two regions of the Principality were each supervised overall by a central treasurer who received a salary of £200 per annum. Price Vaughan, a commissioner, acted as solicitor in London 'attending appeals there' for both north and south Wales Propagators.[29] The Propagators were further assisted by a wide circle of minor officials who carried out much of the day-to-day work. They were often men of humble circumstances who helped to fill a vacuum created by a paucity of reliable personnel. These men were almost universally disliked, and one sequestrator, Jenkin Williams, of the eastern hundreds of Glamorgan, was deemed capable of 'every villainy and barbarity'.[30]

The attempt to implement the Propagation Act gave rise to a wide variety of problems. There was little uniformity in respect of doctrine, ideas about church organization, or the question of state-supported ministers. The treatment of ejected ministers was often hard. They should have received one-fifth of the rent set; but the accounts for south Wales for 1650-3 show that though £1,866 7s. 6d. was paid towards widows and children of ejected ministers the sums were far from being paid regularly or generally granted. Of the former incumbents of sequestered livings in Glamorgan—twenty under the Act and thirty-five before— only twenty-nine were in receipt of fifths in 1650, six in 1651 and nine in 1652. Under these conditions ejected clergy were invariably forced to look for alternative sources of subsistence. Nathaniel Gamage of Eglwys- ilan, Hugh Gore of Oxwich, and Francis Davies of Llan-gan kept private schools. Others had to live on greatly reduced incomes and some left their areas altogether, as did Edward Gage of Rhosili, who having tried un- successfully to become a farmer, emigrated to Ireland, while Dr. Gordon of Porteynon, Gower, removed to Kent, where he died.[31]

Ejection was an easy matter, but finding replacements proved a dismal failure. In spite of strenuous efforts to recruit substitute ministers in England and especially at the universities, very few were forthcoming. Resort was made to the new schoolmasters to help in the work of preaching, and even some of the commissioners and officials themselves did their share of preaching. Very few men could be found sufficiently qualified to preach in Welsh. Of new appointments to settled livings there is very little evidence, and only twelve ministers are known to have settled in south Wales, four of whom were in Glamorgan.[32]

There are known to have been about ninety itinerant preachers in Wales, including most of the twenty-five approvers named in the Act, which meant that about sixty-three were recruited. It appears that William Seaborne and Richard Symonds, approvers named in the Act, confined their activities to Glamorgan. David Walter worked mainly in the Swansea district, though he often preached in Llandaff cathedral. Of the recruited itinerants William Erbery, Henry Nicholas, and Walter Williams devoted their energies to preaching in Glamorgan, while fifteen others divided their time between Glamorgan and another adjacent county—usually Carmarthen.[33] The majority of the itinerants were not learned men and expressed a wide variety of puritan views. Their unconventional and unorthodox methods of preaching made them objects of criticism and often derision. Those at work in Glamorgan were described as 'rambling teachers' and 'hackney preachers'. Nathan Jones of Merthyr described the activities of preachers in his area: 'preach they cannot unless they be sent, and teach they cannot what they never learnt'. In addition to the deficiencies in the education of the preachers, the actual system had serious limitations, now that 'the sinecure rector makes room for the fleeting preacher' supplied 'with fresh horses at every stage'. There were so few preachers that an itinerant went 'now and then' only to Michaelston-super-Ely near Cardiff, and only 'once or twice a quarter' to Merthyr Dyfan, also near Cardiff.[34]

There was great disagreement among the preachers as to the appropriate means of ministerial support. William Erbery, of Cardiff, in many ways epitomized the divergent views as to whether or not preachers should receive payment from the state. After he had received £200 from the Glamorgan treasurer in 1650 and 1651, God began to 'rot in his soul', and men 'to hit him in the teeth', regarding the sources of his maintenance. After many months of painful self-doubts he decided to 'lose a hundred a year' and become 'an Independent indeed'. Yet the majority of preachers had little doubt that it was perfectly consistent with their convictions and scriptural authority to accept state support.[35]

There was thus an official propagation by approved ministers and preachers who worked alongside a smaller number of preachers who comprised what has been described as the unofficial propagation. These included preachers who disapproved of the system of state support and a growing body of preachers, especially Baptists, who deplored the strong ties between church and state.

In addition to the appointment of ministers, the commissioners under the Propagation Act were enjoined to establish new schools in Wales. The need for schools was greater in Wales than in the more developed regions of England, where educational establishments had burgeoned during the previous century. In Wales only a handful of grammar schools had been founded since the reign of Henry VIII and were in the main closely associated with the established church. Their facilities were in any case monopolized by the wealthy and provided very little opportunity for poor scholars or those living in rural areas.[36]

The immediate motives for the advancement of education in Wales under the Propagation Act were to remove 'ignorance and profaneness' among the young and thus complement and help to sustain the work of the preachers. The approvers were empowered to select suitable men to act as schoolmasters at a salary of not more than £40 per annum, which was to derive from the sequestered revenues of the church.[37] Within three years the zeal of the Propagators had led to the establishment of sixty new schools in Wales, of which thirty-three were founded in south Wales, including eight in Glamorgan; at Cardiff, Cowbridge, Llantwit Major, Merthyr, Neath, Penmark, St. Mary Hill, near Bridgend, and Swansea.[38]

The Propagators did not go out of their way to destroy or neglect the existing grammar schools, and there is evidence that money was provided for their maintenance and repair, though they were not left entirely undisturbed, for the Propagators had to be satisfied as to the fitness of the schoolmasters.[39] A small number of private schools were founded as a side-effect of ejections of ministers by the Propagators. For example, Hugh Gore, after his ejection from the rectory of Oxwich, Gower, opened a private school in Swansea.[40] The efforts of the Propagators were not sustained beyond the Interregnum, however, and only a small number of the newly established schools survived the Restoration.

Although the Propagation commissioners devoted themselves to their primary tasks of puritanizing Wales and establishing schools, their sphere of activity was potentially much wider, for in the Propagation Act

T

authority was given to the Propagators to act as commissioners for indemnity in Wales. The central committee in London was active from the summer of 1647. Its purpose was to indemnify those who had suffered in the service of Parliament, and until the Propagation Act, claims from Wales, as from the rest of the country, had to be taken up at Westminster. In August 1649, however, limited powers of examination on behalf of the central committee were conferred on J.P.s throughout England and Wales.[41] In the Propagation Act any five or more of the commissioners were 'constituted a committee of indemnity . . . for the hearing and determining of all matters and things properly relievable' by the central committee of indemnity in London.[42] The Welsh commissioners were empowered to hear complaints and issue warrants to the parties to appear before them. Appeals were to be allowed from the local committee to the central committee in London. Though in December 1651 a petitioner endeavoured to secure a hearing in London because, he claimed, the Propagators had failed to discharge their responsibilities as commissioners of indemnity, the central committee was satisfied that in south Wales the commissioners met fortnightly in that capacity. The Welsh commissioners dealt with a number of personal cases and considered several allegations against persons for holding local offices on behalf of Parliament contrary to two Acts of Parliament in 1647 which proscribed former delinquents from such positions.[43]

All the activities relating to the Propagation of the Gospel in Wales, particularly the payment of ministers and schoolmasters and the salaries and expenses of officials, were to be financed from the sequestered revenues of the church, but how these were to be collected and exploited presented a number of problems. From the outset there ensued conflicts of jurisdiction because already much of the church land in Wales had been sequestered and was being administered by the existing commissioners for sequestration. After a time, although occasional problems occurred during most of the three years of the Act's existence, the general principles emerged that all revenue deriving from church lands should pass into the hands of the Propagation commissioners and that the Propagators should not simply receive and dispose of the money but should collect it and generally administer it themselves.[44]

The activities of the Propagation commissioners and their agents naturally attracted considerable criticism and even open hostility, though in view of the wide range of their responsibilities it is perhaps understandable that the Propagation failed to live up to the expectations of the Act's most ardent advocates. Much of the dissatisfaction against the Propagation and its officials found expression in a pamphlet emanating from south Wales and Monmouthshire which was presented to the House of Commons early in March 1652. It was said to have been signed by 15,000 persons in the interests of 'well affected' but disillusioned puritanism.

The chief sponsors of the petition were Colonel Edward Freeman, attorney-general of south Wales, William Thomas of Brecon, and John Gunter of Tredomen, also of Breconshire. Freeman had already been in conflict with Colonel Philip Jones and had objected to the names of persons appointed as sequestration commissioners in February 1650. Dr. Thomas Richards's careful analysis of the petition has shown that the principal charges of unfair letting of sequestered livings, the high arrears in the commissioners' accounts, the allowing of delinquents and scandalous ministers to act as preachers, and the unworthiness and unfitness of many of the schoolmasters, were largely based on insubstantial evidence and in some cases the allegations were quite without foundation, while the whole must be regarded as inconclusive. The accusations concerning the failure of the itinerant ministers to replace adequately the ejected ministers were more valid; but this was not so much because of their inability as because of the difficulties of their tasks in attending to large areas. The petitioners could cite evidence of only one case to support the allegation that most of the itinerants were illiterate; this was Walter Williams of Glamorgan who, when the Act of Parliament ordering public thanksgiving for the victory at Worcester in September 1651 came down to the county, regretted that 'he could not read the same'.[45]

The petition was referred to the Committee for Plundered Ministers who found little of substance in the allegations against the Propagation. The petition remained, however, the subject of controversy in the Committee throughout the next twelve months up to the time of the dissolution of the Rump Parliament in April 1653. For their part in promoting the petition and their opposition to the Propagation Freeman and Gunter were arrested on the orders of Colonel Philip Jones and imprisoned for a short time. They were both subjected to examination by the Council of State, and Freeman was later dismissed from his post as attorney-general for south Wales.[46]

In spite of the Rump's initial treatment of the promoters of the petition the next few months saw a hardening of Parliament's attitude towards the Propagation, and, in the worsening political situation leading up to the dissolution of the Rump, renewal of the Propagation Act became a key issue in national politics. From June 1650 Parliament was continually discussing the advance of the Gospel in Britain. Conservative politicians in the Rump increasingly saw the itinerants as political agents of revolution and, as Dr. Christopher Hill has pointed out, 'the Propagators were feared less because of their methods of overcoming tough resistance in a tough area than because it was feared that those methods might be extended to the rest of Britain'.[47] This was the atmosphere into which a report on the south Wales petition was introduced into the House on March 23, 1653, just before the expiry of the Act. The House ordered it to be reported on March 25. When the report was read, it proved unfavourable to the petitioners, whereupon Parliament ordered it to be referred back to the Committee for Plundered Ministers. The Act for the Propagation of the Gospel in Wales had expired on March 25 and was scheduled to be re-introduced on the following Friday 'in order to the reviving thereof if the House shall see cause'. Three of the Welsh approvers argued at the door of the House for the renewal of the Act, but it was finally rejected on April 1.[48]

The date of the expiry of the Act and the attempt to renew it coincided with, and contributed to, the tense political situation at Westminster in the spring of 1653. The failure of the Rump to renew the Commission for the Propagation of the Gospel in Wales led to strenuous demands from the army and the radicals like the Fifth Monarchy movement for a dissolution of Parliament. As far as Cromwell and Harrison were concerned, the failure of the Rump to continue the Act finally demonstrated the members' lack of determination to further the cause of the godly reformation to which Cromwell and Harrison were so deeply committed, and became one of the most compelling reasons behind Cromwell's decision on April 20, 1653 forcibly to terminate the proceedings of the Rump of the Long Parliament.

Soon after the dissolution Cromwell wrote to the former commissioners in Wales advising them to continue their work 'and execute things settled by former acts. The Lord will be with you and shall have help from me till those placed in supreme power have further order.'[49] Despite this encouragement the apparatus created by the Propagation Act collapsed, until new proposals for the appointment of ministers were enacted a year later. In the interim, some individuals endeavoured to maintain the appointments and salaries conferred on them by the Propagators by resorting to appeals to other bodies, especially to the Commissioners for Sequestration, the Trustees for the Maintenance of Ministers, and even the Council of State. As far as can be judged from the few known cases they were generally left unsatisfied or granted only modest concessions.[50]

During the period of uncertainty following the dissolution of the Rump, power resided in a temporary Council of State of army officers while alternative forms of government were considered. Eventually it was decided to call a nominated Assembly of Saints on the lines desired by Major-General Harrison. This would consist of a 'body of men fearing God of approved integrity', of 144 members, who were expected to advance the cause of the godly reformation. Under this scheme the number of representatives from Wales was set at six. Although some gathered churches in England and Wales sent in names for consideration the army leaders simply selected those whom they decided were most suitable.[51] Harrison was at the height of his influence with Cromwell and he personally selected the members from north Wales, where he was an intimate of Vavasor Powell. Bussy Mansel was the only one of the six members selected to represent Wales who came from Glamorgan, though Philip Jones secured the one seat allocated to Monmouthshire.[52]

At the opening of Barebone's Parliament on July 4, 1653 Cromwell expressed his admiration for the former Propagators, 'Then, when we came to other trials, as in that case of Wales, which I confess for my own part, I set myself upon . . . how signally that business was trodden under foot in Parliament to the discountenancing of the malignant party of this Commonwealth. And some body will at leisure better impart to you the state of that business of Wales, which really to myself and officers was as plain a trial of their spirits as anything, it being known to many of us that God had kindled a seed there.'[53] Though described as a Parliament of Saints, the members represented a wide range of social backgrounds and political opinions, and only twelve members of the House have been identified as extreme radicals or Fifth Monarchy men, under the leadership of Harrison, though there was a substantial number who shared their aspirations and allowed them to hold the initiative for much of the Parliament.[54]

Throughout the counties of England and Wales, as well as at the centre, there was generally a shift to the left as Barebone's Parliament produced further disruption of local government. During July and August 1653 many counties were purged of their leaders. In reality, however, Barebone's had to govern the counties and rely upon support where it could find it, and 'no more than the Barebone's M.P.s were the local leaders universally radical puritans'.[55] Though there were a number of upheavals in Wales, in Glamorgan itself the structure of local politics remained remarkably stable. Power continued to reside in the hands of the trusted and well-tried leadership of Philip Jones, Bussy Mansel, Rowland Dawkins, and John Price, and their followers.

The short-lived Barebone's Parliament appointed only one body of committeemen throughout England and Wales when in October 1653 small committees, usually of five persons, were nominated for each county to administer relief for poor prisoners. One-third of all those appointed in Wales were former Propagators. The five appointed for Glamorgan included three former Propagators, John Price, Rowland Dawkins, and John Bowen. Price and Dawkins were members of the ruling nucleus, while Evan Lewis—like John Price a brother-in-law of Philip Jones—had been clerk for the Propagation commissioners in south Wales.[56] Only Rice Powell was a newcomer to Glamorgan committees. As far as the traditional governing families were concerned, Barebone's Parliament marked the nadir of their political fortunes during the Interregnum. Cromwell soon became alarmed at the radical legislative proposals produced by Barebone's Parliament, especially in respect of law reform and church maintenance. Eventually, after it had sat for six months Cromwell persuaded the moderate majority to combine to hand over their authority to him on December 10, 1653, thus bringing the

Parliament to a conclusion. Soon after the dissolution of Barebone's Parliament Cromwell accepted the Instrument of Government by which the Protectorate was established without a king or a House of Lords and with himself as Protector.

iii

THE PROTECTORATE

I. The Religious Settlement

After the end of the Propagation and the establishment of the Protectorate no longer was special provision made for the spiritual needs of Wales. By an Act of March 20, 1654 the task of providing and approving ministers throughout England and Wales was entrusted to the Commission for Approbation of Public Preachers, which was based in London.[57] The commission consisted of nine laymen and twenty-nine ministers, of whom only two members were Welsh, Walter Cradock and Jenkin Griffiths. The commissioners were generally men of moderate religious persuasions and represented a wider spectrum of puritan opinion than the former Propagation commissioners. All new ministers had to be approved as fit for the ministry by the Commission for Approbation of Public Preachers commonly known as Triers. They had the power to review all previous appointments and to approve all persons they thought fit and worthy to preach.

To help the Triers there were established in August 1654 throughout England and Wales commissioners for ejecting scandalous ministers. They were appointed on a county basis, except in Wales where the task was assigned to two regional committees, one for the northern and another for the southern counties, with the exception of Monmouthshire, which was given its own committee. In Wales many of the members had been nominated to the earlier Propagation Commission and had sat on many of the committees in recent years. Of the forty-three named for the counties of south Wales four of the most prominent were the familiar Glamorgan leaders, Philip Jones, Bussy Mansel, Rowland Dawkins, and John Price.[58] Also named in the Act for Ejecting Scandalous Ministers were a number of ministers to serve as 'assistants' to the commissioners, sixteen for north Wales and twenty-four for the south Wales counties, who included Walter Cradock, also a member of the Commission for the Approbation of Public Preachers.[59]

The Commissioners for Approbation of Public Preachers granted their approval on receipt of a certificate from a locality guaranteeing the good character of the new minister and subscribed to by any three persons, of whom one had to be a 'Preacher of the Gospel in some constant settled place'. In practice, however, three seems to have been the irreducible minimum, and most ministers were examined by at least five persons, as was the case when a certificate was issued authorising the removal of David Davies from the Baptist church at Llantrisant to Neath.[60]

In practice, the Committee for Approbation of Public Preachers and the Committee for the Ejection of Scandalous Ministers interfered very little with appointments in Wales because the Propagators had carried out their work with great thoroughness. Though the Triers had widespread authority it was in fact limited by the power of patronage exercised by the Protector, by presentation rights vested in the Trustees for Maintenance, and on occasions by rights assumed by the Barons of Exchequer, the central body which co-ordinated and supervised the accounts of a number of bodies, including the Trustees for Maintenance.[61]

The payment of ministers accepted by the Commissioners for Approbation was in the hands of the Trustees for Maintenance, a body of thirteen members established in 1649. It was charged with administering church revenues and from 1654 was brought under the direct control of the Protector and Council. The Trustees for Maintenance did not begin to exercise any authority in Wales until 1653, after the extinction of the Propagation Commission, which had controlled church finances in Wales. The Trustees had a treasury and a treasurer, though the collection of moneys in Wales was vested in four receivers, James Ramsey, Griffith Bowen, John Weston, and John Cox. It was their duty to collect rents and profits and to receive rents from sequestered church lands. They probably began work in December 1653, and in June 1654 Col. Philip Jones was asked to advise with the trustees 'from time to time concerning the tithes of Glamorgan and to be let by them that they may get the best information concerning the same'. The receivers were paid £50 a year plus expenses incurred in carrying out their duties. Trustees could dispose of these revenues for the maintenance of ministers and schoolmasters, but every order they made was subject to the approval of the Protector and the Council of State.[62]

The attempt under the Propagation to supply 'the spiritual hiatus of the countryside had been admittedly a failure', and the Approvers turned to more orthodox methods of ministering to the localities in Wales. Many of the old itinerants were themselves appointed to more settled duties together with the new appointments, of whom at least eighteen, or just under one-quarter of those approved in south Wales and Monmouthshire, have been identified as working in Glamorgan.[63] Early in the Protectorate the supply of new ministers was inadequate, and the Triers were obliged to accept a system little removed from the old itinerant procedure.[64] This system remained in operation throughout the Protectorate, and though the supply of new ministers improved during the period it must be concluded that it was only partially successful, for the Protectorate religious settlement never adequately supplied the religious needs of the Principality.[65]

The Commission for Approbation of Public Preachers was silent about the schoolmasters who were expected to act as complementary agents in puritanizing Wales, and, with the collapse of the Propagation Commission, the procedure for financing schoolmasters was transferred to the Trustees for Maintenance of Ministers in London. The Triers, however, endeavoured to maintain the educational system established under the Propagation and sanctioned a number of original orders of the Propagation Commissioners. In June 1654 the Trustees for Maintenance of Ministers issued an order that all arrears of stipends which had been granted by the Propagators should be paid to the schoolmasters on production of the original order for the particular grant. In spite of these directives some of the county officials in Wales were unwilling to pay arrears owing to the schoolmasters on the ground that their powers had ceased with the end of the Propagation Act, and such payments were obtained only on the direct intervention of the Trustees for Maintenance of Ministers.[66]

The Act for Ejecting Scandalous Ministers of August 1654 laid down specific orders for the commissioners in the counties, with the assistance of the ministers named in the Act, to examine all schoolmasters who were ignorant and scandalous, inefficient, or negligent, as defined in the Act.[67] The great effort during the Propagation years to establish schools in Wales was seriously undermined during the Protectorate, though it is a matter of some conjecture exactly why by 1660 there remained in existence only twenty-one out of more than sixty schools established under the Propagation.[68] As far as the evidence allows us to judge, it appears that ejection accounted for the decline of only a small number of schools in Wales. Among the schoolmasters ejected under the Act for Ejecting Scandalous Ministers of August 1654 was one Hugh Jones of Glamorgan, who had been accused of drunkenness as early as 1652. There is little doubt that a number of masters were attracted away from teaching by larger salaries to become ministers. Other schools failed because they were established in remote parts of the country. William Thomas, M.A., formerly schoolmaster at Cowbridge, was found 'supplying there' as minister in 1656. He proceeded to St. Mary Hill, near Bridgend, in June 1658, and after the Restoration returned to his former profession by 'keeping school at Swanzey'. In most of these transformations the schools fell into decay. Of the seven or eight ejected clergy allowed by the Propagators to supervise the new schools only three succeeded under the Protectorate in retaining their places, including Moor Pye of Swansea.[69]

Throughout south Wales only seven schools continued in existence beyond 1660, of which two only remained in Glamorgan. This sorry situation was reflected in a letter of Dr. Hugh Lloyd, bishop of Llandaff, in October 1662. The bishop appealed to the clergy of his diocese to subscribe 'to the good worke of the free schooles'. 'This county hath eminently contributed to the primitive Christianity of all Wales, its strange wee should now come short of all parts of Wales in the maine acts of it, for of all counties therein, Glamorgan is (notwithstanding the present conditions and estates both of the laytie and cleargie thereof) most unfurnisht of meanes either to propagate to others, yea, or to continue to itself religion and learning. Of old, Christian schooles began here, and (to our great shame) it was not, before the dissolution, so utterly destitute of them, as now it is.'[70]

In spite of its inadequacies state maintenance was valued by most Protectorate preachers and supported by many lay persons, a number of whom were among the 762 signatories to the *Humble Representation and Address* from south Wales and Monmouthshire written by Walter Cradock in 1656, in support of the Protector and his government.[71] Even some who dissociated themselves from state support were found among the signatories to the pamphlet because of its political pronouncements.[72] In fact, only a small number of ministers abjured the state system and preached independently outside it. Though it was said in a pamphlet of 1652 that there were about eighty unpaid preachers in Wales in addition to those receiving state maintenance, sixty-nine preachers have been identified as preaching unsupported during the Protectorate. Their stronghold was the southern part of south Wales; and twenty-two of them are known to have been at work, mostly in Glamorgan. Baptists of various shades of opinion and practice formed the preponderant majority, and eight of the twenty-two were associated with the Ilston church in Gower. Some of these preachers came from the Llantrisant/Gelli-gaer community of Baptists, including the former sequestrator, Captain Thomas Evans, and Thomas Edwards, 'the fierce anabaptist of Gelli-gaer', agent to Edward Prichard of Llancaeach, another member of this church, who had been a governor of Cardiff and was frequently named to Glamorgan committees between 1647 and 1654. Closely associated with this group were those at Eglwysilan, dubbed by Clement Walker as a 'nursery of anabaptists'.[73]

The most militant of those who rejected state support were the millenarian Fifth Monarchists. Fifth Monarchy ideas developed after the battle of Worcester in September 1651 and became particularly active after the creation of the Protectorate. Barebone's Parliament, it was hoped, would correct all the ills in society and prepare the way for the Fifth Monarch and the second coming of Christ to rule in person on the earth. After its failure the Fifth Monarchists began to turn against the state and against Cromwell in particular. Except for Wales, Fifth Monarchy was essentially an urban movement in which London was always dominant. In Wales Fifth Monarchy relied heavily on the personal influence of Vavasor Powell, Morgan Llwyd, and Major-General Harrison, and was confined almost exclusively to the Radnor and Wrexham regions. South Wales was one of the large parts of the country where Fifth Monarchy ideas made no impression, for there the Puritan movement was dominated by the effective political and religious leadership of Philip Jones and Walter Cradock.[74] Vavasor Powell was one of Cromwell's sternest critics and in 1655 claimed that there were twenty thousand saints in Wales ready to hazard their blood in defence of their cause, though when the attempted royalist risings took place in March of that year Powell made no attempt to help the conspirators. In December 1655 Powell produced his tract, *A Word for God*, signed by 322 persons in Wales, nearly all of whom came from the north. The solitary signature of note from south Wales was that of Jenkin Jones, a preacher and friend of Powell. Only three of the six Welsh M.P.s in Barebone's Parliament signed the pamphlet, and Bussy Mansel, the one Glamorgan member of that Parliament, who was always a moderate in religious views, did not give his support. Only six of the former Propagation officials signed the tract and they, too, were nearly all from north Wales. Opposition to the Protectorate declined in Wales soon after the publication of the *Word for God*, and a number of the signatories apostatized and accepted livings in the national church they had recently denounced.[75]

While Fifth Monarchy made no headway in south Wales, Quakerism was more successful in securing support during the 1650s. From 1653, at least, Morgan Llwyd was attracted to Quaker doctrine, and he sent two observers to the centre of George Fox's activities at Swarthmore, Yorkshire, to find out about his teachings. Thereafter determined efforts were made to convert the Welsh and were attended by a fair measure of success in south Wales, and in Glamorgan in particular. The long-standing attacks made by a number of Puritan ministers on existing forms of worship and ministry prepared the way for the advancement of Quakerism in south Wales. Those ministers who even before, and during, the Propagation refused to accept tithe came near to expressing views held by Quakers; the most prominent of them was William Erbery, of Cardiff, who in 1653 was criticized for preaching 'very dangerously and schismatically'. Cardiff was the first place in Glamorgan where Quakerism was introduced, probably by John ap John, a Denbighshire Quaker, in 1655. Soon afterwards he journeyed to Swansea, where he was successful in gaining a few sympathizers, one of whom William Bevan, a merchant, gave the Quakers a site for their meeting house in the town. By the autumn of 1655 there was established in Cardiff a group of active converts, who clashed with the incumbent of St. Andrew's Church in a celebrated dispute, carried on principally by a Cardiff hatter, Francis Gawler.

In spite of the difficulties experienced by Quakers in Glamorgan their numbers grew and by the time Thomas and Elizabeth Holme arrived in Cardiff there were about ten convinced Friends there. The Quakers were particularly successful when directing their propaganda against the Baptists in Glamorgan, from whom they recruited some of their earliest members. This provoked the Baptists, at a denominational meeting at Brecon in 1656, to encourage John Miles of Ilston, Gower, the founder of the first Baptist church in Glamorgan, to write a pamphlet directed against the Quakers. No Quaker in south Wales attempted to answer it, and it was left to George Fox himself, possibly influenced by Miles's attack, to come to south Wales to reply when he visited Glamorgan in 1657. As antagonism between puritans and Quakers grew, the puritan ministers began to refuse to bury Friends in their churchyards and it became imperative for Quakers to secure their own burial grounds. It seems that Swansea Friends used part of the ground given by the merchant William Bevan in 1656, and three years later they acquired a plot at Loughor for the purpose. Cromwell's death in 1658, and determination by the authorities to deal severely with anything likely to cause disturbance made them much stricter in their dealings with Quakers. On several occasions civic authorities in Swansea and Cardiff harassed the local Quakers, including Elizabeth Holme, who spent some time in Swansea 'dark house', for testifying against puritans in the town.[76]

The end of the Propagation Act in March 1653 and the religious developments of the Protectorate did not stem criticism of the activities of the former Propagation commissioners. Opponents kept up their charges against the Propagators, ably supported by the propaganda of the dispossessed Anglican clergyman, Alexander Griffiths. Philip Jones, the dominant committeeman in Glamorgan and overlord of south Wales, remained the principal target of the critics. Jones himself was charged with a wide variety of misdemeanours and especially of his harsh treatment of ejected clergy in Glamorgan and of misappropriation by him and his supporters of sequestered church lands. Cromwell, though sympathetic to the Propagation commissioners, supported demands for an investigation into the workings of the Propagation commission and alleged abuses, to which ends an Act was passed on August 30, 1654. Thirty-three commissioners were appointed with wide powers to try to get at the truth of the charges against the commissioners.[77] Philip Jones, in fact, helped to draft the Act and placed his supporters among those who investigated and 'passed' the Propagation accounts of Glamorgan at Neath on August 10, 1655, which did little to satisfy his critics.[78]

The sequestration of church revenues placed large sums of money at the disposal of the commissioners in Wales, and Alexander Griffiths asserted that the total was £40,000 a year.[79] An official investigation at the Restoration of sequestered church revenues in south Wales during the Propagation years produced figures—corresponding closely with sums alleged by Griffiths in 1654—which showed the potential annual revenue in the six south Wales counties and Monmouthshire was £18,500, of which the value of 151 parishes, vicarages, and impropriations in Glamorgan was put at £4,000 per annum.[80]

[297]

The surviving evidence of actual income from sequestered church property in south Wales suggests that only about one-half of the possible revenue was realized during the Propagation era. The Neath accounts showed that the revenue from church property in Glamorgan in 1650 was £2,833 8s. 10d., or under three-quarters of the potential yield.[81] The Propagation commissioners themselves admitted that the realized income in south Wales of £9,518 5s. 8d. in 1650, and of £10,418 5s. 2d. in 1651, was just about one-half of the expected total.[82] The Neath accounts provide no clear evidence of misappropriation of funds but they, and the figures for south Wales, do support the view that the estates were under-let and inexpertly managed, which is perhaps not surprising when the general inexperience of the Propagators and their minor officials is taken into consideration. Although the evidence in 1654–5 was insufficient to substantiate the allegations against the Propagators, the determination of their critics to worst their former adversaries never wavered, and in 1659 the allegations achieved prominence once more when, in the unsettled political situation, the charges against Jones and his colleagues were renewed (below, pp. 304–5).

II. GOVERNMENT AND POLITICS

The Protectorate witnessed further centralization of government, the most important manifestation of which as far as the localities were concerned occurred in February 1654, when the power to sequester delinquents' estates was removed from the small local committees established in 1650 and placed in the hands of one official in each county who was directly answerable to the central committee for compounding in London.[83] Once again south Wales was treated differently from the English counties, where the power of sequestration over the whole region was conferred on six men—Josias Berniers, Edward Winslow, Richard Moore, John Upton, John Carver, and Rice Williams. Estates were to be let on leases of not more than a year and former commissioners could be summoned and punished if they had defaulted.[84]

In spite of the Protector's determination to keep a close control of the localities and retain power in the hands of small circles of trusted local committeemen he was prepared to be conciliatory where expedient and, in parts of the country, neutrals, Presbyterians, and even former royalists became J.P.s again.[85] There was, however, little evidence of these shifts in the personnel of Glamorgan politics in this period; power and authority remained the preserve of the now well-tried and trusted ruling group under the leadership of Colonel Philip Jones.[86]

The Instrument of Government provided for a redistribution of Parliamentary seats to the effect that over England and Wales county representation was quadrupled and borough representation was more than halved. In Wales itself county representation was doubled and borough representation was all but eliminated, though the total number of M.P.s was raised from the 1640 figure of twenty-four to twenty-five.[87] Each county was given two seats, except for Merioneth which was given one, and borough representation was allowed only to the port towns of Cardiff and Haverfordwest, with one seat each. The vote in counties was given to those possessing estate, real or personal, worth £200 per annum, thus replacing the forty-shilling freeholder franchise. Although the new franchise allowed owners of property other than land a vote, the qualification was set so high that the effect must have been to reduce the size of county electorates. The intention, it must be assumed, was that the Parliaments elected by these more exclusive county electorates would be composed of men of moderate political opinions who would share the aspirations of, and would co-operate with, Cromwell and the Grandees.[88]

In the first Protectorate Parliament Glamorgan was represented by members derived from the small nucleus of local governors who had controlled Glamorgan politics since at least 1648. The two county members were Colonel Philip Jones and Edmund Thomas of Wenvoe, who had become an enthusiastic supporter of the Protectorate, while Jones's brother-in-law, John Price of Gelli-hir, served for Cardiff.[89]

Pretty well unceasing attacks on the Instrument of Government in the first Protectorate Parliament persuaded Cromwell to dissolve Parliament at the earliest opportunity—January 22, 1655. The dismissal of Parliament provided a new impetus to the royalists to try to exploit the discontent in the country to put into operation their conspiratorial plans for widespread risings in March 1655 in a concerted effort to overthrow the Cromwellian régime. A combination of keen government intelligence, ill-prepared royalist plans, and the general inertia of the country at large, was sufficient to render the risings perfunctory in their outcome. Wales was an area expected to lend support to the risings, but in the event gave none at all. Even before the risings took place Cromwell was persuaded he must deal more firmly with dissident elements in the country and he began to turn from his conciliatory approach to a more oppressive one. Central to the Protector's new policy was the reorganization of the militia in the counties in order to place the burden for defence and security more squarely on the localities rather than persevere with an unpopular and expensive standing army.

In common with most appointments during this period no separate group of militia commissioners was nominated in March 1655 for each county in south Wales but on a regional basis, though the sixteen Monmouthshire commissioners were nominated separately. Twenty-two commissioners were named for the six counties of south Wales headed by Philip earl of Pembroke, Sir Erasmus Phillips, and the two Glamorgan stalwarts, Colonel Bussy Mansel and Colonel Rowland Dawkins. Also nominated from Glamorgan were John Price, M.P. for Cardiff and brother-in-law of Philip Jones, Edward Stradling, John Herbert, and

Henry Morgan.[90] On March 24, the Council of State wrote to Col. Dawkins, along with militia commanders throughout England and Wales, urging his militia to be diligent in following the royalist uprisings and to keep a close watch on strangers.[91]

The apparent failure of Cromwell's conciliatory policy, the insurrections of March 1655, and the general unpopularity of the régime, led quickly to the introduction of the rule of the major-generals, which marked the high point of central government control over the localities during the English Revolution. In October 1655 England and Wales were divided into ten—later eleven—military districts comprising groups of counties over which a major-general was appointed with complete authority in his region under Cromwell and the Council of State. Their activities were to be financed by a 10 per cent, or decimation, tax upon all former royalist delinquents. They were not simply military despots and were expected to work alongside the existing local militias, county committees, and J.P.s. The tasks which the major-generals were expected to perform were wide-ranging, though they were especially concerned to ensure that the local militias established in March 1655 were kept in good order and to seek out and prevent any designs by opponents of the government.[92]

By the summer of 1656 the whole of Wales, Herefordshire, and Shropshire, were under the command of Major-General James Berry, who already, in August 1655, had been charged with overall responsibility for ensuring the efficiency of the militias of north and south Wales and Shropshire. Initially, on October 11, 1655, Berry was given the command of Shropshire, Worcestershire, Herefordshire, and north but not south Wales, which was put for a few months under the authority of Colonel Rowland Dawkins. In July 1656, however, Berry was commanded by the Council of State to act as Major-General in south Wales and Monmouthshire also, with Colonel Dawkins and Captain John Nicholas, governor of Chepstow, as his deputies. In April 1656 Dawkins and Nicholas were described as major-generals of south Wales and Monmouthshire. Dawkins was awarded a salary of £300, and Nicholas one of £200, a year, though in June of that year their salaries were equalized. While Berry was authorized to receive £666 13s. 4d., per annum, both Dawkins and Nicholas were to receive exactly half each—£333 6s. 8d. Berry spent very little time in south Wales. His routine work was carried out by his subordinates throughout his whole region, though he did make one tour of the south Wales counties during February and March 1656.[93]

The major-generals were ordered to enforce social and economic regulations and to see that assemblies were prohibited because they could be used to plan and disseminate news of royalist conspiracy. It was with these possibilities in mind that the Council of State wrote in July 1656 to Rowland Dawkins, 'Deputy Major-General for the County of Glamorgan', to enquire into allegations 'that many people out of several parts, do frequently meet and assemble unlawfully at Caerphilly in Glamorgan, under colour of holding a market and faire without any authority, at which meetings many disorders are committed', and to examine the situation, 'that soe the public peace may not be prejudiced or disturbed'.[94]

Increasing centralized control over towns, as well as the counties, in England and Wales, was an important aspect of government policy towards the localities during the Interregnum. It began with the creation of the Committee for Corporations in 1649 and reached a peak with its successor, the Committee for Municipal Charters. The latter was certainly at work in 1656 but probably came into existence soon after the appointment of the major-generals in September 1655.

Governments from the beginning of the seventeenth century had experienced the independent spirit of corporations, for many were possessed of a substantial measure of self-government and were invariably suspicious and independent of outside interference in their affairs. In this period loyal supporters of the government were often in a precarious majority or even a minority in town assemblies, and the governments of the Interregnum endeavoured to ensure the authority of its committed supporters by closer central control of towns where possible. The Protectorate government tried to secure the co-operation of certain independently minded towns, though with mixed success, through the enforced revision of their charters, whereby it restricted the rights of the town assemblies, and adopted the same principles in the charters granted to the few newly incorporated boroughs.[95]

In February 1656, almost certainly through the influence of Colonel Philip Jones, Swansea received from the Protector a charter which was intended to secure the loyalty of the town. Though in a minority on the aldermanic bench during the Commonwealth and early Protectorate periods, the committed government supporters managed to ensure the loyalty of the town under the dominant influence of Philip Jones. It was not until October 1655 that the government supporters became the majority group on the bench comprising seven members of the twelve.[96] Under the charter of 1656 the portreeve became described as mayor. Three of the leading Glamorgan committeemen, Philip Jones, Rowland Dawkins, and John Price, all of whom had close connexions with Swansea, were named in the grant. Jones was created high steward of the town, Dawkins was named as senior alderman, and Price was appointed one of the common council. The traditional power of the burgesses to engage in the election and appointment of officials was reduced, for it was now vested in the council of twelve aldermen and twelve capital burgesses which was dominated by the influential aldermen. The authority of the lord of the town which had been reduced during the early-seventeenth century, was largely resurrected, which gave added influence to Philip Jones in his capacity as high steward. On May 3, 1658 Swansea was granted a supplementary charter empowering the burgesses to return one member to represent the borough in Parliament, as a result of which Swansea returned its first M.P. to Richard Cromwell's Parliament in 1659.[97]

Oliver Cromwell decided to call his second Protectorate Parliament to meet in September 1656. The government was under considerable financial pressure because of the Spanish War, and Cromwell hoped to exploit the traditional anti-Spanish feeling in the country when the Parliament assembled. In the preceding elections the major-generals worked tirelessly on behalf of the government to try to secure the return of a compliant House. Major-General Berry was active in electioneering and was himself elected for three shires in his area, Worcestershire, Herefordshire, and Monmouthshire, but chose to sit for Worcestershire.[98]

There were no surprises in the elections in south Wales at which the loyal government supporters, Philip Jones and Edmund Thomas of Wenvoe, were returned for Glamorgan, while John Price was returned for Cardiff, as in the first Protectorate Parliament.[99] From the beginning of the Parliament Major-General Berry was doubtless deeply involved with affairs in London and his work was probably executed by his subordinate major-generals in south Wales, Rowland Dawkins and John Nicholas, until the major-generals were disbanded at the beginning of 1657.

Cromwell and his supporters shared expectations of a co-operative and fruitful second Protectorate Parliament which assembled on September 17, 1656. In spite of the success of the major-generals in encouraging the return of government supporters to the Parliament a substantial minority of those elected were unacceptable to the Protector, and about one hundred M.P.s were excluded from its sitting. Ironically, the major-generals were soon victims of the more conservative House of Commons which refused in January 1657 to continue the decimation tax upon which their survival depended.

In February 1657, following the discovery of a Leveller plot to murder Cromwell, there ensued a move to persuade him to take the Crown, proposals which were embodied in the Humble Petition and Advice. After much heart-searching and under pressure from the Army, Cromwell rejected the offer of the Crown but accepted the revised petition in June 1657 which created an hereditary protectorship and an 'Other House', of forty members who were to be selected by the Protector. During the Parliamentary recess between June and December 1657 Cromwell selected members of the 'Other House', two of whom were the Glamorgan M.P.s, Philip Jones and Edmund Thomas. Many of the members of the 'Other House' were former M.P.s, which deprived Cromwell of the leadership of some of his most loyal and influential supporters in the Commons.[100]

Cromwell's search for settlement was reflected in his return during 1657 to a more conciliatory policy towards the localities. Although throughout England and Wales power continued to reside in the hands of small groups of trusted committeemen, increasingly during 1657 local assessment committees and commissions of the peace began to be widened to include members of the traditional governing county families, the great majority of whom had been denied office or had opted out of local politics, often from the time of the First Civil War. Cromwell's policy was only partially successful. For although most of the 'county' families welcomed the relative stability afforded by the Protectorate they were never sufficiently reconciled to the régime to help in the achievement of permanent settlement in the localities. The government, however, probably well appraised of the nature of local politics in south Wales by Philip Jones, made virtually no concessions to the traditional governing families in Glamorgan, with the exception of the appointment of Sir Edward Mansel as an additional assessment commissioner in June 1657, while at the same time the rise to prominence in Glamorgan politics of Edmund Thomas, M.P., was reflected in his first official appointment to a Glamorgan committee.[101]

In spite of the efforts of Oliver Cromwell and his supporters, both nationally and locally, hopes of a political settlement being achieved during 1657–8 were short-lived. In the second session of Parliament, which began in December 1657, the powers of the 'Other House' were subject to almost constant criticism in the Commons, urged on by Republican M.P.s, so that Cromwell was obliged to dissolve the Parliament in February 1658. Cromwell's own death on September 3, 1658 was the most serious setback to the prospects of a lasting political settlement, though cautious optimism concerning such a favourable outcome survived for a while after the peaceful succession of his son, Richard, as Protector.

The Council of State, following age-old practice at the beginning of a 'reign', proceeded to call a Parliament for January 27, 1659, and at the same time abandoned the electoral arrangements established in the Instrument of Government. As the Humble Petition was extremely vague concerning the composition of Parliament and the conduct of elections, the Council of State revived the forty-shilling freeholder franchise qualification and the pre-1654 distribution of Parliamentary seats throughout the country.[102] The Principality reverted, therefore, to its traditional arrangements with each county returning one member for the shire and one for the county town, with the exception of Glamorgan. In Richard Cromwell's Parliament only, Glamorgan's representation was one county member, and a further two members, one each for the boroughs of Cardiff and Swansea, the latter as a result of the charter granted by Oliver Cromwell in 1658 which enfranchised Swansea. The county returned Evan Seys of Boverton, serjeant-at-law, while John Price, Philip Jones's brother-in-law, continued to represent Cardiff as he had done since 1654.[103] Swansea's member was William Foxwist, a Welsh circuit judge and a loyal Cromwellian, whose election, there can be little doubt, was secured by Philip Jones, in his capacity as high steward of the

[303]

town.[104] No writs were issued for 'real lords' to attend the Upper House, and the Council of State continued with the members created by Oliver Cromwell, so that Philip Jones and Edmund Thomas sat as members of the 'Other House'.

During Richard Cromwell's Parliament Philip Jones, comptroller of the young Protector's household, was subject to a renewed attack in respect of his activities as the leading Propagation commissioner in south Wales by his long-time adversary, Colonel Edward Freeman, now M.P. for Leominster, and David Morgan, who had displaced Rowland Dawkins as M.P. for Carmarthen, after a disputed election. These two combined with prominent Republican supporters in the Commons to embarrass Jones by obtaining another investigation into the management of Propagation funds. The House committed the measure to Evan Seys and Colonel Edward Freeman, who could be expected to prosecute the charges with great vigour.[105] Coincident with, and possibly related to, the Parliamentary attack on Philip Jones, appeared a pamphlet in the name of the 'distressed and oppressed' inhabitants of south Wales which set out the familiar allegations concerning the activities of the former Propagators, and of Jones in particular, including the assertion that as much as £150,000 remained unaccounted for by the Propagators.[106]

The dissolution of Richard Cromwell's Parliament on April 22 put an end to the work of the Propagation critics for the time being, though it was resumed once more two months before the Restoration of Charles II. The same group was also responsible for securing the expulsion from Parliament in February 1659 of Edmund Jones of Buckland, Philip Jones's 'main agent and instrument in south Wales', on a fabricated charge of delinquency. It also attempted to have the election of William Foxwist as M.P. for Swansea examined on the ground that there seemed to be no election return from the sheriff of the town.[107]

iv

THE RESTORATION OF THE COUNTY COMMUNITY

Any expectations that Richard Cromwell's Protectorate might produce lasting political stability and settlement were soon dissipated. He, like his father before him, failed to establish good relations with the traditional governing families in the localities. The Protectorate, whose Council of State and effective government were dominated by a small group of civilian and anti-military members, soon came under pressure from General Fleetwood and the army officers. On April 22 Fleetwood forced the Protector to dissolve Parliament, whereupon he quickly restored the Rump Parliament with its surviving former members.

The fall of Richard Cromwell's Protectorate was the prelude to a year of intense political uncertainty and instability. The revival of the

Rump Parliament resulted in widespread weeding-out of former prominent supporters of the Protectorate, both nationally and in the localities.
By the summer of 1659 the long-dominant political figures in Glamorgan
and south Wales, Philip Jones, Rowland Dawkins, and John Price, whose
leadership had hitherto gone unchallenged for more than a decade, were
all deprived of their positions. The political leadership of Glamorgan and
south Wales was now taken up by their former colleague, Bussy Mansel,
whose assumed radicalism and membership of Barebone's Parliament,
must have been an advantage at this time.

In this atmosphere, Philip Jones, one of the most prominent protagonists of the Protectorate and former comptroller of the Protector's
Household, soon found himself under renewed attack. A pamphlet of
May 1659 asked concerning Jones, 'Whether a knave or coward hath
most honesty? And whether both centred in one, born to 51 li per annum
(bred accordingly in the Welsh mountains) which in 10 years he hath
multiplied to 5000 li per annum. An oppressor of his countrey, a
Parliament Breaker . . . A Presbyterian, an Independent, a Cavalier,
a Defrauder of the Publique Revenue; and thorough-passed Protec-
torian.'[108] The high point of the attack came in a pamphlet written and
presented to Parliament by Bledry Morgan on May 18, 1659. Morgan,
a former Carmarthenshire treasurer and dealer in sequestrations, undoubtedly acted in concert with Colonel Edward Freeman and other
long-standing adversaries of Jones from the Propagation era. Jones was
accused of abusing his authority during the Protectorate and for the last
ten years 'appeared the chief and only man to recommend and bring in
persons of all places of Authority, Profit, or Trust, Ecclesiastical, Military,
or Civil in South Wales . . . who contrary to the several Ordinances and
Acts of this Parliament . . . recommended, nominated, and brought into
authority there, divers notorious Cavaliers in Arms, Compounded
delinquents, and other disaffected persons'.[109]

Jones decided to sit in the restored Rump as he was entitled to do,
though by now his influence had declined considerably. On May 23 he
used his position to answer his critics and denied the charges. The
pamphlet was referred to a committee, the majority of whose members
were Republicans, to hear the charges and examine witnesses. A number
of enemies of Philip Jones were called from south Wales to give evidence
before the committee. Bledry Morgan then tried, unsuccessfully, to get
Jones excluded from a proposed Act of Indemnity and Pardon for
supporters of the Protectorate, after which attempts were made to pin
charges of bribery on him.[110] Although the accusations and charges
against Jones were never effectively substantiated, the efforts to discredit
him were attended with a good deal of success. Soon after May 1659
Jones quietly withdrew from national politics. He was fined for non-
attendance in Parliament and was cashiered. He probably retired to
Hertfordshire where his brother-in-law, John Price, owned property,

from where he could safely observe the changing political climate and wait on events. Jones and Bussy Mansel were among a number of active politicians of the Interregnum régimes whom the royalists attempted to recruit in 1659 to assist the restoration of the Stuarts, though whether any arrangements were ever concluded is uncertain.[111]

Renewed royalist agitation in the summer of 1659 led to steps being taken by the Rump Parliament for raising and reorganizing the country's militia to meet the contingency. In July militia committees were nominated for the counties of England and Wales. In south Wales, as in England on this occasion, the committees were appointed on a county basis, though the whole of north Wales was put under a joint committee. The committees in south Wales were reduced in size by about one-third compared with the Assessment Committees of 1657. In Glamorgan, although some of the lesser figures of the Protectorate period were kept on as committeemen, there was a purge of the leading personnel of recent years. The Glamorgan commissioners were led by Bussy Mansel, but the omission of Philip Jones, Rowland Dawkins, and John Price, reflected the changed political leadership of Glamorgan under the Rump. At this time Jones also forfeited the governership of Cardiff castle to Captain Mark Grimes, probably a nominee of the republican Sir Arthur Haselrigg, and Dawkins was deprived of the command of Tenby garrison. Many of Jones's dependants also lost their places in south Wales politics, including William Watkins, Jones's agent, and Edmund Jones and Roger Games, in Radnorshire.[112]

When the south Wales militia was mustered during July, commissions were issued to Bussy Mansel for the west Wales counties and Edmund Thomas for Glamorgan, Brecon, and Radnor. Mansel and Thomas were authorized to nominate officers as they thought fit and to draw the troops together. Thomas's commission was probably withdrawn shortly afterwards, however, and the whole force put under the command of Mansel.[113] Little happened in south Wales, as Bussy Mansel described in a letter to Samuel Moyer at Westminster: 'By the care of our small forces in South Wales, it was so kept from insurrection that there will be little work for sequestration commissioners.' Early in September after the failure of the insurrections the militia force was disbanded.[114] Following upon the abortive risings under the overall leadership of Sir George Booth, an Act was passed on August 27 for sequestration of those in any way involved in the attempted insurrections. On September 19 seven sequestration commissioners were chosen for the counties of south Wales on the recommendation of Bussy Mansel, though only one, Robert Thomas of Tregros, was from Glamorgan.[115] On October 13, 1659 the Rump was dissolved a second time by the army, now under General Lambert whom Parliament had dismissed from his command the previous day; but under pressure from General Monck, the commander in Scotland at the head of reliable troops, the Rump was re-instated on December 26. Although the political situation was still very uncertain, restoration was in the air. At Michaelmas the corporation of Swansea set aside Cromwell's charter. The town assembly abandoned the title of mayor established in 1656, and reverted to the customary usage by describing the town's chief official as portreeve.[116]

The uncertain last weeks of republican ascendancy in the Rump were reflected in the composition of the county assessment committees appointed towards the end of January 1660. The Glamorgan commission was effectively headed by Bussy Mansel, while Philip Jones, Rowland Dawkins, and John Price, the most prominent supporters of the Protectorate in Glamorgan, were again left off, though other less influential committeemen who had co-operated with the governments of the Protectorate were re-appointed.[117]

Monck crossed the Tweed on January 2, 1660 and a month later, without opposition from Lambert, whose forces had broken up, he arrived in London. On February 21 Monck recalled the surviving Presbyterian M.P.s, excluded from the Long Parliament in December 1648, to sit in the Rump, thus producing a more moderate House and the virtual certainty of the return of the monarchy.

At the prospect of the restoration of Charles II to the throne, throughout the country—except for uncompromising supporters of the Commonwealth and Protectorate régimes—prominent county committeemen during the Interregnum endeavoured to adjust to the rapidly changing political climate, while members of the once-influential governing families began cautiously to re-assert themselves. The fluid nature of politics in the spring of 1660 was apparent in the composition of the county militia committees issued on March 12 by the re-furbished Rump. Philip Jones, Rowland Dawkins, and John Price, rejected in recent months, were appointed again in Glamorgan, along with their long-standing colleague, Bussy Mansel, and Jones's adversary, Colonel Edward Freeman, recently restored attorney-general of south Wales.[118] On March 14, Jones, Dawkins, and Price, were also added to the assessment committee established in January, before the re-admission of the Presbyterian M.P.s.[119] Despite the brief re-appearance of Philip Jones and his colleagues and the heterogeneous nature of the forty-two-man militia commission, it contained, significantly, a substantial group of representatives of Glamorgan's traditional governing families, whose presence signalled the imminence of their return to the leadership of the county community.

Early in 1660 there occurred a renewed attempt to deal with the alleged financial abuses of the former commissioners for the Propagation of the Gospel in Wales, which continued to excite controversy after more than a decade. On the last day of its sitting in March the Presbyterian-inspired Rump passed an Act for taking account of Welsh tithes and church livings, and on April 5 the Council of State appointed a commission to investigate on its behalf in Glamorgan, though because of the imminence of the Restoration it appears to have been appointed too late to have been implemented. The names of the commissioners, however, including Bussy Mansel and Colonel Edward Freeman, confirmed the revived fortunes of the traditional governing families.[120]

In the elections for the Convention Parliament called for April 25, 1660 to prepare for the return of Charles II, one of the leaders of the restored county community, Sir Edward Mansel, was returned for Glamorgan, while his cousin, the remarkably shrewd former Barebone's M.P., Bussy Mansel, survived a disputed election to continue his political career as M.P. for Cardiff.[121]

The Restoration of Charles II seems to have been received with enthusiasm in Glamorgan. The restored governing families in Glamorgan and throughout south Wales despatched their *Humble Address* of welcome and support for the new King on June 16 signed by seventy-six of their members including the important Glamorgan knights, Sir John Aubrey and Sir Richard Bassett, 'with many more Gentlemen that this paper cannot contain'.[122] The borough of Swansea, which more than a year earlier had set aside Cromwell's charter, financed celebrations on May 11 which included a dinner and entertainment at which Colonel Edward Freeman was the honoured guest.[123] The Restoration government adopted a conciliatory policy towards nearly all former participants in Interregnum politics both at the centre and in the localities, except for a small minority adjudged deserving of harsher treatment. This was evident in the case of Glamorgan, where the restoration of the political ascendancy of the traditional governing families was achieved with the minimum of social and political dislocation. Even in the borough of Swansea there were no obvious attempts to displace aldermen who had supported the governments of the Interregnum. It was not until 1662 that Rowland Dawkins and Matthew David, two of the most prominent of the town's aldermen during the Interregnum, were dismissed from the aldermanic bench, probably not as a result of local pressure but at the instigation of the commissioners acting under the 'Act for the Well Governing and Regulating of Corporations' of December 1661, by which it was hoped to bring the often independent corporations under closer central control and to rid them of those whose loyalty to the Restoration government might be suspect.[124]

Although a small minority of those appointed to Glamorgan committees during the Interregnum—often men of parochial gentry or even humbler social status—faded out of local politics there was in fact a fair measure of continuity in the personnel of politics in Glamorgan following the Restoration. A number of middle-ranking Interregnum committeemen such as Humphrey Windham, John Gibbs, Herbert Evans, and

Edmund Gamage, were immediately appointed J.P.s in the first commission of the peace of the new reign, while they and a number of other former committeemen were nominated commissioners of assessment for Glamorgan at the end of 1660.[125] Some of them became deputy-lieutenants and even high sheriffs later in the century. Even Glamorgan's four prominent political activists throughout the Interregnum achieved the transfer from Interregnum to Restoration political society relatively smoothly. During 1662, however, proceedings were instituted in south Wales against Philip Jones, Rowland Dawkins, and John Price—though not against Bussy Mansel—as part of countrywide investigations into the financial administration, including in Wales the conduct of Propagation finances, of former supporters of the governments of the Interregnum, though in the absence of sufficient evidence of their alleged misdemeanours the prosecutions were dropped.[126]

The relative ease with which past supporters and those who had co-operated with the governments of the Interregnum, were absorbed into the county community of Glamorgan—and elsewhere—at the Restoration helped to reduce, if not entirely eradicate, much of the political tension of the previous twenty years and to preserve much of the nature and character of pre-1640 county society in England and Wales into the later-seventeenth century and beyond.

CHAPTER VII

The Economic and Social History of Glamorgan, 1660-1760

By MOELWYN I. WILLIAMS

i.

POPULATION

IN pre-industrial Glamorgan, geographical and geological facts dictated the distribution of population, and determined social structure. Climatic and soil conditions were the 'natural' factors that shaped the general pattern of Glamorgan farming and determined whether stock rearing or tillage was to become the chief mode of husbandry. Moreover, the standard of life attainable within the pastoral-agricultural economy of the county depended not only on the contemporary state of local husbandry but also on the size and age-distribution of the native population, that is to say, on the number of productive workers relative to the number of dependants.

According to the Glamorgan hearth tax list for 1670, the total number of households within the 121[1] parishes accounted for therein amounted to 9,083. Therefore, on the assumption that each household at that time was made up of the generally accepted averages of between 4.5 and 5 persons, the total population, accordingly, would have amounted to between 40,874 and 45,415.

A close examination of the hearth tax lists reveals that the distribution of households varied in general accordance with the main farming regions of the county, with the greatest concentration to be found in the more fertile lowland regions of the Vale and along the southern coastal regions of the Gower peninsula, where mixed farming predominated. These regions included the major semi-urban areas of Cardiff, Neath and Swansea, as well as the agricultural townships of Cowbridge, Llantwit Major, and Bridgend. The upland regions, moreover, were at this time sparsely peopled—a situation consistent with their geographical features, which generally permitted of only pastoral farming. This general pattern of the distribution of households continued until the middle of the eighteenth century when the growth and progress of non-agrarian undertakings began to reverse it, albeit very slowly.

[311]

It is now generally recognized that there was a steady increase in the population of England and Wales throughout the greater part of the sixteenth century, with a slowing down in the later seventeenth century, and a possible check in the 1720s and 1730s. Then followed a continued cumulative increase which started after about 1750. In Glamorgan there was a slight decrease in the population between 1700 and 1710, and an increase during the next ten years, which was followed by a substantial decrease in the 1720s. Thereafter, with the exception of a slight decrease between 1760 and 1770, the population increased quite steadily, until in 1801 it had reached a total of 71,525.

ii.

SOCIAL STRATIFICATION

Broadly speaking, the population of Glamorgan during our period may be said to have comprised the landowners, the clergy, freeholders, tenant-farmers, farm labourers, traders and rural craftsmen.

The landowners, who included baronets, knights, esquires[2] and gentlemen, owned the land but they did not necessarily occupy it. At the beginning of the eighteenth century, out of a list of 169 principal proprietors of land in Glamorgan, about 36 were absentees.[3] These included the duke of Beaufort, the earl of Plymouth, Viscount Windsor, Lady Charlotte Edwin, and Sir Charles Tynte, who resided in England, while others, like Charles Morgan Esq., or Philip Lewis Esq., resided in the adjoining Welsh counties of Brecon and Monmouth. The resident gentry of the period were individuals who owned and farmed the home farm and possessed other farms, which they had acquired either by inheritance or purchase, or through marriage, in other parishes. Charles Button, Esquire, of Columbar, for example, had all his 'purchased estate partly intermixed with the antient estate' of his family. Richard Deere, Esquire, of Wenvoe, who lived in an eight-roomed house, held land in thirteen different parishes, and when he died in 1699, his personal estate was valued at £1,104 16s. 4d.[4] There were, however, the smaller fry whose lands were not very extensive, and who were entirely dependent on agricultural and allied pursuits for their livelihood.

Closely allied to the gentry were those who, whilst heavily dependent on agriculture, were becoming increasingly active entrepreneurs in industrial or non-agricultural undertakings. Typical of this group was William Thomas, Esquire, of Dan-y-Graig, Swansea, who, besides his 'coaleworks' at Llansamlet, possessed extensive livestock which comprised '940 head of sheep, 100 milk kine, 70 oxen, 20 steers and heifers, 19 working horses and mares, 6 saddle horses', and after his death in 1665, his estate was valued at £891.[5] Similarly, Griffith Price, gent. of Llangyfelach, held lands in several places and possessed '14 oxen, 18 kine, 31 young beasts of two years old, 10 calves, 110 sheep and 30 lambs', and owned besides 'coales by the pitts at Trewyddfa and by the waterside' (worth £9), and 'one lighter bote' (worth £5). When he died the inventory of his goods was valued at £162 12s. 4d.[6]

During our period an increasing number of persons were becoming involved in trade and commerce, and constituted a group which, from the value of their goods, could stand four-square with the gentry. Numerous business men who had set up in the urban and semi-urban centres such as Neath and Swansea, bought up land and houses in the countryside, and Edward Jenkins, a Cardiff apothecary, was only one of many Cardiff business men during our period who possessed lands and other property in the parishes of Llancarfan and Llanbethery.[7] Moreover, the wealth of the mercers, drapers, maltsters and mariners, often equalled that of the gentry of the countryside.[8]

The 'freeholders' of the county owned the land they occupied, and they constituted the 'yeoman' class. Many of them were, in fact, of the same birth as the minor gentry 'but of less condition'. It is for this reason that caution must be exercised in using the status nomenclatures such as 'gentleman' and 'yeoman'. These terms, although they often defined the actual social status of a person were, nevertheless, frequently adopted by those who merely considered themselves 'gentlemen' or 'yeomen', and wanted to be regarded as such by their neighbours because of the 'traditional' status of the family. But during our period, as indeed had been the case a century earlier, it would appear that birth and gentility were being replaced by the size of the money bag as a factor which gave people a 'feeling of otherness' or, perhaps, the prospects of being associated with a higher class on the social ladder. Numerous wills, indeed, reveal this consciousness of class. Joshua Ward, a grocer of Caerphilly, typified many of his contemporaries when he made provision in his will for his daughters to be maintained and kept in school till they arrived at the age of 15 or 16 years 'with all such necessaries as is fit for the children of their quality'.[9] Samuel Sherbourne, a mariner of Cadoxton, near Neath, also made provision towards his son's schooling 'and all other necessarys befitting his rank and quality'.[10] The wishes of testators regarding their burial again reflected a real consciousness of class or station which they often desired to be perpetuated after their day. This may have been the intention of Evan Thomas, yeoman, of Bonvilston, who ordered his executors 'to provide and bring two large tomb-stones[11] about four inches thick from the parish of Llantrisant and cause the same to be laid upon mine and my wife's graves'.[12] Again, Katherine Lougher, a widow of Tythegston, bequeathed a sum of money to the local vicar 'for preaching a sermon' at specified times and dates after her decease.[13]

Next to the 'yeomen' were the tenant farmers, the occupiers who paid rent for the land they occupied. The farm labourers or cottagers, however, formed a class entirely apart from the rest of the agrarian hierarchy, for their main or only means of livelihood was by selling their labour to those who required it. It may be argued that the social, economic and cultural life of the county during our period must be viewed in relation to the alignment of the above 'classes' to the land.

It has been said that the history of Wales in the seventeenth century is necessarily, in the main, the history of a class for, 'of those below the class of "gentry" we can know little at first hand. They had neither the leisure nor the education to leave their own account of themselves.' It was further contended that the *gwerin* (i.e. the peasantry), namely those 'with no estate above what they get by daily labour' was still a relatively small class, 'while the term gentry as understood in Wales was a highly elastic and comprehensive one, embracing all who could put up any sort of colourable claim to descent from the old princes and *uchelwyr*'.[14]

More recently[15] it has been strongly argued that in England also there was only one class in pre-industrial society—the term class being used to denote a 'number of people banded together in the exercise of collective power, political and economic', and which in the main represented the landed and propertied classes. Indeed this was, in a sense, also true of Glamorgan where since *circa* 1536–1542 the political representation of the county and boroughs at Westminster was controlled by only a few of the landowning families.[16] From about 1700 to 1832 'the county seat had been occupied either directly or indirectly by Mansels, Talbots, Tyntes, Beauforts or Windsors'. And the same control was exercised by the same group of families in the boroughs. Throughout the eighteenth century the Windsors controlled Cardiff, Cowbridge and Llantrisant, the Mansels of Margam controlled Kenfig, the Mackworths Aberavon and Neath, while Swansea and Loughor 'were firmly in the pockets of the Beauforts'. In short, from 1710 to 1832, during which there had been twenty-eight parliaments, only five families shared the representation.[17] It should also be remembered that at that time the franchise was enjoyed by the forty-shilling freeholders who, with others qualified to vote, formed an electorate numbering 'well over a thousand', but 'nearly all the voters were tenants or dependants of the local magnates and squires'.[18] Together they constituted only a small minority of the total population.

It has been estimated that 'about a twenty-fifth, at most a twentieth, of all people alive in the England of the Tudors and Stuarts, the last generations before the coming of industry, belonged to the gentry and to those above them in the social hierarchy'.[19] That is to say, about four or five persons out of every hundred owned most of the wealth and, in consequence, controlled the economic, social, and political affairs of the country. In Wales, after 1660, 'a gulf was beginning to yawn between a narrow and exclusive group of greater gentry on the one hand, and on the other the small squire, yeoman or freeholder, of equally ancient lineage but fewer acres'.[20]

According to a survey published in 1690,[21] the gentry of Glamorgan numbered about 219, and were distributed within the ten hundreds of the county as indicated in column 1 of the following list. Assuming that these figures represented the heads of different families, then on the basis of the hearth tax computations, the percentage of the gentry to the total population in each hundred would be as shown in column 2 below. In other words, two or three households out of every hundred in Glamorgan exercised almost complete control over the fortunes of the county.

	1	2
Dinas Powys	34	3.4
Cowbridge	24	2.0
Ogmore	16	2.6
Neath	15	1.5
Newcastle	15	1.0
Caerffili	28	3.7
Miskin	13	1.3
Kibbor	14	2.0
Llangyfelach	4	0.5
Swansea	15	1.3

Again, the list of Glamorgan subscribers to the Voluntary Gift to Charles II[22] provides further evidence which shows that almost every parish had its 'gentleman' and that in the richer agricultural areas of the Vale many parishes had more than one 'gentleman'. The 26 parishes constituting the Hundred of Dinas Powys could claim, between them, 34 gentlemen, and the 21 parishes of the Hundred of Cowbridge had 24. Further, the list of contributions serves to emphasize the economic gulf that separated the 'gentlemen' from the squireen and yeomen. For example, the list of subscriptions for the parishes of Gelli-gaer and Merthyr Tydfil received on August 16, 1661, is headed by Sir William Lewis of Y Fan with a sum of £10, and is followed by a hundred and forty subscriptions which ranged from 6d. to 10s.—the majority of the subscriptions being 6d. or 1s. There was, undoubtedly, a clear distinction between the 'county' and 'parish' gentry.

In the 'Rowle of the Commissioners subscription' taken on November 8, 1661, at Bridgend, Sir Edward Mansel, of Margam, (who was taxed on 32 hearths in 1670) headed the list with £100; Sir John Aubrey of Llantriddyd (taxed on 20 hearths); Bussy Mansel, Esquire (taxed on 22 hearths) and William Herbert of Swansea (taxed on 18 hearths) each contributed £30, while Herbert Evans, Esq., Neath (taxed on 10 hearths) contributed £20, and Richard Lougher, Esquire of Tythegston (taxed on 10 hearths) contributed £7; Thomas Button, Esquire of St. Nicholas (taxed on 10 hearths) gave £10, and Martin Button Esquire, his son (taxed on 12 hearths), subscribed £5.[23] The above contributions serve to confirm that the number of hearths bore a direct relationship to the wealth or status of the heads of households. In other words, the size of a house was a fairly reliable index to the wealth of the occupier. Those who possessed the greatest number of hearths were generally the highest subscribers to the Voluntary Fund. There were exceptions, however, where individuals assessed on only one hearth in 1670 subscribed sums greater than others who were assessed on more than one hearth. For example, Rees ap Evans, of Mwyndy, near Miskin, taxed on one hearth in 1670 subscribed 20s. Incidentally, occupiers of one hearth were not, of necessity, the agricultural 'proletariat'. By and large, it may be said that no 'gentleman' subscribed less than 5s., and no yeoman appears to have paid more than 10s.

The Glamorgan lists generally do not reveal the status of each subscriber, except in the case of the 'gentleman' and 'esquire'. But the list of subscribers for the Hundred of Neath does give the status of each contributor. In the Neath area, where industry and commerce had already created a semi-urban economy, the wealthier groups were the gentry, and the mercers, drapers, and maltsters, who virtually belonged to the same class. The rural craftsmen were the poorest, and the yeoman and husbandman fell between these two extremes.[24]

The same pattern of social stratification emerges from an examination of the Glamorgan hearth tax list of 1670. This reveals that about 60 out of every 100 households lived in houses with only one hearth; 20 households out of every 100 had two hearths, and about one in every 100 lived in houses with seven and more hearths. Although it is probable that some of these houses were, in fact, inns, it is beyond doubt that the largest houses were generally owned by those who possessed the greatest wealth.

The great gulf that existed between the wealthy classes and the great majority of the people is again thrown into high relief by the distribution of personal wealth, as reflected in the probate inventories for the period 1693 to 1760, and tabulated Table I. The grouping adopted in the Table has no special significance.

Throughout the period of seventy-five years or so covered by these figures, it would appear that about 17 out of every hundred testators were, on an average, worth not more than £10; 24 persons in every hundred (or about 1 person in 4) were worth £21 to £40. In other words, 62 per cent of testators who had died between 1693 and 1760 were worth less than £40, while another 31 per cent were valued at between £60 and £200. The remaining 7 per cent obviously comprised the 'gentry', the great landowners and commercial classes of the county, whose personal wealth ranged from £200 to £2,000 and more.

The occupiers of land in Glamorgan, who were neither freeholders nor copyholders, were tenant-farmers whose tenure varied according 'to the legal nature of the act or instrument which creates and regulates their interest in the soil',[25] namely, the lease. As we have seen (12–16,

TABLE I

Distribution of wealth as indicated in the Probate Inventory Values, 1693–1760

Value of inventory in £	No. of testators in each category (Percentages are given in brackets)			Total for whole period	
	1693–1710	*1711–1726*	*1726–1760*		
1–10	290 (17½)	134 (18)	178 (15¼)	602	(17.6)
11–20	332 (21)	201 (27½)	307 (27)	840	(24)
21–40	367 (23)	133 (18)	186 (17)	686	(20)
41–60	168 (10½)	50 (7)	91 (8)	309	(9)
61–80	112 (7)	45 (6)	73 (6½)	230	(6.7)
81–100	86 (5)	47 (6½)	64 (6)	197	(5.7)
101–150	94	45	90	229	
151–200	43	28	46	117	
201–300	49 (3)	24 (3½)	38 (3½)	111	(3)
301–400	13 (.8)	8 (1)	16 (1½)	37	(1)
401–500	13 (.8)	4 (.5)	4 (.4)	21	
501–600	6 (.4)	5 (.7)	5 (.4)	16	
601–700	5	1	6	12	
701–800	1	–	2	3	
801–900	4	1	2	7	
901–1000	1	–	–	1	
1001–2000	3	1	6	10	
2000+	1	1	1	3	
	1,588	728	1,115	3,431	

chap. I), leasehold tenure developed in Glamorgan during the sixteenth and seventeenth centuries, and *circa* 1650 leasehold rents predominated in some manors, although customary rents remained predominant in others. Leases for terms of years were numerous in the lordship of Gower.[26] There were tenants whose leases extended over a period of seven, fourteen, or twenty-one years, or for one or more lives, and in Gower, leases for three lives were frequently granted. Leases for lives, as they fell in, could be easily manoeuvred by the landlord. Charles Button, of St. Nicholas, for example, was well aware of this, for he once declared that 'leases for lives, as they drop in, are better worth than when purchased'.[27] The leases of Penrice and Margam estates show that after about 1740, tenure was for life or lives.[28] This is not surprising, for in a survey of Gower estates in 1720, it is revealed that leases for one, two, and three lives 'frequently fall in hand and are often renewed and altered which bring a constant yearly proffit besides herriots and dutys which are yearly 471 hens and 164 geese paid in kind and some, besides these, pay money . . . '.[29] In other parts of Glamorgan, especially in the Vale, tenants held their farms from 'year to year', or 'at will',[30] and during the latter part of the eighteenth century the number of tenants-at-will had increased considerably.

With the progress of leasehold tenure, landlords were not slow to seize every opportunity of increasing their income from their estates either by shortening leases, or by advancing rents, or by charging heavy entrance fines. When granting new leases, the landlords were able to improve their estates indirectly by inserting specific clauses which compelled tenants to carry out certain improvements on their tenements so that 'whenever their mutual contracts expired' the demands of both landlord and tenant at once came into conflict.[31]

In addition to the payment of rents and fines, and the honouring of covenants, tenants were also obliged to render certain specified duties which it was the lord's privilege to demand. For example, in 1727, William Thomas, of the parish of Margam, was granted a lease on Bryn-y-gurnos, Hafod-y-porth, of 27 acres, on payment of £5 yearly, and had to do yearly 'suit of court, suit of Mill . . . where the lord shall appoint, 2 Gees and 2 capons or 3/– in lieu thereof at the elecion of the Lord, 1 days plowing, 2 days reaping in corne harvest, 2 days carrying of hay, 2 days carrying of ffurzes and 2 days carrying of wood, yearely to digg, or cause to be digged, 5 perches of ditch in length and breadth in the meeres of Margam upon the demeasne lands there yearely on demand, to carry or cause to be carryed thornes, furzes, ffrith, ffearnes, rushes, and other necessaries for repairing of the burrough of Margam four dayes in every year (that is to say) one day in every quarter of a yeare with one man and horse from sunriseing unto sun setting of every of the s^d dayes yearely for stopping out of the waters and sounds there to carry or cause to be carryed 2 Crannocks of lime and 4 Crannocks of coale to the manor house of the s^d Lord at Margam . . . '.[32]

The payment of the 'heriot', which continued throughout our period, represented another of the lord's privileges and rights, namely to seize one or more beasts, usually the best, at the death of each tenant, or upon alienation. Where a tenant held lands of more than one landlord, he was liable to pay the heriot to each one of them. Griffith Hugh of Llandeilo Tal-y-bont, for instance, who died in 1661, possessed six oxen 'four of which were seized upon by his severall landlords'.[33] Despite the hardship which often followed the payment of the heriot, it was taken for granted, and often delivered to the lord at the expense of the tenant. An item in the funeral expenses of Jenett Thomas, who died in 1681, was the payment of 6d. to Lodwick Robert 'for going unto Margam with the heriot'.[34]

Another incident attendant on landownership was the payment of mises. At a Court Leet held at Swansea, April 26, 1757, according to the ancient custom of the Manor of Gower Anglicana, it was affirmed that 'there is due and owing unto the Most Noble Henry Duke of Beaufort upon his entry into the said manor after ye decease of the Most Noble

Charles Noel Duke of Beaufort his late father . . . the sum of twenty six pounds thirteen shillings and four pence, being their shares and parts of the sum of Mises to be paid by the tenants, occupiers and freeholders of the said manor . . . '.[35] These sums were to be collected by tenants 'who have power to distrain the goods, cattle, and chattels of all who refuse to pay'.[36]

It is beyond the scope of this study to dilate on the variety of payments made, and of duties rendered, by tenant farmers on different Glamorgan manors, and sufficient has been said to show that the landowners held their tenantry in economic subjection. The landowners' interests, as exercised through the lease, undoubtedly conflicted with those of their tenants—a situation which made for at least two divergent social classes in pre-industrial Glamorgan. But the Church, no less than the landlords, also enjoyed certain rights and privileges which placed an additional burden upon the cultivators of the soil, and in turn influenced, in no small degree, the standard of farming.

The Church, as represented by the clergy, constituted a social class which, in the eyes of the peasantry, must have been as distinct as the landlords. For the demands of the clergy were often identified with those of the secular landlords, and were equally at variance with the interests of the peasantry. In his study of Glamorgan monasteries, Professor Glanmor Williams found no evidence 'to suggest that as landlords, they differed significantly in their methods or attitude from surrounding laymen'.[37] The payment of tithes, for example, 'caused an immediate conflict of interests between the cultivators and the local representative of the Established Church'.[38]

In the second half of the seventeenth century, there were between 70 and 80 members of the clergy who held livings in Glamorgan[39] and who enjoyed, either directly or indirectly, the economic benefits accruing from the tithes which were levied, not on clear profits, but on the total produce. Tithes were payable in most parishes in kind, but sometimes in cash. In the parish of Betws, for example, 'for tythe of cows for six months (payable the last Monday of May and the last Monday in every month during the continuance of the six months) the whole milk of three days from the cows every month was apprehended to be due', but in practice it was always paid in the form of cheese.[40] Again, at Cadoxton-juxta-Barry, tithes were due on wheat, oats and barley, wool, lambs, cows, calves, horses, pigs, geese, eggs and honey, and the produce of orchards and gardens. In addition 'Easter offerings', which amounts were specified, were payable by every inhabitant of the age of sixteen and upwards.[41] The 'vicar or minister' of the parish of Merthyr Mawr was entitled to two eggs for every cock, drake or turkey cock, and one egg for every hen, duck or turkey hen, payable on Good Friday. There was a tithe on fish, and a 'garden tithe' of a 1*d.* on every householder and ½*d.* on every cottager, but a public gardener was to pay 'in kind

[319]

v

as he sells his stuffe'.[42] In the parish of Sully, which lies on the sea coast, we find that 'for every vessel trading from or constantly belonging to the several port or ports of Sully and Barry Island there was due and payable to the Rector or Tythingman for each vessel the yearly sum of 2s. 8d.'. Moreover, 'tithe oar'[43] found or raised in the parish of Sully or Barry Island was 'immemorially due and payable by the tenth pound or tenth measure'.[44]

Enough has been said to indicate how tight a grip the clergy had on the economic life of the peasantry. The payment of tithes was by no means less irksome to the cultivators of the soil than the payment of rent or other dues to the lay landowners. Both rent and tithes were in conflict with the interests of the small peasant farmers, and were inimical to an improved standard of husbandry which the landowners were anxious to encourage whenever possible. There were, then, serious divergences of interest, not only between the Church and the farmers, but ultimately between the Church and the landowners who naturally 'had no love for an institution which discouraged farmers from improving their farms'. It is not surprising, therefore, that in a later period 'the landlords composing the Board of Agriculture supported their tenants' demand for the reform of the tithe'.[45]

Members of the clergy, moreover, tended to identify themselves, on the whole, with a social class that stood aloof from certain other sections of the community. For instance, when the vicar of Llanbleddian and Cowbridge was requested to reply to the visitation queries of 1763, he stated that there were in his parish 80 families, among which there were no Dissenters except 'Methodists of all trades and denominations—tinkers, thatchers, weavers, and other vermin'.[46] These discriminations echoed the views current at the beginning of the seventeenth century, and expressed by William Vaughan in a paragraph in which he described as 'odius' the 'trades of Butchers, cookes, fishmongers and hunters' and as 'base' 'pedlars and chaundlers', for 'these kind of men have no voice in the common-wealth, and no account is made of them, but only to be ruled and not to rule others'.[47]

From the above discussion there now emerges a picture, in broad outline, of an agrarian society made up of a complex stratification of social 'classes' and status 'groups'. Some of these were distinguished by objectively measurable material wealth and possessions, such as houses, etc. But whether we think in terms of 'status groups' or 'social classes', the fundamental causes of all these social differences hinged upon the system of landownership and the various restrictions and obligations the landlords were able to impose upon their tenantry. For it may be argued that if land is owned by a class other than those who till and live on it 'then there is a conflict between those who produce the crops and those who collect the rents, and this "conflict" is as real as that between labour and capital for the dividends of industry'.[48]

But the general picture we have presented of the agrarian society of Glamorgan conceals the individual hopes and aspirations of the majority of the people who constituted the peasantry—the small producers on the land who, with the help of simple farm implements and the labour of their families, produced mainly for their own consumption and for 'the fulfilment of their duties to the holders of political and economic power'.[49] In the daily struggle to fulfil their legal obligations, their way of life was conditioned by the requirements of the farm. Their festivals took place at slack periods of the agrarian year, and in the Vale of Glamorgan, wakes and revels (or 'riots' as they were sometimes called) and the accompanying singing, morris dancing, bull baiting, cock fighting, etc. took place in October.[50]

It seems fairly clear, on the surface, that the peasantry took for granted their obligations to their landlords and to the clergy. There is no evidence of overt class conflicts during our period. But it should not be assumed that social 'conflicts' (as understood and implied in this context) must, of necessity, be expressed overtly in physical violence or open hostility. Indeed, the migration of workers from agriculture to industry (which occurred from time to time during, and particularly at the end of, our period) may only have been a manifestation of 'conflict' whereby people were showing a strong desire for economic and personal independence, a less monotonous existence, and a higher standard of life. Further, class conflicts may be reflected in differences of religious adherence or persuasion. The increasing number of non-conformists in Glamorgan during the eighteenth century was almost certainly connected with the fact that the gentry 'had lost touch with their tenantry' and that they 'were Anglican . . . '.[51] The Anglican Church, as we have seen, was often represented in the eyes of those who produced crops and reared livestock, as another landlord, in fact an ecclesiastical landlord who demanded the payment of tithes in much the same way as the secular landlord demanded his rent and other dues.

We shall see that the pattern of life in Glamorgan was gradually changing during our period, and that the whole structure of the economy was being modified as new opportunities for alternative employment arose in industry, commerce, and the professions.

iii.

THE STATE OF AGRICULTURE

Throughout the seventeenth and eighteenth centuries, agriculture dominated the economic and social life of Glamorgan. The vast majority of the inhabitants earned their livelihood either by cultivating the land and tending their flocks, or in occupations ancillary to these tasks.

Agriculture, it is said, supported 'about three-quarters of the population of the whole country in the early eighteenth century',[52] but in Glamorgan this proportion must have been even higher. The diverse physical occupational tasks connected with agriculture were performed within a social environment that had been conditioned by the established system of landownership, while the general standards of living attained in these circumstances depended on the application of the most practicable methods of husbandry that were currently possible in the production of goods and commodities, and in their subsequent sale or exchange at the various fairs and markets established to facilitate these economic transactions.[53] Yet in the final analysis everything depended on the physical characteristics of the county, the liberality or niggardliness of Nature, the fertility of the native soil, and the geniality of local climate. These were the basic determinants of the type of farming that was possible, and it may be said that in Glamorgan, as in Wales generally, the physical factors made it a stock-breeding rather than a grain-producing area.

However, we must not lean too heavily on such conventional generalizations because, as we shall show, they contain lacunae which are exposed only after a detailed and systematic study of local records. For instance, too much weight has been given in the past to the general observations made on the Welsh agricultural scene by English 'travellers', 'antiquaries', and 'geographers' whose excursions into Wales hardly ever deviated away from the main highways. Consequently, when we examine the conventional histories of 'Welsh' agriculture, it is sometimes difficult to distinguish between pre-industrial conditions in north Wales from those prevailing in the south. Similarly, the agricultural conditions obtaining in one county have often been assumed to apply to other counties. Glamorgan had its own physical peculiarities, with different soil distribution and marked local variations in climatic conditions, besides the important influences exerted on local production by the proximity of the English markets which could be reached through its small ports.

Geographically Glamorgan comprises two fairly distinct regions traditionally referred to as the Vale (*Y Fro*), and the hill districts (*Y Blaenau*). The comments made by Leland, Merrick, Camden, and Speed on the characteristics of *Bro* and *Blaenau* have already been noted (above, pp. 2–7). In the middle of the seventeenth century Thomas Fuller observed that 'The north of this county is so full of mountains that almost nothing is to be had; the south is so fruitful a valley nothing at all is wanting therein'.[54] But by the end of the century a Glamorgan bard had put it on record that one Hopkin Thomas Philip, of the parish of Llandyfodwg had grown 'strong robust wheat' where deer once roamed in the woods in the northern parts of Glamorgan:

Ceir amlhau lle bu'r Ceirw mlith
Coed ar donn caderdew wenith.[55]

[322]

Circa 1542, corn crops were grown on a limited scale in the lower valley plains[56] where, by the eighteenth century, 'pretty large crops of corn'[57] were produced—a fact corroborated by the probate inventories of the period. But, by and large, the inhabitants of the *Blaenau* earned their living mainly by rearing livestock, and in producing cheese, butter, and wool for the market.

It is worth noting that with the industrialization of Glamorgan, fertile valleys, where cattle once grazed and corn crops waved in the highland breezes, were transformed into 'built-up' areas, losing all semblance of their former pattern of settlement. The most notable of the 'built-up' areas is the Rhondda Valley, which is co-extensive with the former parish of Ystradyfodwg. In 1670 its population cannot have been far in excess of about 500. As late as 1807 it was seen by Malkin to exhibit 'such scenes of untouched nature as the imagination would find it difficult to surpass, and yet', he added, 'the existence of the place is scarcely known to the English traveller'.[58] Even in 1831 there were still only 1,045 persons in the parish, but between 1861 and 1871, the population soared from 4,000 to 16,925, and by 1921 it had reached a staggering total of 162,717—the majority of whom earned their livelihood in the mining and distribution of coal. This was, indeed, a far cry from the days when the majority of the inhabitants were engaged in the rearing of cattle and sheep. The way of life which these occupations imposed upon the pre-industrial community of Rhondda and other similar upland regions of Glamorgan is reflected in some detail in the inventories of farmers' wealth.

Working on a fairly wide canvas, we find that the average (median) number of cattle possessed by farmers in the five upland parishes of Aberdare, Merthyr, Ystradyfodwg, Llanwynno and Llandyfodwg was as follows:

TABLE II

Stock in the Glamorgan hills

Parish	Period	Number of samples	Median number of cattle
Aberdare	1688–1723	12	35
Merthyr	1683–1725	7	15
Ystradyfodwg	1665–1718	37	39
Llanwynno	1670–1720	31	31
Llandyfodwg	1677–1728	7	49

Looked at from another angle, the following table shows the general distribution of cattle as reflected in the inventories of 133 hill farmers for the periods stated:

TABLE III

Number of cattle on Glamorgan hill farms for the periods 1660–1699 and 1700–1735

Number of cattle	No. of farms		Total
	1660–1699	1700–1735	
1–20	21	14	35
21–40	30	17	47
41–60	12	15	27
61–80	9	4	13
81–100	5	1	6
101–200	3	2	5
Total number of farms	80	53	133

In the mixed farming regions of the Vale we find that the herds were considerably smaller. Whereas Table III indicates that out of 133 examples of hill farms, 82 had up to 40 head of cattle, Table IV shows that of 126 examples in the Vale, 111 farms had up to 40 cattle.

TABLE IV

Number of cattle on Vale of Glamorgan farms for 1660–1699 and 1700–1735

Number of cattle	No. of Farms		Total
	1660–1699	1700–1735	
1–20	47	14	61
21–40	35	15	50
41–60	8	2	10
61–80	3	–	3
81–100	–	2	2
Total number of farms	93	33	126

But the quality of the herds was very different in the two areas. The natural differences of the hills and the Vale were reflected in the prices of their animals, as shown in the following table:

TABLE V

Average (median) price of cattle (kine) and sheep per head in the Vale and Blaenau between 1660 and 1760

Vale of Glamorgan		Blaenau	
Cattle (kine)	Sheep	Cattle (kine)	Sheep
£3 10s	5s	£1 10s	3s

The inventories also emphasize the size of the sheep population of the Glamorgan hills, and the relatively large quantities of wool which were accounted for reveal the importance of wool in the pastoral economy of the *Blaenau*. The range of flocks kept in five upland parishes is reflected in the following table:

TABLE VI

Number of sheep on Glamorgan hill farms for the periods 1660–1699 and 1700–1735

Number of sheep	Period		Total
	1660–1699	1700–1735	
1–20	10	7	17
21–40	10	5	15
41–60	10	4	14
61–80	6	5	11
81–100	9	3	12
101–200	13	10	23
201–300	12	7	19
301–400	3	2	5
501–1000	5	5	10
Total number of farms	78	48	126

Although the sheep of the hill regions far outnumbered the cattle, the major part of the farmers' capital was tied up in their cattle. Nevertheless, the traffic in sheep was as brisk as that in cattle. Sheep gave rise to the by-products of wool and mutton. The hill sheep were small, and the wool inferior, but their meat was sweet. Again, the sheep of the Eglwysilan Downs, with their fine wool, greatly resembled the Southdown in shape and colour. The woollen manufactory set up at Caerphilly towards the end of the eighteenth century used up much of the locally grown wool.[59] Sheep shearing was often carried out twice a year in many parts of the county. For instance, Jenkin Thomas, of Llangynwyd, who died in 1727, bequeathed unto his wife, among other things, 'two stones of wool, one being of May and ye other of Michaelmas wool'.[60]

In sharp contrast to the hill farms, the sheep population of the Vale farms was, apparently, much smaller. The following table reflects the general picture, and shows that out of 109 examples, only 30 farmers had flocks of 100 sheep and over, whereas Table VI shows that in the hills, out of 129 examples, 60 had flocks exceeding 100.

TABLE VII

Number of sheep on Vale of Glamorgan farms for 1660–1699 and 1700–1735

Number of sheep	Period		Total
	1660–1699	1700–1735	
1–20	12	2	14
21–40	12	10	22
41–60	12	5	17
61–80	7	5	12
81–100	8	6	14
101–200	16	8	24
200 and over	3	3	6
Total number of farms	70	39	109

There was a great demand for the wool from the Vale of Glamorgan sheep. Newton Down was once famous for its excellent breed of sheep, and their fleeces were claimed to be the finest in Wales, and equal to the finest in England. Equally famous were the fleeces of the sheep that grazed upon the Ogmore Downs, the Golden Mile near Bridgend, St. Mary Hill, and Stalling Down near Cowbridge.

Sheep milking was commonly practised in many parts of Glamorgan during this period, and it was continued by some farmers until well into the nineteenth century. For instance, Thomas William of Canton, near Cardiff, had '10 milch sheep'.[61] John Howell of Llantrisant, who died in 1692, had '17 milch sheep',[62] whilst Robert Williams, yeoman, of Llancarfan, had '30 milking ewes' worth £6, at the time of his death in May 1709.[63] In the parish of Monknash, on the sea coast, Robert Jenkin, yeoman, who died in 1687, had as many as 53 milk ewes valued at £17 13s. 4d., besides '49 fatt weathers (£24), 29 store weathers (£10), 3 rams (£1), 7 fatt ewes (£2 12s. 6d), and 37 tuggs (£7 8s.)'.[64]

CATTLE BREEDS

Contemporary wills help to fill in the sketchy picture we have of cattle breeds in the county in the seventeenth and eighteenth centuries. In Gower, the most frequently mentioned cattle are the reds and blacks,[65] whereas in the rest of the county the reds, blacks and browns, which resembled the Gloucestershire breed,[66] seem to have predominated. Cattle of different colours are mentioned in some wills. John Harry, yeoman of Pendoylan, had one 'white cow'[67] in 1657, while Gronow William of Margam, who died in 1662, possessed, *inter alia* '1 black-cow short taild', '1 blacke heiffer', '1 yellow heiffer', '1 black cow with a white starre on the forehead', '1 red heiffer of a year old, white footed', and '1 young cow of a brownish colour'.[68] Red cattle were to be seen in the Coychurch area in 1696,[69] and Miles David of Penmark, mariner, who died in 1663, possessed '1 red cow with a white list on he(r) backe', '2 heiffers whereof one is black and the other red' and '2 red heiffers'.[70] Again, Mathew Jenkin of Llanishen, yeoman, who died in 1664, bequeathed to various persons 'one reed barren cow', 'one reed yearlinge hayfer', 'one black yearlinge hayfer', 'one yellow cow and one black spoted hayfer of three yeare old'.[71] Morgan John of Welsh St. Donat's, who died in 1663, owned 'one red sparked yerlinge' and 'one black sparked yerlinge'.[72] And as a final example we may refer to the cattle owned by Gibbon Morgan, a yeoman of the parish of Aberdare, high in the Glamorgan hills, who was buried in 1682 according to the 'Canons of the true Catholique and Appostolique Church' having bequeathed '1 heffer of a red coller', '1 whitefoot cow' and '1 white belly cow' to his friends and relatives.[73]

The physical characteristics of cattle were often echoed in the names by which they were distinguished from each other. Morgan Thomas of Rhigos, near Aberdare, for example, bequeathed each of his seven cows by name—*y fuwch sidan ddu* (the black silky cow), *y fuwch nebwen gron* (the round white-faced cow), *y fuwch fraith wen* (the mottled cow), *y fuwch nebwen* (the white-faced cow), and *y fuwch corn las* (the blue-horned cow). In the Cardiff area in 1730, such names as *Cefnwen* (white-backed), *Pengron* (round headed) and *Seren* (star) were common.[74]

The spotted cattle undoubtedly testify to a widespread practice of cross-breeding, or perhaps some degree of experimentation in inbreeding local types or other breeds, as in fact Robert Bakewell and his colleagues did in leading the way to the production of finer meat-yielding animals. Indeed, Owain John of the parish of Coychurch, yeoman, who died in 1672, must have been one of many yeomen who endeavoured, from time to time, to improve their herds, for in his will he had divided his cattle thus—to Evan Owain 'one red cow wth her caulf . . . and one yeolow steere by me formerlie bought from the place called Cwm Garne', and to his daughter 'one heiffer of my owne breed y[t] now is in my dayrie'.[75] The Llanwynno mountain pastures also sustained a fine breed of horned cattle supposed to be the true Glamorgan breed, and found to be preferable to those crossed with any other.[76]

CATTLE HIRING

The practice of hiring out of cows in many parts of Glamorgan is high-lighted in numerous wills. For instance, Thomas David of Flemingston, who died in 1719, bequeathed unto Jane Mathew, 'one cow that's now at Rent wth John Claxon of Llanbethery'.[77] Again, William Clayton, yeoman of Penarth, who died in 1714, worth £61 10s. had 9s. 0d. due to him from John Vaughan of Penarth, for 'the hire of a cow'. Thomas Evans, Esquire, of Neath, when he died in 1676 (worth £211 10s. 2d.) had as many as six oxen and three cows 'out wth Rees Mathew' as well as several score of sheep with various other people.[78] In a previous century, George Owen[79] had calculated that farmers who leased their cattle did so at a considerable loss. However, where the owner had no land upon which to graze cattle, renting them out would obviously be a source of a regular income.

The hirer of cows enjoyed the immediate advantage of not having to find ready money or to borrow money to purchase them, and for an annual rental of about 5s. or 6s. he was provided with milk, butter, and cheese, in addition to the manure—a valuable item in the seventeenth- and eighteenth-century farming—to fertilize the pasture. Moreover, the cow provided a basis for breeding, and the increase of stock, if any, would bring added advantages to both owner and hirer. The renting of cows must be regarded as another facet of the way of life in a pre-industrial community which established the cow as the key animal, guaranteeing the present and future life of the farmer.

HORSES, GOATS AND PIGS

Horses were fairly numerous and were bred for the market as well as for draught purposes. Some oxen were employed alongside horses in many upland parishes, but not as extensively as they were in the Vale.

The place of the goat in the pastoral economy of the Glamorgan hills is a subject which has hitherto received little attention. Numerous herds of goats were to be found on many of the upland farms of the county, and it is certain that they were an integral part of the business of hill farming where cattle were bred mainly for beef. One of the qualities of the goat lay in its ability to convert into milk herbage that no other animal could utilize, and on this account alone its contribution to the provisioning of the households of marginal farmsteads was highly valuable. Indeed, the goat has been referred to as 'the symbol and mascot of subsistence agriculture' for it was 'first and foremost a household provider',[80] requiring nothing that is chargeable to keep them.[81]

[328]

Herds of varying sizes are accounted for in the probate inventories of the period. For example, William Thomas of the parish of Llandyfodwg, who died in 1677, possessed 60 goats valued at £10, in addition to '100 beastes of all sorts' valued at £150, and '300 sheepe' worth £45; his 'implements of husbandry' were valued at £5, and his total estate was worth £306.[82] Again, Watkin Richard (gent.) of the same parish who died in 1698, had 34 goats, 141 head of cattle 'of all sorts', 540 sheep and 74 lambs.[83] Most of the herds recorded, however, were much smaller, and consisted of from 4 to 8 goats, and examples of these were found in several parishes, extending from Llanfabon, in the east, to Cadoxton-juxta-Neath in the west. In the former parish the value of the goat is emphasised by William Rowland who died in 1676, having bequeathed to his daughter 'four milch goats'.[84] In general, their distribution coincided with those areas where the soil may have been too poor and too steep for the rearing of dairy cattle. Indeed, goats did not figure in any of the inventories of the farmers of the Vale of Glamorgan, where dairy and mixed farming was practised extensively. In the hill districts, however, where beef and bacon dominated the 'household provisions' lists, the goat was kept mainly for its milk,[85] although kid meat must have figured in the highland farmer's diet.

But in addition to their value as 'a household provider', goats were undoubtedly a source of commercial profit, and their movements from one locality to another were attested in the charges of 5d. per score imposed 'on drovers of calves, hogs, sheep, goats and lambs'.[86] Moreover, the lists of cargoes shipped across from the small ports of Glamorgan to Bristol and Minehead often included numerous packs of goat and kid skins. On January 23, 1666, for instance, the *Lyon* of Cardiff had as part of her cargo unloaded at Bristol '200 kid skins in the haire'.[87] Again, on June 24, 1683, the *Five Brothers* of Newton had on board '1 pack of goats rawskins' for Bristol,[88] and on November 2, 1686 the *Blessing* of Aberthaw sailed for Minehead with '6 goat skins'.[89] The skins were undoubtedly made up at Bristol into best-quality shoes and gloves.

It is interesting to observe from the inventories examined that the hill farmers kept smaller herds of pigs per head than those in the dairy farming areas. This was, perhaps, to be expected, for dairying and the rearing of pigs are often complementary—the pigs fed on the skimmed milk and whey. Bacon and pork were produced by the dairy farmers for the market, but some ended up as 'flitches' and 'sides' of bacon in the farmhouse.

In the upland regions the average number of pigs per head accounted for in the inventories was about three or four, whereas in the middle regions of the county, and particularly in the region around Cardiff, the average number of pigs was appreciably larger. These regions were nearer the more populous parishes of the Vale, and also more contiguous to the markets of the West of England. Farmers in these areas obviously produced for the market as well as for domestic consumption. Indeed, in 1697 Edward Lhuyd was informed that cattle, sheep, and hogs were exported from Sully, and local pig drovers, such as Evan William[90] of Coychurch, helped to drive the pigs to the ports of the Vale. The traffic in pigs continued until at least the year 1800 when the Rev. John Skinner described the arrival of a cargo boat 'from the opposite coast' at Uphill thus: 'We awaited its arrival on the beach, and were shortly afterwards greeted by the harmonious sound of Welsh gutterals, for the boatmen soon engaged in a business which gave the language every possible variety to the ear of a stranger . . . they proceeded to discharge their freight, consisting of many score pigs, into the water. The swinish multitude, at all times refractory, did not seem inclined in the present instance to forego their rights as terrestrial animals, and it was not till forced by repeated blows, kicks and execrations from four stout fellows at their tails that they leaped into the water'.[91]

MANURES

Seaweed, sea-sludge, shells, and sand were the principal manures used on the lands bordering the sea coast. At one time it was also usual about St. Donat's, Llantwit Major and St. Athan, 'to water land by way of manuring with sea water, and it was esteemed good and produced very fine wheat and grass'.[92] Marl and compost, too, were used in conjunction with farmyard manure which, according to most inventories, was collected and piled 'about the house' and priced in the same way as household goods and livestock. In the inventory of the goods of Margaret Nicholls of St. Brides, who died in 1666, we find that the 'dung and soile in several places about ye house and other places thereunto belonging' was valued at 3s. 4d.[93]—the equivalent of one and a half bushels of oats.

But by far the most common and most universally used form of manure in the Vale of Glamorgan was lime. Many observers thought that local farmers were 'injudicious' and 'indiscriminate' in the manner they used lime on every sort of soil, frequently misapplying its properties and rather injuring the farms 'by the mistaken donation'.[94] The extensive use of lime as manure involved the use of coal for burning the lime before application. But the Vale farmers were also favourably situated in respect of supplies of coal and lime, and consequently the cost of haulage added little to their production costs.[95] Perhaps it was, therefore, inevitable that lime was used sometimes to such excess 'so as to form in some degree a new separate stratum instead of a perfect union with the soil which it is intended to fertilise'.[96] John Fox observed that within the districts he visited in Glamorgan, farmers applied 450 bushels of lime on an acre which was burnt from 1s. 2d. to 2s. 6d. or 3s. a crannock and would 'last good' for four years.[97] In 1769, in other parts of the Vale, 66 crannocks of lime were applied to the acre.[98] But in the Baglan area, lime was so dear that few were able to purchase it 'the limestones being brought hither in boates from the Mumbles 3 leagues off'.[99]

IMPLEMENTS OF HUSBANDRY

The implements and tools of husbandry used by Glamorgan farmers in the seventeenth and eighteenth centuries were fashioned out of local timber and wrought iron in style and design which varied from one area to another. Some of these designs, particularly in the case of certain forms of agricultural transport, continued well into the nineteenth century. But although many of the implements were crude and primitive, they continued in use, not because more refined forms were unknown, but 'because the experience of past generations had proved that certain devices were better suited to the particular needs of different regions'.[100]

In the upland areas of Glamorgan, where there was relatively little tillage, agricultural implements constituted an insignificant part of the farmers' working capital equipment. In these areas, too, we find that many farmers shared their implements and tools, and an occasional will reveals how highly valued was the most commonplace of implements—the plough and its accessories. For example, Thomas ab Thomas of Aberdare, who died in 1673, had bequeathed to his nephew Harry Thomas 'all the implements of the plow except two iron link chains' which he was to lend to the testator's wife during her lifetime, and she, in turn, had to ensure that 'the said two link chains' be delivered to Harry Thomas 'weighing the same weight that she received them from him'.[101]

In the arable regions of the Vale of Glamorgan most farmers seem to have been adequately equipped for all the essential operations of cultivation—ploughing, harrowing, rolling, and hoeing. The usual complement of agricultural implements accounted for in inventories is illustrated in the inventory of Richard Lougher of Tythegston, who died in 1663, possessing 'one waine and a paire of wheels, one paire of harrows, one plow, two yokes and two chaines', all of which were valued at £1 10s.[102] Mary Rosser, a widow of Llantriddyd, who died in 1680, left 'one long waine, two iron chaines with strakes and nails,[103] one pair of treces (i.e. traces), one sull (a plough) and one waine-rope'.[104]

Harrows were sometimes described in detail, as in the inventory of Alexander Edward of Pennard, Gower, in which was listed 'a single harrow with twenty-five iron teeth'.[105] The most common harrow used in Glamorgan during our period was the chain harrow. There were also numerous references in inventories to the 'drag'. Cecil Lewis of Llanilltern, owned a 'plow and plow sheare, 3 yokes, 3 chains, 1 drag and an old pair of harrows, an old pair of wheels and a dung pott'.[106]

Specific references to rollers in the inventories are rare, but Edward Lewis, yeoman, of Rhoose in the parish of Penmark, possessed, according to his inventory, '2 Rowlers, 2 axles and 2 carrs'.[107] At this time rollers would be either of wood or stone.

Cars, and the long-wain in particular, were very common items in the inventories of the farmers of the Vale. For instance, Hugh Hyett of Llantwit Major possessed a long-wain, iron bond wheels, a butt, harrows, a sull (i.e. a plough), and other implements,[108] while Gronow Thomas of St. Brides Major, whose inventory was made up in 1734, owned one long and one short-wain and wheels.[109] Howell Griffith of Coychurch owned a long waggon which, as the inventory states, the local Welsh 'commonly call *crywun*' (i.e. *crywyn*).[110]

The Glamorgan ploughs were often described by late-eighteenth century observers as 'awkward' and too heavy for the 'generality' of the soils. In 1796 John Fox described them as 'old-fashioned, long and clumsy'.[111] The plough, or the sull, as it was called in many parts of Glamorgan, was usually drawn by yoked oxen. The inventories of the Vale farmers frequently refer to 'yokes' and 'bows', as well as to working-oxen. For instance, George Hill of St. Athan, when he died in 1666, owned among other things 'seven fat oxen' valued at £28, and 'four plough-oxen' valued at £10.[112] It was probably considered more economical to employ oxen rather than horses at the plough because the latter required a great deal of fodder. Such economic considerations were the realities which prompted farmers to use oxen although the ploughing operations were slower and the movement of the oxen prevented a neat furrow, which, to an observer, would betray a degree of slovenliness on the part of the ploughman. Horses were used more generally in the upland regions, but in the Vale oxen were used for all kinds of draught purposes. For instance, early in the seventeenth century Jenkin Spencer, of Aberthaw, was paid 6d. for every draught of wine (being two hogs-heads) drawn by his oxen from the harbour to the Booth cellars, 'of which 12 oxen were used'.[113] Again, oxen were used for hauling coal in some of the upland parishes. In 1676 William Rowland of Llanfabon, yeoman, had two oxen, one of which was called 'Collier'.[114] At the end of the seventeenth century both horses and oxen were employed for haulage work at the Coed-frank collieries owned by the Hoby family of Neath Abbey.[115]

In their implements of husbandry, as in their household furniture and utensils, the Glamorgan peasantry were greatly dependent on local timber supplies. The inventory of Evan Llewellyn of Llantwit Faerdre, shows that when he died in 1742, he possessed an old harrow, a car, as well as 'four pieces of oake for making new cars and a ladder'.[116] The same feature is exhibited in the inventory of Elisha Flanders, of Penmark, who possessed 'a sett of harrow lawrells, a set of volleys for a wayne and other sawed timber'.[117]

There is ample evidence to show that many of the poorer farmers and cottagers depended on their better equipped neighbours for assistance in cultivating their holdings. Mary Rees of Wick died in 1740 owing Thomas Morgan, of the same parish, a sum of £5, 'for lime and dung and ploughing three acres of ground twice'.[118]

CROPS

Contrary to the impression sometimes conveyed by conventional generalizations, we have shown earlier that cereal crops were grown on a limited scale in the northern valleys of Glamorgan. Some wheat was certainly grown, but barley and oats preponderated, with barley in larger proportions than oats. Although many of the upland areas were on subsistence level, many farmers undoubtedly produced occasional small surpluses which found their way to the 'market'. In 1677 Andrew Yarranton observed that the corn markets along the English border, particularly at Hereford, had suffered because 'formerly Wales took away their corn when plentiful, but since the Welsh took to break up their Mountains and sow them with corn, they have corn sufficient for themselves and much to spare'.[119] However, the inhabitants of the hills of Glamorgan consumed very little wheaten bread, but oaten bread was quite general, and many farmers like William Rowland, yeoman of Llanfabon, who died in 1676, possessed 'a tripod and one-iron plate for bakeing oaten bread'.[120] The farmer's first concern at this period was not what crop to grow for the market, but what crop could be most economically grown to feed his family and his livestock.

Unfortunately, the inventories are not very helpful in revealing the size and kind of crops grown in the hills. Most of these documents refer to 'corn crops'. However, from a small sample of sixteen hill-farm inventories, the pattern of cropping suggested was as follows:

TABLE VIII

Corn grown on sixteen upland farms in Glamorgan, 1660-1699

Crop	Acres sown	Percentage of total
Wheat	9½	11
Oats	21½	26
Barley	52½	63
Total	83½	100

At the end of the eighteenth century, if we are to believe Iolo Morganwg, wheat was 'abundant' on the mountain slopes of Aberdare and Taff Vales, and 'nearly to the summit of Cefn Merthyr, Cefn Celystan, the highest mountains in Glamorgan wheat, barley etc. grew and ripened well'.[121] By this time, however, the expanding populations of the Dowlais and Merthyr industrial complexes provided a real incentive for local farmers to get the utmost from their cultivable lands, particularly during the lean years which coincided with the Napoleonic Wars.

In the richer low-lying regions of the Vale (*Y Fro*), the general pattern of farming was obviously quite different. Here was to be found a combination of mixed and dairy farming. The general fecundity of this region had, from an early date, earned for it the commendation and admiration of contemporary observers (above, pp. 2–7). Leland, Merrick, Camden, and others had praised its genial and prosperous fertility, but as Merrick had observed its classical open fields had given way to enclosures in the sixteenth century.[122] So that by the seventeenth century the open fields in the Vale had disappeared and the manorial system of cultivation which had given rise to its nucleated villages and its complicated network of roads had long since decayed.[123] Nevertheless, it was here, on the rich lias rock foundation of the Vale, that the population of the county was densest in pre-industrial times, supporting almost double the population of the hill districts. The farms in the Vale were generally occupied in 'mixed husbandry'—corn growing, grazing, breeding, and dairying. They varied in size; the smaller farms ranging from about 30 to 100 acres, and being situated mainly in the northern parishes of the Vale. The farms in the southern sector of the Vale, particularly near the coastal belt, were generally larger and carried larger flocks of sheep. Even in the late-eighteenth century a farm of £50 per annum was deemed a large one 'and consisted then in the Vale of from 110 to 150 statute acres, and the rent from 7s. to 10s. per acre'.[124] At the beginning of the nineteenth century, Walter Davies observed that farms from 300 to 500 acres became numerous, and from 100 to 200 acres still more so; yet the general run of the smaller farms was still from 30 to 100 acres. The largest farms in the Vale of Glamorgan were at Boverton, one of 800 acres, and at Beaupré, one of 600 acres. However, the Board of Agriculture generally regarded as medium-sized a farm of 300 acres, and as large, a farm exceeding 500 acres.[125] Therefore, the farms in the Vale of Glamorgan were, by English standards, either medium-sized or small.

In contrast to the hills, the Vale produced greater quantities and varieties of corn crops, which included wheat, rye, oats, barley, as well as pulses—peas and beans. Pilcorn and muncorn are sometimes mentioned too. An analysis of the crops grown on 129 farms in five parishes in the Vale during the period 1660–1735 has produced the following figures:

TABLE IX

Crops grown in 129 Vale of Glamorgan farms, as shown in 70 inventories for period 1660–1699, and 59 inventories for period 1700–1735

Crop	1660–1699		1700–1735	
	Acres sown	Percentage of total (Approx.)	Acres sown	Percentage of total (Approx.)
Wheat	404	52	211¾	47
Oats	160	21	94¼	21
Barley	168	22	114¼	25
Peas	38	5	27½	6
Beans	2½	0.3	3¼	0.6
Total	772½		451	

GENERAL STANDARDS OF HUSBANDRY

In 1768, Arthur Young observed that 'about Cowbridge and Bridgend in Glamorganshire the husbandry is the most imperfect I ever met with; and totally contrary to the most common ideas in more informed counties'. Young further observed that there were many farms around Bridgend with suitable soil that did not grow turnips, and that 'one farmer from England' in the parish of Candleston had 'sowed two acres and was at great pains to hoe them well and keep them clean'. The neighbouring farmers, apparently, 'ridiculed him infinitely and really thought him mad', but 'were surprised to see what a crop he gained' as well as the vast profits he earned from selling it 'by the sack to all neighbouring towns'.[126] This practice the farmer continued, but was not emulated. Young also lamented the fact that Glamorgan gentlemen farmers did 'not on a large scale practise a better husbandry, that the force of numerous examples might influence the farmers to change their bad methods'.[127]

It would be very unwise to base our conclusions about the standards of husbandry prevailing in Glamorgan in the middle of the eighteenth century on the limited observations and impressions recorded by Young, whose reports may be criticized on precisely the same grounds as Edward Williams (*Iolo Morganwg*) condemned John Fox's report of Glamorgan to the Board of Agriculture in 1796.[128] Both visits were of short duration, and their respective journeys hardly deviated from the main turnpike roads and the village inns *en route*. Had Young penetrated more deeply into the Vale of Glamorgan, he would have discovered that the Rev. Willis of Gileston had already introduced turnips 'for feeding sheep' about the year 1740.[129] Indeed, it is worth pointing out here that John Aubrey, writing between 1656 and 1691, was of the opinion that all

[335]

the turnips that were brought to Bristol *circa* 1600 were from Wales, and that by 1680 'none come from thence, for they found out that the red sand about Bristoll doth breed a better and bigger turnip'.[130] We have not been able to corroborate Aubrey's statement in the Welsh port books of the seventeenth century.

If, however, the growing of turnips was to be Young's criterion in assessing the standard of agriculture in the county, then it should be stated that turnips were not suited to all ecological conditions. The absence of turnips from a local agricultural system did not necessarily imply a backward state of husbandry or a lack of native enterprise. On the contrary, we know very little about the progress made by many unidentified individuals in improving the quality of their livestock following the enrichment of leys by the controlled sowing of clover which, as we shall see, had been practised fairly widely in the county almost a century previous to Young's 'tour'. For the main purpose of growing both clover and turnips was to supply the livestock with more adequate winter feed.[131] Indeed, 'it is quite remarkable', as one writer has observed, that none of the reports of the Royal Society's 'Enquiries' into the state of English agriculture under Charles II makes any mention of turnips.[132]

Although the general methods of husbandry in Glamorgan through-out the greater part of our period were based on empirical knowledge—custom and tradition—yet the need for improvements must have occupied the attention of many of the wealthier and more ambitious members of the farming community, men who not only had the knowledge, but also the necessary capital and security of tenure for experimentation. We cannot ignore the fact that the inventories of many farmers contain references to books on agricultural and veterinary topics. For example, Morgan Thomas, gentleman, of Old Castle-upon-Alun in St. Brides Major, possessed many 'bookes on husbandry' which he bequeathed to his cousin in 1667.[133] Such books must surely have made some impression on their readers, which they translated into practice.

Clover, that is, cultivated or sown grasses, is said to have been introduced into Glamorgan by Sir Edward Stradling of St. Donat's and Mr. Seys of Boverton near by, around the years 1680 or 1690.[134] In this connection we may note that on March 3, 1694, the master of the *Elizabeth* of Aberthaw had entered as part of his cargo from Minehead to Aberthaw, 50 bushels of 'evir' seeds, and on the April 3 following, the *Blessing* of Aberthaw brought back from Minehead '50 bushells of evir seeds and 300 weight of clover seeds'.[135] But remembering the deficiencies of these official trade records, we should not be surprised if clover seeds were imported at a much earlier date. It should also be borne in mind that it was not until 1677 that Andrew Yarranton could report 'a great improvement by clover' in Herefordshire, which seed 'he had sent into those parts'.[136] Glamorgan pioneers were obviously not far behind their English counterparts in applying new methods of husbandry, and indeed their progressive outlook was not recognized by later English observers.

By the beginning of the eighteenth century 'cloved hay' and 'clover' are frequent items in the farm inventories. One of the earliest extant references is in 1718 in the inventory of John Deer, weaver of St. Athan, who had 'one little mow of cloved hay' valued at £1, and 'a small parcell of hay' valued at 15s.[137] In parts of Gower clover had taken deep root by the beginning of the eighteenth century. It appears from an early eighteenth-century terrier that the tithes payable to the rector at Cheriton included 'clover seed, clover hay, and other grasses'.[138] By the early-nineteenth century even the upland farms of the parish of Ystradyfodwg had numerous fields referred to locally as *cae clovers* (clover field) and *ynys-y-clovers* (clover meadow).[139]

Progress of Agriculture

The evidence which we have gathered from probate and other original sources does not suggest that there occurred any 'revolutionary' changes in the agrarian conditions of the county during our period. It was not until after the establishment of the Glamorgan Agricultural Society in 1772 that any positive measures were taken on an 'official' basis to encourage radical reforms in local husbandry. However, we have shown that there were many unidentifiable farmers who endeavoured to improve the quality of their livestock and the standard of their husbandry. There were also more positive signs of 'improvement' which can be detected on those lands contiguous to centres of growing population.

The small industrial complexes of the late-seventeenth and early-eighteenth centuries, which were centred mainly on the Baglan-Neath-Swansea area, had attracted much immigrant labour, as well as local workers, and these men and women had to be fed. The need to feed more mouths in this region provided an incentive to local farmers to improve their husbandry. In a deposition concerning a local litigation, it was stated that by 1694 some lands in the Cadoxton-juxta-Neath area had been improved 'by grubbinge up stumps and rootes of trees and other husbandry and management' with the result that a certain Morgan William Bevan, it was said 'doth now, in 1694, pay £5 rent yearly for a tenement of land which was formerly and until the defendents did manure and improve it held att 30s.'.[140] At the same time, it was said that there were in the area 'three or four coaleworks open employing many cutters of coal'.[141]

In the absence of more positive signs of improvement, it is easy to rush to the conclusion that, because their implements were old and cumbersome, and their system of husbandry contrary to more 'enlightened' ideas, the peasantry of Glamorgan farmed on a subsistence level. But this would be far from the truth. The Welsh peasantry were no more 'ignorant', 'prejudiced', 'bigoted' and 'obstinate' than their English counterparts, for, like them, they regarded every 'improvement' as a 'questionable innovation'.[142] Similarly in English farming, we are told that the 'experts' wrangled and fought over new ideas, while the poor bewildered farmer 'determined to trust to tradition and the benevolence of nature'.[143] It should also be emphasized that the agrarian economy of Glamorgan did not function as an independent unit; it was, in truth, firmly geared to the Bristol market.

iv.

RURAL INDUSTRIES

Spinning and Weaving

When enquiring into the economic conditions that prevailed in Glamorgan in pre-industrial times, we must not lose sight of the uncertainties that attended life in a pastoral-agricultural economy. People were forever conscious of the long term effects of bad climatic conditions. Professor Ashton has suggested that 'the prodigality or niggardliness of the landlord mattered less than the prodigality or niggardliness of nature; what was happening at Westminster or in the City was of small account compared with what was happening in the heavens'.[144] A late harvest, a single crop failure, or an outbreak of disease amongst the livestock were all factors which affected adversely the economic and social welfare of individual farmers (especially small farmers) for several years afterwards. The burden of arrears of rent and the payment of tithes, sometimes aggravated by sickness and incapacity, taxed to the limit the normal resources of the individual. And it was during years of adversity that the peasant farmer and his family strained every muscle, and exploited every subsidiary or supplementary occupation, in order to help balance the household budget. Spinning, weaving, and stocking-knitting, were among the traditional by-industries of the countryside in which the peasantry of the pastoral and mixed-farming regions were invariably employed. Wool was converted into articles of clothing for personal and domestic use and for sale at the fairs and markets—the proceeds of such sales representing the 'real' wages, or at least part of them, of the small domestic producers.[145]

The probate inventories of our period show that most farmhouses and cottages were equipped to card and spin wool, grown on the backs of the highland and lowland sheep, which was then woven into cloth or flannel by the local weavers. Almost every parish in the county had its weavers and tuckers. Weaving continued to be domestic in character, and it was not until about 1770 that a woollen factory was established at Bridgend under the patronage of the Glamorgan Agricultural Society.[146] But while the domestic system prevailed, the peasant farmers in the hills and in the Vale manufactured their own cloths, and what surplus cloth or flannel they had was sold, some in the local fairs and markets, and some in the remoter markets of Bristol and the West of England.

Llanbleddian was one of several Glamorgan villages which were once noted for their weavers. The economic condition of many of them is mirrored in their inventories. David Williams, for instance, who died in 1701 was worth £13 2s. 6d., and possessed 'three weavers loomes wth their appurtenances' valued at £6 10s. 0d., and appears to have been fully occupied as a weaver.[147] His neighbour, John Richards, a tucker, died in 1725, and possessed '18 yards of flannen at 6d. per yard (9s.); 5 yards of cloth at 2/6 per yard (12s. 6d.); and a stone of wooll'[148] worth 5s.

Weavers were also prominent in the parishes of St. Andrews, St. Athan, and Llantwit Major, where the craft was carried on in the same families from one generation to another. John Tucker, of St. Andrews, had in his 'shop' '1 weaver's loome, 3 slaices, warping bars and a trow'.[149] John Deer, a weaver of St. Athan, who died in 1718, bequeathed to his grandson, William Deer, 'my looms with all their appurtenances and all other implements belonging to my trade or mystery (sic) of weaving'. But he also had a small farm with a few cattle and sheep.[150] Edward Rawling, of Llantwit Major, another weaver, owned 'a paire of looms and slayes' which were undoubtedly employed by his three sisters Elinor, Neast, and Sara who, at the time of his death in 1676, inhabited the same dwelling house which they inherited jointly.[151]

The upland parishes of Gelli-gaer, Llangeinor, Llangynwyd, Llan-dyfodwg, Llanwynno, and Ystradyfodwg, all had their weavers and tuckers. Edward Gamage of Abergarw, in the parish of Llangeinor, was described as 'clothier', and owned a 'tucking mill'.[152] Higher up in the *Blaenau*, in the 'village' of Aberdare there was once a well-known tucking mill which, in 1694, Mary Mathew bequeathed to her son Miles Mathew, together with 'all the water courses thereunto belonging bought from Morgan David Jenkin, William Morgan and David Morgan'.[153] The mill was later leased at a yearly value of £15.[154] In the parish of Llangynwyd, Evan Maddock, weaver, owned looms to the value of £1 5s. 0d., and 'two stones of wooll' worth 10s. He possessed cattle, sheep, a working horse and 'implements of husbandry' worth 6s. 8d. When he died in 1704, his estate was valued at £23 2s. 0d.[155]

Cardiff, Neath, and Swansea, had their weavers and tuckers, who depended on the surrounding countryside for their supplies of wool. Some serges were made in the parish of Loughor where, for example, in 1675 Timothy Woodlack, described as 'a sarge weaver' owned '1 paire of worsted comes and implements belonging to the trade of weaver' as well as 'wool and pinions'.[156]

'Pinions' and 'thrums' were items not infrequently referred to in the inventories of our period, and were closely connected with the process of weaving. 'Pinions' were the short refuse wool from the weaver's shop, and 'thrums' referred to the waste ends of the warp which remained attached to the looms when the weaver cut off the web. These short ends were frequently used up in the making of mops, mats, and sometimes caps. 'Screeds', too, were items often mentioned in contemporary documents, and referred to the fragments which were cut, or broken off, the main piece of textile material.[157] 'Pinions', 'thrums', 'screeds' and mats are frequently listed as part of the cargoes which were shipped from Glamorgan to Bristol. For instance, on July 23, 1674, the *Five Brothers* of Newton sailed for Bristol with, *inter alia*, '2 packs screeds' and '60 packs of matts'.[158] Whilst on August 29, 1683, the *Elizabeth* of Aberthaw carried, as part of a cargo destined for Minehead, '1 fardle of pinions'.[159] These several items must surely have represented the waste material that came from the homes of the Glamorgan weavers.

We know little about the position of the local weavers and allied rural craftsmen during our period, or of the way they functioned from the initial stage of procuring their raw materials to the final act of disposing of their finished products. Neither have we evidence regarding the Glamorgan weavers' standards of cloth making and, consequently, it may be assumed that, as in Wales generally, they 'were content to work in the traditional fashion and were little affected by the improvements introduced into the English cloth industry'.[160]

KNITTING

'In the mountainous part of each county', wrote the Rev. Walter Davies in 1814, 'women are industriously employed in knitting stockings, many of them coarse, which are brought to fairs and bought for the use of the inferior military, etc.'.[161] Indeed, almost 'every female' in the interior parts 'was acquainted with the arts of carding and spinning wool',[162] and it is said that occasionally many families had been rescued from starvation by their labours. In north and mid-Wales men, young and old, could also lend a hand in the knitting operations, and during the long winter evenings whole families would gather together, sometimes in each other's houses, to take part in the *Noswaith Weu* (i.e. Knitting Night), or *Cymorth Gwau* (Knitting Assembly), knitting stockings (frequently to the accompaniment of literary and musical competitions)[163] in readiness for the fairs and markets where the hosiers would buy them for ready cash.

In general, the custom of stocking-knitting in Wales was to be found among the small peasant farmers of the pastoral highlands who kept four or five milch cows, a horse, four or five calves, two or three fat pigs and thirty to fifty mountain sheep. In Glamorgan, however, stocking-knitting was carried on not only in the scattered homesteads and hamlets of the pastoral regions, but also in the mixed-farming areas of the Vale, where, as we have seen, the farms were generally small, yielding marginal returns which were often inadequate to sustain the average household.

The evidence we have gleaned from the probate inventories of the period makes it abundantly clear that in Glamorgan stocking-knitting, although only a subsidiary industry in the countryside, was geared to the requirements of a fairly wide market. The small 'parcels' of stockings which formed part of the inventories of so many small farmers, cottagers, widows, and spinsters, were quickly bought up either at the fairs and markets, or by factors who operated in the rural areas. Without a doubt it was for such a market that Mary Miles of Bonvilston in the heart of the Vale, had knitted the '15 paires of stockings' accounted for in her inventory and which, for probate purposes, were valued at 6s.[164] It was for similar reasons that Ann Howell of Peterston-super-Ely had spun and carded her wool to knit the '15 paires of stockings' accounted for in her inventory, along with her spinning wheel and cards.[165] Again, the inventory of John Gamage, yeoman, of Llantwit Faerdre, in the lower hill districts, shows that in addition to his corn, poultry and bees, he possessed 'stockings ready for sale'.[166]

It is in the hill districts proper that we find the greatest number of examples of stocking-knitters. Typical of these was Elias Jenkins of Llangeinor, whose inventory, made up in 1716, included 9 cows, 6 steers, 2 heifers and a bull, two two-year-old beasts, five yearlings, 192 sheep and twenty-eight lambs, together with 'six paires of stockings for sale'.[167] Again, Thomas William, Llanwynno, gentleman, whose inventory was made up in 1714, possessed '6 dozen women's stockings' valued at £1 8s. 0d., as well as '20 yards of home-made cloth undressed'.[168]

At the end of the eighteenth century it was estimated that a pair of stockings would sell at 10d., which yielded a profit of about 4d. A woman would by 'close application, card, spin and knit about four pairs of full sized stockings per week'[169] and would in the process use up about 'two pounds of wool of such as the dealers refuse'.[170] Earlier in the century, *circa* 1764, as much as 1s. 6d. was paid for knitting a pair of yarn hose.[171] In this connection, however, it is worth noting that in north Wales stockings were made in two grades, namely, those made for sale (i.e. *sanau gwerthu*) and those made for personal use which were, usually, the superior in quality.[172]

Monthly markets were organized to enable small farmers and cottagers to sell the products of their spare-time knitting. At Llantwit Major, for example, 'cotton and yarn stockings, Welsh wigs, etc. were manufactured and sold at the monthly markets'.[173] These markets undoubtedly provided a source of ready cash for many families who were thus enabled to buy provisions and to pay their rents. It was precisely with this end in view that John Franklin of Llanfihangel near Cowbridge (an estate agent, and himself a proprietor), established the March fair at Cowbridge, called Franklin's Fair '. . . to provide farmers with some means of raising money to pay their Lady Day rents'.[174]

But the market for knitted stockings was not merely a local one. Throughout the greater part of our period vast numbers of 'fardles' and 'bags' of stockings were regularly exported from the small ports of Cardiff, Sully, Aberthaw, and Newton to Bristol and Minehead. For example, of the 42 shipments despatched from Cardiff to Bristol in 1666, 22 included various quantities of stockings.[175] The extent of the Glamorgan stocking trade may be partly assessed from the following table, which shows the total number of 'bags and fardles' of stockings exported from Aberthaw and Newton to Bristol and Minehead for the years stated, and as indicated in the official port books:—

Year	Total No. bags and fardles of stockings	Approximate No. of pairs
1667	73	8,989
1670	90	11,070
1672	103	12,669
1674	115	13,795
1678	97	11,736
1680	124	15,752
1683	351	50,193
1685	139	19,877
1686	92	13,156
1688	186	26,598
1689	108 (+ 100 dozen)	16,044
1692	57 (+ 30 dozen)	8,181
1694	75	10,725
1695	129	18,447
1696	92	13,156
1697	66	9,438
1698	70	10,010
1699	49 (July-Dec. only)	7,007
1701	70	10,010

In 1721 stockings were still being shipped across the channel from Aberthaw to Minehead and Bristol.[176] It is fairly certain, too, that the stockings were not exported on the off-chance that they would find a market in the West of England. They had already been bought up by the Welsh and English hosiers from the cottagers, both at their homes and at the local fairs and markets. Locally, men like Richard John of St. George's, whose probate inventory shows that he owned 'A packe of stokins' worth £10,[177] must have acted as dealers buying the knitted stockings from local inhabitants and selling them at a profit direct to English customers.

Evidently, English hosiers from Exeter were also closely connected with the Glamorgan countryside, for we find that Edward Marcus, Thomas Chrichard, John Punch, and Christopher Pike, all hosiers of 'ye Citty of Exon' were debtors to Margaret Roberts, widow of Llanharry, who, in 1696, made one bequest to her son of 'ten pounds sterling wch is due to me from Edward Marcus, a hosier in ye Citty of Exon'.[178] It seems likely, too, that John Bomand, a weaver of St. Bride's Major, and Thomas William, gentleman, of Llanwynno, acted as local hosiers, for their 'goods and chattells' included a 'parcul (sic) of stockings' (valued at £5)[179] and 'six dozen women's stockings' (valued at £1 8s. od.) respectively.[180]

TANNING

An important feature of the rural economy of Glamorgan during our period was the tanning industry. The principal factors which determined the establishment of tanneries were an adequate supply of hides, a plentiful supply of oak bark, and sufficient water. All these pre-requisites were to be found both in the lowland and mountain districts of the county. The raw hides came in abundant quantities from the local butchers, and when tanned were sold to local saddlers, cordwainers, and glovers, and exported to the West of England markets. 'The Glamorgan Vale cattle', it was said, 'had the thinnest hides of any known, being excellently adapted for coach and cart-harness'.[181] Lime was another essential requirement in the process of tanning, and this, too, was to be found in great abundance in the Vale.[182] The first stage in the treatment of a raw hide was to remove the hair and 'face', and this was accomplished by soaking it in the lime-pit for two weeks, which caused the pores of the skin to open and the hair to drop out.[183]

The tanner occupied a prominent position in the economic life of pre-industrial Glamorgan. He generally made a comfortable living, and, by and large, it may be said that he was a small entrepreneur producing and putting on the market his own product in much the same way as the early pioneers of the iron and coal industry. He certainly required more capital than other craftsmen, for it took him a period of eighteen months to complete the processing of the hides. Many tanners, however, besides owning their tanneries, reared their own livestock and cultivated their own farms. There were others who belonged to the small, but growing, class of industrial capitalists, such as John Williams of Llanrhidian who, in addition to his coal mines and coastal vessels, possessed 'tanne fatts and a mill to grynde bark'.[184]

In the town of Cardiff there were numerous tanners whose inventories suggest that they were relatively wealthy persons. For example, in 1686, Arthur Yeomans,[185] an alderman of Cardiff, left an estate valued at

£100 10s. 0d. of which his shop and 'the pelts in the pitt and work house' amounted to £10.[186] The inventory of the goods of another Cardiff alderman, Cradock Nowell, who died in 1709, shows that 'his stock in the tann yard' was valued at £200, and represented twenty per cent of his total personal estate valued at £910.[187] It is significant that neither of them possessed wealth in the form of crops or livestock.

Tanning was an industry 'native to the town' of Bridgend, which was neatly situated in the fall line between the hills and the Vale. The most notable of its tanners was Walter Coffin, whose tanyards formed the basis of the wealth which enabled Walter Coffin 'the younger' to become one of the foremost pioneers in the coal industry of the Rhondda Valley.[188] Walter Coffin, senior, by his energy and business acumen, had become a rich man. His leather was famous throughout the county, and he had become a considerable landed proprietor.[189] Another well-known tanner from Bridgend was Michael Williams, who obtained some of his supplies of raw skins and hides from the Margam estate. Between July 20, 1706 and July 7, 1711 he bought 800 skins and 200 hides at a cost of £121 19s. 2d.[190]

A prominent tanner of the market town of Cowbridge was William David, whose inventory shows that at his death he possessed:

	£	s.	d.
In his tannpitt—7 dickers of leather, being 70 hides at £4 per score	14	0	0
In his lime pits—4 dickers of skins, being 40 hides at 20s. per dicker	4	0	0
The mill and stone where the bark is ground	1	0	0
In bark	1	0	0

His total personal estate was valued at £28.[191]

In the Vale and *Blaenau* there were many local tanners who were also dependent on small-scale farming. Estance Prees, tanner of St. George's, for example, possessed 'hides and bark' valued at £18 15s. 0d., as well as livestock to the value of £4 11s. 0d. The total value of his personal estate was put at £34 17s. 3d.[192] Again, Adrian Briant, tanner of Llangynwyd, possessed '30 hides in his tanhouse' valued at £7 10s., whereas his livestock was valued at £15 10s.[193]

Local tanners made great demands upon the local supplies of oak bark. For example, in 1730, Walter Coffin bought eight and a half tons of bark at 3s. 6d. per ton from the Margam estate.[194] By 1738, it appears that the price of bark had advanced considerably, for in that year a certain Thomas Lewis had contracted to pay Thomas Mansel of Margam, 25s. a ton 'for bark fallen in this barking season on his estate' (Gower excepted).[195] The following is an account[196] of the quantities of bark bought of the Lord Mansel of Margam by Mr. Philip Prichard in the same year, 1738:

	£	s.	d.
4½ tons of bark that was stript att S. Mary Church in the year 1736 and wayd in yᵉ year 1738 att £1 5s 0d per ton or 1s 3d per hundred	5	12	6
Also for 6½ tuns and 4 hundred that was stript in the years 1736 and 1737 att the same rate	8	7	6
Also for 28 tunns 5 hundred & 18 pounds that was stript and wayd in yᵉ year 1738 att the same rate	35	7	0½
Also for one ton of timber had from Penllwin Evangwent in ye year 1738	1	10	0
	£50	17	0½

In addition to local demands for oak bark, limited quantities were exported from Glamorgan to the West of England. Between 1728 and 1767 a total of 1,816 tons of oak bark was exported from Cardiff alone.

The products of the Glamorgan tanneries are well attested in the records of its coasting trade. Tanned hides were sent regularly from Newton and Aberthaw to Minehead and Bristol. On May 8, 1634, for instance, the *Speedwell* of Newton sailed for Bristol with a cargo partly made up of '23 dicker of curried leather, and eleven bundles containing eighteen hundreds of white leather'.[197] But the exports of raw hides were on a much more considerable scale than those of tanned hides. There were, too, instances of leather being imported from Bristol to Aberthaw and other places. The *Jane* of Aberthaw arrived from Minehead on September 13, 1662, with '14 bands of tanned leather' and 'half a dozen red leather skins'. And on September 26 in the same year the *Margaret* of Newton arrived in Newton bay with 'five hundred weight of tan'd leather'.[198] This was probably leather of a special quality which could be manufactured more cheaply in the West of England.

Closely related to the trade of the tanner was that of the cordwainers and glovers, whose products were supplied to local and external markets. More often than not these trades were carried on in conjunction with small-scale farming. For instance, William Rees of Pile and Kenfig, cordwainer, besides his small pieces of leather (£1), implements belonging to his trade (4s.), and 'seven paires of shooes' (at 2s. per pair), possessed 1 cow, 1 horse, ewes and lambs, grain and corn.[199] But Richard Thomas of Kenfig, cordwainer, was apparently engaged wholly in his trade. His inventory included a stock of leather (£5 3s. 4d.), his implements 'for yᵉ trade' (2s. 6d.), his 'steale heampe' (5s. 4d.), his stock of pitch (2s. 8d.) and '6 pare of ready made shoes' (8s. 8d.).[200] According to the 'prisers' of the above inventories, a pair of shoes in the parish of Pile and Kenfig cost between 1s. 4d. and 2s., and these prices seem to have remained fairly steady for many years. Valuers of the goods of another cordwainer, Lewis William of Merthyr Tydfil, in 1749 assessed '14 pairs of shoes ready made in his shop of different sizes' at 34*s*.,[201] or approximately 2*s*. 6*d*. a pair.

The inventories of the period provide ample evidence of the work of the glovers. Although mostly concentrated in the towns, there were numerous glovers to be found in the purely rural villages and townships of Glamorgan. In Llantwit Major we have evidence of the domestic system as applied to the trade of glover. John Morgan, glover of that parish, bequeathed to his son David Morgan, 'the too (*sic*) paire of loumes which is in the shop loft and one halfe of the slaies . . . ' and to his son Jenkin Morgan, '1 paire of loomes which is in William Philpots shop and the other haulfe of the slaies' and the 'shuttles, temples and other implements' he divided between the two sons. His 'leather and pelts' were worth £2, and his '3 paire of loumes and slaies' etc. were worth £2 13*s*. 4*d*. He also had 1 pig, 1 horse, an acre and a half of barley, and 1 acre of peas.[202]

The shoes and gloves made by the cordwainers and glovers were sold locally in the village shop, in the towns, and also exported for sale in the West of England. Shoes appear very infrequently in the trade records, but substantial quantities of gloves are often accounted for. The *Elizabeth* of Aberthaw, to mention but one example, sailed for Minehead on January 20, 1682 with 'a trusse of cordufin (i.e. cordovan) gloves' as part of the cargo. These gloves had been made from cordovan, or 'tanned horse leather'.[203]

Closely allied with tanning was the process of 'tawing', that is, whitening skins and dressing white leather. James Roberts of Laleston,[204] described as a 'tawer', was one of many who were engaged in the process of whitening skins, with their stocks of alum and salt, which were readily available in many of the village shops. John Thomas, a shopkeeper of Laleston, for example, had a stock of alum which was probably sold at 1*s*. per lb. in 1710.[205]

KELP AND SOAP ASHES

During the pre-industrial period, many of the inhabitants of Glamorgan, when not employed in work relating to food production, or in the traditional industries of the countryside, found part-time employment in those small enterprises which grew up in response to new economic opportunities afforded by the Bristol and West of England markets.

The Welsh port books, and those of Bridgwater and Minehead, show that throughout the seventeenth and early-eighteenth centuries, varying quantities of 'kelp' (or 'kilp') were exported to Bristol from the small ports of Sully and Aberthaw. 'Kelp' was the calcinised ashes of seaweed extensively used in the manufacture of coarse glass bottles, which were in great demand in Bristol during the seventeenth century for the export of beer, cider, perry etc.[206] One of Edward Lhuyd's correspondents, *circa* 1696, stated that Sully afforded 'sea ore which is converted into kelp transported to Bristol for yᵉ use of Glasshouses'.[207] In this connection it should be realized that it required about twenty tons of seaweed (sea-ore) to produce one ton of kelp. So that when the *William and Margarett* of Aberthaw sailed to Bristol on October 29, 1693,[208] with 4 tons of kelp, it meant that at least 80 tons of seaweed had been collected and burnt to produce that quantity of kelp. These preliminary operations, no doubt, required the employment of many hands.

Locally, the glassworks at Swansea must have required considerable quantities of kelp. We find that in the year 1686, that part of Swansea castle which 'had been lately converted' for use as a glass works was taken over by John Maun who, henceforth, had the control of the '. . . working tooles and instruments, potts, utensils, ashes, kilpes and other such like materialls belonging to the grade of Glasswerke' in consideration that he should render and deliver unto his previous partner Robert Wilmott, gentleman, of Gloucester, '35 gross of good, sufficient and merchandisable bottles . . . ' in a manner as not to exceed 4 gross bottles by the week or in any one week.[209]

Kelp belonged to the lord of the manor,[210] and as late as 1770 it was 'an object of emolument to the landholders' and furnished employment at certain seasons for many of the peasants living on the sea coast.[211] Around the coast of Swansea Bay in 1748, seaweed was allowed to be collected and gathered by persons other than burgesses, in return for which 'they have, when required, with themselves, their servants and cattle, gathered and carried stones up to the beach where wanted to defend the open and unenclosed ground'.[212] The seaweed thus gathered was probably used either as manure, or sold to local soap makers; men like Griffith Jenkins, a merchant of the town of Swansea who, in 1690, manufactured his own soap in the 'soap house' for which he held a 'coal lease'. When he died, his personal estate was valued at £221 11s. 0d., of which £99 10s. 0d. was in 'ready money'.[213] He must have been one of the very early pioneers of soap manufacturing, for more than a century afterwards it was observed that some works for the manufacture of soap 'had been recently erected in the neighbourhood of Swansea'.[214]

In the same category as kelp were ringo roots [215] which were gathered by local peasant folk in large quantities along the sea coast and exported to Bristol from the small ports of Newton, Sully, and Aberthaw.[216] The roots, which were gathered along the seashore at Baglan and Aberavon, were 'accounted in London as good if not the best of any sent there'.[217] It is not easy to establish the monetary value of these roots, but the inventory of Evan Kerry of Swansea, who died in 1666, shows that he possessed a hundred and fifty ringo roots which were valued at 10s.[218] According to John Gerarde, the intrinsic value of the ringo root lay in its many medicinal qualities or 'virtues'. The leaves, when 'kept in pickle and eaten in sallads with oile and vinegar', made a pleasant sauce for meat, 'wholesome for the stoppings of the liver, milt, kidnies and bladder'.[219] At the beginning of the seventeenth century they were candied at a Colchester factory by an Englishman named Robert Burton, who 'produced on a large scale aphrodisiacs compounded of ringo roots or sea holly'.[220]

Another plant which grew 'in great plenty' along the Glamorgan coasts, and which was gathered for the market by many of the local inhabitants, was the *Crithmum maritimum*, or rock samphire. During his tour of the neighbourhood in 1798, Richard Warner learned of 'a hazardous practice[221] common among the inhabitants of the villages of the sea coast of Glamorgan near Llantwit Major in proper season' (June to August) namely, 'the gathering of *Crithmum maritimum*'.[222] This 'object of profit' helped to supplement the earnings of many of the inhabitants, who sold it for use in pickling.

Again, 'fern-burning' became a profitable source of employment in many areas, as the demands of the expanding soap industry increased. Some of the cargoes carried from the port of Aberthaw to Bristol included soap ashes. On October 29, 1693, the *William and Margarett* of Aberthaw carried '400 strikes of sope-ashes' to Bristol, and on November 14, 1720, the *Fonmon* of Aberthaw sailed with 'one tunn of ash' to the same destination.[223] A common source of alkali for both soap-making and glass-making industries of the eighteenth century was obtained from plant ashes. In 1753 John Tyrer, a soap boiler from as far afield as Priscot in Lancashire, was granted permission 'to cut and burn fern at Keven Drim, Coppavach, Brinbach, Graigvawr and Gelliwastad . . . Commons' in west Glamorgan.[224] All these small undertakings in the countryside show how sensitive were the inhabitants of Glamorgan to the economic opportunities afforded them by the requirements of the English manufactories at Bristol and elsewhere during the seventeenth and eighteenth centuries.

The rural activities we have discussed in this section were subsidiary to agriculture, yet the rewards they brought to many of those engaged in them, however small, often supplemented their earnings from the land. To what extent crises of subsistence were thus averted is a subject upon which we can only speculate.[225]

v.

INLAND AND COASTAL TRADE

We have already discussed the nature of the pastoral-agricultural economy of Glamorgan during the period 1660–1760, the livestock the peasants reared, the crops they grew and harvested, the tools and implements they employed in alliance with Nature in order to achieve their economic ends. But production was, in fact, a prelude to the process of distribution

—the exchange and selling of goods and services. How, then, were the ordinary everyday business affairs of the countryside transacted in pre-industrial Glamorgan, and through what channels were they directed?

Although there was still a considerable degree of subsistence farming among the poorer peasants, there were, nevertheless, clear indications that 'commercial agriculture' was gaining momentum. Indeed, the break-up of the old manorial ties and restrictions had encouraged commercial farming in Glamorgan since Elizabethan times, and with the growth and development of the port of Bristol, the commercial activities of the county became more conspicuously orientated to the West of England markets. Yet it would seem that the poor peasantry and cottagers still thought, not so much in terms of what they could buy with money, but of what they could grow and make for themselves. It may be said of the Glamorgan peasant, as of his English counterpart, that he 'did not work simply for money: he worked so as to avoid, as far as possible, the need for money'.[226]

It is probable that the wages of agricultural labourers, or cottagers, were still paid mainly in kind, but it is difficult to establish how far there were money payments, and to what extent there was payment in kind, or even in exchange of services. There is evidence of all three methods operating in Glamorgan, in much the same way as in Leicestershire[227] during an earlier period. Even in 1741, wages due to non-agricultural workers in the Neath and Briton Ferry areas were often paid in goods.[228]

MARKETS AND THE USE OF MONEY

In the sixteenth century there were at least 28 weekly markets and periodic fairs in Glamorgan.[229] In 1692 there were 45,[230] and by 1760 there were, apparently, 60.[231] It is interesting to observe that several of these fairs were held on Church festivals, and even on Sundays. For instance, the Whitsun Fair at Llandaff was held from the Saturday to Tuesday of Whitsuntide, and a market was held every Sunday. The Llandaff Fair was suppressed about the year 1880, owing to the rowdyism which prevailed there on Whit Monday. It had degenerated into a mere pleasure-fair with the usual booths, tents, roundabouts, and swing-boats.[232] Professor A. H. Dodd has estimated that in the seventeenth century there was a fair or market somewhere or other in Wales about four days out of every seven.[233] The increase in the number of these distributive agencies may be attributed to the expansion of a 'money economy' in the limited context of an increase in the relative volume of money payments made within the sphere of local distribution of goods. In a wider context, Professor M. M. Postan has suggested that the so-called 'money economy', in the true sense of the term, depended for its development 'not so much on a general increase in production as on those subtler historical changes which led men away from domestic self-sufficiency and directed them towards shops and market places'.[234] But in all probability all except the bigger farmers depended heavily on the immediate sale of their surplus goods in the weekly markets, if only to obtain ready money for the payment of taxes and rents. The weekly markets were held almost exclusively for the sale of foodstuffs which obviously pre-supposed the use of money. The same was true of the periodic fairs. We have already noted how the March Fair had been established in Cowbridge by John Franklin with a view to providing the local farmers with an opportunity of raising cash to pay their Lady Day rents (above, pp. 341–2).[235] It is certainly true to say that 'what the local market was to the husbandman each week, the regional fair was each year'.[236]

Money was also necessary to purchase goods which fell outside the compass of home production. It may be said that in Glamorgan, as in other parts of the country, 'production was largely for subsistence, and only small surpluses were brought to the local market towns for sale. Yet, these small surpluses converted into rent and tithe formed the economic basis of the ruling class and the support of the Established Church.'[237]

The impression is sometimes conveyed in works on economic history that only large farms—by which perhaps may be meant farms regularly dependent on hired labour for their cultivation—yielded an excess of products for the markets. Such a view is, however, inconsistent with the evidence given here, and it does not in any case follow from any correct economic principles. Any product of a farm, however small, not directly required for consumption by the farmer or his family, may reach the market, though it does not represent any net revenue as profit or rent for the producer. What he purchases with the proceeds of selling may represent his 'real' wages, or at least part of them. The large farmer could often afford to store the products of his holding, and sell in the market when prices were high. In contrast, the small farmer depended to a great extent upon the immediate selling of his products and, consequently, these would reach the market more frequently than the products of the large farmers.

Almost every village in the county had its shop, and the range of articles offered to the inhabitants was quite remarkable. The list of goods which John Thomas, shopkeeper of the parish of Laleston, possessed at the time of his death in 1710 is typical, and worth mentioning, more particularly because the population of the whole parish at that date cannot have been above 350, and of this total at least 120 persons would have been classed as paupers to whom the shop goods would have been, without a doubt, beyond their means. For instance, he sold shalloon (a woollen material chiefly used for linings) at 12d. per yard; damask stuff at 16d. per yard; worsted stuff at 6d. per yard; serges at 15d. per yard; broad coloured linen at 8d. per yard; coloured dimity (stout cotton cloth woven with stripes and figures) at 10d. per yard; plush at

2*s*. 6*d*. per yard; blue broad calico at 18*d*. per yard; crepe at 10*d*. per yard; etc. In addition there were earthenware, wick-yarn, tar, nails, candlesticks, knives and scissors, and 'Manchester goods such as buttons, thread, mohair and inkle-tape'. A significant item in the inventory was described as 'fresh goods bought at St. Paul's faire in Bristol and not sold or disposed of at ye time of ye deceadents death as appeared by ye notes of his severall correspondents att Bristoll' which were valued at £94 1*s*. 0*d*. The total value of the inventory was £193 2*s*. 2½*d*.[238]

Again, in the parish of St. Andrews, Walter Hart, described as a blacksmith, died in 1696 worth £220 1*s*. 4¾*d*.[239] But besides being a blacksmith, he was also a farmer, and kept a shop. He owned 4 milch cows and 3 yearlings, corn worth £5, 16 sheep, 5 pigs, 1 horse and a mare. He had 7 stones of cheese at 3*s*. per stone, and a firkin of butter worth 16*s*., as well as 2 stones of wool. In his shop he sold fustian, German hollands, broad dowlas, 'Oxenbrigge', kerseys, knives, combs, looking glasses, white sugar at 8*d*. per lb., currants at 5*d*. per lb., 'Malligoe (Malaga) raisons' at 4*d*. per lb., starch, copperas, oil and aniseed water. His inventory was valued at £220 1*s*. 4*d*., but his shop goods amounted to £40 5*s*. 0*d*., while his desperate debts were £39 7*s*. 7*d*.

Besides the small village shops were those located in the market towns of Swansea, Neath, Cardiff, Cowbridge, and Llantrisant which, taken together, formed a net-work of distributive centres offering an incredibly wide range and variety of goods and commodities within the county's preponderantly agrarian economy. At these centres, business was, with few exceptions, transacted on a cash basis.

We must not, however, overlook the itinerant 'Scotchmen' or pedlar merchants in this context. They were, indeed, familiar figures in pre-industrial Glamorgan, carrying in their packs a variety of wares, including gloves, pins, combs, hooks, etc., sometimes brought over on coasting ships from Bristol. For instance, on November 24, 1720, the *Blessing* of Aberthaw carried, as part of its cargo to Minehead, 'one pack of Scotchman's goods'.[240] It was through these itinerant Scotchmen that many sophisticated items of consumption found their way into the humblest cottage in the Glamorgan hills and vale. Like the local tradesmen, they, too, required cash for their wares, but were often compelled to give credit. For example, when Richard David, of Gallcwm, Margam, died in March 1700, he owed 'to a Scotchman' the sum of 13*s*.[241]

It seems fairly clear that there were larger sums of 'ready money' in the possession of Glamorgan testators after about 1700 than previously. These sums obviously varied considerably between one social group and another, and, indeed, between members of the same social stratum, but the proportions of ready money to total wealth were often quite striking. Ann Pranch, of Peterston-super-Ely, who died in 1716 worth £315, possessed £200 in ready money,[242] while Mary Howell, spinster, of Llanwynno, was worth £16, of which £12 was in 'ready cash'.[243]

Again Edward Gamage, archdeacon of Llandaff and rector of Coychurch, who died in 1685, was equipped materially in much the same way as a gentleman farmer, even down to his 'timber vessels for brewing' and was worth £495. Of this sum £100 was in ready money, and £200 was owing to him 'by bond'.[244] David Price, M.A., one of the prebendaries of the cathedral church of Llandaff 'and vicar choral there', was also conscious of the growing importance of money in 'matters temperal', for of his total personal wealth of £109 15s., he had £65 14s. put aside 'in money and gold'.[245] One of the outstanding sums of ready money we have noted was that of £969 3s. 0d. held by Blanche Robothom, a widow of the town of Cardiff, whose total inventory was valued in 1734 at £2,291 14s., but her debts amounted to £1,270.[246]

The complications of 'commercial agriculture' must have compelled many Glamorgan farmers and small business men to seek professional assistance in the management of their affairs. One of the claims on the estate of Thomas Richards, of Waterton in Llancarfan, was a debt 'to an accountant' for '6 years wages at £10 a year'.[247]

The floating of the National Debt in 1693, by opening up a vast new field of investment[248] must have eventually changed the attitude of the humblest folk no less than the mercantile and financial classes towards the use of money. To some, 'interest' was looked upon as a form of 'rent', paid for the loan of money, and these terms were often interchanged in wills. To put money 'out on rent' became fashionable with all and sundry. We have innumerable examples of individuals, like Mary Thomas, widow, of St. Hilary, who left a gross personal estate valued at £103 10s., of which £100 was 'upon interest'. Yet her wearing apparel and all her linen was worth only £2, while the rest of her belongings, worth a mere £1 10s. 0d. consisted of simply 'one sheet, one feather bed wth its appurtenances, one iron crock, one little brass pan and one chair'.[249] Again, in 1699, Jenkin John, yeoman of Coychurch, died leaving personal estate worth £132, of which £111 was 'in money upon interest',[250] while Llewellin Robert, yeoman of the near-by parish of Pendoylan, who had 7 sons and 1 daughter, died in 1703 worth £263 10s., but £200 of this sum was 'upon interest'.[251]

It is interesting to observe that from about 1700 onwards, there seems to have been a growing tendency among testators to bequeath the interest accruing from money either already invested, or to be invested. Thomas David, yeoman of St. Brides Major, died in 1723 leaving to his wife £5 per annum to be paid quarterly out of 'the rent or interest of £100'.[252] How different was this testator's bequest to the more conventional bequests in kind,—livestock, furniture, agricultural implements, etc! It was, indeed, a far cry from the outlook on life held by Thomas Johns, a farmer-mariner of Gileston who died in 1595, having charged his executors to dispose of his bedstead 'and with the price thereof to buy sheep and the sheep to be sett to increase' for his grandsons.[253] Or, indeed, the provisions made on a more grandiose scale by Sir John Herbert, Principal Secretary to His Majesty James I, who held lands in Swansea, Llangennith, Rhosili, Llanmadog, Penmaen, Llangyfelach, Cheriton, Penrice, Llanrhidian, Bishopston, Oystermouth, Llansamlet, and Ilston, which he 'did reserve and keep undisposed to be sold to the best advantage towardes the payment of my debts, legacies for preferment of my grandchildren, rewards and annuities to my servants, my funeral expenses etc'.[254] But even in 1705 there were still many testators like George Thomas, a labourer of Roath, who died worth £15, having bequeathed 'a rick of hay towards the reparation of the house'.[255]

Debts were usually divided into two categories, namely 'sperate' which afforded some prospect of being recovered, and 'desperate' which did not. However, it is impossible to establish any degree of correlation between 'good' and 'bad' debts, and their proportions varied to such an extent from one inventory to another, that to work out an average proportion of 'sperate' to 'desperate' debts would be rather futile.[256] It may be true to say, however, that debts, in general, were relatively larger in the semi-urban areas of Swansea, Neath and Cardiff, than they appear to have been in the purely rural areas, and possibly merchants and tradesmen in the towns stood to carry more 'bad' debts than farmers and village shop-keepers.

The 'debts' we have discussed were probably 'deferred payments' for goods sold to the customers or dealers at the town shops or at local fairs and markets. For instance, Rhys Lewis of Cogan, who died in 1696, bequeathed unto his nephew John David the sum of £5 that was 'to be paid unto him as soon as my executrix is satisfied of a debt due unto me from dealers over in Somersetshire or elsewhere in England'.[257] But sometimes it became necessary to obtain a short-term loan to settle some of the larger debts, particularly when creditors insisted on prompt payment. This may have been the case with Edward Lewis, of Cottrell in the parish of Bonvilston, whose gross personal estate, when he died in 1683, was valued at £342 16s. 4d. Debts due to him amounted to £135, but the debts he owed were £329 18s. 0d., which included £18 for the 'use of £300 for one year'[258]—that is, at a rate of interest of 6 per cent. 'Credit' was not a new feature of the agricultural economy of the county. Business transactions in Glamorgan had been conducted along much the same lines as in England, where the granting of 'credit' had been a common business procedure since medieval times.[259]

From this necessarily brief discussion on 'debts', the general picture that emerges shows that the 'cash-nexus' had already taken deep root in the agrarian economy of Glamorgan, and must have contributed to the accentuation of the feeling of otherness between rich and poor, for the old adage, 'the rich lend, the poor borrow', was clearly reflected in the contemporary wills and inventories. We see, possibly, in the debts of large sections of the population a manifestation of the breaking up of the self-sufficiency of local markets and, perhaps, the growing commercialization of the economic activities of the Glamorgan countryside. Such manifestations appear to have coincided with the growth of the trade with Bristol and the West of England, and with the growth of 'heavy' industry locally.

It is worth observing here that the Exchequer King's Remembrancer Port Books disclose that large sums of money were, from time to time, accounted for in the 'coquets' issued to masters of vessels carrying cargoes from Glamorgan to Minehead, and Bristol in particular. For instance, on January 23, 1666, the *Speedwell* of Cardiff had, as part of its cargo for Bristol, '800 pounds in money'. On May 31 following, the *Lyon* of Cardiff sailed with '4000 pounds in money for Bristoll'. Later in the same year, on November 6, we find the *Mayflower* of Cardiff bound for Bristol with '2,000 pounds in money'.[260] Again, on July 10, 1675, the master of the *Anne* of Newton had '1,300 pounds of money' entered as part of his cargo for Minehead.[261] On November 10, 1679, the *Elizabeth* of Aberthaw crossed to Minehead with 'baggs of money containing £90',[262] and on July 23, 1683, the *William* of Aberthaw set out for Bristol with '500 pounds in money'.[263] It is also recorded that Lord Mansel of Margam despatched 300 pounds in money by boat to Bristol in 1661.[264] These sums of money were, undoubtedly, in respect of debts incurred by Glamorgan merchants and other customers in the West of England. It may be argued, from the evidence submitted, that the seventeenth-century masters of the Glamorgan coasting vessels transacted business in Bristol in much the same way as the north Wales drovers—the so-called 'Spanish Fleet of Wales'—who acted as 'agents for the transmission of large sums to London, whether for private or for public purposes'.[265] From the evidence we have examined, it seems quite clear that during the period under review money was becoming increasingly a unit of account, a medium of transactions, and a store of value within the agrarian economy of the county.

EXPORTS

As we have already seen (above, pp. 59–60), sixteenth-century observers listed some twenty ports, havens and creeks at various points along the Glamorgan coast between Cardiff and Loughor. Six of these were situated within the more limited stretch of coastline that skirted the Vale of Glamorgan, namely Ely, Sully, Barry, Aberthaw, Ogmore and Newton. 'In all this coaste of Kardyff and Glamorganshier', states an early-Elizabethan document, 'is grete ladying of butter and cheese and other provysion partely into other shiers of Wales where lacke is thereof and partely into Devon and Cornewall and other places. And here goeth a& muche lether and tallowe to the shippes of Bristoll and so fourthe overseas . . . '.[266] When Defoe visited Glamorgan, almost

150 years later, he observed that 'the low grounds were so well cover'd with grass and stock'd with cattle that they supply the city of Bristol with butter in very great quantities salted and barrell'd up just as Suffolk does the city of London'.[267]

Since Elizabethan times, the ports of Glamorgan, particularly those situated along the coast of the Vale, had provided an outlet through which the surplus products of their pastoral-agricultural hinterland could reach the Bristol and other West of England markets. Fortunately we have in the extant port books, despite their many deficiencies, a general record of the cross-channel trade between Glamorgan and the West of England for the greater part of our period.[268] These records present a picture of an agrarian society producing goods, not only for the local markets, but also for the markets of the West of England. It does not follow, however, that every small farmer in the county afforded surplus products to be sent coastwise. Proximity to the English markets not only provided additional chances and opportunities to sell the surplus farm products that came from the Glamorgan countryside, but also served to keep prices above the level that would have prevailed if 'demand' had been limited to the local markets.

At this point it should be explained that to conceive of a market simply in terms of a local centre for buying and selling of goods and articles may be quite misleading, and in the commercial links between Glamorgan and Bristol in the seventeenth and eighteenth centuries we see a reflection of the wider significance of the term. It has been said that 'no definite area can be assigned as large enough or small enough for a market. A local community, a city, a province may be a market'.[269] The final consideration in defining the extent of an effective market turns around the level of prevailing prices, and the demand of the Bristol market certainly kept prices at a favourable level for the Glamorgan farmers. 'London affects the price of meat everywhere', remarked Arthur Young, 'and though veal and butter were cheap in Wales', he continued, 'yet the prices of them were by no means those which arose from home consumption alone, as I plainly perceived by the great quantities of provisions brought up in all the little ports of the Severn by the Bristol market boats'.[270]

From the fifteenth century, and even earlier,[271] the Welsh store-cattle trade with England had been steady and on an extensive scale, in which the Welsh drovers acted as trading agents with London business houses as well as discharging their primary duties as selling-agents for stock.[272] Glamorgan cattle were either driven on the hoof from local fairs to the English markets at Barnet and Smithfield, and elsewhere, or to the local ports such as Cardiff and Aberthaw, whence they were shipped to Bristol and Minehead, or to Sully where they were sent to Uphill[273] near Weston-super-Mare, and then driven overland to Bristol, Bath, Exeter, and sometimes as far south as Plymouth and Portsmouth[274] in order to be fattened.

There were many cattle fairs in the county, and one of the most famous of the livestock fairs was held annually on August 26 at St. Mary Hill, standing about four miles north of Bridgend. Cattle, sheep and horses were brought here in large numbers from the neighbouring farms, and then sold to dealers who came from all parts of the country. Then the local drovers—men like Walter Edwards of Ystradyfodwg—would be engaged to drive the cattle to England, journeying there *via* Aberdare and Merthyr, and then across the Brecon Beacons and into Hereford. Another important cattle fair in the seventeenth and eighteenth centuries was *Marchnad-y-waun*, near Merthyr Tydfil, which stood hard by a place called Waun Newydd where extensive grazing took place. Llantrisant fair was another important centre for the sale of cattle from the upland parishes of Llanwynno and Ystradyfodwg. Other cattle fairs of note were held at Penrice, in the Gower peninsula, at Neath, Cowbridge, and Llandaff, near Cardiff where, in 1768, Arthur Young recorded that he 'met such numbers of butchers with calves that I inquired if that little town could consume such a quantity of veal (it was market day); they told me the boats were ready in the river to buy for Bristol'.[275]

As already stated, large numbers of Glamorgan cattle were sent coastwise to the West of England. In this regard the Welsh 'port books' reveal an aspect of the south Wales cattle trade which has been generally overlooked. Miss Skeel referred to the conveyance of cattle from Tenby, in Pembrokeshire, to Bridgwater, Watchet, and Minehead. She also noted that 'in 1670 a considerable number of bullocks (over 206) were shipped during January–June from Aberthaw to Minehead'.[276] In fact, over 450 bullocks were shipped from Aberthaw to Minehead during Michaelmas 1669 to Michaelmas 1670,[277] and during two previous years, 1667 and 1669, the number of bullocks shipped from Aberthaw to the same destination was 700 and 850 respectively.[278] Moreover, in 1666, at least 1,160 oxen and cows were exported from Sully to Uphill.[279] It is interesting to observe that '31 Iresh oxen and cowes' were also shipped to Minehead from Aberthaw in 1662.[280]

It has been rightly contended that the Welsh cattle trade 'furnished England with meat and Wales with money',[281] but it also furnished England with working oxen, thus enabling many English farmers to maintain a level of farming that might not have been possible without the supply of Welsh store cattle and working oxen. The inventories of some Essex farmers show that Welsh runts formed part of their stock. For example, John Mariage, who died in November 1686, had 'five Welsh runts', and Richard Horsnaile of Writtle, who died in 1690, possessed '11 little Welch runts (£14 13s. 4d.)', and '43 Welch sheep and lambs (£8 12s.)'.[282] Kent farmers, too, fattened cattle which had been brought down from the Welsh mountains to the local fairs.[283]

It may be argued that the Glamorgan cattle trade with the southern and western counties of England manifested a traditional regional agriculture interdependence, where Welsh farmers reared store cattle to be finished off into prime beasts on English pastures—a pattern of production in which modern agricultural economists would see an example of a 'vertical division of labour'.[284] Indeed, the contribution made by the hill farmers of Glamorgan to the rural economy of west and south-west England in the seventeenth and eighteenth centuries is a subject worthy of a more detailed investigation.[285] The fairly regular coastal traffic in Glamorgan livestock from Elizabethan times down to the beginning of the nineteenth century shows how closely aligned was the pastoral economy of Glamorgan to the Bristol market.[286]

In addition to the livestock, calf skins, sheep skins, goat skins, coney skins, and even dog skins frequently went coastwise to Minehead and Bristol. In 1666[287] over 3,500 hides and calf skins, 450 tanned hides, as well as several fardles of buck skins went from Cardiff alone to Bristol. Again, when the *Five Brothers* of Newton sailed for Bristol in January 1672, the cargo included 'two fardles of deere skins' and 'two fardles of conie skins'.[288] These items continued to figure prominently in the lists of cargoes leaving the Glamorgan ports until well into the eighteenth century.

Wool was exported in varying quantities from Glamorgan, and the trade records help to explain the significance of the large holdings of wool which many of the contemporary inventories disclosed. For example, Jenkin Griffith of Llangeinor, at the time of his death in 1679, had a quantity of wool valued at £9, which represented about 360 lb. of wool.[289] Llewellyn Edwards, of Ystradyfodwg, had 2,000 lb. of wool worth £50 when he died in 1688,[290] whilst William Bowen of Wick, whose inventory was made up in 1729, had £30 worth of wool, that is about 600 lb.[291] Such quantities were obviously held for commercial purposes. It seems fairly clear that some proportion of the annual wool crop would be sold direct at local fairs and markets to native consumers to be made up into cloth and into stockings. What remained was shipped across the channel to various centres such as Minehead, Bristol, Colston, Milverton, and Exeter, either through the farmer-dealer-merchant link, or direct to the clothier.[292] On October 11, 1616, the *Harte* of Aberthaw sailed to Minehead with '30 stones of Welsh wool' for Thomas Chilcott of Milverton 'a clothier'.[293]

Butter and cheese were exported in great quantities to Bristol and Somersetshire, and, as in the case of wool, the large holdings of these commodities accounted for in contemporary inventories made sense only when considered in relation to the coastal trade. It is said that Glamorgan butter stood 'highest in fame at the markets of Bristol, Bath, etc., than any other county, Welsh or English'.[294] The 'butter in casks' valued at £19, and the '88 cheeses' which Morgan David of Llantrisant had when he died in 1760, were almost certainly destined for the West Country.[295] Similarly the '4 firkins and a tub of butter' valued at £6, and the '25 stone of cheese' valued at £3 2s. 6d., belonging to William Thomas, also of the parish of Llantrisant in 1740, were for shipment to England.[296] In the earlier part of the century (1637–1639), butter was sent from Glamorgan to Rochelle and Bordeaux, the ships (the *Long Thomas* and *Jonas* of Aberthaw) returning with 'wines, salt, acquabiters and nutts'. The export of butter provided work for local coopers, and in the parish of St. Athan, for example, Richard Jones, cooper, was paid 'for the cooping and nailing of every kilderkin of butter 1 penny, and for standing of every such kilderkin in the cellars before the shipping, 1d.' There were, apparently, about 12 cellars at Aberthaw, traditionally known as the Booth Cellars, which were used for the 'cellarage of wines, salt, and other goods as were brought home and landed . . . '.[297] In passing, it should be noted that although some of the trade was illegal, it provided work for the local people, who certainly benefited from the casual earnings they received for unloading and hauling contraband cargoes ashore, and stocking them in the cellars. It was said that as many as thirty persons were employed at a time on this work at Aberthaw. On one occasion it was stated that about twenty men and about twelve women were employed for about nine days 'for the unloading of the *Long Thomas* of Aberthaw (burthen 80 tons), and the carrying of salt to the house of George Savour, for all of which time there was VI^d a day paide to every of the men and 4^d to every woman . . . '.[298]

A full account of exports from the ports and creeks of Glamorgan during our period of study would require a separate volume. Sufficient has been said, however, to present a qualitative account of the principal agricultural exports from Glamorgan to the West of England. They consisted of the surplus products of the pastoral-agricultural hinterland, as well as the products of the rural industries. In fact, the evidence examined shows that the commercial activities of the eastern part of Glamorgan between 1666 and 1730 were very similar in character to what they had been in Elizabethan times. But this was in sharp contrast to the state of commerce in the rest of Wales, for 'of the total outward sailings from Welsh ports in 1688, both on coasting and foreign sides' it has been estimated that on a general average 'about 90 per cent were coal shipments'.[299] If, as has been contended, the pre-eminence of Welsh coal was the chief *raison d'être* of Welsh maritime activity in 1688, this was certainly not true of that stretch of coastline between Cardiff and Newton. Nevertheless, the port books show that farther west along the Glamorgan coastline there was a fairly regular export of coal from Swansea, Neath, Briton Ferry, and, to a lesser extent, Newton, during our period. This was only to be expected, for it was a reflection of the groundswell of industrial enterprises, which we shall discuss presently.

Most of the coal and culm exports went in English bottoms. The *John, Betty*, and *Primrose*, of Minehead; the *Marygold, Swift, Endeavour,*

Truelove, Mayflower and *Lyon* of Watchet; the *Samaritan* of Bridgwater; the *Exchange* of Porlock and the *Blessing* of Ilfracombe sailed constantly from Neath and Swansea, carrying from between 10 and 34 chaldrons of coals at a time. Most of the coal produced in Glamorgan was probably sent coastwise, as was the coal and culm sold from the customary lands of Thomas Price of Trewyddfa, near Swansea. Between September 1732 and September 1733, of the total of 194 weys of coal and culm produced at Trewyddfa, 28 weys only were 'sold at the pit', while 166 weys were 'sold to sea'.[300]

Out-going cargoes sometimes included quantities of lead and iron ore. On November 6, 1666, the *Mayflower* of Cardiff sailed for Bristol with 6 tons of lead ore on board, while on November 20 the *Lyon* of Cardiff carried 12 tons of the ore to the same destination.[301] Similarly, in July 1680 the *Speedwell* of Newton sailed to Bristol with 12 tons of lead ore, as well as 2 tons of freestone. Such exports, however, were very rare. But it should be noted that local supplies of lead were limited, and the local efforts to win the ore were short-lived.

IMPORTS

In-coming cargoes from the West of England to the ports of Glamorgan invariably included some of the following goods: broadcloth, serges, kerseys, canvas, mercery ware, leather, 'sacke', Spanish wine, tobacco, perfumes, oil, pitch, rosin, soap, oxbows, reap-hooks, shovels, earthenware, salt, fruit, etc. For example, on June 9, 1662, the *Elizabeth and Jane* of Aberthaw arrived from Minehead with '4 hogsheads of French wine, 9 pieces of serge, one broadcloth, one piece of kersey'. Again, on September 26, 1662, the *Margaret* of Newton left Minehead with '3 packs of mercery wares, 1 pack of candle wax, 4 pockets containing 8 pieces of lockrams, and a truss containing 6 serges, five hundred-weight of tan'd leather, 3 rolls cont. 250 ells of Vittry and Hall canvas'.[302] On February 11, 1700, the *William* of Aberthaw returned from Bristol loaded, *inter alia*, with 108 hides and bends of leather, ½ ton of soap, 40 trusses of linen, 10 dozen sieves, 200 shot, 2 baskets of tobacco pipes, and earthen ware, 2 dozen chairs, 12 runlets of oil, brandy and vinegar, 1 bag of cordage, 2 hundredweight of pitch and rosin, 1 tun of grocery, 3 hampers of Spanish wine, 10 bags of tobacco containing 1,821 pounds.[303]

The goods imported into Glamorgan eventually found their way to the shops in the villages and market towns, and they are reflected in dozens of shop inventories of our period. It was principally through these distributive centres that all those who could afford them acquired the most sophisticated articles of consumption that the Bristol market could offer. The multifarious items which were imported into Glamorgan from the West of England signalled the growing needs of certain sections of an agrarian society which was closely geared to the West of England. Perfumes and powders, which were held in high esteem in the seventeenth century, may have represented the personal requirements of the more well-to-do classes of the community in much the same way as did brandy, 'sacke', Spanish wine[304] and tobacco. Woollen cloths, such as bays, Dunsters, Barnstaples, Bridgwaters, serges and kerseys, probably represented the needs of the rising middle classes in the matter of dress and costume. It has been argued that it was the gentry and the well-to-do who obtained 'every article of consumption both in and out of the house' from Bristol—the Welsh metropolis.[305] But the importation of 'lockrams', 'dowlas' and 'Vittry canvas' suggests that the poorer classes also benefited from the Bristol trade. Lockrams were pieces of coarse, loosely woven, linen fabrics of various qualities used in making shirts, neck wear etc. for the poorer sections of the community. In the seventeenth century, 'dowlas' was another coarse linen fabric used by the poorer people for making shirts and aprons.[306]

The ramifications of the trade of the ports and creeks of Glamorgan are a positive warning against regarding the county as an isolated and self-sufficing community. The evidence of the port books and that of the probate inventories reveal a circulation of commerce with 'an influence far beyond the ports from which or to which goods were shipped'.[307]

In the final analysis, however, it must be emphasized that agriculture and its ancillary occupations still remained the economic foundation of society in Glamorgan during our period. Most of the people who participated in industry and commerce had a direct interest in agriculture. Moreover, it is clear that behind the activities of the ports and creeks were groups of men who, together, formed a complex organization which served both the agricultural hinterland and the small, but scattered, local industrial ventures. But, as we shall show, agriculture remained their sheet anchor.

vi.

THE GROUNDSWELL OF INDUSTRY 1660–1760

The word 'industrial' was not current in the seventeenth century.[308] Even in the early decades of the nineteenth century, the terms generally used in published and unpublished writings relating to Wales to describe the organization by which raw materials were converted into more elaborate articles for sale were 'works' and 'manufactories'.[309] Consequently, when we apply the term 'industry' during our period 'we must rid our imagination of the accretions of two centuries that have associated it with urban life, with a clear division of capital in the shape of factories, plant, and machinery . . . '.[310]

Although our period falls outside the normally recognized stages of 'industrialization',[311] we shall see that throughout the century that preceded the year 1760, numerous small-scale 'works' and 'manufactories' had been established in many areas of the county, more particularly in the neighbourhood of Briton Ferry, Neath, and Swansea, where the unmistakable features of urban and industrial life were already discernible. The year 1760 does not, as is sometimes implied, herald the beginning of the industrialization of Glamorgan; it is merely an arbitrary date to mark a quickening of the pulse of existing industrial activities. The population of Glamorgan in 1670, as we have shown earlier, cannot have been in excess of 50,000. In 1801, it was still only 70,879, of which 7,700 persons, or nearly one in every ten, resided in the industrial neighbourhood of Merthyr, while another 6,821 resided in Swansea, and a mere 1,870 in Cardiff. But by 1851, the population total stood at 231,849, and by 1901 it had reached a staggering total of 859,931. Looked at from another angle, we find that in 1831, 24 per cent of all the families in the county were still employed in agriculture, as compared with the 34 per cent engaged in trade, manufactures, and handicrafts.[312] But in 1891 only 2.2 per cent of the whole population was engaged in agriculture, whilst industrial occupations claimed 41.1 per cent of the people.[313] It could be argued, therefore, that in some respects the industrial 'revolution' in Glamorgan did not, in fact, take place until the nineteenth century. J. U. Nef has suggested in another context that the rise of industrialism in Great Britain may be more properly regarded as a long process extending from the middle of the sixteenth century, and culminating in the industrial state at the end of the nineteenth century 'than as a sudden phenomenon associated with the late-eighteenth and early-nineteenth centuries'.[314] However, we are at present only concerned with the impact of the growth of industry on the agrarian economy of Glamorgan during the seventeenth and eighteenth centuries.

TIMBER AND METALS

The growth of early metallurgical enterprises in Glamorgan depended almost entirely on the abundant supplies of timber that were available over large areas of the county (above, pp. 5–6, 52, 56). Rice Merrick had early drawn attention to the growing demand for timber for use in the smelting of iron. In later years, the increasing demand for timber in local smelting works gave a new value to agricultural produce, and enhanced the value of neighbouring woodlands and coppices from which charcoal could be produced for iron smelting, and pit-wood and pit-props could be cut.[315] It has been estimated that the wood from an acre of forest was required to produce three tons of iron.[316] Therefore, the presence of an iron works often resulted in the deforestation of extensive tracts of land, some of which, in turn, became accessible for agricultural use.

Forges and furnaces had been set up in many parts of the county long before 1760, including those of the Elizabethan and early-Stuart period (above, pp. 52–4). A survey of Hafod-y-porth and Margam in 1633 refers to the existence of two iron mines in the manor, one at

Bryn and the other at Cwmafan. The surrounding country was covered with timber, a feature reflected in place-names such as Forest Nant Herbert, Forest Adam, Argoed, Tewgoed, and Wernderi. The neighbourhood of Coety, near Bridgend, was also a centre of early industrial activity. When Ann Gamage of Penyrallt, in the parish of Coety, died in 1679, she had bequeathed to her son two chattel leases, one of which she described as 'situated by the gwayth irhan'[317] (i.e. *gwaith haearn*=iron works). Almost a century previously Robert Sidney had encouraged the making of iron on his estates, and in 1611 his forest of Coed-y-mwster, of about 500 acres, which stood almost adjacent to the parish of Coety, was let at 4*s.* per acre (above, p. 54). But, over half a century earlier than that, a local bard, Thomas ab Ieuan ap Rhys, had lamented the fact that there was neither shelter nor firewood available in Coed-y-mwstwr because of the iron works:

> ny chair klydwr, ynghoed mwstwr
> na phrenn ar dan, gan waith haearn.[318]

The prolific supplies of timber and coal with which Nature had favoured Glamorgan had, further, originated and fostered a considerable degree of regional economic interdependence, which is particularly manifested in the history of the Cornish copper mines.[319] For example, we find in the late-sixteenth and early-seventeenth centuries, that John Otes had received from Glamorgan 'a freight of timber and necessaries for the works' at St. Ives,[320] while timber from the same source had also been exported to the mines at St. Just 'for to bind the work'.[321] Another instance of regional interdependence may be found in the activities of Sir Humphrey Mackworth of Neath and the Company of Mines Adventurers formed in 1695 for smelting copper, and the extraction of silver out of lead ore. He 'built at great expense' in the Neath area 'a number of workhouses for smelting lead and copper ore, for extracting silver out of lead, and for making lytharge and red lead'.[322] Much of the lead ore was produced from the lead mines of Cardiganshire, and shipped in relatively large quantities to Neath,[323] where it was subsequently manufactured.

The multifarious demands on local arboriculture are again manifested in a number of contracts drawn up in 1729 between Bussy Mansel, of Margam, and the Commissioners for H.M. Navy, to deliver quantities of timber to the naval stores at Portsmouth and Plymouth.[324] The wider economic significance of such an undertaking lay in the immediate demand that arose for local labour to prepare and to convey the timber from the 'woods' to the quay side. A contract was, in fact, subsequently entered into with William Morgan Evan of Llansamlet, yeoman, 'to hall (*sic*) draw and carry the said timber' from the wood called Craigvelen to the Upper Coal Bank near White Rock in Llansamlet. These operations involved 'finding, providing and procuring a good and sufficient way or

passage through Y Vaerdre in Llangyfelach to yᵉ highway near Mel-
ynyvrane in Llansamlet and to repair the same as occasion arises'.[325]
These sundry tasks provided additional opportunities for employment,
particularly for the unskilled workers within the agricultural economy.
In this way, too, much of the 'hidden' unemployment of the countryside
was temporarily relieved. Moreover, the stripping and carrying of bark
from the felled trees, before they were carried away, were operations
in which both women and men were employed. In April 1740, on parts of
Lord Beaufort's estates, Sussi Lewis and Margarett Hopkins were each
paid 1s. for 'loading the carts with bark from St. Hillings to Swansey
Key (sic) (for) 2 days at 6d. per day'. Similarly, William Rosser and his
wife, who were employed on the same work 'with their two horses',
were paid 1s. 4d. per day.[326] Many of those who were engaged in unskilled industrial operations were also part-time agriculturalists, sometimes
employed on haulage work, for which they often used their own horses
and carts. The furnace which had been erected at Whitchurch in the
late-seventeenth century,[327] for example, had attracted local agriculturalists, who became employed as hauliers. Typical of this group was Morgan
Howell, yeoman, of Whitchurch, who, at the time of his death in 1722,
had 'money due to him for lime and for carrying coals and stones to the
furnace'.[328]

New smelting furnaces continued to be erected during the first
half of the eighteenth century, and these were often detrimental to local
agriculture. Farmers whose lands were situated near to these new enterprises frequently suffered losses because of the damage to their crops
and lands. In an account of the estate of William David of Pentyrch,
who died in 1742, it is stated that he had 'half an acre of barley in the
ground, which was grazed and trod down by the horses belonging to
the new furnace, and for that reason was not worth above 12 shillings'.[329]

The fuel requirements of the many smelting works in Glamorgan
had, by the first half of the eighteenth century, resulted in a serious
dwindling in local supplies of timber. In 1779 there were, behind Margam
house, about 'three hundred acres of woodland'.[330] But in 1759 an
indenture made out between Jane Talbot (and others) and William Coles,
of Neath, regarding the felling of timber for charcoal to be used in the
Aberafan forge, stipulated that the timber was to be cut in proper season
for barking and stripping, and that the horses carrying charcoal had to
be muzzled in such manner as that they shall not graze or browse the lands
or young growth in the woods where the said timber and wood shall be
fallen ... '.[331] The indiscriminate felling of timber belonged to the past.

An indication of the extent to which the demands of industry had
changed the face of the county by the end of the eighteenth century
is given by the Rev. Walter Davies, who observed that formerly, Glamorgan estates were sold at an inferior price 'in consequence of their being
crowded with timber', but by about 1800, the situation had so changed

'that a few straggling trees and even coppices of sapplings are to be taken at an exclusive valuation by the purchaser of an estate by auction'. The valleys lying in close proximity to the iron works had been 'stripped of their grown timber' although the more remote areas of Ystradyfodwg, Llanwynno, Glynogwr, and Llangynwyd were still heavily wooded.[332]

COAL AND METALS

Long before its adoption into the smelting processes, coal had been utilized in the burning of lime for use in local agriculture, and for domestic purposes. In the wills of the seventeenth and eighteenth centuries, home-consumed coal was always classified as either 'lime-coal' or 'fire-coal'. Hopkin Popkins, for instance, who died in 1666, owned several mines in Llansamlet and Llangyfelach, and desired that his son, David Popkins, should ensure that this wife 'shall have her fire-coal and lime-coal' from the coal works at Llangyfelach.[333] But by the second half of the seventeenth century, coal had been recognized as a valuable commercial commodity and, in consequence, a number of small capitalists had emerged who were intent on exploiting local coal deposits within the limits imposed upon them by contemporary mining techniques.[334] As early as 1642, Richard Seys, who owned Clyne Forest and Clyne Moor, obtained a grant 'for digginge of coales in Clyne Forest and elsewhere'.[335] But without a doubt, the most notable of the early industrial capitalists was Sir Humphrey Mackworth who, it is said, estimated that his coal works in Neath had brought him a return of over £40,000 between 1695 and 1705.[336]

From the early decades of the seventeenth century, many local peasant farmers as well as 'gentlemen farmers' had been gradually getting richer than their neighbours by judiciously combining agriculture with commercial and industrial activities. For instance, when John Williams, of Llanrhidian in Gower, died in 1655, he possessed lands called 'Hugh John Rise' and 'Thomas Halling' and the 'Crosse', and owned 'one halfe of the coale worked now in Kaerodyn'. He was the owner of a 'barke called the *Endeavour* of Burry and half parte of the lighter called the *William* of Burry and a littell lighter called the *Flower*', as well as 'my great boate'.[337] Much earlier in the century, Hopkin Price, of Neath, had owned lands called '*Keven Sayson Yssa*' and '*Kydynogge Vawr*', together with 'mynes and vaynes of cooles' in the parish of Llansamlet.[338] In the eastern half of the county, the inventory of the possessions of Edward Herbert of Cogan, near Penarth, a 'gentleman farmer', shows that he possessed agricultural stock valued at £76, and held 'one grant under ye Earl of Pembroke of ye coaleworks and lyme-kilnes within ye parish of Merthyr Didvill (*sic*) for 99 years'.[339] Again, William Edward, yeoman of Eglwysilan, bequeathed to his wife 'all that coale-workes, pitts, and veins of coale, together with the lime kilns and quarries of stones . . . situated . . . in a place called Tule Dowlais . . .

wth in the parish of Merthyr Tidvill'. He possessed cattle valued at £21, 2 mares, 2 young colts, 35 head of sheep, and poultry. His total personal estate was valued at £63, of which his wearing apparel accounted for £5, and his household stuff £10.[340] Griffith Roberts, of Penprisk near Coychurch, possessed 'a winde tree for the cole-pitt and coule',[341] besides his agricultural goods. In 1637 there were two coal works called Bryn-y-wrach and Bryn-y-menin, near Bridgend, from which Thomas Carne received the sum of 50s. yearly.[342] These 'works' were, apparently, still in existence in 1712, for the inventory of the goods of Edward Phillips of Llantrisant refers to 'his share and proporcon of a lease on Bryn-y-menin coalwork', which were valued at £5.[343]

Seventeenth-century mining ventures in the eastern regions of Glamorgan were probably more numerous than we have hitherto imagined. Some of these had undoubtedly attracted the attention of Andrew Yarranton[344] who, in a letter dated July 28, 1679, and addressed to an unnamed lady,[345] asked for detailed information regarding certain coal mines owned by her in order to advise her regarding the marketing of the coal and lead which were to be brought by river to Cardiff.[346] Moreover, lead was being mined in the Llantrisant area *circa* 1661, where Christopher Wright and John Nash, both 'lead-miners', subscribed 2s. and 1s. respectively, to the 'Voluntary Gift' of Charles II.[347] The ore was extracted at Cae'r Mwyn Park (which formed part of the present Higher or New Park, standing about half a mile south of Llantrisant) and Green Close. The Cae'r Mwyn project is said to have employed about eighteen to twenty miners and labourers. Again, in the eighteenth century, a valuable lead mine was worked at Tewgoed, in the parish of Llangan, and it was said that the lead work on the porch of Llanmaes House was a product of that mine.

There had been considerable prospecting for coal in the parishes of Neath and Baglan during the second half of the seventeenth century. By the year 1696, there were, in the parish of Baglan alone, 'severall veines of coale to the number of 40 at least, in which from time to time there hath beene a world of coale dig'd'.[348] During the first half of the eighteenth century, the search for coal was prosecuted with increased vigour. Between 1700 and 1740 'there were seven collieries operating at Britonferry, and sixteen more at Swansea'.[349] That the countryside was now being exploited in the interests of coalworking is instanced in the operations carried out in 1724 on the lands of Henllan, in Cadoxton-juxta-Neath, where several workmen were employed for many months 'to search for coale in a great many places and in a great many fields closed, and meadows, upon the s^d tenement'. In these operations about 'thirty holes were bored' and 'four or five pitts' were sunk, for which work the workmen were paid at the rate of from 4s. od. to 6s. od. per week.[350] In the Gower peninsula, too, the search for coal was being carried out with growing intensity.[351]

In passing, it is worth noting that the problems involved in disposing of industrial waste were already present in Glamorgan even at the beginning of the eighteenth century. In the 1730s, for example, we find John Popkins, one of the chief coal proprietors in the Swansea district, paying £1 per annum to Lord Beaufort 'for liberty to lay Rubbish near his coal works'. Similarly, Richard Lockwood enjoyed the same liberty about his coal works at Napley on payment of 10s. per annum.[352] Although these early rubbish heaps did not assume such Himalayan proportions as the tips of today, the same general indifference, apparently, obtained concerning their proximity to places of beauty and to dwelling houses. The fact that Dr. Richard Pococke could refer to Neath in 1756 as 'a small town which depends on the colliers, copper works, and great markets for cattle which are bought up here by English graziers'[353] shows clearly that 'industry' had already cast its long shadows over much of the landscape. In 1769 Sir Harbottle Grimston visited Sir Humphrey Mackworth's magnificent residence at the Gnoll, and observed that 'If I were to consider the beauty of the place abstracted from its trade and manufactory, I should condemn the copper works, the coal mines, and the different engines to get rid of superfluous water, as being too much within the view of the house, but as from hence the riches of the place are collected', he continued, 'the man who owes his support to it should look with satisfaction on the source and rather consider them as appendages on the beauty of his place than blemishes'.[354] Such an attitude surely reflected a new ethos. Mineral wealth was at a premium, and was to be sought at the expense of the countryside. The stage was set for the coming despoliation of the natural beauty of Glamorgan.

Meanwhile the intensive exploitation of the county's coal deposits to provide fuel for metal smelting had begun. The smelting of one ton of copper, for example, required about 20 tons of coals. If, then, by the end of the eighteenth century two-thirds of all the copper smelted in the kingdom were being worked in Swansea,[355] the demand for coal must have reached correspondingly high proportions. This quickening of the tempo of industrial activity in and around the town of Swansea in the eighteenth century is well attested in contemporary documents. In 1717 works were first erected upon the 'river of Swansea' (i.e. the Tawe) for the smelting of copper and lead ores. These works were situated above the town, and about two miles beyond the Extent of the Corporation, 'to which works there is every year imported several hundred tons of ore and other goods and landed upon a wharf . . . whence they also annually ship off great quantities of goods . . . '.[356] Again, in 1720, another works was erected upon 'Swansea river' for copper smelting.[357] These activities called for the extension of harbour facilities, and local blacksmiths and anchor smiths were kept fully employed in making tools for the new industries and essential equipment for ships, etc.

In addition to copper smelting, coal mining was gaining momentum, and by 1720 along the Swansea river, such locations as 'Mr. Popkins' coal place', 'Walter Hughes his coal bank', 'Mr. Seys' coal bank' and 'Thomas Evans' coal bank' were well established.[358] 'Coal works' in the Swansea area were increasingly developed during the early decades of the eighteenth century, as so many of the borough leases testify. In the 1750s, the burgesses of the town were still granting coal mining leases. For instance, in 1758 all the veins, mines and seams of coal on the tenement of lands called Waunwen were leased to three colliers and a blacksmith for 21 years from December 25. A rent of five shillings was to be paid on every wey (i.e. 10 tons) of coal or culm containing 72 bags, each of 24 Winchester gallons, 'such rent to be accounted and paid every fortnight, plus 4 horse loads of coal or culm weekly to be delivered to the Portreave'. The lessees were further 'to employ a competent number of workmen for working and winning the coal' and 'to sell at the Pit's mouth to the Burgesses of Swansea such coal as they might require for their dwelling houses at the price of 4d. per bag of 24 gallons'.[359]

As we have already shown, the importance of a multiplicity of non-agricultural undertakings within an agrarian economy lay in the fact that many agricultural workers, particularly the unskilled workers with no special attachments to the land, were provided with alternative means of a livelihood away from the land. Wherever 'works' were introduced, the countryside soon began to lose its traditional character. In the Neath area, for instance, the backward state of the roads encouraged the employment of mules and oxen in transporting coal from the pits, and local farmers were not slow to employ their horses in carrying iron-ore, coals etc., and they drove them 'becoming in great measure day-labourers'.[360] The wages they received compared favourably with what they might have earned on the land, for between April 10 and May 8 1742, the agent to the Margam Estate paid Walter Rees the sum of 15s. 4d. for '23 days driving the coal horse at 8d. per day'.[361] The 'coal horse' had by now become a valuable part of the capital of many small farmers who dwelt near the coal mines or iron works, and the landlords, in turn, were not slow to insert clauses in the leases of tenant farmers whereby they were expected to keep 'at customary rates, a certain number of horses for the use of their masters' coalworks'.[362] Some horses carried the name 'collier', indicating the nature of the work to which they were put.[363] Oxen, too, were employed in hauling coal. For example, William Rowland, of Llanfabon, had two oxen, one called 'Collier'.[364]

During our period, the demand for industrial labour was obviously very localized, since on account of the primitive state of inland transport, most of the seventeenth- and early-eighteenth-century collieries were worked in, and around, those areas of the coalfield most contiguous to the 'ports', and the contemporary official trade records show clearly that during the second half of the seventeenth century, the exports from the Welsh ports of Neath, Swansea, Briton Ferry, and Aberavon consisted mainly of cargoes of coal. Indeed, it has been estimated that 'of the total outward sailings from Welsh ports in the year 1688, both on coasting and foreign sides, on a general average about 90 per cent were coal shipments', which certainly lends authority to the assertion that the 'pre-eminence of Welsh coal was the chief *raison d'être* of Welsh maritime activity in 1688'.[365] This assertion, however, was not true of the ports lying between Cardiff and Newton.

INDUSTRY AND AGRICULTURE

It may be argued that the period between the first operations of the Mines Royal at Neath and the feverish activity of the Mines Adventurers *circa* 1704 witnessed a process of industrial nucleation in the Neath and Swansea areas. Although the dominant features of the economy remained agricultural, conspicuous changes were taking place in certain areas along the sea coast from Baglan to Swansea, where the early coasting trade in coal had later developed in conjunction with the exchange of Welsh coal for ores for the manufacture of copper. The task of extracting coal, like that of smelting copper and iron, involved the employment of many categories of workers. For example, there were the hewers, the porters carrying coal to the exits of the mines and to the waterside, and from the waterside to the ships. Again, the making and mending of barrows and trams for carrying the coal called for the services of local carpenters and blacksmiths,[366] and the need for considerable supplies of candles for use in the mines engaged the local chandlers whose work was also closely aligned with the production of leather. Tallow supplies were as important to the chandler as hides were to the tanner, the saddler, and the glover.

How, it may be asked, was the increasing demand for labour, following the development of various local non-agricultural undertakings, satisfied? Unfortunately, there are no statistical records to indicate the numbers nor the origins of industrial workers employed in Glamorgan at this period, and conclusions must, of necessity, be based on relatively scanty evidence. It would be rash to assume that the labour force employed in the early industrial undertakings was recruited entirely from the ranks of local agricultural workers. There were, as yet, no real incentives to attract large numbers away from agriculture and rural industry. Indeed, between 1550 and 1700 it has been estimated that work was not available to miners for half the days of the year.[367] The techniques of mining engineering had not been mastered, and explosions, fires, and floods were daily hazards, resulting in frequent stoppages. Around the year 1698, one pit in the Baglan area was 'fired . . . four severall times within this 12 months and some sindg'd everytime but not to endanger their lives'.[368] Moreover, demand was seasonal, and the difficulties of transportation led to short-time working. Nevertheless, despite the hazards and uncertainties of industrial employment, it is fairly certain that there was a hard core of unskilled workers who had been drawn away from local agricultural occupations, and who regarded themselves as non-agricultural workers. Indeed, as early as the sixteenth century there were men in the western coastal regions of Glamorgan who described themselves as 'cole workers since the beginning of their labour',[369] and by the end of the seventeenth century there had emerged, in those areas, a class of workers that may be regarded as constituting a nucleus of an industrial 'proletariat' entirely divorced from the land, and wholly dependent on non-agricultural work for a livelihood. Included in this class were many female workers who often helped to supplement the earnings of their men-folk. In 1742, for example, Lord Mansel's agent at Margam made payments 'to Richard David for cutting and filling coal' and 'to his whife (sic) for gathering stones out of the coal . . . '.[370] By the end of the century the employment of women in industry had become quite common, and at the beginning of the nineteenth century on the banks of the Neath canal could be seen 'little companies of them chipping the large coals into small pieces for the furnaces without shoes or stockings, their clothes hanging about them, released for the sake of ease, from pins and strings, and their faces as black as the coals, except where channelled by the streams of perspiration that trickled down them . . . '.[371]

The complete dependence of the small industrial proletariat on non-agricultural employment is revealed in 'a petition of the cutters and drivers of coal on behalf of themselves and the rest of the colliers belonging to the several works at Briton Ferry and Baglan'[372] sent to Lord Mansel of Margam in the early-eighteenth century. In the face of a threat by his Lordship's agent 'to reduce . . . working coal at the several works to a much lesser quantity weekly' on account of a decline in trade, the men declared that if this were permitted 'not only ourselves but our families must perish for want of food, *having our dependence under God on your* (Lord Mansel's) *employment*'. The petition was signed by thirty-five coal cutters who, with the exception of two, had Welsh names. Indeed, most 'colliers' whose depositions appear in extant records of seventeenth-century litigations between rival parties had Welsh names.[373]

The industrial proletariat of eighteenth-century Glamorgan included a sprinkling of condemned criminals such as those who were employed by Sir Humphrey Mackworth and his partners at Neath. But whether or not the workers were criminals whose sentences were revoked conditionally on binding themselves as labourers in the mines, they 'were not persons likely to be accepted as social equals by the older inhabitants of the districts in which they settled'.[374] In May 1705, the principal inhabitants of Neath complained bitterly that the workmen who were employed in the coal works and smelting works 'are for the most part disorderly livers, often spending two or three daies together in drinking and other debaucherys; and some of them after y^t they have married wives and gott children have left them a Burthen on the Burrough and Parish: and others after that they have debauched young women and gott them with child, and others after they have run in debt have removed into other places and left the parish and their creditors in the lurch'.[375] The way of life of the industrial workers and the immorality allegedly associated with it marked them as a distinctly new class in the social and economic life of Glamorgan.

The coal works also attracted many part-time workers such as the hauliers who, in season, helped to transport coal overland, but continued to look upon agriculture as the basis of their subsistence. But in general, the demand for local labour varied according to the numbers of immigrant workers. Mackworth invariably supplemented local labour supplies by encouraging immigrant labour. He was also accused of giving more responsible and better paid jobs to Englishmen, some of whom received 9s. to 16s. a week, while local labourers' wages amounted to 2s. 6d. to 8s. per week.[376] Native labour, however, seems to have been employed intermittently, and was supplementary to other employment.

As already stated, the major part of the coal extracted from the Glamorgan coal seams in the seventeenth and eighteenth centuries was despatched coastwise. Mariners were engaged extensively in the transportation of coal from the pits to the consumer,[377] and although Glamorgan coal was transported mainly in English coasters that were manned by English seamen, the intermediary tasks of loading coal for shipment into the 'colliers' were performed by local workers.[378]

The arrival of the various vessels and their crews had the effect of temporarily increasing the population in the immediate neighbourhood of the ports. Almost invariably the masters of vessels and their crews were delayed two to three days at a time for the completion of the loading operations, and if the weather became inclement, and the tides difficult, the delays were longer.[379] In the meantime, the seamen had to be boarded and lodged, and their requirements undoubtedly stimulated local business, albeit on a small scale. At the beginning of the eighteenth century, when the extraction of coal was being prosecuted with increased vigour, Daniel Defoe visited Glamorgan, and he observed that around Swansea there was 'a very great trade for coals and culm which they export to all parts of Somerset, Devon and Cornwall, and also to Ireland itself', and consequently 'one sometimes sees a hundred sail of ships at a time loading coals here'. It was observed also that the coal trade at Neath was 'considerable'.[380]

The periodic visits of English seamen to the shores of Glamorgan resulted in numerous marriages between local Welsh girls and English seamen.[381] The network of family relations between Glamorgan and the

West of England counties is a feature of the social life of Glamorgan which is amply demonstrated in the wills of the period. There are numerous examples of testators who had settled in Glamorgan making provision for their kinsmen across the channel as naturally as if they lived in the same county. Christopher Lock, for instance, who had established himself as an innkeeper in Swansea, bequeathed twelve pence apiece 'to my kinsman William Locke of Attaunton in the County of Somerset, clockmaker, and to his brothers James and George and to his sister Bridgett and to Martha Mawdy . . . '.[382] Some of the extant Glamorgan wills are those of miners who had come from Somerset to Swansea and other districts in the county.[383]

The diversity of services required in the production and distribution of coal from the local works is revealed in the following 'Account of the coal works in the Lordship of Havod-y-porth'[384] *circa* 1739:

	£	s.	d.
Piloting vessels over the bar at Aberavan		7	6
Expenses in treating severall masters of vessells at the Corner House		4	6
To Mary Kollicks for meat and drink to ye pilots	2	1	3
To Catherine Morgan for shop goods to the use of ye colliers	6	6	0
To Mr. Plow for shop goods to the same use	11	4	6
To Griffith John	3	6	9
To William Griffith to pay John Thomas for Candles	6	2	11
To Mrs. Lewis of Aberavan for meat and drink to severall colliers and masters of vessells	21	16	11
Making packs and saddles for ye cole horses		14	0

Increasing activity in the mines and in the ports created additional demands for local farm produce, and these, in turn, stimulated local agriculture. For instance, in May 1715, thirty stone of cheese at 4*s.* per stone was sold to the colliers in the Margam area, and butter was sold at 7*s.* per gallon.[385] Moreover, in 1718, the following quantities of corn were delivered 'to the colliers at Britton Ferry'.[386]

	£	s.	d.
July 29 . . . . . . 21 Bushells 3 pecks of wheat at 5/- per bushell	5	8	9
Sept 5 . . . . . . 41 Bushells of barley at 2/6 per bush	5	2	6
Oct 24 . . . . . . 43 Bushells of barley at 2/6 per bush	5	8	9
Oct 20 . . . . . . 48 Bushells of barley at 2/6 per bush	6	0	0
Total value	22	0	0

We have seen that during the second half of the eighteenth century there was a further growth and extension of small pockets of industrialism in many parts of Glamorgan, especially in the hinterland of Swansea and along the coastal areas between Baglan, Neath, and Landore. But as the supplies of local timber for fuel diminished, the iron trade declined until it was found that coal was even better for smelting purposes than wood. Thus from about 1756 to 1810 most of the great south Wales iron works were established, and they eventually extended from Blaenavon in Monmouthshire to Hirwaun in the northern reaches of the Glamorgan hills.[387]

Merthyr, which was to become the centre of a world-famous industrial complex, was but 'a village with about 40 houses' in 1696.[388] In 1760 the inhabitants were still mainly 'hedgers, ditchers, farm labourers, few craftsmen, a shopkeeper, several publicans, the parson and the squire'. There were at that time, about ninety-three farms in the parish of Merthyr, but in 1765 the first furnace was built at Cyfarthfa, and almost immediately twenty of these farms were engulfed by the 'Cyfarthfa works'. Dowlais was equally ruthless, and some farms there were converted into agents' houses and warehouses, while many others were 'tipped over' and 'so undermined the foundations of others by coal and iron works that they eventually tumbled down'.[389]

In the neighbouring parish of Aberdare, coal and iron were being mined upon the lands called Abernant-y-Wenallt in 1741, and sold in considerable quantities 'to the furnace, particularly coal to the several parishes of Penderin, Ystradfellte, and Aberdare'.[390] Industry was on the march in Aberdare as well as in Merthyr, and the scale of the subsequent exploitation of local coal and iron-ore deposits in these relatively virgin areas, and of the obvious impact on agrarian life, may be gauged from the following population figures, which show that within a period of 130 years, from 1670 to 1801, the population of Merthyr had outstripped that of Swansea and, as stated earlier in this chapter, represented about 10 per cent of the total population of the whole county:

	1670 (estimated)	1801	1841	1861
Cardiff	1,670	1,870	10,077	32,954
Swansea	1,500	6,821	19,115	33,972
Merthyr	110	7,700	34,977	49,794

Although there was no industrial 'revolution' in Glamorgan during our period, there is, nevertheless, ample evidence to show that where small industrial undertakings existed, they always tended to modify the traditional economic life of the contiguous agricultural areas. Wages in industry were almost certainly kept in advance of those prevailing in agriculture, and in time there grew up a competitive market for labour. But this did not manifest itself clearly until the end of the eighteenth century. Nevertheless, there was already a distinct economic and social cleavage between the small industrial nuclei of Glamorgan and the larger agricultural-pastoral communities of the surrounding countryside. With the more vigorous and conspicuous industrial developments of the late-eighteenth and early-nineteenth centuries, the gulf between rural and urban, between agriculture and industry, became more pronounced. New communities came into existence. For instance, in 1698, the lower parcel of Baglan contained eighty houses 'most of them cottages for poor colliers'.[391] Again, at Aberavon in 1725, at both forge and furnace, the chief workers were provided with a 'house and firing free'.[392] In 1796, Merthyr Tydfil and Aberavon had regular markets because of the iron and copper works established near them having 'brought from different parts of the country such numbers of workmen and their families, as to create a consumption of great quantities of the necessaries of life, and cause a public market once a week'.[393] An irreversible trend in the social and economic life of the county had commenced. Yet, in the meantime, the economic and social life of Glamorgan continued to gravitate toward Bristol and the West of England rather than towards the homeland—a fact which should be borne in mind when analysing the historical background of Welsh nationhood.

Note: The material for this chapter has been taken from the author's Doctoral Thesis (Leicester, 1967), entitled 'Agriculture and Society in Glamorgan, 1660–1760'.

CHAPTER VIII

Glamorgan Politics from 1660-1790

i

GLAMORGAN POLITICS FROM 1660-1688

By IEUAN GWYNEDD JONES

KING Charles II was proclaimed in the Convention Parliament on Tuesday, May 8, 1660. On the previous day, just two weeks after the Commons had assembled on the basis of the new elections authorized by the restored Rump, the wording of the Proclamation had been agreed between the two Houses, and the members of the Lower House instructed to send it to their constituencies 'to the intent the same may be proclaimed in the respective Counties, Cities and Boroughs; which the several Sheriffs, Mayors, Bailiffs and other Head Officers are required to do with Speed accordingly'. Speed was of the essence of the situation, for though the Convention, dominated as it was in that first session by General Monk—the architect of the Restoration —and secure in the protection of his guards, felt confident and secure enough to recall the King without condition and, by implication, to repudiate the supremacy exercised by its immediate predecessors, there could be no certainty that 'the whole nation was in a manner become courtier'. Republicans and sectaries had been swept aside at the elections, but they still existed as organized groups. Fifth Monarchists were active along the Welsh border, in central Wales, and in the hills of Glamorgan— even, it was rumoured, in Cardiff itself—and though these had opposed Cromwell and the successor governments they were not likely to favour the unconditional return of the King.[1]

The two members responsible for sending the Proclamation to Glamorgan were Sir Edward Mansel, Bart., of Margam, the knight for the shire, and Bussy Mansel, Esq., of Briton Ferry, the member for Cardiff and the associated boroughs of Llantrisant, Cowbridge, Kenfig, Neath, Swansea, and Loughor, whose contributory status had been restored. These two cousins in all probability represented fairly accurately the state of opinion and the configuration of political power in the county at the time of their election, even as their subsequent parliamentary careers can be taken as an index of the changes of the next twenty-eight years. Sir Edward, the fourth baronet, was scarcely old enough to have taken any part in the Civil Wars, and his membership of committees during the later years of the Protectorate signified no more than that general tendency among the old leading families to co-operate with *de facto* government in order to exert a moderating influence from within the administration at the county level. He had also been named as a Commissioner for Glamorgan under the Militia Act of March 1660, which had been one of the final pieces of legislation passed by the Rump before it dissolved itself. This Act required each Commissioner to give a declaration acknowledging the just and lawful nature of 'the War undertaken by both Houses of Parliament in their Defence against the Forces raised in the name of the late King'. But this had been but a yell of defiance by the upholders of the 'Good Old Cause' in the moment of defeat; unenforceable, and such that the Glamorgan Commissioners, even if they had agreed with it, could safely ignore.[2]

Even as Sir Edward was representative of that branch of the family and of the gentry as a whole which had remained as loyal as circumstances allowed to the old order in Church and State, so his cousin Bussy Mansel was as representative of those families who had conformed. He was untypical in the extent to which he had identified himself with Parliament during the Wars and with the governments of the Commonwealth and Protectorate. From 1645 onwards he had been active in south Wales as a soldier, sequestrator, propagator and ejector: he had been one of the six members for Wales in the Barebone's Parliament, and a commissioner for the providing of the safety of the Lord Protector in 1658. With Colonel Philip Jones he had been one of the most powerful men in south Wales, bringing to his posts not merely the kind of administrative ability characteristic of the Colonel but also that social respectability which Cromwell increasingly sought after 1653. With the eclipse of Philip Jones in the months preceding the Restoration and the attacks on him by his enemies his authority in south Wales increasingly devolved on Bussy Mansel. On July 13 he replaced the old Parliamentary general, Rowland Dawkins, in command of the militia in south-west Wales, and a few weeks later he was given the command of all the south Wales militia, horse and foot, 'to lead them against the enemy if need be'. This gave him the key position in south Wales, and he was ordered by the President of the Council 'immediately to repair to Wales to order the security of those parts', and evidently he was still in command as late as September. But already he was covering his retreat and providing for probable eventualities. There is evidence that he was corresponding with the King at Brussels in April 1659, possibly involved in making preparations in south Wales for his return. Whatever the connection, he appears to have sued out a pardon in accordance with the terms proposed by the restored Rump, and to have been granted one without delay.[3]

Unlike that for the county, the borough election had been contested and had resulted in a double return of Bussy Mansel and Herbert Evans, Esq., of the Gnoll, Neath. The report from the Committee of Privileges and Elections on June 27 suggests that the election had been dominated by the burgesses from the Swansea side of the county and that the Cardiff burgesses, probably with the connivance of the sheriff, Richard David (or Davies) of Penmaen, Gower, had been prevented from voting by 'the great Concourse of People'. Whatever the reason, the Cardiff electors were not present and 'the Sheriff and Bailiffs of some of the Out Boroughs proceeded to the Election, and returned Bussy Mansel'. Cardiff and the eastern side of the constituency appeared to be in eclipse and the political initiatives in those months of transition seemed firmly in the hands of the gentry of the western side. The reversion to the ancient distributive and elective franchise and the loss by Swansea of the separate representation accorded to it under the Instrument of Government may have had something to do with this.[4]

The debates for this most critical Parliament are badly reported and there are no means of knowing what, if anything, the two Glamorgan members contributed to its deliberations. Bussy Mansel, whose duties, however, would have kept him in south Wales, was probably aligned with the majority of members who were 'old parliamentarians' and who seemed, at least superficially and during the first session, to dominate the House. Sir Edward was new to Parliament and probably identified with those young and enthusiastic royalists who, though not occupying key positions, accepted the leadership of the Court managers whose tactical skill frustrated the rather confused and nebulous objectives of the majority. One can presume that on the more general issues before Parliament the two members saw eye to eye: on the unconditional recall of the King, the land settlement with its underlying principle that there should be no disturbance of voluntary sales of land as between private persons, the indemnity, and the confirmation of judicial proceedings. On the really contentious issues such as the attempt by the presbyterian majority to establish religion on a new basis of comprehension, there could have been no agreement. Sir Edward belonged to that 'royalist' minority which could afford to wait and see, in the meantime preventing any final decisions by delaying action or merely by leaving the presbyterians to argue themselves into a state of impotence.[5]

As significant were the administrative changes quietly taking place while the Convention sat and in the interval before the assembling of the Cavalier Parliament in March 1661. John Corbet, 'late reputed' justice for the counties of Glamorgan, Brecon, and Radnor, was ordered to hand over the judicial seal to Sir Richard Lloyd, a royalist lawyer with impeccable credentials, and Edward Freeman, one of Philip Jones's implacable enemies, displaced Evan Seys of Boverton as Attorney General. Lesser offices were petitioned for and granted with remarkably little delay to royalist families and their dependants, and the lower reaches of administration purged of 'the creatures' of Philip Jones and his associates.[6] Sir Edward Mansel himself was soon recognized with the grant

[377]

of the office of chamberlain and chancellor of the counties of south-west Wales and steward of the Honour of Pembroke in reversion after the earl of Manchester—the first of those rewards for loyalty and the first recognition of his leading position among the ruling families which were to culminate in the grant of the vice-admiralty of south Wales in 1662. The sheriffs who had been pricked in the last year of the Republic were continued in office for a further year by the Convention, and this gave Richard David (Davies), of Penmaen the opportunity to play a crucial rôle in the elections to the Cavalier Parliament. Of greatest importance was the office of lord lieutenant, for it combined executive with military functions and was therefore the embodiment of royal power in the shires, evidence of the reality and the effectiveness of the Restoration in the localities. Traditionally this office had been reserved to the paramount families, peers of the realm, and as early as June 1660, and again the following month, the gentry of Glamorgan and Monmouthshire petitioned that Henry, Lord Herbert of Raglan should be named as lord lieutenant of the two counties. The family had repossessed most of the lands in south Wales confiscated during the Interregnum for the recusancy of its head, and Lord Herbert, himself a Protestant, was now in high favour, having suffered imprisonment for his complicity in Booth's rising. But although he was made lord lieutenant of Gloucestershire and Herefordshire the choice of the new lord lieutenant fell on Richard Vaughan, the second earl of Carbery, of Golden Grove, Carmarthenshire. His commission in September 1660 made him lord lieutenant for the whole of Wales, and in the following January he was made President of the Council in the Principality and Marches of Wales. This made him viceroy of Wales, with command over the militia and the garrisoned castles of the country. The choice of deputies was his, and he immediately and with vigour set about the task of ensuring the success of the Restoration in his lieutenancy by appointing as his deputies men on whom the administration could rely in the re-establishing of royal authority, in furthering its civil and religious policies, and in continuing that purge of subversive elements which had already begun. This could not have been an entirely easy task. With two notable exceptions, the nineteen names submitted early in September included members of all the leading families whatever their actual political records, and included that of Bussy Mansel. The two exceptions were Philip Jones and Edmund Thomas of Wenvoe. The latter had sat for the county in the parliaments of 1654, 1656, and 1658, was a Cromwellian lord, and had given outstanding services to the Commonwealth. Like Philip Jones he had increased his estate during 'the troubles', and in 1677 his heir was reputed to be worth £2,000 per annum—considerably more, if this were so, than the neighbouring Fonmon estate. Lord Carbery's list sent for approval later in September included eleven of these names and was headed by William, Lord Herbert of Cardiff and Sir Edward Mansel.[7]

At the lower, but in practice the much more important, level of local government, the list of j.ps. appointed in September 1660 shows to what an extent the old families resumed their *ante-bellum* powers and public functions. The attempts of Cromwell to turn the clock back had resulted, as we have seen, in persuading a number of the gentry to cooperate in his régime: his choice of personnel had necessarily been restricted in such circumstances to only a section of the prominent private individuals whose status in the county gave them the kind of authority he sought, and he had been compelled, as his commissions indicate, to raise men from a slightly lower social rank to fulfil the onerous duties that his government required. Such men as these latter were conspicuously absent from the new commission—the first of Charles II— and the roster, while including the names of at least eight who had appeared on the 1656 list, was eloquent of the return to power of the traditional families. The earl of Pembroke, though he had served as an *ex officio* justice throughout the Interregnum, was appointed *custos rotulorum*, replacing the notorious Philip Jones, who was now fighting off his enemies and desperately seeking to make his peace with the new government. Philip Jones's reappearance in the commission in August 1672 marked the final success of these efforts and the ability of the closely-knit mesh of interlocking family relationships, so characteristic of the Glamorgan ruling class, to contain the tensions of, and to present a united front to, the incipient anarchy of the times. But in these early months of adjustment it was the old royalist families which possessed the initiative—men who, though more or less compromised, could argue that not principle but expediency had motivated their cooperation with the usurpers, and who were now determined to demonstrate in their localities the quality of their loyalty.

This resumption by the county families of their pre-war positions was possible because the majority of them still retained most of their estates intact. Few families had emerged from the war unscathed, and such as had were invariably families which had early thrown in their lot with Parliament. Royalist families had suffered sequestration of their estates, and some had had to part with land in order to pay the heavy fines imposed on them for their delinquency, but there is no evidence that families had been destroyed in the process, even if some had been somewhat impoverished. Under the land settlement estates confiscated outright were to be returned: in this way the earl of Worcester re-entered into the Glamorgan estates confiscated by Parliament and given to Cromwell. Lands sold privately were confirmed to their new owners. But if Glamorgan could show no examples of royalist families displaced by this legislation it could boast an outstanding example of a Roundhead officer who had succeeded in building up one of the largest estates in the Vale on the basis of private purchases. Philip Jones of Llangyfelach spent more than £15,800 in direct purchases of land during the Interregnum, and, at his death, after having parted with lands in other counties, his estates included large properties centred on Fonmon and others around Swansea and in Gower, bringing him an annual income of £1,000 *p.a.*—considerably more than that enjoyed by his neighbours. This may have occasioned jealousy, but there is no evidence that the attempt to impeach him in Parliament or to exclude him from the indemnity was supported by the Glamorgan members. On the contrary, as his biographer explains, he was quickly accepted into the ranks of the gentry, being named as high sheriff in 1671 and appointed a j.p. in the following year. With this outstanding exception, the pattern of gentry estates had not been radically changed as a result of the Wars. A somewhat impressionistic 'List of Glamorganshire Gentry' drawn up in 1677, probably by Sir Edward Mansel for the use of Sir John Williamson, reveals that there were 12 estates of £1,000 or over, 11 of between £500 and £1,000, and 9 of less than £500 annual value. The annual incomes given are probably grossly underestimated, but the pattern of ownership is very similar to that to be found in the list drawn up by Richard Symonds in the early years of the War. The leading families are the same, and with the exceptions already noted, there do not appear to have been any very startling changes in the rankings.[8]

If the elections to the Convention had shown that by then 'Cavalier had become a less odious name', the elections to Charles's first parliament —the Cavalier or Long Parliament—which met on May 8, 1661, showed a distinct preference for men of a fairly moderate disposition. By no stretch of the imagination could William, Lord Herbert of Cardiff, heir presumptive to the earldom of Pembroke, who was returned as knight for the shire instead of Sir Edward Mansel, but without a contest, be termed a 'royalist'. Like his father he had co-operated with the Cromwellian régime and had declared for a return of the monarchy—he had been implicated in Booth's Rising—only when the inner contradiction of the Republic threatened to produce anarchy. His return could be regarded as the entry of the premier family into its rightful inheritance with the active consent of the subordinate families with an interest in the return, possibly as much the expression of local loyalties as of political commitment. There may well have been political overtones to the rather complicated elections to the borough seat. Three men were involved in this episode, namely, Sir Richard Lloyd of Esclusham, Denbighshire, and Dulasau, Caernarvonshire, the newly appointed chief justice for the counties of Brecon, Glamorgan and Radnor, Robert Thomas of Betws and Llanfihangel, and William Bassett of Broviscin. On May 24 it was reported to the House that there had been a double return of Lloyd for Cardiff and for the Radnor county seat, and because he chose the latter constituency a writ was issued for a new election for Cardiff. At this subsequent election William Bassett was returned, whereupon Robert

Thomas petitioned on the grounds that the original election had been contested between him and Lloyd and that he (Thomas) had been returned by 105 votes to 40. For his part Lloyd admitted that he had known nothing about the election until informed of it by letter, and the upshot was that the House accepted the recommendation of the Committee that the second election should be voided and Robert Thomas declared duly elected.[9]

It is impossible to discover what lay behind this curious episode, involving as it did the unusual expedient of bringing in a candidate from outside regardless of the fact that he had no county connections, possibly without his knowledge, and returning him in his absence and contrary to the votes cast. It may be significant that the sheriff was Herbert Evans of Neath—the member for the county to the Convention who had been unseated on petition—who may have been working for the Worcester interest against that of Pembroke. What cannot be ignored is the undoubted fact that the two candidates represented differing attitudes to the political issues which would inevitably engage the new parliament. On the one hand there was the exuberant and committed royalism of a law officer of the crown, and on the other, the more calculated and pragmatic attitudes of one who had been a somewhat unsteady royalist in the past and who still maintained friendly relations with that most notorious of republicans, Philip Jones. For the moment there were no 'party' relationships; all were 'royalists' in the sense that there was concord between the King and the ruling classes. Local connections based on family relationship formed the basis of politics, but the Civil Wars had been about liberties, property, and religion, and from that ferment Glamorgan had not emerged unscathed.

The new Parliament was to last for eighteen years, and during this long and eventful period in which relations between it and the King were to worsen steadily in ways very reminiscent of the political history of the reigns of the first two Stuarts, Glamorgan was represented by only three men. Robert Thomas—Sir Robert on succeeding to the baronetcy in 1673—continued in the borough seat without a break until the dissolution of 1678, and Lord Herbert as knight of the shire until he succeeded to the earldom in 1670, when he was followed without a contest by Sir Edward Mansel.[10] None achieved eminence as a parliamentarian; indeed, the evidence would seem to indicate that they were neither active in debate nor particularly busy in committees. That they were undemonstratively, though not uncritically, loyal we can infer from their behaviour in the last sessions of the Parliament and during the Exclusion Crisis, and from the way in which they assisted in their roles as j.ps. at home in putting into effect the legislation in the passing of which they had had a share. A Mr. Thomas, possibly the member for Cardiff, sat on the committee for the Bill for Regulating Corporations which was passed after long debates and considerable obstruction in the second session. By this Act all officials of corporations were to take the oaths of allegiance, supremacy, and non-resistance to the King, take the sacrament according to the rites of the Church of England, and repudiate the Solemn League and Covenant. In this way the government was engaged in establishing as direct a control over the chartered towns as it already exercised over administration in the counties, and though it achieved only a part of its purpose the powers conferred on it by the Act were later to form the basis of the full-scale attacks on the municipalities in 1681 and again under James II. While it is true that the Glamorgan boroughs had already fallen under the control of patrons favourable to the Court, it was under this Act that the duke of Beaufort was able to launch his attacks against them at the end of the reign when the loyalty of their 'natural' patrons was suspect.[11]

Of far greater moment and of enduring importance was the penal legislation designed to re-establish the Church of England on a secure and exclusive basis—the so-called 'Clarendon Code'. Implicitly, this legislation was a partial defeat for the religious policies of the King and of his Chancellor, Lord Clarendon. In accordance with the Declaration of Breda, a measured toleration 'for tender consciences' was what they had envisaged as the ideal religious policy and which, at least initially, they struggled to achieve. The Commons rejected both toleration and its alternative, comprehension, in favour of penal Acts designed to harry the old puritans out of the Church and to make it impossible for them subsequently to organize themselves for religious purposes. The keystone in this arch of the new establishment was the Act of Uniformity (1662), and its pillars the Conventicle Act of 1664 and the Five Mile Act of 1665. None of the Glamorgan members sat on any of the committees which prepared these Bills, but in the intermittent though sometimes prolonged campaigns against the sectaries which the Acts stimulated they and their fellows in Glamorgan were required to be vigilant and active. How vindictive they were and with what energy they used the militia under their command to break up the conventicles and their authority as justices to search out and prosecute the nonconformists is told in another chapter (see below pp. 466–79). The intensity of the persecution, and likewise, perhaps, its relative lack of success, was probably due less to religious zeal than to an apparently ineradicable belief that Dissent equalled sedition and to a conviction that the extremist religio-political groups were still plotting the armed overthrow of the restored monarchy. And if the actual situation in the hilly parishes of the north and west and in the towns seldom if ever provided hard evidence of such treasonable activities, the newsletters which circulated from hand to hand and the peremptory orders of the London government kept the atmosphere tense and from time to time explosive.

Glamorgan's situation on the sea and the growing commercial life of its ports involved the county indirectly in the foreign policy of the Crown, and this also contributed to the tensions endemic during the first part of the reign. The spasmodic wars against the Dutch—Britain's greatest commercial and naval rival—created a constant demand for seamen to man the ships of the royal navy. As Vice-Admiral for south Wales, Sir Edward Mansel had the onerous duty of providing the quotas of men required from the county. Resistance to impressment was common; it was deeply resented in the port towns whose trade depended on their shipping, and whose commercial life was increasingly disturbed by the activities of enemy privateers operating in the Bristol Channel and along the sea routes to the west. As distrust of the King's policies grew and the full implications of the alliance with France came to be understood, this local resentment was something it could feed on and which in due course would be reflected in the activities of the county's members in Parliament.[12]

Up to January 1670—before, that is, the return of Sir Edward Mansel for the county in place of Lord Herbert—the two members may be described as belonging to the opposition groupings, or at least not to have been members of the Court Party after the fall of Clarendon. Lord Herbert seems to have maintained an independent position. Robert Thomas may have been a supporter of the duke of Buckingham—one of the members of the 'Cabal' who was in favour of toleration for Dissenters. With the return of Sir Edward Mansel the Court Party gained a supporter who was to remain consistently loyal throughout the Parliament. Though not a pensioner or the holder of any office in the King's household or government, he was carefully cultivated by Sir Joseph Williamson, the Secretary of State and the chief manager of the Court Party under Danby. He was on Williamson's list of correspondents, receiving the newsletters sent out regularly when Parliament was in recess and accepting the government whips when the House was in session. Hopefully, he was listed as a speaker on the government side in 1675–7, but there is no evidence that he ever did so. Probably he was more of an accession to the government side than was Robert Thomas to the as-yet-unorganized Country Party. As a defaulter for some months he suffered the disgrace, in February 1671, of having to appear at the Bar of the House to explain his prolonged absences. His excuse was that he had been disabled from attending 'by reason of a Quartan Ague, which held him till about Christmas; and since, by a Hurt received in his Hand, and the Danger of a Gangrene, and the Loss of his Hand thereupon likely to ensue'. This excuse was accepted, but worse was immediately to follow, for no sooner had he taken his seat than a petition which had been presented to the House by his father, Sir Edward Thomas, on February 14, 'complaining of Miscarriages, Frauds and Abuses, committed by his said Son', was read. The petition, after Sir Edward had been called in,

[383]

z

was committed to Sir Trevor Williams and twenty others, to whom another eleven were added on March 6, and it was not until April 1 that the matter was disposed of and the petition dismissed. No details of this curious and, so far as Glamorgan was concerned, unprecedented case survive. Whatever lay behind the rupture between father and son could scarcely have enhanced his reputation or added to his effectiveness as a member.[13]

Commitment to clear and definite political views and support for specific courses of action as advocated by political parties became the major characteristics of national politics in the course of the final sessions of the Cavalier Parliament. The revelations of the King's duplicity in his foreign policy combined with the publicly-avowed adherence of his brother, James duke of York, the heir apparent, to Roman Catholicism, created the widely-felt suspicion that the King and his advisers were involved in a conspiracy to undermine the Protestant establishment and to introduce absolute monarchy, modelled on that of Catholic France, in its place. The need of the King's ministers to control Parliamentary business had led to the gradual formation of a Court Party held together less by ties of personal loyalty and conviction than by a rather loosely organized system of rewards and pensions, places and personal influence— a veritable 'sink of iniquity' to those who, for whatever reason, lay outside its golden circle. In its turn this had stimulated the organization by those who opposed the royal policies of an opposition party—the Country Party. These parties—the immediate forebears of the Tory and Whig parties respectively—were coming to be organized on a country-wide basis, their strength and effectiveness depending not only on leadership at the centre but on public opinion in the country at large. To take advantage of this public opinion, to shape it and influence it and to organize it behind candidates so as to deploy it in Parliament became the object of the opposing parties.

In these developments the gentry of Glamorgan could not but be involved. The county lay within the sphere of influence of the marquis of Worcester who had succeeded Lord Carbery in his presidency and lieutenancy in 1672. A member of the Privy Council, he was high in royal favour and an intimate of the duke of York, and the enormous power he possessed was deployed with energy and an over-weening arrogance in favour of the Court. Himself precariously a Protestant, his family remained Catholic and it was believed that he fully concurred in the religious policies of the Court. Nor was he the only holder of high office with Glamorgan connections. From 1680 to 1684 one of the Secretaries of State was Sir Leoline Jenkins of Cowbridge. A distinguished lawyer of unimpeachable integrity and a firm Anglican, he was one of that small élite of new-style administrators who were bringing to government business a new efficiency and expertise. Between them these two had an unrivalled knowledge of Glamorgan and they worked closely together to further the interests of the Court.[14]

Both were most active in the aftermath of the Popish Plot. This hideous episode had a profound effect on Glamorgan opinion despite incontrovertible evidence that Roman Catholicism was extremely weak within its borders. An official list of 1680 names only five families as compared with the 189 names for Monmouthshire and 188 for Breconshire. Furthermore, the persons named were of the minor gentry and whatever influence they possessed there is no evidence to suggest that they were disposed to assert it in county affairs. The 1677 list of gentry already referred to states that Thomas Carne of Nash, whose brother, Howell, was named as a recusant, had an estate of £300 and described him as being 'an honest Gentleman wholy addicted to husbandry'. John Turberville of Pen-llin was richer by £200 but 'a Stranger in his Country liveinge in Berkshire', while his cousin of Sker had an estate of £300 and was also 'a Stranger'. No doubt families such as these—and the Lords' List is obviously incomplete—exercised their patronage to protect their co-religionists lower in the social scale, but all had enjoyed a kind of toleration by connivance and the potentially savage recusancy laws had been applied only intermittently by their kinsmen and neighbours, the justices of the peace.[15]

It was the Plot scare which shattered the post-Restoration period of relative calm, and it was the so-called 'evidence' of deep complicity in the plotting provided by the Monmouthshire men, John Arnold, John Scudamore, and William Beddloe, aided and abetted by Christopher, the younger brother of Edward Turberville of Sker, that initiated the vicious period of priest-hunting in Glamorgan which was to end with the execution of two and the imprisonment of others. The initiative was not a local one; the order to seek out papists came from the government and was directed to the j.ps. of the hundred in which recusants were known to reside. In fact, only three priests were known to be active in Glamorgan at that time. Fr. Philip Evans, S.J., was discovered hiding at Sker House by William Bassett, arrested along with his protector, and taken to Cardiff where, after a charade of a trial, he was condemned and executed. Fr. John Lloyd of Pen-llin was tried and convicted at the same assize, and in May 1679 two women, together with Christopher Turberville and Howell Carne and four others, were presented for refusing the Oath of Supremacy. The j.ps. most prominent in these events were William Bassett, Richard Bassett, Richard Loughor, Sir Edward Stradling, and Humphrey Wyndham of Dunraven, the father-in-law of Sir Trevor Williams of Llangibby, the leading Monmouthshire antipapist. To Christopher Turberville fell the invidious distinction of becoming Glamorgan's equivalent of Monmouthshire's Beddloe.[16]

Politics were involved in the Plot at very profound levels. At the most superficial level it was an opportunity to attack the marquis of Worcester at what appeared to be his most vulnerable point, namely, the religion of his family. The strength of Catholicism was held to be a reflection of his patronage—a patronage doubly to be feared and resented by reason of his avowed Protestantism. To faithful Anglicans his active toleration of Catholics (his steward was a practising Catholic) was the concomitant of his arrogant use and display of power within his lieutenancy, 'an arbitrary Lord who pricks Mayors as the King pricks Sheriffs', 'who commands from St. David's to within 60 miles (of London)', and whose sister, the Catholic Lady Powys, 'dispences commands in North Wales'. The traditional attachment of the Glamorgan gentry was to the Pembrokes—indeed, some of the leading families were their kin, and this ruthless exercise of power by the Somersets cut deep and bitterly into their sense of loyalty and cohesion. Above all it was feared, for its intent and direction seemed, in microcosm, the equivalent in regional terms of the despotic tendencies of a centralizing and Catholicizing state. In such a situation men were obliged to take sides, and while maintaining traditional allegiances to address themselves to national issues. So the ancient Pembroke connection was revivified while underneath opinion polarized against the Court and in favour of the liberties of the ancient constitution and the Church as established. In the circumstances of an election the conflict would be given the appearance of one between ex-roundheads and ex-cavaliers.[17]

The extent of this polarization of opinion and of commitment to party can be seen in the elections to, and inferred from the activities of the Glamorgan members in, the Exclusion Parliaments of 1679, 1680 and 1681. There were two general elections in 1679 and in both Bussy Mansel was returned instead of Sir Edward Mansel. The latter had remained, so far as one can tell, loyal to the Court throughout the developing crises of 1678, and it cannot be without significance that he was replaced by the ex-republican, that most perfect exemplar of Whiggery from the most puritan side of the county. Sir Robert Thomas was opposed for the borough seat by Thomas Stradling, who unsuccessfully petitioned against the return. Unfortunately, nothing is known about this contest, but there is no doubt that during the crisis of the late years of the Cavalier Parliament Sir Robert had moved closer to the Country Party, to their anti-popery and their attacks on Danby, and that he had favoured measures to ensure a Protestant succession by excluding the duke of York. In the Parliament of 1679 both these members were supporters of Shaftesbury and both voted for exclusion.[18]

Equally significant were the elections to the last Parliament of the reign—the 'Oxford Parliament' of 1681. Sir Robert Thomas retired and the borough seat was taken by Sir Edward Mansel while Bussy Mansel transferred to the county seat. The election of Sir Edward did not signify the return of a Tory, but rather a shift in the allegiance of one who throughout his parliamentary career had been identified as a supporter of the Court. It was probably his deep resentment at the attempts of the Court, through the marquis of Worcester, to purge the county commission of its disaffected justices that accounted for this change. This purge had begun, apparently on the sole initiative of Worcester in August 1677, when Richard Seys and Marmaduke Gibbs and possibly Martin Button had been taken out of the commission along with some of the leading Monmouthshire members of the anti-papist, anti-Worcester faction. On that occasion Sir Edward Mansel and William Morgan of Tredegar—families allied by marriage—had written directly to the King to protest. Some of the ejected justices had been recommended by Sir Edward, and their presumed disloyalty would necessarily reflect back on him. It was certainly taken as an indication that he had himself fallen from favour or was in imminent danger of doing so. Sir John Williamson, acting on the King's instructions, wrote to Worcester on two occasions asking for reasons 'why they ought not to be returned into ye Commission of ye Peace', and the matter was discussed between the King and Worcester on March 15. Worcester must have had his way, for in the commission of May 5, 1679 the three Glamorgan names still do not appear. Confirmation of his own fall from grace came with the omission of his name— conveyed to him in a curt letter from the marquis on March 15—from the roster of February 18, 1680. Sir Robert Thomas, Evan Seys, Humphrey Wyndham, and Thomas Mansel were also purged round about the same time.

Personal motives may very well have been present in the earlier and localized omissions of 1679. The purgings of 1680 were in a different category and part of a deliberate policy by the King to draw the teeth of county opposition preparatory to new elections. A contested election in the borough, the return of two Whigs, the canvassing of Sir Edward Mansel as a successor to the violent anti-papist William Morgan in the Monmouth county seat, and the return of Sir Edward as an opposition member to the Oxford Parliament showed to what an extent opposition had grown and how extensive were its ramifications. Nor was opposition confined to the traditional political families or limited in scope to the relatively clear-cut issues involved in the question of exclusion. The conflict within the political nation and the consequent instability in local government which this threatened and might in certain circumstances imply, made possible the resurgence of old republican ideologies. Not the least important effect of the Popish Plot panic had been the radicalizing of anti-popery feelings and the deflection of attention away from the activities of Protestant recusants. There is evidence that John Arnold, the leading Monmouthshire anti-papist, had moved towards extreme republicanism. In 1680 he was said to be cultivating Samuel Jones of Brynllywarch, 'a common preacher at conventicles' who, it was alleged, was responsible for the collection of money 'from many ill-affected persons to promote their dangerous designs against the present Government'. Both Arnold and Samuel Jones had compelled the informer to swear 'that he should be true to the Presbyterian government without king or House of Lords', and to preserve secrecy.[19]

By 1682 a reaction in favour of the King had set in, doubtless inspired by a fear that these upheavals were indeed threatening the peace of the county. Rumours of seditious meetings, of old roundheads rearming, of Cardiff burgesses ready to fight for Sir Edward Mansel even against the King if need be, of the monarch becoming a topic 'of mirth and rebaldry', poured into Sir Leoline Jenkins's office. The natural reaction of the governing gentry, without the need for promptings from above, was to close ranks in defence of a government which, though ill-advised, was still legitimate. For them puritan republicanism was as anathema as popish, royalist absolutism, and they hoped for a middle way beginning with the reassertion of traditional authority in the localities.[20]

It was this shift in public opinion in favour of the Crown as the best preservative of peace and in reaction to the threat of anarchy and a resumption of civil war which enabled the King, by consummate political action, to save his crown, and it was the failure of the Rye House Plot and the flight of Shaftesbury which provided the signal for the reaction. Sir Leoline and the Marquis investigated closely the suspected complicity of some Glamorgan persons in the Plot, and they commended the conduct of those justices who had been most active against them. Worcester—created duke of Beaufort in November 1682—ordered his deputy lieutenants to disarm sectaries, and Jenkins circulated details of 'the horrid Plot' admonishing his correspondents to keep all suspected persons under observation. Indeed, the Rye House Plot sparked off another witch-hunt, the victims this time being Whigs and Dissenters. Despite vague rumours that Sir Edward Mansel was implicated there was no evidence that Glamorgan men were involved, and Beaufort and Jenkins could, with due caution, accept as genuine the protestations of loyalty which eventually they received from the county.[21]

The boroughs, some of them traditionally centres of dissidence and obviously highly sensitive to the flux of opinion, likewise protested their loyalty. But already they were under attack. Loyal toasts were drunk at the corporation elections in Cardiff in 1682, and the bells of Swansea were rung to celebrate the King's recovery from an illness. Yet Jenkins knew of the existence in Cardiff of a faction antagonistic to the government centred on John Richards, one of the bailiffs. This was considered to be so serious as to warrant moving the Great Sessions from the town, but evidently the loyal party were sufficiently in control not to justify proceedings as yet to curb the powers of the corporation. In any case, the borough had a still powerful protector in its lord, and his intercessions may have succeeded in delaying the inevitable. Other towns were less fortunate. The borough of Cowbridge had already surrendered its charter and been re-incorporated in April 1681, and Neath and Swansea were dealt with likewise in 1684. The new charter for Neath confirmed and strengthened the control of the constable by retaining in his hands the final choice of portreeve and all lesser offices, and by giving him the ultimate power to fill vacancies in both the aldermanic bench and among the capital burgesses. Five of the substantial gentry of the immediate locality—including Sir Edward Mansel—were named as aldermen. Swansea had already come under attack from its lord, the cause being the 'admitting of some of our dissenting Brethren not qualified by law to be sworn Aldermen here'. Four aldermen had been elected in 1680 and that year the almost unprecedented number of 15 burgesses had also been admitted. It was probably these threatening motions which prompted an investigation into the old charters by the two stewards, William Herbert and David Evans, which cost the corporation 16s. 6d. for wine and drink and a shilling for the 'mayd' who assisted them at the common coffer. Nothing further appears to have been done at that stage, but Swansea's turn came a few years later as part of the government's general attack on borough charters throughout the country. Swansea surrendered its charter of 1656 in July 1684. The new one followed that of Cromwell closely in that the lord, through his stewards, gained more control over the appointment of officials and above all by constituting the 12 aldermen and 15 capital burgesses a self-elective body and depriving the burgesses at large of any share in the election of the mayor, aldermen, and common council.[22]

The King was dead, his brother James enthusiastically proclaimed as his successor, and the first (and only) Parliament of the new reign elected before the new charter reached Swansea. Meanwhile also, the duke of Beaufort, now at the summit of his power, had been confirmed in his lieutenancy of all the counties of Wales and the Marches, and his son, the marquis of Worcester, headed the list of deputies for Glamorgan. Serving with him were Sir Edward Mansel, Sir Edward Stradling, Sir Charles Kemeys, Sir John Aubrey, Sir Richard Bassett, William Herbert, and David Jenkins (the son of the Judge)—a list which reflected the solidly loyalist complexion of the county. Nor were there as yet any violent changes in the roster of justices: Sir Edward Mansel was back and a Wyndham included. Sir Robert Thomas had by this time retired from political affairs and was preoccupied with the sale of his Llanfihangel estates to London financiers, mainly to Sir Humphrey Edwin, a prominent Whig merchant. Bussy Mansel was not named. This, perhaps, was to be expected of one whose mercurial career seems always to have responded to the heat engendered by political change. But now the times were quiet, the accession of the new King welcomed, and the purging of the corporations by his brother having their desired effect. The March elections passed uneventfully with no contests. Sir Edward Mansel continued as knight of the shire and the borough returned, not Bussy Mansel, but Francis Gwyn of Llansannor. An experienced politician, a lawyer of note and an office-holder, it is virtually certain that he was the nominee of the Court and that Sir Edward, now again on good terms with Beaufort, had arranged his election, apparently in his absence and without having to bribe the Cardiff burgesses. The key position of Sir Edward in Swansea, Neath and Kenfig would have ensured the votes of the burgesses of those towns.[23]

The first indication locally of a determination on the part of the King to adopt a more thorough-going policy came in December 1686 when some of the county's Catholics were added to the Commission of the Peace, namely, Richard Carne and the two Turbervilles. This was in direct contravention of the Test Act of 1673 which an otherwise compliant Parliament had refused to repeal. The second and more radical indication of change was the King's Declaration of Indulgence of April 4, 1687 by which liberty of public worship was given to all Catholic and Protestant recusants. By this the penal laws were suspended and the Oaths of Supremacy and Allegiance and the Test Acts avoided by means of dispensations to any persons 'employed in any Office or Place of Trust either Civil or Military, under Us or in our Government'. This was the culmination of a policy which, as James explained to Beaufort, was intended to ensure that his 'Catholick subjects may be in the same condition the rest of my subjects are'. Negatively, and by implication at first, this involved an attack on the Church of England as established in 1559 and in 1662. At his accession he had unequivocally sworn to protect the Church: now he gave his assurance that he would protect Anglicans in the exercise of their religion—an assurance which, it was observed, might leave the Church as a corporation open to attacks by prerogative power. Likewise, he sought to allay the fears of the gentry that they would be disturbed in their possession of Church lands. But taken with the existence of a large standing army, the dispensations to army officers who were Roman Catholics (the Carnes and Stradlings came into this category), the campaign against chartered corporations, the dilution of the bench and the addition of the clause of dispensation in the Commission of the Peace of August 29, the Declaration seemed to be the penultimate move in a conspiracy to destroy the Church and to subvert the liberties of the nation.

Nor were the Nonconformists beguiled into accepting this bid for their cooperation. There is no evidence that any of the Glamorgan Dissenters had petitioned James for relief in 1686, and the only Address thanking him for this *de facto* toleration originated in the town of Swansea 'with other Places adjacent in Glamorganshire'—locations vague enough to mean much or little and lacking that specificity which the King desired. Not only were the Dissenters by now quietist and introspective, intent on the inner life of the the newly-gathered congregations, but they also had room to fear the threat involved in the combination of Catholicism and politics.[24]

The Declaration of 1687 was part of a larger strategy the aim of which was the creation of conditions in which the King's allies could ensure the return of a Parliament which would legislate what he was now enforcing by prerogative. The corporations of Swansea, Neath, and Cowbridge had already been remodelled. Now it was the turn of Cardiff, where stronger action was called for in order to strengthen the Tory elements against the Whigs—that is, to consolidate the power of Beaufort and weaken that of Pembroke. Cardiff had already ceremoniously surrendered its old charter to Beaufort when he had visited the town at the end of his Progress in August 1684. The draft of the new charter drawn up on December 10, 1686 was modelled closely on those which were being granted at the same time to numerous other towns in England and Wales. It created what was in effect a closed corporation and included the now standard proviso empowering the King to remove officers. To sugar the pill the Corporation had restored to them certain market rights which had been lost to Caerphilly for the restitution of which they had petitioned at the Restoration. This remodelling of the corporate towns, the opening-up of the Commission to men of his own faith, and the lifting of restrictions on the religious and public lives of Dissenters gave the government a large measure of control over the machinery of local government.

It remained to influence the personnel. Late in October the King instructed Beaufort to call before him all the deputy lieutenants and justices within his lieutenancy, either jointly or separately, and ask each one to give his answer to three separate questions. First, would he, if chosen to sit as an M.P. in the next parliament, vote for the repeal of the Penal laws and Test Acts? Second, would he assist in the election of a candidate pledged so to vote? Third, would he support the Declaration by 'living friendly with those of all persuasions, as subjects of the same Prince, and good Christians ought to do'? He was also instructed to make a return of Catholics and Dissenters fit to be approved as deputy lieutenants or added to the Commission of the Peace. Accordingly, Beaufort invited all the deputies and justices to meet him at Ludlow.

The results of this inquiry throw a great deal of light on the complexion of political opinion in Glamorgan at that time. Of the six deputy lieutenants not one attended. Sir Edward Mansel and Sir John Aubrey excused themselves on account of the length of the journey. Sir Richard Bassett and William Herbert absented themselves without explanation, David Jenkins was 'very infirm', and David Evans 'came part of the way and having a dangerous fall had to return'. Of the 18 justices, only William Herbert put in an appearance, and his answers were scarcely helpful, namely, 'Refuses y[e] 2 first. Consents to y[e] 3[d]'. Beaufort assumed that the only Dissenter among them, Rowland Dawkins (currently employed by him to survey his Swansea estates), would consent to all three—an assumption for which there is no evidence either one way or the other. Four of the justices were Catholics, but as two of them were not resident in Glamorgan, these also were numerically in a small minority. Of the remaining eleven, ten were absent and therefore unclassifiable, and the eleventh, Francis Gwyn, explained that he was not yet sworn. His record shows that far from supporting the King he was probably deeply involved with the supporters of William of Orange. Finally, Beaufort noted that 'No Catholick of Note or Estate' was out of the commission, and the list of Dissenters not in the commission consisted of only four names headed, ominously enough, by Sir Humphrey Edwin, the London merchant and leading Whig who had recently purchased Llanfihangel. The others were John Watkins, Martin Button, and William Phillips. The conclusion was inescapable: there were neither enough Catholics nor Dissenters to support the King's policies in the county, and that in turning against the Anglicans and Tories James had left himself without a power-base from which to work and in particular to achieve the kind of representation he would wish to see in the new Parliament. The charters granted to the towns since the Restoration could not be expected to work in his favour: far from entrenching the power of the Crown they effectively consolidated the power of the gentry whom he had now alienated. It was not laziness or a lack of application to his electoral activities alone which accounted for the pessimism of the duke of Beaufort but rather the realities of a worsening situation.[25]

However bad the prospect in Wales generally and in Glamorgan in particular, in the remainder of England they were by no means unpromising, and James pressed ahead with his preparations for a Parliament which should in due course confirm by statute those changes in Church and State which he was now hurriedly making. The Court of High Commission, which had been abolished in 1641, was revived as the 'Ecclesiastical Commission' and deployed, not as its predecessor had been, against the enemies of the establishment but against the Church itself. Above all, the King pressed on with his policy of toleration. The Declaration of Indulgence was renewed in April and published with an Order in Council commanding the clergy to read it from their pulpits on two successive Sundays. The Order made a qualitative difference: it brought home to the localities, at the level of the individual parish and beneficed clergyman, their kinsmen and patrons, the enormity of the the King's actions. Unfortunately, we know little about the condition of the Church in Glamorgan at this time, and least of all about its manpower. That most of the parishes were poor and the bulk of the clergymen impoverished and inferior in status to the gentry is certain. We can be fairly confident that they would have looked not only to their ecclesiastical superiors but also to their patrons for guidance in the terrible dilemma in which they now found themselves. The lead was given promptly by the Church itself at the highest level when the Archbishop and six other bishops—including William Lloyd of St. Asaph—petitioned against the King's compelling them to publicize the Declaration and against his use of the dispensing power. Their imprisonment, trial, and acquittal was thus vindication not only of the Church as a corporate body but also of the law as against an unrestrained executive power, and of Parliament as against prerogative. In this situation clergy and gentry were united and there is no indication that in Glamorgan there was a split between them.

From now on the crisis developed apace. The birth of a son, the Pretender, to James and his Catholic wife shortly before the Seven Bishops' trial added a new dimension. It encouraged James in his policies but drove some of the political leaders to near despair. Already some prominent Whigs and Church leaders were in voluntary exile at the court of William of Orange urging him to take action against his uncle. Now a small group of leading Whigs and Tories decided to invite William over, and it was the tardy confirmation of this treachery and of William's advanced preparations for an invasion which brought about a sudden change of policy amounting to a dismantling of the recent policies and a turning back for support to the traditional allies of the Crown, the Tory and Anglican gentry. But these concessions were coming too late, and if their intention was to open a rift between Whigs and Tories in the localities there was now little possibility for this to happen in Glamorgan. The progress of the King from Badminton through the border counties in August had given the gentry and the Dissenters every opportunity to show their solidarity with him, but such testimonies of support had not been forthcoming. Nor was the King's reliance on a standing army an encouragement to their cooperation. Colonel John Carne was commissioned in October to raise a company of foot soldiers for a special regiment to be called the Prince of Wales's regiment. But recruitment would be a slow process and later in the month orders were issued to the deputy lieutenants through Beaufort to call out the militia. This had a dual purpose: to prepare the country for invasion, including any kind of armed rising in the localities, as also to anticipate and to frustrate the issuing of similar commissions not directly authorized by the King. What was no longer possible was the issuing of generalized orders for the preventative arrests of suspected persons as had been the case during the last invasion of the duke of Monmouth in 1685. The most that could be done or hoped for was to warn the deputies of the presence of Sir Rowland Gwynne, who was moving through south Wales 'to make disturbances', and to instruct them to arrest him, and to issue general warnings against the activities of disaffected persons.[26]

There is no evidence that the militia was raised in Glamorgan: what evidence there is suggests that little notice was taken of the orders issuing from the King via Beaufort. Ten days passed between the receipt by Sir Edward Mansel of an order to be communicated to all the other deputy lieutenants regarding preparations for calling out the militia before Sir Humphrey Mackworth heard of it at his home in Neath, four miles distant from Margam. This precipitated a sudden burst of activity which, however, soon subsided into the now customary silent inactivity. The gentry did nothing, and this was fatal for James. His admonition to Beaufort 'to keep Wales quiett' was only too faithfully observed in Glamorgan, and though none of its gentlemen appeared to have followed the marquis of Worcester with '2 or 300 horse . . . out of yᵉ County of Monmouth to yᵉ Prince who is sayd to be at Oxon or thereabouts', it was clear by then where their loyalties lay. Sir Edward Mansel thought it 'expedient' to send a letter to the Prince, and Bussy Mansel concurred. In this quiet undemonstrative way the reign came to an end in Glamorgan, and with it the end of an era.[27]

ii

GLAMORGAN POLITICS, 1688–1790

By PETER D. G. THOMAS

I. INTRODUCTION

THE POLITICAL STRUCTURE IN GLAMORGAN

Between the Glorious Revolution of 1688 and the Industrial Revolution of the later eighteenth century the political domination of Wales rested entirely with the landowners. They were no longer threatened with prerogative interference from above, and not yet troubled by democracy from below; while there was no significant class of moneyed men to challenge their supremacy, as in England. Political interest now centred almost exclusively on the Parliamentary representation, for this was both the symbol and the substance of power in each county. Ministers of the Crown tended to bestow all official patronage at the suggestion of the local M.P. All manner of influence in each shire therefore stemmed from the representatives of the county and borough, whether the nomination of squires to the bench of magistrates and to commissions in the local militia, or the appointment of their *protégés* to church livings, customs posts, and the like. Such favours comprised the means by which local politicians built up and maintained an 'interest', the contemporary term for influence; for effective power still lay with the traditional leaders of rural society. In Glamorgan the county electorate numbered well over a thousand, but nearly all the voters were tenants or dependants of the local magnates and gentry. In the borough constituency the county town of Cardiff had been joined by no less than seven out-boroughs —Aberavon, Cowbridge, Kenfig, Llantrisant, Loughor, Neath, and

Swansea. The first five of these, however, were hardly more than glorified villages. Cardiff itself was a market town. Only Swansea and Neath thriving as seaports and centres of industry, represented an urban economy. But in any case, the prosperity or otherwise of the boroughs was irrelevant to the size of the electorate: Swansea had only 64 burgesses in 1831, when the census showed a population of 13,256. Each borough was governed by a council or a court leet which deliberately restricted the Parliamentary franchise. Swansea in the eighteenth century had about 60 burgesses; Neath had 31 in 1759, Aberavon 20 in 1780; the total number of voters in the constituency was probably under 500. The electorate was kept small as a matter of policy, because by the opening decade of the eighteenth century all eight boroughs had come under the hold of only four patrons, who exercised power as respective lords of the manor, and who preferred to decide the Parliamentary representation by consultation rather than conflict.[28]

During the seventeenth century, indeed, increasing competition had thinned the ranks of Welsh families with Parliamentary ambitions. In Glamorgan the hold of the Mansel family on the representation of both constituencies was apparent after 1660. Sir Edward Mansel, fourth baronet, of Margam sat for the county in 1660, from 1670 to 1678, in 1681, and again in 1685. Though listed regularly as a supporter of the Court during Charles II's reign,[29] he had nevertheless been among the Welsh squires purged from local county offices in 1680;[30] and when hostility grew to the policies of James II, Sir Edward was regarded as one of the M.P.s opposed to that monarch.[31] Sir Edward Mansel was clearly the leading figure in Glamorgan towards the end of the seventeenth century. Head of a junior branch of the family at Briton Ferry was his cousin, Bussy Mansel, who boasted a record of more consistent opposition to the Court. A zealous partisan of Parliament in the Civil War, Bussy had held many official positions in the period of the Protectorate and Commonwealth. M.P. for Cardiff Boroughs in 1660, his only subsequent service at Westminster had been, significantly, in the Exclusion Parliaments of 1679 to 1681, as member for the county in the first two and for Cardiff in the third. An avowed Whig, Bussy had discreetly declined election in 1685 for James II's Parliament, and the Mansel interest in the borough constituency had helped to secure the return of a Glamorgan squire who was already an experienced Tory politician, Francis Gwyn of Llansannor.[32] To the contemporary observer, therefore, it might well have seemed that control of both shire and borough seats had passed to the great house of Mansel.

That the Mansels were the most influential family in Glamorgan there can be no doubt. Vast estates gave them direct control of over two hundred county voters, about one-sixth of the electorate, and many lesser squires were attached to the Mansel interest. In the borough constituency the Margam branch controlled Kenfig, while both Margam and Briton Ferry had influence in Aberavon. Sir Edward Mansel's two daughters, moreover, made marriages of political significance. Already by 1688 the elder, Martha, was wife to Thomas Morgan of Tredegar, a Whig squire who owned important estates in Monmouthshire and Breconshire. In 1706 the Morgan family interest was extended to Glamorgan, when Thomas Morgan's uncle John purchased the estate of Ruperra from Sir Edmund Thomas, second baronet, of Wenvoe; and on John Morgan's death in 1715 the seat was merged into the main Tredegar inheritance. Of potentially greater significance for the Glamorgan political scene was the betrothal, in 1694, of Sir Edward Mansel's younger daughter, Elizabeth, to Sir Edward Stradling, a young baronet who possessed the valuable estate of St. Donat's, estimated in 1738 to be worth £5,000 a year.[33] Her brother, Thomas, opposed the match, suggesting an alternative husband; but Sir Edward reproved his son and heir for this behaviour, and completed negotiations with Stradling's mother, agreeing to settle £5,000 on the bride.[34] The alliance, however, did not have the political consequences that might have been expected. After this inauspicious beginning, relations between Thomas Mansel and his new brother-in-law were rarely cordial and sometimes openly hostile. Stradling's subsequent share in the Parliamentary representation of Glamorgan clearly stemmed from his own personal consequence rather than his Mansel connections.

For the superficial impression of an all-powerful Mansel family in Glamorgan was misleading. The political structure of the county, indeed, was more complex than that of any other Welsh shire. Those with influence included a non-resident nobility as well as a numerous squirearchy. Prior to 1688 the two peerage houses of most importance in Glamorgan had been the earls of Pembroke and the marquesses of Worcester, who in 1684 had attained the rank of duke of Beaufort. In 1688 the first duke, whose Welsh seat was Raglan in Monmouthshire, was lord lieutenant of Glamorgan. The electoral influence there of the master of Raglan was considerable. The family estates ensured a county interest of over a hundred votes, and control of the boroughs of Swansea and Loughor. The so-called 'Cardiff Castle interest' of the earls of Pembroke was virtually dormant after the death of the seventh earl in 1683, when his south Wales estates were inherited by his daughter, Charlotte. Until her marriage in 1704 to Thomas Windsor, Viscount Windsor in the peerage of Ireland, the family influence was wielded by her uncle, the eighth earl, and he evidently exercised this power in favour of the Mansel family. Contemporaries were nevertheless aware that the Cardiff Castle interest, when exerted on its own behalf, might well prove to be dominant in the borough constituency, for it prevailed in Cowbridge, Llantrisant and in Cardiff itself, where the two bailiffs acted as returning officers. Only in these boroughs, and also in the Mansel stronghold of Kenfig, was the significant creation of voters possible; in the other four Parliamentary boroughs of Glamorgan burgess-ship involved such extensive material privileges that its expansion for electoral purposes was difficult and unpopular.[35]

Although the representation of the borough constituency might seem merely to involve negotiation among a few patrons, management of county and borough alike was in practice a task requiring tact and judgement. The gentry of Glamorgan were not disposed to accept any appearance of dictation, and the underlying theme of county politics during the century after 1688 was the frequent and sometimes successful resistance of the smaller squires to the decisions of the great landowners. A remarkable number possessed the means and ambition to enter Parliament themselves. During the eighteenth century county members were to come from the families of Fonmon Castle, Cefnmabli, Hensol, Llandaff Court, Wenvoe, Ewenni and Llanfihangel; while the seats of Llantriddyd, St. Donat's, and the Gnoll supplied borough members. Llanfihangel, an estate often of Parliamentary significance, had recently changed hands; sometime before 1687 it was purchased by Sir Humphrey Edwin from Sir Robert Thomas of Betws, borough member from 1661 to 1681. Edwin was a Whig merchant prominent in the City of London, where he became Lord Mayor in 1697:[36] though he did not concern himself with Glamorgan elections, three of his descendants were to sit for the shire. Another important newcomer to Glamorgan was Sir Humphrey Mackworth, who in 1686 had married the heiress of Sir Herbert Evans of the Gnoll; two years later he was in residence at that estate.[37] Mackworth soon exploited several coal mines in the district, and undertook copper-smelting at nearby Neath; and these industrial enterprises were continued and expanded by his son and grandson.[38] Although other landowners in the county were also coal proprietors, only the Mackworth family represented in Glamorgan politics at this time any significant economic interest other than land. The Gnoll estate gave Sir Humphrey a voice in the borough constituency, through control of Neath and an influence in Aberavon which he was soon to cultivate at Mansel expense. The Mackworths thus obtained a fourth important interest in the borough constituency, to join those of the Mansel family, the duke of Beaufort and Cardiff Castle.

II. The Mansel Supremacy, 1688–1722

The political structure of Glamorgan was virtually unaffected by the events of the Glorious Revolution, for the gentry of south Wales, like their fellows in England, flocked to the standard of William of Orange. Of the leading Glamorgan squires only Thomas Carne of Nash was actively loyal to James II. Ill-health prevented the personal attendance of Sir Edward Mansel on the Protestant hero, but a joint letter was despatched from Bussy Mansel and himself.[39] Sir Edward now decided to retire from Parliament, though he continued to play a dominant role in Glamorgan politics. In 1689 Bussy Mansel therefore took the county seat, while Sir Edward's son, Thomas, became borough member. But Thomas did not altogether share his elders' approval of the events of 1688. He voted in 1689 against the offer of the throne to William and Mary; and during the alarm of 1696 over the Jacobite conspiracy known as the Fenwick plot he, unlike Bussy, refused to sign the Association for the defence of William III.[40] Glamorgan at the time remained as quiet as most of Britain. The deputy lieutenants of the county returned the names of only three gentlemen who were papist, and therefore suspect as traitors, to the earl of Pembroke as Lord Lieutenant; none of them, Thomas Turbervill of Pen-llin, Christopher Turbervill, and Evan Thomas of Betws, can be identified with certainty.[41]

Meanwhile, the Mansel hold on the Parliamentary representation of Glamorgan remained as yet a matter merely of vigilance and of propriety, formal observance of the expressed will of the county. No evidence has survived on the election of 1690, when both Mansels retained their seats; before the next one, in 1695, a general meeting of the county at Bridgend duly endorsed the nomination of Bussy and Thomas Mansel.[42] But by the 1698 election an unexpected difficulty had arisen: Thomas Mansel's dislike of the new political system after 1689 had hardened into a refusal to stand for Parliament again, a decision greatly to the annoyance of his father. In a letter of July 20 Sir Edward urged on his son the impolicy of such a step.[43]

> Entail not a perpetual trouble on yourself and posterity, for the Borough once lost out of the family will not so easily be recovered. For my part I am old and would not willingly end my days as I began them, in trouble; besides, being out, you will not have so much for your power to oblige. Creditors will be sharp. Neither would I have you give so clear a demonstration of being an enemy to the present Government which is Protestant.

Sir Edward's immediate reason for concern was his belief that a canvass for the borough constituency had been made by Sir Charles Kemys of Cefnmabli. An influential Glamorgan squire, Kemys had been returned for Monmouthshire in 1695, but he was about to lose his seat in 1698.[44] On August 2, however, Kemys wrote to deny that he had 'made interest for standing for Parliament men in Glamorgan'.[45] Thomas Mansel remained obdurate, and Sir Edward Stradling replaced his brother-in-law as borough member, a solution that was to produce difficulty in the future. Bad feeling between Kemys and the Mansels persisted after the election. Sir Charles wrote again to Sir Edward Mansel on October 28, repeating his denial of any intention of standing for a Glamorgan constituency, but voicing his own grievance at exclusion from the county meeting on the subject of the election, an interesting revelation of Mansel tactics. 'Why I was not thought worthy to be sent to amongst the rest of the gentlemen in order to the general meeting at

Cowbridge is past my understanding.'[46] Sir Edward's own son-in-law, Thomas Morgan, wrote to support Kemys. 'My neighbour Sir Charles is with me at this present time, and is very much concerned to find you are of opinion he designed to undermine the house of Margam.'[47] The breach was apparently never healed. In 1700 Sir Charles Kemys was vainly trying to wrest control over the borough of Cardiff from friends of the Mansel family;[48] but his schemes came to nought with his death in 1702.

By that time the high-handedness of the Mansels had led to a quarrel with their own in-law, Sir Edward Stradling. On the death of old Bussy Mansel in May of 1699 Thomas Mansel had agreed to fill the vacancy in the county representation, but soon he was again informing his father of his determination to withdraw from the House of Commons. It was knowledge of this circumstance that in 1700 led Bussy's son, another Thomas Mansel, to announce his candidature for the county, while Stradling proposed to continue as borough member. It transpired, however, that the declarations of Thomas Mansel of Margam were not to be taken at face value. There was speculation in Cardiff over the possibility of a county contest between Margam and Briton Ferry.[49] Wiser counsels prevailed after Thomas Mansel of Briton Ferry had made this apology to his namesake on January 6, 1701. 'I saw a great many letters from you to the old gentleman wherein you mentioned you had no thoughts of standing this Parliament, which made Sir Edward Stradling and myself offer ourselves to the county gentlemen, and am heartily sorry you did not let us know your thoughts sooner.'[50] The agreement for the general election of that month could not be altered; but at the next election, in December of the same year, Stradling found that his seat at Westminster was sacrificed to the cause of Mansel unity. The two Thomas Mansels then shared the Parliamentary representation of Glamorgan, Margam taking the county and Briton Ferry the borough. The same arrangement continued for the general elections of 1702 and 1705; and the deterioration of relations between the Mansels and Stradling was marked by the latter's demands for the belated payment of his wife's marriage dowry.[51]

The alienation of Stradling was a singularly ill-timed event for the Mansel family, as several circumstances at the beginning of the eighteenth century indicated that the Mansel supremacy in Glamorgan would soon be challenged. The Lord Windsor who in 1704 acquired by marriage the Cardiff Castle interest of the earls of Pembroke laid no claim himself to a Glamorgan seat, representing the borough of Bramber from 1705 to 1708 and Monmouthshire thereafter; but he was soon to show his intention of participating in county politics. The revival of the other leading aristocratic interest in Glamorgan also occurred at the same time. The second duke of Beaufort, who had succeeded his grandfather in 1700, came of age five years later; and he at once formed an alliance

[399]

AI

with Sir Humphrey Mackworth,[52] who was by then a declared enemy of the Mansel family. In the decade of the sixteen-nineties there had been frequent consultation between the Mansels and Sir Humphrey over the appointment of officials in the boroughs of Neath and Aberavon.[53] Mackworth, however, contrived to tilt the balance of power in the latter borough in his own favour, and soon after 1700 he was evidently in effective control of both. By 1705 an attack by Sir Humphrey on the Mansel interest was generally anticipated in Glamorgan; for Sir Edward Mansel received from a friend this comment on political affairs in the county.[54] 'Tis plain Sir Humphrey Mackworth aims at nothing less than Universal Monarchy in Glamorganshire, but the attempt cannot succeed while there are such fruits of his Empire. Besides, the people are too sensible of their happiness under their present Guardians and their misery under the little sway he has already over them to vest him with more.'

Mackworth was doubtless aware that in 1705 he would lose his seat for Cardiganshire, where his political attention had previously been concentrated; and he probably hoped to win the borough constituency in Glamorgan. But his campaign there against the Mansel family completely failed; even in his own borough of Neath Thomas Mansel of Briton Ferry secured promises of 15 votes.[55] There is no indication that Sir Humphrey carried his challenge to a poll; but the quarrel between Mackworth and the Mansels continued in ways characteristic of the time. Sir Humphrey sought to have friends of the Mansel family removed from the Commission of the Peace.[56] A Mansel retaliation was an attempt forcibly to enlist into the army some of Mackworth's employees at his copper works.[57] One notable humiliation Sir Humphrey was able to inflict on Sir Edward Mansel. Some of Mackworth's men who were carrying lead ore over Margam land were attacked by servants of Mansel. Instead of having to defend an action for trespass Sir Humphrey, as M.P. for Totnes, appealed to the House of Commons; and in February 1706 the Committee of Privileges ruled that he had suffered several breaches of Parliamentary privilege.[58]

Opposition to the Mansel family was thus already becoming formidable when the circumstances of national politics sparked off an electoral storm in Glamorgan. Hitherto, decisions on the Parliamentary representation had depended on personal and family rather than political factors. Alignments and attitudes at Westminster had been irrelevant, for in Glamorgan there was no significant Whig-Tory party division. The undoubtedly Whiggish views of Bussy Mansel had not hindered his return as shire member, even though the political complexion of the county was Tory. The men of most influence represented, indeed, all shades of Tory opinion. The dukes of Beaufort were openly Jacobite. Sir Humphrey Mackworth was prominent among the High Tories, men zealous to enforce and increase the civil disabilities of Protestant Dissenters (below, p. 481). The correspondence of Sir Edward Stradling, too, reveals him as an extreme partisan in the Tory attack of 1701 on the former Whig ministers.[59] Moderate Tories of varying hue included the eighth earl of Pembroke, Lord Windsor, Sir Edward Mansel, and both the members of Parliament. Bussy's son, Thomas, was a court Tory, and there had recently been a significant change in the political views of Thomas Mansel of Margam. At first so hostile to the new order of the Revolution Settlement, he came to be influenced about the turn of the century by his close friend, Robert Harley, M.P. for Radnor Boroughs and founder of a new moderate Tory group in Parliament. Soon after the beginning of Queen Anne's reign, in 1702, Harley realized the need for cooperation with the Whigs in a vigorous prosecution of the War of the Spanish Succession. By 1704 the ministry comprised a coalition of Whigs and Harleyites, opposed mainly by Jacobites and High Tories; and in April of that year Thomas Mansel himself took the post of Comptroller of the Queen's Household.

This new political situation soon led him into electoral difficulties in Glamorgan. The death of Thomas Mansel of Briton Ferry in January 1706 caused a borough by-election the next month. To fill the vacancy Sir Edward Mansel and Thomas Mansel of Margam recommended not Sir Edward Stradling but a local Whig baronet, Sir John Aubrey of Llantriddyd. The nomination was accepted without demur by the borough officials of Cardiff, and Aubrey was duly returned.[60] There was evidently a widespread feeling in Glamorgan, however, that the seat should have been given to Stradling. Open opposition began to the hegemony of the house of Mansel, and by September of the same year rival candidates had appeared for both county and borough, even though the next general election was not due until 1708. Thomas Mansel faced a serious crisis, and one of his friends sent this gloomy report on Glamorgan affairs to Robert Harley.[61]

> The gentlemen of the county proposed to him some terms of elections, that they would agree him to be knight of the shire next parliament, but would have Sir Edward Stradling for the borough, which he refusing, Captain Jenkins has declared he will oppose him for the County, and Sir Edward Stradling will stand for the Borough; and they are now as busy on all sides making of interest and spending of money as if the election was next month . . . I fear in my heart Mansel will be hard put to it.

Mansel's opponent in the county was Richard Jenkins of Hensol. He and Stradling, Mansel's own brother-in-law, soon obtained formidable support, the backing of Lord Windsor, of the young duke of Beaufort, and of Sir Humphrey Mackworth.[62] It seemed as if the Mansel family would now pay dearly for their failure to avoid the appearance of dictation in their earlier political management of Glamorgan. But Thomas Mansel did not lack resources, or resource. By this time the entire Mansel interest was in his hands. He had succeeded his father in his baronetcy and the

Margam estate in November 1706; while he controlled Briton Ferry in the name of his five-year-old third son Bussy, who had been bequeathed that estate by the other Thomas Mansel, his godfather. Sir Thomas Mansel himself, moreover, also had important allies. He had immediately been promised assistance by his kinsmen, the Morgans of Tredegar and Ruperra.[63] Sir Edmund Thomas of Wenvoe was a staunch supporter, and another baronet, Sir Edward Mansel of Stradey and Trimsaran, was active in canvassing the county. Ministerial influence, too, secured the appointment of a friend, Richard Carne of Ewenni, as sheriff for the election year of 1708. In the borough constituency, where Mansel faced a formidable coalition of hostile patrons, he conducted a vigorous and enterprising campaign. In his own borough of Kenfig, Mansel arranged for his friends to send in quotas of their tenants to be sworn as burgesses.[64] He also contrived to undermine the influence of opposing patrons in their boroughs. In particular, he organised a successful counter-attack on Mackworth. In Aberavon, burgesses were won over by gifts of coal and other necessaries.[65] Favourable burgess creations were engineered in Neath, and also in Cardiff, where the bailiffs were completely under Mansel's direction. Stradling informed Mackworth in March 1707 that Lord Windsor would need to resort to legal action to void the numerous new burgess creations there and restore his own authority.[66] But this had not been achieved by 1708, when the Mansel party anticipated that the conduct of the poll in both constituencies would be in favourable hands.[67]

How far this electoral alignment in Glamorgan did represent a division between supporters and opponents of the ministry is not altogether clear. But in February 1708 the Harleyites, including Mansel, resigned their offices and joined the High Tories in opposition to what became a Whig administration; and it may have been this circumstance that led the Tories of Glamorgan to seek a compromise of the electoral dispute. At the beginning of April Sir Thomas Mansel arranged with his most influential opponent, the duke of Beaufort, to send a joint letter to the sheriff, addressed to the gentlemen of Glamorgan. The draft of the letter survives among the Mansel papers, and shows that they sought to appeal to the contemporary dislike of contested elections.[68]

> Having with very great concern taken into our consideration the manifold inconveniences and disorders that are like to ensue at the next Election for the County and Town, and doubting that tumults and quarrels may arise from so great a concourse of people (especially from the great numbers concerned in the Election for Cardiff) and the great hazard of entailing disputes and animosities on several Gentlemen's families, and others concerned in the Elections; we could heartily wish that such a temper and such expedients might be found as might prevent the Inconveniencies aforesaid, and reconcile all differences; and for our own parts, we will very willingly submit all private considerations of our own to the peace and good neighbourhood of the county . . . We have the same zeal for the support of Her Majesty and Her Government, and the same concern for the preservation of the Constitution, as by law established in Church and State, and as we agree in the same end we hope we shall have no difference about the means of pursuing it. We

heartily wish this may have a good effect towards a reconciliation of all our friends but if it should not we hope at least both elections will be carried on with decency and good manners, that the door may not be shut against a future good understanding and agreement.

The sheriff had received this letter by April 13. First reactions, however, were unfavourable, Mansel being told by a supporter that 'your friends do not seem to approve of your joining with the Duke'.[69] Nor was the sheriff optimistic when replying to Mansel on April 15.[70]

> I wish with all my heart it could have the good effect proposed, but Captain Jenkins showed so little regard to the letter when I mentioned it to him; his answer was this, that he thought the election was no man's birthright, and that opposition of this nature was very common in other parts of the Kingdom . . . So that unless his Grace and you take further measures in this affair the elections must come on and I very much dread the ill consequences the great concourse of people may have especially where disputed elections are so new.

Events thereafter were complex and obscure. It would seem that despite his fine words Richard Jenkins was the first candidate to withdraw his pretensions; and by May 7 he had even promised his support to Sir John Aubrey in the borough. Mansel thereupon renewed his efforts to persuade his brother-in-law Stradling to agree to a compromise.[71] He clearly achieved a temporary success, for Robert Harley was informed by a Welsh correspondent, 'There is a strange jumble in Glamorganshire, old friends turned foes, and old foes made friends, Sir Thomas being entirely reconciled to his brother Stradling.'[72] But this state of affairs must have ended almost at once, for on May 11 Aubrey wrote to Mansel asking him to be at Cardiff for the election with 'as many of the old burgesses' as he thought fit.[73] At the same time Samuel Edwin, eldest son and successor in 1707 to Sir Humphrey Edwin, was urging Jenkins to stand again for the county.[74] The move failed; and Mansel, who was returned unopposed in the shire, triumphed also in the borough. The result was reported thus to Harley. 'Sir Edward Stradling and his brother are again at the utmost variance, and Sir John Aubrey carried his election by the favour of the latter. All Sir Edward's party forsook him because he would not agree to cast lots.'[75]

Before another general election was due, Queen Anne had dismissed her Whig ministers early in 1710, and Harley formed a new administration in which his close friend Sir Thomas Mansel held office as a Lord of the Treasury. Sir John Aubrey, a staunch Whig, could hardly have expected Mansel's support in the circumstance of a national upsurge of Toryism, and there is no evidence that he stood at the election later in the year. 'The Whig interest at present is very low in that country', Sir Edward Stradling commented when accepting Mansel's offer in May of the borough seat. The situation, however, was complicated by the fact that in 1710 Stradling was sheriff of Glamorgan, a circumstance that was thought to debar him from election for any constituency in the county. He therefore made this suggestion to Mansel. 'If a dissolution happens and that I cannot stand, we have no way left but choosing you for town and country.'[76] Mansel could then postpone his decision on which seat to take until Stradling's term of office was over. Robert Harley himself offered an alternative solution, that John Laugharne, Tory M.P. for Haverfordwest, might be willing to change seats so as to accommodate Stradling.[77] But consultation with the foremost Tory lawyer of the day, Sir Simon Harcourt, then M.P. for Cardigan Boroughs, had already established that Stradling was eligible to sit for Cardiff;[78] and at the general election of October 1710 both he and Mansel were returned without opposition. The whole episode illustrates a surprising ignorance of electoral law even among leading politicians.

In 1710 Sir Thomas Mansel's arrangements had not been challenged; but that his rule in Glamorgan may still have been arousing widespread discontent is hinted by the events of the county by-election of 1712. Mansel, who in June 1711 resumed his former post of Comptroller of the Queen's Household, received one of the dozen Tory peerage creations made to pass the Peace of Utrecht, becoming Lord Mansel on December 31, 1711. Another went to Viscount Windsor, then M.P. for Monmouthshire, who on the same day received a British peerage as Lord Mountjoy. For the first time since 1670 there was no Mansel candidate to take the county seat, as the new Lord Mansel's eldest son, Robert, was still under age. The vacancy was filled at the by-election of January 31, 1712 by Robert Jones of Fonmon Castle, the brother-in-law of Samuel Edwin of Llanfihangel. Although the grandson of the Colonel Philip Jones who had governed Glamorgan for Oliver Cromwell during the Commonwealth, he was a Tory. His election was perhaps a Mansel concession to Glamorgan malcontents, in return for a promise to support the ministry; for Richard Carne of Ewenni sent this account of the proceedings to Lord Mansel. 'Yesterday was our election day, when there was as great an appearance as I have seen at any time. Our new Knight appeared very great and I hope he will do so behave, for he has given us great assurances that he will be diligent and an honest voter.'[79]

Lord Mansel's personal influence, however, was strengthened after the death of the second duke of Beaufort in 1714, for there followed another minority in the Raglan family. Under his guidance, Glamorgan continued to return Tory members even after the accession of the Hanoverian dynasty in 1714 put control of the government into Whig hands. Sir Edward Stradling and Robert Jones retained their respective seats without known opposition at the general elections of both 1713 and 1715. When Jones died in December 1715, his place as county member was filled by Sir Charles Kemys of Cefnmabli, son of the Mansel enemy who had died in 1702, and head of a small group of Jacobites in Glamorgan.[80] The return of such a member for the shire was perhaps another concession by Lord Mansel to the independence of the local squirearchy. Kemys was to represent the county without disturbance for eighteen years, but the next borough election raised the issue of Mansel hegemony once again. When it became known by 1720 that Sir Edward Stradling was intending to retire from Parliament, Samuel Edwin, who had unsuccessfully fought Minehead borough in 1715, was proposed as his successor. Since Robert Mansel had come of age in 1716 and was also looking for a seat, this move had apparently been made by the faction hostile to Lord Mansel. Indeed, he seemingly heard of the suggestion only at third-hand, when John Turbervill of Llangattog informed him that Sir Edmund Thomas of Wenvoe had mentioned the project.[81] In these circumstances the return at the general election of 1722 of Stradling's elder son, Edward, as member for Cardiff was probably a compromise solution. In the meantime Robert Mansel had won a Minehead seat at a by-election of December 1721, despite the disapproval of his father, who had refused support because the venture involved spending money outside the county.[82] But Lord Mansel was perhaps not displeased that, when his son retained the seat in 1722, Samuel Edwin was again an unsuccessful candidate.

III. The Whig Challenge and 'The Independent Interest', 1722–50

This election marked the end of the first phase in the political history of Glamorgan since 1688. The threat to Mansel rule now took on a different guise, as a challenge was made by the local Whigs. Too much of a contrast, perhaps, should not be read into the changed situation. Certainly the new attack was one mounted by Whigs against a Tory ascendancy; but later in the century, when party terminology no longer obscured the basic conflict in the county between aristocracy and gentry, the struggle was remembered as a fight by 'the independent interest' for the political freedom of Glamorgan.[83] Lord Mansel did not live to see the new challenge, for he died on December 11, 1723. As Robert Mansel had already predeceased him, on April 29, the title and Margam estates passed to Robert's four-year-old son Thomas. The mother of this young second Lord Mansel, who soon remarried to become Mrs. John Blackwood, undertook the management of her son's affairs. But in Glamorgan politics she allowed herself to be guided by his younger uncle, Bussy Mansel, who himself had come of age to enjoy his own estate of Briton Ferry only in 1722. It was therefore Bussy Mansel who was faced with the refusal of the Whig families of Glamorgan to submit, in an age of Whig supremacy, to a Tory monopoly of the Parliamentary representation. Various circumstances at this time combined to strengthen the Whig interest in Glamorgan. A notable Whig newcomer to the county was Charles Talbot, M.P. for Durham City and Solicitor-General in Walpole's ministry from 1726 to 1733. In 1708 he had married Cecil, heiress daughter of Charles Mathew of Castell-y-Mynach; and she had inherited, also, the important Hensol estate from her uncle, Richard Jenkins. Another influential Whig who now turned his attention to Glamorgan was Commodore Thomas Matthews of Llandaff. After an active and distinguished naval career since the reign of William III, Matthews settled down in 1724 to the life of a country gentleman. He was a kinsman of Charles Mathew, and his own family of Llandaff Court had a tradition of hostility to the Cardiff Castle interest dating back to the sixteenth century (above, pp. 187–91). Always willing to assist the hitherto dormant Whig cause in Glamorgan, too, were the brothers William and Thomas Morgan of Tredegar and Ruperra, sons of John Morgan, who had died in 1720; for the bond of kinship with the Mansels had by now worn thin.

The general election of September 1727 saw the first move by the Glamorgan Whigs, with a candidate in the borough constituency. There Bussy Mansel had become the member at a by-election in January 1727 on the death of Edward Stradling. He was detained in London throughout the campaign by the fatal illness of his first wife, who died on September 3, only two days before the borough election. However, his elder brother, Christopher, promised to appear at Cardiff on his behalf, and he had a close electoral alliance with the county member, Sir Charles Kemys.[84] Before a contest was expected they had agreed to share their election costs, and had then intended to cut this expense to a minimum by holding the county and borough elections on the same day, attended only by about twenty 'double voters'. This plan had been frustrated by the insistence of the borough officials on a separate election day, and the hope of economy was finally wrecked by the appearance of a Whig opponent in the borough.[85] In a letter of July 29 to Kemys, Mansel announced that he had persuaded Mrs. Blackwood to give him the Margam interest in the county, and then urged vigorous action on his own behalf. 'I need not desire you to do me all the service you can, because I know you will: only remember that our enemies have a great advantage when one is not present, and I would not for a thousand pound be thrown out by *such* a Gentleman.'[86] Mansel's opponent was evidently Thomas Matthews; for when thanking Kemys for his assistance after his election on September 5, he mentioned the possibility of a petition to Parliament from 'the commodore'.[87] Mansel, absent in London, appears to have taken the threat more seriously than Sir Charles Kemys, on the spot in Cardiff; for when the question of paying the election bills arose, Kemys proved indignant at the idea that the earlier agreement bound him to share Mansel's expenses for the contest, voicing this complaint.[88]

I leave the Welsh to judge whether it would not hurt upon me to pay for the expense of three or four hundred men, who had no vote in the county. Especially when the opposition Mr. Mansel met with was entirely owing to the mismanagement of his own agents. Therefore by God as I will not be shuffled, I would not willingly have the Welsh convinced I shuffle others.

The matter was eventually referred for arbitration to Sir Edward Stradling, who ruled that Sir Charles Kemys ought to pay half the cost. In 1731, however, Mansel had to remind Kemys that the bills had not all been paid. 'That the poor people may not suffer, to whom the money is due, be pleased to nominate whom you please and I will stand to a second reference.'[89] The outcome of this dispute is not known; but in February 1733 Bussy Mansel thought it expedient to suggest a reconciliation. It was widely known that Sir Charles Kemys would be retiring from Parliament at the next general election through ill-health, and Mansel hoped to succeed him as county representative. He therefore wrote to propose a meeting. 'I will readily admit that in quarrels between friends there are generally faults on both sides.'[90] Sir Charles Kemys accepted the olive branch;[91] but that the dispute still rankled was to be apparent from his attitude at the general election of 1734.

The election took place against the background of national controversy aroused by Walpole's Excise Bill of 1733. In Glamorgan the local Whigs made a bid for both seats. The story of the borough contest is soon told. Here, Thomas Matthews was again the Whig candidate, and he had commenced his campaign before the end of 1732. The fear of the Tories was that he might contrive to obtain a majority in the county town of Cardiff itself, and then secure the disfranchisement of all the out-boroughs by a partisan decision of the House of Commons; for this was exactly what had happened to the Montgomery group of boroughs at the general election of 1727. Some difficulty, moreover, was found in the choice of a Tory candidate to replace Mansel. In December 1732 Sir Edward Stradling told Sir Charles Kemys that Mrs. Blackwood had been pressing his second son, Thomas, to stand.[92] By early 1733 Stradling had withdrawn, and Sir Edmund Thomas, third baronet, of Wenvoe, then newly of age, came forward in his stead, writing to Sir Charles Kemys on March 29, 1733. 'You are the first in the county to whom I have declared my design, as I should be particularly glad that my first attempt of this nature might have your approbation. The Duke of Beaufort has already honoured me with the promise of his assistance.'[93] But young Thomas was presumptuous. An even more important patron than the duke of Beaufort decided to exert his influence, for Lord Windsor sponsored the candidature of his only son, Herbert, on the Cardiff Castle interest. He secured the support of Thomas Stradling, and perhaps his earlier withdrawal, by the post of constable of Cardiff Castle.[94] And at the borough contest of 1734 it was Herbert Windsor who defeated Thomas Matthews in a poll for which the voting figures, as in 1727, are unknown.

The main interest centred on the county election. Here the danger of regarding this contest purely as a Tory-Whig clash is shown by the

first move of Charles Talbot of Hensol, in July 1733. He was then the
Solicitor-General in Walpole's ministry, and before the end of the year
became Lord Chancellor with the peerage title of Lord Talbot. Yet
his initial approach was to the retiring Jacobite member, asking support
for his eldest son, Charles.

> I shall be unwilling to take any measures opposite to your interest if you are
> determined to stand; but if you choose to give yourself ease, it would be a great
> encouragement to my son to offer his service to the county could he hope for the
> vote and interest of Sir Charles Kemys.

The attempt to exploit the bad feeling between Kemys and Bussy
Mansel met with some success; for Sir Charles scrawled this draft reply
on Talbot's letter.[95]

> As to Mr. Talbot's offering his service to the county I must beg leave to be
> intent on that head till the Gentlemen of our county meet and consult about a
> proper person to represent them, at which time I shall be unwilling to take any
> measures opposite to yours or your son's interest.

The answer foreshadowed Kemys's attitude of neutrality during
the contest. The only concession Bussy Mansel could obtain from his
former ally was an order to the Cefnmabli agents that the tenants were
to be 'at their own liberty to give their votes which way they had a mind
to, or stay at home'. Both sides were informed of this decision, but the
Hensol family secured most of the votes. Sir Charles Kemys, indeed,
was allowing personal pique to overcome his political sympathies; for
all the other information on the election indicates a fight between the
Tory families of the county and the Whig supporters of Walpole's
ministry. Bussy Mansel was backed by the traditional Tory interest,
headed by the duke of Beaufort, Lord Windsor, Sir Edward Stradling,
and Herbert Mackworth of Gnoll, who had succeeded his father, Sir
Humphrey, in 1727. The Whig candidate, Charles Talbot, died on
September 27, 1733, to be replaced by his younger brother, William.
Particularly active on his behalf were Thomas Matthews and Thomas
Morgan of Tredegar.[96] At the poll, too, old Sir John Aubrey, the Whig
borough member of Anne's reign, appeared in his support.[97] Not only
were the known adherents of Talbot Whigs, those of Mansel Tories;
a political flavour dating from past party traditions was also imparted
to the election by the charge that the Tory candidate was hostile towards
the religious liberty of Protestant Dissenters. Bussy Mansel felt it expedient
to issue this 'Declaration to Dissenters' in reply.[98]

> Whereas it has been invidiously represented in order to determine persons
> to oppose my interest in the ensuing election that I am an enemy to the religious
> and civil rights of my countrymen, I assure all gentlemen that have votes in this
> country and particularly the Protestant dissenters, that if I have the honour to
> represent this county, I shall always have a tender regard to those just privileges
> they at present enjoy.

As government supporters the Talbot family obtained the advantage of a partisan sheriff for the election year of 1734, William Bassett of Miskin. The poll took place at Cardiff. It began on Thursday, May 23, and continued until Monday, June 3. The total number of votes cast then would have given Bussy Mansel a majority of 823 to 678, and he later claimed that the scrutiny of the poll afterwards had been demanded by his opponent.[99] But a contemporary account of the election shows that he himself insisted on a scrutiny after the sheriff had declared Talbot the victor. William Bassett's ruling had allowed 455 freehold votes for Talbot, and only 288 for Mansel, as he had marked as questionable 535 for Mansel and 223 for Talbot.[100] The scrutiny lasted another week, until on June 10 the sheriff finally made his return, declaring Talbot elected by 658 votes to 577, a majority of 81. He had struck off the poll 246 of Mansel's votes, and only 20 for Talbot. The Tory landowners had undoubtedly created many new leasehold voters in the previous July; but the indignant Bussy Mansel at once resolved to appeal to the House of Commons.[101] His petition, complaining of the sheriff's conduct, was read in the House on January 28, 1735. A motion to hear the case at the Bar of the House, however, was rejected by the Walpole ministry on a party vote; the case was referred to the Committee of Elections, and no report was ever made.[102]

Three years later this bitter contest had an ironic sequel. Lord Talbot died on February 14, 1737; William Talbot succeeded to his title and estates; and Bussy Mansel obtained the county seat in the next month without opposition. The death of Lord Windsor on June 8, 1738 led to a by-election also in the borough, for his son Herbert inherited his titles. The candidate proposed by the Tory borough patrons for this vacancy was Sir Thomas Stradling of St. Donat's.[103] Stradling had succeeded his father Sir Edward on April 5, 1735. But, before the by-election took place, he was killed in a duel in France, on September 27, 1738, bequeathing his estates to Bussy Mansel for life. The other patrons thereupon agreed on Herbert Mackworth as the next member. To his indignation, however, Mackworth found that he was expected to provide an entertainment for the voters; and peevishly wrote instructions to his agent on November 18, 1738.[104]

> I must needs say at the same time that this is a compliment to Lord Windsor, than in any way necessary . . . I dont remember that he made any such treat at Neath or Swansea or any other borough when he stood himself, nor heard of Mr. Stradling's doing before he was Sir Thomas, whilst he was the intended candidate. Indeed, the treating so many boroughs would make this as expensive or more than a county election and money quite thrown away when all the several lords are agreed in the recommendation. However, I agree to such a treat as you advise at Cardiff in respect to Lord Windsor.

Herbert Mackworth was elected on February 16, 1739, and continued to represent the borough constituency without opposition until his death in 1765. Bussy Mansel seems to have anticipated a quiet tenure of the county seat, too, and made a rather formal canvass in the summer of 1740, preparatory to the general election of the next year.[105] He was assured of the support of the duke of Beaufort and the new Lord Windsor, and, through them, of that of Sir Charles Kemys Tynte of Cefnmabli.[106] Tynte, a Somersetshire ally of the duke, had inherited that estate on the death of his uncle, Sir Charles Kemys, in 1735. In September 1740, however, Mansel was faced with a surprise opponent, in the person of Charles Edwin of Llanfihangel, who had succeeded his father Samuel in 1722. The young second Lord Mansel, due to come of age in December, was informed of this event by one of his agents on September 23. 'This country is in as great a ferment as seven years ago . . . The party has spirited Mr. Edwin to oppose Mr. Mansel.'[107] Bussy Mansel himself wrote to his nephew four days later. 'Contrary to my Expectation Mr. Edwin opposes me for this County, and though I am sure he has no chance for it but by getting a sheriff who will make a false return, yet I am forced to be active in getting as great a majority as possible.'[108] Bussy Mansel's confidence stemmed from the fact that the opposition had been instigated solely by Thomas Morgan of Tredegar, and not by all the Glamorgan Whigs. But his nephew proved unco-operative. Lord Mansel was offended because his uncle had not asked promptly for the Margam interest, and he had a deeper grievance over the way in which Bussy had come into possession of the Stradling estate. He refused to announce support for his uncle, and Bussy was therefore obliged to write him a pressing letter on October 9.[109]

> If your Lordship does not declare immediately in my favour you will put me to much trouble and expense, and, if you will give yourself a moment's time to reflect, I am sure you will think it hard I should be put to any unnecessary expense after having laid out full £4,000 to support the family interest during your minority; not that I would have you imagine that your Lordship's interest and mine could ever choose a member for this county without the assistance of many of our friends. This is truth, and whoever tells you otherwise deceives you.

Lord Mansel's other uncle, Christopher, also wrote to reprove his nephew for his obduracy.[110] By November he had yielded to this family pressure and agreed to support Bussy in the election.[111] In the next month the latter's fear of suffering foul play again from a government-nominated sheriff was removed by the appointment for 1741 of Rowland Dawkins of Kilvrough. Although Charles Edwin was still a candidate in January 1741, he clearly withdrew before the poll; for on May 14 Bussy Mansel wrote to Dawkins, 'As you were so kind to tell me I might have the election where I would, there being no opposition, I would desire it might be at Cardiff, as I fancy that place will be most agreeable to you.'[112] Edwin himself fought Westminster as an opposition Whig, and he was returned unopposed there in December after the original election had been voided.

1741, however, did not mark the end of the Whig challenge in Glamorgan. Within four years the county was the scene of a brief and violent by-election contest. The vacancy arose unexpectedly, after the deaths in rapid succession of the young second Lord Mansel on January 29, 1744, and of his uncle and successor, Christopher, on November 26 of the same year. Bussy Mansel then became the fourth Lord Mansel, adding the Margam estates to those of Briton Ferry and St. Donat's. As soon as the news of the third Lord Mansel's death in Sussex reached London on November 28, there was an immediate flurry of activity. Thomas Matthews, the first candidate in the field, was a man then very much in the public eye. He had resumed his naval career in 1736; and, during the War of the Austrian Succession, he had been created an admiral in 1742, by virtue of his seniority, and sent at the age of 66 to take command of the British fleet in the Mediterranean. There, in February 1744, his numerically superior squadron fought an indecisive battle off Toulon with a Franco-Spanish force. The national outcry in Britain at this apparent failure caused Matthews to resign his command and return home, and a court-martial had been appointed to investigate the affair.[113] While serving in the Mediterranean, Matthews had asked Lord Talbot for help to enter Parliament; and, despite the cloud over his head, he promptly sought out Lord Talbot the same day, and obtained the promise of his support for Glamorgan.

The morning of November 29 saw canvassing on behalf of another candidate, Sir Charles Kemys Tynte. Although Tynte himself was in Bath, his claims were urged by two Tory friends from Somerset, Thomas Prowse and Thomas Carew. Also keenly interested in the Glamorgan election was the most influential Welsh Tory, Sir Watkin Williams Wynn of Wynnstay, M.P. for Denbighshire; and it was Wynn who reported developments to the duke of Beaufort on his arrival in London the next day, November 30. The duke enthusiastically agreed to support Tynte, and wrote to both Lord Windsor and the new Lord Mansel, who was home at Briton Ferry.[114] Wynn also met Charles Edwin, but he evasively declined to engage himself to either side.[115] When Bussy Mansel heard of his brother's death he, too, at once urged Sir Charles Tynte to stand.[116] But it was only with reluctance that Tynte yielded to pressure, and commenced his canvass on December 4.[117]

The Glamorgan election coincided with a critical period in British politics, the reconstruction of the ministry by Henry Pelham and his brother, the duke of Newcastle, after the resignation of Lord Carteret on November 24.[118] The Pelhams were negotiating at this time with Tories as well as opposition Whigs; and some of Tynte's friends hoped that ministerial pressure might be brought on Matthews to withdraw, a view expressed by Thomas Prowse to Tynte on December 1. 'As great Professions are now made with regard to Tories, and as this is required as a Pledge of their sincerity, you will readily agree with me that such a request is likely to be granted by People who perhaps intend doing not much more, than barely granting a trifle.'[119] One of the Tory leaders, Lord Gower, did persuade Henry Pelham to offer Matthews a seat then vacant at Portsmouth, but the Admiral declined to reply, and Pelham refused to intervene directly in the contest.[120] The ministers, indeed, might be presumed to favour Matthews, though an opposition Whig, rather than his Tory opponent. And the Glamorgan contest shows the survival of old party alignments at the county level in disregard of national developments. The local Whigs, government and opposition alike, maintained their traditional alliance against the Tory families. Thomas Morgan of Tredegar, the leading ministerial supporter in south Wales, had promptly placed his Ruperra interest behind Matthews;[121] and on December 25 he reported events to the Lord Chancellor, Lord Hardwicke. 'Admiral Matthews has met with success in canvassing and if promises will hold good till after the election I think he stands very fair to be chose but I dont love to be so positive beforehand.'[122]

Matthews had gained a considerable advantage in starting his campaign first, for it was a point of honour to keep an election promise, even if given under a misapprehension.[123] Sir Edmund Thomas of Wenvoe, himself then M.P. for Chippenham, was one of several squires who apologised to Tynte for their prior commitment to Matthews.[124] Tynte did obtain the support of Herbert Mackworth and many other gentlemen of the county.[125] But it was soon apparent that the issue was very much in the balance. This was the moment for calculating Charles Edwin to make his move. He approached the duke of Beaufort with a proposal that Thomas Prowse reported to Tynte on December 6.[126]

> Mr. Edwin consents to give you his Interest at the present Election upon these conditions. He fully intends to cultivate his Interest and offer Himself a Candidate at the next Election for Westminster, but in case he should not be chosen there, he expects that the Duke of Beaufort, Lord Windsor, Lord Mansel, and all the rest of your friends in Glamorganshire will engage to give him their Interest at the next general election for that county.

The bargain was a hard one, but Edwin was able to obtain a grudging acceptance of his terms by December 22.[127] At first Tynte's friends now assumed that the agreement would guarantee his success; but it soon transpired that his opponents had failed to observe the election convention that a landlord should control the votes of his dependants. News came that tenants of both Lord Windsor and the duke of Beaufort had been deluded into supporting Matthews.[128] Moreover, during the negotiations between Tynte and Edwin, a number of the latter's tenants had also been persuaded to promise Matthews their votes.[129] Charles Edwin, fearful of having the agreement voided, strove to repair the damage, and wrote to Tynte on December 29. 'If you find any of my tenants refractory you may assure them there is to be a list sent me of such persons who do not go according to my desire.'[130] Despite these alarms, canvass registers promised a satisfactory majority for Tynte. One estimate gave him a majority of 615 to 415.[131] Another calculation allowed Tynte 817 votes, Matthews 490, and classed 207 as neuter.[132]

But the Tory magnates had the painful memory of 1734, when a paper majority had proved worthless against an unscrupulous sheriff. Apprehensions grew about the conduct of the sheriff, Matthew Dacre of Ashall, especially after he had spent three days with Thomas Matthews at Swansea.[133] Lord Mansel, the duke of Beaufort, and their friends thought the best safeguard against injustice would be the attendance at the poll of Sir Watkin Williams Wynn and other gentlemen of influence in order 'to keep the sheriff honest'.[134] The duke promised Tynte, 'If you find they are likely to begin their old tricks, I will do what I can to get Sir Watkin Williams Wynn to come among you. I don't think it would be amiss for you to get it hinted to Lord Talbot that you expect him.'[135] Wynn, however, refused to take so active a part in an election where he was not directly concerned; his attitude was explained by Thomas Prowse to Tynte on December 25.[136]

> Sir Watkin has been very hearty in this affair, but in two or three instances when I pressed him to speak in your behalf, he declined doing it in Person, as the Election was out of his Province (North Wales), and therefore I believe an application to him to attend you will be to no purpose: and, to say the truth, a gentleman's appearance at a County Election where he has not the least concern very often offends even that side he has come to support.

Lord Mansel disagreed with this view. 'I am sorry to differ in opinion with our friend Mr. Prowse as to Members of Parliament appearing at your Election. I know there is nothing so common, and I also know it would have been of service to you, but it is now too late to think of that.'[137] On December 31 Lord Mansel saw the sheriff and obtained a promise that justice would be done.[138] The promise proved quite worthless and all the fears about the sheriff were to be justified. History, indeed, repeated itself.

After the poll, which began on January 2, 1745 and lasted for several days, the sheriff declared a majority of 47 votes for Thomas Matthews, 688 to 641. His own conduct of the proceedings, however, was blamed by the defeated party for the result, Tynte at once writing to Lord Mansel. 'I think that rascally sheriff ought to be punished with the utmost severity, but I hope you dont expect me to petition. My pocket, my Lord, is too small.'[139] Lord Mansel warmly commiserated with Sir Charles in his reply on January 10. 'You have met with worse usage at this contested election than I did at mine ten years ago. I could not have conceived that that rascal Basset of Miskyn could have been equalled, but I now find that the present rascally sheriff outdoes him infinitely.'[140] The threatened cost did deter Tynte from petitioning, but his campaign expenses nevertheless amounted to £2,500. Tynte, who had virtually been coerced into his candidature, now contended with justice that he should not be expected to pay the whole bill.[141]

> I am convinced that no one harbours so ill an opinion of me that I attempted to get into Parliament to gain any thing by my seat, therefore I think it extremely hard, that I should be expected to pay a greater share of the election expenses for offering my self to be a Slave in Parliament, in hopes to serve poor England in general and the county of Glamorgan in particular.

Lord Mansel, Lord Windsor and the duke of Beaufort agreed to share the burden according to their respective interests, and the Mansel agent, David Rees, was appointed to determine the proportions. 216 of Tynte's votes he attributed to the Mansel interest, and 125 to that of the duke of Beaufort. The other 300 he reckoned to be independent or under Lord Windsor's influence. Rees therefore calculated that Lord Mansel should pay £842 10s. and the duke of Beaufort £487 10s., while Tynte and Lord Windsor were to share the other £1,170.[142]

Sir Charles Tynte entered Parliament only two months later. The third duke of Beaufort died on February 24. He was succeeded by his brother, Lord Charles Noel Somerset, then M.P. for Monmouth Boroughs, and Tynte was elected for the vacant seat on March 14. The Tories, too, were soon able to satisfy their spite against Matthews, for on April 10 in the House of Commons they carried a hostile motion on his behaviour at Toulon.[143] At his trial the next year Matthews was cashiered and dismissed the service for not pressing home his attack at Toulon.[144] Thomas Matthews, moreover, was unable to retain his hard-won Glamorgan seat at the general election of 1747. Charles Edwin then reaped the advantage of the bargain he had made with the Tory magnates at the by-election, for the agreement was honoured even though it had failed to achieve its purpose. Edwin obtained the county seat without a contest, Matthews being returned for the Whig borough of Carmarthen. The triumph of the local Whigs in 1745 had thus proved to be as short-lived as their success in 1734. Their unscrupulous tactics could not destroy the political domination of Glamorgan by the Tory peerage alliance of Mansel, Beaufort, and Windsor. But in 1750 the death of Bussy, fourth Lord Mansel, saw the extinction of the male line of his family, and the permanent division of the Mansel interest. By the will of the third Lord Mansel, Margam passed to the Reverend Thomas Talbot, son of his and Bussy's sister, Mary, and brother-in-law, John Ivory Talbot. The Briton Ferry estate Bussy bequeathed to his only daughter, Barbara, who in 1757 was to marry George Venables Vernon of Derbyshire. Although the influence of the Margam and Briton Ferry estates was to prove virtually unimpaired under their new owners, the end of the house of Mansel marked the passing of an era in Glamorgan political history.

IV. THE BREAK-UP OF THE
TRADITIONAL SYSTEM, 1750–1780

In a wider sense, too, the middle of the century marked the end of another phase in Glamorgan politics. The old party names of Whig and Tory now came to lose whatever significance they had still retained with respect to the electoral alignments of the county. More important was the immediate cause of this development, the collapse of the hitherto dominant electoral coalition. Already bereft of Mansel leadership, this alliance of peers was further weakened by the death of the fourth duke of Beaufort in 1756, for there followed a nine-year minority before his son came of age. The third member of the aristocratic triumvirate, Lord Windsor, himself died in 1758, and the management of the Cardiff Castle interest passed to his widow. This dissolution of the traditional political system in the county means that a veil of obscurity hangs over the next political events in Glamorgan; they can be recorded rather than explained.

At the general election of 1754 Charles Edwin and Herbert Mackworth were again returned without incident.[145] But a problem was posed by the death of Edwin in June of 1756: his estate of Llanfihangel remained with his widow, Lady Charlotte Edwin, until her own death in 1776; then it was inherited by his nephew, Charles Wyndham of Clearwell in Gloucestershire, who thereupon assumed for himself the surname of Edwin. The significance of that event lay in the future. Meanwhile the ensuing county by-election of 1756 reflected the temporary eclipse of the leading interests in Glamorgan. One candidate in the field by early August was Thomas William Matthews, son, and successor in 1751, of the admiral; he had resigned his own commission as major in the army on his father's disgrace in 1746. The only opponent appearing to challenge him was Charles Van of Llanwern, a Monmouthshire squire who, in 1754, had married the younger daughter of Thomas Morgan of Tredegar and Ruperra. But this candidature was not a move by the Morgan family to extend to Glamorgan their electoral power in Monmouthshire and Breconshire. Van stood against the better judgement of his father-in-law; and though vigorously backed by the Monmouthshire M.P., Capel Hanbury of Pontypool, he won little support in Glamorgan. Bias and ignorance of the local scene render almost valueless, though not uninteresting, the opinion from distant St. Petersburg of Hanbury's brother, Sir Charles Hanbury-Williams, the famous wit and diplomat.[146]

> Nothing has surprised me more, than the flights of young Mr. Van; it is the mother of whom he is the picture, that works within him. Good God! If old Van was to hear that his son stood for a county, and kept thirteen bay coach horses, he would rise out of his grave to disinherit him. Major Mathews is certainly an unpopular and disagreeable man, and if Mr. Van spends his money freely, I should not despair of his election.

[415]

Charles Van's presumption was punished by a heavy defeat at the poll in December, when Matthews triumphed by 954 votes to 212. A petition submitted by Van to the House of Commons on January 20, 1757, however, declared that Matthews lacked the property qualification necessary for a county member, a landed estate worth at least £600 a year; and that he himself, intending to contest the return on that ground, had declined to poll a great number of his voters. Van subsequently withdrew this rather improbable complaint, on February 15, before any report on his petition had been made by the Committee of Elections.[147]

The contest highlights the lack of the customary leadership of the great Tory landowners, for a son of one of their former Whig foes had defeated the son-in-law of another. The poll figures show that on this occasion Matthews had obtained curiously overwhelming support, but this near-unanimity proved transitory. New electoral alignments were soon to emerge, culminating in a revival of the same coalition of aristocratic interests that had ruled Glamorgan earlier in the century. During the next decade Glamorgan politics were complicated by a variety of factors, both national and county; and it soon became apparent that the success of Matthews in 1756 had been opportunist and temporary.

The renewed impact of wider considerations than local enmities came with the return to the political arena of his native county of the Sir Edmund Thomas of Wenvoe Castle who had vainly and briefly aspired to the Cardiff seat in 1734. Since that abortive venture Thomas had taken a more active part in national politics than any of his Glamorgan neighbours. He was M.P. for Chippenham from 1741 to 1754, and his career illustrates an important facet of eighteenth-century political life, the 'reversionary interest'; certain politicians would support the heir to the throne if he opposed the ministry, in hope of future favours after his own accession. Thomas had acted on this principle, attaching himself to the party of Frederick, Prince of Wales, and acting as a Groom of the Bedchamber to the Prince from 1742 until his death in 1751. His allegiance, unshaken by this catastrophe, was then transferred to Frederick's son, George; and in 1756 the Princess Dowager of Wales appointed him to a post in her household.

Sir Edmund Thomas clearly had excellent prospects of office on the eventual accession of the young Prince of Wales; and, though he had not stood for Chippenham in 1754, he was now anxious to return to the Commons. It was some eighteen months before the next election was due that he opened a canvass in Glamorgan, during the autumn of 1759. Thomas began with the advantage that Lord Talbot of Hensol also belonged to the party of the Prince of Wales, while Sir Charles Tynte was a close personal friend. He secured a promise of support, too, from Lady Windsor.[148] But the path to Westminster was not clear. Matthews was determined to retain his seat, and by September of that year Thomas had learnt of the hostility of George Venables Vernon of Briton Ferry.[149]

The next month, however, Vernon suddenly left the county, and Thomas informed Tynte, 'I hear he denies he engaged to Matthews, but only in general against me and the family of Morgan'. Thomas did not, indeed, feel assured of the Ruperra interest of Thomas Morgan. 'I can't yet discover what Mr. Morgan will do, but I hardly think, everything considered, he will act against me, especially as many of his best friends are very determined in my favour.' He was already optimistic about his prospects. 'I really think if Mr. Matthews perseveres in this affair, he will make a worse figure than Mr. Van, who had so many disadvantages.'[150]

Sir Edmund Thomas had thus virtually ensured his election for Glamorgan long before the certainty of official support was afforded by the death of George II in October 1760, and the accession of his grandson as George III. The supporters of the reversionary interest thereupon reaped their rewards. Lord Talbot was among those showered with favours; his appointment as Lieutenant of the Glamorgan militia in January 1761 merely presaged further honours in March, when he obtained an earldom, nomination to the Privy Council, and the important office of Lord Steward of the Royal Household, a post he retained until his death in 1782. Sir Edmund Thomas was given political office in March, as a Lord Commissioner of Trade; and by then electoral help from the government was no longer needed. On February 24, 1761 Matthews announced that he would not be standing at the general election. Thomas informed Tynte on March 6 that 'everything in this country is at present in entire quiet', but he was annoyed by a newspaper advertisement alleging that, to avoid a contest, Matthews and himself had made a bargain to cover the next general election as well.[151] Thomas was sufficiently indignant to send a copy of the same notice to Lord Bute, the favourite of the new King.[152] Formerly tutor of George III when Prince of Wales, Lord Bute was to become his first minister the next year: much has been written of his intervention at the general election of 1761, but Sir Edmund clearly owed little or nothing to his assistance in Glamorgan. Thomas met with no further difficulty there, and he was able to thank his constituents on April 16 for 'a unanimous election'.[153]

Two years later, however, Sir Edmund Thomas was alarmed to learn the unexpected news that he would have to submit himself for re-election. In the change of ministerial offices consequent on Lord Bute's resignation in April 1763, Thomas was transferred from his post at the Board of Trade to the position of Surveyor-General of Woods North and South of Trent. Acceptance of any office of profit under the Crown automatically vacated the seat of an M.P., and Thomas was at first greatly concerned about his electoral prospects in Glamorgan. Learning of his new post on April 12, he wrote to explain the situation to Lord Bute the next day.[154]

> The suddenness of this communication and the shortness of the time, exposes me to extreme great embarrassments beyond what I can express, and to various diffi-

culties; being in no way whatever prepared for so critical and (to me) important event; I have consulted some few friends here (I mean such as have concerns in it) in as guarded a way as I could, and more particularly and necessarily Lord Talbot; who though determined if it be thought necessary, to give me all assistance, and to go down himself with me . . . yet foresees very great inconvenience in regard to myself from the re-election; and though not apprehensive of a failure of success, yet seems to think it certain, from the frenzy of the times and knowledge of some individuals there, that an opposition will certainly be raised; how troublesome and expensive that may be, the events may only show, but the latter is certain.

Sir Edmund was afraid not only of personal hostility towards himself in Glamorgan, but also of the effect of a recent tax on cider, much resented in the western counties of England; it was not a propitious time for a ministerial supporter to face re-election nearby. His fears were exaggerated, but not unfounded. On April 25 he wrote to Lord Egmont, a confidant of Lord Bute, that 'though I have all the support that I could possibly expect from the principal persons of this country . . . , yet as I foresaw, there will not be wanting endeavours to stir up an opposition to me, and a young inconsiderate warm young man is already feeling the ground for it and getting a meeting'. Anonymous letters from London had been sent to kindle a flame in Glamorgan. Lord Talbot was prevented by the business of his office from accompanying Thomas to the county, 'but he assured me if an opposition started he would immediately set out. Now the great object is to prevent one, in the bud, which a respectable appearance of my friends in the county now might do.'[155] Lord Egmont forwarded this plea to Bute the same day. 'Your Lordship will perceive that Sir Edmund Thomas believes the personal appearance of Lord Talbot to be essentially requisite to blast the intended opposition at the County meeting, and he plainly solicits your Lordship's interest . . . to prevail on Lord Talbot to give that attendance.'[156] Bute evidently informed the King of the situation; for two days later George III wrote to him. 'I have seen Talbot and insisted on his instantly going to Glamorganshire he tried to get off but I would not let him.'[157] This royal intervention proved to be unnecessary. The county meeting called by the enemies of Thomas unanimously resolved that there should be no further opposition to him;[158] and his letter to Bute on May 17 announcing his election six days before contrasts markedly with his consternation of a month earlier.[159]

> After some little efforts against me at first, I was re-elected last Wednesday without any opposition, and had the pleasure of finding a very friendly and steady disposition in the county towards me. I am very sensible how much I am obliged to your Lordship, . . . in regard to the motions of a noble friend, but we found everything quiet and easy, as all had been settled two or three days before his arrival.

The nature and extent of the opposition to Sir Edmund Thomas in 1763 remains a mystery, but his enemies probably included George Venables Vernon of Briton Ferry. Usually resident on his Newick estate in Sussex, Vernon was a close friend and electoral ally of the duke of

Newcastle, the veteran politician now in unaccustomed opposition to government. Returned for the borough of Bramber at a by-election of May 1762, Vernon attached himself at Westminster to the duke's political connection, headed from 1765 by the marquess of Rockingham. Though already in the Commons, Vernon coveted the county seat for Glamorgan; and, securing the support of the Talbot family now resident at Margam, he planned to win it by a revival of the old Mansel interest. Vernon opened his campaign before the end of 1766, though no election was due until 1768; and on November 13 Newcastle wrote this letter to the fourth earl of Plymouth, who owned the estates of St. Fagan's and the Van in Glamorgan and was Lord-Lieutenant of the county.[160]

> Mr. Vernon, who married my Lord Mansell's daughter, is my near neighbour in Sussex, and a particular friend. He is, as I understand by him, encouraged to offer his service at the next county election, for the County of Glamorgan, where the Mansell family were formerly chose. Mr. Vernon has the whole Mansel interest, his wife's, and Mr. Talbot's interest for him; and the favour I have to ask, is, that your Lordship would do him the honour, to let him have your interest, which is very considerable there.

Newcastle's picture of the revival of an old family claim was misleading, for Vernon had acquired the lesser of the two Mansel seats in Glamorgan. Lord Plymouth's reply, evidently, was not encouraging, for Newcastle forwarded his answer to Vernon with this comment: 'Though it is not so favourable, as I could wish, it is not so bad as I feared it might have been; for I have been since informed that your antagonist is my Lord Plymouth's relation.'[161] Soon afterwards Lord Plymouth apparently quarrelled with Sir Edmund Thomas, for on January 23, 1767 he called on Newcastle to promise Vernon 'all the assistance in his power, at the next election for the county of Glamorgan'.[162] Thomas had meanwhile been driven to retaliate, issuing a circular letter on December 24, 1766 to the gentlemen, clergy and freeholders of Glamorgan. 'Having seen letters from Mr. Vernon, soliciting the favour of gentlemen to approve of him as a candidate for the county of Glamorgan for the next general election, I hope I shall not be thought to make too early an application for the continuance of that honour.'[163] Vernon countered by making the hypocritical distinction between a private and a public canvass; his election notice asserted that he was now forced to open his campaign, 'the peace and tranquillity of the county, which I flattered myself would have been preserved by waiting the result of a General Meeting ... being interrupted by the early canvass of a declared candidate and his friends'. At the instigation of Vernon's party the sheriff of Glamorgan, 'taking into consideration the ill effects of a contested election', called a general meeting of the county for June 10 at Cowbridge.[164] But this failed to restore peace to Glamorgan. Vernon promptly issued a circular claiming the support of a 'a majority of the gentlemen present'. In reply Thomas

[419]

alleged that Vernon, seeing a majority of two to one against him, had refused to agree to any vote by the meeting.[165]

The campaign therefore continued during the summer of 1767. Another letter from Vernon on July 12 announced 'the very great encouragement I have met with on my canvass, in every part of the county'.[166] When Sir Edmund Thomas fell ill, his son, Edmund, canvassed in his stead; and on September 16 a circular by Thomas sought to depict the contest as a struggle of independent freeholders against influential landowners; for he announced his reliance on 'the same laudable spirit of freedom, which hath so often marked out and distinguished the County of Glamorgan in its choice of representatives'.[167] Vernon countered with an implicit reminder of the contrast between Sir Edmund's rôle as a placeman in Parliament with his own record of opposition. 'The spirit of freedom and independency has been, and ever shall be, the characteristic of my conduct.'[168]

Suddenly the political scene in Glamorgan was transformed by the death of Sir Edmund Thomas on October 10. This event not only removed Vernon's opponent, it also made necessary an immediate by-election. At first Vernon thought that the way would now be clear for his own return, writing to Sir Charles Tynte on October 12: 'No opposition is yet declared and it seems to be the general opinion there will be none. We have gained several new voices, . . . so that I am in great hopes all may be quiet. As soon as I have finished my applications here I shall hasten to London, in order to apply for permission to vacate my seat.'[169] Vernon soon found he had been too optimistic. Even before he left Glamorgan he learnt that a new opponent was in the field. John Aubrey of Llantriddyd, grandson of the borough member of Anne's reign, had come forward, with the support of Lord Talbot and those families which had traditionally adhered to the old Whig interest in the county. Aubrey's candidature, too, evidently found favour at Court; for he had the backing not only of the Lord Steward of the Royal Household but also of Lord Bute's heir. Styled Lord Mountstuart, in November 1766 he had married Charlotte, the eldest daughter and eventually sole heiress to the late Lord Windsor. With the Cardiff Castle interest at his command, Lord Mountstuart was to play an increasingly active role in Glamorgan politics. He had no personal ambitions in either county or borough, for he was already in the Commons as M.P. for Bossiney, and represented that borough until in 1776 he received a British peerage as Baron Cardiff of Cardiff Castle; thereafter he continued nevertheless to style himself Lord Mountstuart. At this by-election of 1767, however, Lady Windsor had already promised her interest to Vernon, and pressure from her new son-in-law to declare for Aubrey was unavailing.[170] But the influential connections of Vernon's opponents sufficed to prevent his candidature; for he was refused the Chiltern Hundreds or any other office that would enable him to vacate his Bramber seat to stand for Glamorgan.

The candidature of Aubrey was yet another move by Lord Talbot in his persistent challenge to the influence of the families long dominant in Glamorgan. It was as irrelevant to the alignments in national politics as that of Admiral Matthews in 1745 had been. Now the support of the electoral interest managed by Lord Talbot had been transferred from a courtier to a man whose political connections were with opposition; for Aubrey was a friend of George Grenville, leader of a Parliamentary group hostile to the Chatham ministry then in office. Vernon, too, was acting with the Rockingham group in opposition to the administration; yet earlier, even though challenging such a Court M.P. as Sir Edmund Thomas, he had applied on January 31, 1767 for approval of his candidature to the proud and awkward earl of Chatham. 'I have received very great encouragement to offer myself a candidate at the next general election, for the county of Glamorgan, where Mr. Vernon's family have ever had a very considerable interest, and I have now the honour to be supported by most of the principal noblemen and gentlemen in the county. Your Lordship's concurrence herein, would make me particularly happy.'[171] Any reply from the famous statesman is unknown and also irrelevant, for long before the election Chatham had vanished into temporary political retirement.

This time Lord Talbot's unscrupulous reliance on official favour to overcome local influence failed. Aubrey's canvassing letter was published on October 20.[172] It was answered on November 12 by one from Richard Turbervill of Ewenni. A sixty-year-old squire whose father had married the heiress of Richard Carne of Ewenni, Turbervill informed the Glamorgan electors that 'doubts have risen whether G. V. Vernon may be able to vacate his present seat in Parliament; in that case I do, for the peace and quietness of this my native county . . . offer myself a candidate ONLY for the present vacancy'.[173] Eight days later another election notice from Turbervill announced that Vernon would certainly not be able to stand at the by-election, and Vernon confirmed this on November 24.[174] The expedient of a stopgap candidate proved entirely successful. On December 6 John Aubrey announced his withdrawal;[175] and the outcome of a year's electoral campaign in Glamorgan was the unopposed return of Richard Turbervill at Bridgend on December 16. But on the very same day George Venables Vernon renewed his canvass for the general election, 'my worthy friend Mr. Turbervill having declared his intention of not serving any longer than during the present Parliament'.[176] The strength of the revived Mansel interest was shown by Vernon's uncontested return for the county at that general election, in 1768. The celebrations at his election on April 6, however, were marred by a fatality resulting from the lavish nature of the entertainment on the occasion; for the inquest next day on a certain Morgan Thomas attributed his death to excess of food and drink.[177]

[421]

Vernon's success represented the triumph of the alliance of aristocratic interests dominant earlier in the century, although this fact was to be made apparent by later events rather than by the contemporary evidence to hand. The control of this oligarchy was for the moment unchallenged in either constituency. The borough member since the death of Herbert Mackworth in 1765 had been his son, another Herbert; and at the general election of 1774 both Mackworth and Vernon retained their seats without opposition. Vernon was then one of the many M.P.s caught unawares by the sudden dissolution of Parliament on September 30; he found it necessary in consequence to conduct his canvass through the press, inserting an advertisement of October 3 in the metropolitan and country papers.[178]

That was a mere formality; but a subsidiary campaign for the reversion of the county seat began when news came of the serious illness of Lord Vernon, father of George Venables Vernon. The prospect of a vacancy in the representation of Glamorgan arising from Vernon's succession to the peerage was sufficient to produce at least one candidate avowedly in the field. On 20 October Thomas Pryce of Dyffryn, one of the lesser squires of the county, issued this circular letter to the freeholders of Glamorgan, asking their attendance at the county meeting already arranged at Bridgend on October 24.[179] 'The very dangerous state of health in which Lord Vernon is at present, will in all probability entitle Mr. Vernon to a seat in the House of Lords before the day fixed upon for electing a Representative for this County. If this event should happen, I am desired by several of my friends to offer myself a candidate in his place.' Pryce followed up this public declaration by a private canvass. He explained his unseemly haste in a letter to Charles Morgan, a younger son of Thomas Morgan, who was now master of the Tredegar estates and M.P. for Breconshire. His friends had urged him to lose no time, 'Mr. Jones having declared his intention'; this prospective rival was probably Robert Jones of Fonmon Castle, grandson of the earlier county member and also brother-in-law of Charles Wyndham. Pryce, however, had not been able to obtain a definite promise of the Margam interest; 'Before I declared I waited on Mr. Talbot . . . all I could get from him was a dependance of his support in opposition to any foreigner.'[180] Pryce's request was reinforced by another from his father-in-law, Sir William Owen of Orielton in Pembrokeshire.[181] But Lord Vernon disappointed such expectations by recovering his health, and the anticipated vacancy never occurred. The Bridgend meeting endorsed Vernon's candidature;[182] and he later returned thanks to his constituents for 'a unanimous election'.[183]

V. A CHALLENGE TO OLIGARCHY, 1780–1789

That this episode of Pryce's abortive candidature had a deeper significance than the presumption of a single squire was shown by the events in Glamorgan at the next general election, in 1780. Campaigns had already started in many constituencies, though perhaps not in Glamorgan, when the death of Lord Vernon on August 21, 1780 meant that his son could no longer stand for the county. Thomas Pryce of Dyffryn at once declared his candidature for the vacancy, on September 2. A county meeting for September 20 at Cowbridge was announced by the sheriff, Peter Birt, who had recently purchased Wenvoe Castle from the now impecunious Thomas family. Pryce asked his friends to attend there. But on September 8 Charles Edwin, the former Charles Wyndham who had now inherited Llanfihangel, made this announcement. 'Presuming on the high honours frequently conferred on my ancestors, of electing them your Representatives in Parliament, I beg leave to offer myself a candidate at the approaching election.'[184] The family tradition was largely mythical: only Edwin's uncle, the member from 1747 to 1756, had hitherto sat for Glamorgan. His candidature was based less on this flimsy claim than on the firm support of the electoral coalition that had long dominated Glamorgan politics. He, like Vernon, depended on the old triple alliance of the Raglan interest of the dukes of Beaufort, the Windsor interest of Lord Mountstuart, and the former Mansel interest now shared by the new Lord Vernon of Briton Ferry and Thomas Mansel Talbot of Margam, son and successor of the Reverend Thomas Talbot. A detailed analysis of the political structure of the county at this time was contained in a notable pamphlet published in support of Pryce during the election campaign, *A Calm Address to the Independent Resident Gentlemen, Clergy and Freeholders of the County of Glamorgan.*[185] The anonymous author began by detailing the support for Edwin.

> Mr. Charles Edwin confessedly stands upon the interest of his own and those of the following six great estates. The Duke of Beaufort, Lord Plymouth, Lord Mountstewart, Lord Vernon, Sir Charles Tynte and Mr. Talbot. A combination among these seven, among whom the Peers alone form a majority, is held, by themselves, sufficient to command the county . . . Instead of representing seven hundred, the supposed majority of the county, he will at most be the representative of seven.

There followed a scathing account of these men and their motives. Edwin owed his candidature to an agreement giving his own interest in Gloucestershire to the politically ambitious fifth duke of Beaufort. Lord Mountstuart had fallen in with this plan in the eventual hope of the duke's interest in the Cardiff Boroughs constituency for his son John, then aged twelve. Savage treatment was accorded to Lord Vernon. 'The late representative of the county, now a peer, has already begun to show the contempt in which he always held his constituents . . . Little as he has been used to visit Briton Ferry, less will he be at that beautiful residence for the future. His graceless manner will not again be exhibited to our laughter. No more sour claret for his tenants and acquaintances. The house itself will be suffered to tumble into ruins.' More significant than such attacks, however, was the evident hope of the author that

Thomas Mansel Talbot of Margam might in the future be detached from the alliance.

> Mr. Talbot is very little known in public life, and totally untried in public; if he had submitted to declare he stood upon no grand alliance, might have been thought worthy of a seven years' choice. He proposed himself a candidate whenever a vacancy should happen by Lord Vernon's death. He pledged his honour he would stand. Nay, he said, he would go through thick and thin with his engagements. These engagements he has now dropped. It is true he was drunk when he publicly made them. But he has neither tongue, heart nor head to speak in public but when he is drunk. . . . He spends much money in the county, but it is highly indecent in him and may be detrimental to his future interest to declare for Mr. Edwin before the sense of the county should be better known at the general meeting.

The pamphleteer meanwhile advocated an immediate challenge to the oligarchy. 'To oppose this command of property, there certainly are men and estates enough in the county if united.' An obvious head of such an opposition was the man who had defeated the same coalition of interests nearly fifty years earlier, in 1734. 'Lord Talbot is well known by his detachment from such an injurious clan of domination. He opposed in person the whole interest whilst a commoner with effect. That independent interest which brought him in, he surely will not desert. The Morgans of Tredegar are well known by their successful opposition to the ambitious views of the Duke of Beaufort in two adjoining counties. We have among us others of great property and character, all enemies to the combination.' There followed a list of such squires, and the author concluded by urging support of the alternative candidate already declared, Thomas Pryce of Dyffryn, 'a gentleman who resides amongst us and stands upon the country interest'. The penetration and accuracy of this survey of the Glamorgan political scene were to be revealed by the story of the county by-election nine years later. But in 1780 the hopes of the pamphleteer were disappointed. Thomas Pryce seemingly withdrew his candidature again, for in an address from Cardiff on the day of election, October 4, Charles Edwin thanked his constituents for a unanimous return.[186]

Already on September 15 Mackworth had given thanks to the borough electorate for 'the most disinterested choice and cordial unanimity'.[187] At Westminster he was one of the few Welsh M.P.s of the century to participate regularly in debate, and he may even have made more speeches than any other representative of the Principality until that time; in one Parliament alone, that from 1768 to 1774, he is recorded as making over a hundred speeches.[188] Unlike the almost silent Vernon, who always voted with the Rockingham group in opposition, Mackworth was an independent member who afforded judicious support to the ministry headed by Lord North after 1770. He received a baronetcy in 1776; and though he had earlier opposed coercion of the American colonies, he supported the government's assertion of British sovereignty once the War of American Independence had begun.[189]

In the Parliament of 1780 Sir Herbert Mackworth continued to vote for North until his fall in 1782, while Charles Edwin sided with the opposition. When the complex political situation of the next year ended with the ministry of the younger Pitt, Mackworth was in opposition under Charles James Fox, and Edwin an adherent of Pitt. The new minister held a general election in 1784 to consolidate his position; and the heated political atmosphere of the time may have affected the electoral situation even in Glamorgan. The small group of patrons who had returned both members in 1780 were Foxites, with the exception of the duke of Beaufort; and it is surprising that this comment on the Cardiff constituency should have been included in the government analysis made for the election. 'Lord Mountstewart has the influence here. It is said he will not bring Sir H. Mackworth in again.'[190] The remark was optimistic, for Sir Herbert was once more returned without opposition.[191] In the county, however, public opinion probably helped Edwin to retain his seat. Nothing is known of the background to his return, but he perhaps owed this success as much to popular support as to the magnates who had given him the seat in 1780, and were now hostile to his political views. The opinion of the self-styled 'independent gentlemen, clergy and freeholders' of Glamorgan was strongly in favour of the King's appointment of Pitt as his minister; and, after his re-election, Edwin presented to George III a loyal address from the county with 697 signatures.[192]

The county election of 1784 may thus have been in some sense a prologue to the dramatic by-election five years later. By the beginning of 1789 Charles Edwin was contemplating retirement from Parliament. His health was failing, or so it was thought; in fact he lived until 1801. Edwin hoped to bequeath the county seat to his son, Thomas Wyndham, an ambitious and forceful young man who already at the age of twenty-five had attracted attention, largely unfavourable, by taking the chair at the Quarter Sessions of the county.[193] It was rumoured in Glamorgan that Edwin had asked his fellow-Pittite, the duke of Beaufort, to support his son, but without success.[194] Despite this disappointment Wyndham opened a canvass early in 1789, two years before the next general election was due.

The coalition of magnates who had sponsored Edwin in 1780 had no intention of allowing their traditional command of Glamorgan to be flouted in such a manner. The rival candidate put forward by the duke of Beaufort, Lord Mountstuart, Lord Vernon and Lord Plymouth was the Honourable Thomas Windsor, brother of the last-named peer, a captain in the navy, and a follower of Fox. There followed a vigorous campaign, enlivened by the publication of several anonymous pamphlets. The electoral storm that had threatened the county oligarchs in 1780 now blew up into a veritable whirlwind. Notable in the torrent of propaganda were the productions of 'A Friend to the Independence of

Glamorgan', usually identified as Robert Morris of Clasemont. Morris had earlier been a prominent radical in London, where he was the first secretary of the Bill of Rights Society in 1769. He had now returned to his native Glamorgan, and his first pamphlet on May 13 urged the county electors to throw off their shackles; the question at issue, he declared, was 'whether a few non-resident Lords shall name, or the freeholders elect, a member to represent the county of Glamorgan in Parliament'.[195] Thereafter, the cause of Glamorgan independence was championed in a stream of pamphlets and songs, which throw a good deal of light on the alignments within the county. Lord Talbot, hitherto the acknowledged leader of the independent interest in Glamorgan, had died in 1782, but his heiress daughter, Lady Dynevor, followed family tradition by pledging the influence of the Hensol estate to Wyndham.[196] Thomas Mansel Talbot of Margam, whose defection from the side of oligarchy had been anticipated in 1780, now placed himself at the head of 'a general union of the resident Country Gentlemen', a role of rare moment for the Margam family and perhaps the decisive move in the contest.[197] Other squires of influence who joined the popular side included Sir John Aubrey of Llantriddyd, Robert Jones of Fonmon, and the John Morgan who in 1787 had succeeded his brother Charles as master of Tredegar and Ruperra.[198] Sir Herbert Mackworth may well have done the same, for he was already aware that Lord Mountstuart intended the Cardiff seat for his son at the next general election.[199] Certainly, few of the resident gentry of the county supported Windsor; and two who did so, Richard Aubrey of Ash Hall and Peter Birt of Wenvoe Castle, were pilloried in a popular song.[200]

> 'Dick Aubry and Birt,
> Fell into the Dirt,
> When Wyndham for Liberty stood.'

Abuse was showered on the absentee aristocrats, who soon discovered how unwise their choice of candidate had been—a naval officer with no property in Glamorgan and whose attendance in Parliament would necessarily be irregular. The song 'Wyndham, Peace and Liberty' denounced a tyrant lord, a Scottish thane, an oppressive duke and a venal Windsor.[201] Lord Mountstuart was portrayed in local propaganda as a grasping Scot who sought to enclose the common lands of Glamorgan;[202] and a printed broadside of June 20, 1789 by 'a Supporter of Rights' in Swansea generalized this issue, declaring that 'down with the enclosures' was the popular cry.[203]

Another weapon to the hand of the pamphleteers was the connection of the popular candidate with the Pitt ministry. A circular address from 'a determined enemy to Mr. Pitt' purported in sarcasm to support Captain Windsor, reminding its readers that Wyndham's father was a Pittite in the Commons.[204] The duke of Beaufort was singled out for particular attack. Though high in favour under the Pitt administration, he was cooperating with 'a Junto of Opposition Lords' to force upon the county a man 'who with all his family and connections are determined Foxites'.[205] The duke's three allies, Lords Mountstuart, Vernon and Plymouth, were indeed followers of Charles James Fox; but the political alignment at Westminster was often still irrelevant to most elections of the time; and it was the duke of Beaufort himself who was named as the sponsor of Thomas Windsor in the hostile song 'The Naval Candidate's Inland Expedition'.[206]

The climax of the campaign came at a county meeting held at Cowbridge Town Hall on July 21, presided over by the sheriff, John Llewellyn of Penllergaer. On a motion by Thomas Mansel Talbot, seconded by John Morgan of Tredegar, Thomas Wyndham was nominated as Parliamentary candidate for the general election or any earlier election. The meeting thanked Wyndham for 'his determination to stand forth in support of the Independent Interests of this County', and Talbot for 'his patriotic and spirited exertions in support of the Independence of the County of Glamorgan'. The resolution was then carried 'that we will not at the next or any other future occasion consent on our parts to be represented in Parliament by any person who is not a resident in the county'. Finally, to rub salt into the wounds of the aristocratic party, the meeting also carried the proposal of Robert Morris that 'the conduct of Captain Windsor, after he had appealed to a County Meeting, in not attending so respectable a call of the county by the High Sheriff is disrespectful to the county at large'.[207]

Charles Edwin decided to take immediate advantage of the wave of popular feeling. He promptly vacated his seat by obtaining a formal appointment to an office of profit under the Crown; and the writ for a by-election in Glamorgan was issued on August 10.[208] The evidence of public opinion in the county, together with the loss of the Margam and Llanfihangel interests, deterred the aristocratic sponsors of Thomas Windsor from pushing his candidature further; and no challenge was made to the return of Thomas Wyndham on September 4. Wyndham was again returned without opposition at the general election of 1790, and he continued to represent the county until his death in 1814. The electoral revolution of 1789 thus proved more permanent than the earlier setbacks to the dominant oligarchy; but the enduring power of the Margam influence was to be reflected in the representation of the county in the nineteenth century.

The next year, by contrast, saw confirmation of the control over the borough constituency by the 'Cardiff Castle interest' now held by the Stuart family. An analysis of the constituency by the *Calm Address* in 1780 had publicized the precarious nature of Sir Herbert Mackworth's tenure of his seat. He commanded only the few voters of Neath, for he had lost to Thomas Mansel Talbot his hold on Aberavon. It was, moreover, in these boroughs and in Swansea and Loughor, the two ruled by the duke of Beaufort, that the privileges of burgess-ship made any significant increase of the electorate impossible. Effective power in the constituency was wielded by Lord Mountstuart, who could create new voters in Cardiff, Cowbridge, and Llantrisant; though the pamphleteer reminded him that Thomas Mansel Talbot could do the same in Kenfig. 'Kenfig is entirely under Mr. Talbot's influence. He has already a numerous set of voters there. He can make as many more as he pleases and when he has made them, he can command them . . . Let Lord Mountstuart now judge whose interest is worth his courting for the Boroughs.' In fact, Lord Mountstuart did obtain a promise of support from Talbot well before the election of 1790. His son, the Honourable John Stuart, had come of age in 1788, and his father's intention that he should replace Mackworth as borough member was known in Glamorgan at the time of the county by-election of the next year. 'A Friend to the Independence of Glamorgan' then urged Talbot to join Mackworth instead.[209] Despite Talbot's role in the county election, there is no evidence that he heeded this exhortation to oppose the aristocratic oligarchy in the borough constituency. As a precautionary measure, Lord Mountstuart arranged for the admission of 111 new burgesses in Cardiff during 1789. The only other borough for which evidence of such activity had been found was Swansea, and here the course of events is obscure. Thirty-four new burgesses were created in 1789, despite the difficulties of such a step. In 1790 the burgesses of Swansea, resentful of Stuart neglect to canvass them, professed to know of no candidate for the constituency, and put forward one of their own number, Gabriel Powell; this venture was presumably short-lived, for nothing more is heard of it. The indignation of the displaced member, Sir Herbert Mackworth, was reflected in a resolution by the burgesses of Neath to support him or any other candidate in opposition to Stuart. But Sir Herbert made no serious attempt to defend his seat; and Stuart's election in 1790 cost his father only £289.[210]

VI. Looking to the Future

By 1790 the political stage in Glamorgan was set for another scene in the history of the county, the era of agitation and discontent preceding the Reform Act of 1832. Soon the by-election of 1789 was to be hailed by T. H. B. Oldfield, the famous critic of the unreformed electoral system, as a welcome example of political vitality.[211] But that result was significant rather in terms of the past than the future, the triumph at last of the smaller gentry over the county magnates. The landed interest was still dominant; and, in particular, the traditional power of Margam was to maintain its importance far into the next century. Already, however, there were political portents of the new social environment developing in the era of the Industrial Revolution. The grievance of enclosures, revealed in the propaganda of the 1789 election, foreshadowed the clash of economic interest always latent in the countryside. In the borough constituency, too, the change of member in 1790 involved the replacement of an industrialist by an aristocratic nominee; and it is possible that some of the inexplicable events of that election reflected resentment at the rule of landed patrons among the men concerned with trade and industry in Swansea and other towns. The political calm stemming from the social stability of the eighteenth century would soon be over.

CHAPTER IX

Religion and Education in Glamorgan, 1660-c.1775

By E. T. DAVIES, GLANMOR WILLIAMS and GOMER ROBERTS

INTRODUCTION

DIVISIONS in religion had been one of the major causes of the Civil War in England and Wales. The Puritans, once their armies had been victorious in the field, had taken advantage of their successes to reduce the Church of England from its position of power and privilege and to foster the dissemination of their own beliefs. In Glamorgan, like other counties, many Anglican incumbents had been removed from their livings and reduced to penury, a number of Puritan ministers and schoolmasters had been installed, and every encouragement had been given to sectarian convictions to take firm root among congregations of Presbyterians, Independents, Baptists, and Quakers. Yet the Puritans, of whatever complexion they were, remained a minority; and in the spring of 1660, when the restoration of the monarchy was as popular as it was imminent, most of the population, hardly less than the deprived Anglican clergy, wanted to see the Church of England brought back along with the King. Clearly, when Charles II returned from his 'travels', one of the most delicate as well as urgent responsibilities facing him and his ministers would be the satisfactory settlement of the religious issue.

Before he left exile Charles had issued the Declaration of Breda on April 4, 1660, in which he expressed approval of religious toleration: there was to be 'a liberty to tender consciences; . . . no man shall be disquieted or called in question for differences of opinion in matter of religion', and the King would be ready 'to consent to such act of parliament as, upon mature deliberation, shall be offered to us for the full granting that indulgence'.[1] Unfortunately, he did not find it possible in practice to implement these enlightened principles. The differences between the opposing groups had become too wide to be bridged, and old wounds inflicted in the name of religion too deep to be healed. The Convention Parliament, which met in 1660, approved the Declaration of Breda, but the Cavalier Parliament (1661–79) contained a large majority of devoted Royalists completely out of sympathy with Puritanism and too suspicious of its potential for subversion to allow a

[431]

policy of toleration, to succeed. The Church of England was restored, but the aim of 'comprehending' all the king's subjects within it went unfulfilled. Those who dissented from the Church of England were placed under a series of legal constraints and handicaps. Even when persecution ended and toleration was allowed, not all the legal disabilities on Protestant Nonconformists, still less Roman Catholics, were removed. What was to be the long, and often unedifying, breach between 'Church' and 'Chapel' had become a prominent, and has remained hitherto a permanent, feature of the life of Glamorgan, like that of the rest of England and Wales.

i.

THE CHURCH OF ENGLAND AND SCHOOLS
1662–1774

By E. T. DAVIES

I. The Bishops and Their Diocese

Ecclesiastical Glamorgan in 1662 was divided between two dioceses, those of Llandaff and St. David's, two archdeaconries, Carmarthen and Llandaff, and into three deaneries: Llandaff and Groneath (alias Cowbridge) in the archdeaconry of Llandaff and the diocese of Llandaff, and Gower in the archdeaconry of Carmarthen and the diocese of St. David's. The ecclesiastical boundaries had been fixed in the Middle Ages and these three deaneries formed part of greater units, that of the diocese of Llandaff extending to the river Wye on the east, while St. David's was one of the most unwieldy dioceses in the Church, comprising the whole or part of six Welsh counties: Glamorgan, Carmarthenshire, Pembrokeshire, Cardiganshire, Brecknockshire, and Radnorshire; together with a few parishes in Herefordshire. The physical task of-administering these dioceses in conditions which had not fundamentally changed since they had been created was such that any comparison with later and more favourable circumstances is unhistorical; the truth is that the seventeenth- and eighteenth-century bishops of Llandaff were probably as assiduous in their duties as had been their mediaeval predecessors.

When Hugh Lloyd, rector of Llangattock, Brecknockshire, and archdeacon of St. David's, was elected to the see of Llandaff on October 16, 1660, and was consecrated on the following December 2, he inherited an administrative and financial problem from his predecessors which was not to be eased for nearly two centuries. Had the county and diocesan boundaries coincided in Glamorgan the physical task of administration would have been easier, but the problems which were not to be removed until parliament took action after 1836 would still remain. A diocese in those days was an area within which a bishop exercised certain ecclesiastical functions but it was not itself a legal corporation. It consisted of an aggregate of ecclesiastical corporations, called parishes, which owned property and certain legal rights, and was administered by ecclesiastical officers who could sue and be sued in the courts; and the only other independent body in the old diocese of Llandaff was the cathedral chapter. But the diocese itself had no independent existence in the financial sense: it had no funds of its own nor any central body with administrative authority. As with finance, so with administration: authority was divided and the diocese as a unit had neither the legal, administrative, nor financial capacity or authority for executive action. The only authority was that vested in the bishop and delegated by him to archdeacons, rural deans, chancellors, and incumbents, apart, of course, from the legal powers vested in patrons of livings. There were no diocesan committees nor any means of consultation apart from ruridecanal chapter meetings and the annual meeting of the cathedral chapter in Llandaff at Peterstide; while the laity had no means whatever of making their views known on purely ecclesiastical matters. The diocese of Llandaff was, like every other diocese in the Church, an essentially mediaeval institution and was to remain so until the reforms of the nineteenth century.

Moreover, the bishops of Llandaff had obligations outside their diocese which made a severe demand on their time, for, unless they were content to neglect their duties and to accept the consequences of not being seen and known at the centres of power, the translation to another diocese which most of them desired would never be effected. In practice, this meant that the bishops had to spend the winter and spring of every year in London in attendance at Convocation (until that body was suspended in 1717), or as Lords Spiritual of the Realm in the House of Lords. The leading authority on these matters in this period writes: 'At the heart of the problem of episcopal administration lay the distraction from the proper business of diocesan oversight involved in the residence of bishops in London during the greater part of each year'.[2] There were times when the journey could not be made, and then apologies had to be sent. Bishop Francis Davies wrote to Archbishop Sheldon from his palace in Mathern (Mon.) on October 8, 1670: 'I am att present by my owne, but more by that sad indisposition of those few servants I am so disabled for a journey, that I do most humbly begg your Grace his favourable dispensation to me for not attending the next convocation. I have hitherto constantly waited, as in Duty I ought, nor would I have ye Confidence to be dispensed with now, but that I have seen it granted to others who were not God be thanked in more need of it than I am'.[3]

This quotation raises another problem with which the bishops of Llandaff had to contend, namely, the inconvenience of their residence in south-east Monmouthshire. Not only was it inconveniently situated, but its cost of upkeep was out of proportion to the income of the bishops. Bishop Beaw (1679–1705), the last of the episcopal tenants of Mathern palace, complained to Archbishop Tennison in a letter, written from Adderbury on August 21, 1699, of the financial demands made upon him, including, among other matters, 'for reparation of a barn burnt down by fire, £50', and 'for reparation of a Gout as they call it on a mound against ye breaches of the Severn Sea, £50'.[4] Such items for the repairs of a mediaeval residence were quite out of proportion to the income of the bishops. At the end of the seventeenth century the official income was returned as £154 14s. 1d.,[5] but this had risen to a little under £400 by the days of Bishop Tylor (1706–24), who is credited with having improved it by an Act of Parliament of 12 Anne which provided that the treasurership of the cathedral chapter should be annexed to the bishopric thus adding a further £12 2s. 10d. annually to the income of the bishops.[6] Thus it was that the bishop of Llandaff became the treasurer of the cathedral, the last episcopal holder, Bishop Ollivant, resigning this office on April 27, 1867. But even with the improvement in their financial condition toward the beginning of the eighteenth century the bishops of Llandaff were badly off financially, and this made it necessary for them to seek ecclesiastical posts elsewhere, usually the deaneries of Hereford, Wells, Exeter, and later, that of St. Paul's, or a canonry at Christ Church, Oxford.

This doleful description of the bishopric of Llandaff is not yet complete, for the most surprising feature has yet to be mentioned, viz., the fact that the bishops had not a single living in their gift in Glamorgan. They held the advowson of Bishopston (Llandeilo Ferwallt) in the deanery of Gower, and the bishops of St. David's had the patronage of Llanddewi and Llangyfelach in the same deanery. This lack of control of the bishops over appointments to parishes must be borne in mind when assessing their responsibility for complaints which were to be made later. It was not in their power to correct abuses of which they themselves were conscious and unable to amend.

It is not surprising that Llandaff was the least prized of all the dioceses in the Church in the eighteenth century, and that for a long time it was considered but as a stepping stone to better things. It is against this situation, which neither the bishops nor any other clerical body had the legal authority or financial means to reform, that the record of the bishops and their clergy must be assessed. It is unhistorical to judge the former in the light of the circumstances in which their successors of the second half of the nineteenth century and later have performed the duties of their office; the comparison must be made with their predecessors who had to administer the same ecclesiastical system, while the blame for this state of affairs must rest with the political authority who did nothing to reform it and the laity and clerical corporations who drained the diocese of its already meagre financial resources. When so assessed, the record of the eighteenth-century bishops of Llandaff can be seen in a different light and bears favourable comparison with that of their predecessors.

There is no evidence whatsoever that their canonical duties were neglected except for the later years of Bishop Beaw; their administrative functions were very frequently delegated; and the most serious charge that can be brought against them is that their personal contacts with their clergy and laity were too transient to form the basis of a true pastoral relationship.

The first three post-Restoration bishops of Llandaff were resident in the sense already explained (i.e., they lived in their official residence in the diocese), and they were Welsh-speaking. Hugh Lloyd (1660–67), Francis Davies (1667–75), and William Lloyd (1675–79) mark the first period in the history of the diocese after 1662. Ordinations were held in Llandaff cathedral, St. Margaret's, Westminster, and in the chapel of Mathern palace, while although Confirmation records for the old diocese have not survived, it is reasonably certain that they were held in conjunction with the triennial visitation.

Ordinations ceased in Llandaff cathedral in 1669 and were not held there again until 1730, although they were held in Mathern until 1697. Beaw was the last bishop to live in Mathern; he withdrew more and more to the living of Adderbury in Oxfordshire from whence he visited his diocese during the summer months and London in the winter; but his diocesan activities became reduced as he passed into extreme old age. His successor, John Tylor, was dean of Hereford at the time of his appointment in 1706 and he retained this latter office and continued to live in Hereford which was the base for his diocesan activities, except for ordinations which were held in Hereford cathedral. Similarly, Robert Clavering, Tylor's successor in 1724, was a canon of Christ Church, but he was soon appointed to succeed John Tylor, not only at Llandaff but also as dean of Hereford. This connection was continued when John Harris, a Pembrokeshire man and dean of Windsor, was elected to succeed Clavering in 1729 both as bishop and as dean, but he moved from Hereford to the deanery of Wells, and he proved to be an assiduous bishop in the eighteenth-century manner. Mathias Mawson, who succeeded Harris in 1738, was master of Corpus Christi College, Cambridge, but he was translated to Chichester within a year. The two succeeding bishops were deans of English cathedrals: John Gilbert (1740–48) was dean of Exeter, and Edward Cresset was dean of Hereford at the time of his appointment to Llandaff but resigned the former office. Cresset was almost unique in the line of eighteenth-century bishops of Llandaff in that he welcomed his appointment, for he wrote to the duke of Newcastle: 'Although the revenues of the see may not be very considerable, I think my private fortune cannot be better employed than in his majesty's service, by enabling me to attend parliament. And on all occasions to shew myself a steady and hearty friend to our happy establishment in church and state'; and he went on to say: 'The situation of Llandaff is so convenient to me that I shall never desire to leave that neighbourhood'.[7] He was bishop of Llandaff from 1749 to

1755, and there is no evidence to believe that his episcopal duties as laid down by the Canons of 1604 were not fully carried out. But it was clear that the diocese of Llandaff had become a political and an ecclesiastical pawn. Bishop Ewer (1761–69) accepted the bishopric, and was consecrated, but delayed his coming in the hope that something better than Llandaff would be offered him; but having assumed his duties, he carried them out conscientiously, although his permanent place of residence seems to have been in Berkshire. Things were to get worse before they got better: the lowest point in the fortunes of the diocese was reached in the episcopate of Jonathan Shipley, who was bishop for only five months in 1769 when he was translated to St. Asaph, before he had time to hold an ordination, visitation, or confirmation in his diocese.

These men fitted into the pattern of the eighteenth-century episcopate. Their duties were determined by canon law, and there is no evidence that they were not fulfilled. They were non-resident in the sense that after 1697 they did not occupy their official residence for those summer months which they and their contemporaries spent in their dioceses; they were not non-resident in the sense that their dioceses never saw them. It is true that, after William Lloyd's translation to Peterborough in 1679, Llandaff was to lack a Welsh-speaking bishop until 1883 (although it should not be forgotten that Bishop Harris was a Pembroke-shire man), yet the language question, although not entirely absent from the mind of the bishops and the laity, was not nearly so prominent as it was to become in the nineteenth century. The real indictment is not against these bishops personally but against the ecclesiastical system which paid too little attention to their essential episcopal duties, and perpetuated the mediaeval tradition of the close connection between Church and State, thus making it obligatory for a bishop to spend as much time on his parliamentary as on his ecclesiastical duties. This made it difficult for a bishop in those days to establish a pastoral relation-ship with his clergy and laity. To what degree such a relationship was established it is difficult to estimate, for the official records do not reveal these matters; but it is significant that when Bishop Clavering was translated to Peterborough at the end of 1728, William Morgan, deputy registrar at Llandaff, sent a letter to Chancellor William Beaw (son of the former bishop), dated January 3, 1728–29, in which he wrote: 'The news of our good Bishop's translation has fill'd all our hearts here with inexpressible sorrow; for we can never be so happy as since we had him for our Diocesan; he always had at heart the interests of his poorer Clergy and pittied their narrow circumstances, which perhaps even our own Countreymen may not be so aware of; however since it was our misfortune to be deprived of him I heartily wish his Lordship's next removal may be to the best See in the Kingdome'.[8] The records of the old diocese of Llandaff throw no light on what William Morgan was referring to in his letter, but it is clear that Clavering's episcopate possessed important features which have been preserved for us only in one letter. If we knew more it is certain that the general reputation of the eighteenth-century bishops of Llandaff would benefit as the result of assessing them against their contemporary background and its problems which they could do little to remove.

II. THE CLERGY AND THEIR PARISHES

The distribution of parishes and parish churches remained unchanged in the three Glamorgan deaneries from the Middle Ages until the Industrial Revolution opened up the uplands and made necessary a vastly increased spiritual provision for a quickly growing population. As with the diocese, so with the parishes: we are dealing with what were essentially mediaeval institutions as far as their economics and administration were concerned.

Clerical Incomes. The source of the income of the parish priest had not changed since pre-Reformation time: glebe land, tithes, surplice fees, and offerings were the four main sources of the income of the majority of the clergy. But it is not easy to ascertain their real income, for most of the lists published reproduce the figures in the 'King's Books' which were used for taxation purposes and do not necessarily reflect the real income of the clergy. Thus *A Book of the Valuations of all the Ecclesiastical Preferments in England and Wales,* published in 1680, virtually reproduced the incomes shown in *Valor Ecclesiasticus* of 1535. According to the former list, the most financially desirable livings in Glamorgan were those of Merthyr Tydfil (£20 5s. 9d.), Gelli-gaer (£20 7s. 9d.), Coychurch (£21 1s. 8d.), Coety (£21 11s. 4d.), and Swansea (£20). The real values of the parishes were not revealed until after 1707.

By 6 Anne cc. 24 & 34, all benefices under the value of £50 per annum were discharged from the payment of first fruits and tenths, which had been introduced into the Church of England in the reigns of John and Henry III, paid to Rome until 1534, and transferred to the Crown in that year. This payment was a tax upon clerical incomes, and when the governors of the Corporation of Queen Anne's Bounty began to administer those payments which the Crown had restored to the Church for the augmentation of poorer livings, a realistic assessment of the value became necessary. Unfortunately the reply to the circular letter which Bishop Tylor sent to all rural deans on August 21, 1707, 'to inform yourselves of the clear improved Yearly Value of every Benefice with Cure of Souls within (your deanery) the clear improved Yearly Value thereof doth not exceed *Fifty Pounds*',[9] is missing, but it is possible to give a picture of the value of benefices in eighteenth-century values twenty years later. By 1728 the majority of Glamorgan livings had been discharged from the payment of tenths and first fruits as their value did not exceed £50 per annum; only 15 remained subject to this tax. The income of the discharged livings ranged from the £8 per annum of Penarth to the £49 annual income of Llandow, the average annual income of discharged livings being £35, which was appreciably higher than the official returns. But it should be remembered that this is what the incumbent received; the assistant curate who had charge of a parish in the place of an absentee incumbent received far less than this average. No doubt it was of this latter class that Thomas Price, rector of Merthyr Tydfil, wrote: 'Many poor clergymen are not able to purchase more than bare food and raiment for their families'.[10]

The eighteenth century saw a gradual but steady improvement in the economic status of the local clergy, but it would be true to say that it was still low by English standards, and the prospect of raising minimum stipends to £60 per annum was thought to be 'the Work of Ages'. The curse of many livings was the financial drain to lay impropriators who enjoyed considerable income from tithes 'which were torn away from the clergy without any manner of Default or Forfeiture committed, or possible to be committed *by them*, or on their part; and their new Proprietors have ever since contented themselves to this very Day, with paying only the poor pecuniary Stipend or Pittance that was antiently alloted to the *Vicar* or *Curate* before the Reformation'.[11] Gradually things got better: increased rent from glebe and from land bought by the governors of the Corporation of Queen Anne's Bounty augmented the poorer livings.

It is possible to turn from these general considerations to specific cases of the sources of clerical income. In 1717 the rector of St. Athan had a parsonage house (covered with thatch), consisting of a hall, parlour, kitchen, buttery (with chambers above), a garden, two orchards, a ruinous barn, a cowhouse, two cottages attached to the parsonage, together with 43 acres of glebe land, and a parcel of land for which he paid 4*d*. per acre to the lord of the manor. Part of his tithe was received in kind, and part had been commuted for money payment. In theory, the tithes were paid in kind, but 'if the Rector for the time being does not think fit to receive the Tythe in kind from the Occupier of any Lands within the said Parish that then the Occupier if an Indweller shall pay yearly at All Saints one shilling in the Pound, & if an Outdweller shall and ought to pay twenty pence in the pound for all such Lands as he holds'. The Easter offerings came to 1½*d*. per head for every inhabitant of the parish; 4*d*. was due to the rector for the churching of every woman, and 5*s*. for the solemnization of marriage after banns. These marriage fees were higher than those charged in Merthyr Mawr where they were 2*s*. but in this latter parish the churching fee was 6*d*. The vicar of Llanbleddian received 1½*d*. for each Easter communicant, 4*d*. for each garden in his parish, 5*s*. as a marriage fee, 1*s*. for publishing the banns of marriage; 6*s*. 8*d*. for every parishioner buried in the middle chancel (with double fees for those outside the parish), and 26s. for every stranger buried in the church. But the main source of his income was from the letting of his glebe, for which he received £100 per annum.[12]

It was as well for the vicar of Llanbleddian that he was well provided with glebe land or else his income would have been considerably lower, for the rectors of the parish were the dean and chapter of Gloucester cathedral, and this body, of course, had a financial interest in their appropriated parish. This was not their only appropriation in Glamorgan: Aberdare, Cardiff (St. John's and St. Mary's), Welsh St. Donats, Llantwit Major, Llantwit Faerdre, Llancarfan, Llantrisant, Llanwynno, Penmark, Roath, and Ystradyfodwg were all sources of income for Gloucester cathedral. Its extent in the eighteenth century is not known, but in the days of tithe commutation award after 1836 it amounted to £3,148 13s. 2d. per annum, which was money originally intended for the maintenance of the parish priest. The dean and chapter of Gloucester were not the only ecclesiastical corporation to take rectorial tithe from Glamorgan: their counterpart of Bristol derived part of their income from Penarth and Lavernock. The bishops of Llandaff derived no income from Glamorgan parishes, but the archdeacon and chapter of Llandaff held Caerau, Eglwysilan, St. Hilary, Llandaff, Llanedern, Llanfabon, Merthyr Mawr, Pendoylan, Pen-tyrch, Whitchurch, and Ystradowen. Between the lay impropriators and the ecclesistical appropriators nearly one-half of the tithe income left the parishes, leaving the parishes that much poorer, but many of them were saved from almost complete destitution by rents received from property purchases by the governors of the Corporation of Queen Anne's Bounty.

The lot of assistant curates was worse than that of incumbents. At the beginning of the eighteenth century a bishop was empowered to insist upon a minimum stipend of £20, but there are many examples where even this was not attained: the assistant curate of Cadoxton-juxta-Neath was paid £10 in 1753; and when Elias Thomas offered himself for ordination in the summer of 1764, William Thomas, incumbent of the above parish, in commending the ordinand to the bishop, wrote: 'And I hope my Lord will consider, upon a just Representation of the slender Incomes of the Clergy in Wales in general, that a Polite and well bred Man would never stoop to accept such a Pittance as the beneficed Clergy here (I speak of the Generality) can afford to give a Curate. He is a better Schollar, to my knowledge, than three Parts in four of the *Shirgars* that swarm in our Diocese; and to crown the whole, as it never, I believe, entered into his head to go out of Wales . . . In short, I verily think he will make a very humble, useful, Drudge; for he aspires at nothing higher than a Curacy.'[13] The assistant curate who served a parish for an absentee incumbent (who in turn served another parish to eke out a living), had himself to serve more than one parish in that lowly capacity to make a living. Poverty was at the root of absenteeism and pluralism in Glamorgan at this time. By the end of the century other factors accounted for the perpetuation of this state of affairs.

The origins and attainments of the clergy. Thomas's reference to Carmarthenshire men among the Glamorgan clergy suggests that most of the clerics were not natives of their county and diocese. Certainly there were few ordinations during the century where all the candidates were of the diocese; many natives of the surrounding counties of Carmarthenshire and Brecknockshire were ordained to Llandaff. In the summer ordination of 1746, of five candidates, two were from the county, and the remainder from beyond, and in the corresponding ordination a year later there were ten candidates, of whom five were Glamorgan men and the remainder were 'Shirgars'; and a year later, of eight candidates, three were Glamorgan men.[14] An examination of this question, shows that the Glamorgan clergy were made up of a hard core of natives of the county with a liberal addition of men from the surrounding counties, but scarcely any from north Wales.

The educational attainments of the local clergy in this period show that from 1660 the majority of ordinands were university graduates of either Oxford or Cambridge. This persisted thoughout the eighteenth century, and of the colleges, Jesus College, Oxford, supplied the majority of the clergy, but most Oxford colleges are represented in the ordination lists. This does not mean that the clergy received a theological training for their work: the first recorded example of an ordinand producing a certificate that he had attended divinity lectures is not forthcoming until 1813. Of those who had attended university, the majority were men from the county or diocese itself; Carmarthenshire men holding degrees were not as numerous as those who came from Glamorgan or Monmouthshire. But the more interesting question concerns the education of those clergy who had not been to a university, and here the evidence is scanty until the end of the century when the divinity schools attached to Cowbridge, Usk, and Abergavenny grammar schools produced a steady flow of ordinands. There were undoubtedly men who had received tuition in country parsonage houses and local village schools; as for example, Rees Davies, of whom the parishioners of Llanmaes complained in 1734 that 'though he was not brought up in any university but in County Schools he is given so much to Law that he makes the whole Parishioners unsafe'.[15] It was not until the third quarter of the eighteenth century that the bishops of Llandaff began seriously to undertake the task of educating their clergy.

Having been ordained, and instituted to their parishes, many of the clergy could look forward to nothing higher than an assistant curacy, and most of them became little more than names in ecclesiastical documents, performing the routine canonical duties in rural parishes, visits to the local market town, attendance at the ruridecanal chapter meetings; while the more fortunate and prominent served as magistrates, visited assizes and quarter sessions, and a still fewer number attended the annual cathedral chapter meeting in Llandaff at Peterstide. Among them are a few who will merit attention for their literary contributions: Thomas Wilkins, rector of Marychurch, David Lewis, vicar of Llangattock-juxta-Neath, Thomas Richards, of Coety, Dr. John Richards, rector of Coety with Nolton, John Walters, of Llandochau and St. Hilary, are the most prominent among the clerics who contributed to the cultural and literary history of the county (below, Chapter X).

It can be taken for granted that the majority of the clerics in those days in these parts fulfilled their duties to the best of their ability, in spite of the fact that, outside the towns, their difficulties were great. Very few assistant curates could eke out a living by the charge of one parish in the absence of its incumbent; usually they had to serve two or more parishes, and in view of these difficulties the evidence shows that ecclesiastical life in Glamorgan did not fall short of eighteenth-century standards in rural parishes, and, as was the case elsewhere, town standards were higher. It would be an easy matter so to quote from the records of the consistory court as to give the impression that all the clergy sooner or later appeared to answer charges before it. This would be to give a false picture: the majority of the clergy knew the court by name only; but there was a steady trickle of clerical offenders who appeared before it. Until the middle of the eighteenth century the most frequent canonical offence was that of officiating at clandestine marriages. This has been attributed to 'a parcel of strolling curates in south Wales', who, having little hope of an incumbency, 'for a crown or at most for a guinea, would marry anyone under a hedge'.[16] But it was not only the unbeneficed curate who so offended: on February 23, 1671 Theophilus Price, vicar of Cardiff and rector of St. Athan, was charged with this offence. His sentence of suspension was remitted, but he was cautioned about saying the daily offices, 'according to the form of the Anglican liturgy', in the church of St. John if he was well and was at home.[17] A year later the sentence of suspension against John Cooke, rector of Llansannor, was enforced for the same offence,[18] and it was for defiance of the sentence of suspension that Robert Jones was charged before the court for taking duties in St. Lythans, and was excommunicated by Bishop Lloyd in Mathern palace on December 6, 1678.[19] Occasionally the charge was the general neglect of duties, as when Thomas David, curate of Ystradyfodwg, was charged before the consistory court in July 1743 with a general neglect of duties in his parish, general misconduct, especially tippling, and that he 'did not on Candlemas Day, nor Ash Wednesday, nor on any day in passion Week last except on Easter Eve officiate in the said parish church of Ystradyfodwg aforesaid nor offer yourself ready for that purpose by ordering the Bell to be rung or toll'd'. It was further alleged that Davies was so addicted to card playing that 'You always keep a pack by you for that purpose'.[20] The real significance of such cases (and there were more of them) is that they reveal that in a century when general personal and social standards were low, clerical standards could not be abandoned with impunity. The first half of the eighteenth century does not reveal the hard-drinking, fox-hunting parson who has been thought typical of the time, but the second half of the century did produce John Carne, parson of Llysworney, who was considerably more interested in his bloodstock than he was in his parishioners. But he was an exception.

Parish administration and church repairs. The position of the laity in the Church was as eloquent a testimony as any that the Church was still essentially a mediaeval institution. It is true to say that they had no voice whatsoever in purely ecclesiastical affairs, but, as the parish was a civil as well as an ecclesiastical unit, the churchwarden had secular as well as religious duties to perform. The 89th Canon of 1604 had laid down that all churchwardens and quest-men should be chosen annually by the joint consent of the minister and parishioners, and, failing this, that the incumbent should choose the one and the parishioners the other; and this was the rule generally followed. There were exceptions: in Cowbridge in 1720 it was claimed that it was customary for the vicar to nominate the one and for the bailiffs to elect the other churchwarden. Thomas Carne and Thomas Wilkins had resisted this arrangement whereby John Valence and John Tudor had been appointed church-wardens on Easter Monday, and an application was made to the consistory court that the arrangement should stand and that Carne and Wilkins should pay the cost of the application.[21] This was not the last disputed election in Cowbridge.

The Canons of 1604 were based on the principle that every citizen was a baptized member of the Established Church, and in spite of an incipient Nonconformity, both Protestant and Roman Catholic, this presumption was justified. But although the ecclesiastical colour of Glamorgan in the post-Restoration period, and up to the end of the eighteenth century, was decidedly 'Church', it could no longer be taken for granted that the choice of the parishioners in the vestry would result in a churchman becoming churchwarden; and consequently his ec-clesiastical allegiance might well be elsewhere. This was particularly true when it is recalled that the maintenance of the church fabric, its ornaments, its vestments, and even the bread and wine of the sacrament, were provided from the church rate. With the exception of very few parishes which obeyed the letter of the Prayer Book by taking a collection at the offertory in Holy Communion, church collections were unknown. This probably did great harm to the Church, for it is unlikely that churchmen, and especially Nonconformists, were anxious to tax them-selves adequately in the Vestry for the ecclesiastical as well as the civil needs of the parish. The church rate was not objected to on principle until the nineteenth century (except by the Quakers), but the cases which went to the consistory court show that there were technical and legal niceties which were not overlooked even by those who voiced no conscientious objection to the payment.

It was this dependence upon the church rate for the maintenance of the fabric that accounted for the slow deterioration in the ancient parish churches which necessitated such extensive repair and rebuilding in the next century. It was not that nothing was done, but that not enough was done. The chancellor's visitation in 1727 showed that Llandow needed a Welsh Bible and Prayer Book, that the windows were unglazed, the nave unpaved, and new seats were needed. Llysworney churchwardens reported 'a want of Ladders to ye bellfry Loft, & the seats out of repaire; ye pulpitt fallen to decay & ye want of a large and convenient reading place for the minister'. The roof of St. John's church, Cardiff, was uncovered. In the following visitation (1728) every churchwarden, without exception, in the Groneath deanery reported that repairs were needed to their churches. In 1732 the churchwarden of Cadoxton-juxta-Neath testified to 'the want of a napkin ffor the communion table, the want of a new Chalice in the chapel of Croynant & the windows of the chapeles of Abberpergwm and Croynant want of glazing'. For the 1742 visitation there were many parishes which could not produce registers, terriers, or copies of the Act against immorality. It is almost with relief that one reads that all that the churchwardens of Aberdare had to complain of in 1748 was that 'one of the church windows (is) out of repair', and Baglan five years later was even milder: 'the surplice out of repair'.[22] The revealing feature in these visitation returns is that the same reports recurred annually, evidence that little, if anything, was done in many churches to repair the ravages of wind and rain.

We are fortunate in being able to trace the finances of one country parish church throughout the eighteenth century. The accounts of the parish of Betws in 1710 amounted to £2 1s. 6d., and two years later 3s. 9d. was spent on a lock for the church door and 1s. for 50 tiles. Little was spent on the church fabric: in 1725 £2 5s. 0d. was spent on a Bible and Prayer Book, and ten years later the churchwardens spent £4 12s. but little of it on the maintenance of the fabric. In 1739 £1 1s. 11d., in 1745, 17s. 11d., in 1749, 18s. 1d. were spent on the church, and in 1750 a coat of white lime put the expenses up to £1 14s. 8d. In 1764 7s. was spent on '6 days Work in Repairing the Wainscott above the Reading Pew', and the whole operation cost 10s. In 1771 a church rate of 5d. in the £1 had to be levied for an expenditure of £4 5s. 6d., but the amount to be raised dropped to £1 10s. 0d. in the following year. More work was done in 1776, when £7 12s. 0d. was spent, a fair proportion of it on minor repairs and restoration of the stonework. Three years later the parishioners decided to undertake the re-seating of the church, and a little pointing and paving were done at the same time. In 1780 it was decided to repair the pulpit and the gallery, for which a church rate of 4*d*. in the £1 was levied, but even so the general account for the expenditure on the church amounted to only £3 11*s*. 2*d*.[23] Here is a brief history of the expenditure on an ancient parish church for the better part of a century. Little was done to the fabric itself, for it must be remembered that the above figures included items for bread and wine, cleaning the church, and ecclesiastical fees at visitations, in addition to the service books already noted.

Ecclesiastical authority did not acquiesce in this neglect. Churchwardens were charged with neglect as also were rectors, owners of tithes, lessees, and farmers of tithes. In 1746–47 the following parishes in Glamorgan were involved in such cases before the consistory court: Michaelston-super-Avon, Cadoxton-juxta-Neath, Llantwit by Neath, Aberdare, St. Fagans, Whitchurch, Llantwit Major, Newton Nottage, Coychurch, Eglwys Brewis, Llanwynno, Cardiff, Betws;[24] and in 1750 other charges were brought against certain parishes for the same kind of neglect. In 1765 Giles Tibbs and Richard Morgan, churchwardens of the parish of Neath, were charged with neglect of the churchyard wall which 'is now left open to the Highway whereby the Hogs Pigs and Cattle get therein and root up and destroy the Graves or Burying Places in the said Churchyard and by Reason whereof the same is become a great Nuisance and very offensive to the parishioners and Inhabitants of the said parish'.[25] But in spite of such charges and proceedings the neglect of our Glamorgan churches went on, except in those parishes which could afford more extensive repairs. It is known that St. John's, Cardiff, was extensively repaired in the 1730s, and in 1766 Aberavon church was restored, partly by the aid of the royal brief which raised £1,025 towards the cost. Between 1730 and 1732 Llantwit-juxta-Neath spent about £100 on its church, while in 1765 Wick church was re-seated, and the same necessary work was carried out in Cowbridge in 1777, and in Newcastle and St. Brides Major the following year.[26]

The condition of Llandaff cathedral. Of all the restorations of the eighteenth century, that of Llandaff cathedral was the most famous, or notorious, not only in the old diocese of Llandaff, but beyond it. The Church in the diocese and in Glamorgan suffered during this period and after from the sad decline in the fortunes of Llandaff cathedral. The Chapter Act Books reveal that the condition of the fabric had given rise to anxiety since the end of the sixteenth century, and the period of the Civil Wars, Commonwealth, and Protectorate put an end to the small efforts which had been made to maintain the cathedral structure. The benevolence of £100 granted to Charles II on June 30, 1662, could have been better spent in other ways, but on September 26 of the same year a grant was made out of a fine from the rectory of Llantilio

Pertholey 'towards the rebuilding and repayreinge of the school house'. At the same chapter meeting the chancellor and registrar, who had held their courts in the 'Ladies chappell' were now instructed to repair 'the ancient Consistory roome' for their activities; and on November 18, 1668 the chapter agreed that the room over the consistory room should be converted into a registry for the custody of records. But the problem of the cathedral church itself remained, and it was on June 30, 1665, that the chapter decided to make an appeal to the nobility and gentry 'toward the good of this Cathedral Churche as many Chappters have done in respect of their respective Churches successfully'. The result of this appeal is not known, but there is no evidence that anything of significance was done to the cathedral, but there is a reference in the Chapter Act Books on June 30, 1679, to 'the New House lately built by this Chapter lying and being in the Churchyard of this Cathedral Church', and it was this which housed the cathedral library. Five years later, on June 30, 1684, it was decided to furnish this house for chapter meetings which had hitherto been held in a local inn, and this was done to prepare for 'the changes (that) are likely to be very great which must arise upon the necessary repairs of this Church and the adorning the same to the honr of God'.

A great storm in 1704 and a still greater catastrophe on the night of February 6, 1722–23 virtually completed the ruin of the cathedral church. Before the final blow the building had become the concern of Archbishop Tennison, who inspired George Bull, archdeacon of Llandaff and, later, bishop of St. David's, to bring the matter before the chapter, but it was not until 1728 that a message was sent to the chapter from Bishop Clavering 'recommending the speedy repairing of the Cathedral Church and declaring thereby that he would subscribe £100 to the same and order and direct their Proctor General to subscribe the sum of £200 toward carrying on the repairs of the said Church which are to be allowed him out of the fund of the Chapter'. But it was Clavering's successor, Bishop Harris, who undertook the restoration of the cathedral, beginning in 1730. On July 20 and September 23 of that year John Wood, of Bath, was commissioned to survey the fabric, and his report showed that it was in a serious condition and that its reconstruction would cost £6,366 13s. 2d. Other contractors were invited to make surveys, and they recommended less ambitious schemes at a lower cost, but on June 24, 1734, the chapter entered into a contract with John Wood for a partial reconstruction at a cost of £1,700. This modified scheme was necessary because it had become obvious that the original scheme of reconstruction could not be carried out, for the appeal for funds had been disappointing. The response to Bishop Harris's appeal resulted in private benefactions of £891 15s. 7½d., of which a large proportion had been given by Clavering, Harris himself, and the members of the chapter. A brief, sanctioned by the justices in Quarter Session and sent to Lord Chancellor

Ockham, realized £1,265 2s. 0½d. by 1737, less expenses amounting to £364 14s. 6d., thus leaving a net sum of £1,792 3s. 2d. to meet an account of £6,366.

Before 1737 it was clear that the restoration originally intended by Wood could not be carried out, but when the chapter had entered into contract with the famous architect on June 29, 1734, it had been their intention to make the money go as far as possible on the reconstruction of the existing fabric. In 1736, however, Wood was engaged on the construction of an Italian temple within the old cathedral, and what emerged can best be described in the words of one of the historians of the cathedral: 'He (Wood) recast the six eastern bays of the church in his own style; the decrepit walls were lowered; a new roof, concealed by plaster vaulting, was placed upon them, the Gothic work in the Choir was hidden behind classical work, mainly Ionic, in plaster; new stalls and screens were added on the traditional lines, and a large portico surmounted the elevated communion table.' In itself the Choir was not unpleasing, and was pronounced 'exceeding fine'.[27] Thus was effected the strangest 'restoration' of any cathedral church in the kingdom, and Llandaff presented this mixture of classical and gothic until the following century.[28] Little wonder that when Bishop Sumner presented himself at Llandaff cathedral for his enthronement in 1826, he turned to his chaplain and said: 'I didn't know that such a place existed'.

This plight of the cathedral, and the decline in its services, affected its status in the county and diocese, and the absence of a bishop's residence in the cathedral city meant that the diocese had no effective centre. It was suggested that the see should be removed to Cardiff whose inhabitants 'have within these few years beautify'd their Church and furnished it with an organ, at their no small expense'.[29] In a letter to Browne Willis, the antiquarian and historian of Llandaff cathedral, a writer who signed himself 'Ecclesiophilus' said that the condition of the cathedral was so decayed 'that its members like Rats in a Sinking Ship, are upon the Point of Deserting it & removing their See and their Habitations to Cardiff'.[30] The writer believed that this move should be checked at once, or else St. David's would be moved to Carmarthen or Brecon, Bangor to Caernarvon or Beaumaris, and St. Asaph to Denbigh or Wrexham. Willis's correspondent urged him to do for Llandaff what he had already done for St. David's and so prevent the removal of the see to Cardiff. On March 10, 1717, William Wotton wrote to Willis confirming the design to abandon Llandaff, and said that the prospect had been put aside for the time being. Apparently the reasons for the proposed change were the desirability of having a cathedral in a populous centre rather than in a village, the smallness of the chapter's financial resources and the inconvenience of Llandaff itself, especially in the matter of accommodation. Wotton replied to these objections and said that the Cardiff church (St. John's) was not big enough to hold its own parishioners, and 'it

[446]

certainly had no Room to Spare for Cathedral uses'.[31] This low estimate of Llandaff as a diocesan centre persisted until the middle of the nineteenth century.

Religion and worship in the parishes. For a general picture of the state of the Church in the three Glamorgan deaneries we must rely entirely on the replies given to the queries issued by the bishops in preparation for their triennial visitations. For the deanery of Gower there were nineteen returns to the bishop's queries in 1755, the three missing parishes being Llan-giwg, Llanrhidian and Porteynon. For these nineteen parishes there were eleven clergy, most of them curates and serving more than one parish. There was a great deal of non-residence on the part of incumbents, for there were only four who lived in their parishes: the incumbents of Swansea, Llangyfelach, Penmaen, and Penrice, but all the clergy were resident in one of the parishes they served, and no curate served more than two parishes, usually adjacent to each other. There were, therefore, eleven resident clergy to serve nineteen parishes. Of these parishes the most flourishing was Llangyfelach with 160–200 communicants, followed by Llandeilo Tal-y-bont with a monthly average of 100 communicants. All the parishes had one service per Sunday, with two services on that day in Swansea, Penmaen, and Llangyfelach (this, of course, meant one service in the parish church and the other in one of the chapels). As might have been expected most of the services were held in English, except in Llandeilo Tal-y-bont and Llangyfelach where the services were conducted in Welsh, and in Loughor and Swansea where both languages were used. The frequency of Holy Communion was higher than might have been expected. Swansea, Llandeilo Tal-y-bont, Llangennech, and Llangyfelach had monthly celebrations in addition to those at the great Festivals, while Loughor had 13 such services per year; Oystermouth had seven, while the other parishes maintained the traditional custom of celebrating Holy Communion four times a year, at the great Festivals.[32] Set against its contemporary background, this is by no means an unattractive picture of a rural deanery; on the contrary: the ideals of the Prayer Book were not lost sight of in any parish, with the result that very few cases of moral turpitude came before the consistory court from the deanery of Gower during this period.

According to the visitation returns of 1763 and 1774 in the two deaneries of Groneath and Llandaff the most flourishing parishes were those of Cadoxton-juxta-Neath, with a resident incumbent and about 200 communicants, and Neath with Llantwit and the chapel of Resolven (in ruins). The adjoining parishes of Aberavon with Baglan did not see their parson except during the long vacation, for during term time he lived in an Oxford college of which he was a fellow, and paid his curate £20 per annum. Likewise the incumbent of Coychurch, Daniel Durel, lived in Cowbridge where he was master of the Free School, while the famous Dr. John Richards resided in Coety although he had no parsonage house. He served Coety with Nolton, and Newcastle, while his curate ministered in Betws, Laleston, and Tythegston. John Rogers, rector of Marcross, lived in Eglwysilan and served in addition Llanfabon and St. Martins' Chapel. He paid £12 to the curate of the parish adjacent to Marcross to take services there, which was the same as the rector of Llanharry paid a neighbouring curate to look after his parish while he lived in Wiltshire. The curate of Ystradowen received £14 per annum for doing duty in Llansannor, whose rector lived in Abergavenny as master of the grammar school. Another absentee incumbent was James Scott, of Gelli-gaer, where Nonconformity flourished. Scott lived in Southampton and left a large parish in charge of the curate who was able to report that 'the church is full of people every Sunday'. Nearby, in Eglwysilan, Lewis Rogers, rector of Marcross, acted as resident curate at £30 per year to the vicar who lived in Abergavenny and held the living of Llanddewi (?Skirrid). Rogers had to undertake this extra cure because he said of Marcross: 'This living is too small to maintain my family'. The vicar of Llantrisant (R. Harris), strove manfully with three curates, to serve the most unwieldy parish in Glamorgan, consisting as it did of 'Llantwit Minor, Talygarn, St. John's, Llanwynno, Aberdare, and Ystradyfodwg', a parish appropriated to the dean and chapter of Gloucester. Cardiff St. John's had its resident vicar, but the number of 40–50 communicants seems very small, and Roath, whose vicar, in the absence of a parsonage house, lived in Lisvane, claimed 40 communicants of whom only 8–10 'received' regularly, and about 24 'received' in Llandaff cathedral where there were two services per Sunday, two on Wednesdays, Fridays, and Holy Days, a celebration of Holy Communion on the first Sunday of the month and on Holy Days—all within John Wood's Italian temple.

In regard to language, with the exception of most of the churches in the Vale of Glamorgan, services were held in Welsh and in English in the great majority of parishes. Generally, the use of the Welsh language decreased as one travelled from west to east in the diocese of Llandaff, but even in 1774 there were parishes in the deanery of Llandaff where services were held exclusively in the Welsh language, e.g., Ystradowen, Whitchurch, Caerau, Llaniltern, Pen-llin, while most of the parishes adjacent to these were bilingual in the services.[33]

There was not a church in Glamorgan which did not have at least one service per Sunday, and in the country churches, which comprised the great majority, it was impossible to provide more as there were very few clergy in the county who were not responsible for more than one church, and the care of three churches, with difficult transport conditions, was by no means unusual. At the root of this was the pernicious system whereby parishes, already poor, had much of their income drained away to laymen and ecclesiastical bodies, and especially to the former, who paid a pittance to clergy to perform ecclesiastical duties and carry out their pastoral functions. Thomas Mansell Franklin, who took the tithes of Margam, was more honourable than most in giving the vicar of Margam £40 per annum. When we add these adverse economic and financial factors to an administrative system which the Church itself was powerless to reform, the Church in Glamorgan acquitted itself creditably up to the middle of the eighteenth century. But it was in the realm of education it made its greatest contribution during this period.

III. Schools and Education

(a) Unendowed schools

The outstanding characteristic of education in Glamorgan in this period, as it had been for centuries past, and as it was to be for another century to come, was its development within an ecclesiastical framework. Directly or indirectly all education was a province of the Church, and no man could hold school except under licence from the bishop. In practice, however, ecclesiastical control was not complete, for there were cases of unlicensed schoolmasters in Glamorgan and, in any case, after Bates' Case in 1670 it was no longer necessary for the patron of a school to seek a bishop's licence for the schoolmaster.

The bishops' concern with schooling was revealed in the Articles of Enquiries sent out by Bishop Lloyd in 1662 preparatory to his first visitation. Section VI (II) dealt with schools: 'Doth any man keep a publick or private School in your Parish, who is not allowed thereunto by the Bishop? Present such, if there be any in your Parish or Chappelrie. Doth your School-master teach his Scholars the Catechism of Religion, set forth by Authority? Doth he cause them upon Sundaies and Holidaies orderly to repair to your Church or Chappel, and see that they behave themselves there quietly and reverently during the time of Divine Service and Sermon?' There is reason to believe that the county was badly off for schools in 1660: the Puritan experiment had, unfortunately, come to an end, and Bishop Lloyd said in 1662 that Glamorgan was 'utterly destitute of schools'. This state was temporary, for on January 21, 1713/4, William Lewis, curate of Margam, was able to inform the S.P.C.K., that 'there is hardly a parish in that part of the world where there is not a private school for teaching children to read'. Most of these would have been unendowed schools and their origin is unknown in most cases, nor is it possible to tell whether they had a continuous life: apart from episcopal licences and visitation returns they have left few records. Space will not permit a description of all the unendowed schools of the county, but the following places in Glamorgan had unendowed schools in the period covered by this chapter:

[449]

Deanery of Gower: every parish in this deanery possessed an unendowed school, with the exception of Llanddewi in Gower and Reynoldston. There were schools in Bishopston, Cheriton, Ilston, Llandeilo Tal-y-bont, Llan-giwg, Llangennith, Llangyfelach, Llanmadog, Llanrhidian, Loughor, Nicholston, Oxwich, Oystermouth, Pennard, Penmaen, Penrice, Porteynon, and Rhosili.

Deanery of Groneath and Llandaff: Aberavan, Aberdare, Bonvilston, Briton Ferry, Blaen-gwrach, Cadoxton-juxta-Barry, Cilybebyll, Glyncorrwg, Llandough, Llandyfodwg, Llanfabon, Llangynwyd, Llanharan, Llantrisant, Llantwit Major, Margam, Merthyr Tydfil, Neath, Newton Nottage, Pen-tyrch, Pyle and Kenfig, St. Mary Hill, St. Nicholas, Ystradowen, and Ystradyfodwg.[34]

(b) ENDOWED SCHOOLS (I) PRIMARY

The schools hitherto dealt with in this section were those which depended upon the goodwill of an incumbent who taught the children of the parish as part of his duty as parish priest, or those which eked out a living for a man or a woman who made a small charge for those attending the school. It is certain that the children were taught to read English, drilled in the Catechism of the Established Church, possibly taught 'accounts' (or arithmetic) and, if the local incumbent were a scholar, it is possible that the rudiments of Latin would be taught to the brighter boys.

More detailed knowledge is obtainable of those schools which were endowed by a local benefactor, and of this class the following provided primary, or elementary, education, i.e., they were non-classical and, consequently, were not grammar schools.

Within three years the borough of Cardiff benefited from two charities which were to serve as the basis of its educational system throughout the eighteenth century. On January 6, 1707, Jane Herbert of Whitefriars, in Cardiff, bequeathed the sum of £500 for purchasing an absolute estate of inheritance in the names of Sir Edward Stradling of St. Donat's, Edward Herbert of Whitefriars, and George Howells of Bovill, and their heirs for ever, 'in trust for a perpetual endowment of a free-school, to be established and kept within the town of Cardiff, and likewise for establishing a yearly salary, arising out of the rents and profits of the said lands, to the master of the said school for the time being', who was to teach 15 boys of poor parentage. With the bequest a property of 80 acres, known as Tir-y-pont Ton, in the parish of Merthyr Tydfil, was purchased, and this yielded £25 per annum in rent to the schoolmaster.

Three years later, on December 5, 1710, Craddock Wells, alderman of the borough of Cardiff, gave property in the High Street of Cardiff and in the hamlet of Canton, together with £28, to purchase three-and-a-half acres of property contiguous to the Canton property, upon trust to educate, freely, poor boys and girls of Cardiff who would be nominated yearly; 'and he further directed that such boys and girls should be well instructed to read, write, and cypher, and that each of the said boys would wear a blue bonnet, and each of the girls some badge to distinguish them from other children of the school where they should be taught'. It is clear that this school received fee-paying pupils, and there is evidence that sufficient Latin was taught here to justify its description as a grammar school in 1771.

In Llantwit Major, Margaret Seys bequeathed £200 in 1700 for teaching ten poor children, but, like so many other local charities in those days, the money was not applied for this pupose, for, although it appears that a school was opened in the parish, the bequest was later withdrawn. Likewise, the bequest of £100 by the Reverend John Cooke of St. Fagan's for teaching five poor children, three of the parish of St. Fagans and two of the hamlet of Chapel Llaniltern, was partly misapplied, for only half of the bequest was ultimately applied to its original purpose.

Endowed Schools (II) Grammar

The origin of grammar school education in Glamorgan is not easily traced. It is known that the vicar choral taught Latin in 1662 in a school attached to Llandaff cathedral, but there is no record that this was continued. The Reverend Evan Llewelyn, M.A., kept a classical school in Loughor before he moved to Aberavon, and it is likely that the school kept in Margam by the Reverend John Walters sometime in the 1740s gave a classical education, as also did the Craddock Wells's school in Cardiff in 1771. But there were two endowed schools which gave a grammar education: the Cowbridge Free School, and the Bishop Gore School in Swansea.

It is probable that there was a connection between the Cowbridge Free School and an earlier school in Llantwit Major. There was a school in this latter parish in the sixteenth century endowed by the Stradling family, and it is possible that this was transferred to Cowbridge, at first to temporary premises and then to a school house supplied by Sir John Stradling. This property was bought by Sir Leoline Jenkins who in 1685 'devised to the principal, fellows, and scholars of Jesus College, Oxford, all his lands, tenements, and hereditaments, and the free-school, and school-house, with its appurtenances in Cowbridge, and charged his said lands first, with the yearly payment of £100, for ever'. The master of the school was to be nominated by the principal of Jesus College and he was to receive £10 per year and the use of the school house for teaching five scholars who were to be known as pensioners (and later as monitors) and a further £10 per annum for teaching ten poor children from Cowbridge and the neighbouring parishes; and such duties were not to be conjoined with the cure of souls, but the master 'should keep wholly to the business of the schools'. The five pensioners were to be given an annual grant of £6 for four years, and three of them were eligible for an exhibition of £10 per year at Jesus College for four years, while the number of fellowships at the college was increased by two, and in the filling of them 'a respect should be had *caeteris paribus* to those bred at Cowbridge school'. The school was exclusively classical in its education, and the boys attended a neighbouring school 'for instruction in a general English education'.

Although it is abundantly clear that the work of Sir Leoline Jenkins was to strengthen and extend a school which had already existed for some generations, there is no evidence that the grammar school provided for Swansea in 1682 was based upon an earlier foundation. The benefactor in this case was Hugh Gore, bishop of Waterford and Lismore in Ireland, and a native of the borough of Swansea, who 'for the love he bore to the corporation, town, and burgh of Swansea, and to the burgesses and inhabitants thereof', on September 13 and 14, 1682, granted to Bussy Mansel, of Briton Ferry, certain properties in the parish of Llandyfodwg 'upon special trust and confidence to nominate and appoint, in writing, under his and their hands and seals, one discreet and well-learned man to supply the room of schoolmaster of the said free grammar-school in the said town and borough, to instruct in the Latin and Greek tongues, without reward than hereafter provided, 20 poor children and youths sons of the poorer sort of the burgesses, and that were the burgesses of the said corporation and burgh'. Mansel and his heirs had the right of nomination to the schoolmaster's office, and should a vacancy happen during the minority of the heir-at-law of Bussy Mansel, the bishop of St. David's should have the right of nomination and appointment. It was this arrangement which led to the building of Swansea's first grammar school on land belonging to Mansel in Goat Street. But by the end of the century the school did not benefit the poor of Swansea, as had been originally intended, for free education was restricted to the classics and the 'general English course of education' was charged for at £4 per year.[35]

(c) The Schools of the Welsh Trust (1672–81)

Hitherto the schools dealt with were those which had their origin among the local benefactors; in the case of the unendowed schools, founded by those who taught for a living or, in the case of the clergy, by those who regarded the teaching of children as part of their parish duties. It will also have been noticed that the grammar school curriculum was restricted to the classics, while the endowed and unendowed primary schools offered little else than the reading of the Bible and Catechism, in English, with some arithmetic. The inspiration which lay behind most of these schools was religious, and this was particularly true of the three classes of schools which have yet to be described in this section.

It was generally believed during the second half of the seventeenth century that the problems of belief and conduct could best be approached through schools, and that a reformation of manners would be effected through the provision of education. This belief was not confined to this country; indeed, it found its earliest expression in Germany. In an age when the social structure was accepted without question, both the re-formation of manners and problem of work were believed to depend upon the early instruction of the children of the poorer classes. 'Instruction in Bible and Catechism during the formative years of childhood, before the infant population was ready for apprenticeship or service, would build up a God-fearing population and, at the same time, would inoculate the children against the habits of sloth, debauchery and beggary, which characterised the lower orders of society'.[36] Many of the local endowments were thus inspired, for a large number of them provided for the apprentice-ship of boys after their education was over; but the three main agencies through which the Established Church worked on a very extensive scale were the 'Society for the Reformation of Manners' (1692), the 'Society for the Promotion of Christian Knowledge' (1699) (to be referred to henceforth in this section by its well known initials: S.P.C.K.), and the 'Society for the Propagation of the Gospel in Foreign Parts' (1701) (better known as S.P.G.). A great deal of eighteenth-century philanthropy and piety found its expression in the support given to these societies. The work done through them represents what was, in fact, a revival of religion, but it has not so been recognized because the marks of a religious revival have since been determined by the religious 'enthusiasm' which charac-terized the better known Methodist revival both in Wales and in England. Furthermore, the term 'charity schools' sounds cold, if not offensive, to modern ears, but the definition of charity as 'doing good to the souls and bodies of men' by Robert Nelson, the non-juror, and a prominent figure in the eighteenth-century movement, shows clearly the religious impulse which inspired the whole conception of providing schools and work for the children of the poorer classes.

The first Charity Movement to benefit Glamorgan was the Welsh Trust, whose founder was the Reverend Thomas Gouge, an Anglican clergyman who was ordained in 1634 and was incumbent of St. Sepulchre's, London, which he resigned rather than accept the Act of Uniformity (1662). Before, and especially after, his resignation, he devoted himself to acts of charity and education, and in the years following 1662 he collected large sums of money donated by both Churchmen and Dissenters which, after 1671, he devoted to the task of evangelizing in Wales. In 1672 the Welsh Trust was formed, and continued its work until the death of Gouge in 1681.

Details of the schools set up under the auspices of this Trust are lacking, but a Report of the Trust gives a list of the schools, together with the number of those who attended them, in Glamorgan in 1675. Here is the list: Cardiff (50), Margam (20), Cunffig (Kenfig) (20), St. Nicholas (12), Llancarfan (20), Llantriddyd, bracketed with St. Mary Hill (20), Penmark, bracketed with St. Hilary (20), Wenvoe (14), Cowbridge

(40), Swansea (20), Neath (40), Llandeilo Tal-y-bont (20), Bridgend (20), and Betws (15). In the majority of these schools those locally responsible were the clergy and the churchwardens. Another account for 1678 gives the following list of schools under the Trust: Cardiff (24), Margam (20), Cunffig (20), St. Nicholas (12), Llancarfan (20), Llan-triddyd (20), St. Mary Hill (20), Penmark (20), St. Hilary (10), Wenvoe (14), Cowbridge (40), Swansea (20), Neath (40), Llandeilo Tal-y-bont (20), Bridgend (20), and Llongebellan [?Llangyfelach] (10); and from the 1678 list it is clear that those mainly responsible for the administration of these schools were the clergy and the churchwardens.[37]

In addition to the provision of schools, the Welsh Trust also disseminated the Welsh translation of the Bible, *The Whole Duty of Man* and the *Practice of Piety*. It is interesting to note that although the language of the schools was English the literature distributed was in Welsh. We have an account of this work in 'An Account of the Distribution of the fore-mentioned Books in several Towns and Parishes in North and South Wales where they have been given to Poor people that could read Welsh', and in this work the Welsh Trust continued the work begun by the Dissenter, Stephen Hughes and his friends, both Anglican and Nonconformist. Here is an account of Welsh books distributed in Glamorgan by the Trust: Llansamlet (28), Margam (27), Llangyfelach (51), Llanwynno (13), Eglwysilan (11), Lyfavand and St. Brides (33), Betws (27), Llanfabon and Tythegston (35), Newcastle (5), Llangynwyd with Leckwith and Tragans (196), Loughor (5), Penarch with Gower-land and Aberduer [?Aberdare] (92), Pen-tyrch (8), and Llan-giwg (6).[38]

(d) The S.P.C.K. Schools (1699–1724)

The activities of the Welsh Trust ceased with the death of Thomas Gouge in 1681, and Glamorgan did not again benefit from an outside charitable movement until the foundation of the Society for the Promotion of Christian Knowledge in 1699, which from the outset received powerful local support, especially from Sir Humphrey Mackworth, the Neath industrialist, who was one of its five founder members.[39] If Mackworth was the leading lay supporter of the society in the county, its chief clerical supporter was James Harris, vicar of Llantrisant, prebendary of Llandaff, and fellow of Jesus College, Oxford, who founded the society's first two charity schools in Wales in his own parish in 1699 and worked unremittingly for the society until his death in 1728. Another active cleric was Thomas Price, rector of Merthyr Tydfil, to whom must be given the credit that the Welsh translations of the society's publications were sent to prisons in north and south Wales, even though nothing seems to have come of his plea that such publications should be translated into the south Wales dialect. The society received the active support of Bishops Tylor and Harris, of Francis Wyndham, of the Dunraven castle family, William Lewis, curate of Margam, William Hopkins, rector of Llantriddyd, Robert Powell, of Cowbridge (one of the two Leoline Jenkins' Fellows at Jesus College and master of the Cowbridge Free School from 1704 to 1721), and Morgan Evans, chancellor of Llandaff. The activities of the S.P.C.K. were twofold: to inspire the founding of schools and the provision of literature. One of these schools has already been listed in a previous section, viz., the Jane Herbert Charity founded in Cardiff in 1707. In 1706 Sir Humphrey Mackworth and the Company of Mines Adventurers provided £20 a year for a Charity School in Neath for the children of their workmen, which may be regarded as the fore-runner of the many 'Works' Schools' which came to south Wales with the Industrial Revolution. It has also been noted that James Harris, vicar of Llantrisant, established two schools in his parish in 1699, and these were conducted by the curate whom Harris kept for this purpose. It was Harris, too, who founded the last S.P.C.K. school in Glamorgan. This was in Llanwynno in 1724, and the society's records reveal that the number of children was increased in the Llantrisant school. Margam had an S.P.C.K. school in 1705 at the expense of a private patron, originally intended to educate 12 children, but by 1711 the number had dropped to three or four. A year later, in 1706, Cowbridge saw the establishment of an S.P.C.K. school by Francis Wyndham, for the teaching of 10 boys and 10 girls. Thomas Lewis, Y Fan, Caerphilly, founded three schools in Merthyr Tydfil in 1713–14, but Lewis's charities came to an end in 1715, presumably because of the £10,000 fine he is said to have incurred for his Jacobite sympathies. Llanharan obtained a school for 20 boys in 1718, and two years later Llantwit Major was given an endowment of £5 for the same purpose by Robert Powell, whom we already know as master of the Cowbridge Grammar School and who was rector of Llysworney and vicar of Llantwit Major from 1721 to 1731.

From two charities on the Glamorgan–Monmouthshire border both counties benefited. The first was set up by Edward Lewis, of Gilfach Fargoed, in the parish of Gelli-gaer, by will on March 19, 1715. Among the provisions of this charity a school of the value of £40 was to be built near Gelli-gaer church, 'and that every year after the same should be built, his said trustees should pay to a schoolmaster £10 yearly out of the rents, and likewise should lay out £15 yearly for coats and caps for 15 poor boys of the said parish, to be taught by the same master to read, write and cast accounts, and the rest of the profits for improving the said charity for the use of the said master and boys'. The property belonging to this charity was situated in the parish of Gelli-gaer which alone benefited educationally from the Lewis Charity.

The other border educational charity was that of Anne Aldworth, of the parish of Bedwas, who by will, dated August 19, 1729, left pro-perties in Llandaff, Ely, Eglwysilan and Bedwas for the education of five poor girls each from the parishes of Eglwysilan and Bedwas 'in reading, writing, sewing, needlework or any other useful science'. Both the Aldworth and Lewis charities greatly increased in value when the coal measures they contained were worked, and the Aldworth charity supported three schools by the beginning of the nineteenth century: one in the parish of Eglwysilan, a school room in the town of Caerphilly and a third in the parish of Bedwas.

The adjacent parishes of Lisvane and Llanishen benefited from a charity set up in 1728, comprising of part of the tithes of the former, for the education of poor children in the two parishes by a person who was to be paid £5 annually for his services. This was the Mary Lewis's Charity.

There were no educational charities in mid-Glamorgan, but the parish of Neath had two eighteenth-century charities for this purpose. The first was set up by John Davies on September 25, 1719 when he gave £200 to the minister, churchwardens, and overseers of the parish to educate 20 children of the poorer inhabitants; and in 1795, William Cross bequeathed the interest of £100 for the education of five children, sons of some of the burgesses of Neath. Farther west, in 1733, Mary Williams bequeathed property called Clynymarch in the parish of Llangyfelach to be subject to the sum of 40s. per year for building and maintaining a school in Rhyndwyclydach and to pay a schoolmaster for teaching English to six poor children of the district. No school house was built under the terms of the bequest, but one was built later by public subscription. Probably before the middle of the eighteenth century, Thomas Price, of Penllergaer, of the same parish of Llangyfelach, bequeathed 45s. per annum for ever for the education of five poor boys in the newly erected school at Llangyfelach. This bequest was a charge on Abergwenlais farm; and Price also gave a further 45s. per annum for the education of a further five poor boys, the annuity this time being charged to his personalty.

Apart from Swansea itself, the hundred of Swansea had to be content with two educational charities only, that of Catherine Rees, set up in 1728 by providing £100 for the education of six poor children 'as had their legal settlement in the said parish of Bishopston, and that their education should not surmount 2s. the quarter', and in 1794 Francis Gibbs, of Porteynon, bequeathed £40 to the churchwardens of that parish, the interest to be devoted to the 'teaching such of the poor parishioners' children, to read and write'.[40]

These schools continued the policy of the schools of the Welsh Trust in the use of the English language as a means of instruction, and this in an age when the children of Glamorgan, with the exception of those of Gower and the Vale of Glamorgan, must have been largely monoglot, especially in the upland parishes. Dr. Mary Clement sums up the educational scheme in these S.P.C.K. schools thus: 'A study of the curriculum of a typical Charity School shows that it was more varied than might be expected. Reading was, of course, the main subject taught, and the Bible and the Prayer Book, together with *The Whole Duty of Man* for the senior scholars, were the basic text-books. There were four classes in the larger schools. The first learnt the rudiments of reading and spelling, the second read the Psalter and the New Testament, the third read the whole Bible and learnt to write, while, in the fourth, arithmetic was introduced for the boys, and the girls were taught plain needlework, knitting, weaving, and spinning. From the earliest stages the Catechism was to be learnt and was generally taught on two days a week.' The schools were under the supervision of the local clergy, who often taught in them to eke out their stipends, while all the schoolmasters had to be members of the Church of England; and where it was difficult to find competent schoolmasters locally, provision was made whereby they could be trained in London in the methods used in the Charity Schools there. This method of training a master for the Neath Charity School was advocated in 1719. Such, in the briefest outline, was the provision made for educating children against a background of apathy and indifference. Thomas Price, rector of Merthyr Tydfil, testified 'that the parents show an aversion to teaching their children', and similar evidence was forthcoming from other quarters. The Society was very much in advance of its time in giving clothes and food, and in some cases boarding allowances, to poor children.

In addition to the schools, it was the S.P.C.K. which provided Glamorgan with its first public library. This was the diocesan library set up in Cowbridge in 1711 and whose books were available to any clergyman or schoolmaster living within ten miles of that town, any trustee, and to any person giving 10s. in cash or in books to the library.[41] The books were provided by the Society and were obviously not intended for popular consumption. For this latter public the Society did great work in issuing Welsh translations of English theological and devotional literature, notably *The Feasts and Fasts of the Church of England* (1712), *The Companion to the Altar* (1715), *The Husbandman's Manual* (1711), *The Truth of the Christian Religion* (1716), and a new edition of the Welsh Bible in 1718.

(e) The Welsh Circulating Charity Schools (1738–77)

Apart from the provision of literature, the work of the S.P.C.K. in Glamorgan came to an end with the founding of the Charity School by James Harris in Llanwynno in 1724, but thirteen years later the county saw the most widespread system of primary education that it had ever seen and was to see for yet a century. This was the Welsh Circulating Charity School movement, initiated and largely maintained by Griffith Jones, rector of Llanddowror, Carmarthenshire, 'the most distinguished figure in the history of education in Wales'.

The educational succession from the schools of the Welsh Trust, those of the S.P.C.K., to those of Griffith Jones, is obvious. They all fit into the eighteenth-century pattern of a reformation of morals by the provision of a free religious education to the children of the poorer classes, although, as has been shown, the schools of the S.P.C.K. showed a marked advance over those of the Welsh Trust in their general approach to the problem. But the connection between the circulating schools and their predecessors is closer than their approximation to a general pattern, for Griffith Jones, the founder of the former, was a most prominent member of the S.P.C.K. since 1713 and had himself been responsible for the foundation of many of the Society's schools in west Wales, a task in which he enjoyed the powerful support of his brother-in-law and patron, Sir John Philipps, of Picton castle. Hence, when the new schools first appeared in Glamorgan during the winter of 1738–39, their relationship to their predecessors was obvious, yet, at the same time they revealed those significant differences which made them so much more successful.

The fact that they were circulating schools, meeting during the winter months in a given district, and returning to the same parish, in some cases year after year, if requested, was a new feature of primary education, for it enabled children to attend school at a time of year when their parents were less reluctant to excuse them from the tasks of husbandry. Moreover, after the children had been taught in the daytime, the schools were frequently open to adults in the evening, and this gives them the distinction of being the pioneers in adult education in Wales. But without doubt their great success was due to the fact that they taught in a familiar language their pupils understood. Their predecessors, from the Puritan schools of 1649–53 to the S.P.C.K. schools had been conducted through the medium of the English language, and where English was the customary language, Jones wisely used it as a medium of instruction. It will be noted from the list of schools in the Appendix to this section that most of the Gower schools were English. But where the majority of Glamorgan children would very probably still be monoglot Welsh in 1738, to instruct them in English would have been as fruitless as if charity schools in England were carried on in French. In a sense, the Welsh Circulating Charity Schools might be regarded as having made a retrograde step in comparison with their predecessors. Their aim was simple and direct: it was for the good of the souls of children that they should be taught to read as quickly as possible so that they could read their Bible, Prayer Book, and be instructed in the Church Catechism. There is no reference to arithmetic, husbandry, sewing or needlework, nor any provision for apprenticeship when school days were over. It cannot be denied that Robert Nelson's definition of charity as doing good to the souls and bodies of men covers more than Jones attempted, but it may well be that the latter's limited objective was one reason for his success. His aim was religious; indeed, narrowly so, but because he taught thousands to read, the significance of his great work had consequences which Jones had never intended, probably not foreseen, and certainly would have condemned.

The Appendix to this section gives a list of the Welsh Circulating Charity Schools from their first appearance in Glamorgan in 1738–39 to their disappearance in 1777. The lists are based on Griffith Jones's reports of the activities of the schools issued annually in *Welch Piety*. There are gaps in the records: 1767–68, 1769–70, and the period 1774–77, when this movement came to an end. In all 699 'sessions' were held in Glamorgan, and up to the time of Griffith Jones's death in 1761 the schools had been held in about 300 districts in the county. They were held wherever accommodation could be found for them, and the names in the Appendix show that they were held in parish churches, farms, and cottages. They came to a parish at the invitation of the incumbent or curate, and it was he who was responsible for seeing that they were conducted according to the rules laid down by Jones. Quarterly reports were sent to Llanddowror, and it is from these that we learn the little we know of the history of the schools in any particular district.

It is clear from the reports sent by the clergy to Griffith Jones that these schools achieved their intended results. William Thomas, incumbent of Cadoxton, Neath, wrote at the end of 1739 that, as the result of the Circulating Schools 'we hope to see Religion again flourish in these Parts; Christians walking worthy of that glorious Name, in Imitation of those of the first and purest Ages of the Church'; and on July 16, 1741, P. Thomas, curate of Gelli-gaer reported: 'Our churches in general in this Neighbourhood are now near as full again of Auditors . . . our solemn Assemblies are thronged . . . we have a Monthly Communion about us here in several Parish Churches, where, within a very few Years past, it could hardly be administer'd so often as thrice a Year, for want of Persons to receive it'; and David Williams, of Eglwysilan, wrote four days later that divine worship 'has since become more numerously attended'. John Price, vicar of Llangyfelach, wrote on September 9, 1747, strongly supporting the use of the Welsh language in these schools, and went on to say: 'Here I observed, that the Parents of such Children as were taught to read, and have learnt some Portions of the *Exposition* on the *Church Catechism*, seem more civilized in outward Behaviour, and more frequently attend the publick Service'. On April 23, 1751 John Thomas, of Llanharry, wrote: 'it appears, that about eighteen Persons, who before were common Swearers, Profaners of the Lord's Day, Scoffers and given to Drinking, were greatly reformed by means of this School'.

Such were the results that the founder of the Welsh Circulating Charity Schools had intended, but it is regrettable that he did not receive more help from his fellow countrymen to finance his venture. Contrasted with the support given to the S.P.C.K., Jones received little help from Glamorgan and the old diocese of Llandaff: not one of the contemporary bishops or any of the leading laity are associated with this work, and it is likely that Jones received little, if anything, more than the collection occasionally taken in parish churches at the Holy Communion for this work.

It has been acknowledged for some time past that the Established Church in Glamorgan was not the moribund institution that was once thought by denominational historians, a view even half accepted by Church historians. In the light of the great difficulties she had to contend with, her record will bear comparison with that of most eighteenth-century dioceses, and this, in turn, has been shown to be comparable with any preceding century. But when the scope of ecclesiastical history is extended so as to include educational development, it is clear that a real religious revival took place in the Welsh Church during the first half of the eighteenth century. This was a revival based on the sober piety and strong moral emphasis of the Prayer Book and Church Catechism, embodying the Anglican ideal of godliness and sound learning. But before the end of the 1730s this revival coincided with, and partly overlapped, another and very different type of revival, which also began in the Established Church, but which, because of its nature, was quite incompatible with the discipline and ethos of the Prayer Book. The real indictment against the Established Church in Glamorgan, as elsewhere, was its failure to continue a religious work which began in 1675 and was allowed to come to an end in 1777.

Such is the religious implication of the work of education which went on in Glamorgan during this period; the cultural implication was more far-reaching. With the exception of Griffith Jones's schools, organized primary education in the county was conducted through the medium of the English language in an age when the county was largely Welsh-speaking. This English tradition was to persist throughout the eighteenth and following centuries. It is a mistake to believe that the anglicizing influence of education began in 1870; on the contrary, as far as is known, the educational pattern of primary education had always been English. The reforms of 1870 accelerated and extended English influences through education.

APPENDIX A

WELSH CIRCULATING CHARITY SCHOOLS IN GLAMORGAN, 1738–1774

The figures denote the number of pupils. The lists for 1774–1777 are missing. A few localities in the lists given below have been wrongly included in Glamorgan in issues of *The Welch Piety*. Schools clearly belonging to parishes in other Welsh counties have been identified as such. ES English school.

1738–39

Ystrad Dyfodwg	43
Gelly Gare	70
Trane Hamlet in Llantrisant	53
Ymlaen y Glais, Veynor Parish (Brecs.)	70
Ymlaen y Glais	39
Merthyr Tydfil	54
Llanguke	56
Llanishan	56
Ystrâd Gynlas (Brecs.)	70
Llangattwg	84
Llanharen	100
Capel Newydd, Cwm Nêdd	54
Ynys y Bool, Llanwynno	49
Llangrallog	60
St. Nicholas	61
Coyty alias Coychurch	56
Pen yr Aly, Coed Fraink Cadoxton	48
Near Pool y Pant	46
Eglwysilian	70
Ponty Ty Prîdd	40
Bedwellty Cwm Syrewi (Mon.)	46
Pentyrch	41

1739–1740

Coyty	58
Llandidwg, Bridgend	66
Penyfan, Newcastle, Bridgend	52
Gelligâr	45
Llantrisant Village	67
Llansamled	64
Cefnseison, Llanilltyd	55
Aberdâr	67
Llanwynno	20
Llanylltyd Feirdref	51
Merthur Tudful	55
Pont Cadifor, Merthur Tudful	45
Eglwys Helen	45
Eglwysilian	39
Aberdâr	60
Llanguke	84
Llangyfelach	116
Waun Cygurwen, Llanguke	45
Llangrallog	70
Llanddiddan, Nr. Cowbridge	62
Glynogwr	46
Bettus, Nr. Neath	53
St. Goris	37

Ynysfach, Llanylltydfawr	56
Tonnau, Llanylltyd	58
Ynys Bowys, Llangranog (Cards.)	41
Croynant Chappel, Cadoxton	74
Laleston	55
Llandilo-tal y bont	107
Henffig near Margam in Modlen	53
Llanblethian	64
Llanhary	44
Pentyrch	38
Meline, Ystrad Mynach (Mon.)	34
Waynfawr, Bedwellty (Mon.)	36
Llanfabon	66
Ystrad Gynlas	50
St. Andrews	47

1740–1741

Llansamlet	90
Llanguick	96
St. John	118
Gellygron, Llanguick	135
Wenallt, Llantwid	67
Tylloyd, Cadoxton	73
Ynysfach, Llantwid	56
St. Michael	104
Llangynwyd	69
Llandilo talybont	53
Illan	49
Ton y planwydd, in Cadoxton	48
Casllychwr	41
Ystrad Gynlas (Brecs.)	94
Llantrisant	41
Dinas Llantrisant	29

1741–1742

Gellifelgaws, Cadoxton	42
Abertridwr, Eglwysilan	40
Llisfân	21
Kil bebyll	30
Gilfach yr Haidd, Llanguick	47
Tonnau, Llantwit	77
Hawdd-dre, Baglan	93
Llanynewn Chapel, Llanrhidian	120
Penylan, Swansea	53
Neath	50
Cadoxton Village	53
Llangynwyd	43
Alltgrig, Llanguick	52
Michaelston	74

Tŷ yn Ffram, Margam	70
Cygerwen, Llanguick	51
Flimston	47
St. Mary Church	32
Siggai, Llantwit	47
Berthyn, Llanddeiddan	21
Coychurch	38
Newcastle, Bridgend	47
Penheolfawr, Llanfabon	59
Near Ynys y pool, Llanwynno	42

1742–1743

Penylan, Swansea	73
Penylan, Swansea	61
Pentre Estyll, St. John's Parish	50
Bettus, Llangynwyd	54
Llan St. Fred, alias St. Bride minor	52
Pentile, Baglan	82
Tynycroft, Baglan	106
Tynygraig, Llansawel	58
Trisaint, East Margam	71
Pentretrybaid, East Margam	76
Llysfane	52
Llansamlet	62
Aberdâr Parish	103
Cwm, Llansamled	58
Llanguinor	50

1743–1744

Tynygraig, Llansawel	65
Near Brombill, Margam	17
Tewgoed, Michaelstone on Avan	66
Llansamled	56
Cnap y llwyd, Llangyfelach	68
Felin Wen, Llangyfelach	81
Cast'llychwr, alias Loughor	65
Neath Abbey, Cadoxton	50
Pentre Estyll, Near Swansea	32
Llanrhidian Parish	74
Newton, Osyter Mouth	89
Newton	28
Nottage	40
Margam	100
Penyprisk, Coychurch alias Llangrallo	52
Llangynny	105
Cadoxton Village	53
Penrise	68
Penrise	76
Baglan, Near Abaravon	36

1744–1745

Newton, Oystermouth	66
Lunnon Village, Ilston	91
Blaenrhondda, Cadoxton	39
Penrhyw, Margam	47
Machyn (Mon.)	34
Llantwyn, Hyttri	31

Cwm llwydrew, Machyn	44
Reeding, Cadoxton	59
Britton Ferry, Llansawel	54
Pilton, Rosilly	58
Hills, Portynon	8y
Penlan, Near Swansea	51
Penlan, Near Swansea	53
Llanguick	57
Llanguick P.C.	42
Margam Village	63
Newcastle, Bridgend	84
Ty yn Rheol, Llanelltyd, alias Lantwit	63
Clyn y Castell, Llantwit	38
Chapel glyn Castell	32
Garnlwyd, Llangynnwyd	38
Felinwen, Llangyvelach	57
Gelliwastod, Llangyvelach	56
Windmill, Llanrhidian	66
Ystrad-dafodwg	32
Cefncribwr, Llandidwg	44
Cwm, Llansamled	48
Kilbebyll	18
Llusendy, Bettus	43
Newton Nottage	40
Crinant, Cadoxton	41
Cygerwen, Llanguick	52
Brynylloi, Bettus	40
St. Nicholas	48
Ygadles-Issa, Aberdare	77
Ynnys y Bowys	67
Llanfabon Church	34
Molton, Llancarfan	33
Llanmaes	55
Llanblithian Village	41
Blaencrymlyn, Coy Church	24

1745–1746

Newton, Oystermouth	55
Lunnon Village, Ilston	85
Swansey	201
Felin Wen, Llangyfelach	54
Cwm Dwr, Llangyfelach	48
Golwyn Village, Golwintown	40
Melyn Gwryfon, Near Neath	58
Llanwnno P.C.	38
Ty yn y wain, Lantwit	41
Tucking Mill, Micklestown	51
Neath Town	78
Penprise, Llangrallog	40
Penprise, Llangrallog	38
Llanbedr, near Llanharan	46
Pomprenlwyd, Penderin (Brecs.)	39
Cwmmanllwyd, Kilbebyll	20
Bryncaled, Lalestown	50
Gadless, Aberdare	61
Coity	23
Ynys Bowys, St. Andrew's	

Wilton, Llantwit maj.	45
Llanguick, P.C.	24
Llwyncelyn, P.C. (?Mon.)	34
Llwyncelyn, P.C. (?Mon)	28
Aberdare P.C.	46
Pantymoch, Margam	34
Kefn Cribwr, between Tythegstown and Lalestown	53
Reeding, Cadoxton	14
Kennickstown, Llangeni	67
Hills, Ryalstown	51
Welch Moor, Llanrhidian	66
Peskedwyn Llandilotalybont	41
Cwmdwr, Llangyfelach	44
Cefn Cribwr, Lalestown	32

1746–1747

Cwm maenllwyd, Cilbebyll	26
Cwm, Llansamlet	49
Neath	79
Michaelston	54
Kenicston, Llangenni	84
Llanrhidian near Welch moor	49
Llantrisant Village	40
Mynydd Cadle, Llangyfelach	55
Gelli Fedi, Llanbedr fynydd, alias Peterston super Montem	49
Denys Powys, St. Andrew	46
Llanguic	24
Wilton, Llantwit major	40
Llanharan Village	43
Bwrthing, Llanblethian	109
Swansea Town.	102
Ty ar y cefn, Laleston	41
Mynydd bach, Tythegston	50
Aberdare P.C.	59
Ty uchlaw'r Eglwys, Michaelston	62
Bwlchaufynydd, Michaelston	57
Ynysfach, Llantwit	43
Cenffig, Pyle	12
Newton Nottage	84
Fernhill, Rosilly	52
Fonmon Village, Penmarc	61
Craigtrewyddfa, Llangyfelach	69
Lynon, Ilston	51

1747–1748

Cwm, Llansamlet	46
Ynysy Maerdy, Britton Ferry	47
Burthen, Llanblethian	60
Silly Village	55
St. Andrews	40
Aberdare	71
Aberdare	61
Bryn, Michaelstone	60
Cadoxton Village	22
Olchfa, Swansea	46

Dunvant, Llanrhidian	18
Penprisc, Coychurch	51
Llangenith	34
Lynon, Ilston	45
Swansea Town.	74
Craig-trewyddfa, Llangyfelach	64
Danygraig, Llangyfelach	76
Near Bath newydd	75
Ty'r Cyrnel, Tythegston	49
Ystrad-dafodog P.C.	53
Penhydd-waelod, Margam	48
Nottage, Newton	50

1748–1749

Ynys y Maerdre, Briton Ferry	47
Cross Wen, Eglwys Ilan	82
St. Andrews	39
St. Andrews	36
Llwyn Owen, Baglan	55
Penprisc, Coychurch	29
Llangewydd, Laleston	43
Llwynhelyg, Laleston	55
Tŷmaen, Laleston	56
Tŷ Rhos, Gelligâr	39
Llanguic P.C.	15
Croynant, Cadoxton	24
Penyddwaelod, Margam	55
Llantrisant Village	6
Colwinston Village near Cowbridge	72
Tre' Oes, Llangan	48
Ty ucha, Llangyfelach	49
Craig-tre' wyddfa, Llangyfelach	61
Bryn-Cettyn, St. Brides' Minor	55
Heolybryn Cettyn, St. Brides' Minor	57
Abertwrch, Llanguic	59
Alltwen, Cilbebyll	37

1749–1750

Cross-Wen, Eglwys Ilan	47
Llantrisant Village	50
Talygarn, Llantrisaint	58
Tre-Oes, Llangan	51
Tŷ-Picca, Colwinstown	82
Near Cappel Talygarn, Llantrisaint.	51
Cwm-dwr, Llangyfelach	65
Cors Eynon, Llangyfelach	45
Bryncoch, St. Brides' Minor	52
Green y quills, Lower Hamlet, St. Brides' Minor	57
Tŷ'r Cornel, Tythegston	58
Tŷ'r Cornel, Tythegston	49
Abertwrch, Llanguick	31
Alltwen, Kilbebyll	61
Cefn-hengoed, Gelligâr	44
Pontgynon, Llanwonno	44
Neuadd, Llanguke	43

1750–1751

Cigerwen, Llanguick	49
Aberlonga, Ystrad-Owen	22
Croes-Eynon, Llangyvelach ..	47
Danygraig, Llangyvelach	78
Craig-Trewyddfa, Llangyvelach ..	65
Llanhary Village	44
Persondŷ, Llanhary	48
Pwll y Gath, Pile	58
Abertwrch, Llanguick	41
Ty-issa, Michaelstone in Avan Parish	45
Pontyr-un, Merthyr Tydvil	36
Pont-cynon, Llanwonno	36
Cwmmawr, Llwchwr Parish	53

1751–1752

Cors-Einon, Llangyvelach	29
Craig Trewyddfa, Llangyvelach ..	41
Velin-wen, Llangyvelach	22
Llusendy, Llandyvoduck	41
St. Bride's Minor	27
Pont yr ynn, Merthyr Tydvil ..	29
Dyffryn, Merthyr Tydvil	13
Upper Hamlet, Laleston Parish ..	59
Aburlonga, Ystrad Owen	19
Coity Village	65
Llanblethian Village	11
Aberbargoed Bridge, Gelligâr ..	41
Llusendy, Bettus Parish	55
Llusendy, Coychurch	32

1752–1753

Llandyfodoc near the Church ..	27
Alms-house, Coychurch Village ..	30
Maes-teg, Llantwit-Vardre	28
Roath P.C.	42
Aberbargoed Bridge	8
Cwmcyllen, Gelligâr	36
Laleston Village	49
Kefen Cribwr	12
Cwm, Llanwonno	29
Pwll-ffawydd	31
Old Castle, Bridgend	28
Gelliveddgar, Upper Hamlet Coychurch	32
Whitchurch	30
Ty-taldon, Merthyr Tydful	34
Aberdare P.C.	33

1753–1754

Ryddry P.C.	16
Llisfane Parish	22
Aberdare P.C.	21
Village of Coyty	40
Village and Parish of Laleston ..	38
Tŷ'r Bont, Merthyr Tydvil	50
Ffillocks, Llandaf Parish	18

Pwllffawydd, Llanwonno	25
Tyn y Garddau, Coychurch Upper Hamlet	18
Bridgend-End, Llanvihangelvedw ..	16
Village of Peterston super Ely ..	38
Ty dan y graig, Ryddry	41
Lluest y Nant, Llanwonno	24
Llanharan Village	27
Merthyr Mawr Village	34
Angel Town, Newcastle Bridgend ..	36
Penydaren, Gelligâr	32
Hamlet of Forest, Merthyr Tydvil ..	47

1754–1755

Fedw-fach, Gelligare	25
Penydarren, Hengoed Hamlet, Gelligare	27
Merthyr Mawr Village	37
Angel Town, Newcastle Bridgend ..	31
Tybach danygraig, Llysvane ..	51
Llangewydd, Laleston	31
Gelligare Village	30
Coychurch Village	32
Melin pwll y glaw, Michaelstone upon Avon	34
Llandyvodog P.C.	28
Llanishen Almshouse, Llanishen ..	44
Cadoxton Village	66
Cross-wen, Radyr	30
Cefndonn, Llwydgoed Hamlet, Aberdare	35
St. Fagans Village	14
Old Castle, Bridgend Village.. ..	30
Kenffig Hall	32
Michaelston super Avon P.C. ..	43

1755–1756

Cadoxton Village	55
Craig trewyddfa, Llangevelach ..	60
Llwydgoed Hamlet, Aberdâr ..	26
Coyty Village	52
Cyffyg Hall, Cynffyg	32
Hirwaen, Aberdâr	26
Llanishen Almshouse	43
Llantrissent Town	29
Newcastle Bridgend	31
Cwmdare, Aberdâr	26
Byeastown, Coyty	30
Brombil, West Margam	38
Monachty, Llanwonno	25
Village, Newton Parish	37
Hamlet of Bayden, Llangynwyd ..	44
Gwarcaeau, Havod Hamlet, Margam	38
Danygraig, Llangevelach	50

1756–1757

Ty dan ylan, Llangevelach	50

Cwmrhydy filast, Llangevelach	54
Cnapllwyd, Llangevelach	56
Brombil, West Margam	36
Near Baiden Chapel, Llangynwyd	44
Laleston Village	27
Bridgelyn, Eglwys Ilan	20
Llantrissent Town	26
Tŷ yn y cwm, Merthyr Tydvil	58
Byeaston, Coyty	38
Cefncribwr, Tythegston	40
Newton Village, Newton	36
Cross-Brombil, Margam	36
Angel-Town, Newcastle Bridgend	30
Monachdy-barn, Llanwonno	18
Dyffryn House, Aberdare	26
Nottage, Newton	32
Rhydyreithnen, Llantwit Vardre	38
Carffilly Town, Eglwys Ilan	39
Colwinston Village	28
Tynynycwm, East Margam	35
Llantwit Vardre P.C.	21
Near Pont yr Ynn, Merthyr Tydvil.	36
Trevorŷg, Llantrisant	22
Cae helyg, St. Brides' Minor	38
Brychton, Wick	27
Heol y Sheet, Pile	39

1757–1758

Corse Eynon, Llangevelach	43
Another school near Corse Eynon	40
Clwydyvedw, Gelligare	50
Sheet lane, Pile	38
Michaelstone upon Avon	18
Gwar y Caeau, Havod Hamlet, Margam	33
Newcastle, near Bridgend	30
Landow Village, Landow Parish	29
Glyn Tâf, Eglwys Ilan	41
Llantwit Vardre P.C.	15
Llanishan Village	45
Pont Cynnon, alias Cynnon Bridge, Llanwonno	22
Goston, Llangan	36
Kenffig Hall	34
Treguff, Llancarvan	31
Coyty Village	38
Velin vach, St. Brides' Minor	42
Middle Stormy, Tythegston	37
Glyn Gwynn, Llanwonno	28
Lysworney Village	36
Aberavon Town	36
Ystrad Owen P.C.	30
Tongwynlais, Whitechurch	44
Michaelston-le-pit P.C.	29
Bagland P.C.	33

1758–1759

Clyngwyn, Llanwonno	26

Ystrad Owen P.C.	30
Newton Town	42
Melin y Cwm, Gelligâr	36
Tŷn y Cae, Whitechurch	13
Pandy House, Merthyr Tydvil	40
Byeaston Village, Coyty	34
Penlline Village	43
Llangan P.C.	30
Llanhary Village	29
Home Mill, Ystradyvoduck	27
Pont yr Ynn, Merthyr Tydvil	23
St. Mary Hill Common	28
Llanmaes Parish	39
Nottage, Newton	32
Baydon Chapel, Llangynwyd	32
Brombil, Margam	43
Tre'r Rhingyll, Llanblethian	31
Howelwormwood Hamlet, Merthyr Tydvil	28
Penybont newydd, Gelligâr	43
Coyty Village	26
Pant mawr, Havod Hamlet, Margam	30
Colwinston Village	38
Tonntraethwg, Llantrissent	21
Talygarn Chapel, Llantrissent	30
Llanharan Village,	28
Llwynhelyg, Upper Division, Laleston	28

1759–1760

Aberdare Village	31
Colwinston Village	26
Llanharan Village	33
Dyffryn Mill, Margam	42
Llwynhelyg, Upper Hamlet, Laleston	29
Near Talygarn Chapel, Llantrissent.	32
Peterston Super Montem	33
Llwydgoed Hamlet, Aberdare	42
Bryncethin, St. Brides' Minor	21
Coyty Village	44
Old Castle Bridgend, Coyty Parish	21
Cefnmachen, Llangwinor	42
Llanblethian Village	25
Trallwm, Trissent Hamlet	28
Garthgynyd, Gelligâr	21
Felin Fâch, St. Brides' Minor	40
Burthin Village, Llanblethian	28
Gilfach, Llangynoyd	30
Penbrysge, Coychurch	20
Pencoed, Coychurch	30
Tyr plwyf, Llanginor	28
Cwm-brombil, West Margam	38
Penyrheol, Llandilotalybont	52
Bolgoed (Brecs.)	59
Llandilotalybont P.C.	77

1760–1761

Penycoed P.C.	30

Pentre bâch, Aberdâr..	21
Hendre, Gelligar	46
Ty'r Eglwys, Llangeinwr	14
Pandy, Bettus	24
Penlline Village	25
Landow Village	26
Coyty Village ..	37
Cilfach, Llangynwyd	26
Troedy Rhiw, Llangynwyd ..	35
Cwmgwinau, Margam..	44
Penlline Village	36
Forest, Merthyr Tydvil	21
Blaentwyn, Gelligar	45
Hendredenny, Eglwys Ilan ..	50
Gwyddonor, Gelligâr	30
Coychurch P.C.	20
Golden Mile, Colwinston	27
Newton Town ..	32
Penrhiw'r Havod, Margam ..	30
St. Brides Major	14
Penlline Village	28
Langan P.C. ..	29
Velin yr home, Ystrad havodog	27

1761–1762

Home-mill, Ystradyvaduck ..	27
Ty pant y gwaith, Merthyr Tydvil ..	15
Newton Town ..	34
Penlline Village	26
Havod, Margam	32
Langan Village	26
Dyffryn, Margam	31
Corner House, Cwmdu, Llangynwydd	26
Coyty Village ..	43
Llanharan Village	43
Goston Village, Llangan	26
Brombil, Margam	33
Corner House, Cwmdu, Llangwynwydd	30
Cwm y fuwch, Pentyrch	26
Cwm y fuwch, Pentyrch	13
Newcastle, Bridgend	35
Gravel Pit, Margam ..	32
Llwyngwladus, Middle Hamlet, Llangynwyd..	32
Goston Village, Llangan	26
Llanharan Village	32
Coyty Village ..	31
Coedsaeson fach, Llandeilo Talybont	48

1762–1763

Abbey, Cadoxton	102
Pyle P.C.	38
Llangynoyd P.C.	23
Llwydgoed Hamlet, Aberdare	35
Landow Village	28
Cwmbrombil, Margam	36

Laleston Village	28
Higher Hamlet, Coychurch ..	30
Llwydgoed Hamlet, Aberdare	26
Newcastle, Bridge End	12
Pen y fai, Bridge End	30
Llwyn helyg Upper Hamlet, Laleston	35
Laleston Parish	28
Landow Village	25
Coyty Village ..	40
Cwm brombil, Margam	41
Upper Hamlet, Coychurch ..	30
Tregyff Village, Llancarvan	34
Tregyff Village, Llancarvan	22
Newton Town ..	32
Goytre Havod, Margam	43
Ffynnon Ralph, Aberdare	32
Ffynnon Ralph, Aberdare	25
Penprysc, Coychurch	30
Penprysc, Coychurch	30
Coyty Village ..	30
Newton Town ..	32
Goytre, Margam	33

1763–1764

Not known

1764–1765

Craig trewyddfa, Llangevelach	45
Night School ..	27
Gorseinon	84
Gorseinon	34
Gorseinon Village	34
Horton Village Penrice (E.S.)	61
Landenny Village (E.S.) (Mon.)	39
Penrice Village (E.S.)	48
Overton Village, Porteynon (E.S.) ..	41
Cigwaun Bridge, St. Mary	27
Penydd Waelod, Margam	36
Cwmbrombil, Margam	36
Cwmbrombil, Margam	25
Varteg Vawr, Margam	25
Varteg Vawr, Margam	24
Almshouse, Langemon	26
Langynwyd Village	32
Langynwyd Parish	32
Llanvabon P.C.	36
Cwrt y wiwer, Llanvabon	30
Glyn-rhymney, Llanvabon	25
Rhyddry P.C. ..	48
Tregŷff, Llancarvan	27
Langan Village	25
Langan Village	24
Hirwaen Common, Aberdare	29
Hirwaen Common, Aberdare	36
Aberaman, Aberdare ..	26
Dynain, Eglwys Ilan ..	27
Efel issa, Llantruit verdre	37

Coyty Village	53
Coyty Village	42
Llanferney Village	28
Lanferney Village	24
Almshouse near Bettus Church ..	33
Almshouse near Bettus Church ..	29
Boverton, Llantwit-major	32
Lanmadock Village (E.S.)	71

1765–1766

Tre'r doinaw, Llangevelach	66
Gelliaur, Llangevelach ..	37
Tŷ yn y berth, Llangevelach ..	45
Tre'r doinaw, Llangevelach (night school)	16
Porteynon Village (E.S.)	44
Llanmadock Village (E.S.)	44
Reynoldstown Village (E.S.) ..	45
Oxwich Village (E.S.)..	37
Llwyn Hen, Llanguick	49
Tŷ'r Cwm, Llansamlet	93
Tŷ'r Cwm, Llansamlet	60
Night School	26
Keven hengoed, Gelligare	45
Keven hengoed, Gelligare	30
Newcastle, Bridgend	37
Llantwyt-verdre P.C.	30
Llantwyt-verdre P.C.	31
Dderwen-deg, Llŷsfân	31
Dderwen-deg, Llŷsfân	31
Aberamman, Aberdare ..	25
Cwrdd-dû, St. Brides' Minor ..	31
Cwrdd-dû, St. Brides' Minor ..	32
Beverton, Llantwyt Major	23
Pyle Village	48
Pyle Village	42
Penlline Village	25
Penlline Village	25
Ffynnon Iago, Margam	30
Ffynnon Iago, Margam	30
Ynys-y-bwl, Lannwno	32
Ynys-y-bwl, Lannwno	27
Llwydgoed, Aberdare	27
Llwydgoed, Aberdare	20
Home-mill Landyvadog	26
Penprysc, Coychurch	28
Tregyff Village, Lancarvan ..	27
Tŷ yn y Ton, Michaelston ..	29
Tŷ yn y Ton, Michaelston ..	30
Tyllwyd, Lantrissent	27
Caerfilly Hill, Eglwys Ilan ..	47
Caerfilly Hill, Eglwys Ilan ..	35
Nantgrynwydd, Langynwyd ..	36
Lanbyderry Village	32
Lanbyderry Village	24
Tythegstone Village	14
Coal-book, Margam	42

Bryncethin, St. Brides' Minor ..	29
Luestynant, Lanwono	37

1766–1767

Taldy, Llandeilo talybont	50
Penllwyn, Llandeilo talybont ..	32
Cwm, Llansamlet	32
Glaswen, Cilbebyll	28
Night School, Cilbebyll	37
Middleton Village, Roshilly (E.S.) ..	39
Middleton Village, Roshilly (E.S.) ..	34
Llanmadock Village (E.S.)	39
Oxwich Village (E.S.)..	37
Caegyrwen, Llanguwck	60
Michaelston P.C.	35
Cenffyg Village	24
Cenffyg Village	30
Danylan, Cenffyg	29
Lluestynant, Llanwono	30
Cwmcleidach, Llanwono	21
Ragged, Llantrisent	24
Llwyn y Piau, Llantrisent	13
Castella, Llantrisent	21
Llantrisent Town	28
Caerphily Town	38
Caerphily Town	46
Llanvabon P.C.	42
Llanvabon P.C.	24
Ddrysiog, Margam	29
Trisient	26
Abertwrch, Llantwil	36
Abertwrch, Llantwil	32
Melin y Cwrt	15
Vedwhir, Cadoxton	39
Velin Rheolau, Cadoxton	31
Croynant Chapel, Cadoxton ..	25
Abey, Cadoxton	37
Llancatle, Llancarvan	25
Penline Village	17
Cwm Bagland P.C.	32
Cwm Bagland P.C.	21
Tŷ'n y Cae, Llysfaen	30
Coyty Village	33
Coyty Village	44
Llanferney Village	26
Llanferney Village	22
Neath Town	46
Neath Town	35
Pile Village	28

1767–1768

Not known

1768–1769

Brombil, Margam	23
Bath, Llangevelach	90
St. Hilary Village	22

Kenvass issa, Cadoxton	.. ..	18
Danygraig, Cadoxton	.. ..	18
Llangynnwyd Village	.. ..	43
Llangynnwyd Village	.. ..	27
Gelly Village, St. Mary Hill	.. ..	42
Gelly Village, St. Mary Hill	.. ..	20
Neath Town ..	.. .. ..	21
Lanferney Village	.. ..	27
Lanferney Village	.. ..	21
Cryddfan, Llantwit	.. ..	58
Cryddfan, Llantwit	.. ..	21
Coyty Village ..	.. ..	34
Coyty Village ..	.. ..	34
Llangeinor Almshouse	.. ..	31
Llangeinor Almshouse	.. ..	29
Penhaul, Pendaulwyn	.. ..	24
Penhaul, Pendaulwyn	.. ..	21
Michaelstone P.C.	.. ..	16
Penon, Llancarvan	.. ..	31
Penon, Llancarvan	.. ..	27

1769–70
Not known

1770–1771

Pentwyn, Newcastle Bridgend	..	30
Brynchwyth, Coychurch	.. ..	28
Penryse, Coychurch ..	.. ..	34
Penylan, Coychurch ..	.. ..	32
Llanbyddery Village, Llancarvan	..	28
Crynant, Cadoxton ..	.. ..	70
Crynant, Cadoxton ..	.. ..	47
Pandybach, Coychurch	.. ..	33
Pandybach, Coychurch	.. ..	31
Penylan, Coychurch ..	.. ..	30
Llangorse, Coychurch..	.. ..	25
Tŷ'n y Pant, Newcastle	.. ..	43

Tŷ'n y Pant, Newcastle	.. ..	41
Tredaniel, Newcastle ..	.. ..	31
Tresaeson, St. Mary Hill	.. ..	38
Hendafarn, St. Mary Hill	.. ..	62
Hendafarn, St. Mary Hill	.. ..	32
Tirbach, Llanguke ..	.. ..	85
Tirbach, Llanguke ..	.. ..	52
Nanty vedw, Llanwonno	.. ..	36
Nanty vedw, Llanwonno	.. ..	22
Coychurch Village	.. ..	
Felinfach, St. Brides' Minor ..	..	
Bryncoch, St. Brides' Minor	..	34
Pontrhydycyff, Llangynwydd	..	55
Pontrhydycyff, Llangynwydd	..	31
Llanbythery Village, Llancarvan	..	39
Llantrisiant ..	.. .. ..	40

1772–1773

Nantygroes, Aberdare	.. ..	34
Nantygroes, Aberdare	.. ..	29
Hirwen, Aberdare ..	.. ..	49
Hirwen, Aberdare ..	.. ..	47
Ty'r Cwm, Aberdare	.. ..	44
Gelly lwch, Llanwonno	.. ..	17
Llantwit Faerdre P.C.	.. ..	48
Llantwit Faerdre P.C.	.. ..	40
Coyty Village ..	.. ..	41
Coyty Village ..	.. ..	45
Mardy House, Radir	.. ..	33
Gelly heblyg, Bettus	.. ..	41
Gelly heblyg, Bettus	.. ..	23
Old Castle, Bridgend ..	.. ..	30
Tyn y gwarrau, Lly-	.. ..	34

1773–1774

Coyty Village ..	.. .. ..	32
Coyty Village ..	.. .. ..	33

ii

THE DISSENTERS IN GLAMORGAN, 1660–c. 1760

By GLANMOR WILLIAMS

I. PENAL CODE AND PERSECUTION, 1660–1688

Very soon after Charles II had landed in Dover on May 25, 1660 the first rumblings of the storm of persecution that was soon to break on Puritans were heard. On June 22 an order was issued for churchwardens to retain in their own hands tithes and other income from those parishes which were the subject of conflicting claims between the Anglican incumbents who had been ejected and their Puritan successors. Among the petitions received from such Anglican clergymen seeking restoration to their livings were five from Glamorgan clerics, including Francis Davies and Hugh Lloyd, both of whom were subsequently to be bishops of Llandaff. Later, in September, Parliament passed an Act for the Confirming and Restoring of Ministers, under the terms of which a number of Puritan ministers, especially Baptists, who were obnoxious to both Presbyterians and Anglicans, were evicted, and eight Anglican priests were restored. In October 1660, 18 Quakers, who were even more widely detested than the Baptists, were imprisoned in Cardiff gaol for refusing to take the oaths of allegiance and supremacy when required to do so by the justices of the peace. In April 1661, 18 Catholic recusants appeared before Great Sessions for not attending church services.[42]

Despite these measures against ministers and congregations some hope of a church settlement comprehensive enough at least to include the Presbyterians and the more moderate Independents was held out by the summoning of the Savoy Conference between Anglican and Presbyterian leaders, which was in session between April and July 1661. There seems little doubt that some leading Glamorgan Puritans like Samuel Jones of Llangynwyd, who was left free and unmolested at this time, or Marmaduke Matthews, who continued to hold his living at Swansea, pinned their faith on the successful outcome of this conference. However, the failure of the participants to agree and the election of the strongly Royalist Cavalier Parliament, which met in 1661, presaged a darker future for the Puritans. The Act of Uniformity passed on May 19, 1662 insisted that all ministers must accept and use the newly-revised Anglican Book of Common Prayer, must be ordained by a bishop, and must take an oath of loyalty to the King on pain of deprivation. Lecturers and schoolmasters, too, must be approved and licensed by bishops and also accept the Prayer Book, or be subject to three months' imprisonment for unlawfully exercising their functions. All were given until the Feast of St. Bartholomew (August 25, 1662) to conform. Hugh Lloyd, bishop of Llandaff (1660–67) and William Lucy, bishop of St. David's (1660–78), followed up the passing of the Act with very searching articles of visitation designed to secure uniformity (above, p. 449).[43]

Up until this point a handful of leading Puritans in Glamorgan had either escaped being ejected from their livings, like Samuel Jones or Marmaduke Matthews, or had been ejected from one living only to be transferred to another, like Daniel Higgs. These three now refused to accept the Act of Uniformity and all were permanently ejected. In all 23 (possibly 24) ministers had been turned out of Glamorgan livings during the period from the Restoration to 'Black Bartholomew', a far larger number than for any other county in Wales (see Appendix B, pp. 497–8). All but four of these had been deprived *before* the Act of Uniformity. Five of those ejected subsequently conformed, one other may have done so, and the fate of another remains a mystery. Two Puritan schoolmasters were also turned out. A number of the leading Puritan laymen were more pliable than the Puritan ministers. Among those who found it possible to conform, despite the prominent part

[469]

they had played in administration and politics under the Commonwealth and Protectorate, were Colonel Philip Jones, Edmund Thomas of Wenvoe, and Bussy Mansel. Rowland Dawkins of Cil-frwch, however, was stauncher in his loyalty than his erstwhile comrades; though he somehow contrived to retain his place on the commission of the peace, he refused to have his children baptized in the parish church and, as late as 1687, when replying to questions put to him by the duke of Beaufort he was described by the latter as a 'Dissenter'.[44]

In 1664–65 the Cavalier Parliament had further shots in its locker to direct against Nonconformist ministers and their congregations. In 1664 it passed the Conventicle Act, under the terms of which any gathering for worship except in accordance with the Prayer Book became a 'conventicle' (i.e., an illicit and seditious assembly) if it consisted of five persons or more over and above the normal members of the household. Stiff penalties were prescribed for those found guilty of meeting in conventicles: up to three months' imprisonment or a fine of £5 for the first offence; double the penalty for the second offence; and transportation for seven years for a third offence. The Act was to be in force for three years. It was followed in 1665 by the Five Mile Act, which forbade any ejected Puritan minister to come within five miles of any city, corporate town, or parliamentary borough, to dwell within five miles of any parish in which he had previously ministered, or to preach in any conventicle.

Persecution of Dissenters had actually preceded the enactment of this legislation. As early as February 1661 the constables of Glamorgan had been ordered by the high constable of the county to see that sufficient watch was kept in their parishes that 'none of those called Quakers or Anabaptists be suffered to go from one parish to another, or gather together any meetings or conventicles'. Because the Quakers were much the most meticulous of the Dissenters in recording their sufferings and because they were probably the most hounded of the sects, we know more about their ordeals than those of any other group. As a consequence of the order of February 1661, 41 of them from the east of the county were imprisoned, and attacks on their meetings and further imprisonments of their members continued at intervals throughout 1661 and 1662. During this time persecution was extended to Quakers in the north of the county at Merthyr Tydfil and also to those in Swansea and its environs. But others besides the Quakers suffered; along with many Quakers from the west of the county, a number of other Nonconformists from the rural deanery of Gower were haled before the consistory court of the archdeacon of Carmarthen. Dr. R. L. Hugh has traced the names of a large number of people from many parishes in the hundreds of Swansea and Llangyfelach, both of which fell within the archdeacon's jurisdiction, who appeared within his court between the years 1662 and 1668. 96 people were cited for refusing to attend church and a further 8 for not attending Easter communion; 17 were accused of refusing to have their children baptized in the parish church, 33 of not paying church rate, and 6 of keeping conventicles. Not all of these were necessarily Dissenters. While we can readily identify Marmaduke Matthews, who was three times accused of keeping conventicles, as the eminent Puritan minister, or William Bevan, also accused of keeping conventicles, as the leading Swansea Quaker, or Rowland Dawkins, alleged not to have had his children baptized in the parish church, as the old parliamentary commander, many of the other people included in the lists may not have been there on account of Dissenting principles at all.[45]

Neither should we overemphasize the severity of the punishments which the courts imposed. Mr. Walter T. Morgan has shown that the consistory court's heaviest penalty, excommunication, was in practice largely ignored. The famous Puritan, Stephen Hughes, who had been excommunicated in December 1667 for preaching at a conventicle and for keeping a school without a licence, could nevertheless untroubledly co-operate with William Thomas, dean of Worcester and a future bishop of St. David's (1678–83), in the publication of religious books. Excommunication might have had more effect if it had not been that the writ of *de excommunicato capiendo*, under which the excommunicate could be arrested and kept in prison until he obeyed the court's mandate, was so difficult to obtain as to make the process rarely if ever exercised. Neither is there much evidence to show that churchwardens were active in employing their powers to impose the statutory fine of 12*d*. for each wilful absence from the service at the parish church. Nor can we tell, in the absence of Quarter Sessions records for this period, how vigorously the justices of the peace were harrying Nonconformists in Glamorgan. A letter of March 8, 1666 from Bishop William Lucy to the deputy-lieutenants and justices of the peace suggests that they had to have their attention forcefully drawn to their duty by him before there could be any hope of their taking action. He wrote anxiously seeking their support in wiping out meetings of Dissenters at Llangyfelach, 'dangerous to the King and kingdom and an affront to the established religion'. The continued existence of the church at Llangyfelach and letters from Lucy of the year 1673 (below, p. 473) suggest that he had little joy of his appeal to the secular authorities. On the other hand Sir John Aubrey, J.P., in April 1664, before the Conventicle Act was passed, sent a troop of soldiers to break up a religious meeting at Kenfig at which Jacob Christopher was preaching; and in 1668 the magistrates would waste no time in coming down heavily on Vavasor Powell (below, p. 472).[46]

After the first Conventicle Act expired in December 1667 Dissenters enjoyed a short respite. Leading personalities among them may have taken advantage of this breathing-space to visit Glamorgan in order to put new heart into the rank and file. That most lion-hearted of the Welsh Puritans, Vavasor Powell, made his way to Monmouthshire and from there to Merthyr Tydfil, where he preached in the churchyard to a large and expectant congregation. For his pains, he was arrested on a warrant made out by Edmund Thomas of Wenvoe and Dr. William Bassett of Beaupré. Brought to Cowbridge and later to Cardiff to undergo examination, he defended himself with his customary courage, dexterity, and knowledge of the law. Another prominent visitor to Glamorgan in the same year was the great Quaker leader, George Fox, who held what he described as a 'large and precious meeting' at Swansea and also visited Merthyr and Cardiff.[47]

The relative ease and freedom which Dissenters enjoyed during 1668 and the early part of 1669 soon induced feelings of alarm and suspicion among Anglicans. In June 1669 Archbishop Sheldon issued inquiries designed to discover the number, location, leaders, and size of Nonconformist congregations. The returns to his inquiries gave a somewhat curious and obviously incomplete picture of the Dissenters of Glamorgan. In the first place, returns for the diocese of St. David's are missing, and this at once excludes some of the strongest centres of Dissent, which fell within the two westernmost hundreds of Swansea and Llangyfelach. Even for the rest of Glamorgan the returns of the diocese of Llandaff seem to be far from comprehensive. They reveal the presence of conventicles at Merthyr Tydfil (said to number from 300 to 600—almost certainly an exaggeration), Llanedern (about 40), Baglan (about 20), Newton Nottage (20–30), and Eglwysilan and Betws, for neither of which was any estimate of membership given. There were also three Quaker meetings at Llandaff (40–100), and at Merthyr and Neath (no estimate of membership). However, no mention is made of congregations at Cardiff or other known foci of Dissent (see Appendix C). In addition, although the returns supply the names of some leading ministers like Samuel Jones, Robert Thomas, Lewis Thomas, John Powell, and Thomas Quarrell, they say nothing of others as active as John French of Cardiff, Joshua Miller of Wenvoe, Watkin Cradock of Newton Nottage, or Jacob Christopher of Kenfig. Nevertheless, whatever may have been the omissions for Glamorgan and other counties, the reports were alarming enough to the authorities in Church and State. They were soon followed up by the Second Conventicle Act, due to come into force on May 10, 1670 and, in some of its provisions, more rigid and constrictive than the Act of 1664.[48]

No further relief came the way of Dissenters until Charles II, by personal inclination always favourable to toleration, proclaimed his Declaration of Indulgence on March 15, 1672. Under its terms, penal laws were suspended, and all Dissenters except Roman Catholics were allowed to worship in a limited number of approved places under the guidance of licensed preachers. Although some Dissenters had grave reservations about the propriety of the use of royal powers in this way and were suspicious of the true intentions behind the measure, there was a rush to secure licences. Between April 1672 and February 1673 a larger number of licences (42) were issued for Glamorgan than for any other Welsh county, and 26 different places within the county were authorized for worship (Appendix C). Of the Welsh preachers who obtained a general licence to preach, only one, John Powell, was likely to have been active in Glamorgan; but doubtless Stephen Hughes was not the only licensed preacher within Glamorgan who, much to Bishop Lucy's vexation, cheerfully ignored the fact that he was licensed to preach only in his own house and one other and who preached at any meeting where he was welcome—in Carmarthenshire as well as Glamorgan. Of the 26 congregations licensed, 8 were Congregationalist, 7 Presbyterian, 6 Independent, and 5 Baptist. Evidently, in the freer air of the Indulgence, denominational differences had re-asserted themselves and become more clear-cut again, and the kind of mixed congregations of Independents and Baptists who had met together at Baglan or Newton Nottage in the harsh climate of the 1660s were now tending to go their separate ways. Notably absent from the congregations licensed in 1672–73 were the Quaker meetings, though they certainly continued to exist at Merthyr, Cardiff, and Swansea, together with a new one founded by John ab Evan and his family at Tref-y-rhyg near Llantrisant. Dissenters also opened schools in 1672–73 even though the Indulgence made no provision to allow them to do so. It may well have been at this time that Samuel Jones, former fellow of Jesus College, Oxford, ventured to open his celebrated academy at Brynllywarch, and William Thomas, also M.A. of Jesus College, opened a school at Swansea.[49]

The short-term effect of the Indulgence was undoubtedly to give the Dissenters a much-needed fillip. The revival of their fortunes, their growing boldness, and their blatant disregard of ecclesiastical censure, evoked indignation and alarm among staunch Anglicans, whose reactions found typical expression in the irate letters written by Bishop William Lucy of St. David's to Archbishop Sheldon in February 1673. What had particularly incensed Lucy was the defiance of men whom he had excommunicated but who had, nevertheless, been given licences to preach as Dissenting ministers; and he hinted darkly at the support being given them by 'leading men of the country', 'friends in court', and others with 'great purses'. In view of this and other similar Anglican reaction the Indulgence was inevitably short-lived. When Charles II, desperate for money, faced a hostile Parliament in February 1673, he was soon forced to cancel his concessions on March 7, 1673. Whatever advantages the Indulgence had brought to Dissenters, it had also been the means of compiling an official register of licensed Dissenting congregations and had given persecuting authority very much fuller and more accurate information upon which to work.[50]

The rise in the number and morale of Dissenters following the Indulgence, which was not officially revoked until the beginning of

1675, continued to cause deep disquiet among Anglicans, and in 1676 Archbishop Sheldon determined to embark on an inquiry to test the numbers of Dissenters. However, just about a year previously, the eminent Welsh Puritan and pastor of the thriving Nonconformist church centred at Brecon, Henry Maurice, had compiled for the benefit of his friend, Edward Terril of Bristol, 'a catalogue of all the congregational churches . . . in Wales', with the names of their pastors and other officers, and it is interesting to compare Maurice's picture of Dissent with that provided by Sheldon's inquiry. Though Maurice's information about some of the Glamorgan churches is decidedly hazy and though he provides no statistics, he does present a scene of lively activity in the churches which he identified at Merthyr Tydfil, Swansea, Baglan, Llangyfelach, Gelligaer, and Llangynwyd. On the other hand, the returns made to Archbishop Sheldon in 1676 are unquestionably a serious underestimate of the numbers of Dissenters. In the whole diocese of Llandaff they were said to number 905, of whom 298 were found in Glamorgan; and in the diocese of St. David's there were reckoned to be 2,398, of whom 300–400 were traced to those parts of Glamorgan which lay within the diocese. There were many more Dissenters within the county than these figures suggested. The powerful church at Merthyr, possibly the strongest in Wales at this time, was not included at all, nor was Samuel Jones's congregation at Llangynwyd. Other churches may not have been reported because they had leaders like John French of Cardiff, who attended public worship at St. Mary's parish church before preaching to his own congregation at his home. Even those congregations which were included in the returns were often estimated at a figure which appears to have been well below their real numerical strength. Whereas as recently as 1669, before the impetus given to Nonconformity by the Indulgence, the churches at Baglan and Llanedern and the Llandaff Quakers were returned as having 20, 40, and 40 members respectively, in 1676 they were said to number only 3, 13, and 3. Even the 292 Dissenters assigned to Swansea in the returns—the largest single congregation recorded in Wales—may not have fully represented their numerical strength in this particularly robust centre of Dissenting activity.[51]

It was not only the strength of Protestant Nonconformist numbers that was revealed in these inquiries of 1676. Roman Catholics were also included; and the returns showed the continued existence in Glamorgan of at least 21 of these recusants. The figure was small, but not altogether surprising in the light of the growth of Puritanism and the strict repression of Catholics during the years of Puritan supremacy. Nor was the lot of the unfortunate Catholics made any happier at the Restoration in spite of their unswerving devotion to the Royalist cause and the great sacrifices made by many of them on its behalf. In Glamorgan they were among the first to be imprisoned for their beliefs in 1661. Later, during

1668–69, they may have won some sort of respite like Nonconformists of the Protestant sort, for Vavasor Powell told the Glamorgan magistrates in 1668 that they would have been better employed in directing their attention to the emboldened Catholic recusants than to him. By 1670, however, there were in all 14 penal statutes bearing down on Catholics.[52]

Despite these stringencies, the 1670s saw a handful of missionary priests continuingly active in Glamorgan visiting the homes of the old stalwart Catholic families of the Turbervilles at Sker and Pen-llin and of Howel Carne at Colwinston. Two of the priests, John Lloyd (d. 1679) and Philip Evans (1645–79), were to be at the eye of the storm when the fabrications of Titus Oates and the hysteria of the Popish Plot convulsed the country in 1678–79. John Lloyd, a native of Breconshire and a secular priest trained and ordained at Valladolid, had come back on the mission to south Wales as early as 1654, while Evans, a Monmouthshire man, was a Jesuit educated at St. Omer and ordained at Liége in 1675, who had in the same year come back to south Wales. Both were informed against and included in Sir John Trevor's 'abstract' of Roman priests in April 1678, but each declined to leave Wales. At the height of the Oates furore Lloyd was arrested at John Turberville's house in Pen-llin on November 20, 1678, and Evans at Christopher Turberville's house at Sker on December 4, 1678, following the offer of a £50 reward for his capture made by the priest-hunting magistrate, John Arnold of Llanthony. Both priests were committed to Cardiff gaol until being brought to trial on May 8–9, 1679 at the Great Sessions in Cardiff. It is commonly said that great difficulty was experienced in getting witnesses to testify against them and that only an old woman and her daughter came forward; but Great Sessions records show that in fact recognizances were taken from a number of witnesses. On July 22, both men were barbarously hanged, drawn, and quartered at Cardiff, and met their death with exemplary dignity and fortitude. The only Catholic martyrs to be executed in Glamorgan, by a sad irony they died for their faith in the reign of one of the two Stuart rulers most sympathetic to their beliefs. A contemporary Catholic narrative recorded some of the moving last words attributed to Philip Evans: 'I die for religion and conscience' sake. Sure this is the best pulpit a man can have to preach in . . . if I had never so many lives, I would willingly give them all for so good a cause'. A Protestant broadside, in its frenzied outbursts against these 'abettors of the traitorous hellish design of re-establishing popery in these nations', conveys much of the contemporary sense of unreasoning panic which Oates had succeeded in arousing. In the event, the Popish Plot proved to be the deathblow to recusancy in south Wales. Though a handful of adherents lingered on, all the heart had gone out of the old faith until it was revived again with the advent of a wave of Catholic immigrants in the nineteenth century.[53]

The years from 1680 to 1686 were to be a bad time not only for Roman Catholics but for Protestant Dissenters too. Following his difficulties with Whig Parliaments over the Exclusion crisis, 1679–81, Charles II determined to do without Parliament and to depend wholly on Tory and Anglican support. Abandoning any attempts to gain concessions for Roman Catholics, he also reacted more hostilely against Dissenters, especially in the atmosphere of revulsion against them which followed the failure of the Rye House Plot of 1683. It was no coincidence that the year 1684 should provide evidence of a much sharper turn of the screw on Dissenters. Among the Margam manuscripts is one of 1684 containing a warrant for the appearance before the Great Sessions of a number of prominent Nonconformists from the hundreds of Swansea, Llangyfelach and Neath, including among them their most distinguished representatives, such as Samuel Jones, Stephen Hughes, Robert Thomas of Baglan, and Robert Morgan of Llandeilo Tal-y-bont. It seems very likely that they never actually appeared before the court, having 'either removed themselves for some time into such countries where the process would not run, or else so secured themselves in their houses as they could by no means be taken, to the great obstruction of justice, and encouragement of other factions, dissenters, or fanatics'. Yet the pressure to conform at this time was sufficiently great to compel at least two well-known Dissenters, Watkin John and Richard Cradock, to yield to it—though only temporarily, it seems, for when Cradock died in 1690 he was still minister at Cilfwnwr church. Tensions were increased in 1685 by the suspicion that Dissenters and erstwhile Puritans might be implicated in the Monmouth Rebellion. In Glamorgan, Bussy Mansel, Rowland Dawkins, and Lewis Aylward (at whose house in Kenfig Dissenting meetings had regularly been held) were among eight men delivered to the custody of the governor of Chepstow castle as possible 'disaffected and suspicious persons'. They were, however, discharged on July 25, 1685 free of any complicity.[54]

But for the Monmouth Rebellion and the apprehensions it aroused, James II might have taken steps early in his reign to secure a measure of toleration for those who would not conform to the Church of England, having in mind especially the interests of his fellow Roman Catholics. From the time that he ascended the throne James made no secret of his own Catholic beliefs or his desire to see his co-religionists relieved of the civic and religious disabilities under which they laboured. He exerted strenuous efforts to advance them in office and favour and to build up an army increasingly dependent on Catholic officers. Such policies served only to alienate the Anglicans, who should have been the natural allies of a Stuart monarch, and by 1687 James had lost their sympathy to such an extent that he had no option but to revert to the extra-parliamentary approach adopted by his brother in his Indulgence of 1672. On April 4, 1687 he issued his own 'gracious Declaration to all his loving subjects for liberty of conscience'. In some respects it was more liberal in its terms than the Declaration of 1672. One licence now sufficed for both preacher and place of worship, and it could be obtained simply by giving the relevant information to the nearest justice of the peace, who appeared to have had no powers to refuse any valid notification. Yet the reactions of Dissenters to the Indulgence were distinctly cool. They, like the Anglicans, could not but note James's declared wish 'that all the people of our dominions were members of the Catholic Church', and they viewed with growing concern his friendship with Louis XIV, whose own attitude towards Protestants had been only too plainly revealed in the Revocation of the Edict of Nantes. Nevertheless, some Dissenters quickly showed themselves eager to avail themselves of the new freedom, however tainted its source. As early as April 15, 1687, that stalwart Independent minister, Robert Thomas of Baglan, gave notice to Sir Edward Mansel of Margam, his nearest justice of the peace, that he wished to maintain worship at his own house at Pen-y-gisla at Margam and at the house of Mary Thomas, widow, in the parish of Llangyfelach. There may have been a number of others who did the same without any record of their actions having survived. A handful of Dissenters were so pleased by James II's magnanimity that they went so far as to offer the king addresses of gratitude. One of these, dated October 1687, emanated from an amorphous group of Presbyterians, Independents, and Baptists dwelling in the three south-western counties of Wales 'and [in the] town of Swansea and other places adjacent in Glamorganshire'; but its initiators and authors cannot be identified. Many Dissenters, however, were plunged into deepening gloom and insecurity, fearing the total destruction of all they held dearest, as the constitutional crisis between James and his subjects reached its climax in 1688 (below, pp. 481–82).[55]

Because the Indulgence of 1687 and its successor of April 1688 were so quickly swallowed up in the revolution of 1688 it is difficult to assess their consequences. In one major respect, however, they were to have a permanent effect: the degree of freedom they conferred was never revoked. In practice, James II's Indulgence brought to an end the era of the persecution of Protestant Dissenters.

The three decades which had passed since the Restoration had been a 'time of troubles' for all Dissenters. They were obliged to worship in fear and trembling, to conceal themselves from the malice of spies and informers, to endure ostracism, excommunication, fines, imprisonment and distraint of goods, and to face the suspicion and hostility of magistrates and bishops, constables and churchwardens. Some had had to suffer much more than others; those most severely oppressed were the Roman Catholics at one end of the religious spectrum and Quakers at the other. Admittedly the pressure was not unrelieved; there were serious limitations to the efficacy of ecclesiastical and secular procedures, and the penal acts were strictly enforced only in spasms—from 1664 to 1667, 1670 to

1672, and 1680 to 1686. Nevertheless, Dissenters could only rarely and briefly feel themselves unburdened by anxiety. Some found the strain too much, gave way, and conformed. Others compromised, conformed occasionally, or rendered passive obedience, like John French, who attended the parish church at Cardiff before conducting a conventicle in his own house. Attempts were made to win over moderate leaders, notably John Powell and Samuel Jones. The latter was pressed hard in 1665 by the bishop of Llandaff and his archdeacon to accept a living at their hands, to which he replied with a series of searching questions designed to demonstrate how impossible it was for him to agree to their request. Similarly, in 1680, he penned another set of equally probing questions to persuade a fellow-minister not to agree to conform occasionally. Jones's loyalty to his convictions was the admiration even of Anglicans. Yet leaders like he were not the only ones to stand fast. There were many other more obscure adherents who were just as steadfast, like that Edward Harry commemorated in the church book of Mynydd-bach as a 'serious professor and a member for fifty years together', who 'continued honest and faithful in God's ways even to the last'.[56]

Under persecution Dissenters had, of course, exercised their imagination and ingenuity to find ways of minimizing the consequences of the Penal Code. Denominational differences tended to break down; it became almost impossible to distinguish between Presbyterians and Independents; and mixed congregations of Baptists and Independents met together at Baglan, Llangyfelach, Merthyr Tydfil, and Eglwysilan, though the freer air of 1672 seems to have revived denominational differences again. Another means of fortifying individual congregations and strengthening the links between them was the revival of the successful itinerant system of the 1650s. Stephen Hughes made wide and numerous forays from Swansea into Carmarthenshire, and Henry Maurice from Breconshire into Glamorgan; Thomas Quarrell visited five secret meeting-places on the borders of Glamorgan and Monmouthshire and John Powell three; and Lewis Thomas and Robert Morgan looked after the strict Baptists of west Glamorgan and neighbouring Carmarthenshire as well as serving those of Craig-yr-allt near Hengoed and others at Blaenau Gwent. Such contacts were not restricted to Wales and Welshmen. Close links were maintained between south Wales and the west of England, and especially with the great Dissenting nerve-centre of Bristol.[57]

Other ways of softening persecution were found by taking advantage of loopholes in the law. Excommunication, as we have seen, was a blunt weapon largely disregarded, while the more damaging writ of *de excommunicato capiendo* was much more difficult to obtain in Wales than in England, being obtainable only at Great Sessions and not directly from the sheriff. Even when it was successfully procured it could sometimes be overriden by a writ of *supersedeas* from the Lord Chancellor, as

Bishop William Lloyd of Llandaff (1675-79) seems to have discovered to his vexation and dismay. Neither were the lay courts necessarily very much better in ensuring the apprehension and appearance before them of offending Dissenters, who seem to have been able to leave their habitations or barricade themselves inside them with comparative immunity, judging by the fate of the Margam warrant of 1684 already referred to.[58]

A discreet choice of the location of dwellings and places of worship could also afford protection and advantage. Ministers, when ejected, moved from parishes in which they had laboured but often contrived to remain within easy reach of their former flock. Thomas Joseph, turned out of Llangeinwyr in 1660, went only as far as Bridgend, John French left Wenvoe for Cardiff, Joshua Miller St. Andrew's for Wenvoe; while Samuel Jones, despite being ejected, never seems to have left Llangynwyd, nor Marmaduke Matthews Swansea. Care could also be taken to choose out-of-the-way places for worship, like Samuel Jones's retreat at Cildeudy, or the Merthyr Nonconformists' refuge at Blaencannaid, where they had the added protection of a vigilant lady who gave warning of the approach of unwanted visitors. Still more significant was the way in which many churches were located near the borders of counties, so that pastors and members could evade the jurisdiction of sheriffs and justices by slipping across the county boundary. Close co-operation existed between Baptists and Independents on either side of the Glamorgan/Carmarthenshire boundary; churches in east Glamorgan were hand-in-glove with their co-believers in Monmouthshire; and in the north of the county Merthyr Dissenters came under the aegis of the Brecknock church. Possibly the most important consideration of all was that Dissenters foregathered in those places where they hoped for a measure of protection from influential landowners, which was as important for them as comparable patronage had been for Roman Catholic recusants in the sixteenth century. Robert Thomas, pastor at Baglan, was himself the eldest son of an influential landed family there, and his mother was a Williams of Blaen Baglan. In the same area, Bussy Mansel, though he had conformed, was still sympathetic to Dissenters (below, p. 485). At Llangynwyd Samuel Jones must have owed much to the goodwill of his father-in-law, Rees Powell, head of the Llwydarth family and a justice of the peace. The Baptists of Craig-yr-allt numbered among their members two influential laymen, Colonel Edward Prichard of Llancaeach and Captain Thomas Evans; the latter being considered for appointment to the commission of the peace in 1687. One would also give much to know more about the attitudes of Philip Jones of Fonmon and Edmund Thomas of Wenvoe—certainly Joshua Miller was an active minister on the latter's own doorstep in Wenvoe. Another old parliamentary commander, Rowland Dawkins, clung to his Puritan beliefs and must have been a great comfort to the Dissenters of Gower. But the most remarkable case of all is the complaisance of the justices and corporation at Swansea, where at least four ejected Puritan ministers—Stephen Hughes, Daniel Higgs, Marmaduke Matthews, and William Thomas—were resident and very active. As a 'city of refuge' Swansea was to south Wales what Bristol was to the west of England or Manchester to the north. The kind of freedom which Dissenters enjoyed in the town is best illustrated by this remarkable description given by Edward Calamy of Marmaduke Matthews's activities: this 'very pious, zealous man . . . went from house to house to instruct the inhabitants of the town . . . [he] preached at a little chapel at the end of the town by the connivance of the magistrates . . . would often go out on market-days to the country people and speak to them about spiritual matters'.[59]

Thus did the Dissenters contrive to limit the damage inflicted upon their cause by persecution. Dr. Thomas Richards, indeed, went further and declared that the 'Penal Code was the salvation of Puritanism. These dark days were also its golden age. Puritans now said farewell to that materialism which had disgraced their liberty, and eased themselves of the dangerous company of opportunists and self-seekers.' While there is a large measure of justification for such a verdict, its enthusiasm needs perhaps to be tempered somewhat. The code had borne hard upon the Dissenters and had depleted their numbers. The persecuted who suffered most—the Quakers and the Roman Catholics—were reduced to so pitiful a remnant as to be virtually a spent force in Glamorgan by 1689. Moreover, even those who survived in sufficiently large numbers to face the future with confidence—the Presbyterians and Independents (almost indistinguishable now) and the strict Baptists—had had to endure grave losses. They had lost many of their more well-to-do members who were unwilling to see their social status and hopes of office jeopardized by too close an association with Dissent. It does not do simply to dismiss all of these as ambitious worldlings well lost; some of them were reluctant Anglican converts who, in a hierarchical landed society, could have been a source of strength to Dissent had they remained within its fold. Furthermore, the first generation of Puritan ministers, most of them learned men and university graduates, were fast disappearing from the scene. Their successors were being debarred from grammar schools and universities, and this exclusion, despite the excellence of some Nonconformist academies, must be accounted a loss. Nor was it the only loss to education, because although there was a measure of co-operation between Anglicans and Dissenters in the work of the Welsh Trust for schools and literature, there can be little doubt that had a concerted attack on illiteracy and ignorance been launched by all religious men of goodwill it would have produced more effective results. But possibly the most grievous of all the effects of the Penal Code was that it tended to produce a 'siege mentality' on the part of many Dissenters; the psychology of small, embattled 'in-groups', struggling for survival. This, more than anything else, prevented them from taking full advantage of toleration when it eventually came. Nevertheless, it had been a massive achievement on their part to survive as well as they had done. Buffeted and weakened they may have been, but they came through far too strong in numbers to be in danger of being extinguished. In 1689 they could look forward with some hope and confidence to the more genial climate of toleration.[60]

II. UNCERTAIN FREEDOM, 1688–1715

James II's own undisguised adherence to the Roman Catholic Church and the political and religious policies pursued by him had aroused widespread and deep-seated fears among his subjects; among none more than Protestant Nonconformists. The latter's feelings of desperate alarm during the autumn of 1688 before William of Orange landed at Torbay on November 5 were subsequently recalled in graphic terms by a leading Welsh Dissenter, James Owen: 'We were', he declared, 'as Isaac bound to the altar. The bloody knife was at our throat; all things were ripe for execution. An army of papists and debauched Protestants were within our gates ready to enslave us. The fatal conjunction of England and France threatened the utter extirpation of the Protestant interest.' Such fears were perhaps exaggerated and the language in which they were expressed overdramatic; yet Owen's words give us a vivid insight into the state of mind of the Dissenters and the warmth of their welcome to the Dutch prince whom they regarded as their deliverer.[61]

Not that everyone saw William, or the Parliament which recognized him as king, in so favourable a light, and some Glamorgan men did not forbear to voice in public their criticism. Thomas Mansel of Margam, M.P. for Glamorgan Boroughs, voted against the offer of the throne to William and Mary (above, p. 398). Edward Llewellin, gentleman, formerly of Newton Nottage, was brought before Great Sessions in 1689 on a charge of having said, in Welsh, of King William, 'Never was there such a fool of a king as this!', and of Parliament, 'Parliament is doing a thing which it has no power to do'. In 1690, Mark Jenkin, a yeoman of Llantrisant, was similarly presented for declaring his support for King James and uttering treasonable words against William III. As late as 1695 Edward Carne, gentleman, of Cowbridge was bound over to answer a charge of having spoken contemptuous words against the King and his government. However, the events of the following year, 1696, were to show that William in reality enjoyed a wide degree of support in the county. The discovery of a plot to assassinate him had led to an almost universal attestation throughout the realm of a Bond of Association for the defence of the sovereign and the country. The Association Roll for Glamorgan was subscribed by 760 men, who included among them deputy-lieutenants, magistrates, officers of the militia, municipal officials, Anglican clerics, leading Dissenters, and a number of relatively obscure individuals. Among those who signed was that Edward Llewellin who had been so contemptuous of William in 1689, but Thomas Mansel of Margam refused to do so (above, p. 398).[62]

One of the first acts of policy implemented by William and Mary and, as far as Dissenters were concerned, the most important and welcome, was the Toleration Act enacted in May 1689. Its provisions allowed Dissenters to worship freely in licensed places of meeting under the guidance of ministers licensed for the purpose. Licences could be obtained, at sixpence a time, from any one of three recognized places for registration: the bishop's court, the archdeacon's court, or Quarter Sessions. To disturb Dissenting worship was made an offence punishable by a fine of £20. Freedom of worship was accompanied by other valuable privileges: legacies bequeathed to Dissenters could no longer be declared invalid; funds raised by Dissenters to sustain the weaker churches, needy ministers, or ministerial education, were no longer in danger of being confiscated; and couples married at properly-licensed Dissenting places of worship in the presence of witnesses could not be accused of adultery.[63]

On the other hand, the liberty being offered to Dissenters was still a strictly conditional one in some respects. They were obliged to take an oath of loyalty to the king as head of the Established Church as well as sovereign, they had to repudiate the authority and doctrine of the pope, accept the 39 Articles, keep the doors unlocked during their meetings for worship, continue paying tithes, and serve as church-wardens and overseers, if appointed to those offices. Furthermore, the Corporation Act of 1661, still on the statute book, excluded Dissenters from municipal office, and the Test Act (1673) prevented them from holding civil or military office under the Crown. These statutes affected only the wealthier and more ambitious Dissenters, who learnt to evade their restrictions by the practice of occasional conformity. Interestingly enough one of the most celebrated exponents of this tactic was a man who had a close connection with Glamorgan, Sir Humphrey Edwin (1642–1707). The son of a Carmarthenshire felt-maker who moved to Hereford, Edwin was first apprenticed at Hereford and later in London. He became an extremely wealthy City wool-merchant, and some time before 1687 bought the estate of the Thomas family of Llanfihangel and became constable of Ogmore castle and owner of the lordship. Knighted in 1687 and sheriff of Glamorgan in 1688, he crowned his career by becoming lord mayor of London in 1697. As lord mayor he scandalized Tories and High Churchmen when, after attending communion service at his parish church on the morning of Sunday October 31, 1697, he proceeded in the afternoon to his own Presbyterian place of worship in full civic regalia, accompanied by a shocked and reluctant sword-bearer. He repeated the performance a week later. Sir Humphrey was to die in Wales in 1707 and his memory is perpetuated on a tablet in Llanfihangel Church.[64]

The freedom conferred upon Dissenters became more restricted during the first years of the eighteenth century. The victory of the Tories in the elections of 1701 and 1702, the death of William III in March 1702 and the accession of Anne combined to give the High Church party a position of much greater strength from which to harass the Dissenters. There followed a protracted and embittered struggle in Parliament over the issue of occasional conformity. One of the leading Tory and High Church critics of the practice was Sir Humphrey Mackworth of Neath (1657-1727), who published a pamphlet, *Peace at Home* (1703), in which he advanced familiar High Church arguments against occasional conformity. Thanks to the Whig majority in the House of Lords, the Tories were frustrated until 1711 when, as the result of Whig miscalculation, an Act was passed against occasional conformity. Potentially much more damaging to the Nonconformist cause than the attacks on occasional conformity was the increasing pressure being brought to bear against Dissenting academies and schoolmasters. Under the terms of the Schism Act, hurried through Parliament during May and June 1714, no schoolmaster would be allowed to teach unless he accepted the Book of Common Prayer and was in possession of a bishop's licence; a licence which no bishop might confer unless he was satisfied that the recipient was a communicant of the Church of England. The object of the Act was perfectly summed up by Bolingbroke, who declared that it was not intended 'to distress the consciences of the existing generations of Nonconformists, but to prevent any fresh generation from being brought up in error'. What saved Dissent from undergoing another difficult time of pressure and tribulation was the death of Queen Anne on August 1, 1714 and her replacement by the Hanoverian dynasty and the Whig ascendancy.[65]

Nonetheless, whatever may have been the shortcomings of the régime set up under the Toleration Act, and no more matter how much more restrictive it became in Queen Anne's reign, it undoubtedly offered Dissenters an atmosphere of markedly greater reassurance and hope. Even in 1688, before the Toleration Act was itself passed, a number of new ministers had been ordained among the Nonconformists, including two in Glamorgan—David Richards at Merthyr Tydfil and John Higgs in Swansea. In 1689 and the years that followed, Dissenters began to take advantage of some of the new opportunities open to them. The major denominations—Presbyterians, Independents, and Baptists—proceeded to take action at the centre designed to help their co-religionists throughout England and Wales. In 1689 the Presbyterians and Independents joined together to set up a General Fund, though this arrangement lasted only until 1693. In 1695, however, the Congregationalists established their own fund, administered by the Congregational Fund Board. Under its auspices money was raised among wealthy members of the denomination in and around London to be disbursed for the assistance of their poorer brethren in the provinces. In April 1696 George Griffiths and Lewis Lloyd were given £30 from the fund, and a further £20 in June, to share among the churches in south Wales. The money was used to found churches and augment ministerial stipends; and though we have no details of the recipients in south Wales, some of the money must, pretty certainly, have come to Glamorgan. The county did, without doubt, receive some of the grants made from the fund to candidates for the ministry. The Presbyterian Fund Board supported twelve students at Brynllywarch in 1690; and in 1696 and 1697 allowances of £3 were made from the Congregational Fund to young men studying there. Samuel Jones of Brynllywarch died in 1697 and was later succeeded by Rees Price of Tyn-ton—father of the illustrious Richard Price. Rees Price had done much of Samuel Jones's work during the last two years of his life, and he may have been the 'Mr. Price' whose case was considered by the Congregational Fund Board in March 1698. Ministerial students studying in Glamorgan under Price were awarded sums ranging from £4 to £10 by the Board during the years from 1699 to 1702. Among Welsh students studying at English academies who received help was the young Glamorgan man, Samuel Price, brother to Rees Price.[66]

Baptists, too, took advantage of their newly-found freedom to strengthen their organization. A General Assembly of the Baptists of England and Wales was convened in London in 1689, at which Robert Morgan, one of the two ministers of the Swansea Baptists, was present. His church is the only Welsh Baptist church to be included in the list of churches drawn up by the Assembly. The 1690 Assembly's list, however, included Craig-yr-allt (near Hengoed) as well as Swansea. From 1693 onwards the Baptist General Assembly was divided into two, with the western half, to which the Welsh churches belonged, meeting at Bristol. By 1700 the Welsh Baptist churches were strong enough to set up their own Welsh Assembly, which for some years held its annual meeting alternately at Swansea and Llanwenarth, and later went the rounds of the Baptist churches in Wales.[67]

Locally, as well as at the centre, fresh life and energy were burgeoning among the Dissenters. Within a short space after the passing of the Toleration Act, new chapels were erected in those centres where Dissent had survived in strength throughout the years of persecution. Not surprisingly, in view of the town's history as a 'city of refuge', Swansea had one of the first chapels to be built. It was raised in 1688, or soon after, and already by 1697 was proving too small for its congregation, who then built a new place of worship on the site of the present Unitarian chapel in High Street. Services in Swansea were conducted in English, but a few miles away the powerful Welsh Independent church of Mynydd-bach worshipped in Welsh at Tirdwncyn, though no chapel was built at Mynydd-bach until 1762. Two other early chapels in the west of the county were built at Gellionnen (1692) and Chwarelau-bach near Neath (1695) by members of the church founded at Cadoxton-juxta-Neath. Both were reputedly built with some help from Bussy Mansel, who still retained enough affection for his former beliefs to help provide Dissenters with land, stone, and timber for their chapels. On the very westernmost edge of the county, at Cwmllynfell, there may have been yet another early chapel (it was certainly in existence by 1715) built by yet another offshoot of the prolific Cadoxton church. Away at the opposite end of Glamorgan, in the north-east, another old and numerous church had long existed in the Merthyr Tydfil district. Soon after 1688 its members raised a chapel at Cwm-y-glo on land belonging to the Jenkinses of Hensol and continued to worship there until a new chapel was built at Ynys-gau in Merthyr in 1749. The other early Presbyterian/Congregational chapel was built in another long-standing centre of Nonconformity, Cardiff. Hitherto services had probably been held in the house of the minister, John French, but in 1696 land was leased in Womanby Street by John Archer from Sir John Thomas, Bt., of Wenvoe, and on it Trinity Chapel was built.[68]

The Baptists were slower to build chapels. The earliest chapel accredited to them in Glamorgan was the one formerly belonging to the Congregationalists at Swansea, which was taken over by the Baptists in 1698 when it became too small for its previous owners. Baptists from the western end of the county, however, went on meeting in private houses in Swansea, Loughor, Llangyfelach, and Kenfig. The other main Baptist centre of strength lay in the church of Craig-yr-allt near Hengoed in east Glamorgan. For many years its members, numbering several hundreds, continued to meet in a number of private houses in the parishes of Eglwysilan and Llanfabon until eventually, in 1710, they built a chapel at Hengoed, a convenient centre in Gelli-gaer parish.[69]

Glamorgan Quakers, attenuated in numbers and repeatedly harassed by legal actions brought against them for refusing to pay tithes, could do little to build meeting-houses. In the Cardiff area there were so few of them that when new trustees were needed for the Quaker burial ground in the town in 1696, only three out of 13 could be recruited from Cardiff itself, and this once-vigorous centre of Quakerism remained lifeless and inconspicuous throughout the eighteenth-century history of the sect. The little Quaker group at Tref-y-rhyg had suffered a crippling blow when its leader, John ab Evan, and his family emigrated to America in 1683, and though it took on a new lease of life when he and his wife and daughter returned in 1704, it remained too small to have its own meeting-house. At Quaker's Yard near Merthyr Tydfil, where the Quakers had their own burial ground, members were similarly few and dwindling in number. Only in Swansea, under the leadership of William Bevan and later his son, Silvanus, were the Quakers sufficiently flourishing to have their own meeting-house and to maintain a good deal of their earlier vitality and commitment.[70]

By the year 1715 we are able to form a reasonably accurate impression of the location of and attendance at Dissenting causes in Glamorgan. It is drawn from a list of churches, together with some details of the numbers attending them, compiled in that year by Dr. John Evans. The information given by him for Glamorgan may be tabulated as follows:

Place	Denomination	Minister	Average attendance	Social and Political standing
Swansea Cardiff	Independent Presbyterian	George Denbury Rice Protheroe, ordained 1702	250	15 votes
Cwmllynfell	Independent	Llewellyn Bevan, Roger Howell, John Davies removed	600	15 single and 14 double votes
Neath, Tirdwncyn, Blaen-gwrach	Independent	Thomas Davies, David Thomas removed	1,006	50 votes, several double votes
Cildeudy near Bridgend	Independent	Rees Price, John Thomas		
Cilibion and Pitton, Gower	Independent	David Jones	200	40 voters
Gwynfe (Carmarthenshire)	Independent	Llewellyn Bevan, Roger Howell, John Davies removed	550	21 voters
Swansea	Baptist	Morgan John		
Llanfabon	Baptist			
Near Kenfig	Baptist			
Cefnhengoed parish of Gelli-gaer	Baptist	Morgan Griffith	700	2 gentlemen, 40 yeomen, 12 tradesmen, 85 farmers, 140 labourers, 20 votes for co. of Glamorgan, 22 for co. of Monmouthshire, and 60 for the boroughs
Hendref	Baptist	Morgan Griffith	300	12 yeomen, 5 tradesmen, 30 farmers, 70 labourers, 12 votes for the county, 70 votes for the boroughs

The total average attendance recorded is 3,606; and this figure would include the many 'listeners' as well as church members. From this total the 550 for Gwynfe and other districts in Carmarthenshire should be excluded at once. The church at Hengoed must also have included a large number of Monmouthshire people, but these are probably offset by a number of attenders at Monmouthshire churches who are specifically said in the return for that county to have been from Glamorgan. As against the number that must be deducted from the 3,606, we have to take account of the attendance of the five Glamorgan churches for which no figures are provided. An average of 100 for each of these groups would be a reasonable and cautious estimate remembering the average of 500 for each of the other Glamorgan churches listed, or the average of 230 for the very carefully-detailed 13 churches of neighbouring Monmouthshire. Moreover, the powerful church at Merthyr Tydfil, with an attendance probably of some hundreds, is not included at all in Dr. Evans's statistics, nor are the small groups of Quakers within the county. All in all, therefore, the attendance at Dissenting churches in Glamorgan in 1715 can hardly have been less than 3,500 and was probably nearer 4,000. Assuming that the population of the county at this time was about 50,000 (above, pp. 311–12), this would mean that Dissenters formed about seven to eight per cent of the total population, or as much as eleven to thirteen per cent of an estimated adult population of 30,000. Such a proportion would be distinctly higher than the average estimate of six per cent of the total population for Wales as a whole, or the four to five per cent estimate for England. Yet when we consider that Glamorgan was one of the Welsh counties which had, from the outset, responded most readily to the Puritan appeal and had withstood persecution strongly, the high concentration of Dissenters there cannot be regarded as surprising.[71]

Dr. John Evans's statistics also give some interesting insights into the social status of those attending Dissenting worship. Unfortunately, he gave details for only two of the Glamorgan congregations, those of the Baptist churches at Cefnhengoed and Hendref. But the kind of social composition of membership shown for these two is broadly similar to that given in the much fuller details available for Monmouthshire, and it is unlikely that the social origins of other Glamorgan congregations differed in any significant respects. What the figures reveal is that a large proportion of Dissenters were drawn from among the more substantial members of society, including among them a sprinkling of parish gentry and a large number of yeomen, farmers, and tradesmen, many of whom were prosperous enough to be voters in parliamentary elections. This element made up half or more of the congregation. In fact, the proportion of labourers in the two Glamorgan Baptist churches was decidedly higher than in nearly all the Monmouthshire churches, while the proportion of freeholders, farmers, and tradesmen ordinarily tended to be higher in the Presbyterian and Independent churches than among the Baptists.

Geographically the churches were widely distributed in many parts of the county. However, four features stand out about their location: in contrast with the licensed meetings of 1672, there were none in the Vale of Glamorgan proper; the Dissenting churches in the main towns were relatively less important than they had been; Dissenters were found in markedly larger numbers in the upland and more completely Welsh-speaking areas of the county; and the heaviest concentration of them all was to be found in the west of the county, in the hundreds of Neath, Llangyfelach and Swansea, where industrialization had also made most progress (above, chapter vii). How is such a pattern to be explained? To some extent it may well have been the result of the increased efforts made ever since the time of the Propagation Act to spread and intensify preaching in Welsh and also to extend literacy among Welsh speakers. It is impossible to measure precisely the effects of the schools established or the books published in Welsh under the auspices of the Propagation Act, the Welsh Trust, the S.P.C.K., and Nonconformist ministers, or by more informal voluntary effort, but they must considerably have augmented the number of those literate in Welsh and in English as well as multiplying the number of books available to them. The efforts of the Trust and the S.P.C.K., were, of course, directed at Anglicans as well as Nonconformists, but whereas it was, on the whole, a minority of devoted Anglican clergy and laymen who were impressed with the urgent need for wider preaching and literacy, the Dissenters were, as a body, committed to these ideals.

Other reasons may account for the success of the Dissenters outside the towns and the Vale. There is evidence of a good deal of prejudice against the Dissenters, especially the Quakers and Baptists, in the towns. They were suspected by magistrates and municipal authorities, e.g., Cardiff Baptists were repeatedly refused a licence for worship in the town by Quarter Sessions. At times they were the target of mob violence, connived at if not instigated by the authorities, and it was for this reason that Bussy Mansel advised the church members at Neath to build their chapel some distance outside the town at Chwarelau-bach, where the town mob was less likely to break their windows or interrupt their services. On occasions, too, they were the object, in seaport towns, of unwelcome attention from the press-gang, as the Baptists discovered when they met for their Assembly at Swansea in 1706 and had to disperse surreptitiously in order to avoid being forcibly haled off to sea. A further reason which could help to explain the greater success of Dissent in the upland areas is the contrast between the parish organization there and in the Vale. In the latter the parishes were small and compact, with a high concentration of resident Anglican incumbents, whose religious authority and prestige served to underpin the rule of the mainly Anglican magistrates, whereas the upland parishes were large, sprawling, ill-provided with communications, and often neglected by absentee incumbents, who entrusted their spiritual duties to a handful of badly-paid curates. Such differences in parochial organization were reinforced by others in the economic and social structures of the two areas. A point much emphasized in recent years in relation to early-Stuart England is that the inhabitants of those regions in which manorial tenures and open-field farming had been the norm were inclined to be more docile and submissive in politics and religion than the freer and less landlord-ridden inhabitants of woodland and pastoral districts. This could be equally relevant to the religious history of late-seventeenth century Glamorgan in explaining the distribution of Dissenters. The more dispersed population of the uplands, having a much larger proportion of small freeholders in its midst and very much less under the dominance of predominantly Anglican landlords and justices of the peace mainly resident in the lowlands, were in a position to take a much more stubborn and independent line in their religious convictions than the tenant farmers of the Vale. It may not be too much to suggest that the Dissent of the uplands was only the latest manifestation of a centuries-old tradition of maintaining a separate 'moes a defod' (above, p. 85). That this kind of response to Puritan or Dissenting beliefs came late in upland Glamorgan, as compared with many wooded and pastoral regions in England, was inevitable in view of the slowness with which such doctrines came to be presented in a language which the Welsh-speaking inhabitants of the county could understand. Then, finally, there was the apparent correlation between Dissenting strength and industrial progress. This, too, was to be expected when we remember that it was in west Glamorgan that there first emerged an industrial or semi-industrial population alienated to a large extent from the ethos and ties of rural society, and reluctant to accept the authority or religious beliefs of a Tory and High Church landlord, or, indeed, of a Tory and High Church industrialist like Sir Humphrey Mackworth.[72]

III. The Eighteenth-Century Dissenters

Despite the presentation at Great Sessions between the years 1715 and 1721, and again in 1745, of a number of men from Cardiff and other parts of Glamorgan for publicly proclaiming their sympathy for the Jacobite cause, the first of the Hanoverian dynasty was peacefully and well received by the population of the county. Among no section of the community was he more thankfully welcomed than the Dissenters. The Assembly of the Welsh Baptists regularly referred to their 'deliverance' at his hands, and Baptist churches regularly held meetings of thanksgiving for his accession (not to say Anne's death!) on the first Sunday of August every year and the first Wednesday of every month. The Dissenters' confidence in George I and his Whig ministers was further consolidated in 1719 by the passing of the Act for Strengthening the Protestant Interest, which repealed the Schism Act of 1714 and deprived the Act of 1711 of its force against Dissenters. Toleration for Protestant Nonconformists was now firmly and, as it turned out, finally established in England and Wales. Some restrictions remained, of course. Before they could conduct worship Nonconformists were still obliged to license their meeting-places, and no Nonconformist minister could exercise his functions without obtaining a licence. The earliest surviving example of such a licence in Glamorgan is one obtained in 1719–20 from Quarter Sessions for holding meetings at the house of James Davies, called Cilfach Maen Isa, in the parish of Gelli-gaer; and many other later licences have been traced. The handicaps imposed by the Test Act were also still in force; and some magistrates and other officials continued to be hostile and prejudiced against Dissenters. When under pressure the latter derived great help from the Protestant Dissenting Deputies, founded in 1732 to ensure that their co-religionists were not deprived of their legal rights.[73]

Two main Nonconformist denominations now existed to enjoy the rights conferred upon them by the Hanoverians: the Independents (or Congregationalists) and the Baptists. Quakers entered upon a long period of decline until the end of the century, and Presbyterians, following the failure of their efforts to set themselves up as an established church, had virtually become indistinguishable from Independents. Dr. John Evans, in his list of 1715 for Glamorgan, recognized only the church at Cardiff as Presbyterian, and even this was soon to become regarded as the Independent church at Trinity Chapel. Vestiges of Presbyterian practice, however, still survived among the Independent churches in the widespread custom of electing elders: the church at Mynydd-bach, for example, clung to the four-fold Calvinistic ministry of pastors, supported by 'teaching' elders, 'ruling' elders, and deacons. Between the Independents and the Baptists, on the other hand, differences had become sharper, and their mixed congregations of the early days of persecution had long since disappeared. Three issues, in particular, separated the two denominations. First, the Baptists laid special emphasis on the absolute need for adult baptism; an issue which caused much controversy in Glamorgan from about 1725 onwards and was hotly argued out in public at Merthyr Tydfil in 1728 between Edmund Jones of Pontypool, who championed infant baptism, and Miles Harry of Blaenau Gwent, who upheld the cause of adult baptism. Secondly, the Baptists were, in general, more rigid in the high Calvinism of their theology. Thirdly, the Baptists were more closely-knit together by their General Assembly, which on the whole exercised a healthy influence in maintaining discipline and trying to reconcile differences, e.g. between 1730 and 1750 it helped to prevent the badly-split church at Hengoed from tearing itself apart (below, p. 494). The self-sufficiency of individual Independent churches should not be overstressed, however; although they maintained their autonomy and no assembly was established until 1778, there was, in practice, a good deal of close co-operation between them in the ordination of young ministers and in financial help for one another.[74]

Despite these differences between them, the Dissenting churches of both denominations had much in common. They were all deeply concerned with the need for care in the education of ministers and their ordination. Even before the end of persecution, ministerial education had become a serious problem for the Dissenters, as many of the leading Puritan ministers who, in their youth, had been educated at the universities began disappearing from the scene. As early, perhaps, as *c.* 1672 Samuel Jones had founded his famous academy at Brynllywarch, which he maintained until his death in 1697. Jones's reputation as a master of Greek, Latin, and oriental languages, and a philosopher, moralist, and theologian well abreast of contemporary scholarship was thoroughly deserved. His gifts as scholar and teacher were brilliantly reflected in his pupils, who numbered such outstanding leaders as the Independents, James Owen, Philip Pugh, Rees and Samuel Price, and the Baptist, David Rees. When Jones died, a new academy was set up at Abergavenny by Roger Griffith, to which some of the Presbyterians at Brynllywarch emigrated; but in 1702 Griffith joined the Anglican Church. The real continuator of Jones's work in Glamorgan was Rees Price, who taught his pupils at Tyn-ton. He continued to take ministerial students there until the 1730s, despite the opening in 1704 of the new academy at Carmarthen, to which a growing number of young Dissenters were attracted. The Baptists, for their part, had no academy in south Wales and were heavily dependent on the one which existed in Bristol from 1710 onwards. During the régime of the illustrious Bernard Foskett there, from 1720 to 1758, 64 preachers were educated, of whom half came from Wales. Among them were a number of men with Glamorgan connections, including Griffith Davies, minister at Swansea from 1736, the brothers Peter and David Rees of Swansea—both to be well-known ministers in England, and Thomas Llewellyn, the most celebrated of them all. Not until *c.* 1732–34 was a Baptist academy founded at Trosnant near Pontypool, but even then many of its *alumni*, including Thomas Llewellyn, completed their education at Bristol.[75]

Individual churches remained few in number, though they might have branches or offshoots which, in the fullness of time, would become separate churches. The prolific church at Cadoxton, for instance, had branches at Mynydd-bach, Gellionnen, Cwmllynfell, and Blaen-gwrach, all of which had become separate churches by the eighteenth century. The membership of such churches was usually drawn from a wide area. At Mynydd-bach the church book recorded baptisms of children from points as widely scattered in west Glamorgan as Cwmllynfell, Sketty, Forest, Gelliwastad, Loughor, Clydach, Cadle, Cors y llan and Clas. Blaen-gwrach, again, was a very early centre of Nonconformist worship, but only in 1718 did it become a separate church. By 1734 it had a total of 59 members drawn from widely-scattered localities: the Swansea Valley, Ystradfellte, Cwmdulais, and Glyncorrwg, as well as the Neath

Valley and the immediate vicinity of Blaen-gwrach. The Baptists of Hengoed found it difficult to maintain the coherence of their far-flung membership, spread as it was over an extensive area in east and north Glamorgan. They tried to overcome the problem by bringing all the members together for the monthly communion services in May, June, and July—known as *pen mis mawr Hengoed* ('the great end of the month at Hengoed'). The practice turned out to be a mixed blessing, however; for the purveyors of food and drink came to descend on Hengoed in large numbers, thereby encouraging many to resort there for pleasure rather than worship. The most effective means of maintaining contact with such dispersed congregations still depended on the extraordinary willingness of the ministers to travel long distances to keep in touch with their flock. The career of Henry Davies (?1696–1766) provides one of the most striking examples of the devotion of a Nonconformist minister to his calling. He became minister of Blaen-gwrach c. 1718 and kept a school there. Not content with looking after the needs of his own scattered membership, he became one of the new 'evangelical' type of Dissenting minister, tirelessly itinerating the hill-country of Glamorgan. He founded a new church at Llanharan c. 1734, and he penetrated into the Rhondda Valleys. Here, he founded a new church at Cymer (Porth) about 1738, left Blaen-gwrach to become its minister, and in 1743 built a new chapel, the first Nonconformist place of worship to be built in the Rhondda. Typically, he met his death on a preaching tour when, at the age of about 70, he was drowned trying to ford the River Rhondda on horseback.[76]

Early church covenants surviving from the eighteenth century give us a clear indication of the ideals cherished by these Dissenting congregations. Their members were, in general, thoughtful and responsible individuals, who set considerable store on intellectual understanding and theological knowledge. They were expected to be able to give a careful and reasoned account of the basis of their convictions. Not surprisingly, they laid emphasis on the need for education. A minister regarded it as part of his responsibility to act as schoolmaster as well as pastor, and almost every church had some sort of school attached to it in which its members could be taught to read. At Mynydd-bach early in the eighteenth century a school was conducted every Sunday afternoon, where the scholars were taught to read, to absorb theological instruction, and to participate intelligently in worship. The chief textbooks used for the purpose were the Shorter Catechism of the Westminster Assembly and William Perkins's Catechism. Dissenting ministers and their congregations were also active in the publication and purchase of the much larger output of Bibles and other literature in Welsh which characterized the period.[77]

The church covenants also show that members were required to maintain a high standard of personal morality, discipline, and commitment. They were expected to set an example to one another as well as to those outside the church in the matter of conduct and behaviour becoming a Christian, were to attend worship regularly, and to maintain concord and unity within the church. They were to follow an occupation compatible with their profession of faith and to marry fellow-believers. It was their duty to visit the sick, console those in mourning and distress, and generally to succour their fellow-members. They collected regularly to help the poor in their midst and to support worthy causes elsewhere. In all these matters they were to look upon themselves as their brothers' keepers, to sustain the weak and correct the errant. Church discipline, always condemned by Puritans as being too flabby in the Anglican Church, seems to have been regularly and strictly applied. For the more flagrant lapses the punishment was expulsion from membership. The church book of Mynydd-bach records the turning out of gross or persistent offenders for such transgressions as sexual delinquency, blasphemy, mendacity, and 'idle, vagrant life, together with a total negligence of the means of grace'. In view of the high standards they demanded, Dissenters admitted new members only after care and deliberation, and there would always be many 'listeners' as well as members in their congregations. One such 'listener', the highly intelligent and original self-taught poet, Siôn Llewelyn, recorded in verse his reactions to his own period of probation, when he was kept waiting from the month of June until St. Andrew's feast (November 30) before knowing whether or not he would be admitted to membership of the church at Merthyr Tydfil:

> Treulio'r dyddiau hynny'n chwerw,
> Rhai'n fy nhaflu, rhai'n fy nghadw,
> Fe ddywedai rhai mor ffôl dan chwerthin,
> 'Na rowch un law i Siôn Llewelyn.'
> Fe dd'wedai'r gwir addolwyr cynnes,
> 'Os yw e 'nawr yn rhodio'n addas,
> Oni phrofir i'r gwrthwyneb,
> Mae'n rhaid ei dderbyn i gymundeb.'

('Those were bitter days I spent, with some wanting to reject me, others to keep me. Some said amid foolish laughter, "Don't give a hand to Siôn Llewelyn." The true and ardent worshippers said, "If he now walks uprightly and no one can prove to the contrary, he must be accepted to communion." ')[78]

The services held by Dissenters reflected the nature of their convictions and ideals. Public worship might be conducted only once on Sundays, because ministers frequently had more than one congregation to serve. The order of service was simple: there would be reading from the Bible accompanied by explanatory comment; prayers were extempore and often long and earnest; and psalms were sung, though hymns were gradually becoming more popular in the eighteenth century, especially after the spread of Methodist influences. The core of the service and its virtual *raison d'être*, however, was the sermon. Normally the preaching was clear, well-ordered, carefully-reasoned, and expository in style, and might frequently be strongly theological in content. Yet it has recently been rightly emphasized that too sharp a contrast has often been drawn between the 'dryness' of Dissenting preaching and the fervour of that of the Methodists; the former was not, in fact, necessarily lacking in warmth, feeling, or urgency. The monthly communion service occupied a place of marked and, it seems, growing importance during this period. Communion was usually ministered only by the minister of the church, and was preceded in the previous week by a service of prayer and preparation. Nor was worship restricted to the public services; on the contrary, the head of every household was enjoined by the church covenant to ensure that he maintained regular devotions at home for his family and servants, brought his children up in the faith, and ensured that none of his household desecrated the sabbath. Moreover, despite the building of chapels, the old Nonconformist tradition of meeting for worship in private houses still retained much of its vigour in the eighteenth century.[79]

The emphasis placed by Dissenters on the place of reasoned intellectual and theological convictions, combined with the greater freedom they now enjoyed and the more widely-ranging speculation among contemporary thinkers of many kinds, led to fierce and prolonged controversies in the eighteenth century. The differences over adult baptism have already been referred to. More damaging to the denominations were the rifts in the ranks of each between the supporters of Calvinism and Arminianism. The seedbed of most of the Arminian ideas which flourished in Wales was the Carmarthen Academy, to which so many young ministers went for their education. The academy was a lively centre of intellectual innovation, in which there pullulated ideas drawn from a variety of sources: John Locke, the Deists, Samuel Clarke, the universities of Holland and Scotland, and contemporary science. As a result, a number of students there adopted Arminian beliefs concerning free will and election. One of them, Charles Winter, in 1729 took these ideas back with him to the Baptist church at Hengoed, where he acted as assistant to the venerable minister, Morgan Griffith, with whom he got on well despite the latter's staunch Calvinism. In 1730 the Welsh Baptist Assembly met at Hengoed, and bitter debates between Calvinists and Arminians ensued. An open split at this point was prevented only by the skilful mediation of David Rees, a London minister but a native of east Glamorgan. Winter continued as assistant to Griffith until the latter's death in 1738 and again under his successor, Griffith Jones, until the latter's emigration to America in 1749. But in 1750 Winter and 24 of his supporters were expelled from the church at Hengoed and formed their own church of General Baptists at Craigfargoed in 1753.[80]

Among the Independents of Glamorgan the first storm centre of controversy was the church at Cwm-y-glo, Merthyr Tydfil. This church was, until 1730, a joint pastorate with distant Cefnarthen near Llandovery, and it had two ministers. The senior of the two, Roger Williams, had been minister since 1698, and was an Arminian, whose views were shared by part of his congregation. The other, James Davies (d. 1760), had come to Cwm-y-glo in 1724. Like Henry Davies of Blaen-gwrach (no relation) he was an energetic and ardent itinerant evangelizer. He was also a firm Calvinist, with whom one wing of the church agreed. Not until after the death of Roger Williams in 1730 did things go seriously awry. Two years later, the Arminian members of the church chose Richard Rees, a well-to-do freeholder of Gwernllwyn Uchaf, Dowlais, and a product of Carmarthen Academy, as James Davies's co-pastor. Rees's preaching was very much to the taste of the Arminians of Cwm-y-glo, among whom Siôn Llewelyn was a leading light and who recorded his views of Rees thus:

> Gŵr llawn o ddeall, dysg a doniau,
> Llariaidd, gwresog ei rasusau;
> Mi glywn y gŵr yn rhoi ergydion,
> Ac yn dechrau hela hoelion,
> 'Nôl eu hiro yn olew'r Ysbryd,
> Fe gerddai'r hoelion hynny'n hyfryd.

('A man full of understanding, learning and gifts; of gentle and warm graces; I heard him striking blows and driving in the nails; after lubricating them with the oil of the Spirit, those nails went in beautifully.')

Relations between James Davies and Richard Rees and their rival followings became increasingly tense, and in 1747 Rees and the Arminians hived off to form a new church at Cefn-coed-y-cymer, which eventually moved all the way to Unitarian beliefs. The rest of the members at Cwm-y-glo, their lease having expired, themselves moved in 1749 to Ynys-gau in Merthyr Tydfil. Here, James Davies was joined by his son, Samuel, as co-pastor in 1750. Samuel, too, had been at Carmarthen Academy and, like so many others, had imbibed Arminian principles there. His preaching led to further dissensions in the church and left his father discredited and friendless at the time of his death in 1760.[81]

Three Independent churches in the west of the county began to be affected by Arminian beliefs about the third quarter of the century. They reached Gellionnen towards the end of the ministry of Roger Howell (d. 1742); but it was Josiah Rees (1714–1804), another of Carmarthen's *alumni*, who was the main influence in directing the church in an Arminian direction. Arminianism was brought to Swansea by Solomon Harris (1726–85), yet another Carmarthen product, who was ordained at Swansea in 1751; while Blaen-gwrach was won over by Thomas Morgan who came there as minister in 1773. All three churches passed through the customary three phases of eighteenth-century

[495]

Arminians: first they became Arminian in belief, then Arian, and finally Unitarian.[82]

By the middle of the eighteenth century the Dissenters had become firmly established in Glamorgan as a sizeable minority of the population. Furthermore, the rigorous standards they were expected to achieve in order to be admitted to church membership and to maintain it afterwards gave them an influence that was out of proportion to their actual numbers. They had already increased their membership considerably since 1689 and, in Glamorgan, had achieved more success than in most counties in England and Wales. In the long run, the Independents and the Baptists were to be the most numerous and influential sects amid the county's vastly-swollen population of the nineteenth century. For most of the eighteenth century, however, their numbers grew relatively slowly, and new churches were being founded only at rather long intervals. The reasons for this are not far to seek. The Dissenters were showing many of the symptoms of what some religious sociologists have described as the transition from a sect to a church, i.e., that their membership was increasingly dependent on those who had been born and brought up into their faith rather than been converted to it. With such a change came something of a loss of the crusading impetus of the first generation; and nowhere could this be more clearly observed than among the Quakers, who had been transformed from the fiery, aggressive, outgoing zealots of the 1650s into the placid, respectable, in-group quietists of the eighteenth century. Added to the effects of the transition from sect to church were the consequences of a long period of persecution and uncertainty, from which Dissenters tended to emerge with a cautious defensive mentality born of the need to conceal their activities, or at least to maintain them with discretion, and to test the reliability of members. New members, as might be expected, were accepted only after due care and circumspection, which tended to reinforce the inherent emphasis placed by Dissenters on respect for individual conscience and reason, and the need for proper deliberation upon full realization of the responsibilities which church membership imposed. Within such a framework of values and beliefs there was not much scope for sudden gusts of emotion or 'instant' conversion. Moreover, much of their energy became introverted and absorbed in acrimonious doctrinal controversies among themselves, thus limiting still further their capacity to win over the unconverted. Finally, their close connection with Dissent in England, valuable though it had been in the era of persecution and in the years of reconstruction after 1689 and still continued to be in some respects, could also be a source of weakness by draining away some of their brightest talents. A number of the most gifted young ministers and leaders, after being educated at academies in England, subsequently settled there in charge of Dissenting churches; Peter and David Rees and Thomas Llewellyn from among the Baptists, and Samuel Price, Richard Price, and David

Williams from among the Independents. Even if, like Thomas Llewellyn, they continued to maintain close and helpful contact with their native country and county, their brilliant gifts were employed primarily in the land of their adoption.[83]

The Dissenters have also tended to suffer, of course, by comparison with the drive, urgency, and success of the early Methodists. Yet it is essential to keep the scene in proper perspective. Not only were the earliest generation of Methodists in the first flush of enthusiasm and achievement, but their activities also happen to be more fully and vividly documented than those of the Dissenters. Moreover, there was a great deal that was admirable in the latter's emphasis on the place of the intellect and the reason; the appeal primarily to emotion has not been wholly for the health of religion in Wales. However much we may rightly admire the gifts and successes of the early Methodists they were not alone in having a conscientious concern for the religious needs of the people at large. There were in south-east Wales Dissenters who were profoundly convinced of the need for intensive itinerant evangelizing among the mass of the populace, and men like the Independent, Edmund Jones of Pontypool, and the Baptist, Miles Harry of Blaenau Gwent, were already giving a lead when the Methodists first appeared. In Glamorgan itself, though the Baptists, on account of their convictions concerning adult baptism, were not well-disposed to the Methodists, most of the leading Independent ministers—David Williams of Watford, James Davies of Merthyr, Henry Davies of Cymer, Joseph Simmons of Neath, and Lewis Jones of Bridgend—welcomed and assisted the earliest efforts of Howell Harris, as indeed did a number of Anglican ministers (see below, pp. 499–504). No single group in the Christian community of the eighteenth century had a monopoly of conscience, idealism, or good intentions.[84]

APPENDIX B

MINISTERS AND SCHOOLMASTERS EJECTED IN GLAMORGAN, 1660–1662

This list is based on information drawn from the following sources: E. Calamy, *An Account of the Ministers Ejected*, vol. II; R. T. Jones and B. G. Owens, 'Anghydffurfwyr Cymru', *Y Cofiadur*, 32 (1962), 3–93; *Llandaff Records*, vol. II; T. Rees, *Protestant Nonconformity*; T. Richards, *Religious Developments, 1654–1662*. (Abbreviations used: c. conformed; e. ejected; Lland. Reg. Llandaff Registers; p. presented.)

Davies, David	E. Neath under Act of September, 1660.
Davies, Griffith	E. Gelli-gaer, September 1660–summer 1662. However, Lland. Reg. July 1662 records the death of ( ) Davies, previous incumbent.
Davies, Rees	E. Flemingston, 1660. C. and p. May 10, 1661 Michaelstone-le-pit which he held until his death, 1680.
Ellis, Edmund	E. St. Fagan's, 1660, to make way for 'lawful' parson.
Flower, Benjamin	E. Cardiff, 1660, to make way for 'lawful' parson.
French, John	E. Wenvoe, 1662.

Griffith, Evan	E. Oxwich, 1662. C. later and held livings in Gloucestershire.
Higgs, Daniel	E. Rhosili, 1660. P. Porteynon. E. Porteynon, 1662.
Hiliard, Thomas	E. Newton Nottage, 1661. C. later, according to Calamy, but there is no proof of this. Lland. Reg. records death of previous but unnamed incumbent of Newton Nottage, October 1661.
Jones, James	E. Llangyfelach, 1660. Patent Rolls, July 4, 1660, record him as moved to Cilybebyll; but Lland. Reg. and NLW MS. 16260 record Owen Evans at Cilybebyll April 27, 1631–June 5, 1662, when succeeded by William Phillips, who was there until 1695.
Jones, Jenkin	E. Cadoxton-juxta-Neath, according to Calamy; but this seems unproven (*DWB, s.n.*)
Jones, Morgan	E. Llanmadog under Act of September 1660. C. later and licensed as schoolmaster, 1663.
Jones, Morgan	E. Newcastle (Bridgend), 1660.
Jones, Samuel	E. Llangynwyd, 1662.
Joseph, Thomas	E. Llangeinwyr under Act of September 1660.
Matthews, Marmaduke	E. Swansea, 1662.
Matthews, Mordecai	E. Llancarfan, 1660. C. and p. Reynoldston, April 16, 1661.
Miles, John	E. Ilston, 1660.
Miller, Joshua	E. St. Andrews, 1660, to make way for 'lawful' parson.
Nicholls, Henry	E. Coychurch, 1660, to make way for 'lawful' parson. C. and p. Neath, 1667. Died 1670. But, note, a Henry Nicholls also p. St. Brides and Michaelston-super-Ely, March 16, 1671/2.
Powell, John	E. St. Lythan's, 1660. Charles II named his successor.
Proud, Thomas	E. Cheriton under Act of September 1660.
Thomas, Howell	E. Glyncorrwg, 1660.
Thomas, William	E. St. Mary Hill, 1661.

Schoolmasters

Llywelyn, Evan	E. Swansea.
Seal, George	E. Cardiff.

APPENDIX C

LICENCES ISSUED IN GLAMORGAN UNDER THE DECLARATION OF INDULGENCE OF 1672

Place	Licence	Date of issue	Sect
Baglan	Robert Thomas at his own house	July 16	Congregationalist
Bishopston	The house of Henry Griffith	April 20	Congregationalist
Bride's, St.	The house of Widow Williams	June 15	Baptist
Bridgend	Thomas Joseph at his own house	June 15	Baptist
Cardiff	John French at his own house	June 15	Presbyterian
Cildeudy	The house of Rees Powell	November 18	Presbyterian
Cowbridge	Samuel Jones at the house of Eve Christopher	September 30	Presbyterian
Eglwysilan	Thomas John at the house of William John	August 10	Independent
Gelli-gaer	The house of Lewis Rees	August 10	Congregationalist
Goetre-hen	Samuel Jones at the house of Rees Powell	April 30	Presbyterian

Place	Licence	Date of issue	Sect
Kenfig	Jacob Christopher at the house of Lewis Alward	July 16	Independent
Llanfabon	The house of William Rowlands	August 10	Congregationalist
Llangewydd	The house of Llewellyn Morgan	June 15	Baptist
Llangynwyd	Samuel Jones at his own house	April 30	Presbyterian
Margam	Samuel Jones at his own house	June 15	Independent
Merthyr Tydfil	Henry Williams at the house of Howell Rees	February 3, 1673	Independent
Neath	The house of Elizabeth Morgan	November 18	Presbyterian
Newton Nottage	Watkin Cradock at his own house	July 16	Independent
Newton Nottage	Howell Thomas at the house of William Andrews	June 15	Baptist
Nicholaston	The house of Robert Gethin	April 20	Congregationalist
Rhosili	The house of Richard Bevan	April 20	Congregationalist
Swansea	Daniel Higgs at his own house	April 17	Congregationalist
Swansea	The house of Stephen Hughes	April 20	Congregationalist
Swansea	Marmaduke Matthews at his own house	April 12	Independent
Swansea	Lewis Thomas at the house of William Dykes	September 30	Baptist
Wenvoe	Joshua Miller at the house of Morgan Thomas	June 15	Presbyterian

The details given above are derived from the table printed in Thomas Richards, *Wales under the Indulgence*, p. 158.

iii

CALVINISTIC METHODISM IN GLAMORGAN, 1737–1773

By GOMER MORGAN ROBERTS

HOWELL HARRIS AND THE BEGINNINGS OF METHODISM IN GLAMORGAN, 1738–1740

The pioneer of Methodism in Glamorgan was Howell Harris of Trevecka, the fiery evangelist who preached throughout Wales between 1735 and 1750, establishing societies and organizing the movement which bears the imprint of his personality to this day. On February 16, 1738 Harris received a letter from the Rev. Philip Thomas, curate of Gelli-gaer, informing him that his patron had reprimanded him for consorting with the revivalist, and warning him that he would not receive priest's orders unless he would 'be more true to the Church' than he was.[85] It is evident that Harris had visited Thomas's parish, probably during the summer of 1737. Evidence of an early visit to Glamorgan is found in Harris's handwriting on the back of a letter written in April 1738.[86] It seems that he had promised to write to the Rev. David Williams of Pwll-y-pant, the Independent minister of Watford and Cardiff, in June

1738, and had arranged a visit to the parishes of Llantrisant and Eglwysilan. In a brief note he mentions Morgan Evan of Ffynnon Rhingyll in the latter parish, and Thomas Phillips, dyer, of Dyffryn Crawnon. There is a reference, too, to 'Caerffyli Fair (a fortnight before Augt)'. David Williams had sent him a letter on May 17, 1738 informing him that he had been announced to preach in two places in Eglwysilan, viz., at Bwlch-y-cwm on Whitsun Wednesday, and the following day at Maesdiofal above Senghennydd.[87] David Williams was a man of liberal views and had worked in harmony with Philip Thomas, the Methodist curate of Gelli-gaer.

Very little is known of Harris's first visits to the county. He was acquainted, too, with the Rev. Henry Davies, the Independent minister of Blaen-gwrach in the Vale of Neath (above, pp. 491–92). Writing from Nantcelyn, Ystradyfodwg on June 9, 1738 he informed Harris that many people had been disappointed because they did not hear him at Aberdare and Lan, Llanwynno.[88] Harris had been taken ill, and that explains why he did not fulfil his intention of preaching in those places. David Williams wrote to him on June 12, informing him of the great expectations which had been raised at Llanwynno, Llantrisant and St. Nicholas. 'The two days' service with us', he wrote, 'has been attended with marvellous success. The churches and meetings are crowded, sabbath-breaking goes down; it is looked upon as a very abominable thing; dancing has been much interrupted, profane swearing and cock-fighting are exclaimed against. But you do not imagine that the devil is mute and still; no, he both speaks and acts, but I think there seems to be more against him than for him in this part of the country. Your friends are more numerous than your adversaries; you are preached against in some places, but it turns to the reproach of them who attempt it.'[89]

During his illness Harris had received many appeals to visit the county. One letter, dated June 23, 1738, came from Howell Griffith of Treferig Uchaf, Llantrisant. 'My Heart and house', he writes in a postscript, 'is always Ready for you and all Godly men of what denomination soever.'[90] Henry Davies informed him on July 11: 'I have one good news to tell you—young people come together from 40 to 60 to read, pray and exhort one another near the place where they formerly transgressed on the Lord's day. I hear that Counsellor Williams near Neath is for your coming to his house and another serious clergyman who is hated by most of his brethren for his doing good.'[91] Counsellor Williams's identity is unknown to me, but the Rev. William Thomas, the curate of Llanilltud Nedd, was probably the 'serious clergyman'. Other letters were addressed to Trevecka in July 1738 by Williams and Davies. Williams, writing on July 14 made arrangements for Harris to visit various places—St. Nicholas, Llanedern, Eglwysilan, &c. 'I should have told you', he wrote, 'that you are expected from our parish to

Gelly-gaer. The curate, who called the other night at our house, is for promoting it all he can; though he may act a little behind the curtains, being now about to receive priest's orders. He is the friendliest of all the clergy hereabouts, preaches with much life, and endeavours to do all the good he can in the parish. I would not advise you to anything prejudicial to the cause, which I hope I can say I have at heart; but I may tell you, that you need not be so *shy* of conversing with Dissenters in these parts, as in some places, for, blessed be God, prejudice is falling off more and more here.'[92] In another letter, written on July 28, Williams suggested that it would be better for Harris to postpone his visit 'till after ye harvest'. He also suggested a preaching tour, beginning at Basaleg, on to Llanedern, Eglwysilan, St. Nicholas and towards Llantrisant (to hear the Rev. Richard Harris, the vicar, on a Sunday), and thence to Gelli-gaer. 'Dont forget St. Nicholas', he wrote, 'because you are so much expected there, and otherwise it will be given out by some that you are afraid to come there.'[93] Henry Davies wrote him a letter on the same day, and gave him some very interesting information concerning the Neath area. 'That serious, zealous, and pious man, Mr. William Thomas, clergyman at Lantwit-juxta-Neath', he wrote, 'is very desirous to see and to have your company. He came to hear you at the Abbey, but was disappointed, and so many thousands more. He was reproved by a bitter clergyman who lives at Neath. The clergy are divided one against another in our parts. A captain of the cock matches, who heard you at Bettws [possibly Cwrt y Betws, near Neath], promises never to follow that wicked game any longer; and another *dux omnium malorum*, near the sea side, did cut off the heads of his cocks when he went home after he heard you. I have seen him last Lord's day, and he appears a serious hearer. He did invite me to his house. I find there is much reformation in many since you have been this way, which calls loud upon you to come again as soon as possible. A great gentleman's lady, a lawyer below us, is very much for to come to hear you, and he is contrary.'[94] There is a gap in Harris's diary during July 5–29, 1738; but it is evident, from Henry Davies's letter, that he had been preaching in the Neath area during the month.

In August 1738, Harris took a short journey through the county.[95] He came from Blaenau Gwent to Gelli-gaer, and then travelled towards Llanbradach and Pentwyndela in Llanedern, and Llanishen. One of his converts in this district was Thomas William of Melin Corrwg in Eglwysilan, who was soon to become an exhorter and one of Harris's chief supporters in Glamorgan. At Mynydd Llwyndiddan (between Llanishen and St. Nicholas) he met with some opposition from a local clergyman and a lawyer. A constable was ordered to apprehend him, but nothing untoward happened. On Sunday, August 6, he attended the ministry of the Rev. Richard Harris, vicar of Llantrisant. The vicar inveighed against him and denounced his preaching with such force that he felt quite despondent. He made up his mind not to preach any more, and after the service he approached the vicar to confess his faults and endured his reprimands in silence. He had no heart to address the immense crowd that had gathered together to hear him, and eventually he wended his way broken-hearted towards Treferig Uchaf, the home of Howell Griffith. The next morning he met Henry Davies, who inspired him to go forward. From thence he went cross-country towards Neath, where he addressed a gathering of three thousand people at Neath Abbey. Here he enjoyed the fellowship of Henry Davies, William Thomas, the curate of Llanilltud Nedd, and Joseph Simmons, the Independent minister. Simmons lived near Neath Abbey, where he kept an academy for young preachers; and Harris stayed the night with his new friend. Someone at Neath gave him five shillings and six pence as a gift, and the man's generosity rejoiced his soul. On his way towards Llanelli he heard that the press-gang was after him.

After this short preaching tour Harris received many letters from his correspondents in Glamorgan. Howell Griffith, writing on September 16, alluded to 'Our Society'. 'I keep it at my tenant's house and my own house every Sabath night, and another at the next parish att the Cymer in the lower end of Ystradyvodwck parish and that mightily encreases.'[96] The last-named society, kept possibly at Garth-y-fforest (now called Pen-y-graig) was the incipient Independent church of Cymer. These gatherings in private houses must have been the first Methodist societies in Glamorgan. Further information concerning these early societies is derived from Henry Davies's letter, dated September 21. 'This week', he wrote, 'I have been down towards Cowbridge. Esquire Rees [Hopkin Rees, near St. Mary Hill] and his lady and other serious Christians are for your coming here. I beg you would come over to Aberdare, Llanwonno, and near Esquire Rees's house. You know you had much assistance of the good and great God at Ystradyfodog, and now, blessed be God, there are some fruits appearing at Ystrad. There are some 40 or 50, and near Llantrisant they come together to read and pray and sing Psalms. There is a visible reformation in young and old, though much opposition.'[97] David Williams, too, wrote on October 17. 'Meetings here are crowded', he reported. 'There be sixteen that have bespoke communion next time at Cardiff. Doors are opening in places not expected. I have been last Saturday night at Lan-st-fred [St. Bride's-super-Ely] where came together by Night an Hundred & fifty people at least . . . I hope God has a kindness for that young woman in Caerphilly. She lately contriv'd to meet me with a few friends in a private House . . . She stole away last Thursday night to ye meeting in our House.'[98] In a further letter, dated December 29, Williams alluded to meetings at Ynys Angharad, Pont-y-pridd, and Pentre-bach ('where people crowded to hear'). A churchman, it is stated, lived there. 'It is an exceeding large house where you can make a thousand to hear, and there I am desired to bring you and no place more needful.'[99]

Just before Christmas Harris came to Llachart-fawr near the old Gellionnen Chapel, and afterwards to Ton-y-planwydd near Neath. On January 5, 1739 we find him at Ty'n-y-faen in Coychurch, and the next day with Hopkin Rees at St. Mary Hill.[100] His next call was at Collennau in Tonyrefail, the home of the Prichard family, which was to become a strong pillar of Methodism in Glamorgan for many years. It was a Sunday, and he attended morning service at Llanhari. He met Henry Davies in the afternoon, and in hearing him praying was in much straitness of spirit. The same day he received a letter from the celebrated George Whitefield, which rejoiced his soul. On Monday he was at Treferig with Howell Griffith, and crossed the mountain to Cymer, preaching on the way. Then he went to Ynys Angharad, and during the week he preached at Parc (Eglwysilan) and Ty'n-y-coed. At Llanbradach-fach a Baptist opposed him, but he was in no mood to quarrel. Before the end of the week he was at Werndomen, a farm near Caerphilly, where once again the Baptists caused him some trouble.[101] James Davies, the Independent minister of Cwm-y-glo, near Merthyr, wrote him a letter on January 13, inviting him to 'spend hours one day again at Rhiw'r Ychen, another at Gwaelod-y-garth [in the same district] where [you were] before at Merthyr'.[102] Harris, probably, had preached there in June 1738 on his way to Monmouthshire.

On February 7, 1739 David Williams informed Harris of 'three societies now going on not far from Cardiff'. He adds: 'The Society in Cardiff present their love and service.'[103] This early society had been revived by William Seward of Badsey, Worcs., in 1738; it met at the house of Thomas Glascott, and in 1740 it became a *Wesleyan* Methodist Society.[104] Early in March 1739 George Whitefield came to Cardiff. On his way he had met the Rev. Nathaniel Wells, the rector of St. Andrew's who served occasionally at St. John's, Cardiff. Wells was no friend of the Methodists—at least, not of the *Calvinistic* Methodists. (Later, he became the friend of the Wesley brothers; it was he who first invited Charles Wesley to Wales, possibly to weaken Harris's influence!). He refused to enter the boat at the New Passage because of Whitefield's presence. Whitefield came to Cardiff on March 7, and on arriving he preached in the Town Hall from the judge's seat to a congregation of about a hundred hearers; after the service he saw Howell Harris for the first time. On the morrow Whitefield preached again in the Town Hall to a large assembly, Harris sitting close to him. 'I did not observe any scoffers within', wrote Whitefield in his journal, 'but without some were pleased to honour me so far, as to trail a dead fox, and hunt it round about the Hall.' After the service he and Harris, together with two Dissenting ministers, went to public worship. He preached again in the afternoon, 'and prayed with the Religious Society, whose room was quite thronged'.[105]

It would be tedious to follow Howell Harris on his preaching tours in Glamorgan. He varied his journeys, of course, proceeding sometimes from the direction of Blaen Glyn Tawe towards Swansea or Neath; on other occasions he would come from Merthyr or Gelli-gaer (from Monmouthshire) towards Cardiff. He would follow the highway to the west from Cardiff, taking in his stride the Vale of Glamorgan and then proceeding towards Llansamlet and Pontarddulais. Sometimes he would strike up to the highland parishes of Ystradyfodwg and Aberdare. In his trail he left small groups of converts here and there, and before long these groups would be organized into societies.

During his travels in Glamorgan Harris became friendly with all sorts of people. We have already noted four Nonconformist ministers; to these we may add another name, the Rev. Lewis Jones, the Independent minister of Bridgend, who wrote a letter on February 7, 1741, in which he referred to a letter sent by Daniel Rowland of Llangeitho to Henry Davies.[106] We have noted, too, two Anglican clergymen who favoured his ministry. In a letter to Howell Harris, dated October 6, 1750, Susanna Young of St. George's referred to 'ye Minister of Wenvoe, Mr. Hodges, who is a gospel preacher'.[107] The Rev. John Hodges, the rector of Wenvoe, is better known by reason of his association with the Wesley brothers. He was a member of the first three Wesleyan Methodist conferences, but he was friendly with the Welsh Methodists too. A few of Harris's lay supporters have been mentioned, but no reference has been made to John Deer of St. Nicholas and Thomas Price, the squire of Plas y Watford near Caerphilly. The latter was a member of David Williams's congregation, and one of the trustees of the chapel erected near Plas y Watford in 1739. He was a justice of the peace—William Williams of Pantcelyn styled him 'Price y Justis' in an elegy he composed in memory of Grace Price, his daughter-in-law. Harris, Whitefield and the two Wesleys enjoyed his hospitality at Plas y Watford, and they all found him a sound defender of Methodism.

CHAPELS AND SOCIETIES, 1740–1742

Towards the end of 1740 relations between Howell Harris and David Williams became strained. In November Harris wrote a long letter to his friend (it is not clear *when* the letter was delivered) complaining that Williams 'had more oratory than Demonstration of spirit & experience & heart searching Doctrine' in his ministry to the young converts. He charged him with being unsound in his views on the doctrine of Assurance. He set forth thirty-two questions, demanding an answer forthwith. 'It is not enough to *allow* that there *are* people who have Assurance', he wrote, 'and then to say that this assurance is not an absolute necessity for salvation.'[108] David Williams, in a letter written in December

1740, expressed surprise 'that one who formerly made it his business to expose Biggottry should himself be a great example of it'. He reminded Harris 'that yᵉ Interest of Religion and yᵉ Interest of a Party are very different things'.[109] This correspondence marked the end of the friendship between the two men. In his diary under March 27 Harris wrote: 'Mr. David Williams continues to be in the gall of bitterness, and things have been set in this light before the ministers'.[110] Harris seems to have been proud of his long letter to Williams. He read it, for instance, at Watford in the monthly society held there in March, 1741, and the following day he recorded in his diary: 'Having sat up all night with the brethren from 8 miles round, reading a letter I had wrote to Mr. David Williams about assurance and weak faith, and agreed upon it'.[111]

Harris had written to Thomas Price on February 16, 1741. 'I fear Satan yᵉ great Divider of yᵉ Brethren is sowing his Tares', he wrote, 'O let us lift up strong cries to yᵉ maker of unity, to heal our Breaches.'[112] Price, it must be admitted, was in a difficult position. He was a trustee of David Williams's chapel at Watford, but he cast in his lot with Harris. Henry Davies—on March 17, at least—was friendly. Writing to Harris on that date he urged him to do his utmost to persuade George Whitefield to visit Glamorgan.[113] Howell Griffith, in a letter dated May 7, 1741, had heard that Whitefield was due to visit Cardiff that week, but he had been misinformed. In the same letter Griffith referred to a 'Society at ty newydd about a mile below Llantrissent Town' where many people congregated.[114] The early Methodists were very careful in naming their places of worship. 'Chapel' had an ecclesiastical flavour, and 'Meeting-house' savoured of Nonconformity; in consequence they favoured non-committal terms such as 'New House', 'Society House', 'New Room' or 'School-house'. Harris preached at the 'New House near Llantrisant' in March 1742.[115] Was this place an edifice specially built for the purpose of worship? There are no records available, so the question must remain an open one.

Howell Harris began to think of building places of worship in 1741. 'Riches I don't desire', he confided to his diary in November, 1741, 'and had I 10,000*l* I must give it away in building Society Houses.' Thomas Price of Watford put theory into practice, and he referred to the project in a letter he wrote to Harris on October 24, 1741. 'According to our last agreement', he wrote, 'we have been discoursing about building a Society house, the Brethren all of whom excepting two or three are unanimously resolved to go on with it; we have also fixed a spott of ground with Bro. Thos. Evans ye which he gives us gratis, and lyes very convenient between the Pentyrch and Lantaf and our Societies; we have also subscribed in the private bands about 12 pounds towards it but as we see that will be a great deal too little to carry on ye great work which will att least cost between thirty or five and thirty pounds building.' He urged Harris to acquaint the Methodist societies in other counties of the design, and to desire their contributions.[116] On January 24, 1742

Harris and his brethren at Watford 'consulted about building a Society House' there, and they agreed to build on the site at Waun-fach, Groes-wen. In February at Llanddewibrefi, Cardiganshire, Harris 'made a Collection towards a School House in Glamorganshire'.[117] Thomas Price had some qualms with regard to the safety of the New House, inasmuch as it would not be licensed as a Nonconformist meeting-house. He evidently shared his fears with Harris, and on September 30 the matter was dealt with in a letter. 'As for your Query', wrote Harris, 'what is to be done with the House? As 'tis yᵉ Lord's and no one can legally tear it down; the Building of it as a dwelling House, or as yᵉ Property of any of you, and then only converted to publick Use, will as much entitle it to his Majesty's Protection as it 'twere licensed.' Where did the threat come from? 'If tis unlawful', wrote Harris, 'Let it be drawn down in a legal Manner in his Majesty's Name, to whose Protection no Mob can fly, tho' Headed by Men of the highest Rank.'[118] The legal deed had been signed on June 16, 1742 by Thomas Price, William Morgan, and Thomas Evans. The assignment referred to a 'building lately erected for a Society or Meeting House for and towards public worship of God or a school for the education of children'.[119] It was still in the process of being built in the autumn, for on October 20, 1742 Harris recorded in his diary, 'Then I said of Wales . . . They have now a House a-building, & have made 20l. towards it, & want 15l. more'.[120] By the end of the year the building was completed, the first Methodist place of worship in Wales.

The Welsh Methodists, from the beginning, had been much concerned with ordering their societies. Harris and the other Methodist leaders were staunch members of the Church of England, and they counselled the new converts to communicate in their parish churches. This policy became a bone of contention later on, owing to the tendency of many converts to communicate in the meeting-houses. The converts, after all, had to owe allegiance to some ecclesiastical body or other. However, much freedom was allowed, and that eased the situation. In the ordering of the societies Harris favoured Presbyterianism. 'Independency, to me', he declared at the end of 1741, 'is not right'.[121] David Williams of Pwll-y-pant, was present in a preliminary conference of ministers of all denominations held at Glyn, Defynnog, in October 1740, where rules for the societies were discussed. A system of Monthly and Bi-Monthly Societies was organized. In the Monthly Societies stewards and exhorters met to compare notes and to discuss matters concerning the societies within a certain area. In the Bi-Monthly Societies these local leaders met the superintendents to report on the state of the various societies.[122] Early in March, 1741, Harris was at Tonna, near Neath, organizing Monthly Societies. Some of the converts here wanted to join with Lewis Jones, the Independent minister of Bridgend, but Harris resisted them. A few days afterwards he was at a Bi-Monthly

Society at Watford, where rules were discussed; it was agreed that the leaders were to meet in future every two months in Glamorgan.[123]

THE REVIVAL GAINS GROUND, 1741–1742

In the meantime the religious awakening was gaining ground in Glamorgan. In May and June 1741 Harris spent a fortnight preaching in the county. In Bridgend he heard 'that Lord Mansel of Margam' had forbidden him to preach at Hafod, a house on his estate. He enjoyed the hospitality of Lewis Jones, the Dissenting minister. In the Swansea area he was welcomed by John Rosser of Wig Uchaf, Cwmbwrla.[124] Rosser was a member of the Independent church which met at Tir-dwncyn, but a mixed gathering of Methodists and Nonconformists met at his house.[125] In a letter dated August 30, 1741 Howell Griffith informed Harris that Charles Wesley had been during the previous week at Fonmon Castle in the Vale, the home of Robert Jones.[126] The squire of Fonmon was the friend of Harris and the Wesleys and always gave them a hearty welcome to his mansion. But in the struggle between Arminianism and Calvinism Robert Jones favoured the former, and sided with the Wesleys.[127] John Deer, too, (in a letter to Harris dated September 15, 1741) referred to Charles Wesley's visit, and he added these ominous words, 'I need not tell you what doctrine he do preach'.[128] Susanna Young, the schoolteacher of Drope near St. George's, in a letter dated October 30, 1741 alluded to the preaching of Herbert Jenkins of Monmouthshire and James Beaumont of Radnorshire (two well-known Methodist exhorters) in Cardiff, Dinas Powys and Tre-hyl in St. Nicholas.[129]

On October 12, 1741 Joseph Simmons of Neath (who kept a school in Swansea at the time) wrote a letter to Harris. 'I earnestly desire', he urged, 'you would be pleased to give a turn to the lower part of Gower once again among the English, who have a great desire to hear you.' In a postscript he added, 'If Mr. Whitefield is with you, please to bring him to Swanzey if you can prevail with him.'[130] Whitefield was in Scotland, but he had a mind to visit Wales in the near future on an affair of the heart. In November 1741 an interesting event in the annals of Methodism took place in Glamorgan. George Whitefield came to Plas y Watford on November 13, and on the following day he and Mrs. Elizabeth James of Abergavenny were married at St. Martin's Church, Caerphilly, the Rev. John Smith officiating.[131] Henry Davies wrote a letter to Harris on November 1. 'Our faithfull friend Howell Griffith, & other Christian friends', he wrote, 'is very desirous of having your company in our neighbourhood.' He added, 'The Pious old woman of Abernant & her son is desirous of your coming to their House: Her Husband is Dead.'[132]

In May 1742 Howell Harris went to Llansamlet on the invitation of John Richard, who had been converted under his ministry some time previously. Richard had sent him a Welsh letter on January 3, 1742 informing him that some of his brethren had urged him to form a private society. He invited Harris to the parish in order to instruct them in regulating the society.[133] Six or more societies met there in May, and they decided to provide for the necessities of Richard William Dafydd of Llandyfaelog, Carmarthenshire, who visited them occasionally.[134] In a letter to Thomas Price on May 15, 1742 Harris referred to the societies between Neath and Margam which were under Dafydd's care. 'He is very poor in the world', he wrote, 'having a wife and two Children, but a Sweet Soul full of God.'[135] A Monthly Society had been arranged for the district, to meet near Neath about the end of May.

There was some trouble at Watford in July 1742, when Thomas Price was 'for going from the Church', but later he was 'made easy about staying'.[136] Harris wrote to Howell Griffith from London on September 2, explaining how matters were ordered in Whitefield's congregation in Moorfields. The single men met together in bands, and the married men met apart; so, too, with the women, but once a week they met together.[137] In the Monthly Meeting at the 'New House', Groes-wen, on November 17 Morgan John Lewis of New Inn and Thomas Price 'differ'd about settling the class Bands'. Lewis thought that the men and women should meet apart, but Price insisted on adopting the London society scheme.[138]

In October 1742 Harris wrote two letters to Whitefield. In his first letter he referred to 'Mr. Thomas . . . Curate to Mr. Hodges of Wenvo'.[139] He administered the Sacrament every Sunday, and many Methodists, presumably, communicated there. In his second letter he observed that 'Mr. Thomas of Kelly Gâr assists Mr. Hodges at Wenvo'. He alluded, of course, to Philip Thomas of Gelli-gaer, who, in or about 1741, became curate to the Rev. John Hodges of Wenvoe. Harris referred, too, to 'another old man, one Mr. Price, near Swanzey, that preaches ye Truth . . . He loves us sweetly and receives us to his Communion.'[140] He was the Rev. John Price, vicar of Llangyfelach, who was very friendly with the Methodists in his neighbourhood.

METHODIST ASSOCIATIONS AND EXHORTERS, 1743–1744

We have already noticed the tendency among some Methodists to leave the communion of the Church of England and become Dissenters. Harris abhorred the idea and fought against it with all his might. He thought that Whitefield might be able to help him in combating this disaffection. A General Association of the leaders of Welsh and English Calvinistic Methodism had been arranged, and Harris hoped that this meeting would settle this matter once and for all. This association was held at Plas y Watford and the 'New House' at Groes-wen early in January 1743.[141] It was thought, until recently, that this meeting was the first Welsh Methodist Association, but modern research has established the fact that the first formative associations of Welsh Methodism were held in Carmarthenshire in 1742. However, the famous Watford Association was the first joint association of the Welsh and English movements, and therein lies its importance. The members gathered together on January 5 in the 'New Room' at Groes-wen, and afterwards at Plas y Watford. George Whitefield was chosen moderator, and the following brethren (amongst many others) were present: Daniel Rowland of Llangeitho (who preached a sermon on the occasion), John Powell (rector of Llanmartin and Wilcrick, near Newport), William Williams of Pantycelyn, and Howell Harris (representing the Welsh movement); and Joseph Humphreys and John Cennick (representing the English societies). Their main task at Watford was the appointment of private exhorters to visit and superintend the societies in the various districts. The following appointments were made to the work in Glamorgan:

Howell Griffith; Llantrisant and Glynogwr.
Richard Thomas; Llanedern and to assist at Watford.
John Belcher; Visitor of the Single Brethren at Watford.
William Price; Visitor of the Married Brethren at Watford.
Thomas Evans to the care of outward things at Watford.
William Price and William Morgan; Visitors of the Married Men at Watford.
Thomas Price to the care of Watford.
Henry Harris to help Thomas Price.
William Powell to the care of the societies at his house.
Thomas Lewis; Pen-tyrch and 'New House'.
Richard Jones and John Deer; Aberthin, Llanilid and Aberddawan.
Morgan John; Palleg (near Ystradgynlais), Creunant, and Cwmaman (Carms.).
John Richard was approved.

It was agreed that all who had scruples about receiving the Sacrament either in Church or meeting-house should continue to receive in Church till God would open a plain door for leaving the Church.

Many of the names in the above list are known to us already. Howell Griffith was an educated man if we can judge by his letters; he died December 26, 1753, aged 49.[142] Richard Thomas lived at the Ball House, across the river Rhymni opposite Llanedern, near Cardiff; he died there in 1751.[143] John Belcher (or Bellchamber) was a native of Eglwysilan.[144] Thomas Evans and William Morgan were two trustees of the 'New House' of Groes-wen. William Powell was a native of Caerphilly and was a member of the Groes-wen Society; he lived at one time in Brynllefrith, Llanfabon, and the early Methodist society of that parish met at his house.[145] Very little is known of Thomas Lewis; probably he was a Glamorgan man.[146] Richard Jones and John Deer were members of the Tre-hyl Society, St. Nicholas; Deer died in 1743.[147] Morgan John, it is thought by some, was Morgan John Lewis of New Inn, but that is hardly possible as they are mentioned separately in some association minutes. In a letter to Whitefield written on January 25, 1743 Harris observed that on the previous Sunday (at St. Nicholas and Pen-tyrch)

[509]

he had settled John Deer, Richard Jones and John Yeoman ('three very solid souls') to overlook five societies in the district; and that on the previous night, at Watford, Thomas William, Thomas Lewis and William Edward were appointed to overlook '6 more societies between them alternately'. Richard Thomas, John Belcher and Evan Thomas Jacob were chosen to visit '5 more Societies by turns'.[148] Very little is known of Evan Thomas Jacob, but William Edward was the famous bridge-builder. He was a member of the Groes-wen Society.

Details concerning the work in Glamorgan are found in the minutes of subsequent associations.[149] At Llanddeusant, on February 3, 1743, Thomas Price of Llandeilo Tal-y-bont was ordered to be silent until the next association. It was arranged that John Jones of Caeo, Carmarthenshire, should settle near Neath in order to superintend the societies in Creunant, Hafod (Margam), Neath, &c. John Richard of Llansamlet was to assist him, together with George Phillips at Neath and Hafod. John Jones might be identified with the hymnist of that name whose hymns were printed in Pantycelyn's *Aleluia* in 1747. George Phillips was a native of Neath; he was described 'a Thunderbolt of a Methodist preacher' by William Thomas (the Glamorgan diarist) when he died in 1762.[150] At Glanyrafon-ddu, March 1, it was 'agreed that John Richard of Llansamlet should take care & exhort in the Societies of . . . Casllwchwr, Llandremôr, Llangyfelach, Llansamlet, Neath, Havod [Margam], Creinant, Palleg. That he should see these once a fortnight—one every day, and to be assisted by John Jones of Cayo, who is to visit 'em once a month to go about one week & to work the other'. George Phillips was to assist at Neath and Hafod, Morgan John at Palleg and Creunant, and Edward Meurig at Casllwchwr on trial. Hopkin John of Llangyfelach was to remain at home and come to the next association to be catechized. Thomas William of Eglwysilan was present at the Watford Association on April 6, 1743, and he was appointed to superintend the Glamorgan societies as far as Llantrisant. He was to be assisted by E. Evans, William Powell, Thomas Price, William Edward, Thomas Lewis, Richard Jones, John Yeoman, and Howell Griffith. John Powell, the rector of Llanmartin, was elected moderator of the Monthly Societies of Glamorgan and Monmouthshire. At Watford on May 11, Thomas Price was confirmed as the steward of the Groes-wen Society as before, and he was urged to assist Thomas William in his rounds. The men and women were to meet apart. At Llandremôr Uchaf (near Pontarddulais) it was agreed that John Richard should be superintendent over the societies at Neath, Creunant, Palleg, Casllwchwr, Llandeilo-fach, and Llansamlet, and be assisted by George Phillips. John and Edward Meurig, 'if they are not turned out by their Parents, should exhort privately under the Inspection of John Richard'.

John Richard, early in his career as an exhorter, rebelled against the authority of the association. It had been decided at Watford in April

1743 that every superintendent should keep a book containing the names of their private exhorters, together with the names of every member of the societies under their care. It was decided, too, that the members should be divided into groups or classes on the London pattern. These arrangements did not commend themselves to John Richard. He complained that the proposals were popish and unscriptural, and moreover he asserted that the appointment of superintendents to particular districts was not right. He had a mind to go where God called him, let the brethren say what they would. The matter was discussed at the Trevecka Association on June 29, and Whitefield was appointed to reply to his complaints. Whitefield wrote in conciliatory terms, but Richard was unrepentant. His contumacy was discussed at the Rhiw'r Adar Association in July, and all the Welsh societies were warned not to accept him on the grounds that he was a disturber of the peace. He attended the Gellidochlaethe Association in November, and according to Harris's diary he read the names of those under his care. His wife fell ill and his worldly circumstances became desperate. He capitulated at last and wrote a letter to his brethren expressing his sorrow for being so stubborn and pig-headed. He was allowed to visit the societies once again, and in the Trevecka Association in May 1744 it was agreed that Thomas Jones should engage himself in Richard's service. He was a bookbinder by trade, and in the minutes of the Nantmel Association October 18, 1744 we find this note: 'Agreed that Brother Richard Tibbot should go to Brother John Richard to learn ye trade of Book-binding'.[151]

Henry Davies of Cymer was present at the Watford Association on January 4, 1744. A letter was received from the Cnap-llwyd Society (near Morriston) requesting that George Phillips might go there occasionally to assist them; the request was granted. At Llandremôr Association on April 19 a similar request was made by the Gorseinon Society with regard to Richard William Dafydd; he and his brother were allowed to go there. This brother was David Williams of Llandyfaelog—afterwards of Llyswyrny—who was to play a prominent part in the Methodist movement in Glamorgan.[152] An association was held at Watford on April 25. After a long discussion it was agreed here that the private exhorters should not exhort publicly, excepting William Edward of Groes-wen. A strong call for his service came from Llantrisant and Groes-wen. Edward Lloyd was nominated to catechize at Groes-wen, and other brethren in the various societies, viz. Samuel Jeremiah at Llanedern, William Thomas at Aberthin and Llanhari, Edward Edwards at Dinas Powys and St. Nicholas, Christopher Basset at Aberddawan, Howell Griffith or Morgan Howell at Llantrisant, William Hughes at Newton Nottage, and Jenkin Lewis at Hafod (Margam). John Belcher was elected a general superintendent instead of Herbert Jenkins over the districts cared for by John Richard, Thomas William, Thomas Price and Morgan John. He was directed to meet these brethren once a fortnight.

[511]

Richard Jones of St. Nicholas was reproved for worldliness and unfaithfulness. He was warned that if he did not reform he would not be allowed to visit the societies any longer. William Rees was excommunicated for his Antinomian tendencies. At the Trevecka Association on June 27, it was agreed, after consultation, that someone should assist Morgan John, Thomas Price, Thomas William, and John Richard. John Belcher was urged to assist them until the next association. The association held at Watford on September 28, 1744 was notable on account of so many thorny matters being discussed there. It was reported that Howell Griffith had been guilty of a misdemeanour. He expressed his deep contrition and in consequence was readmitted on condition that he would exercise more care in future. Harris had been deputed to interview Richard Jones of St. Nicholas, and he, too, would be readmitted on reforming. He avowed this two days later before the societies at St. Nicholas, and it was arranged that he and Thomas Lewis of Pwll-y-meirch were to exchange places on alternate Sundays. Stewards were chosen for the societies at St. Nicholas, St. Andrews, Aberthin, and Aberddawan. It seems that Thomas William had spoken against the cassock and gown—meaning, presumably, the clergy—but he confessed that he did not object to these things as such but against making idols of them. William Powell also confessed that he had charged Thomas Price and John Belcher with unorthodoxy in some principles. Powell had been careless, too, in exhorting the people not to respect the preachers more than the ordinary members. He defended himself by arguing that it was not seemly to idolize the preachers. The members of this association must have had an uncomfortable session!

Some of John Richard's reports to the association have survived.[153] They are written in Welsh, and one of them, written on June 20, 1744, may be translated as follows:

Hafod, Margam. I believe that they grow daily in the knowledge of the impossibility of being justified before the bar of righteousness except through the righteousness of the man Christ Jesus.

Llansamlet. They are made more industrious in God's work by being made free in their souls from prejudice, and made to love one another more.

Creunant. I was there lately and they complained that there was great negligence in coming together in their midst, and this is a cause of distrust, and a lack of sympathy with one another.

Gorseinon. They are mostly under a necessity of being sanctified, that they might believe that their souls are righteous before God; they are unable to confess this yet, but this is the language of their hearts. They live quite blamelessly.

Cnap-llwyd. They have fallen out with one another—a debate as to where to hold the society. I have reason to believe, as they are so disobedient, that they have never experienced a conviction of sin.

Another unsigned report written in 1744 (by Thomas William, probably) gives us an idea of the strength of some societies.[154] Groes-wen Society was the strongest with 62 members ('most of them under grace: four were admitted lately'). St. Nicholas could boast of 22 members; three had died there lately, viz., Edward Evan, Evan William and Joan Rhaglan. There were 21 or 22 members at Aberthin, and 21 at Llantrisant together with eight on probation. Gelli-gaer Society consisted of only six or seven members; it was the weakest society in his round, or district. John Richard reports to Howell Harris in January 1745 that he and James Ingram (a Brecknockshire exhorter) had visited Newton in Gower. Ingram addressed the Gowerites in a language they could understand, but Richard, being a monoglot Welshman, had to be quiet. 'I never felt the need of the English language', he confessed, 'as at that time.'[155]

CRISES AND CONTROVERSIES, 1745–1747

The year 1745 saw a great crisis in the Methodist movement in Glamorgan. The exhorters of Groes-wen became convinced that a separation from the Church of England would solve many of their problems. On March 30, 1745 a Welsh letter, signed by Thomas Price, William Edward, Thomas William, John Belcher and Evan Thomas, was sent to the Caeo Association, Carmarthenshire, which met in the beginning of April. 'We see that God, from the outset', they argued, 'has given His Church an order . . . We think it is your duty to sympathise with us in this weighty matter; because it was at your advice we became messengers of God in an irregular way; and for all we know God has given us a measure of success; and will you, as good stewards of God's house, strive to carry on this great work until order is attained? It is most unlikely that any body of people ever remained in this fashion for all time. We have been expecting to get your views on this matter for nearly two years, and we do not see any indications that you have deliberated on this question as it deserves; but we fear that too many of the prejudices of your upbringing cling to you. We are of the opinion that you are too much attached to the Established Church.' It was a daring attack on the policy of the clerical leaders of Methodism. The new converts required 'a number of men to minister the Word and ordinances to them regularly [and] to undertake their oversight as shepherds over flocks'. They were unwilling to remain as they were. It was a plea, of course, for ordination. 'Brethren', they wrote, 'it pains us to hear that you cannot grant us liberty to exhort because we are not ordained, and that, as far as we can see, you do not care whether we shall be ordained or not. If your sympathy fails us, we feel that we must turn our eyes to some other direction; and may God direct us.' They appealed to apostolic practice; the laying of hands was practised in the early church in the case of all who ministered the Word—bishops, elders and deacons alike.[156]

The letter must have caused no little consternation at Caeo. No official reply to this communication exists, but Howell Harris had some pungent observations on the matter in his diary. He spoke of 'symptoms of pride and self appearing in the exhorters', and evidently he lashed out at them. He came to the Watford Association, held on April 25, with much trepidation, but he faced the problem squarely with the Glamorgan exhorters. 'I never looked on the Societies as Churches', he told them, 'but as little branches of a Church.' He had never thought of the exhorters as ministers to dispense ordinances; he never thought of the Methodists 'as a sect, but a people in a Church, called to reform' it. He made a powerful plea for staying within the Established Church and he succeeded in his efforts to quell the dissenting faction. He persuaded the societies into accepting his views, and pacified the exhorters by the power of his logic and the magic of his oratory. No one else could have succeeded as Harris did on that occasion. There was a low rumbling underground, so to speak, for a long time afterwards. Harris reproved the pride of John Belcher, and argued with Thomas William and endeavoured to overcome his scruples.[157]

It has been affirmed that Thomas William and William Edward (and possibly others) were ordained by the Groes-wen Society in 1745, but there is no evidence in support of this assertion. As a matter of fact, Thomas William, writing in Welsh to Howell Harris on February 8, 1746, complained that Thomas Price and John Belcher would not co-operate with him at Llantrisant. They had brought charges against him—(a) 'If I had a congregation to ordain me that I would dissent'; and (b) 'That I had gone so dark that I could see no error in the Church of England'.[158] Now, these words can hardly be applied to a man who *had* been ordained. This letter, incidentally, explains a phrase in Harris's diary on January 2, 1746, written at Aberthin. 'I heard', he wrote, 'how the Lord brings Thomas William again, and had prevented their being divided and scattered at Llantrisant.'[159]

Howell Harris preached a sermon on the mystery of Christ at Graig-wen, Eglwysilan on January 3, 1746, in which he aired those peculiar views concerning the Person of Christ which were beginning to fill his mind. A private society was held afterwards and he dealt with Thomas William's case; he was assured by all present that they had 'no scruple to dissent' any longer. But another difficulty arose. Someone stood up and opposed the substance of the sermon just delivered and William Edward also spoke against it. Harris argued that if they did not accept his doctrine they must be heretics! The matter was put before the society and it was accepted, but William Edward continued to oppose. Harris insisted on silencing him and threatened to turn him out, but Edward denied his authority to do so. It was a very stormy society meeting.[160]

Repercussions of this affair were felt at the association held in the following week at Glyn, Defynnog. Harris noted in his diary that 'Thomas William, that had been, by means of a scruple, led in heart from us this four years . . . is now brought to see his error'. It was agreed to readmit him, on trial, till the next association. William Edward was defiant, but he confessed (according to the association minutes) 'that he mistook the meaning of Mr. Harris, and is sorry for offending him, and is convinced he had done wrong in proposing a question to the staggering of many Christians, asking, Is the manhood of Christ an object of our worship? and other expressions that were bad'.[161] Presumably Edward also was readmitted. Thomas William began to itinerate once again, and in the letter from him to Howell Harris dated February 8, 1746, referred to above, he gave an account of his ministry. He complained that the brethren at Groes-wen accused him of publishing himself in the societies; in consequence he had decided to remain silent until the next association. The brethren were prejudiced against him because he had refused to dissent.

In an association held at New Inn, Monmouthshire on March 10, Thomas William's case was dealt with once again. Howell Harris wrote in his diary: 'We settled that Bro. Price, Bro. Thomas William, and Bro. John Belcher should act henceforth in connexion, and that they should do what they can to remove the prejudice against Thomas William, and that he should not go to the Vale of Glamorgan without having an outward call there.'[162] This resolution dealt with three of the signatories of the Caeo remonstrance. William Edward dissented owing to the differences that had arisen between him and Harris, but two years later he rejoined his old friends. Evan Thomas, the fifth signatory, was with the Methodists in July 1745; he is mentioned in connection with the Mynydd Islwyn Society in a report given to the Blaen-y-glyn Association— 'There are signs of the Lord's blessing Bro. Evan Thomas among them'.[163] In a letter to Harris written at New Inn on July 21, 1746, Thomas William reported that the Lord 'has Brok't Down the Parting Wall of Pre Judice that were Between Mr. Price, Mr. J. Belcher & others of the Brethren Effectually Towards Unworthy me'.[164] In another letter, dated September 14 from Gelli[dochlaethe], he informed Harris that Thomas Price had desired him to go to Margam, Neath and Pontarddulais in his stead. He had also been at Aberddawan, Pen-prysg, Nottage, Cynffig and through Gower.[165]

Reference has been made to Howell Harris's peculiar views on the Person of Christ. In 1746 he openly preached a brand of Patripassianism and was intolerant towards all other views. Harris was strong-willed and imperious by nature—almost dictatorially so—which made co-operation between him and others difficult on occasions. It soon became a struggle for supremacy in the associations between him and Daniel Rowland, the beginnings of which may be traced as far back as the associations in Trevecka in June and Gellidochlaethe in October 1746. In the latter Harris charged Belcher with causing a breach 'by carrying a railing accusation to Bro. Rowland'. Belcher, he asserted, was so 'puffed up' that he 'could not labour with him till he should be humbled'.[166] Belcher

[515]

and Thomas Price approached him after the association and (according to Harris's diary) they fell upon his neck and begged his pardon. But for a long time afterwards Harris suspected Price of carrying tales to Rowland. Many of the Glamorgan exhorters opposed Harris, and we are not surprised to read that the association advised him to avoid coming there. But Harris could not resist coming to the midst of his enemies and lashing out at them when the opportunity arose.

Methodist Societies, 1747-1749

The letters of Thomas William provide an occasional glimpse of the life of the Glamorgan societies from 1747 onwards. Writing to Howell Harris in 1747 he gave an account of his stewardship.[167] A new society of six or seven members had sprung up at Aberafan. He met Gwen David of Gellidochlaethe in Neath; they had a discussion concerning her impending marriage. There was an unruly element in the Neath Society but Richard Rees and George Phillips had matters well in hand. At Nottage some were disposed to join the Baptists. Thomas William was at Groes-wen in August, and he complained that the members of the society had allowed William Edward to preach there. Sleep had overcome them; John Belcher had informed him that he could hardly keep them awake on a Sunday evening. In another letter, written on September 1,[168] he reported that an agreement had been reached in Groes-wen concerning William Edward. At a Monthly Society at St. Nicholas the following brethren were present: John Belcher, Thomas Lewis, Evan Watkins and Richard Jones. Watkins was a strong pillar at St. Nicholas but Richard Jones was unstable. He went to the east as far as Mumbles and Llwyn-onn in Gower, and then towards Llandeilo-fach, where a Baptist was causing trouble. He wrote his letter at Pwll-y-glaw in Cwmafan; he was anxious to reach home that evening to hear William Williams, Pantycelyn, preaching at Llantrisant. He wrote later that he had heard Pantycelyn preaching at Llantrisant and Groes-wen. Daniel Rowland and Pantycelyn had been preaching in 'Mr. Wesley's Room' in Cardiff, but nobody (he added dryly) was converted there. He met Samuel Jeremiah, the exhorter, at Llanedern; he was one of the first called in those parts, and was often called to Dinas Powys and St. Nicholas. His wife was a scold, and he had a houseful of children.

There were eleven Glamorgan exhorters present at a Monthly Society at St. Nicholas on January 15, 1748, viz., Thomas Price, John Belcher, William Powell, Thomas Lewis, David Williams, Evan Watkin, Richard Jones, Samuel Jeremiah, Richard Thomas, Joshua Simons and Thomas William—William Edward and Evan Thomas were absent. Belcher had excommunicated John Butler of the Dinas Powys Society for drunkenness. He then went towards the west where he met George Phillips at Neath. He called at Gellidochlaethe; Gwen David was now married and expecting her time. He saw her husband, too, Henry Thomas, a native of Laugharne in Carmarthenshire who came to the district as one of Griffith Jones's circulating schoolmasters and soon began to exhort with the Methodists. He failed to preach on Wednesday, January 27 at Llangatwg as it was market day at Neath. He went on to Newton near Mumbles, and Llwyn-onn, where a few people met every Wednesday night.[169]

In another letter, endorsed September 21, 1748 by Howell Harris, he was at a Monthly Society at St. Nicholas, where eleven exhorters were present. Some time was spent in examining Morgan Evan who had been seduced by Thomas Prosser's doctrine—Prosser was a Wesleyan exhorter from Cardiff who was imbued with the Quietist tendencies so prevalent in those days in Moravian circles. He steered clear of Llantrisant; Thomas Price and Belcher, he reported, had the work well under hand there. He had hardly anything to report of Pen-prysg, Llyswyrny and Tre-os.[170] He had no good to report of Llansamlet in January, 1749; John Richard had been entangled but he hoped that he had been set free. He called at Rhos-fawr in the parish of Llangyfelach, the home of John Powell, one of the best Methodists he had ever met.[171]

In October he was at Aberddawan where the society had received a new lease of life under the leadership and influence of Christopher Bassett of Breaksea Point. Alas, he says, Alice his wife was more of a hindrance to him than a help. He urged Bassett to exhort on Sundays at Aberddawan.[172] In Cardiff a young girl who had been a member of the society had robbed her mistress, who 'was some sort of member' in Mr. Wesley's society.[173] This statement suggests that there were *two* societies in Cardiff, one of them Wesleyan, and the other Calvinist. The Llantrisant Society complained that John Belcher was somewhat addicted to drink, but Thomas William thought that the charge was quite groundless and he reproved them. Thomas Price, afterwards, from the Monthly Society at Aberthin on December 28, 1748, wrote a sharp letter of reproof. Belcher was present at the meeting at Aberthin, and so were Thomas Price, Thomas Lewis, David Williams, Richard Jones and Thomas William. Reference is made in his letters to a society at Bryn-bach, in the vicinity of Swansea or Loughor. This particular society was divided into four bands or classes; one of these bands was led by John Evans, the tanner, and was of a Dissenting tendency. In a postcript to his letter Thomas William informed Harris that Howell Griffith had repented of his sin, and he begged to be reinstated on trial.

Thomas William wrote in the same gossipy strain during the year 1749. He alluded to a Monthly Society held at St. Nicholas on Whit Tuesday, with nine exhorters present, including some who had been absent of late, viz., Joshua Simons, Evan Thomas Jacob, Evan Watkin, and David Thomas—the latter was a Monmouthshire exhorter who had moved lately, on his marriage, to Dinas Powys. Abraham Williams of New Inn was also present. John Wesley had been the previous week in *his* societies at Cardiff, Llantrisant and Llanwynno.[174] Wesley was on his way to his brother's wedding to Miss Sarah Gwynne of Garth. 'Brinbach seems to be settled', he wrote on September 1, 'and Cnap Llwyd is better than ever; at Llansamlet there are some converted added daily.' There had been a Monthly Society at Groes-wen, and the brethren who exhorted at the societies of Cardiff, Llantrisant, Cwmcynon, and Pen-tyrch were present. One from Cwmcynon testified that nobody had kept a private society in that area since the previous winter.[175]

There was a time when Howell Harris was in favour of administering the Sacrament in private houses. He allowed this as far back as 1742 in a letter to Herbert Jenkins. But the early Methodists communicated in their parish churches. It appears however, that the Lord's Supper was being administered at Groes-wen in 1749. Harris was there on January 19; 'I met the preachers and stewards', he said, 'and shewed the latter their places and work . . . and called them all to account here for giving the Sacrament here in this house, as it affected the whole Body, without consulting us all; and if they want to do what seems to me to hurt the work several ways, I would withdraw from them'.[176] Evidently it was a very recent innovation or else Harris would have protested far earlier. Who administered the Sacrament there? Was it William Edward?[177]

Up to that period the 'New House' at Groes-wen was the only place of worship built by the Methodists in Glamorgan. Jenkin David, it is said, had also placed a 'weaver's cottage' on his estate at Gellidoch-laethe at the disposal of the Creunant Society, but when is not known.[178] In the year 1749, however, another place of worship was built by the Aberthin Society, near Cowbridge, for the use of its members. On May 27 Harris and Rowland were together at Aberthin settling 'about a New House', and the former's patience was much tried 'for Rowland and he could not agree as to its form and cost'. It is evident that the Aberthin Society had a sprinkling of Independents among its members, but how many no one can tell. The deeds of Aberthin are held today by the Calvinistic Methodists. One document, dated November 23, 1749, conveys 'all that out cottage or dwelling house with the curtilage and Garden . . . commonly called . . . Ffynnon Vaire' in Aberthin to Daniel Rowland, Howell Davies (of Pembrokeshire), Howell Harris. Thomas Evans (Abertridwr, one of the trustees of Groes-wen), Richard Jones (St. Nicholas), Alexander Bassett (Llanfleiddian), and John Bellchamber (i.e. Belcher, of Eglwysilan)—all Methodists. The 'New House' was registered by the Independent group at Llandaff in 1750; they called themselves 'protestant Dissenters of the Independent persuasion' and it is stated in the application 'that the Late Dwelling house of Elizabeth Lewis at Byrthun . . . is now Erected and fitted for a meeting-house, a place of public worship'. The list of names attached to the application is headed by Henry Davies (of Cymer) and David Williams—of Llyswyrny. Nine other men signed the application.[179]

[518]

HOWELL HARRIS'S SECESSION, 1749–1752

The relations between Harris and Rowland worsened during the year 1749, and matters did not improve when Harris began to associate with Mrs. Sidney Griffith of Cefn Amwlch, Caernarvonshire. Harris paid a short visit to Glamorgan in the beginning of October 1749. He was at Groes-wen on the eighth and the following day he and Thomas Price went to Cardiff. They discussed the situation and Harris offered to relinquish his position in the association to Rowland, but Price assured him that Rowland would not accept that proposal.[180] There was a stormy meeting at the New Inn Association on January 31, 1750, but (according to Harris's diary) when Rowland and Thomas Price left the meeting 'the Lord came down'. In this association Belcher, William Powell and Thomas Price were appointed to visit north Wales.[181] On February 28 Harris was preaching at Llangatwg near Neath when Peter Williams of Carmarthen contradicted him openly and in the private society. By then Harris had made up his mind to separate. He saw John Richard and George Phillips at Llansamlet and spoke his mind to them; here he 'had again a great combat with Peter Williams'.[182] On the last day of March he preached at William Powell's house at Llanfabon, and afterwards had a conversation with Thomas William with a view to arranging a private meeting with Powell, John Richard, and others. Thomas William accompanied him to Llantrisant and Aberthin. In the latter place he held a private society and heard complaints concerning William Powell. 'Satan came in', he wrote, 'I turned two out and another three walked out.' They went afterwards to Fonmon Castle where they met Henry Lloyd of Rhydri, a prominent Wesleyan Methodist preacher. Harris proposed to him a meeting of Calvinist and Wesleyan Methodists to take spiritual counsel. He had a stormy meeting at Dinas Powys—'I turned out one exhorter and admitted another.' He preached at Cardiff where Thomas Price heard him; they left Cardiff together for Plas y Watford but the two men could not agree. He preached a powerful sermon at Groes-wen, but in the private society afterwards he turned out one of the stewards. On the morrow he had a verbal duel with Thomas Price and David Williams, Llyswyrny, concerning the two stewards that had been turned out at Aberthin, but Harris stubbornly refused to reinstate them.[183]

Thomas William, in a letter to Harris dated May 9, 1750, referred to the situation at Aberthin. The two stewards, it seems, were William Thomas Lewis and Alexander Bassett (one of the new trustees). Thomas Price, it is stated, had reinstated Lewis but Bassett refused to be reinstated until he had seen Harris. Thereupon David Williams accepted Thomas Millar to the stewardship.[184]

The crisis came to a head in the important association held at Llanidloes on May 9, 1750.[185] Five Glamorgan exhorters were present, viz., Thomas Price, Belcher, Thomas William, John Richard and David Williams. Once again it was agreed to send Price, David Williams and John Richard to north Wales. On the way home, at Erwd, Harris, Thomas William, John Richard, and others discussed the future and made plans to meet in a month's time. Harris visited Glamorgan again at the end of May, preaching at Aberthin where he once again, in the private society, turned out many stewards there. He saw Thomas Price at Watford and informed him that he would go out on his own, and those whom God chose would follow him. He met David Williams at New Inn, but the meeting was not a pleasant one.[186]

On June 23, 1750 Daniel Rowland and his supporters met in conclave at Llantrisant; it was decided there to separate from Harris and his followers. Harris heard the news on the following day on his way to Llansamlet, where, at Waunllysdy, he met eight exhorters 'and began laying ye foundation of God's house'. John Richard and Thomas William prayed fervently, and afterwards they settled their policy. Rowland by then had secured all the Methodist meeting-houses; in consequence Harris and his followers could no longer meet at Aberthin and Groes-wen. They met at St. Nicholas on July 26 for their first separate association, or council, as they afterwards called their meetings. Four Glamorgan exhorters, at least, were present, viz., Thomas William, John Richard, Henry Thomas of Gellidochlaethe, and George Phillips of Neath. It was decided to carry on the work of reviving religion in Wales, and that every member should worship according to the rites and ordinances of the Established Church. It was decided that William Powell and Thomas William should report on the work in Glamorgan and Monmouthshire in the next meeting, and John Richard to do likewise in the west. Thomas William and David Thomas (of Dinas Powys) were to arrange the next meeting at Builth with the exhorters, the former, in the meantime, was to visit north Wales. Before leaving for the north, on August 1, Thomas wrote a letter to Howell Harris. He had seen John Richard and had given him a good dressing down because of his fickleness. Richard told him that Henry Thomas was holding fast but that John Belcher and David Williams were weak. Richard was in a better frame of mind after the redoubtable Thomas William had finished with him but it is quite evident that his faith in Harris was weakening.[187]

On his way north, on August 28, Thomas William wrote another letter (in Welsh) to Harris, in which he referred to the situation in Glamorgan in the following terms:

> In Margam they are in a deep torpor; in Cefn Cribwr and Nottage I think some will be for us and others will choose them [i.e., the Rowlandites]; Tre-os and Pen-prysg are holding their ground. You have heard, it is likely, that they are about to break [into] the house at Pen-prysg and that Jenkin has placed three locks there to keep it intact. They have broken into the house at Llantrisant but I have heard more of the voice of freedom at Bro. Philip's, where the Society now meets, than I have heard for many years. The people are flocking there to hear . . . They

of St. Nicholas who have renounced the flesh are holding their ground, and at Dinas Powys they are standing together; the small Society at Tal-y-garn are coming up . . . I am in haste, will you please send Roger Williams [of Brecknock] into Glamorgan to stay there until the next association.[188]

The references to the 'houses' are intriguing; they show that places other than Aberthin and Groes-wen were used exclusively by the Methodists to hold their society meetings.

The Harrisians met at Builth on September 26–27, 1750 and John Richard preached at one of the services. One hundred exhorters were present and they were classified according to their fitness or abilities. Thomas William, John Richard and William Powell were placed in the first class, and Henry Thomas in the second. It was decided to send William Powell and Henry Thomas to north Wales.[189] There was another meeting on January 2, 1751 at Diserth near Llandrindod; Thomas William preached there and William Powell and John Richard were present. Harris pressed the exhorters present to leave all things and to dedicate themselves completely to the work, asking all who promised to obey to stand upon their feet. 'The Lord is doing a great work', whispered Powell as many stood up, but John Richard walked out.[190] Harris visited Glamorgan in February and preached on the ninth at Hafod Margam; on the following day, at Dyffryn Uchaf, the home of William Thomas (a future exhorter), he declared that the Lord had left the Hafod Society. In Neath 'John Richard asked to come in to open his scruples & was permitted but he stayed behind & failed to come on' because he 'was entangled by means of his wife'. At Gellidochlaethe he complained that Hafod, George Phillips's house at Neath, and Richard's house at Llansamlet were closed against him.[191]

The Harrisians met at Neath on April 10–11, 1751. John Richard asked permission to come in and this was granted, but he could not join with his old friends.[192] Thomas William began to feel despondent and in a letter to Harris in May he wrote, 'Today, the 15th of May, I feel a particular tenderness and longing for Glamorgan, especially for my Parish. What if there is nothing for the Lord here? Will He have anything? Is there not a Remnant?' He offered to bring horses to meet his brethren at Nantgarw.[193] Harris visited the area in a few days and endeavoured to whip up enthusiasm for his cause. At Llanwynno six exhorters came to hear him, all of them antagonistic. William Edward could not withstand the temptation to hear him at Cardiff.[194] Thomas William, in a postscript to a letter he wrote in July 1751, reported that he had lately been at Llantrisant, praying and singing with two or three people, one of them an ex-schoolmaster of Rhyding, near Neath.[195] Thomas William, in September 1751 made one more attempt to win John Richard's allegiance to the movement. He called at his house in Llansamlet, but after a long discussion with him he failed to make any impression. Richard was afraid, he says, that Harris and his followers were party men.[196]

Thomas William wrote a long letter (in Welsh)[197] to Harris on September 24, 1751, extracts of which may be translated as follows:

> As regards the work in Glamorgan . . . The House of John Powell, Rhos-fawr, he is so carnal and the people are so lazy that it would be better, he says, if we did not come there . . . Llandeilo-fach, the Lord is at work there and gives His own strength to exhort. And at Cefn Golau I believe God is speaking there; the man of the house is undissembling; he asked me to come three miles further because he is moving to Pen-clawdd, a dark and pagan place. A door has been opened at Pentre'r Estyll, but I had no freedom to exhort there, except in my bonds. There is a door open at Llansamlet, close to John Richard's house, but the congregation, mostly, are publicans. Neath—here Owen the Tinker, one of the trustees of the house, met Harry Lloyd [of Rhydri, the Wesleyan] and invited him to his house, that is the New House, to preach. He came and exhorted there for a while and sent two others who made such a noise and commotion that many of the townspeople came together to break George Phillips's windows; he went to law but he only gained a small sum of money after all his trouble. When I passed through Neath I was impelled to converse with George . . . I think that the Lord is turning His face to some at Margam; the last time I was there I was so straitened that I could hardly say a word . . . As regards Cefn Cribwr, a woman who was wont to receive us, and two other professors died suddenly; they were the only three in the locality . . . At Pen-prysg they are dark and weak; Jenkin Thomas has a spirit of seeking, and, William Hughes in Self—his wife has a pretty good voice. William Thomas and his servant, near Aberthin, are truly seeking, and Will is being made free . . . Around Ffwl-y-mwn [i.e., Fullmoon—Fonmon] they are weak and carnal and in consequence they are hanging to us. And Llantrisant, similarly, are carnal. There are a few souls in Cardiff and God gives freedom to bring Salvation to them. As regards Nant-garw I experienced God speaking there . . . In Llanilltud [Faerdre] six or seven souls are cleaving somewhat to us and they receive something from our ministry. Thomas Harry near Pont-y-tŷ-pridd is trying to bestir himself. I have been exhorting twice at Ynys-y-bŵl in Llanwynno, and God was speaking loudly on the two occasions. William Philip, the man who contradicted you at Caerphilly when you withstood David Williams ten or twelve years ago, and Evan Williams of Mynydd Meio, have risen against David Williams of Pwll-y-pant; they have left his congregation and now attend at Groes-wen. Edmund Jones (Pont-y-pŵl) is to be at Groes-wen next Sunday. Daniel Rowland has been in this locality. He preached at Neath and they heard some authority with him . . . but when he came to other places some were hardened in the hands of the Devil . . . some were shaken . . . I have been conversing with John Richard; I fear that he is going further away from God's work; there is in him a pretty deep root of Self and rebellion against God. Rowland administered the Sacrament at Groes-wen . . .Thomas Jones is full of poison and has drawn John Richard down from the place he was when I wrote before. I hear from William Powell that he intends to form a party, and that he cannot join with them [i.e., the Rowlandites]. Mr. Price sent his kind regards to me on October 1st, and said *that he was the same as ever.*

Thomas William was the only Glamorgan exhorter present at an association held at Trevecka on October 2, 1751.[198] William Powell's defection was a hard blow, and a few days after the association Harris wrote him a letter. 'Dear William', he asked, 'Where are you? what are you doing? cant you Determine who shall Rule, ye Saviour or Self? Reason no more but come away, 'tis no time to Confer with Flesh & Blood. I write to you from the Lord's Head Quarters in ye Field of

Battle; come & take your Place & let not yᵉ Enemy Triumph . . . Madam Griffith Joyns with me to call you to yᵉ Field.'[199] Harris was preparing for a journey to north Wales, an undertaking fraught with dangers so he imagined. He made his will on the thirteenth, appointing Thomas William his executor and his daughter's guardian, and bequeathing unto him his papers and books and his bay and white horses'.[200]

On January 1, 1752 Harris's followers held a meeting at Llanllugan, Montgomeryshire. Thomas William was now suspected of wavering, but it was he who kept the minutes of this association. It was decided there to send Thomas Dafydd, a Montgomeryshire exhorter, on a visit to Glamorgan and other places in south Wales.[201] Soon after the association, in mid-January, Harris took a journey in Glamorgan from Llandeilo-fach through the Vale to Gelli-gaer, calling at most of the old centres. He was weak in body and tired in spirit. He could hardly stand on his feet at Pentre Estyll near Swansea, where a large congregation hung upon his words, including six exhorters who had left him. He came to Porth y Fynachlog, near Neath, 'the place I came first to in all this country 14 years ago'. At the end of a service held at Thomas William's house one David Bowen announced that Richard Tibbott, the Montgomery exhorter who had just defected, would preach at such-and-such a time. The announcement so exasperated Harris that he cried out that such a meeting would only be in the devil's service. This journey was his last in Glamorgan for many years; he did not set his feet in the county again until the year 1764. Another meeting was held at Trevecka in the second week of February 1752. At this meeting Thomas William, his faithful henchman, was excommunicated from his following until his spirit had been restored. He was the last Glamorgan exhorter to support Harris's cause.[202]

William Powell wrote a letter to Harris on May 17, 1752, excusing himself for not coming to the associations of Harris's people. He wrote half-heartedly that the matter was a burden on his soul. 'Last association', he said, 'I found God would not let me come there, the Night before the association . . . God did put his hand upon me that I could not Rise from the bed.' He believed that 'when we Seperated from yᵉ clergy' God was with them, but some steps were taken 'that God dont Approve of'. He was 'waiting for a Commission to go to the high ways and hedges carrying a message from God to poor sinners . . . I am Determin'd to be alone to see what God will do and be a member in the Church of England'.[203]

Howell Harris, from 1752 onwards, confined himself to Trevecka, establishing the religio-industrial community which came to be known as the Trevecka Family. Evan Moses, a tailor by trade from Aberdare, joined the Family in 1752 and soon became Harris's right-hand man until the latter's death in 1773. He used to visit the fairs in north and south Wales recruiting men and women for the Family. After Harris's death he was one of the trustees of Trevecka, and was a 'Father' to the community until his death in 1805.[204] Many Glamorgan people joined the Family from time to time. Anne and Margaret Miles, two sisters from Llanilltud Faerdref came there in 1753; the former dying at Talgarth in 1795 and the latter in 1815. David Miles, from the same place, went there soon afterwards, with his wife and child; he died in 1783. Janet Davies of the same parish came there in 1758; she was the wife of Hugh Davies, one of the Trevecka soldiers who fought at the Battle of Quebec; she died in 1782 aged 50. Rhoda Evan of Llanwynno went there in 1759; she was the chief singer of the Family and died of a fatal accident at Trevecka in 1767 aged 31. One could name others, such as James Williams who came from Glamorgan with his wife and two daughters in 1776, and Barbara James and two others who went there in 1777. Mary John, from the vicinity of Swansea, came there in 1772. Anne Gibbon, of Peterston-super-Ely, died at Trevecka in 1776 aged 18. Then there was Thomas David of Llan-giwg, and Isobel Davies, an old woman from Glamorgan, who died in 1777.

METHODISM IN GLAMORGAN AFTER 1752

Let us now follow the fortunes of Calvinistic Methodism in the county after the disruption in the movement. Thomas William rejoined his brethren at Groes-wen, and possibly it was after 1752 that he and William Edward were ordained. Many Methodist societies seceded after 1752 and some exhorters were ordained by their fellow-members. Henry Thomas of Gellidochlaethe was ordained in 1752 and the 'house called Godre'r Rhos' was registered by Richard Rees (an old member of the Neath Society) in the same year as a meeting-house. In 1754 Jenkin David of Gellidochlaethe conveyed the house to 'Henry Thomas, Dissenting Preacher', Richard Rees, Cwmdulais, John Evans, and Joseph Simmons, 'Dissenting Minister'.[205] The incumbent of the parish in a visitation return in 1763 refers to 'a little Cot' in Creunant, 'where a few constantly meet every Sunday & where one Henry Thomas holds forth to them'.[206] Henry Thomas was a faithful member of the 'associated ministers' who met at Rhydymaerdy near Loughor.[207] He relinquished the ministry a few years before his death (at the age of 90); he died in 1802 and was buried at Godre'r Rhos.

David Williams, Aberthin, came originally to Glamorgan as a servant in the employ of Christopher Bassett of Aberddawan. In 1754 he married Elizabeth, the daughter of Evan Prichard of Collennau, Llantrisant—a staunch Methodist. Shortly afterwards, we are told, on the advice of Daniel Rowland, he was ordained by the Aberthin Society. He did not cease to be a Methodist; he still attended the associations and when he died in 1792 he was buried at Salem, Pen-coed, the first to be laid in that graveyard.[208] Neither was Aberthin lost to the Methodists;

after many vicissitudes the little chapel (now disused) still belongs to the Calvinistic Methodists (Plate VIII).

In Thomas William's letter to Howell Harris in September 1751, quoted above,[209] reference is made to the 'New House' in Neath—the home of George Phillips, the exhorter—and 'one of the trustees of the house' is named. The 'house of George Phillips' at Neath was registered in the Quarter Sessions in 1756.[210] Phillips died on June 11, 1762 and eleven days afterwards Anne, his widow, wrote a letter to Howell Harris. She and her four children were in trouble because of 'a Great deal of Debt' she could 'not recover since the building of the house'. Some 'Professors', she wrote, had advised her to sell the building, but she would not do this without consulting with Harris. She may have been answered, but the letter has not survived.[211] It is quite evident that the Methodists had a place of worship in Neath, and that this house had been used for the purpose up to the year 1762.

In Llansamlet, after 1752, the Methodists gathered at two cottages called 'Y Cwm', about half-a-mile from Waunllysdy. John Richard was still with them, and in January 1758 he and seven others, 'being Members of a Protestant dissenting Congregation me[et]ing at Cwm' applied at the Quarter Sessions to certify Richard Tibbott of Montgomeryshire (an ex-exhorter) 'to excercise his Gifts & Talents amongst us as our Minister'. We have no evidence that Tibbott settled at Llansamlet in 1758. Had he done so it would be interesting to speculate what the situation would be today.[212] The parish of Llansamlet, to this day, is a stronghold of Methodism; but if Tibbott had been prevailed upon to settle there in 1758 the parish, perhaps (like the Mynydd-bach district across the river Tawe), would be a stronghold of Independency.

Apart from these sporadic signs of life the evidence of any activity in the Glamorgan Methodist societies is very meagre. But judging from the situation in later years it is certain that the Rowlandites consolidated their position after Howell Harris had retired to Trevecka. Many societies succumbed, of course, but others were revived and new societies were formed. David Williams was a strong pillar in the Vale. Christopher Bassett, Richard Jones of St. Nicholas, and Samuel Jeremiah held firm—the first two names are found in a list of subscribers for a volume of Daniel Rowland's sermons in 1772. New men came to the forefront, such as William Thomas of Dyffryn Uchaf, Margam. Thomas had been converted under the preaching of Howell Harris in 1739 and he began to exhort after 1750—at least we have no record of him in the pre-disruption associations. He attended the communion services at Llangeitho and when he moved to Tŷ-draw, Pyle, in 1760 he rallied the members of the old societies of Cefn Cribwr and Cynffig and welded them into a new society.[213]

In the Bishop's Queries to the clergy of the diocese of Llandaff in 1763 Methodism is not specifically mentioned and it is quite evident that many of the clergy did not regard Methodism as Dissent; but in a few instances the incumbents have given information about Methodism in their returns.[214] Lewis Jones of Bridgend is named as the Dissenting teacher in the Coety return, 'but they run after every strolling Methodist yᵗ comes here'. There are no Dissenters at Llanfleiddan 'unless the strolling Methodists may be deemed as such'. The 'Methodist meeting House at Aberthyn', of course, was in the parish, where 'Methodists of all Trades and Denominations' congregated—'Tinkers, Thatchers, Weavers, and all other Vermin!' A few families in St. Mary Hill were 'Methodically Inclin'd, but they do attend the Church as well as any of the other Inhabitants'. There were a few Methodists at Bonvilston, but they too attended 'divine Service as regular as the other inhabitants of the Parish'. 'Many of our Parishioners are called Methodist', reported the incumbent of Pen-tyrch, 'Their Meeting House is not Licens'd. The usual Teachers there, I am told, are Samuel Jeremiah, Edward Thomas, William Edwards [of Groes-wen], and others.' There were some Methodists at Peterston-super-Ely, all of them attending divine service regularly. 'There are some Methodists' at St. Nicholas, all attending the church services. 'We have a meeting house for the Methodists but not Licens'd; there are several Teachers belonging to it.'

Howell Harris Returns, 1763–1769

By the year 1763 Howell Harris had rejoined his old friends. An association of Methodist preachers had been held at Neath in May 1761 and Evan Moses of Trevecka was there. In May 1762 Harris was recalled to the ranks of the leaders of Welsh Methodism, and the following year he began to itinerate once again in south Wales. He travelled from Cardiff to Llansamlet in the beginning of June 1763.[215] William Thomas, the Glamorgan diarist, refers to this visit; under June 1 he writes: 'This day a great Meeting of the Methodists at Aberthin. Then Daniel Rowland &c. preached, and in the evening Howel Harris preached, being the first [time] he preached amongst them since the great division.'[216] It was a Monthly Association meeting. In Swansea a crowd of four thousand people heard him preaching. He met the society at Llansamlet and had a three hours conference with John Richard. It seems that Richard and his wife were at loggerheads with one another, and Harris vainly attempted to bring them to a better frame of mind. He was in the county again in February–March 1764, preaching in Swansea and Gower. He was still dissatisfied with John Richard—'I think his spirit puffed up'; he heard that certain brethren in Swansea were 'openly exposing John Richard on lying'. William Powell (of Cnap-llwyd?) went with him to Gower. Powell informed him that his wife had hindered his coming to Trevecka, and explained his reasons for leaving John Richard.[217] William Thomas, the diarist, recorded another meeting at Aberthin in October 1764, when William Williams of Pantycelyn and

Daniel Rowland preached there to very large congregations. The diarist reported that the Methodists were very active during those years; Rowland, he said, is 'continually about preaching' and so were the exhorters. The Aberthin and Groes-wen meeting-houses had been licensed, he stated, and 'several of ye exhorters licensed themselves when the Militia came about'.[218]

Howell Harris's next visit to Glamorgan was in January 1765, when he travelled from Cardiff to Gower. He preached in one of the chapels of Cardiff to a full congregation. He called with Mrs. Jones of Fonmon castle and at all the old centres.[219] William Thomas, the diarist, refers to this visit. Harris preached in Cardiff, Tre-hyl, Llantrisant and Cowbridge 'in a very convincing manner', but 'nevertheless [he] had the form of a Moravian preaching about the blood of God'—evidently Harris had not changed his Patripassian views! Harris went about, he said, 'in his chaise & 2 horses', with the words 'God is my peace' written on the chaise.[220]

In January 1766 he set out once again in his chaise towards Glamorgan. He met some of his old converts at Mr. Thomas's house at Llanbradach-fawr, including Thomas Price of Plas y Watford. He went about 'from place to place', says William Thomas, 'and a great crowd meeting him everywhere'.[221] He preached for two hours to a vast congregation at Llantrisant. He attended morning service at Cowbridge church and in the evening visited St. Nicholas.[222] He was in the county again in May, preaching as before in Llanbradach and Watford (in the Independent chapel)—by-passing Groes-wen! He preached with zest to huge congregations at Cardiff, St. Nicholas, Llantrisant, Cowbridge, Bridgend (in a 'Methodist chapel'), Margam (by the door of an inn), Neath Abbey (to many thousands), and Swansea. We see him once again in the county before the end of the year, in December. He came through the Vale of Neath to Cefnygelli, and he heard the Rev. William Davies, the curate, preaching at Llanilltud Church, near Neath. He took the Sacrament at Neath Church (St. Thomas'?), and afterwards preached at the old abbey ruins. He discoursed on the road near Margam, at the White Hart Inn in Pyle, and at a Meeting-house near Bridgend. He called at all the old centres—Pen-prysg, Aberddawan, &c.— preached at 'the Room' at Cardiff. He wended his way to Llys-faen, 'by the famous New Bridge on the Taf' (built by his old friend William Edward), and to Llantrisant church. He discoursed at the Meeting-house at Cymer, and 'came through the ford, where Mr. Henry Davies was drowned [on July 28, 1766], to a public house near New Bridge'. At Llanbradach he 'felt the old authority of 30 years ago to cut'. He returned to Trevecka via Merthyr Tydfil. 'Great crowds frequented him everywhere', said William Thomas, but his comment on this tour is unfavourable. 'He went about as Zinzendorf the Moravian of Germany in his chaize', he said, 'seeing he himself had swallowed much of that doctrine.'[223]

There is a gap in Howell Harris's diary in 1767 and very little is known of his movements for that year; but William Thomas reports a visit in June, when he preached at Dinas Powys 'and at St. Lythan's Down', presumably 'by Morris the weaver's house', as in 1766.[224] He paid his last visit to Glamorgan in July 1769. He came to Llanbradach feeling weak and tired, but he preached to a thousand people and to a much larger congregation at Caerphilly. He discoursed in English and Welsh. He travelled, preaching on the way, through Llys-faen, and Cardiff (where he was ill and in pain); his voice was quite hoarse when he addressed the people at Baduchaf. A huge crowd awaited him at Llantrisant. After preaching at Cowbridge he dined at Fonmon and preached that night at Aberddawan. His next call was Llan-gan, where he 'discoursed in Mr. Jones' Parish with much Power'. He referred, of course, to the Rev. David Jones who had been instituted rector of Llan-gan in 1767. In Bridgend, on July 4, he notes in his diary, 'I heard that Mr. Jones is not bold for ye Lord but Lodges in a Carnal house & has no Prayer there but is one with ye world & for that Reason is called a Moravian'. Was he referring to Jones of Llan-gan? It is not quite clear whom he meant. The following day, in the morning, he heard 'an excellent sermon from Mr. Jones in Llanilltud Church [Neath] where ye church was crowded'. In the afternoon he discoursed in English and Welsh to a congregation 'att least I think 10,000' in the Abbey court. In Swansea he discoursed 'on ye Green' to another vast crowd. He stood on 'ye Turnpike Gate' and addressed them in Welsh and English, 'being quite exhausted in strength & Spirit & my voice hoarse'.[225]

Undoubtedly these last visits of Howell Harris did much to repair the breaches caused by the disastrous disruption between the leaders of Welsh Methodism. At Creunant, for instance, Mary Thomas of Hendre Gyngan left £200 to the little Methodist society which had survived there after the defection at Godre'r Rhos, and in 1769 a small chapel was built to accommodate the society.[226]

METHODISM, 1769-1773

Methodism is often referred to in the 1771 visitation returns for the diocese of Llandaff. At St. Andrew's there were a 'few Methodists, but they come at the stated times to Church'. At Llantrisant there was 'an itinerant Methodist preacher that now & then comes hither'. A number of people called themselves Methodists at Pen-marc, and at Llanilid 'we have several Methodists'. There were 'three families of Methodistical Dissenters' at Llanfihangel near Cowbridge, and at Cowbridge itself 'a medley of Persons, who resort indiscriminately to Church, Meeting of Independents, and to the Societies of Methodists'. They are described in the same terms at Colwinston, 'yet they communicate nowhere'. David Williams of Llyswyrny is denominated a Presbyterian, and a 'medley of visionaries meet every Sunday from different parishes' at Aberthin. 'The House', it is stated, 'is more frequented by Methodists than Presbiterians.' 'Some of the Methodists come here sometimes', reported John Hodges of Wenvoe, 'but very seldom'—he himself had left the Methodists before 1771. In Llantwit Major 'there are People who call themselves Methodists, who congregate in an House in this Parish', and 'several Methodists', in Llyswyrny, 'meet once a week in the House of one David Williams'. The Dissenters and the 'People called Methodists follow the same Teachers indiscrimately' in Pyle and Cynffig, 'and in whatever else they may differ, all agree in the Love of Novelty and Dissension'. At Margam the Dissenters and the Methodists 'hold meetings from House to House wherever they can find entertainment'. There were 'some People of low Rank' in Ewenni, 'called *Jumpers*'—a reference to enthusiastic modes of worship by the Methodists.

Strangely enough, Methodism is not mentioned by David Jones in his return for Llan-gan, although there must have been many Methodists in the parish; Jones evidently regarded them as loyal churchmen. At Eglwysilan there was 'a House belonging to the Methodists (Groes-wen), or Independents as they call themselves', and their teacher was William Edward, 'licensed, as I am informed'. The incumbent complained, 'We are continually pestered by itinerant Preachers, who make it their Employment to pervert the whole parish. They preach in all places alike without making any distinction whatever'.[227] There were Methodists in other Glamorgan parishes, of course, in 1771, but the incumbents were queried with regard to the growth of Dissent in the various parishes, and like David Jones of Llan-gan they did not regard the Methodists as Dissenters.

Howell Harris, in 1771, was confined by ill-health to his home at Trevecka, but he was still interested in the religious awakening in Glamorgan. Writing in September 1772, a few months before Harris' death, Edmund Jones of Pont-y-pŵl informed him 'that there is an awakening on both sides [of] the river Rumney, [but] Chiefly on the Glamorgansh-[ire] side of it from Hengoed down towards the sea, & abt. [Caer]fily. Great add[itions to the churc]h at Croes wen . . . But D. Wms. of Watford with his [Arm]inianism loses ground.'[228] Harris died in July 1773, leaving the work in the hands of new men, lay and clerical, younger in years and different in outlook. It was their task to consolidate the gains made by him and his fellow-revivalists, and to build up a church. The end of his life is a convenient date to mark the completion of the first phase in the history of Calvinistic Methodism in the county of Glamorgan.

APPENDIX D

EARLY CALVINISTIC METHODIST EXHORTERS IN GLAMORGAN

(Names printed in italics denote the exhorters who sided with Howell Harris at the beginning of the Methodist Disruption.)

Bassett, Christopher (fl. 1744–1784), of Breaksea Point, Aberddawan.

Belcher (or Bellchamber), John (fl. 1721–1763), Eglwysilan.

Dafydd, Richard William (fl. 1740–1752), of Llandyfaelog, Carms.; settled at Swansea at the end of his life.

Deer, John (d. 1743), St. Nicholas.

Edward, William (1719–1789), Bryn-tail, Eglwysilan; ended his life as an Independent minister.

Edwards, Edward, Dinas Powys (?).

Evans, E.

Evans, Thomas, Abertridwr.

Griffith, Howell (1704–1753), Treferig Uchaf, Llantrisant; buried at Llantrisant.

Harris, Henry, Groes-wen.

Howell, Morgan, Llantrisant (?).

Hughes, William, Pen-prysg (?).

Jacob, Evan Thomas.

Jeremiah, Samuel, Llanedern.

John, Hopkin, Gorseinon; he lived for a season at Swansea, and ended his days at Llangyfelach. He is sometimes known as Hopkin John Hopkin.

John, Morgan.

Jones, John, of Caeo, Carms. He settled near Neath.

Jones, Richard (fl. 1743–1772), St. Nicholas.

Lewis, Jenkin.

Lewis, Thomas, (d. 1746).

Lloyd, Edward, Groes-wen.

Meurig, Edward and John, Casllwchwr.

Morgan, William, Groes-wen.

Moses, Evan (1726–1805), of Aberdare; he became the head of the Trevecka 'Family' after Howell Harris's death.

Phillips, George (d. 1762), Neath.

Powell, William (fl. 1742–1752), Caerphilly, afterwards of Brynllefrith, Llanfabon.

Price, Thomas (fl. 1739–1783), Plas y Watford, Caerphilly; buried at Capel Martin, Caerphilly.

Price, Thomas, Llandeilo Tal-y-bont.

Price, William, Watford (?).

Richard, John (fl. 1742–1764), Llansamlet.

Simons, Joshua.

Thomas, David, of Monmouthshire; he settled at Dinas Powys in 1749.

Thomas, Edward.

Thomas, Evan, Groes-wen.

Thomas, Henry (1712–1802), of Laugharne, Carms. He settled at Gellidochlaethe, Creunant *c.* 1740, and ended his life as an Independent minister; he is buried at Godre'r Rhos, Creunant.

Thomas, Richard (d. 1751), Ball House, Llanedern.

Thomas, William (1723–1811), Dyffryn Uchaf, Margam; afterwards of Tŷ-draw, Pyle.

Watkins, Evan, St. Nicholas.

William, Thomas (1717–1765), Melin Corrwg, Eglwysilan. He ended his life as an Independent minister; he was buried at Cymer, Rhondda.

Williams, David (1717–1792), born at Llandyfaelog, Carms. He settled at Llyswyrny and was ordained by the Aberthin Society; he was buried at Salem, Pen-coed.

Yeoman, John, St. Nicholas (?).

APPENDIX E

EARLY METHODIST SOCIETIES IN GLAMORGAN

(Where possible, dates are given—at least the dates of the earliest references to the societies; in a few cases the dates are tentative. See also Map V.)

1. Aberafan (1747).
2. Aberddawan (1743).
3. Aberthin (nr. Cowbridge, 1743).
4. Blaen-taf Fawr (1743).
5. Bridgend (before 1766).
6. Bryn-bach (nr. Swansea, 1744).
7. Cadoxton (Barry, 1749).
8. Cardiff (1738).
9. Casllwchwr (1743).
10. Cefncribwr (c. 1745).
11. Cefngolau (nr. Swansea, 1751).
12. Cnap-llwyd (Morriston, 1743).
13. Cowbridge (1749).
14. Creunant (Gellidochlaethe, 1743).
15. Cwm Cynon (Aberdare, 1749).
16. Cynffig (1749).
17. Dinas Powys (1743).
18. Eglwysilan (Parc, 1738).
19. Ffwl-y-mwn (Fonmon, 1751).
20. Gelli-gaer (c. 1737).
21. Glynogwr (1743).
22. Gorseinon (1743).
23. Groes-wen (nr. Caerffili, 1742).
24. Gwaelod-y-garth (Merthyr, c. 1738).
25. Llanbradach Fawr (c. 1738).
26. Llandeilo Fach ('house of John Wallter', 1743).
27. Llandremôr Uchaf (nr. Pontarddulais, 1743).
28. Llanedern (1743).
29. Llanfabon (1743).
30. Llan-giwg.
31. Llangyfelach (1743).
32. Llanhari (1743).
33. Llanilid (1743).
34. Llanilltud Faerdre (c. 1740).
35. Llanilltud Fawr (1771).
36. Llanishen (c. 1739).
37. Llan-maes (1749).
38. Llansamlet (1742).
39. Llantrisant (1738).
40. Llanwynno (1749).
41. Llwyn-onn (Gower, c. 1745).
42. Llyswyrny (1748).
43. Margam (Hafod, 1742; Dyffryn, 1747).
44. Moulton (1749).
45. Nantgarw (1751).
46. Neath (1742).
47. Newton (Gower, 1745).
48. Nottage (Porth-cawl, 1743).
49. Pen-clawdd (Gwenffrwd, 1747).
50. Penmarc.
51. Pen-prysg (Pen-coed, 1748).
52. Pontgynon (1749).
53. Porthceri (1749).
54. Rhos-fawr ('house of John Powel', nr. Swansea, 1751).
55. Rhuthun (nr. Pen-coed, 1743).
56. St. Andrews (1744).
57. St. Nicholas (Tre-hyl, 1743).
58. Sully (1749).
59. Tonna (nr. Neath, c. 1740).
60. Treferig Uchaf (nr. Llantrisant, 1738).
61. Tre-os (1749).
62. Watford, Plas y (nr. Caerphilly, 1743).
63. Wenfô (c. 1740).
64. Wig Uchaf (Cwmbwrla, c. 1738).
65. Ynys Angharad (Pont-y-pridd, c. 1738).
66. Ynysybwl (1751).
67. Ystradyfodwg (Cymer, 1748).
    Tal-y-garn (1750).

APPENDIX F

EARLY CALVINISTIC METHODIST PLACES OF WORSHIP IN GLAMORGAN

(Inclusion in this list does not mean that an edifice had been built in the places mentioned; it might mean that a dwelling-house had been adapted and used for society meetings and preaching services. There were many other meeting-places, where Howell Harris and others often visited, but these places are not included.)

1. LLANTRISANT, 1741: 'Tŷ Newydd', 'New House', a mile or so below Llantrisant, possibly the farm-house situated where the road to Pendeulwyn leaves the main Llantrisant—Cardiff road.

2. Y GROES-WEN, built in 1742 by the Methodists.

3. GELLIDOCHLAETHE, near Creunant, a weaver's cottage near the old mansion given in the 1740s by Jenkin David to the Methodist Society; it is called 'a little Cot' in the 1763 Visitation Returns, and is the 'meeting-house, called *Godre'r rhôs*' in the 1771 Return (it was by then, of course, an Independent meeting house). It was registered in the Quarter Sessions in 1752.

4. ABERTHIN, near Cowbridge, built in 1749 and is still standing, but disused during the last few years.

5. PEN-PRYSG, near Pen-coed, 1750: 'the house at Pen-prysg', mentioned by Thomas William in 1750.

6. NEATH, 1750: the house of George Phillips, the exhorter, also mentioned by Thomas Williams in 1750 (the trustees of the house are mentioned by him in 1751). It is also called the 'New House'. After Phillips's death in 1762, Anne Phillips, his widow, wrote a letter to Howell Harris (dated June 2, 1762), imploring his advice with regard to the house. 'I am left', she writes, ' . . . under a Great deal of Debt which we could not recover since the building of the house.' The house of George Phillips had been registered in the Quarter Sessions in 1756 as a meeting-house.

7. LLANSAMLET, 1751: the house of John Richard, the exhorter. It is also called 'New House'. After 1752 the Llansamlet society met at two cottages called 'Y Cwm', about half a mile from Waunllysdy. (The present chapel is still called Capel y Cwm.)

8. ST. NICHOLAS, 1763: a 'meeting House' used by the Methodists is mentioned in the 1763 Visitation Returns; it was called Tre-hyl, possibly the house of John Deer, the exhorter, who died in 1743, and probably the St. Nicholas society had gathered together there throughout the years. The present chapel at St. Nicholas is still known as Tre-hyl.

9. PEN-TYRCH, 1763: A Methodist 'Meeting House' (but not licensed) is mentioned in the 1763 Visitation Returns.

10. BRIDGEND, 1766: it is stated that Howell Harris preached in a 'Methodist chapel' at Bridgend in 1766. In the 1774 Visitation Return mention is made of two places in the town where 'all the Jumpers, and the Methodists, or rather Whitefield & Wesley' congregate.

11. CREUNANT, 1769: a small chapel was built for the Methodists at Creunant in 1769. It was built near the brook, not far from the present chapel; it was afterwards adapted as a cottage and quite recently it was sold to the occupant.

BIBLIOGRAPHY

(a) Manuscript Sources

1. National Library of Wales. Trevecka MSS., including Trevecka Letters, Howell Harris's Diaries, Reports of Associations, etc.
2. National Library of Wales. Church in Wales Records: visitation returns of the diocese of Llandaff.
3. Cardiff Central Library. Cardiff MS. 4.877. William Thomas's diary.

(b) Printed Sources

Bennett, Richard. *Methodistiaeth Trefaldwyn Uchaf* (Bala, 1929).
Bevan, Hopkin. *Ychydig Hanes neu Goffadwriaeth, &c.* (Swansea, 1838).
Jenkins, D. E. *Calvinistic Methodist Holy Orders* (Caernarvon, 1911).
Jones, J. Morgan and Morgan, William. *Y Tadau Methodistaidd* (2 gyf. Abertawe, 1895–1897).
Jones, M. H. *The Trevecka Letters* (Caernarvon, 1932).
Roberts, Gomer, M. *Emynwyr Bethesda'r Fro* (Llandysul, 1967).
Idem (ed.), *Hanes Methodistiaeth Galfinaidd Cymru*. I 'Y Deffroad Mawr' (Caernarfon, 1973).
Williams, W. Samlet, *Hanes Methodistiaeth Gorllewin Morgannwg* (Caernarfon, 1916).

Journal of the Calvinistic Methodist Historical Society (JCMHS) (1916 ff).
Articles as follows:

Volume

II   'Capel cyntaf y Methodistiaid' by Richard Bennett
V   'Y Burthin—an early Methodist Society' by M. H. Jones
VI   'An account book, Aberthyn chapel' by M. H. Jones
XXI   'Caerphilly and early Methodism' by James Davies
XXVII   'John Richard, Llansamlet' by Gomer M. Roberts
    'Howell Harris's visits to Llansamlet and district' by Tom Beynon
XXVIII   'Capel y Groes-wen; Cymdeithasfa'r Groes-wen, 1743' by Tom Beynon
XXIX   'Llythyrau ac adroddiadau Thomas William' copied by Tom Beynon
XXXI   'Llawysgrifau Evan Moses' by K. Monica Davies
XXXIV   'The diary of William Thomas' by W. W. Price
    'Pennod yn hanes Richard Tibbott' by Gomer M. Roberts
XXXV   'Extracts from William Thomas' diary' by Gomer M. Roberts
    'Richard Thomas, Morgannwg' by William Griffith
    'David Williams, Llyswyrnwy', by Gomer M. Roberts
XXXVI   'The Deere family of Trallwn, Llanilid' by T. J. Hopkins
    'Glamorgan visitation returns, 1763, 1771' by Gomer M. Roberts
XXXIX   'Plas y Watford a'i berchennog' by J. Price Williams
XL   'Glamorgan visitation returns, 1774' by Gomer M. Roberts
XLVII   'Evan Moses o Drefeca' by R. T. Jenkins
LI   'Howel Harris's friends and supporters in east Glamorgan' by T. J. Hopkins
LVI   'Teulu Thomas Price, Plas y Watfford' by D. Emrys Williams

Y Cofiadur (1923ff.)
Articles as follows:

Number

12   'Yr Annibynwyr Cymreig a Hywel Harris' by R. T. Jenkins
17   'Henry Thomas, Gelli Dochlaethe' by Gomer M. Roberts
27   'Annibynwyr a llythyrau Trefeca' by Gomer M. Roberts

Bathafarn (1946 ff.)
Articles as follows:

Volume

9   'Glimpses of early Methodism in and around Cardiff' by A. H. Williams
15   'The first Methodist society in Wales' by A. H. Williams
17   'The first Methodist society in Wales: a postscript' by A. H. Williams
18   'That Cardiff society again!' by A. H. Williams

Gower (1948 ff.)
Volume

X   'Early Methodism in Gower' by Gomer M. Roberts

CHAPTER X

The Literary History of Glamorgan from 1550 to 1770[1]

By CERI W. LEWIS

INTRODUCTION

FEW features are likely to impress themselves more forcibly on the student of the literary history of Glamorgan than the marked decline which becomes increasingly evident from the mid-sixteenth century onwards in the standard of poetry composed in the strict metres. This type of syllabic verse, distinguished by the intricate pattern of consonantal alliteration and internal rhyme known as *cynghanedd* in Welsh, had obviously lost much of its creative impulse and vigour by this period; the style and language of the bards had become stultified and, with a few rare exceptions, their traditional verses, especially when set against the works of those enlightened scholars and littérateurs who had been imbued with the ideals of the Renaissance and the new humanism, seemed by comparison dull, stereotyped, and uninspiringly monotonous. Nor was this phenomenon confined to Glamorgan, for there are indisputable indications of decadence in the works of many bards in the other major historic regions of Wales. Tradition, especially one as rich and resilient as that represented by the Welsh bardic order, died hard, and some poets occasionally succeeded in rising above the general level of artistic mediocrity. But they were disappointingly few in number and only rarely does one encounter some vestigial traces of the exquisite felicity of phrase, the pregnant economy of expression, the unmistakable distinction of tone and sure sense of style and rhythmical balance which so clearly characterize the works of the great masters who sang in this medium in the fifteenth century, when verse of this genre undeniably reached its highest pitch of artistic refinement and elegance.[2]

Not only had the *awdl* and *cywydd* manifestly lost their long preeminence and artistic refinement by the mid-sixteenth century, but the very principle which lay at the root of the canonical twenty-four metres was being seriously challenged at that time by an entirely different method of scansion, represented by verse composed in the so-called free metres.[3] Whereas poetry composed in the strict metres rigidly adhered to a prescribed number of syllables in each line, the metrical pattern of

[535]

free verse was basically determined by the number of accentual beats which it contained. This type of verse had probably flourished for centuries among those whom that Renaissance scholar and Catholic exile, Gruffydd Robert (*c.* 1522–*c.* 1610), called 'the unskilled folk' (*y bobl annhechnennig*),[4] the ordinary, untutored people who could not appreciate all the refinements of the stylized and highly ornate poetry in the strict metres which was mainly addressed to the nobility. There is much evidence to suggest, however, that verse composed in the free metres was becoming increasingly popular from the mid-sixteenth century onwards among those who belonged to the literate upper strata of native Welsh society. This verse was composed either on old Welsh metres devoid of *cynghanedd* or on various airs, frequently of English origin, which were then in vogue.[5] Some bards, deeply disturbed no doubt by the threat which this new tendency constituted to their position and livelihood, refer bitterly in their compositions to the unprecedented demand which had arisen in their day for these airs and carols.[6] But there were others among the bardic fraternity who occasionally sang on the new metres.[7] This tendency can be found in the works of such Glamorgan bards as Meurug Dafydd and Llywelyn Siôn or Edward Dafydd of Margam (below, pp. 543–546, 554–558).

THE CRISIS CONFRONTING THE WELSH BARDIC ORDER IN THE SIXTEENTH AND SEVENTEENTH CENTURIES

The decadence which characterizes the verse composed by the professional poets and the greater attention given to the free metres both reflect, in their different ways, the major crisis which confronted the bardic order. No attempt to analyse its causes should ignore either the deeply-ingrained conservatism of the bards themselves or the senility of the tradition which they represented. That tradition, as Sir Philip Sidney clearly recognized in his celebrated *Apologie for Poetry*, was 'not more notable in soone beginning then in long continuing',[8] and had reached a most venerable age long before the middle of the sixteenth century. No literary movement can be expected to continue indefinitely. Even the strongest of literary traditions will ultimately die when the particular social conditions which once created and fostered it no longer prevail. No new development of major significance had occurred since the fourteenth century in the conventions of strict-metre panegyric verse, except that the sixteenth-century bards, largely in response to the great demand for pedigree-making in the Tudor period, tended to incorporate more genealogical and heraldic data in their *cywyddau mawl* ('poems of praise').[9] This strongly suggests that all the thematic and artistic possibilities of this literary genre had by then been discovered and exhaustively exploited. This stagnant conservatism is reflected even in the metrical pattern of this poetry, for of the twenty-four measures in the metrical repertoire of the professional bards, most poets showed a marked predilection for only a few of these. It would have been far better if the professional bards had been more prepared to experiment with new literary forms and metres, as suggested by Gruffydd Robert, who had hinted vaguely at 'such metres as the Italians use'.[10] He had advocated not only a relaxing of the rigid metrical rules of the bards but also the adoption of the free metres for the composition of epic poetry. His exhortations, however, fell on deaf ears, for the period produced no new literary form of major significance. In that respect Wales presented a striking contrast to Elizabethan England, where the sonnet enjoyed a vogue second only to that of the drama.

Nor, with a few notable exceptions, were the bards influenced in any significant way by the great currents of thought and intellectual inquiry of the Renaissance and the new humanism. The humanist scholars, who passionately longed to see the native indigenous culture enriched with classical learning and the Welsh language used as a medium for all kinds of new scholarship, made a number of concrete proposals to arrest the gradual decline of Welsh poetic art.[11] In the first place, they besought the bards to refrain from flattering their patrons for material gain and from issuing false pedigrees, and urged on them the necessity to satirize as well as to praise.[12] Secondly, the bards should seriously endeavour to make up for the alleged lack of substance in their work by gaining from printed sources a knowledge of the liberal arts and sciences, which could then profitably become the theme of their compositions.[13] Thirdly, the artistic decadence of the strict-metre verse of this period could effectively be arrested by a skilful exploitation of the classical art of rhetoric.[14] Fourthly, the bards should renounce unreservedly the reticence and secretiveness for which their order had been so long renowned and explain the mysteries of their esoteric craft to all who wished to understand them.[15] These proposals, however, evoked little response, and it is therefore hardly surprising that some Renaissance scholars, such as Siôn Dafydd Rhys (1534–1619?), were firmly of the opinion that it was the bards' stubborn obscurantism which, above all else, was responsible for the ultimate disintegration of their organization 'until in the end there was left neither art among them, nor a man skilled in art that was worthy of mention; and until, by long following of this evil practice, the Bards did draw and hale themselves clean out of all desert and dignity'.[16] But in fairness to the bards it must readily be conceded that most of those who belonged to the Welsh middle class were either clearly unable or stubbornly unwilling to take over the duties of literary patronage from the rapidly-defecting nobility. Nor should it be forgotten that the whole social and intellectual milieu of sixteenth-century Wales, a country which had no university of its own or any other national institution of any real significance and whose only capital was London, to which it was a remote and relatively unimportant province, was singularly unconducive to the successful adoption of the type of cultural programme envisaged by the Welsh humanists.

Upon an organization which thus contained within itself the seeds of its own ultimate destruction there impinged a number of powerful solvents from without. Not the least widespread of these in its effects was the inflation of the late-sixteenth and early-seventeenth centuries in England and Wales alike.[17] Naturally, when the professional bards continued to receive the shelter and hospitable board to which there are so many glowing references in medieval panegyric verse, they were to a certain extent cushioned against the inflationary spiral. But when, as was frequently the case, their remuneration was in coin, this inflation must have struck the bards a severe economic blow, and they bemoan the alleged niggardliness of their patrons almost as frequently as they complain about the unprecedentedly sharp rise in the domestic price-level.[18] But patrons of any kind were becoming increasingly difficult to find, and the poets themselves were adamant that the main reason for the inexorable decline of their order was that the glorious days of noble patronage were virtually at an end.[19] Although the effects of the Act of Union could not have been as sudden or as cataclysmic as has sometimes been supposed,[20] it can hardly be doubted that the Welsh gentry gradually became more and more anglicized, losing their native speech, their interest in the life and culture of Wales and even, to some extent, their sense of nationality as well. One of the most powerful of the social influences operating in Tudor Wales was the so-called 'cult of gentryhood', and this was preeminently an English cult. Such educational facilities as did exist were directed to obliterating the native language and culture.[21] Indeed, the sons of many of the Welsh gentry went to schools in England and afterwards to the universities or to the Inns of Court. Although the process of cultural re-orientation was inevitably a slow and gradual one, many of the Welsh gentry came to regard their own native language and culture as something inherently inferior and began to look disdainfully on the bards. Although the picture drawn by the latter may at times have been an excessively sombre one, for bards were still being patronized during the sixteenth and early-seventeenth centuries,[22] there can be no doubt that, in general, it is a fair and accurate portrayal of contemporary trends. In any case, their diatribes against those anglicized gentry are frequently echoed in the works of the sixteenth-century humanists. The decline of the bardic order was a natural concomitant to the progressive anglicization of the gentry and the gradual disappearance of patronage, for such a professional art as the medieval Welsh bards had practised could not adequately be sustained by zealous amateurs in a rapidly-changing society. Moreover, the difficulties in which the bards found themselves were aggravated by the dissolution of the monasteries. There can be no doubt that the bards were generously patronized by the religious houses, of which the monasteries at Neath and Margam were two outstanding examples.[23]

Nor were the new intellectual currents of the age less hostile to the Welsh poetic tradition. That tradition had been indissolubly linked with the ideal of heroic panegyric, an ideal which had as its philosophic basis the medieval hierarchic conception of the world according to which every man had a permanent, pre-ordained position in society.[24] Although 'the transition from the spirit of the declining Middle Ages to humanism was far less simple than we are inclined to imagine',[25] it is nevertheless true that the restlessly-inquiring spirit of the humanists directly challenged and ultimately undermined the medieval conception of an ordered unity. In the final analysis, the whole intellectual and social ethos of the sixteenth and seventeenth centuries, with their emphasis on individualism and private enterprise, often to the detriment of the common weal,[26] was as alien to the native Welsh poetic tradition as it was to Dante's *Divina Commedia*. It is little wonder that the bards rapidly lost confidence in the social function of their art. In that respect their verse presents a striking contrast to medieval Welsh bardic poetry, which exudes an assurance of tone that strikes the reader as forcibly as does its great artistic accomplishment. The bards, it is true, still had a trade of sorts to pursue, they were still called upon, from time to time, to trace pedigrees or to compose eulogies to some of the gentry, who might be inclined, such was the force of habit and custom, to patronize the native literary tradition. But their work had lost its *raison d'être*, and it was therefore inevitable that the time-honoured Taliesinic tradition should rapidly degenerate into 'a matter of *vers de société*, lacking any significance wider than that of the events it commemorated'.[27]

One interesting piece of evidence effectively illustrates the great change that had taken place in Glamorgan. It comes from Sir John Stradling's account of the dispute over the burrows of Merthyr Mawr (above, pp. 23, 121). Stradling states that the defendant, Griffith Williams, brought two heraldic bards to the court 'to trye pettigrees'. One of these was the Glamorgan bard, Meurug Dafydd:

> . . . Hee would be counted a bard, and a poet: . . . Of his skill in poetry I am not able to Judge, but I cann tell you for a truth howe ould William Basset of Bewper, a good learned esqr judged of yt, who was a man very iudiciall in deede. This bard resorting a brode to gentlemens howses in the loytringe time betweene Christmas and Candlemas to singe songes and receave rewardes, comminge to Bewper hee presented the good ould squier with a cowydh, odle or englyn (I knowe not whither) containinge partelie the praises of the gentleman, and partelie the pettygrees and matches of his auncesters. The gentleman havinge perused the rhyme, prepared in his hand a noble for a reward and called the poet who came with a good will; of whome he demaunded whether he had reserved to himself any copie of that rhyme; no by my fayth (sayd the rhymer) but I hope to take a copie of that which I delivered you: Then replyed the gentleman, hould, here ys thy fee, and by my honestie I swere yf there bee no copie of this extante, none shall there ever bee, and therewith put it sure enough into the fier.[28]

Some of these details may well be apocryphal, and Stradling obviously had a special reason for pouring scorn on the Glamorgan bard. But that Meurug Dafydd addressed verses to the family mentioned in Stradling's account is beyond question, for an elegy which he sang to this same William Bassett in 1586 has fortunately been preserved in Llanover MS. B 5, 116–19. But however sceptical one may be of some of its details, the story strikingly illustrates the level to which the Welsh poetic tradition had sunk by that period, and not in Glamorgan alone: the flames which devour Meurug Dafydd's composition in John Stradling's vivid account symbolically engulf the whole Taliesinic tradition which had continued unabated for a thousand years or more.

That the professional bards were sometimes confused with the unskilled minstrels and hucksters who roamed the country in such large numbers only served to add to the scorn which was poured on them from so many quarters. For various reasons, the number of vagabonds increased substantially during the sixteenth century (above, pp. 89–92). But the London parliament frequently found it difficult to make a clear distinction between the trained bards of the classical Welsh tradition and the English minstrels and ballad-mongers who roamed the country entertaining in fairs and taverns.

Given such distinctly adverse circumstances as these, it was almost inevitable that considerable disorganization should have arisen among the Welsh bards; hence the two famous *eisteddfodau* which were held at Caerwys, in Flintshire, the first in 1523, the second, under a commission granted by Elizabeth I herself, in 1567, with a view to introducing a more stringent discipline into the bardic order by revising its statutes and carefully scrutinizing the qualifications of its members.[29] But these efforts were of little avail and the bardic order, unable to adapt itself to a changed society, continued to decline. Caught in a maelstrom of forces that were as mercilessly hostile in their effects as they were widely diverse in origin, the bards could only hope to struggle along from day to day, clinging desperately to those patrons who were still prepared to support them in the traditional manner and eagerly accepting the largesse of those among the aspiring *nouveaux riches* who were not averse to buying pedigrees and eulogies if they might thereby add to their newly-acquired material gains an air of social respectability.[30] As Edward Dafydd of Margam so bitterly complained in 1655, the world in which the poets of his day lived and moved was a singularly uncongenial one: 'Nid yw'r byd hwn gyda'r beirdd'.[31] That anguished *cri de cœur* is echoed in the works of many bards who sang outside Glamorgan.[32] Nor can these complaints be construed as a case of special pleading on their part, for their plight was noted by less partial contemporary observers. By this time, wrote the author of *The Three Antiquities of Bryttaen*, though obviously not without an element of exaggeration, 'all the greate knowledge of the Bards, there credyt and worth is altogether decayed and worne out, soe that at this time they are extinguish [*sic*] amongest vs./And the *Prydyddion*, at this time likewise are of noe estimatione . . .'.[33]

i.

POETRY COMPOSED IN THE STRICT METRES DURING THE LATE-SIXTEENTH AND SEVENTEENTH CENTURIES

One significant indication of the extent to which the native bardic tradition had declined in Glamorgan by the second half of the sixteenth century is that only rarely were the works of its bards included in manuscripts transcribed in north Wales. This tendency contrasts strikingly with the practice of the preceding period, when their compositions were obviously regarded as constituting a vital part of the nation's rich literary heritage, and northern scribes frequently included in their manuscripts the compositions of Ieuan Gethin, Gwilym Tew and Lewis Morgannwg,[34] or even the works of far less famous Glamorgan bards, alongside the works of famous bards from Gwynedd and Powys. After *c.* 1550, however, only rarely are copies of the works of such late-sixteenth-century Glamorgan bards as Dafydd Benwyn, Meurug Dafydd or Llywelyn Siôn found in manuscripts transcribed in north Wales. This is not to imply that all literary intercourse between the various regions had abruptly ceased, for there is ample evidence that many bards from various parts of Gwynedd, Powys, and Deheubarth continued to visit Glamorgan down to the early part of the seventeenth century. Rather it suggests that the great majority of the copyists were firmly convinced that the compositions of the contemporary Glamorgan bards were not of sufficient literary merit to be included in their manuscripts.

Fortunately, however, many of the Glamorgan bards themselves now began to practise the difficult and exacting art of manuscript transcription. Before *c.* 1550, with the two notable exceptions of Gwilym Tew and Lewis Morgannwg, not one of the bards can legitimately be regarded as copyists, and even those two famous chiefs-of-song made no serious attempt to prepare a comprehensive collection of their own compositions. But many of the bards who sang in Glamorgan from *c.* 1550 onwards were diligent copyists, and some of them included in the manuscripts which they transcribed substantial and extremely valuable collections of their own compositions. The zeal which they and some members of the bardic fraternity in other parts of Wales displayed in a country where the prevailing conditions were distinctly inimical to the rapid development of the printing-press[35] doubtless reflects, in part, their response to the urgent appeals of the humanists who passionately longed to see priceless literary material preserved and the works of the bards disseminated to a far wider circle. Fortunately, therefore, the literary historian has ample material at his disposal to pinpoint the major landmarks in the literary history of the region. For example, Llanover MS. B 5 contains a substantial collection of Meurug Dafydd's work, probably in his own hand. Dafydd Benwyn made an equally extensive collection of his own work. Some of his compositions, transcribed by the bard himself, occur in Llanstephan MS. 164 and Cardiff MS. 10, while the remainder can be found in two other substantial collections, one in Jesus College MS. 13, the other in Cardiff MS. 2.277 (= Baglan MS. 1), which was transcribed early in the seventeenth century by a certain 'Risiart Twrbervil', probably one of the descendants of the famous Turbervilles of Coety. Occasionally, one finds that a bard of little renown has filled a whole manuscript with copies of his own work and of the *cywyddau* composed by some of his contemporaries. The work of Sils ap Siôn in Llanover MS. B 6 is a notable example of this. Moreover, one of the bards, Llywelyn Siôn of Llangewydd, was himself a professional copyist of great importance who was from time to time commissioned by some of the local landed gentry to transcribe not only prose texts but also substantial collections of strict-metre verse, including the works composed by some of his contemporaries. But he rarely forgot to include some of his own work in the collection.

THE LOCAL GENTRY AS PATRONS OF THE BARDIC TRADITION

Many of the gentry of the region were a turbulent and undisciplined brood. Nevertheless, they included in their number some who obviously took a keen and intelligent interest in literary life and in the activities of the bards. Many of the gentle families, including those that were unquestionably of foreign descent, spoke Welsh. Indeed, according to the bards, some of the English ladies who became associated with these families by marriage made successful efforts to master the vernacular. For example, Lewis Morgannwg commented admiringly on the bilingual proficiency of Barbara, the daughter of Robert Bret of Somerset and wife to Sir George Mathew of Radyr[36]: 'Doetha merch, dwy iaith o'i min'. She spoke the vernacular, declared the poet, though doubtless with more than a touch of poetic hyperbole, without any discernible diffidence or trace of corrupt accent:

> Dilediaith, di-ŵyl ydyw,
> Ym mrig iaith Gymräeg yw.[37]

Indeed, some of these families, including the Bassetts, the Turbervilles, the Flemings and Gamages, now had more Welsh than foreign blood in their veins and a number of them were obviously fond of giving their children Welsh names.[38] The picture which emerges from Iolo Morganwg's manuscripts[39] is that of a circle of literature-loving gentry, who periodically organized *eisteddfodau* to study Welsh prosody and who took a passionate interest in the fortunes of the bardic order and the ancient druidic traditions with which, so Iolo claimed, it was historically linked. Fanciful and over-romanticized though some of these details undoubtedly are, nevertheless there were quite a few among the local gentry who were still fond of seeing accredited heraldic bards visiting their mansions and delivering eulogies or elegiac verses, into which were skilfully woven a wealth of interesting details concerning their pedigrees and coats-of-arms. But whether they could fully understand this type of verse and appreciate its deeper significance is very much open to question. Nevertheless, there were some among their number whose cultural attainments were quite impressive. To this group belonged Sir Edward Stradling, Sir Edward Mansel, Rice Merrick, and Anthony Powel (below, pp. 594–605).

The active part played by Sir Edward Stradling in the dissemination of Welsh culture is well known. It is noteworthy, however, that even such men as Sir Edward Stradling made no serious attempt to publish any of the strict-metre verse transcribed during this period. Nor did the gentry of north Wales: all alike seem to have deliberately eschewed the 'stigma of print'.[40] It is not until the closing years of the seventeenth century that we find a Glamorgan bard seriously contemplating the use of the printing-press.

The poets can conveniently be divided into two main classes. The first consisted of the professional bards who regularly went on itinerancy to the homes of the local gentry. To this group belonged such poets as Dafydd Benwyn and Meurug Dafydd, Tomas ab Ieuan ap Rhys,[41] or Edward Dafydd of Margam. Secondly, there were the gentlemen-bards from the Uplands (*Blaenau*), 'singing on their own food', to whom the composition of poetry was pre-eminently a pleasurable pastime. To this class belonged Hopcyn Tomas Phylip of Gelli'r-fid, in the parish of Llandyfodwg, Tomas ap Llywelyn of Rhigos, Gronwy Wiliam of Hendre Forgan, Watcyn Powel of Pen-y-fai, or clerics such as Morgan Powel of Llanhari and Dafydd Williams (Dafydd o'r Nant), the vicar of Pen-llin, near Cowbridge. It must not be imagined, however, that all the gentlemen-poets were averse to receiving patronage, and there were probably quite a few among the clergy who were heavily dependent on it.

THE PROFESSIONAL BARDS:
MEURUG DAFYDD (*fl. c.* 1560–*c.* 1593)

One of the most prominent members of the first class mentioned during the second half of the sixteenth century was Meurug Dafydd, who came from the district of Llanisien, near Cardiff. A bardic disciple of Lewis Morgannwg, he was obviously singing as early as 1560–1, for some of his work, written in his own hand, is ascribed in Llanover MS. B 5 to the third regnal year of Elizabeth I (*y 3 o Rhaynad Elizabeth*).[42] Nevertheless, the greater part of his strict-metre compositions, which were written by him in the aforementioned manuscript, clearly belong to the period 1580–93. However, the date 1534 is appended to one of his love-poems in this manuscript.[43] There is no valid reason for rejecting

[543]

this date, for the *cywydd* referred to occurs in the bard's autograph. This suggests that he was born about 1510–15, and he must therefore have been an octogenarian when he wrote some of the verses contained in Llanover MS. B 5. Even so, nothing composed by Meurug Dafydd which can confidently be ascribed to the period between 1534 and *c.* 1560 has so far been discovered.

He went on itinerancy to most of the important families who lived in Glamorgan and Gwent, although it seems that he was pre-eminently an *habitué* of the Lewis families of Rhiw'r-perrai (Ruperra) and Y Fan, near Caerphilly, to whom he probably regarded himself as some kind of household bard. His pedigree does not seem to have been recorded by the heraldic bards, but he may well have been of gentle lineage, for it is generally assumed that he was the 'Meyric David of Llanishen' who married Joan, the grand-daughter of Sir Christopher Mathew of Llandaff.[44] Although the general standard of his work is undeniably inferior to that achieved by the great *penceirddiaid* who sang during the fifteenth century, the golden age of the *cywydd*, he was a figure of considerable importance in the bardic history of Glamorgan, and Iolo Morganwg's manuscripts abound with references to him.

Dafydd Benwyn (second half of the sixteenth century)

Another prominent figure was Dafydd Benwyn. The late T. C. Evans ('Cadrawd', 1846–1918), was convinced that Dafydd Benwyn was a younger brother of Tomas ap Llywelyn of Rhigos, because he had composed a *cywydd gofyn* ('poem of asking') on behalf of the latter's father, Llywelyn ap Dafydd, soliciting the gift of a gown.[45] But there is no real foundation for this claim. Cadrawd was obviously unaware of the practice sometimes adopted by the bards of composing poems in which they vicariously solicited gifts of various kinds for their patrons. Following this poem in Jesus College MS. 13 is the composition which Dafydd Benwyn addressed to the two gaolers of Cardiff beseeching the release of his nephew.[46] Sils ap Siôn, a contemporary to Dafydd Benwyn, explicitly stated that the latter came from Llangeinwyr (Llangeinor), in the ancient commote of Glyn Ogwr.[47] This is further corroborated by the fact that Dafydd Benwyn refers to Ieuan ap Siancyn ab Ieuan ap Madog, of Betws Tir Iarll, as his 'neighbour'.[48] He came, therefore, from Tir Iarll, the home of his two bardic teachers, Rhisiart Iorwerth (or Rhisiart Fynglwyd) and Lewis Morgannwg, and the cradle of all that was best in the rich bardic tradition of Glamorgan.[49]

Dafydd Benwyn was unquestionably the most prolific of all the Glamorgan bards who sang in the strict metres. In addition to a large number of *englynion* on a wide variety of themes, Cardiff MS. 2.277 contains over 180 of the *cywyddau* and *awdlau* which he sang to the leading families of Glamorgan and Gwent, including some which are never mentioned in the work of any other Glamorgan bard. Although he was the bardic disciple of two prominent and gifted poets, the bulk of his work is undeniably commonplace and stereotyped. Nevertheless, his muse could occasionally produce verse of a far higher standard. Of particular interest from this standpoint are the *cywydd* soliciting the gift of a horse from Rhisiart Tomas ap Gruffudd Goch of Ynys Arwed, in the Vale of Neath, and the elegies to the said Rhisiart, to Lleision ap Rhys of Llanisawel (or Briton Ferry), and to Tomas Lewys of Baglan.[50] But these occasions are disappointingly rare. Nevertheless, his work is important for two reasons. In the first place, it sheds much valuable light on the genealogies of many important families in both Glamorgan and Gwent. Secondly, his verse contains the Welsh forms of various place-names in those areas where he regularly went on bardic itinerancy, forms for which one searches in vain in most of the official Latin records relating to this period. It has often been claimed, on the basis of some elegiac *englynion* addressed to him by Siôn Ieuan ap Rhys Fychan, that Dafydd Benwyn died in 1590.[51] These verses occur in Cardiff MS. 2.277, but no date is mentioned in that source.[52] The same manuscript contains an elegy composed by Dafydd Benwyn in 1581 to 'Sion jevann Rys ychan [*sic*] o gelli gaer'.[53] This obvious inconsistency is difficult to explain satisfactorily, unless it is another example of the amusing bardic practice of composing elegies to living persons.[54]

LLYWELYN SIÔN (*c.* 1540–*c.* 1615–17)

A man of quite a different background from the poets mentioned above was Llywelyn Siôn. Born at Llangewydd, in Trelales (Laleston), near Bridgend, he was, according to tradition, a landed gentleman. That he was keenly interested in the subject of husbandry is shown by the letter which he addressed in 1596 to Wiliam Prys, the *cwndidwr* from Llanisawel (Briton Ferry),[55] probably the earliest extant Welsh letter which is unquestionably of Glamorgan provenance.[56] The claim that it was Llywelyn Siôn who was pre-eminently responsible for systematizing and preserving the 'Mysteries of the Bards of the Isle of Britain' is really a figment of Iolo Morganwg's fertile imagination. It is extremely unlikely that he ever received any formal instruction from leading *penceirddiaid*, nor does he appear to have been closely associated in his younger days with Meurug Dafydd and Dafydd Benwyn, both of whom were his contemporaries. His bardic teacher, according to one of his *cywyddau*, was Tomas ap Llywelyn ap Dafydd ap Hywel (*fl. c.* 1580–1610) of Rhigos, and it is probably of some significance that Morgan Powel of Llanhari, another prominent literary figure in this period, was a cleric in Laleston *c.* 1563. It seems, therefore, that Llywelyn Siôn was initiated into the bardic craft by this small but unusually enthusiastic circle of literary-minded gentlemen and clerics.

His literary output, however, was astonishingly meagre. Only about fourteen of his strict-metre compositions, including both *awdlau* and *cywyddau*, are now extant.[57] The fact that the poems attributed to him are so extraordinarily few in number suggests that he did not go as frequently as did other bards on itinerancy in Glamorgan and Gwent. Although he was obviously not of much importance as a creative artist, his great renown rests pre-eminently on the fact that he was one of the ablest professional copyists of his age. This was probably the main reason why he became elevated in Iolo Morganwg's manuscripts into one of the most important and influential figures in the latter's picture of Glamorgan, as a scribe to whose industry and acumen latter-day literary historians were largely indebted for preserving much of the early literature connected with the ancient druidic traditions of the Isle of Britain. Although it is extremely difficult to fix Llywelyn Siôn's dates with any degree of precision, it appears that he was somewhat younger than both Meurug Dafydd and Dafydd Benwyn. The date 1613 occurs in his autograph in Llyfr Hir Llanharan ('The Long Book of Llanharan'),[58] probably the most famous of all the manuscripts which he transcribed, and he must by then have been well advanced in years. The suggestion that he died *c.* 1615–17 probably originated with Iolo Morganwg, but it cannot be very wide of the mark.

In addition to the three figures mentioned above, there were many other peripatetic bards of lesser repute. They included in their number such gentlemen-bards as Hopcyn Tomas Phylip, Tomas ap Llywelyn of Rhigos, and Goronwy Wiliam of Hendre Forgan, or the cleric-poet Morgan Powel of Llanhari. But they are chiefly renowned in the literary tradition of the region as *cwndidwyr* (below, pp. 566–576).

Sils ap Siôn (*fl. c.* 1570–*c.* 1590)

A particularly interesting member of this second class of poets was Sils ap Siôn. A reference contained in the *cywydd* which he composed on the theme of husbandry suggests that he lived somewhere near Radyr and Llandaff, a fact which Iolo Morganwg was quick to perceive. In Llanover MS. C 53 the latter quotes the pedigree of a certain 'Giles ap John', who was related to one of the well-known Miskin families, that of Llywelyn ap Cynwrig,[59] and it is quite possible that this was the Glamorgan bard. A small collection of his work, probably in his own hand, is preserved in Llanover MS. B 6. The greater part of his work consists of *cywyddau* addressed to his friend and neighbour, William Evans (d. 1589–90), treasurer and chancellor of Llandaff, and to Rice Merrick of Cotrel. Apart from these compositions, his work contains no panegyric or elegiac verses similar to those usually written by the peripatetic bards, which tends to confirm the view that he was probably a landed gentleman.

His work contains one extempore *englyn* composed when a group of bards assembled before the aforementioned William Evans and Thomas Lewis of Llandaff, who had obviously been chosen to act as adjudicators, 'to sing in verse for the mastery' (*i gany ar wawd am y vaistrola[eth]*).[60] Sils ap Siôn himself recorded the *englyn* which he sang on that occasion.[61] The homes of the church dignitaries at Llandaff were undoubtedly centres of great importance in the bardic history of Glamorgan throughout the sixteenth century. But it was from 1550 to *c.* 1590, when William Evans was intimately associated with the cathedral church, that Llandaff achieved its greatest renown as a centre of bardic activity. Dafydd Benwyn, for example, described him as the 'Ifor Hael' of Llandaff, thus equating him with the medieval Maecenas of that name immortalized in the poetry of Dafydd ap Gwilym.[62] In Llanover MS. B 6 Sils ap Siôn has left us a collection of strict-metre verse, consisting of *awdlau*, *cywyddau*, and *englynion*, in praise of the chancellor by eight different bards. The contents of these verses suggest that he was keenly interested to see the bardic order flourish and prosper. His name is also clearly associated with the only *eisteddfod* known for certain to have been held in Glamorgan before the eighteenth century. The brief description which Sils ap Siôn gives us of this bardic assembly at Llandaff suggests that it was not unlike the kind of literary contest which later became known as an *eisteddfod* in the eighteenth century (below, pp. 624–626).[63]

In a later period the manuscript transcribed by Sils ap Siôn came into Iolo Morganwg's possession. He then proceeded to write a fictitious and highly romantic account of this *eisteddfod*, which unfortunately misled a number of literary historians of the nineteenth century. Iolo claimed that William Evans had established a famous bardic 'chair' at Llandaff in 1558, which was held annually on the Feast of St. Teilo (February 9) and Whit Monday. He even presumed to fix the precise date when the *eisteddfod* to which Sils ap Siôn referred had been held: the year, he claimed, was 1564, and he gave a list of the bards who had assembled there. On another occasion he quoted nine verses composed in order to counsel the bards who had attended the *eisteddfod* which William Evans had organized at Llandaff in 1561.[64] The plethora of fabricated details which Iolo Morganwg ingeniously wove around the simple but irrefutably authentic entry contained in Sils ap Siôn's manuscript (plate XI) provides us with an instructive example of the way in which his exceptionally perverse mind worked.

Although the entry in Llanover MS. B 6 is the only extant authentic record of any *eisteddfod* held in Glamorgan prior to the eighteenth century, it is more than likely that bardic assemblies of this kind constituted a vital part of the literary life of the region in the sixteenth and seventeenth centuries. Iolo Morganwg was again fully aware of this and his manuscripts abound with colourful details of various mythical bardic 'chairs' or *eisteddfodau*. His volume, *Cyfrinach Beirdd Ynys Prydain*

(1829), contains references to a grandiose series of meetings allegedly held by the bards in the sixteenth century in order to systematize the Welsh metres, a series which reaches its climax with what is probably the most remarkable and colourful of all the many *eisteddfodau* recorded in Iolo Morganwg's manuscripts, the bardic assembly which he claimed had been held at Beaupré (Y Bewpyr) in 1681.[65] He had also discovered in early authentic manuscript-sources a series of verses in the *englyn* measure composed by the bards who had assembled at the second *eisteddfod* held at Caerwys in 1567, and so he proceeded to write scores of poems and triads which, he asserted, the bards had composed and proclaimed in their professional assemblies in various places in Glamorgan. Although it would be extremely unwise to state categorically that no such bardic assemblies were ever held, it is beyond question that Iolo Morganwg was the author of many of the *englynion* and *cywyddau* which are associated in his manuscripts with many of these *eisteddfodau*.

Nevertheless, enough genuine evidence has survived to suggest that the second half of the sixteenth century and the early part of the seventeenth was a period of intense literary activity in Glamorgan. The contemporary verse proves that there were very few mansions of importance in the region that were not periodically visited by the peripatetic bards. Meurug Dafydd, for example, sang to the influential Herbert family, to the Bassetts of Beaupré, the Lewis families of Y Fan and Rhiw'r-perrai (Ruperra), the Stradlings of St. Donat's, the Mansels of Margam, the Gamages of Coety, the Morgans of Tredegar, as well as to many of the prominent gentry of Gwent. The circle with which his contemporary, Dafydd Benwyn, became familiar was an even wider one. Indeed, he appears to have visited homes which are rarely, if ever, mentioned in the strict-metre verse of the preceding period, including Y Cotrel and Dyffryn (both situated in the parish of St. Nicholas in the Vale), Treglement (or Clemenston, near St. Bride's Major), Rhydlafar (in St. Fagans), Y Rhws (Rhoose), Llancaeach (near Gelli-gaer), Splott (near Cardiff), Brynhelygen and Caerewigau (both of which are situated in Pendoylan), Llandŵ (Llandow), St. Bride's-super-Ely (Llansanffraid-ar-Elái), and many more besides. Unquestionably, the outstanding example of a professional bard is Dafydd Benwyn, by far the most prolific and, in certain respects, probably the most interesting of all the peripatetic bards who lived in Glamorgan in this period.

Many interesting references occur in contemporary manuscripts to the payment received by the bards for their verses. Meurug Dafydd, according to John Stradling, received a 'noble' for the panegyric which he addressed to William Bassett. 'Here is an elegy', wrote the same bard on another occasion, 'for the composition of which not a single penny was received'. But it was not always the patrons who were to blame, for there were obviously occasions when the poets lamentably failed to fulfil their promises. For example, Sils ap Siôn explicitly states in a note written above the elegiac *cywydd* which he sang to William Evans of Llandaff that he had composed it 'when the other bards were indolent, having been paid in advance'.[66]

LITERARY INTERCOURSE BETWEEN GLAMORGAN AND OTHER PARTS OF WALES *c.* 1550–*c.* 1620

Glamorgan bards were familiar with much of the strict-metre verse composed by their contemporaries in north Wales. Llywelyn Siôn, for instance, included in his invaluable transcriptions the compositions of some of the famous northern bards of his period, including those of Siôn Tudur, Wiliam Llŷn, and Wiliam Cynwal. Indeed, Wiliam Cynwal, although he probably never visited Glamorgan, composed an *englyn* in praise of Meurug Dafydd, while Llywelyn Siôn seems to have been involved in some sort of contention with a certain cleric from north Wales called Sir Huw Robert. Llywelyn Siôn's autograph also occurs in Peniarth MS. 182, which was transcribed by Sir Hugh Pennant *c.* 1514, although it is extremely difficult to determine the precise whereabouts of this manuscript when it eventually came into the Glamorgan scribe's possession.[67] There is little evidence, however, to suggest that any of the bards who lived in Glamorgan in this period ever went on itinerancy to north Wales, as many of their predecessors had done in the medieval period. On the other hand, the homes of some of the more prominent members of the Glamorgan gentry were visited periodically by bards from other parts of Wales. The poet who undoubtedly caused the greatest stir in the region during this period was Siôn Mowddwy (*fl. c.* 1575–1613), a bard who sang the praises of many members of the gentry in many parts of Wales, from Mostyn to Glamorgan. It appears that he spent a considerable time in Glamorgan, a fact which probably inspired the various details concocted about him by Iolo Morganwg in Llanover MS. C 18.[68] Although there is no historical foundation for any of these statements, they nevertheless show that Iolo Morganwg had grasped that Siôn Mowddwy was a figure of considerable importance in the literary history of the region. Sometime during the period 1575–80 this bard indulged in flyting poetry with Meurug Dafydd concerning the rights and privileges of the peripatetic bards in Gwent, which Iolo Morganwg ingeniously attempted to use as a means of proving the genuineness of the Glamorgan classification of the Welsh strict metres. It is difficult at this stage to determine the exact cause of this bardic disputation. But it seems to have originated in the kind of disagreement which so frequently occurred when one poet endeavoured to oust another from his established position as the accredited 'household bard'. Both poets poured scorn on one another in the traditional manner, and each imputed serious faults and deficiencies in the metrical art of his adversary. But by far the most interesting aspect of this disputation is the letter which Siôn Mowddwy addressed to Meurug Dafydd. The reference contained in this letter to a certain man, such as Meurug Dafydd, who had lamentably failed to master the bardic craft, in spite of having been permitted to borrow a copy of the bardic grammar for over two years and being personally instructed by Siôn Mowddwy himself, gives us a rare insight into the manner in which the older bardic teachers taught their young disciples.[69] Characteristically, Iolo Morganwg forged a reply by Meurug Dafydd. In this document he attempted to show that the contention had originated in a bitter disagreement between the bards of Glamorgan, who faithfully adhered to the local classification of the Welsh metres 'as it occurs in the manuscript-books of the magnificent teachers of old', and the bards of Gwynedd and Deheubarth, who accepted the new classification devised by Dafydd ab Edmwnd (*fl.* 1450–90) at the famous *eisteddfod* held at Carmarthen *c.* 1451.[70]

Heraldic bards from other parts of Wales also visited Glamorgan during this period with a view to collecting the pedigrees of some of the local landed gentry. It is possible that Wiliam Llŷn visited Glamorgan, although he does not appear to have addressed a single poem to any of the region's gentry. In Peniarth MS. 140, written for the most part by Wiliam Llŷn, sometime before 1569,[71] he states that he had been given the pedigree of Lleision ap Rhys of Llanisawel (Briton Ferry) by Tomas ap Hywel of Tir Iarll.[72] This tends to corroborate the view that he had visited the region in his eager search for important genealogical data. Moreover, pages 372–7 of the same manuscript were written in 1573 by a certain 'R.T.', probably Rhisiart ap Tomas ap Gruffudd Goch of Ynys Arwed, who was one of the descendants of the famous Aberpergwm family. Another prominent figure who spent some time in the region was Thomas Jones ('Twm Siôn Cati', *c.* 1530–1609), the poet-genealogist from Fountain Gate, near Tregaron, Cardiganshire, who is known to have assisted both George Owen (*c.* 1552–1613) and Lewys Dwnn (*c.* 1550–*c.* 1616) as well as the officers of the Heralds College.[73] Again, the *cywyddau* contained in Peniarth MS. 96 prove beyond any doubt that Lewys Dwnn visited the region on a number of occasions between 1599 and 1605 in his search for pedigrees and that he called at a number of important mansions, including those at Y Cotrel, Llandaff, and Beaupré. During his visits he was shown the 'old Records and manuscripts of the religious houses' by Sir Edward Stradling, Sir Edward Mansel, Rice Merrick, and Anthony Powel.[74] There clearly was, therefore, considerable social and literary intercourse during this period between the Glamorgan bards and those who came from other parts of Wales. That this is true also for the early-seventeenth century is shown by the *englynion* written on the alleged 'qualities of the men of Gwynedd' by a certain Tomas Lewis (*fl. c.* 1610–30) of Llechau (possibly in Llanhari), who had obviously been deeply offended by some of the lesser itinerant bards from the northern province.[75]

The General Standard of the Strict-metre Verse

Analysis of the general artistic standard of the strict-metre verse composed during this period reveals clearly the extent to which the bardic tradition had declined in Glamorgan. The subjects or themes on which the Glamorgan bards sang were generally very similar to those of strict-metre poets in other parts of Wales, and the manuscripts transcribed in the region during this period contain scores of eulogies and elegies couched in that consciously measured, formal style which had been one of the outstanding characteristics of Welsh bardic poetry for centuries, of poems soliciting gifts of various kinds (*cywyddau gofyn*) and expressing gratitude for the patrons' largesse, of love-poems and poems of contention (*cywyddau ymryson*). The *awdl* was obviously a very popular literary form. The bards were familiar with much of the matter contained in the traditional bardic vocabularies, and a copy of one of these, transcribed by Meurug Dafydd, has fortunately been preserved.[76] They had obviously studied the bardic grammar associated with Einion Offeiriad and Dafydd Ddu of Hiraddug, and a few, at least, among their number were familiar with the contents of Siôn Dafydd Rhys's famous grammar.[77] But in spite of all the praise lavished by Iolo Morganwg on various Glamorgan bards, no early copy exists of any work on Welsh versification which is irrefutably of Glamorgan provenance.[78] This is remarkable in view of the indefatigable industry and catholic range of interest displayed by Llywelyn Siôn as a professional copyist.[79] Nevertheless, it is obvious that the Glamorgan bards had assiduously studied the works of the great chiefs-of-song in the strict metres and they had clearly mastered some of the basic rudiments of this unusually difficult art. But their work, in general, hardly bears comparison with the superb artistry and technical accomplishment displayed by such acknowledged masters as Iorwerth Fynglwyd and Lewis Morgannwg. Their verses reflect a lack of sensitiveness to the niceties of the literary language, an inadequate sense of style, a diffuseness and lack of rhythmical balance which contrast strikingly with the standard achieved in the fifteenth and early-sixteenth centuries. Some compositions are even marred by elementary errors in the rules of *cynghanedd*. Nor can these faults be attributed to textual corruption, for they occur even in those verses which were transcribed by the authors themselves. The language, too, had lost much of its former brilliance and had been corrupted by the intrusion of dialectal forms, although the professional bards succeeded, on the whole, in avoiding the more patently vulgar forms and phrases which abound in the free-metre *cwndidau* or religious carols, some of which were composed by professional bards. In general, their work suggests that they were a comparatively unskilled circle of bards who bravely, but vainly, attempted to imitate the art of the old masters: the same stereotyped imagery, compound epithets, and turns of phrase often occur in their verses. But in attempting to capture some of the artistry displayed by their more accomplished forebears they frequently wrote lines or couplets which are completely devoid of meaning. The following short extract from the elegy which Dafydd Benwyn sang to a certain Siôn ap Tomas of Llandŵ (Llandow), in the Vale of Glamorgan, is typical of much of that bard's prolific output and illustrates a few of the faults and weaknesses mentioned:

> Wylwn od aeth o Landŵ,
> Os henwaf, eisiau hwnnw,
> Bwrw i fedd braw a fu yn,
> Braw tost ar burwaed Iestyn.
> Bwrw Siôn bob awr ysy wg,
> Briwfawr gŵyn Bro Forgannwg,
> Bwrw anap uwch bro Einion,
> Briwo'n sir bwrw yna Siôn;
> Nefrber waed, wyler alaeth,
> Oedd ddewr iawn, i ddaear aeth;
> Iawn ach y Based yn oedd,
> Ach Lleision uwch holl oesoedd.[80]

Yet some of the verse possesses quite substantial merits. For example, parts of the *cywydd* which Meurug Dafydd sang to Aberafan have a delicate loveliness which immediately elevates it above the general level of artistic mediocrity.[81] No less commendable are the *cywyddau* which Tomas ap Llywelyn of Rhigos, Morgan Powel, the cleric-poet from Llanhari, Gronwy Wiliam of Hendre Forgan, and Llywelyn Siôn addressed to one another.[82] There is a touching poignancy in some sections of the poems written by these bards on the theme of senility, yet they are not completely devoid of an element of humour and they occasionally exhibit some deft and delicate touches of craftsmanship. But they are hardly representative of the great bulk of verse composed during this period, and whatever artistic merits they may occasionally reflect, cannot reasonably be compared with the works of their more talented northern contemporaries. There is scarcely a poem written by a Glamorgan bard which is worthy to be included in an anthology of the best strict-metre verse composed during this period.

The period reviewed above drew to a close towards the end of the first quarter of the seventeenth century. No elegy was composed to any of the bards referred to, apart from the *englynion* which Siôn Ieuan ap Rhys Fychan of Gelli-gaer is supposed to have sung when he heard of the death of Dafydd Benwyn.[83] It is astonishing that, although Dafydd Benwyn sang elegies in the traditional manner to Maredudd ap Rhoser and Hywel ap Sir Mathau, who came from outside the county, neither he nor his fellow-poets composed elegies to any of their bardic contemporaries in Glamorgan. The decline in the native bardic tradition was probably proceeding at an appreciably more rapid pace in Glamorgan than in north Wales, and from this time onwards the local bards were given a cold reception in the homes and mansions of most of the gentry.

It is also significant that Dafydd Benwyn and his contemporaries left very few disciples after them. A detailed comparison of Dafydd Benwyn's prolific output, undistinguished though much of it may be, with the depressing dearth of strict-metre verse in seventeenth-century Glamorgan strikingly illustrates the rapid decline that had taken place. Most of those who sang during the seventeenth century were figures of little renown or significance. Nor were they nearly as numerous as some scholars have occasionally been led to believe, for many of the bards mentioned in various studies published in the nineteenth century were figments of Iolo Morganwg's imagination. This cannot be said of Ieuan Tomas, however, the author of four elegies which were included in the substantial collection of *cywyddau* transcribed by Tomas ab Ieuan of Tre'r-bryn in Llanover MS. B 1. The information which can be gathered about Ieuan Tomas is meagre in the extreme, but it is known that he sang to Sir John Carne of Ewenni towards the beginning of the seventeenth century as well as to Anthony Powel, who died in 1618–19.[84]

TOMAS LEWIS (*fl. c.* 1610–30)

Another bard who flourished in this period was Tomas Lewis of Llechau. He probably succeeded in acquiring Sils ap Siôn's manuscript, Llanover B 6, after the latter's death, for spaces left vacant in this manuscript were filled by him with *englynion* of his own composition. Iolo Morganwg tried to elevate him into one of the great masters of Welsh poetry. He also maintained that Tomas Lewis had written an extremely important and erudite work entitled 'Yniales'. But there is no historical warrant for any of these pretentious claims: his few modest attempts at composition prove that Tomas Lewis could boast of very little skill or accomplishment as a bard.

WATCYN POWEL (*c.* 1600–55)

A person whose background was markedly different from that of many of the literary figures mentioned above was Watcyn Powel, the gentleman-bard and genealogist from Pen-y-fai, near Bridgend. He was a nephew to Anthony Powel of Llwydarth and belonged to that rapidly-diminishing group of cultured, literature-loving gentlemen who usually 'sang on their own food'. Six of his *cywyddau* were included by Tomas ab Ieuan of Tre'r-bryn in *Y Byrdew Mawr*. These compositions suggest that he was by no means inferior to any of his contemporaries in poetic craftsmanship and that he was decidedly more talented than most. He was probably the last in that long distinguished line of Glamorgan gentry who could compose a *cywydd* in the traditional manner, as the following extract from Edward Dafydd's elegy in which he bemoaned the death in 1655 of Watcyn Powel and the passing of the old teachers and heraldic bards clearly testifies:

> Darfod o'u hamod mae'r heirdd—athrawon,
> A threio arwyddfeirdd;
> Dwyn dynion dawn dianeirdd,
> Nid yw'r byd hwn gyda'r beirdd.
>
> . . . .
>
> Ni chlywir, cwynir hyd Gonwy,—ergyd
> I'r gerdd gymeradwy,
> Na da fiwsig difaswy,
> Na mawl ym Mhen-y-fai mwy.[85]

Two elegies written on the occasion of Powel's death are extant, one by Edward Dafydd, the other by Dafydd o'r Nant, as well as two *englynion* which Dafydd Edward of Margam sang to his memory.[86]

Edward Dafydd (*c.* 1600/2–78?) and His Bardic Disciples

By far the most famous of all the bards who sang in Glamorgan in the seventeenth century was Edward Dafydd of Margam. It was he, according to Iolo Morganwg, who had arranged and systematized 'Dosbarth Morgannwg', that is, the Glamorgan classification of the Welsh metres as they occur in *Cyfrinach Beirdd Ynys Prydain* (1829).[87] Iolo further maintained that this special metrical system had been confirmed at the great *gorsedd* of bards held at Beaupré in 1681, with Edward Dafydd playing an influential rôle. None of these claims, however, can find a place in any sober literary history. Indeed, Edward Dafydd seems to have been a figure of little renown in his own day, and it is extremely unlikely that any of his contemporaries in Gwynedd had ever heard of him. He was probably a comparatively undistinguished figure even in his native county in the eighteenth century; for example, Thomas Richards did not include Edward Dafydd's name in the list of 'British Authors' printed at the end of his dictionary of 1753 (below, pp. 630–633). Undoubtedly, it was Iolo Morganwg who transformed the Margam bard into one of the most famous figures in the literary history of the region. He even attributed to this poet some of his own best compositions, including the splendid *cywydd* in which the summer is sent as a messenger to his beloved Glamorgan.[88] There may, however, have been some foundation for Iolo's claim that Edward Dafydd had been instructed in the bardic craft by Llywelyn Siôn. But the series of verses in the *englyn* measure which the latter is supposed to have addressed 'to Edward Dafydd of Margam when he was 15 years old' are all the product of Iolo Morganwg's gifted pen.[89] It is also possible that Edward Dafydd had been a bardic disciple to Watcyn Powel of Pen-y-fai. On the basis of an elegiac *cywydd* which he sang in 1623 to Sir Rawleigh Bussie (or Bussy), who was buried in the bard's native parish of Margam,[90] his birth has usually been ascribed to the beginning of the seventeenth century, but this is very tentative.

Much of Edward Dafydd's work, which occasionally reflects his royalist and Anglican sympathies, occurs in his own hand in Cardiff MS. 5. 44 ('Llyfr Hir Llanharan', plate XII), one of the last of the many important manuscripts transcribed by Llywelyn Siôn, in Llanstephan MS. 164, immediately after the copy made by the latter of 'y Baibil ynghymraec', and in Llanover MS. B 20, which at one time had been in the possession of Iolo Morganwg.[91] Another collection of the Margam bard's poetry may also be contained in Llanover MS. B 12, although the authorship of a number of the poems attributed in this source to a bard called Edward Dafydd poses some difficult problems. A number of the Margam bard's cywyddau can also be found in manuscripts written by scribes of a slightly later period, such as Tomas ab Ieuan of Tre'r-bryn, in Llanover MS. B 1. He was also the owner of Cardiff MS. 2. 277 (= Baglan MS. 1), which contains a substantial collection of the poetry of Dafydd Benwyn. This is not to imply, however, that he had ever been one of the latter's bardic disciples, as some literary historians have suggested. Rather it means that he had somehow succeeded in acquiring a number of the manuscripts formerly owned by the preceding generation of Glamorgan bards.[92] Llyfr Hir Llanharan had once been in the possession of the Powel family of Tir Iarll, and it is probable that Edward Dafydd wrote his own compositions in empty spaces which he found in this manuscript on those occasions when he called at the family mansion during the course of his bardic itinerancies. His work in general suggests that he was by far the most talented of the itinerant bards who sang in Glamorgan in the period after c. 1620–5. But in spite of all the pretentious claims made by Iolo Morganwg concerning his rôle at the gorsedd allegedly held at Beaupré in 1681, his extant work contains nothing which can confidently be ascribed to a date later than 1665.[93] Two persons called 'Edward David' were buried at Margam in 1678, the first on May 14, the second on July 10. One of these may well have been the Glamorgan bard.[94] In that case, not a single line of poetry composed by him during the last thirteen years of his life is now extant. Although it is not entirely inconceivable that the work which he may have composed during this period has been irretrievably lost, it is far more likely that the gentry families who had once patronized him were by then no longer prepared to reward the bards.

Edward Dafydd sang to most of the prominent landed gentry of Glamorgan—to the Bassetts, the Mathews, the Flemings, the Powels of Tir Iarll and, inevitably, to the Mansels, whose family home was situated in the bard's native parish. Indeed, both he and his son probably regarded themselves as some kind of household bards to the Mansels. But it was only very rarely, to judge from his extant work, that he went on itinerancy to any of the neighbouring counties. He was probably the

last of the Glamorgan poets to visit these regions, for it seems that from
c. 1650 onwards the bards received little welcome even in the homes of
those minor gentry who had generously patronized Dafydd Benwyn and
his contemporaries. As Edward Dafydd so poignantly declared, 'This
world is not with the poets'. Although there were still a few minor
itinerant bards who addressed elegies in the traditional manner to some of
the local gentry down to the beginning of the eighteenth century,
Edward Dafydd was the last of the Glamorgan professional bards of any
significance, as Iolo Morganwg realized.[95]

His work in general shows that he was familiar with many of the
intricate details relating to Welsh versification, including *cynghanedd*, the
traditional bardic vocabulary, the classification of the Welsh syllables and
diphthongs, the syntactical parentheses and figures of speech, and the
cymeriadau, that is, the device whereby the lines in an *awdl* or *cywydd* are
linked together by beginning each line with the same letter or word, by
alliterating or rhyming the first word in each consecutive line, or by
permitting the sense to flow from one line into another.[96] His work
includes examples of nine of the canonical twenty-four measures, namely,
englyn unodl union, *englyn proest gyfnewidiog*, *englyn proest gadwynog*,
cywydd deuair hirion, *cyhydedd hir*, *toddaid*, *hir-a-thoddaid*, *tawddgyrch
cadwynog*, and *cadwynfyr*.[97] He was also familiar with much of the
traditional stock-in-trade of the old Welsh *cyfarwyddiaid* (or storytellers).
Moreover, he had a fairly extensive knowledge of the pedigrees of a
number of the leading aristocratic families of south Wales. The greater
part of his work consists of eulogies and elegies addressed to various
members of these families and, true to the time-honoured tradition of
Welsh strict-metre panegyric verse, he invariably sang to 'those abstract
virtues which ought to be found in a nobleman, and which no doubt
were found in many of them—courage and generosity above all, kindli-
ness, protection for the weak and the poor, the gift of government, and
at times education and culture'.[98] His verses are therefore unmistakably
formal and stereotyped in theme, language and style, and only rarely
does he strike a distinctly personal note. But at its best his work displays
a vigour and technical accomplishment reminiscent of some of his more
immediate predecessors, as the following extract from his *cywydd* to
Sir Richard Bassett of Beaupré clearly shows:

> Pwy'n farchog pennaf orchest?
> Pwy'n ail Lawnslod ffonnod ffest?
> Hyr wyd i wŷr, hir dy wart,
> Hiroesog fych, Syr Rhisiart;
> Urddedig o wraidd ydwyd
> A bwysi dalm, Based wyd;
> Llin Mawnsel, cansel y caid,
> Llin Urien o'r llwyn euraid;
> Ergyd trwm, irgoed tramawr,
> Ar fryn a fu o'r Frân fawr . . .

Cymro er hwylio helynt,
Crair o gorff cwncwerwyr gynt; . . .
Eryr y Bewpyr euraid
Yn dy blas, Duw yn dy blaid;
A'th arglwyddes, santes sir,
Ail Anna a foliennir.[99]

Some sections of his work, however, are marred by the same faults as those of the preceding generation of bards—errors in syntax, a tendency to use dialectal words or forms, obscurity in expression, a failure at times to comprehend the correct meaning of obsolete vocabulary and, occasionally, some elementary errors in the rules of *cynghanedd*. Although some of these faults can be found in his traditional panegyric and elegiac verses, they occur far more frequently in the verses attributed to Edward Dafydd in Llanover MS. B 12, some of which were undoubtedly composed during the period of the Civil War. The late Professor G. J. Williams obviously accepted these as part of the Glamorgan bard's canon.[100] But they are far more debased in both style and language than the bulk of the work attributed to Edward Dafydd in other sources and, although the problem has not been satisfactorily resolved, there are some grounds for doubting whether he was the author of a number of the verses attributed to a certain Edward Dafydd in Llanover MS. B 12. This latter manuscript once belonged to a certain Jenkin Richards from the upper reaches of Gwent (*Blaenau Gwent*), who transcribed in it a very interesting collection of poems which mercilessly castigate the Puritans. Among the verses attributed to Edward Dafydd is a *cywydd* which openly expressed unbounded admiration for General George Monk ('Siors Mwnk') and welcomed Charles II on the latter's return to England.[101] The author of this poem, which has usually been attributed to Edward Dafydd, was undeniably a staunch and fervent Royalist. But, although the evidence is not conclusive, there are certain features in the style of this composition which are not characteristic of the Margam bard's work. Nevertheless, it was mainly on the basis of this poem that Iolo Morganwg attributed to Edward Dafydd the well-known 'Cywydd y Ffanaticiaid' ('Poem of the Fanatics'), which contains some interesting references to the Puritans.[102] Eight otherwise famous Baptists who were active in south Wales from 1654 to 1660 are mentioned in this poem. The general accuracy of these descriptions suggests that the portrayal of ten unusually obscure figures who are also mentioned in this 'Dunciad' may also be correct in its basic essentials.[103] But, as the late Professor G. J. Williams has shown, there is considerable doubt regarding the authorship of this poem, for Iolo Morganwg's manuscripts contain a number of compositions written in a similar vein, and if these were to be accepted as authentic, they would radically transform the picture presented to us by more responsible historians of the early beginnings of Nonconformity in south Wales.[104] Llanover MS. B 12 also contains a number of *cwndidau* which are attributed to Edward Dafydd. Some of these were included in 'Caniadau Gwent a Morganwg', an unpublished selection of verse prepared by the late Dr. L. J. Hopkin-James.

DAFYDD EDWARD AND HOPCYN Y GWËYDD

Edward Dafydd was succeeded by two bards in Margam, both of whom had undoubtedly been instructed by him. One of these was his son, Dafydd Edward. Two elegiac *englynion* which the latter composed on the death of Watcyn Powel of Pen-y-fai, in 1655, occur in Llanover MS. B 20.[105] He wrote his name in Cardiff MS. 2. 277 (= Baglan MS. 1), which, at one time, had been in his father's possession.[106] The same source contains a composition by him in the measure called *englyn unodl union* followed by a note which states explicitly that it had been transcribed by Edward Dafydd.[107] The following *triban* which is attributed in the same source to Dafydd Edward was also probably transcribed by his father:

> Nyd hawdd gan vagad gredü
> pann el y korff /n/ llydü
> y bydd pob kymal yny le
> pyn delo ve yddy varnü.[108]

The fact that references to other compositions by him occur in the Margam collection of manuscripts suggests that he also regarded himself as some kind of household bard to the Margam family. And, significantly, in a series of *englynion* written by the bard in the year 1682 Sir Edward Mansel is addressed as 'my master' (*fy meistir*).[109] Very little is known, however, about Dafydd Edward. A letter which a certain 'W. Lewis', of Margam, addressed in 1696 to Edward Lhuyd contains an explicit reference to 'an old MS. of Welsh Poetry consisting of Cywyddion [*sic*] and Marwnadau etc., wch was lately in ye possession of David Edward a Bard of this Parish'.[110] It is difficult to determine whether this implies that Dafydd Edward had died sometime before the letter was written. Nor is it at all certain that he was the gentleman-farmer of that name whose burial was recorded on May 4, 1692 and whose will was proved on June 27 at Llandaff, for another 'David Edward' was buried on February 4, 1693–4.[111] The Glamorgan bard does not appear to have lived the peripatetic life of the Welsh *clerwr*. Nor would that be at all surprising if he were in fact the gentleman-farmer referred to.

The second poet to succeed Edward Dafydd in Margam was Hopcyn y Gwëydd ('Hopcyn the Weaver'), a bard of little ability and of even less significance. A number of *englynion* which he composed on the 'Birth of Edwd Stradling esquire' in 1699[112] suggest that he occasionally visited some of the noble mansions situated in the Vale.

DAFYDD WILLIAMS (d. *c.* 1693–4)

The only bard of any repute in Glamorgan towards the end of the seventeenth century was Dafydd Williams, the vicar of Pen-llin, near

Cowbridge, and another of Edward Dafydd's bardic disciples. He is probably better known by his bardic title of Dafydd o'r Nant. Edward Lhuyd, who was acquainted with him and with his work, described him as 'acris ingenii poëta, & apud suos merito Celebris'.[113] But in spite of Lhuyd's enthusiastic appraisal, there is no reference to him in Thomas Richards's dictionary. He was ordained as a deacon on January 13, 1660–1, and was received into holy orders on March 3 that year. About eighteen months later he became vicar of Pen-llin (or Llanfrynach).[114] He probably had some family connection with this place, for the entry of his ordination as deacon refers to him as David Williams 'de Penline' and he may, therefore, have been able to exercise some local influence in order to secure his appointment as vicar. His pedigree shows that he was of gentle lineage, which may have told decisively in his favour.[115] Edward Lhuyd maintained that he died *c.* 1690,[116] but this is obviously incorrect, for a poem which he composed in 1691 occurs in Llanover MS. B 22.[117] The appointment of his successor is recorded in September 1694,[118] which suggests that Dafydd o'r Nant died *c.* 1693–4.

His work can be found in Llanover MS. B 20 and in Cardiff MS. 5. 44 (Llyfr Hir Llanharan).[119] Moreover, the contents of Llanover MS. B 22, which are in his own hand, show that he had both diligently collected and assiduously studied the works of the older bards. Of particular interest are the notes which he wrote on the vaticinatory poems (*cywyddau brud*) inasmuch as they reveal that he seriously expected to see some of the old bardic prophecies fulfilled one day. The earliest extant example of his work is a poem of 1655 to Watcyn Powel of Pen-y-fai, and it seems that the latter and Edward Dafydd of Margam were his bardic teachers. The date of this composition suggests that he was born *c.* 1630–5, and he must obviously have been initiated into the bardic craft before taking holy orders. His duties as a cleric do not seem to have prevented him, however, from going on bardic itinerancy, for his work contains a number of interesting panegyrics and elegies addressed to the Powels of Maes-teg and Ton-du, the Mansels of Margam, the Gamages and Bassetts, and the Jenkins family of Hensol Castle. These verses prove that he had mastered many of the technical intricacies of the old strict-metre verse. But he was not a professional bard; he was an enthusiastic cleric who 'sang on his own food'. He was also a classical scholar. His work contains references to famous figures in the literature and history of both Greece and Rome,[120] and on one occasion—probably in 1683—he co-operated with Tomas Roberts, the parson of Llanilid, in making a translation into Welsh on the *cywydd* measure of one of Martial's epigrams.[121] Indeed, Iolo Morganwg maintained that the Glamorgan cleric-poet was the author of a Welsh composition on the Latin hexameter. But the style and language of the example quoted by Iolo are far more characteristic of his own work than that of Dafydd o'r Nant.[122] His work contains little to substantiate the view that he was a creative pioneer in the field of Welsh metrics; he was probably quite content with the old metres of the classical Welsh tradition. But although he had diligently studied these compositions, much of his work reflects those faults which mar Welsh strict-metre verse in general in the seventeenth century. Indeed, his work is inferior in this respect to that of Edward Dafydd of Margam. An epenthetic vowel is frequently included in the rhyme pattern,[123] or counts as one of the syllables in a particular line.[124] There are many examples of local dialectal forms in his verses, such as *cenel*, *iddi* for *i'w*, *ym hunan*, *yndi*, or *o maas*; *hw-* occurs frequently for *chw-*, and the diphthongs of the standard literary language are often levelled with vowels, exactly as they are in colloquial speech (e.g. *gwad* is written for *gwaed* 'blood', *gore* for *gorau* 'best', etc.).[125] There are frequent errors in syntax, especially in the use of the prefixed and infixed personal pronouns,[126] nor is he always certain of his mutations in a particular phonetic context.[127] Some metrical faults can also be detected in his verses,[128] which, significantly, he invariably composed on the two measures called *cywydd deuair hirion* and *englyn unodl union*. He probably could not compose an *awdl* and it appears that Edward Dafydd of Margam was the last Glamorgan bard who could. He was nevertheless familiar with the traditional verses composed by the Welsh professional bards, as the following short extract from the elegy which he sang to Dafydd Morgan of Bryncethin clearly testifies:

> Dewr ydoedd, diwair odiaith,
> Mwynlan, diofan ei daith;
> Ni thrôi [ei] gefn, ŵr trefnol,
> Na'i wyneb, er neb, yn ôl.
> Ni adai i ffrynd fynd ar feth,
> Ŵr diofan, iôr difeth;
> Collai 'i wad, hoywgad hygar,
> A'r hyn y ceid, o ran câr.
> Mwynaidd, gweddaidd wrth y gwan,
> Trugarog, tiriog eirian;
> Llew i gryf, llywiog â'r on,
> Abl da gawr, o blaid gwirion.[129]

He had a fairly extensive knowledge of the pedigrees of the gentry families to whom he addressed his verses, but he sang the praises of no one outside Glamorgan. Another interesting feature of his work is that it occasionally reflects his royalist sympathies and his uncompromising hostility to Catholics and Puritans alike.[130] That his work, in spite of the many faults which it contains, is incomparably superior to the verses composed by the minor bards who followed him in the late-seventeenth and early-eighteenth centuries is a clear indication of the abysmal depths to which the native bardic tradition had sunk by that period.

To Dafydd o'r Nant, however, belongs the unique distinction of being the first Glamorgan bard, as far as we can tell, seriously to consider the use of the printing-press as a means of disseminating his work to a wider public, something which was quite exceptional in that period. Very little use of the printing-press had hitherto been made by the bards. Dafydd o'r Nant's career, however, constitutes a significant landmark, for in a series of *englynion* which he addressed in 1690 to a certain Job Watkins, a clerk in the Chancery in London, the bard, who was then obviously well advanced in years, expressed the fervent hope that, in spite of the fact that they were not acquainted with one another, the addressee might find some means of assisting him in publishing a miscellaneous collection of his work which he had gathered together in a manuscript-book of quite substantial proportions:

> Mae llyfran tewlan i'm tŷ—o'm llafur,
> Llefain wyf am allu,
> O dyro nerth, cyfnerth cu,
> Iôr groywffawd, i'w argraffu.

The book, apparently, would include verses of both a religious and moral nature as well as panegyric and elegiac verses (*odlau gwŷr*):

> Dwyfawl a moesawl ymhob mesur—sydd
> Yn ei swydd i'm llyfyr,
> A salmau ac odlau gwŷr
> Diwaelion yndo welir.[131]

Some of the more influential Glamorgan gentry, we are told, had already promised the bard their assistance; but the contents of these *englynion* fail to make it clear whether the support which Dafydd o'r Nant sought from Job Watkins was financial or otherwise. In any case, it is extremely unlikely that his ambition was ever fulfilled, for no such work is now extant, nor are there any authentic references to its publication, either during the bard's lifetime or after his death. Nevertheless, Dafydd o'r Nant deserves an honourable mention as the first, in all probability, of all the many bards who lived and sang in Glamorgan seriously to consider the possibility of using the printing-press. His career thus forms an interesting and vital link between the practices of the bards of the classical Welsh tradition and the proposals of the humanists, who earnestly desired to see the works and esoteric lore of the bards made available to all. Iolo Morganwg claimed that Thomas Richards had informed him that the library (*llyfreugell*) of Tre-groes mansion, near Pen-coed, contained a large volume in which the Glamorgan bard had transcribed all his own work 'ready to be printed' (*wedi ei barattoi i'w argraffu*).[132] It is difficult to understand, if this was the case, why Thomas Richards made no reference of any kind to Dafydd o'r Nant in his list of Welsh bards. It is, therefore, quite possible that Iolo Morganwg concocted the whole story about the unpublished manuscript at Tre-groes after he had read the *englynion* by Dafydd o'r Nant which occur in Llanover MS. B 22.

The End of the Bardic Order in Glamorgan

That arch-romantic, Iolo Morganwg, drew a singularly enchanting picture of the bardic life of Glamorgan:

> The Bards in Glamorgan, so late as 1700, taught reading and writing in Welsh from house to house, and some of them practised physic, taught Archery, Graffting fruit trees, &c. and for this they were rewarded with presents of corn, Cheese, Butter–wool–Bacon–Beef–fat geese–Christmas Presents of mead, Bragod, &c.[133]

There is no real historical basis, however, for this description, charming though some of its details may be. The small circle of bards, including Llywelyn ab Ifan of Coychurch, Tomas Morgan of Tyle Garw (in Llanhari), Miles Wiliam, Tomas Lleision of Llanddunwyd (or Welsh St. Donat's), and Tomas Wiliam of Tregolwyn (Colwinston), who continued after the death of Dafydd o'r Nant to visit 'gentlemens howses in the loytringe time betweene Christmas and Candlemas to singe songes and receave rewardes', were little better than unskilled hedge-side rhymesters, as some of their more percipient contemporaries were not slow to realize. In the letter which he addressed to William Wynn in November 1734 John Bradford (1706–85), of Betws Tir Iarll, an antiquary and poet (below, pp. 614–616), expressed his great astonishment that the authors of poetry whose standards were so pitiably low should have received the patronage and commendation of some of the more influential local gentry, a view which was fully endorsed by the contemporary 'grammarians'.[134] It is impossible to dissent from this verdict, for the frequent errors in both the language and metrical art of the eulogies and elegies as well as the serious faults so frequently in evidence in the *englynion*, written usually on distinctly moral and didactic themes, reveal clearly the abysmal depths to which the ancient Taliesinic tradition had now sunk.[135] Another significant indication of this decline is that some of the verses which were addressed to the local gentry were sometimes composed in the free metres, a practice which the great chiefs-of-song who flourished in the golden age would have unreservedly condemned. The passing of this pathetically inept, though not unenthusiastic, generation of bards, the last of whom had almost certainly died by the middle of the eighteenth century, marked the final disintegration of the old bardic order in Glamorgan.

ii.

POETRY COMPOSED IN THE FREE METRES

The steady, inexorable decline of the time-honoured Taliesinic tradition was largely responsible for the increasing popularity of a new kind of poetry, that composed in the so-called free metres. There are frequent and interesting references in Iolo Morganwg's manuscripts to this type of verse, which, he repeatedly claimed, constituted one of Glamorgan's most distinctive contributions to the literary heritage of Wales (*Ante*, III, 521). He even went so far as to claim that it was to this particular class of verse that the *cwndidau* belonged, 'the poetry of nature and good sense' in which the *bardd teulu* had endeavoured to impart some form of religious instruction to the people.[136] But there is no historical warrant for any of these claims. He became convinced also, as a result of his study of the old Welsh triads, that the composition of love-poetry in the free metres was one of the most important functions associated with the office of the *bardd teulu*,[137] and so he proceeded to postulate the theory that the composition of romantic eclogues and amatory verses constituted one of the most important elements in the development of free-metre verse in Glamorgan. The reference, tantalizingly obscure though it is, to 'cwndide llelo' in the elegiac poem which Hopcyn Tomas Phylip sang sometime before 1560,[138] to his bardic teacher, Tomas ab Ieuan ap Rhys, suggests that there is some foundation for this claim, although hardly any of this verse has survived in written form.[139] Iolo Morganwg, however, was hardly the person to be daunted by a serious dearth of authentic literary material. His manuscripts contain scores of poems, many of which are compositions of substantial artistic merit, which he himself had written and later attributed to various bards, ranging from the *pencerdd* Gwilym Tew in the fifteenth century to John Bradford and Wil Hopcyn in the eighteenth. Hence he included the *dyri(f)*, a song or carol in free metres, having regular syllabic accentuation with occasional touches of *cynghanedd*, among what he considered to be the twenty-four distinctive 'attributes' of the Glamorgan classification of the Welsh metres, and he attempted to justify this with quotations from the *cerddi teuluaidd* (or poems in the free metres) which he claimed had been composed at various times during the seventeenth century by such bards as Edward Dafydd of Margam, Dafydd Williams (Dafydd o'r Nant) or Lleision Ifan.[140] But many of the poets to whom he refers are unquestionably figments of his own over-active imagination, and Iolo himself was the author of many of the free-metre poems which occur in his manuscripts. Occasionally, however, he seems to have taken some old traditional free-metre verses and refurbished them with lines and phrases of his own composition.[141]

Nor, according to Iolo Morganwg, was the free-metre verse of interest to the literary scholar alone. It also provided the social historian with some interesting details of the happy day-to-day life of the common folk and gave him an extremely valuable insight into the 'gentleness' (*mwynder*) and uninhibited *joie de vivre* of the Vale and Uplands alike. The following remarks are typical of his views:

> Convivial songs of great merit are also pretty numerous in S[outh] W[ales]. Some of them perfect Paterns [*sic*] of excellence. A May Song by Will Tabwr about 1660, may be instanced as one of these, others of the same period have great merit. Several also of this description by Will Hopkin, a finely natural Poet of the earlier part of the last century are worthy of notice. many of these songs have a good deal of delicate humour. Summer songs or May songs, Harvest Songs, etc. are to be found in S[outh] W[ales] but not as in N[orth] W[ales] prophanely [*sic*] devotional. they are of a cheerful & innocently convivial cast.[142]

But Wil Tabwr exists nowhere outside Iolo's own manuscripts. However, distortions of this kind should not blind us to the central fact that he had perceived that the extant poetry composed in the accentual metres sheds much more light on contemporary social conditions than do the stereotyped, highly formalized *awdlau* and *cywyddau*. The *cwndidau* are an excellent example of this.

Iolo Morganwg was also correct in assuming that the accentual poetry which comes increasingly into prominence as the old strict-metre verse began to decline was not something which suddenly developed *in vacuo*. Although the greater part of the extant free-metre poetry composed in Glamorgan belongs to the period after *c.* 1550, it is in origin much older, for some kind of verse written in the accentual free metres probably existed in Wales throughout the centuries (*Ante*, III, 521–3). It is more than likely, therefore, that in the accentual verse we witness the emergence of an 'inferior' kind of poetry that had been popular among the lower strata of native Welsh society for many centuries, a phenomenon which has been compared with the sudden popularity of the *cywydd* measure and love-poetry composed in the strict metres in the fourteenth century.[143]

The earliest extant examples of poetry composed in the free metres by bards who sang in Glamorgan and in other parts of south Wales have already been examined (*Ante*, III, ch. x). One outstanding characteristic of the bardic tradition of Glamorgan, which clearly differentiates it from the other regions of Wales, is that the free metres seem to have been used far more frequently there. It is also significant that much of this free verse was written in indigenous Welsh metres, which constituted an important part of the canonical strict-metre system when *cynghanedd* was introduced into them.[144] In tracing the development of free-metre verse in Glamorgan literary historians have generally tended to concentrate heavily on the religious compositions known as *cwndidau*. But one of the most prominent of the *cwndidwyr*, Tomas ab Ieuan ap Rhys (*fl. c.* 1510–*c.* 1560), employed the free metres not only when he sang on distinctly religious or moral themes but also when he addressed panegyrics and elegies to some of the leading gentry of the region. And he did this during the very period when his cousin, the celebrated *pencerdd* Lewis Morgannwg, sang to them in the traditional manner in stately *awdlau* and *cywyddau*. The poetry composed by Tomas ab Ieuan ap Rhys contains some interesting examples of elegiac verses, composed in the measure called *cywydd deuair fyrion*, devoid of *cynghanedd*, to men of rank, such as John Gamage and Tomas ap Wiliam Siancyn, or the cleric Sir Siôn Watcyn of Llanilltud.[145] The employment of the accentual metres, even when addressing the landed gentry, is another striking feature which differentiates the bardic history of Glamorgan from that of the other major historic regions of Wales. The same bard's canon also includes a *cwndid gofyn* ('poem of asking'), while one of the accentual carols in which he eulogises the celebrated Dunraven family develops into a prognostication.[146] But Tomas ab Ieuan ap Rhys was probably the only professional bard in Glamorgan to compose this type of poetry during the first half of the sixteenth century,[147] for the *penceirddiaid* who flourished in that period seem on the whole to have consciously eschewed the free metres. They probably regarded the employment of these measures as a degradation of the art for which they had been specially trained. A great change occurred in the period after *c.* 1550, however, for some of the professional bards, such as Meurug Dafydd and Llywelyn Siôn, employed the free metres in their religious *cwndidau*. But their steadfast refusal to use these measures whenever they sang eulogies or elegies to the landed gentry reflects their strong bias against the accentual metres. The same is also true of Edward Dafydd of Margam in the seventeenth century. But, if he was the author of the verses attributed to him by L. J. Hopkin-James in his unpublished volume, 'Caniadau Gwent a Morganwg', the Margam bard was obviously not averse to composing religious *cwndidau* in the free metres, especially in the measure called *awdl-gywydd*, devoid of *cynghanedd*, in which he sustained the same main rhyme throughout.[148] And not one genuine example has survived of a *cwndid* composed by Dafydd Benwyn, the most prolific of the Glamorgan bards who sang during the latter half of the sixteenth century.[149]

An interesting link with the strict-metre system is provided by some of the vaticinatory verse composed within the region, for the free metres were sometimes used for the composition of prophetic poems which, with the notable exception of the metre, bear a striking resemblance in many respects to the *cywyddau brud* ('prophetic poems'). Although it is difficult to date with any degree of precision many of the vaticinatory poems composed in the free metres, the places specifically mentioned in some of them prove conclusively that they are the work of Glamorgan bards. Tomas ab Ieuan ap Rhys, for example, wrote vaticinatory poems (*daroganau*) not only in the strict metres but also in the measure called *triban Morgannwg*. Indeed, his vaticinatory verses contain some of the earliest extant examples of a *triban* composed by a Glamorgan bard:

> Ar y Filltir Aur bydd ymledd,
> A rhowto'r Sais o'r diwedd,
> A thorri pen y pennaf ar frys
> Wrth ffynnon Llys y fronedd.[150]

It is frequently forgotten that Tomas ab Ieuan ap Rhys's great renown in the bardic tradition rests mainly on the reputation which he had acquired as an author of prophetic verse rather than on his religious *cwndidau*.

Among the most interesting of the poems composed in the free metres are those which have a direct connection with particular occasions or circumstances. Perhaps the most notable example of this is the composition on the measure called *awdl-gywydd* in which some anonymous poet, who probably sang sometime during the reign of Elizabeth I, expressed his great sorrow and regret when the Wood of Glyn Cynon was cut down to provide charcoal for the manufacture of iron:

Aber da llan wna i gid
    plwy merthyr hyd llan vadon
mwia adfyd a fy erioed
    pen dored koed glyn kynon ...

llawer bedwen glas /i/ chlog
    ynghrog /i/ bytho r sayson
sydd yn danllwyth mawr o dan
    gen wyr yr hayarn dvon.[151]

THE RELIGIOUS CAROLS OR *Cwndidau*

But by far the best-known of all the poems composed in the free metres in Glamorgan are undoubtedly the *cwndidau*,[152] or carols as they were popularly known in the region.[153] The majority of these belong to the period from the first half of the sixteenth century to approximately the middle of the seventeenth.[154] But although the earliest extant examples known for certain to have been composed in Glamorgan cannot be earlier than the first half of the sixteenth century, the use of the term itself in a *cywydd gofyn* ('poem of asking') by the Carmarthenshire bard, Ieuan Deulwyn (*fl. c.* 1460), suggests that verses of this kind were already being composed in the fifteenth century at the very latest.[155] Glamorgan was undeniably the main centre for verse of this genre, but it constituted an integral part of the literary tradition of other parts of south Wales, notably Gwent and Carmarthenshire. Nevertheless, the great majority of the *cwndidwyr* were natives of Glamorgan, and it is to the indefatigable industry of its scribes that we owe the preservation of much of this large volume of verse. For example, Llanover MS. B 9, a bulky compilation transcribed by Llywelyn Siôn, contains a valuable collection of these poems.

The composition of the *cwndidau* during the sixteenth and seventeenth centuries probably reflects to a certain extent the efforts being made to compensate in some degree for the shortcomings of the priests and mendicants as preachers in the vernacular. In one of his *cwndidau* Hopcyn Tomas Phylip earnestly entreated the young generation of his parish to listen attentively to his efforts to instruct them:

Gwrandewch ieuenctid   fy mhlwyf i gyd
Mi rof newid   ywch ar gwndid
Dros fy llafur   yn ei wneuthur
'Rwy'n chwenychu   i chwi ddysgu.[156]

Most of the *cwndidwyr* mercilessly attacked the wickedness of the age and endeavoured to show that the hardships endured by the common folk were the direct result of sinful living. And some were not averse to borrowing liberally from the religious poetry of Siôn Cent (1367?–1430?), whose work set the pattern for a great deal of the moral and didactic verse composed during the late-medieval period in Welsh. A particularly interesting feature of some of the *cwndidau* composed by the Catholic poet, Llywelyn Siôn, is that he, unlike most authors of this type of verse, made no secret of his spiritual allegiance. The Reformation changes were extremely distasteful to him, and he bitterly attacked Luther, Calvin, Zwingli and Beza, who, he asserted, had been dispatched by the Devil to replace the four evangelists, Mark, Matthew, Luke and John, sent by God to disseminate the true faith, which had been in the land for many a year. And, sad to relate, there were already too many disciples of the four persons sent by the Devil and these were growing worse from day to day, so that neither the Lord's Mother nor His saints were held in any esteem:

Marc, Matho lân,   Luc a Ieuan
A ddodai sêl,   ar Dy chweddel,
A'th ddisgyblion,   i gyd o'u bron
I'r byd a fu,   yn pregethu.
Fe fu'r Ffydd hyn   lawer blwyddyn
A'r saint bob tro   yn cytuno.
Fe ddaeth heb gêl   gan y Cythrel
Bedwar'n eu lle   o'i wŷr ynte,
Luther, Calfin,   Beza, Zwinglin,
Felly gelwir   y pedwargwyr,
Ac mae digon   o ddisgyblion
O'u dysgeidiaeth   hwy'n mynd waethwaeth.[157]

To Llywelyn Siôn and his like the Protestant religion was an alien faith imposed by the Saxons, not the true faith to which his fellow-countrymen had steadfastly adhered from time immemorial.

Inevitably, these 'Welsh sermons in song' contain a wealth of scriptural themes and allusions.[158] For example, one of Tomas ab Ieuan ap Rhys's religious carols is really nothing more than a metrical version of the parable of the sower,[159] while a certain Siôn Siancyn of Pen-llin refers explicitly to the thirty-first verse of the sixth chapter of the Gospel according to St. Luke:

Ond mae Luc a'i eiriau pêr
'N y chweched chiapter droson
Yn dwedyd fel y rho'r dyn
Y caiff e'r un taliadon.[160]

Naturally, many of the *cwndidau* began by addressing the poet's fellow-parishioners. The following quotation, taken from a carol composed by an anonymous cleric, is a typical example:

Clywch fy mhlwyf hyn,   'ddwy bob blwyddyn
Ar gerdd newydd   yn rhoi rhybudd,
Ac yn fynych   'ddwyf i'n chwennych
Rhybuddio'r byd   yn y pulpud.

But he seems to have been most poorly rewarded for his pains:

> Cerdd sen angall   rhyw ddyn arall
> Hi a fydd ym mhen   pob rhyw fachgen.[161]

Some of these verses were intended to be sung on special festive occasions; for example, to be sung as Christmas carols:

> Fy nghyfeillion   cywir, ffyddlon,
> Clywch fel y mae   fy nghaniadau;
> Dyma'r plygain   cywir cywrain
> Y ganed un   mab Duw Frenin.[162]

Thomas Jones, the incumbent of Llandeilo Bertholau, refers to the Christmas season even in the carol which he composed to express his gratitude for Bishop William Morgan's translation of the Bible into Welsh[163] (below, pp. 571–572). The eighteenth-century poet, Lewis Hopkin, likewise described a Christmas carol, composed in the measure called *awdl-gywydd* with the same rhyme throughout, as 'Can, Neu, Gwndid, i'w ganu ar Blygain Ddydd Nadolig Crist'.[164]

Nevertheless, some of these poems were of a distinctly secular nature. Undoubtedly, 'the unskilled folk' to whom the Catholic exile, Gruffydd Robert, referred composed carols and songs for special festive occasions and wrote amatory poems—the 'cwndide llelo' mentioned by Hopcyn Tomas Phylip—and humorous and ribald verses in exactly the same metres as those used for the composition of the religious *cwndidau*. For example, in the *cywydd* which Dafydd Benwyn addressed to the two gaolers of Cardiff beseeching the release of his nephew, the bard makes it clear that the latter was very much a man of the world, idling in taverns and frequently gambling and paying court to all the maids of the county. He was also an uncommonly productive versifier, being particularly fond of singing *cwndidau*, which, with head held erect, he daily produced 'in bundles':

> Cwnnu'i ben, canu beunydd
> Cwndidau yn bynnau y bydd.

It is more than likely that the contents of these verses were humorous and ribald rather than religious. He himself was probably the author of some, for Dafydd Benwyn comments admiringly on his nephew's manifest expertise in composing poems on the *triban* measure:

> A saer gwych, heb fesur gwan,
> Trabalch ar englyn triban.[165]

The Authors of the *Cwndidau*

The *cwndidwyr* can conveniently be divided into three main classes, although it is not always easy to make a sharp and rigid distinction between them. First of all, there were the professional poets who had received, albeit in varying degrees, some formal training in their craft. To this group belonged such poets as Tomas ab Ieuan ap Rhys, Meurug Dafydd, Llywelyn Siôn, and Edward Dafydd, the last of Glamorgan's professional bards. Secondly, there were the gentlemen-poets, who usually 'sang on their own food', although some were not averse to receiving patronage occasionally. Undeniably, the most famous member of this class was Tomas ap Llywelyn ap Dafydd ap Hywel (*fl. c.* 1580–1610) of Rhigos, in northern Glamorgan. One clear indication of his great reputation is that verses were addressed to him by many bards, including Siancyn of Defynnog, Llywelyn Siôn of Llangewydd, Gronwy Wiliam (d. 1593) of Hendre Forgan, and Morgan Powel, the vicar of Llanhari. This proves conclusively that his life spanned the latter half of the sixteenth century and the beginning of the seventeenth, although there are references in some of these verses which suggest that he was appreciably older than the poets who had composed them. According to one pedigree, he was related to the family of Rhys Brydydd, the Powels of Tir Iarll, and the famous Aberpergwm family.[166] He therefore claimed descent from Rhicert ab Einion ap Collwyn. The cleric-poet, Morgan Powel of Llanhari, informs us that he was a comparatively affluent member of the landed gentry:

A goludog mewn gloywdir,
A theg berchen tai a thir.[167]

Some of the various *cywyddau* which were addressed to him suggest that in his younger days he had been a happy, jovial character, fond of the sensual pleasures of life, and an author of love-poetry. It seems also from these poems that he was afflicted with blindness in his old age. Not surprisingly, in view of his lineal connections with the celebrated *pencerdd*, Rhys Brydydd, he had received some instruction in the bardic craft, and it appears that Llywelyn Siôn regarded him as one of his bardic teachers. A number of *cywyddau* composed by Tomas ap Llywelyn survive in various manuscripts, but there can be no doubt that it was his religious *cwndidau* which won for him a secure and revered place in the bardic tradition. Probably the two most widely-known of his compositions, both written in the measure called *traethodl*, are one describing a contention between the Tavern and the Church[168] (above, p. 231) and another a prognostication for the year 1610, which is heavy-laden with moral and religious advice.[169] But there is no historical basis for Iolo Morganwg's claims, accepted unquestioningly by many writers in the nineteenth century, that Tomas ap Llywelyn was one of the great pioneers of Nonconformity in south Wales, that he had translated the Bible from English into Welsh many years before 1588, that he was a Puritan licensed to preach by Archbishop Grindal, and that he had attracted large congregations at Rhigos in northern Glamorgan, Blaencannaid in Merthyr Tudful, and elsewhere within the county.[170]

An equally interesting member of the second class of *cwndidwyr*
mentioned above was Hopcyn Tomas Phylip (d. 1597) of Gelli'r-fid, in
the parish of Llandyfodwg in the commote of Glyn Ogwr.[171] According
to some pedigrees, the deeds relating to the family property, and the
testimony of the bards, he was one of the descendants of Iestyn ap
Gwrgant.[172] As the bard Siôn Mowddwy declared:

> Dewr nerthol, duwiol yw'r dyn,
> Dwystal, o aelwyd Iestyn.[173]

The peripatetic bards who visited Gelli'r-fid were invariably given a warm
and hospitable welcome, as the *cywyddau* addressed to Hopcyn and his
family by Dafydd Benwyn, Siôn Mowddwy and Dafydd Llwyd Mathau
eloquently testify. These bards referred in the traditional manner to his
martial prowess, his unstinting generosity, his great learning, his singleness
of purpose and his mastery of Welsh prosody. Siôn Mowddwy explicitly
referred to his undisputed expertise as a poet:

> Awdur dysg, da yw'r dysgwr,
> Urddas gwych yw'r ddysg i ŵr;
> Parod ddadl, prydydd ydyw,
> Pwyll iawn gerdd, pwy well nag yw?
> Gramadegydd, grym dygiad,
> Gŵr i Dduw'n rhoi'i gerdd yn rhad.[174]

Nor were these claims unduly extravagant, for some of the *cywyddau*
which he composed prove conclusively that he was far more skilled than
his bardic teacher, Tomas ab Ieuan ap Rhys,[175] in composing poetry in
the strict metres. But in his religious *cwndidau*, which are, in general, pious
exhortations to 'cease from evil and learn to do good' and which amply
testify to his extensive knowledge of the Bible and the Apocrypha, he made
liberal use of the colloquial forms and expressions which had long since
become one of the distinguishing features of the free-metre tradition.[176]

Another literary-minded gentleman who indulged his taste for
composing religious carols was Wiliam Prys, squire of Ynys-y-maerdy in
Llan(i)sawel (Briton Ferry), who belonged to the same line as Ieuan
Gethin ab Ieuan ap Lleision, the celebrated fifteenth-century bard from
Baglan.[177] He seems to have derived considerable pleasure from the
company of the bards. A Welsh letter addressed to him in 1596 by
Llywelyn Siôn is extant,[178] and Edward Dafydd of Margam sang an
elegy to him in which he is respectfully described as the head of the
nobility (*brigyn y bonedd*).[179] Unfortunately, only one of his carols has
survived, a poem written on the measure called *cywydd deuair fyrion* in
which the author, who was then obviously well advanced in years,
contritely confesses his former sins and abjectly throws himself on the
divine mercy.[180]

No account of this class of poets would be complete without a
reference to Tomas ab Ieuan ap Madog of Betws Tir Iarll, which seems
to have been the cradle not only of the strict-metre poetry composed in

Glamorgan but of much of the free-metre verse as well. His family pedigree is quoted by the heraldic bards, while references to certain members of the family, including the poet himself, occur in various deeds in the Margam collection.[181] His brother, Ieuan ab Ieuan ap Madog, was one of the leading scribes of the period and a friend to both Llywelyn Siôn and Anthony Powel. An entry in one of the Margam deeds suggests that Tomas ab Ieuan ap Madog died childless sometime before 1569.[182] Hopcyn Tomas Phylip sang an elegiac *cwndid* to him in which he commented on the sweetness of the panegyric verses which the deceased had been so fond of composing:

> . . . pwy mwy a gan mor velys
> m]oliant i wr lle rhoe serch, ne wraig ne verch wrsibys.[183]

His work shows that, like his friend, Tomas ab Ieuan ap Rhys, he employed the free metres not only when he sang on unmistakably religious themes but also when he composed panegyric and elegiac verses. But there is no certain proof that he ever went on bardic itinerancy.

The third class of *cwndidwyr* comprised the cleric-poets, such as 'Syrr Sion Jwng' (John Young), 'Syrr Risiart y Vwalchen', possibly the *nom-de-plume* of Richard Wiliam, said to have been a clergyman in a parish situated somewhere in east Glamorgan who lived, according to Iolo Morganwg, from about 1590 to 1630, or Morgan Powel of Llanhari.[184] To this class also belonged Thomas Jones who, in one of his *cwndidau*, described himself as 'the son of an old prelate who is a clergyman':

> O daw gofyn ar awnaeth hyn
> mab hen brelad sydd offeyrad.[185]

He composed two very interesting poems on the measure called *awdl-gywydd*, one to express gratitude for the Welsh Bible,[186] the other his joy at the defeat of the Spanish Armada,[187] both in 1588. It is clear, therefore, that many clerics used the *cwndid* as a convenient medium for imparting some form of spiritual instruction to their parishioners, and there were probably many others among the clergy who directly commissioned or actively encouraged the composition of many of these religious verses or carols whose patrons are otherwise cloaked in a veil of tantalizing anonymity. This does not mean, however, that all the cleric-poets were loath to accept patronage, and some may have found it quite indispensable if they were to persevere with their literary pursuits.

THE METRES USED IN THE COMPOSITION OF THE *Cwndidau*

The *cwndidau* are a significant landmark in the history of Welsh prosody and the development of Welsh free verse. The two metres used most frequently in these compositions were the *cywydd deuair fyrion* (or 'the short metre' or 'carol couplet', as it was sometimes called) and the *awdl-gywydd* (*Ante*, III, 532). The former consists of two rhyming lines of four syllables each. This measure was rarely used in the strict-metre system, but it was probably very popular throughout the centuries among the lower grades of bards and wandering minstrels. In the latter half of the sixteenth century, however, we find that the measure, devoid of *cynghanedd*, was used even by a bard of the status of Llywelyn Siôn, and at least one example occurs where this measure was employed in the composition of an English *cwndid*.[188]

The measure known as *awdl-gywydd* consists of lines of seven syllables, the end of the first line rhyming with the middle of the second, which has the main rhyme at its end, this being sustained throughout the composition. Here is an example from the poem by Thomas Jones of Llandeilo Bertholau to the Welsh Bible, and even here he begins by addressing his fellow-parishioners and refers explicitly to the Christmas season:

> F'annwyl blwyf, drwy Grist a'i r*ad*,
> A gaf i genn*ad* heno
> I adrodd dau air ar goedd w*awd*
> O ddysg i'n br*awd*, y Cymro?
>
> Mae fy mryd fal dyn di-dd*ig*
> Nad êl Nadol*ig* heibio
> Heb ryw gyngor, dewch yn n*es*,
> A wnelo l*es* i Gymro.[189]

This is another measure, called 'Messir chwech' in one of the old Glamorgan manuscripts,[190] which never became popular among the professional bards but which was probably used quite frequently by those lower orders known usually in Welsh as *y glêr*. It was certainly the measure used most frequently by the *cwndidwyr* of the second half of the sixteenth century and by Edward Dafydd of Margam in the seventeenth.

Surprisingly, however, the measure known as *triban Morgannwg*, the great popularity of which among the bards of the region is clearly indicated by the term itself, does not occur very frequently in the works of the Glamorgan *cwndidwyr*. This is the measure known as *englyn unodl cyrch* in the bardic grammars, and consists of stanzas of four seven-syllable lines which have the rhyme sequence *a a b b a*, the second *b* rhyme occurring in the middle of the fourth line.[191] Undoubtedly, this was another measure used by the inferior class of itinerant bards and minstrels, for one extant copy of the bardic grammar strictly enjoins the highest grade of bard, called *prydydd* in the text, not to use it, such was its brevity and unadorned simplicity: 'A'r mod hwnnw ar ynglynn ny pherthyn ar brydyd y ganu namyn ar deuluwr diwladeid, rac y hawsset a'y vyrret'.[192] This was another measure which was ultimately taken over into the strict system and made more polished and ornate by the introduction of *cynghanedd*, although it never ceased to be popular among the lower grades of bards and wandering minstrels, especially in south Wales, where it was sometimes described as '[mesur] gwyr deheubarth'.[193]

But the term most generally used in free verse was *triban* or *triban Morgannwg*. The Welsh mystery-play *Y Tri Brenin o Gwlen* ('The Three Kings of Cologne'), an early-sixteenth-century work which is unquestionably of Glamorgan provenance, was written in this metre.[194] But there is only one example in the work of Tomas ab Ieuan ap Rhys, and this occurs, as we have already seen, not in a religious carol but in one of his vaticinatory compositions. Only one certain example has so far been discovered among the numerous free-metre poems composed by Glamorgan bards of a religious *cwndid* written entirely in this metre. This is 'Gochel y Drwg' ('Avoid Evil') by Hopcyn Tomas Phylip, from which the following stanza has been taken:

> Na fydd ddiog i wneuth*ur*
> Rhyw dda rhag bod yn seg*ur*,
> Can's seguryd a fag chw*ant*
> A drwg fydd pl*ant* o nat*ur*.[195]

But the rhythmic accentuation of this poem is obviously quite unlike that which usually occurs in the measure known as *triban Morgannwg*. The metre was undoubtedly used for the composition of amatory verses—the 'cwndide llelo' mentioned above—although most of these poems have unfortunately disappeared, probably because the professional copyists deemed them unworthy of preservation in their manuscripts. Many of the examples which have frequently been quoted of this type of verse are almost certainly the product of Iolo Morganwg's pen. Among the few early authentic examples which have survived is the following stanza, written by a seventeenth-century Glamorgan scribe in the margin of his manuscript. It obviously comes from the beginning of a love-poem which has otherwise been lost:

> Ceiliog du'r fwyalch*en*
> Sy â'i drigfa ym mrig celynn*en*,
> A ei di droso'i at deg ei ll*un*
> Heb weud wrth ddy*n* o'r ddaer*en*?[196]

Some interesting examples also occur in the works of the Glamorgan bards of the measure called *traethodl*, consisting of rhymed couplets with seven syllables in each line. It represents an early stage in the development of the strict-metre measure called *cywydd deuair hirion*, and was therefore less elaborate and ornate than the latter. The *traethodl* was at least as old as the fourteenth century, for it occurs in the work of Dafydd ap Gwilym. It was never popular among the *cwndidwyr*, but here is a brief example from the prognostication for the year 1610 composed by Tomas ap Llywelyn of Rhigos:

> Gwell gan gall na'i wenieithio
> Ddangos ei feiau iddo.
> O synnir ar y gorau,
> Nid oes neb heb ei feiau.
> Gwell fydd gan ddiog, lle bo,
> Fod yn segur na gweithio.[197]

This metre, also employed by him in his poem on the Tavern and the Church,[198] had probably been very popular with the lower-grade itinerant bards for many centuries. Once again, when it was taken over into the canonical strict-metre system, it was deliberately made into something far more complicated and ornate by introducing *cynghanedd* into each line and by applying the rule that an accented syllable at the end of one line in each couplet should rhyme with an unaccented syllable at the end of the other.[199] This was the measure called *cywydd deuair hirion* in the strict system, which became increasingly popular from the latter half of the fourteenth century onwards.

The first three measures mentioned above, namely, the *englyn unodl cyrch*, the *cywydd deuair fyrion*, and the *awdl-gywydd*, were never popular among the professional bards, in spite of the fact that they were included in the traditional classification of the Welsh strict-metre system. But although they were, in general, deliberately eschewed by the more accomplished bards, who usually only used them when they composed an *awdl enghreifftiol* ('exemplifying ode'), they were probably very popular among the lower-grade itinerant bards and minstrels, who sang in these measures, devoid of *cynghanedd*, all through the centuries. And it is highly significant that when these metres occur in free verse they are not drastically dissimilar to the corresponding measures which occur, albeit rarely, in the strict-metre compositions, except that the more skilled professional bards have deliberately made them much more intricate and ornate by introducing *cynghanedd* and prescribing an exact number of syllables for each line, which varied according to the particular measure used. Another interesting link with the strict-metre system is provided by the work of Tomas ab Ieuan ap Rhys, who, as we have already seen, belonged to that class of *cwndidwyr* who had received a certain amount of formal instruction in the bardic craft, for in addition to the very popular *cywydd deuair fyrion* and *awdl-gywydd* his compositions contain, significantly, some examples of the metres called *cyhydedd fer*,[200] *cyhydedd nawban*,[201] *toddaid*,[202] and *cyhydedd hir*.[203] In some of these verses we find attempts, though not always without blemish, at composing in *cynghanedd*. The work of his bardic disciple, Hopcyn Tomas Phylip, also contains an interesting example of the metre called *cyhydedd fer*,[204] while variant forms of the *cyhydedd hir* occur in the compositions of some other *cwndidwyr*.[205] Therefore, the metres which occur most frequently in the *cwndidau* were old indigenous Welsh metres, which amply confirms that much of the free verse composed in Glamorgan during the sixteenth and seventeenth centuries represented a long and uninterrupted tradition, distinguished by its own special diction and literary conventions. This body of verse, therefore, forms a chapter of great importance in the history of Welsh metrics. Unfortunately, the old indigenous free poetry, as distinct from the verses composed on English airs and set to *cynghanedd*, later went out of fashion. Hence the sudden appearance of this type of verse in Glamorgan in the sixteenth century 'does no more than afford a glimpse of it before it died'.[206]

THE ARTISTIC STANDARDS OF THE *Cwndidau*

But important as the *cwndidau* undoubtedly are in the history of Welsh metrics, most of them in the matter of art fall well below the high standards achieved by the bards of the classical Welsh tradition. There are, undeniably, a few compositions, such as the elegy composed by Tomas ab Ieuan ap Rhys to John Gamage or the anonymous 'Coed Glyn Cynon', whose poignant dignity and occasional flashes of delicate fancy leave a lasting impression on the reader. Yet the great bulk of this verse is marred by an inadequate sense of style and an unmistakable slackness and diffuseness in expression. Both the language and style of these poems are far simpler and more debased than anything written in the traditional strict metres. There is sometimes considerable irregularity in the length of the lines and it is only as the result of a great deal of elision or even violence to the natural stress-accent that this metrical unevenness can be overcome. Liberal use is made of forms which occur, many of them to this day, in the Glamorgan dialects (e.g. *kroelon, troelo, ody, rhog, mogi, canddo* for *cadno* 'fox', and the plural *cenddi, trydy, heddy, ar ywcha, grwdgio*, etc.); the initial consonantal clusters *gwl-* and *gwr-* are simplified to *gl-* and *gr-* respectively (e.g. *glyb* is written for *gwlyb* 'wet', the standard literary form); initial *chw-* becomes *wh-* or *w-*; an epenthetic vowel is often included in the rhyme pattern (e.g. *pobol* rhymes with *gwrthol, drychevenn* with *llenn, llaidir* [*sic*] with *tir, Dwnrheven* with *ffyrfafen*); the unaccented diphthongs *-ai* and *-au* at the end of a word are levelled with *-e*, and the diphthong *-oe* is levelled with *-o*, exactly as they are in the local dialects (e.g. *rhinwedde* is written for the plural noun *rhinweddau* 'virtues', *gwele* occurs for *gwelai*, the 3rd singular imperfect of the verb *gweled* 'to see'); and the reduced form of a diphthong is occasionally made to rhyme with a vowel (e.g. *gweithredodd*, written for the plural noun *gweithredoedd* 'acts, deeds', rhymes with the noun *modd* 'mode, manner, means'). By far the most blameworthy of all the Glamorgan *cwndidwyr* was Tomas ab Ieuan ap Rhys, for many of the features referred to above occur not only in the religious carols which he composed but also in those poems which he wrote in the more formal *toddaid* measure or the *cyhydedd fer* and *cyhydedd nawban*, or when he addressed panegyric verses to some of the gentry. His work, the general style and diction of which seem to have a far stronger affinity with the tradition of *y glêr* than anything that occurs among the compositions of the other Glamorgan *cwndidwyr*, is a quarry of considerable value for making a diachronic study of the local dialects. Even so, it is well to remember that the differences between his poetry and the free-metre work of a northern poet such as Llywelyn ap Hywel ab Ieuan ap Gronwy, of Anglesey, are

[575]

LI

not nearly as marked as one who is familiar with the two dialects would at first be led to expect.[207] This again confirms the view that the free verse was not something which suddenly appeared *in vacuo* in the sixteenth century, written entirely in the spoken language of that period and hence incorporating all the corruption and idiosyncrasies, the numerous phonetic developments and various semantic changes which help to distinguish the local dialects from one another. Rather was it the product of an old tradition which had persisted unabated for many centuries and had retained its own distinctive diction and literary modes.[208] In spite of all its artistic blemishes, 'it was the poetry of literary men, not what may, hesitatingly, be called folk poetry'.[209] And, significantly, many of Tomas ab Ieuan ap Rhys's successors, who had received some degree of formal instruction in the bardic craft, tried hard, though not always successfully, to avoid many of those debased linguistic and stylistic features which so obviously mar the compositions of Tomas ab Ieuan ap Rhys. His successors were also strongly averse to composing poetry of this kind when they addressed eulogies to men of rank and social status.

Nor is it only from the metrical and linguistic standpoint that the *cwndidau* are interesting and important: they generally tell us much more about the manners and customs of the period and the changing conditions of life and society than does the strict-metre poetry composed in *cynghanedd*, the primary function of which was to portray the ideal of an ordered, hierarchic and essentially homogeneous society.

iii.

WELSH PROSE

The prose texts composed and transcribed in Glamorgan during the Middle Ages constituted one of the region's most important and most distinctive contributions to the literary heritage of Wales.[210] However, by the end of the sixteenth century the creative literary energy of these medieval prose works had lost much of its former drive and momentum. No literary-minded gentleman or cleric of means made any serious effort to have the interesting corpus of medieval prose texts printed. However, during the very period when a professional scribe of the calibre of Llywelyn Siôn was energetically transcribing much of this uncommonly rich and varied material one of the Glamorgan clerics set about the task of translating *Certain Sermons or Homilies* into Welsh under the title *Pregethau a osodwyd allan trwy awdurdod i'w darllein ymhob Eglwys blwyf a phob capel er adailadaeth i'r bobl annyscedig. Gwedi eu troi i'r iaith Gymeraeg drwy waith Edward Iames* (1606). The translator, Edward James (*c.* 1570–*c.* 1610?), had been born in Glamorgan and educated at Jesus College, Oxford, where he gained his B.A. on June 16, 1589 and his M.A. on July 8, 1592. On February 2, 1595–6 he was appointed vicar of Caerleon (Caerllion-ar-Wysg), and he later served as rector of Shire-newton and of Llangattock-nigh-Usk (Llangatwg Dyffryn Wysg), before becoming vicar, on July 12, 1599, of the parish of Llangatwg Feibion Afel in Monmouthshire. Four years later, on July 23, 1603, he became vicar of Llangatwg in the vale of Neath (Cadoxton-juxta-Neath), where he served for three years, until he was eventually appointed chancellor of Llandaff in 1606.[211] But although he thus belonged, late in his career, to that distinguished line of cultured church dignitaries at Llandaff, no bard, as far as can now be ascertained, ever sang his praises. The fact that he served as a cleric in the Llandaff diocese during Bishop William Morgan's episcopacy may be significant, for it is possible that it was the latter who actively encouraged Edward James to translate the church homilies into Welsh. In undertaking this worthy task James was not in any way a pioneer, for sometime during the previous century an anony-mous member of the very talented school of translators had translated some of the homilies contained in John Mirk's celebrated *Liber Ffestialis* into Welsh under the title *Darn o'r Ffestifal*.[212] There are some striking differences, however, between the language of Edward James's translation and that which characterizes many of the Glamorgan prose texts trans-cribed by Llywelyn Siôn. Although he was obviously not averse to using occasionally some forms and expressions which occur in the Glamorgan dialects, Edward James's linguistic standards were generally those adopted in the Welsh translation of the Bible by Bishop William Morgan (*c.* 1545–1604), who generally took as his medium the majestic and manifestly purer language of the classical *cywyddwyr*.

iv.

MANUSCRIPTS AND SCRIBES

A change no less remarkable than that which distinguished the prose tradition occurred also during the same period in the fortunes of those manuscripts which were almost certainly of Glamorgan provenance. The Welsh manuscripts which were transcribed during the medieval period rarely provide an incontrovertible indication of their original ownership or of the particular place or area where they were first compiled. Nevertheless, although much research remains to be done, a detailed analysis of various linguistic features contained in the medieval Welsh manuscripts strongly suggests that many of them, particularly those containing copies of Middle Welsh prose works, had been compiled and transcribed in Morgannwg and were probably deposited in various places within the region during the fifteenth and early-sixteenth centuries.[213] It is extremely difficult, however, to trace the later history of these manuscripts with any degree of precision. A number of them undoubtedly fell into the hands of Thomas Wilkins (below, pp. 584–589); but not even an antiquarian as zealous and as well-informed as Wilkins could possibly hope to gather into his net all the rich and varied material that had been transcribed in Glamorgan during the medieval period, for it is obvious that quite a few of these manuscripts had already been transferred to north Wales by approximately the beginning of the last quarter of the sixteenth century.[214] Probably the most outstanding example is the priceless thirteenth-century manuscript called *Llyfr Aneirin* ('The Book of Aneirin'), which is now retained in Cardiff Central Library. In the fifteenth century it had been in the possession of Gwilym Tew (*fl. c.* 1460–80), whose interest was obviously aroused by its contents, for he set about collecting the obsolete and difficult words which it contained and valiantly attempted, albeit unsuccessfully, to interpret their hidden meaning.[215] But a little over a century later its contents were being diligently transcribed and studied by some of the more renowned northern scribes and antiquarians, such as Sir Thomas Wiliems (1545–6 to *c.* 1622) of Trefriw.[216] It is conceivable that a number of the Glamorgan manuscripts had been taken to north Wales by various professional poets during the course of their bardic itinerancies, and had, after their death, fallen into the hands of such famous antiquarians as Robert Vaughan (1592?–1667), the collector of the well-known Hengwrt library. But probably the most potent of all the various factors that eventually resulted in the transference of these manuscripts from Glamorgan to north Wales was the widely-embracing antiquarian activities of the unusually accomplished group of scholars that had arisen in the Vale of Clwyd and its confines.[217] A number of the more prominent antiquarians of this period visited Glamorgan, obviously with a view to acquiring some, at least, of the more valuable manuscript material which could still be found in the region. Robert Vaughan, for example, refers specifically to the manuscript-book of 'Walter the archdeacon', namely, *Brut y Brenhinedd*, a Welsh version of Geoffrey of Monmouth's *Historia Regum Britanniae*, which was then in the possession of 'Mr Turbervil' in Morgannwg, to the Red Book of Hergest, unquestionably the most important single manuscript compilation of medieval Welsh literature, which at that time was in the possession of 'Sr tho: Mansel' in Margam, and to a copy of *Brut y Tywysogyon* ('The Chronicle of the Princes') and 'Rhol Jolo Goch', which was in the possession of 'Wil Meuric o Sain Nicolas', the son of Rice Merrick of Cotrel.[218] One of the greatest of Welsh scholars, Dr. John Davies (*c.* 1567–1644) of Mallwyd, was fortunate enough to acquire a collection of some of Dafydd ap Gwilym's famous *cywyddau*, which had been transcribed sometime before 1577, 'from the book of Mr Wm Mathew' of Llandaff,[219] and in 1631 he made a very important copy of 'Gwassanaeth Meir', the Middle Welsh metrical version of the *Officium Parvum Beatae Mariae Virginis*.[220] This copy was taken from a manuscript-book 'which had been written in Llanhari', in Glamorgan, about the year 1537.[221] Three years later, in 1634, he borrowed the Red Book of Hergest from Sir Lewis Mansel of Margam.[222]

In a letter to Owen Wyn of Gwydir on May 19, 1639, Dr. John Davies wrote: 'Concerning Dauid ap Gwillims workes, I haue begonne such a collection of them as you write of, but could not perfecte it, because I knewe I wanted many of his poemes. Mr. Willm Mathewe of the Castle of Landaffe had a booke written in paper wth an ould hand wch had many of them, whereof I gotte copie of the one half *when I dwelt in those parts*'.[223] This may have been sometime between 1595 and 1601, when William Morgan, with whom he was closely connected, was bishop there.[224]

That John Jones (*c.* 1578–83 to 1658?) of Gellilyfdy, in the parish of Ysgeifiog, Flintshire, unquestionably the most accomplished calligrapher and transcriber of manuscripts of his day, had also visited Glamorgan during this period is beyond doubt. He refers specifically to the fact that he visited Cardiff in September 1612 in order to transcribe parts of the *Liber Landavensis*, or 'the book of Teilo' (*llyfyr Teilaw*), as he preferred to call it.[225] Indeed, he may have been partly responsible for the transference from Glamorgan and from other parts of south Wales of quite a few of the important manuscripts which are now contained in the impressive Hengwrt collection in the National Library of Wales at Aberystwyth. During his visit in 1612 he prepared a short catalogue of those manuscripts which were known to be in the possession of some of the local gentry at that time.[226] These included, *inter alia*, a collection of strict-metre *cywyddau* which was in the possession of Llywelyn Siôn of Llangewydd; a 'text', the contents of which are not specified, owned by Hopcyn ap Hywel of Pen-y-fai, the father of the bard Watcyn Powel (above, pp. 553–554); a Welsh book in the possession of Anthony Powel, who was almost certainly the gentleman-antiquary from Llwydarth and a brother to Hopcyn ap Hywel;[227] an anthology of *cywyddau* which was the property of Rhys ap Rhisiart Tomas of Glyn Nedd, a cultured gentleman whose father had once owned the famous manuscript known as *Y Cwta Cyfarwydd* ('The Short Guide');[228] another collection of strict-metre verse, composed in the popular *cywydd* measure, which was in the possession of the son of Ieuan Siancyn Tomas ap John of Y Gadlys, near Aberdare; a work, the precise contents of which are not specified, owned by Lambrook Stradling, a grandson to Sir Edward Stradling (d. 1535), who lived in Roath, near Cardiff;[229] a collection of *cywyddau* which was the property of Rhys ap Jankyn Rhys of West-plas (West Place) in Coety; the 'book of Caradog of Llancarfan' in the possession of Mr. Wiliam Hughes of Caerleon-on-Usk; *Y Cwta Cyfarwydd*, which by that time had been acquired by a 'Mr hugh sanfford gwas Iarll penvro';[230] and a Welsh version of Geoffrey of Monmouth's *Historia Regum Britanniae* in the possession of Christopher Turberville of Pen-llin, a son-in-law to Sir John Carne of Ewenni.[231]

There were at least three classes of people in Glamorgan in the sixteenth century who took a keen and intelligent interest in the contents of the medieval manuscripts and who were themselves copyists. First of all, there were a number of cultured, literary-minded gentry. They have reasonably been compared by the late Professor G. J. Williams with that altruistic gentleman from Powys, Ieuan ab Wiliam ap Dafydd ab Einws. Many of the old religious texts which he had so painstakingly transcribed were to be found, he claimed, in printed editions in England. But this was not the case in Wales, and hence it was absolutely imperative that texts of this nature should be disseminated in manuscripts 'as an example to the people that they might improve their lives'.[232] It was undoubtedly motives such as these which prompted some of the Glamorgan gentry to transcribe medieval religious texts, and obviously inspired the composition of the numerous religious *cwndidau*. The intellectual activities of this group, however, were not confined to religious and devotional literature, for there were also among the local gentry a number of enlightened scholars and antiquarians (below, pp. 592–608).

The second class comprised the professional bards. As far as can now be ascertained, no Welsh bard attempted to make a substantial collection of his own work before approximately the middle of the fifteenth century. Among the earliest and most notable examples in this respect are Gutun Owain (*fl. c.* 1460–*c.* 1498) of Powys and Lewis Glyn Cothi (*fl.* 1447–86) of Deheubarth.[233] About the same time Gwilym Tew transcribed in Peniarth MS. 51 the literary material which was regarded as an indispensable part of every chief-of-song's repertoire (*Ante*, III, 506–9). In general, however, very few of the more prominent professional bards were diligent copyists or chroniclers. No manuscripts now exist which are known to have been transcribed by such celebrated Glamorgan chiefs-of-song as Rhisiart ap Rhys, Iorwerth Fynglwyd, or Rhisiart Iorwerth,[234] although the latter, according to the late Dr. Gwenogvryn Evans, made a copy of the poems which he addressed to the Dwnn family.[235] The most famous *pencerdd* in the region during the first half of the sixteenth century was unquestionably Lewis Morgannwg (*fl.* 1520–65),[236] but it is extremely unlikely that he transcribed any of the extant manuscript material, apart, possibly, from some pedigrees that occur in Peniarth MS. 132.[237] Nevertheless, there is considerable evidence that he had an important collection of manuscripts in his possession, and after his death these probably passed to his two bardic disciples, Meurug Dafydd and Dafydd Benwyn. But the second half of the sixteenth century witnessed a remarkable change in this respect, for in that period we find that a number of professional bards, such as Meurug Dafydd, Dafydd Benwyn (plate XI), and Sils ap Siôn, made valuable collections of their own compositions and, occasionally, of some of the strict-metre poems of other bards as well. The copies which they transcribed sometimes contained substantial collections of pedigrees. A notable example occurs in Cardiff MS. 10, which was transcribed by Dafydd Benwyn.[238] But it seems unlikely that any of the Glamorgan bards made collections similar to those transcribed in north Wales by such celebrated heraldic bards as Gruffudd Hiraethog (d. 1564) or Simwnt Fychan (*c.* 1530–1606), where the coats-of-arms of some of the more prominent gentry are noted together with the relevant genealogical details. There is nothing in the extant works of the Glamorgan bards to suggest that they had any expertise in the art of heraldry, nor does any convincing proof exist that there were in their midst any skilled copyists.

THE PROFESSIONAL SCRIBES

It was the third class, however, consisting of a small but exceptionally industrious group of professional scribes which was by far the most important in the sixteenth and seventeenth centuries. In order to appreciate the full significance of their work, it must be remembered that although nearly two hundred Welsh books had been printed during the century and a half that had elapsed since 1546, the year when Sir John Prys's *Yny lhyvyr hwnn* ('In this book'), the earliest Welsh printed book, appeared, they were mainly, apart from some important grammars and dictionaries, works of a distinctly religious or devotional nature. No serious efforts had been made to publish the great wealth of prose and poetry that had been composed during the Middle Ages. On the other hand, one should not overlook the small collection of *cywyddau* published by the Renaissance scholar and grammarian, Gruffydd Robert (*c.* 1522–*c.* 1610), during his exile in Italy. 'Exemplifying odes' (*awdlau enghreifftiol*) were also published by Siôn Dafydd Rhys (1534–1619?) in his famous grammar, *Cambrobrytannicae Cymraecaeve Lingvae Institvtiones et Rvdimenta* (1592), the first occasion when complete compositions by Glamorgan bards, as distinct from select quotations from their works, appeared in print, while extensive quotations from the works of the bards were also included in *Eglvryn Phraethineb sebh Dosparth ar Retoreg* (1595) by Henry Perri (or Parry, 1560/1–1617), a native of Maes Glas, Flintshire. Moreover, a portion of one of the *cywyddau* which Iorwerth Fynglwyd, probably the most accomplished of Glamorgan strict-metre bards, addressed to his patron, Rhys ap Siôn of Aberpergwm, was included in Bishop Richard Davies's epistolary greeting in William Salesbury's Welsh translation of the New Testament (1567). One of the earliest of the Welsh poets to publish a collection of his own work was Wiliam Midleton (*c.* 1550–*c.* 1600), but he was a gentleman of independent means. Generally speaking, however, the professional bards rigidly adhered to the time-honoured practice of making manuscript-collections of their own strict-metre compositions together with some of the works composed both by their predecessors and by their contemporaries. Naturally, the literature-loving gentry would commission one of the professional scribes to prepare a similar collection for them. An interesting reference occurs in Mostyn MS. 131, 78, to a certain

'L'n ap Math', which may conjecturally be interpreted as 'Llywelyn ap Mathau', who transcribed in 1567, on behalf of Sir Edward Stradling of St. Donat's, a series of *englynion* which Gruffudd ap Nicolas, Owain Dwnn and Gruffudd Benrhaw had addressed to one another.[239] Unfortunately, little is known of the activities of the professional scribes. The exemplary neatness of the copy which 'Risiart Twrbervil' so carefully transcribed towards the beginning of the seventeenth century in Cardiff MS. 2. 277 (= Baglan MS. 1) of Dafydd Benwyn's compositions suggests that he may have been one of their number.[240]

LLYWELYN SIÔN (*c.* 1540–*c.* 1615–17?)

Undoubtedly, the most outstanding member of this class in Glamorgan was Llywelyn Siôn of Llangewydd, in Laleston (Trelales), near Bridgend, whose place in the bardic history of the region has already been discussed (above, pp. 545–546). Iolo Morganwg was well aware of Llywelyn Siôn's renown as a professional scribe. 'Llywelyn Sion', he wrote, 'seems to have been a transcriber by trade, for there are in Glamorgan several copies of the same work in his handwriting . . .'.[241] Iolo, with characteristic acumen, was probably the first to grasp this important fact. However, surprisingly little is known for certain about Llywelyn Siôn's career as a professional scribe. But the extant manuscripts which he transcribed show that he had received some degree of formal instruction in this exacting art, and he placed far greater emphasis on this aspect of his career than he did on his activities as a bard and *clerwr*.

At least thirteen manuscripts transcribed by him are still extant. These include seven extremely valuable collections of strict-metre verse, consisting of both *awdlau* and *cywyddau*,[242] a very important collection of *cwndidau*,[243] a transcription of pedigrees,[244] and four precious collections of prose texts.[245] Some of his work also occurs in four other manuscripts.[246] Two or three of the manuscripts which he transcribed can legitimately be regarded as notebooks which he kept for his personal use. One particularly interesting feature of those manuscripts which contain collections of strict-metre verse is that there is no marked variety in their contents or, on the whole, in the order in which the various items are arranged, a fact which suggests that he always kept close at hand a personal collection of verse of this kind from which he could easily make a selection whenever he was commissioned to transcribe a manuscript containing works of this nature. Towards the end of his life, between *c.* 1600 and *c.* 1613, he tended to use rather long, narrow parchment, and hence the three most famous of the many manuscripts transcribed by him are appropriately known as the Long Book of Shrewsbury (*Llyfr Hir Amwythig*),[247] the Long Book of Llywarch Reynolds (*Llyfr Hir Llywarch Reynolds*),[248] and the Long Book of Llanharan (*Llyfr Hir Llanharan*).[249] He was not invariably an exact and faithful copyist, for considerable variations can occasionally be detected in the various copies which he transcribed, with couplets sometimes being incorrectly transposed. The notes in some of these manuscripts suggest that at least two of them were transcribed at the behest of the Powels, one for the Kemeys family, and one for the Carnes of Nash (*Yr As Fach*). Surprisingly, however, not one of his manuscripts can confidently be connected either with Sir Edward Stradling or with Rice Merrick, the two scholars most passionately interested during this period in the history of Glamorgan (below, pp. 594–603).

Llywelyn Siôn was undeniably one of the greatest professional scribes of his day. Although his output may not have been nearly as prolific as that of John Jones of Gellilyfdy or Robert Vaughan of Hengwrt, the contents of his manuscripts are, on the whole, arranged far more systematically and he does not appear to have been influenced in any significant degree by some of the more prevalent literary prejudices of the period. It is to his devotion and indefatigable industry that we are largely indebted for the preservation of the compositions of a number of the minor poets who sang in Glamorgan in the second half of the sixteenth century, as well as the works of many bards who sang in other parts of Wales during this period. The fullest and most important collection of *cwndidau*, that contained in Llanover MS. B 9, is in his autograph (plate XII). The prose texts transcribed by him are of exceptional importance (*Ante*, III, 550–4). His transcript of *Y Drych Cristianogawl* ('The Christian Mirror'), a summary of some of the basic tenets of the Church on the nature of sin and justification and on the importance of the sacraments, is extremely valuable, for the copy which occurs in his hand in Cardiff MS. 3. 240 is at once the earliest and the only complete version of the Welsh text in its three parts.[250] The copy which he transcribed *c.* 1590 in Llanover MS. B 17 of the Welsh version of *Chwedleu Seith Doethon Rufein* ('Tales of the Seven Sages of Rome') is strikingly different from the other versions, of which there are at least nine in all, found in other manuscripts,[251] while the only surviving Welsh version of the *Gesta Romanorum*, a popular work which contained a collection of moral stories about various saints which were probably often used by preachers in their sermons, is preserved in his autograph in Llanover MS. B 18.[252] The manuscripts transcribed by Llywelyn Siôn reflect some interesting facets of the literary life of the region during his day, and to his zeal and devotion we owe the preservation of many of our most valuable literary treasures in an age when these were frequently lost or destroyed. But in spite of all the frequent references made by Iolo Morganwg to the many treatises on the ancient druidic and bardic lore which he claimed to have discovered in Llywelyn Siôn's manuscripts, these latter contain nothing which deals with any aspect of Welsh poetic art. No copy occurs in Llywelyn Siôn's hand of any version of the prosodic grammar used by the teachers in the bardic schools, or of a transcript of the famous 'Statute of Gruffudd ap Cynan'.

There is, therefore, a considerable body of evidence that there existed in Glamorgan a number of gentry who were prepared to commission professional scribes to make copies of substantial collections of Welsh poetry and prose. This enlightened interest had virtually ceased, however, long before the beginning of the eighteenth century, although, as the career of Edward Lhuyd amply confirms, there were still some among the local gentry who were prepared even in that period to support and encourage research into Welsh history and antiquities. Striking though the general decline during the second half of the seventeenth century may have been, the picture is nevertheless not one of unrelieved gloom. The famous Powel family—'y Poweliaid Doethion' ('the Wise Powels'), as they were frequently called, according to Iolo Morganwg— were a notable exception. According to Edward Lhuyd, 'Mr George Powell of pen y vay', a grandson of Watcyn Powel, the celebrated poet and antiquary, had a collection of old manuscripts.[253] And in Iolo Morganwg's day some of them had passed to the Rev. Gervase Powel in Llanharan, and it was there that he and Evan Evans (or 'Ieuan Fardd'), the talented eighteenth-century antiquary from Cardiganshire, pored avidly over the contents of the 'Long Book of Llywelyn Siôn'. This was why Iolo claimed that it was at Llanharan that he had seen a copy of *Cyfrinach Beirdd Ynys Prydain*.[254] After the various branches of the cultured Powel family of Ton-du and Y Goetre-hen (in Llangynwyd Isaf) had become extinct, their manuscripts came ultimately, according to Iolo, into the hands of John Bradford (1706–85) of Betws Tir Iarll. This probably explains why Iolo frequently maintained that a great deal of the material relating to the literary history of Glamorgan which he himself had undoubtedly forged derived ultimately from the manuscript-books of both Anthony and Watcyn Powel acquired by John Bradford.

Thomas Wilkins (1625–6 to 1699)

Fortunately, however, at this critical juncture, when most of the local gentry no longer took any interest in the native literature and culture and when the bardic order was in its last death throes, an astonishingly rich and varied collection of much of the old manuscript material was preserved by the Rev. Thomas Wilkins of Llan-fair (St. Mary Church), a descendant of one of the Norman lords who had settled in the Vale in the twelfth century. The Norman family from which he was descended was originally surnamed 'de Wintona' and it settled, apparently, at Llandough (or, possibly, Llandow), in Glamorgan. In spite of its foreign extraction, the family, which changed its name in the fourteenth century to 'Wilcoline' or 'Wilkyn', and in the seventeenth to 'Wilkins', became thoroughly Welsh in both speech and sentiment. For some generations before Thomas Wilkins's birth the family had settled in St. Mary Church.[255] Born in 1625–6, Thomas Wilkins went to

Jesus College, Oxford, in 1641, and took the degree of B.C.L. in 1661. Like his father and grandfather before him, he became rector of St. Mary Church (Llan-fair). In addition to St. Mary Church he also held the rectories of Gelli-gaer (1666) and Llan-maes (1668), as well as a prebend at Llandaff.[256] His death occurred on August 20, 1699, and he was buried on the following Tuesday, at the age of 74. His will was proved on September 8, 1699.

In any discussion of Thomas Wilkins's career particular attention must be paid to Cardiff MS. 3. 464, the only manuscript, as far as we are now able to judge, which is entirely in his own hand (plate XIII). It contains a miscellaneous collection of various matters relating to the history of Glamorgan, and the greater part of it seems to have been written during the period 1657–60, when he was still a comparatively young man. Thomas Wilkins was pre-eminently an antiquary and historian who had been inspired by Rice Merrick's researches and, like his northern compatriots, Robert Vaughan (1592?–1667) of Hengwrt and William Maurice (d. 1680) of Cefn-y-braich, in Llansilin, he was a dedicated bookworm who devoted himself to collecting and preserving as many as possible of the ancient manuscripts which were scattered over many parts of Glamorgan. The magnificent private library which he assembled at St. Mary Church with such industry and devotion is one of the first in Glamorgan about whose contents the literary historian can speak with any degree of authority. Although it cannot seriously be compared with the very substantial collections at Hengwrt and Cefn-y-braich, it has authoritatively been claimed that it constituted the most important collection of manuscripts ever amassed by an individual within Glamorgan.[257]

It is difficult to determine the precise number of manuscripts contained in Wilkins's magnificent collection, for a number of those which had formerly been in his possession were housed in the mansion at Hafod Uchdryd, in Cardiganshire, which was destroyed in a fire in 1807. Fortunately, however, he referred in his will to a number of the books contained in his library. A copy of the edition of the Welsh Bible which appeared in 1690 and 'B. Jewell's works' were bequeathed by him to the churches of Llan-fair and Llan-maes respectively. The will also referred to a number of English books which he left to his eldest son, who also inherited his father's manuscripts. Although this is the only explicit reference that occurs to Wilkins's manuscripts, it is really not too difficult to gain some idea of the main contents of his library. Of all the numerous manuscripts transcribed in south Wales during the Middle Ages, probably the richest in content and unquestionably the most famous was the Red Book of Hergest. Its history, however, is very obscure. It is impossible to determine when it was removed from Hergest, but Sir John Prys (1502?–55) obviously had an opportunity to peruse some of its contents c. 1550. Its whereabouts at that time are uncertain, but in an address written c. 1565–8, a copy of which is now preserved in

NLW. MS. 6434, William Salesbury stated that he had himself seen the Red Book of Hergest about three years previously 'in Ludlow with Sir Harry Sydney, lord president', and that the manuscript had been borrowed by a certain Siancyn Gwyn of Llanidloes. By the first half of the seventeenth century, however, the manuscript was in the possession of the Mansel family at Margam, but it is impossible to determine exactly how they had acquired it. Its later history is very obscure, but by the summer of 1697, when Edward Lhuyd was in Glamorgan, the manuscript was in the possession of Thomas Wilkins, although he was certainly not its rightful owner. In a letter written at Cowbridge in September 1697 Lhuyd states that he had been 'detained by Mr Wilkins of Lhan Vair in this neighbourhood these 2 months: for so long a time the copying an old Welsh MS. took up; which had he been willing to restore to ye owner, we might have bought for twenty shillings'.[258] The 'old Welsh MS.' to which Lhuyd referred was the Red Book of Hergest. It is impossible to determine whether Wilkins had succeeded in buying it prior to his death in August 1699, but some two years later his eldest son wrote his name in this priceless manuscript before presenting it, in 1701, to Jesus College, Oxford (Jesus Coll. MS. 111). Thomas Wilkins had also acquired *Llyvyr Agkyr Llandewivrevi*, which was also presented to Jesus College, Oxford. Two other manuscripts from his collection were donated at the same time, namely, Jesus College MS. 29 and Jesus College MS. 27. It is not clear when these manuscripts were donated. Professor G. J. Williams believed that the Red Book of Hergest, *Llyvyr Agkyr Llandewivrevi*, and possibly Jesus College MS. 3 ('The Book of Llywelyn the Priest') were all donated together.[259] But this is impossible, for Jesus College MSS. 119 (*Llyvyr Agkyr Llandewivrevi*), 27 and 29 are all recorded in Bernard's catalogue of 1697, and they must therefore have been presented to Jesus College sometime before the death of the elder Wilkins.[260] If Professor G. J. Williams was correct, however, in assuming that the 'Book of Llywelyn the Priest' was included among the donations made by the Wilkins family to Jesus College, Oxford, this further substantiates the claim that the manuscript was of Glamorgan provenance.[261] The fact that the signatures of both Morgan Lewis of Llantrisant and Thomas Carne occur in Jesus College MS. 29 provides us with a hint of the way in which it was eventually acquired by Wilkins. The former belonged to the influential Lewis family of Y Fan, while the latter was evidently a member of the prominent Carne family of Nash. Early in the seventeenth century these two families became connected by marriage,[262] and Thomas Wilkins married Jane, daughter of Thomas Carne of Nash, while Wilkins's second son, Roger, married Elizabeth Lewis, who belonged to the Llanisien branch of the famous Fan family.

Wilkins had also in his possession at least two other works transcribed on parchment, namely, Hafod MS. 16, a medical treatise which had been written c. 1400, and 'Gwassanaeth Meir', the Middle Welsh version of the *Officium Parvum Beatae Mariae Virginis*, which was later removed, sometime between 1755, when it is known to have been in Glamorgan, and 1778–88, in very obscure circumstances, to Shrewsbury School, where it is still retained. Moreover, Wilkins had somehow acquired a copy of *Brut y Brenhinedd* ('The Chronicle of the Kings'), contained in Peniarth MS. 162, which had been transcribed in the fifteenth century, a copy of *Brut y Tywysogyon* ('The Chronicle of the Princes') and of *Brut y Saesson* ('The Chronicle of the Saxons'), contained in Peniarth MS. 253, which is attributed to the third quarter of the sixteenth century; a transcript of one of the versions of the Laws of Hywel Dda, contained in Peniarth MS. 258, which is dated to the second half of the fifteenth century and which, at various times, had belonged to the bard Dafydd Benwyn and to a certain 'Jevan sienkin Tomas ap Sion o blwyf Llangonwyd [*sic*] vawr y morganwg'; and a copy of a substantial number of important Middle Welsh prose texts, which are contained in Hafod MS. 8, the first part of which was written not later than 1561, and the second part not later than 1577.[263] Of greater interest, perhaps, is that Thomas Wilkins had also in his impressive collection a number of the Welsh prose texts composed in Glamorgan during the sixteenth century, including the earliest surviving transcript of *Y Marchog Crwydrad* made c. 1585, in Llanstephan MS. 178, by Ieuan ab Ieuan ap Madog of Betws Tir Iarll, and the copies of *Dives a Phawper* and *Y Drych Cristianogawl*, both of which occur in the hand of Llywelyn Siôn, in Cardiff MS. 3. 240.[264] Furthermore, it seems more than likely that he once owned the other manuscripts copied by Glamorgan scribes which are nowadays kept in the Hafod collection in Cardiff Central Library. These included Hafod MS. 4, in which the only other surviving transcript of the Welsh translation of Henry Parker's *Dives et Pauper* occurs, a valuable collection of strict-metre verse contained in Hafod MS. 20, both of which were transcribed by Llywelyn Siôn, and a miscellaneous collection of prose texts contained in Hafod MS. 22, a bulky compilation of over 700 pages in two hands of the second half of the sixteenth century, one of which was undoubtedly that of Anthony Powel (c. 1560 to 1618–19).[265] Wilkins also had the poetical works of Dafydd Benwyn contained in Jesus College MS. 3, which was transcribed early in the seventeenth century, and Cardiff MS. 2. 278, containing the genealogies of many prominent families in south Wales which Sir Joseph A. Bradney published in 1910 under the title *Llyfr Baglan*.

The list given above, however, does not include all the manuscripts which Thomas Wilkins had in his library. Nor was he in any sense a jealously possessive owner; when Edward Lhuyd and his enthusiastic assistants visited the county in 1697, they spent at least two months eagerly transcribing material from the valuable store of manuscripts in St. Mary Church, and they were obviously permitted to borrow some of them, including, surprisingly, the priceless Red Book of Hergest.[266] Indeed, Iolo Morganwg claimed that Wilkins was the only gentleman who generously permitted Edward Lhuyd to make liberal use of the contents of his library.[267] Nor was Wilkins's eldest son any less generous, for it appears that he loaned other manuscripts to Lhuyd in 1701, when the latter made a copy of one of the works on the history of Glamorgan.[268] When Lhuyd died on June 30, 1709, he had many works from Wilkins's library in his possession. Surprisingly, both Jesus College and the University of Oxford refused to purchase his manuscripts, which were eventually sold to Sir Thomas Sebright. A number of these were donated in 1778 to Thomas Pennant (1726–98), who described them as 'a vast collection', but their subsequent history is very obscure.[269] The remainder of the Sebright manuscripts were later sold and scattered. Among the buyers were Sir Watkin Williams-Wynn of Wynnstay, who tragically lost most of the manuscripts which he had bought in a fire in a London book-binder's shop, and Thomas Johnes (1748–1816), the enlightened landowner and man of letters of Hafod Uchdryd, near Cwmystwyth, Cardiganshire,[270] which became a veritable Mecca for many Welsh scholars and antiquarians. Iolo Morganwg, who visited Hafod Uchdryd in 1799, later claimed that 'about 180 volumes of ancient Welsh Manuscripts' were preserved there, and it is unlikely that this estimate was very wide of the mark.[271] Much of this material, amounting in all to about a hundred manuscripts, according to Iolo Morganwg, was irretrievably lost when the Hafod mansion was destroyed in 1807. If Iolo's estimate be accepted, approximately eighty volumes were saved.[272] Twenty-six of these are now retained in Cardiff Central Library and another three, designated the 'Wrecsam Manuscripts', in the National Library of Wales. At least two of these manuscripts had once been in Wilkins's possession, and it seems more than likely, therefore, that the other manuscripts transcribed by Llywelyn Siôn and Anthony Powel which are now contained in the important Hafod collection in Cardiff Central Library had also belonged to him at one time. There is also some evidence to support Iolo Morganwg's claim that the manuscripts acquired by Thomas Johnes contained other works which were originally of Glamorgan provenance, including 'a very curious Manuscript History of Glamorgan in folio written in the time of Queen Elizabeth by Rice Meyrick of Cottrel Esqr with the arms of ancient families finely blazoned in rich colours'.[273] This claim is partly substantiated by the fact that Wilkins's work on the history of Glamorgan shows that Rice Merrick's manuscripts had come into his hands. There is, therefore, considerable evidence to suggest that among the many manuscripts lost when Hafod was destroyed there were quite a few which Edward Lhuyd had borrowed at an earlier date from Wilkins.

When the Sebright collection was sold in April 1807 a number of the manuscripts were bought by the Hengwrt family. The magnificent collection of Welsh manuscripts amassed by this family remained at Hengwrt until 1859, when it was bequeathed in the will of Sir Robert Williames Vaughan to W. W. E. Wynne (1801–80), the antiquary and genealogist of Peniarth, Merionethshire. The bulk of the Hengwrt–Peniarth library became the property in 1909 of Sir John Williams (1840–1926) and this was one of the crucial factors which resulted in the establishment of the National Library of Wales at Aberystwyth. Hence a number of the books which were once owned by Wilkins are now kept there as part of the impressive Hengwrt–Peniarth collection. It would be quite wrong to assume, however, that Edward Lhuyd had succeeded in acquiring all the manuscript-volumes that once formed a part of Wilkins's collection. Many of the latter's manuscripts remained in the possession of his eldest son. Unfortunately, however, these were later carelessly dispersed and although a few of them, such as the Middle Welsh translation of 'Gwassanaeth Meir', the collection of the poetical works of Dafydd Benwyn which is now retained in the library of Jesus College, Oxford, the Baglan genealogies, and the transcripts of both *Y Drych Cristianogawl* and *Dives a Phawper*, were fortunately preserved, many of Wilkins's literary treasures have since vanished, perhaps for ever. Even so, this was the finest collection of Welsh manuscripts ever assembled by an individual within Glamorgan, the only Welsh library in any part of the southern regions which can even remotely be compared with the magnificent collections gathered at Hengwrt and Wynnstay in north Wales.[274]

Tomas ab Ieuan of Tre'r-Bryn
(second half of the seventeenth century)

Tomas ab Ieuan of Tre'r-bryn, in the parish of Llangrallo (Coychurch), was probably the last of the region's industrious and commendably devoted scribes. According to Iolo Morganwg, who ascribed to him a fairly prominent and influential rôle in the picture of the literary life of Morgannwg which he depicted in his writings, Tomas ab Ieuan was one of the descendants of Rhys Brydydd, one of the most talented chiefs-of-song who lived in Tir Iarll in the second half of the fifteenth century.[275] This claim, however, must be treated with the greatest reserve, although it must be allowed that details about Tomas ab Ieuan's life and career are meagre in the extreme. He undoubtedly lived during the second half of the seventeenth century, for two of the manuscripts which he transcribed, Llanover MS. B 8 and British Museum MS. 14878, can confidently be ascribed to the years 1674 and 1692 respectively.[276] A deed drawn up in 1659 proves conclusively that he acquired the Tre'r-bryn estate as a direct result of his marriage in that year to Rebecca Howell, daughter of Howell Rees of Tre'r-bryn.[277] According to some of the descendants of the family, who still lived until comparatively recently at Tre'r-bryn, Tomas ab Ieuan had come, at some unspecified date, to Glamorgan from Carmarthenshire. It seems that he had four sons, the youngest of whom, 'Evan ap Evan', acquired 'the customary hold estate of Tre Bryn'. The latter's son, Tomas ab Ieuan, or Tomas Bevan, still lived in Tre'r-bryn about the middle of the eighteenth century, and his name occurs in the list of subscribers to *Creulonderau ac Herledigaethau Eglwys Rufain* (1746) by Thomas Richards (below, pp. 630–633). He may also have been the 'Thomas Bevan, *of* Penycoed, *Esq.*' who subscribed to Richards's dictionary in 1753. That the manuscripts transcribed by Tomas ab Ieuan were still retained at the family home towards the end of the eighteenth century cannot seriously be doubted, for the manuscripts of 'The Widow Bevan, at Tre'r Bryn, near Cowbridge—The Collection made in 1684, by Thomas Bevan' were proudly recorded in 1795 as one of the most important collections to be found throughout the whole of south Wales at that time.[278] In a short note written *c.* 1791–5 on the cover of one of the manuscripts which had been acquired by the British Museum, Iolo Morganwg supplies us with some further interesting details:

> This book was written by Thomas ab Ifan of Tre'r Bryn. I have several in the same hand and one very large volume of Cywyddau, which was given me by his grandson whose name was also Thomas ab Ifan. he died about 20 years ago. there are now at Tre'r Bryn a large chest full of MSS. by the same hand. When John Rhydderch was in Glamorgan about (I think) 1725, he borrowed many MSS. which he never returned.[279]

But by the beginning of the nineteenth century this valuable collection had unfortunately 'been scattered like Chaff before the wind',[280] and it seems more than likely that many of Tomas ab Ieuan's manuscripts have been irretrievably lost. Fortunately, however, a number are still extant.[281] These include:

(1) Llanover MS. B 1, or '*Y Byrdew Mawr*', as Iolo Morganwg obviously preferred to call it, a bulky compilation bound together as two volumes and consisting of strict-metre *cywyddau* which had been transcribed from the manuscripts of Llywelyn Siôn together with the compositions of some seventeenth-century bards. The various headings agree, on the whole, with those which occur in the manuscripts of Llywelyn Siôn.

(2) Llanover MS. B 2, consisting of another substantial collection of *cywyddau* and *englynion*, transcribed in 1684.

(3) Llanover MS. B 8, containing a collection of *cywyddau brud* and *daroganau* ('vaticinatory poems') which, as the scribe himself indicates on page 125a, was copied in 1674.

(4) Llanover MS. B 29, containing a copy of Dr. John Davies's *Botanologium*.

(5) British Museum MS. 14878, consisting of verses attributed to 'Cattwn Ddoeth' and Taliesin, the works of a number of

sixteenth-century bards and some miscellaneous triads. Tomas ab Ieuan states that he had transcribed it in 1692.

(6) Peniarth MS. 447, a work transcribed in English in 1683 and containing the genealogies of many of the leading families of Glamorgan and Gwent. The contents of this manuscript reveal that the scribe was familiar with English works on the art of heraldry.

There are also some interesting references in Iolo Morganwg's writings to other manuscripts which he invariably claimed were the product of Tomas ab Ieuan's pen. These, according to Iolo, were housed at Hafod Uchdryd and were consumed in the fire of 1807. There seems to be no valid reason to doubt this claim. It is not unreasonable to assume, therefore, that Edward Lhuyd had succeeded in acquiring, during his stay in Glamorgan, a number of Tomas ab Ieuan's manuscripts, which eventually found their way to Hafod Uchdryd in Cardiganshire. Indeed, Iolo Morganwg claimed that he had seen there, towards the beginning of June 1799, 'other books' which were indubitably in Tomas ab Ieuan's autograph.[282] The source of many of the documents in Iolo's own manuscripts is frequently attributed by him to the work of Tomas ab Ieuan of Tre'r-bryn. Although many of the assertions and statements made by Iolo Morganwg must be treated with the greatest caution, Professor G. J. Williams was firmly convinced that he rarely specified a clearly identifiable source for any of his claims and transcripts unless he had already seen material of a fairly similar nature in the works of the scribe or scholar to whom he explicitly referred.[283] This is almost certainly true of the many references that occur in his writings to Tomas ab Ieuan. The latter had transcribed an interesting manuscript-book of genealogies, and it was probably this fact which prompted Iolo to claim that it was from his work that the two copies published in *Iolo Manuscripts* of 'Achau Saint Ynys Prydain' ('The Genealogies of the Saints of the Isle of Britain'), which unfortunately did much to corrupt a number of currents of Welsh historical scholarship in the nineteenth century, were ultimately derived.[284] Iolo referred also to a copy of *Brut y Tywysogyon* ('The Chronicle of the Princes'), in Tomas ab Ieuan's autograph, which he claimed he had seen alongside *Brut Aberpergwm* in the private library of Thomas Richards of Llangrallo. But perhaps the most remarkable of all the various transcripts which he claimed to have discovered in Tomas ab Ieuan's manuscripts are 'Doethineb Catwg Ddoeth'[285] and 'Trioedd Beirdd Ynys Prydain', which were published in the third volume of the *Myvyrian Archaiology*. This attribution is not difficult to explain. One of Tomas ab Ieuan's transcripts, British Museum MS. 14878, contains material attributed therein to 'Cattwn Ddoeth' as well as a series of triads, and so when he had concocted the material which was eventually published in the *Myvyrian Archaiology*, it was natural that Iolo should claim that it had been taken from the manuscripts transcribed at various times during the second half of the seventeenth century by Tomas ab Ieuan.[286]

[591]

If the family at Tre'r-bryn had, sometime between 1791 and 1795, 'a large chest full of MSS.' in Tomas ab Ieuan's hand, it is probably safe to assume that the latter was passionately interested in the vernacular literature, in genealogy, early Welsh history and antiquities, and that he was, moreover, impelled by a burning desire either to collect or to transcribe all the literary material of any significance which happened to engage his attention. The exemplary neatness of his autograph and the systematic order in which the various items that he copied were usually arranged strongly suggest that he had received some training in the art of manuscript transcription. He can be regarded, therefore, as the last of that diligent group of professional scribes to whom we are largely indebted for the preservation, during an acutely critical period, of a number of the priceless treasures of the Welsh literary heritage.

v.

ANTIQUARIAN AND SCHOLARLY ACTIVITIES

The poets of the classical Welsh tradition were, by time-honoured custom, under a strict obligation to keep and cherish a three-fold 'memory of the Island of Britain'. The first of these strands was 'the History of the notable Acts of the kings & princes of this land of Bruttaen and Cambria'; the second was the language of the Britons; and the third was 'the genealogies or Descents of the Nobi[li]tie, there Division of lands and there Armes'.[287] That a detailed knowledge of the pedigrees of the nobility and gentry, of their coats-of-arms and estates, formed an important element of the traditional bardic lore is amply confirmed by the antiquarian activities of the Glamorgan bards.[288] The most renowned of these was unquestionably Lewis Morgannwg, who deserves to rank as one of the most talented heraldic bards of the sixteenth century. His manuscripts, which probably contained a great wealth of genealogical data, passed on his death to Meurug Dafydd and Dafydd Benwyn.[289] A detailed analysis of the verses composed by the latter and of the interesting collection of genealogies that occur in his hand in Cardiff MS. 10 reveals that he had made an impressively detailed study of the history of many of the leading families of Glamorgan and Gwent. His contemporary, Meurug Dafydd, must also have won some renown in his day in this particular field (above, p. 539). Both these poets were heavily indebted to Lewis Morgannwg for much of the extensive genealogical lore which they had acquired. Some of the most famous heraldic bards in both north and south Wales visited Glamorgan from time to time, and some members of the local bardic fraternity, such as Dafydd Benwyn, were frequently involved in acrimonious disputations with Thomas Jones ('Twm Siôn Cati', c. 1530–1609). Another prominent figure in the literary life of this period, Hywel ap 'Syr' Mathew (d. 1581), the soldier and poet-genealogist from the Teme valley in Radnorshire who had helped to instruct Lewis Dwnn in the art of heraldry, went on bardic circuit in Glamorgan, and Dafydd Benwyn addressed a series of elegiac *englynion* to him.[290] Unfortunately, however, there is no extant work by a Glamorgan bard which contains not only extensive collections of genealogies but also precise details of the coats-of-arms of the gentry, and hence it is no longer possible to make a balanced appraisal of the expertise which they may have acquired in the art of heraldry. It is obvious, nevertheless, that many of the details about the descendants of Iestyn ap Gwrgant, Einion ap Collwyn, Gwaethfoed, and Maenarch, as well as many of the pedigrees of the Anglo-Norman families, derive ultimately from the work of the heraldic bards; and many of the detailed pedigrees published by G. T. Clark in *Limbus Patrum Morganiæ et Glamorganiæ* (1886) are ultimately based on the extensive genealogical lore of the professional bards, although some of it was manifestly corrupted by oral transmission over the centuries. Many of the details contained in the account of the conquest of the kingdom of Morgannwg in 1091 by twelve Norman knights under Robert fitzHamo (or Fitzhamon) derive ultimately from the same source.[291] The claim that this saga owes its origin to the fertile imagination of some of the local historians, especially Sir Edward Stradling and Rice Merrick, cannot be accepted, for it is obviously based on an older tradition. An explicit reference to the discord between Iestyn ap Gwrgant and Rhys ap Tewdwr in a *cywydd* by Ieuan Rudd (*fl. c.* 1470), a Glamorgan bard from Glyn Rhondda, proves conclusively that some of the basic elements in this saga are at least as old as the second half of the fifteenth century.[292] Indeed, in an unpublished version of this story written by Rice Merrick it is claimed that the account there given of the dissension which arose between Iestyn ap Gwrgant and Rhys ap Tewdwr had been taken from the 'Records of the auncient Abbey of Neth'.[293] Thomas Wilkins, who was not usually given to wild flights of fancy, was equally adamant that he had seen an account of the story 'in an Antient Manuscript'.[294] It seems, therefore, quite possible that some elements in the story may be based on a very old tradition carefully preserved over the centuries by the heraldic bards. It is significant that Rice Merrick states unequivocally that his particular version of the story is given 'as continuall fame and memory from antiquity hath preserved in both their Signories', that is, in Morgannwg and in Deheubarth. Merrick was probably referring obliquely to the work of the heraldic bards when he later emphasized that 'The fame and remembrance whereof from one generation to another, as well among the men of Dehybarth as of Morganwg, have beene preserved as a thing notable and worthy to be remembred'.[295] It is also significant that Merrick refers to variant versions of the saga with which he was familiar and attempts to determine which one of these is most likely to be authentic. There is, then, much evidence to suggest that with the passing of the professional bards a considerable amount of extremely valuable genealogical data as well as a great body of traditional lore and legend relating to the early history of Glamorgan was tragically lost for ever.

THE SIXTEENTH-CENTURY HISTORIANS:

SIR EDWARD STRADLING (*c.* 1529–30 TO 1609)

There can be no doubt, however, that it was largely as a result of the publication in 1584 of *The Historie of Cambria, now called Wales*, edited by Dr. David Powel, the well-known Ruabon antiquary, that the saga of the conquest of Morgannwg by Robert fitzHamo and his twelve knights became widely known. The greater part of the text consisted of an English translation by the celebrated physician and antiquary, Humphrey Llwyd (1527–68), of one of the Middle Welsh versions of *Brut y Tywysogyon* ('The Chronicle of the Princes'). But the work also included, amongst other things, a treatise written by Edward Stradling, 'The Winning of the Lordship of Glamorgan or Morgannwc', which contained a description of the lordship, an account of the way in which it had been conquered by the Normans, and the genealogies of the alleged descendants of Robert fitzHamo and the twelve knights.[296] It is extremely difficult to fix the precise date of composition, but several factors suggest that it was written sometime between 1561 and 1566, when the author was still a comparatively young man: William Cecil is never addressed as Lord Burghley but invariably as master of the wards and liveries, a position which he held from January 10, 1561; it appears that the author's father, Sir Thomas Stradling, who died on January 27, 1571, was still alive; and the work contains no reference, either explicit or implicit, to Edward Stradling's own marriage on November 19, 1566 to Agnes (1547–1624), daughter of Sir Edward Gage, although matrimonial details abound in the account of the Stradling lineage. One copy of this treatise, transcribed apparently in 1572, eventually reached Blanche Parry, a distant relative of Edward Stradling who served as lady-in-waiting to Queen Elizabeth. It was upon this particular copy that Dr. David Powel, who had probably met Blanche Parry at court during the period when he was busily engaged in tracing William Cecil's pedigree, based the version that was published twelve years later in *The Historie of Cambria*. But before passing this copy to the Ruabon antiquary Blanche Parry had seen fit to add a few notes to the effect that its author, following the death of his father, Sir Thomas, was now the acknowledged head of the Stradling family.[297]

Sir Edward Stradling's scholarly attainments secured for him a reputation far transcending the bounds of his native county. The magnificent library at St. Donat's became at once the envy and the quarry of many historians and antiquarians in both England and Wales. Archbishop James Ussher, who came to St. Donat's in 1645, when he was fleeing before the Parliamentary forces, avidly studied many of the works which it contained, particularly those 'ancient, rare and curious' books and manuscripts that dealt with the history of Wales. Not only did Sir Edward possess old records, but he had also written, according to Lewis Dwnn, 'about the whole island of Britain'.[298] He was the proud owner of printed books and manuscripts as early as 1567, and he generously loaned various items from his impressive collection to other scholars and antiquarians. Lord Mountjoy borrowed a book in 1577 and promised to send Sir Edward in return some new chronicles and a book that was likely to arouse his interest.[299] It is difficult, however, to determine precisely what Welsh manuscripts were contained in the library at St. Donat's. Although there is some evidence to suggest that Sir Edward had commissioned scribes to copy works,[300] it is impossible to prove that any of the important texts transcribed by Llywelyn Siôn had ever been in his possession. But the library undoubtedly contained administrative records of great importance, including *The Register of Neath*, an excerpt from which was copied by Sir John Stradling (1563–1637) and is now kept in the Bodleian Library, Oxford.[301] This short extract, which had been transcribed, according to the copyist, from the cartulary of Neath abbey, suggests that the *Register* contained historical narrative and comments of great importance. The cartulary of Neath abbey may have passed into the possession of the Stradling family at the dissolution of the monasteries. That it had been at one time in the possession of Sir Edward is beyond question, for Rice Merrick sent a letter to him in 1574 asking permission to borrow the *Register* 'wherein att my last being wth you I found somewhat of Justyn'.[302] It was still in the possession of the Stradling family when William Dugdale was busily engaged in compiling material for his famous *Monasticon*.[303] The subsequent history of this extremely important cartulary, however, is a mystery. Included also among the administrative records retained at St. Donat's was an inquisition of 1399, which Lord St. John sought leave to borrow in 1592.[304] Sir Edward was equally generous in providing authors and scholars with information from his own writings, and in 1574 Rice Merrick returned a book written by Sir Edward 'wherein the state of Glamorgan for a longe tyme in many things ys preserved from oblivyon'.[305] It is impossible to tell at this stage, however, whether Sir Edward had written a fuller and more comprehensive history of Glamorgan than that contained in 'The Winning' mentioned above. But an interesting reference occurs in Peniarth MS. 120, 436, to 'A Bk: written by Sir Edw: Stradling in Latin to Mr Camden'. It is conceivable that Sir Edward helped Camden to gather material for the chapter on Glamorgan which he intended to publish in *Britannia*. There is some evidence to suggest that Camden knew of the work which Sir Edward had written on the Norman conquest of Glamorgan,[306] and the latter's heir, Sir John Stradling, regarded William Camden as his

[595]

'verie lovinge good frend'.[307] Rice Merrick was heavily indebted to Sir Edward, for it is obvious that parts of his well-known work, *A Booke of Glamorganshires Antiquities*, owed much to one of the manuscript versions of 'The Winning', the work which Merrick had probably borrowed *c.* 1574 from Stradling.[308] Moreover, when Sir Edward Mansel attempted to write a work on the same theme early in the 1590s, his treatise was, in essence, only a variation on the basic theme of the work written by Sir Edward Stradling, although there are some striking differences at times in matters of detail.[309]

A scholar-gentleman like Stradling was obviously the person best qualified to supply Queen Elizabeth in the 1560s with a powerful body of historical data which could effectively contest the claims made by William, earl of Pembroke, to far-reaching powers as lord of Cardiff. This issue remained a burning one for the first ten years or so of the Queen's reign, and it is known that Sir Edward, accompanied by his friend Anthony Mansel, journeyed to London to testify on her behalf. It was probably during such a visit to the court that Stradling went with the Queen and her entourage to the royal retreat at Havering-atte-Bower, in Essex. There he obviously became acquainted with her principal secretary and counsellor, Sir William Cecil, who was also deeply interested in history and antiquarian studies. Cecil was passionately anxious to acquire for himself a respectable pedigree that would effectively cloak his rather obscure family origins. He therefore besought Stradling to bring his own pedigree with him during his next visit to London.[310] That the Stradlings claimed, as did the Cecils, to have had ancestors who actively assisted Robert fitzHamo only served to deepen Cecil's interest. It appears that, as a result of the statesman's entreaties and inquiries, Edward Stradling set about compiling his treatise sometime between 1561 and 1566, and eventually sent to Cecil an account of the conquest of Glamorgan. Several copies of this work were made during the years that followed, and some of these may even have been circulated among various members of the Stradling family. One copy was translated into Welsh towards the end of the sixteenth century.[311] This translation, in spite of the errors contained in it, is interesting for at least three reasons: it is one of the few Welsh documents now extant that deal with the history of the Norman subjugation of Morgannwg; it contains the Welsh forms of many place-names in the Vale, forms that rarely occur in the Latin deeds and documents written during the medieval period or in the works of the sixteenth-century Glamorgan historians; and it has a very interesting introduction which points clearly to the motives that prompted its compilation. Another copy eventually reached Blanche Parry in London,[312] and it was this which evidently provided the basis for the version which Dr. David Powel of Ruabon ultimately published in 1584. Edward Stradling had cleverly conjured for himself and his family a long and honourable lineage, one far gentler and infinitely more impressive than either its early continental origins or its later English associations warranted.[313] Inspired by Stradling's imaginative enterprise, Cecil quickly proceeded to produce a pedigree for himself whose roots lay deep in the Welsh border and in the Norman conquest of Glamorgan. Whether he was personally acquainted with Powel or not it is difficult to tell, but he obviously saw in his work an excellent opportunity to win widespread publicity for the impressively lengthy lineage which he had blazoned for himself. Dr. David Powel, therefore, published a postscript to the treatise on 'The Winning' which had been ingeniously compiled from documents said to have been in the possession of both Cecil and his Herefordshire kinsman, William Sitsyllt. Powel thus became, albeit unwittingly, the publicist and propagandist of the genealogies which both Cecil and Stradling eagerly sought to claim for themselves, and he also helped to make widely current an historically misleading account of the Norman conquest of Glamorgan which was to be accepted almost without challenge for the next three hundred years. Unfortunately, the treatise on 'The Winning' is the only work by Sir Edward Stradling which seems to have survived, and hence it is no longer possible to make a balanced appraisal of his contribution as an historian.

Rice Merrick (Rhys Meurug, d. March 1, 1586–7)

The most important of the older historians of Glamorgan was Rhys Meurug, or Rice Merrick as he is more popularly known, the sixteenth-century landed gentleman, attorney and scholar of Cotrel, the stately old mansion which was situated approximately half a mile to the west of the village of St. Nicholas.[314] The genealogical tracts and some of the compositions of the bards reveal quite clearly that he belonged to one of the native Welsh families of Meisgyn (Miskin). In 1546 the manor of Trehill, consisting of approximately a third of the original fee of St. Nicholas, which had formerly been subject to the jurisdiction of an extinct family called Cotrel, had been granted to Rice Merrick's father, Meurug ap Hywel ap Philip, by Walter Herbert of Dunraven. This had passed by 1554 to his son, *Reseus Mirick de Pencoid in parochia Sancti Fagani generosus*. As the latter is described as *Receus Miricke de St. Nicholas* in a deed dated 1563, it appears that at some time between 1554 and 1563, impelled perhaps by his antiquarian and historical interests, he had moved to a new residence situated near to the remains of Cotrel Court. In 1575 he bought the adjoining manor of Bonvilston from William Bassett of Beaupré. During the course of their lives Rice Merrick and his father, Meurug ap Hywel ap Philip, had managed to acquire freeholds in both the aforementioned manors, and by the time of his death Rice possessed the solid nucleus of an estate which at a later date was to include the western part of the parish of St. Nicholas, the greater part of Bonvilston, and small sections of Llancarfan and Pendoylan.[315]

The family pedigree reveals that Rice Merrick's father had married a daughter of William ap John of Bonvilston. In a deed dated 1528 he is described as *Meurick ap Hoell ap Philip de Bovilleston ffrankelanus*. His father, Hywel ap Philip, came from Llantrisant, and so the surviving evidence suggests that Meurug ap Hywel had moved to Bonvilston and had settled there on the occasion of his marriage *c.* 1520. And it was there, in all probability, that Rice, who seems to have been his only son, was born. In 1550 Rice Merrick still resided at Bonvilston, but by 1554 he had taken up residence at Pen-coed in the parish of St. Fagans. His marriage to Mary, daughter of Christopher Fleming of St. Andrew's Major, probably took place about this time and it was to Pen-coed that he may well have taken his new bride. Rice Merrick refers explicitly to this early-fifteenth-century house as one of the ancient properties in the lordship of Miskin which had been retained by the native Welsh inhabitants after the period of the Norman incursions into Glamorgan.[316] That Rice Merrick took a special interest in the indigenous Welsh families of Miskin lordship is hardly surprising when his own ancestors claimed to be able to trace their descent from them. His pedigree shows that he claimed descent in the direct male line from Caradog Freichfras, a rather shadowy figure who exercised jurisdiction in the northern part of what is now the county of Radnor. If one may safely rely on the various details contained in the extant family pedigree,[317] Rice Merrick's father, Meurug ap Hywel, was sixth in descent from the valiant Cadwgan Fawr of the thirteenth century. Many of the details contained in this pedigree agree with those given by the late-sixteenth-century bards in their verses, and so it is not unreasonable to assume that when he moved from Bonvilston to the southern part of the lordship of Miskin, Rice Merrick appropriately went to reside in an area where his ancestors for some eight generations or more had proudly lived upon their freehold tenements.

Rice Merrick probably began to practise as an attorney when he was still a comparatively young man, for he has left it on record that he was appointed Clerk of the Peace by two successive *custodes rotulorum* of the county of Glamorgan, namely, William, the first earl of Pembroke (d. 1570), and Henry, the second earl of Pembroke.[318] Moreover, some of the estreat rolls for the manor of Glynrhondda show that in 1583 Rice Merrick was deputy steward to William Mathew and in 1585 to George Herbert.[319] In view of the close connection between the manors of Glynrhondda and Miskin it is more than likely that he also acted as deputy steward for Miskin. He may have begun his researches into the history and topography of Glamorgan when he was still a comparatively young man, and his appointment as Clerk of the Peace afforded him an excellent opportunity to visit almost every part of Glamorgan in his search for deeds, documents, inscriptions and local traditions, the fruit of which was his celebrated *Morganiæ Archaiographia* or, as he obviously preferred to call it, *A Booke of Glamorganshires Antiquities*. It was first published by Sir Thomas Phillips at his private press in Middle Hill, Worcestershire, in 1825, but it is best known in the second edition, by James Andrew Corbett in 1887.[320] The editors of these two editions used a seventeenth-century copy, transcribed sometime between 1660 and 1680, which is now kept in the library of Queen's College, Oxford. The claim made by J. A. Corbett that this is the 'only known MS.' is incorrect, however, for another unpublished copy of Merrick's work is retained in Cardiff Central Library.[321] This copy, which was made *c.* 1674–5, corresponds fairly closely with the one that is now housed in Queen's College, although it was probably not transcribed from the latter. It contains some very interesting additional matter, including a variant version of the dissension between Iestyn ap Gwrgant and Rhys ap Tewdwr which was based, we are told, on 'the Records of the auncient Abbey of Neth'. The original autograph copy of Rice Merrick's *magnum opus* has been lost, but it appears from some of the references contained in Thomas Wilkins's work that it was one of the literary treasures which the latter had in his possession in St. Mary Church. Frequent quotations from the manuscript occur in his work and some of these reveal quite clearly that the original contained matter of considerable importance not included in either of the printed editions. Moreover, it seems fairly certain that this was one of the Glamorgan manuscripts which Edward Lhuyd managed to acquire, for Iolo Morganwg claimed that he had seen the manuscript at the mansion of Hafod Uchdryd in 1799: 'a very curious Manuscript History of Glamorgan in folio written in the time of Queen Elizabeth by Rice Meyrick of Cottrel Esqr with the arms of ancient families finely blazoned in rich colours'.[322] This was obviously not the one used in preparing the printed version, for the latter does not contain the coats-of-arms in 'rich colours'. Nor is this the only piece of evidence to suggest that the final copy prepared by Rice Merrick is no longer extant. On page 90 of the printed edition the author sets out to discuss the ten hundreds contained in the county of Glamorgan, but only three of those listed by him are discussed, namely, Cardiff, Caerphilly, and Dinas Powys. Although accounts of the other seven hundreds mentioned by Merrick do not occur in the seventeenth-century manuscript on which the two printed editions were based, he had written descriptions of them, for about a hundred years later they were seen, and fortunately copied in part, by Edward Lhuyd's enthusiastic assistants.[323] Lhuyd had designed the rough notes made by his assistants to be the basis of a more detailed account of the county of Glamorgan which, unfortunately, he was unable to complete. There can be no doubt, however, that Rice Merrick was the author of this work, which was probably written *c.* 1584–5. In a reference to 'court Colman' the author states that it had been bought by John Gamage of Coety, but that it was 'now parcell of yᵉ possessions of Mr. Robert Sidney *in jure uxoris*'.[324] John Gamage died in September 1584 and his daughter, Barbara, married Robert Sidney towards the end of that year or the beginning of the following, which suggests that the work had been written sometime towards the end of the sixteenth century. The list of the justices of the peace contained in the third part of Lhuyd's *Parochialia* suggests a similar date.[325] It is also highly significant that parts of the latter, such as the descriptions of the Vale and Uplands, correspond to the descriptions contained in the printed version which was edited by J. A. Corbett, while the same sources, including 'ye register of ye Abbey of neth', are sometimes cited in both works. Nor should it be overlooked that the author of this work describes the scanty remains of 'Cottrell Court' which were still visible in his day.[326] It is clear, therefore, that the third part of Edward Lhuyd's *Parochialia* contains an important section of the work written by Rice Merrick, and as the latter died on March 1, 1586–7, it may well be that he was struck down before he had managed to complete it.

The *Booke of Glamorganshires Antiquities* falls naturally into three parts. In the first, after attempting to explain what is meant by the names *Morgannwg* and *Gwlad Forgan* and outlining the main character-istics of the Vale (*Bro*) and Uplands (*Blaenau*), the author proceeds to discuss the dissension that arose between Iestyn ap Gwrgant and Rhys ap Tewdwr and the subsequent conquest of Glamorgan by the Normans. In the second part, he shows how the subjugated territory was divided between the knights and what territories were retained by some of the indigenous Welsh inhabitants, the descendants of Iestyn ap Gwrgant and Einion ap Collwyn. He then proceeds to discuss the history of the Norman families who came to settle in Glamorgan. This section contains some interesting and important observations on the fortunes of the vernacular in the Vale. In the third part he essays a description of the ten hundreds contained in Glamorgan as they were in his own day, but only three of those listed by him are discussed, although parts of the remainder undoubtedly occur in the manuscript which was owned by Edward Lhuyd.

When the relevant sections of Lhuyd's *Parochialia* and the *Booke of Glamorganshires Antiquities* are read in conjunction, some very interesting and valuable features emerge. Particular attention is paid to rivers and streams; and among the many houses noted are the homes of poets and their patrons.[327] Merrick was obviously fascinated by place-names and could not resist the temptation to explain many of the forms noted by him, explanations which, in some instances, probably have their origin in the works of the heraldic bards.[328] Some interesting references are also made to old customs and practices which were still prevalent in certain areas in the latter half of the sixteenth century.[329] Rice Merrick was the only Glamorgan historian living in the sixteenth century to display any kind of interest in matters such as these, and no serious attempt was made to complete the work which he had so magnificently begun until the days of Iolo Morganwg. Merrick's work is a more important contribution to Welsh historiography than has usually been realized. It is also, in some respects, an interesting and instructive example of what Renaissance scholars called 'chorography', to wit, a study of local history with special reference to surviving physical remains.[330]

A detailed examination of the various references that occur in his work reveals quite clearly that he had studied his sources with great care. He was obviously familiar with, and occasionally extremely critical of, the works of English historians such as Stowe, Fabian, Bale, Leland, Daniel, and Camden, and he knew also of the works written by some of his compatriots, such as Sir John Prys and Humphrey Llwyd. He had consulted Welsh manuscripts, 'old Bookes & pamphletts in the Brittaine tongue',[331] many of which were probably the works of the old heraldic bards. The only manuscript to which he refers explicitly, however, is *Y Cwta Cyfarwydd*.[332] He had studied the *Liber Landavensis* and one of the versions of 'Caradog's Book', that is, *Brut y Tywysogyon* ('The Chronicle of the Princes'). Nor had he overlooked the writings of Giraldus Cambrensis which, in that period, could only be found in manuscript form. He may also have consulted 'Llyfr Llywelyn Offeiriad', which was transcribed in the first half of the fifteenth century, because the explanation of the word *Morgannwg* given in this latter source is similar to the one offered by Merrick himself.[333] A letter which he addressed to Sir Edward Stradling in 1574, the only one by him which is now extant, reveals that he sought leave to borrow manuscripts and valuable documents, such as *The Register of Neath*, from his acquaintances and fellow antiquarians.[334] The cartulary of Neath abbey has long since disappeared, and a similar fate has befallen another document of which he made extensive use, namely, the 'Survey' which Lord 'Hugh Spencer' is said to have made in 1320. His attention must have been drawn, sometimes fortuitously, to many valuable documents of this nature when he was actively discharging his official duties as 'Clarke of the Peace'. Moreover, he questioned many of the older inhabitants of the county about such matters as the practices followed in the courts of Glamorgan, the troubles experienced by Edward II in Llantrisant, and the appalling devastation caused by Owain Glyndŵr. In the account which he gives of the visit made by Dafydd ap Gwilym to the home of Sir Mathew (or Mayo) le Soor, who was sheriff of Glamorgan in 1346, the author attributes to the poet a couplet which occurs in no other known source.[335]

The *Booke of Glamorganshires Antiquities* was not the only product of Merrick's scholarly pen. He refers in that book to other works which he had written or compiled, such as 'that booke which treateth of

Cambria', 'Treatice of Wales', and 'Short Treatice of the Bishoprick of Landaph'. Unfortunately, no copies of these works have survived. Frequent references also occur to another work which Merrick calls 'Peramb',[336] probably an abbreviation for 'Perambulation'. This may have been a work describing in detail his journeys through Glamorgan and containing material similar to that found in the section on the hundreds and in Lhuyd's *Parochialia*. It appears, if one may judge from the foliation cited by Merrick, that this was a work of quite substantial proportions.[337] He was renowned both as an historian and genealogist not only in his native county but also in Deheubarth and north Wales. Lewis Dwnn, one of the most distinguished Welsh genealogists of the period, sang to his great learning and scholastic attainments:

> Glain dysg, glain addysg, glân wyd,—Rys Meurug,
> Mawredd Cymru'th wnaethpwyd,
> Gŵr odiaeth, gorau ydwyd,
> Grym yr iaith a'r gramer wyd.[338]

According to the same authority, he had compiled 'one of the finest books in Wales about the whole island of Britain' (*vn or llyfrau teccaf yng Nghymru am holl ynys Brydain*),[339] a reference probably to his very important collection of genealogies, and Dwnn, who had visited Cotrel in Rice Merrick's day, also includes him among those who had generously shown him sundry old records. It is evident that Merrick was an authority on the lineage of old Glamorgan families and it was to him that Dafydd Benwyn and some of his bardic contemporaries, such as Sils ap Siôn, went for instruction in the art of compiling genealogies. Both these poets composed elegies to him, and the former also addressed panegyrics to other members of the Cotrel family. Sils ap Siôn in his elegy bemoans the passing of a scholar who had frequently assisted the poets in their search for genealogies:

> Ba wiw i feirddion dorri calonnau
> Yma fynychu i 'mofyn achau?[340]

The Cotrel family was renowned for generous hospitality over a long period to the peripatetic bards, and as late as 1601, fourteen years after Rice Merrick's death, Lewis Dwnn sang the praises of his three sons, Morgan, William, and John.[341] There are frequent references in Lewis Dwnn's work to Rice Merrick's impressive collection of pedigrees, which was also seen by the celebrated grammarian Siôn Dafydd Rhys.[342] This collection is also frequently mentioned by Thomas Wilkins, into whose hands it may eventually have passed after Merrick's death, and there is some evidence to suggest that, at one time, it may have been in the possession of the earl of Clarendon.[343] The subsequent disappearance of this work has deprived us of a large and valuable body of evidence.

Upon his death on March 1, 1586–7 Rice Merrick was buried in the south aisle of Cowbridge church. Unfortunately, the magnificent monument which was erected to commemorate his burial place has long since disappeared from the scene.[344] Rice Merrick seems to have had seven daughters, and one of these, Elnor,[345] married Roger Williams, who was rector of St. Nicholas from 1582 to 1626.[346] He was probably the 'Roger Willms clarke' who transcribed the collection of genealogies and miscellanea contained in Llanover MS. E 4.[347] Most of Rice Merrick's manuscripts were probably acquired after his death by this scholarly cleric and it may have been from one of his descendants that they eventually passed into the possession of Thomas Wilkins. This valuable collection probably included the final autograph version of Merrick's work on Glamorgan, which eventually found its way to Hafod Uchdryd and was completely destroyed in 1807.

ANTHONY POWEL (c. 1560 TO 1618–19)

Anthony Powel, the gentleman-genealogist of Llwydarth in the parish of Llangynwyd, plays a prominent and highly influential rôle in the picture of the literary life of Glamorgan which emerges from the writings of Iolo Morganwg, who characteristically attributed to him a variety of works, including a copy of *Brut y Saesson* ('The Chronicle of the Saxons'), a copy of a chronicle giving an account of Iestyn ap Gwrgant, a work on grammar and Welsh poetic art, a history of some early bardic *eisteddfodau*,[348] a collection of triads, a history of the Glamorgan bards in a manuscript called 'Llyfr Cofion Llwydarth',[349] a collection of genealogies, and much else besides. Iolo Morganwg also claimed that Anthony Powel was an accomplished bard, and among the various compositions attributed to the latter is an *englyn* which, it was claimed, he had sung when he went, together with Dafydd Benwyn, Llywelyn Siôn and other bards, to an *eisteddfod* of some kind held on 'Craig y Ddinas'.[350] It was further claimed that Anthony Powel and his brother [*sic*], Watcyn, were among the earliest Unitarians in the county.[351] It was probably a reference he had seen in Lewis Dwnn's *Heraldic Visitations* which impelled Iolo to elevate Anthony Powel into an important and influential figure in his literary forgeries.

Powel claimed descent from Rhicert ab Einion ap Collwyn and belonged to the same branch of the family as did Rhys ap Siôn of Aberpergwm.[352] His grandfather, Hywel ap Siôn Goch, resided at Llwydarth, and so did his father when Rice Merrick wrote his description of the district in 1584–5.[353] It seems that the surname 'Powel' was first adopted by his father and his uncles; their descendants formed the Powels of Tir Iarll, a well-known and important family whose various branches resided at Llwydarth, Maes-teg, Pen-y-fai, Genau'r Glyn, Llanharan, Llyswyrny, Ton-du, and other parts of Glamorgan. Dafydd Benwyn addressed a panegyric on the *cywydd* measure to Anthony Powel's father into which he skilfully wove details of the lineage of

Anthony's mother, Sioned, daughter of Hopcyn ap Madog, 'of the line of Aaron' (*o hil Aron*),[354] one of the most famous families in Betws Tir Iarll. She was, therefore, a cousin to both Tomas ab Ieuan ap Madog, the well-known *cwndidwr*, and his brother, Ieuan ab Ieuan ap Madog, the copyist, a fact which undoubtedly helps to explain some facets of her son's literary career. A number of references to Anthony Powel occur in the official papers of the Mansel family, and in one of these, the 'Court Roll of the Manor of Havod-porth and Margam', dated September 24, 1605, he is described as 'steward of Thomas Mansell, Knt., Lord of the Manor'.[355] In discharging his duties as steward he certainly had a splendid opportunity to examine not only official deeds and documents but also the Welsh manuscripts that were contained in that family's private library, including the famous Red Book of Hergest.

Anthony Powel, like many other members of his family, was passionately interested in many aspects of Welsh literature and scholarship. Lewis Dwnn includes him among the gentlemen who had shown him the 'old Records and books of the religious houses' (*hen Regords a llyfrau y tai o grefydd*), and further claims that he had written 'about the whole island of Britain'.[356] This is probably a reference to Anthony Powel's genealogical work. But it seems that the only collection of genealogies in his autograph now extant is Llanover MS. E 3, or 'Llyfr Du Pantylliwydd', a manuscript which belonged in the eighteenth century to Thomas Truman of Pantylliwydd in Llansanwyr (below, pp. 638–639). This manuscript contains an important collection of genealogies, the coats-of-arms of the gentry, and a copy of the Welsh 'Book of Heraldry' which had been translated into the vernacular in the fifteenth century, the only copy of that translation which can be shown to have been written in Glamorgan. The only other work by Anthony Powel which is now extant is that contained in Hafod MS. 22, a substantial compilation of more than 700 pages in two hands of the second half of the sixteenth century, one of which is unquestionably Powel's.[357] This manuscript contains an extremely important collection of Welsh prose works. Whether or not he was the 'A. Powel' from whose manuscript-book Siôn Dafydd Rhys transcribed parts of the life of 'Sant y Catrin' it is impossible to tell.[358] There is much to suggest, nevertheless, that he was one of those members of the gentry who commissioned and encouraged the professional scribe Llywelyn Siôn, and the manuscript known as 'Llyfr Hir Llanharan' may have been transcribed for him. In the following century this manuscript was in the possession of the Powels of Maes-teg and Ton-du, and in Iolo Morganwg's day it belonged to the Rev. Gervase Powel of Llanharan. The manuscript known as 'Llyfr Hir Amwythig' ('The Long Book of Shrewsbury') may also have been in the possession of this family in the seventeenth century. Nevertheless, although his nephew, Watcyn Powel, addressed a *cywydd* to him, the only professional bard who appears to have sung the praises of Anthony

Powel was Dafydd Benwyn in a series of *englynion* in which he eloquently extolled the unstinting generosity of the Llwydarth family.[359] He makes no reference of any kind, however, to Powel's scholarly attainments or to his renown as a genealogist and historian. This is not to imply, however, that Anthony Powel's contemporaries were completely ignorant of his prowess as a scholar, for it would be impossible to deduce solely from the Glamorgan bards' strict-metre verse that Rice Merrick was an historian of any significance.

Anthony Powel died on January 17, 1618–19, and a copy of the inscription on his gravestone in Llangynwyd occurs in Iolo Morganwg's manuscripts.[360] Ieuan Tomas, one of the lesser bards of the period, sang an elegy to him in which he compared his learning with that of Homer.[361] It was probably Anthony Powel who aroused the interest of his nephew, Watcyn Powel, in certain aspects of Welsh scholarship. The elegies addressed to the latter after his death in 1655 by Edward Dafydd and Dafydd o'r Nant reveal quite clearly that he was a learned genealogist and an acknowledged master of the art of heraldry.[362] It is possible to infer from a comment made by Edward Lhuyd[363] that Watcyn Powel's manuscripts, as well as those once owned by Anthony Powel, were in the possession of his descendants at Pen-y-fai towards the end of the seventeenth century. Their subsequent history, however, is obscure. The 'Long Book of Llywelyn Siôn' was in the possession of that branch of the Powel family which resided at Llanharan in the second half of the eighteenth century, but it is impossible to identify at this stage the other manuscripts in that family's private library.[364] Some of these manuscripts may later have passed into the possession of John Bradford (below, pp. 614–616).

THOMAS WILKINS (1625–6 TO 1699)

The only other historian of any significance who lived in Glamorgan in the seventeenth century was Thomas Wilkins. One manuscript of his work, called *Analectica Glamorganica*, or *Analectica Morganica Archaeographia, Fragments of ye Antiquityes of Glamorganshire*, is Cardiff MS. 3.464, the contents of which consist mainly of miscellaneous English notes which Wilkins, who probably began the work in 1657, has entered rather haphazardly. Although various details were added by him in the years that followed, he never seems to have attempted to reduce all this material to some semblance of order. Profoundly disturbed by the disappearance of many old and valuable documents, he set out conscientiously to gather everything connected with the history of Morgannwg.[365] It is obvious that he was familiar with the works of a number of sixteenth- and seventeenth-century historians, for they are listed by him. But his chief authority was unquestionably Rice Merrick, 'my President', as he respectfully called him, and he probably had the autograph manuscript of Merrick's work on Glamorgan in his private collection. He quotes also from other manuscripts which unfortunately are no longer extant, such as 'an antient Brittish Manuscripts' [*sic*] which related the history of the Turbervilles, the history of the lordship of Tal-y-fan and the dissension between Ifor Bach and the lord of Glamorgan, all of which he assures the reader 'was guaranteed under the hand of Wiliam, Abbot of Margam' (*a hyn yn warrantedig dan law Wm Abad Margam*).[366] Wilkins, though writing in English, twice cites his authority in this manner in *Welsh*. This suggests that the Margam source to which he refers had been written in the vernacular. He refers also to the substantial compilation of genealogies made by Rice Merrick and to another 'Antient Manuscript' which contained a history of the quarrel between Iestyn ap Gwrgant and Rhys ap Tewdwr.[367] Very few references occur in his work, however, to his magnificent collection of Welsh manuscripts, which included many of the important medieval Welsh prose texts, the strict-metre compositions of the poets of the princes and the poets of the nobility, and the works which had been turned into Welsh in the fifteenth and sixteenth centuries by the talented school of Glamorgan translators. Nor does he seem to have used the works of the bards when compiling the genealogies of the aristocracy. He quotes an *englyn* from the work of Meurug Dafydd and a couplet from one of the best-known *cywyddau* which Iorwerth Fynglwyd addressed to Rhys ap Siôn of Aberpergwm. The manuscript also includes a copy of one of Siôn Tudur's *cywyddau*, and a quotation from Henri Perri's *Eglvryn Phraethineb* (1595). But the only Glamorgan bard whose history is discussed in any detail is Lewis Morgannwg. It is difficult to determine, therefore, what scholarly use, if any, Wilkins made of his valuable collection of Welsh manuscripts. Nevertheless, the reply sent by Edward Gamage, the rector of Llangrallo (Coychurch), to Edward Lhuyd's 'Parochial Queries' suggests that Wilkins was regarded during his lifetime as something of an authority on the Welsh language: 'we have not many skilled in ye Welsh, I suppose ye best is ye Rd Mr Tho: Wilkins rector of St Mary Church & Lanmaes, & one of ye prebends of Landaffe'.[368] The scribes and scholars who laboured in Glamorgan in the seventeenth century seem to have been generally preoccupied with historical, genealogical and heraldic matters, and the Welsh language itself received but scant attention in their writings.

A detailed scrutiny of the manuscripts transcribed during this period reveals that, in addition to the scholars mentioned above, there were a number of lesser-known figures who also had a penchant for historical research. One of these was Rice Lewis, who wrote an essay *c.* 1596–60 on the manors of Glamorgan; a copy of this work, called 'A breuiat wth notes conteyninge all the Lordshippes and Mannors [*sic*] within the countie of Glamorgan', occurs in Cardiff MS. 4. 196. Another work on the same basic theme, written *c.* 1680, occurs in Cardiff MS. 3. 1.[369]

Moreover, many compilations of genealogies made during this period are still extant, including Llanover MS. B 13 (or 'Llyfr Achau Llanganna'), a Welsh manuscript written *c.* 1600; Cardiff MS. 4.213 (or Baglan MS. 3), a compilation made *c.* 1610–30; NLW. MS. 7 and NLW. MS. 8, written *c.* 1678. Unfortunately, little is known about these Glamorgan genealogists, although one of their number, Philip Williams of Dyffryn Clydach in the Neath valley, a gentleman who claimed to be one of the descendants of Rhys ab Iestyn ap Gwrgant, was described by Edward Lhuyd as 'a Glamorganshire Herald' who had supplied him with details of the history of the Carnes taken 'out of his manuscript of the Glamorgan families'.[370] He also contributed to the fund raised to support Edward Lhuyd in his researches,[371] and he seems to have had a collection of strict-metre *awdlau* and *cywyddau*.[372] This may have been one of the compilations transcribed by Llywelyn Siôn.

Nor should we overlook the encouragement and assistance which a number of Glamorgan gentry gave Edward Lhuyd. Lhuyd himself openly acknowledged this generous assistance in a letter of May 2, 1695 to his friend, John Lloyd of Rhuthin:

> Some gentlemen in Glamorganshire have invited me to undertake a *Natural History of Wales*; with an offer of an annual pension from their County of about ten pounds for the space of seaven [*sic*] years; to enable me to travail &c.: but I know not how the gentry of other countrey's [*sic*] stand affected. If the like encouragement would be allow'd from each county, I could very willingly spend the remainder of my days in that employment: and begin to travail next spring. Nor should I onely regard the Natural History of the countrey, but also the antiquities and anything else (as far as may be consistent with my capacity) which my Lord of Bangor and other competent judges shall think convenient to be undertaken.[373]

He published shortly afterwards *A Design of a British Dictionary, Historical & Geographical; With an Essay entitl'd, 'Archaeologia Britannica'; And a Natural History of Wales.* Although it was the production of a '*Natural History of Wales*' that the Glamorgan gentry had suggested to Lhuyd, it may safely be inferred that they were no less anxious that he should undertake also a study of the history and antiquities of the country, for he was generously permitted by Sir Thomas Mansel to borrow all the charters of Margam abbey.[374] Lhuyd stated in 1696 that the Glamorgan gentry had subscribed 'as much as a third part of all Wales as far as I can yet learn'.[375] The list of subscribers published in *Archaeologia Britannica* (1707) contains the names of six members of the Mansel family, Sir John Aubrey of Llantriddyd, Thomas Button of Cotrel (one of Rice Merrick's descendants),[376] Gervice Powel 'of Milton' (a member of that branch of the Powel family that had settled in Maes-teg), Sir Edward Stradling, and a number of other Glamorgan gentlemen. But Lhuyd's chief patron was Sir Thomas Mansel, to whom he dedicated the *Archaeologia Britannica*: 'I have a Great while long'd for so Publick an Occasion of expressing my due Sense of Your Generosity, and manifesting Your Laudable Aim at the promoting of

Learning in General'. Nevertheless, it is extremely doubtful whether the Glamorgan gentry took much interest in the linguistic matter contained in the *Archaeologia Britannica*: they were far more interested in the study of botany and geology and in promoting research into the history and antiquities of Wales and the other Celtic countries. As one of Edward Lhuyd's acquaintances reported to him, 'Yᵣ Learned & curious booke had not ye reception in these parts as it deserved, not one in twenty that I conversed with giving it any tolerable character'.[377]

vi.

THE EIGHTEENTH-CENTURY POETIC REVIVAL

By the end of the seventeenth century the bard had obviously lost both the status and the esteem which he had once enjoyed, while many of the gentry had become heavily anglicized and had lost interest in their cultural heritage. This period was a particularly bleak one in the history of Welsh literature as a whole. Very little of the old literature had been printed. Most of it still remained in hundreds of manuscripts in the homes of a comparatively small number of gentry. These manuscripts were often regarded, even by those who owned them, as mere curiosities, interesting enough in their own way, but having no connection of any significance with Welsh scholarship and the native culture. The eighteenth century, however, witnessed a great revival in the history of Welsh literature and scholarship: it was a period when poets, antiquarians and lexicographers made a detailed analysis of the old literary language, of the compositions of the bards from the sixth century onwards, of the rich learning preserved in the old manuscripts, and of various aspects of the history of Wales.[378] Glamorgan played a prominent part in this revival, which fortunately prevented a complete and irreparable break in the indigenous poetic tradition.

In the letter which he addressed in November 1734 to William Wynn (1709–60), the antiquary and poet whose name is associated with the literary revival in north Wales, John Bradford stated that there were seven grammarians, in addition to bardic disciples, in the county of Glamorgan in his day and that they looked with great disdain on the older generation of rhymesters who, unfortunately, were both praised and rewarded by some of the local gentry for corrupting the language.[379] John Bradford obviously meant by the term 'grammarians' the small circle of bards in the Uplands of Glamorgan. These poets had diligently studied the various versions of the bardic grammar and they had devoted themselves wholeheartedly to mastering the literary language. The 'grammarians' and their bardic disciples to whom John Bradford referred were probably Dafydd Hopcyn from Coety, Rhys Morgan from Pencraig-nedd, Lewis Hopkin, John Bradford himself, Edward Evan (or Evans) of Aberdare, Dafydd Nicolas of Aberpergwm, Dafydd

Thomas of Pandy'r Ystrad, and possibly Wil Hopcyn of Llangynwyd. There were certain features which they had in common: they were all ardent *eisteddfodwyr*, not unlike John Rhydderch and his associates in north Wales; they were all trained artisans, and although there were some among them who composed panegyric and elegiac verses couched in the traditional style of the bards, there is no convincing proof that they ever went on bardic itinerancy; most of them were men of culture who took a keen interest not only in the traditional lore of the bards and in various aspects of Welsh scholarship, but also in the works of many contemporary English poets, or, as in the case of Dafydd Nicolas, in the works of some of the classical authors; and, finally, they were all staunch Nonconformists, a feature which distinguishes them clearly from the most prominent members of the bardic circle in north Wales.[380]

The literary revival represented by this cultured fraternity of bards owed its initial impetus to the brilliant, even if tragically short, career of Edward Lhuyd (1660–1709).[381] It has been suggested that the vital link in this respect was Dafydd Lewys of Llanllawddog, who became vicar of Cadoxton-juxta-Neath on August 21, 1718 and was buried there on April 21, 1727. The publication by him in 1710 of *Flores Poetarum Britannicorum*, the collection made by Dr. John Davies of Mallwyd (*c.* 1567–1644) of notable lines from the compositions of the *cywyddwyr*, together with a second edition of Wiliam Midleton's work on the craft of Welsh poetry, proves that he had a fairly detailed knowledge of the works of the strict-metre poets. He was also acquainted with such notable scholars as Iaco ab Dewi (1648–1722), Moses Williams (1685–1742) and Samuel Williams (*c.* 1660–*c.* 1722), on all of whom the work and ideals of Edward Lhuyd had made a deep and indelible impression.[382] During the nine years which he spent as vicar of Cadoxton-juxta-Neath Dafydd Lewys probably communicated much of their enlightened enthusiasm to Rhys Morgan of Pencraig-nedd and his bardic associates, and he doubtless brought to the attention of the Glamorgan bards the high artistic standards and technical accomplishment of the old chiefs-of-song. This probably accounts, in a very large measure, for the poetic revival that occurred in the northern hill country of Glamorgan during the first half of the eighteenth century, the repercussions of which were inevitably felt in the Vale also.

This literary revival took place in a distinctly Welsh milieu, for there can be no doubt that in the eighteenth century, and especially during its second half, the Welsh language made fairly rapid strides. Iolo Morganwg was well aware of the transformation that had taken place in the fortunes of the language within the county during his lifetime. In one of his letters, which he claimed had been written in August 1751 by Rhys Morgan of Pencraig-nedd, he attributed this astonishing transformation to the great success of the Welsh circulating schools and to the influence of the Nonconformists, with their emphasis on the Welsh sermon and Welsh services.[383] The influence of the circulating schools, though they do not appear to have been very numerous in the anglicized coastal areas, played a vital rôle in the spread of the Methodist movement. The Methodist religious revival, which affected almost the whole of Wales during the eighteenth century, penetrated also to Glamorgan (above, pp. 499–529). Through the Methodist revival the old cultural connections of the Vale with the other parts of Wales, which had been maintained without any significant interruption throughout the Middle Ages by the itinerant professional bards, were once again resumed or appreciably strengthened.[384]

It was also during this period that Welsh books began to flow from the press in constantly increasing numbers. Many of these books contained details of the alphabet and some elementary instructions for reading. The works, at once secular and popular, which were produced by the press prove that the ability to read Welsh was greatly on the increase in this period. The publication of collections of free-metre carols and of *englynion* and *cywyddau* in the strict metres helped to re-awaken interest in the ancient craft of the bards, while the publication in 1716 of Theophilus Evans's famous work, *Drych y Prif Oesoedd*, a second edition of which appeared in 1740, created widespread interest in some early aspects of Welsh history. In 1680 Thomas Jones, that enterprising publisher from Tre'r-ddôl, near Corwen, began publishing his almanacs, and thereafter they appeared regularly, without interruption, for thirty-two years. The almanac was a publication of considerable importance during the eighteenth century, for in addition to the usual calendar, general prophecies, details of bardic *eisteddfodau* and of fairs which were to be held in various parts of Wales and the border, it contained a substantial amount of poetry in both the strict and free metres. Almanacs certainly received a warm welcome in Glamorgan, not least among the local bards, most of whom periodically published some of their compositions in these popular publications, and the itinerant booksellers who helped to distribute them penetrated to every part of the county.

Another extremely influential publication which appeared during this period was John Rhydderch's *Grammadeg Cymraeg* (1728), a work based ultimately on Siôn Dafydd Rhys's celebrated grammar and on the 'Pum Llyfr Cerddwriaeth', the definitive version of the old bardic grammar.[385] The Glamorgan bards seem to have been well aware of the activities of John Rhydderch (1673–1735), who was closely associated from 1701 onwards with most of the local *eisteddfodau* held during his lifetime. Moreover, the almanacs which he himself published provided him with a splendid opportunity to give widespread publicity to these bardic assemblies and to publish some of the works composed by the poets who attended them. His almanac for 1727 contains *englynion* composed by Lewis Hopkin, when he was only nineteen years of age, verses which prove conclusively that he knew of John Rhydderch's work on the bardic grammar which eventually appeared the following year.[386] But the clearest indication of the detailed attention which the eighteenth-century Glamorgan bards gave to the various bardic grammars is provided by their 'exemplifying odes' into which they skilfully wove an example of every one of the twenty-four strict metres. Compositions of this nature occur, for example, among the works of Lewis Hopkin, Edward Evan and Dafydd Thomas of Pandy'r Betws.[387] This tends to confirm Iolo Morganwg's claim that Siôn Dafydd Rhys's grammar, many copies of which were probably still circulating in Glamorgan in the eighteenth century, was the work most frequently studied by the local bards. This work contained 'exemplifying odes' by Gwilym Tew, Lewis Morgannwg, Simwnt Fychan, and Wiliam Midleton. These compositions were included by John Rhydderch in his grammar of 1728. And, significantly, the example which he published by a contemporary bard came from the pen of Rhys Morgan of Pencraig-nedd, who composed an 'exemplifying ode' on the theme of the Welsh language.

THE GRAMMARIANS

The first of the Glamorgan grammarians mentioned above, Dafydd Hopcyn of Coety, is a very obscure figure. Iolo Morganwg, in his well-known 'Bardic pedigree' of the region, refers to Dafydd Hopcyn as a bardic disciple (*awenydd*) in the year 1680 and as the head of the local poets in 1730.[388] The extant parish registers throw no light on his history, nor does his name occur among those poets who attended the *eisteddfodau* held by Rhys Morgan and his associates.[389] But it must not be assumed that he was one of the figments of Iolo Morganwg's imagination. It has been claimed that it was he who transcribed the collection of *cywyddau* contained in Llanover MS. B 3, which for some inexplicable reason is called 'Llyfr Llanfihangel Iorwerth'. This manuscript contains (on page 4) an elegiac *cywydd* which Dafydd Hopcyn is said to have sung in 1734, while another *cywydd* by him, entitled 'Cywydd o Ymddiddan rhwng mab a merch ieuangc', was published in *Trysorfa Gwybodaeth* (1770), 68–70. Although there are some clear indications in both these compositions that he was rather uncertain of his craft at times, the two strict-metre works by him which have survived are manifestly superior to the verses produced by the unskilled rhymesters of the late-seventeenth century.

RHYS MORGAN (*c.* 1700–*c.* 1775)

Fortunately, much more is known about Rhys Morgan of Pencraig-nedd in the parish of Cadoxton in the Vale of Neath. He was probably born towards the end of the seventeenth century, for his name occurs in the list of subscribers to the volume *Llun Agrippa*, which Jenkin Jones, the Arminian minister, published in 1723. According to Iolo Morganwg, who cited John Bradford as his authority, Rhys Morgan was a carpenter, weaver, harpist, and Nonconformist preacher.[390] It is fairly certain that he was a member of the so-called 'Old Meeting-house' (*Hen Dŷ Cwrdd*) in Blaen-gwrach, for two persons bearing the name 'Rees Morgan' occur in the list of members in 1734, the one an elder, the other a deacon.[391] One of these was probably the bard from Pencraig-nedd. He may have been instructed in the bardic craft by one of the disciples of Edward Dafydd of Margam, but by far the greatest influence on him was Dafydd Lewys of Llanllawddog, vicar of Cadoxton. The fact that Rhys Morgan came into contact with John Rhydderch accounts to some extent for the attempts made by him and his bardic contemporaries in Glamorgan to arrange *eisteddfodau* similar to those being held in north Wales. He sent some of his compositions to be published in the Welsh almanacs: for example, he published in the *Almanac* of John Jones ('Philomath') for 1739 eight *englyn*-stanzas addressed to the chief bard of the *eisteddfod* held at Bala on Whit Monday, 1738. Another eight *englyn*-stanzas by him appeared in Siôn Prys's *Almanac* for 1758, stanzas which were addressed to George Varier, a 'Clock maker' from near Pontneddfechan (Pontneathvaughan). He had made a detailed study of the old bardic grammars, and the example published in John Rhydderch's grammar of an 'exemplifying ode' by a contemporary bard was the work of Rhys Morgan.

His career had some turbulent phases. He was imprisoned *c.* 1740–2 for alleged fraud.[392] In 1745, when the Young Pretender landed, Rhys Morgan was in prison once again, where he composed a humorous and spirited *cywydd* for presentation to the duke of Cumberland in which he offered the services of himself and his fellow-prisoners. Much later, when he was well advanced in years, he published this *cywydd* in *Trysorfa Gwybodaeth* (1770), where he explained that he had been imprisoned by Lord Mansel of Margam.[393] A copy of the *cywydd* was also published in Gwilym Howel's *Almanac* for 1775.

The date of Rhys Morgan's death has not been recorded. His work was never gathered together into a single volume, and the few compositions by him which are still extant are scattered in various publications, such as John Rhydderch's *Grammadeg Cymraeg* (1728), *Trysorfa Gwybodaeth*, various eighteenth-century almanacs, *Y Fel Gafod* (1813), and in some of Iolo Morganwg's manuscripts.

LEWIS HOPKIN (*c.* 1708–71)

The most talented of this small circle of bards and the one who possibly exerted the greatest influence on the literary life of the county in the first half of the eighteenth century was Lewis Hopkin. He was probably born *c.* 1708 in the parish of Llanbedr-ar-fynydd (Peterston-super-montem), the son of Lewis Hopkin and one of the descendants of Hopcyn Tomas Phylip of Gelli'r-fid, the celebrated *cwndidwr*. No record of Lewis Hopkin's baptism occurs, however, either in the registers of Peterston-super-montem or of Llantrisant parish.[394] When he was still a young man, he moved to the parish of Llandyfodwg, where many of his ancestors had been born, and it was there, at Hendre Ifan Goch, that he made his home until his death in 1771. He was trained as a carpenter, but he acquired considerable expertise in other crafts as well, including those of glazier, stone-cutter, and wire-worker. In the latter part of his life he took to farming and he also owned a fairly large country shop. According to his son:

> He was a man of universal genius both for literature and mechanics. He was employed by many in surveying, planning, measuring, calculating, writing all sorts of law instruments, and doing innumerable little ingenious jobs mostly gratis, for he never coveted money. He could exercise any trade that he had seen better than most of its professors, he could and did build a house, finish and furnish it himself.[395]

Lewis Hopkin became a Nonconformist and was a member (and, according to some authorities, a deacon) of the congregation of Independents at Cymer, Porth (above, p. 492). According to his son, Lewis Hopkin was the first member of the family to become a Nonconformist, and he married Margaret, the daughter of Thomas Bevan, who belonged to a family of staunch Quakers. Lewis Hopkin was obviously a figure of considerable importance in the lively Nonconformist circles of upper Glamorgan. 'He was esteemed by all that knew him', declared his son, 'for his wisdom, integrity, ingenuity, and piety, in which he was so zealous in his latter years, that he kept meetings on Sabbath-day evenings from house to house to expound the scriptures to the edification of many'.[396]

Lewis Hopkin was a prominent figure in the literary revival. As a boy, he had received, according to Iolo Morganwg, the type of education which was usually given in his day in English, writing, and mathematics. As a result of his own efforts, he acquired a fairly good knowledge of Latin, to which he also added a wide acquaintance with English literature, which he held in high esteem.[397] Much of his reading was of a devotional and poetical character, and he devoted himself wholeheartedly to becoming a master of the Welsh bardic craft. He also played an important rôle in organizing bardic *eisteddfodau*. Some of his poems appeared in various eighteenth-century almanacs and in the journal called *Trysorfa Gwybodaeth* (1770), while the elegiac *cywydd* which he addressed to the Rev. David Jardine of Abergavenny was published by John Ross at Carmarthen in 1769. In 1813, over forty years after his death, his son-in-law, John Miles of Pen-coed, published a valuable collection of his work under the title *Y Fel Gafod*.

Although his verse is not of the highest merit, it nevertheless reflects the determined efforts which he had made to study the literary language and to master the intricate rules relating to *cynghanedd* and the twenty-four strict metres. He was the bardic teacher of Edward Evan of Aberdare, and Iolo Morganwg informs us that he, too, had received some instruction in the bardic craft from Lewis Hopkin. According to Iolo Morganwg, Lewis Hopkin and his bardic contemporaries, John Bradford, Dafydd Nicolas, and Edward Evan, had a fairly extensive knowledge of eighteenth-century English literature and of the works of English literary critics of that period. This claim is partly confirmed by the splendid translation which Lewis Hopkin made of the 'Ballad of Chevy Chase' and 'The History of Lavinia'.[398] The letters which he addressed to his son in English reflect a devout and cultured mind and prove that their author could write that language fairly well.[399] He also composed some verses in English. Many of the books that had previously been in his possession were retained until comparatively recently in the farmhouse of Llanbed Fawr, not far distant from the ruins of the church of Peterston-super-montem. The collection is an extremely interesting one, for it includes Welsh books of the eighteenth century, various English works, some of which are of a distinctly devotional and religious nature, works on law and medicine, the *Spectator*, and some Latin and French works. It is difficult to determine precisely how much knowledge he had of Latin and French, but there is much to suggest that he had a fairly extensive knowledge of the English literature of his day. He seems to have travelled a great deal, visiting London twice and Bristol frequently, where he had some influential friends.

Lewis Hopkin was undoubtedly a very important figure. He had become familiar with many of the acknowledged leaders of the Presbyterian and Independent movements; he was also acquainted with some of the gentry of the county; but he was equally at home with the Nonconformist preachers in the Uplands or in the company of the bards who sang and caroused in the taverns of Pyle, Pen-coed, and Cymer. He was probably the most important figure in the literary life of Glamorgan in the early-eighteenth century, prior to the advent of Iolo Morganwg, and his extant work suggests that he was the most accomplished poet of his day. He died in November 1771 and was buried with his children and forefathers in Llandyfodwg churchyard. William Thomas, the schoolmaster from Llansanffraid-ar-Elái (St. Bride's-super-Ely), wrote in his diary on December 3, 1771: 'Was burd at Glyn Ogwr since ye 27 Nov last Lewis Hopkin of about 63 yrs of age of a lingring disease. One of the best Welsh poets in all South Wales and author of several Welsh poems.'[400] Among the elegies addressed to him are those composed by Edward Evan of Aberdare in *Afalau'r Awen* and by Iolo Morganwg, under the title, *Dagrau yr Awen* (1772).

JOHN BRADFORD (1706–85)

Although Lewis Hopkin was manifestly the most versatile and possibly the most influential of the small circle of bards, the person who figures most prominently in Iolo Morganwg's voluminous writings was John Bradford, the weaver, fuller, and dyer who lived in Betws Tir Iarll. The Bradford family came from Bradford-on-Avon to settle at Betws during the first half of the seventeenth century and they had their own coat-of-arms. Little definite is known of John Bradford, or of his father, Richard, but it seems that he devoted himself wholeheartedly in his younger days to studying the ancient Welsh bardic traditions and collecting Welsh manuscripts. There is some evidence that he had acquired some of the valuable manuscript-volumes of the cultured Powel family of Tir Iarll. He was undoubtedly acquainted with the works of many English authors and literary critics. If he regularly received *The Gentleman's Magazine*, he must have been well acquainted with the literary life of eighteenth-century England.[401] And, like the other members of this closely-knit bardic fraternity, he, too, was a Nonconformist. His name occurs in the list of subscribers to Jenkin Jones's *Llun Agrippa* (1723), although he was only seventeen at the time. He corresponded with William Wynn, Llangynhafal,[402] and with Lewis Morris (1701–65), the famous poet and scholar, who described the Glamorgan bard, in a characteristically sarcastic manner, as 'ye Prime of South Wales Poets';[403] and John Bradford occasionally visited Lewis Morris after the latter had moved to Cardiganshire.[404] He was elected a member of The Honourable Society of Cymmrodorion in London. In 1740 he addressed a series of *englynion* to Theophilus Evans, when the latter published the second edition of *Drych y Prif Oesoedd*. He was also one of the most *avant-garde* rationalists in Glamorgan, and the works of some of the more prominent eighteenth-century Deists made a deep impression on him. He was probably a member in the chapel at Betws where Samuel Jones (1628–97) of Brynllywarch was once pastor. This may be highly significant, for the latter had married a daughter of Rees Powel of Maes-teg. This may explain how John Bradford managed to acquire some of the valuable collection of manuscripts of the Powel family.

Among those who received some degree of instruction from John Bradford was Iolo Morganwg, who invented all kinds of stories about his teacher's impressive erudition and of his vital connection with the druidic and Unitarian bardic system which, he claimed, had persisted throughout the centuries in his native county, and especially in the ancient region of Tir Iarll. Many of these stories, however, were ingeniously concocted by Iolo himself. The fact that John Bradford's son, Richard, was blind probably explains why Iolo dared to state in his work, *Poems, Lyric and Pastoral* (1794), that the manuscript-copy of the allegedly ancient bardic triads which he had forged was still in the possession of 'Mr. Richard Bradford, of Bettws, near Bridgend, in Glamorgan'.[405] It may also explain why he informed some of his London associates that the original copy of *Cyfrinach Beirdd Ynys Prydain* was still preserved there.

John Bradford was buried on June 6, 1785 and his will was proved at Cowbridge on October 11 that year. He left the bulk of his possessions to his son, Richard. No reference was made, however, to his valuable collection of books and manuscripts.[406] A month after his death William Thomas of St. Bride's-super-Ely wrote in his diary in July 1785: 'Was lately buried at Betws near Bridgend John Bradford a fuller and dyer of 80 yrs of age. a great disbater [*sic*] and a Nominated Deist or a freethinker'.[407]

Dafydd Nicolas (1705?–74)

Another poet of this group who is frequently mentioned in Iolo Morganwg's manuscripts was Dafydd Nicolas. According to the late T. C. Evans he was the 'David Nicholas' who was baptized in Llangynwyd on July 1, 1705, and kept a school at one time in the parish.[408] It is more than likely, however, that he lived for a while in Ystradyfodwg and, possibly, in Glyncorrwg and Cwm-gwrach.[409] In his younger days Dafydd Nicolas was probably an itinerant schoolmaster in various parts of the Uplands of Glamorgan. Towards the middle of the century, or, possibly, a little earlier, his marked ability attracted the attention of the Williams family of Aberpergwm, and from then until his death on February 8, 1774 Aberpergwm became his home. It was often stated in the nineteenth century that he was kept and maintained there as a sort of 'family bard', the last, it was claimed, to fulfil this age-old function in any part of Wales.[410] But William Davies (1756–1823) of Cringell, Llantwit-juxta-Neath, a responsible and industrious antiquary, stated unequivocally in 1795–6 that Dafydd Nicolas served as a '*Private Tutor* at Aberpergwm'.[411] And it is surely significant in this connection that no panegyric or elegy addressed by him to any member of the Aberpergwm family is now extant.

Although Iolo Morganwg referred to him in his manuscript as a 'self-educated' and 'self-taught' man, Dafydd Nicolas certainly won considerable renown as a classical scholar. William Davies of Cringell was firmly convinced that he fully deserved the high reputation which he had acquired 'as a poet, as well as a classic scholar' and Davies saw in the well-known poem 'Ffanni Blodau'r Ffair'—or, to be more precise, 'Fanny blooming fair', as Dafydd Nicolas himself had written—an apt and commendably judicious imitation of Horace.[412] Moreover, according to a tradition that was current in the Neath valley towards the end of the eighteenth century, Dafydd Nicolas had translated a part of the *Iliad* into Welsh.[413] Iolo Morganwg also claimed that Dafydd Nicolas had a firm grasp of Latin, Greek, and French, and that he was easily the most talented of all the Welsh poets he had ever known.[414] Although the few verses which he composed in the strict metres reflect little artistic merit,[415] his compositions in the free metres have won for him a secure place in the literary history of Glamorgan. Two lyrics, entitled 'Callyn Serchus' and 'Ffanni Blodau'r Ffair', were attributed to him by Miss Maria Jane Williams in *Ancient National Airs of Gwent and Morganwg* (1844), and his name is also traditionally associated with the words of 'Y 'Deryn Pur'.[416] These are three beautiful love-lyrics which were to be sung to the accompaniment of various airs, both old and modern. They show quite clearly that he had an ear for the music of words and that he took an infinite delight in the rhythmical cadences and unfeigned spontaneity of his metres. Not inappropriately, therefore, he has been described as 'the Ceiriog of the eighteenth century', and some well-informed critics are firmly of the opinion that his free-metre verse was the best work produced by a Glamorgan bard in the first half of the eighteenth century.[417] The authorship of a long letter, dated April 3, 1754, is attributed to Dafydd Nicolas in Llanover MS. C 35, 165–74.[418] This is an unusually interesting document, for it attempts to analyse the technique of composing verse in the free metres. The only extant copy of this letter is the one which occurs in Iolo Morganwg's hand in Llanover MS. C 35, and its style and diction strongly suggest that it is one of Iolo's inspired forgeries.[419] It was probably Dafydd Nicolas's prowess as a classical scholar and as a free-metre bard which prompted Iolo Morganwg to attribute the letter to him.

DAFYDD THOMAS (d. 1735)

In *Llyfr Ecclesiastes* (1767) Edward Evan maintained that Dafydd Thomas of Pandy'r Ystrad was a native of Cardiganshire who had moved to Glamorgan in 1727, when, according to Iolo Morganwg, he was between twelve and fifteen years of age.[420] He settled in Betws Tir Iarll and became a member of Rees Price's congregation at Tŷ'n-ton, Llangeinwyr. It is possible that a number of these early-eighteenth-century bards had received some instruction under Rees Price, and so it is hardly surprising that Dafydd Thomas soon devoted himself to studying the contents of the bardic grammar and to mastering Welsh strict-metre prosody and *cynghanedd*. About 1730 he began composing poetry under the tuition of John Bradford, and an 'exemplifying ode' that occurs in Llanover MS. B 19 is attributed by Edward Gamage of St. Athan (Sain Tathan) to 'Dafydd Thomas o blwyf y Bettws'. This ode points clearly to his mastery, when still a young man, of the traditional twenty-four strict metres. Sometime before 1734 he entered into a marriage with a widow, but he was eventually forced to leave her.[421] He moved to the parish of Ystradyfodwg, where he set up house in Pandy'r Ystrad, and it was there, according to Edward Evan, that he died in 1735. Some of his *englynion* were published in *Y Fel Gafod*.[422] He also left a translation in the *cywydd* metre of the first chapter of the book of Ecclesiastes. This led ultimately to the publication in 1767 of a translation of the entire book, *Llyfr Ecclesiastes*, by his bardic associates,

Lewis Hopkin and Edward Evan. A letter outlining the history of Nonconformity in Glamorgan attributed to him is yet another of Iolo Morganwg's many forgeries.[423]

Edward Evan (1716–17 to 1798)

Perhaps the most romantic and undoubtedly the best-known of all the Glamorgan grammarians was Edward Evan, especially after Iolo Morganwg had claimed in 1789 that they two were the only survivors of the Welsh bardic fraternity. 'Besides Edward Williams [i.e., Iolo Morganwg]', wrote a certain 'J.D.' from Cowbridge in *The Gentleman's Magazine* in November 1789, 'there is, I believe, now remaining only one regular Bard in Glamorgan, or in the world: this is the Rev. Mr. Edward Evans, of Aberdare, a Dissenting Minister. These two persons are the only legitimate descendants of the so-long-celebrated *Ancient British Bards*; at least they will allow no others this honourable title.' Moreover, his verse enjoyed a vogue among the Welsh inhabitants of the Uplands equalled only by that of Vicar Prichard (1579?–1644), and four editions of his poetry appeared during the nineteenth century.

Born in March 1716 (or, possibly, 1717) at Llwytgoed, Aberdare, he was the son of Ifan ap Siôn ap Rhys, a weaver and smallholder noted for his geniality and fondness for poetry.[424] It is said that Edward Evan was a skilled harpist when he was only eleven years of age, and that later his services were frequently in demand. It was in this capacity that Edward Evan was welcomed by Dafydd Nicolas to the bardic *eisteddfod* held at Cymer on March 1, 1735:

> A Iorwerdd brydferdd ei bryd,
> Delynwr da wyl ynyd,
> Fab Ifan gyngan ei gerdd,
> Difawr ing, dofwr angerdd.

The *englynion* which he sang at this bardic assembly show quite clearly that, although he was only eighteen, he was already beginning to take a serious interest in Welsh prosody.[425] He received very little education in his early formative years, but he was later taught, according to Iolo Morganwg, by a certain James John from Aberdare, a hooper and farmer who was well-read in English and Welsh and a tolerably good poet.[426] After working for a few years as a weaver, Edward Evan was apprenticed, at the age of twenty-three, to carpentry and glazing under Lewis Hopkin at Hendre Ifan Goch, and it was his association with the latter which, above all else, explains the main features of his career as a bard and Nonconformist. Under the guidance of Lewis Hopkin he devoted himself to studying the Welsh strict metres and the contents of the bardic grammar, and he soon set about composing an 'exemplifying ode'. It was also Lewis Hopkin who probably instilled in him a deep love of English literature, and his work contains translations of some of the poems of Pope, Samuel Butler, Bishop Horne, and Dr. Watts. It may also have been under the influence of Lewis Hopkin and the religious congregation at Cymer that he joined the Nonconformists. But his verse, especially his love-poetry, which comprises a substantial part of his popular volume, *Afalau'r Awen*, proves conclusively that he remained an essentially jovial character to the end of his days.

Edward Evan worked for many years as a carpenter and glazier—in seventeen parishes, in all. After his marriage in 1744 to Margaret Thomas of Penderyn, he settled for a while at Cefnpennarisaf, and in 1749 he moved to the farm of Ton Coch, above Dyffryn House, Mountain Ash, where he remained until his death in 1798. About 1748, or, possibly, a little earlier, he joined the Nonconformist congregation at Cwm-y-glo,[427] and when a separate church—'yr Hen Dŷ Cwrdd' ('the Old Meeting-house')—was later established near Aberdare, he became one of its most prominent members and a preacher to boot. According to Iolo Morganwg, he was an orthodox Calvinist in his earlier days, but later took a distinct turn towards Arminianism and, later still, to Arianism. He did not take a prominent part, however, in contemporary theological disputations, although he translated into Welsh the account written by Charles Winter (1700–73) of the dissension at Hengoed[428] (above, p. 494). It seems also that some of Edward Evan's political views were of an unmistakably radical nature. From July 1, 1772 until 1796 he was pastor of the 'Old Meeting-house'.

During his lifetime he published two prose works: *Gwersi i Blant a Dynjon jeuaingc, Mewn Dau Gatecism* (1757), a Welsh translation of one of Samuel Bourn's catechisms; and *Golwg ar Gynheddfau Gwasanaeth, ac Anrhydedd Gwasanaethwyr Crist* (1775), a sermon delivered at one of the Presbyterian gatherings. He also published in 1767, jointly with Lewis Hopkin, a Welsh translation of the book of Ecclesiastes (above, pp. 617–618). After Edward Evan's death, some of his poetry was published at Merthyr Tudful under the title *Caniadau Moesol a Duwiol* (1804). Three enlarged editions were later published under the title *Afalau'r Awen*—at Merthyr Tudful in 1816 and 1837, and at Aberdare in 1874. Edward Evan died, aged eighty-two years, on June 1, 1798, on the very day when, under Iolo Morganwg's influence, a new generation of so-called 'druidic' bards assembled at a *gorsedd* held on Garth Mountain, in the ancient parish of Pen-tyrch, a generation which undoubtedly held him in the highest esteem as one of the two survivors of the 'Ancient British Bards'.[429]

WILIAM HOPCYN (?1700–41)

Another poet traditionally associated with the Glamorgan *eisteddfodau* was Wiliam Hopcyn from the parish of Llangynwyd in Tir Iarll. Unfortunately, however, little definite is known about him, although he became a very popular and highly romantic figure in the works of many nineteenth-century literary historians. Many references to him occur in Iolo Morganwg's manuscripts, where he is delineated as one of the bards who had composed some enchantingly beautiful love-lyrics in the manner of Rhys Goch ap Rhicert.[430] Both Wil Hopcyn and Dafydd Nicolas were regarded by Iolo as the modern representatives of a long and uncommonly rich tradition, and he attempted to buttress this claim by attributing to Dafydd Nicolas many beautiful poems in the free accentual metres, most of which were probably works of his own composition. Strangely, however, only a few verses of this nature were attributed by him to Wil Hopcyn, although c. 1815 Iolo claimed, characteristically, to have discovered in his younger days over twenty of his compositions in a manuscript which was in the possession of Dafydd Rhisiart of Llandough, near Cowbridge.[431] In the 'Bardic pedigree' which Iolo Morganwg claimed he had copied from one of John Bradford's manuscripts it was stated that 'William Hopcin' was an *awenydd*, or bardic disciple, in the 'Bardic Chair' of Glamorgan in 1760.[432] Among the other disciples included in this 'Chair' were Lewis Hopkin, Edward Evan, and Iolo Morganwg himself, which shows conclusively that the last-named firmly believed c. 1785–90, when he prepared this particular list, that Wiliam Hopcyn lived during the second half of the eighteenth century. Iolo informed William Owen [-Pughe] that Hopcyn had died c. 1780, and so this is the date recorded in *The Cambrian Biography* (1803) and subsequently repeated by Edward Williams ('Iolo Fardd Glas'), who lived in Glamorgan and regularly associated with the bards of the region throughout his life.[433] This strongly suggests that even the local inhabitants knew very little of Wil Hopcyn when Iolo Morganwg was working on the 'Bardic pedigree'. But later, when he was well advanced in years, Iolo went to Llangynwyd, saw a gravestone in the local churchyard of a certain 'William Hopkin', who died in August 1741, and then maintained that this was the grave of the celebrated poet.[434] This view was generally accepted by nineteenth-century literary historians, many of whom also claimed that Wil Hopcyn was a tiler and plasterer by trade.

The parish records of Llangynwyd show that a 'William Hopkin' was born there in November 1700, the son of Hopkin Thomas, and that he died in 1741.[435] Furthermore, a reference in one of the Margam manuscripts, dated March 25, 1722, shows that he, his mother, Diane Thomas, and his brother, Jenkin Hopkin, held eight acres of meadow land called 'Gwayne-y-llan' in Llangynwyd. Another document refers to him as collector of taxes in 1723.[436] This may well be the love-poet; but it is well to remember that another person bearing the same name lived in the parish of Llangynwyd in this period and died in 1769.[437] It may well have been this person whom Iolo Morganwg had in mind when he drew up c. 1785–90 his list of the bards of the region. But there is one fact about which the literary historian can feel reasonably certain: the *englynion* by Lewis Hopkin which were published in *Y Fel Gafod*, 109–10, prove conclusively that a poet called 'Will Hopkin' satirized the bards at the *eisteddfod* held at Cymer on March 1, 1735.[438]

Undoubtedly, it was Iolo Morganwg who attributed to Wil Hopcyn the authorship of 'Bugeilio'r Gwenith Gwyn', the charming poem usually known in English as 'Watching the Wheat'.[439] Although the core of the poem may be genuinely old, the late Professor G. J. Williams was firmly convinced that it was Iolo who was responsible for refurbishing the poem in its final form. During the latter part of the nineteenth century the story of Wil Hopcyn and Ann Thomas, the 'Maid of Cefn Ydfa', romantically associated with the poem 'Bugeilio'r Gwenith Gwyn', gained widespread currency as one of the great tragic romances of eighteenth-century Wales. Professor G. J. Williams concluded that, after it had been stripped of successive accretions of fancy and pure conjecture, its hard residual core consisted of a few facts that Taliesin ab Iolo, writing in 1845, claimed to have heard from the parish clerk of Llangynwyd some thirty-four years earlier. Apparently, it was Taliesin ab Iolo who began to relate the tragic love experiences of Wil Hopcyn and Ann Thomas, and to associate the poem called 'Bugeilio'r Gwenith Gwyn' with that tradition.[440] The mental perversity which characterizes so much of Iolo Morganwg's teeming literary output was nowhere in evidence in his son, and the veracity of Taliesin ab Iolo's account was corroborated by Maria Jane Williams, who, in a letter written in 1841 (or 1842), stated unequivocally that she had learned indirectly from an old man that a song known to him as 'Y Ferch o Gefn Ydfa' was the work of Wil Hopcyn. She quoted a part of this song in her letter. It is obviously not identical with 'Bugeilio'r Gwenith Gwyn', nor is it composed in the same metre as the latter, though the words of both poems are undeniably similar in character.[441] Although her unbiased testimony casts further doubt on the attribution to Wil Hopcyn of the authorship of 'Bugeilio'r Gwenith Gwyn', it nevertheless preserves the only work associated with his name on any authority other than that of Iolo Morganwg. Whether these verses are actually a genuine product of Wil Hopcyn's pen or merely associated with him by popular tradition it is impossible to determine, but they are not entirely unworthy of the great acclaim which he has won as a love-poet and are in general agreement with the basic theme of the story related by Taliesin ab Iolo. In the early 1840s Mrs. Mary Pendrill Llewelyn (1811–74), the wife of the vicar of Llangynwyd, began to set about collecting the old *penillion* and *tribannau* of Tir Iarll. She maintained that a number of these songs and stanzas were the authentic work of Wil Hopcyn and were definitely connected with the tragic Cefn Ydfa episode. The tale thus began to assume its final form about 1845, and in the years that followed the various elements usually found in romantic tales of this kind were gradually added—the cruel parents, confining the lovesick maid to her chamber, dispatching messages by a servant to her beloved one, using blood instead of ink, concealing letters in a hollow tree, and the unfortunate maid finally languishing to death after being cruelly forced to marry a wealthy man.[442]

The Learning of the Grammarians

Nearly all the eighteenth-century Glamorgan poets mentioned above paid great attention to technical details connected with the ancient craft of the strict-metre bards.[443] But it is difficult to determine precisely how much attention they gave to the works of the great masters who sang in the strict metres during earlier centuries. Some important manuscripts were still retained in the county during this period, the manuscripts of Meurug Dafydd, Dafydd Benwyn, Sils ap Siôn, and Edward Dafydd, as well as the substantial collections transcribed by Llywelyn Siôn and Tomas ab Ieuan of Tre'r-bryn. But whether any of the early-eighteenth-century Glamorgan grammarians ever managed to acquire some of them it is impossible to tell, and the only substantial collection of *cywyddau* which can confidently be connected with one of their number is that contained in Llanover MS. B 3, which was probably transcribed by Dafydd Hopcyn of Coety. Nevertheless, Iolo Morganwg's manuscripts contain a great deal of interesting material which, he claimed, had been transcribed from the manuscripts of Rhys Morgan, Dafydd Nicolas, and Edward Evan. Much of this material had undoubtedly emanated from his own incomparably fertile imagination. But not all, for he frequently re-wrote and 'doctored' the material which he had discovered in authentic manuscript-sources, including the material which occurred in the works of the early-eighteenth-century bards. Lewis Hopkin certainly had a fairly large library, containing works in both English and Welsh; but the collection does not appear to have included any ancient manuscripts.

John Bradford's work was frequently cited by Iolo Morganwg as the source from which he had transcribed the various triads and treatises on the esoteric lore of the bards, on the druidic doctrines and practices, and on the Glamorgan classification of the metres. And it was in the same source that he claimed to have discovered the enchantingly beautiful love-lyrics of Rhys Goch ap Rhicert and many valuable data concerning the literary history of Glamorgan. It is possible that John Bradford had managed to acquire some of the manuscripts of Anthony and Watcyn Powel. His name also occurs in the Long Book of Llanharan as well as in Llanover MS. B 1 (above, pp. 582, 590, 604). But neither of these manuscripts had ever formed a part of Bradford's private collection. In a letter to William Wynn in 1734 Bradford referred to the manuscripts which he had succeeded in gathering during his visits 'to many old houses', where they were being thoughtlessly damaged and destroyed.[444] Unfortunately, however, these were not explicitly identified by him.

Moreover, it appears from a letter which Lewis Morris sent to Edward Samuel on October 1, 1736 that Bradford had 'an Inclination to Publish some Poems of ye antients', nearly forty years, it should be noted, before Rhys Jones (1713–1801) of Blaenau, Merionethshire, published his *Gorchestion Beirdd Cymru* (1773).[445] The plan never materialized, however, probably because of a lack of subscribers. But Bradford never relented in his anxious search for manuscripts, and there were undoubtedly many small collections to be found in various parts of the county in his day. These were in the possession of minor antiquaries such as Siôn (or John) Phylip and Thomas Phylip of Tre-oes, in the parish of Coychurch, Edward Lewis, the solicitor from Pen-llin, Esaia Powel of Llansanffraid (St. Bride's), near Bridgend, Thomas Robert of Bridgend, and Dafydd Rhisiart of Llandochau, near Cowbridge. Scholars such as Thomas Richards, Morgan Llywelyn of Neath, and genealogists such as Thomas Truman, Pantylliwydd, also had some manuscripts in their possession. Many of these collections were ultimately acquired by Iolo Morganwg, and it is more than likely that most of the early-eighteenth-century grammarians had some knowledge of their contents, which included, *inter alia*, transcripts of strict-metre verse and of religious *cwndidau* as well as copies of the prose-texts which had been written by Llywelyn Siôn and some of the scribes of Tir Iarll. A number of the grammarians were also familiar with many of the scholars and talented littérateurs linked with the great literary revival which took place in Wales in the eighteenth century. John Bradford corresponded with both William Wynn and Lewis Morris. His name also occurs among the subscribers to *Diddanwch Teuluaidd* (1763), the volume in which Huw Jones of Llangwm published for the first time the work of the famous Anglesey poets, Goronwy Owen, Lewis Morris, and Hugh Hughes. Both John Bradford and Thomas Richards of Llangrallo were elected corresponding members of the London Cymmrodorion Society.[446] Nor should one overlook the generous assistance which the Morris brothers gave Thomas Richards to enable the latter to publish his famous dictionary.

In common with the poets in other parts of Wales, the Glamorgan grammarians were very keen to publish their compositions, which they sent periodically to the ever-popular almanacs. Edward Evan and Lewis Hopkin sent some of their verses to the first number of the journal *Trysorfa Gwybodaeth, neu, Eurgrawn Cymraeg*, which appeared in 1770, and their work, together with that of Rhys Morgan of Pencraig-nedd and Iolo Morganwg, appeared in subsequent numbers. John Bradford also sent a *cywydd* taken from one of his manuscripts. And some among their number succeeded in publishing their verse in booklets, such as *Llyfr Ecclesiastes* (1767) and *Cywydd Marwnad y Parchedig Mr. David Jardin* (1769). But by 1770 a new period was clearly beginning in the literary life of Glamorgan, for by then the county had its own printing-press at Cowbridge, John Walters of Llandochau (Llandough), near Cowbridge, had published his dictionary, and the youthful Iolo Morganwg was beginning to manifest an interest in Welsh literature.[447]

[623]

The Bardic *Eisteddfodau*

References abound in Iolo Morganwg's manuscripts to the bardic assemblies which met in various places in Glamorgan—at Ystradowen, Y Pîl (Pyle), Melin Ifan Ddu, Llangynwyd, Ystradyfodwg, and Llanilid, to mention only a few—in the first half of the eighteenth century.[448] It is obvious that many of those who actively supported the *eisteddfod* in the eighteenth century genuinely believed that the institution could be used as an effective means of fostering the native language and culture and restoring the metrical art of the strict-metre bards to its erstwhile high standard. The procedure adopted is described in some detail by John Rhydderch in his *Grammadeg Cymraeg* (1728): the poets, who usually assembled at taverns, selected a dozen men who had some knowledge of the bardic craft and the intricate rules of Welsh versification to act as literary adjudicators and to specify the theme on which the poets were to compose their extempore strict-metre verses in order to decide which one of them 'had the mastery'.[449] This was undoubtedly the procedure adopted by the Glamorgan grammarians. Indeed, it is known that John Rhydderch himself visited Glamorgan, probably in 1734, and he must have encouraged the local grammarians to arrange bardic assemblies similar to those described by him in his grammar.

Although the descriptions given by Iolo Morganwg of these *eisteddfodau* must invariably be treated with the greatest caution and reserve, it can hardly be doubted that they are occasionally based on a hard core of genuine fact, for some of his statements can be corroborated from independent sources. For example, Benjamin Heath Malkin (1769–1842) referred to the *eisteddfodau* held at Ystradowen, a place which was remarkable, *inter alia*

> . . . for the meeting of the Welsh bards, under the immemorial patronage of the Hensol family . . . on the 28th day of May. The last assembly under these auspices took place on the 28th of May, 1720; for though Richard Jenkins, the last of the family, lived till July 1721, it does not appear that the meeting was patronized as usual that year . . . It was, however, continued for some years after his death, though it gradually dwindled into nothing, in consequence of the new family at Hensol looking with indifference on the institution, and withdrawing the accustomed liberality of the patrons.[450]

This Richard Jenkins, according to Malkin, was a talented harpist who had 'inherited undiminished that affection for Welsh poetry and music, which had distinguished the Jenkins's of Hensol from time immemorial'.[451] It is not difficult to understand, therefore, why Iolo Morganwg gave such a prominent place in many of his forgeries to Ystradowen, which, he frequently claimed, was the real centre of the *eisteddfod* movement in the Vale and the cradle and repository of the ancient druidic traditions. He further claimed that bardic assemblies of a similar nature had been held at Pyle. A number of glaring inconsistencies in matters of chronology strongly suggest that most of these details originated in his own over-active imagination.[452] Nevertheless, a reference contained in the *englynion* which Lewis Hopkin addressed to the bards of west Glamorgan proves conclusively that an *eisteddfod* of some kind was held at Pyle, and as these verses were answered by Dafydd Thomas, it may reasonably be assumed that this meeting took place sometime between 1727 and 1735, possibly in the tavern which the latter, or his irascible wife, kept there.[453]

But the first *eisteddfod* to be held in Glamorgan in the eighteenth century of which the literary historian can now be absolutely certain was the one held at Pen-coed on All Souls' day (November 2), 1733. The *englynion* composed by Lewis Hopkin reveal that the meeting had been arranged to impart some instruction to the assembled bards both in the Welsh language itself and in the intricacies of their craft. Having referred to the sad decline which had taken place, he extended his warm greetings to every 'grammarian' and prophesied a new and glorious beginning in the bardic history of the region:

> Gwellir hynt helynt haeledd—gwlad Forgan,
> Glyd fawrgall gyfanedd,
> Gwn, a mwynhau gawn mewn hedd,
> Gwar ganu fel gwyr Gwynedd.

Nothing is known, however, of the activities that took place at this *eisteddfod*. More details have survived of the *eisteddfod* held at Cymer on St. David's day 1735. The theme chosen on this occasion was 'Yr Angau' ('Death'). The *englynion* composed on this theme have also survived, but the victorious bard is not named. Lewis Hopkin referred explicitly to the learned people and strangers who came there to listen, which proves that the meeting was not confined exclusively to members of the bardic fraternity:

> I'n cwrdd i wrando'n cerddi—y daethant,
> Rai doethion i'n perchi,
> Dieithraid têg diwegi,
> Mi wn oll er ein mwyn ni.

Nor was it only this small circle of grammarians which tried to foster the literary life of the region in this period through the medium of the *eisteddfod*. Some references contained in a series of *englynion* in which Lewis Hopkin greeted the poets of Gelli-gaer prove that they, too, carefully studied the bardic grammar, attempted to master the strict-metre system and periodically visited bardic assemblies, some of which Lewis Hopkin himself attended.[454] Dafydd Thomas's name is recorded along with Hopkin's poems, and so it may reasonably be assumed that the bardic meetings at Gelli-gaer were held c. 1730–5. Nothing is known of their activities, however, or of any other *eisteddfod* held in the county for many years after 1735, apart from the bardic meetings mentioned by Iolo Morganwg, but as no reference to them occurs in any other known source, they must be regarded as apocryphal. The extant evidence strongly suggests that the bardic *eisteddfodau* began to decline in Glamorgan after 1735, although some of the local grammarians continued to take a lively interest in the activities of the *eisteddfodwyr* in north Wales (above, pp. 610–612).

THE LITERARY ACHIEVEMENTS OF THE GRAMMARIANS

Hardly any of the compositions of the Glamorgan grammarians were published during their own lifetime. This is not surprising, however, for it was in a later period that the Welsh poets in general began seriously to regard the printing-press as a means of bringing their work to a much wider public. In some cases only fragments of their work have survived. In assessing the aesthetic standards achieved by them, it is therefore essential to bear in mind that many important works by them may have been irretrievably lost. One notable example is the translation which Dafydd Nicolas is said to have made of a part of the *Iliad*. Even the manuscripts used by Rhys Evans and John Miles when they were preparing for publication a collection of the work of Edward Evan and Lewis Hopkin respectively (above, pp. 613, 619) are, unfortunately, no longer extant.

The most conspicuous feature in the work of these early-eighteenth-century bards was their determination to master the various technical details relating to their craft and to demonstrate their mastery by composing 'exemplifying odes' and *englynion*.[455] This emerges very clearly not only from those compositions which they sent periodically to the almanacs but also from their correspondence with some of their compatriots in north Wales. A number of these poets, however, fell far short of the high artistic standards achieved by the great chiefs-of-song who lived during the fifteenth or early-sixteenth centuries. Rhys Morgan's work, for example, is occasionally marred by some elementary errors in both *cynghanedd* and language.[456] Nevertheless, it was the revived interest in the contents of the bardic grammar which helped very largely to create the poetic reawakening of the eighteenth century, and it was this enthusiastic interest which also enabled Lewis Hopkin and Iolo Morganwg to compose *cywyddau* of a standard incomparably higher than that attained by almost any other Glamorgan bard since the early-sixteenth century. Moreover, the publication in London in 1688 of *Y Gymraeg yn ei Disgleirdeb*, a Welsh-English dictionary by Thomas Jones (1648?–1713) and, more importantly, the publication of Thomas Richards's dictionary in 1753 (below, pp. 630–633) provided the Glamorgan grammarians with an excellent opportunity of mastering a great deal of the old bardic vocabulary. The publication of Thomas Richards's dictionary helps very largely to explain Iolo Morganwg's mastery of the old literary language, a mastery clearly reflected in many of the strict-metre verses

which he sang even before he began associating with the northern antiquarians, poets, and littérateurs.[457] The most accomplished of the
early-eighteenth-century Glamorgan grammarians, as far as a mastery
of the old bardic lore is concerned, was Lewis Hopkin. It must have been
from an acquaintance with the works of the old masters, and not merely
from his study of the bardic grammar, that he acquired the pregnant
economy of expression, the unmistakable distinction of tone, the sure
sense of style and rhythmical balance which can occasionally be found in
his best work. The following short extract from the elegy which he
addressed to William Bassett of Meisgyn (Miskin) illustrates some of
these features:

> Ing i'n tir, angau'n taro,
> Awr brudd, ar oreugwyr bro;
> Arwyddion o droeon drwg,
> Fawr gwynion, i Forgannwg.
>
> Oes eisiau yn y Sesiwn
> Y gŵr mawrglod hynod hwn?
> Eisiau'i wyneb sy yno,
> A'i ddoethder a'i fwynder fo;
> Eisiau'i gyngor rhagorol,
> Deg cant a wylant o'i ôl.[458]

The grammarians also paid a great deal of attention to the free
accentual metres. Lewis Hopkin composed a *cwndid*, or Christmas carol,
on the measure called *awdl-gywydd*.[459] As verses of a similar nature occur
in the works of Edward Dafydd of Margam and some of his contemporaries, it may reasonably be assumed that free-metre poetry on old
indigenous Welsh metres had been composed in Glamorgan all through
the centuries. Nevertheless, it is obvious that the eighteenth-century
Glamorgan poets were influenced to a considerable extent by the
interesting collections of free-metre verse and carols which were published
by Ffoulke Owens (1686), Thomas Jones (1696), John Rhydderch
(1720), Dafydd Jones of Trefriw (1759), and by the various editors of
the contemporary almanacs. It was by studying the contents of these
popular anthologies that they became familiar with that distinctive type
of free-metre verse into which *cynghanedd* had been introduced and with
the complex metrical patterns of those accentual poems which were
designed pre-eminently to be sung to various English airs. An example
of this type of verse occurs in the work of Tomas Morgan of Tyle Garw
in the early years of the eighteenth century, a poem in which he sang
the praises of the ancestors of his friend, Edward Gamage of St. Athan
(Sain Tathan).[460] It is hardly surprising, therefore, that a number of the
Glamorgan grammarians composed free-metre verses containing *cynghanedd*, as some of the poems which were published in *Y Fel Gafod* and,
more especially, in *Caniadau Moesol a Duwiol* clearly testify. Edward
Evan composed a number of poems in the style of Huw Morus on both

[627]

amatory and moral or didactic themes. It was verse of this kind which, more than anything else, won for him such widespread acclaim among the Welsh inhabitants of the *Blaenau* during the nineteenth century.

Undoubtedly, it was his free-metre accentual verse which won for Dafydd Nicolas of Aberpergwm a secure place in the literary history of the county. The charming lyric entitled 'Callyn Serchus', one of the three poems attributed to him by Maria Jane Williams, contains *cynghanedd*, and the general aesthetic effect is occasionally reminiscent of that achieved by Huw Morus and his followers. But the best-known of the three poems is undoubtedly 'Y 'Deryn Pur', a poem devoid of *cynghanedd* intended to be sung on one of our most charming national airs. The rhymes contained in this splendid lyric prove conclusively that it was the work of a Glamorgan poet, who had an exceptional talent for composing words on traditional airs. Another free-metre composition attributed to him in the same source is 'Ffanni Blodau'r Ffair', a poem consisting of three verses. At least five versions of this song occur in Iolo Morganwg's manuscripts, most of which consist of eight verses.[461] After making a detailed study of three versions of it Professor G. J. Williams concluded that Iolo Morganwg was responsible for re-writing and refurbishing the song composed by Dafydd Nicolas in the first half of the eighteenth century. He wrote Welsh words for the English ones found in the original version, which began with the words 'O! Fanny blooming fair', polished the language and altered some of the expressions.[462] The three verses of 'Ffanni Blodau'r Ffair' published in *Ancient National Airs of Gwent and Morganwg* bear a much closer resemblance to the version given by Iolo Morganwg in Llanover MS. C 59, 321–3, than to any other known copy and include readings which may well be emendations made by Iolo. Nevertheless, a few obvious differences can be detected, some of which correspond to the readings that occur in other versions of this song quoted by Iolo Morganwg. A few readings, however, are found only in the version printed by Maria Jane Williams, which shares no marked peculiarities with the original version transcribed in the author's own lifetime. It is interesting that some words which occur in the original version were restored by Iolo in a few of his marginal emendations. Moreover, a version of this particular song found in *Melus Seiniau*,[463] a work by John Jenkins ('Ifor Ceri', 1770–1829), the cleric and antiquary who devoted much of his life collecting old airs and melodies, begins with the words 'O Fanny Blodau'r Ffair', not 'O! Fanny blooming fair', the opening words in Dafydd Nicolas's original, and this immediately poses the thorny problem whether Professor G. J. Williams was correct in concluding that it was Iolo Morganwg who was directly responsible for this particular change. Another interesting problem is the precise connection between Dafydd Nicolas's composition and *Fanny Blooming Fair*, which seems to have been one of the most popular English airs in the first half of the eighteenth century. That there is a connection between the Welsh lyric and the English air is indisputable, and Professor G. J. Williams ventured the opinion that Dafydd Nicolas wrote his words to the English tune. A detailed comparison of the Welsh lyric with a copy of the English song now preserved in the British Museum and published *c.* 1736 under the appropriate title of *The Ravished Lover*—with the music composed by William Boyce—reveals that the song printed by Maria Jane Williams is a somewhat simpler, but undeniably improved, version of Boyce's tune.[464]

Other lyrics, some of quite exquisite beauty, are attributed to Dafydd Nicolas in Iolo Morganwg's manuscripts. Although no copies of some of these poems, including 'Gostegiad y Gwynt'[465] and various love-verses or harvest-songs,[466] have so far been discovered in any other source, it must not be concluded that they are therefore Iolo Morganwg's work, although the latter may well have refurbished the original version in certain cases. If these poems are authentic, their author, Dafydd Nicolas of Aberpergwm, was unquestionably one of the most talented and exquisitely lyrical of all Glamorgan bards in the first half of the eighteenth century. There may well have been other Glamorgan poets living in this period who were equally adept at writing words to be sung on some of the old traditional airs. According to Maria Jane Williams, it was in Glamorgan that she had heard both the words and the tunes of many of the compositions which she included in her collection, such as 'Y 'Deryn Du Pigfelyn', 'Y Bore Glas', 'Y Fwyalchen' ('O gwrando, y beraidd fwyalchen'), 'Pan oeddwn ar ddydd yn cydrodio', 'Mab Addfwyn', and 'Holl Brydyddion gloywon glân'. Only two Glamorgan figures are explicitly mentioned by her, however, to wit, Dafydd Nicolas and the harpist who, it was said, had composed 'Y Ferch o'r Scer' about 'eighty or ninety years ago'. The latter seems to have been another of the popular romantic figures of Glamorgan, although little is known about him. 'He was engaged in his youth', according to M. J. Williams, 'to a young woman, but subsequently, in consequence of his having lost his sight, she refused to fulfil her promise to marry him, and he vented his feelings of disappointment and grief in this composition, which is of a very pathetic character.'[467] A number of versions of it exist, including some by Iolo Morganwg. The two verses of the song printed by Maria Jane Williams (pp. 42–3) follow one or other of Iolo Morganwg's versions at all significant points of difference, and this strongly suggests that his transcripts were her source. This is further confirmed by a note written by Taliesin ab Iolo.[468] The five verses of the song which Iolo transcribed on page 214 of Llanover MS. C 12 are attributed by him to 'Thomas Evan', the harpist from Newton Nottage in Glamorgan. The composition in the free metres of amatory verses of this nature seems to have been one of the distinctive features of the literary history of Glamorgan in the eighteenth century.

vii.

THE EIGHTEENTH-CENTURY LEXICOGRAPHERS AND ANTIQUARIANS:

THOMAS RICHARDS (1710–90)

One of the essential requirements of the poetic revival was a substantial dictionary which would enable those who aspired to compose in the traditional strict metres to regain the vocabulary of the old Welsh bards. An excellent Welsh–Latin and Latin–Welsh dictionary had been published in 1632 by Dr. John Davies (c. 1567–1644), one of the most distinguished of the Welsh Renaissance scholars. But unfortunately it was of little use to those eighteenth-century bards and littérateurs who had no knowledge of Latin. The provision of a substantial Welsh–English dictionary was therefore a prime necessity, and it was a clergyman, Thomas Richards of Llangrallo (Coychurch), who published such a dictionary in 1753. He was no doubt the greatest Welsh scholar to arise in Glamorgan in the first half of the eighteenth century. It is not known where he was born or under what circumstances he received his early education. His name was included by Iolo Morganwg in a list of the 'Self educated persons in Glamorgan Vale',[469] but what basis he had for doing so it is impossible to tell. According to the records of the diocese of St. David's, Richards was ordained a deacon on September 2, 1733 and a priest on September 22, 1734. He became curate of Llanismel (or St. Ishmael) and Llan-saint in Carmarthenshire, and he probably remained there until 1738. His history for the next few years is obscure, but in August 1742 he was licensed as 'perpetual curate' of Llangrallo and Llanbedr-ar-fynydd (Peterston-super-montem) in Glamorgan. Years later, in 1777, he became vicar of Eglwysilan, but he never seems to have resided in that parish, being quite content to remain at Coychurch until his death in 1790.

Thomas Richards began his career as a man of letters in 1746, when he published *Creulonderau ac Herlidigaethau Eglwys Rufain*, a translation of an English work by Philip Morant. The poem which Lewis Hopkin composed in praise of this work ('Cywydd Moliant i'r Gorchwyl hwn') shows that Richards had already become acquainted with some of the local grammarians. Richards then began to prepare a Welsh translation of Dr. John Davies's celebrated grammar (1621) and equally-famous Welsh–Latin lexicon (1632), adding to them words which he had seen in Edward Lhuyd's *Archaeologia Britannica* (1707), in William Wotton's work on the Welsh laws, which was published in 1730 by his son-in-law, under the editorship of Moses Williams, as *Cyfreithjeu Hywel Dda ac eraill, seu Leges Wallicae*, and in many old vocabularies. He included also the many words which he had heard in the local Glamorgan dialects or which he had discovered in old manuscripts and printed sources. This important work, entitled *Antiquae Linguae Britannicae Thesaurus: being a British, or Welsh–English Dictionary*, was published in Bristol in 1753, and a second edition appeared in 1759. The English introduction which Richards wrote to this work and the epistolary greeting in Welsh both reveal that he was well aware of the labours of older lexicographers, such as William Salesbury, Henry Salesbury, and 'Sir' Thomas Wiliems. He also had some knowledge of the achievements of the early grammarians, although, surprisingly, he did not mention Gruffydd Robert, and he was undoubtedly familiar with Edward Lhuyd's scholarly work, for he quoted Irish, Breton, and Cornish words which he had seen in *Archaeologia Britannica*. He referred also to the theory which became increasingly popular from the seventeenth century onwards that Welsh was one of the world's oldest languages, which had miraculously kept its pristine purity, and he was obviously familiar with some of the ideas of Paul Pezron (1639–1706).[470] Nor did Richards overlook old Welsh manuscripts: 'I have moreover', he wrote in the introduction, 'in order to render this Performance more compleat, made it my Business to peruse whatever *Welsh* Manuscripts I could come at; and it has been my good Fortune to meet with large Collections of the Works of the Poets, and some antient Manuscripts in Prose'. But unfortunately these manuscripts were not explicitly identified by Richards, who in his will left all his books and manuscripts to Edward Thomas, the squire of Tre-groes in the parish of Coychurch.[471] Their subsequent history is obscure, although Iolo Morganwg cited some of the manuscripts that had formerly been in Richards's possession as the source of many of his forgeries, such as the 'Aberpergwm Brut'[472] and some of the *cywyddau* which he claimed had been written by Dafydd ap Gwilym.[473] Nor is it easy to determine where Thomas Richards managed to have access to the important manuscript collections to which he referred. Although he undoubtedly corresponded with Richard Morris[474] and was greatly assisted by the Morris brothers when he was preparing his dictionary for publication, there is no evidence to suggest he ever saw the manuscripts in their possession or that he visited Hengwrt or any other mansions where substantial manuscript collections were still housed. And the magnificent collection which Thomas Wilkins had so assiduously assembled had been dispersed by this time. But he probably saw some, at least, of the manuscripts of John Bradford and the other contemporary grammarians, and he must have known of the important copies transcribed by Tomas ab Ieuan of Tre'r-bryn in the very parish where he himself served as a perpetual curate. He may also have made some use of the collection of the Powel family at Llanharan.

The publication of Thomas Richards's work in 1753 was an event of great importance, although Goronwy Owen, *more suo*, and some other northern antiquarians were rather critical of his achievement.[475] Their criticism, however, was very ill-informed. At long last those Welsh literati who had no knowledge of Latin were presented with an excellent opportunity of studying the contents of Dr. John Davies's important work. By using Richards's dictionary they were able to understand the difficult and occasionally obsolete words that occurred in the compositions of those bards who were acknowledged masters of the *cywydd* measure. It was, therefore, a work of considerable significance in the poetic revival and frequently used by the bards when they composed their *awdlau* and *cywyddau*. Nor should it be forgotten that Thomas Richards was one of the scholars who helped to arouse the interest of Iolo Morganwg and who urged him to collect Welsh words and expressions from old manuscripts and printed books, a task which remained one of his main interests throughout his long life.

Thomas Richards continued to add diligently to his lexical collections even after the publication of his dictionary, and Iolo Morganwg claimed that he had seen them.[476] Richards probably intended to publish a third edition of his work, and on March 2, 1789, about a year before his death, William Owen [-Pughe] published his 'Proposals for Printing by Subscription, . . . a Welsh and English Dictionary',[477] and he stated that the main purpose of the London publishers, 'E. and T. Williams', was to prepare another edition of Richards's dictionary. Richards must have expended a great deal of time and energy on his researches, for immediately after the second edition of his work appeared in 1759 he began compiling material for an English–Welsh dictionary. 'The Rev. Thomas Richards of Coychurch', wrote Richard Morris in a letter to his brother, Lewis, on November 24, 1759, 'is compiling an English–Welsh Dictionary: Gambold's MS. would be of infinite service to him, but there is no such thing as procuring it for him.'[478] It appears, therefore, that Thomas Richards had written to Richard Morris seeking help and encouragement and, possibly, expressing a desire to have the opportunity of studying Gambold's dictionary. As early as 1707 William Gambold (1672–1728), of Puncheston, Pembrokeshire, was planning an English–Welsh dictionary in which he intended to give not only the Welsh equivalents of the English words but also translations of English idioms and expressions. This work was completed in 1722, but, apart from *A Grammar of the Welsh Language*, which appeared at Carmarthen in 1727, the fruits of his labour were never published, obviously for lack of financial backing. He stipulated in his will that his son, John Gambold, could sell the manuscript of his work and divide the proceeds among his brothers.[479] References occur in the correspondence of the Morris brothers to the efforts made to procure the manuscript for Thomas Richards and to the assistance which the latter received in this matter from John Richards, LL.D., the rector of Coety.[480] John Richards (d. 1769), 'a poor Welshman, but eat up with zeal for ye language',[481] was also interested in collecting material for an English–Welsh dictionary obviously with a view to amplifying the work which had already been published by Thomas Richards.[482] The final outcome of these negotiations is not clear, but there is nothing to suggest that one of the Glamorgan lexicographers managed to acquire Gambold's valuable manuscript. As well as collaborating with his neighbour, John Richards of Coety, Thomas Richards also revised and corrected the English–Welsh dictionary of William Evans (*fl.* 1768–76), published in Carmarthen in 1771, for it is clearly stated on the title-page of the second edition of 1812 that it had been 'Improved by the late Rev. Mr. Richards, of Coychurch'. This was a task which he probably undertook in the last few years of his life. Moreover, according to a notice which occurs in Mathew Williams's *Almanac* for 1790, it was proposed to publish another edition of Thomas Richards's Welsh–English dictionary 'with considerable Additions'. But the Glamorgan lexicographer died on March 20, 1790,[483] and so the plan never materialized.

JOHN WALTERS (1721–97)

The zeal and energy so clearly evident in Thomas Richards's career were undoubtedly communicated to another Glamorgan cleric, John Walters of Llandochau, a devoted scholar who finally managed to acquire William Gambold's unpublished manuscript. Born on August 22, 1721, John Walters was the son of a timber-merchant of the same name from Llanedi, Carmarthenshire.[484] Little is known of his early education—his name is also included in Iolo's list of 'Self educated persons in Glamorgan Vale'—but he went to Basaleg, Monmouthshire, as a schoolmaster. Later, troubled by his deficiencies as a classical scholar, he went to 'Mr. Durell then Master of Cowbridge School to improve himself in Greek & Latin'. He then kept a school at Margam, where he seems to have won the support of the Mansel Talbot family. In 1750 he was ordained a priest and became curate of Baglan. During this period he wrote 'The History of the noble Family of the Mansels', probably his first literary work. In 1754 he was appointed perpetual curate of Llanfihangel Ynys Afan, and in 1759 he became rector of Llandough, near Cowbridge, and vicar of the neighbouring parish of St. Hilary. He may also have discharged some clerical duties in the adjacent parish of Llan-fair (St. Mary Church). In 1795, two years before his death, he was granted a prebend in Llandaff cathedral.

It was probably John Walters who eventually persuaded Rhys Thomas (1720?–90) of Llandovery, Carmarthenshire, one of the most important Welsh printers of the eighteenth century,[485] to set up at Cowbridge towards the end of 1769 or the beginning of 1770 the first printing-press in Glamorgan.[486] The connection between the two men continued without interruption for about twenty years. John Walters's fame as a scholar rests pre-eminently on his large and extremely important English–Welsh dictionary, but the motives which impelled him to prepare this work can only be adequately understood when it is studied in conjunction with the very interesting treatise which Walters published in 1771 under the title *A Dissertation on the Welsh Language, Pointing out it's Antiquity, Copiousness, Grammatical Perfection, with Remarks on it's Poetry*. This work, moreover, provides a fairly clear idea of the author's scholarly attainments and of the literary material at his disposal. It reflects also his burning love for his native tongue:

> I shall not hesitate to profess to the world that I prefer *this* to any of the languages ancient or modern, that I have any acquaintance with . . . for which my affection encreases every hour! Nor would I have the reader by any means imagine, that this preference springs from blind prepossession, or undiscerning partiality; no, but from the best and most impartial judgment, that I have been able to form of the comparative merit of this language, when I had spent many of the best years of my life in the investigation and study of it.

He emphasized that a thorough knowledge of the Welsh language was an indispensable prerequisite for any one who took a serious interest in the history of Britain, and he poured his scorn on those who presumed to deal with the 'Antiquities of Britain without an acquaintance with, or a competent skill in the *Ancient British* Language'. Walters was obviously aware of the works of some of the older authorities who had discussed the different elements contained in various place-names in both Britain and Gaul, such as Camden or Samuel Bochart. He referred also to the view held by Dr. John Davies of Mallwyd that Welsh can be regarded as one of the primitive eastern mother-tongues, and to some of the linguistic discoveries of Edward Lhuyd, although, like most members of the famous Morris circle, he does not appear to have grasped their true significance. He expressed his unstinted admiration of Paul Pezron, who had proved 'by his amazing skill in languages and history, that this *common origin* of the European tongues, was no other than the *ancient Celtic*'. Nor had Bullet's *Mémoires sur la langue celtique* (1754–60) escaped his attention, a work which went even further than that of Pezron by claiming that Celtic was 'a dialect of the original language communicated by the Creator to the first Parents of mankind'. The fact that John Walters was thus greatly influenced by many of the eccentric linguistic and ethnographic ideas that were so popular in his day should not blind us to the true significance of his work. In the second part of this interesting treatise he discussed the unlimited 'copiousness' of the Welsh language. The fact that English and most of the modern European languages were forced to borrow many of their scientific and technical terms from Greek was, in his view, 'a proof of their native poverty and domestic scantiness'. The Welsh language, on the other hand, rivalled 'the celebrated *Greek* itself in it's aptitude to form the most beautiful *derivatives*; as well as in the elegance, facility and expressiveness of an infinite variety of *compounds*'. The truth of all this would immediately be evident to any one who took the pains to consult the English–Welsh dictionary which was then being published 'in *Quarto* by subscription'.

It is on this dictionary that John Walters's renown undoubtedly rests. The work was based on William Gambold's unpublished manuscript, which Walters had somehow managed to acquire sometime, possibly, after the death of Dr. John Richards of Coety in the spring of 1769.[487] Like Gambold and the Renaissance scholars before him, John Walters wished to compile a dictionary which would fulfil the needs of those who were actively engaged in translating English works into Welsh and who earnestly desired to see the vernacular become a fitting medium for all branches of learning.[488] The work was printed at the Cowbridge press, the first part appearing on April 5, 1770.[489] It was warmly received by many of the Welsh literati; and some prominent figures in contemporary England, including Dr. Samuel Johnson, William Seward, Mrs. Thrale, and Dr. Charles Burney, are named among the subscribers. From 1770 to 1776 the numbers appeared fairly regularly, but then the difficulties began to increase and part xiv was not issued until 1783. Confronted with a number of serious financial problems, John Walters, who had bought the press in 1777, had to exercise infinite patience and, ultimately, to suffer bitter disappointment. The remainder of the dictionary did not appear until 1794, and then not from Cowbridge but from London, Walters having secured the altruistic assistance of Owen Jones ('Owain Myfyr', 1741–1814) to bring this about.[490] Walters referred explicitly to William Gambold's unpublished manuscript in the introduction to his dictionary, after the last number had been printed in 1794: 'But it may be say'd, and that with the strictest adherence to truth, that the above-mentioned Manuscript, were it put in print and given to the Public, would by no means supersede the necessity of the present Undertaking. Whosoever hesitates to believe, must examine and compare.' It is difficult to dissent from this view, for although Walters was clearly indebted to Gambold, the greater part of his work was unquestionably the fruit of his own meticulous labour. He often tacitly refuted various explanations suggested by Gambold, he added his own words to elucidate the precise meaning of a particular English word or phrase, and he frequently translated English idioms for which one searches in vain in Gambold's manuscript. Moreover, he coined a very large number of words which have become established as an indispensable part of the Welsh vocabulary; e.g. *adloniant, adnoddau, amaethyddiaeth, amhendant, amlinell, blodeuglwm, beirniadaeth* 'criticism', *braslun, ansefydlogrwydd, anwelladwy, aralleirio, arfbais, argraffnod, briwlaw, brwdfrydog, bytholwyrdd, calediad, canmoliaethus.*[491] They effectively illustrate the inherent 'copiousness' of the language to which he referred in his *Dissertation*. The dictionary is undeniably one of the outstanding landmarks in the history of Welsh lexical scholarship in the eighteenth century.

[635]

Morgan Llywelyn (d. 1777–8)

There are many references in Iolo Morganwg's writings to the gifted antiquaries with whom he became acquainted, such as the Rev. Thomas Bassett of Glanelái, near Llantrisant, rector of the parish of Eglwys Brewys, Watcyn Giles of Llan-gan, Esaia Powel of St. Bride's Minor (Llansanffraid-ar-Ogwr), William Cobb of Cardiff, or Tomas Hopcyn of Llangrallo.[492] Many of these, according to Iolo, were authorities on the literary history of the region and they all assiduously collected old manuscripts and records from which, he frequently claimed, he had taken much of the material contained in his own writings. Unfortunately, however, most of these antiquaries are very obscure figures, and no manuscript has yet been discovered which can confidently be connected with any one of them. But there are two notable exceptions, both of whom exercised a great influence on Iolo Morganwg in his early formative years.

The first of these was Morgan Llywelyn (d. 1777–8) from Neath, whom Iolo included in his 'Early Welsh Poetical Acquaintance[s]'. Indeed, he claimed that Morgan Llywelyn was a descendant of Tomas Llywelyn of Rhigos and a poet of quite exceptional ability.[493] Iolo even attributed some verses to him, although these are astonishingly few in number in view of the great praise which he lavished on Morgan Llywelyn as 'one of the most ingenious Welsh Bards of his age'.[494] Iolo Morganwg spent a great deal of time in Morgan Llywelyn's company *c.* 1770, and he repeatedly claimed to have seen in the latter's manuscripts an excellent collection of Dafydd ap Gwilym's poems, including some which were included in the 'Appendix' to *Barddoniaeth Dafydd ab Gwilym* (1789) but which are now known to be spurious,[495] details of Dafydd ap Gwilym's history compiled by Morgan Llywelyn himself, some letters written by Siôn Mowddwy and Meurug Dafydd and, most important of all, a number of valuable genealogical tracts and Welsh treatises dealing with the Norman conquest of Glamorgan and with the early history of Nonconformity in the Uplands. It has been proved that a number of these works were the product of Iolo Morganwg's pen. To this category belong some of the *cywyddau* attributed to Dafydd ap Gwilym, the details which Morgan Llywelyn had assiduously compiled about that poet's life, and the letter attributed to Meurug Dafydd. It would be wrong to conclude, however, that all the other documents which Iolo claimed he had seen in Morgan Llywelyn's possession were also a figment of his imagination, for the antiquary from Neath had a collection of some of the works of the older bards and manuscript-books which dealt with some aspects of the history of Glamorgan. He was also a quite well-informed scholar who knew much, as Iolo Morganwg claimed, about the early history of Nonconformity in the Uplands.

A Morgan Llywelyn is known to have been a schoolmaster in Neath in 1770 and to have lived in the 'High Street' there. He can confidently be identified from various details in his will, which was proved on March 9, 1778, as the antiquary-poet with whom Iolo Morganwg was intimately acquainted. He is described therein as 'Morgan Llewellyn late of Blaengwrach now of Neath'.[496] Although Iolo Morganwg claimed that all Morgan Llywelyn's manuscripts had completely vanished by the beginning of the nineteenth century,[497] at least two of them are still extant, one being preserved in the library of Jesus College, Oxford, the other in Cardiff Central Library.

The first of these, Jesus College MS. 13, contains a substantial collection of the work of Dafydd Benwyn. Apparently, the manuscript, formerly in the possession of Thomas Wilkins, had been acquired by Morgan Llywelyn from a certain 'John Williams, Clyn y Regos'.[498] Some of the comments written by Morgan Llywelyn in this manuscript suggest that he gave it his most detailed attention while it was in his possession. This is further supported by the verses in the *englyn* measure elsewhere in the manuscript, which were probably composed by Morgan Llywelyn himself, and lend some support to Iolo Morganwg's claim that he was a fairly talented poet. Another interesting feature of this manuscript is that two prominent Nonconformists, Edward Evan and James John of Aberdare, wrote their names on some of its pages.[499] This supports Iolo Morganwg's claim that Morgan Llywelyn was intimately associated with some of the leading contemporary Nonconformists, and it reveals, moreover, that he had some connection with one of the local grammarians.

The second work, Cardiff MS. 4. 33, was transcribed by Morgan Llywelyn himself. It contains an interesting collection of the genealogies of many of the old families, together with an account of the Norman conquest of Morgannwg and of the bitter dissension between Iestyn ap Gwrgant and Rhys ap Tewdwr. This account is substantially similar to that given by Rice Merrick and, apart from the translation which was made of Sir Edward Stradling's 'The Winning', it appears to be the earliest extant Welsh copy of the saga. Probably, one of the sources used by Morgan Llywelyn was the manuscript which Sir Joseph Bradney published under the title *Llyfr Baglan* (1910), a manuscript once in the possession of the Llewellyn family at Baglan in the nineteenth century and, before that, in the collection of Thomas Wilkins. It was transferred in 1905 to Cardiff Central Library. Nor had the substantial collection transcribed by Tomas ab Ieuan of Tre'r-bryn escaped his attention, for in one place he quoted what he had seen 'In Codice manuscripto Tho. Bevan'.[500]

These manuscripts also throw some light on Morgan Llywelyn's personal history. As we have already seen, he resided at Neath when he died some time in 1777 or 1778, but in the list of subscribers to Thomas Richards's dictionary of 1753 he is described as 'Morgan Lewelyn, *of* Blaen-gwrâch, *Gent*'. Blaen-gwrach is situated in the ancient parish of Glyncorrwg, and it was in Blaen-cleirch in that parish that he lived when he transcribed Cardiff MS. 4. 33.[501] He recorded the family pedigree on one of the manuscript's pages.[502] He claimed to be able to trace his descent to Rhicert ab Einion ap Collwyn, and he states that one of his ancestors, Morgan ap Llywelyn, had bought Blaen-gwrach,—probably towards the beginning of the seventeenth century. Moreover, a Llywelyn Morgan is mentioned in the list of founders of the Presbyterian 'Old Meeting-house' at Blaen-gwrach in 1704,[503] and as one of the elders there in the year 1734. His son, Morgan Llywelyn, also named as one of the members, was probably the antiquary with whom Iolo Morganwg later became acquainted in Neath.[504] It is obvious, therefore, why Morgan Llywelyn expressly stipulated in his will that he wished to be buried 'in the south east end of the Meeting yard', that is, in Blaen-gwrach.

There is, therefore, a firm historical basis for many of the claims made by Iolo Morganwg concerning this figure. He is undoubtedly an interesting example of a cultured, literary-minded Nonconformist, the type that seems to have flourished in many parts of the Uplands during this period. He seems to have studied the works of many of the theologians and prominent rationalists of the period, and he was obviously passionately interested in the genealogies of the Glamorgan gentry, in the early history of the region and in the works composed by the local poets and littérateurs. He may have had some knowledge of the ancient bardic traditions, and he may well have communicated a great deal of his learning to the comparatively young and manifestly enthusiastic Iolo Morganwg.

Thomas Truman (*fl. c.* 1750–80)

Another antiquary whom Iolo Morganwg regarded as an authority on the history of Glamorgan was Thomas Truman. His pedigree occurs in Cardiff MS. 3. 1,[505] probably in his own autograph. He came from an English family which originally resided in Northampton. The first member of the family to come to Glamorgan did so as an officer in Cromwell's army, and he appears to have settled at Llantrisant. Thomas Truman, the eighteenth-century antiquary, married the heiress of Panty-lliwydd, and it was there that he and his descendants lived for many years. His name is mentioned in the local parish records of Llansanwyr towards the middle of the eighteenth century as 'Overseer of the Poor', and his will was proved at Llandaff in May 1786.

He obviously had a penchant for historical and genealogical research, for he was the owner of Llanover MS. E 3, or 'Llyfr Du Pantylliwydd', a manuscript in the autograph of Anthony Powel which consisted of a collection of genealogies and other data taken from the works of the old heraldic bards. Furthermore, Cardiff MS. 3. 1, parts of which, as we have already seen, are in his autograph, also consists mainly of genealogies, and it is quite possible that this material was transcribed from two manuscripts which are now deposited in the National Library of Wales, Aberystwyth.[506] But many details, including some which were connected with the history of his own family, were added by Thomas Truman himself, probably about 1770-1.[507] Nor were these the only manuscripts in his possession, for John Dorney Harding, the author of a history of the castles of Glamorgan and Monmouthshire, acknowledged the fact that he had been 'favoured by Mr. Truman, of Bryntêg, near Bridgend, with the perusal of some valuable MS. compilations made by that gentleman's grandfather; from one of which, a kind of Historical Account, that appears to have been carefully collected from local tradition, and personal knowledge, he has made some quotations'.[508] This suggests that Thomas Truman, in addition to collecting and transcribing various genealogical tracts, diligently recorded those ancient traditions which helped to elucidate the early history of Glamorgan. It is hardly surprising, therefore, that Iolo Morganwg, who described him as a learned antiquary and skilful genealogist,[509] referred to him frequently in his writings whenever he dealt with the history and antiquities of the Vale,[510] or discussed the information which could be gathered from parish registers about the history of old families of the region. It is extremely difficult to determine precisely how much attention Thomas Truman paid to the vernacular literature, but his name occurs in the list of subscribers to the first edition of Thomas Richards's dictionary. According to David Jones (1834-90), Wallington, Thomas Truman was a 'stonecutter, and original *lapidary* verses of his may be found in various churchyards'.[511] It is quite possible, therefore, that it was while pursuing his trade as a monumental mason that Iolo Morganwg first became acquainted with Truman. As masons, both of them had a splendid opportunity to collect the data recorded on monumental inscriptions and to search the parish registers of the Vale. Iolo Morganwg frequently referred to Truman as his 'dear friend',[512] and he probably borrowed 'Llyfr Du Pantylliwydd' from him *c.* 1770, a manuscript which is now preserved in the Llanover collection. Many of Iolo's forgeries were attributed by him to manuscripts which he claimed he had seen in Thomas Truman's possession.[513] One of the most interesting documents taken, he insisted, from this source is the treatise on the Norman conquest of Glamorgan which was attributed to Sir Edward Mansel (d. 1595).

The eighteenth century, therefore, was a period of intense activity in the literary history of Glamorgan, for there arose a small but talented circle of poets; a few devoted and diligent lexicographers; and a number of enlightened antiquarians. To all of them Iolo Morganwg was deeply indebted: it was the local grammarians who first instructed him in the intricate art of the strict-metre bards; the lexicographers who aroused his interest in dialectology, which remained one of the ruling passions of his long life; and the antiquaries who instilled in him that deep and abiding love for his native county which usually coloured, or even at times substantially distorted, many of his pronouncements on the history and literature of Glamorgan. Between them they helped to create the most remarkable figure in the whole history of Welsh literature.

[639]

NOTES

CHAPTER I

[1] W. G. Hoskins, 'Harvest fluctuations and English economic history, 1480–1619', *Agric.HR.*, XII (1964), 28–46; idem, 'Harvest fluctuations and English economic history, 1620–1759', ibid., XVI (1968), 15–31.

[2] Leland, *Itin. Wales*, pp. 16, 19, 26.

[3] *Merrick's Glam. Antiqs.*, pp. 9–11; cf. also extracts from Peniarth MS. 120, ff. 462–96, written by Merrick and transcribed in 'Parochialia', *Arch. Camb.*, Supplement, 1911, pp. 116–17.

[4] William Camden, *Britannia*. Ed. Edmund Gibson (London, 1695), p. 610. Cf. John Speed, *The Theatre of the Empire of Great Britaine . . .* (London, 1627). See also G. J. Williams, *Iolo Morganwg* (Caerdydd, 1956), pp. 1–79, and *Ante*, III, 11–12; 453–4; for the comments of modern geographers, E. G. Bowen (ed.), *Wales* (London, 1957), pp. 402–29, and F. V. Emery, 'West Glamorgan farming, c. 1580–1620', *NLWJ.*, IX (1956), 392–400, esp. pp. 393–4; and *NLWJ.*, X (1957), 17–32. For early maps of Glamorgan, see F. J. North, 'Glamorgan on maps—and maps of Glamorgan', *Glam. Hist.*, II (1965), 13–29.

[5] *Merrick's Glam. Antiqs.*, pp. 11–2; *Val. Eccl.*, IV, 348–9; Camden, *Britannia*, p. 610; Speed, *Great Britaine*, p. 105; Emery, *NLWJ.*, X, 17–32; Megan Thomas, 'Glamorgan, 1540–1640: Aspects of Social and Economic History' (M.A. Thesis, University of Wales, 1973), pp. 72–4.

[6] Speed, *Great Britaine*, p. 105; R. Flenley (ed.), *Calendar of the Register of the Council in the Marches of Wales, 1569–91* (Cymmr. Record Ser., London, 1916), pp. 98, 108–9, 123, 155; NLW, Llandaff P.R., 1603; Emery, *CAgH*, IV, 134; ibid., IV, 187, quoting *The Book of Husbandry by Master Fitzherbert*; Leland, *Itin. Wales*, p. 16; William Harrison, *The Description of England*. Ed. G. Edelen (Ithaca, N.Y., 1968), p. 311.

[7] Leland and Churchyard quot. in D. J. Davies, *The Economic History of South Wales prior to 1800* (Cardiff, 1933), p. 59; *A Relation . . . of the Island of England . . . about the year 1500*. Transl. by C. A. Sneyd (Camden Soc., 1847), p. 18; Leland, *Itin. Wales*, pp. 18, 22; John Major in C. H. Williams, *English Historical Documents, 1485–1558* (London, 1967), pp. 203–4; *Merrick's Glam. Antiqs.*, p. 11 and *Arch. Camb.*, Suppl., 1911, pp. 116–17; B. E. Howells, 'Pembrokeshire farming, c. 1580–1620', *NLWJ.*, IX (1956), 324–6.

[8] Leland, *Itin. Wales*, pp. 16, 20; D. R. Phillips, *The History of the Vale of Neath* (Swansea, 1928), p. 231; Survey of Tir Iarll, Clark, *Cartae*, VI, 2113–15; H. J. Randall, *The Vale of Glamorgan* (Newport, 1961), p. 36; *Merrick's Glam. Antiqs.*, p. 12; Button quot. in D. G. John, 'Contributions to the Economic History of South Wales' (D.Sc. Thesis, Univ. of Wales, 1930), I, ch. vi, p. 8; E. D. Lewis, *The Rhondda Valleys* (London, 1959), p. 22.

[9] *Val. Eccl.*, IV, 348–55, esp. 348, 349, 350, 353; Leland, *Itin. Wales*, pp. 16–32; *Merrick's Glam. Antiqs.*, p. 10; the so-called quotation from Edward Mansel may be found in *Cardiff Records*, IV, 22, D. J. Davies, *Econ. Hist. S. Wales*, p. 57, and Emery, *CAgH*, IV, 134, but see *TLlM.*, pp. 200–3 for Iolo's authorship. Emery, *NLWJ.*, X, 17–32.

[10] F. G. Payne, *Yr Aradr Gymreig*, (Caerdydd, 1954), pp. 177–8, 183; 'David Jones of Wallington's notes on Glamorgan Wills', Cardiff City Library MS. 2. 1307, I, 135–9, 207–12, II, 23–32; Phillips, *Vale of Neath*, pp. 210–11, cf. also for John Llewelyn Williams, Clark, *Limbus*, p. 105; David M. Cole, 'The Mansells of Oxwich and Margam' (M.A. Thesis, Univ. of Birmingham, 1966), pp. 180–1.

[11] Emery, *NLWJ.*, X, 18–25, where a wealth of detail is supplied. For the value of rabbits, H. J. Randall and William Rees, 'The Storie of the Lower Borowes of Merthyr Mawr', *S. Wales and Mon. R.S.*, I (1932), 73, 155.

[12] For the importance of open fields in Glamorgan, see Margaret Davies, 'Rhosili open fields and related South Wales field

patterns', *Agric.HR.*, IV (1956), and 'Field patterns in the Vale of Glamorgan', *Trans Cardiff Nat. Soc.*, LXXXIV (1954–5). For the villages, see Randall, *Vale*, ch. iii; Williams, *Iolo Morganwg*, p. 25.

[13] Randall, *Vale*, pp. 31–2, 47; Randall and Rees, *S. Wales and Mon. R.S.*, I, 51, 119, 140–2; Leland, *Itin. Wales*, pp. 29–30; Merrick, *Arch. Camb.*, Suppl. 1911, p. 124; L. S. Higgins, 'The parish of Newton Nottage in the seventeenth century', *Morgannwg*, VII (1963), 52, 55; J. D. Davies, *Historical Notices . . . of West Gower*, Part II (Swansea, 1879), pp. 48, 53; Clark, *Cartae*, VI, 2172ff., 2209.

[14] Eric Kerridge, *Agrarian Problems in the Sixteenth Century and After* (London, 1969), p. 31, quot. John Norden, *The Surveior's Dialogue* (1618), p. 27. An excellent example of a court book, that for the manor of Ewenni from 1634–69, survives in the Ewenni Collection of MSS., GRO, D/DE 1.

[15] Rice Lewis's 'Breviat' is kept at NLW, and is now Bute MS., Box 99D. It has been transcribed with notes by William Rees in *S. Wales and Mon. R.S.*, III (1954), 94–145. Among many surveys in print are those in Clark, *Cartae*, VI, 2113, 2156, 2177, 2200, 2205; and C. Baker and G. G. Francis (eds.), *Surveys of Gower and Kilvey*, *Arch. Camb.* Suppls., 1861, 1864, and 1870. A number of surveys will be found in NLW, Bute MSS., 83g, 86c, 93E2, 99c. Others will be found in CCL, MSS. BRA, 247; 34.34; 35.34, Bushby MS. I, 7; ibid., III, 1 and 2. Cf. also GRO, Fonmon Collection D/DF/M 11–15, M 95–107, M 270–86; E 26–35; GRO, Carne MSS., M 41–3; GRO, Ewenni MSS., D/DE 523/1–7. For a useful study based on seventeenth-century surveys, Higgins, 'Newton Nottage', *Morgannwg*, VII, 48–73.

[16] Rice Lewis, *S. Wales and Mon. R.S.*, III, *passim*, and esp. p. 108. For the main grants to Herbert, *CPR*, *1547–8*, pp. 193–4, 333; ibid., *1548–9*, p. 368; ibid., *1549–51*, p. 416; ibid., *1550–3*, pp. 31–2, 122, 128; cf. *Cardiff Records*, I, 457ff.; Gareth E. Jones, 'The Glamorgan Gentry, 1536–1603' (M.A. Thesis, Univ. of Wales, 1963), p. 67. For Herbert's rents, NLW, Bute MSS., 2, 4, 8–31. See also Tresham Lever, *The Herberts of Wilton* (London, 1967), chap. i.

[17] Rice Lewis, *S. Wales and Mon. R.S.*, III, *passim*; Randall and Rees, ibid., I, introd.; R. A. Griffiths, 'The rise of the Stradlings of St. Donat's', *Morgannwg*, VII (1963), 15–47; Glanmor Williams, 'Sir Rice Mansel of Oxwich and Margam', ibid., VI (1962), 33–51.

[18] T. I. Jeffreys-Jones, 'The Enclosure Movement in South Wales during the Tudor and Early Stuart Periods' (M.A. Thesis, Univ. of Wales, 1936), chap. 12; Lewis, *S. Wales and Mon. R.S.*, III, 102; NLW, Bute MS., 99/C; GRO, Carne MSS., D/DC/M 41–3; Harrison quot. J. T. Cliffe, *The Yorkshire Gentry: from the Reformation to the Civil War* (London, 1969), p. 49; Cole, 'Mansells', chap. iv.

[19] Jeffreys-Jones, 'Enclosures', p. 199; GRO, Carne MS., D/DC/M 41–3; NLW, Bute MS., 99/C; T. J. Hopkins, 'The village and parish of Pendoylan', *History on My Doorstep*. Ed. S. Williams (Cowbridge, 1959), pp. 77–86; Higgins, *Morgannwg*, VII, 52; Cole, 'Mansells', p. 169; NLW, Bute MS. 99/C.

[20] *HMC. De L'Isle and Dudley MSS.*, IV, 315–6; Cole, 'Mansells', pp. 169–73; Clark, *Cartae*, VI, 2187; ibid., VI, 2157; Baker and Francis, *Gower Surveys*, pp. 169, 179; Clark, *Cartae*, VI, 2155–6; Megan Thomas, 'Glamorgan', p. 146.

[21] PRO, E112/149; cf. T. I. Jeffreys-Jones, *Exchequer Proceedings concerning Wales in Tempore James I* (Cardiff, 1955), p. 209; D. M. Cole, 'Mansells', p. 169.

[22] Kerridge, *Agrarian Problems*, pp. 76–7, 163, quot. Edward Coke, *The Compleate Copyholder* (1641). For the survival of copyhold, see B. Ll. James, 'Marcross, Monknash, and Wick', *Saints and Sailing Ships*. Ed. S. Williams, (Cowbridge, 1962), p. 60; D. J. Francis, 'Llanharry: a Border Vale mining village', *Glam. Hist.*, VI (1969), 165; and J. B. Davies, 'The parish of Pentyrch', ibid., I (1963), 79.

[23] For typical leases, see Clark, *Cartae*, V, 1803–4, 1814–15, 1824–5, 1844, 1877, 1911, 1912, 1914, 1929–30, 1960–1, 2090–1, 2092; cf. *Penrice and Margam MSS.*, *passim*. George Owen, *The Description of Pembrokeshire* (Cymmr. Record Ser., 1892–7), I, 190.

[24] NLW Bute MS. 99/c; Megan Thomas, 'Glamorgan', p. 178.

[25] *Stradling Correspondence*, p. 112. For

Pembrokeshire, see Howells, *NLWJ.*, IX (1956); Megan Thomas, 'Glamorgan', p. 228.

[26] Higgins, *Morgannwg*, VII, 53; Jeffreys-Jones, 'Enclosures', pp. 274–80.

[27] For climate, see Emery, *CAgH.*, IV, 114; *New Cambridge Modern History*, IV, 72ff.; Hoskins, *Agric.HR.*, XII, 28–46; ibid., XVI, 15–31. E. H. Phelps Brown and S. V. Hopkins, 'Seven centuries of the prices of consumables . . . ' in E. M. Carus-Wilson (ed.), *Essays in Economic History*, II (1962), 179–96; Peter Laslett, *The World We Have Lost* (London, 1965), chap. 5; F. J. Fisher, 'Influenza and inflation in Tudor England', *Econ.HR*, ii, XVIII (1965), 120–9. For the possible origins of influenza in Wales, *CSP Ven.*, IV, 541.

[27A] Most of the earliest Glamorgan registers still extant are available in NLW, where either the originals or facsimile copies are kept. They include: Llyswyrnwy Parish Register, 1588–1752, Pendoylan P.R., 1569–1672, St. Donat's P.R., 1571–1758, and the following facsimile copies: NLW 9042E (Llandough-juxta-Cowbridge, 1583–1812), NLW 9043E (St. Marychurch, 1584–1761), and NLW 5244E (Wenvoe, 1585–1739). For a list of Llandaff registers, *A Digest of the Parish Registers: Llandaff Records*, Vol. I (Cardiff, 1905). For the poetry, *Hen Gwndidau*, pp. 34–6, 59–60, 99–100, 103–4; cf. below, note 31.

[28] For indexes of prices, Carus-Wilson, *Essays in Economic History*, II, 168–96 and *CAgH.*, IV, appendices A and B, ibid., chap. ix.

[29] Ibid.

[30] For inflation, see R. B. Outhwaite, *Inflation in Tudor and Stuart England* (London, 1969); Peter Ramsey, *Tudor Economic Problems* (London, 1965); idem, *The Price Revolution in Sixteenth-Century England* (London, 1971); E. H. Phelps Brown and S. V. Hopkins, 'Wage-rates and prices', *Economica*, XXIV (1957), 289–306 and 'Builders' wage-rates, prices and population: some further evidence', ibid., XXVI (1959), 18–38. Y. S. Brenner, 'The inflation of prices in early sixteenth-century England', *Econ.HR*, ii, XIV (1961), 225–39 and 'The inflation of prices in England, 1551–1650', ibid., XV (1962), 266–84; J. D. Gould, 'The price revolution reconsidered', ibid., XVII (1964), 249–66; C. E. Challis, 'The debasement of the coinage, 1542–1551', ibid., XX (1967),

441–66; F. P. Braudel and F. Spooner, 'Prices in Europe from 1450 to 1750', *Cambridge Economic History of Europe*, IV (Cambridge, 1967), 378–486.

[31] *Hen Gwndidau*, pp. 25, 34–6, 59–60, 61–2, 77–9, 97–100, 103–7, 111–12, 114–15, 120–2, 141, 148, 170–2.

[32] PRO, DL 42/107, LR 2/206, DL 44/981, DL R and S 13/4; and for a detailed analysis, Jeffreys-Jones, 'Enclosures', appendix to chap. 8.

[33] A very full account of the Gower encroachments, together with many of the relevant documents, exists in W. R. B. Robinson, 'The litigation of Edward, earl of Worcester, concerning Gower', *BBCS*, XXII (1968), 357–88, XXIII (1968–70), 60–99; *Stradling Correspondence*, p. 101; G. E. Jones, 'Glamorgan Gentry', p. 131; Randall and Rees, *S. Wales and Mon. R.S.*, I, *passim*; Rice Lewis, ibid., III, 108; Megan Thomas, 'Glamorgan', chap. ii.

[34] G. E. Fussell, *The Old English Farming Books . . .* (London, 1947).

[35] Baker and Francis, *Gower Surveys*, pp. 138, 227, 240; *Merrick's Glam. Antiqs.*, pp. 11, 104, cf. *Arch. Camb.* Suppl., 1911, p. 117; Emery, *NLWJ.*, IX, 399ff.; *Stradling Correspondence*, p. 49.

[36] *Cardiff Records*, I, 296ff.; *Stradling Correspondence*, pp. 257–9; P. McGrath, *Merchants and Merchandise in Seventeenth-Century Bristol* (Bristol Record Soc., XIX, 1955), p. ix; E. A. Lewis, *Welsh Port Books, 1550–1603* (Cymmr. Record Ser., 1927), *passim*; *CAgH*, IV, 528.

[37] Cole, 'Mansells', p. 180; *Cardiff Records*, I, 296; Clark, *Limbus*, pp. 40–1; Jeffreys-Jones, 'Enclosures', pp. 238–44; Cardiff Central Library, Bushby MSS., III, i–ii, surveys of Neath Citra, 1590, 1611, 1628, 1638, 1654; J. B. Davies, *Glam. Hist.*, I, 83; Megan Thomas, 'Glamorgan', pp. 187–9; Emery, *NLWJ.*, X, 29.

[38] *Merrick's Glam. Antiqs.*, p. 10; William Rees, *South Wales and the March, 1284–1415* (Oxford, 1924), pp. 174, 191, 198, 200; Jeffreys-Jones, 'Enclosures', chap. xi. For comparable conditions in Pembrokeshire, Howells, *NLWJ.*, IX, 315–16, 326–30.

[39] Jeffreys-Jones, 'Enclosures', chap. xi; Megan Thomas, 'Glamorgan', pp. 92–4.

[40] Emery, *NLWJ.*, x, 29; Jeffreys-Jones, 'Enclosures', pp. 347–63, 372, 432–4; PRO, Req., 82/46; E134/12 Eliz.; STAC. 5, P54/4;

C24/15/24; G.D. Owen, *Elizabethan Wales: the Social Scene* (Cardiff, 1962), pp. 87–9; Megan Thomas, 'Glamorgan', pp. 99–100.

[41] Winstanley quot. in Christopher Hill, *Puritanism and Revolution* (London, 1968), p. 154. Owen, *Pembrokeshire*, I, 190. For examples of deeds and documents conveniently in print, Clark, *Cartae*, V and VI, *passim*; *Penrice and Margam MSS.*, *passim*. For examples of marriage contracts, ibid., III, 36, 38, 39, 46–7, 106, 145, 148; IV, i, 211, 213–14; IV, ii, 123, 125, 134.

[42] Clark, *Limbus*, p. 250; ibid., p. 35 (Morgan), 93 (Loughor); 286–7 (Herbert of Swansea); and 341 (Aubrey). Phillips, *Vale of Neath*, pp. 384–6.

[43] *DWB.*, s.n. Carne; J. D. H. Thomas, 'Judge David Jenkins, 1582–1663', *Morgannwg*, VIII (1964), 14–34; B. Ll. James, 'The parish of Llantrithyd', Ed. S. Williams, *The Garden of Wales* (Cowbridge, 1961), pp. 94–105; Phillips, *Vale of Neath*, pp. 374–6.

[44] Rice Lewis, 'Breviat', *S. Wales and Mon. R.S.*, III, 108; NLW, Bute MSS., 2, 4, 8–31.

[45] R. A. Griffiths, *Morgannwg*, VIII, 15–47; Glanmor Williams, 'The Stradlings of St. Donat's', Ed. S. Williams, *Vale of History* (Cowbridge, 1960), pp. 85–95.

[46] Cole, 'Mansells', *passim*; Williams, *Morgannwg*, VI, 33–51.

[47] Randall, *DWB.*, s.n. Lewis; Clark, *Limbus*, pp. 40–2.

[48] J. B. Davies, *Glam. Hist.*, I, 77–87; Cole, 'Mansells', pp. 98–101.

[49] Williams, *Morgannwg*, VI, 40; Phillips, *Vale of Neath*, p. 386; *Stradling Correspondence*, pp. 97, 101, 113, 127, 133–4, 149; Cole, 'Mansells', pp. 54–5; NLW, Penrice and Margam Correspondence, L1, 4, 5, 6, 7; Robinson, *BBCS*, XXII, 357–88, XXIII, 60–99; *HMC. De L'Isle and Dudley MSS.*, III, 241–2, 399; IV, 141, 294–5.

[50] Cole, 'Mansells', pp. 177–81.

[51] Jones, 'Glamorgan Gentry', pp. 136–8; Megan Thomas, 'Glamorgan', pp. 222–3.

[52] The tables are based on the following sources: 1540: PRO, S.C.6/Henry VIII/7493; 1570: NLW, Bute MS. 99/C; 1588–9: Bute MS. 2; 1595–6: Bute MS. 7; and 1631: Bute MS. 165.

[53] This paragraph is based on Cole, 'Mansells', chaps. ii–iv.

[54] Ibid., pp. 150–67; cf. Megan Thomas, 'Glamorgan', chap. iii.

[55] Below, pp. 227–8, 243–5.

[56] W. Rees, *Cardiff* (Cardiff, 1962), pp. 73–4; Rice Lewis, *S. Wales and Mon. R.S.*, III, 104, 108; Leland, *Itin. Wales*, pp. 19, 27, 28; *Merrick's Glam. Antiqs.*, pp. 11, 12, 114; NLW, Bute MSS., 8–31.

[57] Cole, 'Mansells', pp. 192–3; Stradling, *S. Wales and Mon. R.S.*, I, 52–3, 113; *Stradling Correspondence*, pp. 18–19; Glanmor Williams, 'The affray at Oxwich Castle', *Gower*, II (1949), 6–11; William Rees, 'Wreck de Mer', *S. Wales and Mon. R.S.*, IV (1957), 178–80; *CSPD*, *1629–31*, pp. 52, 65, 106, 398, 407–9, 412, 485, 488, 492, 495; cf. *APC*, *1630–1*, pp. 164, 166, 183, 187. For a more peaceful episode, NLW, P and M Orig. Correspce, L7.

[58] L. Stone, *The Crisis of the Aristocracy, 1558–1641* (Oxford, 1965), p. 467; Robinson, *BBCS*, XXI, 46–7; Cole, 'Mansells' pp. 20–1 205.

[58A] For rentals and accounts, NLW, Bute MSS., 99 A, B and C.

[59] *Ante*, III, chap. vii; Davies, *Econ. Hist. S. Wales*, p. 41. For a map showing estimated populations of Glamorgan hundreds, Emery, *CAgH.*, IV, 146–7.

[60] PRO, E179/221/238; Griffiths, *ante*, III, 358–9; W. R. B. Robinson, 'The first subsidy assessments of the hundreds of Swansea and Llangyfelach, 1543', *WHR.*, II (1964), 125–46, esp. pp. 142–3 and Table II. The other subsidy assessments for the county will be found in PRO, E179/221/237, 35 Henry VIII (11 mm. Hundreds of Cardiff, Caerphilly, Dinas Powys and Llantrisant); E179/221/238, 36 Henry VIII (18 mm. Hundreds of Cardiff, Caerphilly, Cowbridge, Dinas Powys, and Miskin); E179/221/239, 37 Henry VIII (16 mm. Hundreds of Cardiff, Caerphilly, Cowbridge, Dinas Powys, and Miskin); E179/221/246, 37 Henry VIII (39 mm. Hundreds of Cardiff, Caerphilly, Llangyfelach, Swansea, Neath, and Newcastle). *Merrick's Glam. Antiqs.*, pp. 92–5; Speed, *Great Britaine*, p. 105; Clark, *Cartae*, V, 1864–70, VI, 2138–9; *CSPD*, *1603–10*, p. 446; Rees, *Cardiff*, p. 43.

[61] L. Hopkin-James, *Old Cowbridge* (Cardiff, 1922), p. 35; Rees, *Cardiff*, p. 75; W. S. K. Thomas, 'The History of Swansea from the Accession of the Tudors to the Restoration Settlement' (Ph.D. Thesis, Univ. of Wales, 1958), p. 125; UCS,

Swansea Corporation Records, Book of Orders, pp. 54, 98.

[62] *CAgH.*, IV, 122–3; *Merrick's Glam. Antiqs.*, p. 114; Rice Lewis, 'Breviat', *S. Wales and Mon. R.S.*, III, 99; Rees, *Cardiff*, p. 71; Owen, *Elizabethan Wales*, p. 48.

[63] For a list of fairs, *Merrick's Glam. Antiqs.*, p. 115; UCS, Swansea Corporation Records, Churchwardens' Accounts, 1558–1694, for 1611 and 1614. PRO STAC. 5, K/10/8, H/58/30.

[64] For the information in this paragraph see Thomas, 'Swansea, 1485–1660', chap. ii. Evan ap David's will, PRO, PCC Weldon 31.

[65] *Cardiff Records*, III, 121–4, 338, 342–7, 348–52; Rees, *Cardiff*, p. 47; Owen, *Elizabethan Wales*, p. 116; Thomas, 'Swansea, 1485–1660', chap. ii; *CAgH*, IV, 147.

[66] Cowbridge, Hopkin-James, *Old Cowbridge*, pp. 27–38; Kenfig, Thos. Gray, *The Buried City of Kenfig* (London, 1909), pp. 156–78; Neath, W. de G. Birch, *A History of Neath Abbey* (Neath, 1902), pp. 260–5; Swansea, L. W. Dillwyn, *Contributions towards a History of Swansea* (Swansea, 1840), pp. 15–18, and W. H. Jones, *History of the Port of Swansea* (Carmarthen, 1922), pp. 13–15. UCS, Swansea Corporation Records, Common Hall Book, 1549–1665, *passim*; Book of Orders, *passim*. *Cardiff Records*, II, 157–8, 162, 164–5, 166–7, 172, 275.

[67] *Ante*, III, 375; Cole, 'Mansells', p. 182; *Cardiff Records*, III, 418; PRO E112/61/ Glam. 23, cf. E. G. Jones, *Exchequer Proceedings concerning Wales* (Cardiff, 1939), pp. 220–1. *Cambrian Journal*, 1863, p. 168.

[68] L. A. Clarkson, 'The leather crafts in Tudor and Stuart England', *Agric.HR.*, XIV (1966), 25–39; *ante*, III, 376; UCS, Swansea Common Hall Book, 1549–1665, *passim*; *CAgH.*, IV, 147; Emery, *NLWJ.*, X, 21–2.

[69] The fullest account of early coal-mining and other industrial ventures in Glamorgan, to which this and subsequent sections on industry owe much, is William Rees, *Industry before the Industrial Revolution* (2 vols. Cardiff, 1968), I, chaps. i and ii. Also, B. M. Evans, 'The Welsh Coal Trade during the Stuart Period, 1603–1709' (M.A. Thesis, Univ. of Wales, 1928); Phillips, *Vale of Neath*, pp. 56, 231ff.; C. D. J. Trott, 'Coalmining in the

Borough of Neath in the 17th and early 18th centuries', *Morgannwg*, XIII (1969), 47–74; W. G. Thomas, 'The coalmining industry in West Glamorgan', *Glam. Hist.*, VI (1969), 201–27; D. T. Williams, *The Economic Development of Swansea and the Swansea District to 1921* (Cardiff, 1940), pp. 16–26. For the history of British coalmining generally, J. U. Nef, *The Rise of the British Coal Industry* (2 vols. London, 1932).

[70] Sidney quot. Rees, *Industry*, I, 67; Owen, *Pembrokeshire*, I, 88.

[71] Emery, *CAgH.*, IV, 158; idem, *NLWJ.*, IX, 395–6; Trott, *Morgannwg*, XIII, 51; Rees, *Industry*, I, chap. ii.

[72] Ibid.; Baker and Francis, *Gower Surveys*, pp. 295, 299.

[73] Owen, *Pembrokeshire*, I, 90–1; D. G. John, 'Contributions', Part II, chap. i; D. T. Williams, *Econ. Devel. Swansea*, pp. 19–20.

[74] For the iron industry in general, H. R. Schubert, *History of the British Iron and Steel Industry from 450 B.C. to A.D. 1775* (London, 1957); Rees, *Industry*, I, chap. iv. See also C. Wilkins, *History of the Iron, Steel, and Tinplate Trades of Wales* (Merthyr Tydfil, 1903), chaps. i and ii; W. Llewellin, 'Sussex ironmasters in Glamorgan', *Arch. Camb.*, IX (1863); T. Bevan, 'Sussex ironmasters in Glamorgan', *Trans. Cardiff Nats. Soc.* LXXXVI, (1956); Davies, *Econ. Hist. S. Wales*, pp. 74–6; D. G. John, 'Contributions', I, chap. vi; D. Morgan Rees, *Mines, Mills, and Furnaces . . .* (London, 1969), pp. 52–6; idem, 'Industrial archaeology in Glamorgan', *Glam. Hist.*, V (1968), 193–205; T. J. Prichard, 'Upland Glamorgan', p. 247ff.

[75] Rees, *Industry*, I, chap. iv; *HMC. De L'Isle and Dudley MSS.*, I, 318–21; Rees, *Glam. Hist.*, V, 194–5; Owen, *Elizabethan Wales*, pp. 159–60.

[76] Rees, *Industry*, I, 249–51; *HMC. De L'Isle and Dudley MSS.*, I, 318–21.

[77] Rees, *Industry*, I, 259–62; *Cardiff Records*, I, 362–3; *APC., 1616–17*, pp. 38, 47; *HMC. De L'Isle and Dudley MSS.*, V, 155, 205.

[78] Rees, *Industry*, I, 263–4.

[79] Ibid., I, 252–8; Rees, *Glam. Hist.*, V, 194–5.

[80] Rees, *Industry*, I, 265–6.

[81] Llewellin, *Arch. Camb.*, IX, 81–119; Bevan, *Trans. Cardiff Nats. Soc.*, LXXXVI, 5–12; Rees, *Mines, Mills*, pp.

52–6; idem, *Glam. Hist.*, V, 193–5; D. G. John, 'Contributions', I, chap. vi.

[82] Owen, *Elizabethan Wales*, p. 160.

[83] For the companies in general, W. R. Scott, *The Constitution and Finance of the Joint Stock Companies* (2 vols. Cambridge, 1910–12); for copper, M. B. Donald, *Elizabethan Copper* (London, 1955); Rees, *Industry*, II, chaps. vi and vii, especially, pp. 429–37. For Neath, G. G. Francis, *The Smelting of Copper in the Swansea District* (London, 1881); R. O. Roberts, 'The development and decline of copper . . .', *Trans. Cymmr.*, 1956, pp. 78–115; D. G. John, 'The organization and activities of the chartered companies . . .', *Trans. Neath Antiq. Soc.*, ii, IV (1933–4), 67–80; Lionel Williams, 'A sixteenth-century example of regional interdependence and alien participation . . .', *Morgannwg*, III (1959), 3–20.

[84] Rees, *Industry*, II, 429–37; Williams, *Morgannwg*, III, 3–20; John, *Trans. Neath Antiq. Soc.*, IV, 70; Owen, *Elizabethan Wales*, pp. 154–5; Megan Thomas, 'Glamorgan', p. 251.

[85] D. T. Williams, *Econ. Devel. Swansea*, p. 11; UCS, Swansea Common Attorneys' Accounts, for 1623, 1633, 1635; Swansea Common Hall Book, 14 December 1652; Jones, *Port of Swansea*, p. 36; Thomas, 'Swansea, 1485–1660', pp. 58–60, appendices D and E; Lewis, *Port Books 1550–1603*, pp. 38, 45; 14, 17–9, 46; 5, 15, 20, 37; 5, 23; *Stradling Correspondence*, pp. 272–3; Davies, *Econ. Hist. S. Wales*, p. 64; Moelwyn Williams, *Saints and Sailing Ships*, p. 17.

[86] Rees, *Cardiff*, p. 73; *Cardiff Records*, III, 418; Davies, *Econ. Hist. S. Wales*, p. 63; *CAgH.*, IV, 159; Randall and Rees, 'Lower Borowes', *S. Wales and Mon. R.S.*, I, 73, 155–6 (mats); 118–9 (fishing).

[87] Lewis, *Port Books, 1550–1603*, *passim*; PRO, E112/149/41; Davies, *Econ. Hist. S. Wales*, pp. 30, 63–4; *Cardiff Records*, III, 418; Williams, *Iolo Morganwg*, quot. NLW, Llanover MS. C27, p. 35.

[88] Lewis, *Port Books, 1550–1603*, introduction; *Cardiff Records*, II, 157, 162–3.

[89] H. J. Randall, *Bridgend*, pp. 2–3; W. R. B. Robinson, 'Dr. Phaer's report on the harbours and customs administration of Wales under Edward VI', *BBCS*, XXIV (1972), 485–502; idem, 'The establishment of royal customs in Glamorgan and Monmouthshire under Elizabeth I', ibid., XXIII (1970) 347–96; Lewis, *Port Books, 1550–1603*, pp. ix–xiv.

[90] Robinson, *BBCS*, XXIII, 347–96.

[91] For an outline of the medieval arrangements, William Rees, 'The port books of . . . Cardiff . . . Swansea and Neath', *S. Wales and Mon. R.S.*, III, 69–70; Robinson, *BBCS*, XXIII, *passim*; Lewis, *Port Books, 1550–1603*, pp. xv–xvi; B. M. Lansdowne MS. 46, f. 102, quot. Thomas, 'Swansea 1485–1603', p. 43; *Stradling Correspondence*, pp. 123, 325–6; Randall and Rees, 'Lower Borowes', *S. Wales and Mon. R.S.*, I, 115–6, 123–4; E. G. Jones, *Exchequer Proceedings*, pp. 216–7; Jeffreys-Jones, *Exchequer Proceedings James I*, p. 218; *Cardiff Records*, I, 399; II, 161, 166.

[91A] *Cardiff Records*, I, 361; PRO, E112/107/62, E112/149/43, 149/41, cf. Jeffreys-Jones, op. cit., pp. 253, 214–6; PRO, STAC., 8/26/6; PRO, E112/149/50, cf. Jeffreys Jones, op. cit., p. 218; *CSPD, 1611–18*, p. 587; *APC, 1618/9*, pp. 336, 428, 440.

[92] Lewis, *Port Books, 1558–1603*, *passim*; Rees, *S. Wales and Mon. R.S.*, III, 69–91; Moelwyn Williams, *Saints and Sailing Ships*, pp. 11–17; idem, 'Some aspects of the economic and social life of the southern regions of Glamorgan, 1600–1800', *Morgannwg*, III (1959), 21–30.

[93] Jones, *Port of Swansea*, pp. 25–35; Thomas, 'Swansea, 1485–1660', pp. 88–100; *Cardiff Records*, III, 47–8; Emery, *NLWJ*, X, 25–6; Williams, *Vale of History*, p. 91.

[94] Lewis, *Port Books, 1550–1603*, *passim*; P. McGrath, *Merchants . . . in 17th century Bristol*, introd.; *APC, 1630–1*, p. 125; Flenley, *Council in the Marches*, pp. 108–9.

[95] Williams, *Saints and Sailing Ships*, pp. 14–8; Williams, *Morgannwg*, III, 30–1; Megan Thomas, 'Glamorgan', pp. 260–1; drovers' licences, *Penrice and Margam MSS.*, IV, i, 217, 220; Cole, 'Mansells', p. 181.

[96] Robinson, *BBCS*, XXIV, 495; Defoe quot. in Williams, *Morgannwg*, III, 28; P. McGrath, *Records relating to the Society of Merchant Venturers in . . . Bristol in the 17th Century* (Bristol Rec. Soc. Pubs., XVII, 1952), pp. 119–25; *Cardiff Records*, I, 399; II, 161, 166; *CSPD, 1625–6*, p. 213.

[97] Williams, *Morgannwg*, III, 28–9; Robinson, *BBCS*, XXIV, 495; PRO, E112/

61 Glamorgan 17; Lewis, *Port Books, 1550–1603*, pp. 30–4, 41–3.

98 Nef, *British Coal Industry*, I, 53, II, appendix D; B. M. Evans, 'Coal Trade', p. 31; Rees, *Industry*, I, 107–14; Rees, *S. Wales and Mon. R.S.*, III, 69–88; PRO, E112/149/41; D. T. Williams, *Econ. Devel. Swansea*, pp. 16–23; Thomas, 'Swansea, 1485–1660', pp. 49–87; Lewis, *Port Books, 1550–1603, passim*.

99 Ibid., pp. 30–3, 41–3 (iron), pp. 20, 48 (lead); Thomas, 'Swansea, 1485–1660', pp. 57–8; T. S. Willan, *The English Coasting Trade, 1600–1750* (Manchester, 1938), p. 69.

100 Lewis, *Port Books, 1550–1603, passim*; Megan Thomas, 'Glamorgan', chap. vii; Thomas, 'Swansea, 1485–1660', p. 87; Williams, *Saints and Sailing Ships*, pp. 13–14.

101 Lewis, *Port Books, 1550–1603, passim*; Willan, *Coasting Trade*, pp. 12, 47; Thomas, 'Swansea, 1485–1660', p. 78; Nef, *British Coal Industry*, I, 116; Williams, *Saints and Sailing Ships*, p. 16; Rees, *Cardiff*, pp. 72–3; Megan Thomas, 'Glamorgan', p. 241.

102 Lewis, *Port Books, 1550–1603, passim*; Rees, *S. Wales and Mon. R.S.*, III, 69–88; Willan, *Coasting Trade*, pp. 43–9.

103 Lewis, *Port Books, 1550–1603, passim*; Owen, *Elizabethan Wales*, pp. 128–9; PRO, PCC Dorset 18.

104 For piracy in general, Carys E. Hughes, 'Wales and Piracy' (M.A. Thesis, Univ. of Wales, 1937); David Mathew, *The Celtic Peoples and Renaissance Europe* (London, 1933), chap. xv; E. R. Williams, *Some Studies of Elizabethan Wales* (Newtown, 1924), chaps. viii–xi; *Cardiff Records*, I, 349–59.

105 As above, note 104, especially Hughes, 'Piracy', pp. 213–47; cf. also Rees, *Cardiff*, pp. 93–4; Owen, *Elizabethan Wales*, pp. 144–7; letter, misdated 1598, from Burghley to Edward Mansel, *HMC. Hatfield MSS.*, VIII, 560.

106 E. R. Williams, *Elizabethan Wales*, chap. x; *Cardiff Records*, II, 157–8; *Stradling Correspondence*, pp. 251–2, 286–7, 78–83, 291–6.

107 Ibid., pp. 179–80, 230–1; D. B. Quinn, 'A merchant's long memory', *Gower*, IX (1956), 8–11; Owen, *Elizabethan Wales*, pp. 135–7; *CSPD., 1629–31*, pp. 52, 65, 106, 398, 408, 412, 485, 488, 492, 495; *APC., 1630–1*, pp. 164, 166, 183, 187.

108 C. Mervyn Thomas, 'The First Civil War in Glamorgan' (M.A. Thesis, Univ. of Wales, 1963), pp. 30–9; *Cardiff Records*, I, 365; McGrath, *Merchants in Bristol*, pp. 181–2, 187–8.

¹ For population studies in general: Joan Thirsk, *Sources of Information on Population* (Canterbury, 1965). Recent studies on sixteenth-century population in England and Wales include: E. E. Rich, 'The population of Elizabethan England', *Econ.HR.*, ii, I (1948), 247–65; G. S. L. Tucker, 'English pre-industrial population', ibid., XVI (1963), 208–12; J. Cornwall, 'English population in the early sixteenth century', ibid., XXIII (1970), 32–44; I. Blanchard, 'Population change, enclosure, and the early Tudor economy', ibid., pp. 427–43. For the population of Wales, David Williams, 'A note on the population of Wales, 1536–1801', *BBCS.*, VIII (1935–7), 359–63; E. G. Bowen (ed.), *Wales*, pp. 230–2; *CAgH.*, IV, 142–7 (including two useful maps); Leonard Owen, 'The population of Wales in the sixteenth and seventeenth centuries', *Trans. Cymmr.*, 1959, pp. 99–113.

² W. R. B. Robinson, 'The first subsidy assessments . . . of Swansea and Llangyfelach, 1543', *WHR.*, II (1964), 125–46, is particularly valuable.

³ Chantry certificates of 1545–6 are printed in E. D. Jones, 'A survey of South Wales Chantries', *Arch Camb.*, LXXXIX (1934), 135–45; cf. also chap. iv, note 38. For the multiplier, Cornwall, *Econ.HR.*, XXIII, 43. Bishops' returns for 1563 and 1603, BM, Harleian MS., 595, ff. 1–17b (Llandaff) and 77–92 (St. David's). The 1563 returns for Gower are printed in Glanmor Williams, 'Gower parishes in the sixteenth century', *Gower*, I (1948), 42–6. For the parish registers, chap. i, note 27A.

⁴ This table was published by the late Leonard Owen, *Trans. Cymmr.*, 1959, p. 110. It is reproduced here by the courtesy of the editor of *Trans. Cymmr.*, Professor I. Ll. Foster, Jesus College, Oxford.

⁵ For instance, the late Leonard Owen never really made it clear why he chose a multiplier of 5⅓ for Glamorgan.

⁶ Emery, *CAgH.*, IV, 144; Robinson, *WHR.*, II, 142.

⁷ Important general studies of the gentry are R. H. Tawney, 'The rise of the gentry', *Econ.HR.*, XI (1941); H. R. Trevor-Roper, *The Gentry, 1540–1640* (*Econ.HR.* Supplement, 1953); M. Finch, *The Wealth of Five Northamptonshire Families* (Northants Record Soc., 1956); J. E. Mousley, 'The fortunes of some gentry families of Elizabethan Sussex', *Econ.HR.*, ii, XI (1959); A. Simpson, *The Wealth of the Gentry* (Cambridge, 1961); Howell A. Lloyd, *The Gentry of South-west Wales* (Cardiff, 1968); and J. T. Cliffe, *The Yorkshire Gentry . . .* (London, 1969). Leland, *Itin. Wales*, p. 30.

⁸ For details, *Limbus, passim. TLIM.*, pp. 183–5. It is noticeable that the late Sir John Edward Lloyd was so unconvinced of the reality of Einion ap Collwyn's existence that he refused to include him in *DWB.*

⁹ *TLIM.*, pp. 194–200 and Griffiths, *Morgannwg*, VII, 15–47 (Stradling); *Limbus*, p. 369 (Button); *Penrice and Margam MSS.*, II, nos. 547–53, cf. C. A. Maunsell and E. P. Statham, *A History of the Family of Maunsell . . .* (4 vols. London, 1917–20) for Mansel; *Limbus*, pp. 406–7 (Kemeys).

¹⁰ *TLIM.*, p. 82; *Stradling Correspce.*, pp. 288–9; *HMC. Hatfield MSS.*, I, 82; VIII, 287–8; S. R. Meyrick (ed.), *Lewys Dwnn's Heraldic Visitations of Wales* (2 vols. Llandovery, 1846), I, xxii–iv; Gareth E. Jones, 'Tudor Glamorgan: some gentry interests', *Glam. Hist.*, IV (1967), 221–30.

¹¹ Thomas Smith, *De Republica Anglorum.* Ed. L. Alston (Cambridge, 1906), pp. 32–40; cf. Lawrence Stone, *The Crisis of the Aristocracy, 1558–1641* (Oxford, 1965), p. 49; *Limbus*, p. 250.

¹² Ibid., p. 89; *Hen Gwndidau*, p. 170; R. Symonds, *Diary of the Marches of the Royal Army during the Great Civil War.* Ed. C. E. Long (Camden Soc., 1859), pp. 216–7.

¹³ *Penrice and Margam MSS.*, IV, i, 10; *Limbus, passim, s.n.* Mansel, Stradling, Kemeys, Thomas of Betws, Herbert of Swansea, Aubrey, Lewis Y Fan, Mathew of Llandaff and Radyr, Carne of Ewenni, Morgan of Ruperra. Glamorgan esquires in BM, Harleian MS., 6804, ff. 180–1.

[14] *TLlM.*, pp. 203–13 and chaps. iii and iv; Phillips, *Vale of Neath*, chap. xvii.

[15] T. J. Hopkins, 'Rice Merrick (Rhys Meurug) of Cottrell', *Morgannwg*, VIII (1964), 5–13. Merrick, David Jenkins, Leoline Jenkins, and Philip Jones, *DWB.*, *s.n.*

[16] Peter Thomas in a valuable series of articles on Glamorgan medical men, *Glam. Hist.*, I, ff., found none worthy of mention before the eighteenth century. For the Nichol family, *Limbus*, p. 421.

[17] For yeomen generally, M. Campbell, *The English Yeoman under Elizabeth and the Early Stuarts* (New Haven, 1942). Laslett, *World We Have Lost*, p. 38; *Merrick's Glam. Antiqs.*, pp. 40, 46, 101–5; NLW, Llandaff P.R., 1639; Hopkins, *History on My Doorstep*, pp. 84–5; Flenley, *Register*, p. 87; Smith, *CAgH.*, IV, 802.

[18] Robinson, *WHR.*, II, 125–46, table I; Megan Thomas, 'Glamorgan', pp. 57ff. Emery, *NLWJ.*, IX, table 2; Emery, *CAgH.*, IV, 153–4.

[19] For labourers generally, Everitt, *CAgH.*, IV, chap. vii; cf. G. E. Fussell, *The English Rural Labourer* (London, 1947).

[20] Megan Thomas, 'Glamorgan', p. 112; GRO, D/DC/M 41–3 (Boverton), D/DF/M 277, 288 (Fonmon) and M 278 (Penmark).

[21] Statute of Artificers, R. H. Tawney and Eileen Power, *Tudor Economic Documents* (London, 1951), I, 342; Owen, *Pembrokeshire*, I, 42–3; CCL MS., 2. 148, vol. V, 48; Williams, *Iolo Morganwg*, p. 26.

[22] E. M. Leonard, *The Early History of English Poor Relief* (Cambridge, 1900); Harrison, *Description of England*, chap. x; *Hen Gwndidau*, pp. 105–6, 111–12, 10–11, 54; GRO, MS. History of the Mansel Family, D/DC F48; PCC, Gore 160 (John Stradling); Holney 21 (Thomas Stradling), Dorsett 222 (Edward Stradling), Hele 94 (Agnes Stradling); *Stradling Correspce.*, pp. 160–2, 169–71.

[23] W. G. Hoskins, 'English provincial towns in the sixteenth century', *TRHS.*, v, VI (1956), 1–19. The only town in Glamorgan for which enough material exists is Swansea, see Thomas, 'Swansea, 1485–1660', chap. ii, but conditions in Haverfordwest seem to have been similar, B. G. Charles, *Calendar of the Records of the Borough of Haverfordwest, 1539–1660* (Cardiff, 1967).

[24] D. Hollis, *Calendar of the Bristol Apprentice Book, 1532–42* (Bristol Record Soc., XIV, 1949), *passim*; cf. McGrath, *Bristol Merchants*, appendix i; Thomas Jones, 'The place-names of Cardiff', *S. Wales and Mon. R.S.*, II (1950), 25–8.

[25] *Cardiff Records*, II, 156–8; III, 58, 67; UCS, Swansea Book of Orders, fl. 78–9, 106, 186, 198; UCS, Swansea Churchwardens' Accounts, 1558–90, *passim*; UCS, Swansea Common Hall Book, 1549–1665, ff. 86–95; cf. Thomas, 'Swansea, 1485–1660', pp. 126–39; Thomas Dinely, *An Account of the Progress . . . of the First Duke of Beaufort through Wales, 1684*. Ed. Charles Baker (1864), p. 172.

[26] Symonds, *Diary*, pp. 216–7; *Limbus*, pp. 7–28 (Mathew); *TLlM.*, p. 215 (Powel); BM, Vespasian MS. FXIII, f. 180; *Limbus*, p. 439 (Stradling); *TLlM.*, p. 81.

[27] Joan Thirsk, 'Younger sons in the seventeenth century', *History*, LIV (1969), 358–71; Thomas Wilson, 'The state of England, 1600'. Ed. F. J. Fisher, *Camden Soc.*, iii, LII (1936), 24; PCC, Barrington 31 (Lewis), Gore 160 (Stradling); CCL. MS. 2. 1307, I, 190–4 (Thomas).

[28] NLW, Llandaff P.R. 1597 (ap Richard); CCL. MS. 2. 1307, I, 176–7 (Giles); PCC, Lee 74 (Mansel), Dale 45 (Thomas).

[29] Wilson, *Camden Soc.*, iii, LII, 24; PRO SP12/107/4; Owen, *Pembrokeshire*, III, 302–59; NLW, P and M Orig. Correspce., L47.

[30] Smith, *Republica Anglorum*, p. 43; Clark, *Cartae*, V, 1924–6; *Limbus*, p. 218; *Penrice and Margam MSS.*, III, 98, 103, 111; Emery, *NLWJ.*, X, 31.

[31] PCC, Dorsett 19; Wilson, *Camden Soc.*, iii, LII, 24–5; Stradling, *S. Wales and Mon. R.S.*, I, 80, cf. for other complaints of lawyers' sharp practice, Jeffreys-Jones, *Exchequer Proceedings*, pp. 210, 216; *Limbus*, pp. 218–9, 341; Phillips, *Vale of Neath*, pp. 374–5.

[32] Smith, *Republica Anglorum*, p. 46; *Sermons or Homilies to be Read in Churches in the Time of Queen Elizabeth* (London, 1817), p. 96.

[33] NLW, P and M Orig. Correspce., L3; HMC. *Hatfield MSS.*, XII, 576–7; PRO, STAC 8/183/36.

[34] W. T. MacCaffery, 'Place and patronage in Elizabethan politics', *Elizabethan Government and Society*. Ed. C. H.

Williams, S. T. Bindoff and J. Hurstfield (London, 1961), pp. 95–126.

[35] NLW, P and M Orig. Correspondence, L29, 44.

[36] PCC, Dorsett 97 (Stradling); Vaughan quot. *Limbus*, p. 233. For seventeenth-century comment on Glamorgan houses and tombs, Dinely, *Beaufort Progress*, pp. 165–216.

[37] John Steegman, *A Survey of Portraits in Welsh Houses: II. South Wales* (Cardiff, 1962), pp. 81–120.

[38] Thomas Richards, *Religious Developments in Wales, 1654–1662* (London, 1923), p. 134; Jones, 'Glamorgan Gentry', p. 136; NLW, P and M Orig. Correspce., L6; Phillips, *Vale of Neath*, pp. 385–6; *Stradling Correspce.*, p. 133; PCC, Dorsett 97.

[39] *Limbus*, p. 14.

[40] For the subject of crime and punishment generally, Harrison, *Description of England*, chap. xi. Senghennydd: Estreats of Fines, 25–39 Eliz., NLW, Bute MSS., Box 91, E 3–14; Court Book of Ewenni Manor, 1634–69, GRO, D/DE 1; David Jones of Wallington's notes of Great Sessions records relating to Glamorgan, CCL MS. 2. 1148, vols. I–IX, esp. VI, 91–3, II, 124, III, 132–7; NLW, P and M Orig. Correspce., L31.

[41] Ibid., L47; Glanmor Williams, 'The affray at Oxwich Castle, 1557', *Gower*, II (1949), 9–10; Stradling, *S. Wales and Mon. R.S.*, I, 106–7.

[42] *Stradling Correspce.*, p. 115; Stradling, *S. Wales and Mon. R.S.*, I, 49, 46; Gareth E. Jones, 'A case of corruption', *Glam. Hist.*, V (1968), 121–32; Flenley, *Register*, p. 90.

[43] NLW, P and M Orig. Correspce., L5; H. D. Traill and J. S. Mann, *Social England* (6 vols. London, 1903), III, 191.

[44] Stone, *Crisis of Aristocracy*, chap xi, esp. p. 613; Joan Thirsk, 'The family', *Past and Present*, no. 27 (1964). For Margam settlements and others, above chap. i, note 41; Clark, *Cartae*, V, 1774–6, 1778–80, 1797–1801, 1816–18, 1831–2, 1836–40, 1847–51, 1987–90, 1994–6; *HMC. De L'Isle and Dudley MSS.*, III, 422, IV, 140–1.

[44A] *Stradling Correspce.*, p. 8; T. J. Prichard, 'Upland Glamorgan' (M.A. Thesis, Univ. of Wales, 1973), pp. 206–8.

[45] PCC, Dorsett 97 (Stradling), Bucke 23 (Bassett); CCL MS., 2. 1307, I, 147–51 (Fleming); *Stradling Correspce.*, p. 8.

[46] Ibid., pp. 138, 221; PCC, Dorsett 97; PRO, E112/149/45, cf. Jeffreys-Jones, *Exchequer Proceedings*, p. 216; PRO, STAC 5/G17/32, P34/7; STAC 8/156/28, 158/15, 281/9. Griffith's suit was STAC 5/G17/32.

[47] PRO, STAC 8/158/15; *Limbus*, pp. 435, 377, 49, 495.

[48] The Sidney letters are preserved in *HMC. De L'Isle and Dudley MSS.*, *passim*. For the Lloyds, Owen, *Eliz. Wales*, p. 16; Thomas ab Ieuan ap Rhys, *Hen Gwndidau*, pp. 25–7; PCC, Meade 53 (Carne), Barrington 31 (Lewis), Byrde 84 (Mansel) and Hele 94 (Stradling).

[49] The families examined for this purpose were Bassett of Beaupré, Bassett of Llantriddyd, Carne of Ewenni, Carne of Nash, Evans of the Gnoll, Gwyn of Llansannor, Lewis Y Fan, Loughor of Tythegston, Mansel of Margam, Mathew of Radyr, Mathew of Castell-y-mynach, Powel of Llwydarth, Price of Briton Ferry, Prichard of Llancaeach, Seys of Boverton, Stradling of St. Donat's, Thomas of Betws, Turberville of Pen-llin, Van of Marcross, and Williams of Blaen Baglan.

[50] General studies include Joan Simon, *Education and Society in Tudor England* (Cambridge, 1966); K. B. Charlton, *Education in Renaissance England* (London, 1965); L. Stone, 'The educational revolution in England, 1540–1640', *Past and Present*, July 1964, pp. 41–80; W. Prest, 'The legal education of the gentry', ibid., December 1967, pp. 20–39.

[51] Clark, *Cartae*, V, 2046–7 (Mansel); ibid., VI, 2220–1 (Lewis); PRO, STAC 8/158/15, cf. ibid., 281/9; Merrick, *Arch. Camb. Suppl.*, 1911, p. 137; CCL MS. 2. 1307, I, 190–4 (Thomas).

[52] Iolo Davies, 'A Certaine Schoole': A History of Cowbridge Grammar School (Cowbridge, 1967), chap. i. For Evan Seys, see W. R. Williams, *The Welsh Judges* (Brecknock, 1899), p. 100; Leoline Jenkins, *DWB.*, *s.n.*

[53] Much of the content of this and the preceding paragraph is based on the research of my former pupils, Mr. Gareth E. Jones and Mr. C. Mervyn Thomas, to both of whom I am most grateful. See also, A. L. Rowse, *The Elizabethan Renaissance: the Life of the Society* (London, 1971), p. 24; *HMC. Hatfield MSS.*, II, 173–4 (Mansel); Worcester, *DWB.*, *s.n.*

Somerset; and *Cardiff Records*, I, 366 (Mathew and Prichard).

⁵⁴ *DWB.*, *s.n.* Carne, Herbert and Mansel.

⁵⁵ *TLlM.*, pp. 67–98, 123–6, 158–62. Dafydd Benwyn's verse is collected in CCL MS. 2.277 (Baglan MS.1).

⁵⁵ᴬ *Stradling Correspce.*, *passim*, and esp. pp. 229–30, 266–8, 322–4; NLW, P and M Orig. Correspce., L13; *Stradling Correspce.*, pp. 239–40; Phillips, *Vale of Neath*, p. 523.

⁵⁶ *Stradling Correspce.*, *passim*, and esp. pp. 314–15, 330, 167–8; PCC, Dorsett 97, cf. also Griffiths, *Morgannwg*, VII, 37–47; Williams, *Vale of History*, pp. 85–95.

⁵⁷ *DNB.*, *DWB.*, *s.n.* Stradling; cf. also *S. Wales and Mon. R.S.*, I, introd.; Glanmor Williams, 'Sir John Stradling of St. Donat's', *Glam. Hist.*, IX (1973), 11–28.

⁵⁸ W. G. Hoskins, 'The rebuilding of rural England', *Past and Present*, no. 4 (1953), 44–59; M. W. Barley, *The English Farmhouse and Cottage* (London, 1961); Cyril Fox and Lord Raglan, *Monmouthshire Houses* . . . (3 vols, Cardiff, 1951–4); Barley, *CAgH.*, IV, chap. x and Peter Smith, ibid., chap. xi. Stradling, *S. Wales and Mon. R.S.*, I, 77.

⁵⁹ Leland, *Itin. Wales*, pp. 18–33; *Merrick's Glam. Antiqs.*, pp. 98–100; NLW, Bute MS. 132, E 20; GRO, D/DF/M 288; Smith, *CAgH.*, IV, 804.

⁶⁰ Turbervill, *Ewenny Priory*, pp. 93–101; Jones, *Glam. Hist.*, IV, 223–6; Dinely, *Beaufort Progress*, pp. 182–6.

⁶¹ J. B. Davies, 'The parish of Pentyrch', *Glam. Hist.*, I, 82–3; *Limbus*, p. 40.

⁶² Leland, *Itin. Wales*, p. 21; *Merrick's Glam. Antiqs.*, pp. 113–4 for full lists; *Stradling Correspce.*, pp. 26, 71, 152, 225–6, 249, 264, 281, 290, 309, 312; Dinely, *Beaufort Progress*, p. 185; Williams, *Vale of History*, p. 90.

⁶³ Ex inf. Mr. Peter Smith; idem, *CAgH.*, IV, 802.

⁶⁴ *Limbus*, pp. 35, 40; *Cardiff Records*, III, 121–2; Thomas, 'Swansea, 1485–1660', pp. 119–21 and appendix G.

⁶⁵ Gerald, quot. Smith, *CAgH.*, IV, 773; Iorwerth C. Peate, *The Welsh House* (Liverpool, 1944), p. 106.

⁶⁶ NLW, Bute MS. 132, E 21, inventory of household stuff at Cardiff castle; Owen, *Eliz. Wales*, p. 38; Turbervill, *Ewenny Priory*, pp. 93–101 (Carne); W. S. K. Thomas, 'A Swansea Inventory (John

Moris)', *Gower*, X (1957), 58–61; PCC, Holney 21 (Stradling), Kitchin 23 (Carne); *Cardiff Records*, III, 121–3 (Collins); PCC, Dale 19 (Williams), Hele 119 (Edwards); *Cardiff Records*, III, 123–4 (Davies).

⁶⁷ For an unusually full inventory of a prosperous tradesman conveniently in print, *Cardiff Records*, III, 121–3; NLW, Llandaff P.R., 1627 (Moses David); ibid., 1632 (Owen Griffith).

⁶⁸ For costume in general, D. C. Calthrop, *English Costume* (London, 1923); F. W. Fairholt, *Costume in England* (2 vols. London, 1896). *Hen Gwndidau*, pp. 107, 137.

⁶⁹ J. D. Davies, *West Gower*, IV, 320–1; *Cardiff Records*, III, 119.

⁷⁰ Owen, *Eliz. Wales*, pp. 42–4; *Cardiff Records*, III, 123.

⁷¹ J. D. Davies, *West Gower*, IV, 320–1; *Penrice and Margam MSS.*, IV, i, 14–5; PCC, Holney 21 (Stradling); *Penrice and Margam MSS.*, IV., iii, 5; *Cardiff Records*, III, 113, 117.

⁷² Quot. in J. Hurstfield and A. G. R. Smith, *Elizabethan People: State and Society* (London, 1972), p. 23.

⁷³ For food and drink generally, Harrison, *Description of England*, chap. vi; J. C. Drummond and A. Wilbraham, *The Englishman's Food* (London, 1939); and Rowse, *Eliz. Renaissance*, chap. v. *Stradling Correspce.*, *passim*, esp. pp. 158, 303; *Hen Gwndidau*, pp. 10–11, 21.

⁷⁴ Owen quot. in Davies, *Econ. History S. Wales*, pp. 82–3.

⁷⁵ Owen, *Eliz. Wales*, pp. 41–2; Traill and Mann, *Social England*, III, 540–2.

⁷⁶ For the subject in general, see Trefor Owen, *Welsh Folk Customs* (Cardiff, 1959); Iorwerth C. Peate, *Tradition and Folk Life: A Welsh View* (London, 1972); Charles Redwood, *The Vale of Glamorgan: Scenes and Tales among the Welsh* (London, 1839); M. Rhys, 'Unpublished traditions of Glamorganshire', *The Cambrian Journal*, II (1855), 68–72, 115–24; G. J. Williams, 'Glamorgan customs in the eighteenth century', *Gwerin*, I (1957), 99–108. Iolo Morganwg quot. in Williams, *Iolo Morganwg*, p. 37, see also pp. 35–72 for general customs; *Hen Gwndidau*, pp. xliii, 54.

⁷⁷ *Stradling Correspce.*, p. 172; *Hen Gwndidau*, p. 54; Flenley, *Register*, pp.

102–3, 151, 164, 167, 169, 170, 204; Williams, *Iolo Morganwg*, pp. 50–6; Owen, *Eliz. Wales*, pp. 53–7; Thomas, 'Swansea, 1485–1660', pp. 143–4.

[78] Owen, *Eliz. Wales*, pp. 53–4; *Hen Gwndidau*, pp. 138, 97.

[79] Williams, *Iolo Morganwg*, pp. 59–66, 43–6; Thomas, 'Swansea, 1485–1660', pp. 145–6.

[80] *Hen Gwndidau*, pp. 83, 86, 82, 89–90; Flenley, *Register*, pp. 102–3, 145, 151; *Hen Gwndidau*, p. 86.

[81] Trefor Owen, *Folk Customs* is an excellent introduction to the whole subject. The book has a useful bibliography and, even more valuable, a guide to the collections preserved at the Welsh Folk Museum at St. Fagan's. See also the works by Dr. Iorwerth Peate and Professor G. J. Williams listed in note 75.

[1] This section does not attempt a full account either of conditions before the Union or of the Acts of Union themselves. For a detailed analysis, see *ante*, III, chap. xi, and also W. R. B. Robinson, 'Early Tudor policy towards Wales', *BBCS.*, XX (1962–4), 421–38; XXI (1964–5), 43–74, 334–61. The most complete account of the Union is in P. R. Roberts, 'The "Acts of Union" and the Tudor Settlement of Wales' (Ph.D. Thesis, Univ. of Cambridge, 1966).

[2] Robinson, *BBCS.*, XXI, 338–42. Thomas Wright, *The History of Ludlow and its Neighbourhood* (Ludlow, 1852), pp. 383–5.

[3] T. B. Pugh, *The Marcher Lordships of South Wales, 1415–1536* (Cardiff, 1963), pp. 3–48. T. B. Pugh and W. R. B. Robinson, 'The sessions in eyre in the lordships of Gower and Kilvey', *S. Wales and Mon. R.S.*, IV (1957), 111–22.

[4] *Ante*, III, 561–9. Roberts, 'The "Acts of Union"'; Penry Williams, *The Council in the Marches of Wales under Elizabeth I* (Cardiff, 1958), pp. 11–15.

[5] Ibid., pp. 15–21. The statutes of 26 Henry VIII cc. 4–6, printed in Ivor Bowen, *The Statutes of Wales* (London, 1908), pp. 51–62.

[6] Quot. in W. Ogwen Williams, *Tudor Gwynedd* (Caernarvonshire Historical Soc., 1958), p. 6. See also *L and P.*, *Addenda*, I, no. 1193; XII, i, no. 93; XV, no. 494.

[7] 27 Henry VIII c. 5; Bowen, *Statutes*, p. 67.

[8] 27 Henry VIII cc. 5, 24, 26; Bowen, *Statutes*, pp. 67–93. See William Rees, 'The Union of England and Wales, with a transcript of the Act of Union', *Trans. Cymm.*, 1937, pp. 27–100.

[9] 34 & 35 Henry VIII c. 26; Bowen, *Statutes*, pp. 101–33. The process of creating the various acts was a good deal more complicated than my summary suggests; but I am here concerned only with the final effects upon Glamorgan. For a fuller discussion, see Robinson, *BBCS.*, XXI, 334–61; Roberts, 'The "Acts of Union"'; and *ante*, III, chap. xi.

[10] Monmouthshire remained separate from the system set up for Wales.

[11] The Act speaks of Pembroke and Glamorgan as if they were already counties: though they might be so in name, they bore little resemblance to the shires of England, Rees, *Trans. Cymm.*, 1937, p. 32.

[12] William Rees, 'Gower and the March of Wales', *Arch. Camb.*, CX (1961), 1–29; *ante*, III, 571–2.

[13] 27 Henry VIII c. 24; 1 & 2 Philip and Mary, c. 15; Bowen, *Statutes*, pp. 73, 141.

[14] 32 Henry VIII c. 27. Robinson, *BBCS.*, XXI, 350–7.

[15] Robinson, loc cit., p. 357. See above, pp. 161–4, 175–7.

[16] 34 & 35 Henry VIII c. 26, s. 4; Bowen, *Statutes*, p. 102.

[17] See below, Section II, for the working of these institutions.

[18] 34 & 35 Henry VIII, c. 26, s. 128; Bowen, *Statutes*, p. 132; Rees, *Trans. Cymm.*, 1937, pp. 69–74. Also, 27 Henry VIII c. 26, s.20.

[19] Rees, loc. cit.; Ogwen Williams, *Tudor Gwynedd*, pp. 37–44. For a full discussion of the effect of the Union upon Welsh law, R.R. Davies, 'The twilight of Welsh law, 1284–1536', *History*, LI (1966), 143–64.

[20] Ogwen Williams, 'The survival of the Welsh language after the Union of England and Wales', *WHR.*, II (1964), 67–93.

[21] Glyn Roberts, 'Wales and England: antipathy and sympathy, 1282–1485', ibid., I (1963), 375–96.

[22] The most useful accounts are: T. G. Barnes, *Somerset, 1625–1640* (Oxford, 1961); W. B. Willcox, *Gloucestershire, a Study in Local Government, 1590–1640* (New Haven, 1940); W. Ogwen Williams, *Calendar of the Caernarvonshire Quarter Sessions Records*. Volume I (Caernarvonshire Historical Soc., 1956), introd.; Joel Hurstfield, 'County Government, 1530–1660', *Victoria County History of Wiltshire*, V (London, 1957), 80–110; J. H. Gleason, *The Justices of the Peace in England, 1558–1640* (Oxford, 1969); T. H. Lewis,

'The justices of the peace in Wales' and 'The administration of justice in the Welsh county', *Trans. Cymm.*, 1943–44, pp. 120–32, ibid., 1945, pp. 151–66.

²³ The Mansel papers are in NLW, Penrice and Margam Orig. Correspce. The Stradling letters have been printed in *Stradling Correspce*.

²⁴ For a full account of the central government, G. E. Aylmer, *The King's Servants* (London, 1961).

²⁵ *APC.*, VI, *1556–8*, 236, 251, 252–4, 273, 276, 282, 316, 347, 427.

²⁶ Ibid., XXI, 183.

²⁷ Ibid., XIV, 278; Flenley, *Register*, pp. 108, 123.

²⁸ *APC.*, XXVI, 310, 378.

²⁹ Ibid., XXII, 429; XXIII, 103.

³⁰ E. G. Jones, *Exchequer Proceedings*; T. I. Jeffreys-Jones, *Exchequer Proceedings, temp. James I.*

³¹ I. ab Owen Edwards, *Catalogue of Star Chamber Proceedings*; cf. Penry Williams, 'The Star Chamber and the Council in the Marches of Wales, 1558–1603', *BBCS.*, XVI (1956), 287–97. One other agency of central government deserves mention—the customs officials; see W. R. B. Robinson, *BBCS.*, XXIII, 347–96. I am grateful to Mr. Robinson for allowing me to see this article in typescript.

³² Penry Williams, *Council in the Marches*, pp. 50, 53.

³³ Ibid., chap. v.

³⁴ The Great Sessions heard cases of felony and murder; but the major conflicts of the shire did not often reach them. For examples of their work see *Cardiff Records*, II, chaps. v, vi; III, chap. iii; and K. O. Fox, 'An edited calendar of the first Brecknockshire Plea Roll of the Courts of King's Great Sessions in Wales, July 1542', *NLWJ.*, XIV (1965–6), 469–84. There is other material on the Great Sessions in Williams, *Council in the Marches*, pp. 25–6; E. J. Sherrington, 'The plea rolls of the courts of Great Sessions, 1541–75', *NLWJ.*, XIII (1963–4), 363–73; W. Ll. Williams, 'The King's Court of Great Sessions in Wales', *Y Cymmrodor*, XXVI (1916), 1–87; W. R. Williams, *History of the Great Sessions, with lives of the Welsh Judges* (Brecon, 1899).

³⁵ *L and P.*, XIX, i, nos. 273, 276; ibid., XIV, i, no. 654 (14).

³⁶ See above, p. 176.

³⁷ *L and P.*, XX, i, no. 1105.

³⁸ G. Scott Thomson, *Lords Lieutenants in the Sixteenth Century* (London, 1923), pp. 24–42.

³⁹ Williams, *Council in the Marches*, pp. 112–14.

⁴⁰ Flenley, *Register*, pp. 55, 60, 67–9, 70–4.

⁴¹ PRO, SP 12/89/42.

⁴² Ibid., 98/23; 124/50; 125/34, 39; 133/19, 20. Flenley, *Register*, pp. 168–71. G. Scott Thomson, 'The origin and growth of the office of deputy-lieutenant', *TRHS.*, iv, V (1922), 154–5.

⁴³ *APC.*, XLV, *1629–30*, p. 213; Flenley, *Register*, pp. 218–20, 226–7.

⁴⁴ 4 & 5 Philip and Mary cc. 2 & 3.

⁴⁵ PRO, SP 12/92/53; cf. ibid., 125/34. Flenley, *Register*, pp. 200–8: these instructions for Denbighshire probably applied also to Glamorgan. For the militia in general see L. O. J. Boynton, *The Elizabethan Militia, 1558–1638* (London, 1967), *passim*.

⁴⁶ For the work of the sheriff see Barnes, *Somerset*, chap. v; Ogwen Williams, *Caerns. Quarter Sessions Records*, I, 23–9; Willcox, *Gloucestershire*, pp. 38–49; C. H. Karraker, *The Seventeenth-Century Sheriff* (Chapel Hill, 1930), chaps. i–v.

⁴⁷ *Stradling Correspce.*, nos. 8–9; see above, p. 194.

⁴⁸ George Owen, 'Dialogue of the Government of Wales', *Cymmr. Rec. Ser.*, (London, 1906), part iii, pp. 62–3, 69–81. J. E. Neale, *The Elizabethan House of Commons* (London, 1949), *passim* and especially chap. iii. I am grateful to Professor Glanmor Williams for drawing my attention to Owen's remarks.

⁴⁹ Barnes, *Somerset*, p. 126; *Stradling Correspce.*, no. 215; Owen, 'Dialogue', p. 67.

⁵⁰ *Stradling Correspce.*, nos. 233, 192–5; cf. nos. 7, 45, 49–54.

⁵¹ Ibid., nos. 79, 90; cf. nos. 84, 89. Also *APC.*, XXI, 183; XXII, 514, 541.

⁵² Barnes, *Somerset*, pp. 129–30, 135–42; Willcox, *Gloucestershire*, pp. 45–8.

⁵³ Owen, 'Dialogue', pp. 69–74, 80–83; *Stradling Correspce.*, nos 29, 64, 207; *APC.*, XXII, 429; XXIII, 103. See also *Stradling Correspce.*, nos. 42, 183, 212, 213; *APC.*, XXII, 514, for the office of gaoler.

[54] The principal works used are: Barnes, *Somerset*, chap. iii, Willcox, *Gloucestershire*, pp. 55-71; Williams, *Caerns. Quarter Sessions Records*, pp. lxxxvi-cviii; Hurstfield, *V.C.H. Wilts.*, V, 80-110.

[55] Barnes, *Somerset*, p. 53.

[56] 39 Eliz. cc. 3 & 4. E. M. Leonard, *Early History of English Poor Relief* (London, 1900), pp. 318-26.

[57] Hurstfield, *V.C.H. Wilts.*, V, 94-7; Flenley, *Register*, pp. 95-6. 14 Eliz. c. 5.

[58] Flenley, *Register*, pp. 177-9; cf. pp. 227-9.

[59] Ibid., pp. 122-3; cf. pp. 153-6.

[60] Ibid., pp. 123-7, 146-8, 100-1, 116-17, 158-60.

[61] Barnes, *Somerset*, p. 67. See above, pp. 194-5, for the burden of the 1630s.

[62] PRO, SP 12, vol. 96; vol. 104, p. 56. Flenley, *Register*, p. 142. Barnes, *Somerset*, pp. 80-5.

[63] PRO, SP Dom. Chas. I, 412/31.

[64] Flenley, *Register*, pp. 108-9.

[65] *APC.*, VII, 278-90. For an extended account of Tudor piracy, see Carys Hughes, 'Wales and Piracy', above, chap. I, note 104.

[66] *APC.*, IX, 298; PRO, SP 12/110/2, 3; 111/35; 112/5. For some of the vicissitudes of this commission, see above, pp. 186-7.

[67] *Stradling Correspce.*, no. 11.

[68] Ibid., no. 178. For other examples see nos. 12, 169, 206.

[69] Ibid., no. 66.

[70] Ibid., no. 67.

[71] Ibid., no. 201.

[72] Ibid., nos. 153-5; cf. also nos. 26, 87, 149, 198, 203-4, 214, 226, 230, 245, 256.

[73] W. S. K. Thomas, 'Municipal government in Swansea, 1485-1640', *Glam. Hist.*, I, 32.

[74] UCS, Swansea Corporation Records, Book of Orders, 1569-1682, p. 210.

[75] Thomas, *Glam. Hist.*, I, 33; UCS, Book of Orders, pp. 74, 194.

[76] Ibid., pp. 46, 78.

[77] Thomas, *Glam. Hist.*, I, 34. UCS, Swansea Common Hall Book, f.29.

[78] UCS, Book of Orders, p. 154.

[79] UCS, Swansea Common Attorneys' Books, *passim*; Book of Orders, pp. 51, 151, 25, 26.

[80] UCS, Common Attorneys' Books, *passim*.

[81] UCS, Swansea Benevolences, 1563-1569, *passim*.

[82] UCS, Book of Orders, pp. 78, 210; Common Hall Book, ff. 11, 21, 45-8.

[83] UCS, Benevolences, *passim*. W. S. K. Thomas, 'Tudor and Jacobean Swansea: the social scene', *Morgannwg*, V (1961), 37-42.

[84] UCS, Book of Orders, pp. 178, 182, 187, 146, 159, 50; Common Hall Book, ff. 79, 103-8.

[85] UCS, Book of Orders, f. 78; Common Hall Book, f. 11.

[86] UCS, Book of Orders, p. 106; cf. also pp. 131, 139, 186, 202; Common Hall Book, f. 70.

[87] Thomas, *Morgannwg*, V, 42-4; UCS, Common Hall Book, f. 11.

[88] Thomas, *Morgannwg*, V, 47-8.

[89] NLW, P and M Orig. Correspce., L3, 6.

[90] William Rees, *Cardiff*, p. 39. *Merrick's Glam. Antiqs.*, pp. 95-6.

[91] Rees, *Cardiff*, p. 49. For the influence of the earl, below, sections III and IV.

[92] Ibid., pp. 42-7, 78-82; *Cardiff Records*, I, 50-72.

[93] Owen, 'Dialogue', pp. 83-9. J. P. Dawson, *A History of the Lay Judges* (Cambridge, Mass., 1960), chap. iv.

[94] See the map of Glamorgan families (map 3). The material for office-holders is drawn from the following sources. For justices of the peace my final lists were taken from J. R. S. Phillips, *The Justices of the Peace in Wales and Monmouthshire, 1541 to 1689*, to be published by the History and Law Committee of the Board of Celtic Studies. I am most grateful to Dr. Phillips for allowing me to use his lists in typescript: they enabled me substantially to correct and supplement my own. The names of sheriffs are given in PRO *Lists and Indexes*, no. 9 (1898), and of Members of Parliament in *Return of the Name of Every Member of the Lower House . . . 1213-1874* (3 vols. Parliamentary Papers, 1878). The copies of these latter two volumes in the reading-room at the PRO contain useful additions and corrections. There is no single available list of deputy-lieutenants; their names have been discovered from a variety of sources, of which the most important are: PRO, SP 12/133/19, 20; *APC.*, XIX, 248, 304, 309; ibid., XXV, 13-7; NLW MS. 7895E; PRO SP Dom., Charles I, 18/5, 81/46, 116/9.

[95] See the accompanying family tree of the Herberts.

[96] *DWB.*, pp. 916–9. Robinson, *BBCS.*, XX, 421–38; XXI, 43–74, 334–61. Idem, 'The earls of Worcester and their estates, 1596–1642' (B.Litt. Thesis, Univ. of Oxford, 1958). I am grateful to Mr. Robinson for allowing me to look at the typescript of this thesis. Idem, *BBCS.*, XXII, 357–88; XXIII, 60–99. *Ante*, III, chap. xi.

[97] Rice Lewis, 'Breviat', *S. Wales and Mon. R.S.*, III, 120–22. *DWB.*, pp. 350–4.

[98] Ex inf. Professor A. H. Dodd and the History of Parliament Trust.

[99] *DWB.*, p. 350 and references therein cited. For evidence to establish that George Herbert was the elder brother, Robinson, *BBCS.*, XXI, 338, n.3.

[100] *DWB.*, p. 350.

[101] Above, pp. 172–4.

[102] Glanmor Williams, *Morgannwg*, VI, 35–51.

[103] *DWB.*, pp. 611–3.

[104] *Limbus*, pp. 84–5. See above, p. 173. For Bussy Mansel, *DWB.*, p. 612.

[105] *APC.*, XIX, 304, 309.

[106] *DWB.*, pp. 67–8; *Limbus*, p. 374; *APC.*, XIX, 304, 309; Lewis, *S. Wales and Mon. R.S.*, III, 126–7; Aylmer, *The King's Servants*, pp. 318–9.

[107] *DWB.*, pp. 1121–23. For the competition over Barbara Gamage's marriage above, pp. 183–6.

[108] Quot. Griffiths, *Morgannwg*, VII, 31.

[109] *DWB.*, pp. 925–7; Griffiths, *Morganwg*, VII, 15–47; Glanmor Williams, *Vale of History*, pp. 85–95.

[110] *Limbus*, pp. 348–59. Beaupré is a corruption of Y Bewpyr.

[111] *DWB.*, p. 17; *Stradling Correspce.*, nos. 20, 244; *Limbus*, pp. 340–43.

[112] *DWB.*, p. 60; Lewis, *S. Wales and Mon. R.S.*, III, 136; *Limbus*, p. 369.

[113] *DWB.*, pp. 617–18; *Limbus*, pp. 7–10. See above, pp. 186–8.

[114] *DWB.*, p. 546; Leland, *Itin. Wales*, p. 18; *Limbus*, p. 38.

[115] *DWB.*, p. 532; *Limbus*, pp. 412–15.

[116] See note 94.

[117] Above, p. 153.

[118] Huntington Library MS. EL, 7196, 7215.

[119] The names of the sheriffs are taken from PRO *Lists and Indexes*, no. ix: *List of Sheriffs for England and Wales* (London, 1898).

[120] See J. R. S. Phillips, *Justices of the Peace*, introd., for a full discussion of the problems.

[121] Cf. Gleason, *Justices of the Peace*, chap. iv, esp. p. 49.

[122] Above, p. 166. Cf. Gleason, *Justices of the Peace*, chap. v.

[123] The names of members are taken largely from the official *Return of Members of Parliament* (1878).

[124] On Mathew and Sidney, see above, pp. 181–8. *Stradling Correspce.*, nos. 15, 68. NLW, Bute MSS. Box 132, parcel B.

[125] Violet A. Rowe, 'The influence of the earls of Pembroke on parliamentary elections, 1625–41', *EHR.*, L (1935), 242–56; L. Stone, 'The electoral influence of the second earl of Salisbury, 1614–68', ibid., LXXI (1956), 394–400; A. H. Dodd, 'Wales's parliamentary apprenticeship, 1536–1625', *Trans. Cymm.*, 1942, pp. 42, 71. The outsiders were Philip, Lord Herbert, returned once; his son, once; Sir Robert Mansel, three times.

[126] Dodd, loc cit., p. 71.

[127] NLW, Bute MSS., Box 132, parcel C.

[128] But although a Herbert, he may not have been elected by Pembroke influence. He was certainly opposed to Pembroke on national issues. See Mary Frear Keeler, *The Long Parliament, 1640–1641, a biographical study of its members* (Philadelphia 1954), pp. 212–13.

[129] Dodd, loc. cit., pp. 9, 21.

[130] Ibid., pp. 31, 35, 38, 42, 50, 60, 62, 65, 70, 71. Idem, 'Wales in the Parliaments of Charles I', *Trans Cymm.*, 1945, pp. 21–3, 26–8, 33, 37–40, 48–9.

[131] T. J. Hopkins, 'Rice Merrick of Cottrell', *Morgannwg*, VIII (1964), 5–13.

[132] It is worth remarking that of the six families which have emerged from this analysis as dominant in Glamorgan, five are described by Professor Glanmor Williams, as 'the main beneficiaries from the sale of monastic lands in Glamorgan', *WHR.*, III, 37. The only dominant family not to have benefited from the dissolution were the Aubreys, who of course entered the county too late. But one should not conclude that the dissolution created the dominant families: men like Mansel and Carne, possibly the others, benefited because they were already powerful in the county.

[133] PRO, STAC 2/8, ff. 139–49. For a fuller account of the incident, Gareth E.

Jones, 'Glamorgan Gentry', pp. 318–22; idem, 'Local administration and justice in sixteenth-century Glamorgan', *Morgannwg*, IX (1965), 29–30.

[134] PRO, STAC 2/9, f. 65; *ante*, III, chap. xi; *L and P.*, XV, nos 129, 146.

[135] PRO, STAC 4/4/29; *Cardiff Records*, IV, 74–9; Griffiths, *Morgannwg*, VII, 34–5.

[136] Jones, *Morgannwg*, IX, 31–2.

[137] Glanmor Williams, *Gower*, II, 6–11; J. Davies, *West Gower*, IV, 165–95; PRO, STAC 2/20/160; 2/24/365; 4/1/26; *APC.*, VI, 236, 251, 252–4, 273, 276, 282, 316, 347, 427; *CPR. Eliz.*, I, 112.

[138] Pugh, *Marcher Lordships of South Wales*, pp. 47–8, 145–7; *ante*, III, chap. xi.

[139] Quot. Pugh, *Marcher Lordships of South Wales*, p. 48. I have followed Mr. Pugh's explanation of these events.

[140] PRO, SP 12/195/126; *Cardiff Records*, I, 347.

[141] Ibid., III, 72ff., 267ff. NLW, Penrice and Margam MS. no. 3356.

[142] *Cardiff Records*, III, 278–94.

[143] NLW, P and M Orig. Correspce., L43. This letter is dated only 15 May. It must be prior to 1571, when Stradling died.

[144] *Cardiff Records*, I, 393–6.

[145] See above, p. 198. NLW, Penrice and Margam MS. no. 2411. *Cardiff Records*, V, 191ff. *Ante*, III, chap. xi, n. 122.

[146] Flenley, *Register*, pp. 88, 91–2. The early part of the dispute over the coroners is described, ibid., pp. 88–92.

[147] Ibid., pp. 85–90.

[148] PRO. STAC 8 (i.e. Star Chamber Proc. James I) 188/30. When I consulted this document, it was misplaced into the reign of James I. The authorities at the PRO told me that they would attach it to STAC 5 (i.e. Star Chamber Proc. Elizabeth) /J9/39—depositions in the same case.

[149] *Stradling Correspce.*, no. 255.

[150] NLW, P and M Orig. Correspce., L8. This is clearly a reply to Grove's letter, although it is undated.

[151] Accounts of these disputes are found in NLW, P and M Orig. Correspce., L11–19, 42, 56; also in Penrice and Margam MSS., nos. 3441, 5746–8, 5819–22, 6060–2. See *Stradling Correspce.*, nos. 58–60, 120.

[152] NLW, Penrice and Margam MS. no. 3475; see also no. 3441.

[153] NLW, P and M Orig. Correspce., L16.

[154] *Stradling Correspce.*, nos. 58, 59.

[155] NLW, Penrice and Margam MS., no. 5746.

[156] *Stradling Correspce.*, no. 60.

[157] For a fuller account and for references, see Penry Williams, 'Controversy in Elizabethan Glamorgan: the rebuilding of Cardiff Bridge', *Morgannwg*, II (1958), 38–46.

[158] Signatories to the shire's first petition are given in NLW, Penrice and Margam MS. no. 2770.

[159] Ibid.

[160] NLW, P and M Orig. Correspce., L44.

[161] Ibid., L29.

[162] Rees, *S Wales and Mon. R.S.*, IV, (1957), 178–80. PRO, STAC 5/P51/39, M12/23; SP 12/168/7, 24, 32; 169/14, 15.

[163] Williams, *Council in the Marches*, pp. 242–6, for details and sources. See genealogical table at p. 185 for Barbara Gamage's relatives.

[164] *Stradling Correspce.*, no. 22.

[165] *APC.*, XIV, 143, 168, 203. PRO, SP 12/195/59. *Stradling Correspce.*, nos. 27, 70, 229.

[166] Ibid., no. 70.

[167] Ibid., no. 229. For further details, see Carys Hughes, 'Wales and Piracy', p. 253 ff.

[168] PRO, SP 12/200/19, 32, 43, 51; 204/7; 211/16. BM Harleian MS. 6994, f. 82. *APC.*, XV, 88, 232.

[169] PRO, SP 12/200/51.

[170] Ibid., 204/7.

[171] PRO, STAC 5/L47/6, f. 19. For an earlier dispute between Lewis and Mathew, see above p. 187, and also STAC 5/A1/10.

[172] Stradling, 'Lower Borowes', *S. Wales and Mon. R.S.*, I, 98–113. Also, PRO, STAC 5/A2/24.

[173] Stradling, *S. Wales and Mon. R.S.*, I, 102.

[174] Ibid., p. 103.

[175] Ibid., pp. 110–3.

[176] PRO, STAC 5/A2/24.

[177] Stradling, *S. Wales and Mon. R.S.*, I, 107.

[178] PRO, STAC 5/L8/3.

[179] Ibid., L25/6.

[180] Ibid., M25/32; M8/30; R8/19; L25/6.

[181] Ibid.

[182] Ibid., M51/37.

[183] Stradling, *S. Wales and Mon. R.S.*, I, 68, 108–9, 112.

[184] PRO, STAC 8/296/26. For another case of minor violence involving Mathew, ibid., 183/36 (Countess of Pembroke v. Roger Jones *et al.*, cf. above, p. 100).

[185] The Star Chamber proceedings for the reign of Charles I are either missing or are not available to researchers. There is thus a gap in the material; but even allowing for this there seems to have been a decline in violent feuding.

[186] *Limbus*, pp. 12–5; *APC.*, *1613–14*, pp. 87, 185–6, 446–7, 539.

[187] BM, Stowe MS. 39, ff. 44–5.

[188] PRO, STAC 8/195/16, 198/11, 202/36, 239/19, 241/18, 251/24, 254/22, 299/12, 301/23, 302/19, 304/38.

[189] Ibid., 234/6.

[190] Ibid., 270/11.

[191] PRO, SP Dom. James I, 48/121.

[192] PRO, SP 12/260/40; 268/124; 271/37.

[193] *APC.*, *1613–14*, pp. 111–12, 433–4; ibid., *1615–16*, pp. 89–90, 228–31, 516–19; ibid., *1616–17*, pp. 305–6; ibid., *1618–19*, pp. 118–19, 363–6; ibid., *1619–21*, p. 215; ibid., *1621–3*, pp. 89, 225; ibid., *1623–5*, pp. 8, 206.

[194] PRO, SP Dom., Charles I, 56/8.

[195] Ibid., 42/114, 53/84. But contrast the more gloomy reports in 18/5; cf. Barnes, *Somerset*, pp. 163–8.

[196] Barnes, *Somerset*, pp. 172–81; *APC.*, *1630–1*, pp. 213–14.

[197] PRO, SP Dom., Charles I, 193/64.

[198] *APC.*, *1623–5*, pp. 351, 371–2, 378, 467, 472; *1625–6*, pp. 42–5; *1627*, pp. 455–7, 500–1.

[199] PRO, SP Dom., Charles I, 81/46.

[200] Barnes, *Somerset*, p. 259; *APC.*, *1628–9*, pp. 419–21; Boynton, *Elizabethan Militia*, chap. viii.

[201] PRO, SP Dom. Charles I, 202/42, 224/49.

[202] Ibid., 278/29, 293/47, 370/59. See Barnes, *Somerset*, chap. ix for the defects in the militia of a county whose deputy-lieutenants usually reported in optimistic tones.

[203] M. D. Gordon, 'The collection of Ship-Money in the reign of Charles I', *TRHS.*, iii, IV (1910), 141–62; Barnes, *Somerset*, pp. 209–10.

[204] PRO, SP Dom. Charles I, 302/85, 303/120, 311/28, 312/63, 314/46, 330/57.

[205] Ibid., 331/61, 349/118. The receipt for the 1636 levy is dated 15 March 1637.

A. H. Dodd, 'The pattern of politics in Stuart Wales', *Trans. Cymm.*, 1948, p. 38.

[206] PRO, SP Dom. Charles I, 448/62; Dodd, *Trans Cymm.*, 1948, pp. 36–9; *CSPD 1640*, p. 452; ibid., *1640–1*, p. 58; cf. Barnes, *Somerset*, chap. viii.

[207] PRO, SP Dom. Charles I, 413/111; *CSPD 1638–9*, p. 514; Dodd, *Trans. Cymm.*, 1948, pp. 43–4.

[208] Ibid., p. 46; PRO, SP Dom. Charles I, 455/80; also 453/115.

[209] Ibid., 453/115, 454/66, 455/80.

[210] Ibid., 459/28, 29, 30.

[211] *CSPD 1640*, p. 483.

[212] Ibid., *1636–7*, pp. xxxvi–xl, 183; Dodd, *Trans. Cymm.*, 1948, pp. 40, 44–6.

[213] *CSPD 1640–1*, pp. 16, 48. On the events of 1640 in Wales see A. H. Dodd, 'Wales and the Second Bishops' War (1640)', *BBCS.*, XII (1948), 92–6.

[214] Huntington Library MS. HL EL 7545.

[215] *DWB.*, p. 351; Dodd, *Trans Cymm.*, 1948, pp. 41, 51.

[216] Keeler, *The Long Parliament*, pp. 212–3.

[217] For example, in Kent. See A. M. Everitt, *The Community of Kent and the Great Rebellion, 1640–60* (Leicester, 1966), *passim*.

[218] For example, Barnes, *Somerset*, chaps. vii–xi.

[219] Dodd., *Trans. Cymm.*, 1948, pp. 58–9. See also Alan Everitt, 'Social mobility in early modern England', *Past and Present*, no. 33 (1966), p. 64. Professor Everitt suggests that counties where new families predominated tended to support Parliament in the civil war. The example of Glamorgan confirms this: here was a royalist county whose upper ranks had long been stable.

[220] Quot. *Ante*, III, 580.

[221] PRO, SP 12, 200/51.

[222] Cf. W. T. MacCaffrey, *Exeter, 1540–1640* (Cambridge, Mass., 1958), chap. ix.

[223] Compare Cardiff's behaviour in the Cardiff Bridge dispute and in the quarrel over Stradling's and Mathew's piracy commission with its struggle for independence in the suits against the Dowager Countess under James I.

[224] Williams, *Council in the Marches*, p. 279.

[225] PRO, SP 12/107/4.

[226] George Owen, 'Description of Wales', *Cymmrodorion Rec. Ser.*, no. 1, part III (London, 1906), p. 316.

[227] *Stradling Correspce.*, nos. 79, 89.

[228] *APC.*, XXI, 183, 215; XXII, 429, 514, 541; XXIII, 103. *Cardiff Records*, I, 331–42.

[229] Ibid., I, 315–16; Stradling, *S. Wales and Mon. R.S.*, I, 110–13.

[230] PRO, SP 12/112/5; cf. *ibid.*, 110/2, 3, 4; 111/1, 35; 112/27; 122/2; 123/39. For further evidence on the complicity of local officials with pirates, Carys Hughes, 'Wales and Piracy', chap. iii, part C.

[231] Quot. Pugh, *Marcher Lordships*, p. 43.

[232] Quot. ibid., p. 48.

[233] *Merrick's Glam. Antiqs.*, p. 88. I am grateful to Professor Glanmor Williams for this reference.

[234] Ibid., p. 89.

[235] Owen, 'Dialogue', p. 91.

[236] Penry Williams, 'The Welsh borderland under Queen Elizabeth', *WHR.*, I (1960), 30–1. Stone, *Crisis of the Aristocracy*, chap. v.

[237] Above, p. 198.

[1] A very useful work on all aspects of the religious changes in the diocese of Llandaff in the sixteenth century is Lawrence Thomas, *The Reformation in the Old Diocese of Llandaff* (Cardiff, 1930).

[2] For Chapuys's reports on Wales, see *L and P.*, V, 432, 563; VI, 902; VII, 957, 1057, 1141, 1193, 1534.

[3] *L and P.*, VII, 939, 1020, 1169, 1607; X, 45, 46; cf. Clark, *Cartae*, V, 1902–3.

[4] E. J. Saunders, 'Gweithiau Lewis Morgannwg' (M.A. Thesis, Univ. of Wales, 1922), no. xviii.

[5] For Athequa, see *DNB*, *s.n.*; Clark, *Cartae*, V, 1902–3; Thomas, *Llandaff*, pp. 3–12; Garrett Mattingley, *Catherine of Aragon* (London, 1950), pp. 270–2, 307; *CSP Span., Supplement to Vols. I and II*, pp. 234, 325, 375, 411.

[6] *L and P.*, XII, i, 969, for the Gower priest; Thomas, *Llandaff*, pp. 12–17; PRO, E36/63, pp. 17–20; *L and P.*, VII, 769, 1025 (2), 1216 (7); Clark, *Cartae*, V, 1878–9 for Ewenni, and translation in J. P. Turbervill, *Ewenny Priory* (London, 1901), pp. 49–51.

[7] *L and P.*, IX, 806; X, 45–6, 481; XII, ii, 1266.

[8] *DNB*, *DWB*, *s.n.* Carne; *L and P.*, VI, 601, 1111; Glanmor Williams, *Morgannwg*, VI, 33–51.

[9] The best study of the dissolution is David Knowles, *The Religious Orders in England: III. The Tudor Age* (Cambridge, 1959); cf. also Joyce Youings, *The Dissolution of the Monasteries* (London, 1971). For the dissolution in Glamorgan, Glanmor Williams, *Welsh Reformation Essays* (Cardiff, 1967), pp. 91–110. Cromwell's scheme, *L and P.*, VII, 1355. The returns for Wales are in *Valor Eccl.*, IV.

[10] *L and P.*, VIII, 149 (169); IX, 161, 695; cf. PRO, SP 1/95, p. 168; 1/98, pp. 56–7; Thomas, *Llandaff*, pp. 21–8.

[11] *L and P.*, IX, 806; PRO, SP 1/99, p. 35.

[12] PRO, LR 6/151; Glanmor Williams, *The Welsh Church from Conquest to Reformation* (Cardiff, 1962), p. 412.

[13] Turbervill, *Ewenny*, pp. 50–2; Clark, *Cartae*, V, 1927–9.

[14] *L and P.*, X, 1222; XII, i, 311 (43); XIII, ii, 457 i(3); XIV, i, 395; cf. PRO, SP 1/143, pp. 183–4.

[15] Knowles, *Religious Orders*, III, 360–1.

[16] *L and P.*, XIII, ii, 294–5; PRO, E36/115/ff.35, 83; Clark, *Cartae*, V, 1872–6; Thomas, *Llandaff*, pp. 62–73; William Rees, 'The suppression of the friaries', *S.Wales and Mon. R.S.*, III (1954), 7–19.

[17] *L and P.*, XIV, i, p. 602; XIII, i, 575, f. 25b; for the identification of one or two who may have become priests, T. J. Prichard, 'The reformation in the deanery of Llandaff', *Morgannwg*, XIII (1969), 19.

[18] *Cardiff Records*, III, 32–7.

[19] W. de G. Birch, *A History of Neath Abbey* (Neath, 1902), pp. 117–18.

[20] Clark, *Cartae*, V, 1903–4, 1918–23.

[21] Ibid., V, 1936, 1949–50; PRO, Particulars for grants, Henry VIII, nos. 243–4 (Ewenni), 1067 (Llantwit).

[22] *L and P.*, XVI, 1226 (5); XVIII, i, 623(4), 802.

[23] Ibid., XVIII, i, 981(54); PRO, Particulars for grants, Henry VIII, no. 1058 (St. John); no. 329 (Cromwell); *L and P.*, XVII, 220(95); 1012(5); XVIII, i, 474(11); Clark, *Cartae*, V, 1932–3; PRO, Particulars for grants, Henry VIII, no. 567 (Heneage); *CPR, 1547–8*, p. 278.

[24] Clark, *Cartae*, V, 1918–22, 1937–48, 1964–71, 2023–6, 2031–1; cf. also, Williams, *Morgannwg*, VI, 33–51.

[25] Turbervill, *Ewenny, passim*; PRO, Particulars for grants, Henry VIII, nos. 243–5; *L and P.*, XXI, ii, 332.

[26] Clark, *Cartae*, V, 1932–3; *L and P.*, XVIII, ii, 107(62) (Stradling); *Cardiff Records*, II, 16–7; *CPR, 1553–4*, pp. 153–4 (Lewis); *L and P.*, XX, i, 465 (101); XX, ii, 910(82); Rees, *S. Wales and Mon. R.S.*, III, 14–15.

[27] For the influence of these families, see chap. iii.

[28] For fuller details, Williams, *Welsh Ref. Essays*, pp. 104–5.

[29] *Valor Eccl.*, IV, 351; for the condition of Welsh monasteries generally, Williams, *Welsh Church*, chaps. x and xi.

[30] A. G. Dickens, *Robert Holgate* (York, 1955).

[31] Thomas, *Llandaff*, pp. 61–2.

[32] Ibid., pp. 80–5; *DNB, s.n.*

[33] James Gairdner, *Lollardy and the Reformation in England* (4 vols. London, 1908–13), II, 141; Hugh Latimer, *Sermons and Remains* (Parker Soc., 1845), p. 395; *L and P.*, XIII, ii, 345; E. A. Lewis and J. Conway Davies, *Records of the Court of Augmentations relating to Wales* (Cardiff, 1954), pp. 141–2.

[34] *Cardiff Records*, I, 372–80, cf. Thomas, *Llandaff*, pp. 75–9.

[35] For Gamage, PCC, Spert XXII. For translations of the New Testament, Henry Lewis, 'Darnau o'r efengylau', *Y Cymmrodor*, XXXI (1921), 193–216; cf. Williams, *Welsh Church*, p. 418.

[36] *Cardiff Records*, I, 225.

[37] C. H. Smyth, *Cranmer and the Reformation under Edward VI* (Cambridge, 1926). A modern reprint of *Kynniver Llith a Ban* was edited by John Fisher (Caerdydd, 1931).

[38] E. D. Jones, 'A survey of South Wales Chantries, 1546', *Arch Camb.*, LXXXIX (1934), 135–55. The Chantry Certificates of 1549, PRO, E301/74, extracts from which are printed in *Cardiff Records*, II, 293–309; cf. Thomas, *Llandaff*, chap. vi.

[39] *Cardiff Records*, I, 259–60; Lewis and Davies, *Augmentations Proceedings*, pp. 116, 413, 417–18, 420–1.

[40] *Cardiff Records*, III, 43ff., 350–2.

[41] Glamorgan is the only Welsh county for which a fairly full record of church goods survives, PRO, E117/12/17, some extracts from which are printed in *Cardiff Records*, I, 379–86; cf. Thomas, *Llandaff*, chap. vii.

[42] No contemporary record of the Llandaff manor transaction is known to survive. It is first mentioned in *Merrick's Glam. Antiqs.*, p. 101. A copy of the grant exists in Cardiff MS. 840. Babington's jest is recorded by Newell, *Llandaff*, p. 143. Another clumsier version of the same story was given by William Harrison, *The Description of England* (Ed. Ithaca, N.Y., 1968), p. 57.

[43] *TLlM.*, pp. 122–6, 138–41; for Thomas ab Ieuan ap Rhys's poems, *Hen Gwndidau*, pp. 1–48, especially pp. 31–44.

[44] *CSP Span.*, X, 368; *APC*, II, 225–6, 304; III, 6, 411, 433.

[45] *CSP Span., 1553*, pp. 13, 25–6, 129; cf. H. F. M. Prescott, *Mary I* (London,

1952), pp. 172–4. *Hen Gwndidau*, pp. 43–4, 59–60.

[46] Ibid.

[47] *APC*, V, 122; *CSP Span., 1554*, pp. 88, 97.

[48] *CPR, 1553–4*, p. 175.

[49] For Bangor and St. David's, Glanmor Williams, 'The episcopal registers of the diocese of St. David's', *BBCS*, XIV (1950), 45–54. For Lipyngton, E. A. Lewis, *Early Chancery Proceedings* . . . (Cardiff, 1937), p. 209; for Morgan, PRO, C3/122/70.

[50] *Cardiff Records*, I, 213, 235; V, 475–8; John Foxe, *Acts and Monuments* . . . Ed. G. Townsend and S. R. Cattley (8 vols. London, 1838), VII, 28–33.

[51] Ibid.

[52] *Cardiff Records*, I, 379–86; T. J. Prichard, *Morgannwg*, XIII, 16–8; Thomas *Llandaff*, pp. 106–12.

[53] *TLlM.*, pp. 159–60.

[54] *CSP Span.*, I, 86.

[55] Glanmor Williams, 'The royal visitation of the diocese of Llandaff, 1559', *NLWJ.*, IV (1946), 189–97; idem, *Welsh Ref. Essays*, pp. 141–54; Prichard, *Morgannwg*, XIII, 19–22; Thomas, 'Swansea, 1485–1660', p. 221.

[56] BM, Lansdowne, MS. 8, pp. 193, 195, 199, 202; cf. Matthew Parker, *Correspondence* (Parker Soc., 1853), pp. 257–61.

[57] *HMC. Hatfield MSS.*, IV, 215; XI, 144, 232.

[58] *CSPD, 1628–9*, p. 570.

[59] E. J. Newell, *Llandaff* (London, 1902), pp. 143–4; for details of leases, NLW, Church in Wales Records, Ll.Ch./4 (Llandaff Chapter Act Book, 1573–1640), pp. 4–5; *HMC. Hatfield MSS.*, V, 290–1; *Stradling Correspondence*, pp. 280–1; *DNB, s.n.* Godwin.

[60] J. A. Bradley, 'The speech of William Blethin, bishop of Llandaff . . .' *Y Cymmrodor*, XXXI (1921), 240–64; *Merrick's Glam. Antiqs.*, p. 102.

[61] *Cardiff Records*, V, 8–10; Geraint Gruffydd, 'Bishop Francis Godwin's injunctions for the diocese of Llandaff', *JHSCW*, IV (1954), 14–22.

[62] *Cardiff Records*, III, 112–15 (Nicholas); PCC, Hayes 75 (Herbert), Stafford 95 (Evans); NLW, Llandaff P.R. 1611 (Philip); ibid., 1612 for another comparable cleric, Rice Morgan of Wenvoe.

[63] The original returns are in BM, Harleian MS. 595, ff. 1–8. A transcript exists in Clark, *Cartae*, VI, 2144–8.

[63A] For Bleddyn's letters and others, *Stradling Correspce.*, pp. 83–91, 331.

[64] Thomas, *Llandaff*, pp. 118–19, 127; *Stradling Correspce.*, pp. 83–7.

[65] Thomas, *Llandaff*, pp. 118–19, 127.

[66] Gruffydd, *JHSCW.*, IV, 16.

[67] *Hen Gwndidau*, pp. 138, 184–5, 187–92.

[68] Ibid., *passim*, but esp. pp. 98–9, 75, 81–91.

[69] Ibid., pp. 162, 187–8.

[70] John Fisher, 'Wales in the time of Queen Elizabeth', *Arch Camb.*, vi, XV (1915), 237–52.

[71] *CSPD 1581–90*, p. 383; *HMC. Wells Cathedral MSS. 10th Report*, III, 249.

[72] Turbervill, *Ewenny*, pp. 59–61; *CSP Rome*, I, 15–16; PCC, Loftus 21; *APC 1550–2*, pp. 411, 433; David Williams, 'The miracle at St. Donat's', *The Welsh Review*, 1947, pp. 33–8; Griffiths, *Morgannwg*, VII, 34–7.

[73] M. Bateson, 'Original letters from the bishops to the Privy Council', *Camden Society Miscellany*, IX (1893), 81.

[74] PRO, SP 12/66, p. 29; ibid., p. 19; Thomas, *Llandaff*, pp. 129–31; PCC, Holney 21.

[75] J. Strype, *The Life and Acts of John Whitgift* (3 vols. Oxford, 1822), I, 165–6; Beddyn's returns, PRO SP 12/118, no. II, ii, 129–30; F. H. Pugh 'Glamorgan recusants, 1577–1611', *S. Wales and Mon. R.S.*, III (1954), 49–68; W. R. Trimble, *The Catholic Laity in Elizabethan England* (Havard, 1964), chap. iii.

[76] Pugh, *S. Wales and Mon. R.S.*, III, 52–8.

[77] *APC 1591–2*, p. 543; A Leslie Evans, *The Story of Sker House* (Port Talbot, 1956), pp. 14–15; *HMC. Hatfield House MSS.*, XI, 460. The returns for 1603 are in BM, Harleian MS., 280, pp. 162b–164; cf. also Emyr G. Jones, *Cymru a'r Hen Ffydd* (Caerdydd, 1951), pp. 38–40.

[78] Pugh, *S. Wales and Mon. R.S.*, III, 49–68; J. M. Cleary, 'The Catholic resistance in Wales, 1568–78', *Blackfriars*, XXXVIII (1957), 111–25; Trimble, *Catholic Laity*, p. 164.

[79] Pugh, *S. Wales and Mon. R.S.*, III, *passim*. Roland Mathias, *Whitsun Riot* (London, 1963), pp. 15–16.

[80] *HMC. Hatfield MSS.*, VIII, 263.

[81] Mathias, *Whitsun Riot*, pp. 15–18; *DWB, s.n.* David Baker.

[82] Evans, *Sker House*, pp. 15–16; *Cardiff Records*, II, 166–72.

[83] BM, Harleian MS., 6998, ff. 3–16; *Y Bywgraffiadur Cymreig, 1941–1950* (Llundain, 1970), *s.n.* Morgan Clynnog; cf. J. M. Cleary, *A Checklist of Welsh Students in the Seminaries* (Cardiff, 1958), p. 17.

[84] *TLlM*, pp. 156–60.

[85] *CSPD, 1611–18*, p. 500.

[86] *DNB, s.n., DWB, s.n.*; Francis Godwin, *A Catalogue of the Bishops of England*, address to the reader; *HMC. Hatfield MSS.*, XI, 21; *CSPD, 1603–10*, p. 552; Newell, *Llandaff*, p. 155.

[87] *DNB, s.n.*; Newell, *Llandaff*, p. 155; *CSPD, 1611–18*, p. 500.

[88] *DNB, s.n.; DWB, s.n.*; H. R. Trevor-Roper, *Archbishop Laud* (London, 1962), p. 186.

[88A] Newell, *Llandaff*, pp. 157–8.

[89] Ibid., pp. 158–9; *DNB., s.n. DWB., s.n.*

[90] *DNB., s.n.; CSPD, 1611–18*, p. 500; Newell, *Llandaff*, p. 157.

[91] *DNB, s.n.*; Newell, *Llandaff*, pp. 155–7.

[92] NLW, Ll.Ch./4/pp. 53, 35, 64, 79, 81–2, 96–9; NLW, Badminton MS. 1463 (Babington).

[93] NLW, Bute MS. 91/I/1–3.

[94] NLW, Ll.Ch./4/pp. 53, 29, 106, 111, 126–8; *CSPD, 1628–9*, pp. 570–93; *Cardiff Records*, V, 6–19, especially pp. 14–15.

[95] NLW, Ll.Ch./4/ *passim*; *Cardiff Records*, V, 17–19.

[96] Phillips, *Vale of Neath*, pp. 75, 139; Clark, *Limbus*, pp. 351, 357, 471; J. R. Guy, 'The Gamage family: a study in clerical patronage . . .', *Morgannwg*, XIV (1970), 35–61.

[97] Thomas Richards, *Cymru a'r Uchel Gomisiwn* (Lerpwl, 1930), pp. 75–80; PRO, Institution Books, series A, vol. IV, 94–6.

[98] W. J. Gruffydd, *Llenyddiaeth Cymru: Rhyddiaith o 1540 hyd 1660* (Wrecsam, 1926), chap. vi; Margaret Walker, 'Welsh books in St. Mary's Swansea, 1559–1626', *BBCS*, XXIII (1970), 397–402.

[99] Gruffydd, *Llên Cymru*, pp. 105–111. *DWB., s.n.* Edward James.

[100] *TLlM.*, pp. 128–9; *Hen Gwndidau*, pp. 289–91; *DWB, s.n.* Edward Dafydd.

[101] Clark, *Cartae*, VI, 2220–1. For William Evans, *DWB, s.n.*

[102] This table is based on figures drawn from the Glamorgan gaol files of the

Court of Great Sessions, now at NLW, and the Rescusant Rolls (PRO, E377). Printed summaries of some of these returns will be found in *Cardiff Records*, II, 170–3 and Pugh, *S. Wales and Mon. R.S.*, III, 49–68.

[103] *Cardiff Records*, II, 172–3. There was a profoundly recalcitrant recusant in the parish of Colwinston, a yeoman called William Thomas, possibly this offender's father.

[104] Perrott to Salisbury, *CSPD, 1611–18*, p. 123; Pugh, *S. Wales and Mon. R.S.*, III, 49–68, has very convenient tables of Glamorgan recusants.

[105] Cleary, *Checklist of Students*, p. 25.

[106] Idem, *Blackfriars*, XXXVIII, 117.

[107] *Cardiff Records*, II, 145, 159–60, 163.

[108] CCL, David Jones of Wallington's notes of wills, *s.n.* David Hopkins; Phillips, *Vale of Neath*, pp. 76–7, 385–6; *Arch Camb.*, 1851, pp. 238–40; Thomas, 'Swansea, 1485–1660', pp. 238–40.

[109] The letter, ostensibly from Dafydd Thomas of Pandy'r Ystrad, is published in *Hen Gwndidau*, pp. 207–13, cf. also, pp. 214–20. For critical treatment, *TLlM.*, pp. 127–8. For 'romantic' treatment, B. Malkin, *The Scenery, Antiquities, and Biography of South Wales* (2 vols. London, 1807), I, 297–8; Chas. Wilkins, *The History of Merthyr Tydfil* (Merthyr Tydfil, 1867), pp. 82–92; J. Spinther James, *Hanes y Bedyddwyr yng Nghymru* (4 vols. Caerfyrddin, 1893–98), II, 48–68.

[110] *DWB, s.n.* Wroth, Erbery, Cradock; Newell, *Llandaff*, pp. 163–5; William Erbery, *Apocrypha, the second epistle of Paul to the church of Laodicea* (London, 1652), p. 8; J. A. Jenkins, *The History of the Early Nonconformists of Cardiff* (Cardiff 1891), pp. 47–8.

[111] W. H. Hutton, *The English Church from the Accession of Charles I to the Death of Anne* (London, 1913), pp. 59–60; *The Works of . . . Archbishop William Laud* (Oxford, 1853), V, ii, 321, 329; cf. Thos. Shankland, 'Anghydffurfwyr ac ymneilltuwyr cyntaf Cymru', *Y Cofiadur*, I (1923), 32–44; G. F. Nuttall, *The Welsh Saints, 1640–60* (Cardiff, 1957), pp. 21–2.

[112] *Laud's Works*, V, ii, 334–5; 358; PRO, Institution Books, series A, IV, f. 96 (Erbery), 125 (Wroth); Shankland, *Y Cofiadur*, I, 36–7; *CSPD, 1635–6*, pp. 89, 91, 95, 102, 110, 474; Thos. Richards, *Cymru a'r Uchel Gomisiwn*, pp. 38–9; *DWB., s.n.* Wroth; Thos. Richards, *A History of the Puritan Movement in Wales* (London, 1928), p. 28.

[113] Thomas Rees, *History of Protestant Nonconformity in Wales* (London, 1861), p. 209; Wilkins, *Merthyr Tydfil*, pp. 82–3; F. J. Pedler, *History of the Hamlet of Gellideg* (Merthyr Tydfil, 1930), pp. 32–3.

[114] *Laud's Works*, V, ii, 244–5; Shankland, *Y Cofiadur*, I, 37; *DWB, s.n.* Marmaduke Matthews, Ambrose Mostyn; A. H. Dodd, 'Wales in the Parliaments of Charles I', *Trans Cymm.*, 1945, p. 89.

* Initially, I was invited to assist the late Sir Frederick Rees in writing this chapter; but on account of advancing years he left the work on the First Civil War to me but read and approved of what I wrote. The summary of the Second Civil War, he suggested, could be taken from his lecture on 'The Second Civil War in Wales', published in his *Studies in Welsh History* (Cardiff, 1947); a suggestion which I readily accepted. I should like to record my gratitude for Sir Frederick's help and interest.—C. M. THOMAS.

1 F. H. Pugh, 'Recusancy in the diocese of Llandaff' (M.A. Thesis, Univ. of Wales, 1953), p. 30; A. G. Vesey, 'Colonel Philip Jones, 1618–74' (M.A. Thesis, Univ. of Wales, 1958), p. 15; C. M. Thomas, 'The First Civil War in Glamorgan, 1642–1646' (M.A. Thesis, Univ. of Wales, 1963), pp. 172–8.

2 A. H. Dodd, 'Wales in the Parliaments of Charles I', *Trans. Cymm.*, 1945, p. 49; idem, 'Wales under the Early Stuarts', in *Wales Through the Ages*. Ed. A. J. Roderick (Llandybïe, 1960), II, 60.

3 Thomas, 'Civil War in Glamorgan', pp. 28–31 and 39.

4 A. H. Dodd, 'The pattern of politics in Stuart Wales', *Trans. Cymm.*, 1948, p. 41.

5 Ibid., p. 49.

6 Bodleian Library, Clarendon MS., 21, nos. 1630, 1632, 1643, 1644.

7 *CJ.*, II, 29 July 1642, p. 695.

8 *CSPD.*, *1641–43*, pp. 179, 285; A. H. Dodd, *Trans. Cymm.*, 1948, p. 51; idem, 'Wales in the Parliaments of Charles I, 1640–42', *Trans. Cymm.*, 1946–7, p. 85; *CJ.*, II, 10 March 1642, p. 474; 17 August, 1642, p. 724; *DNB.*, XIX, 14–15.

9 Aled Eames, 'Sea Power and Welsh History, 1625–1660' (M.A. Thesis, Univ. of Wales, 1954), pp. 152–3.

10 NLW, Ll/MB/17, Diocese of Llandaff Records, *passim*. A transcript of these records, 'The Book of Results and Orders of the Glamorgan Commissioners of Array', appears as an appendix in Thomas, 'Civil War in Glamorgan'.

11 NLW, *Civil War Tracts*, W.b. 78, pp. 2–5.

12 *Cardiff Records*, IV, 146, V, 489; NLW, Ll/MB/17, p. 28; Richard Symonds, *Diary of the Marches of the Royal Army during the Great Civil War*. Ed. C. E. Long (Camden Soc., 1859), pp. 217–8; C. A. Maunsell and E. P. Statham, *History of the Family of Maunsell (Mansell, Mansel)* (2 vols. London, 1917), II, 161.

13 Edward Hyde, earl of Clarendon, *The History of the Rebellion and Civil Wars in England*. Ed. W. D. Macray (6 vols. Oxford, 1888), II, 342–3.

14 *Thomason Tracts*, E. 240(5); *CJ.*, II, 5 September 1642, p. 732; 27 September 1642, p. 785. NLW, Tredegar MSS., no. 911; W. R. Williams (ed.), *Old Wales* (3 vols. Brecon, 1905–07), II, 230; Arthur Clark, *Raglan Castle and the Civil War in Monmouthshire* (Chepstow, 1953), p. 21.

15 *Thomason Tracts*, E. 119(24), 121(9), 127(28); J. F. Rees, *Studies in Welsh History* (Cardiff, 1947), pp. 64–5; M. Coate, *Cornwall in the Great Civil War and Interregnum, 1642–1660* (Oxford, 1933), p. 35; Eliot Warburton (ed.), *Memoirs of Prince Rupert and the Cavaliers* (3 vols. London, 1849), II, 105–6. *CJ.*, II, 8 October 1642, p. 800.

16 Clarendon, *History*, II, 371, 394–5; *Thomason Tracts*, E. 129(20), 242(2); C. H. Firth (ed.), *The Memoirs of Edmund Ludlow* (2 vols. Oxford, 1894), I, 43; Thomas Carte (ed.), *Ormonde Papers* (2 vols. London, 1739), I, 11.

17 *Thomason Tracts*, E. 124(33).

18 Ibid., E. 127(28).

19 Ibid., E. 242(24), 242(30).

20 Ibid., E. 244(5).

21 Ibid., E. 90(7), 245(7), 244(46); Warburton, *Memoirs*, II, 92; J. Washbourne (ed.), *Bibliotheca Gloucestrensis* (2 vols. Gloucester, 1825), I, part 1, xxxiv; Clarendon, *History*, II, 479–84.

22 Ibid., II, 482–3.

23 *Thomason Tracts*, E.96(2), 97(2), 97(9); *HMC 29, Portland*, I, 703; L. W. Dillwyn, *Contributions towards a History of Swansea* (Swansea, 1840), p. 27; S. R. Gardiner, *History of the Great Civil War, 1642–1649* (3 vols. London, 1886–91), I, 121; Clarendon, *History*, III, 27.

24 Gardiner, *Civil War*, I, 229.

[25] Warburton, *Memoirs*, II, 273, III, 524.

[26] Ibid., II, 281; NLW, Ll/MB/17, p. 25.

[27] Ibid., pp. 27, 28, 35.

[28] Ibid., pp. 29, 37.

[29] Ibid., pp. 51, 61; Gardiner, *Civil War*, I, 255.

[30] *Thomason Tracts*, E.71(32).

[31] Rees, *Studies in Welsh History*, pp. 70, 162–7 (appendix C); Warburton, *Memoirs*, II, 357; A. H. Dodd, 'Caernarvonshire in the Civil War', *CHST.*, 1953, pp. 10–13.

[32] Warburton, *Memoirs*, II, 385–6.

[33] NLW, Ll/MB/17, p. 63; *CJ.*, III, 8 April 1644, p. 453.

[34] NLW, Ll/MB/17, p. 72.

[35] Ibid., pp. 77, 81.

[36] A. H. Dodd, *Studies in Stuart Wales* (Cardiff, 1952), pp. 92–3.

[37] Ibid., p. 93; *Thomason Tracts*, E.3(19).

[38] NLW, Ll/MB/17, p. 84; Symonds, *Diary*, pp. 217–8.

[39] Anthony à Wood, *Athenae Oxonienses*. Ed. P. Bliss (4 vols. London, 1813–20), I, cxliv.

[40] *CSPD.*, *1644–45*, p. 42; *HMC 29, Portland*, III, 130.

[41] *Cardiff Records*, VI, 34–6.

[42] Ibid., VI, xxxvi.

[43] Clarendon, *History*, IV, 47.

[44] Edward Walker, *Historical Discourses upon Several Occasions* (London, 1705), p. 116—error in pagination, *recte*, p. 132.

[45] Symonds, *Diary*, p. 210.

[46] A. H. Dodd, 'Anglesey in the Civil War', *AAFCT.*, 1952, p. 15.

[47] BM, Harleian MS., 6852, f. 290.

[48] *Cardiff Records*, VI, xli–ii.

[49] Gardiner, *Civil War*, II, 242–5; Symonds, *Diary*, pp. 210–11; Clarendon, *History*, IV, 72; Rees, *Studies in Welsh History*, p. 73; *Cardiff Records*, IV, 146–7.

[50] Warburton, *Memoirs*, III, 148–9.

[51] Symonds, *Diary*, pp. 212–5; *Thomason Tracts*, E.298 (15).

[52] Symonds, *Diary*, p. 215; NLW, Mansel Franklen MS. 6574C(f).

[53] Warburton, *Memoirs*, III, 150.

[54] C. H. Firth (ed.), *Memoirs of Edward Ludlow*, I, 124–5.

[55] Warburton, *Memoirs*, I, 526.

[56] *CSPD.*, *1645–7*, pp. 96–7.

[57] Symonds, *Diary*, pp. 238–9.

[58] *CSPD.*, *1645–47*, p. 136.

[59] Symonds, *Diary*, p. 239; *CSPD.*, *1645–47*, p. 120.

[60] *Cardiff Records*, IV, 149; PRO, SP 23/189/624, 628.

[61] *Thomason Tracts*, E.301(14), 304(25).

[62] *CJ.*, IV, 25 October 1645, p. 320; Dillwyn, *Contributions . . . Swansea*, p. 28.

[63] Thomas, 'First Civil War', pp. 172–8.

[64] *CJ.*, IV, 17 November 1645, p. 347; 3 December 1645, p. 364; *CSPD.*, *1645–47*, p. 243.

[65] *HMC 29, Portland*, I, 322.

[66] Ibid., pp. 345–46; NLW, *Civil War Tracts*, W.b. 7863, pp. 3–4.

[67] *HMC 29, Portland*, I, 348–50.

[68] Ibid., p. 348; *HMC Sixth Report*, p. 101a; *Thomason Tracts*, E.327(2).

[69] NLW, *Civil War Tracts*, W.b. 7862, p. 5.

[70] Ibid., pp. 6–7.

[71] *HMC 29, Portland*, I, 351–2.

[72] NLW, *Civil War Tracts*, W.b. 7863, p. 4; *CJ.*, IV, 6 April 1646, p. 501; PRO, SP 23/196/271–2.

[73] Dillwyn, *Contributions . . . Swansea*, p. 28; PRO, SP 23/183/177, 187; PRO, SP 23/186/237.

[74] Ibid., 23/189/612.

[75] Ibid., 196/272, 274, 277, 279, 284.

[76] Ibid., 188/177, 192.

[77] Ibid., 186/191, 192, 198.

[78] Ibid., 186/237, 244.

[79] Ibid., 206/463, 465; 10/805; *CJ.*, IV, 3 March 1646, p. 461.

[80] Ibid., IV, 22 January 1646, p. 414; W. R. Williams, *Great Sessions*, p. 169; Sir W. Scott (ed.), *Somers Tracts* (13 vols. London, 1809–15), V, 131; PRO, SP 23/95/853, 855, 856, 857, 859, 861, 863; *DNB.*, X, 735–7.

[81] PRO, SP 23/206/264, 267, 272–3.

[82] Ibid., 120/57, 59, 61, 63.

[83] Ibid., 135/697.

[84] The documents relating to this affair are printed in J. R. Phillips, *Memorials of the Civil War in Wales and the Marches* (2 vols. London, 1874), II, 335–43.

[85] *CJ.*, V, 5 January 1647, p. 42; *Calendar of the Clarendon State Papers* (4 vols. London, 1872), I, 410; *CSPD.*, *1648–49*, pp. 6–8.

[86] C. H. Firth and R. S. Rait, *Acts and Ordinances of the Interregnum, 1642–60* (3 vols. London, 1911), I, 1053–4; Bulstrode Whitelocke, *Memorials of the English Affairs* (4 vols. Oxford, 1853), II, 278; *CSPD.*, *1648–49*, p. 42; Rees, *Studies in Welsh History*, pp. 101–4.

[87] Thomas, 'Civil War in Glamorgan', pp. 225–8.

[88] J. F. Rees, op. cit., pp. 105–7. The documents relating to these events are printed in Phillips, *Memorials* II, 362–9.

¹ Throughout this period almost exactly the same persons were nominated county commissioners and J.P.s. For the names of J.P.s I am indebted to Dr. J. R. S. Phillips of University College, Dublin, for allowing me to use his valuable study, 'The Justices of the Peace in Wales and Monmouthshire, 1541–1689', to be published by the Board of Celtic Studies of the University of Wales.

² A valuable study of local administration in Wales in this period is T. M. Bassett, 'A Study of Local Government in Wales under the Commonwealth with Especial Reference to its Relations with the Central Authority' (M.A. Thesis, Univ. of Wales, 1941). For this point, pp. 363–84.

³ *F. and R.*, II, 14–16.

⁴ Bassett, 'Local Government in Wales', pp. 146–8.

⁵ NLW., Civil War and Commonwealth Tract, 197. *The Humble Acknowledgement of the Inhabitants of South Wales and County Monmouth*.

⁶ Act for the Settlement of the Militia of the Commonwealth, July 11, 1650, *F. and R.*, II, 397–402; Bassett, 'Local Government in Wales', appendix V, p. xxi, pp. 273–4.

⁷ *CCC.*, I, 172, February 4, 1649–50. Other members may probably be added to the original list of sequestrators, namely Edward Bowen, Matthew Hopkin, *CCC.*, I, 492, and William Jones, Bartholomew Games, and James Watkins, see Bassett, 'Local Government in Wales', p. 178.

⁸ *CCC.*, I, 222, May 14, 1650.

⁹ Ibid., I, 512, 492; Bassett, 'Local Government in Wales', p. 247; *CCC.*, I, 238–9, 295, 158–9; Bassett, op. cit., pp. 149–50; *CCC.*, I, 352.

¹⁰ Ibid., I, 222, 352; PRO., S.P. 23/254: 45; *CCC.*, I, 404–5, 391, 415.

¹¹ Freeman's recommendations with corrections, PRO., S.P. 23/98, p. 81, Nov. 25, 1651. See also *CCC.*, I, 827; Bassett, 'Local Government in Wales', pp. 178–80.

¹² *CCC.*, I, 517.

¹³ Ibid., 522, Jan. 1, 1651–2; ibid., p. 569.

¹⁴ *F. and R.*, I, 960; II, 30, 54 *et seq.*

¹⁵ Hundredal rates quoted by W. S. K. Thomas, 'Swansea, 1485–1660', pp. 260–1, from 'Results and orders of the Commissioners of Array for Glamorgan, 1643–4', i.e. NLW., Ll/MB/17. I owe the NLW. reference to Dr. Ian Roy of King's College, London.

¹⁶ Quoted by Bassett, 'Local Government in Wales', p. 134.

¹⁷ For the Rump Parliament: D. Underdown, *Pride's Purge: Politics in the Puritan Revolution* (Oxford, 1971). The passage of the Propagation Act is discussed, pp. 272–4.

¹⁸ C. Hill, 'Propagating the Gospel', pp. 35–59, in H. E. Bell and R. L. Ollard (ed.), *Historical Essays 1600–1750 presented to David Ogg* (1963). For the thought of Cradock and Powell, G. F. Nuttall, *The Welsh Saints, 1640–1660* (Cardiff, 1957).

¹⁹ Quoted by Hill, 'Propagating the Gospel', p. 43.

²⁰ *F. and R.*, II, 342–8: T. Richards, *A History of the Puritan Movement in Wales* (1920), pp. 81–90, hereafter Richards, *PM*.

²¹ Richards, *PM.*, p. 93.

²² Ibid., pp. 85–6.

²³ Ibid., pp. 100–1.

²⁴ B. Whitelocke, *Memorials of the English Affairs* (1682), p. 442.

²⁵ Richards, *PM.*, pp. 115–33.

²⁶ Ibid., p. 241.

²⁷ Lambeth Palace Library MS. Comm. VIII/1, orders of the Committee for Propagating the Gospel, 1653.

²⁸ Ibid.; Richards, *PM.*, p. 235.

²⁹ Richards, *PM.*, p. 236.

³⁰ Bodleian Library, Oxford, MS. J Walker, c. 4, f. 66.

³¹ Richards, *PM.*, pp. 136–7.

³² Ibid., p. 145.

³³ Ibid., pp. 63, 148–50.

³⁴ Ibid., pp. 154–7.

³⁵ Ibid., p. 162.

³⁶ W. A. L. Vincent, *The State and School Education 1640–1660 in England and Wales* (S.P.C.K., 1950), p. 20.

³⁷ Richards, *PM.*, p. 86.

³⁸ Ibid., pp. 222–34. H. Thomas, *A History of Wales 1485–1660* (Cardiff, 1972),

p. 228, prints a map showing the distribution of schools in Wales before, and as a result of, the work of the Propagators.

[39] T. Richards, *Religious Developments in Wales (1654–1662)* (1923), pp. 64–5, hereafter Richards, *RD*.

[40] Richards, *PM.*, p. 137.

[41] *F. and R.*, II, 235.

[42] Ibid., 347.

[43] This section is based on the series of Order Books of the Committee for Indemnity, PRO., S.P. 24, of which particular use has been made of vols. 1–14, which cover the period from the first Order Book, June 1647 to June 1653, especially S.P. 24/10, pp. 28, 36 (Dec. 3, 1651), p. 76 (Jan. 21, 1651–2); S.P. 24/6, p. 36 (Dec. 13, 1649); S.P. 24/7, p. 1 (July 17, 1650). The Acts of Sept. 9 and Oct. 4, 1647 (*F. and R.*, I, 1009, 1023). Both Dr. Richards and Dr. Hill rightly draw attention to the part of the Propagation Act dealing with indemnity. Dr. Richards, *PM.*, p. 241, could offer no evidence as to whether this part of the Act was ever implemented, while Dr. Hill, 'Propagating the Gospel', p. 44, attributes a greater competence to the Propagators acting as commissioners of indemnity than the evidence allows, when he suggests that the 'political powers entrusted to the commissioners . . . strongly resemble those previously wielded by the Councils in Wales and the North'. Professor Dodd's claim, *Stuart Wales*, p. 148, that 'until it received its *coup de grace* in 1653 the Propagation Commission remained the real government of Wales', should also be modified.

[44] Bassett, 'Local Government in Wales', pp. 245–6; *CCC.*, I, 391–2, 323, 252, 562–3, 574.

[45] The South Wales Petition of 1652 is printed and carefully analysed by Dr. Richards, *PM.*, pp. 246–70. This reference, ibid., pp. 247–9.

[46] Bassett, 'Local Government in Wales', pp. 256–7; *CSPD.*, 1651–2, p. 354; *CSPD.*, 1652–3, pp. 423, 452.

[47] D. Underdown, *Pride's Purge*, p. 330; Hill, 'Propagating the Gospel', p. 47.

[48] S. R. Gardiner, *History of the Commonwealth and Protectorate, 1649–1656* (1903), II, 251.

[49] *CSPD.*, 1652–3, pp. 293–4; *CCC.*, I, 637; Bassett, 'Local Government in Wales', p. 260.

[50] Ibid., pp. 261–2.

[51] A. H. Woolrych, 'The Calling of Barebone's Parliament', *EHR.*, LXXX (1965), 492–513.

[52] W. R. Williams, *Parliamentary History of the Principality of Wales* (Brecknock, 1895), pp. 123, 98. While the letter in *A Collection of the State Papers of John Thurloe* (1742), I, 637, quoted by H. R. Trevor-Roper, 'Oliver Cromwell and his Parliaments', in *Religion, the Reformation and Social Change* (1967), p. 367, n. 1, seems to demonstrate that Bussy Mansel was a radical sympathizer in Barebone's Parliament, the evidence of his long career suggests that his main concern was political survival and that he was a man of moderate political views. He voted for the retention of the tithe in Barebone's Parliament, Richards, *RD.*, p. 177.

[53] W. C. Abbot (ed.), *The Writings and Speeches of Oliver Cromwell* (4 vols., Harvard, 1937–47), III, 32–67.

[54] B. S. Capp, *The Fifth Monarchy Men* (1972), p. 60; A. H. Woolrych, 'Oliver Cromwell and the rule of the Saints', in R. H. Parry (ed.), *The English Civil War and After 1642–1648* (1970), pp. 59–77.

[55] Underdown, *Pride's Purge*, pp. 340–1.

[56] *F. and R.*, II, 753; Dodd, *Stuart Wales*, pp. 152–3.

[57] *F. and R.*, II, 855–8.

[58] Ibid., p. 976, Aug. 28, 1654; Dodd, *Stuart Wales*, pp. 152–3; Richards, *RD.*, pp. 50, 278–81.

[59] *F. and R.*, II, 984.

[60] Richards, *RD.*, pp. 10–11.

[61] Ibid., pp. 9–10, 12, 14.

[62] Bassett, 'Local Government in Wales', pp. 263–6; Richards, *RD.*, p. 83.

[63] Richards, *PM.*, pp. 159–61.

[64] Richards, *RD.*, p. 10.

[65] Richards's conclusion, *RD.*, p. 135.

[66] Richards, *PM.*, p. 244; *RD.*, p. 54; Vincent, *State and School Education, 1640–1660*, p. 106.

[67] *F. and R.*, II, 968, Aug. 28, 1654.

[68] Richards, *RD.*, pp. 54–7; Vincent, *State and School Education, 1640–1660*, p. 96.

[69] Richards, *PM.*, 265–6; *RD.*, pp. 55–7.

[70] A. Wood, *Athenae Oxonienses* (5 vols., 3rd ed., P. Bliss, 1820), IV, col. 835, quoted by Richards, *RD.*, p. 60; and Vincent, *State and School Education, 1640–1660*, p. 111.

[71] NLW., Civil War and Commonwealth Tract, 141. BM. E. 866 (3), *The Humble Representation and Address to His Highness of Several Churches and Christians in South Wales and Monmouthshire*, presented Thursday, January 31, 1656 (7). This pamphlet must, in fact, have been presented at the beginning of the previous year, 1655–6, Richards, *RD.*, p. 180, n. 1.

[72] Ibid., p. 198.

[73] Ibid., pp. 182, 200–3, 198, 184.

[74] Capp, *The Fifth Monarchy Men*, p. 78.

[75] BM. 861 (5), *A Word for God, or a Testimony on Truths behalf; from several Churches, and diverse hundreds of Christians in Wales . . . against wickedness in High Places, with a letter to the Lord General Cromwell*, Dec. 3, 1655. A. H. Dodd, 'A Remonstrance from Wales, 1655', *BBCS.*, XVII (1955–8), 279–92; Richards, *RD.*, pp. 218–19, 224–5; Capp, *The Fifth Monarchy Men*, p. 112.

[76] For this discussion of Quaker activities I have followed M. Fay Williams, 'Glamorgan Quakers, 1654–1900', *Morgannwg*, V (1961), 49–75, esp. pp. 49–59.

[77] *F. and R.*, II, 990–3, Aug. 30, 1654; *CSPD.*, 1654, p. 337; names added Aug. 31, *CSPD.*, 1654, p. 348.

[78] Bodleian Library, Oxford, MS. J Walker c. 13, ff. 16–32.

[79] *Strena Vavasorienses, a new Year's Gift for the Welsh Itinerants or a hue and cry after Mr. Vavasour Powell*, by Alexander Griffiths, printed (Cymdeithas Llên Cymru, Cardiff, 1915), p. 5.

[80] Bodleian Library, Oxford, MS. Clarendon 75, ff. 411–12 (July–Dec. 1661). Griffiths's figures are from his *A true and perfect Relation of the Whole Transaction concerning the Petition of the Six Counties of South Wales and the County of Monmouth, formerly presented to the Parliament of the Commonwealth of England . . .* (1654), N.L.W., Civil War and Commonwealth Tract, 28, p. 23. Griffiths supplies the county totals only, which differ in a few cases from the official investigation figures of 1661. The county figures—with the number of livings, impropriations, etc., in brackets—are as follows, with Griffiths's totals, where different, preceded by G: Monmouth £4,100 (142) G=£4,500; Carmarthen £1,600 (81) G=£2,000; Pembroke £4,000 (145) G=£3,500; Glamorgan £4,000 (151); Radnor £1,800 (50) G=£2,000; Brecon £2,000 (60) G=£2,500;

Cardigan £1,000 (70); Total=£18,500; G total=£20,000.

[81] Bodleian Library, Oxford, MS. J Walker c. 13, f. 16v.

[82] Griffiths, *True Relation*, p. 41; and quoted by Richards, *PM.*, p. 257, n. 2.

[83] *F. and R.*, II, 839–92, Act of Feb. 10, 1653–4; *CCC.*, I, xx–xxi.

[84] *CCC.*, I, 668, Feb. 10, 1653–4; Bassett, 'Local Government in Wales', pp. 179–80.

[85] For the best short discussion of the counties during the Protectorate, D. Underdown, 'Settlement in the Counties, 1653–1658', in G. E. Aylmer (ed.), *The Interregnum: the Quest for Settlement, 1646–1660* (1972), pp. 165–82.

[86] Compare the assessment commissioners of 1652, *F. and R.*, II, 680, who continued to 1657, ibid., 1249, at which time only slight changes were made among the less influential committeemen. Little change is evident among those appointed J.P.s during this period, Dr. J. R. S. Phillips, 'Justices of the Peace in Wales'.

[87] Trevor-Roper, 'Oliver Cromwell and his Parliaments', p. 374; Vernon Snow, 'Parliamentary re-apportionment proposals during the Puritan Revolution', *EHR.*, LXXIV (1959), 409–42.

[88] The most recent discussion of the effect of the distribution of Parliamentary seats and the franchise established by the Instrument of Government is John Cannon, *Parliamentary Reform, 1640–1832* (Cambridge, 1973), pp. 13–19.

[89] Williams, *Parliamentary History of Wales*, pp. 97–9, 109.

[90] PRO., SP. 25/76a, pp. 32–3, Mar. 14, 1654–5. Five members of this commission are noted in *CSPD.*, 1655, p. 79.

[91] *CSPD.*, 1655, p. 93.

[92] For the major-generals, I. Roots, 'Swordsmen and Decimators — Cromwell's Major-Generals', in Parry (ed.), *The English Civil War and After*, pp. 78–90.

[93] J. Berry and S. G. Lee, *A Cromwellian Major-General: the Career of Colonel James Berry* (Oxford, 1938), pp. 117, 166, 290, 157.

[94] Ibid., pp. 183–5.

[95] B. L. K. Henderson, 'The Commonwealth Charters', *TRHS.*, 3rd series, VI (1912), 129–61; A. M. Johnson, 'Politics in Chester during the Civil Wars and the Interregnum, 1640–1662', in P. Clark and

P. Slack (eds.), *Crisis and Order in English Towns, 1500–1700* (1972), esp. pp. 220–31.

[96] For Swansea during the Interregnum, W. S. K. Thomas, 'Swansea, 1485–1660', chap. VI, pp. 277–317. This reference, pp. 297–8. This study includes as an appendix a valuable transcription of the Book of Common Hall of the borough.

[97] The charters are printed in George G. Francis, *Charters granted to Swansea*, pp. 25–47, 49–59. The date of the governing charter is Feb. 26, 1656, and not Feb. 1655, as described by W. S. K. Thomas, 'Swansea, 1485–1660', pp. 302–5. On Oct. 23, 1655, at the beginning of his year of office, the chief official of the town, Lewis Jones, was described as portreeve, in the customary manner (Hall Book, f. 225v). On Mar. 18, 1655–6, Jones, appointed mayor under the charter, was sworn in to office (Hall Book, f. 227v), PRO., A.O. 1/1377/144 m. 12, 'Patents granted between 29 Sept. 1655–29 Sept. 1656' records the patent granted to the mayor, aldermen and burgesses of Swansea, i.e. charter of 1656.

[98] Berry and Lee, *A Cromwellian Major-General*, p. 193.

[99] Williams, *Parliamentary History of Wales*, pp. 98, 107.

[100] Ibid., pp. 97–8.

[101] *F. and R.*, II, 1249, June 26, 1657. There is little substance, as far as Glamorgan was concerned, for Professor Dodd's view, *Stuart Wales*, p. 161, that the commissions of 1657 were 'the most representative Wales had had since the war', including many old families 'tempted back into political life by the apparent stability of the Protectorate'.

[102] G. Davies, 'The Election of Richard Cromwell's Parliament, 1658–9', *EHR.*, LXIII (1948), 488–501.

[103] Williams, *Parliamentary History of Wales*, p. 107.

[104] W. S. K. Thomas, 'Swansea, 1485–1660', p. 305; A. G. Veysey, 'Colonel Philip Jones, 1618–1674', *Trans. Cymm.*, 1966, p. 328; W. R. Williams, *The History of the Great Sessions in Wales, 1541–1830* (Brecknock, 1899), p. 60.

[105] Veysey, *Trans. Cymm.*, 1966, p. 327.

[106] NLW., Civil War and Commonwealth Tract, 274, pp. 1, 5, *The Distressed Oppressed Condition of the Inhabitants of South Wales* (1659).

[107] Ibid., p. 3; Veysey, *Trans. Cymm.*, 1966, p. 328.

[108] BM. E 983 (3), *Twelve Queries humbly proposed to the Consideration of the Parliament and Army* (May 12, 1659), Article IX. See also BM. E 985 (12), *Democraticus turned Statesman* (June 3, 1659); Veysey, *Trans. Cymm.*, 1966, p. 328, has made good use of these sources.

[109] NLW., Civil War and Commonwealth Tract, 170. *Articles of Impeachment of Transcendent Crimes, Injuries, Misdemeanours, . . . committed by Col. Philip Jones: exhibited by Mr. Bledry Morgan; and read in Parliament, the 18th May 1659. Together with Col. Philip Jones's Answer thereunto* (1659); Veysey, *Trans. Cymm.*, 1966, p. 329.

[110] Ibid., p. 329.

[111] Ibid., pp. 330–1; *Calendar of the Clarendon State Papers*, IV, (1657–1660), ed. F. J. Routledge (Oxford, 1932), pp. 253–4, 269–70, 292–3 *et seq.*

[112] *F. and R.*, II, 1328, July 26, 1659; Dodd, *Stuart Wales*, pp. 162, 166; *CSPD*, 1659–60, pp. 36, 221, 293.

[113] *CSPD*, 1659–60, p. 24, July 13, 1659, p. 56, July 30; Bassett, 'Local Government in Wales', p. 324.

[114] *CCC.*, I, 747; *CSPD.*, 1659–60, p. 179.

[115] *CCC.*, I, 747; PRO., S.P. 23/264:52 (Dec. 1659).

[116] W. S. K. Thomas, 'Swansea, 1485–1660', p. 308.

[117] *F. and R.*, II, 1383, Jan. 26, 1659–60.

[118] Ibid., II, 1447–8.

[119] *CJ.*, VII (1651–9), p. 876.

[120] *F. and R.*, II, 1465; GRO., D/DFV/128; Veysey, *Trans. Cymm.*, 1966, p. 332.

[121] Williams, *Parliamentary History of Wales*, pp. 99, 107; L. B. John, 'The Parliamentary Representation of Glamorgan, 1536–1832' (Unpublished M.A. Thesis, Wales, 1934), pp. 92–3.

[122] NLW., Civil War and Commonwealth Tract, 165. *To the King's Most Excellent Majestie. The Humble Addresse of the Lords, Knights, and Gentlemen, of the Six Counties of South Wales, and County of Monmouth. Presented to, and most gratiously receiv'd by his Majestie* (June 16, 1660).

[123] W. S. K. Thomas, 'Swansea, 1485–1660', p. 309.

[124] Ibid., p. 309. Although there is no specific evidence that Dawkins and David were dismissed by commissioners appointed under the Corporation Act, it is

quite possible that they were. 'Lords Commissioners' were entertained by the corporation during the mayoral year 1661–2 (Hall Book, f. 263r). For a general discussion of the Act, J. S. Sacret, 'The Restoration Government and the Municipal Corporations', *EHR.*, XLV (1930), 232–59; A. M. Johnson, 'Politics in Chester, 1640–1662', pp. 230–1.

[125] J. R. S. Phillips, 'Justices of the Peace in Wales'; *Statutes of the Realm*, IV, 222, 343.

[126] Veysey, *Trans. Cymm.*, 1966, pp. 332–3; Richards, *RD.*, pp. 341 ff., 418–19.

[1] Throughout the nineteenth century there was considerable disagreement concerning the number of parishes in Glamorgan. The *Myvyrian Archaiology* (Denbigh, 1870), pp. 748–9, gives a list of 133 parishes, with a note stating that they amounted to 140. An additional note by Iolo Morganwg stated that the correct total was 128. D. W. Jones (Dafydd Morganwg) in his *Hanes Morganwg* (Aberdar, 1874), p. 24, gives a list of 126 parishes, while the 1801 census refers to only 113 parishes under 'Glamorgan'. Rice Merrick (1578) lists the names of 121 parishes, which corresponds with the number accounted for in the hearth tax list.

[2] According to BM, Harleian MS. 6804, ff. 180–1, esquires in Glamorgan in the reign of Charles I numbered 33. And according to Iolo Morganwg's estimate, the number of the principal landlords in Glamorgan *circa* 1790 was 90, NLW MS. 13,114B.

[3] NLW, Penrice and Margam MS. 5092.

[4] NLW, P.R. (Ll.), 1699.

[5] Ibid., 1665.

[6] Ibid.

[7] Ibid., 1736.

[8] Moelwyn I. Williams, 'Cardiff—its trade and its people', *Morgannwg*, VII (1963), 83–6.

[9] NLW, P.R. (Ll.), 1718.

[10] Ibid.

[11] They cost £2.

[12] NLW, P.R. (Ll.), 1715.

[13] Ibid., 1737.

[14] A. H. Dodd, *Studies in Stuart Wales* (Cardiff, 1952), p. 1.

[15] Laslett, *World We Have Lost*, pp. 22–52.

[16] W. R. Williams, *The Parliamentary History of the Principality of Wales* (London, 1895), pp. 95–101.

[17] I. G. Jones, 'Franchise reform and Glamorgan politics in the mid-nineteenth century', *Morgannwg*, II (1958), 48–9.

[18] P. D. G. Thomas, 'Glamorgan politics, 1700–1750', ibid., VI (1962), 52.

[19] Laslett, *World We Have Lost*, p. 26.

[20] A. H. Dodd, 'The landed gentry after 1660'. Ed. A. J. Roderick, *Wales through the Ages*, II (Llandybïe, 1959), 80.

[21] John Adams, *Index Villaris* . . . (London, 1690), pp. 1–404.

[22] PRO, E 179/264/47. This Voluntary Gift was an emergency measure to relieve the shortage of ready money which faced Charles II on his return to power. Individual subscriptions were graded and limited to £400 for peers and £200 for commoners. These sums were hardly ever obtained.

[23] PRO, E 179/264/47.

[24] This conclusion is substantiated by the probate inventories we have examined.

[25] *LCR.*, 1896, p. 278.

[26] Baker and Francis, *Surveys of Gower and Kilvey.*

[27] NLW, P.R. (Ll.), 1714.

[28] *Penrice and Margam MSS.*, Appendix, 1942.

[29] NLW, Penrice and Margam MS., 7463.

[30] John Fox, *A General View of Agriculture in Glamorgan* (1796), pp. 18–9.

[31] Cf. Halévy, op. cit., p. 235.

[32] NLW, Penrice and Margam MS., 5130; cf. ibid., MS. 2192; GRO, D/D M.B.N. 211.

[33] NLW, P.R. (S.D.), 1661.

[34] Ibid., P.R. (Ll.), 1681.

[35] NLW, Badm., (series 1), no. 1737.

[36] Ibid.

[37] Glanmor Williams, *WHR*, II, 41–2; idem, *Welsh Church*, chaps. x and xi. Cf. NLW, Penrice and Margam MS., 2070.

[38] Halévy, op. cit., p. 238.

[39] NLW, Ll/VC/2; SD/VC/7; see also NLW MS., 16,260.

[40] NLW, Ll/Ter/6.

[41] NLW, Ll/Ter/11.

[42] NLW, Ll/Ter/3.

[43] The 'oar' was the seaweed which was collected in great quantities and converted into kelp and exported to Bristol.

[44] NLW, Ll/Ter/135.

[45] Halévy, op. cit., p. 238.

[46] NLW, Ll/QA/1, 1763.

[47] *The Golden Grove* (London, 1608), Book III, chap. 22.

[48] C. C. Taylor, *Rural Sociology* (New York, 1926), p. 132.

[49] Cf. Theodor Shanin, 'The peasantry as a political power', *Sociol Rev.*, March 1966, p. 5.

[50] G. J. Williams, 'Dyddiadur William Thomas o Lanfihangel-ar-Elai', *Morgannwg*, I (1959), 21.

[51] R. T. Jenkins, 'The development of nationalism in Wales', *Sociol Rev.*, XXXII (1935).

[52] J. D. Chambers and G. E. Mingay, *The Agricultural Revolution, 1750–1800* (London, 1966), p. 15; cf. Schlicher van Bath, *The Agrarian History of Western Europe, A.D. 500–1850* (London, 1963), p. 3.

[53] Moelwyn I. Williams, 'Some aspects of the economic and social life of Glamorgan, 1600–1800', *Morgannwg*, III (1959), 22–3.

[54] Thomas Fuller, *The History of the Worthies of England* (London, 1880), III, 542.

[55] Lemuel James, *Hopkiniaid Morgannwg* (Bangor, 1909), p. 208.

[56] Leland, *Itin. Wales*, p. 16.

[57] P. Russell, *England Displayed . . .* (London, 1769), II, 288.

[58] B. H. Malkin, op. cit., I, 82.

[59] NLW MS. 13,147A.

[60] NLW, P.R. (Ll.), 1727.

[61] *Cardiff Records*, III, 135.

[62] NLW, P.R. (Ll.), 1692.

[63] Ibid., 1709.

[64] Ibid., 1687.

[65] Emery, *NLWJ.*, X, 20–1.

[66] E. Lisle, *Observations in Husbandry* (London, 1757), p. 228.

[67] PRO, PCC, 78 Wootten.

[68] NLW, P.R. (Ll.), 1662.

[69] Ibid., 1696.

[70] Ibid., 1663.

[71] Ibid., 1664.

[72] Ibid., 1663.

[73] Ibid., 1682.

[74] *Cardiff Records*, III, 168, 169.

[75] NLW, P.R. (Ll.), 1672.

[76] NLW MS. 13,147A.

[77] NLW, P.R. (Ll.), 1719.

[78] Ibid., 1676.

[79] George Owen, *Taylors Cussion*, part I, fo. 34.

[80] David Mackenzie, *Goat Husbandry* (London, 1957), p. 35.

[81] *Dictionarium Rusticum* (1717).

[82] NLW, P.R. (Ll.), 1677.

[83] Ibid., 1698.

[84] Ibid., 1677.

[85] Goats were also kept because of their peculiar smell which, it was supposed, reduced abortion among cows.

[86] Swansea and Glamorgan Calendar, II, Part I, p. 412.

[87] PRO, E 190/1277/7.

[88] Ibid., 1281/14.

[89] Ibid., 1094/1.

[91] NLW, P.R. (Ll.), Mary William, 1678.

[91] J. Skinner, 'Tour in Wales, 1800', CCL MS. 1, 503.

[92] NLW, I.A.W. MS. 123/10.

[93] NLW, P.R. (Ll.) 1666.

[94] Richard Warner, *A Second Walk Through Wales, 1798* (London, 1799), p. 58; cf. Malkin, op. cit., p. 94.

[95] These circumstances explain, in part, why the 'Rebecca Riots' of the 1840s were not evident in the Vale of Glamorgan.

[96] John Fox, op. cit., p. 35.

[97] Arthur Young, *A Six Weeks Tour . . .* (London, 1768), p. 124.

[98] GRO, D/DC F/L.

[99] Lhuyd, *Parochialia*, part III, p. 31.

[100] J. Geraint Jenkins, *Agricultural Transport in Wales* (Cardiff, 1962), pp. 9–10.

[101] NLW, P.R. (Ll.), 1673.

[102] Ibid., 1663.

[103] Strakes were pieces of iron used as 'tyres' on wooden wheels. These were fastened by means of square nails— 'strake nails'.

[104] NLW, P.R. (Ll.) 1680.

[105] Ibid., (S.D.), 1700.

[106] Ibid., (Ll.), 1726.

[107] Ibid., 1723.

[108] Ibid., 1673.

[109] Ibid., 1734.

[110] Ibid., 1760.

[111] John Fox, op. cit., Appendix, p. 12.

[112] NLW, P.R. (Ll.), 1666.

[113] PRO, E 134/23 Charles I/Mich. 1.

[114] NLW, P.R. (Ll.), 1676.

[115] PRO, E 134/7/William III/Mich. 37.

[116] NLW, Ll/CC/P, 672.

[117] NLW, P.R. (Ll.), 1683.

[118] Ibid., 1740.

[119] Andrew Yarranton, *England's Improvement by Sea and Land* (London, 1677), p. 157.

[120] NLW, P.R. (Ll.), 1676.

[121] NLW MS. 13,147A.

[122] *Merrick's Glam. Antiqs.*, p. 10.

[123] Margaret Davies, *Cardiff Nat. Soc. Trans.*, LXXXIV, 6.

[124] NLW MS. 13,114B; cf. John Fox, op. cit., p. 19.

[125] Walter Davies, *A General View of the Agriculture and Domestic Economy of South Wales* (2 vols. London, 1814), I, 162.

[126] Arthur Young, op. cit., pp. 123–4.

[127] Ibid., p. 127.

[128] Moelwyn I. Williams, 'Glamorgan farming in pre-industrial times', *Glam. Hist.*, II (1965), 180–1.

[129] NLW MS. 13,147A.

[130] John Aubrey, *The Natural History of Wiltshire Written between 1656 and 1691* (London, 1847), p. 3.

[131] Lord Ernle, *English Farming Past and Present* (London, 1961), p. lxxxi.

[132] R. Lennard, 'English agriculture under Charles II . . .', *EconHR.*, IV (1932–3), 45.

[133] NLW, P.R. (Ll.), 1667.

[134] W. Davies, op. cit., I, 575; cf. Moelwyn I. Williams, 'A further contribution to the commercial history of Glamorgan', *NLWJ.*, XI (1960), 343, 343n.

[135] PRO, E 190/1095/9.

[136] Yarranton, op. cit., p. 156.

[137] NLW, P.R. (Ll.), 1718.

[138] G. H. Eaton, 'A survey of the manor in seventeenth-century Gower' (M.A. Thesis, Univ. of Wales, 1936), p. 186.

[139] Tithe Apportionment Schedule for Ystradyfodwg, 1844, *vide* nos. 511, 1303 and 1504 in the Schedule.

[140] PRO, E 134/7 William III/Mich. 37.

[141] Ibid.

[142] John Evans, *Letters Written during a Tour of South Wales* (London, 1804), pp. 186–7.

[143] T. H. Marshall, 'Jethro Tull and the "New Husbandry" of the eighteenth century', *EconHR.*, II (1929–30), 53.

[144] T. S. Ashton, *Economic Fluctuations in England, 1700–1800* (Oxford, 1959), p. 2.

[145] For an illuminating discussion on the location of rural industries, Joan Thirsk, 'Industries in the countryside', F. J. Fisher (ed.), *Essays in the Economic and Social History of Tudor and Stuart England* (Cambridge, 1961), p. 70–88, esp. pp. 86–7.

[146] John Evans, *Letters*, p. 132.

[147] NLW, P.R. (Ll.), 1701.

[148] Ibid., 1725.

[149] Ibid., 1670 and 1691.

[150] Ibid., 1718.

[151] Ibid., 1676.

[152] Ibid., 1749.

[153] Ibid., 1664.

[154] PRO, E 134/15 Geo. II/Hil. 4.

[155] NLW, P.R. (Ll.), 1704

[156] Ibid., (S.D.), 1675.

[157] Moelwyn I. Williams, 'Some aspects of the economic and social life of Glamorgan, 1600–1800', *Morgannwg*, III (1959), 33–4.

[158] PRO, E 190/1279/3.

[159] Ibid., 1281/14.

[160] Caroline Skeel, 'The Welsh woollen industry in the 16th and 17th centuries', *Arch. Camb.*, vii, IV (1922), 223–4.

[161] Walter Davies, op. cit., II, 441.

[162] John Evans, *Letters*, p. 434.

[163] Thomas Pennant, *Tours in Wales*. Ed. John Rhys (Caernarvon, 1883), II, 204. Pennant observed that in Bala (Merionethshire) women and children were to be found 'in full employ knitting along the road'.

[164] NLW, P.R. (Ll.), 1725.

[165] Ibid., 1715.

[166] Ibid., 1722; cf. ibid., 1694 (Margarett Morgan of Whitchurch, spinster).

[167] Ibid., 1716. Further evidence is provided in the inventories attached to the wills of the following: Jane Thomas, spinster, Pentyrch; Harry Lewis, husbandman, Gelli-gaer, 1700; Rees ap John, yeoman, Cadoxton-juxta-Neath, 1713.

[168] NLW, P.R. (Ll.), 1714.

[169] In the seventeenth century stockings were worn to the knee, and they sometimes measured about three feet, Hugh Evans, *Cwm Eithin* (2nd ed., Lerpwl, 1922), pp. 11–2.

[170] John Evans, *Letters*, p. 434; W. Davies, op. cit., II, 442.

[171] GRO, D/DC F2.

[172] Hugh Evans, *Cwm Eithin*, p. 171.

[173] NLW, MS. 13,147A.

[174] CCL, Cadrawd MS. 2.355.

[175] PRO, E 190/1277/7.

[176] Moelwyn I. Williams, 'Contributions to the commercial history of Glamorgan', *NLWJ.*, IX, 350–5.

[177] NLW, P.R. (Ll.), 1674. Note, at 6d. or 8d. per pair, this amount would represent the value of 300 to 400 pairs of stockings.

[178] Ibid., 1696.

[179] Ibid., 1722–3.

[180] Ibid., 1714.

[181] Walter Davies, op. cit., II, 444.

[182] GRO, D/D Au/32 (folio 53).

[183] For an account of the process of tanning, Anna M. Jones, *The Rural Industries of England and Wales*, IV, (Oxford, 1927), 85.

[184] PRO, PCC, 81 Dixy.

[185] He was taxed on four hearths in the hearth tax assessment of 1670 (PRO, E 179/221/294).

[186] NLW, P.R. (Ll.), 1686.

[187] Ibid., 1709.

[188] Elizabeth Phillips, *Pioneers of the Welsh Coalfield* (Cardiff, 1925), p. 156. Note, it is said that Coffin became interested in coal when prospecting for oak bark in the Rhondda Valley, *DWB.*, *s.n.*

[189] Caroline E. Williams, (ed.), *A Welsh Family from the Beginning of the Eighteenth Century* (2nd. ed., London, 1893), p. 69.

[190] NLW, Penrice and Margam MS., 5900. (The skins were of two grades; one was sold at 6*d.* per skin, and the other at 1*s.* 2*d.* per skin. Some hides weighed as much as 136 lb.).

[191] NLW, P.R. (Ll.), 1691.

[192] Ibid., 1700.

[193] Ibid., 1694.

[194] NLW, Penrice and Margam MS., nos. 5607, 5614.

[195] Ibid., no. 6101.

[196] Ibid., no. 6112.

[197] PRO, E 190/1088/9.

[198] Ibid., 1090/1.

[199] NLW, P.R. (Ll.), 1690; cf. ibid., 1704 (David Phillips, cordwainer, also of Pyle).

[200] Ibid., 1684.

[201] Ibid., 1749.

[202] Ibid., 1681.

[203] PRO, E 190/1093/4.

[204] NLW, P.R. (Ll.), 1730.

[205] Ibid., 1710.

[206] William Barnett, *The History and Antiquities of the City of Bristol* (1789), pp. 184–5.

[207] Lhuyd, *Parochialia*, III, 45.

[208] NLW, I.A.W. (collection); cf. Moelwyn I. Williams, *NLWJ.*, IX, 337.

[209] NLW, Badm. MS. (Group 2), no. 1273.

[210] GRO, MS. D/DF 61; Baker and Francis, *Surveys of Gower and Kilvey*, p. 154.

[211] D. J. Davies, *Econ. Hist. S. Wales*, p. 116.

[212] NLW, Badm. MS (Group 2), no. 1961.

[213] NLW, P.R. (S.D.), 1690.

[214] T. Rees, *Beauties of England and Wales* (London, 1815), pp. 608–9.

[215] Otherwise known as Sea Holly, or *Eryngium Maritimum*.

[216] PRO, E 190/1278/12; E 190/1279/3; E. 190/1281/14.

[217] Lhuyd, op. cit., p. 35.

[218] NLW, P.R. (S.D.), 1666.

[219] John Gerarde, *The Herball or General Historie of Plantes* (London, 1636), pp. 533–4.

[220] H. E. Wedeck, *Love Potions through the Ages* (London, 1963), p. 211; B. H. Barton and T. Castle, *The British Flora Medica* (London, 1877), p. 155.

[221] Shakespeare, in *King Lear*, refers to the 'dreadful trade' of gathering this plant.

[222] Richard Warner, *A Second Walk through Wales, 1798* (London, 1799), pp. 72–3.

[223] Moelwyn I. Williams, *NLWJ.*, IX, 337, 349.

[224] NLW, Badm. (Group 2), no. 2737.

[225] Laslett, *World We Have Lost*, pp. 31–2.

[226] Dorothy Davis, *A History of Shopping* (London, 1966), pp. 4–5.

[227] W. G. Hoskins, *The Midland Peasant* (London, 1957), p. 171.

[228] NLW, Penrice and Margam MS., no. 5648.

[229] George Owen, *Taylor's Cussion* (1552–1613); *Merrick's Glam. Antiqs.*, p. 114.

[230] *Almanac* Thomas Jones (Llundain, 1692).

[231] *Almanac* John Prys: 1760.

[232] *Cardiff Records*, III, 2.

[233] A. H. Dodd, *Stuart Wales*, p. 31.

[234] E. M. Carus-Wilson (ed.), *Essays in Economic History* (London, 1954), p. 8.

[235] CCL, Cadrawd MS., 2. 355, p. 106.

[236] *CAgH.*, IV, 543.

[237] *The New Cambridge Modern History*, VII (Cambridge, 1957), 243.

[238] NLW, P.R. (Ll.), 1710.

[239] Ibid., 1696.

[240] Moelwyn I. Williams, *NLWJ.*, IX, 249.

[241] NLW, P.R. (Ll.), 1700.

[242] Ibid., 1716.

[243] Ibid., 1696.

[244] Ibid., 1685.

[245] Ibid., 1688.

[246] Ibid., 1734.

[247] NLW, Ll/CC/P. 642.

[248] H. J. Habbakkuk, 'English land-ownership, 1680–1740', *EconHR*, X (1940), 12–17.

[249] NLW, P.R. (Ll.), 1714.

[250] Ibid., 1699.

[251] Ibid., 1703.

[252] Ibid., 1723. The rate of interest was 5 per cent.

[253] PRO, PCC, 29 Scott.

[254] Ibid., 107 Weldon

[255] NLW, P.R. (Ll.), 1705.

[256] Cf. W. G. Hoskins, 'The Elizabethan merchants of Exeter', *Elizabethan Government and Society*, p. 174.

[257] NLW, P.R. (Ll.), 1696.

[258] Ibid., 1682.

[259] M. M. Postan, 'Credit in medieval trade', *Essays in Economic History*, pp. 61–87.

[260] PRO, E 190/1277/7.

[261] Ibid., 1091/6.

[262] Ibid., 1092/5.

[263] Ibid., 1281/14.

[264] NLW, Penrice and Margam MS., no. 2587.

[265] Dodd, *Stuart Wales*, p. 23.

[266] 'Anglia Wallia. A transcript from the Queen's Remembrancer Roll, 4 Eliz.', *Arch Camb.*, 1911, II, 423–4.

[267] D. Defoe, *A Tour through England and Wales* (Everyman's ed., 1928), II, 55.

[268] Moelwyn I. Williams, *NLWJ.*, IX, 188–215, 334–53; idem, *NLWJ.*, XI, 330–60; XII, 58–81, 266–87, 353–69.

[269] N. S. B. Gras, *The Evolution of the English Corn Market* (Cambridge, 1915), pp. 34–5.

[270] Arthur Young, op. cit., p. 329.

[271] Professor H. P. R. Finberg has presented fresh evidence which carries the history of the Welsh cattle trade back to the middle of the thirteenth century, *Agric.HR.*, II (1954), 12–4—'An early reference to the Welsh cattle trade'.

[272] Caroline Skeel, 'The cattle trade between Wales and England from the fifteenth to the nineteenth century', *TRHS.*, iv, IX (1926), 135–58.

[273] Lhuyd, op. cit., p. 45; Moelwyn I. Williams, *Morgannwg*, III (1959), 3 on.3.

[274] NLW, MS. 13,089E.

[275] Arthur Young, *Six Weeks Tour*, p. 260.

[276] Skeel, op. cit., p. 149.

[277] PRO, E 190/1278/1.

[278] Ibid., 1277/9; 1277/2.

[279] Ibid., 1277/7.

[280] Ibid., 1090/1.

[281] Skeel, op. cit., p. 155.

[282] F. W. Steer, *Farm and Cottage Inventories of Mid-Essex, 1635–1749* (Chelmsford, 1950), pp. 182, 206; cf. also R. Trow-Smith, *A History of British Livestock Husbandry to 1700* (London, 1957), p. 215.

[283] C. W. Chalklin, *Seventeenth-century Kent* (London, 1965), p. 99.

[284] Cf. Edgar Thomas, *Introduction to Agricultural Economics* (London, 1949), p. 72n.

[285] For a fairly full discussion on the Glamorgan cattle trade, P. G. Hughes, 'Porthmona ym Morgannwg', *Trans. Cymm.*, 1946–7, pp. 250–70. On the Welsh cattle trade in general, P. G. Hughes, *Wales and the Drovers* (London, 1943) and C. S. Smith, 'Dafydd was a drover', *Farmer's Weekly*, 4 January 1952, pp. 34–5, 37.

[286] Dunster Castle MSS., Shelf 57, bundle 10.

[287] PRO, E 190/1277/7.

[288] Ibid., 1278/12.

[289] NLW, P.R. (Ll.), 1679.

[290] Ibid., 1688.

[291] Ibid., 1729.

[292] P. J. Bowden, *The Wool Trade in Tudor and Stuart England* (London, 1962), p. 60.

[293] PRO, E 190/1086/2.

[294] NLW MS. 13,089E.

[295] NLW, P.R. (Ll.), 1760.

[296] Ibid., 1740.

[297] PRO, E 134/23 Chas.I/Mich. 1. Note, the freight of every kilderkin of butter from Aberthaw to Bristol was 6*d*.

[298] Ibid.

[299] E. A. Lewis, 'Maritime trade of Wales in Stuart times . . .' in *Times Trade and Engineering Supplement*, 6 December 1924.

[300] NLW, Badm. (Group 2), no. 2065.

[301] PRO, E 190/1277/7.

[302] Ibid., 1090/1.

[303] NLW, I.A.W. MS. 16, transcribed by Moelwyn I. Williams, *NLWJ.*, IX.

[304] Thomas Wyndham, of Dunraven castle, still had his port wine shipped from Bristol to Newton, and carted to Dunraven late in the eighteenth century.

[305] A. H. John 'Iron and coal on a Glamorgan estate, 1700–1740', *EconHR.*, ii, IV (1951), 98.

[306] C. W. and P. Cunnington, *Handbook of English Costume in the Sixteenth Century* (London, 1954), p. 199.

[307] Cf. T. S. Willan, *The English Coasting Trade, 1600–1750* (Manchester, 1938), p. 192.

[308] Charles Wilson, *England's Apprenticeship, 1603–1763* (London, 1965), p. 66.

[309] Walter Davies, op. cit., II, 319, 448; John Evans, *Letters*, pp. 165–8.

[310] Charles Wilson, op. cit., p. 66.

[311] J. F. Rees, *Studies in Welsh History* (Cardiff, 1947), pp. 130–48.

[312] Census, 1831.

[313] Moelwyn I. Williams, 'Observations on the population changes in Glamorgan, 1800–1900', *Glam. Hist.*, I, 117–8.

[314] Carus-Wilson (ed.), *Essays in Economic History*, I, 105.

[315] Cf. J. H. Clapham, *An Economic History of Modern Britain: the Railway Age* (Cambridge, 1926), p. 13.

[316] Davies, *Econ. Hist. S. Wales*, pp. 75–6.

[317] NLW, P.R. (Ll.), 1679.

[318] *Hen Gwndidau*, p. 30, ll. 14–6.

[319] M. B. Donald, *Elizabethan Copper* . . . (London, 1955), pp. 344–5; cf. Lionel Williams, *Morgannwg*, III, 3–20.

[320] M. B. Donald, op. cit., pp. 344–5.

[321] Ibid., p. 354.

[322] BM, 522 M12(2).

[323] Ibid., M12(28).

[324] NLW, Penrice and Margam MS., nos. 6668–6682 (refer to the period 1732–1745). In Neath in the sixteenth century there had been ship-building, *Stradling Correspce.*, pp. 271–2; cf. above, p. 57.

[325] NLW, Penrice and Margam MS., no. 6673; cf. no. 6104.

[326] NLW, Badm. (Group 2) MS., no. 11,763.

[327] NLW, P.R. (Ll.), 1692 Lewis Morgan.

[328] Ibid., 1722.

[329] NLW, Ll/CC/P.660, 1742.

[330] *HMC Earl of Verulam MSS.*, p. 255.

[331] NLW, Penrice and Margam MS., no. 3666; cf. T. S. Ashton, op. cit., p. 43.

[332] Walter Davies, op. cit., II, 19, 27.

[333] NLW, P.R. (S.D.), 1666.

[334] For a detailed account of the extent and methods of coal mining in west Glamorgan, Michael Williams, 'Early coal mining in Clyne Valley', *Gower*, XI (1958), 17–21; *vide* also, BM., 522 M12(37).

[335] For a list of early Gower enterprises, R. P. Roberts, 'The history of coalmining in Gower from 1700–1832' (M.A. Thesis, Univ. of Wales, 1953), pp. 49–79.

[336] B. M. Evans, 'The Welsh coal trade', p. 84.

[337] PRO, PCC, 58 Berkeley.

[338] Ibid., 81 Dixy (1584–1604).

[339] NLW, P.R. (Ll.), 1670.

[340] Ibid., 1697.

[341] Ibid., 1691.

[342] CCL. MS. 4.309/18 (PRO Rentals and Survey Rolls, no. 78).

[343] NLW, P.R. (Ll.), 1712; cf. *Arch. Camb.*, 1878, p. 121.

[344] Author of *England's Improvement by Sea and Land* . . . (1677).

[345] Her brother was a certain Mr. Wharton.

[346] NLW, MS. 19,148B.

[347] PRO, E 179/264/47.

[348] Lhuyd, *Parochialia*, part III, p. 28; *Arch. Camb.* Suppl., 1911.

[349] John, *EconHR.*, XIII, 97.

[350] PRO, E 134/1 Geo. II/Mich. 14.

[351] R. P. Roberts, 'Coalmining in Gower'; NLW, Penrice and Margam MS., no. 6099.

[352] NLW, Badm. (Group 2) MS., no. 11,763.

[353] *Travels through England* (Camden Soc., 1889), II, 200.

[354] *HMC Lord Verulam MSS.*, p. 256.

[355] R. Ayton, *Voyage round Great Britain* (London, 1814), p. 68.

[356] Royal Institution of South Wales, Miscellaneous Collection, pp. 255, 257.

[357] Ibid.

[358] Charles Wilkins, *South Wales Coal Trade* (Cardiff, 1888), p. 37n.

[359] B. and C. L. Lease, no. 84.

[360] Phillips, *Vale of Neath*, p. 212.

[361] NLW, Penrice and Margam MS., no. 5648.

[362] R. P. Roberts, 'Coalmining in Gower', p. 146. For a list of tenants who ought, by their leases, to carry coal, NLW, Penrice and Margam MS., nos. 6821, 6822.

[363] NLW, P.R. (Ll.), 1676.

[364] Ibid.

[365] E. A. Lewis, *Times Trade Suppl.*, 6 December 1924; cf. Moelwyn I. Williams, *NLWJ.*, IX, 198–9.

[366] Nef, *British Coal Industry*, II, Appendix K, pp. 422–3.

[367] R. B. Buzzard and F. D. Kelly, *Coal Miners' Attendance* (National Coal

Board Medical Research Memoranda, no. 2, London, 1963), p. 19; cf. Nef, op. cit.

[368] Lhuyd, op. cit., p. 33.

[369] Exch. Spec. Comm., no. 3441, quot. Nef, op. cit., II, 144.

[370] NLW, Penrice and Margam MS., no. 5648.

[371] Ayton, op. cit., p. 67.

[372] NLW, Penrice and Margam MS., no. 6097. It is worth observing that during the first half of the eighteenth century the few scattered inventories of 'colliers' that have survived do not include 'agricultural' goods. This might reflect from another angle the increasing number of 'colliers' who were divorced from the land and from access to it.

[373] PRO, E 134/1 Geo. II/Mich. 14.

[374] Nef, op. cit., II, 150.

[375] NLW, Penrice and Margam MS., no. 5555.

[376] Ibid., no. 3249.

[377] Nef, op. cit., II, 141.

[378] NLW, Penrice and Margam MS., no. 5648.

[379] A Cornish mariner, named Giles Dudge, wrote on July 21, 1836, from Aberavon to his employers at Hayle complaining 'I beg to inform you . . . we have been down river nine days ready for the sea but we never had one tide in which we might have got out'. (Truro Record Office, Harvey MSS.).

[380] Defoe, *Tour*, II, 55; cf. Wilkins, *Coal Trade*, p. 21.

[381] See the will of Arthur Triplett, mariner, of Cornwall, NLW, P.R. (S.D.), 1745.

[382] Ibid., 1716; cf. also ibid., 1755 (Eliz. Davies of Swansea)—'gave to Silvanus James sone of my kinswoman Jane James late of Penzance, Cornwall . . . .'.

[383] Ibid., P.R. (Ll.), 1721 (Roger Stephens, a miner from Somerset).

[384] NLW, Penrice and Margam MS., no. 6084.

[385] Ibid., no. 6307.

[386] Ibid., no. 2753.

[387] Eliz. Phillips, *Pioneers of Welsh Coalfield*, p. 51.

[388] CCL. MS. 2.59.

[389] Wilkins, *Merthyr Tydfil*, p. 169.

[390] PRO, E 134/15 Geo. II/Hil. 4.

[391] Lhuyd, op. cit., p. 28.

[392] John, *EconHR.*, XIII, 102.

[393] John Fox, *General View of Agriculture*, p. 7.

¹ *C.J.*, 8, p.16; T. Richards, *Puritan Movements*, p.318; *CSPD, Charles II, 1660–61*, p.124.

² *F. and R.*, ii, pp. 1085, 1249, 1455

³ *CSPD., 1659–60*, pp. 23, 56, 223; 1658–59, p. 325; Mansel Family Papers GRO, D/D, BL 5–8, 22.

⁴ W. R. Williams, *Parliamentary History*, p. 107; *C.J.*, 8, pp. 30, 75.

⁵ J. R. Jones, 'Political Groups and Tactics in the Convention of 1660', *Historical Journal*, VI, No. 1 (1963), 159–178.

⁶ *CSPD., 1660–61*, pp. 209, 214, 281; W. R. Williams, op. cit., p. 174, 98; A. H. Dodd, *Studies in Stuart Wales* (1952), *passim*.

⁷ *CSPD., 1660–61*, pp. 240, 368; W. R. Williams, op. cit., p. 99; Cobbett, *Parliamentary History*, IV, p. 102; *A List of the Names and Residences of the High Sheriffs of the County of Glamorgan from 1541 to 1866* (1961), p. 22; PRO, SP 29/4, f. 67, 179. *CSPD.*, 1660–61, pp. 52, 149; Dodd, op. cit., *passim*; F. Jones, 'The Vaughans of Golden Grove', *Trans. Cymm.* (1963), p. 122; M. P. Schoenfeld, *The Restored House of Lords* (1967); *CSPD., 1661–2*, p. 102; PRO, SP 29/42, ff. 120v, 135.

⁸ Seymour Phillips, *List of Justices of the Peace in Wales, 1542–1688* (unpublished); A. G. Veysey, 'Colonel Philip Jones, 1618–74', *Trans. Cymm.* (1963), pp. 316 ff; PRO, SP 29/398, ff. 283–4; Camden Soc., 74, (1859).

⁹ W. R. Williams, op. cit., pp. 99, 107, 174; *C.J.*, 8, pp. 258, 264, 271, 273.

¹⁰ 'Sir Edw. Mansell Bart, of Margam has been chosen knight of the shire for co. Glams, without opposition, in place of Lo. Herbert, called to the House of Peers by the death of his father', John Man (of Swansea) to Sir John Williamson, 9 March 1670, *CSPD., 1670*, p. 106.

¹¹ *C.J.*, 8, p. 276; J. H. Sacret, 'The Restoration Government and Municipal Corporations', *EHR*, XLV (1920).

¹² E.g. *CSPD., 1671–2*, p. 394; 1672, p. 23; UCS, C. Att. Acc., 1672, p. 166; NLW, Penrice & Margam MSS, L88, L110, L111, L113, L115, L116, L118.

¹³ A. Browning, *Thomas Osborne, Earl of Danby*, iii (1951), *passim.*; E. S. de Beer, 'Members of the Court Party, 1670–78', *BIHR*, XI; N.L.W, P & M MS. L141; *C.J.* 8, pp. 175, 187, 205, 210, 214, 228; Dodd, op. cit., *passim*; D. M. Elis-Williams, 'The Activities of Welsh Members of Parliament 1660–1688', (M.A. Thesis, University of Wales, 1952).

¹⁴ For Jenkins see *DWB*.

¹⁵ *HMC, XI R, App., Pt. ii, H of L.*, pp. 222–237; PRO, SP 29/398, f. 184; Margaret Cusack O'Keefe, 'The Popish Plot in South Wales and the Marches of Hereford and Gloucester', (M.A. Thesis, University College of Galway, 1969).

¹⁶ *CSPD., 1678, Addendum*, pp. 524–5; NLW, P & M MS. L151; PRO, SP 44/43, ff. 236–7; O'Keefe, op. cit.

¹⁷ *HMC, 12th R, App., Pt. IV.*, pp. 106, 114.

¹⁸ W. R. Williams, op. cit., pp. 99, 107; *C.J.*, 9, p. 570; J. R. Jones, 'Shaftesbury's "Worthy Men": a Whig View of the Parliament of 1679', *BIHR*, XXX (1957), 241; A. Browning and D. Milne, 'An Exclusion Division List', ibid., XXIII, 205.

¹⁹ *CSPD., 1680–81*, p. 476; A. H. Dodd, 'Tuning the Welsh Bench', *NLWJ.*, VI (1950), 249; Seymour Phillips, op. cit., *sub* August 7, 1677, April 20, 1680 and note on page 43a; PRO, SP 44/43, ff. 192, 195; NLW, P & M MS. L155; *HMC Ormonde*, n.s., VI, 148; A. H. Dodd, *Studies in Stuart Wales*, p. 207; *CSPD., 1679–80*, p. 453; ibid., *1682*, pp. 271–2.

²⁰ PRO, SP 44/62, f. 382; *CSPD., 1682*, pp. 77, 276.

²¹ Ibid., July 1–Sept. 30, 1683, p. 262; NLW, P & M MSS. 7161, L162, L165, L166.

²² *CSPD., 1682*, p. 476; Swansea Common Attorney's Accounts, f. 182; PRO, SP 29/422, f. 141; *CSPD., May 1684–February 1685*, pp. 239, 256; D. Rhys Phillips, *The Vale of Neath*, App. VIII, pp. 668–677; NLW, (Mansel Franklin Collection) MS. 75, No. 116; UCS, Swansea Portreeve's Book 1665–1762, ff. 57, 58, 69; L. W. Dillwyn, *Contributions Towards a History of Swansea* (1840), pp. 12–13.

²³ R. H. George, *EHR*, LV (1940), 47; Swansea Portreeve's Book, f. 73; *CSPD.*,

James II, Vol. 1, 832; NLW MS. 75, No. 116; Seymour Phillips, op. cit., *sub* Sept. 28, 1685; W. R. Williams, op. cit., pp. 99, 108; NLW, P & M MSS. L170, L171, L181; Swansea Portreeve's Book, f. 73. Seymour Phillips, op. cit., *sub* Dec. 17, 1686.

²⁴ *HMC, XII Rep., App., Pt. ix*, pp. 89–90; J. R. Jones, *The Revolution of 1688 in England* (1972), p. 107; Seymour Phillips, op. cit., *sub* Aug. 20, 1687; T. Richards, 'Declarasiwn 1687', *Trafodion Cymdeithas Hanes Bedyddwyr Cymru* (1924), t. 14.

²⁵ T. Dineley, *Account of the Official Progress of the first duke of Beaufort through Wales, 1684* (1888), p. 351. *CSPD., James II*, Vol. II, 1231; ibid., *Charles II, 1660–1661*, p. 564; Bodleian MS. Rawlinson A—139A, ff. 47, 48; for Edwin's political views see N. Luttrell, *A Brief Historical Relation of State Affairs from September 1678 to April 1714*, (6 vols., 1857, reprinted 1969) *passim.*; T. Richards, *art. cit.*, pp. 27–34, 45–46. *HMC 12th Report*, App., IX, p. 91.

²⁶ J. R. Jones, op. cit., p. 160, 167, 169. *CPSD., James II*, vol. III, 1947, 1706; A. H. Dodd, op. cit., *passim.*

²⁷ *HMC, 12th Report*, vii, 214; Luttrell, op. cit., 1, p. 467; *CSPD., James II*, Vol. I, 957; P & M, MSS. L205, L201–L206.

²⁸ Llewelyn B. John, 'The Parliamentary Representation of Glamorgan, 1536 to 1832' (M.A. Thesis, University of Wales, 1934), pp. 17–95. Much general information has been obtained for this chapter from the above thesis, as also from W. R. Williams, *The Parliamentary History of Wales* (Brecon, 1895), and Clark, *Limbus*.

²⁹ A. Browning, *Thomas Osborne, Earl of Danby* (3 vols., Glasgow, 1951), III, 60, 76, 79, 83, 89, 96, 117.

³⁰ NLW, Penrice and Margam MSS., no. L155.

³¹ Browning, op. cit., III, 157.

³² NLW, Penrice and Margam MSS., no. L181. Gwyn, an M.P. almost continuously from 1673 to 1727, was to hold important offices under Tory ministers in the reigns of William III and Anne, but his subsequent career has no direct relevance to the politics of Glamorgan.

³³ *The Gentleman's Magazine*, 1738, p. 546.

³⁴ NLW, Penrice and Margam MSS., nos. L284–8.

³⁵ John, op. cit., pp. 207–8.

³⁶ N. Luttrell, *A Brief Historical Relation of State Affairs from September 1678 to April 1714* (6 Vols. Oxford, 1857), IV, 303; V, 338, 437.

³⁷ NLW, Penrice and Margam MSS., no. L203.

³⁸ D. Rhys Phillips, *Vale of Neath*, pp. 226–28, 233, 238, 265–80.

³⁹ NLW, Penrice and Margam MSS., nos. L206–7.

⁴⁰ Browning, op. cit., III, 172, 212–13.

⁴¹ NLW, Penrice and Margam MSS., no. L304.

⁴² ibid., no. L298.

⁴³ ibid., no. L348.

⁴⁴ ibid., no. L348.

⁴⁵ ibid., no. L350.

⁴⁶ ibid., no. L355.

⁴⁷ ibid., no. L356.

⁴⁸ ibid., no. L395.

⁴⁹ ibid., no. L413.

⁵⁰ ibid., no. L409.

⁵¹ ibid., nos. L504, 516.

⁵² ibid., no. L525.

⁵³ ibid., nos. L234, 240, 352.

⁵⁴ ibid., no. L522.

⁵⁵ ibid., no. L519.

⁵⁶ ibid., no. L519.

⁵⁷ ibid., no. 527.

⁵⁸ Luttrell, op. cit., V, 627; VI, 13.

⁵⁹ NLW, Penrice and Margam MSS., nos. L427, 430.

⁶⁰ ibid., no. L541.

⁶¹ *HMC Reports, Portland MSS.*, IV, 329.

⁶² UCS., Mackworth MSS. (formerly in the Royal Institution of South Wales, Swansea), nos. 910–16. I am indebted to Mr. A. F. Peplow for transcripts of some of these MSS.

⁶³ NLW, Penrice and Margam MSS., no. L558.

⁶⁴ ibid., no. L582.

⁶⁵ UCS., Mackworth MSS., nos. 910–16.

⁶⁶ NLW, Penrice and Margam MSS., no. L570.

⁶⁷ ibid., no. L582.

⁶⁸ ibid., Red Box 29, 9018. I owe this and some other references in these MSS. to Professor G. S. Holmes of Lancaster University.

⁶⁹ ibid., no. L585.

⁷⁰ ibid., no. L1443.

⁷¹ ibid., no. L1455.

⁷² *HMC Reports, Portland MSS.*, IV, 489.

⁷³ NLW, Penrice and Margam MSS., no. L598.

⁷⁴ ibid., no. L595.

[75] *HMC Reports, Portland MSS.*, IV, 490.

[76] NLW, Penrice and Margam MSS., no. L678.

[77] ibid., no. L686.

[78] ibid., no. L679.

[79] ibid., no. L721.

[80] For evidence of his Jacobite sympathies, see P. D. G. Thomas, 'Jacobitism in Wales', *WHR*, I, (1962), 282.

[81] NLW, Penrice and Margam MSS., no. L886.

[82] ibid., nos. L979, 983.

[83] John, op. cit., p. 110.

[84] GRO, Kemys Tynte MSS., 3/2. I am grateful to Dr. R. D. Rees for the loan of a microfilm of these MSS.

[85] ibid., 1/5.

[86] ibid., 3/2.

[87] ibid., 1/4.

[88] ibid., 1/5.

[89] ibid., 1/7.

[90] ibid., 1/13.

[91] ibid., 1/14.

[92] ibid., 1/8.

[93] ibid., 1/9.

[94] ibid., 1/11.

[95] ibid., 1/10.

[96] ibid., 1/12.

[97] NLW, Penrice and Margam MSS., no. L1158.

[98] *Cardiff Records*, IV, 161–62.

[99] GRO, Kemys Tynte MSS., 1/37.

[100] UCS., Mackworth MSS., no. 451.

[101] ibid., no. 455.

[102] *Journals of the House of Commons*, XXII, 330–31.

[103] GRO, Kemys Tynte MSS., 1/15.

[104] UCS., Mackworth MSS., no. 520.

[105] GRO, Kemys Tynte MSS., 1/16.

[106] ibid., 1/17.

[107] NLW, Penrice and Margam MSS., no. L1197.

[108] ibid., no. L1198.

[109] ibid., no. L1200.

[110] ibid., no. L1202.

[111] ibid., no. L1206.

[112] Quoted by John, op. cit., pp. 99–100.

[113] For an account of the battle see H. W. Richmond, *The Navy in the War of 1739–1748* (3 Vols. Cambridge, 1920), II, 1–58.

[114] GRO, Kemys Tynte MSS., 1/18–19.

[115] ibid., 1/22

[116] ibid., 1/20.

[117] UCS., Mackworth MSS., no. 653.

[118] For the political situation at this time see J. B. Owen, *The Rise of the Pelhams* (London, 1957), pp. 239–66.

[119] GRO, Kemys Tynte MSS., 1/22.

[120] ibid., 1/47.

[121] ibid., 1/24.

[122] BM, Additional MSS. 35601, fo. 348.

[123] GRO, Kemys Tynte MSS., 1/28.

[124] ibid., 1/33.

[125] ibid., 1/23–32.

[126] ibid., 1/27.

[127] ibid., 1/35–36, 41.

[128] ibid., 1/37, 44.

[129] ibid., 1/55–56.

[130] ibid., 1/59.

[131] ibid., 1/66.

[132] ibid., 1/68.

[133] ibid., 1/37.

[134] ibid., 1/42–44.

[135] ibid., 1/52.

[136] ibid., 1/47.

[137] ibid., 1/60.

[138] ibid., 1/62.

[139] ibid., 1/69.

[140] ibid., 1/70.

[141] ibid., 1/78.

[142] ibid., 1/83.

[143] Owen, op. cit., p. 265.

[144] Richmond, op. cit., II, 260–8.

[145] BM, Add. MSS. 32995, fos. 75–82.

[146] *The Works of the Right Honourable Sir Charles Hanbury-Williams, K.B.* (3 Vols. London, 1822), III, 104.

[147] *Journals of the House of Commons*, XXVII, 659–60, 709.

[148] GRO, Kemys Tynte MSS., 1/85.

[149] ibid., 1/84.

[150] ibid., 1/86.

[151] ibid., 1/87.

[152] Bute MSS. (Mount Stuart, Isle of Bute. By kind permission of the marquess of Bute), Thomas to Bute, March 8, 1761.

[153] *London Evening Post*, April 21, 1761.

[154] Mount Stuart, Bute MSS., no. 553.

[155] Mount Stuart, Bute MSS., no. 562.

[156] ibid., no. 561.

[157] *Letters from George III to Lord Bute 1756–1766* (ed. R. Sedgwick, 1939), p. 230.

[158] BM, Add. MSS. 38458, fo. 34.

[159] Mount Stuart, Bute MSS., no. 568.

[160] BM, Add. MSS. 32977, fos. 385–86.

[161] ibid., 32978, fos. 141–43.

[162] ibid., 32979, fos. 321–22.

[163] *The Glocester Journal*, February 16, 1767.

164 ibid., May 11, 1767.

165 ibid., June 22, 1767.

166 ibid., August 10, 1767.

167 ibid., September 21, 1767.

168 ibid., October 5, 1767.

169 Wharton (Kemys Tynte) MSS. (Somerset Record Office, Taunton).

170 ibid., Vernon to Tynte, October 26, 1767.

171 PRO, Chatham MSS., 30/8/LXIV, fos. 311–12.

172 *The Glocester Journal*, November 2, 1767.

173 ibid., November 16, 1767.

174 ibid., November 30, 1767.

175 ibid., December 7, 1767.

176 ibid., December 21, 1767.

177 *Cardiff Records*, II, 222.

178 *London Evening Post*, October 8, 1774. *The Glocester Journal*, October 10, 1774.

179 NLW, Penrice and Margam MSS., no. L1301.

180 NLW, Tredegar MSS., no. 66/86.

181 ibid., No. 66/87.

182 ibid., No. 66/88.

183 *The Glocester Journal*, October 31, 1774.

184 ibid., September 11 and 18, 1780.

185 For an almost complete transcript, see John, op. cit., pp. 104–111.

186 *The Glocester Journal*, October 9, 1780.

187 ibid., September 25, 1780.

188 Peter D. G. Thomas, 'Check List of M.P.s Speaking in the House of Commons, 1768 to 1774', *BIHR*, XXXV (1962), 224.

189 W. Cobbett, *Parliamentary History . . . 1066 to . . . 1803* (36 Vols. London, 1806–20), XVIII, 265, 1413; XXII, 850.

190 *The Parliamentary Papers of John Robinson 1774–84* (Ed. W. T. Laprade, London, 1922), p. 95.

191 *Hereford Journal*, April 15, 1784.

192 *London Gazette*, May 1, 1784.

193 Earl of Dunraven, *Dunraven Castle* (London, 1926), p. 89.

194 NLW, Tredegar MSS., no. 72/78.

195 ibid., no. 72/77.

196 ibid., no. 72/79.

197 ibid., no. 72/80.

198 ibid., no. 72/75.

199 John, op cit., pp. 117–18.

200 NLW, Tredegar MSS., no. 72/75.

201 ibid., no. 72/74.

202 ibid., no. 53/58.

203 ibid., no. 72/80.

204 ibid., no. 72/82.

205 ibid., no. 72/78.

206 ibid., no. 72/76.

207 John, op cit., pp. 118–120.

208 *Journals of the House of Commons*, XLIV, 646.

209 John, op. cit., pp. 117–118.

210 John, op. cit., pp. 30–80, 222.

211 T. H. B. Oldfield, *Entire and Complete History . . . of the Boroughs* (1792), III, Wales, 29.

Note.   Parts of the above chapter originally appeared in an article in *Morgannwg* VI (1962) and are reprinted here by kind permission of the editors.   P.D.G.T.

Chapter IX

[1] J. P. Kenyon, *The Stuart Constitution* (Cambridge, 1966), p. 358.

[2] Norman Sykes, *Church and State in the XVIII Century* (London, 1934), p. 93.

[3] Tanner MSS., 146.

[4] Lambeth Palace Library, MSS., 930.49.

[5] *Dioc: Llandavensis Computus* (n.d.).

[6] Browne Willis, *A Survey of the Cathedral Church of Llandaff* (London, 1717), pp. 103-4.

[7] N. Sykes, op. cit., p. 360.

[8] Willis MSS., 104.

[9] NLW., LL Bounty, 131-6.

[10] Mary Clement, *The S.P.C.K. and Wales, 1699-1740* (London, 1954), p. 7.

[11] Browne Willis (ed.) *Thesaurus Rerum Ecclesiasticarum* (3rd Ed., London, 1753), Preface, IV.

[12] NLW., LL Terr 24, 83.

[13] NLW., LL O 82.

[14] NLW., LL O 17-39.

[15] NLW., LL CC G760.

[16] Quoted by N. Sykes, op. cit., p. 221.

[17] J. A. Bradney and R. Rickards, *Llandaff Records*, II, 92.

[18] Ibid., II, 101.

[19] Ibid., II, 108.

[20] NLW., LL CC G953.

[21] NLW, LL CC 180.

[22] NLW, LL VW 4, 15, 42, 52.

[23] *Bettws parish finances and accounts.*

[24] NLW, LL VW 46, 47.

[25] NLW, LL CC G1259.

[26] NLW, LL CC G1377, 1390, 1391.

[27] E. W. Williamson, *Llandaff Cathedral*, p. 18.

[28] E. T. Davies, 'John Wood's Italianate Temple', *JHSCW.*, VI, 70-81.

[29] Browne Willis, op. cit., pp. 34-35.

[30] Willis MSS., 104. The letter is undated, but it was written before 1719 which was the year of Willis's book on Llandaff Cathedral.

[31] Ibid.

[32] NLW., SD QA 61.

[33] NLW, LL QA 1, 6.

[34] NLW, SD VW 14, 21, 24, 26, 27A; SD QA 61; LL QA 1, 6; J. A. Bradney, *Acts of the Bishops of Llandaff*, I-IV; Edward Lhwyd, 'Parochialia', *Arch. Camb.* Supplements, 1909-11.

[35] *Report of the Charity Commissioners, South Wales* (London, 1838).

[36] M. G. Jones, *The Charity School Movement* (Cambridge, 1938), p. 4.

[37] M. G. Jones, 'Two Accounts of the Welsh Trust, 1675 and 1678 (?)', *BBCS.*, IX (1937-9), 74, 78.

[38] Ibid., p. 79.

[39] This section on the S.P.C.K. schools is based exclusively on the writings of Dr. Mary Clement, *Correspondence and Minutes of the S.P.C.K. relating to Wales, 1699-1740* (Cardiff, 1952), and *The S.P.C.K. and Wales 1699-1740* (London, 1954).

[40] *Report of the Charity Commissioners, South Wales* (London, 1838); ibid., *County of Monmouth* (London, 1834).

[41] A description and history of this diocesan library has been given by E. O. T. Lewis, 'The Cowbridge Diocesan Library', *JHSCW.*, IV (1954), 36-44; VII (1957), 80-91.

[42] Important general works on the penal code and its effects on Dissenters are Edward Calamy, *An Account of the Ministers . . . Ejected or Silenc'd after the Restoration in 1660* (London, 1713); Idem, *A Continuation of the Account* (London, 1927); A. G. Matthews, *Calamy Revised* (Oxford, 1934); A. Gordon, *Freedom after Ejection* (Manchester, 1917); S. Palmer, *The Nonconformist's Memorial* (London, 1803); G. Lyon Turner, *Original Records of Early Nonconformity under Persecution and Indulgence* (3 vols. London, 1911-14); for Wales, see R. Tudur Jones, *Hanes Annibynwyr Cymru* (Abertawe, 1965); Thomas Rees, *History of Protestant Nonconformity in Wales* (London, 1861); Thomas Richards, *Religious Developments in Wales, 1654-1662* (London, 1923); idem, *Wales under the Penal Code (1662-1687)* (London, 1925); idem, *Wales under the Indulgence, 1672-1675* (London, 1928). *Cardiff Records*, II, 174-75.

[43] Richards, *Religious Developments*, pp. 396, 470-86.

[44] For a list of the Glamorgan ministers ejected, see Appendix B, pp. 497-98. The information contained in it is drawn

mainly from Rees, *Protestant Nonconformity*, pp. 153–59; Richards, *Religious Developments*, Part II, *passim*; and R. Tudur Jones and B. G. Owens, 'Anghydffurfwyr Cymru', *Y Cofiadur*, 32 (1962), 3–93. For the laymen, Richards, *Religious Developments*, pp. 419–21, and Walter T. Morgan, 'The persecution of Nonconformists in the consistory courts of the diocese of St. David's, 1661–1668', *JHSCW.*, XII (1962), 28–54, esp. p. 52. Cf. also *DWB*, *s.n.* Philip Jones, Bussy Mansel, and Thomas (of Wenvoe).

[45] M. Fay Williams, 'The Society of Friends in Glamorgan, 1654–1900' (M.A. Thesis, University of Wales, 1950), pp. 55–56; idem, 'Glamorgan Quakers, 1654–1900', *Morgannwg*, V (1962), 49–75; J. Besse, *A Collection of the Sufferings of the People called Quakers* (2 vols. London, 1753), I, 744–50; R. L. Hugh, 'Annibyniaeth yng Ngorllewin Morgannwg', *Y Cofiadur*, 18 (1948), 3–58.

[46] Walter T. Morgan, *JHSCW.*, XII, 28–52; Lucy's letter quot. Hugh, *Cofiadur*, 18, 31; Richards, *Penal Code*, pp. 20–21, 76–78.

[47] Ibid., pp. 76–78; Williams, 'Friends in Glamorgan', pp. 65–66.

[48] These returns are now preserved in Lambeth Palace MS. 639; a transcript of the returns relating to Glamorgan is given in Rees, *Protestant Nonconformity*, pp. 200–1; cf. also Richards, *Penal Code*, pp. 63–4 for the Quaker meetings; ibid., pp. 124–5; idem, *Indulgence*, pp. 44–6. Samuel Jones, Robert Thomas, Lewis Thomas, and Thomas Quarrell are all included in *DWB*, *s.n.*

[49] For the text of the Declaration, E. Cardwell (ed.), *Documentary Annals of the Reformed Church of England* (2 vols. Oxford, 1844), II, 333–7; Richards, *Indulgence*, *passim* and esp. pp. 42–3, 69–71, 82, 92, 100–3, 109, 116, 158, 169–75; Williams, 'Friends in Glamorgan', pp. 67–75.

[50] Morgan, *JHSCW.*, XII, 41–5. For a description of Brynllywarch and other details, T. C. Evans (Cadrawd), *A History of Llangynwyd Parish* (Llanelli, 1887), chap. viii; cf. also nn. 66, 75 below.

[51] The most detailed study of the returns of 1676 is to be found in T. Richards, 'The religious census of 1676', *Trans. Cymm.* Supplement, 1925–6, pp. 1–118. For Henry Maurice, *DWB*, *s.n.*

A transcript of Maurice's catalogue is printed in Rees, *Protestant Nonconformity*, pp. 203–10.

[52] Richards, *Penal Code*, pp. 48–51; idem, *Indulgence*, pp. 47–9.

[53] T. P. Ellis, *Welsh Catholic Martyrs* (London, 1933), pp. 119–24; *DWB*, appendix, *s.n.*; E. G. Jones, *Cymru a'r Hen Ffydd*, pp. 85, 89–92; Cleary, *Blackfriars*, XXXVIII, 123–5; Margaret C. O'Keeffe, 'The Popish Plot in South Wales' (M.A. Thesis, University College of Galway, 1969), p. 84 ff.; *Cardiff Records*, II, 174–5; IV, 156–9.

[54] NLW, Margam MS. 2978, cf. W. R. Watkin, 'Bedyddwyr Llangyfelach', *Traf. Cym. Hanes Bedyddwyr*, 1916–19, pp. 49–63 and T. Mardy Rees, 'Robert Thomas, Baglan', *Y Cofiadur*, 18 (1948), 59–69. NLW., Margam MS. 5174, cf. Hugh, *Cofiadur*, 18, 36. NLW, Margam MS. 1137, cf. Rees, *Cofiadur*, 18, 64. Richard Cradock, Robert Morgan, and Robert Thomas are all in *DWB*, *s.n.*

[55] The only detailed study of the working of the Indulgence in Wales is T. Richards, 'Declarasiwn 1687: tipyn o'i hanes a barn Cymru amdano', *Traf. Cym. Hanes Bedyddwyr*, 1924, tt. 1–46; cf. Mardy Rees, *Cofiadur*, 18, 59–69. For the text of the Declaration, Cardwell, *Documentary Annals*, II, 359–63.

[56] T. Richards, 'Bedyddwyr Cymru yng Nghyfnod Lewis Thomas', *Traf. Cym. Hanes Bedyddwyr*, 1916–19, pp. 3–45; Rees, *Protestant Nonconformity*, pp. 260–67; Hugh, *Cofiadur*, 18, 32; G. E. Evans prints extracts from the Mynydd-bach church book (NLW MS. 371B) in 'Llangevelach: Tirdunkin Chapel, Annals and Registers', *Trans. Carmarthenshire Antiq. Soc.*, XV (1921–2), 50–54.

[57] Richards, *Penal Code*, pp. 89–95; idem, *Indulgence*, pp. 36–37, 42–43; Jones, *Hanes Annibynwyr*, pp. 94–5; Joshua Thomas, *Hanes y Bedyddwyr ymhlith y Cymry . . .* Ed. B. Davies (Pontypridd, 1885), pp. 175–8; *Llandaff Records*, II, 104–5.

[58] Richards, *Penal Code*, pp. 33–7.

[59] Richards, *Indulgence*, pp. 98–9; J. Spinther James, *Hanes y Bedyddwyr yng Nghymru* (4 cyf. Caerfyrddin, 1893–8), II, 468–9; Richards, *Penal Code*, pp. 93–5; idem, *Indulgence*, p. 43; A. Leslie Evans, *The Story of Baglan* (Port Talbot,

1970), pp. 35–7; Joshua Thomas, *Bedyddwyr*, p. 176; Calamy, *Account*, II, 732–3.

⁶⁰ Richards, *Penal Code*, p. xi.

⁶¹ Rees, *Protestant Nonconformity*, p. 269.

⁶² *Cardiff Records*, II, 178–82; Thomas Richards, *Piwritaniaeth a Pholitics (1689–1719)* (Wrecsam, 1927), pp. 13–15; idem, 'The Glamorgan loyalists of 1696', *BBCS.*, III (1926), 137–49.

⁶³ Richards, *Piwritaniaeth a Pholitics*, chap. iii.

⁶⁴ Ibid., pp. 39–40, 47–48; cf. *DNB*, *DWB*, *s.n.*

⁶⁵ *DWB*, *s.n.* Mackworth; Bolingbroke quot. G. M. Trevelyan, *England under the Stuarts* (London, 1938), p. 475.

⁶⁶ Tudur Jones, *Hanes Annibynwyr*, p. 106, n. 4, 5; H. P. Roberts, 'Nonconformist academies in Wales (1662–1862)', *Trans. Cymm.*, 1928–29, pp. 1–98; *DWB*, *s.n.* Samuel Jones and Richard Price; Isaac Thomas, 'Y Gronfa Gynulleidfaol ac Annibynwyr Cymru', *Y Cofiadur*, 28 (1958), 3–32.

⁶⁷ Joshua Thomas, *Bedyddwyr*, p. 103; Spinther James, *Bedyddwyr*, III, 1–15.

⁶⁸ Thomas Rees and John Thomas, *Hanes Eglwysi Annibynnol Cymru* (2 gyf. Lerpwl, 1872), II, 48, 38–39, 97, 247–48, 414–15; J. Dyfnallt Owen, *Hanes Eglwys Cwmllynfell* (Caerfyrddin, 1935).

⁶⁹ Joshua Thomas, *Bedyddwyr*, pp. 105–6, 178–83; Spinther James, *Bedyddwyr*, III, 6–11.

⁷⁰ M. Fay Williams, 'Friends in Glamorgan', chap. ii; idem, *Morgannwg*, V, 63–8.

⁷¹ Details of the statistics are printed in Rees, *Protestant Nonconformity*, pp. 286–92. The best discussion of them is in R. T. Jenkins, *Hanes Cymru yn y Ddeunawfed Ganrif* (Caerdydd, 1931), pp. 48–52.

⁷² Thomas Richards, 'Y Bedyddwyr a'r *Dissenting Deputies*, 1732–1812', *Traf. Cym. Hanes Bedyddwyr*, 1959, p. 17; Rees and Thomas, *Eglwysi Annibynnol*, II, 97; Joshua Thomas, *Bedyddwyr*, p. 118; Thirsk, *CAgH*, IV, 111–12; Everitt, ibid., IV, 588–59.

⁷³ *Cardiff Records*, II, 187–92, 201–2; Richards, *Piwritaniaeth a Pholitics*, pp. 134–6; records of old licences in E. Lewis Evans, 'Hen drwyddedau', *Y Cofiadur*, 19 (1949), 66–7; 20 (1950), 72–8; Richards, *Traf. Cym. Hanes Bedyddwyr*, 1959, pp. 17–28.

⁷⁴ Tudur Jones, *Hanes Annibynwyr*, p. 121; R. T. Jenkins, *18fed Ganrif*, pp. 54–5; Spinther James, *Bedyddwyr*, III, 32–3, 44–6; R. L. Hugh, *Y Cofiadur*, 18, 41–4.

⁷⁵ Samuel Jones, James Owen, Philip Pugh, Rees Price, David Rees, and Roger Griffith are all included in *DWB*, *s.n.* Cf. also H. P. Roberts, *Trans. Cymm.*, 1928–9, pp. 14–15; G. Dyfnallt Owen, *Ysgolion a Cholegau yr Annibynwyr* (Abertawe, 1939); Isaac Thomas, *Y Cofiadur*, 28, 3–32; Spinther James, *Bedyddwyr*, III, 51–4. Thomas Llewellyn is included in *DWB*, *s.n.*

⁷⁶ The Mynydd-bach church book is NLW MS. 371B; cf. R. L. Hugh, *Y Cofiadur*, 18, 39 and Evans, *Trans. Carmarthenshire Antiq. Soc.*, XV, 50–4. For Blaengwrach, Rees and Thomas, *Eglwysi Annibynnol*, II, 111, with a correction in R. L. Hugh, *Y Cofiadur*, 18, 68–9; Spinther James, *Bedyddwyr*, III, 106–7. Henry Davies is included in *DWB*, *s.n.*

⁷⁷ The covenant of the Mynydd-bach church, the earliest and fullest of those extant, is set out in Rees and Thomas, *Eglwysi Annibynnol*, II, 4–8; for the school there, Tudur Jones, *Hanes Annibynwyr*, p. 125; for literature, ibid., pp. 130–3 and Spinther James, *Bedyddwyr*, III, 74ff.

⁷⁸ NLW MS., 371B, p. 109; cf. Evans, *Trans Carmarthenshire Antiq. Soc.*, XV, 53 and Tudur Jones, *Annibynwyr Cymru*, p. 109. Siôn Llewelyn quot. Rees and Thomas, *Eglwysi Annibynnol*, II, 248 and *DWB.*, *s.n.*

⁷⁹ Jenkins, *18fed Ganrif*, pp. 55–6; Tudur Jones, *Hanes Annibynwyr*, pp. 111–22; Rees and Thomas, *Eglwysi Annibynnol*, II, 6.

⁸⁰ Jenkins, *18fed Ganrif*, pp. 65–9; Roberts and Owen, n. 75 above, *passim*; Charles Winter and David Rees, *DWB*, *s.n.* Spinther James, *Bedyddywr*, III, 44–6.

⁸¹ Rees and Thomas, *Eglwysi Annibynnol*, II, 248–9; Rees, *Protestant Nonconformity*, pp. 340–1; Wilkins, *Merthyr Tydfil*, chap. x; Roger Williams, James Davies, Richard Rees, and Samuel Davies are all included in *DWB*, *s.n.* (Samuel Davies under the entry for James Davies).

⁸² Josiah Rees and Solomon Harris, *DWB*, *s.n.*; R. L. Hugh, *Y Cofiadur*, 18, 47–51; Rees and Thomas, *Eglwysi Annibynnol*, II, 111.

⁸³ For a useful summary of the differences between a 'church' and a 'sect',

H. Richard Niebuhr, *The Social Sources of Denominationalism* (Meridian Books, 1957). M. Fay Williams, 'Friends in Glamorgan', chap. ii; Jenkins, *18fed Ganrif*, chap. iii; Rees, Llewellyn, Samuel and Richard Price, and David Williams, *DWB*, *s.n.*

[84] Edmund Jones and Miles Harry, *DWB*, *s.n.*

[85] Abbreviation: T.L.: The Trevecka Letters (at NLW). T.L., 106; *JCMHS*, IV, 35 (wrongly attributed to 'J. Tho'-').

[86] T.L., 108; *JCMHS*, Sept. 1920, p. 121.

[87] T.L., 110; *JCMHS*, 1920, p. 123.

[88] T.L., 111; *JCMHS*, 1920, p. 124.

[89] T.L., 112; Rees, *Protestant Nonconformity*, p. 371.

[90] T.L., 114; *JCMHS*, Sept. 1920, pp. 125-6.

[91] T.L., 115; *JCMHS*, 1920, p. 127.

[92] T.L., 116; Rees, *Protestant Nonconformity*, p. 372.

[93] T.L., 117; *JCHMS*, Sept., 1920, pp. 127-8.

[94] T.L., 118; Rees, op. cit., p. 374.

[95] Richard Bennett, *Blynyddoedd Cyntaf Methodistiaeth* (Caernarfon, 1909), pp. 192-3.

[96] T.L., 121; *JCMHS*, Sept. 1920, p. 130.

[97] T.L., 122; *JCMHS*, March, 1921, p. 132.

[98] T.L., 125; Hugh J. Hughes, *Life of Howell Harris* (London and Newport, 1892), p. 56.

[99] T.L., 135; *JCMHS*, March, 1921, p. 142.

[100] 'The itinerary of Howell Harris', *JCMHS*, Dec., 1923, p. 22.

[101] J. M. Jones and W. Morgan, *Y Tadau Methodistaidd* (2 vols., Abertawe, 1895-7), I, 86-89.

[102] T.L., 138; *JCMHS*, March, 1921, p. 145.

[103] T.L., 142; *JCMHS*, 1921, p. 148.

[104] *Bathafarn*, 17 (1962), 35; 18 (1963), 46ff.

[105] Iain Murray (ed.), *George Whitefield's Journals* (London, 1960), 288ff. Cf. also *JCMHS*, LV, 17ff.

[106] T.L., 313, see *Y Cofiadur*, 12 (1925), 54.

[107] T.L., 288, extracts printed in *Y Cofiadur*, 12 (1925), 40-1.

[108] T.L., 303; *JCMHS*, June, 1950, pp. 11ff.

[109] D. E. Jenkins, *Calvinistic Methodist Holy Orders* (Caernarvon, 1911), p. 23.

[110] Ibid., p. 20.

[111] T.L., 314; *JCMHS*, June, 1950, p. 28.

[112] T.L., 321; *JCMHS*, March, 1952, p. 42.

[113] T.L., 336; *JCMHS*, March, 1952, pp. 55-6.

[114] *JCMHS*, December, 1923, p. 40. 'The Society at ty newydd about a mile below Llantrissent Town' is mentioned in T.L., 336, written May 7, 1741 (*JCMHS*, March, 1952, p. 56).

[115] Ibid., II, 58.

[116] T.L., 401; *JCMHS*, XXVIII, 26-7.

[117] *JCMHS*, II, 58.

[118] T.L., 673; *JCMHS*, II, 59.

[119] *JCMHS*, XXVIII, 29.

[120] Ibid., II, 59.

[121] D. E. Jenkins, op. cit., p. 45.

[122] Ibid., pp. 18-19; also M. H. Jones, *The Trevecka Letters* (Caernarvon, 1932), p. 263.

[123] D. E. Jenkins, op. cit., pp. 19-20.

[124] *JCMHS*, XXVII, 165-6.

[125] John Davies, *Y Lloffyn Addfed* (Abertawy, 1852), p. 26.

[126] T. L. 379; *JCMHS*, March 1957, p. 122.

[127] A. H. Williams, *John Wesley in Wales* (Cardiff, 1971), pp. xxii-iii.

[128] T.L., 383; *JCMHS*, March 1957, p. 125.

[129] T.L., 405; *JCMHS*, July 1959, pp. 151-2.

[130] T.L., 392; *Y Cofiadur*, 27 (1957), 5.

[131] *JCMHS*, XXVIII, 17.

[132] T.L., 407; *Y Cofiadur*, 27, 6.

[133] T.L., 454; *JCMHS*, XXVII, 149-50.

[134] Ibid., XXVII, 168.

[135] T.L., 556; see Gomer M. Roberts, *Selected Trevecka Letters (1742-1747)* (Caernarvon, 1956), p. 18.

[136] D. E. Jenkins, op. cit., p. 75.

[137] T.L., 618; G. M. Roberts, op. cit., p. 40.

[138] T.L., 731; *JCMHS*, XXVII, 28-9.

[139] T.L., 685; G. M. Roberts, op. cit., p.52.

[140] T.L., 694; G. M. Roberts, op. cit., p. 56.

[141] *JCMHS*, XXVIII, 29ff.

[142] See introduction to T.L., 336; *JCMHS*, March, 1952, pp. 54-5.

[143] Ibid., XXXV, 42; G. M. Roberts, op. cit., p. 78, n. 7.

[144] *DWB*, *s.n.* Belcher, John.

[145] *JCMHS*, March 1952, p. 68, n. 2.

[146] Ibid., pp. 68–9, no. 4. He died in 1746, see *DWB.*, *s.n.* Lewis, Thomas.

[147] *JCMHS*, XXXVI, 91.

[148] T.L., 788; G. M. Roberts, op. cit., p. 78.

[149] NLW, C.M. Archives, Trevecka MS., 2945 contains the early association records; they have been printed *in toto*, *JCMHS*, XLVIII–LI.

[150] *JCMHS*, XXXV, 37.

[151] Ibid., XXVII, 138ff.

[152] Ibid., XXXV, 59–60.

[153] They have been printed in ibid., XXVII, 149–59; XXVIII, 1–9.

[154] T.L., 1262 (NLW C.M. Archives, unpublished).

[155] T.L., 1284; *Gower*, X (1957), 16.

[156] D. E. Jenkins, op. cit., pp. 103ff.

[157] Ibid., pp. 107, 114ff.

[158] D. E. Jenkins, op. cit., p. 128.

[159] Ibid., pp. 130ff.

[160] Ibid., p. 134.

[161] Ibid., p. 135.

[162] *JCMHS*, LIII, 54.

[163] T.L., 1494 (NLW C.M. Archives, unpublished).

[164] T.L., 1526 (NLW, C.M. Archives, unpublished).

[165] *JCMHS*, XXXI, 93ff.

[166] T.L., 2816A; *JCMHS*, XXXIX, 23ff.

[167] T.L., 2816B; *JCMHS*, XXXIX, 29ff.

[168] T.L., 2819B; *JCMHS*, XXXIX, 70ff.

[169] T.L., 2819C; *JCMHS*, XXXIX, 73ff.

[170] T.L., 2819A; *JCMHS*, XXXIX, 129.

[171] Ibid., p. 131.

[172] Ibid., pp. 134–35.

[173] T.L., 1854; *JCMHS*, XXX, 30.

[174] T.L., 1885 (NLW C.M. Archives, unpublished).

[175] D. E. Jenkins, op. cit., p. 147.

[176] *Y Cofiadur*, 17, 75.

[177] *JCMHS*, V, 34–6; see also Gomer M. Roberts, *Emynwyr Bethesda'r Fro* (Llandysul, 1967), chap. ii.

[178] Jones and Morgan, op. cit., I, 367.

[179] Richard Bennett, *Methodistiaeth Trefaldwyn Uchaf* (Y Bala, 1929), p. 164.

[180] Jones and Morgan, op. cit., I, 372–3; *JCMHS*, XXVII, 173.

[181] Jones and Morgan, op. cit., I, 375ff.

[182] T.L., 1935; *JCMHS*, XXXI, 112–13.

[183] Richard Bennett, op. cit., pp. 171ff.; *JCMHS*, LI, 34–5.

[184] Jones and Morgan, op. cit., I, 379.

[185] Ibid., I, 385ff.

[186] T.L., 1956 (NLW C.M. Archives, unpublished).

[187] Jones and Morgan, op. cit., I, 391.

[188] Ibid., I, 398–9.

[189] *JCMHS*, XXVII, 175.

[190] Jones and Morgan, op. cit., I, 399–400.

[191] T.L., 1988 (NLW C.M. Archives, unpublished).

[192] R. Bennett, op. cit., p. 194.

[193] T.L., 1996 (NLW C.M. Archives, unpublished).

[194] T.L., 1999, Sept. 5, 1751 (NLW C.M. Archives, unpublished).

[195] T.L., 2002; *JCMHS*, XXXII, 60ff.

[196] Jones and Morgan, op. cit., I, 400–1.

[197] T.L. 2014; see Gomer M. Roberts, *Selected Trevecka Letters (1747–1794)* (Caernarvon, 1962), pp. 52–3.

[198] *JCMHS*, XLI, 27–8.

[199] R. Bennett, op. cit., p. 215.

[200] Ibid., pp. 216–17.

[201] T.L., 2030; Gomer M. Roberts, op. cit., pp. 56–7.

[202] R. T. Jenkins, 'Evan Moses o Drefeca', *JCMHS*, XLVII (1962).

[203] *JCMHS*, IX, 16ff.

[204] *Y Cofiadur*, 17, 75ff.

[205] *JCMHS*, XXXVI, 72.

[206] *Y Cofiadur*, 21, 38.

[207] *JCMHS*, XXXV, 60.

[208] See note [195] above.

[209] *Y Cofiadur*, 20, 76.

[210] T.L., 2482; Gomer M. Roberts, op. cit., p. 88.

[211] *Y Cofiadur*, 19, 67; *JCMHS*, XXXIV, 83ff.

[212] Jones and Morgan, op. cit., II, 122ff.

[213] See *JCMHS*, XXXVI, 92–3.

[214] Ibid., XXVII, 176.

[215] Ibid., XXXIV, 45.

[216] Ibid., XXVII, 176–7.

[217] Ibid., XXXIV, 46.

[218] Jones and Morgan, op. cit., I, 417–8.

[219] *JCMHS*, XXXV, 37.

[220] Ibid., Dec., 1927, p. 32.

[221] Ibid., XXXIV, 46.

[222] Ibid., Dec., 1927, p. 32.

[223] Ibid., pp. 33–4; XXXIV, 46; Jones and Morgan, op. cit., I, 420.

[224] *JCMHS*, XXXIV, 46.

[225] Ibid., XXVII, 177; Jones and Morgan, op. cit., I, 423–54.

[226] John Hughes, *Methodistiaeth Cymru* (Gwrescam, 1856), III, 46.

[227] See *JCMHS*, XXXVI, 93–4.

[228] T.L., 2724; *Y Cofiadur*, 27, 17–8.

[1] I should be singularly ungrateful were I not to put on record here how much I owe to the unremitting labours of my former teacher and Head, the late Professor Emeritus Griffith John Williams, whose many brilliant researches into the literary history of Glamorgan have placed all students of Welsh literature under an immeasurable obligation. Some parts of the discussion which follows inevitably owe a great debt to his scholarly labours, especially to his monumental *Traddodiad Llenyddol Morgannwg* (Caerdydd, 1948). My grateful thanks are also due to the staff of the National Library of Wales, Aberystwyth, of the British Museum, London, and of the Central Library and University College Library, Cardiff, for their generous assistance and unfailing courtesy. Last, but by no means least, I am profoundly grateful to my wife, who spent long hours laboriously checking and systematizing the many transcripts which I had made from a variety of MS. sources. Any errors in transcription—and hence in the quotations which occur at various points in this discussion—and any errors in fact or interpretation are, however, entirely my own responsibility.

[2] Saunders Lewis, *Braslun o Hanes Llenyddiaeth Gymraeg* (Caerdydd, 1932), chap. vii; H. I. Bell, *The Development of Welsh Poetry* (Oxford, 1936), chap. v; Gwyn Williams, *An Introduction to Welsh Poetry* (London, 1953), chap. vi; T. Parry, *A History of Welsh Literature*, translated by H. I. Bell (Oxford, 1955), chap. vi; T. Parry, 'Datblygiad y Cywydd', *Trans. Cymm.* (1939), pp. 209 ff.

[3] For the general background, see T. H. Parry-Williams (ed.), *Canu Rhydd Cynnar* (Caerdydd, 1932); *TLlM.*, chap. iv; Brinley Rees, *Dulliau'r Canu Rhydd*, 1500–1650 (Caerdydd, 1952); D. J. Bowen, *Gruffudd Hiraethog a'i Oes* (Caerdydd, 1958), p. 64; and the works cited in n. 2.

[4] G. J. Williams (ed.), *Gramadeg Cymraeg gan Gruffydd Robert* (Caerdydd, 1939), p. 279.

[5] T. H. Parry-Williams, op. cit., pp. lxxxvii ff.; Brinley Rees, op. cit., pp. 9, 10,

11–12, 26, 32–5, 128, 132, 135, 137, 140, 151.

[6] D. J. Bowen, op. cit., p. 64.

[7] T. H. Parry-Williams, op. cit., pp. 102–8, 119–29, 188–203, 244–52, 324–5, 410–22.

[8] Quoted in John Buxton, *Sir Philip Sidney and the English Renaissance* (London, 1954), p. 97.

[9] E. D. Jones, 'Presidential Address', *Arch. Camb.*, CXII (1963), 1–12; D. J. Bowen, op. cit., pp. 64–5.

[10] *Gramadeg Cymraeg gan Gruffydd Robert*, pp. cxxvi, 330.

[11] R. Geraint Gruffydd, 'Wales and the Renaissance', in *Wales through the Ages*, vol. II, ed. A. J. Roderick (Llandybïe, 1960), 45–53.

[12] *Gramadeg Cymraeg gan Gruffydd Robert*, pp. 205–6, 208; W. Salesbury, *Oll Synnwyr Pen Kembero Ygyd* [1547], ed. J. Gwenogvryn Evans (Bangor–London, 1902); G. H. Hughes, *Rhagymadroddion 1547–1659* (Caerdydd, 1951), pp. 15, 75–7, 91–2; Siôn Tudur, 'Cywydd i'r Beirdd' in *The Oxford Book of Welsh Verse*, ed. T. Parry (Oxford, 1962), pp. 223–6.

[13] G. J. Williams, 'Llythyr Siôn Dafydd Rhys at y Beirdd', *Efrydiau Catholig*, IV (1949), 5–11; Thomas Jones (ed.), *Rhyddiaith Gymraeg*, II (Caerdydd, 1956), pp. 155–60 (esp. pp. 158–9 here); G. H. Hughes, op. cit., pp. 11, 92–3; T. Parry, *Hist. Welsh Lit.*, pp. 203 ff.

[14] W. Alun Mathias, 'Llyfr Rhetoreg William Salesbury', *Llên Cymru*, I (1950–1), 259–68; II (1952–3), 71–81; G. J. Williams (ed.), *Egluryn Ffraethineb sef Dosbarth ar Retoreg . . . gan Henri Perri* (Caerdydd, 1930); G. H. Hughes, op. cit., pp. 84–8.

[15] *Gramadeg Cymraeg gan Gruffydd Robert*, pp. 207–8; W. Salesbury, *Oll Synnwyr Pen Kembero Ygyd* (introduction); G. H. Hughes, op. cit., pp. 10, 67–71, 83; Thomas Jones, op. cit., p. 156; *TLlM.*, p. 156 and n. 48; T. Parry, *Hist. Welsh Lit.*, pp. 209–10; D. J. Bowen, 'Agweddau ar Ganu'r Unfed Ganrif ar Bymtheg', *Trans. Cymm.* (Session 1969), pp. 284–335 (esp. pp. 323–7).

s1

[16] For the Welsh original, G. H. Hughes, op. cit., p. 67.

[17] For references on inflation, see above, chap. I, nn. 27, 30.

[18] D. J. Bowen, *Gruffudd Hiraethog a'i Oes*, pp. 62–3.

[19] Ibid. Cf. further *Trans. Cymm.* (Session 1969), pp. 302–7.

[20] W. Ogwen Williams, 'The Survival of the Welsh Language after the Union of England and Wales: The First Phase, 1536–1642', *WHR.*, II (1964), 67–93.

[21] David Williams, *A History of Modern Wales* (London, 1950), pp. 88–9.

[22] See the very interesting receipts of a bard on his round which occur in Rhys Cain's autograph in NLW., Peniarth MS. 178, Part II, 56–62; *RWM.*, I, 993–4. Cf. further T. Parry, *Hist. Welsh Lit.*, pp. 219–20.

[23] *Ante*, III, chap. x, *passim*.

[24] Arthur O. Lovejoy, *The Great Chain of Being* (Cambridge, Mass., 1936). Cf. further Penry Williams, *Life in Tudor England* (London, 1964), chap. iii.

[25] J. Huizinga, *The Waning of the Middle Ages* (Pelican edn., London, 1955), p. 322.

[26] 'Everywhere private interests predominated over public: every one "gaped" for gain': J. B. Black, *The Reign of Elizabeth* (Oxford, 1936), p. 218.

[27] *The Penguin Book of Welsh Verse*, translated with an introduction by Anthony Conran (London, 1967), p. 63.

[28] J. Stradling, 'The story of the lower borowes of Merthyr Mawr', ed. H. J. Randall and W. Rees, *S. Wales and Mon. Rec. Soc. Pubns.*, I (1932), 70–1.

[29] Gwyn Thomas, *The Caerwys Eisteddfodau* (bilingual publication, Cardiff, 1968).

[30] E. D. Jones, op. cit., pp. 4–11 (esp. p. 8).

[31] NLW., Llanover MS. B 20, [3]–[4].

[32] These complaints began in the first half of the sixteenth century and continued unabated throughout the century that followed. Note, e.g., NLW., Mostyn MS. 144, 717; Mostyn MS. 161, 418; NLW., Peniarth MS. 63, 242; Peniarth MS. 73, 61; *Detholiad o Waith Gruffudd ab Ieuan ab Llewelyn Vychan*, ed. J. C. Morrice (Bangor, 1910), pp. 49–51 (no. xx); *Barddoniaeth William Llŷn*, ed. J. C. Morrice (Bangor, 1908), p. 142; *Hist. Welsh Lit.*, pp. 220–2; D. J. Bowen, op. cit., pp. 62–5.

[33] NLW., Llanstephan MS. 144, 16, in the hand of John Jones of Gellilyfdy.

[34] *Ante*, III, 497–9, 506–9, 515–20.

[35] Glanmor Williams, *Dadeni, Diwygiad a Diwylliant Cymru* (Caerdydd, 1964), pp. 22–6. Cf. further E. H. Miller, *The Professional Writer in Elizabethan England* (Harvard Univ. Press, Cambridge, Mass., 1959), p. 152.

[36] Clark, *Limbus*, p. 10.

[37] *TLlM.*, p. 82.

[38] Ibid., p. 82, n. 16.

[39] *Ante*, III, 449–52.

[40] Cf. J. W. Saunders, 'The Stigma of Print', *Essays in Criticism*, I (1951), 139–64.

[41] *Ante*, III, 529–32.

[42] *TLlM.*, pp. 72–3.

[43] NLW., Llanover MS. B 5, 52–5.

[44] Clark, *Limbus*, p. 8.

[45] *Hen Gwndidau*, p. 271.

[46] Phillips, *Vale of Neath*, pp. 530–1.

[47] NLW., Llanover MS. B 6, 30 *b*.

[48] Cardiff MS. 2. 277, 90–3.

[49] *Ante*, III, 501 ff.

[50] Copies of these poems were published in Phillips, *Vale of Neath*, pp. 479–80, 483–4, 510–11, 511–12. Cf. further NLW., Llanstephan MS. 164, 33–5, 48–50, 87–9; Jesus College MS. 13, 170 *b*–172; *Cyfaill yr Aelwyd* (1893), pp. 399–400.

[51] *Hen Gwndidau*, pp. 166–7, the printed version having been taken from NLW., Llanover MS. C 43, 7.

[52] Cardiff MS. 2. 277, 525–6.

[53] Ibid., 529–31.

[54] *TLlM.*, p. 79, n. 8. For further refs. to Dafydd Benwyn and his work: *Iolo Morganwg a Chywyddau'r Ychwanegiad*, pp. 68, 110, 123–4, 140, 141, 168, 186, 199, 200, 202, 212; Phillips, *Vale of Neath*, pp. 412–13, 479–80, 483–4, 510–12, 519, 527–32, 541; *Hen Gwndidau*, pp. 271–3; *TLlM.*, pp. 78–9.

[55] NLW., Llanover MS. B 6, 21 *a*; see also the photo-copy facing p. 278 in *Hen Gwndidau*.

[56] *TLlM.*, p. 79, n. 9.

[57] Ibid., p. 79.

[58] Photo-copy facing p. 277 in *Hen Gwndidau*. See also *Iolo Morganwg a Chywyddau'r Ychwanegiad*, pp. 16, 29, 34, 41, 43, 49, 54, 106, 110–11, 120, 137, 186; Phillips, *Vale of Neath*, pp. 141, 384, 470, 524, 534; *TLlM.*, pp. 79–80.

[59] NLW., Llanover MS. C 53, 259. *Ante*, III, 482–3.

[60] NLW., Llanover MS. B 6, 40 (formerly numbered as 36 *a*).

[61] *TLlM.*, p. 89.

[62] *DWB.*, *s.n.*, p. 414.

[63] *Grammadeg Cymraeg . . . O Gasgliad, Myfyriad ac Argraphiad John Rhydderch* (Mwythig [*sic*], 1728), pp. 188–9.

[64] NLW., Llanover MSS. C 33, 72; C 2, 320; C 40, 165; cf. further *Hen Gwndidau*, pp. 76–7.

[65] *Cyfrinach Beirdd Ynys Prydain* (Abertawy, 1829), pp. viii–xv, 1–10, *passim*. However, another list preserved by Iolo refers to a different series of Glamorgan *eisteddfodau*; NLW., Llanover MS. C 75, 73.

[66] *TLlM.*, p. 84.

[67] NLW., Peniarth MS. 182, 253; *RWM.*, I, 1005: 'llyma vy llaw j ll'n ap sion o blwyf tre lales yng wlad vorgan'. Only rarely did he write *ap* before *Siôn*.

[68] NLW., Llanover MS. C 18, 114.

[69] A copy of this letter and of Siôn Mowddwy's *cywydd* is preserved in BM. MS. 14886, 45–6.

[70] Iolo Morganwg published this reply in *Y Greal* (1806), pp. 208–10. Copies of both letters, in Iolo's autograph, occur in NLW., Llanover MSS. C 34, 501–5, transcribed *c.* 1785, and C 45, 28–32. See also *TLlM.*, p. 86, n. 27.

[71] *RWM.*, I, 891–8.

[72] NLW., Peniarth MS. 140, 368.

[73] *DWB.*, *s.n.*, p. 513.

[74] L. Dwnn, *Heraldic Visitations of Wales*, ed. S. R. Meyrick (2 vols., Llandovery, 1846), I, 7.

[75] NLW., Llanover MS. B 6, 77 *b*.

[76] See BM., Addl. MS. 15,067, 151 *b*. I am grateful to Mr. Gareth O. Watts and Mr. Milwyn Griffiths of the National Library of Wales, Aberystwyth, for confirming this reference. For a brief description of the contents of this manuscript, see *Catalogue of Additions to the MSS. in the British Museum in the Years MDCCCXLI–MDCCCXLV*, p. 82.

[77] *TLlM.*, p. 92.

[78] G. J. Williams and E. J. Jones, *Gramadegau'r Penceirddiaid* (Caerdydd, 1934), pp. xiii–xvi, xlvii–lviii.

[79] The letter which Iolo Morganwg claimed Llywelyn Siôn had addressed to Meurug Dafydd, in which the sender stated that he was transcribing manuscript-books on Welsh poetic art, is manifestly spurious. *Hen Gwndidau*, p. 221; *TLlM.*, p. 93, n. 45.

[80] Cardiff MS. 2. 277, 431–2; *TLlM.*, pp. 93–4.

[81] The copy which occurs in NLW., Llanover MS. B 5 is probably in Meurug Dafydd's autograph. Cf. also Llanover MS. C 38, 509–12; *Iolo Morganwg a Chywyddau'r Ychwanegiad*, pp. 240–1.

[82] Some of these poems were published in *Hen Gwndidau*, pp. 174–84.

[83] Above, p. 545.

[84] *TLlM.*, p. 95, and n. 52; NLW., Llanover MS. B 1, 583 *b*.

[85] NLW., Llanover MS. B 20, 3–4.

[86] Ibid., 3–4, 6–8.

[87] *Cyfrinach Beirdd Ynys Prydain*, p. 1.

[88] NLW., Llanover MS. C 54, 161–5; *Iolo Morganwg a Chywyddau'r Ychwanegiad*, pp. 232–5.

[89] L. J. Hopkin-James, *Caniadau Gwent a Morganwg* [*sic*], pp. 5–6.

[90] Llyfr Hir Llanharan (Cardiff MS. 5. 44), 340 *b*–341 *b*; NLW., Llanover MS. B 1, 508 *a*–510 *a*. The year referred to is noted in Edward Owen (ed.), *A Catalogue of the Manuscripts relating to Wales in the British Museum* (4 vols., London, 1900–22), IV, 964.

[91] *RWM.*, II, 753; *Iolo Morganwg a Chywyddau'r Ychwanegiad*, p. 175.

[92] Cardiff MS. 2. 277, 65, 167, 311, 518; *TLlM.*, p. 98.

[93] NLW., Llanover MS. B 20, 10.

[94] *TLlM.*, p. 98, n. 56. See also *Penrice and Margam MSS. Series I–IV*, III, 44 (no. 1282) and 55–6 (no. 1346).

[95] NLW., Llanover MSS. C 42, 1 ff.; C 29, 256 ff.

[96] Most of the features referred to can be found in the bard's *awdlau*; note, e.g., CCL., Llyfr Hir Llanharan, 334 *b*–335 *b*; 336 *a*–337 *a*; 337 *b*–339 *a*; 339 *a*–340 *a*. Some of the features can also be found in the verses which he composed on the popular *cywydd* measure; see, e.g., Llyfr Hir Llanharan, 340 *b*–341 *b*; NLW., Llanover MSS. B 1, 508 *a*–510 *a*; 514 *a*–515 *a*; B 20, 11–12.

[97] John Morris-Jones, *Cerdd Dafod* (Oxford, 1925), pp. 321–3, 324–7, 328–9, 338–9, 339–40, 342–3, 344–8, and 351–2. Cf. also pp. 232 ff., *passim*.

[98] T. Parry, *Hist. Welsh Lit.*, p. 150.

[99] NLW., Llanover MSS. B 20, 11–12; B 1, 514 *a*–515 *a*.

[100] *TLlM.*, p. 100.

[101] NLW., Llanover MS. B 12, 9–12; *TLlM.*, p. 100.

[102] NLW., Llanover MS. C 65, 155 ff.

[103] Richards, *Religious Developments in Wales, 1654–1662*, p. 189.

[104] *TLlM.*, p. 100.

[105] NLW., Llanover MS. B 20, 4.

[106] Cardiff MS. 2. 277, 430.

[107] Ibid., 474.

[108] Ibid., 349.

[109] CCL., Llyfr Hir Llanharan, 303 *a*.

[110] Bodleian MS. 25202, 60; quoted in *TLlM.*, p. 101.

[111] *TLlM.*, p. 101, and n. 59.

[112] NLW., Llanover MS. B 19, 8–9. Clark, *Limbus*, p. 438.

[113] *Archaeologia Britannica* (1707), p. 255.

[114] *Llandaff Records*, II, 10, 16, 31.

[115] Clark, *Limbus*, p. 179.

[116] *Archaeologia Britannica*, p. 255.

[117] NLW., Llanover MS. B 22, 35–7.

[118] *Llandaff Records*, III, 122.

[119] NLW., Llanover MS. B 20, 5, 6–8, 16–18, 20–1, 22–3, 25–6, 27–8; Cardiff MS. 5. 44, 353 *a*, 353 *b*–354 *a*, 354 *a*–354 *b*, 355 *a*–355 *b*, 356 *a*–356 *b*. See also Llanover MS. B 22, 11–14, 31–2, 33–4, 35–7; Cardiff MS. 2. 614, 25, 114; NLW., Penrice and Margam MS. 5937.

[120] NLW., Llanover MS. B 22, 11–14.

[121] NLW., Llanover MS. B 20, 27–8.

[122] See the example quoted by Iolo Morganwg in NLW., Llanover MS. C 19, 37.

[123] Note, e.g., NLW., Llanover MS. B 20, 22–3 (l. 50); 27–8 (l. 63); Cardiff MS. 5. 44, 354 *a*–354 *b* (l. 26); Llanover MS. B 22, 31–2 (l. 18); Cardiff MS. 2. 614, 114 (ll. 32 and 44).

[124] Note, e.g., NLW., Llanover MS. B 20, 20–1 (l. 70), 25–6 (l. 32).

[125] Examples of the faults referred to can be found in NLW., Llanover MS. B 20, 5 (l. 4), 16–18 (l. 49), 20–1 (ll. 65, 67, 69, and 72), 25–6 (ll. 17 and 33); Llanover MS. B 22, 35–7 (ll. 16 and 42); Cardiff MS. 5. 44, 353 *b*–354 *a* (l. 3), 356 *a*–356 *b* (l. 80); Cardiff MS. 2. 614, 114 (l. 11).

[126] E.g., NLW., Llanover MSS. B 20, 5 (ll. 3 and 4); B 22, 31–2 (l. 28); Cardiff MS. 2. 614, 114 (l. 42).

[127] Cf. 'Ymhob fawrgwys, mab Forgan', in NLW., Llanover MS. B 20, 25–6 (l. 16).

[128] E.g., ibid., 21–2 (ll. 12 and 32), 27–8 (ll. 45 and 64).

[129] Ibid., 25–6.

[130] Cardiff MSS. 5. 44, 353 *a* and 355 *a*–355 *b*; 2. 614, 114; NLW., Llanover MS. B 22.

[131] NLW., Llanover MS. B 22, 31–2.

[132] NLW., Llanover MS. C 59, 264.

[133] NLW., Llanover MS. C 2, 320.

[134] NLW., Peniarth MS. 115, 68. The date 1735 given in *RWM.*, I, 698, should be corrected to 1734.

[135] *TLlM.*, pp. 106–9.

[136] *TLlM.*, p. 110, n. 1.

[137] Ibid., pp. 110–11.

[138] *Hen Gwndidau*, pp. 49–51.

[139] *Ante*, III, 526; *TLlM.*, pp. 117–19.

[140] *Cyfrinach Beirdd Ynys Prydain* (1829), p. 159. Cf. further pp. 160–71.

[141] *Ante*, III, 521–2.

[142] NLW., Llanover MS. C 51, 74–5; *TLlM.*, p. 111.

[143] Bell, *Development of Welsh Poetry*, p. 108.

[144] T. Parry, *Hist. Welsh Lit.*, pp. 165–8.

[145] *Hen Gwndidau*, pp. 10–11, 11–12, 30–1; and cf. *Hist. Welsh Lit.*, pp. 176–7.

[146] NLW., Llanover MS. B 23, 302. This composition was not included in *Hen Gwndidau*.

[147] *Ante*, III, 529–32.

[148] *TLlM.*, p. 143.

[149] A *cwndid* is attributed to Dafydd Benwyn in *Hen Gwndidau*, pp. 164–5, but the only extant copy is that which occurs in Iolo Morganwg's autograph in NLW., Llanover MS. C 35, 138, and hence its authenticity is very doubtful.

[150] *TLlM.*, p. 117, and n. 18.

[151] *Canu Rhydd Cynnar*, pp. 399–401.

[152] Many of these compositions were published in *Hen Gwndidau*, and in *Hopkiniaid Morganwg* [*sic*], ed. Lemuel James (Bangor, 1909). For their origins, *TLlM.*, pp. 120 ff.

[153] Cf. *Hen Gwndidau*, p. 134; *Canu Rhydd Cynnar*, p. 180; G. J. Williams (ed.), *Gramadeg Cymraeg gan Gruffydd Robert* (Caerdydd, 1939), p. 279; *TLlM.*, p. 130.

[154] *Ante*, III, 526–34, for a discussion of the early *cwndidwyr*.

[155] Ifor Williams (ed.), *Casgliad o Waith Ieuan Deulwyn* (Bangor, 1909), p. 82.

[156] *Hopkiniaid Morganwg*, p. 190.

[157] *Hen Gwndidau*, pp. 98–9.

[158] *Hen Gwndidau*, pp. xxxvii–xxxviii.

[159] Ibid., pp. 19–20.

[160] Ibid., p. 100.

[161] This *cwndid* occurs on a loose page in NLW., Llanover MS. B 23, but the author is not identified. See *TLlM.*, p. 131, and n. 65.

[162] NLW., Llanover MS. B 23, 379. This composition is attributed to Siôn Lewis.

[163] *Canu Rhydd Cynnar*, pp. 367-72; *Hen Gwndidau*, pp. 187-92.

[164] Lewis Hopkin, *Y Fel Gafod* (Merthyr Tydfil, 1813), pp.15-17.

[165] Cardiff MS. 2. 277, 226-8; printed by Phillips in *Vale of Neath*, p. 531.

[166] Bodleian MS. 29398, 229.

[167] *Hen Gwndidau*, p. 176 (ll. 5-6).

[168] Ibid., pp. 81-91.

[169] *Canu Rhydd Cynnar*, pp. 203-8.

[170] Benjamin Heath Malkin, *The Scenery, Antiquities, and Biography of South Wales* (2nd edn., 2 vols., London, 1807), I, 297-9, which proved to be a fruitful source for many nineteenth-century historians of the region.

[171] *Hopkiniaid Morganwg*, pp. 18-46.

[172] His pedigree occurs in Wiliam Llŷn's autograph in NLW., Peniarth MS. 132, 305; *RWM.*, I, 829.

[173] Quoted in *TLlM.*, p. 125.

[174] *Hopkiniaid Morganwg*, p. 210.

[175] *Hen Gwndidau*, p. 49.

[176] Iolo Morganwg was the author of the love-poem attributed to Hopcyn Tomas Phylip in *Hopkiniaid Morganwg*, pp. 153-4.

[177] *Ante*, III, 497-9, for a discussion of Ieuan Gethin of Baglan.

[178] NLW., Llanover MS. B 6, 21 *a*; photo-copy in *Hen Gwndidau*, p. 278.

[179] Llyfr Hir Llanharan (=Cardiff MS. 5. 44), 339 *a*-340 *a*, l. 21.

[180] *Hen Gwndidau*, pp. 139-40, although the manuscript-source does not explicitly identify the author as Wiliam Prys.

[181] Ibid., p. 283.

[182] Ibid., pp. 283-4.

[183] *Hopkiniaid Morganwg*, p. 185.

[184] *Hen Gwndidau*, pp. 110-11, 281; 152-3, 280; 176-7, 279-80.

[185] NLW., Llanover MS. B 23, 279; *Hen Gwndidau*, p. 281.

[186] *Canu Rhydd Cynnar*, pp. 367-72; cf. also *Hen Gwndidau*, pp. 187-92 and 281.

[187] *Hen Gerddi Gwleidyddol*, 1588-1660 (Caerdydd, 1901), pp. 7-11.

[188] *Hen Gwndidau*, pp. 152-3.

[189] *Canu Rhydd Cynnar*, p. 367.

[190] *Hen Gwndidau*, p. 67.

[191] J. Morris-Jones, *Cerdd Dafod* (Oxford, 1925), pp. 323 ff.

[192] G. J. Williams and E. J. Jones, *Gramadegau'r Penceirddiaid* (Caerdydd, 1934), p. 48.

[193] *Caniadau yn y Mesurau Rhyddion* (Caerdydd, 1905), p. 64.

[194] *Ante*, III, 525-6.

[195] *Hen Gwndidau*, pp. 60-1.

[196] NLW., Llanover MS. B 12, 55; *TLlM.*, p. 137.

[197] *Canu Rhydd Cynnar*, p. 206.

[198] *Hen Gwndidau*, pp. 81-91.

[199] T. Parry, 'Datblygiad y Cywydd', *Trans. Cymm.* (1939), pp. 209 ff.

[200] *Hen Gwndidau*, pp. 2-3, 21-2. Cf. *Hopkiniaid Morganwg*, pp. 200-1. For a discussion of the metre, see J. Loth, *La métrique galloise* (3 vols., Paris, 1900-2), I, 95-7; *Cerdd Dafod*, p. 334.

[201] *Hen Gwndidau*, pp. 4-5, 14-15, 20-1; J. Loth, op. cit., I, 99-100; *Cerdd Dafod*, pp. 337-8.

[202] *Hen Gwndidau*, p. 29; J. Loth, op. cit., I, 89-90; *Cerdd Dafod*, pp. 339-40.

[203] *Hen Gwndidau*, p. 9; J. Loth, op. cit., I, 97-9; *Cerdd Dafod*, pp. 338-9; *TLlM.*, p. 139.

[204] *Hopkiniaid Morganwg*, pp. 200-1.

[205] *Hen Gwndidau*, pp. 114-17, 140-2, and *Hopkiniaid Morganwg*, pp. 194-6.

[206] T. Parry, *Hist. Welsh Lit.*, p. 170.

[207] *Canu Rhydd Cynnar*, pp. 21 ff., and the refs. cited there.

[208] T. Parry, *Hist. Welsh Lit.*, pp. 172, 183.

[209] Ibid., p. 183.

[210] *Ante*, III, 546-54.

[211] J. Foster (ed.), *Alumni Oxonienses . . . 1500-1714* (6 vols., Oxford, 1888-92), II, 798.

[212] *Ante*, III, 551-2.

[213] *Ante*, III, 535-45.

[214] *Agweddau ar Hanes Dysg Gymraeg: Detholiad o Ddarlithiau G. J. Williams*, ed. A. Lewis (Caerdydd, 1969), pp. 18-19.

[215] NLW., Peniarth MS. 51, 119-23; *RWM.*, I, 399 and 400; Ifor Williams, 'Geirfa o Hen Gymraeg', *BBCS.*, I (1921-3), 216-25.

[216] BM. MS. 31055, 138-43 and 161-3.

[217] G. J. Williams, 'Traddodiad Llenyddol Dyffryn Clwyd a'r Cyffiniau', *TDHS.*, I (1952), 20-32; *idem*, 'Edward Lhuyd a Thraddodiad Ysgolheigaidd Sir Ddinbych', ibid., XI (1962), 37-59; C. W. Lewis, 'Ysgolheictod', in *Gwŷr Llên y Ddeunawfed Ganrif*, ed. Dyfnallt Morgan (Llandybïe, 1966), pp. 164-72; Enid

Roberts, 'The Renaissance in the Vale of Clwyd', *Flintshire Historical Society Publications*, XV (1954–55), 52–63.

[218] NLW., MS. 5262, 66–8.

[219] NLW., Peniarth MS. 49, A; *RWM.*, I, 382–3, 384.

[220] *Ante*, III, 534–5.

[221] NLW., MS. 4973 C.

[222] NLW., Panton MS. 40, 220; *RWM.*, II, 851.

[223] NLW., MS. 14529 E; my italics.

[224] *The Cambrian Journal* (1863), 159; Rhiannon F. Roberts, 'Dr. John Davies o Fallwyd', *Llên Cymru*, II (1952–3), 19–35 (here p. 28).

[225] NLW., Peniarth MS. 267, 329–31; *RWM.*, I, 1081.

[226] NLW., Peniarth MS. 364, I, 160–1; *TLlM.*, pp. 153–4.

[227] *TLlM.*, p. 153, n. 40.

[228] *Ante*, III, 539–40.

[229] Clark, *Limbus*, p. 439.

[230] *TLlM.*, p. 151, n. 28; p. 154, n. 53.

[231] Clark, *Limbus*, p. 377.

[232] *RWM.*, II, 568–79; *TLlM.*, p. 154.

[233] *DWB.*, pp. 323, 544–5.

[234] *Ante*, III, 509–15 and 520–1.

[235] *RWM.*, II, 499.

[236] *Ante*, III, 515–20.

[237] *RWM.*, I, 824.

[238] *RWM.*, II, 133–7.

[239] *RWM.*, I, 88; *TLlM.*, p. 156, n. 49.

[240] Ibid., p. 157, n. 50.

[241] NLW., Llanover MS. C 2, 315.

[242] NLW., Llanstephan MSS. 47, 48, and 134 (=Llyfr Hir Amwythig); CCL., Hafod MS. 20; NLW., MS. 6511; NLW., MS. 970 (=Llyfr Hir Llywarch Reynolds); Cardiff MS. 5. 44 (=Llyfr Hir Llanharan); *RWM.*, II, 323–8, 516–25, 695–712.

[243] NLW., Llanover MS. B 9.

[244] BM., Harleian MS. 2414.

[245] Cardiff MS. 3. 240; CCL., Hafod MS. 4; NLW., Llanover MSS. B 17 and 18; *RWM.*, II, 306.

[246] Parts of CCL., Hafod MS. 5, NLW., Llanstephan MS. 164, and NLW., Llanover MS. B 6 are in Llywelyn Siôn's autograph; *RWM.*, II, 306 and 747; *TLlM.*, pp. 157–8 and n. 52.

[247] This MS. (=NLW., Llanstephan MS. 134) was later acquired by the celebrated antiquarian Moses Williams; *RWM.*, II, 695.

[248] This manuscript (now NLW., MS. 970) was deposited in the library of

Llywarch Reynolds of Merthyr Tudful towards the end of the nineteenth century; *RWM.*, II, 372.

[249] This is Cardiff MS. 5. 44, which belonged at one time to the Powel family of Llanharan.

[250] *TLlM.*, pp. 159–60 and 178.

[251] *Ante*, III, 547–8, 550–1; Henry Lewis (ed.), *Chwedleu Seith Doethon Rufein* (Wrecsam, 1925), pp. 21–30.

[252] *Ante*, III, 552.

[253] NLW., Llanstephan MS. 185, 74; *RWM.*, II, 774; *TLlM.*, p. 160 and n. 58.

[254] *Cyfrinach Beirdd Ynys Prydain* (1829), p. xiii.

[255] Clark, *Limbus*, pp. 471–3. The family lineage was recorded by Thomas Wilkins himself in Cardiff MS. 3. 464, 138.

[256] *DWB.*, s.n., p. 1019.

[257] *TLlM.*, pp. 162–3.

[258] R. T. Gunther, *Life and Letters of Edward Lhuyd* (Oxford, 1945), p. 343.

[259] *TLlM.*, p. 164.

[260] Bernard's *Catalogi librorum manuscriptorum Angliae et Hiberniae in unum collecti cum indice alphabetico*, I, pt. viii, 67. Cf. further C. L. Wrenn, 'Curiosities in a Medieval Manuscript', *Essays and Studies*, XXV (1939), 101–15, *passim*.

[261] *TLlM.*, pp. 148–9 and n. 19, p. 164

[262] Clark, *Limbus*, pp. 57, 375.

[263] *RWM.*, II, 318–20; I, 948; 1071; 1073–4; II, 310–11.

[264] *Ante*, III, 550–4.

[265] *RWM.*, II, 306, 323–8, 329–31.

[266] Ashmolean MS. 1817, 203–4; *TLlM.*, p. 165.

[267] NLW., Llanover MS. C 2, 273.

[268] *TLlM.*, p. 165 and n. 72.

[269] G. J. Williams, 'Wiliam Midleton a Thomas Prys', *BBCS.*, XI (1941–4), 113–14.

[270] *DWB.*, pp. 441–2, 567, 1100.

[271] NLW., Llanover MS. C 16, 270.

[272] Ibid., 137. In NLW., Llanover MS. C 35, 218–19, Iolo Morganwg quotes from 'Havod MS. 107'; see *TLlM.*, p. 166, n. 77.

[273] NLW., Llanover MS. C 16, 270. Edward Lhuyd's MSS. contain quotations from the work by Rice Merrick which is no longer extant.

[274] *TLlM.*, p. 167.

[275] NLW., Llanover MS. C 41, 163.

[276] NLW., Llanover MS. B 8, 125 a; BM. MS. 14878, 96.

[277] *TLlM.*, p. 169 and n. 87.

[278] *Cambrian Register*, I (London, 1796), 444. The information had probably been supplied by Iolo Morganwg.

[279] Quoted in *TLlM.*, p. 170.

[280] NLW., MS. 13221, 145.

[281] For the list which follows, *TLlM.*, pp. 170–1.

[282] NLW., Llanover MS. C 13, 265–84.

[283] *TLlM.*, p. 172.

[284] Taliesin Williams (ab Iolo), *Iolo Manuscripts* (Llandovery, 1848), pp. 100–14 and 115–34.

[285] *The Myvyrian Archaiology of Wales*, ed. Owen Jones, Edward Williams, and William Owen [-Pughe] (2nd edn., Denbigh, 1870), pp. 754–6, 874 ff.

[286] Iolo Morganwg never explicitly stated that he himself possessed those manuscripts in which he claimed to have discovered all this manifestly spurious material. The manuscript from which 'Achau Saint Ynys Prydain' had been taken was in the possession of 'Thomas Hopcin, of Llangrallo', according to Iolo, while Thomas Truman (above, pp. 638–639) was supposed to have the other extant copy. Again, 'Doethineb Catwg Ddoeth o Lancarvan' was allegedly in the possession of James Thomas of Maerdy Newydd near Bonvilston (Tresimwn), *Iolo Manuscripts*, pp. 100, 115; *Myv. Arch.²*, pp. 754, 875; *Iolo Morganwg a Chywyddau'r Ychwanegiad*, p. 172; *TLlM.*, p. 172, n. 95.

[287] G. J. Williams, 'Tri Chof Ynys Brydain', *Llên Cymru*, III (1954–5), 234–9 (esp. pp. 234–5).

[288] *Ante*, III, 535 ff.

[289] CCL., Aberdare MS. I, 80. Cf. Dwnn, *Heraldic Visitations of Wales*, I, 331.

[290] Cardiff MS. 2. 277, 541.

[291] *TLlM.*, pp. 185–90; Ralph Griffiths, 'The Norman Conquest and the Twelve Knights of Glamorgan', *Glam. Hist.*, III, 153–69.

[292] NLW., Llanover MS. B 12, 182.

[293] Cardiff MS. 5. 8, 77.

[294] Cardiff MS. 3. 464, 14.

[295] Rice Merrick, *A Booke of Glamorganshires Antiquities*, ed. J. A. Corbett (London, 1887), p. 17; cited hereafter as *BGA*.

[296] D. Powel, *The History of Wales*, ed. W. Wynne (Merthyr Tydvil, 1812), pp. xxv–xlvi. A manuscript copy of Edward Stradling's treatise is preserved in Cardiff MS. 4. 943. Although it is obviously not the original work, it was probably copied from it between *c.* 1573 and *c.* 1582; see folios 11ʳ, 16ᵛ, 17ʳ, and 18ʳ.

[297] D. Powel, op. cit., pp. xxx, xl, xlvi. Cf. also the details supplied by Blanche Parry on pp. xxix, xxx, and xxxviii.

[298] CCL., Aberdare MS. I, 79.

[299] *Stradling Correspondence*, pp. 47–8, 201–2, 288–9.

[300] NLW., Mostyn MS. 131, 59–78, for a copy of a series of *englynion* which Roger Morris had taken from a transcript written by 'L'n ap Math for Mʳ Edwart ystradling an. do. 1567'.

[301] F. R. Lewis, 'A History of the Lordship of Gower from the Missing Cartulary of Neath Abbey', *BBCS.*, IX (1937–9), 149–54. A further short extract was transcribed in 1595, Clark, *Cartae*, I, 77; G. R. C. Davis, *Medieval Cartularies of Great Britain* (London, 1958), pp. 77–8.

[302] *BGA.*, pp. iv–v.

[303] W. Dugdale, *Monasticon Anglicanum*, V (1825 edn.), 259.

[304] *Morgannwg*, VII (1963), 44.

[305] *Stradling Correspondence*, pp. 167–8.

[306] *TLlM.*, p. 199 and n. 152.

[307] Ibid., p. 200, n. 153.

[308] *BGA.*, pp. 67–82.

[309] At least two copies of the treatise which has been attributed to Sir Edward Mansel have survived in NLW., Llanover MSS. C 27, 211–17, and C 74, 19–55. Both copies were published in *Cardiff Records*, IV, 6–22. In Llanover MS. C 74, 56–8, immediately after the aforementioned treatise, there occurs 'Another account of the coming in of the Normans, in a shorter storry [*sic*] than that before by Sir Edward Mansel of Margam', *Cardiff Records*, IV, 23–9. Some of the details contained in this version strongly suggest that Iolo Morganwg was the author. Note also *TLlM.*, pp. 200–3 and the refs. cited there; W. Rees, 'A Breviat of Glamorgan, 1596–1600, by Rice Lewis', *S. Wales and Mon. Rec. Soc.*, III, 102 and 106.

[310] Cardiff MS. 4. 943, 10ʳ; A. L. Rowse, 'Alltyrynys and the Cecils', *Eng. Hist. Review*, LXXV (1960), 54–5.

[311] Bodleian MS. E Mus. 63; *TLlM.*, pp. 197–8.

[312] D. Powel, op. cit., p. xlvi; *Cardiff Records*, IV, 43; *Stradling Correspondence*, p. 235, n. 1; *TLlM.*, p. 197.

[313] Ralph Griffiths, 'The Rise of the Stradlings of St. Donat's', *Morgannwg*, VII (1963), 15–47.

[314] He signed his name as 'Rys Mirike' in the letter which he sent to Sir Edward Stradling, although the form 'Amerike' also occurs. The bards, however, used the name 'Rhys Amheurug'. See Dafydd Benwyn's ode in Cardiff MS. 2. 277, 10, where 'Rhys ymheyryg' occurs, and note also the name 'rhys amhavrig' used by Bedo Hafesb in Cardiff MS. 10, 112. Cf. further *TLlM.*, p. 203, n. 162.

[315] T. J. Hopkins, 'Rice Merrick (Rhys Meurug) of Cottrell', *Morgannwg*, VIII (1964), 5–13 (esp. pp. 6–9 in this context).

[316] *BGA.*, p. 49.

[317] Clark, *Limbus*, p. 540.

[318] *BGA.*, p. 115.

[319] Hopkins, *Morgannwg*, VIII (1964), p. 13.

[320] Rice Merrick, *A Booke of Glamorganshires Antiquities*, ed. James Andrew Corbett (London, 1887).

[321] This is Cardiff MS. 5. 8.

[322] NLW., Llanover MS. C 16, 270.

[323] *Parochialia*, III, 116–47 (Supplement to *Archaeologia Cambrensis*, 1911).

[324] Ibid., III, 128.

[325] Ibid., III, 138–9.

[326] Ibid., III, 137.

[327] Ibid., III, 122, 123, 126–7, 146; *TLlM.*, p. 211.

[328] *Parochialia*, III, 120, 125, 127; *BGA.*, pp. 52, 54–5, 91, 105–6; *TLlM.*, pp. 212–13.

[329] E.g., *BGA.*, p. 107.

[330] Peter Burke, *The Renaissance Sense of the Past* (London, 1969), p. 29.

[331] *BGA.*, p. 3.

[332] Ibid., pp. 4 and 54.

[333] Jesus College MS. 3 ('Llyfr Llywelyn Offeiriad'), p. 35 *b*; *BGA.*, p. 5; *TLlM.*, p. 149, n. 19; p. 209, n. 183.

[334] *Stradling Correspondence*, pp. 167–8.

[335] *BGA.*, pp. 41, 60, 75–6.

[336] Ibid., pp. 12, 16, 29, 48.

[337] 'Marke Peramb. f. 245' occurs in *BGA.*, p. 29.

[338] Cardiff MS. 10, 113; *RWM.*, II, 137.

[339] CCL., Aberdare MS. 1, 79; *RWM.*, II, 397–8. Cf. also Iolo Morganwg in NLW., Llanover MS. C 34, 19.

[340] Quoted in *TLlM.*, p. 205.

[341] NLW., Peniarth MS. 96, 245ff.; *RWM.*, I, 596.

[342] Cardiff MS. 18, 54; *RWM.*, II, 173.

[343] *Stradling Correspondence*, p. 169.

[344] *Archaeologia Cambrensis* (1890), pp. 321–2; *Llên Cymru*, I (1950–1), 48; Thomas Dineley, *The Account of the Official Progress of his Grace Henry the First Duke of Beaufort through Wales in 1684*, ed. R. W. Banks (London, 1888), p. 346.

[345] Cardiff MS. 4. 33 (here pp. 360–2). But in Clark, *Limbus*, p. 543, this daughter is called Ellen.

[346] C. F. Shepherd, *St. Nicholas* (Cardiff, 1934), p. 44.

[347] The MS. was transcribed *c.* 1613–14. It is stated on the cover that the MS. belonged to 'Rowland [*sic*] Williams', but the name 'Roger Willms' occurs in the rector's own hand on p. 49. See also *TLlM.*, p. 214.

[348] *Cyfrinach Beirdd Ynys Prydain* (1829), pp. 238–40.

[349] NLW., Llanover MS. C 41, 189.

[350] NLW., Llanover MS. C 13, 221.

[351] NLW., Llanover MS. C 34, 335.

[352] Clark, *Limbus*, p. 159.

[353] *Parochialia*, III, p. 126; but see *TLlM.*, p. 215, n. 220.

[354] Cardiff MS. 2. 277, 288–90.

[355] W. de Gray Birch, *Penrice and Margam MSS. Series I–IV*, II, 23.

[356] CCL., Aberdare MS. 1, 79; *RWM.*, II, 397–8. Cf. also Iolo Morganwg's additional comments in NLW., Llanover MS. C 34, 19.

[357] *RWM.*, II, 329. This manuscript is now deposited in CCL.

[358] Cardiff MS. 18, 41; *RWM.*, II, 173.

[359] Cardiff MS. 10, 121.

[360] NLW., Llanover MS. C 75, 128. Cf. further T. C. Evans (Cadrawd), *History of Llangynwyd Parish* (Llanelly, 1887), p. 31.

[361] A copy of this elegy has been transcribed in Cardiff MS. 5. 44 ('Llyfr Hir Llanharan'), 341.

[362] NLW., Llanover MS. B 20, 3 and 5.

[363] NLW., Llanstephan MS. 185, 74; *RWM.*, II, 774; *TLlM.*, p. 220.

[364] *TLlM.*, p. 220, n. 240.

[365] Cf. Thomas Wilkins's remarks in Cardiff MS. 3. 464, 2.

[366] Ibid., 48, 50, 103.

[367] A copy of the history of this dissension occurs in Cardiff MS. 5. 8, where the author, who may well have been Rice Merrick, claims that the account which he gives had been taken from 'the Records of the auncient Abbey of Neth' (p. 77). These 'Records' may possibly have been acquired

by Thomas Wilkins, together with others formerly in Rice Merrick's possession.

368 *Parochialia*, III, p. 15.

369 Thomas Nicholas, *Annals and Antiquities of the Counties and County Families of Wales* (2 vols., London, 1872), II, 591–4.

370 Gunther, *Life and Letters of Edward Lhuyd*, pp. 541–5.

371 See the list of subscribers in *Archaeologia Britannica* (1707).

372 *RWM.*, II, 547, 516–23; *TLlM.*, p. 224, n. 255.

373 Gunther, op. cit., pp. 269–70; *TLlM.*, p. 225.

374 Ibid., p. 536.

375 Ibid., p. 311.

376 Clark, *Limbus*, pp. 370–1.

377 Gunther, op. cit., pp. 42–3.

378 On the general background, see Bell, *The Development of Welsh Poetry*, chap. vii; T. Parry, *Hist. Welsh Lit.*, chap. x; S. Lewis, *A School of Welsh Augustans* (Wrexham and London, 1924); *Agweddau ar Hanes Dysg Gymraeg*, chap. vii; *TLlM.*, chap. vi.

379 NLW., Peniarth MS. 115, 68; *RWM.*, II, 698.

380 *TLlM.*, p. 259 et seq.

381 *Agweddau ar Hanes Dysg Gymraeg*, chap. vii; *TLlM.*, pp. 259 ff.

382 *TLlM.*, pp. 262–3; *DWB.*, s.n., 'Dafydd Lewys', on p. 565.

383 This letter is quoted in full in *TLlM.*, p. 260.

384 For a convenient general survey of the linguistic position, Brian Ll. James, 'The Welsh Language in the Vale of Glamorgan', *Morgannwg*, XVI (1972), 16–36.

385 G. J. Williams and E. J. Jones, *Gramadegau'r Penceirddiaid*, pp. lxi ff.; 89–142.

386 *TLlM.*, p. 265.

387 Lewis Hopkin, *Y Fel Gafod* (Merthyr Tydfil, 1813), pp. 17–21, 22–6; NLW., Llanover MS. B 19.

388 William Owen [-Pughe], *The Heroic Elegies and Other Pieces of Llywarch Hen* (London, 1792), p. lxiii.

389 L. J. Hopkin-James, *Hopkiniaid Morganwg*, p. 90.

390 NLW., Llanover MS. C 43, 34.

391 Phillips, *Vale of Neath*, p. 143.

392 Ibid., p. 543.

393 *Trysorfa Gwybodaeth* (1770), 25–7.

394 L. J. Hopkin-James, *Hopkiniaid Morganwg*, p. 97.

395 Ibid., p. 115.

396 Ibid.

397 Ibid., p. 97.

398 Ibid., p. 100; L. Hopkin, *Y Fel Gafod*, pp. 75–83, 91–8.

399 For a selection of this correspondence, *Hopkiniaid Morganwg*, pp. 118–41.

400 Cardiff MS. 4. 877, 165, in the autograph of David Jones, Wallington.

401 *TLlM.*, p. 240.

402 *TLlM.*, p. 239, n. 31.

403 BM. MS. 14929, 54, Lewis Morris to Edward Samuel in October 1736.

404 *The Cambrian Register* (3 vols., London, 1796–1818), I, 343; *TLlM.*, p. 239, n. 32.

405 Iolo Morganwg, *Poems, Lyric and Pastoral* (2 vols., London, 1794), II, 218–19.

406 *TLlM.*, p. 238, n. 28.

407 Cardiff MS. 4. 877, 235.

408 Evans, *Llangynwyd Parish*, p. 187.

409 See the letter in NLW., Llanover MS. C 35, 165–74, which Dafydd Nicolas is said to have sent to Edward Evan on April 3, 1754, when he lived in Glyncorrwg; published by Phillips, *Vale of Neath*, pp. 547–9.

410 Ibid., pp. 549, 550.

411 *The Cambrian Register*, II, 564–6.

412 Phillips, *Vale of Neath*, pp. 550–1, 738–9; *TLlM.*, p. 294.

413 Phillips, *Vale of Neath*, p. 550.

414 NLW., Llanover MS. C 54, 133.

415 Lewis Hopkin, *Y Fel Gafod*, pp. 98, 100–1.

416 Maria Jane Williams, *Ancient National Airs of Gwent and Morganwg* (Llandovery, 1844), pp. 14–15, 32–3; 10–11.

417 *TLlM.*, pp. 293 and 296; *Y Llenor*, XXVIII (1949), 193.

418 John Williams (ab Ithel), *Taliesin*, I (1859–60), 92–5; cf. Phillips, *Vale of Neath*, pp. 547–9.

419 *TLlM.*, pp. 290–2.

420 NLW., Llanover MS. C 67, 446–7.

421 Ibid.; *Llyfr Ecclesiastes* (Bristol, 1767).

422 Lewis Hopkin, *Y Fel Gafod*, pp. 89–90.

423 This letter has been published in *Hen Gwndidau*, pp. 207–13. On Dafydd Thomas, see further *TLlM.*, pp. 127, n. 45, 228, 244–5, 250, 260, 266, 278, 279, 284; *DWB.*, p. 940.

424 Some interesting facts regarding his life can be gleaned from his book of

verse, *Afalau'r Awen* (4th edn., Aberdare, 1874). Cf. Iolo Morganwg in NLW., Llanover MS. C 72, 142–5, and R. T. Jenkins, 'Bardd a'i Gefndir (Edward Ifan o'r Ton Coch)', *Trans. Cymm.* (1946–7), pp. 97–149. Cf. also *DWB.*, *s.n.*, p. 228.

[425] Lewis Hopkin, *Y Fel Gafod*, pp. 98–9, 101.

[426] *TLlM.*, p. 248 and n. 53.

[427] R. T. Jenkins, op. cit., p. 118; *TLlM.*, p. 249.

[428] Published in *Yr Ymofynydd* (1847), 149–53.

[429] Edward Williams ('Iolo Fardd Glas'), *Cyfaill y Cymru* (1797), pp. 12–13.

[430] NLW., Llanover MSS. C 63, 170 and 171; C 73, 85; C 67, *passim*.

[431] *Iolo Morganwg a Chywyddau'r Ychwanegiad*, p. 174.

[432] William Owen [-Pughe], *The Heroic Elegies and Other Pieces of Llywarch Hen* (London, 1792), p. lxiii.

[433] *Cyneirlyfr: neu Eiriadur Cymraeg* (2 vols., Aberhonddu, 1826), II, 379.

[434] NLW., Llanover MS. C 67, 9; Evans, *Llangynwyd Parish*, p. 105.

[435] *TLlM.*, p. 254.

[436] *Hopkiniaid Morganwg*, p. 68.

[437] *Y Llenor*, VII (1928), 34–5; *TLlM.*, p. 254.

[438] Ibid., p. 251. Cf. also the *englynion* in *Y Fel Gafod*, pp. 101–2, to 'William Hopkin'. Moreover, the *englynion* (ibid., p. 100) which name the poets who attended the *eisteddfod* refer to two bards called 'William'. One of these was probably Wil Hopcyn.

[439] NLW., Llanover MS. C 12, 205. For the text of the poem, as it has become popularly known, *Y Flodeugerdd Gymraeg*, ed. W. J. Gruffydd (3rd edn., Caerdydd, 1940), pp. 45–6.

[440] G. J. Williams, 'Wil Hopcyn a'r Ferch o Gefn Ydfa', *Y Llenor*, VI (1927), 218–29; ibid., VII (1928), 34–46; idem, 'Wil Hopcyn and the Maid of Cefn Ydfa', *Glam. Hist.*, VI, 228–51; *TLlM.*, pp. 251–9.

[441] Daniel Huws, 'Ancient National Airs of Gwent and Morganwg', *NLWJ.*, XV (1967–8), 31–54 (here p. 51).

[442] *Y Llenor*, VII, 44; *Glam. Hist.*, VI, 247.

[443] E.g., *englynion* which Rhys Morgan of Pencraig-nedd published in John Jones's *Almanac* for 1739, and Lewis Hopkin, *Y Fel Gafod*, pp. 31 and 32; *TLlM.*, pp. 266–7.

[444] NLW., Peniarth MS. 115, 68; *RWM.*, I, 698.

[445] BM. MS. 14929, 54.

[446] *TLlM.*, p. 271 and n. 100.

[447] G. J. Williams, *Iolo Morganwg* (Caerdydd, 1956).

[448] NLW., Llanover MSS. C 67, 105–10, 441–7; C 33, 72–3; C 52, 98; C 57, 398 and 429; *Hopkiniaid Morganwg*, pp. 106–7; *TLlM.*, pp. 272–5.

[449] *Grammadeg Cymraeg ... John Rhydderch*, pp. 188–9.

[450] Malkin, *South Wales*, I, 119–20.

[451] Ibid., 117.

[452] NLW., Llanover MS. C 67, 441–7.

[453] Lewis Hopkin, *Y Fel Gafod*, pp. 88–90.

[454] Ibid., pp. 26–7, 90–1, 98–9, 109.

[455] *TLlM.*, pp. 286–8.

[456] E.g., *Y Fel Gafod*, pp. 14–15.

[457] *TLlM.*, pp. 287–8.

[458] *Y Fel Gafod*, pp. 110–16.

[459] Ibid., pp. 15–17.

[460] NLW., Llanover MS. B 19. It became very popular in the nineteenth century.

[461] NLW., Llanover MSS. C 59, 321–3; C 54, 380–2; C 40, 475–7; NLW., Iolo A. Williams MS. 131, 12, and 12 *a*.

[462] *TLlM.*, pp. 293–5.

[463] NLW., MS. 1940, which was completed not later than 1829.

[464] *NLWJ.*, XV (1967–8), 50.

[465] NLW., Llanover MS. C 12, 198–9.

[466] NLW., Llanover MSS. C 12, 121–3; C 40, 473–5, 511; C 59, 386. Quotations in *TLlM.*, pp. 297–9.

[467] Maria Jane Williams, op. cit., p. 82.

[468] *NLWJ.*, XV, 41.

[469] NLW., Llanover MS. C 70, 158; *TLlM.*, p. 301.

[470] P. T. J. Morgan, 'The Abbé Pezron and the Celts', *Trans. Cymm.* (1965), 286–95.

[471] *TLlM.*, p. 303 and n. 160.

[472] *The Myvyrian Archaiology of Wales* (2nd edn., Denbigh, 1870), pp. 685–715; G. J. Williams, *Iolo Morganwg a Chywyddau'r Ychwanegiad*, pp. 168–9, 198, 208, 214; *TLlM.*, pp. 3, 4, 8, 21, n. 13, 172, 182, 186, 303; idem, 'Brut Aberpergwm', *Glam. Hist.*, IV, 205–20; and ante, III, 476.

[473] G. J. Williams, *Iolo Morganwg a Chywyddau'r Ychwanegiad*, pp. 168–9.

[474] BM. MS. 14929, 215–16.

[475] *The Letters of Goronwy Owen*, ed. J. H. Davies (Cardiff, 1924), p. 68.

[476] NLW., Llanover MS. C 52, 353–5.

[477] NLW., MS. 13226, 127–9; *TLlM.*, p. 305.

[478] *The Letters of Lewis, Richard, William and John Morris, of Anglesey*, ed. J. H. Davies (2 vols., Aberystwyth, 1907–9), II, 141; henceforth cited as *ML*.

[479] Ibid., II, 221.

[480] Ibid., II, 419–20; G. J. Williams, *Iolo Morganwg*, pp. 141–2.

[481] *ML.*, II, 420.

[482] *ML.*, II, 221, 439; *TLlM.*, p. 307; G. J. Williams, *Iolo Morganwg*, pp. 141–2.

[483] See William Thomas's diary, as printed in *Cylchgrawn Cymdeithas Hanes y Methodistiaid Calfinaidd* (1949), 48. On Thomas Richards, *DWB.*, *s.n.*, p. 854; *TLlM.*, pp. 300–8; G. J. Williams, *Iolo Morganwg a Chywyddau'r Ychwanegiad*, pp. 168–9; idem, *Iolo Morganwg*, pp. xliv, 106, 133–5, 137, 155, 243–5, 341.

[484] NLW., MS. 6515, a manuscript which, at one time, belonged to the Rev. J. M. Traherne, of Coedrhiglan. For further details, see Cardiff MS. 4. 304, 35–8; *DWB.*, *s.n.*, pp. 1011–12; *TLlM.*, pp. 308–9; G. J. Williams, *Iolo Morganwg*, *passim*.

[485] *DWB.*, *s.n.*, pp. 960–1; G. J. Williams, *Iolo Morganwg*, pp. 142–3, 156, 172, 174, 392–9, 424; Cardiff MS. 3. 167; Cardiff MS. 4. 304; NLW., MS. 6516; NLW., MS. 15415, 69; NLW., Llanover MS. C 54, 119; D. Gwenallt Jones, *Y Ficer Prichard a 'Canwyll y Cymry'* (Gwasg yr Eglwys yng Nghymru, 1946), pp. 25–9; Ifano Jones, *A History of Printing and Printers in Wales to* 1810 (Cardiff, 1925), pp. 84–91.

[486] T. C. Evans (Cadrawd), 'John Walters and the First Printing Press in Glamorganshire', *The Journal of the Welsh Bibliographical Society*, I (1911–15), 83–9; G. J. Williams, *Iolo Morganwg*, p. 142.

[487] After the death of Walters's son, Henry, this MS. went to the private library of the Rev. J. M. Traherne of Coedrhiglan. It is now NLW., Llanstephan MS. 189, which also contains the transcript of a Welsh–English Dictionary by William Gambold. *RWM.*, II, 776; *TLlM.*, p. 308 and n. 174.

[488] G. J. Williams, *Iolo Morganwg*, p. 143.

[489] G. J. Williams and A. Lewis in *Llên Cymru*, III (1954–5), 188–9.

[490] BM. MS. 15030, 172–3. Cf. further Cadrawd in *The Red Dragon*, XI (1887), 269–71, and in *The Journal of the Welsh Bibliographical Society*, I, 83–9; Ifano Jones, op. cit., p. 85; G. J. Williams, *Iolo Morganwg*, pp. 391 ff.

[491] These words are discussed briefly in *Geiriadur Prifysgol Cymru: A Dictionary of the Welsh Language* (Caerdydd, 1950–).

[492] *Iolo Manuscripts*, ed. Taliesin Williams (Llandovery, 1848), pp. 19, 24, 27, 34, 98, 227.

[493] NLW., Llanover MSS. C 49, 123; C 29, 374; C 42, 161.

[494] NLW., MS. 168, 132.

[495] G. J. Williams, *Iolo Morganwg a Chywyddau'r Ychwanegiad*, pp. 166–8.

[496] *TLlM.*, pp. 310–11.

[497] NLW., Llanover MS. C 51, 89–90.

[498] *RWM.*, II, 46–56; *TLlM.*, p. 311, nn. 187 and 188.

[499] E.g., Jesus College MS. 13, 284 *b*; ibid., 282 *b*; ibid., 5, 12, 29, 54.

[500] Cardiff MS. 4. 33, 150.

[501] Ibid., 366. And on p. 78 he refers to himself as 'Scriptor hujus libri'.

[502] Ibid., 78.

[503] Phillips, *Vale of Neath*, pp. 143–4.

[504] Loc. cit. On Morgan Llywelyn, see further *TLlM.*, pp. 309–15.

[505] Cardiff MS. 3. 1, 56. Cf. Clark, *Limbus*, pp. 446–7.

[506] NLW., MSS. 7 and 8.

[507] Thomas Nicholas, *Annals and Antiquities of the Counties and County Families of Wales* (2 vols., London, 1872), II, 591–4. The MS. passed eventually to Sir Isaac Heard, Clarencieux King-at-Arms, and its contents were published in 1845 by Sir Thomas Phillips, Middle Hill; *TLlM.*, p. 316, n. 200.

[508] This history was published in *Trans. Cymm.* (1843), 263–320.

[509] NLW., Llanover MS. C 54, 372.

[510] E.g., the reference in NLW., Llanover MS. C 42, 420.

[511] Cardiff MS. 4. 877, 233. David Jones, however, did not have a high opinion of Thomas Truman's expertise as a genealogist.

[512] E.g., NLW., Llanover MS. C 53, 1.

[513] *Iolo Manuscripts*, ed. Taliesin Williams (ab Iolo), p. 199. On Thomas Truman, see further *TLlM.*, pp. 315–18; G. J. Williams, *Iolo Morganwg* (1956), pp. 12, 16, 156, 306, 309, 424.

INDEX

T1

Seys, William, 282.
Sheldon, Archbishop Gilbert, 433, 472, 473, 474.
Ship Money, 152, 194, 258.
Shirley, Jonathan, bishop of Llandaff, 1769, 436.
Siancyn, Siôn, of Pen-llin, 567.
Sidney family,
　　Sir Henry (d. 1586), 39, 48, 52–4, 67, 69, 101,
　　　151, 182–7, 586.
　　Robert, Viscount Lisle and earl of Leicester
　　　(d. 1626), 11, 30, 39, 41, 54, 109, 112, 166,
　　　169, 172, 184–6, 246, 362, 600.
　　　　Barbara, wife of, 11, 30, 109–110, 112, 166,
　　　　　183–6, 198, 600.
　　　　Katherine, daughter of, 109
　　　　Mary, sister of, 115, 186.
　　　　Sir Philip, brother of, 119, 184–6, 536.
Sils ap Siôn, 542, 544, 546, 547, 548, 553, 580, 602,
　　622.
Simmons, Joseph, 497, 502, 507, 524.
Simons, Joshua, 516, 517.
Siôn Hywel Siôn, 89, 91, 132.
Siôn Mowddwy, 549, 550, 570, 636.
Sker, 93, 124, 210, 385, 475.
Sketty, 50, 491.
Skinner, Rev. John, 330.
Smith, John, archdeacon of Llandaff, c. 1550–1564,
　　218, 229.
Smith, Sir Thomas, 80, 81.
Smythe, Thomas, 55, 56.
Society for the Promotion of Christian Knowledge,
　　449, 453, 454–7, 458, 460.
Society for the Propagation of the Gospel in Foreign
　　Parts, 453.
Solemn League and Covenant, 382.
Somerset, county of, 25, 45, 64, 67, 111, 357, 370,
　　371.
Somerset, family of, 161–2, 164, 314, 386, 396.
Somerset earls of Worcester, later marquises of
　　Worcester, 11, 22–3, 31, 34, 40–1, 60, 82, 90,
　　99, 103–4, 108, 158, 160, 169, 205, 236, 239,
　　245, 386.
　　Charles, first earl (d. 1526), 19–20, 143, 161–2,
　　　163.
　　Henry, second earl (d. 1549), 40, 48, 111, 143,
　　　145, 162–3, 175–6, 197, 205.
　　William, third earl (d. 1589), 22–3, 99, 103–4,
　　　108, 162.
　　Edward, fourth earl (d. 1628), 23, 116, 151, 162.
　　Henry, fifth earl and first marquis (d. 1646),
　　　116–17, 162, 192–3, 195–6, 245, 258, 261–2,
　　　267.
　　Edward, second marquis and earl of Glamorgan
　　　(d. 1667), 193, 195, 261–3, 265–6, 268.
Somerset dukes of Beaufort, 312, 382, 391, 396,
　　400, 423.
　　Henry, third marquis of Worcester and first
　　　duke of Beaufort (d. 1700), 378, 382, 384,
　　　386–7, 388–94, 396.
　　Henry, second duke (d. 1714), 399–400, 401–4.
　　Henry, third duke (d. 1745), 363, 366, 407–8,
　　　410–14.
　　Charles Noel, fourth duke (d. 1756), 319, 414–15.
　　Henry, fifth duke (d. 1803), 318, 423, 424–5,
　　　427–8.
Southerndown, 22, 28.
Spain, 65, 67, 68, 132.
Speed, John, 3, 43, 322.
Spittle, 36.
Splott, 32, 548.
Stalling Down, nr. Cowbridge, 326.

Star Chamber, Court of, 35, 40, 61, 100, 108, 110,
　　147, 148, 149, 189, 191, 199, 200, 201, 258.
Star Chamber suits, 111, 176, 190.
Story of the Lower Burrows, the, 121.
Stradling of Llantwit, family, 93.
　　Robert, 93.
Stradling of Roath, family, 93.
　　Edward, 93.
Stradling of St. Donat's, family, 11–12, 17, 31–2,
　　39–40, 55, 82, 90, 93, 116, 123, 147, 170, 172,
　　174, 178, 180, 198, 210, 220, 228, 237, 259,
　　451, 548, 595–6.
　　Sir Thomas (d. 1480), 120.
　　Sir Edward (d. 1535), 166, 579.
　　Sir Thomas (d. 1573), 7, 30, 31, 41, 123, 130,
　　　131, 134, 150, 166, 171–2, 176, 178, 209–10,
　　　212, 224, 232–4, 237–8, 593.
　　Sir Edward (d. 1609), 12, 13, 23, 24, 31–2, 33,
　　　40, 57, 61, 63, 70–2, 79–80, 100–2, 104, 115,
　　　116–17, 119–20, 123, 134, 135, 137, 153–4,
　　　156–7, 167, 169, 171, 178–82, 184–7, 199,
　　　226, 228–9, 543, 550, 582, 583, 593, 594–7,
　　　601, 637.
　　Sir John, first bart. (d. 1637), 82, 90, 94, 97–8,
　　　107, 115, 119, 120–1, 123, 167, 170, 173–4,
　　　192, 451, 539–40, 548.
　　Sir Edward, second bart. (d. 1644), 167, 196,
　　　228–9, 260, 261.
　　Sir Edward, third bart. (d. before 1661), 259,
　　　299.
　　Sir Edward, fourth bart. (d. 1685), 336, 385, 389.
　　Sir Edward, fifth bart. (d. 1735), 396, 398–9,
　　　401–5, 407–8, 607.
　　Edward, M.P. (d. 1723), 405–6, 558.
　　Sir Thomas, sixth bart. (d. 1738), 409.
　　Stradling, Agnes (*temp.* Elizabeth), 113.
　　　David (*temp.* Elizabeth), 134, 167, 237.
　　　Gwenllian (*temp.* Elizabeth), 110.
　　　Sir Henry (*temp.* Charles I), 120, 259, 275–6,
　　　　280.
　　　Jane (*temp.* Henry VII), 111.
　　　Major-General John (*temp.* Charles I), 259,
　　　　269, 275–6.
　　　Col. Thomas (*temp.* Charles I), 94, 259, 261.
　　　Sir Thomas (*temp.* Charles II), 386.
　　　Walter (*temp.* James I), 115.
Stradling of St. Donat's, correspondence of, 100,
　　104, 119, 125, 135.
Stuarts, dynasty of, 172, 173, 198, 200, 257, 306,
　　314.
Stuart earls of Bute,
　　John, third earl (d. 1792), 417, 418.
　　John, Lord Mountstuart, fourth earl and first
　　　marquis (d. 1814), 420, 423, 425, 427, 428.
　　John, Lord Mountstuart (d. 1794), 428.
Sully, 12, 27, 31, 60, 64, 228, 229, 320, 330, 342,
　　346, 347, 354, 355, 356.
Sussex ironmasters, 52, 53, 54.
Sutton, 22.
Swansea, 11, 12, 24, 40, 42, 43–6, 47–8, 49–51,
　　56–8, 60, 62–3, 75–6, 77, 90–2, 108, 115, 129,
　　139, 252–3, 260, 262, 266–8, 270–1, 272, 274,
　　277, 285–6, 287, 294, 311, 313, 337, 339, 347,
　　351, 353, 361, 363, 365–8, 370–1, 372, 380,
　　388, 423, 426, 428–9, 452, 456, 504.
　　borough, 157–60, 172, 216, 301–2, 303–4, 308,
　　　314, 375, 388, 395–6, 452.
　　burgesses, 92, 158–9, 253, 367, 377, 389.
　　corporation, 91–2, 99, 139, 271, 301, 307, 308,
　　　391, 480.

Y

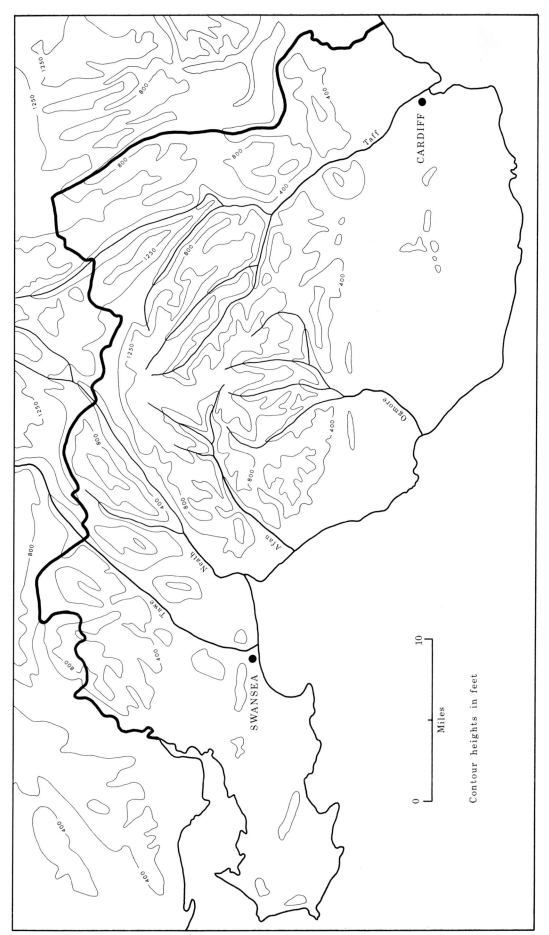

I. Glamorgan: contours and rivers

Contour heights in feet

Miles

0 10

CARDIFF

SWANSEA

Taff

Ogmore

Afan

Neath

Tawe

1250

800

400

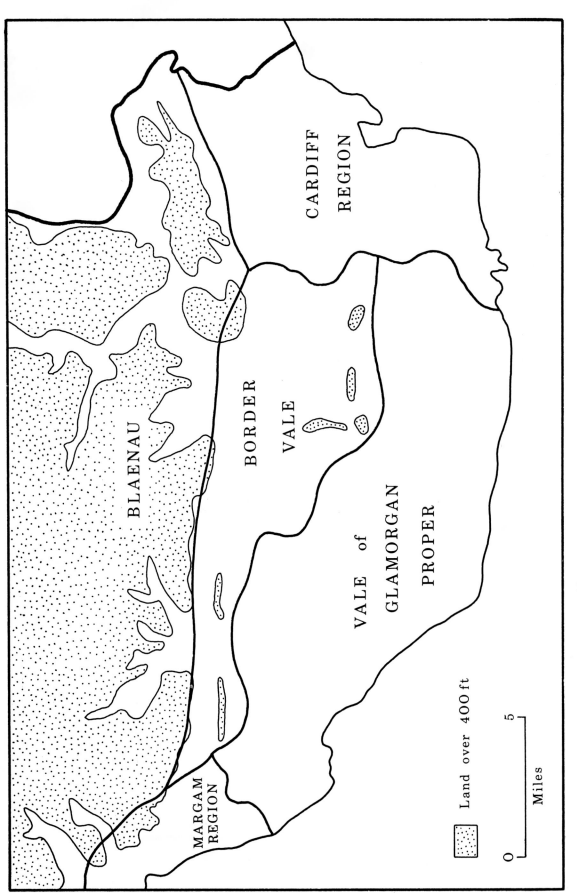

CARDIFF REGION

BLAENAU

BORDER VALE

VALE of GLAMORGAN PROPER

MARGAM REGION

Land over 400 ft

0 5
Miles

II (a). The Vale of Glamorgan, the Border Vale, and the *Blaenau*

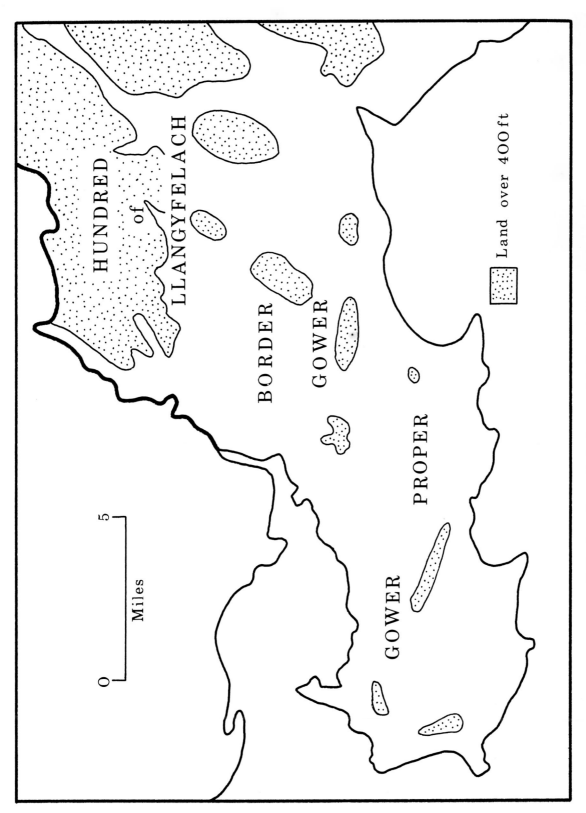

II (b). Gower Proper, Border Gower, and the Hundred of Llangyfelach

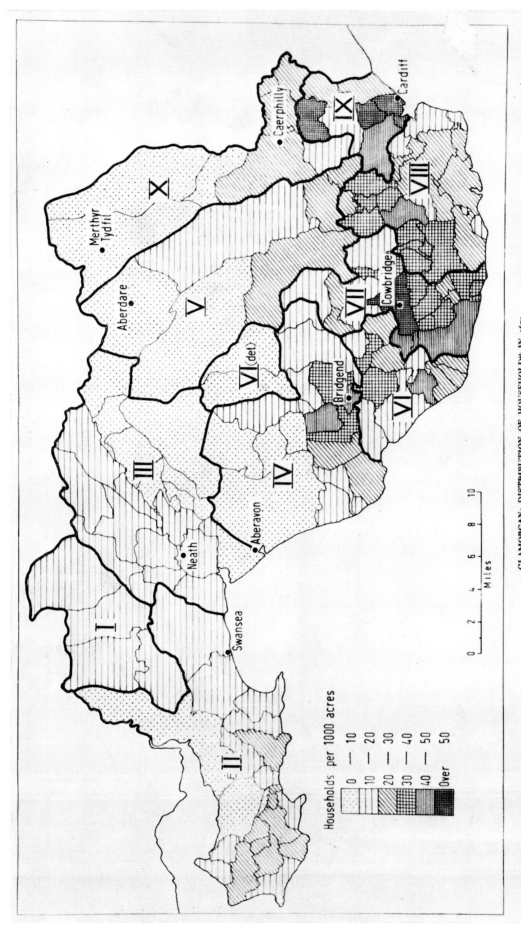

GLAMORGAN: DISTRIBUTION OF HOUSEHOLDS IN 1670
(Based on the Hearth Tax List.)

HUNDREDS—I. LLANGYFELACH. II. SWANSEA. III. NEATH. IV. NEWCASTLE. V. MISKIN. VI. OGMORE.
VI(a) OGMORE (detached.) VII. COWBRIDGE. VIII. DINAS POWYS. X. KIBBOR. X. SENGHENYDD.

III. The distribution of population in Glamorgan, 1670

Taken from Dr. Moelwyn Williams's Ph.D. thesis by courtesy of the author.

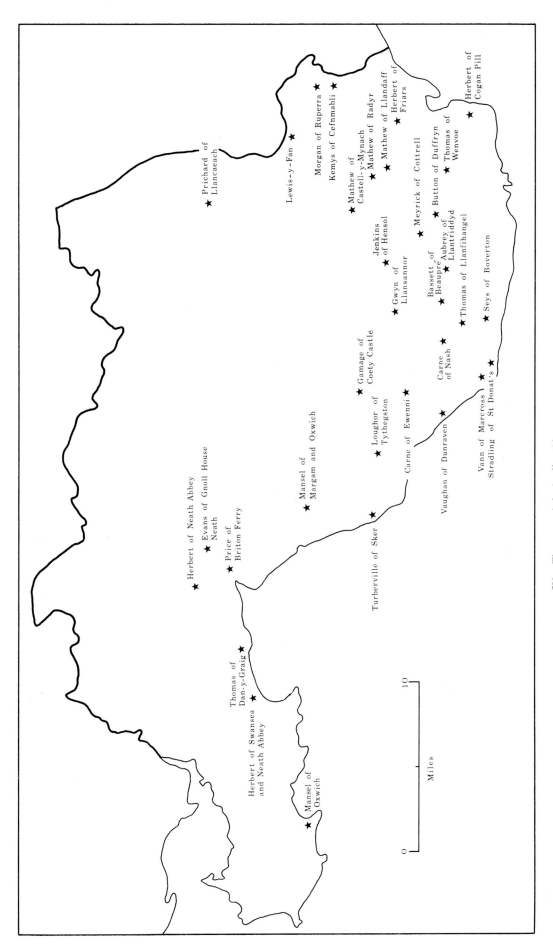

IV. The seats of the leading Glamorgan gentry

Prichard of Llancaeach ★

Lewis-y-Fan ★

Morgan of Ruperra ★
Kemys of Cefnmabli ★

Mathew of Castell-y-Mynach ★
Mathew of Radyr ★
Mathew of Llandaff ★
Herbert of Friars ★

Herbert of Cogan Pill ★

Meyrick of Cottrell ★
Button of Duffryn ★
Thomas of Wenvoe ★

Jenkins of Hensol ★

Gwyn of Llansannor ★
Bassett of Beaupré ★
Aubrey of Llantriddyd ★
Thomas of Llanfihangel ★
Seys of Boverton ★

Gamage of Coety Castle ★
Carne of Nash ★

Loughor of Tythegston ★
Carne of Ewenni ★

Vaughan of Dunraven ★
Vann of Marcross ★
Stradling of St Donat's ★

Mansel of Margam and Oxwich ★

Turberville of Sker ★

Herbert of Neath Abbey ★
Evans of Gnoll House Neath ★
Price of Briton Ferry ★

Thomas of Dan-y-Graig ★

Herbert of Swansea and Neath Abbey ★

Mansel of Oxwich ★

0

10

Miles

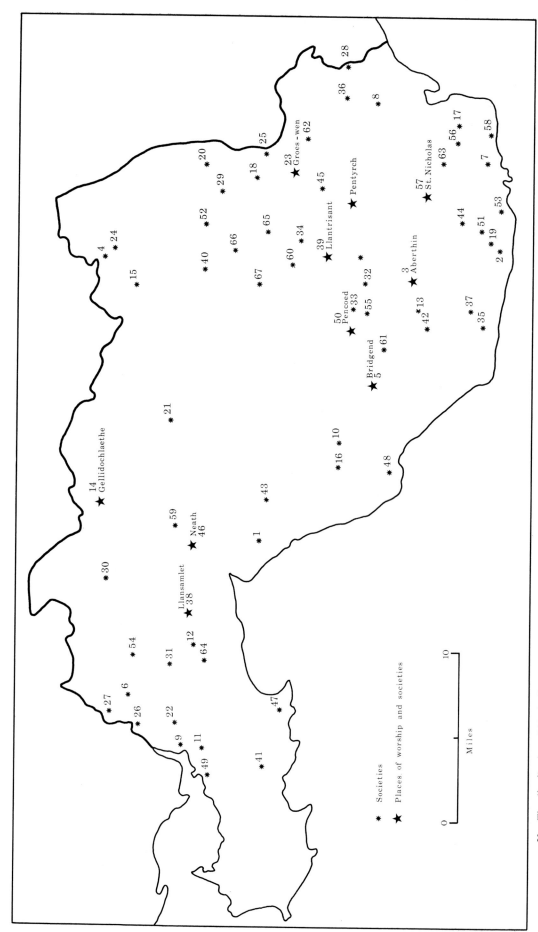

V. The distribution of Methodist places of worship and societies in eighteenth-century Glamorgan. See also Chapter IX, appendices E and F.

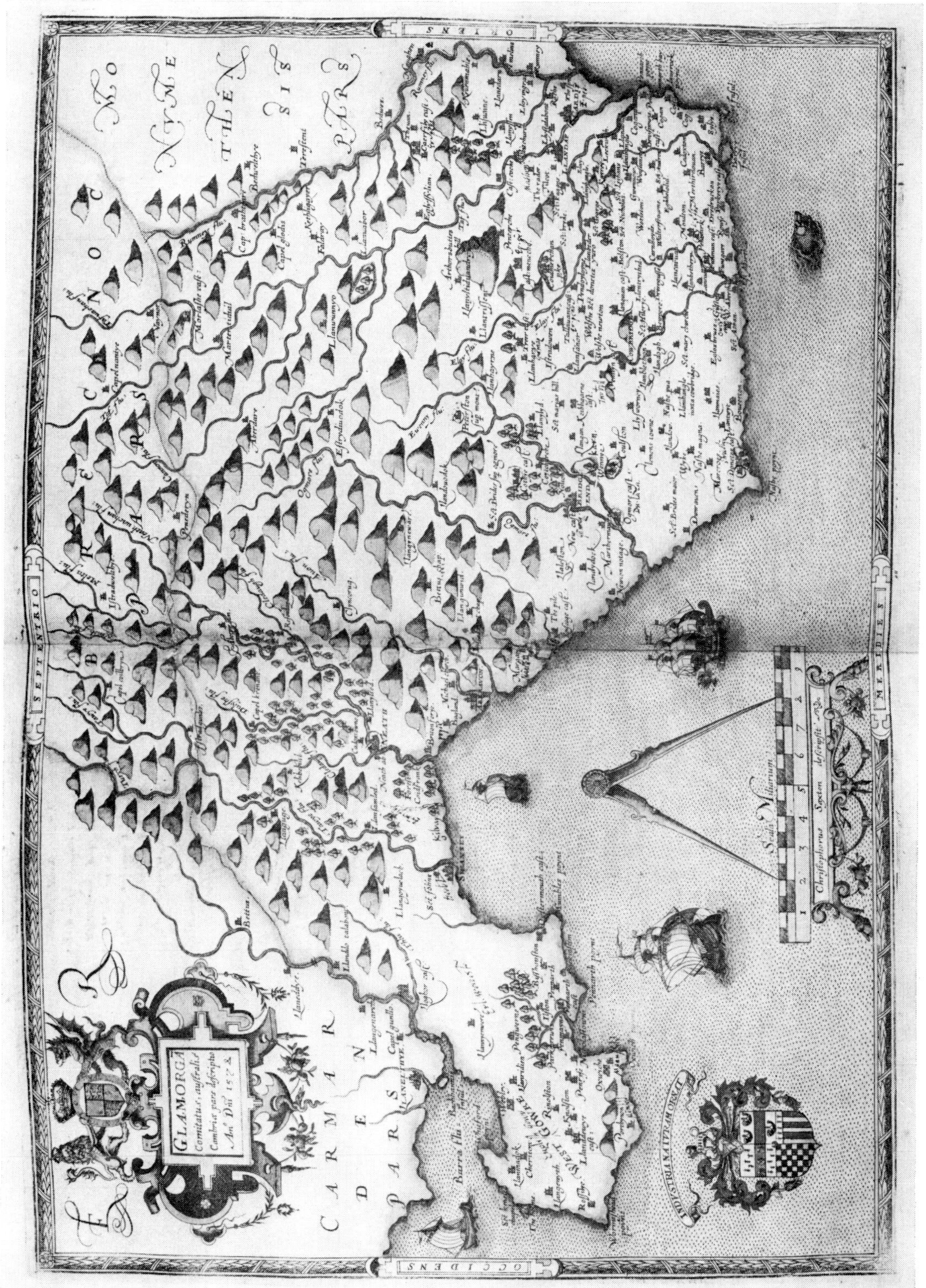

PLATE I

Christopher Saxton's map of Glamorgan, 1578. British Museum MS. Royal 18 D iii

PLATE II

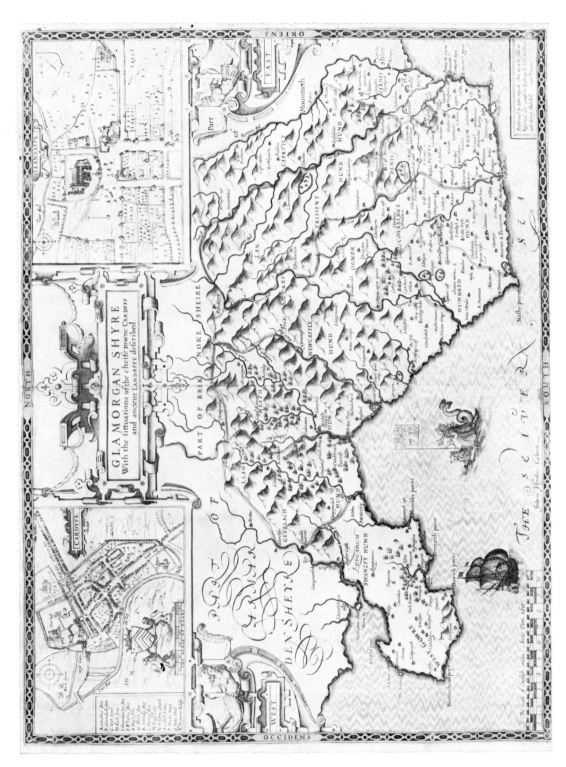

Map of Glamorgan (1611) by John Speed, *The Theatre of the Empire of Great Britaine*

[*Roger Davies, Esq.*

PLATE III

Tomb effigy of Charles, first earl of Worcester (c. 1460–1526) in the Beaufort Chapel, Windsor Castle

[Dean and Chapter, St. George's Chapel

PLATE IV

Possibly Sir Robert Mansel of Margam
and Penrice, *c.* 1630 (1573–1656)

(Artist unknown)

(By courtesy of
Mr. Christopher Methuen-Campbell)

[*Roger Davies, Esq.*

Sir Thomas Mansel of Margam and
Penrice in 1614 (1556–1631)

(Artist unknown)

(By courtesy of
Mr. Christopher Methuen-Campbell)

[*Roger Davies, Esq.*

Sir Thomas Mansel and his wife, Jane,
and daughter, Mary, *c.* 1620

(Artist unknown)

(By courtesy of
Mr. Christopher Methuen-Campbell)

[*Roger Davies, Esq.*

PLATE V

Colonel Philip Jones, parliamentary commander,
c. 1655 (1618–74) (Artist unknown)
(By courtesy of Sir Hugo Boothby, Bt.)

[Stewart Williams, Esq.

Edward Williams ('Iolo Morganwg'),
poet, littérateur, and antiquary
(1747–1826)

[Cardiff Central Library

William Edwards, minister and architect
(1718–89)

[National Library of Wales

Sir Thomas Button, admiral and explorer,
c. 1610 (d. 1634) (Artist unknown)
(By courtesy of Sir Cennydd G. Traherne, K.G.)

[National Museum of Wales

PLATE VI

Tomb of the brothers, Sir William Herbert (d. 1610) and
Sir John Herbert (1550–1617), in St. John's Church, Cardiff

[Crown copyright: R.C.A.M. Wales

Tomb of John Bassett (d. 1554) and his wife, Elizabeth, and of their son-in-law
and daughter, Anthony and Elizabeth Mansel, in Llantriddyd Church

[Crown copyright: R.C.A.M. Wales

PLATE VII

Tombs of the Mansel family in Margam Abbey Church

PLATE VIII

[Roger Davies, Esq.

The old Methodist Chapel at Aberthin near Cowbridge

PLATE IX

A view up the River Neath from Briton Ferry, *c.* 1770
From a print in the National Library of Wales

[National Library of Wales

The Cyfarthfa Iron Works, Merthyr Tydfil, *c.* 1800
From a print in the National Library of Wales

[National Library of Wales

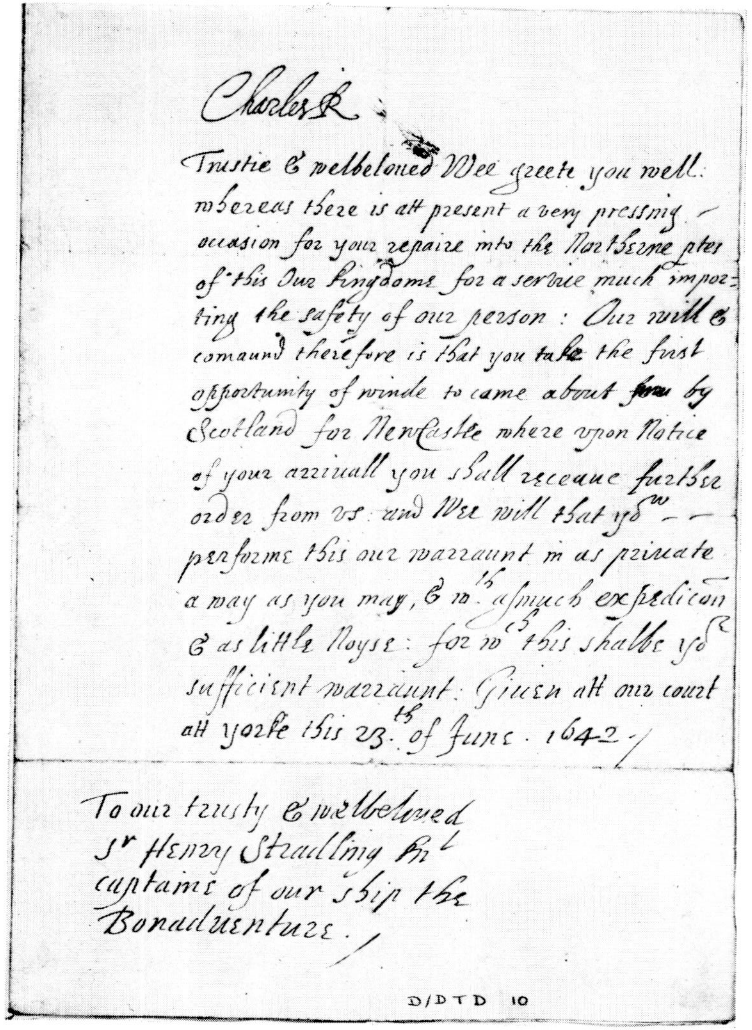

Charles R.

Trustie & welbeloued Wee greete you well: whereas there is att present a very pressing occasion for your repaire into the Northerne parts of this Our kingdome for a service much importing the safety of our person: Our will & comaund therefore is that you take the first opportunity of winde to came about by Scotland for Newcastle where upon Notice of your arriuall you shall receaue further order from vs: and Wee will that you performe this our warraunt in as priuate a way as you may, & with asmuch expedicon & as little Noyse: for which this shalbe your sufficient warraunt: Giuen att our court att yorke this 23th of June. 1642.

To our trusty & welbeloued Sr Henry Stradling Knt captaine of our ship the Bonaduenture.

D/DTD 10

Letter from Charles I to Sir Henry Stradling, June 23, 1642

[*Glamorgan County Record Office*

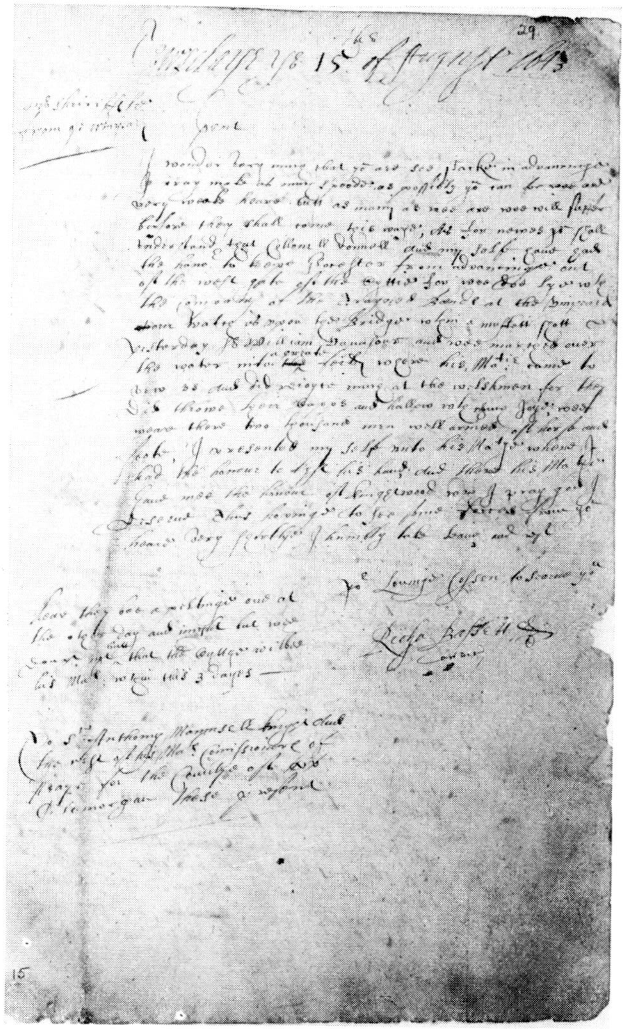

Letter from Sir Richard Bassett concerning the siege of Gloucester, August 15, 1643, in the Book of Results and Orders of the Glamorgan Commissioners of Array, f. 21

[*National Library of Wales*

PLATE XI

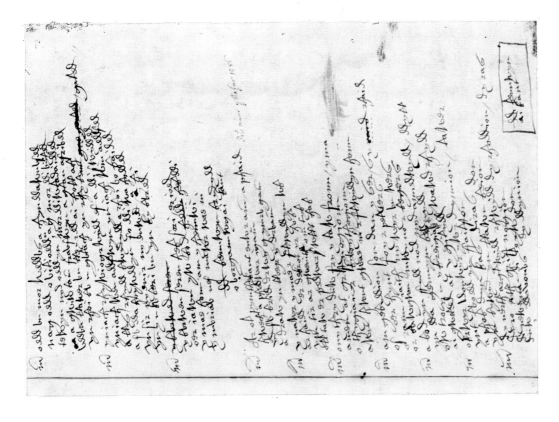

Poetry by Dafydd Benwyn, in the bard's own autograph,
in Llanstephan MS. 164, p. 73

National Library of Wales

The entry transcribed by Sils ap Siôn in Llanover MS. B 6, p. 40
(formerly numbered p. 36 a) recording the bardic *eisteddfod* held
at Llandaff in the late-sixteenth century

[*National Library of Wales*]

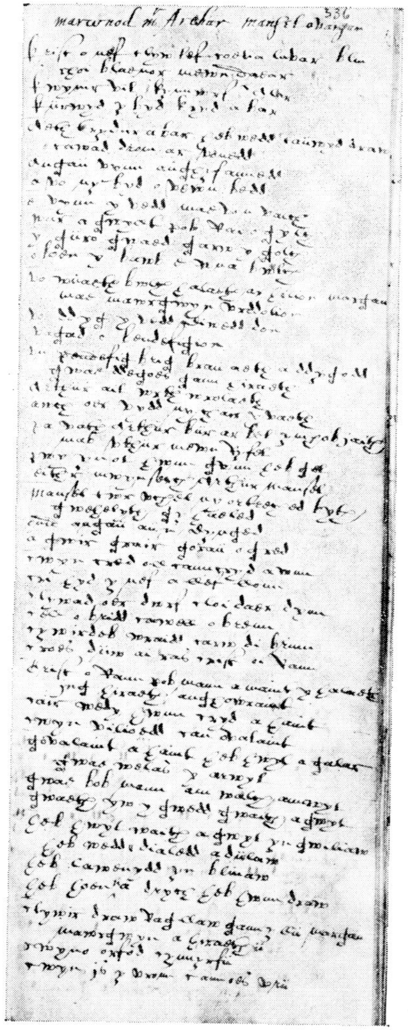

PLATE XII

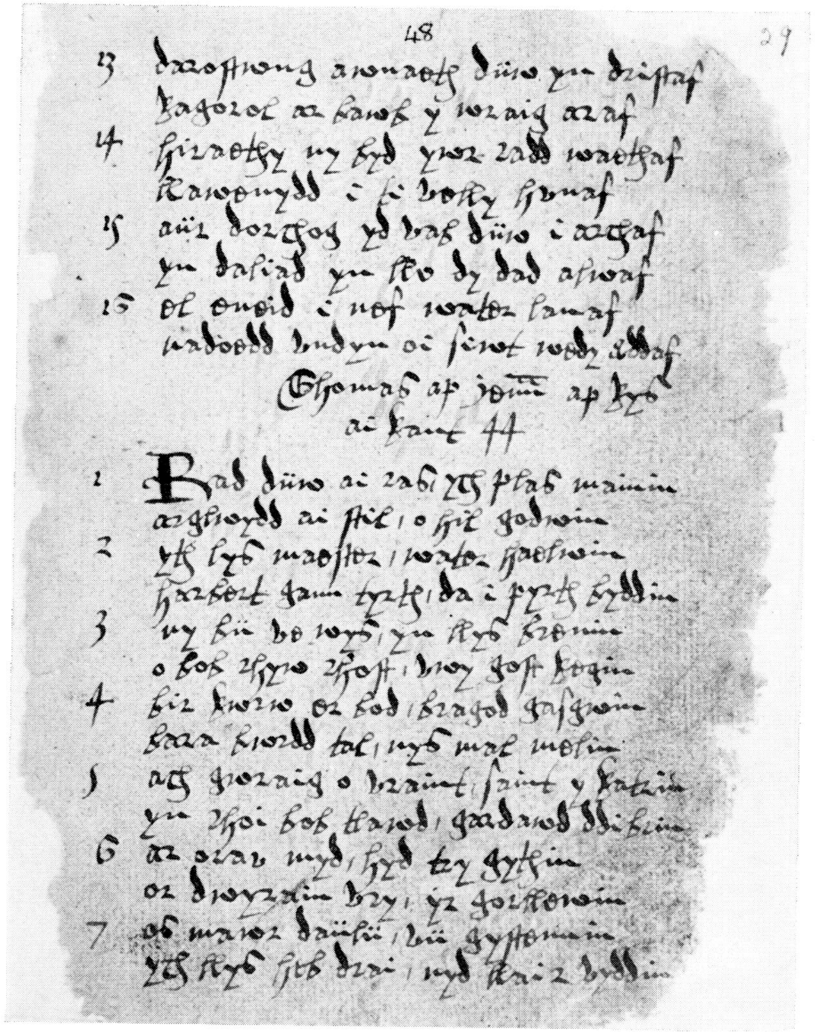

Llanover MS. B 9, p. 29, a source which contains a substantial collection
of *cwndidau* in Llywelyn Siôn's autograph

[*National Library of Wales*]

Part of the elegy by Edward Dafydd of
Margam to Arthur Mansel of Margam,
in the bard's autograph, in Cardiff
MS. 5. 44 ('Llyfr Hir Llanharan')

[*Cardiff Central Library*]

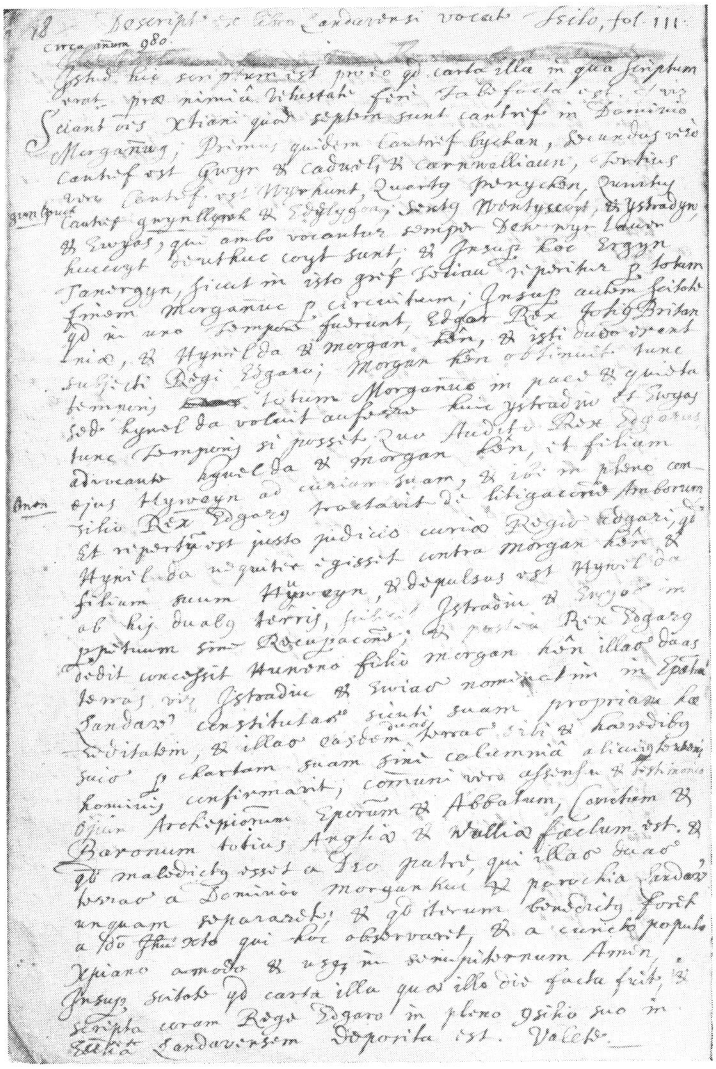

PLATE XIII

Cardiff MS. 3. 464, p. 18, transcribed *c.* 1657–60 by
the Rev. Thomas Wilkins of St. Mary Church

GLAMORGAN HOUSES

(Notes by Peter Smith, M.A., Secretary to the Royal Commission on Ancient Monuments for Wales.)

XIV. ST. DONAT'S CASTLE

Aerial view of St. Donat's Castle, a medieval castle which continued to be the home of the Stradling family throughout the sixteenth and seventeenth centuries, though much modified and improved.

XV. BEAUPRÉ (ST. HILARY)
OXWICH CASTLE

Sixteenth- and seventeenth-century Glamorgan houses may be divided into two main groups, namely the houses of the magnates and the houses of the minor gentry and yeomen. Many of the great houses show that the influence of the Castle was still strong in their design as instanced by Beaupré (St. Hilary), enlarged in the late-sixteenth century out of an earlier house, and Oxwich Castle in Gower.

XVI. LLANMIHANGEL PLACE

Another medieval theme, the first-floor hall, which had its primary accommodation on an upper floor, is also apparent among the major landowners' houses. At Llanmihangel Place the fenestration shows that the main rooms are upstairs, a mural stair leading from a ground-floor entrance to the first-floor hall.

XVII. LLANTRITHYD PLACE

The influence of the first-floor hall is also evident at Llantrithyd Place (near Cowbridge) originally built 1546, with seventeenth-century additions, now too ruined and overgrown for useful photography but well illustrated by drawings made when still intact. Many great sixteenth-century Glamorgan houses are now in ruins—Oxwich Castle, Beaupré, Van, Boverton Place, etc.

XVIII. SKER HOUSE
NEATH ABBEY

The first-floor hall idea is also apparent at Sker, where the hall (now ruined but similar to that at Llanmihangel Place on plate XVI) is clearly indicated by the large first-floor windows.

The great scale of the Glamorgan magnates' houses is also well illustrated by the ruins of the house built by the Herbert family, incorporating the monastic buildings of Neath Abbey. The main living accommodation was again on the first floor.

XIX. RUPERRA CASTLE

The more formal planning which came into fashion with the Renaissance is illustrated by Ruperra Castle built by Sir Thomas Morgan in 1626, a type of plan associated with the architect Smythson. Ruperra figures in the book of plans collected by John Thorpe, the seventeenth-century surveyor. It was a popular type of plan with court officials, another Welsh example being Plas Teg in Flintshire (1610).

XX. LLANSANNOR COURT
GREAT HOUSE, ABERTHIN

The trend to a formally symmetrical elevation is also found in other gentry houses as illustrated by Llansannor Court and the Great House at Aberthin (near Cowbridge). A formal elevation in which large dormered gables played an important part was very popular with the gentry in the late-sixteenth and early-seventeenth centuries. Cf. also St. Fagan's Castle.

XXI. COAT OF ARMS, OXWICH CASTLE
COAT OF ARMS, BEAUPRÉ

Great pride in pedigree was a recognised Welsh characteristic in the Tudor and Stuart period. It is illustrated by that favourite architectural embellishment, the shield of arms, as at Oxwich and Beaupré.

XXII. OUTER GATEHOUSE, BEAUPRÉ
GATEHOUSE, ABERTHIN

The strong sentiment of the magnates and gentry about the feudal past is illustrated by their attachment to the gatehouse, a fashion for which lasted in Wales until the Restoration. The gatehouses at Beaupré (1586) and Aberthin illustrate the idea in Glamorgan. Note the great difference in scale.

XXIII. BLUE ANCHOR INN, ABERTHAW
OLD PLAS COTTAGE, LLANTWIT MAJOR

On a smaller scale altogether are the houses of the substantial yeomen. The origins of these houses can be traced to the hall-house rather than the first-floor hall and castle, although unlike the sub-medieval houses of the borderland counties, very few farmhouses have *direct* evidence of a medieval predecessor. The commonest sub-medieval house in Glamorgan (as in Monmouthshire and Brecon) had its entry directly behind the main fireplace. The plan is illustrated by (*a*) The Blue Anchor Inn at Aberthaw and (*b*) Old Plas Cottage in Llantwit Major.

XXIV. EAST HALL, FONMON
SUTTON, OGMORE

The chimney-backing-on-the-entry plan is also illustrated by (*a*) East Hall at Fonmon and (*b*) Sutton (Ogmore). Note the thatch roof dressed over the dormers. Such would have been the appearance of most houses in the Vale before slates began to be imported from north Wales in the nineteenth century.

XXV. WALTERSTON-FAWR
FFORWEL-UCHAF, ST. GEORGE'S

Less common than the chimney-backing-on-the-entry house, but still fairly numerous, is the central-chimney, lobby-entry house, where the entrance is opposite the side of the main fireplace. The type is illustrated by (*a*) Walterston-fawr and (*b*) Fforwel-uchaf (St. George's). (See also pp. 126–28.)

XXVI. CHURCH HOUSE, LLANDOW
FLEMINGSTON COURT

Comparatively rare is that illustrated by Church House (Llandow) where the main chimney is away from the entry standing between hall and parlour. Also quite rare is the house with its main chimney placed on the side wall of the house illustrated by Flemingston Court. In some areas (for example Pembs.) this arrangement is also found in small farmhouses, but in Glamorgan it usually indicates fairly high status. The shaped heads to the windows and richly-moulded doorway suggest this house may be earlier (? mid-sixteenth century) than those illustrated in plates XXIII–XXV.

XXVII. ST. JOHN'S HOSPICE, NEWCASTLE (BRIDGEND)
WALTERSTON-FAWR (INTERIOR)

The interior of the sub-medieval, middle-sized house is illustrated by The Hospice (Bridgend) and Walterston-Fawr (Walterston). Note the doorway on one side of the fireplace giving onto the lobby-entry, and the doorway on the other giving onto the stairs at Walterston. The winding stone stair by the fireplace is found in great numbers in Glamorgan.

XXVIII. CHURCH HOUSE, LLANDOW (INTERIOR)
ST. JOHN'S HOSPICE, NEWCASTLE (BRIDGEND)

In the earlier sub-medieval houses the cross-passage was retained. The partition separating the passage from the outer rooms is illustrated by Church House (Llandow) and The Hospice (Bridgend). Note the thin stone partition which in most other parts of Wales would have been of some sort of timber construction.

XXIX. WINDOW, CHURCH HOUSE, LLANDOW
WINDOW, SUTTON, OGMORE

A striking feature of Glamorgan (particularly the Vale) is the great wealth of dressed-stone, mullioned windows. Apparently the earlier type had shaped heads and concave mouldings as at Church House (Llandow).

The later type illustrated by Sutton (Ogmore) had a square head and sunk-chamfered mouldings.

XXX. DOORWAY, SUTTON, OGMORE
DOORWAY, BLUE ANCHOR INN, ABERTHAW
DOORWAY, LLANSANNOR COURT

The wealth of good stone detail in Lias limestone and Quarella Sandstone is also illustrated by the doorway. The favoured doorhead was the perpendicular four-centred arch, as at Sutton (Ogmore), but a minority have the more pointed and more Gothic-looking equilateral arch as at the Blue Anchor, Aberthaw.

The yeoman houses usually had a plain chamfered moulding and a diagonal or broach-stop as at the Blue Anchor and Sutton. In the gentry houses both the mouldings and stops were more elaborate, as at Llansannor Court. All illustrate a skill in masoncraft more widespread than in any other Welsh county.

XXXI. THE ROCOCO LIBRARY, FONMON CASTLE

The most elegant example of an eighteenth-century room in Glamorgan.

PLATE XIV

Aerial view of St. Donat's castle, a medieval castle which continued to be the home of the Stradling family throughout the sixteenth and seventeenth centuries, though much modified and improved

[H. Tempest, Cardiff Ltd.

PLATE XV

Beaupré (St. Hilary)

[*Crown copyright: R.C.A.M. Wales*

Oxwich Castle

[*Crown copyright: R.C.A.M. Wales*

PLATE XVI

Llanmihangel Place

Llanmihangel Place (interior)

Plate XVII

Llantrithyd Place

[*National Museum of Wales*

Llantrithyd Place (interior)
(By A. J. Rolfe after Mrs. J. M. Traherne)

[*National Museum of Wales*